BEASTARS
Volume 17

Story & Art by
Paru Itagaki

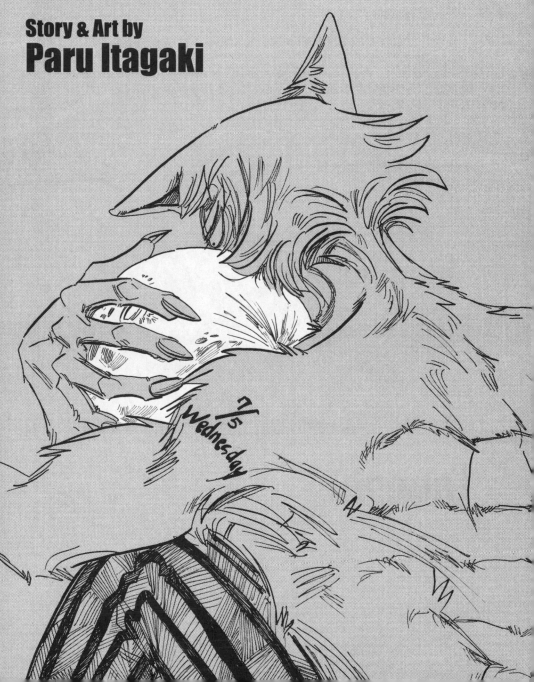

STORY & CAST OF CHARACTERS

Legoshi has been designated a registered meat offender after consensually eating his friend Louis's leg to give him the strength to defeat Riz, the bear who murdered their friend Tem. Now Legoshi has dropped out of school and is working at Bebebe, an udon noodle shop, as well as dating Haru.

Half-carnivore, half-herbivore Melon has no sense of taste—he only kills herbivores for sport. Despite being part carnivore himself, he fears carnivores and can't reconcile himself with his true nature. Legoshi and the lion gang Shishi-gumi agree to a truce so as to join forces against Melon. But first, they must find a gang named Kopi Luwak, led by a civet.

Meanwhile, a suspicious group of bats appears at the nursery for mixed-species children where Gosha volunteers...

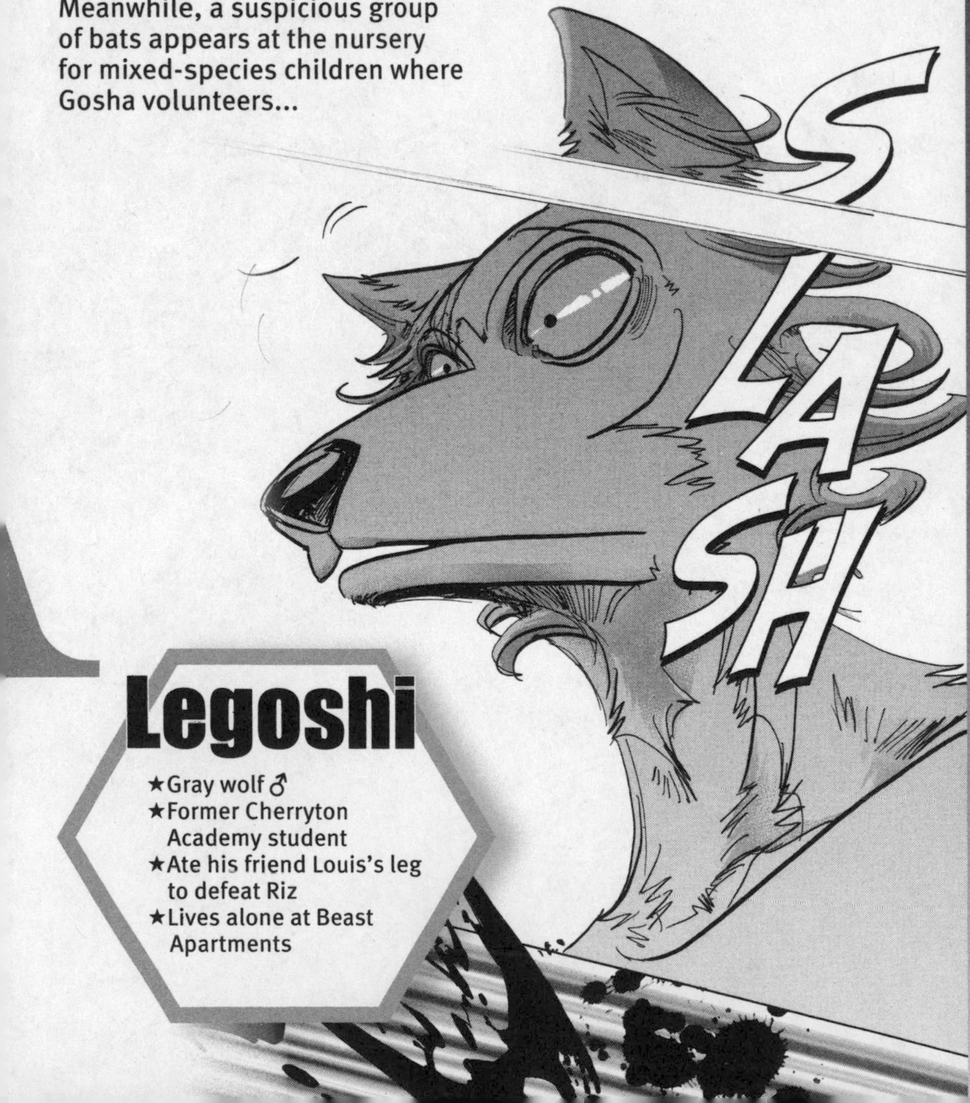
SLASH

Legoshi

- ★Gray wolf ♂
- ★Former Cherryton Academy student
- ★Ate his friend Louis's leg to defeat Riz
- ★Lives alone at Beast Apartments

Louis

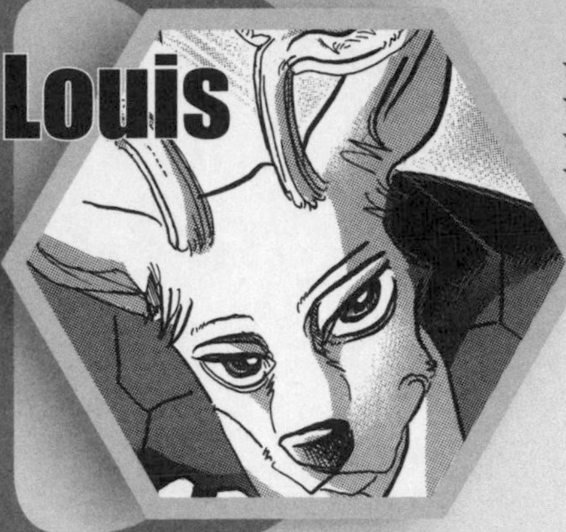

★Red deer ♂
★Former leader of the Drama Club actors pool
★Former leader of the Shishi-gumi lion gang
★Offered his leg to Legoshi so he could defeat Ri

Haru

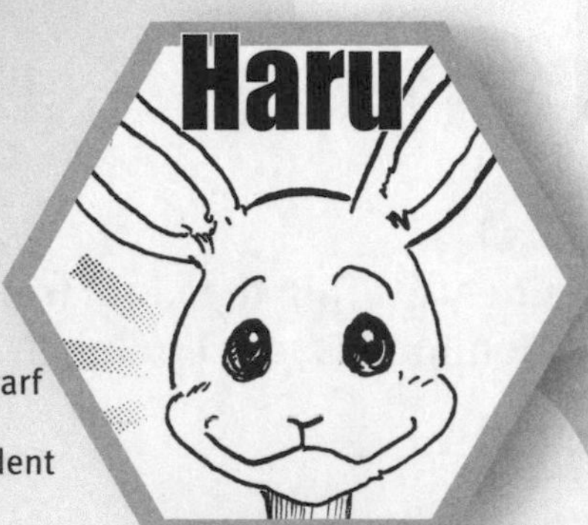

★Netherland dwarf rabbit ♀
★University student

Sagwan

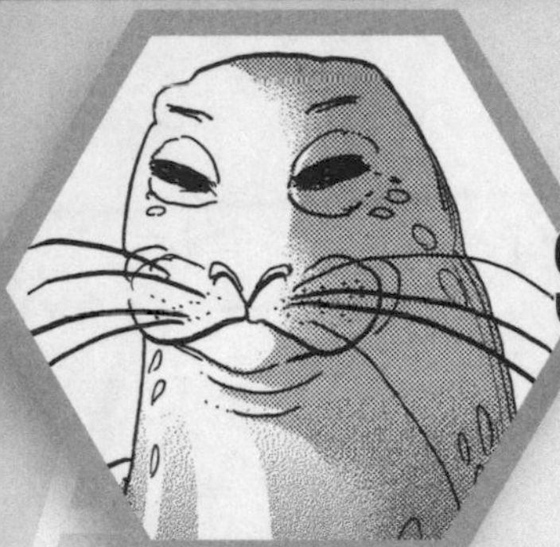

★Spotted seal ♂
★A half-marine, half-land animal
★Resident of Beast Apartments

Yahya

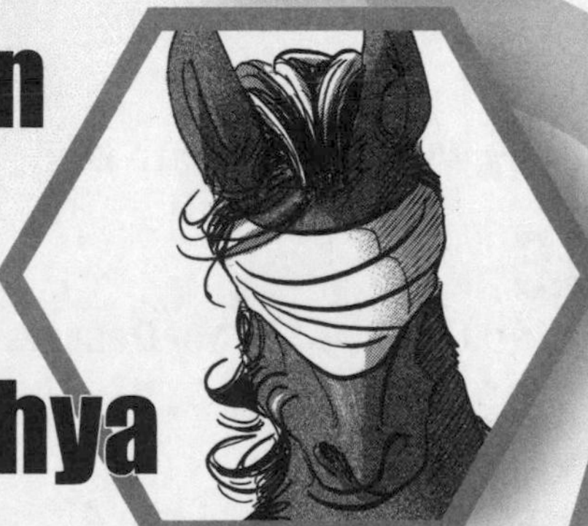

★Horse ♂
★Current Beastar
★Powerful combatant

Gosha

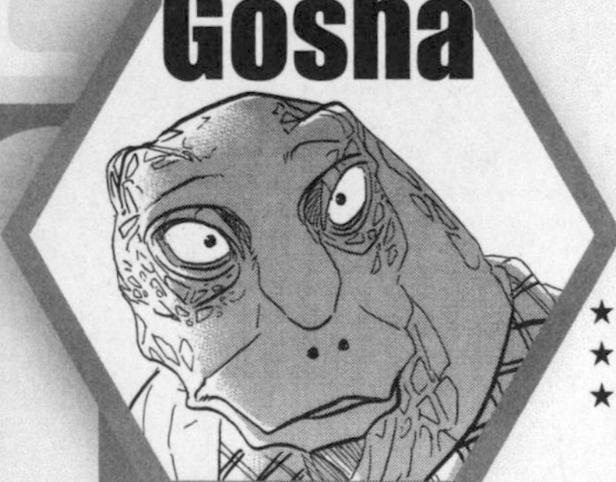

★Komodo dragon ♂
★Legoshi's grandfather
★Has a history with Beastar Yahya

Melon

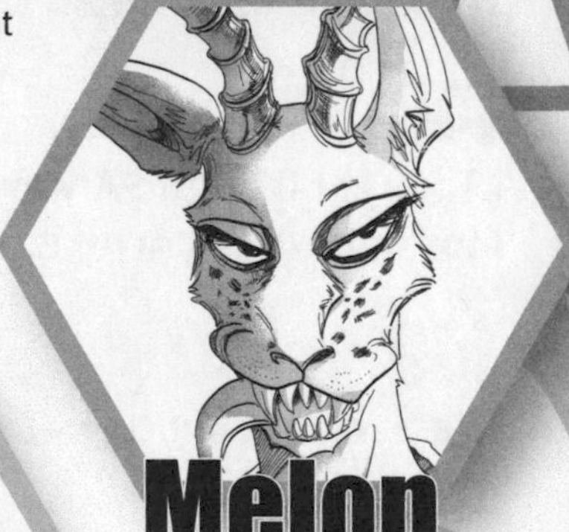

★Half-leopard, half-gazelle ♂
★Elephant poacher who sells tusks on the black market

Leanno

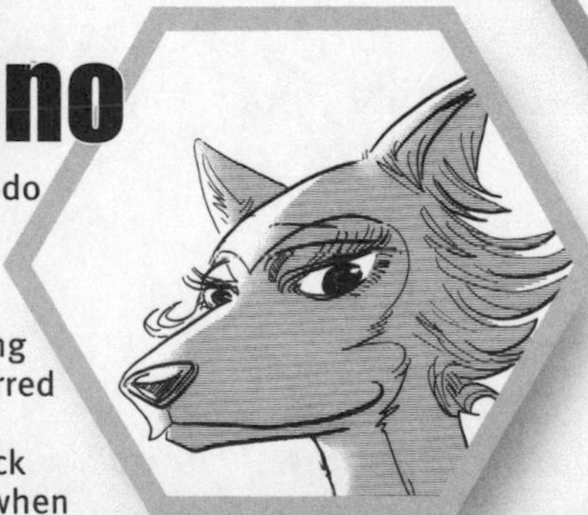

★Half-wolf, half Komodo dragon ♀
★Legoshi's beautiful mother
★Believed her stunning wolf beauty was marred when lizard scales appeared on her back
★Committed suicide when Legoshi was 12

BEASTARS
Volume 17

CONTENTS

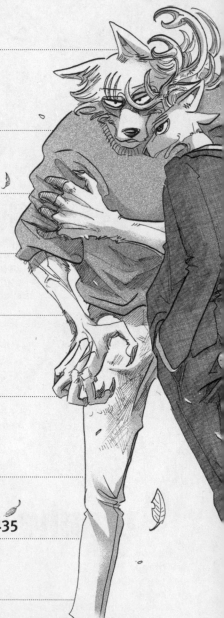

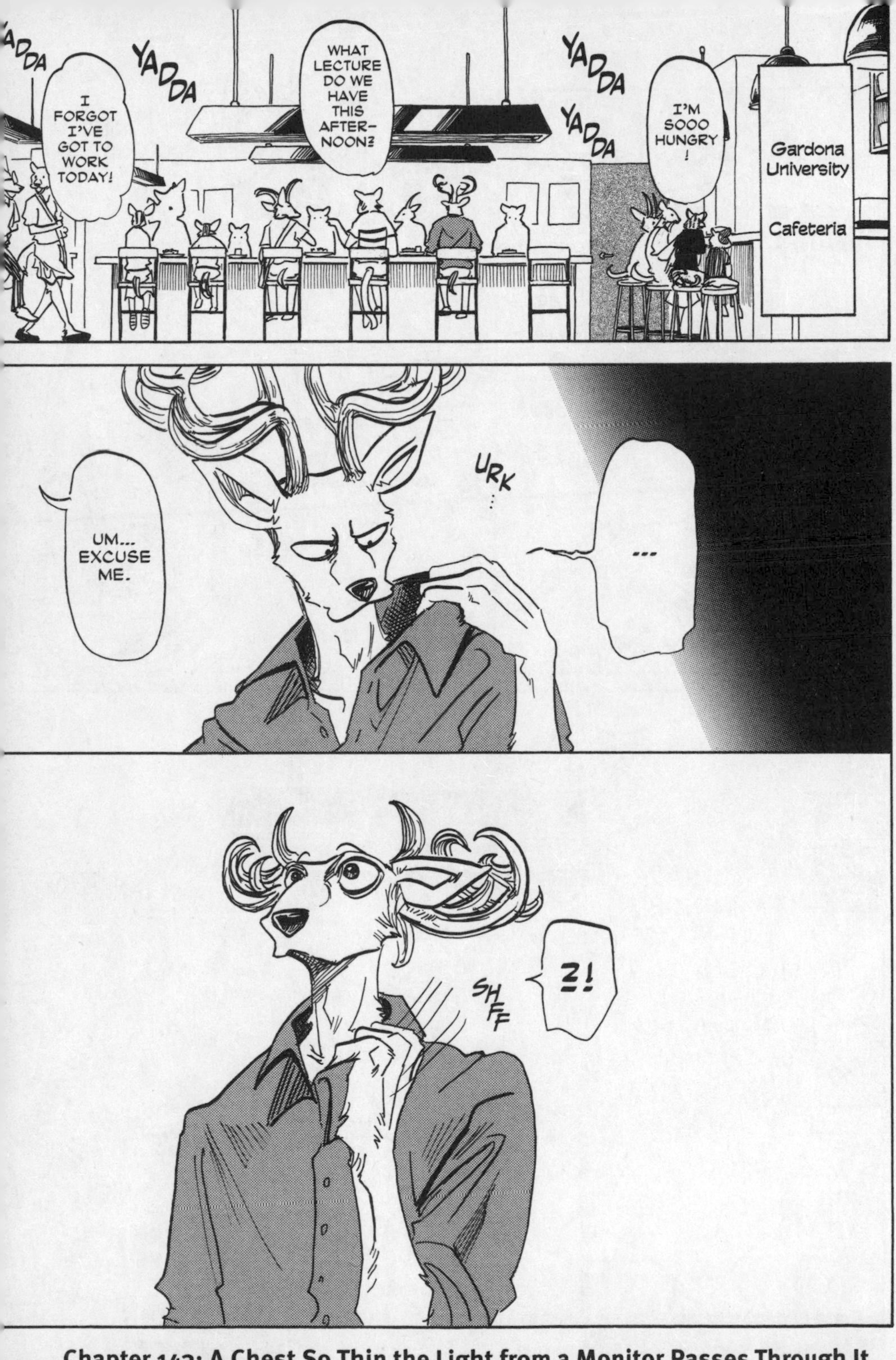
Gardona University Cafeteria
I'M SOOO HUNGRY!
YADDA
YADDA
WHAT LECTURE DO WE HAVE THIS AFTERNOON?
YADDA
I FORGOT I'VE GOT TO WORK TODAY!
YADDA
...
URK...
UM... EXCUSE ME.
?!
SHFF

Chapter 143: A Chest So Thin the Light from a Monitor Passes Through It

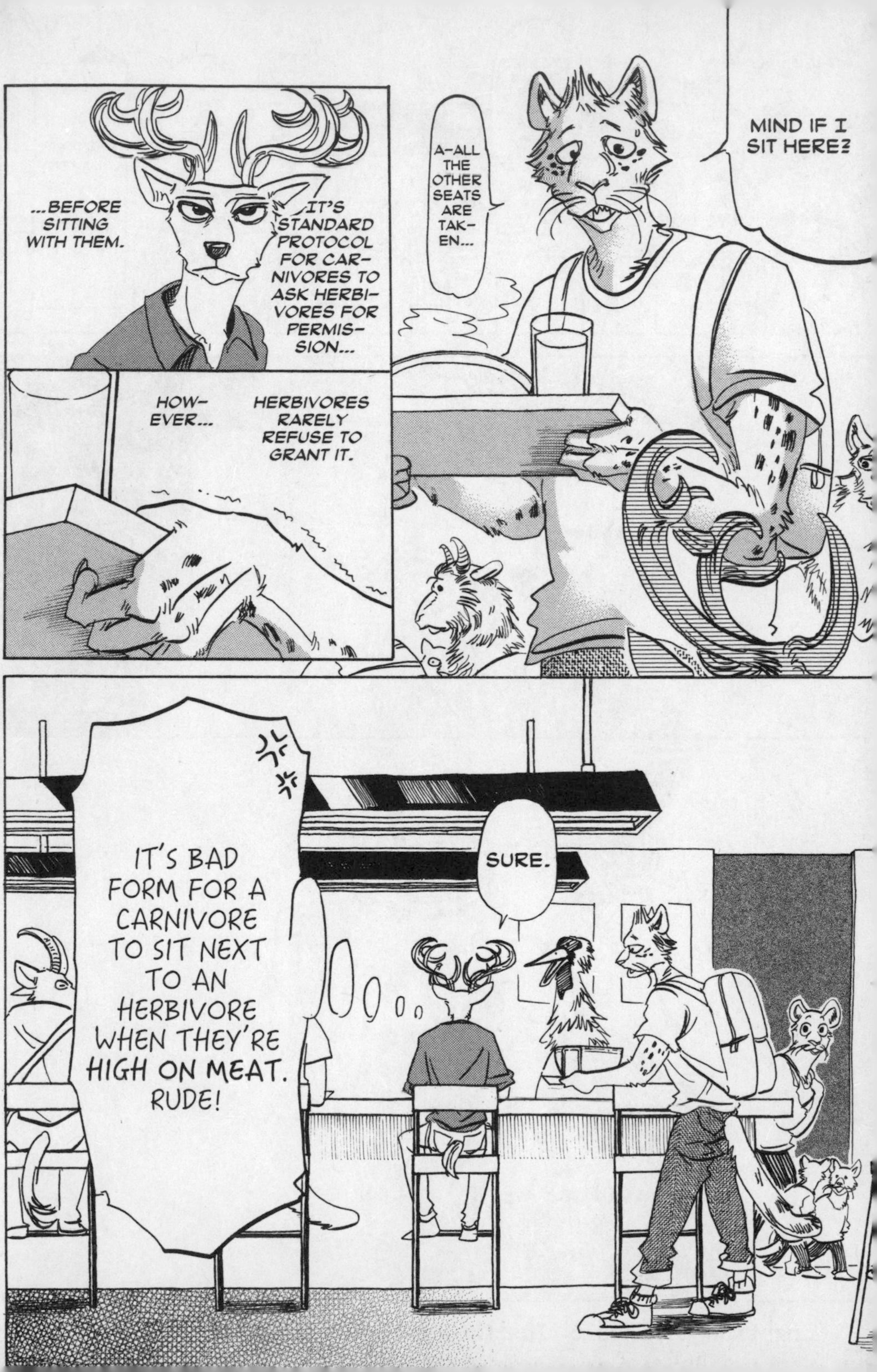
MIND IF I SIT HERE?
A-ALL THE OTHER SEATS ARE TAK-EN...
IT'S STANDARD PROTOCOL FOR CAR-NIVORES TO ASK HERBI-VORES FOR PERMIS-SION...
...BEFORE SITTING WITH THEM.
HERBIVORES RARELY REFUSE TO GRANT IT.
HOW-EVER...
SURE.
IT'S BAD FORM FOR A CARNIVORE TO SIT NEXT TO AN HERBIVORE WHEN THEY'RE HIGH ON MEAT. RUDE!

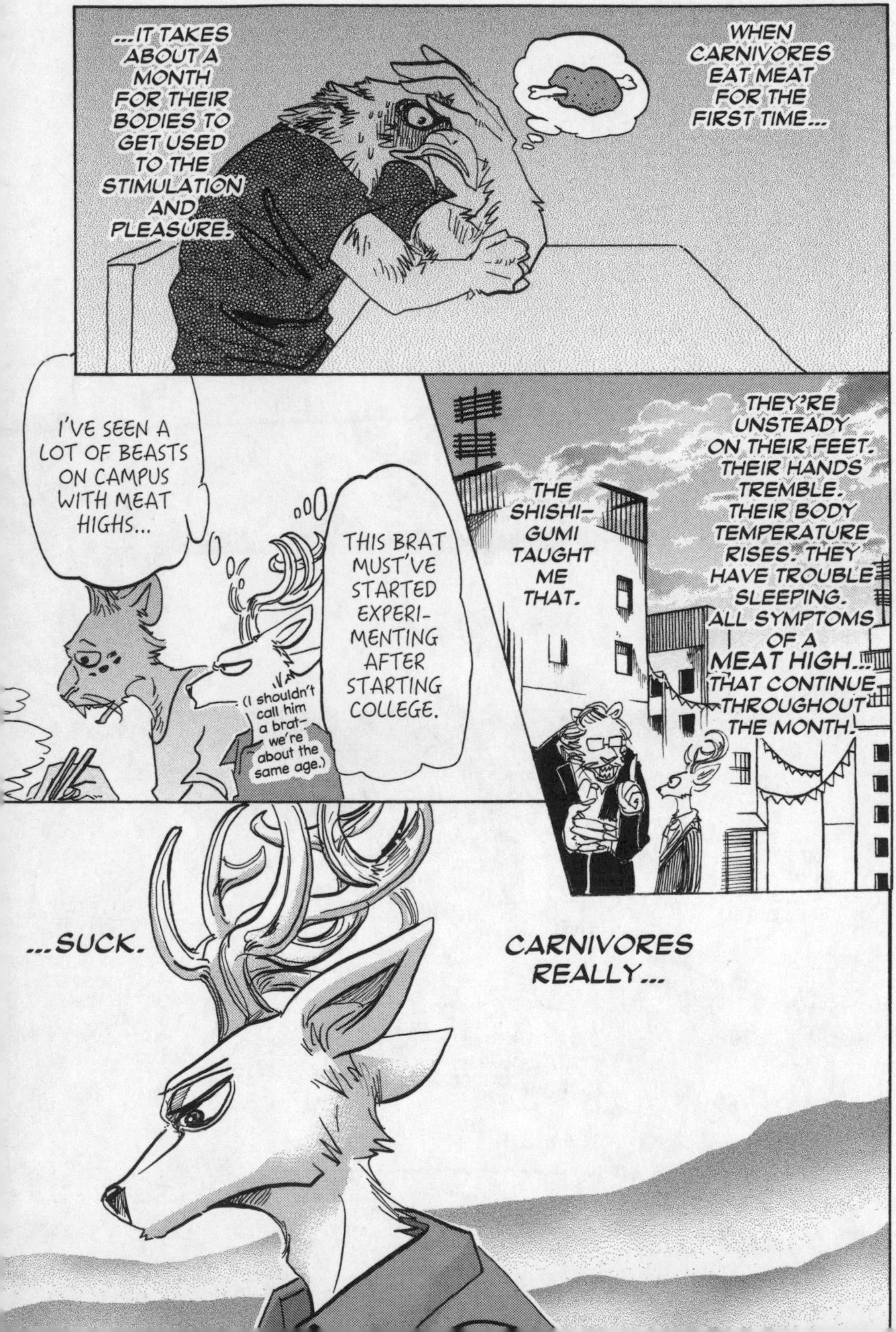
WHEN CARNIVORES EAT MEAT FOR THE FIRST TIME...
...IT TAKES ABOUT A MONTH FOR THEIR BODIES TO GET USED TO THE STIMULATION AND PLEASURE.
THEY'RE UNSTEADY ON THEIR FEET. THEIR HANDS TREMBLE. THEIR BODY TEMPERATURE RISES. THEY HAVE TROUBLE SLEEPING. ALL SYMPTOMS OF A MEAT HIGH... THAT CONTINUE THROUGHOUT THE MONTH.
THE SHISHI-GUMI TAUGHT ME THAT.
I'VE SEEN A LOT OF BEASTS ON CAMPUS WITH MEAT HIGHS...
THIS BRAT MUST'VE STARTED EXPERI-MENTING AFTER STARTING COLLEGE.
(I shouldn't call him a brat- we're about the same age.)
CARNIVORES REALLY...
...SUCK.

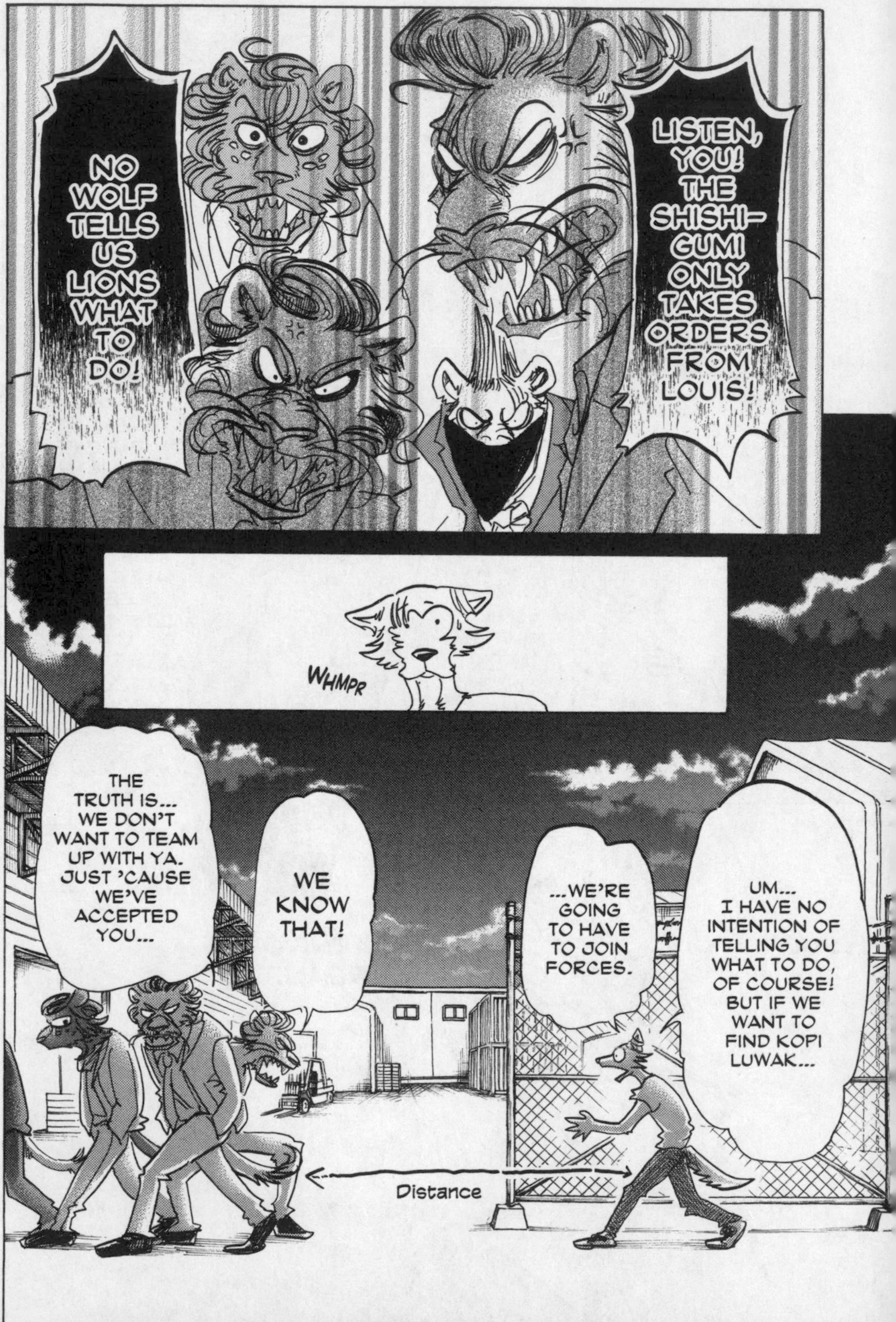
LISTEN, YOU! THE SHISHI-GUMI ONLY TAKES ORDERS FROM LOUIS!
NO WOLF TELLS US LIONS WHAT TO DO!
WHMPR
UM... I HAVE NO INTENTION OF TELLING YOU WHAT TO DO, OF COURSE! BUT IF WE WANT TO FIND KOPI LUWAK...
...WE'RE GOING TO HAVE TO JOIN FORCES.
WE KNOW THAT!
THE TRUTH IS... WE DON'T WANT TO TEAM UP WITH YA. JUST 'CAUSE WE'VE ACCEPTED YOU...
Distance

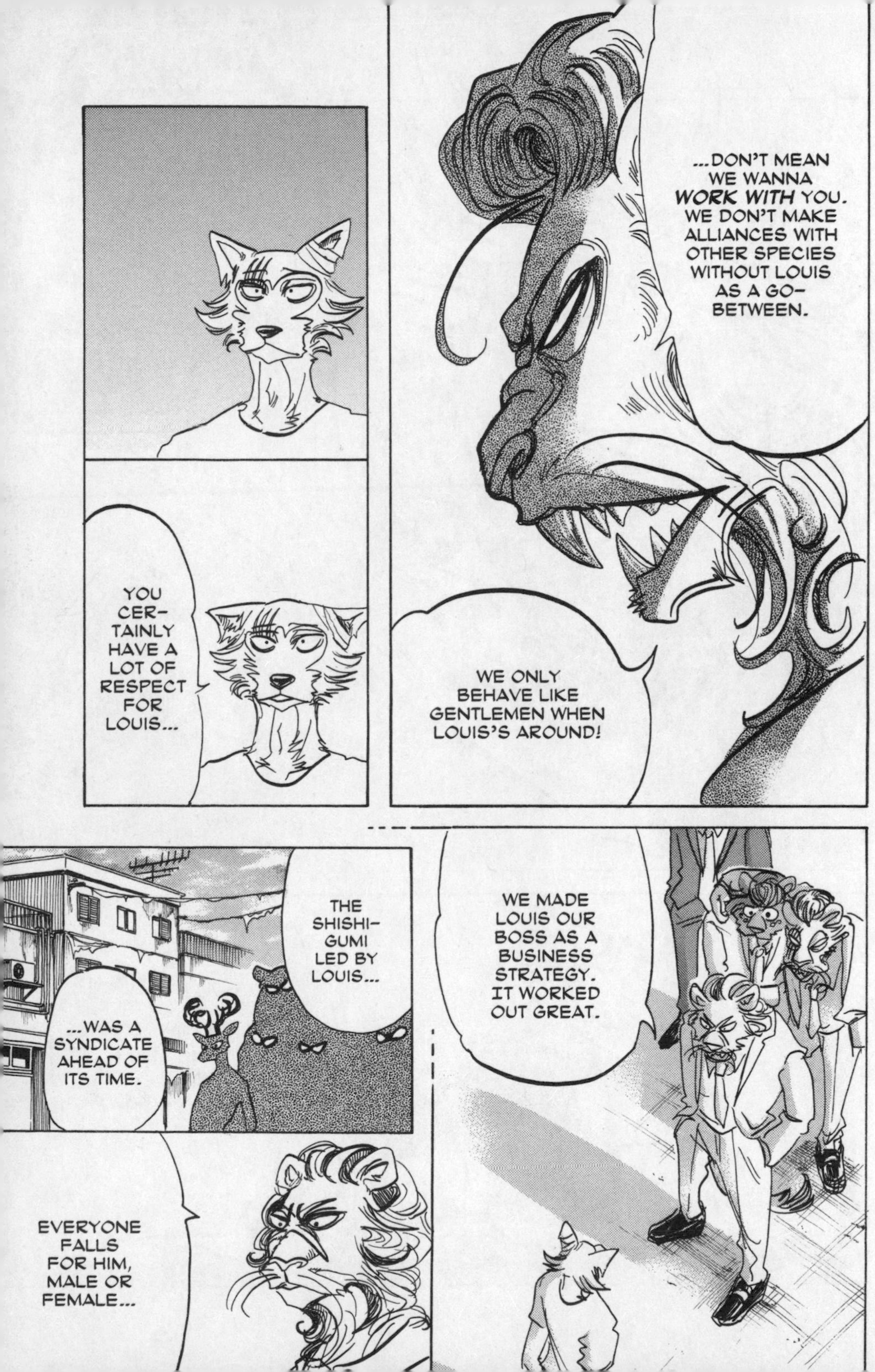
...DON'T MEAN WE WANNA **WORK WITH** YOU. WE DON'T MAKE ALLIANCES WITH OTHER SPECIES WITHOUT LOUIS AS A GO-BETWEEN.
WE ONLY BEHAVE LIKE GENTLEMEN WHEN LOUIS'S AROUND!
YOU CERTAINLY HAVE A LOT OF RESPECT FOR LOUIS...
WE MADE LOUIS OUR BOSS AS A BUSINESS STRATEGY. IT WORKED OUT GREAT.
THE SHISHI-GUMI LED BY LOUIS...
...WAS A SYNDICATE AHEAD OF ITS TIME.
EVERYONE FALLS FOR HIM, MALE OR FEMALE...

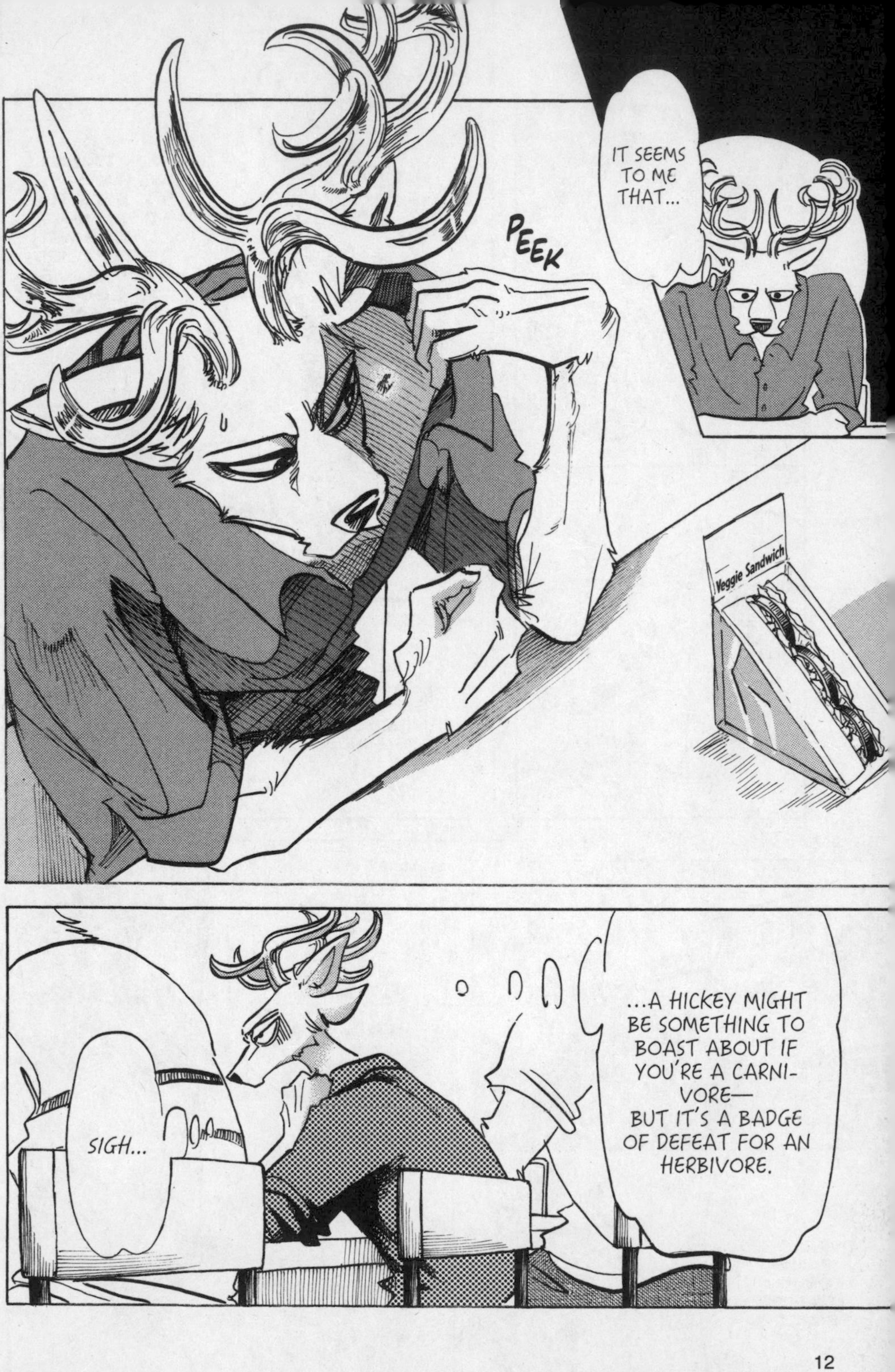
IT SEEMS TO ME THAT...
PEEK
Veggie Sandwich
...A HICKEY MIGHT BE SOMETHING TO BOAST ABOUT IF YOU'RE A CARNI-VORE— BUT IT'S A BADGE OF DEFEAT FOR AN HERBIVORE.
SIGH...

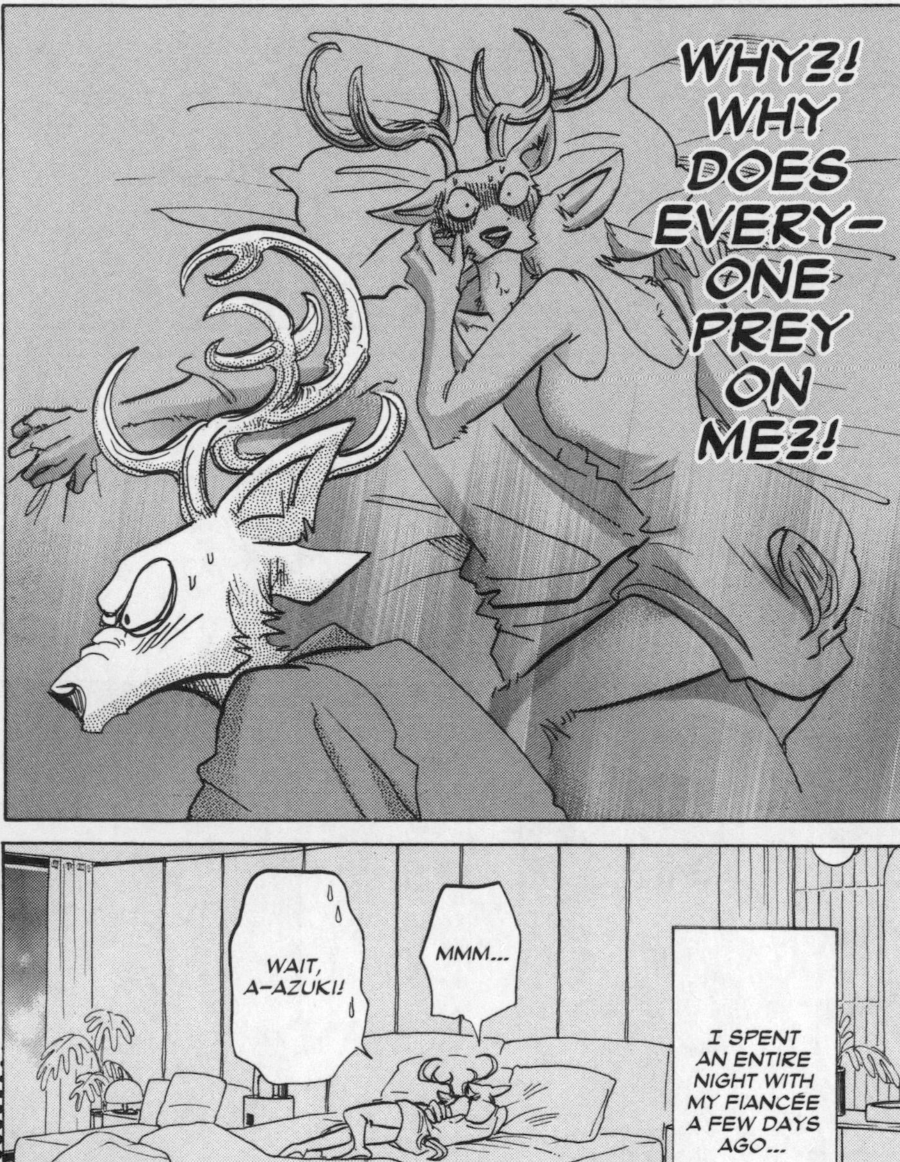
WHY?! WHY DOES EVERYONE PREY ON ME?!
I SPENT AN ENTIRE NIGHT WITH MY FIANCÉE A FEW DAYS AGO...
MMM...
WAIT, A-AZUKI!

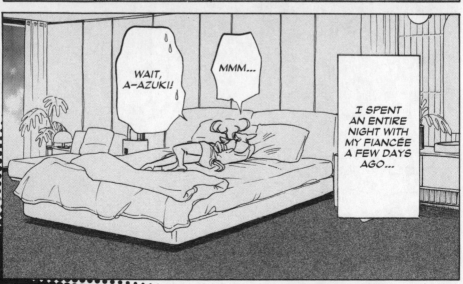

See chapter 136.

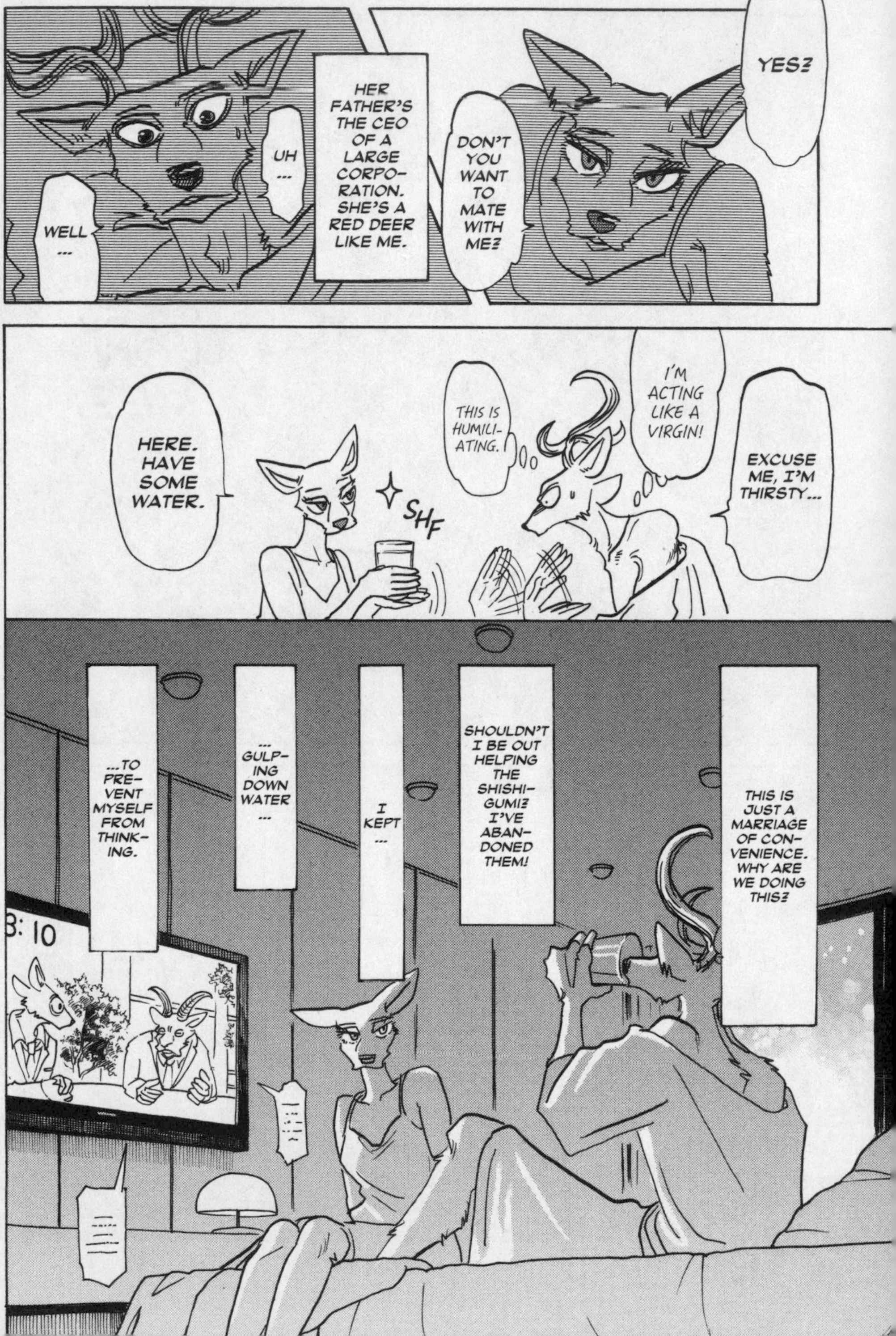
YES?
DON'T YOU WANT TO MATE WITH ME?
HER FATHER'S THE CEO OF A LARGE CORPORATION. SHE'S A RED DEER LIKE ME.
UH ...
WELL ...
EXCUSE ME, I'M THIRSTY...
I'M ACTING LIKE A VIRGIN!
THIS IS HUMILIATING.
SHF
HERE. HAVE SOME WATER.
THIS IS JUST A MARRIAGE OF CONVENIENCE. WHY ARE WE DOING THIS?
SHOULDN'T I BE OUT HELPING THE SHISHIGUMI? I'VE ABANDONED THEM!
I KEPT ...
... GULPING DOWN WATER ...
...TO PREVENT MYSELF FROM THINKING.

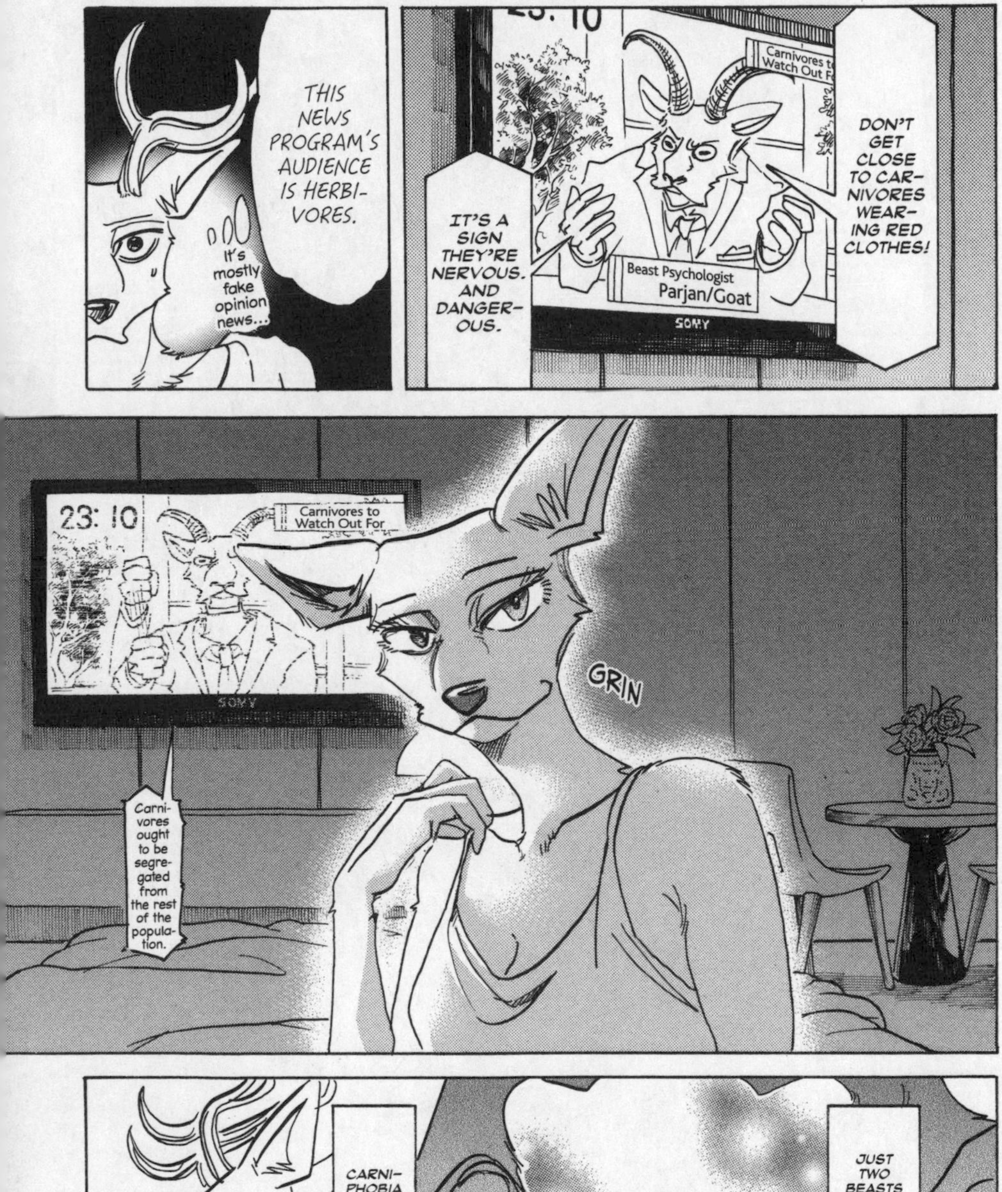
23: 10
Carnivores to Watch Out For
DON'T GET CLOSE TO CARNIVORES WEARING RED CLOTHES!
Beast Psychologist
Parjan/Goat
SONY
IT'S A SIGN THEY'RE NERVOUS. AND DANGEROUS.
THIS NEWS PROGRAM'S AUDIENCE IS HERBIVORES.
It's mostly fake opinion news...
23: 10
Carnivores to Watch Out For
SONY
GRIN
Carnivores ought to be segregated from the rest of the population.
JUST TWO BEASTS PRESSING THEIR SLENDER, FRAGILE BODIES TOGETHER ...
CARNIPHOBIA IS THE BACKGROUND MUSIC OF OUR SOCIETY ...

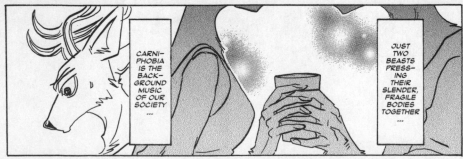

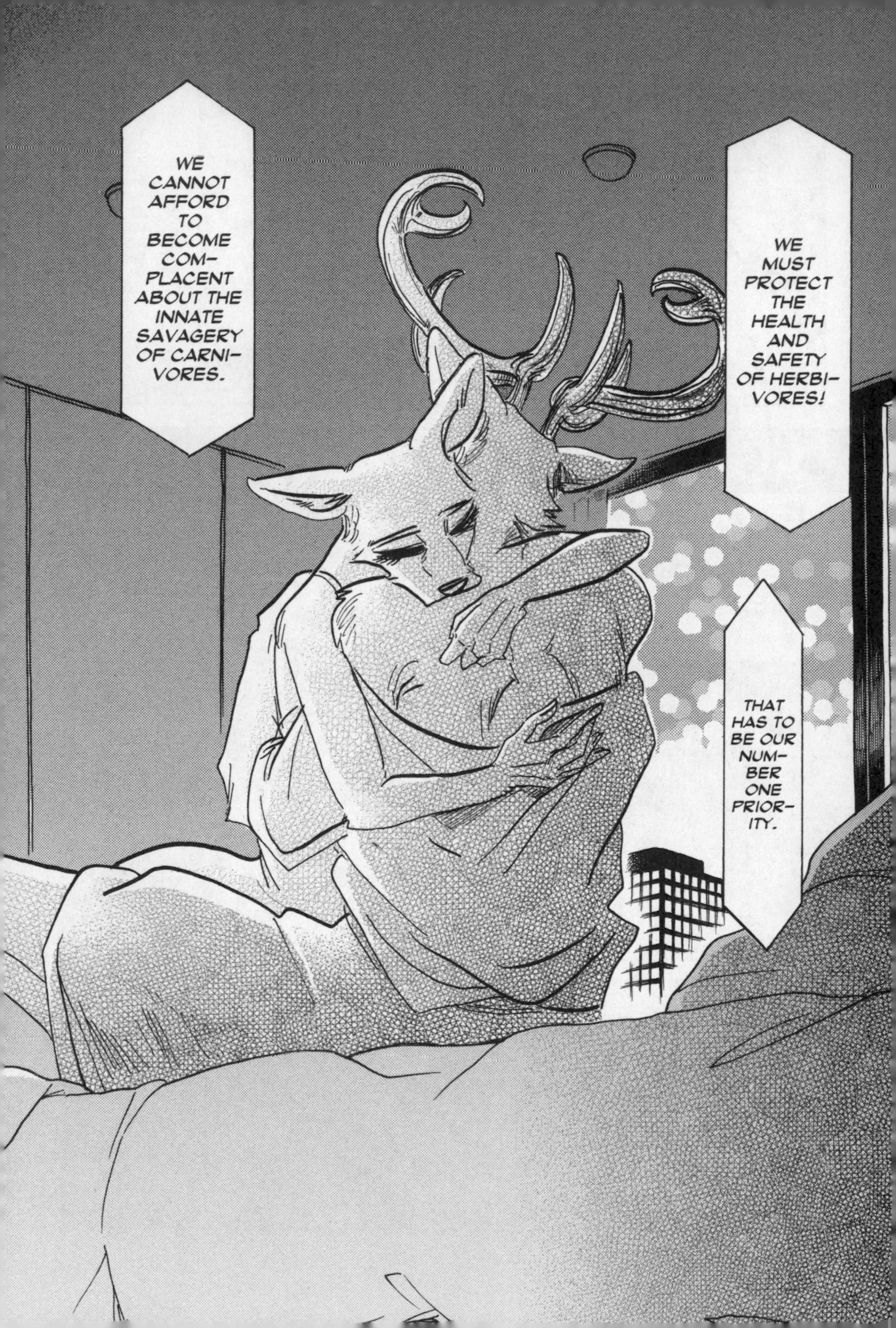
WE MUST PROTECT THE HEALTH AND SAFETY OF HERBIVORES!
WE CANNOT AFFORD TO BECOME COMPLACENT ABOUT THE INNATE SAVAGERY OF CARNIVORES.
THAT HAS TO BE OUR NUMBER ONE PRIORITY.

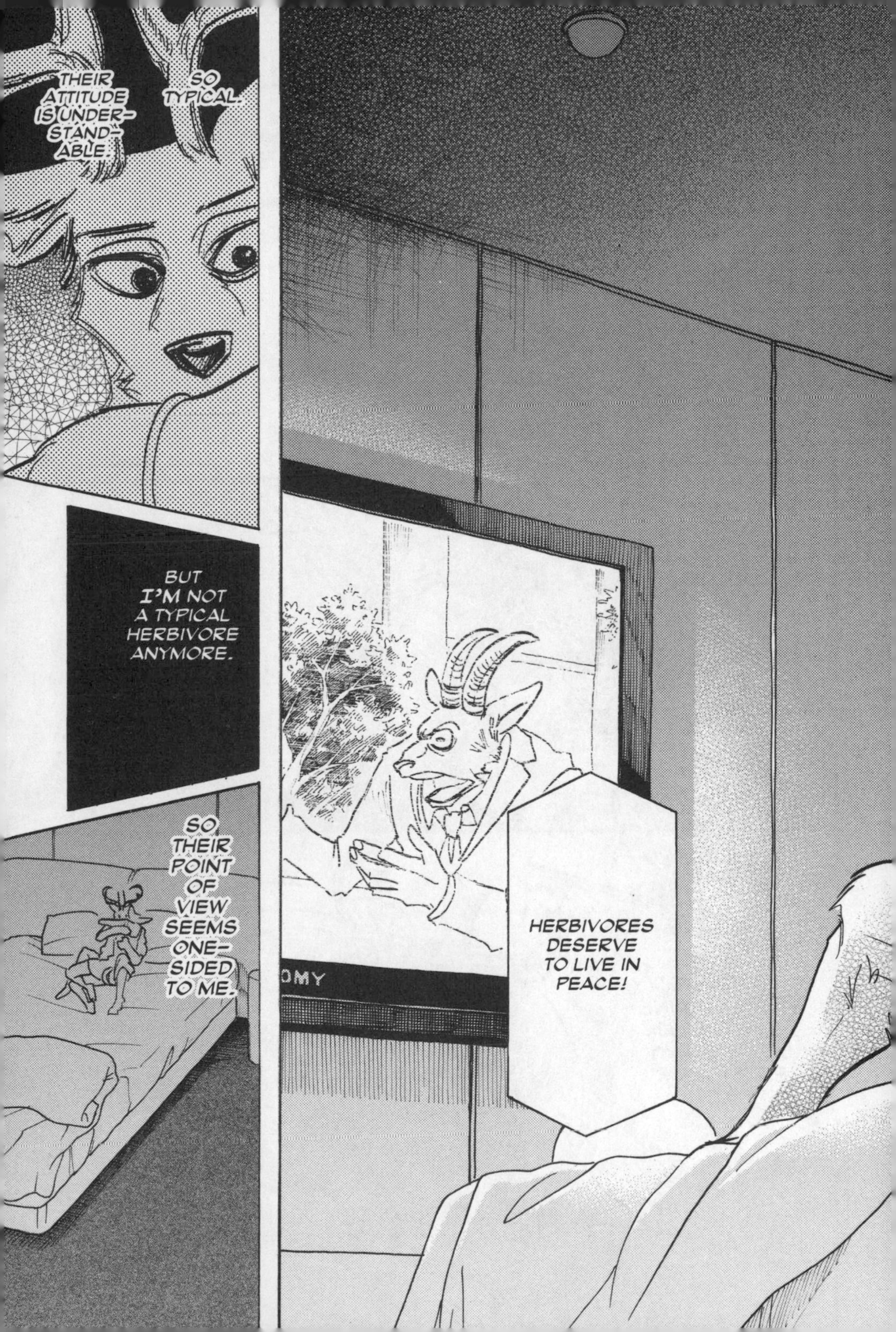
HERBIVORES DESERVE TO LIVE IN PEACE!
SO TYPICAL.
THEIR ATTITUDE IS UNDER-STAND-ABLE.
BUT I'M NOT A TYPICAL HERBIVORE ANYMORE.
SO THEIR POINT OF VIEW SEEMS ONE-SIDED TO ME.

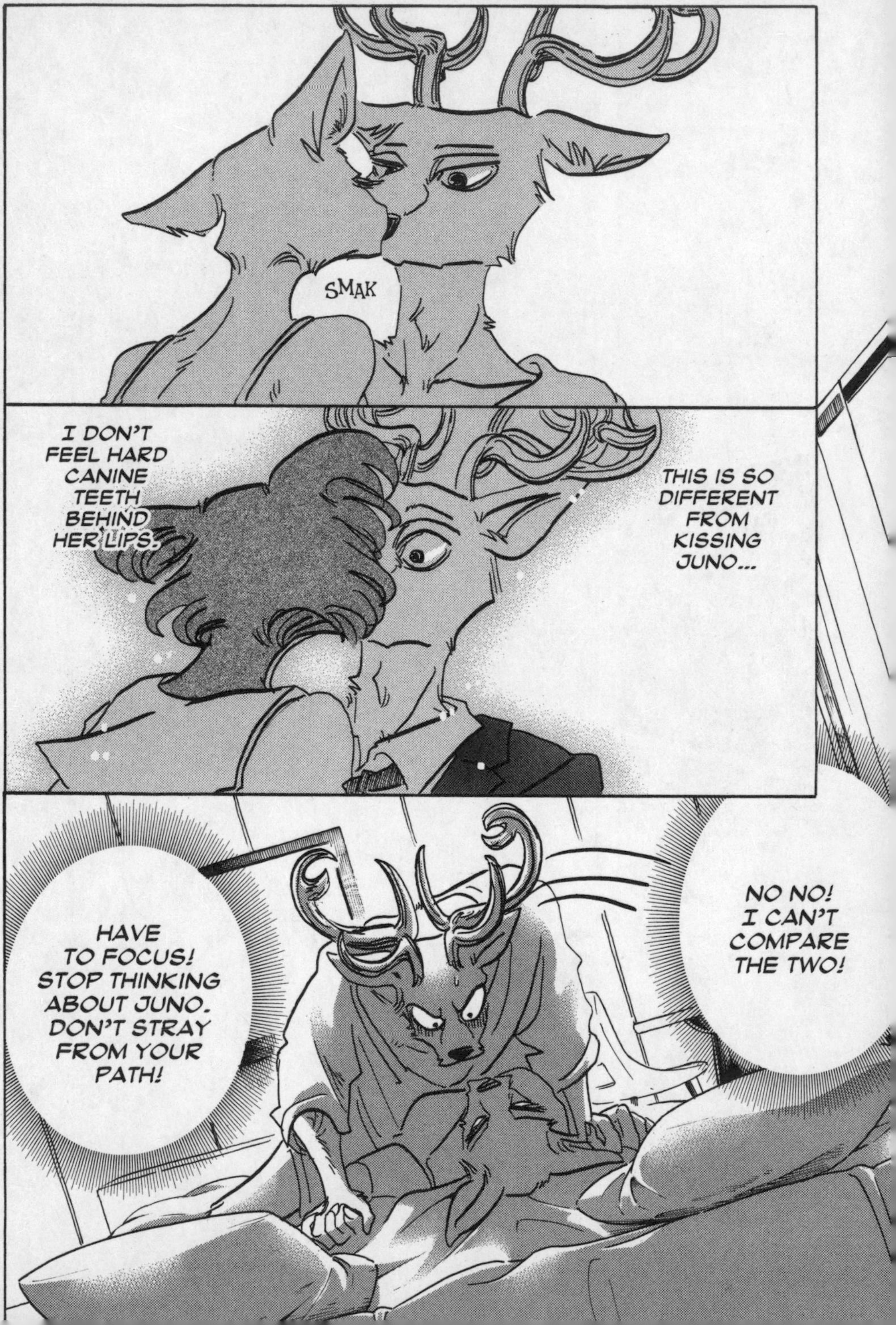
SMAK
THIS IS SO DIFFERENT FROM KISSING JUNO...
I DON'T FEEL HARD CANINE TEETH BEHIND HER LIPS.
NO NO! I CAN'T COMPARE THE TWO!
HAVE TO FOCUS! STOP THINKING ABOUT JUNO. DON'T STRAY FROM YOUR PATH!

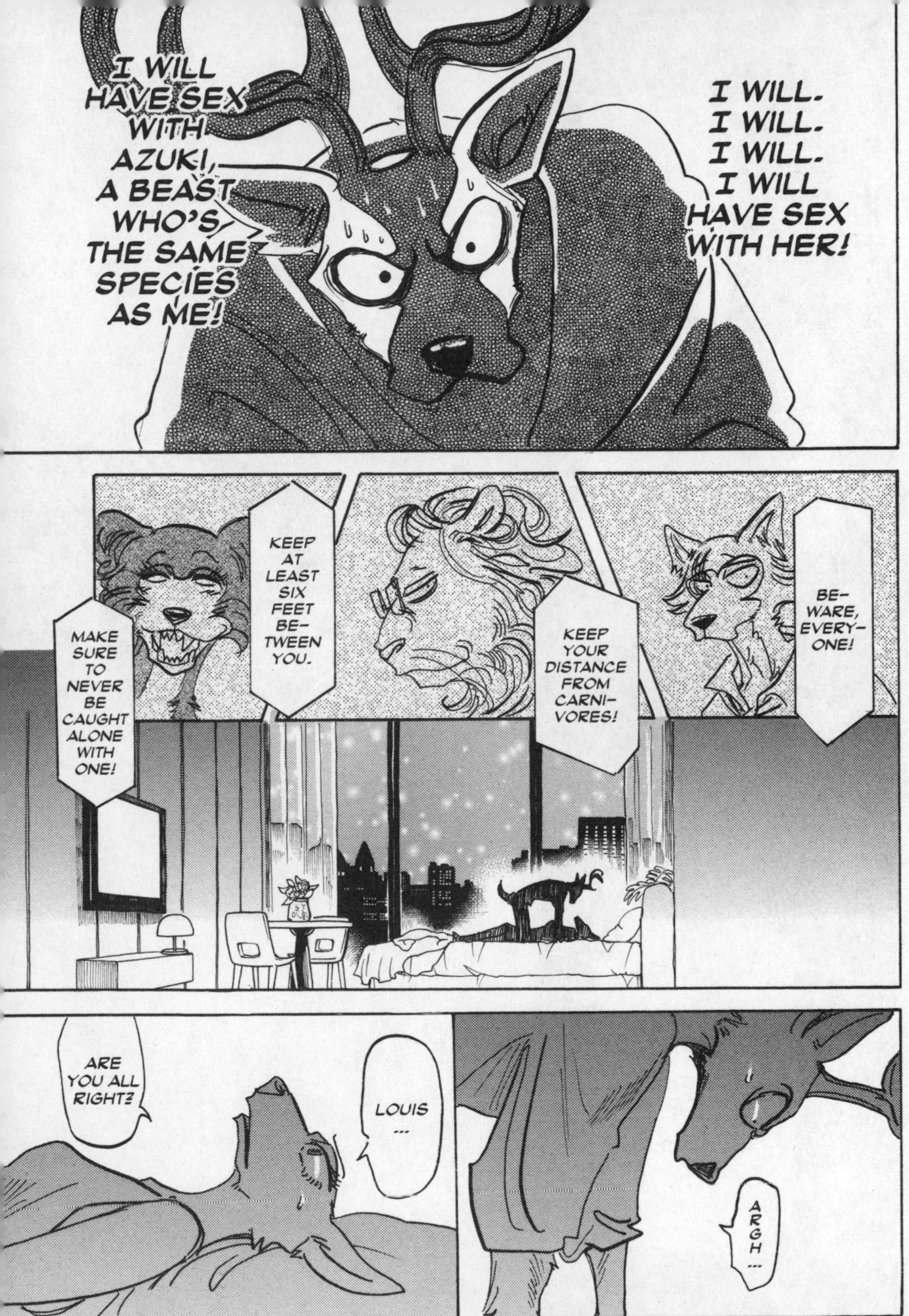
I WILL. I WILL. I WILL. I WILL HAVE SEX WITH HER!
I WILL HAVE SEX WITH AZUKI, A BEAST WHO'S THE SAME SPECIES AS ME!
BE-WARE, EVERY-ONE!
KEEP YOUR DISTANCE FROM CARNI-VORES!
KEEP AT LEAST SIX FEET BE-TWEEN YOU.
MAKE SURE TO NEVER BE CAUGHT ALONE WITH ONE!
ARGH...
LOUIS...
ARE YOU ALL RIGHT?

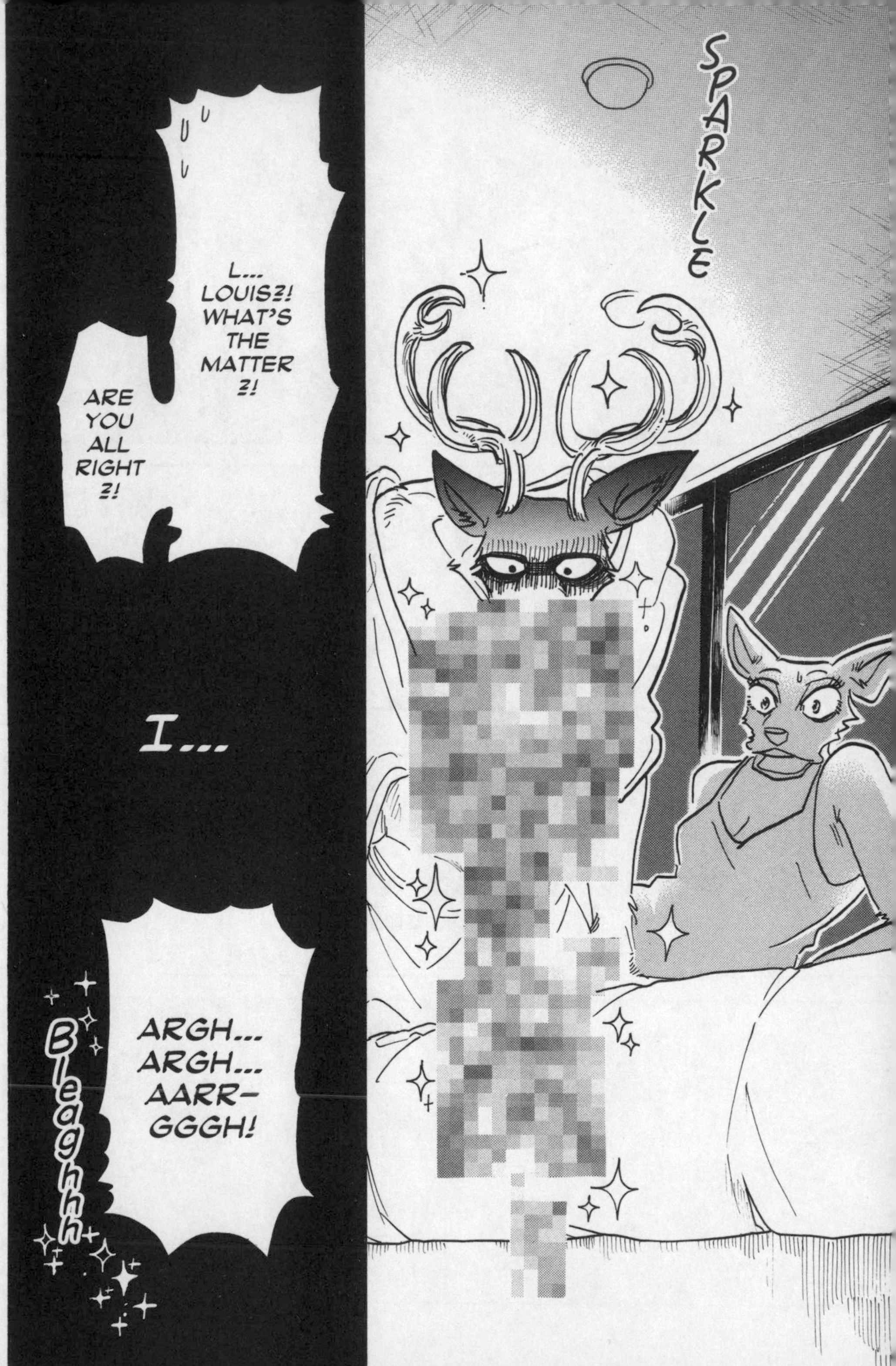
SPARKLE
L... LOUIS?! WHAT'S THE MATTER?!
ARE YOU ALL RIGHT?!
I...
ARGH... ARGH... AARR-GGGH!
Bleaghhh

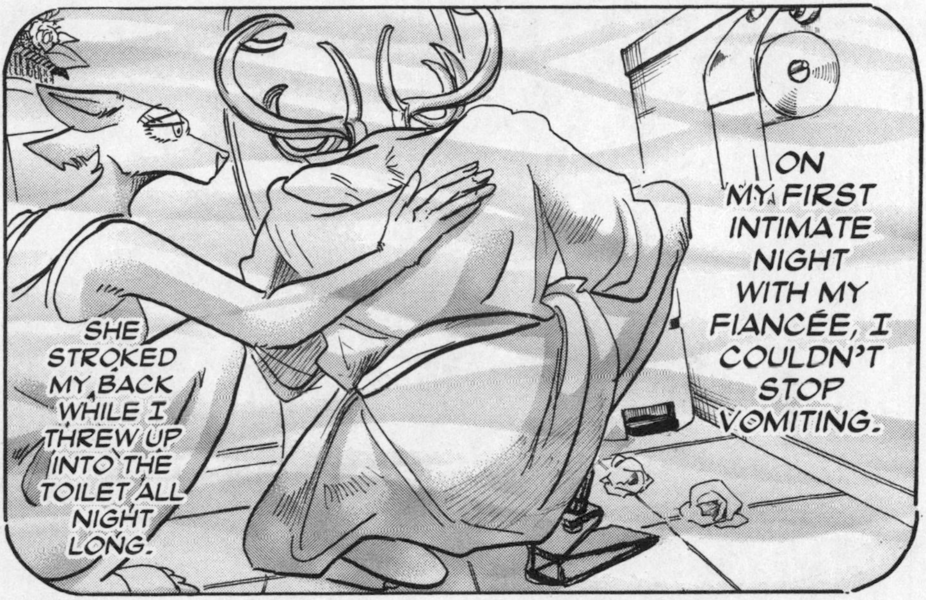
ON MY FIRST INTIMATE NIGHT WITH MY FIANCÉE, I COULDN'T STOP VOMITING.
SHE STROKED MY BACK WHILE I THREW UP INTO THE TOILET ALL NIGHT LONG.
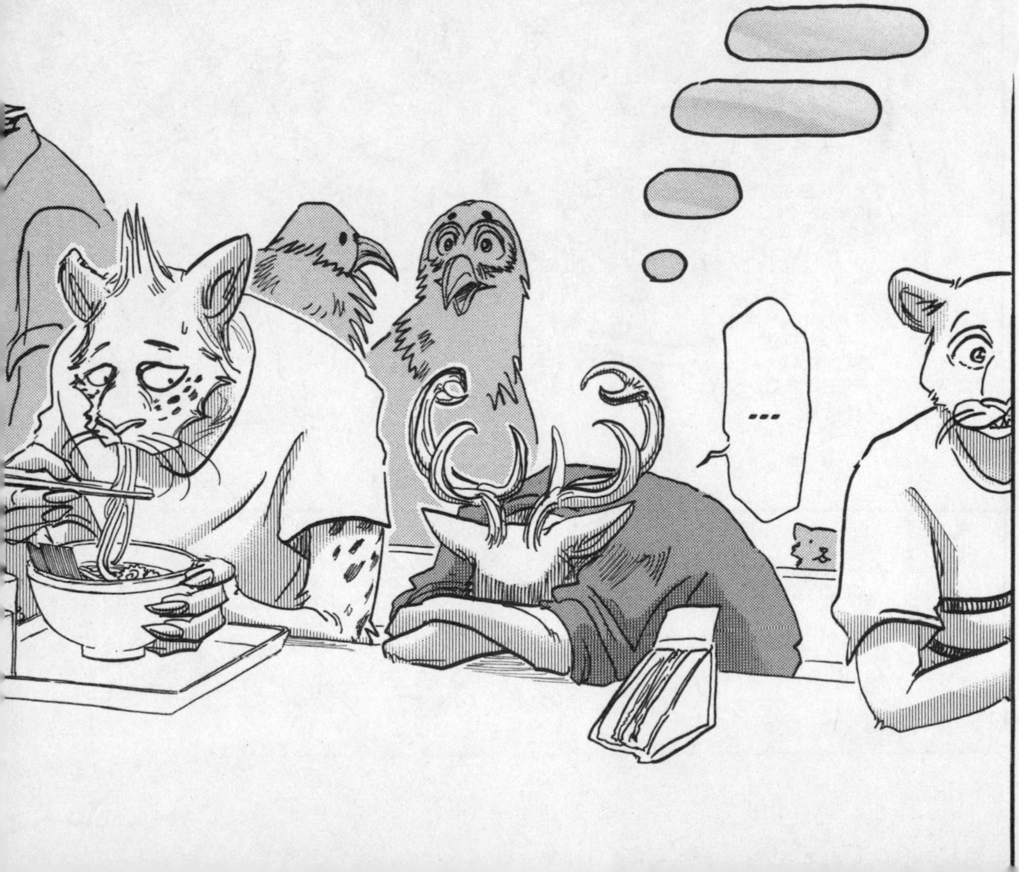
...

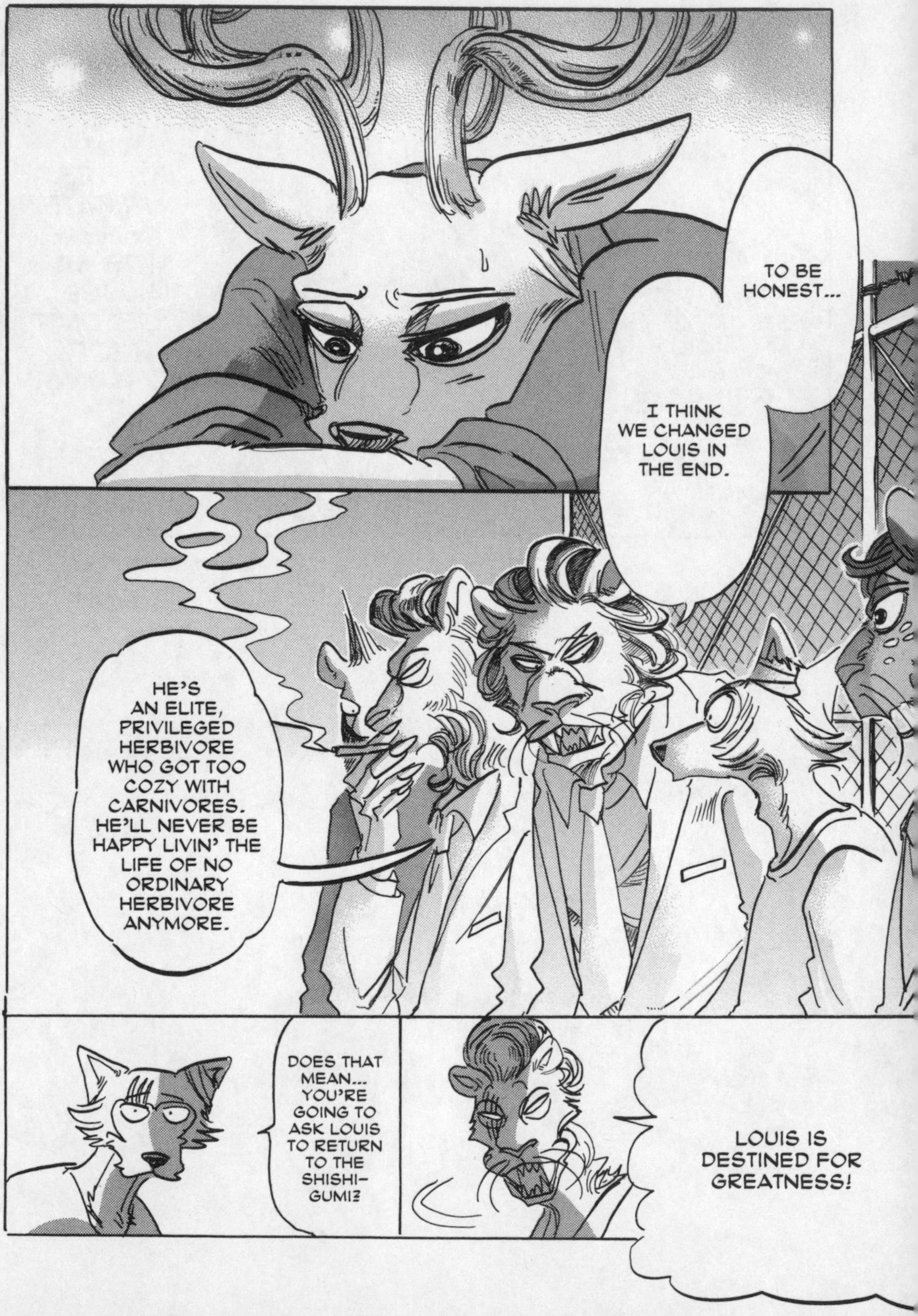
TO BE HONEST...
I THINK WE CHANGED LOUIS IN THE END.
HE'S AN ELITE, PRIVILEGED HERBIVORE WHO GOT TOO COZY WITH CARNIVORES. HE'LL NEVER BE HAPPY LIVIN' THE LIFE OF NO ORDINARY HERBIVORE ANYMORE.
LOUIS IS DESTINED FOR GREATNESS!
DOES THAT MEAN... YOU'RE GOING TO ASK LOUIS TO RETURN TO THE SHISHI-GUMI?

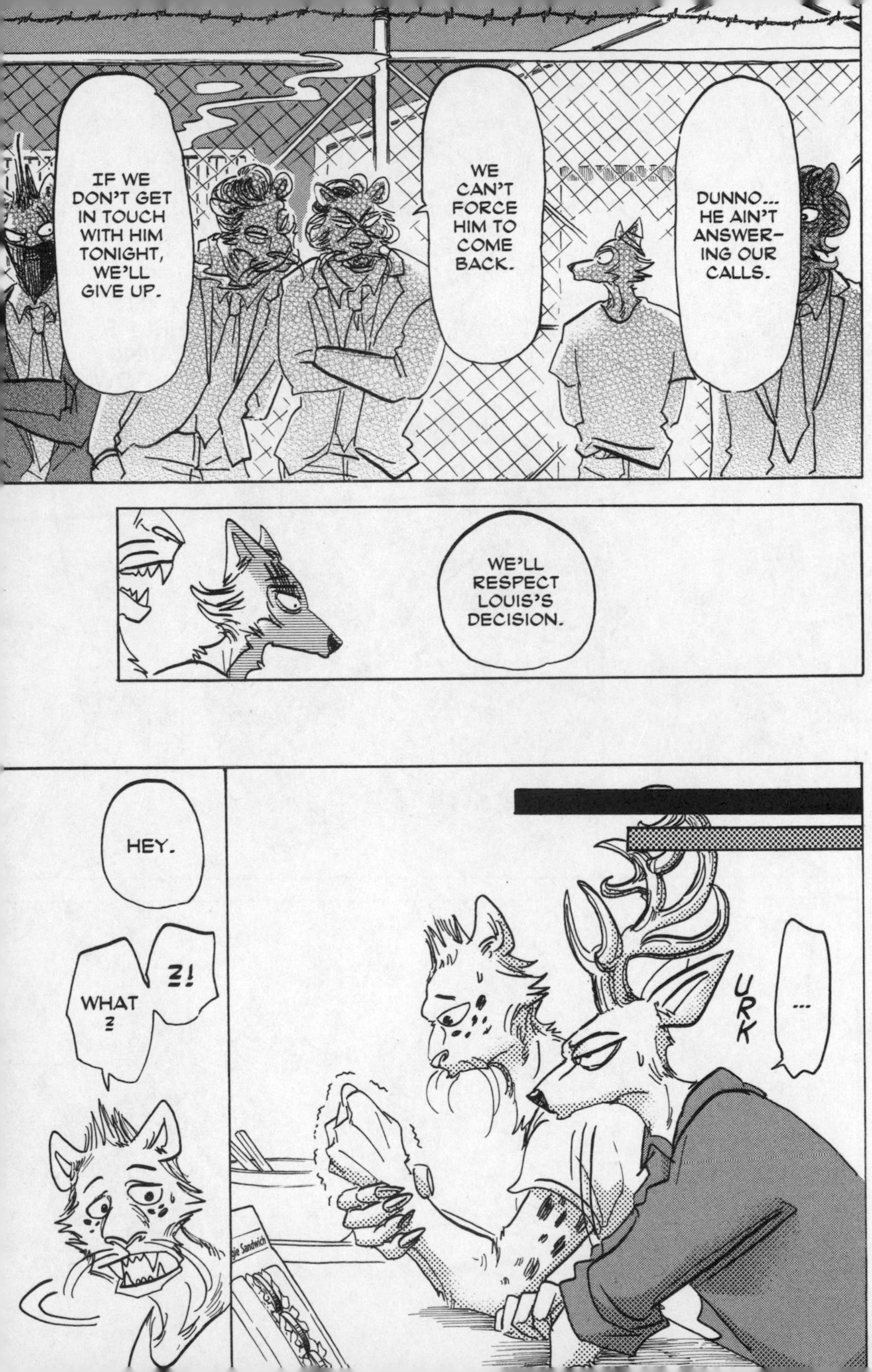
DUNNO... HE AIN'T ANSWER-ING OUR CALLS.
WE CAN'T FORCE HIM TO COME BACK.
IF WE DON'T GET IN TOUCH WITH HIM TONIGHT, WE'LL GIVE UP.
WE'LL RESPECT LOUIS'S DECISION.
...
URK
HEY.
WHAT?!

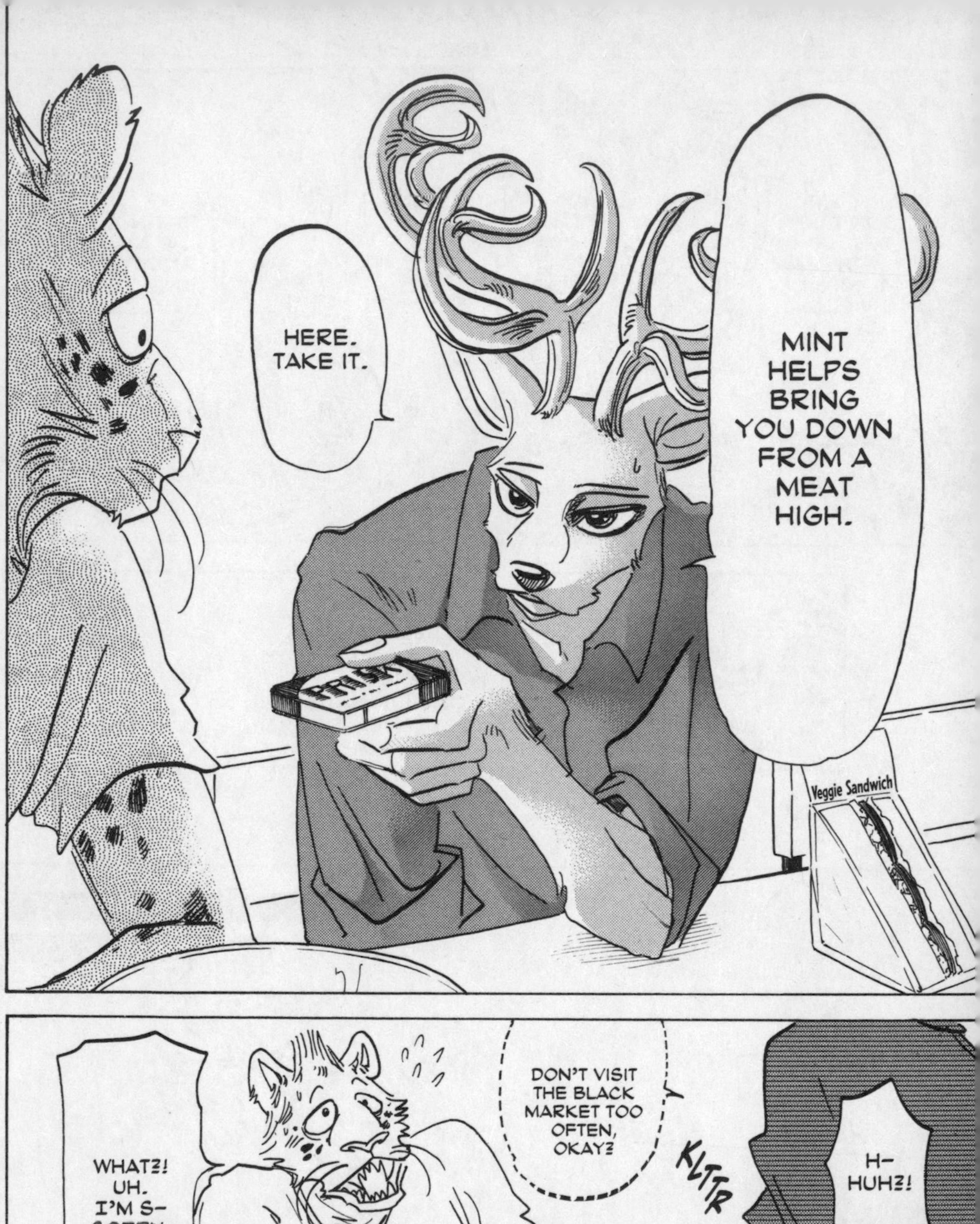
MINT HELPS BRING YOU DOWN FROM A MEAT HIGH.
HERE. TAKE IT.
Veggie Sandwich
H-HUH?!
KLTTR
DON'T VISIT THE BLACK MARKET TOO OFTEN, OKAY?
WHAT?! UH. I'M S-SORRY. THANK YOU...

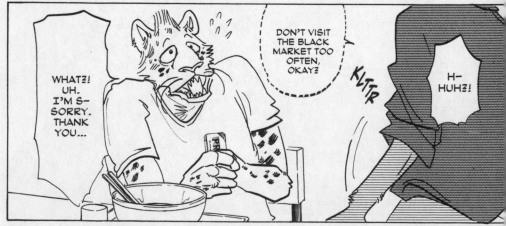

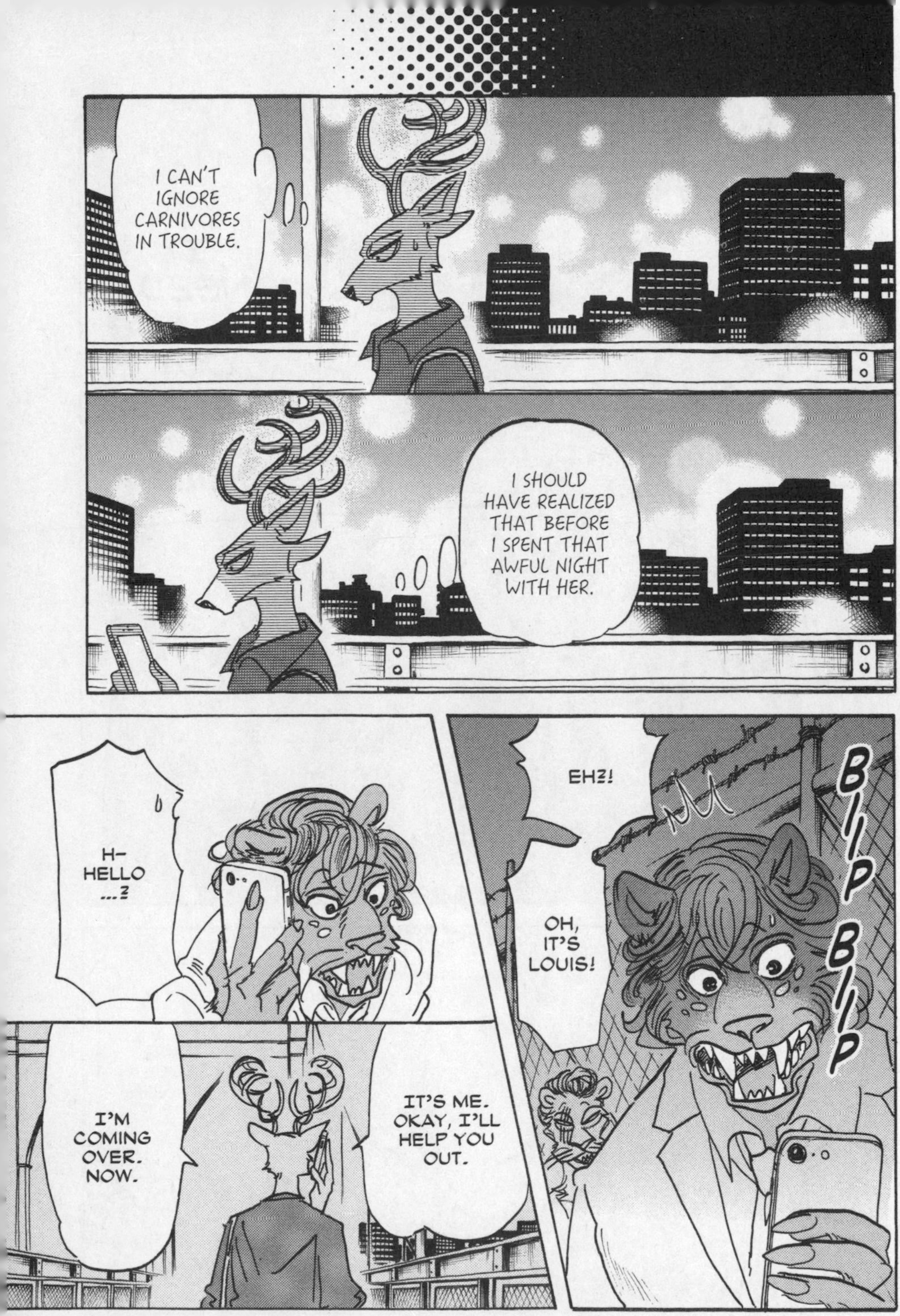
I CAN'T IGNORE CARNIVORES IN TROUBLE.
I SHOULD HAVE REALIZED THAT BEFORE I SPENT THAT AWFUL NIGHT WITH HER.
BIIP BIIP
EH?!
OH, IT'S LOUIS!
H-HELLO...?
IT'S ME. OKAY, I'LL HELP YOU OUT.
I'M COMING OVER. NOW.

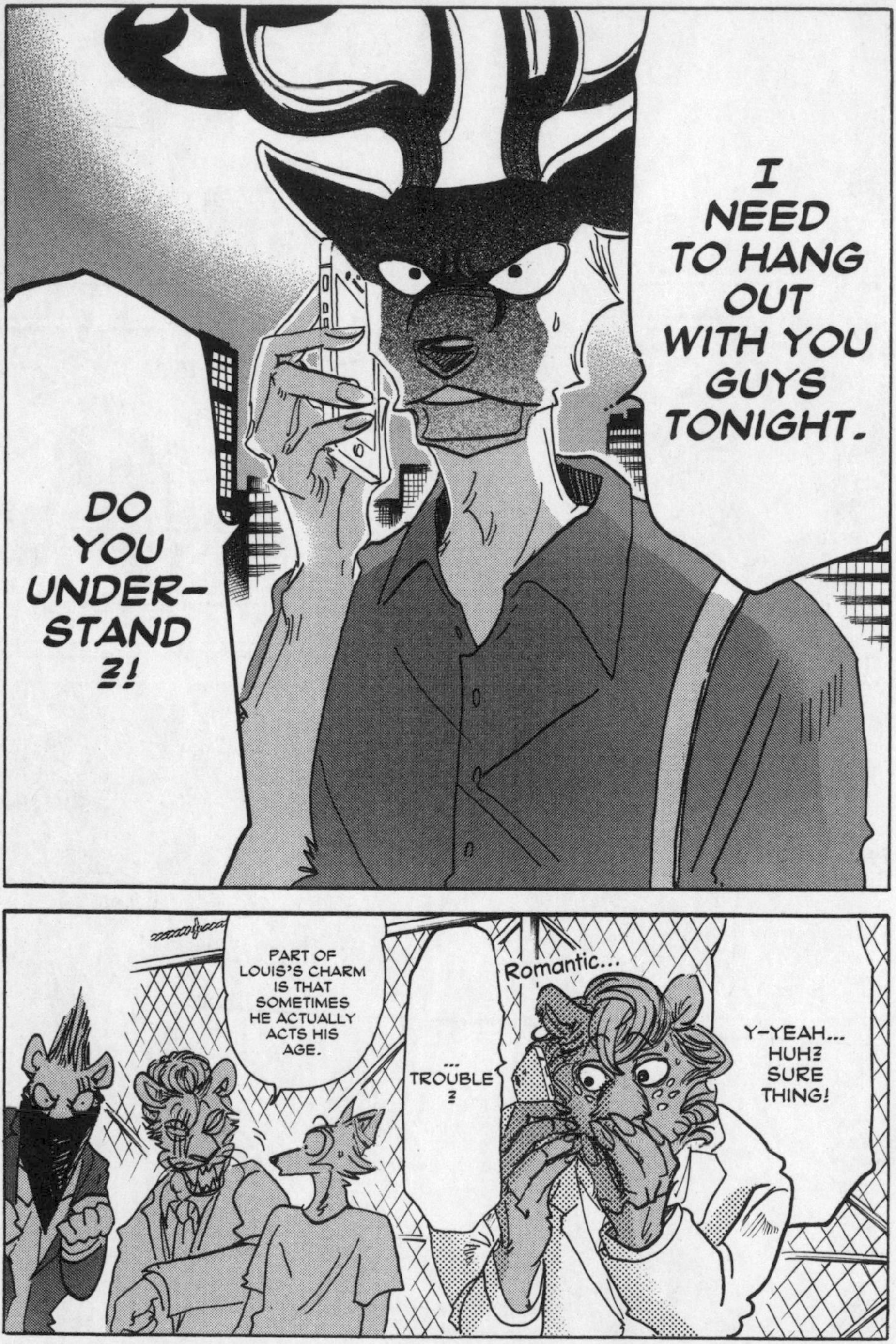
I NEED TO HANG OUT WITH YOU GUYS TONIGHT.
DO YOU UNDER-STAND?!
Y-YEAH... HUH? SURE THING!
Romantic...
PART OF LOUIS'S CHARM IS THAT SOMETIMES HE ACTUALLY ACTS HIS AGE.
...TROUBLE?

Chapter 144: I Am a Felidae

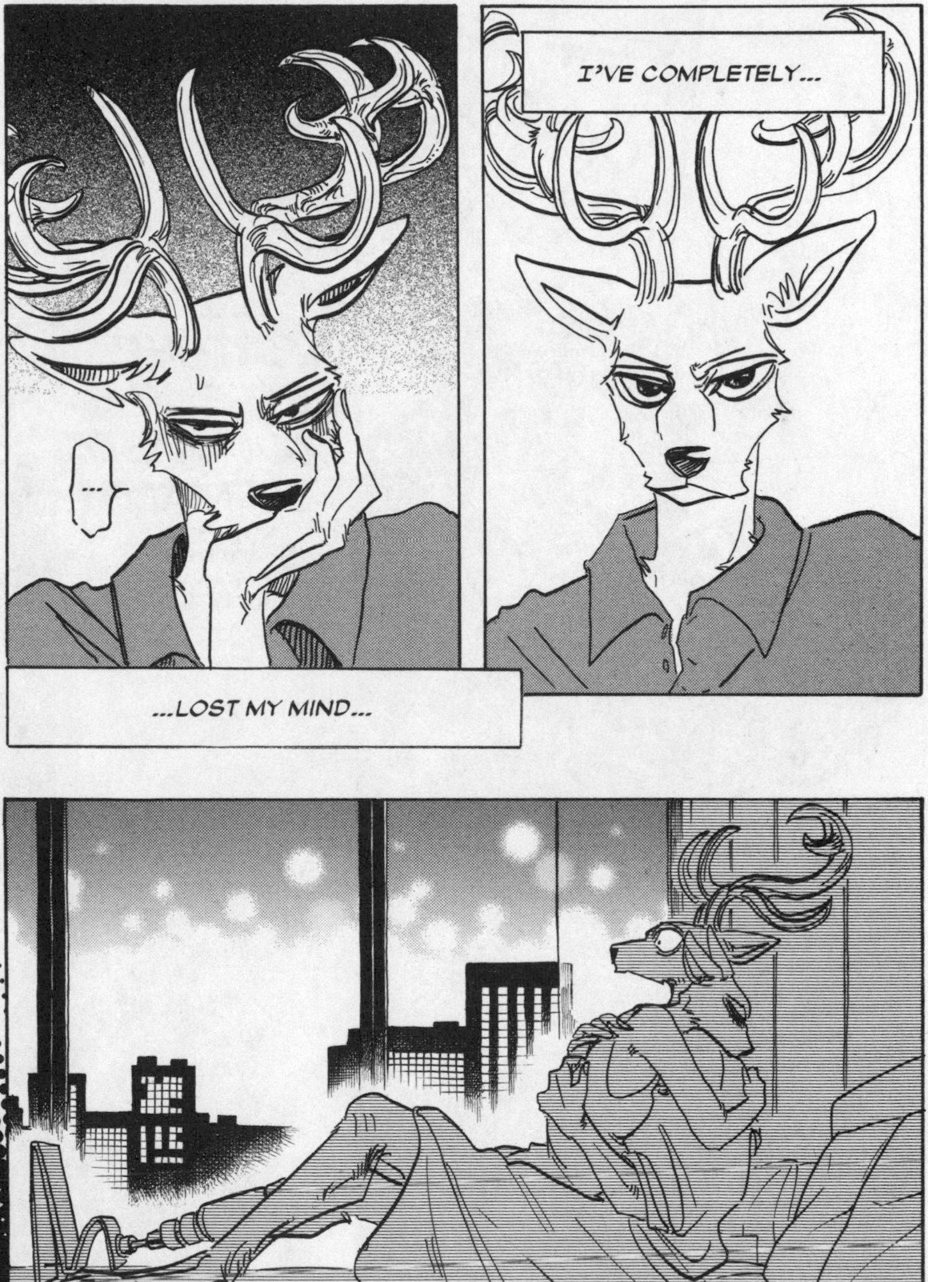
I'VE COMPLETELY...
...
...LOST MY MIND...
INSTEAD OF EMBRACING A FEMALE OF THE SAME SPECIES IN A HOTEL ROOM...

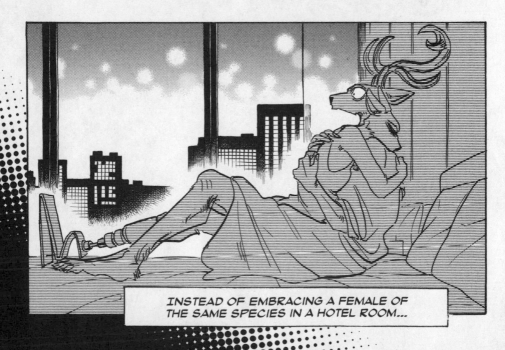

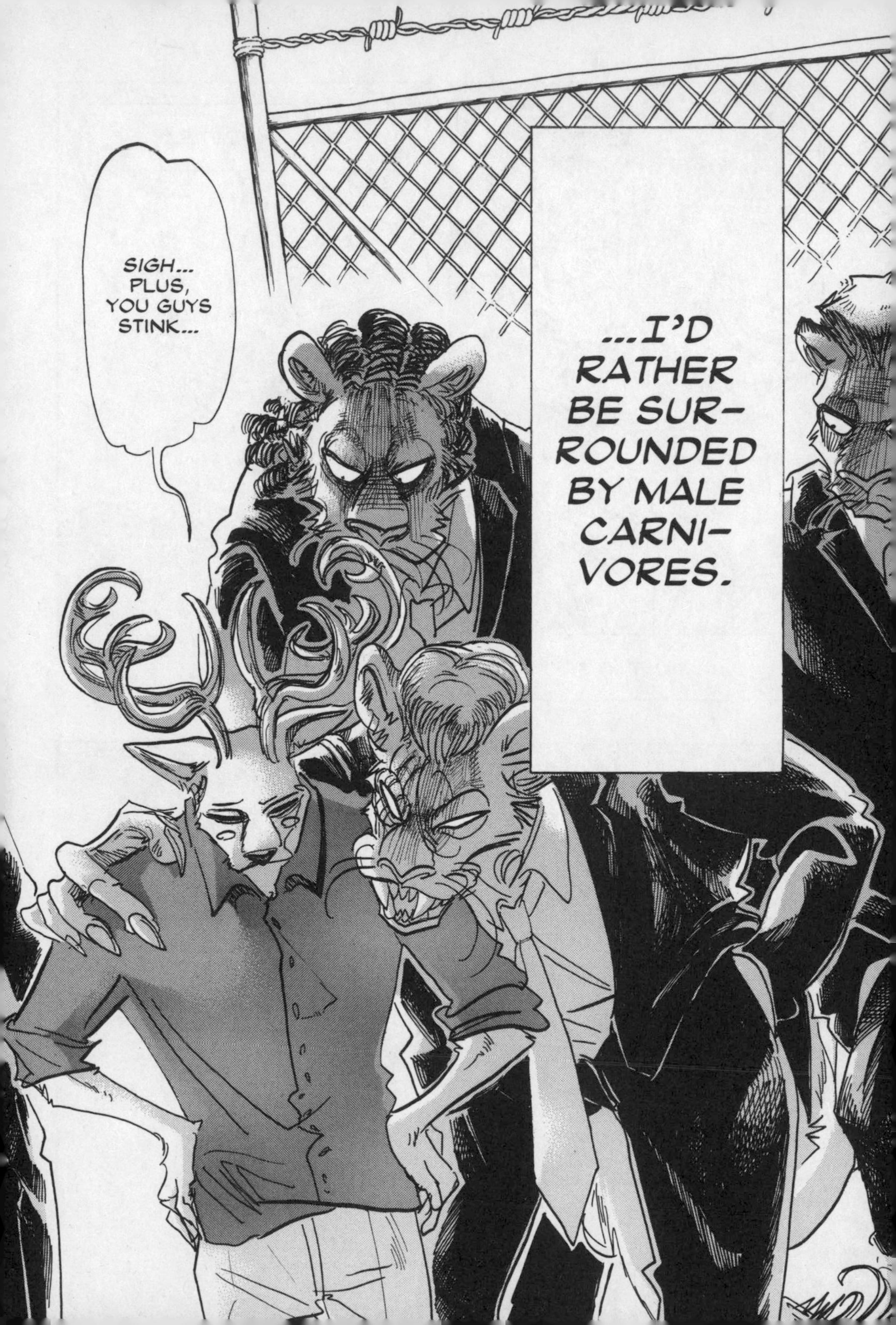
...I'D RATHER BE SUR-ROUNDED BY MALE CARNI-VORES.
SIGH... PLUS, YOU GUYS STINK...

Chapter 144: I Am a Felidae

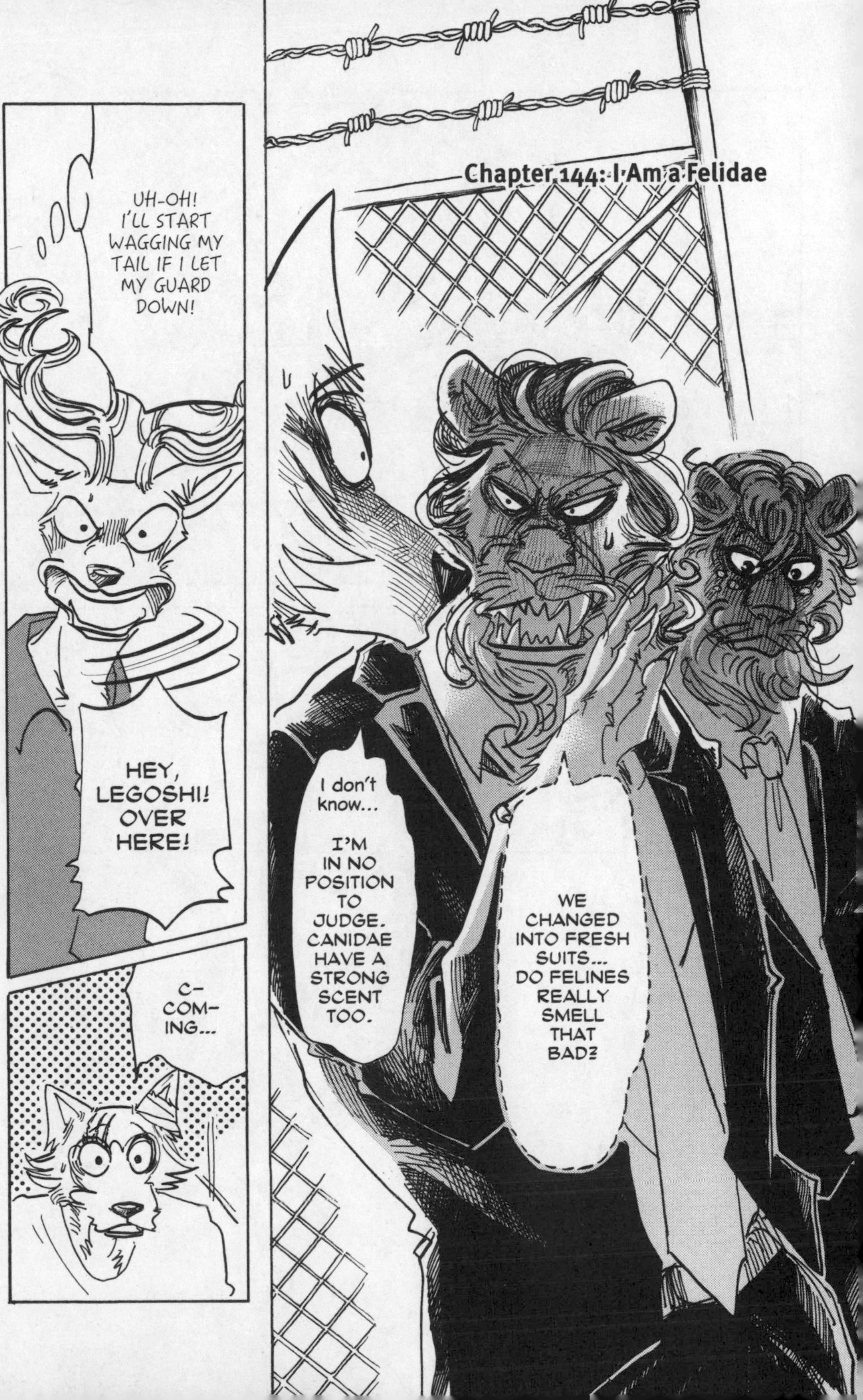
WE CHANGED INTO FRESH SUITS... DO FELINES REALLY SMELL THAT BAD?
I don't know... I'M IN NO POSITION TO JUDGE. CANIDAE HAVE A STRONG SCENT TOO.
UH-OH! I'LL START WAGGING MY TAIL IF I LET MY GUARD DOWN!
HEY, LEGOSHI! OVER HERE!
C-COM-ING...

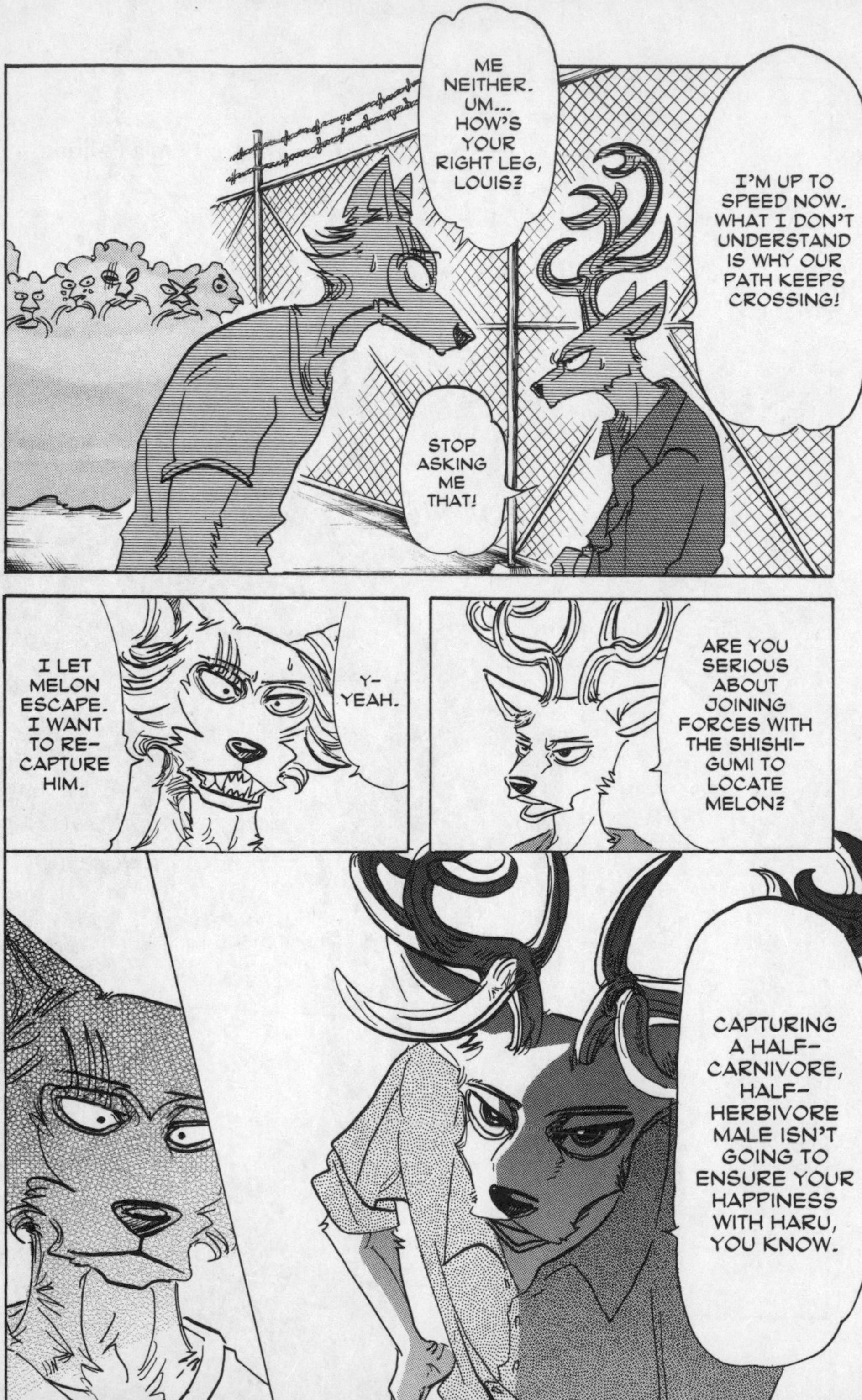
ME NEITHER. UM... HOW'S YOUR RIGHT LEG, LOUIS?
STOP ASKING ME THAT!
I'M UP TO SPEED NOW. WHAT I DON'T UNDERSTAND IS WHY OUR PATH KEEPS CROSSING!
ARE YOU SERIOUS ABOUT JOINING FORCES WITH THE SHISHI-GUMI TO LOCATE MELON?
Y-YEAH.
I LET MELON ESCAPE. I WANT TO RE-CAPTURE HIM.
CAPTURING A HALF-CARNIVORE, HALF-HERBIVORE MALE ISN'T GOING TO ENSURE YOUR HAPPINESS WITH HARU, YOU KNOW.

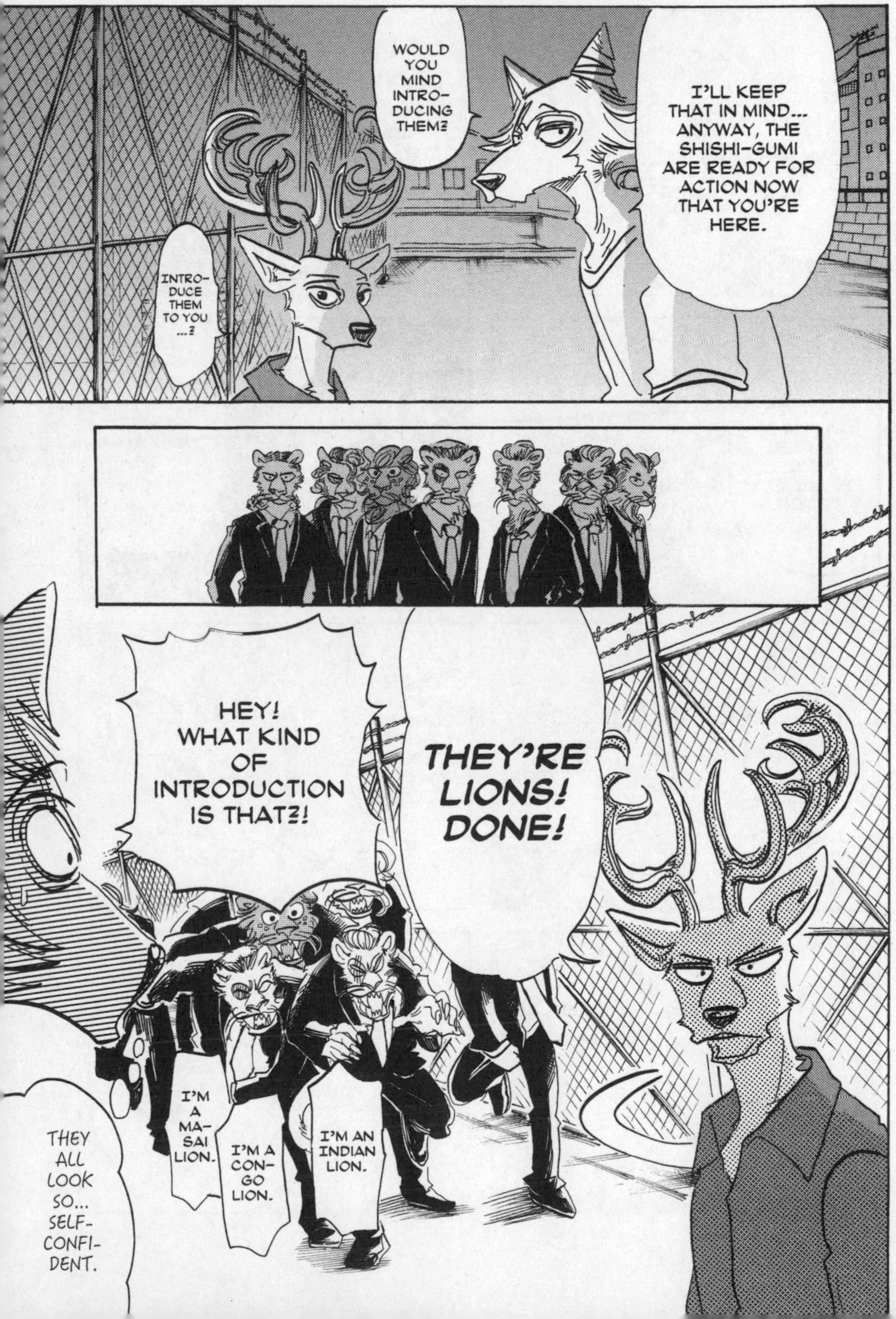
I'LL KEEP THAT IN MIND... ANYWAY, THE SHISHI-GUMI ARE READY FOR ACTION NOW THAT YOU'RE HERE.
WOULD YOU MIND INTRODUCING THEM?
INTRODUCE THEM TO YOU...?
THEY'RE LIONS! DONE!
HEY! WHAT KIND OF INTRODUCTION IS THAT?!
I'M AN INDIAN LION.
I'M A CONGO LION.
I'M A MASAI LION.
THEY ALL LOOK SO... SELF-CONFIDENT.

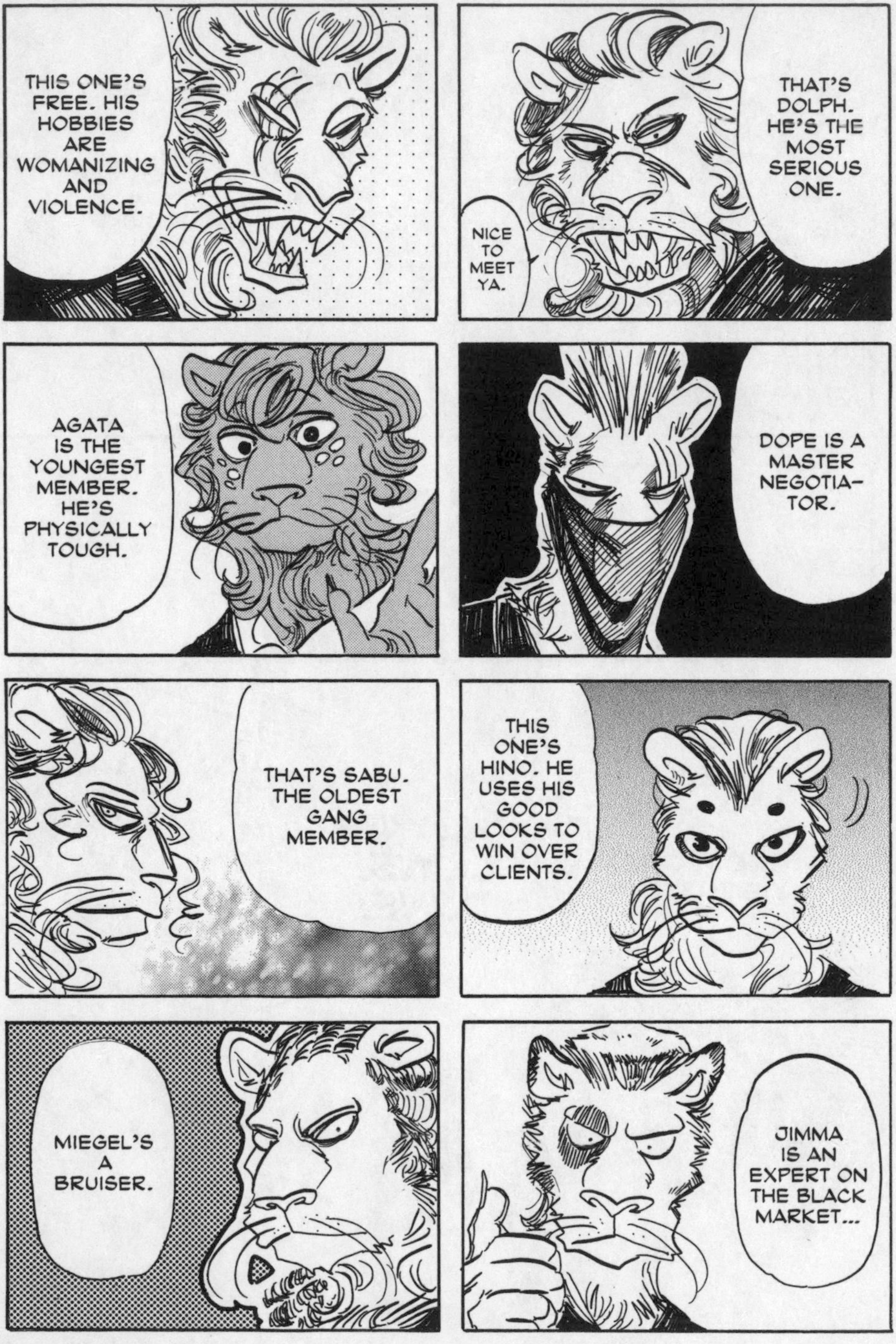
THAT'S DOLPH. HE'S THE MOST SERIOUS ONE.
NICE TO MEET YA.
THIS ONE'S FREE. HIS HOBBIES ARE WOMANIZING AND VIOLENCE.
DOPE IS A MASTER NEGOTIA-TOR.
AGATA IS THE YOUNGEST MEMBER. HE'S PHYSICALLY TOUGH.
THIS ONE'S HINO. HE USES HIS GOOD LOOKS TO WIN OVER CLIENTS.
THAT'S SABU. THE OLDEST GANG MEMBER.
JIMMA IS AN EXPERT ON THE BLACK MARKET...
MIEGEL'S A BRUISER.

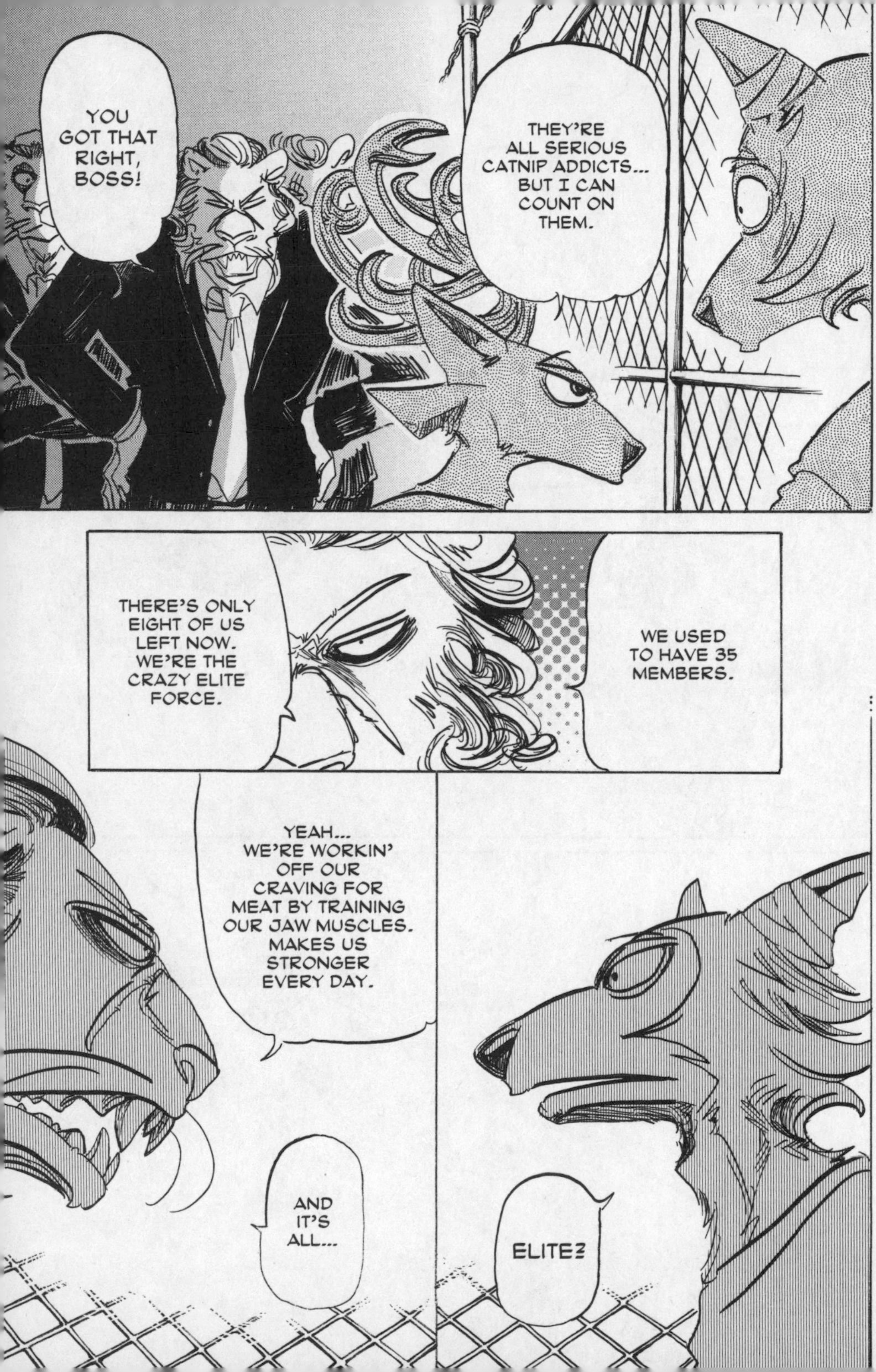

THEY'RE ALL SERIOUS CATNIP ADDICTS... BUT I CAN COUNT ON THEM.
YOU GOT THAT RIGHT, BOSS!
WE USED TO HAVE 35 MEMBERS.
THERE'S ONLY EIGHT OF US LEFT NOW. WE'RE THE CRAZY ELITE FORCE.
ELITE?
YEAH... WE'RE WORKIN' OFF OUR CRAVING FOR MEAT BY TRAINING OUR JAW MUSCLES. MAKES US STRONGER EVERY DAY.
AND IT'S ALL...

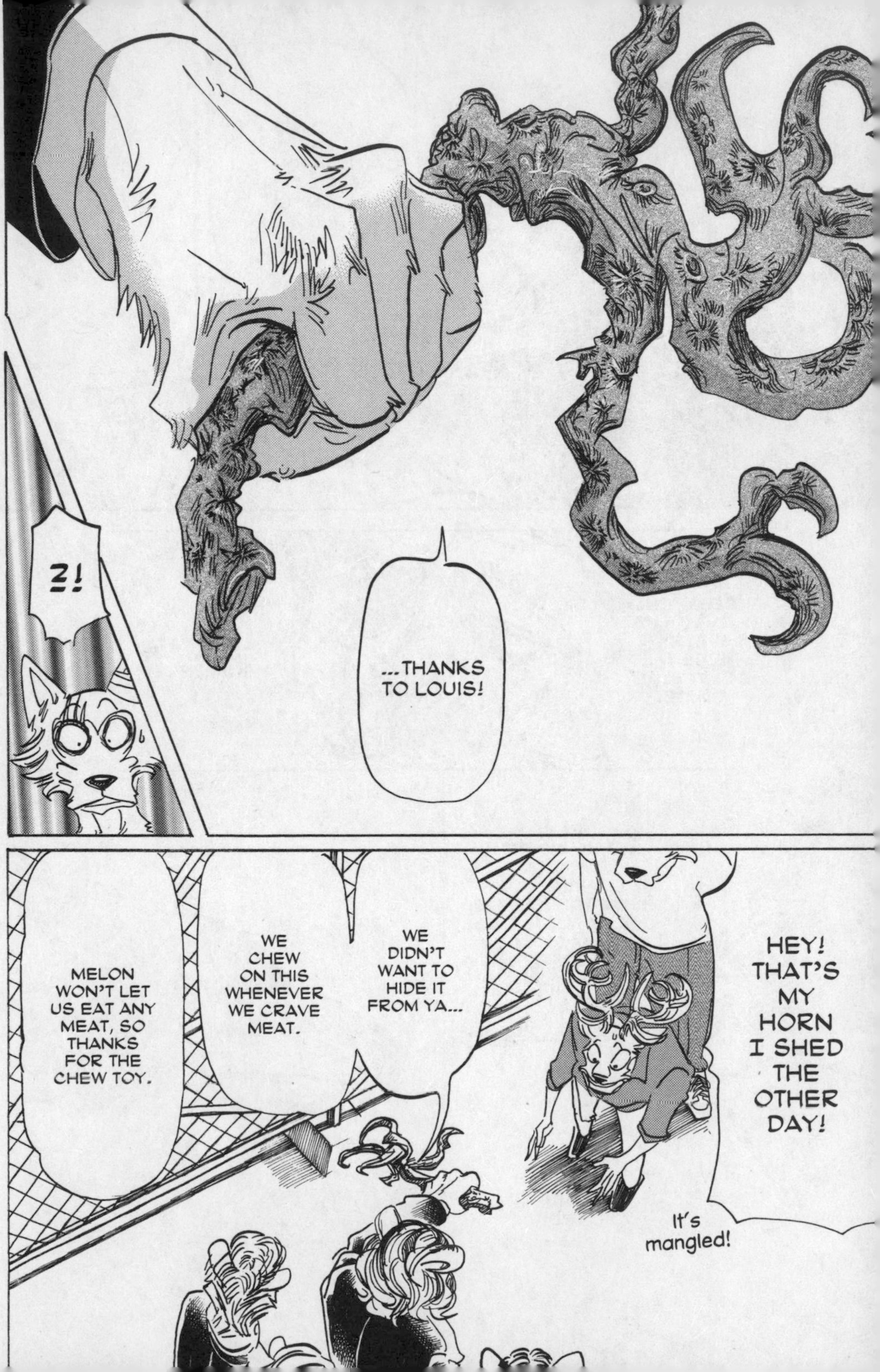
...THANKS TO LOUIS!
!?
HEY! THAT'S MY HORN I SHED THE OTHER DAY!
It's mangled!
WE DIDN'T WANT TO HIDE IT FROM YA...
WE CHEW ON THIS WHENEVER WE CRAVE MEAT.
MELON WON'T LET US EAT ANY MEAT, SO THANKS FOR THE CHEW TOY.

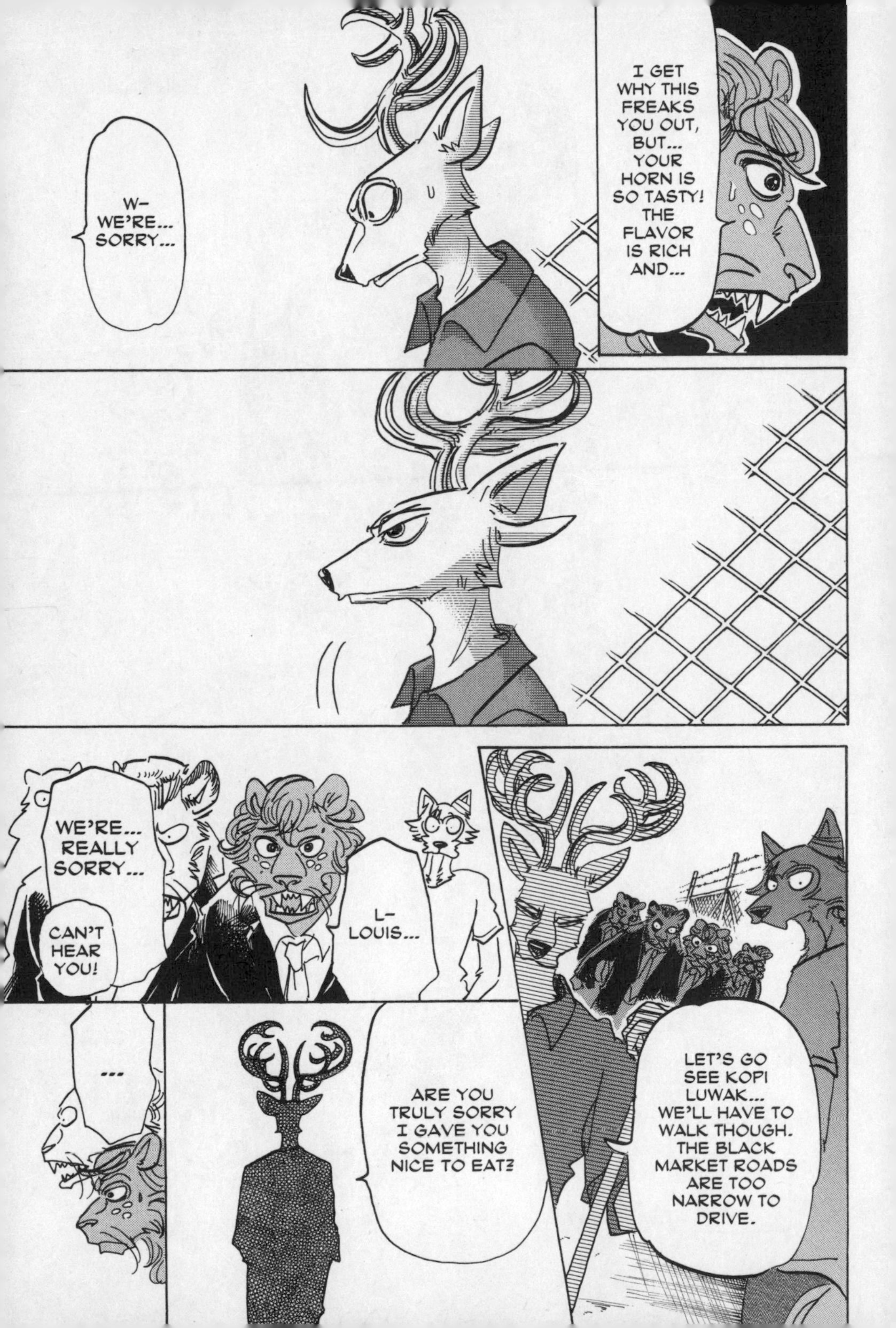
I GET WHY THIS FREAKS YOU OUT, BUT... YOUR HORN IS SO TASTY! THE FLAVOR IS RICH AND...
W- WE'RE... SORRY...
LET'S GO SEE KOPI LUWAK... WE'LL HAVE TO WALK THOUGH. THE BLACK MARKET ROADS ARE TOO NARROW TO DRIVE.
L- LOUIS...
WE'RE... REALLY SORRY...
CAN'T HEAR YOU!
ARE YOU TRULY SORRY I GAVE YOU SOMETHING NICE TO EAT?
...

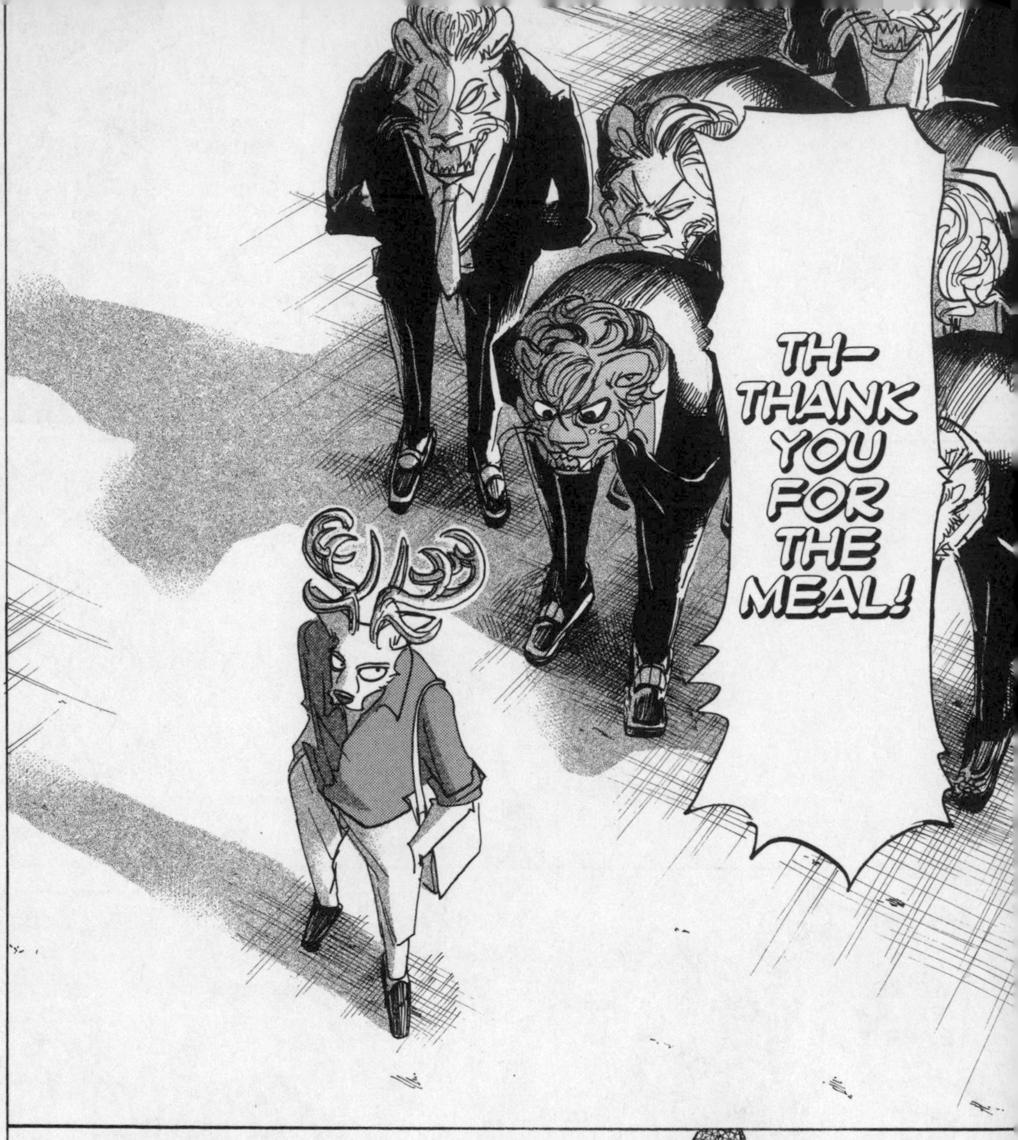
TH-THANK YOU FOR THE MEAL!

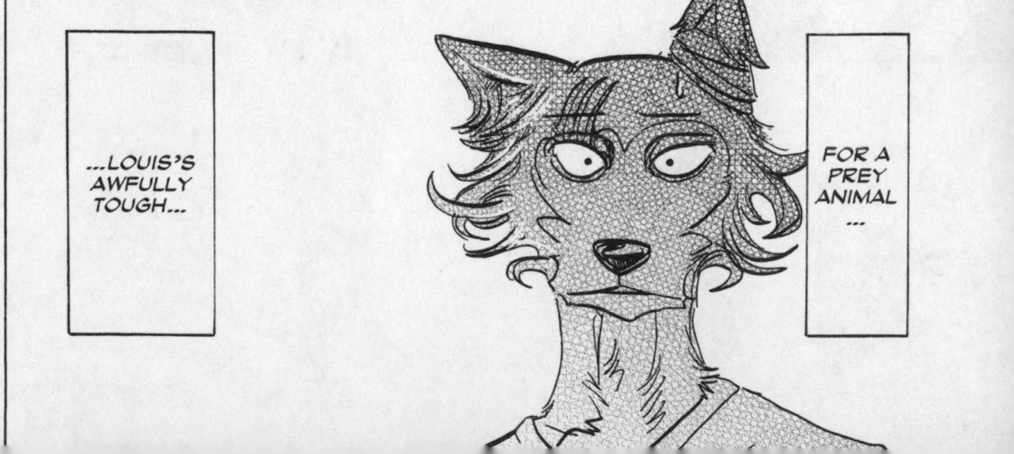
FOR A PREY ANIMAL ...
...LOUIS'S AWFULLY TOUGH...

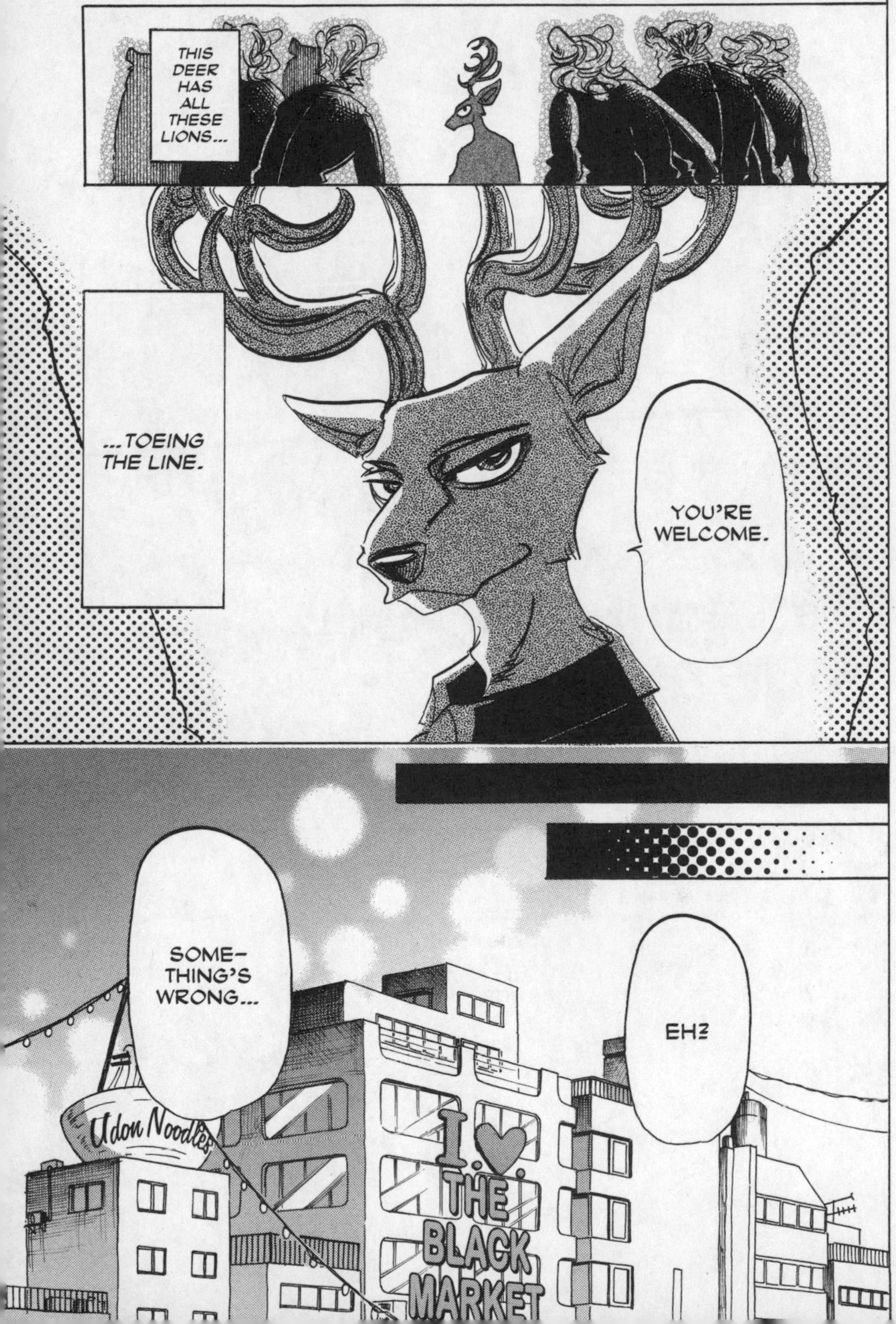
THIS DEER HAS ALL THESE LIONS...
...TOEING THE LINE.
YOU'RE WELCOME.
SOME-THING'S WRONG...
EH?
Udon Noodles
I ♥ THE BLACK MARKET

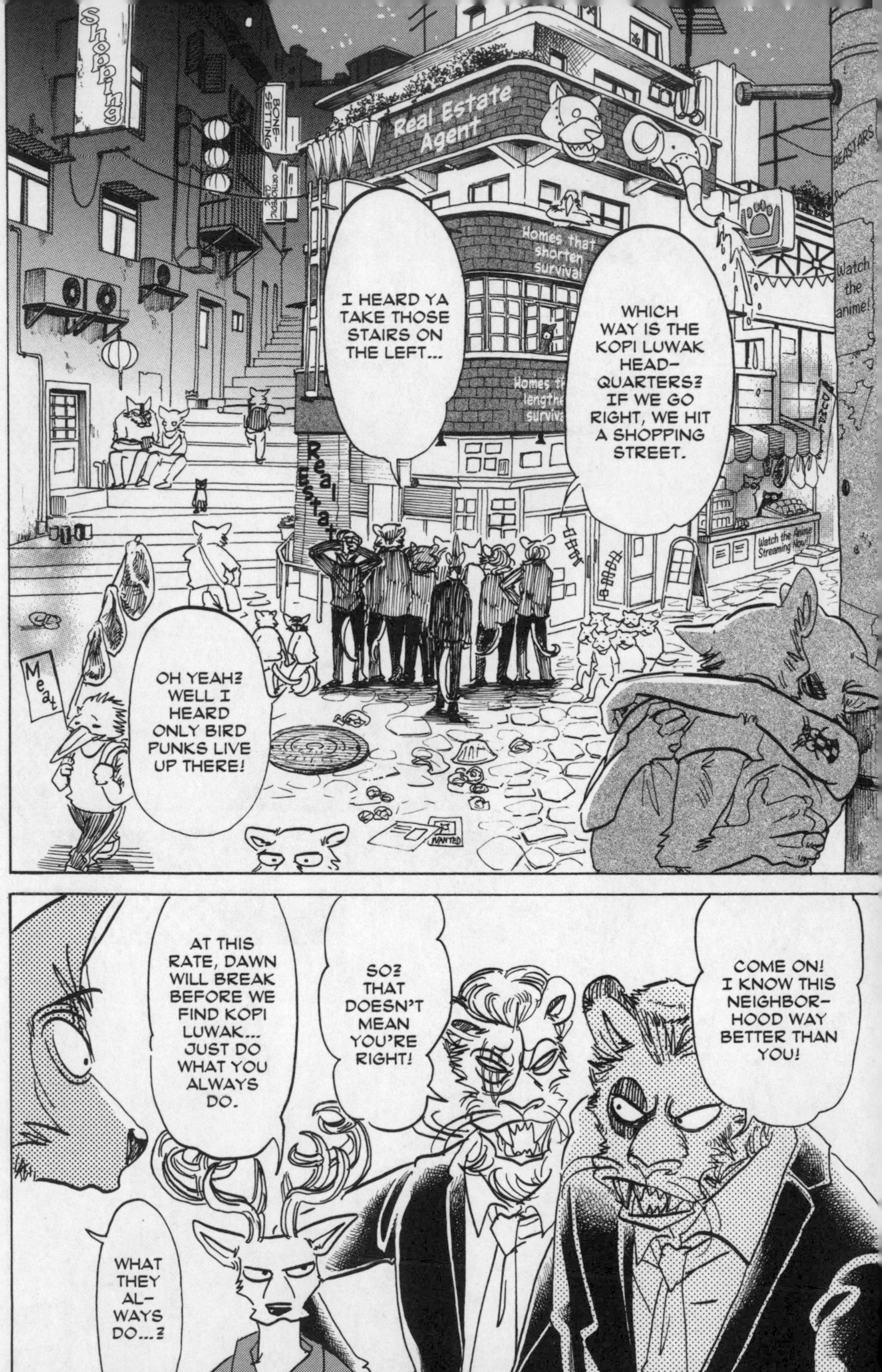
Shopping
BONE-SETTING
ORTHOPEDIC CLINIC
Real Estate Agent
BEASTARS
Homes that shorten survival
Watch the anime!
WHICH WAY IS THE KOPI LUWAK HEAD-QUARTERS? IF WE GO RIGHT, WE HIT A SHOPPING STREET.
I HEARD YA TAKE THOSE STAIRS ON THE LEFT...
Real Estate
Watch the Anime Streaming Now!
Meat
OH YEAH? WELL I HEARD ONLY BIRD PUNKS LIVE UP THERE!
WANTED
COME ON! I KNOW THIS NEIGHBOR-HOOD WAY BETTER THAN YOU!
SO? THAT DOESN'T MEAN YOU'RE RIGHT!
AT THIS RATE, DAWN WILL BREAK BEFORE WE FIND KOPI LUWAK... JUST DO WHAT YOU ALWAYS DO.
WHAT THEY AL-WAYS DO...?

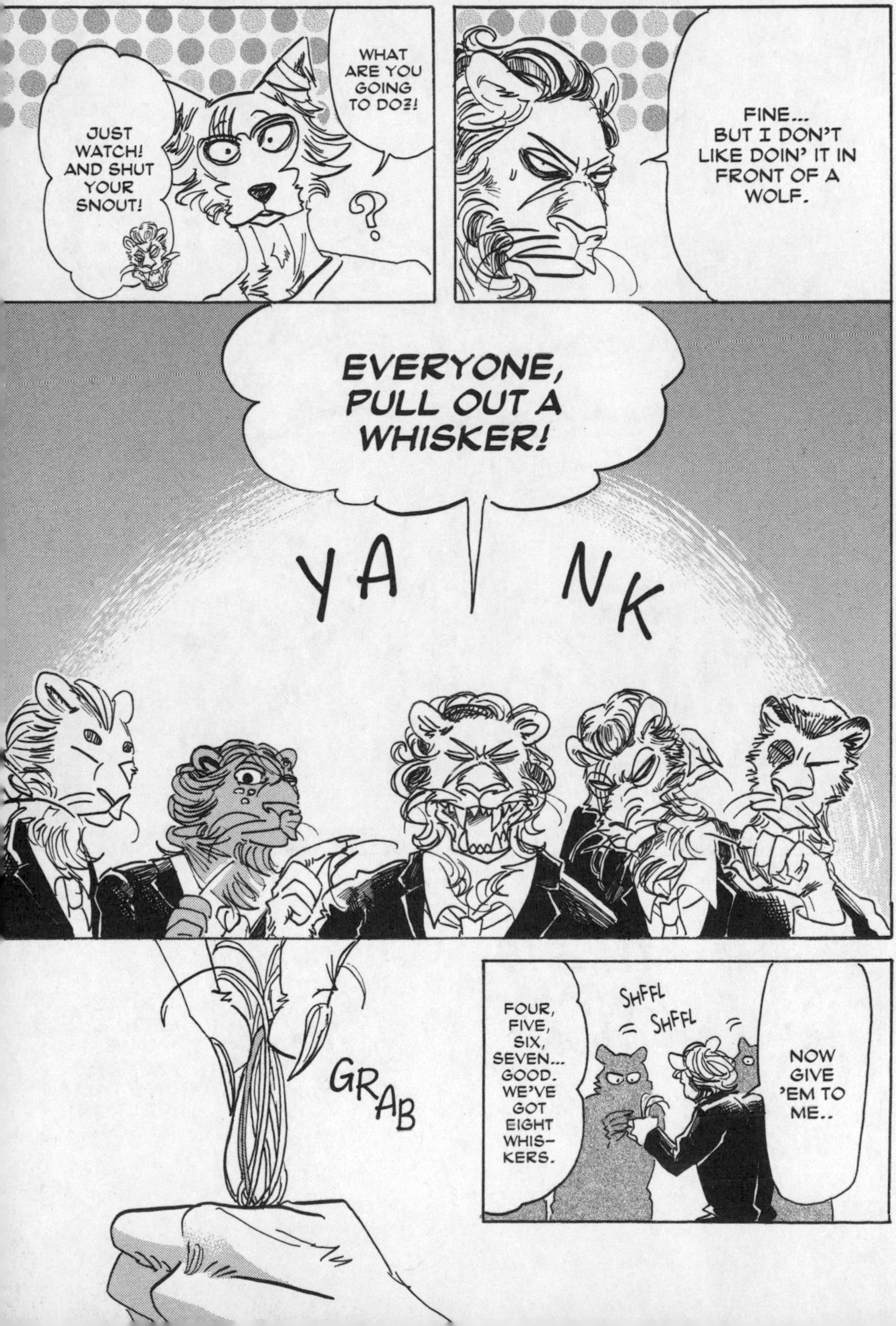

FINE... BUT I DON'T LIKE DOIN' IT IN FRONT OF A WOLF.
WHAT ARE YOU GOING TO DO?!
?
JUST WATCH! AND SHUT YOUR SNOUT!
EVERYONE, PULL OUT A WHISKER!
YANK
NOW GIVE 'EM TO ME..
SHFFL SHFFL
FOUR, FIVE, SIX, SEVEN... GOOD. WE'VE GOT EIGHT WHIS-KERS.
GRAB

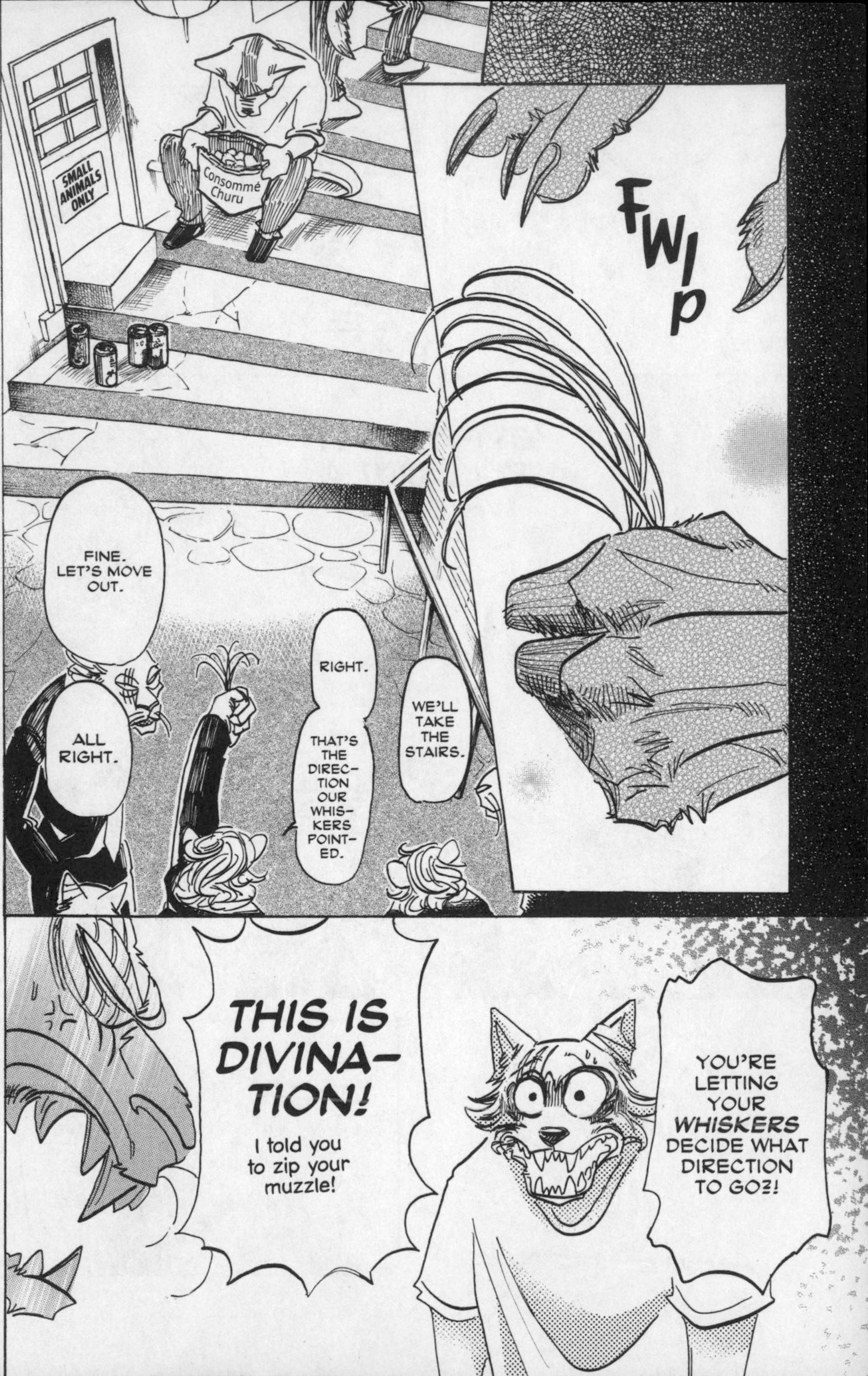
FWIP
Consommé Churu
SMALL ANIMALS ONLY
WE'LL TAKE THE STAIRS.
RIGHT.
THAT'S THE DIRECTION OUR WHISKERS POINTED.
FINE. LET'S MOVE OUT.
ALL RIGHT.
YOU'RE LETTING YOUR *WHISKERS* DECIDE WHAT DIRECTION TO GO?!
THIS IS DIVINATION!
I told you to zip your muzzle!

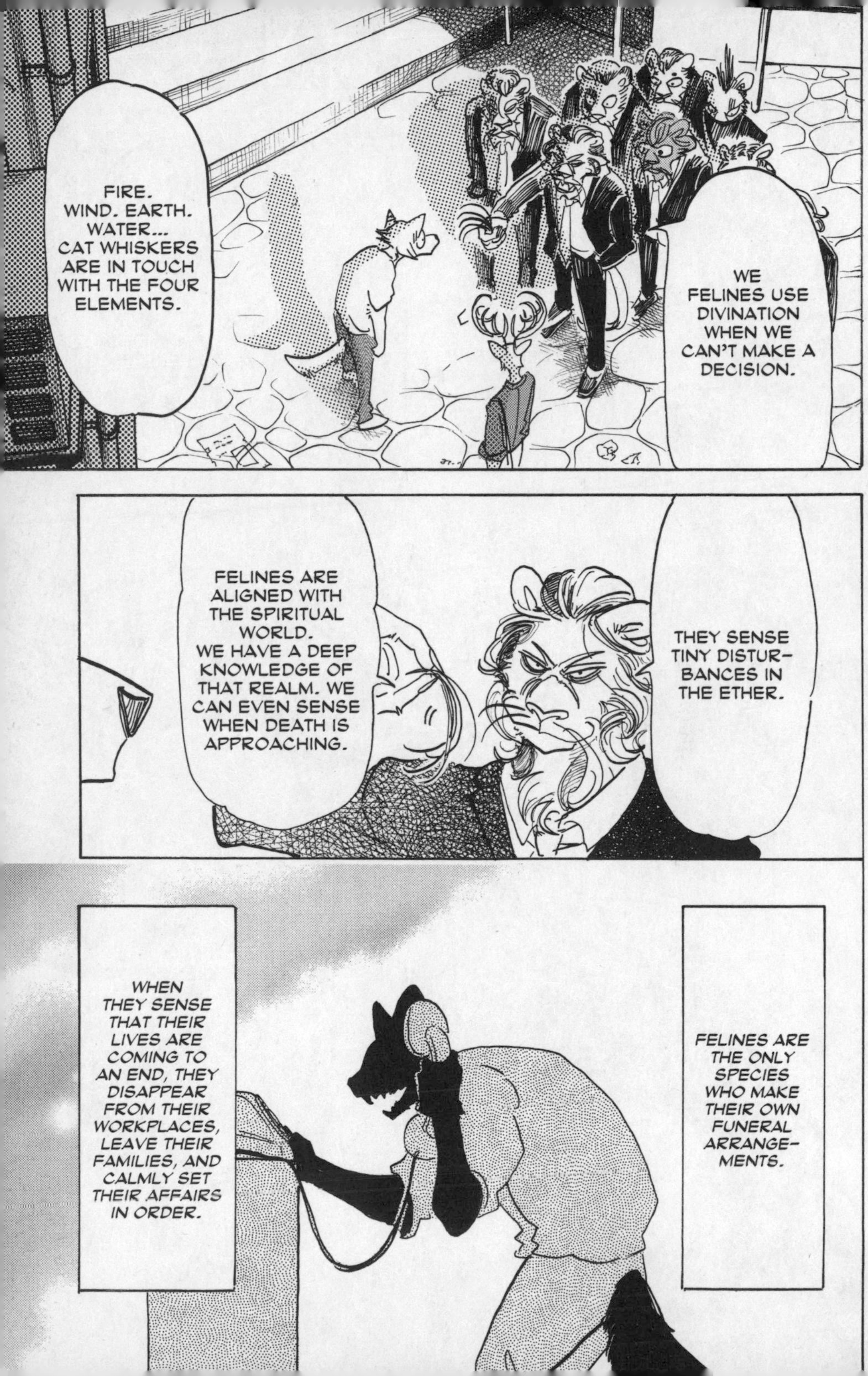
WE FELINES USE DIVINATION WHEN WE CAN'T MAKE A DECISION.
FIRE. WIND. EARTH. WATER... CAT WHISKERS ARE IN TOUCH WITH THE FOUR ELEMENTS.
THEY SENSE TINY DISTUR-BANCES IN THE ETHER.
FELINES ARE ALIGNED WITH THE SPIRITUAL WORLD. WE HAVE A DEEP KNOWLEDGE OF THAT REALM. WE CAN EVEN SENSE WHEN DEATH IS APPROACHING.
FELINES ARE THE ONLY SPECIES WHO MAKE THEIR OWN FUNERAL ARRANGE-MENTS.
WHEN THEY SENSE THAT THEIR LIVES ARE COMING TO AN END, THEY DISAPPEAR FROM THEIR WORKPLACES, LEAVE THEIR FAMILIES, AND CALMLY SET THEIR AFFAIRS IN ORDER.

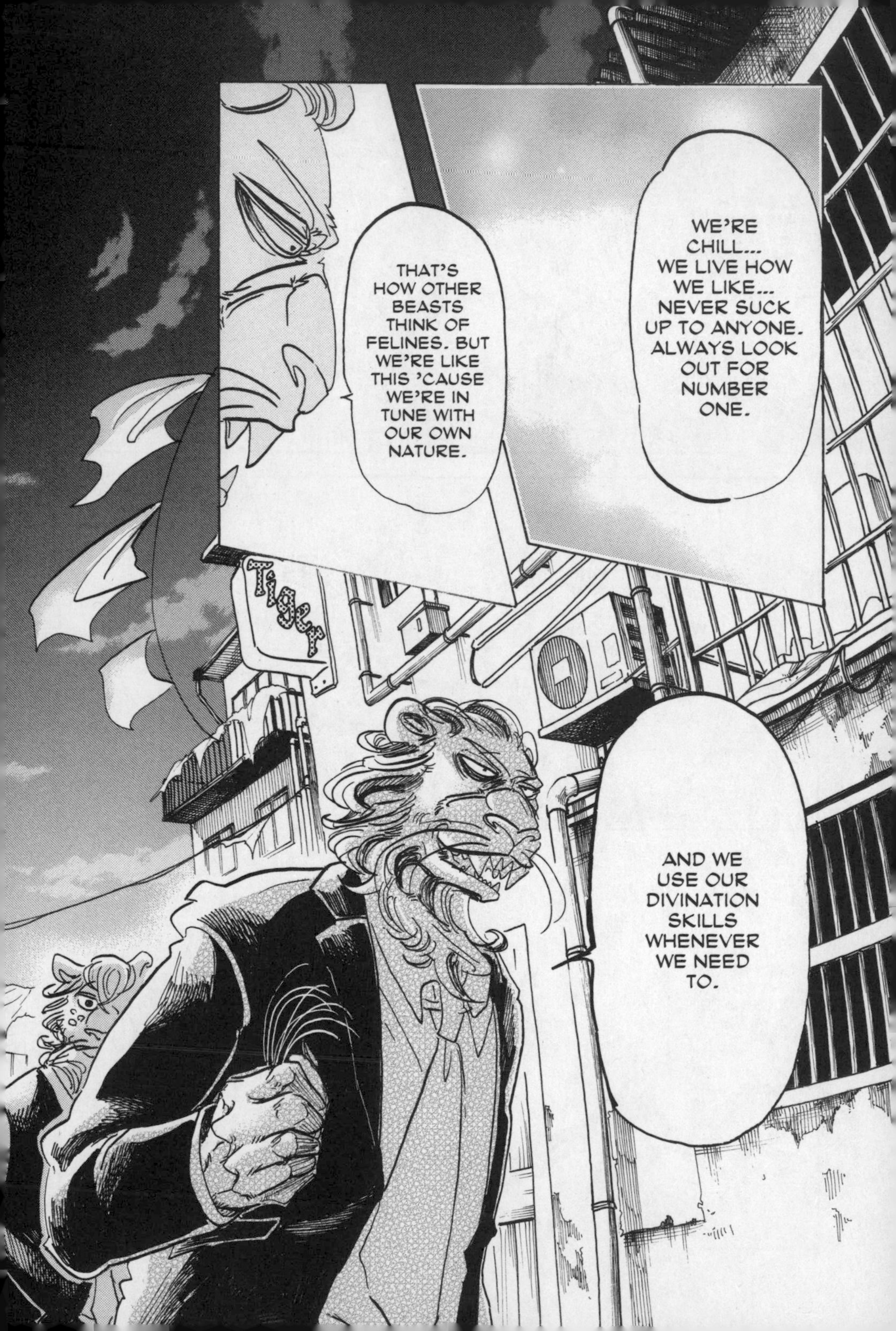
WE'RE CHILL... WE LIVE HOW WE LIKE... NEVER SUCK UP TO ANYONE. ALWAYS LOOK OUT FOR NUMBER ONE.
THAT'S HOW OTHER BEASTS THINK OF FELINES. BUT WE'RE LIKE THIS 'CAUSE WE'RE IN TUNE WITH OUR OWN NATURE.
Tiger
AND WE USE OUR DIVINATION SKILLS WHENEVER WE NEED TO.

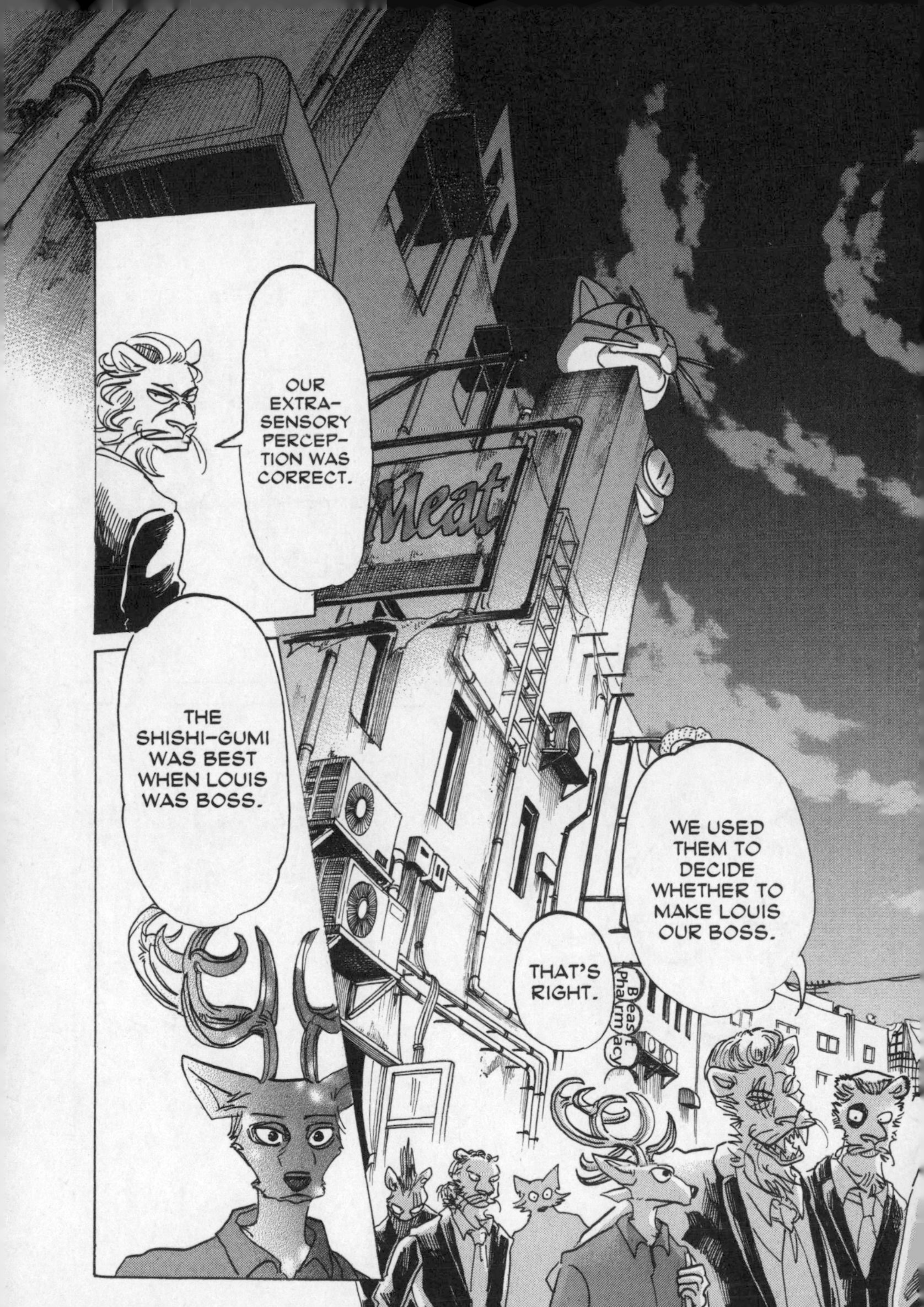
Meat
WE USED THEM TO DECIDE WHETHER TO MAKE LOUIS OUR BOSS.
THAT'S RIGHT.
Beast Pharmacy
OUR EXTRA-SENSORY PERCEP-TION WAS CORRECT.
THE SHISHI-GUMI WAS BEST WHEN LOUIS WAS BOSS.

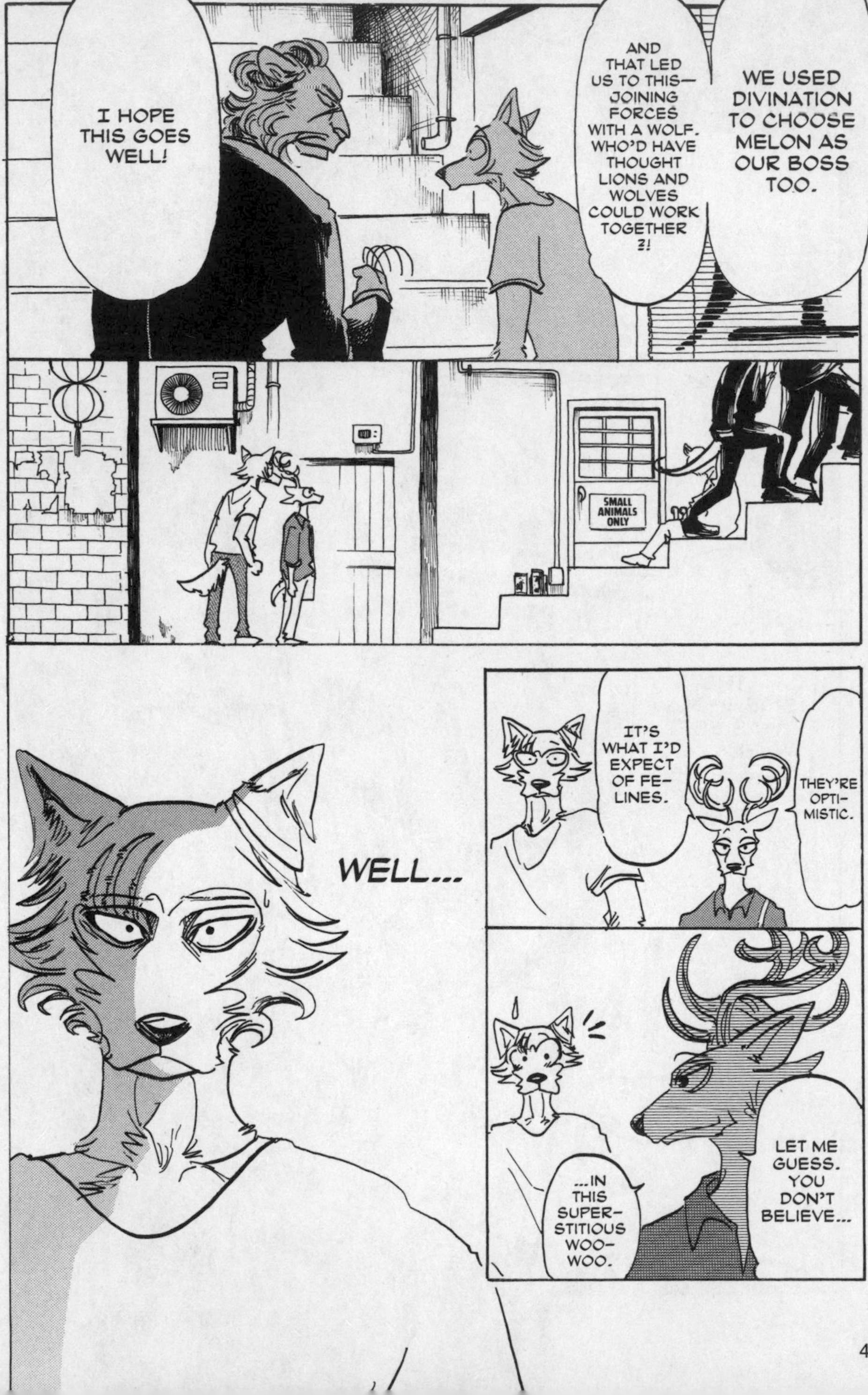
WE USED DIVINATION TO CHOOSE MELON AS OUR BOSS TOO.
AND THAT LED US TO THIS— JOINING FORCES WITH A WOLF. WHO'D HAVE THOUGHT LIONS AND WOLVES COULD WORK TOGETHER?!
I HOPE THIS GOES WELL!
SMALL ANIMALS ONLY
THEY'RE OPTI-MISTIC.
IT'S WHAT I'D EXPECT OF FE-LINES.
LET ME GUESS. YOU DON'T BELIEVE...
...IN THIS SUPER-STITIOUS WOO-WOO.
WELL...

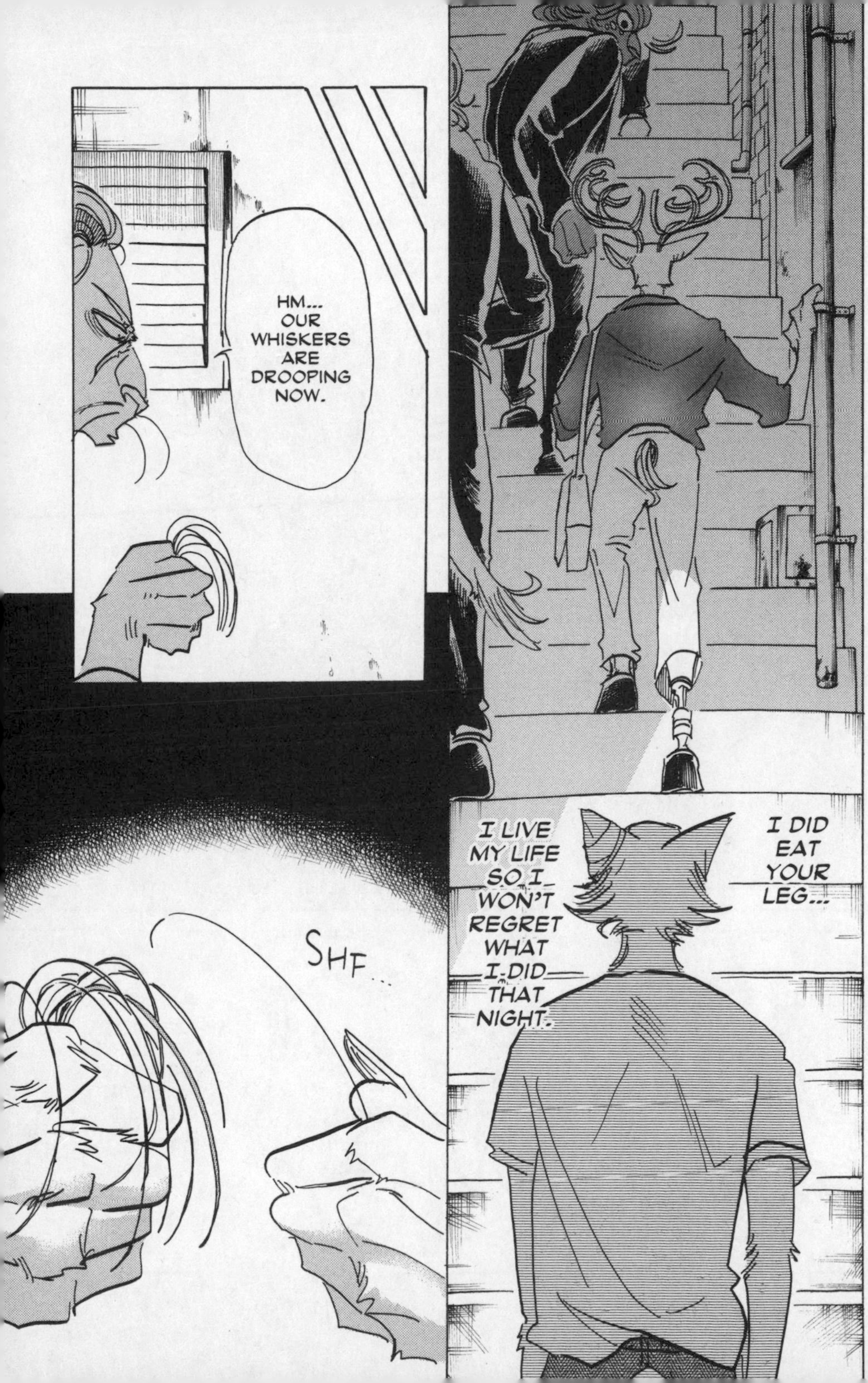
HM... OUR WHISKERS ARE DROOPING NOW.
I DID EAT YOUR LEG...
I LIVE MY LIFE SO I WON'T REGRET WHAT I DID THAT NIGHT.
SHF...

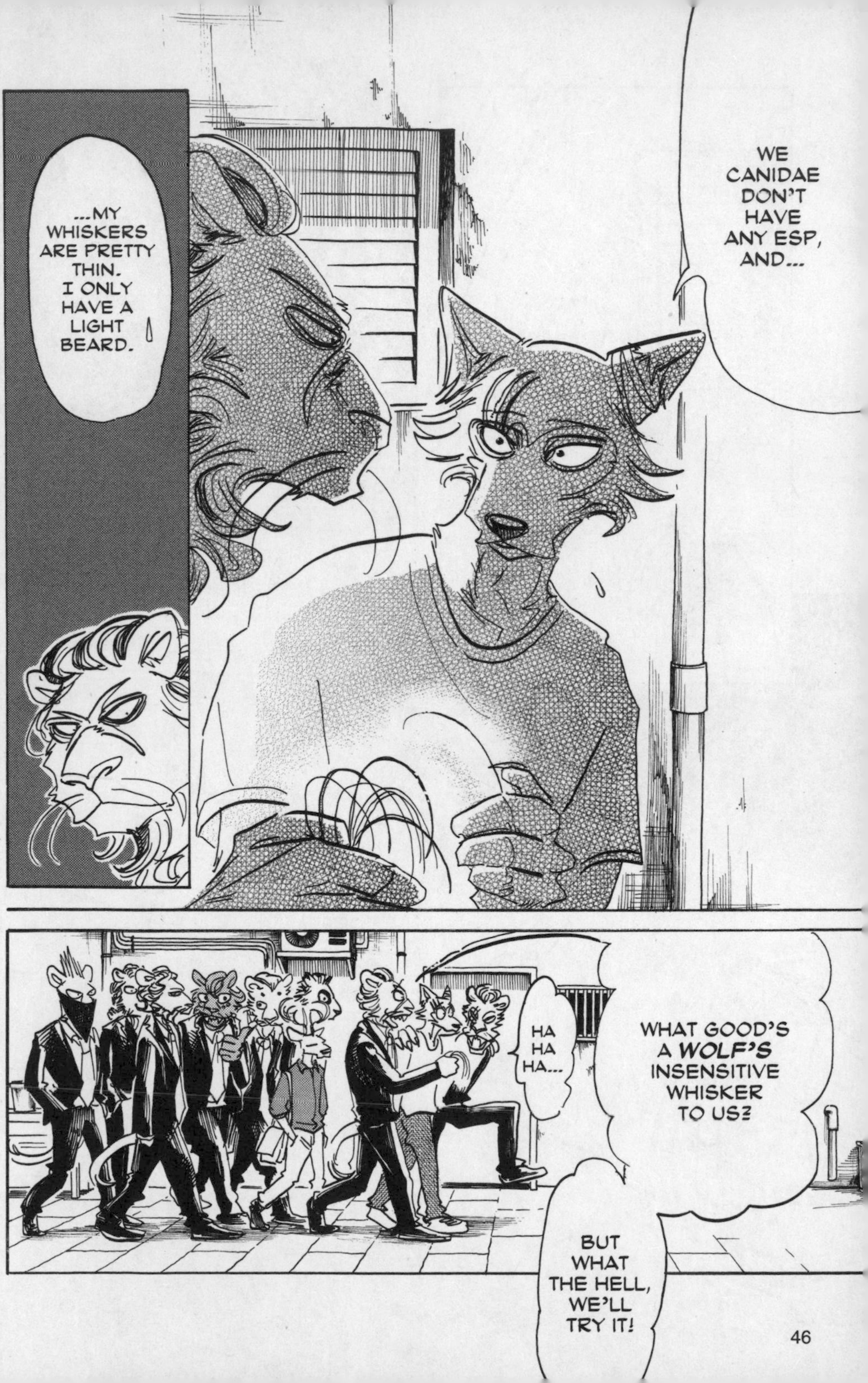
WE CANIDAE DON'T HAVE ANY ESP, AND...
...MY WHISKERS ARE PRETTY THIN. I ONLY HAVE A LIGHT BEARD.
WHAT GOOD'S A ***WOLF'S*** INSENSITIVE WHISKER TO US?
HA HA HA...
BUT WHAT THE HELL, WE'LL TRY IT!

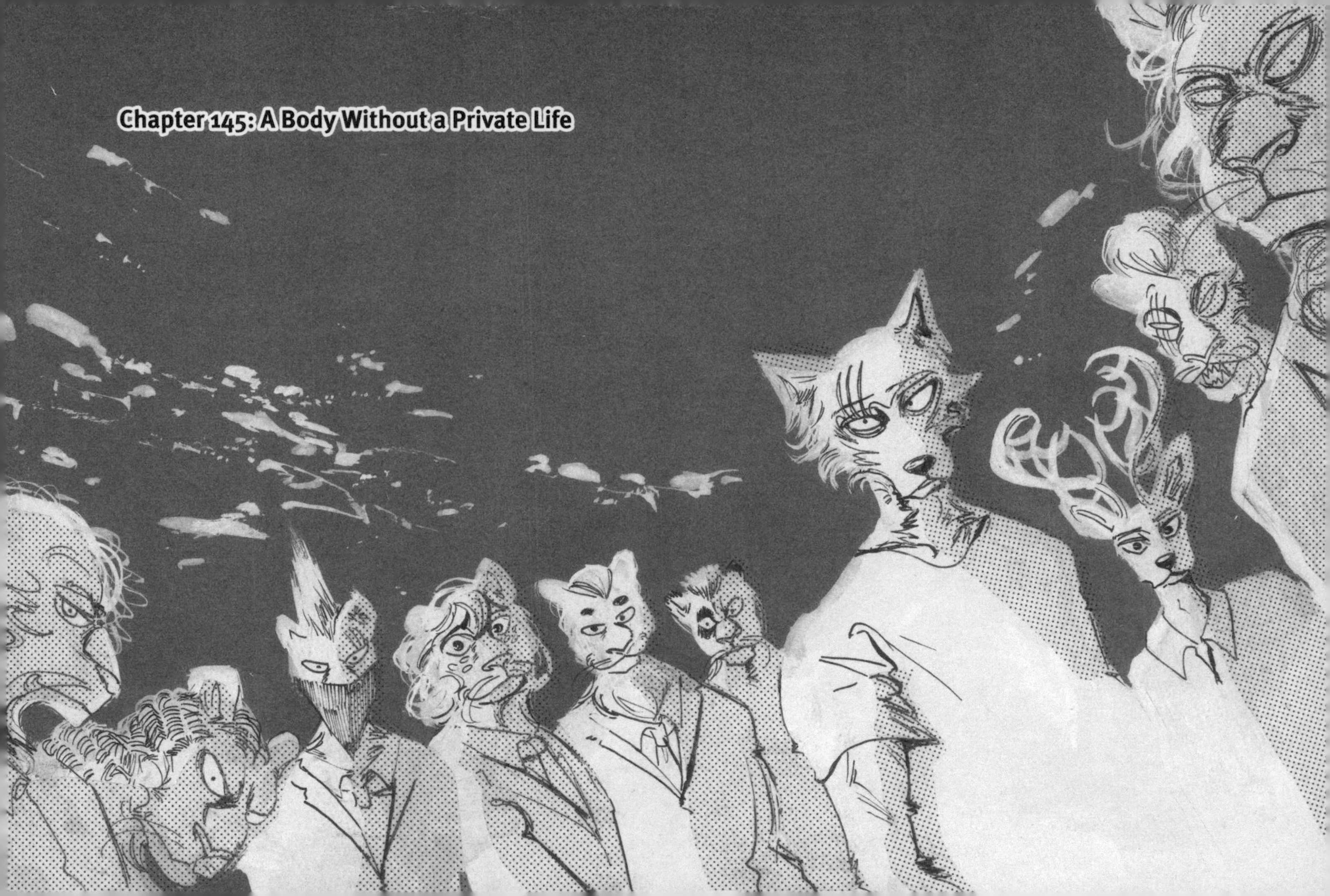
Chapter 145: A Body Without a Private Life

BEASTARS
Vol. 17

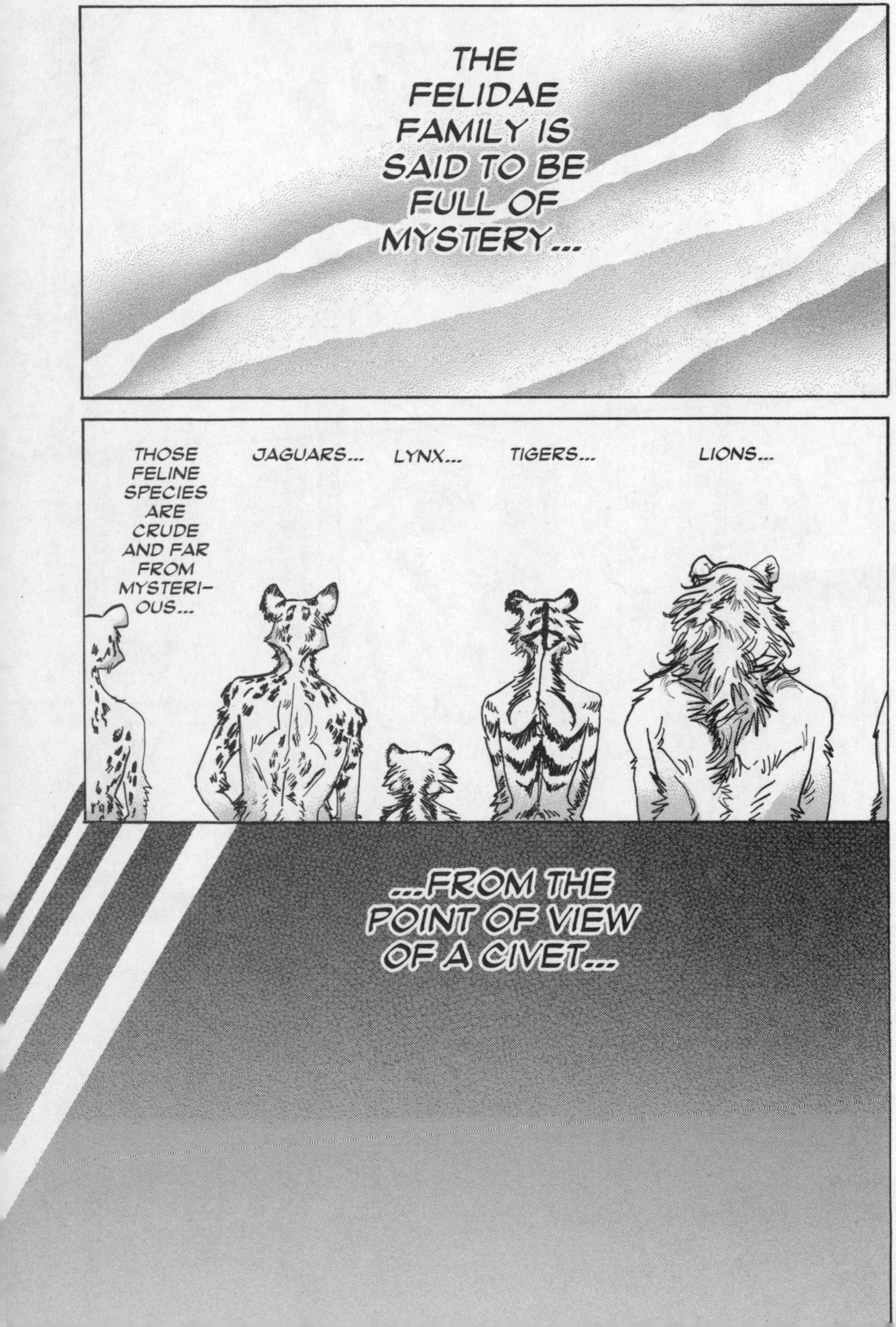
THE FELIDAE FAMILY IS SAID TO BE FULL OF MYSTERY...
LIONS...
TIGERS...
LYNX...
JAGUARS...
THOSE FELINE SPECIES ARE CRUDE AND FAR FROM MYSTERI- OUS...
...FROM THE POINT OF VIEW OF A CIVET...

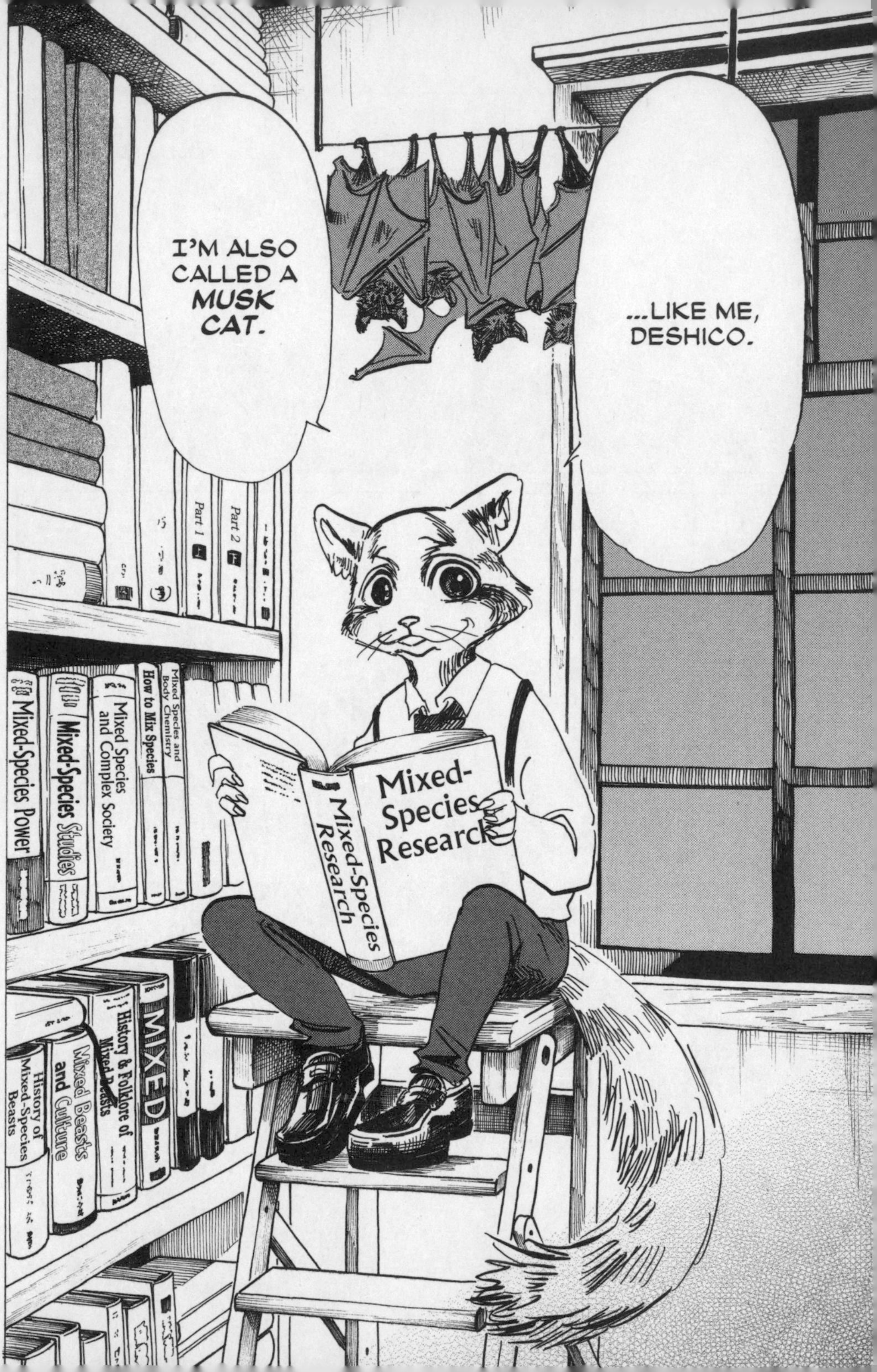
...LIKE ME, DESHICO.
I'M ALSO CALLED A MUSK CAT.
Mixed-Species Research
Mixed-Species Research
Part 1
Part 2
Mixed-Species Power
Mixed-Species Studies
Mixed Species and Complex Society
How to Mix Species
Mixed Species and Body Chemistry
History of Mixed-Species Beasts
Mixed Beasts and Culture
History & Folklore of Mixed Beasts
MIXED

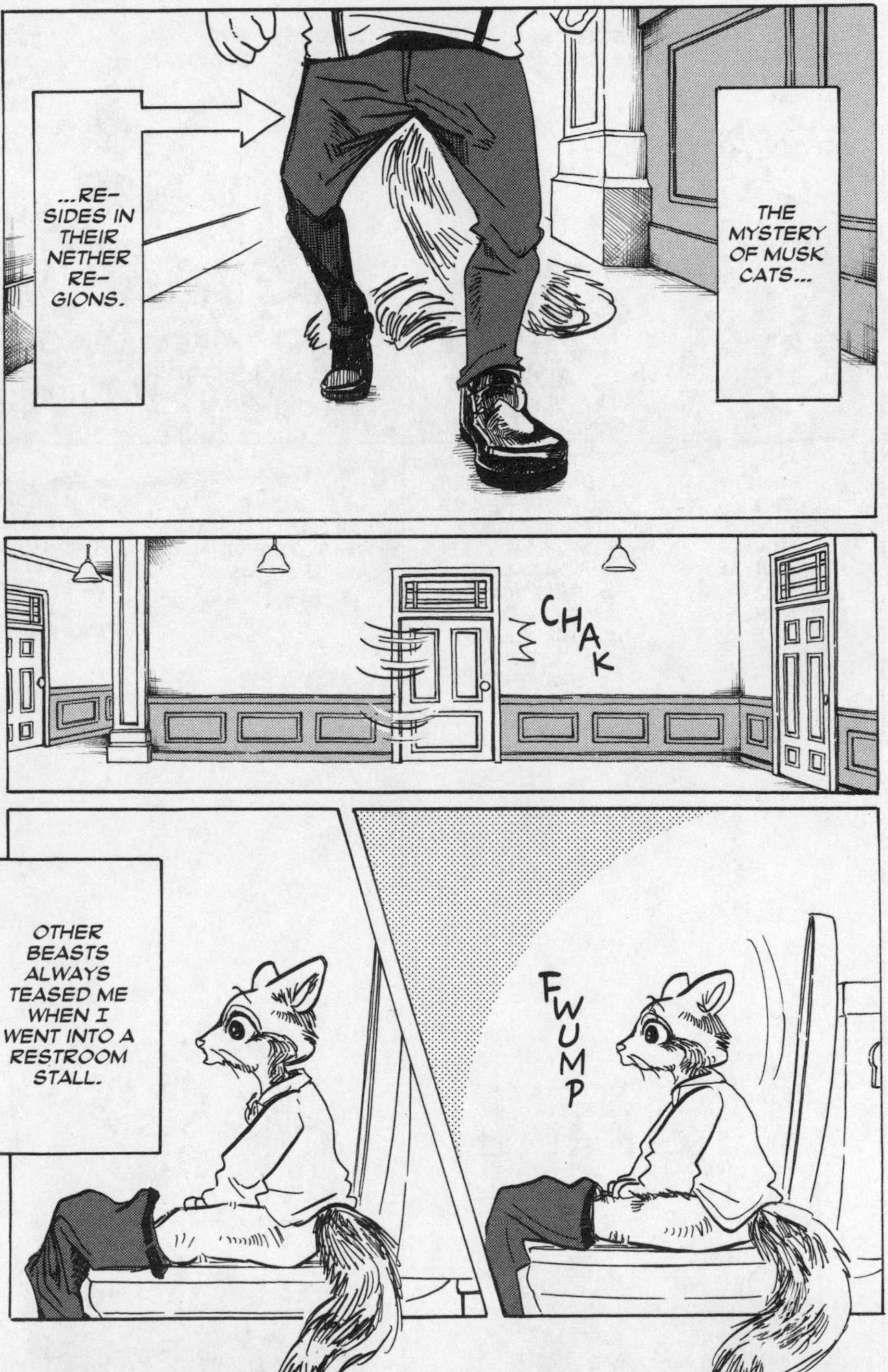
THE MYSTERY OF MUSK CATS...
...RE-SIDES IN THEIR NETHER REGIONS.
CHAK
FWUMP
OTHER BEASTS ALWAYS TEASED ME WHEN I WENT INTO A RESTROOM STALL.

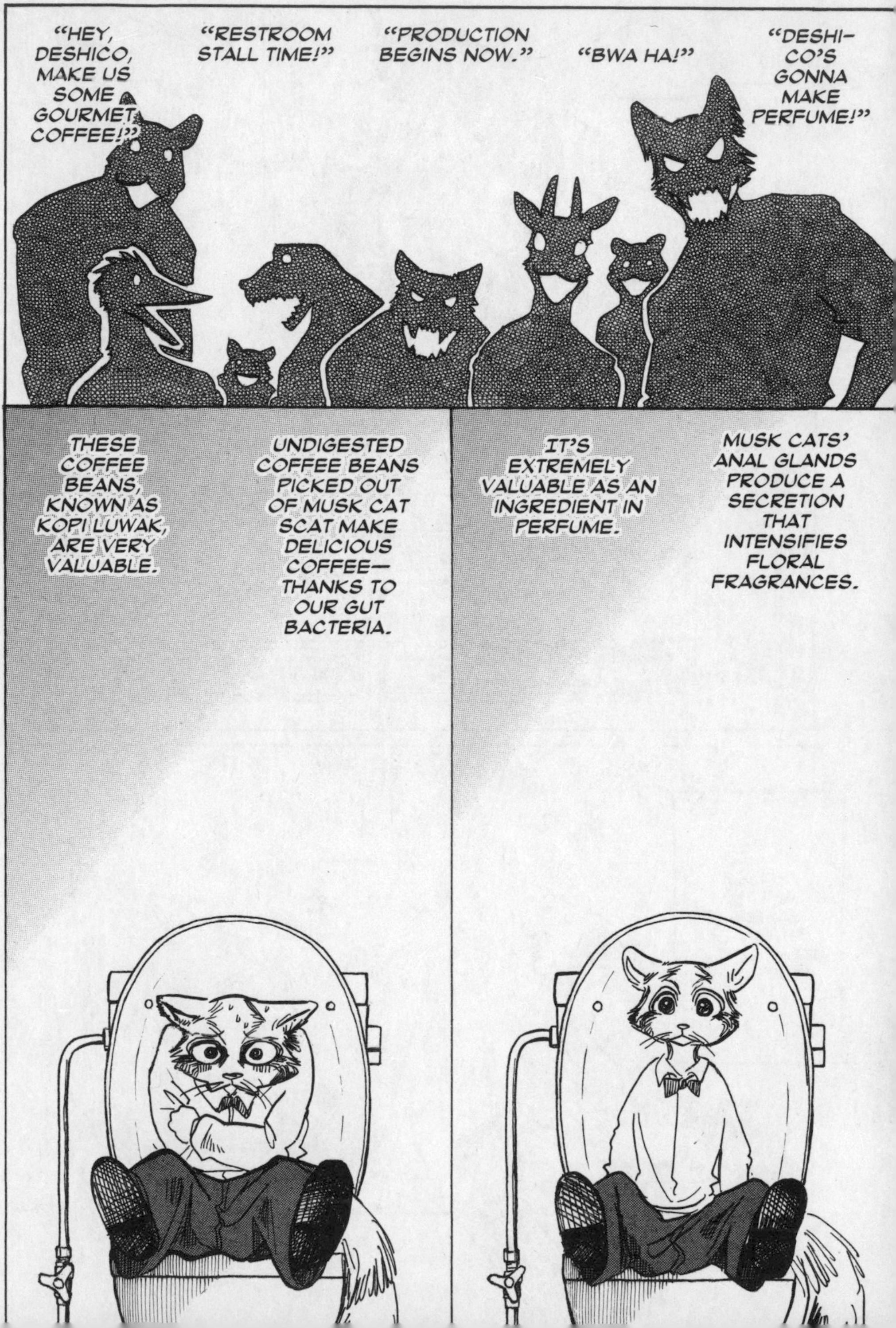
"DESHICO'S GONNA MAKE PERFUME!"
"BWA HA!"
"PRODUCTION BEGINS NOW."
"RESTROOM STALL TIME!"
"HEY, DESHICO, MAKE US SOME GOURMET COFFEE!"
MUSK CATS' ANAL GLANDS PRODUCE A SECRETION THAT INTENSIFIES FLORAL FRAGRANCES.
IT'S EXTREMELY VALUABLE AS AN INGREDIENT IN PERFUME.
UNDIGESTED COFFEE BEANS PICKED OUT OF MUSK CAT SCAT MAKE DELICIOUS COFFEE—THANKS TO OUR GUT BACTERIA.
THESE COFFEE BEANS, KNOWN AS KOPI LUWAK, ARE VERY VALUABLE.

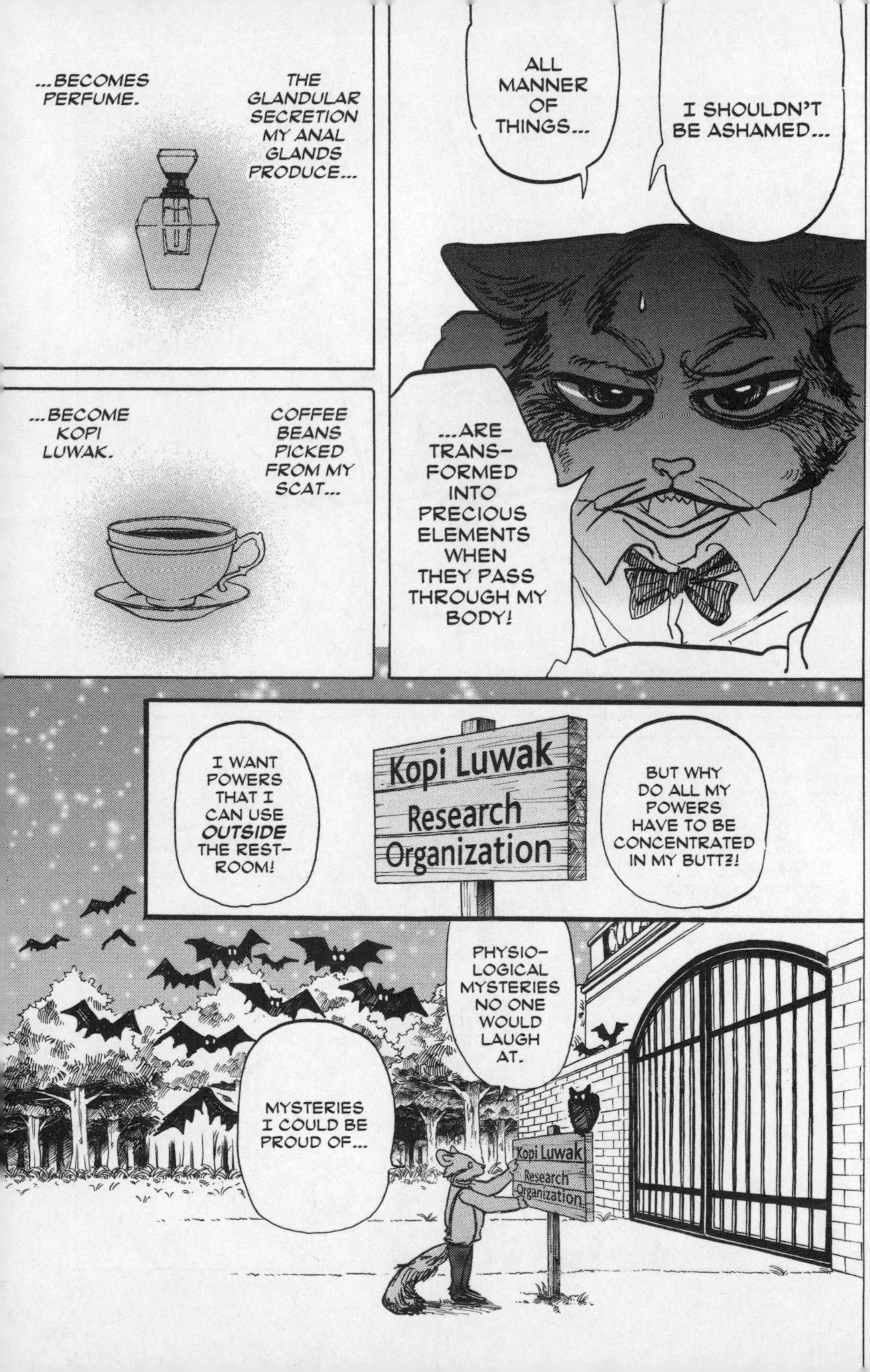
I SHOULDN'T BE ASHAMED...
ALL MANNER OF THINGS...
...ARE TRANS-FORMED INTO PRECIOUS ELEMENTS WHEN THEY PASS THROUGH MY BODY!
THE GLANDULAR SECRETION MY ANAL GLANDS PRODUCE...
...BECOMES PERFUME.
COFFEE BEANS PICKED FROM MY SCAT...
...BECOME KOPI LUWAK.
BUT WHY DO ALL MY POWERS HAVE TO BE CONCENTRATED IN MY BUTT?!
Kopi Luwak Research Organization
I WANT POWERS THAT I CAN USE ***OUTSIDE*** THE REST-ROOM!
PHYSIO-LOGICAL MYSTERIES NO ONE WOULD LAUGH AT.
Kopi Luwak Research Organization
MYSTERIES I COULD BE PROUD OF...

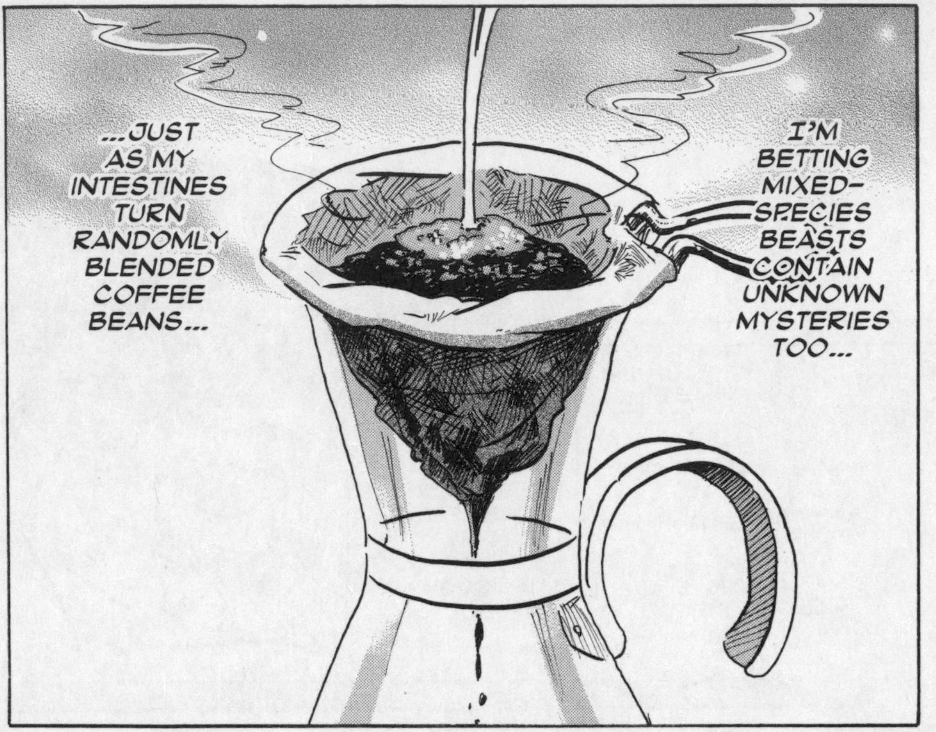
I'M BETTING MIXED-SPECIES BEASTS CONTAIN UNKNOWN MYSTERIES TOO...
...JUST AS MY INTESTINES TURN RANDOMLY BLENDED COFFEE BEANS...

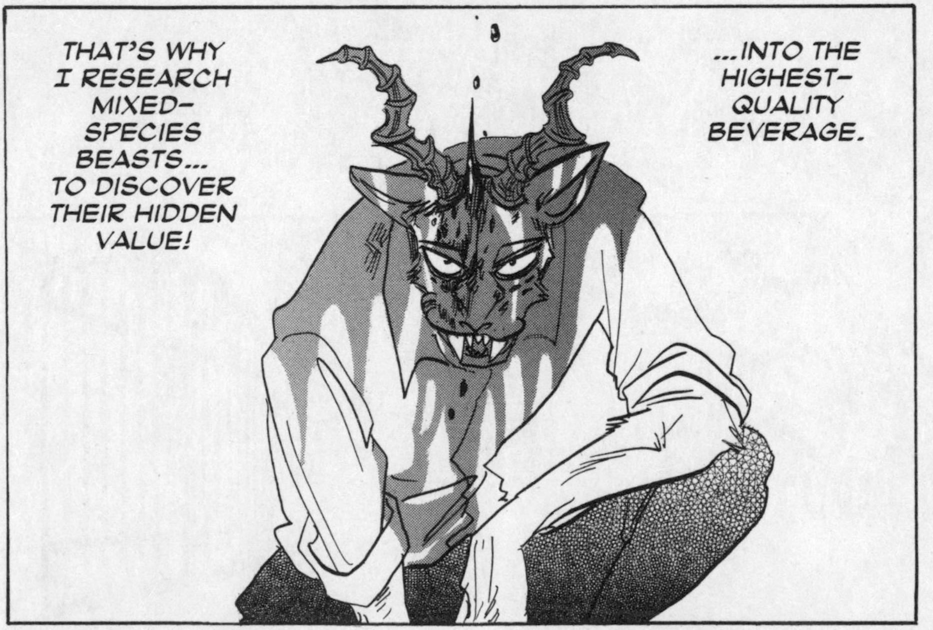
...INTO THE HIGHEST-QUALITY BEVERAGE.
THAT'S WHY I RESEARCH MIXED-SPECIES BEASTS... TO DISCOVER THEIR HIDDEN VALUE!

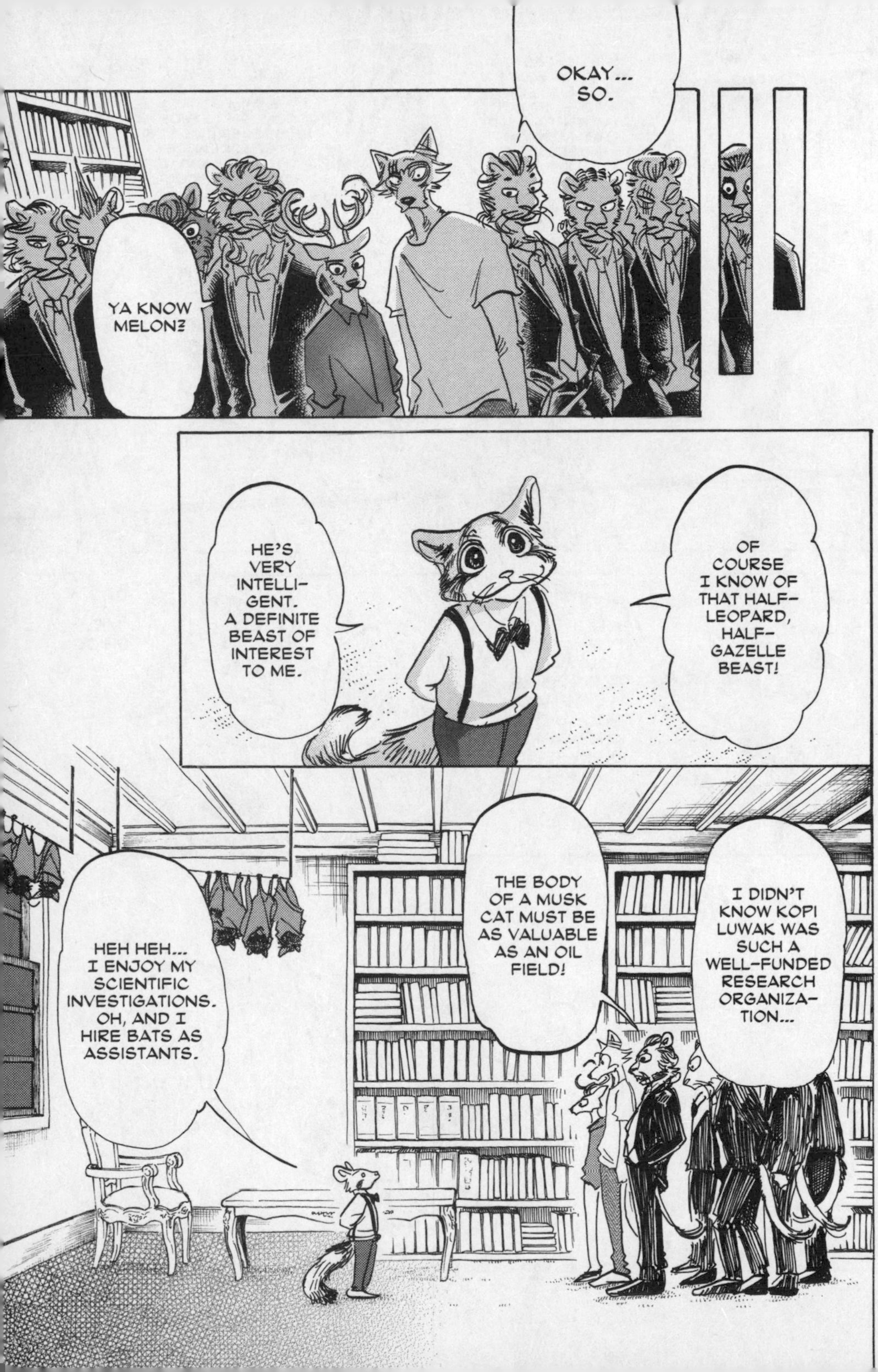
OKAY... SO.
YA KNOW MELON?
OF COURSE I KNOW OF THAT HALF-LEOPARD, HALF-GAZELLE BEAST!
HE'S VERY INTELLI-GENT. A DEFINITE BEAST OF INTEREST TO ME.
I DIDN'T KNOW KOPI LUWAK WAS SUCH A WELL-FUNDED RESEARCH ORGANIZA-TION...
THE BODY OF A MUSK CAT MUST BE AS VALUABLE AS AN OIL FIELD!
HEH HEH... I ENJOY MY SCIENTIFIC INVESTIGATIONS. OH, AND I HIRE BATS AS ASSISTANTS.

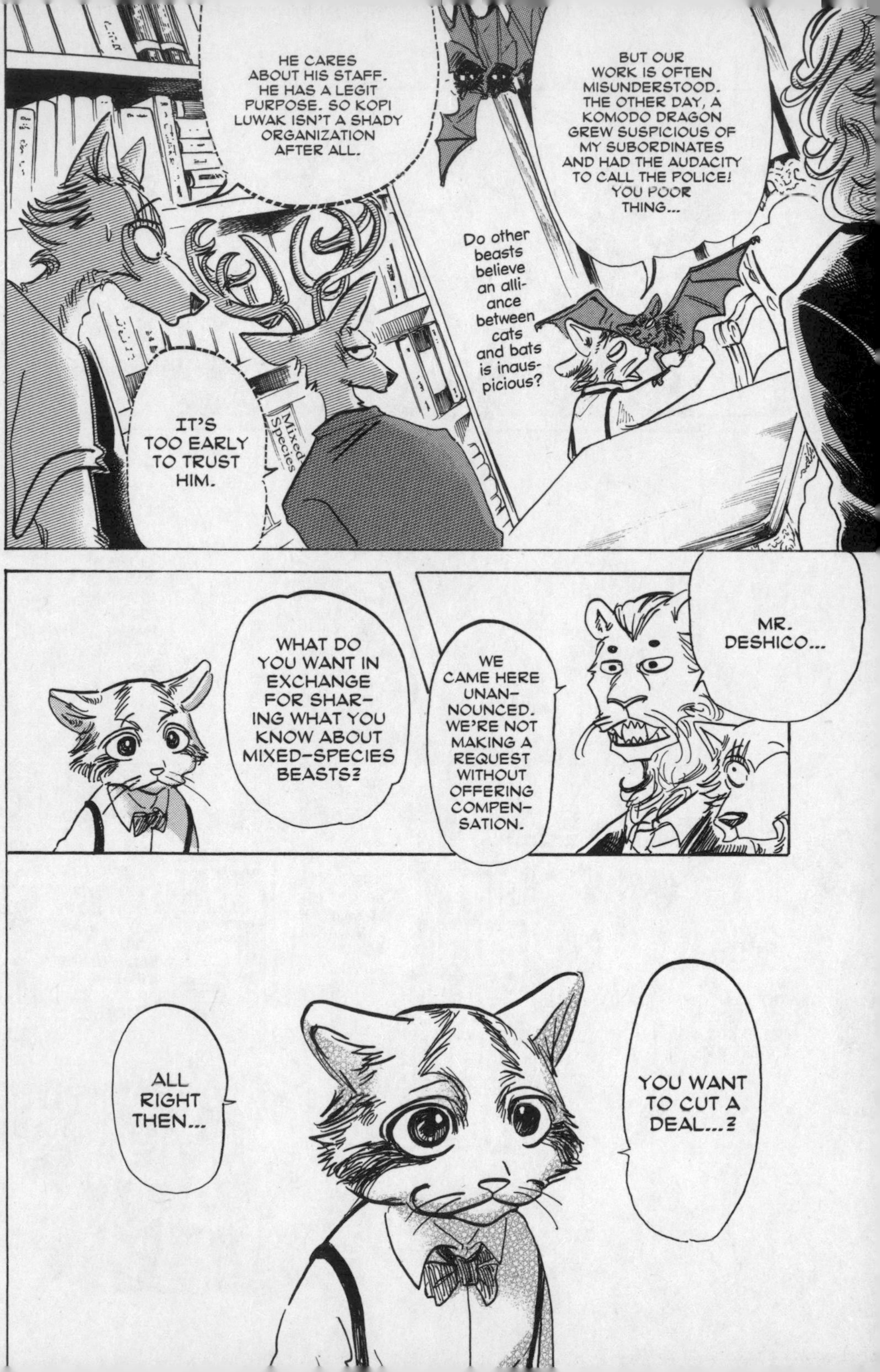
BUT OUR WORK IS OFTEN MISUNDERSTOOD. THE OTHER DAY, A KOMODO DRAGON GREW SUSPICIOUS OF MY SUBORDINATES AND HAD THE AUDACITY TO CALL THE POLICE! YOU POOR THING...
Do other beasts believe an alliance between cats and bats is inauspicious?
HE CARES ABOUT HIS STAFF. HE HAS A LEGIT PURPOSE. SO KOPI LUWAK ISN'T A SHADY ORGANIZATION AFTER ALL.
Mixed Species
IT'S TOO EARLY TO TRUST HIM.
MR. DESHICO...
WE CAME HERE UNANNOUNCED. WE'RE NOT MAKING A REQUEST WITHOUT OFFERING COMPENSATION.
WHAT DO YOU WANT IN EXCHANGE FOR SHARING WHAT YOU KNOW ABOUT MIXED-SPECIES BEASTS?
YOU WANT TO CUT A DEAL...?
ALL RIGHT THEN...

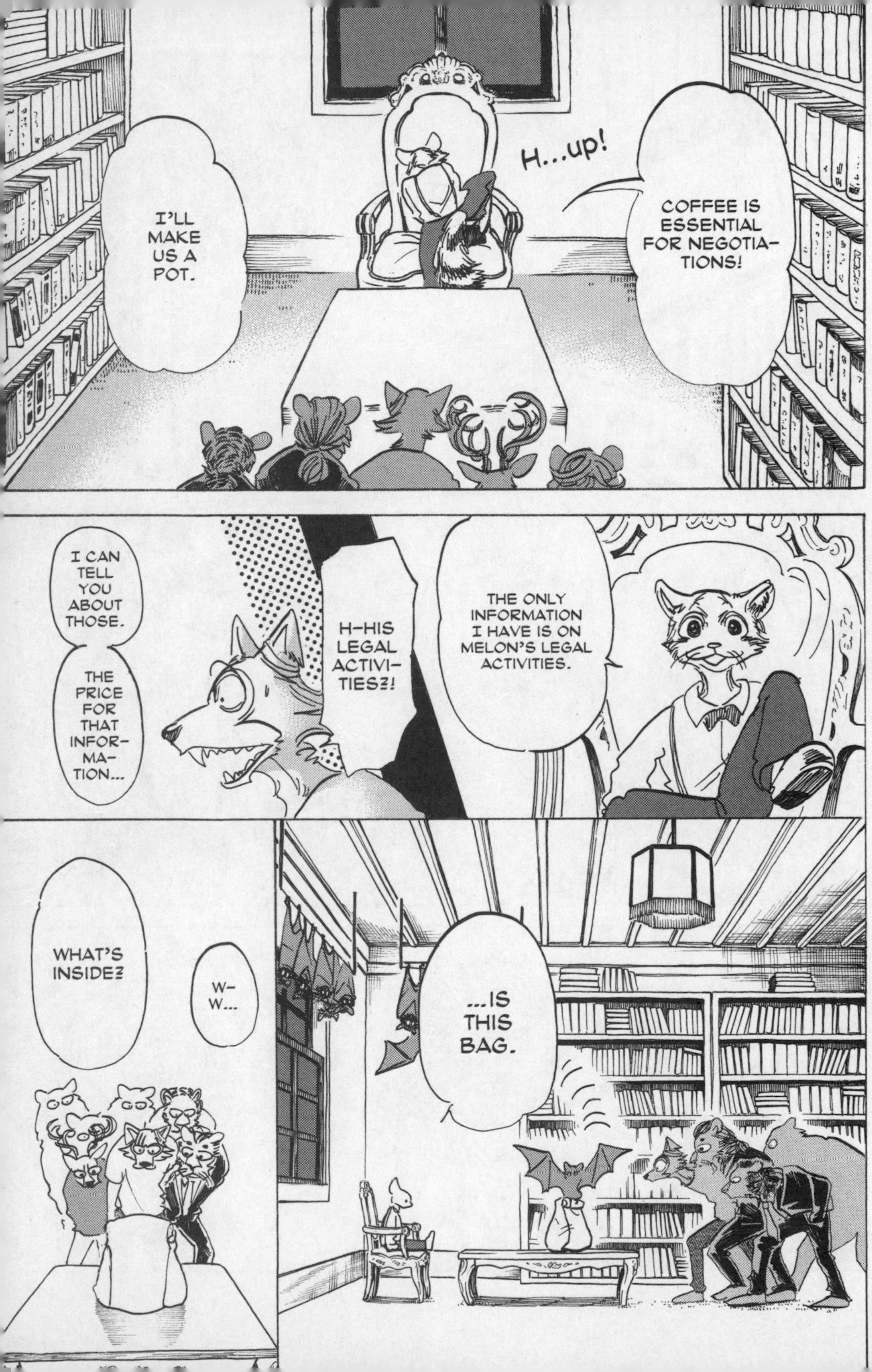
COFFEE IS ESSENTIAL FOR NEGOTIATIONS!
H...up!
I'LL MAKE US A POT.
THE ONLY INFORMATION I HAVE IS ON MELON'S LEGAL ACTIVITIES.
H-HIS LEGAL ACTIVITIES?!
I CAN TELL YOU ABOUT THOSE.
THE PRICE FOR THAT INFORMATION...
...IS THIS BAG.
W-W...
WHAT'S INSIDE?

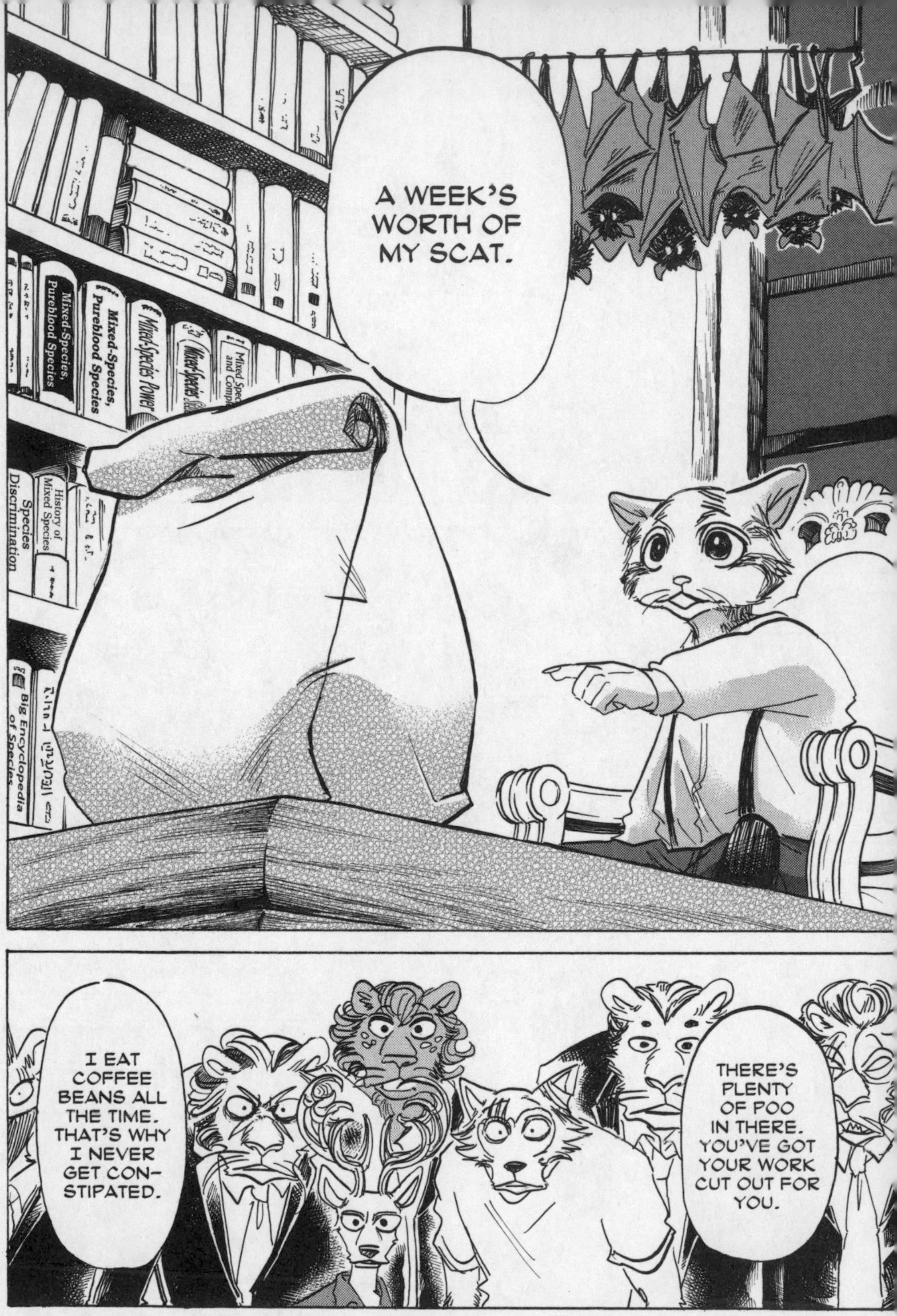
A WEEK'S WORTH OF MY SCAT.
Mixed-Species, Pureblood Species
Mixed-Species, Pureblood Species
Mixed-Species Power
History of Mixed Species
Species Discrimination
Big Encyclopedia of Species
THERE'S PLENTY OF POO IN THERE. YOU'VE GOT YOUR WORK CUT OUT FOR YOU.
I EAT COFFEE BEANS ALL THE TIME. THAT'S WHY I NEVER GET CON-STIPATED.

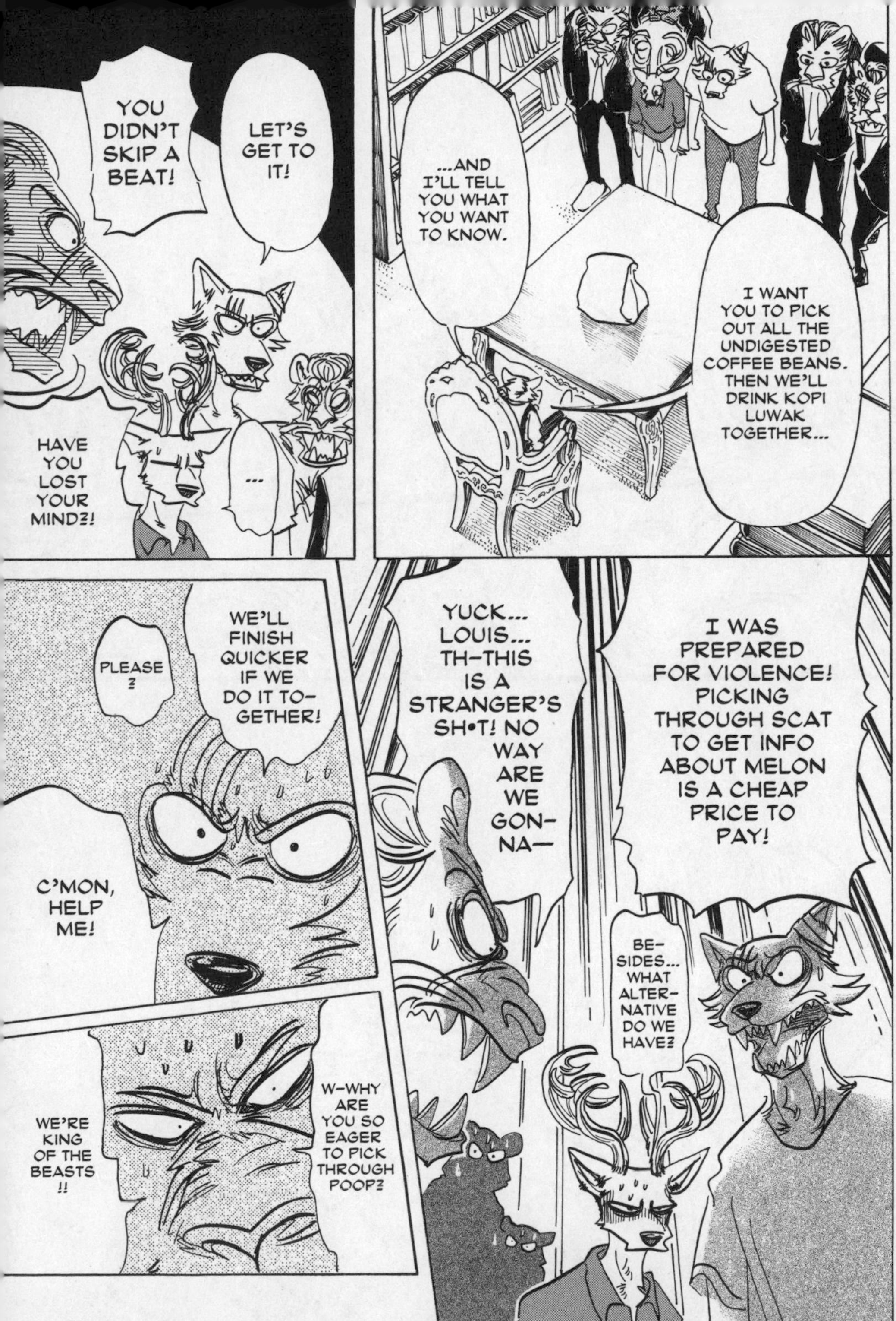
I WANT YOU TO PICK OUT ALL THE UNDIGESTED COFFEE BEANS. THEN WE'LL DRINK KOPI LUWAK TOGETHER...
...AND I'LL TELL YOU WHAT YOU WANT TO KNOW.
LET'S GET TO IT!
YOU DIDN'T SKIP A BEAT!
...
HAVE YOU LOST YOUR MIND?!
YUCK... LOUIS... TH-THIS IS A STRANGER'S SH•T! NO WAY ARE WE GON-NA—
I WAS PREPARED FOR VIOLENCE! PICKING THROUGH SCAT TO GET INFO ABOUT MELON IS A CHEAP PRICE TO PAY!
BE-SIDES... WHAT ALTER-NATIVE DO WE HAVE?
WE'LL FINISH QUICKER IF WE DO IT TO-GETHER!
PLEASE?
C'MON, HELP ME!
W-WHY ARE YOU SO EAGER TO PICK THROUGH POOP?
WE'RE KING OF THE BEASTS!!

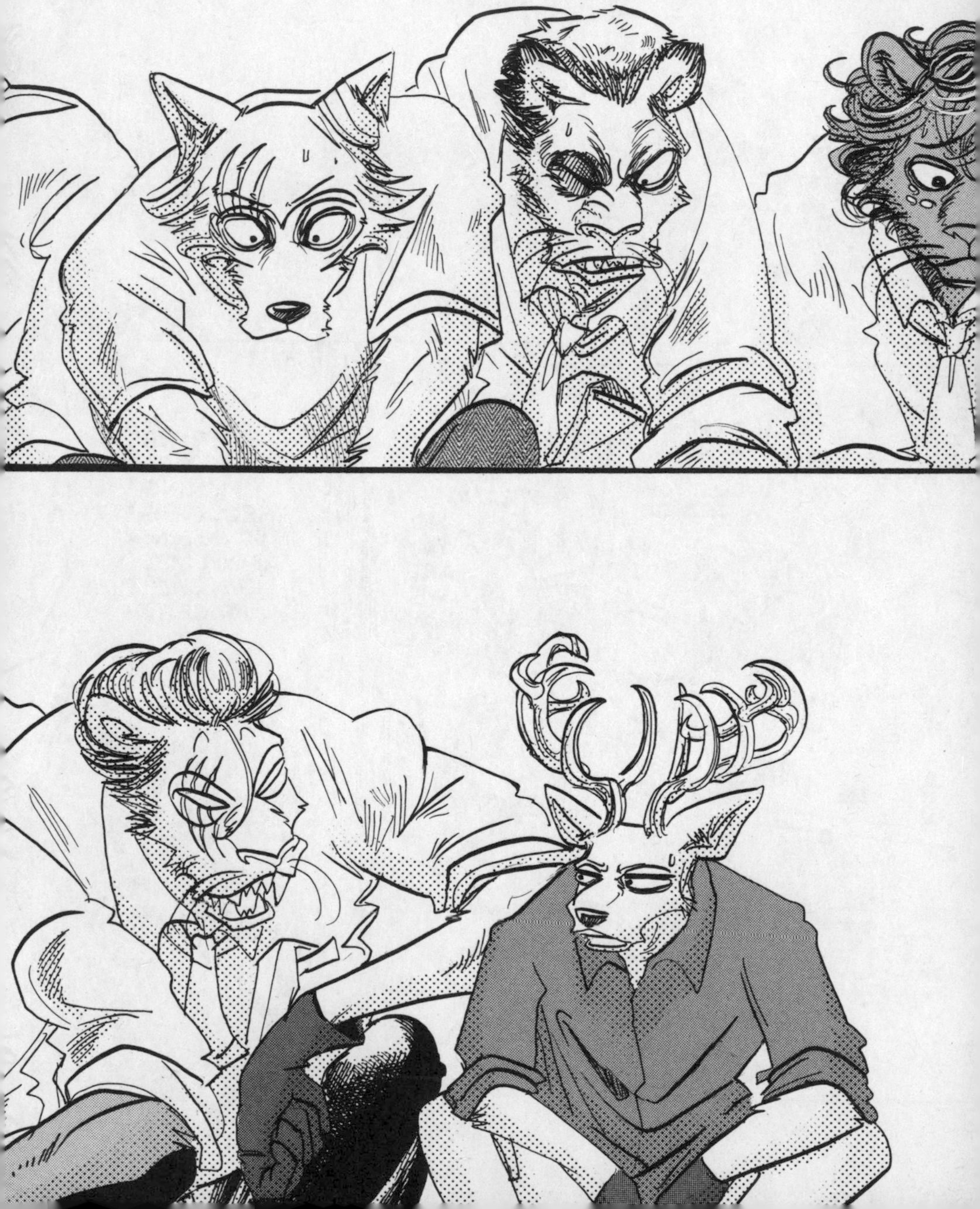

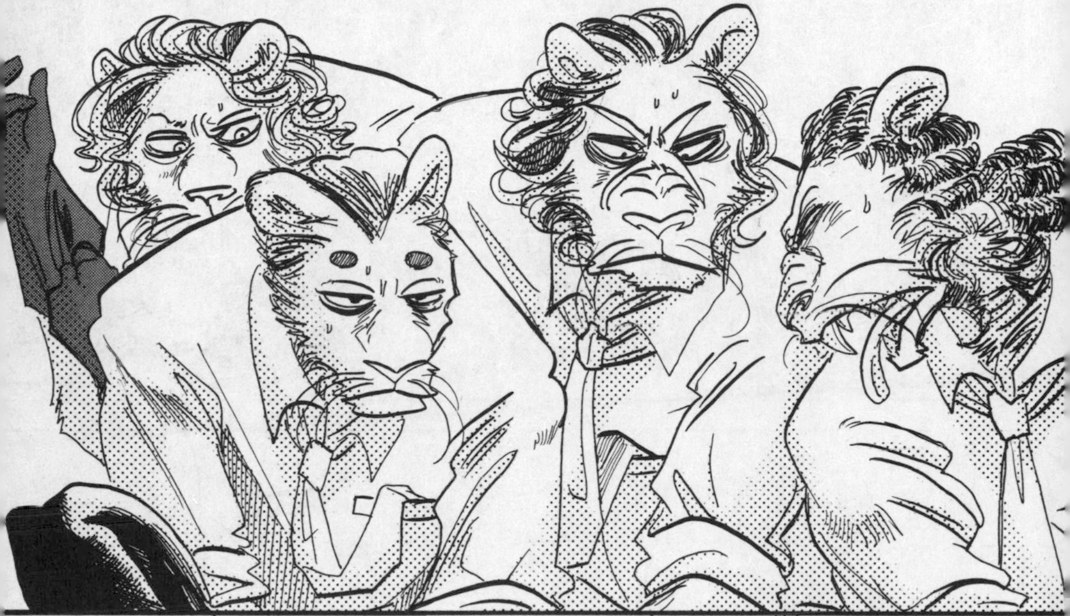
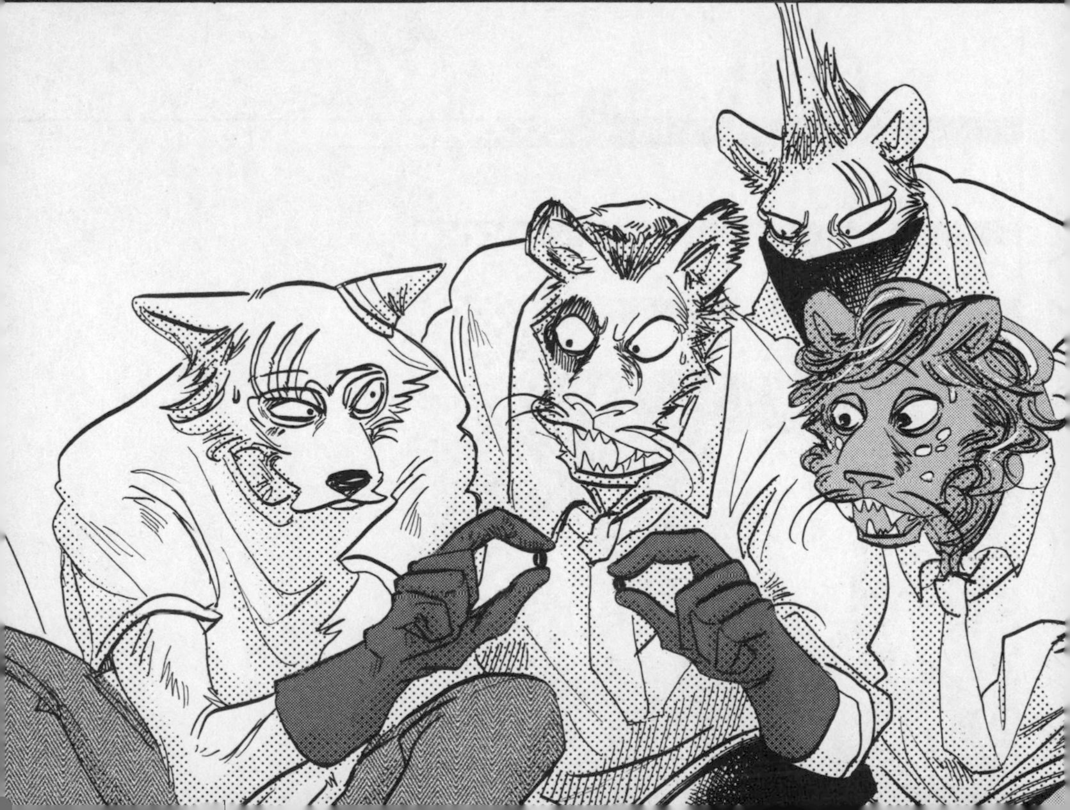

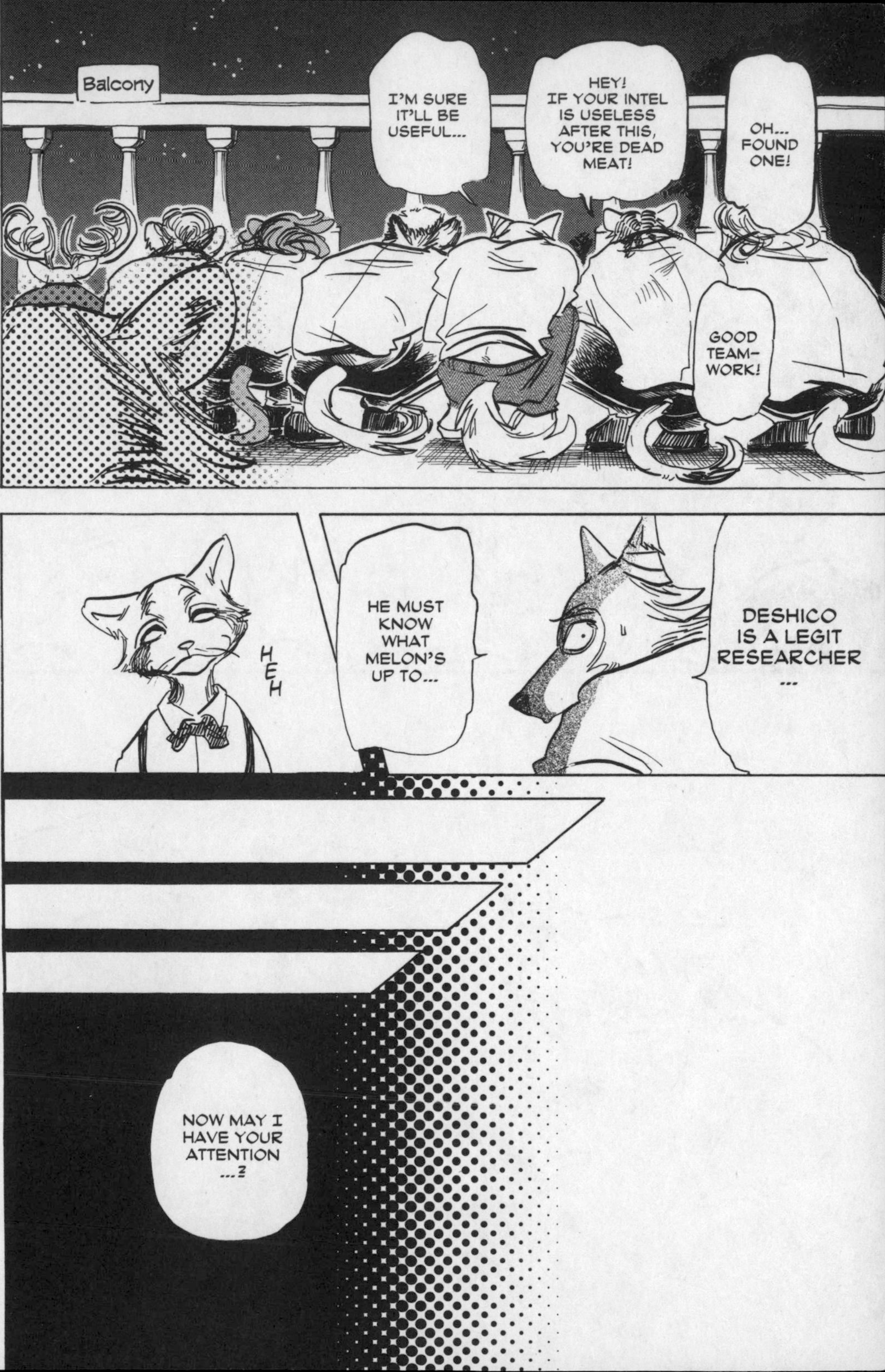
Balcony
OH... FOUND ONE!
GOOD TEAM-WORK!
HEY! IF YOUR INTEL IS USELESS AFTER THIS, YOU'RE DEAD MEAT!
I'M SURE IT'LL BE USEFUL...
DESHICO IS A LEGIT RESEARCHER ...
HE MUST KNOW WHAT MELON'S UP TO...
HEH
NOW MAY I HAVE YOUR ATTENTION ...?

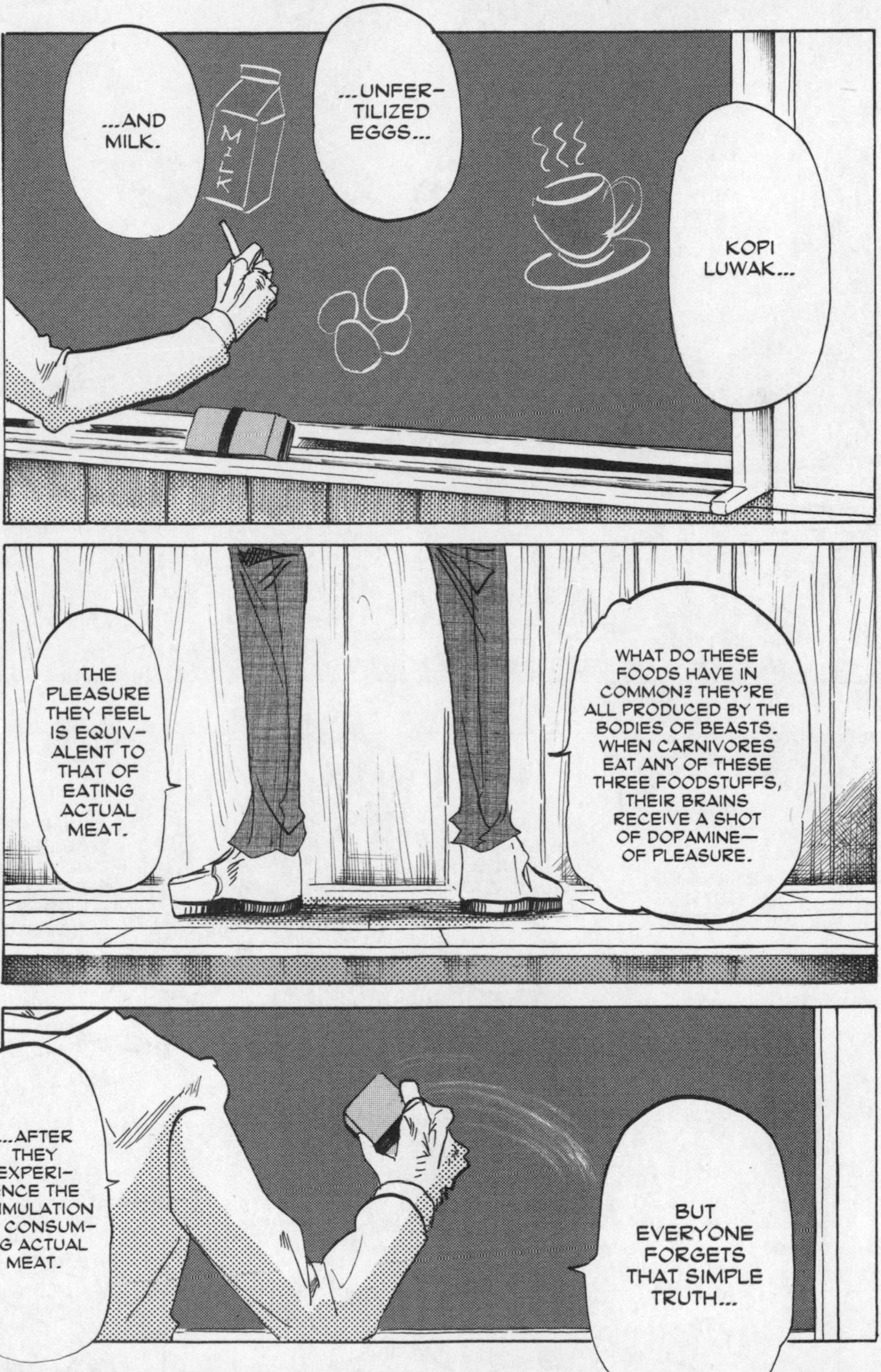
KOPI LUWAK...
...UNFER-TILIZED EGGS...
...AND MILK.
MILK
WHAT DO THESE FOODS HAVE IN COMMON? THEY'RE ALL PRODUCED BY THE BODIES OF BEASTS. WHEN CARNIVORES EAT ANY OF THESE THREE FOODSTUFFS, THEIR BRAINS RECEIVE A SHOT OF DOPAMINE—OF PLEASURE.
THE PLEASURE THEY FEEL IS EQUIV-ALENT TO THAT OF EATING ACTUAL MEAT.
BUT EVERYONE FORGETS THAT SIMPLE TRUTH...
...AFTER THEY EXPERI-ENCE THE STIMULATION OF CONSUM-ING ACTUAL MEAT.

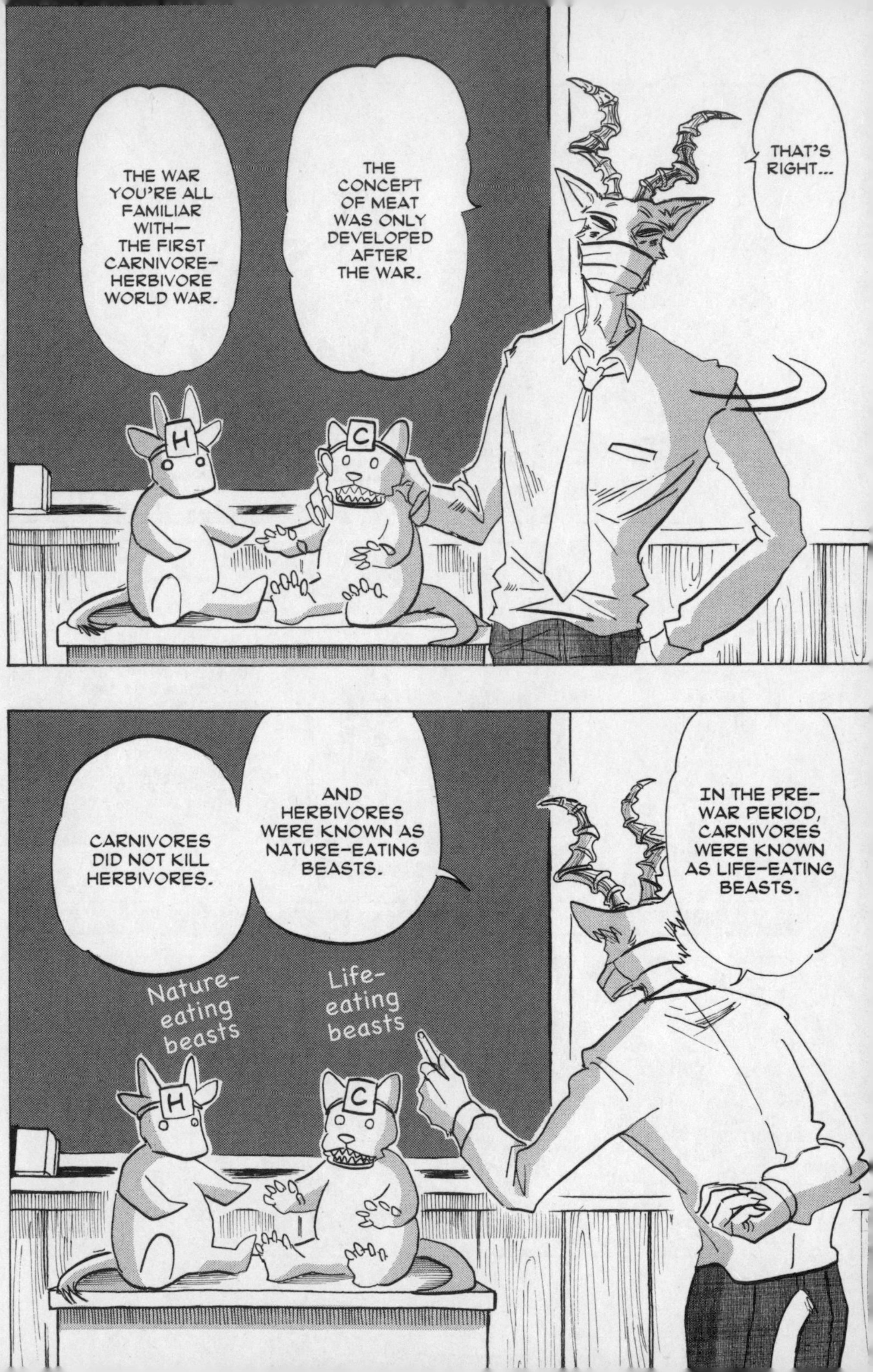
THAT'S RIGHT...
THE CONCEPT OF MEAT WAS ONLY DEVELOPED AFTER THE WAR.
THE WAR YOU'RE ALL FAMILIAR WITH— THE FIRST CARNIVORE-HERBIVORE WORLD WAR.
C
H
IN THE PRE-WAR PERIOD, CARNIVORES WERE KNOWN AS LIFE-EATING BEASTS.
AND HERBIVORES WERE KNOWN AS NATURE-EATING BEASTS.
CARNIVORES DID NOT KILL HERBIVORES.
Life-eating beasts
Nature-eating beasts
C
H

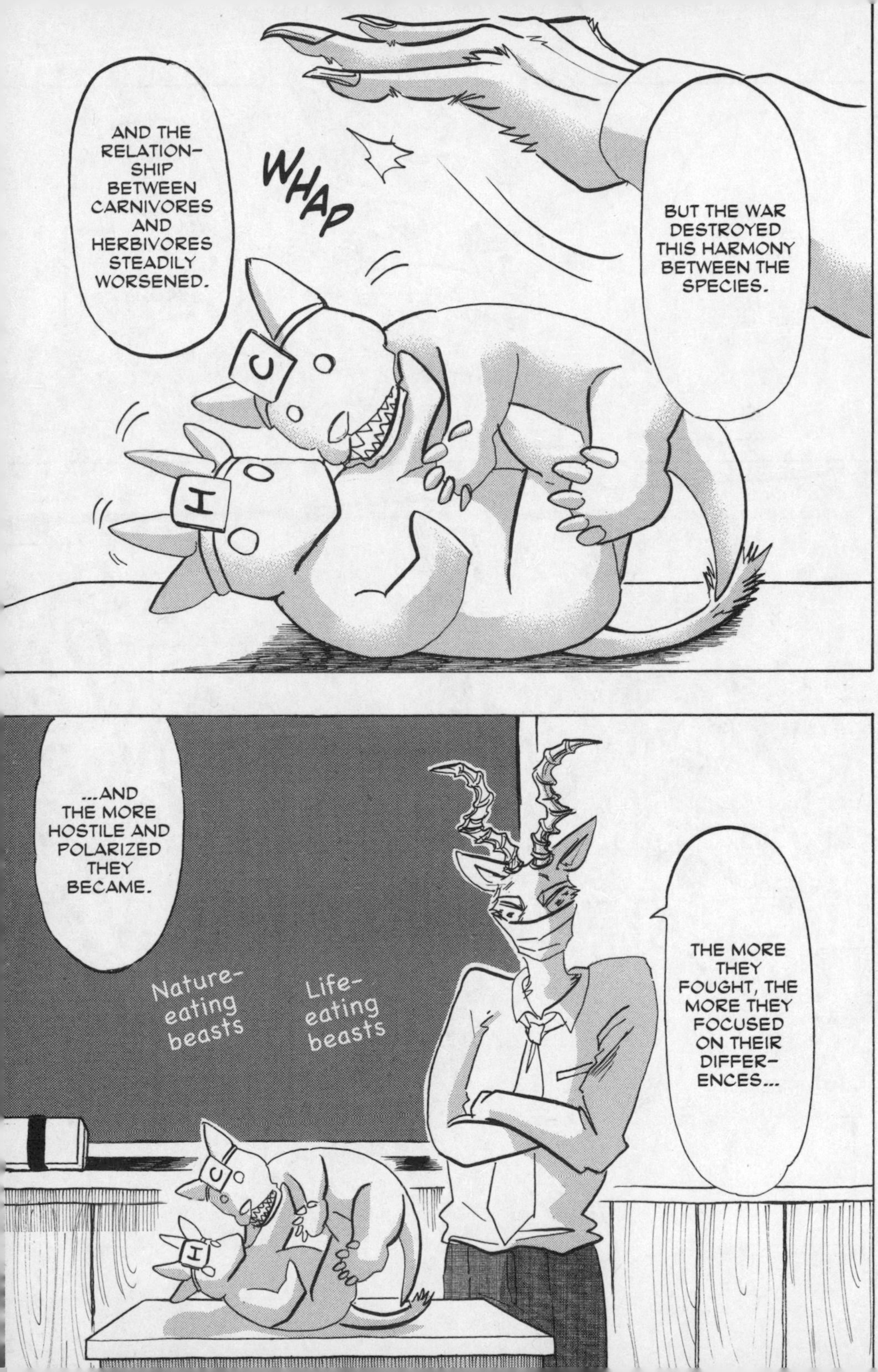
BUT THE WAR DESTROYED THIS HARMONY BETWEEN THE SPECIES.
WHAP
AND THE RELATION-SHIP BETWEEN CARNIVORES AND HERBIVORES STEADILY WORSENED.
C
H
THE MORE THEY FOUGHT, THE MORE THEY FOCUSED ON THEIR DIFFER-ENCES...
...AND THE MORE HOSTILE AND POLARIZED THEY BECAME.
Life-eating beasts
Nature-eating beasts

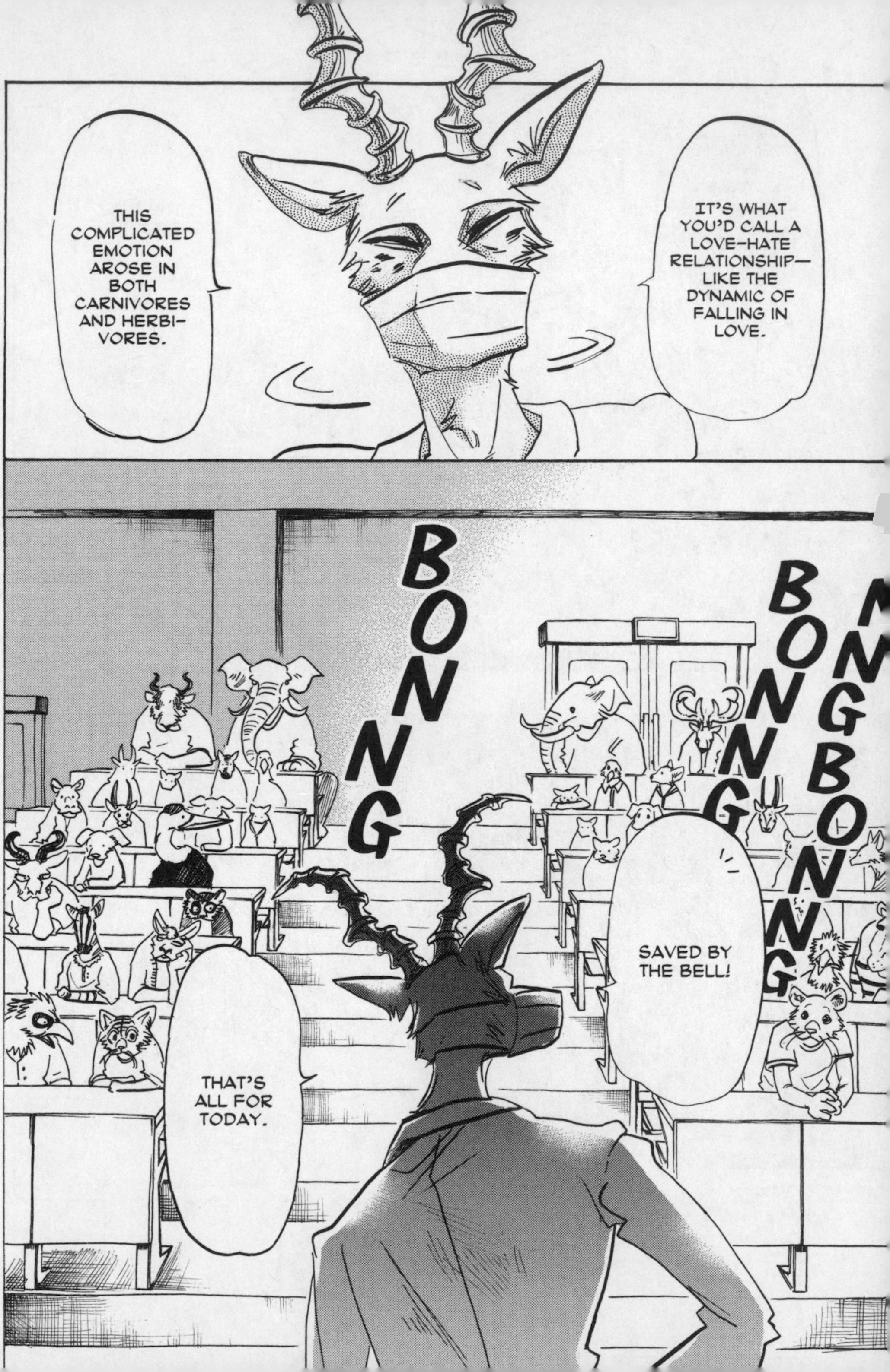
IT'S WHAT YOU'D CALL A LOVE-HATE RELATIONSHIP— LIKE THE DYNAMIC OF FALLING IN LOVE.
THIS COMPLICATED EMOTION AROSE IN BOTH CARNIVORES AND HERBIVORES.
BONNG
BONNG
SAVED BY THE BELL!
THAT'S ALL FOR TODAY.

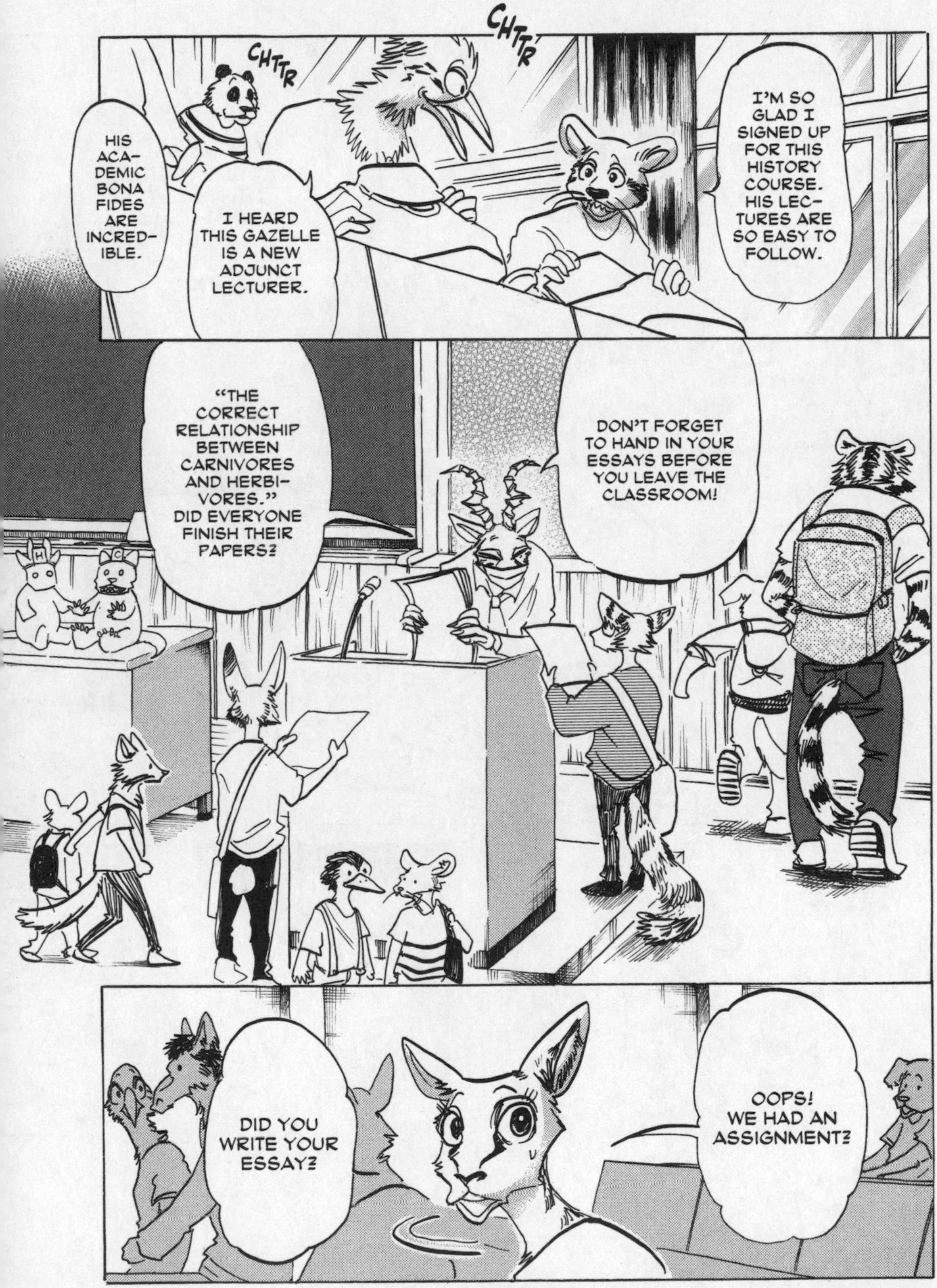
CHTTR
HIS ACA-DEMIC BONA FIDES ARE INCRED-IBLE.
I HEARD THIS GAZELLE IS A NEW ADJUNCT LECTURER.
CHTTR
I'M SO GLAD I SIGNED UP FOR THIS HISTORY COURSE. HIS LEC-TURES ARE SO EASY TO FOLLOW.
"THE CORRECT RELATIONSHIP BETWEEN CARNIVORES AND HERBI-VORES." DID EVERYONE FINISH THEIR PAPERS?
DON'T FORGET TO HAND IN YOUR ESSAYS BEFORE YOU LEAVE THE CLASSROOM!
DID YOU WRITE YOUR ESSAY?
OOPS! WE HAD AN ASSIGNMENT?

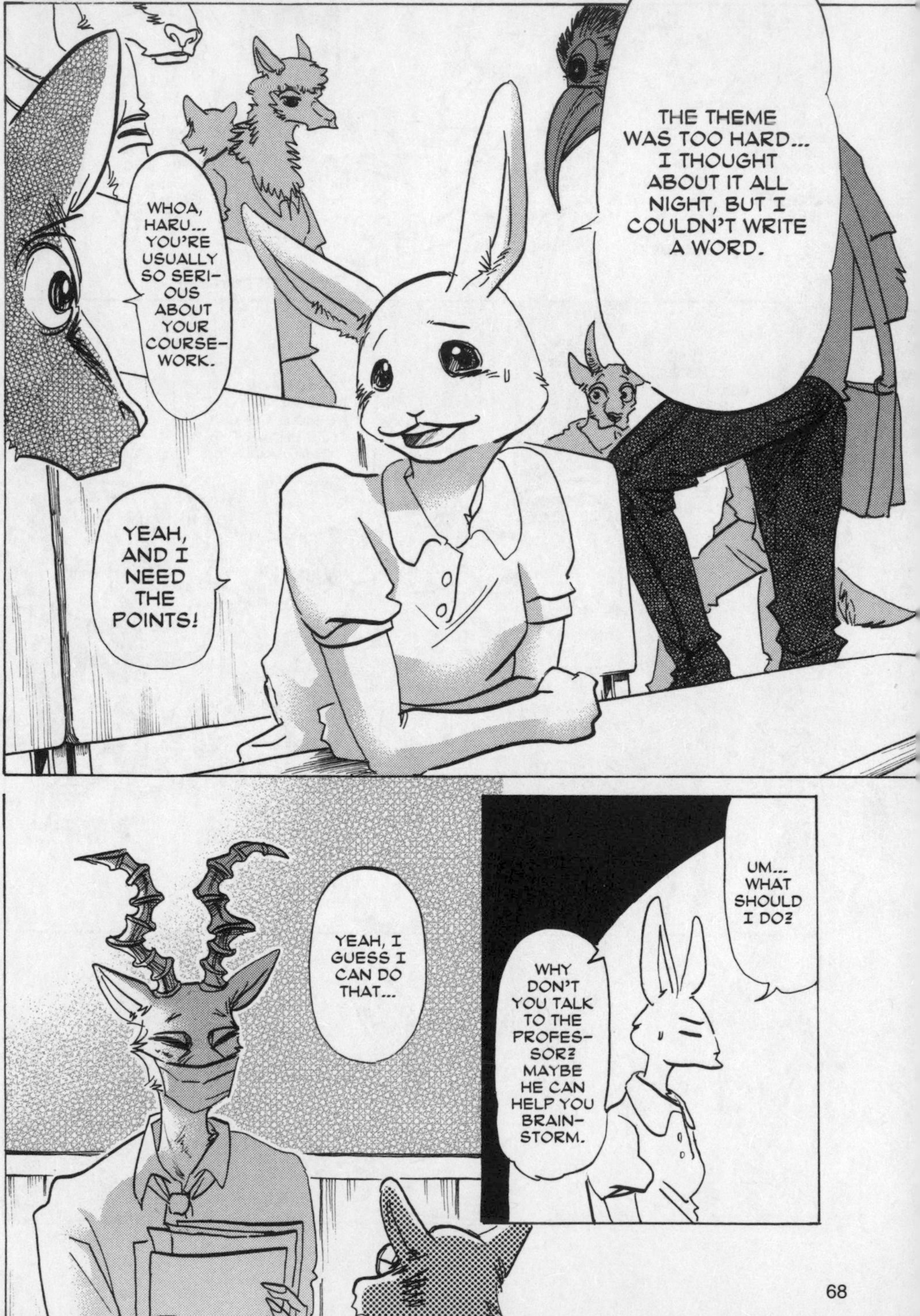
THE THEME WAS TOO HARD... I THOUGHT ABOUT IT ALL NIGHT, BUT I COULDN'T WRITE A WORD.
WHOA, HARU... YOU'RE USUALLY SO SERIOUS ABOUT YOUR COURSEWORK.
YEAH, AND I NEED THE POINTS!
UM... WHAT SHOULD I DO?
WHY DON'T YOU TALK TO THE PROFESSOR? MAYBE HE CAN HELP YOU BRAINSTORM.
YEAH, I GUESS I CAN DO THAT...

Chapter 146: El Niño Occurred in My Desert

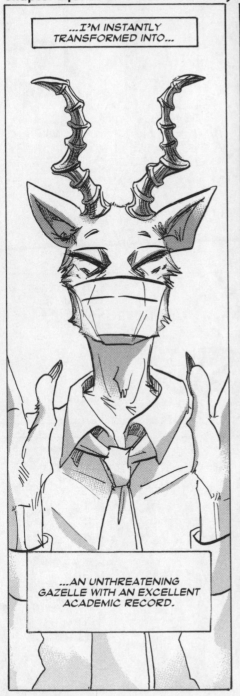

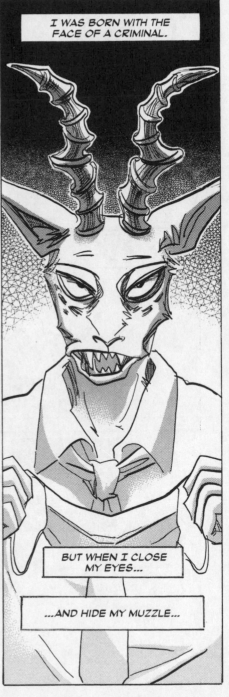

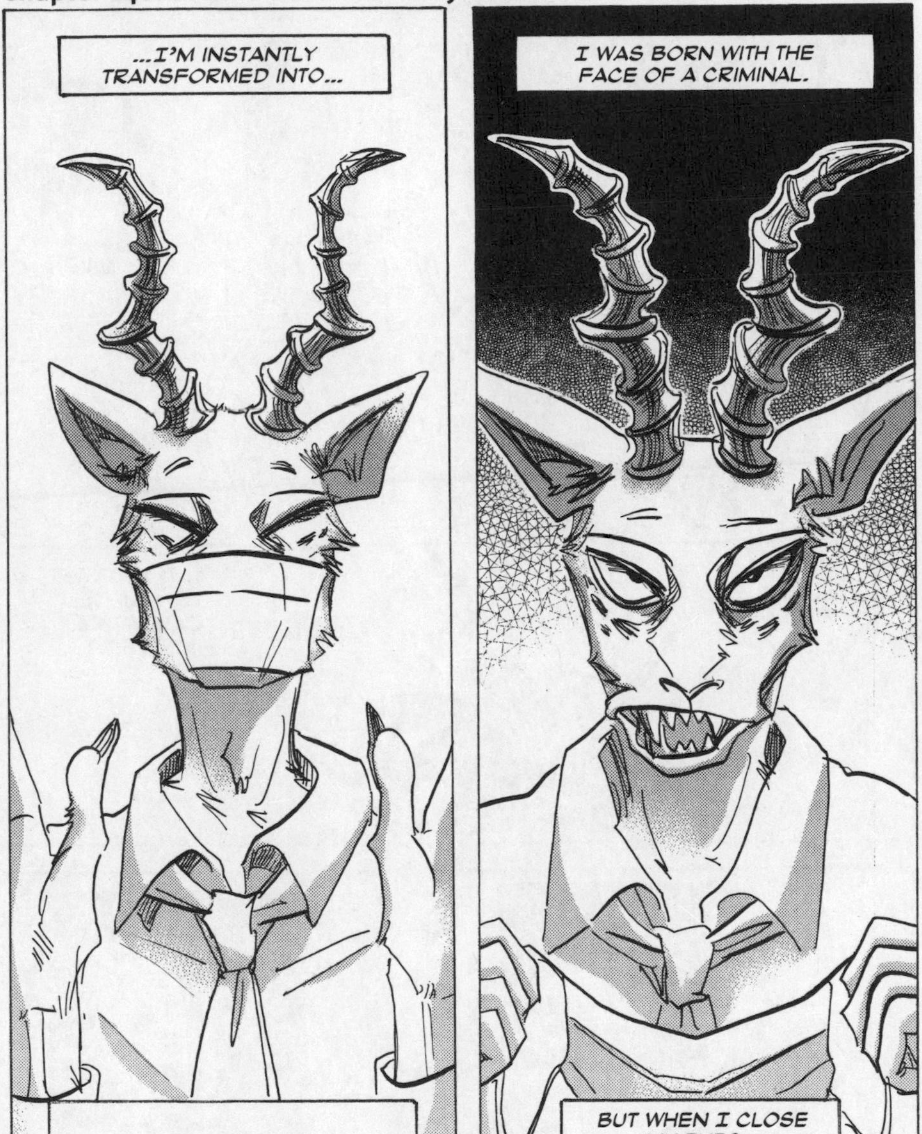
I WAS BORN WITH THE FACE OF A CRIMINAL.
BUT WHEN I CLOSE MY EYES...
...AND HIDE MY MUZZLE...
...I'M INSTANTLY TRANSFORMED INTO...
...AN UNTHREATENING GAZELLE WITH AN EXCELLENT ACADEMIC RECORD.

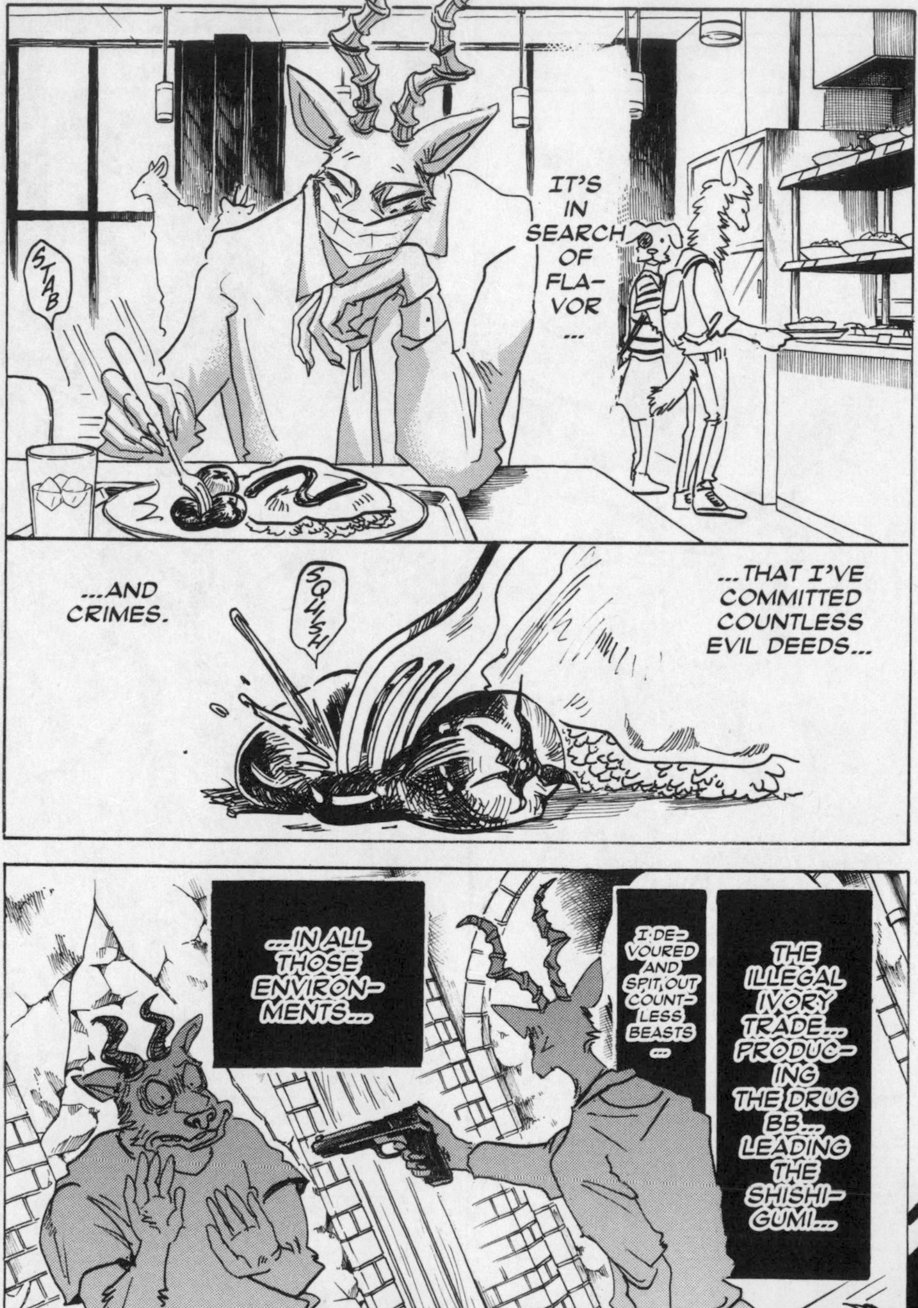
IT'S IN SEARCH OF FLA-VOR...
STAB
...THAT I'VE COMMITTED COUNTLESS EVIL DEEDS...
SQUISH
...AND CRIMES.
THE ILLEGAL IVORY TRADE... PRODUCING THE DRUG BB... LEADING THE SHISHI-GUMI...
I DE-VOURED AND SPIT OUT COUNT-LESS BEASTS...
...IN ALL THOSE ENVIRON-MENTS...

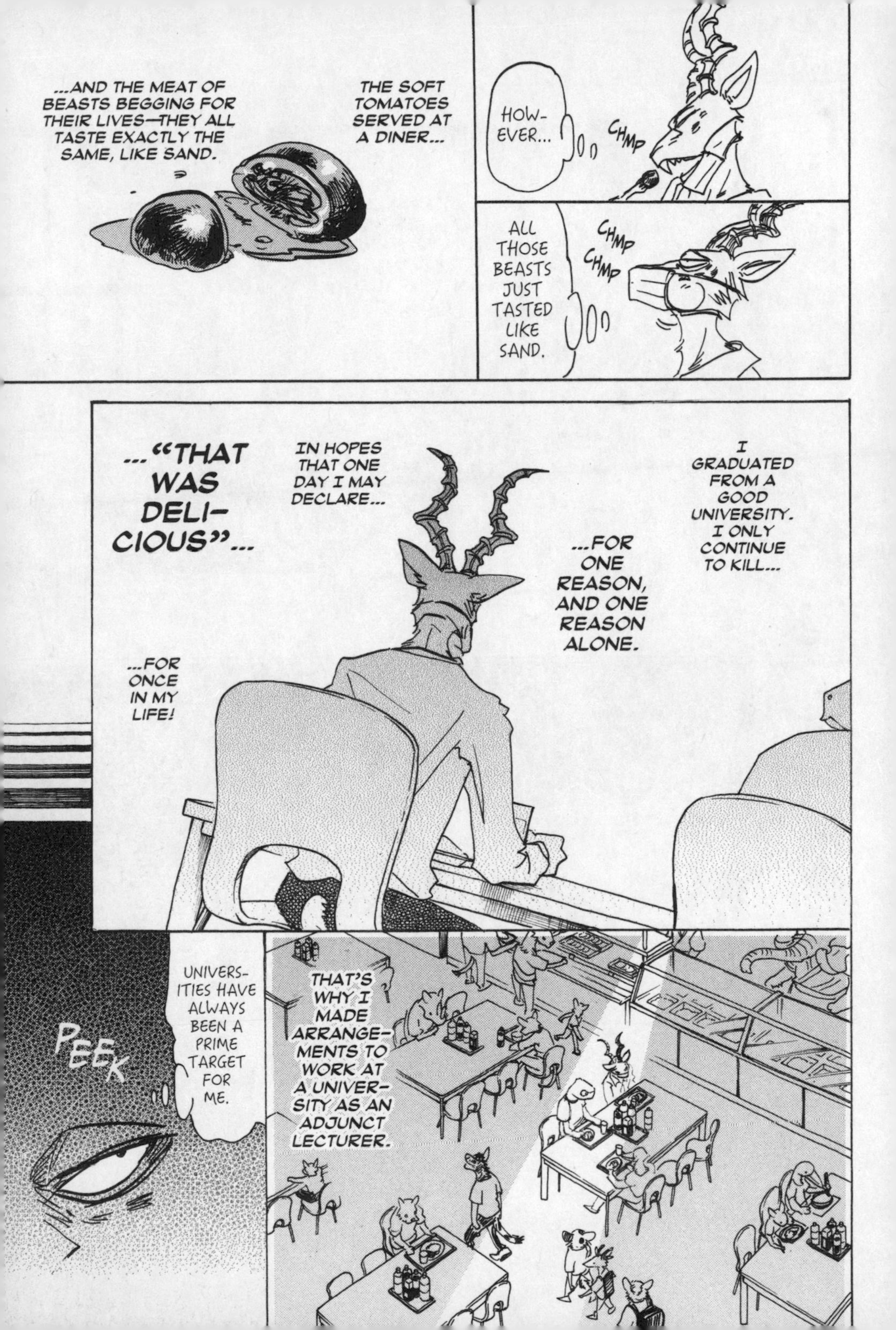
HOW-EVER...
CHMP
ALL THOSE BEASTS JUST TASTED LIKE SAND.
CHMP
CHMP
THE SOFT TOMATOES SERVED AT A DINER...
...AND THE MEAT OF BEASTS BEGGING FOR THEIR LIVES—THEY ALL TASTE EXACTLY THE SAME, LIKE SAND.
I GRADUATED FROM A GOOD UNIVERSITY. I ONLY CONTINUE TO KILL...
...FOR ONE REASON, AND ONE REASON ALONE.
IN HOPES THAT ONE DAY I MAY DECLARE...
..."THAT WAS DELICIOUS"...
...FOR ONCE IN MY LIFE!
THAT'S WHY I MADE ARRANGE-MENTS TO WORK AT A UNIVER-SITY AS AN ADJUNCT LECTURER.
UNIVERS-ITIES HAVE ALWAYS BEEN A PRIME TARGET FOR ME.
PEEK

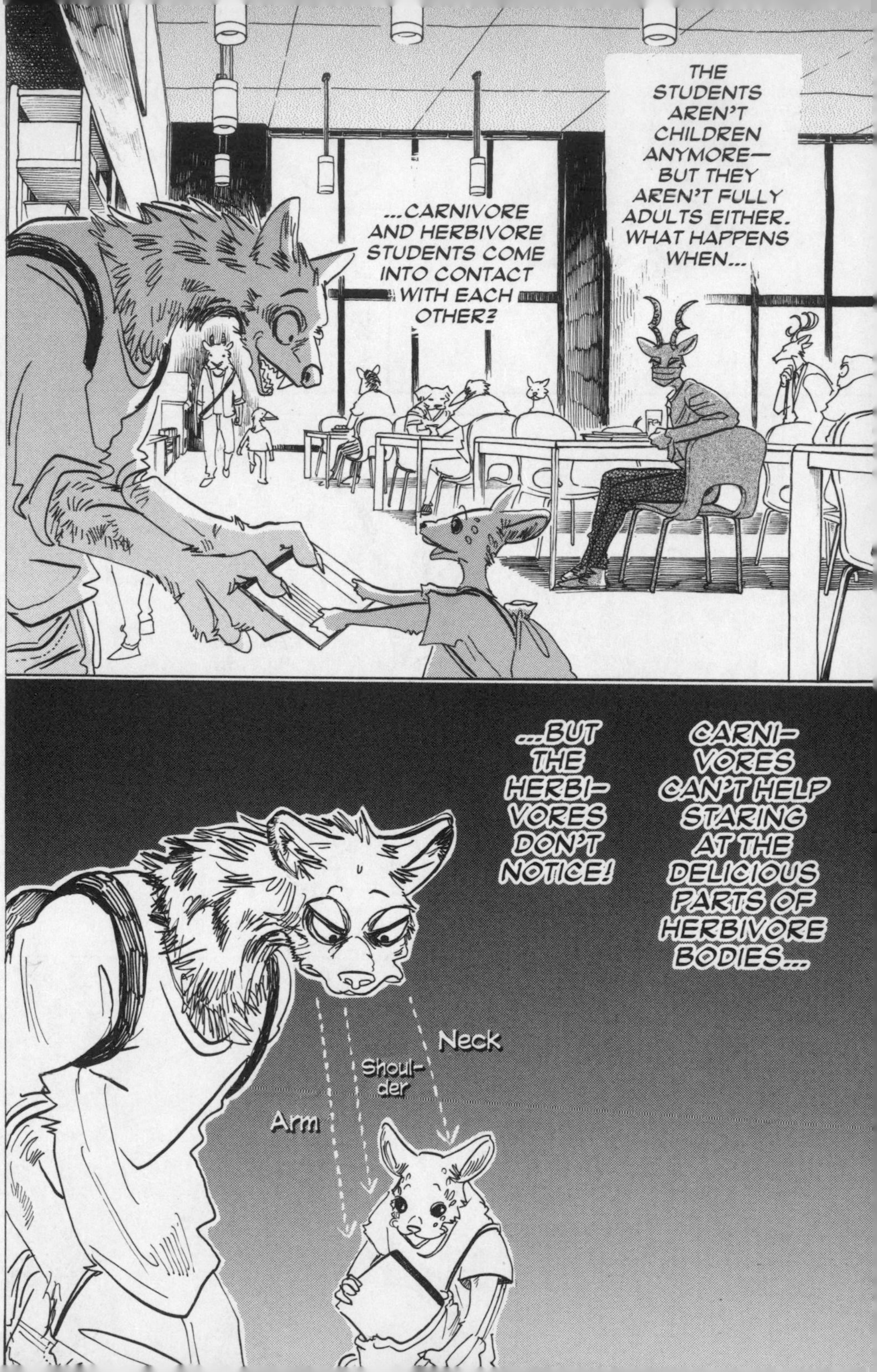
THE STUDENTS AREN'T CHILDREN ANYMORE—BUT THEY AREN'T FULLY ADULTS EITHER. WHAT HAPPENS WHEN...
...CARNIVORE AND HERBIVORE STUDENTS COME INTO CONTACT WITH EACH OTHER?
CARNIVORES CAN'T HELP STARING AT THE DELICIOUS PARTS OF HERBIVORE BODIES...
...BUT THE HERBIVORES DON'T NOTICE!
Neck
Shoulder
Arm

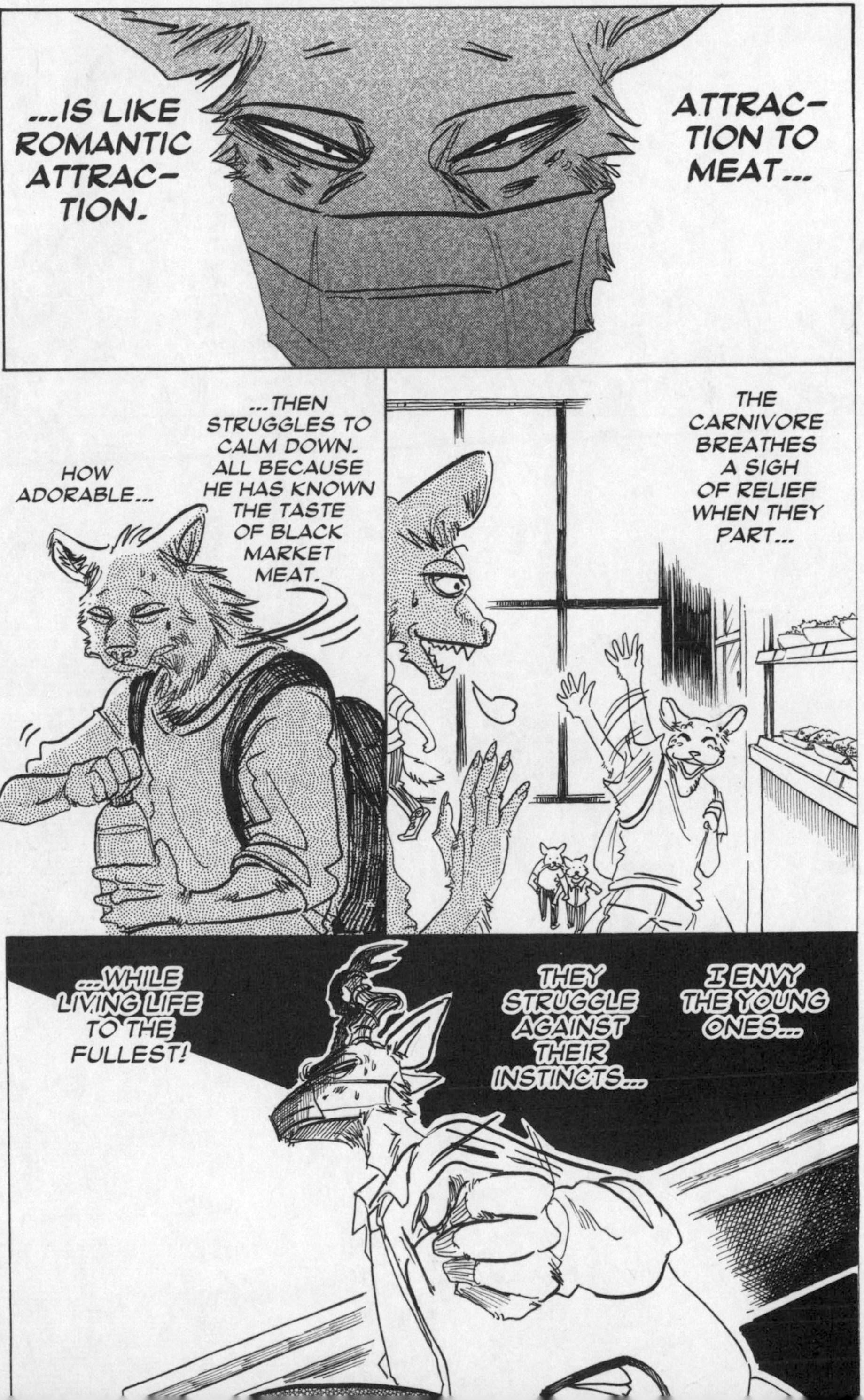
ATTRACTION TO MEAT...
...IS LIKE ROMANTIC ATTRACTION.
THE CARNIVORE BREATHES A SIGH OF RELIEF WHEN THEY PART...
...THEN STRUGGLES TO CALM DOWN. ALL BECAUSE HE HAS KNOWN THE TASTE OF BLACK MARKET MEAT.
HOW ADORABLE...
I ENVY THE YOUNG ONES...
THEY STRUGGLE AGAINST THEIR INSTINCTS...
...WHILE LIVING LIFE TO THE FULLEST!

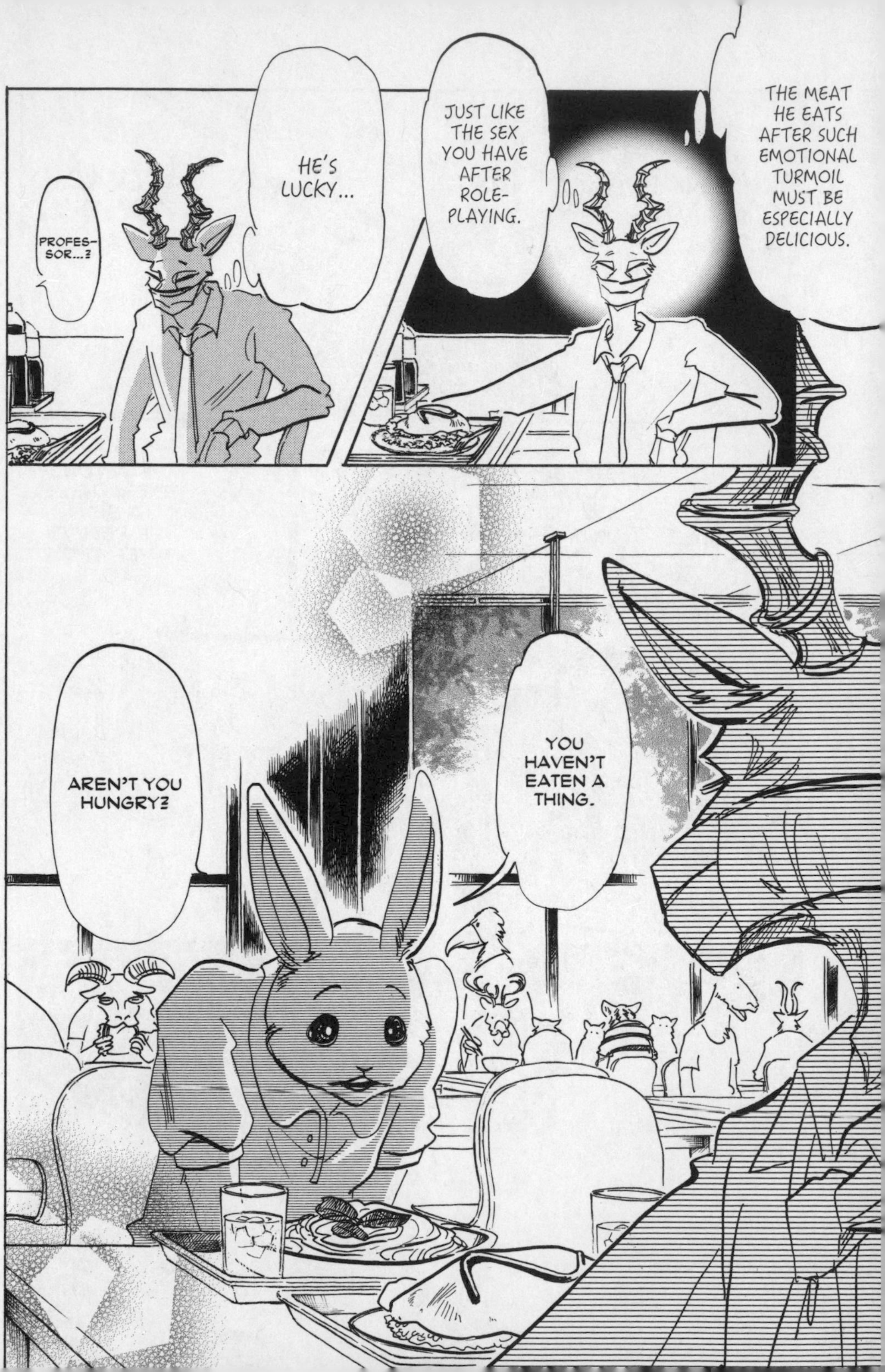

THE MEAT HE EATS AFTER SUCH EMOTIONAL TURMOIL MUST BE ESPECIALLY DELICIOUS.
JUST LIKE THE SEX YOU HAVE AFTER ROLE-PLAYING.
HE'S LUCKY...
PROFES-SOR...?
YOU HAVEN'T EATEN A THING.
AREN'T YOU HUNGRY?

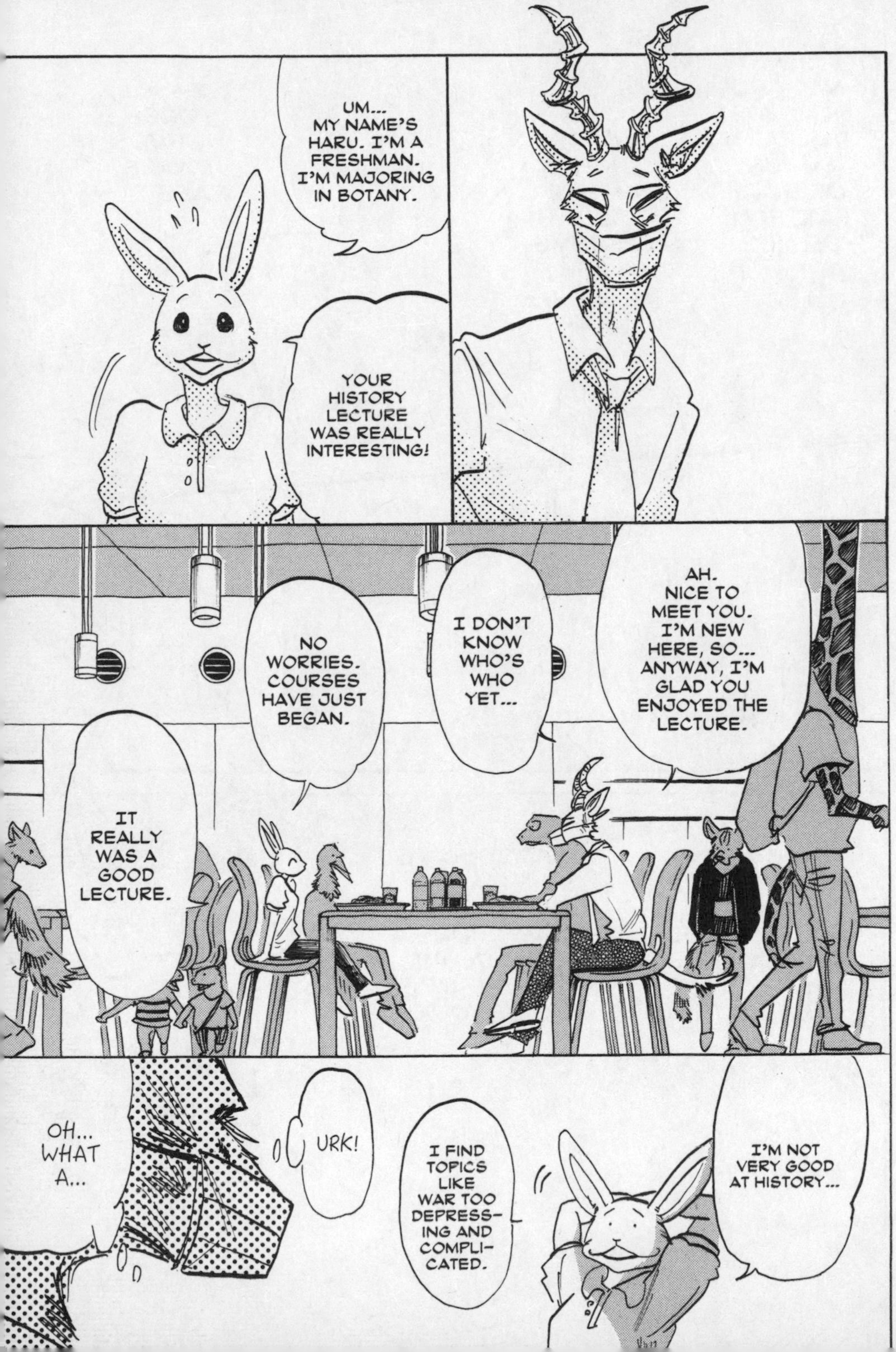
UM... MY NAME'S HARU. I'M A FRESHMAN. I'M MAJORING IN BOTANY.
YOUR HISTORY LECTURE WAS REALLY INTERESTING!
AH. NICE TO MEET YOU. I'M NEW HERE, SO... ANYWAY, I'M GLAD YOU ENJOYED THE LECTURE.
I DON'T KNOW WHO'S WHO YET...
NO WORRIES. COURSES HAVE JUST BEGAN.
IT REALLY WAS A GOOD LECTURE.
I'M NOT VERY GOOD AT HISTORY...
I FIND TOPICS LIKE WAR TOO DEPRESSING AND COMPLICATED.
URK!
OH... WHAT A...

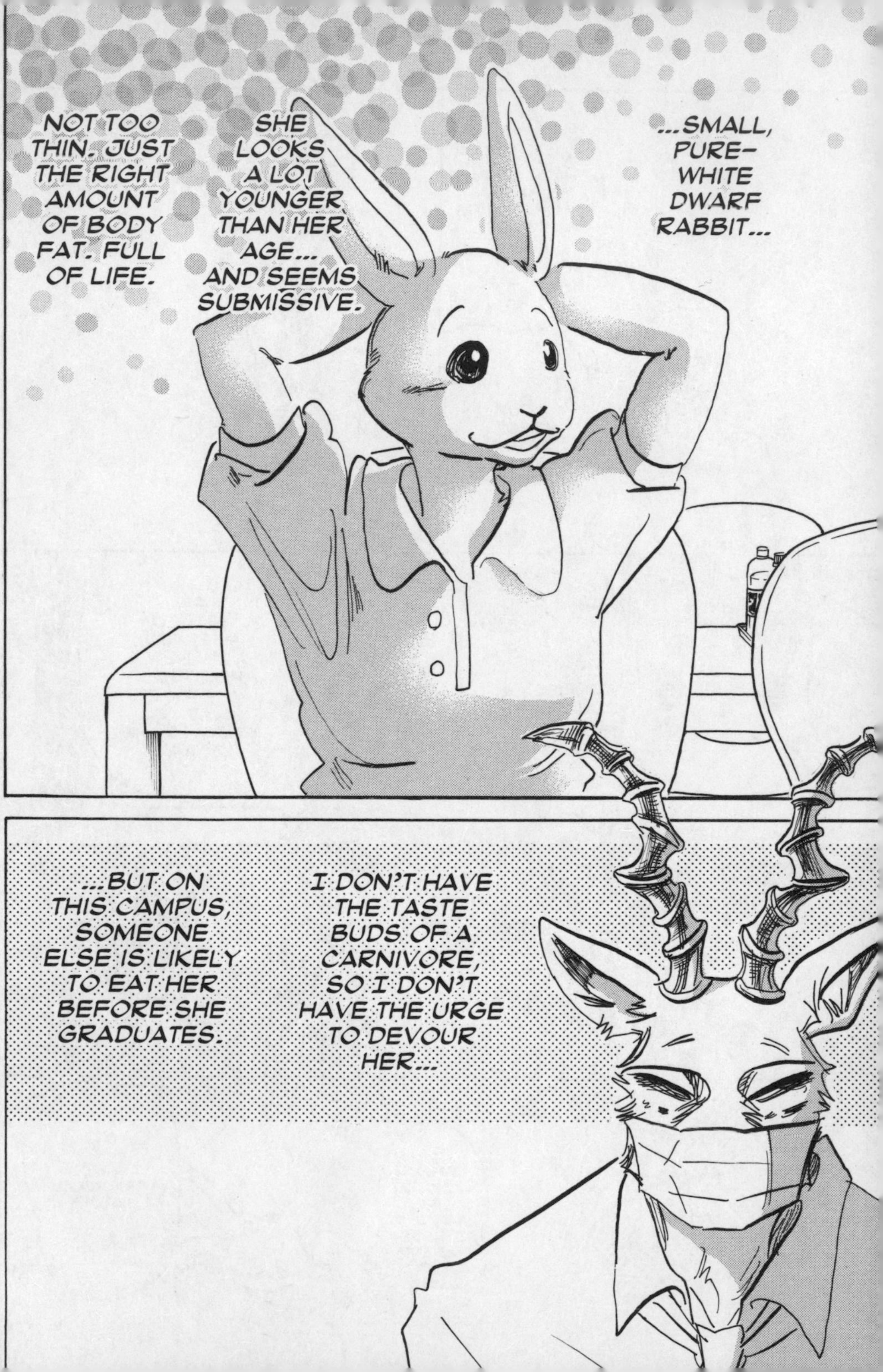
...SMALL, PURE-WHITE DWARF RABBIT...
SHE LOOKS A LOT YOUNGER THAN HER AGE... AND SEEMS SUBMISSIVE.
NOT TOO THIN. JUST THE RIGHT AMOUNT OF BODY FAT. FULL OF LIFE.
I DON'T HAVE THE TASTE BUDS OF A CARNIVORE, SO I DON'T HAVE THE URGE TO DEVOUR HER...
...BUT ON THIS CAMPUS, SOMEONE ELSE IS LIKELY TO EAT HER BEFORE SHE GRADUATES.

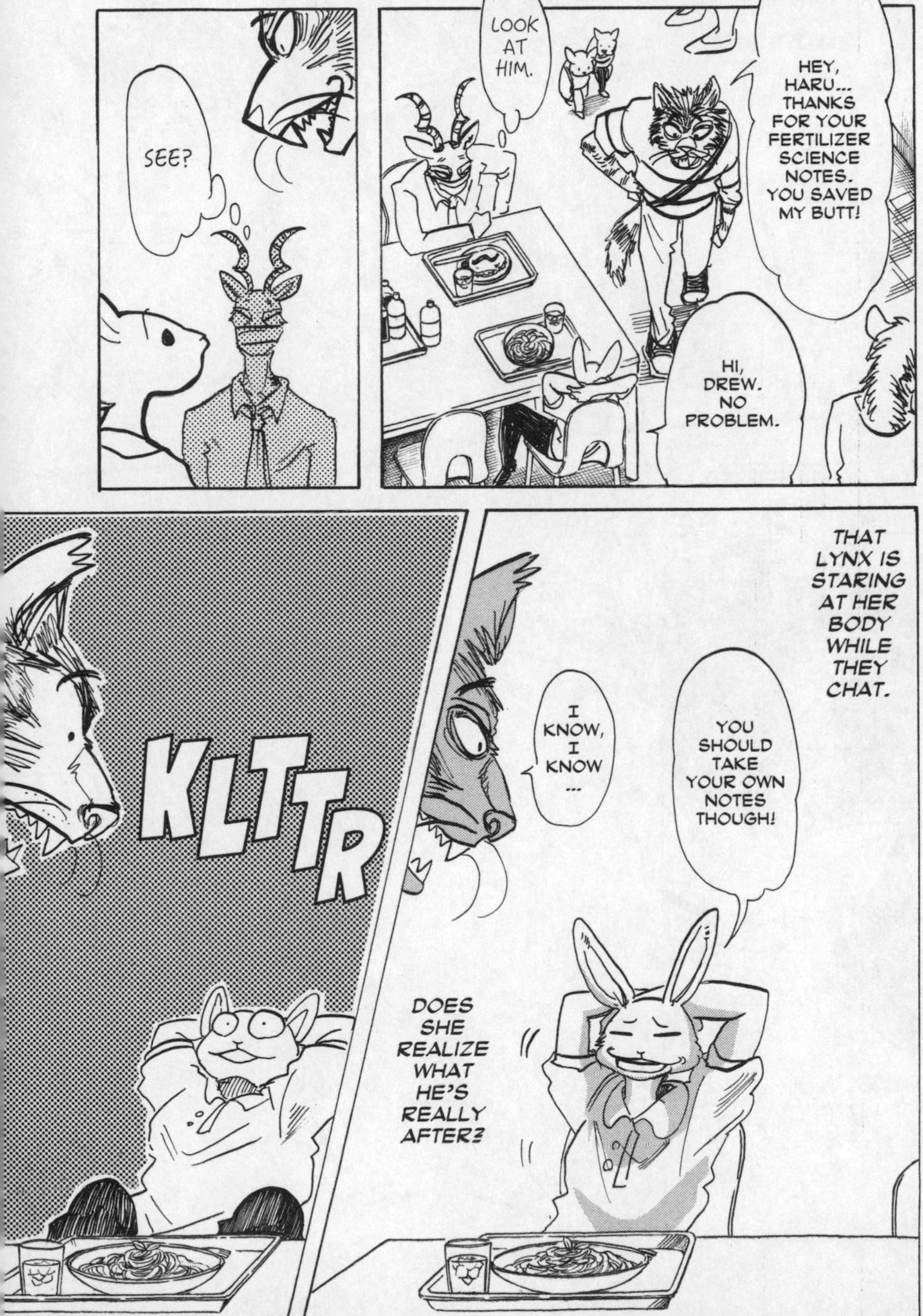
HEY, HARU... THANKS FOR YOUR FERTILIZER SCIENCE NOTES. YOU SAVED MY BUTT!
HI, DREW. NO PROBLEM.
LOOK AT HIM.
SEE?
THAT LYNX IS STARING AT HER BODY WHILE THEY CHAT.
YOU SHOULD TAKE YOUR OWN NOTES THOUGH!
I KNOW, I KNOW ...
DOES SHE REALIZE WHAT HE'S REALLY AFTER?
KLTTR

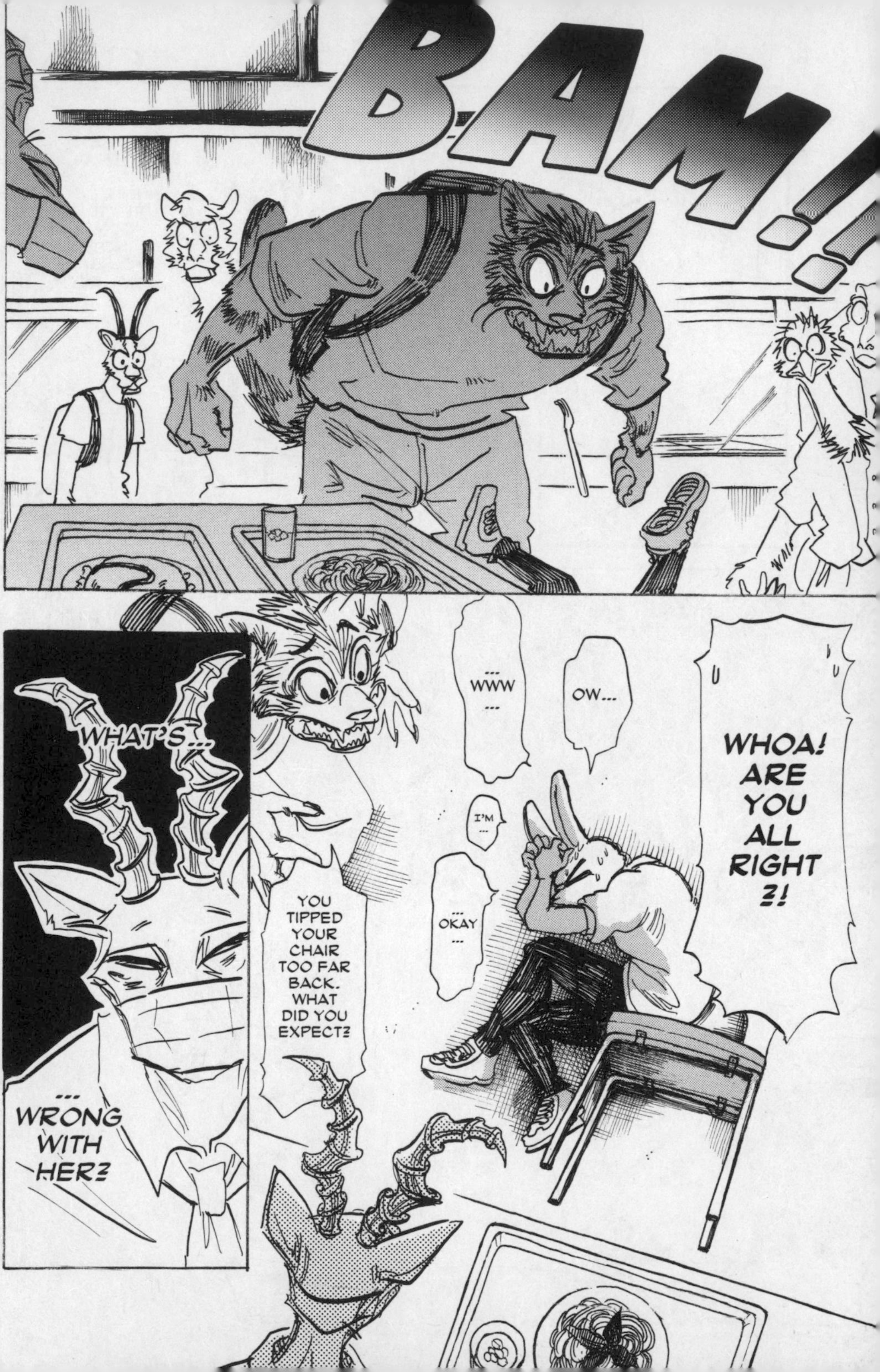
BAM!!!
WHOA! ARE YOU ALL RIGHT?!
OW...
...WWW...
I'M...
...OKAY...
YOU TIPPED YOUR CHAIR TOO FAR BACK. WHAT DID YOU EXPECT?
WHAT'S...
...WRONG WITH HER?

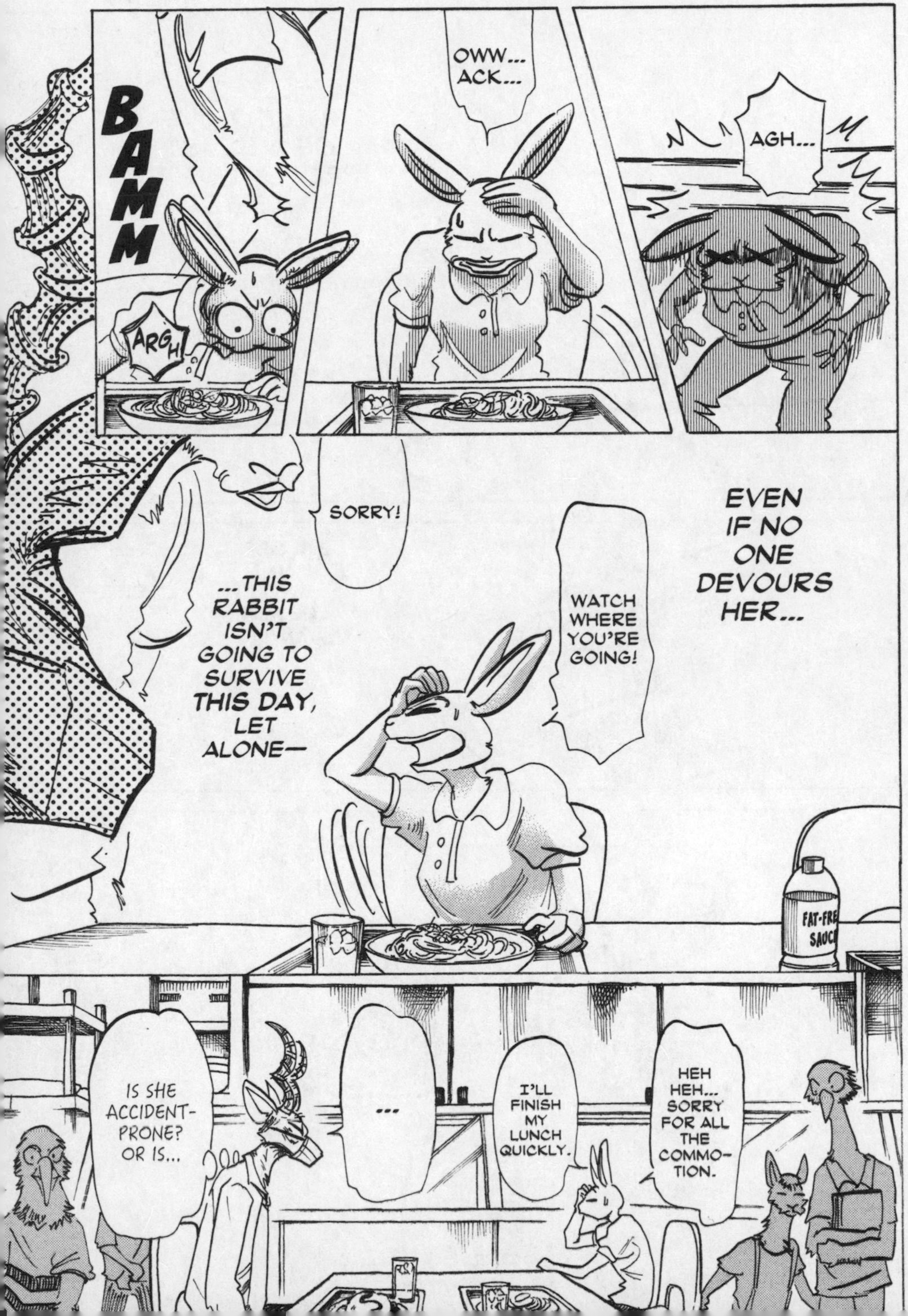
AGH...
OWW... ACK...
BAMM
ARGH
EVEN IF NO ONE DEVOURS HER...
WATCH WHERE YOU'RE GOING!
SORRY!
...THIS RABBIT ISN'T GOING TO SURVIVE THIS DAY, LET ALONE—
HEH HEH... SORRY FOR ALL THE COMMOTION.
I'LL FINISH MY LUNCH QUICKLY.
...
IS SHE ACCIDENT-PRONE? OR IS...

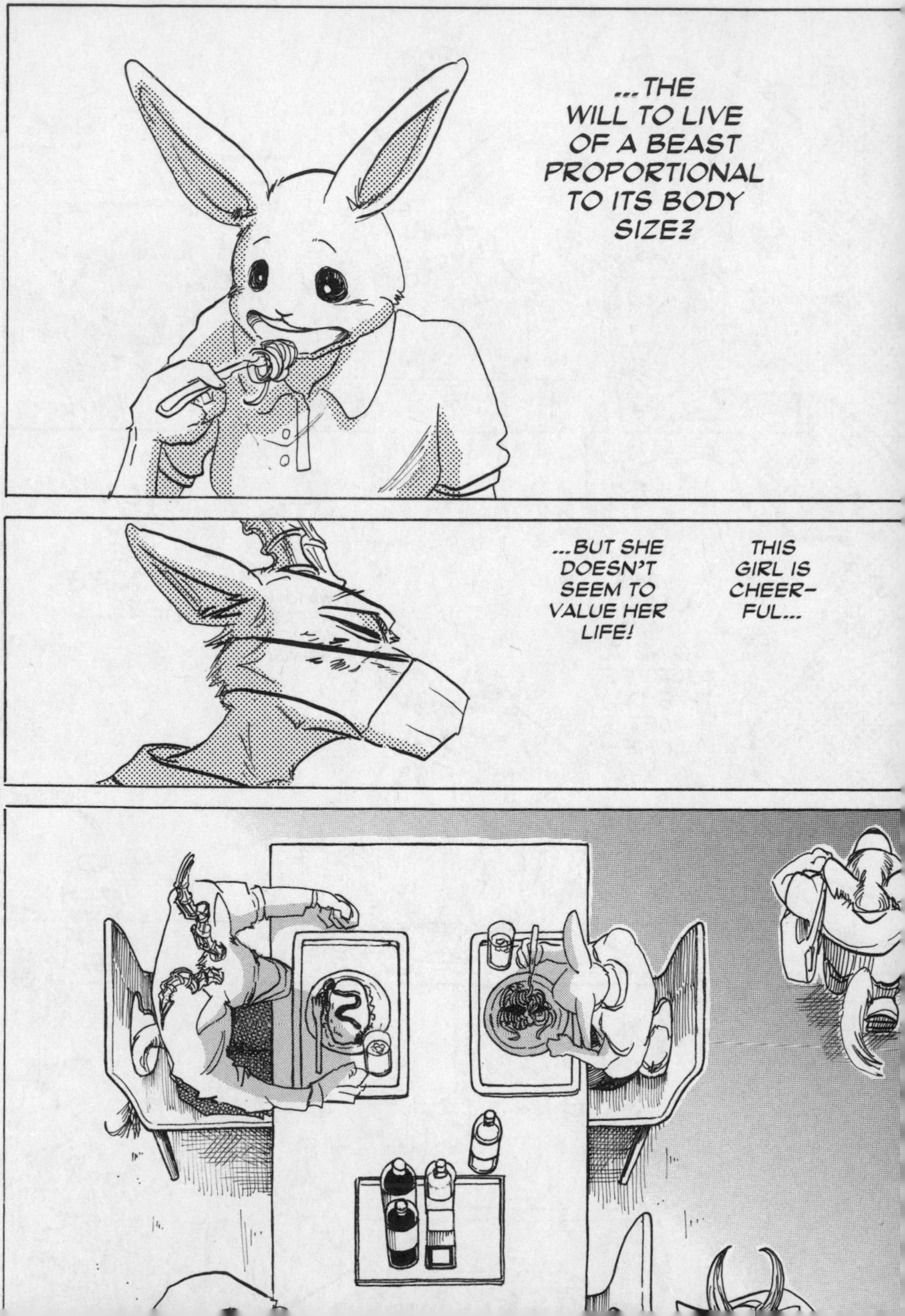
...THE WILL TO LIVE OF A BEAST PROPORTIONAL TO ITS BODY SIZE?
THIS GIRL IS CHEERFUL...
...BUT SHE DOESN'T SEEM TO VALUE HER LIFE!

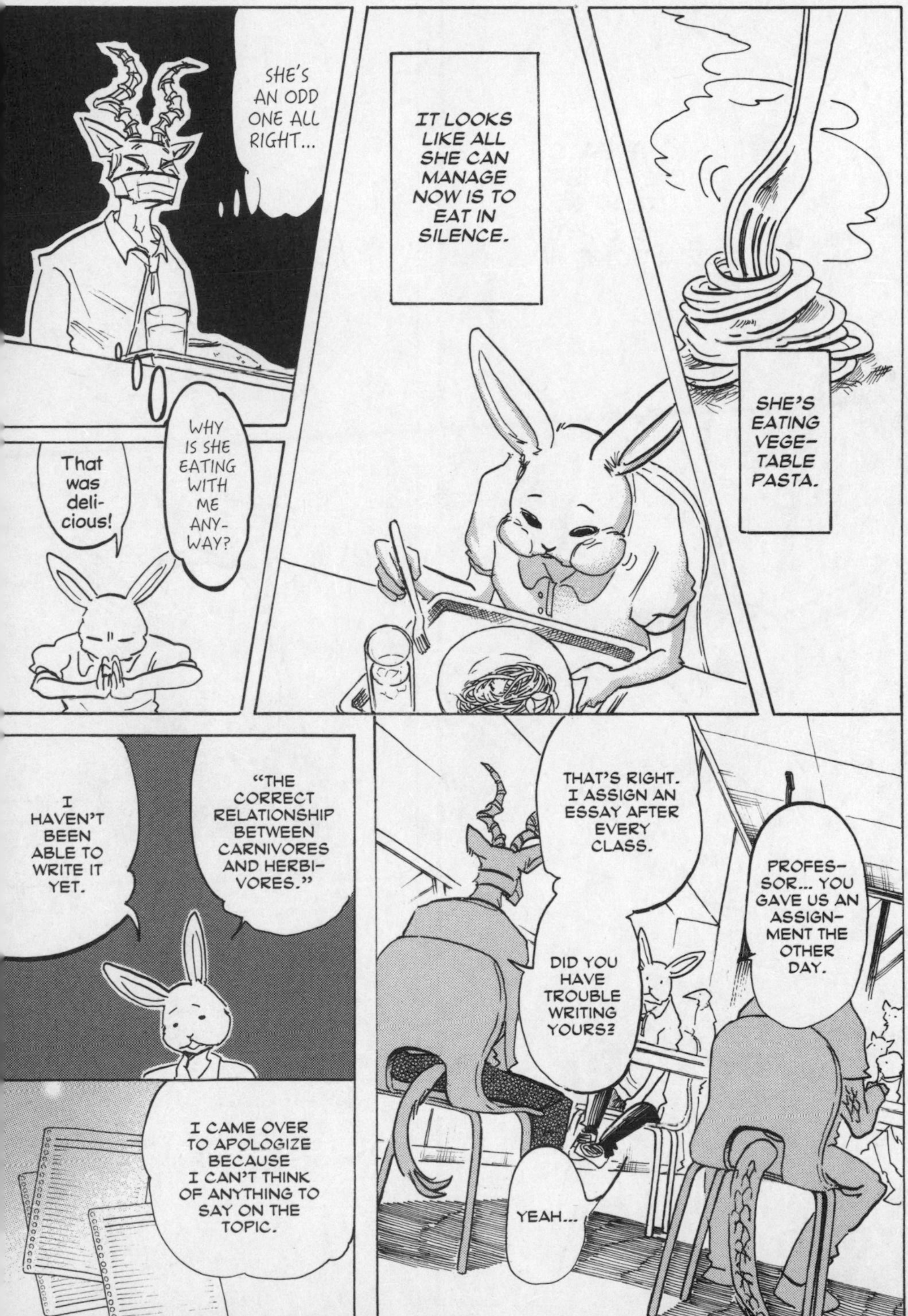

SHE'S EATING VEGETABLE PASTA.
IT LOOKS LIKE ALL SHE CAN MANAGE NOW IS TO EAT IN SILENCE.
SHE'S AN ODD ONE ALL RIGHT...
WHY IS SHE EATING WITH ME ANYWAY?
That was delicious!
PROFESSOR... YOU GAVE US AN ASSIGNMENT THE OTHER DAY.
THAT'S RIGHT. I ASSIGN AN ESSAY AFTER EVERY CLASS.
DID YOU HAVE TROUBLE WRITING YOURS?
YEAH...
“THE CORRECT RELATIONSHIP BETWEEN CARNIVORES AND HERBIVORES.”
I HAVEN'T BEEN ABLE TO WRITE IT YET.
I CAME OVER TO APOLOGIZE BECAUSE I CAN'T THINK OF ANYTHING TO SAY ON THE TOPIC.

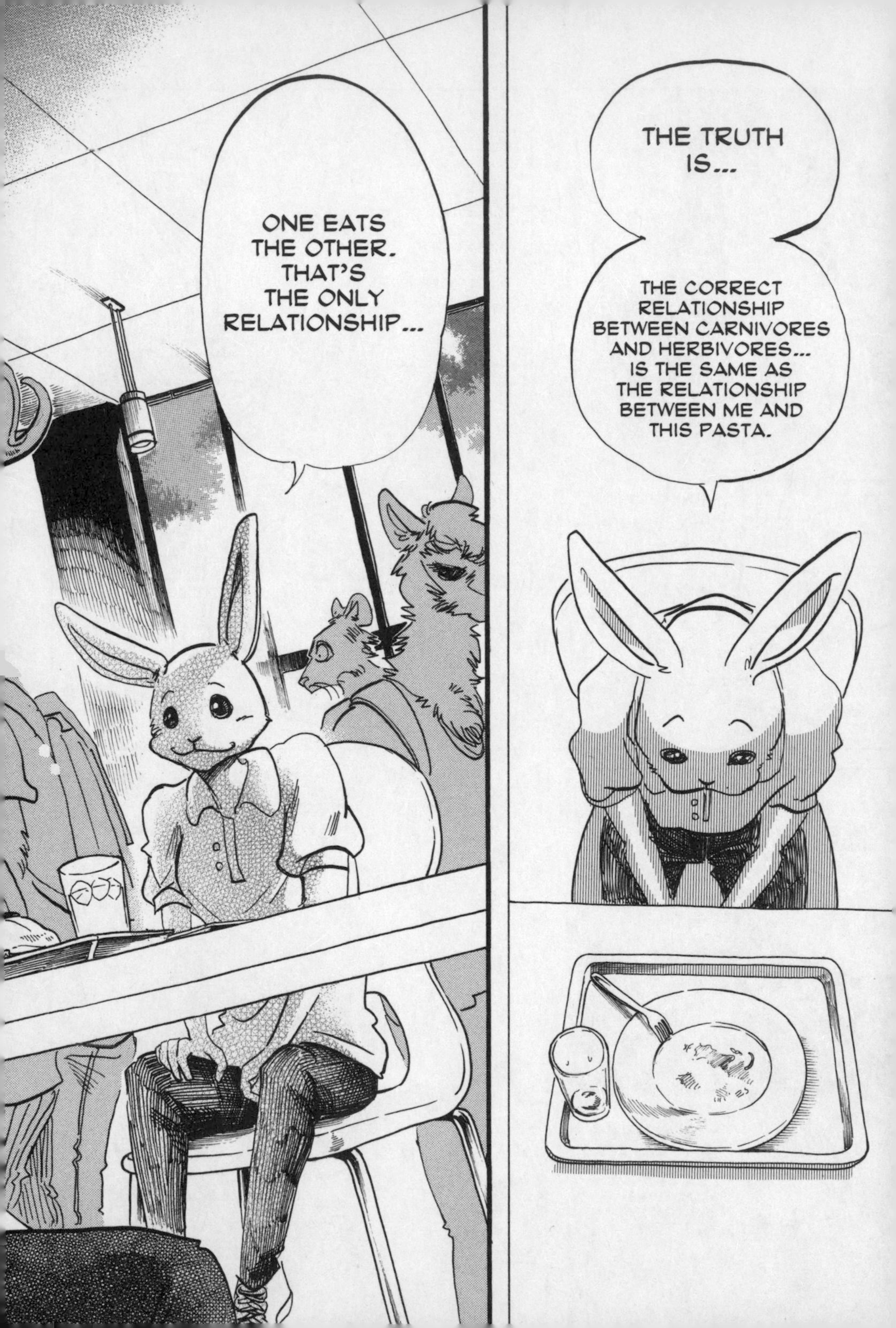
THE TRUTH IS...
THE CORRECT RELATIONSHIP BETWEEN CARNIVORES AND HERBIVORES... IS THE SAME AS THE RELATIONSHIP BETWEEN ME AND THIS PASTA.
ONE EATS THE OTHER. THAT'S THE ONLY RELATIONSHIP...

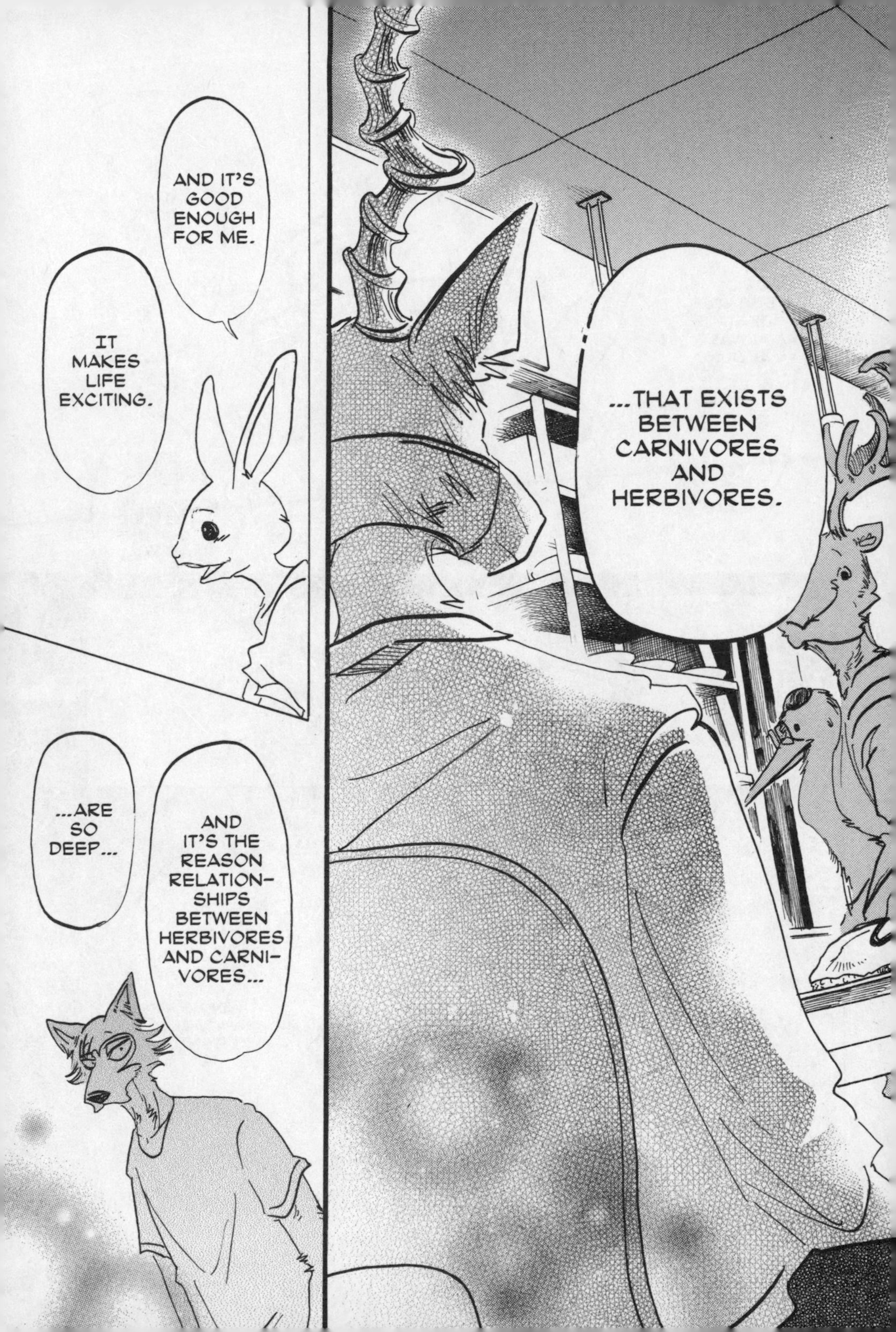
...THAT EXISTS BETWEEN CARNIVORES AND HERBIVORES.
AND IT'S GOOD ENOUGH FOR ME.
IT MAKES LIFE EXCITING.
AND IT'S THE REASON RELATION-SHIPS BETWEEN HERBIVORES AND CARNI-VORES...
...ARE SO DEEP...

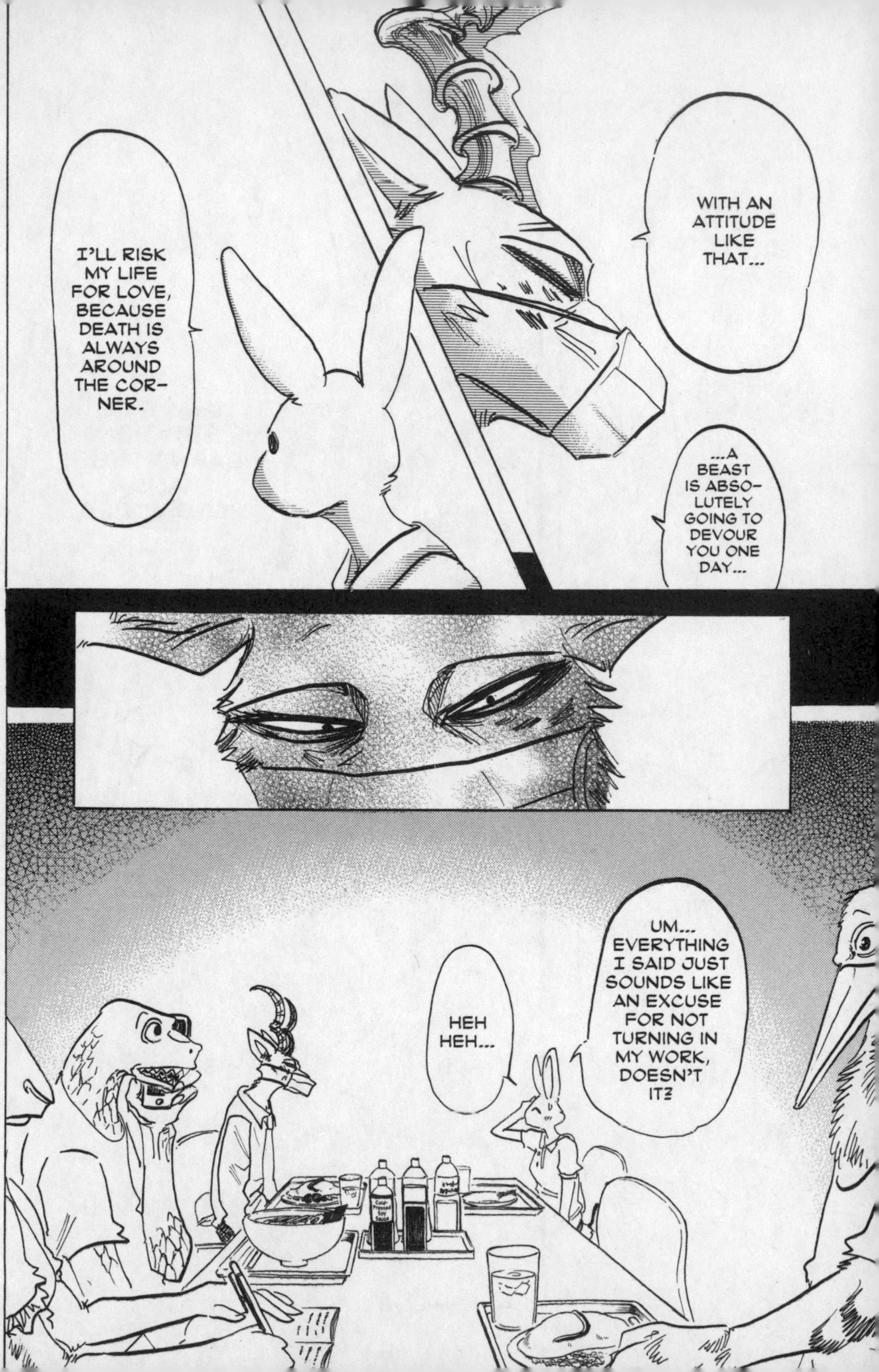
WITH AN ATTITUDE LIKE THAT...
...A BEAST IS ABSOLUTELY GOING TO DEVOUR YOU ONE DAY...
I'LL RISK MY LIFE FOR LOVE, BECAUSE DEATH IS ALWAYS AROUND THE CORNER.
UM... EVERYTHING I SAID JUST SOUNDS LIKE AN EXCUSE FOR NOT TURNING IN MY WORK, DOESN'T IT?
HEH HEH...
Cold-Pressed Soy Sauce

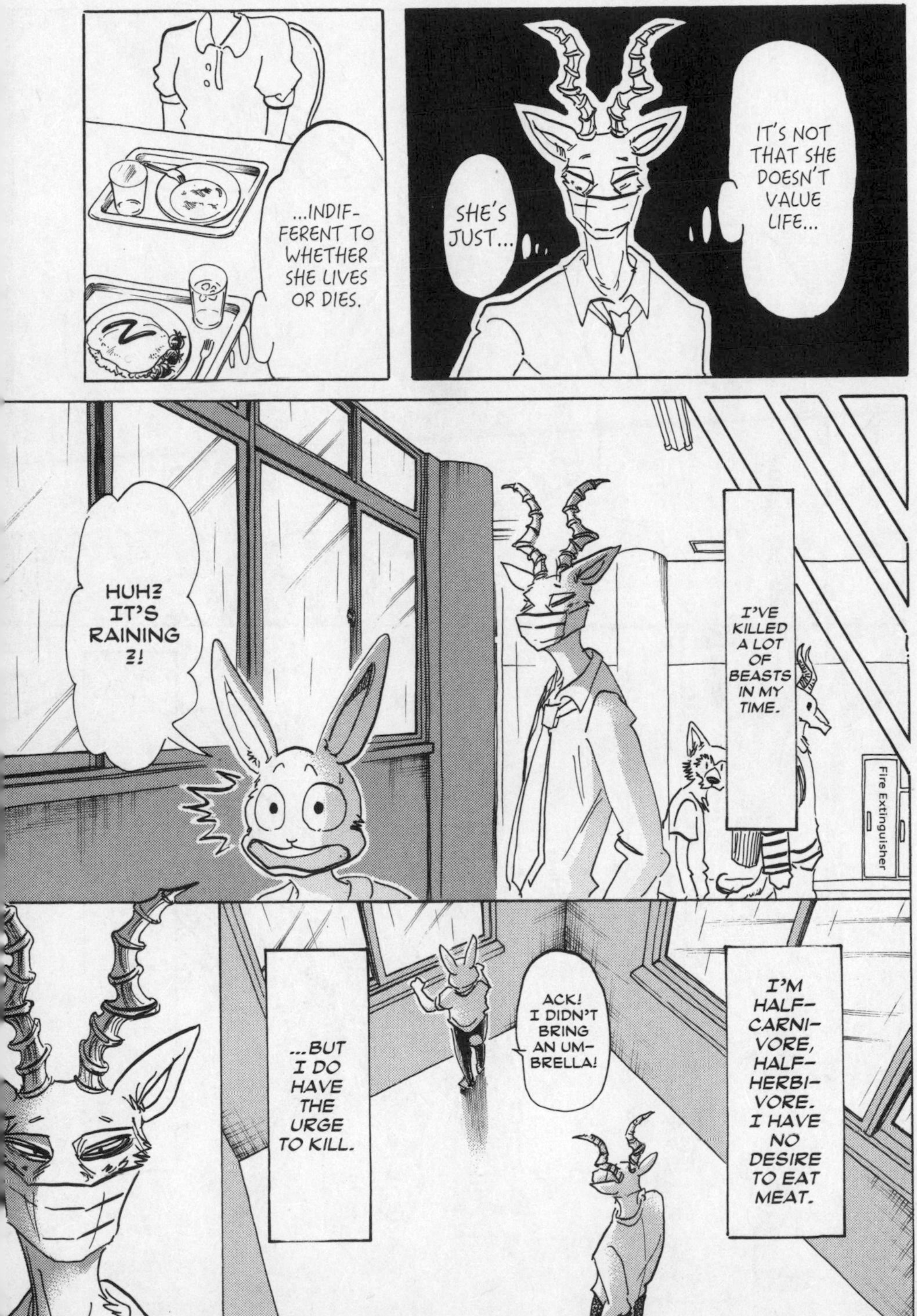
IT'S NOT THAT SHE DOESN'T VALUE LIFE...
SHE'S JUST...
...INDIFFERENT TO WHETHER SHE LIVES OR DIES.
I'VE KILLED A LOT OF BEASTS IN MY TIME.
HUH? IT'S RAINING?!
Fire Extinguisher
I'M HALF-CARNIVORE, HALF-HERBIVORE. I HAVE NO DESIRE TO EAT MEAT.
ACK! I DIDN'T BRING AN UMBRELLA!
...BUT I DO HAVE THE URGE TO KILL.

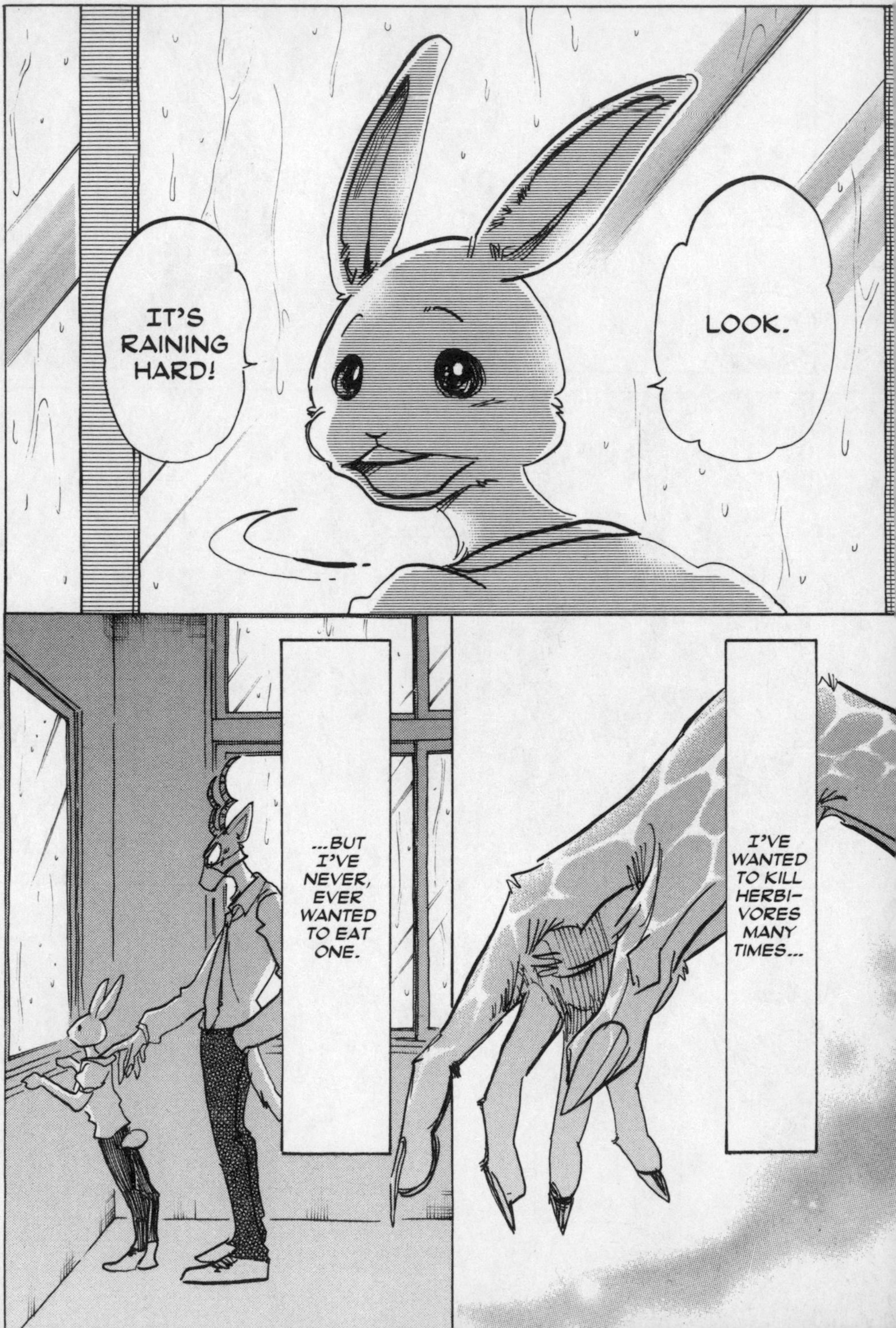
LOOK.
IT'S RAINING HARD!
I'VE WANTED TO KILL HERBI-VORES MANY TIMES...
...BUT I'VE NEVER, EVER WANTED TO EAT ONE.

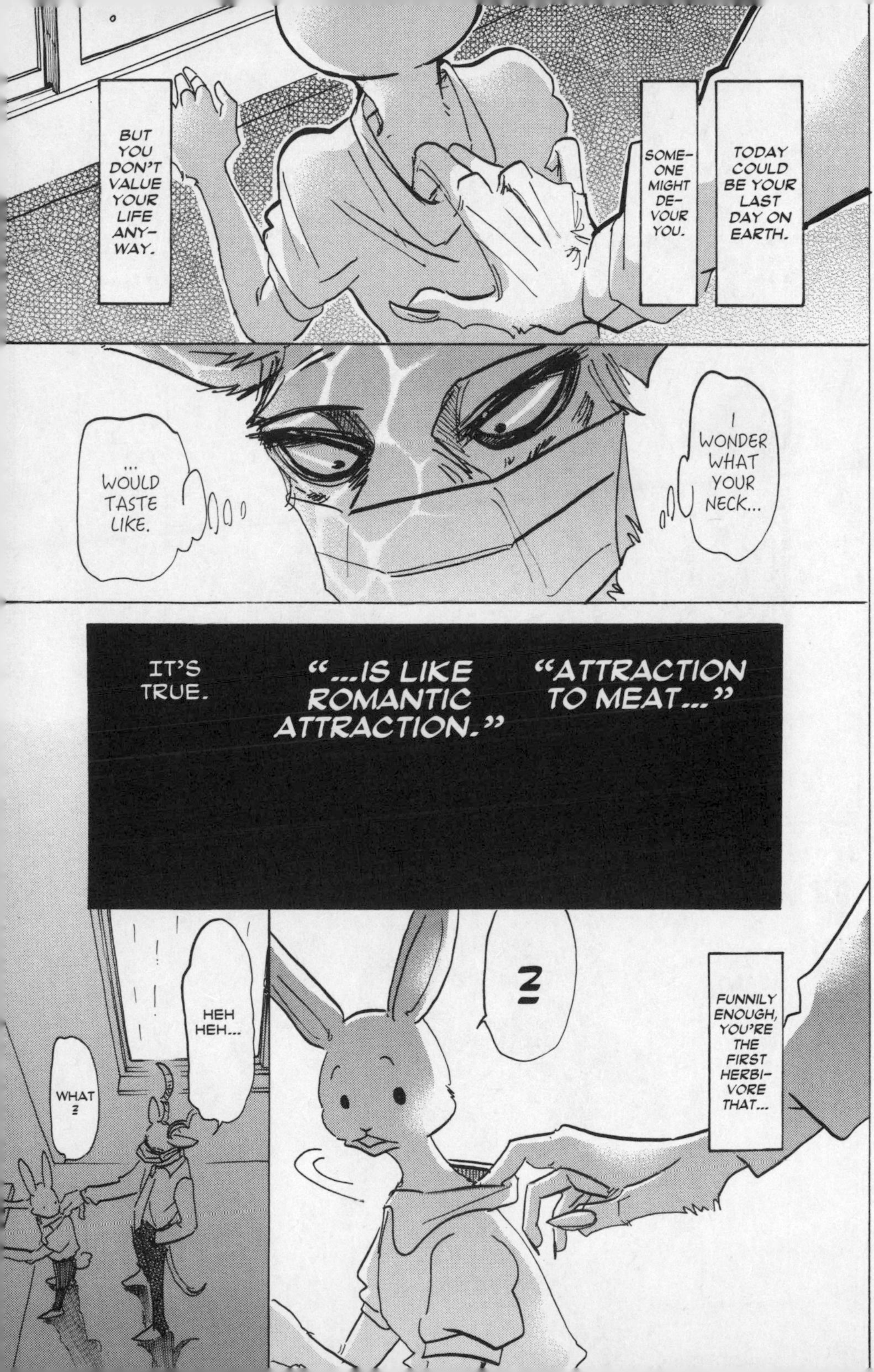
TODAY COULD BE YOUR LAST DAY ON EARTH.
SOME-ONE MIGHT DE-VOUR YOU.
BUT YOU DON'T VALUE YOUR LIFE ANY-WAY.
I WONDER WHAT YOUR NECK...
...WOULD TASTE LIKE.
"ATTRACTION TO MEAT..."
"...IS LIKE ROMANTIC ATTRACTION."
IT'S TRUE.
FUNNILY ENOUGH, YOU'RE THE FIRST HERBI-VORE THAT...
?
HEH HEH...
WHAT?

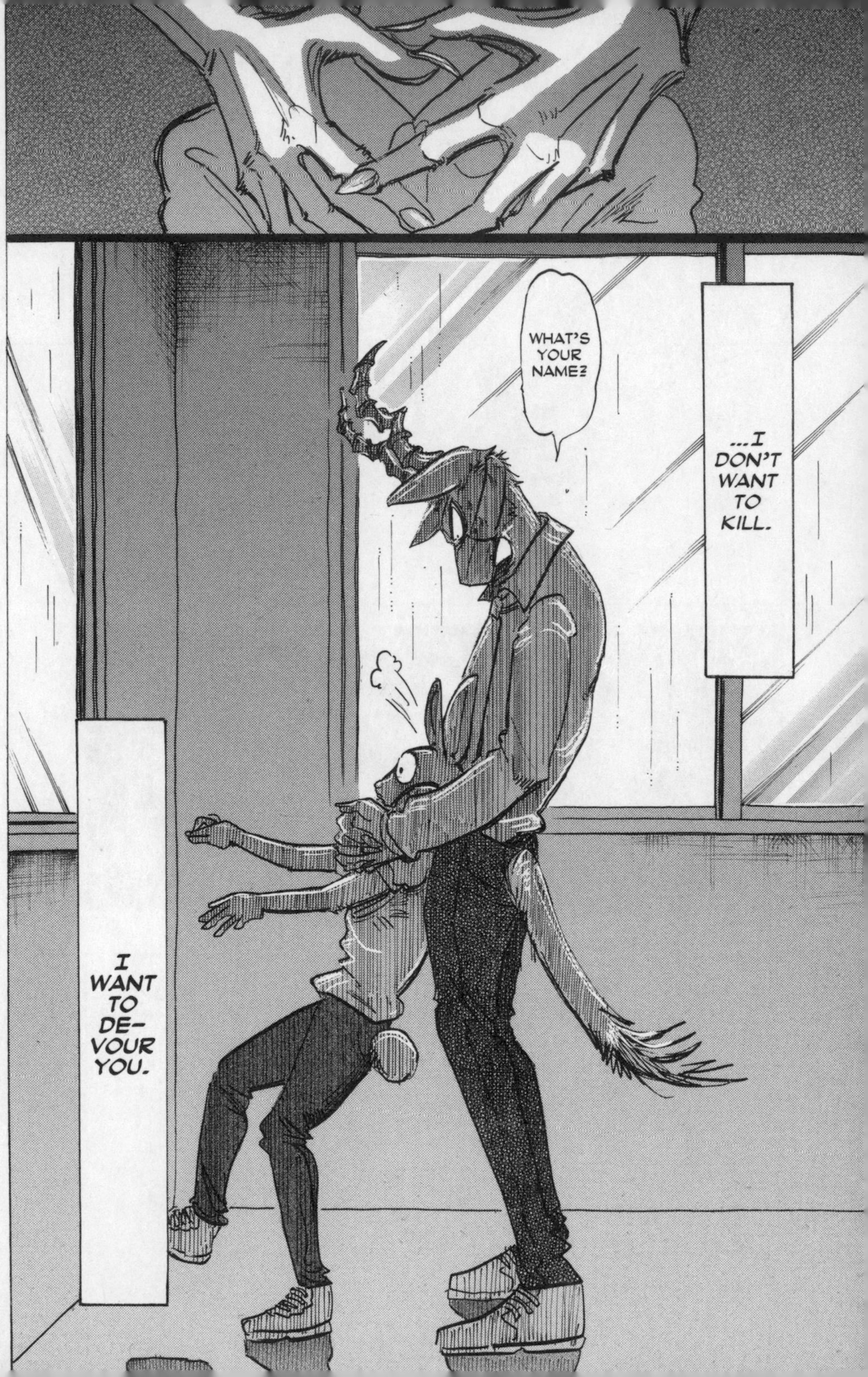
...I DON'T WANT TO KILL.
WHAT'S YOUR NAME?
I WANT TO DE-VOUR YOU.

Chapter 147: Speak Your Words of Love After Wiping Off Your Drool

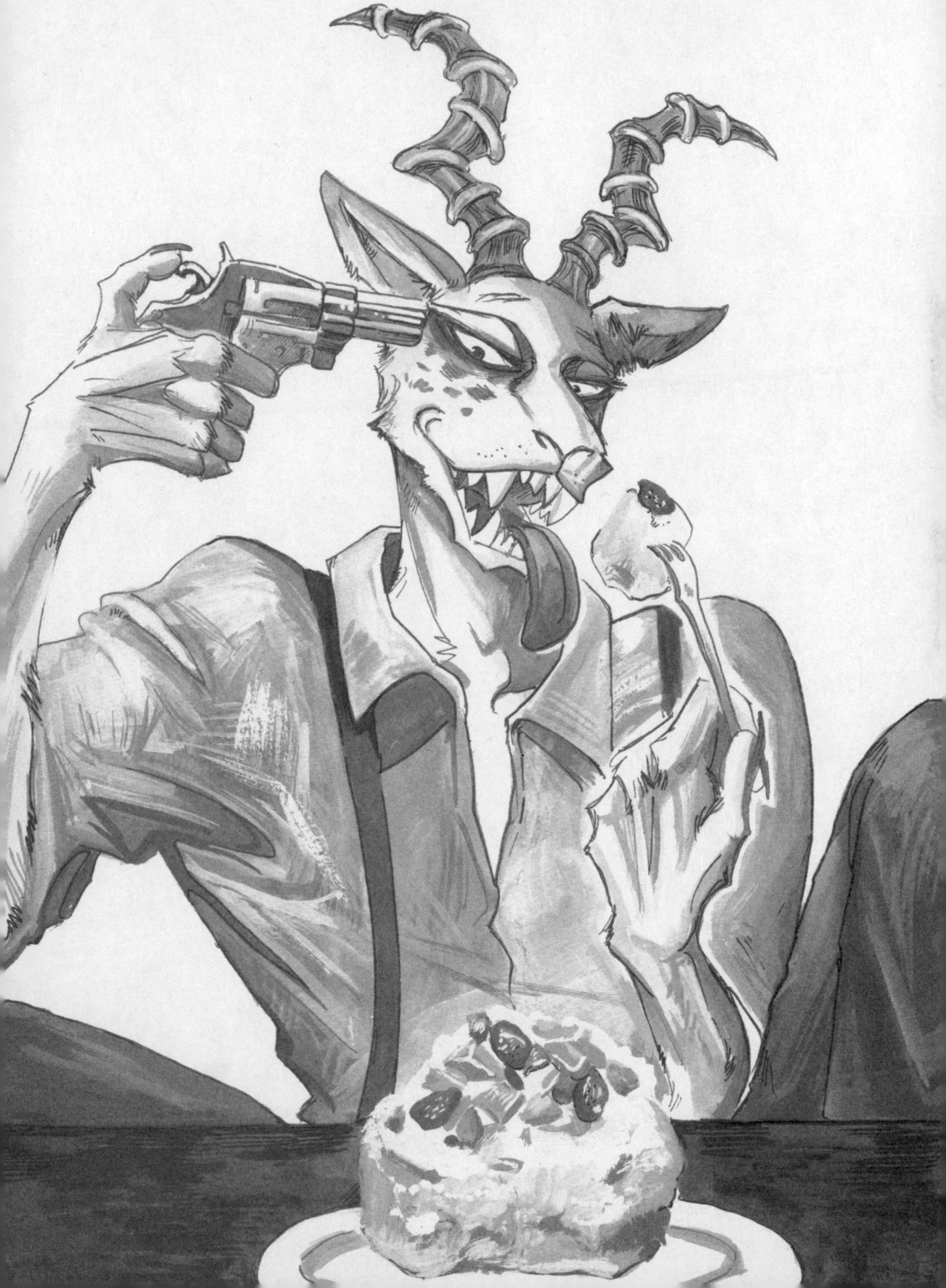

BEASTARS
Vol. 17

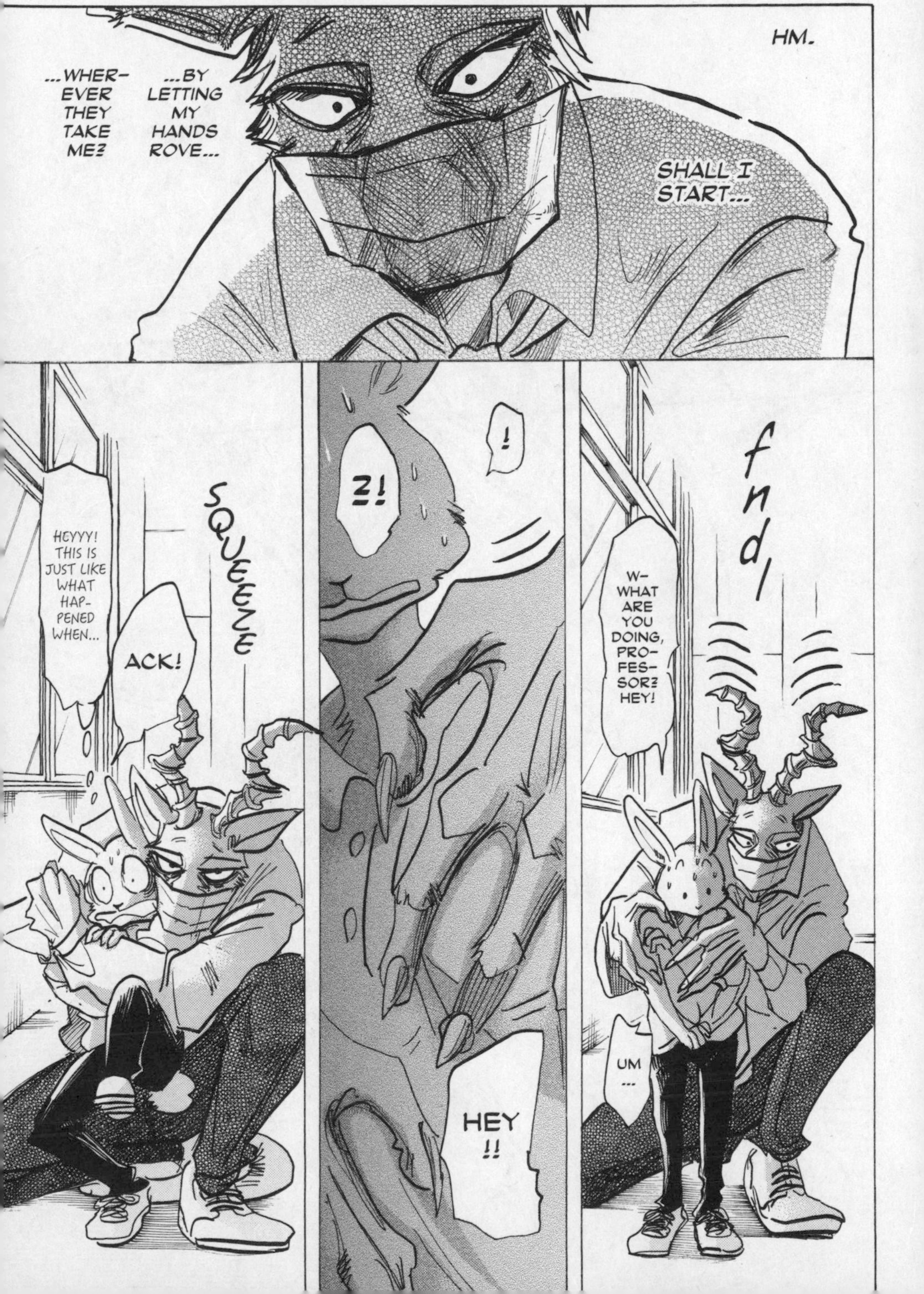
HM.
SHALL I START...
...BY LETTING MY HANDS ROVE...
...WHER-EVER THEY TAKE ME?
fnd/
W-WHAT ARE YOU DOING, PRO-FES-SOR? HEY!
UM...
!
!?
HEY!!
SQUEEZE
HEYYY! THIS IS JUST LIKE WHAT HAP-PENED WHEN...
ACK!

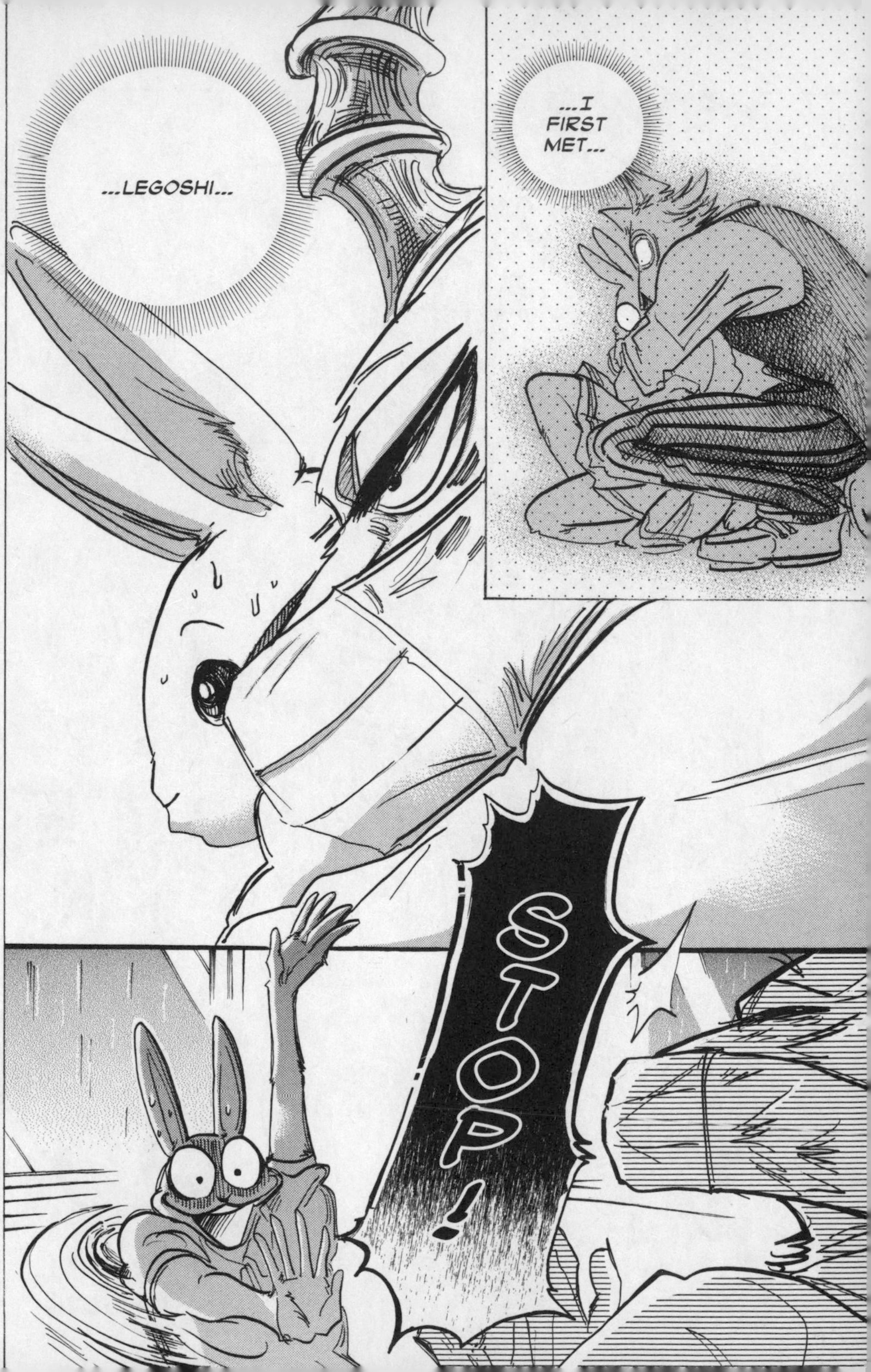
...I FIRST MET...
...LEGOSHI...
STOP!

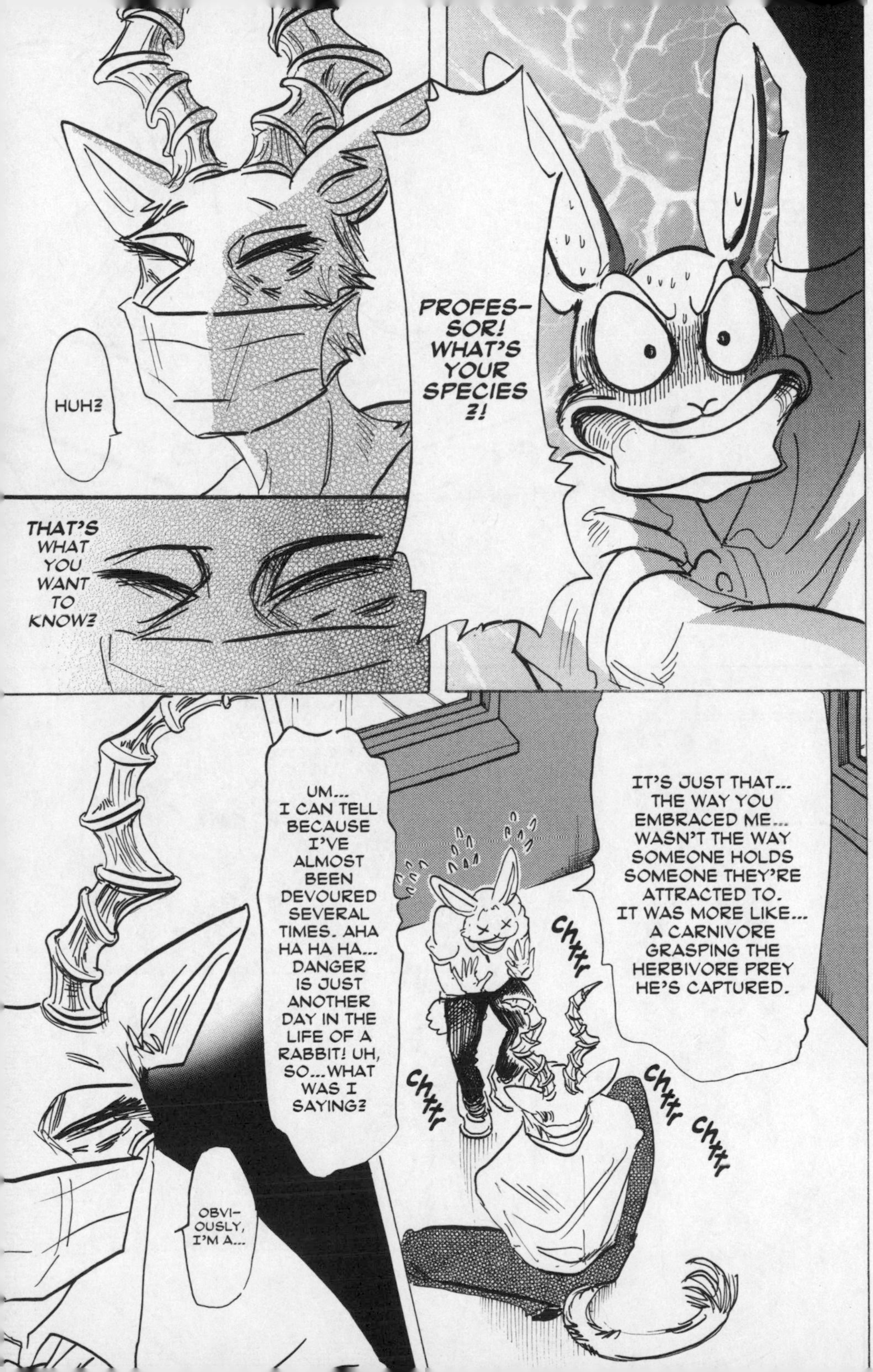
PROFES-SOR! WHAT'S YOUR SPECIES?!
HUH?
THAT'S WHAT YOU WANT TO KNOW?
IT'S JUST THAT... THE WAY YOU EMBRACED ME... WASN'T THE WAY SOMEONE HOLDS SOMEONE THEY'RE ATTRACTED TO. IT WAS MORE LIKE... A CARNIVORE GRASPING THE HERBIVORE PREY HE'S CAPTURED.
UM... I CAN TELL BECAUSE I'VE ALMOST BEEN DEVOURED SEVERAL TIMES. AHA HA HA HA... DANGER IS JUST ANOTHER DAY IN THE LIFE OF A RABBIT! UH, SO...WHAT WAS I SAYING?
Chttr
Chttr Chttr
Chttr
OBVI-OUSLY, I'M A...

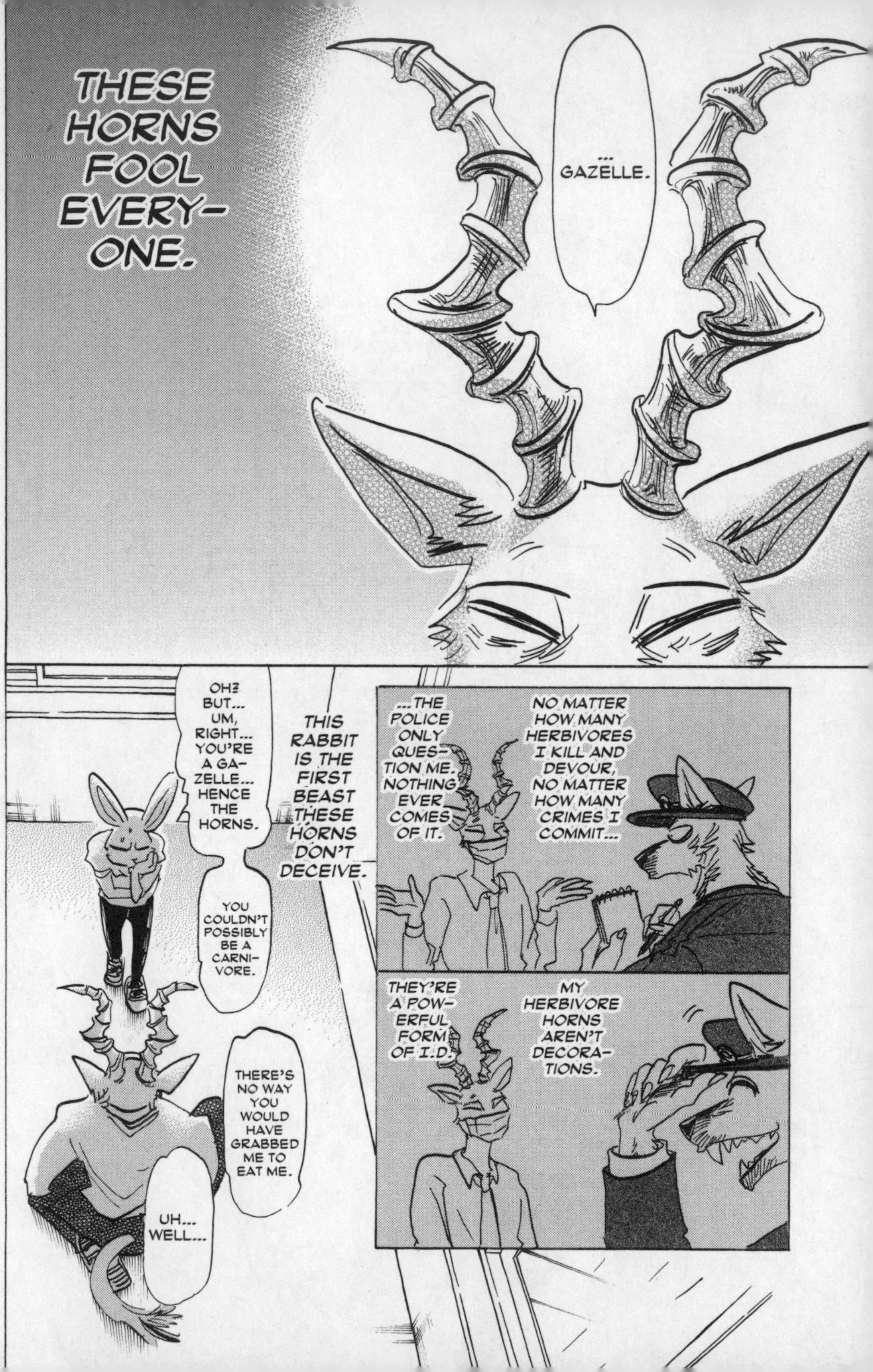
...GAZELLE.
THESE HORNS FOOL EVERYONE.
NO MATTER HOW MANY HERBIVORES I KILL AND DEVOUR, NO MATTER HOW MANY CRIMES I COMMIT...
...THE POLICE ONLY QUESTION ME. NOTHING EVER COMES OF IT.
MY HERBIVORE HORNS AREN'T DECORATIONS.
THEY'RE A POWERFUL FORM OF I.D.
THIS RABBIT IS THE FIRST BEAST THESE HORNS DON'T DECEIVE.
OH? BUT... UM, RIGHT... YOU'RE A GAZELLE... HENCE THE HORNS.
YOU COULDN'T POSSIBLY BE A CARNIVORE.
THERE'S NO WAY YOU WOULD HAVE GRABBED ME TO EAT ME.
UH... WELL...

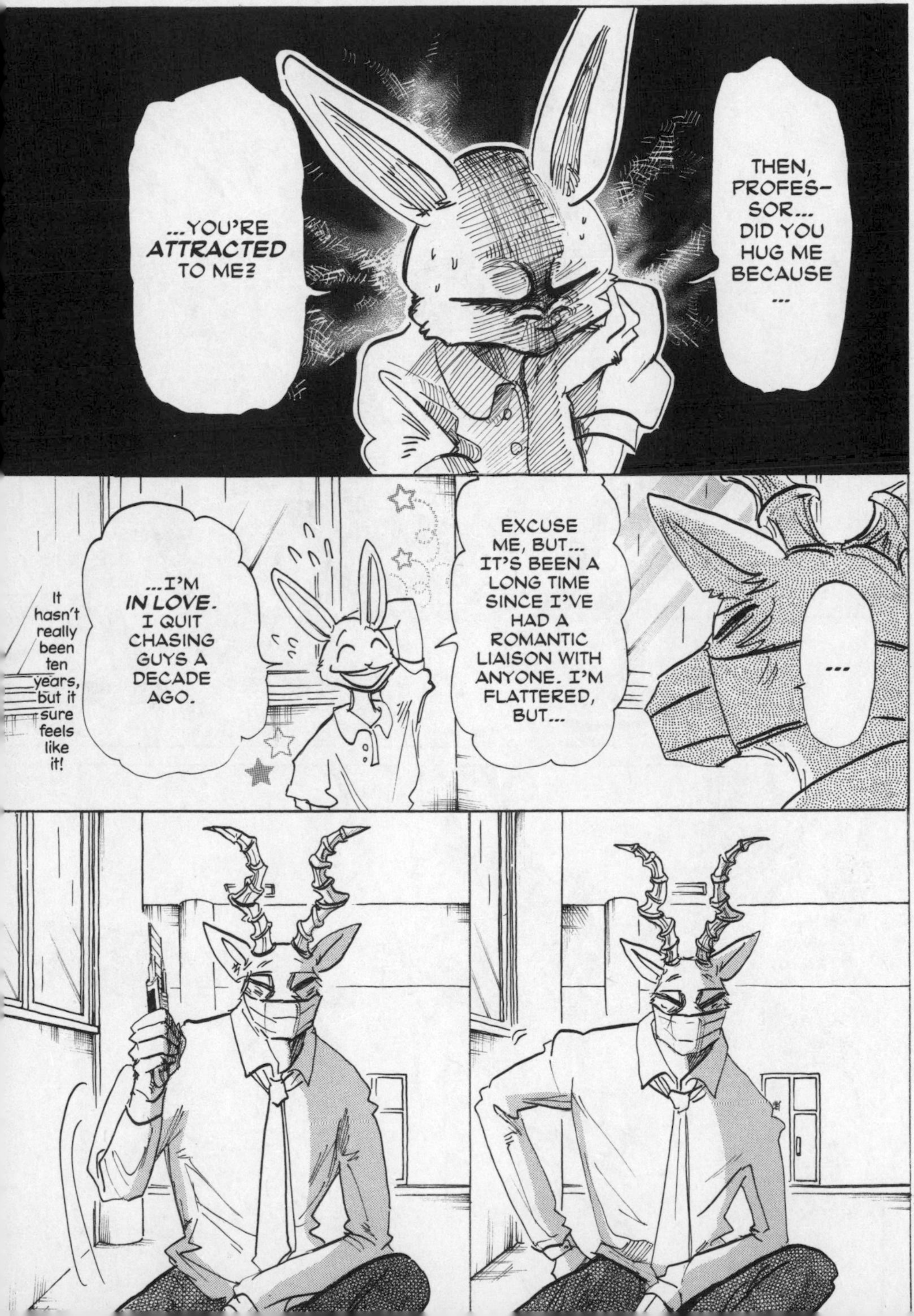
THEN, PROFES-SOR... DID YOU HUG ME BECAUSE ...
...YOU'RE ATTRACTED TO ME?
...
EXCUSE ME, BUT... IT'S BEEN A LONG TIME SINCE I'VE HAD A ROMANTIC LIAISON WITH ANYONE. I'M FLATTERED, BUT...
...I'M IN LOVE. I QUIT CHASING GUYS A DECADE AGO.
It hasn't really been ten years, but it sure feels like it!

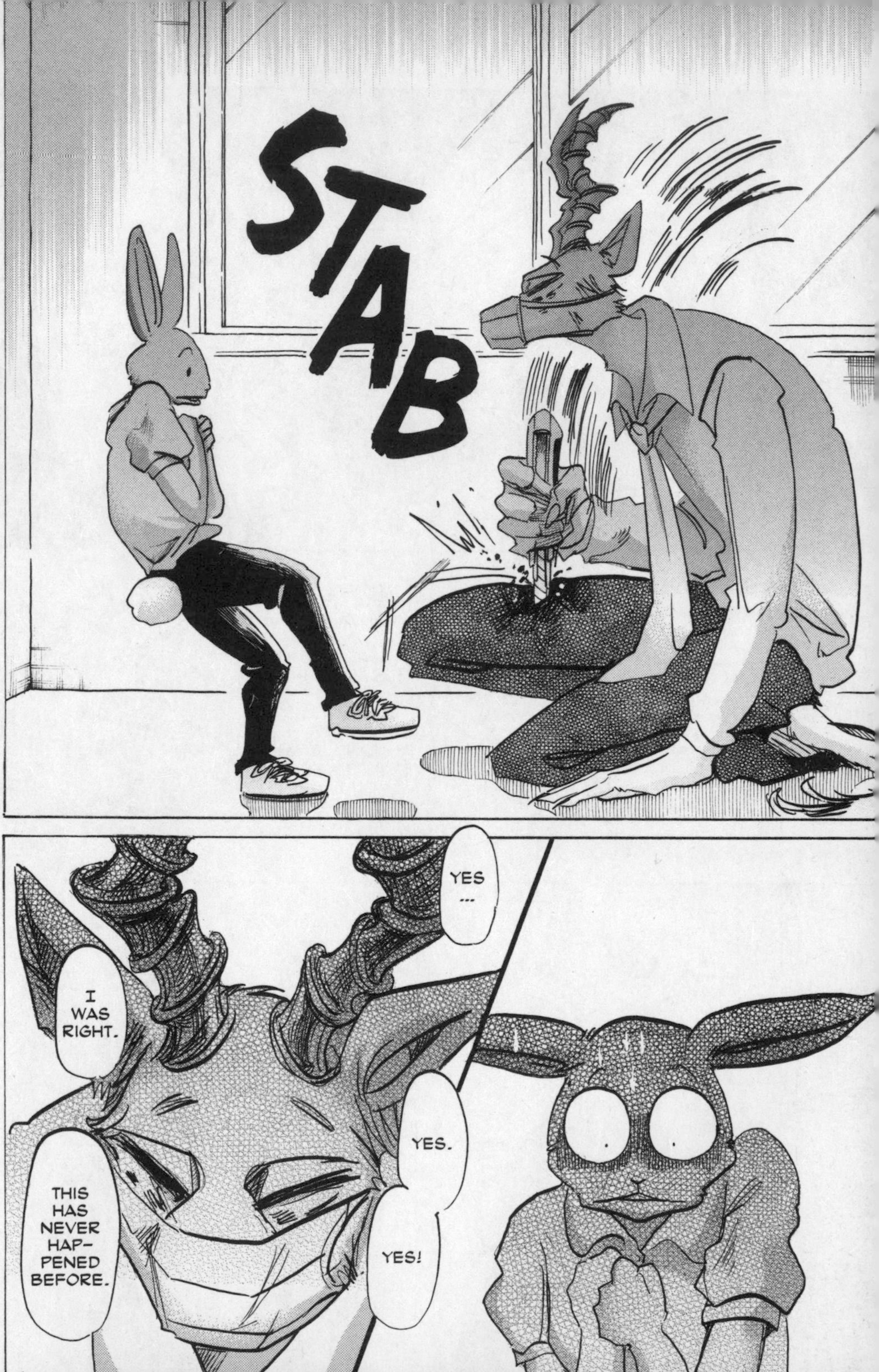
STAB
YES ...
I WAS RIGHT.
YES.
THIS HAS NEVER HAP-PENED BEFORE.
YES!

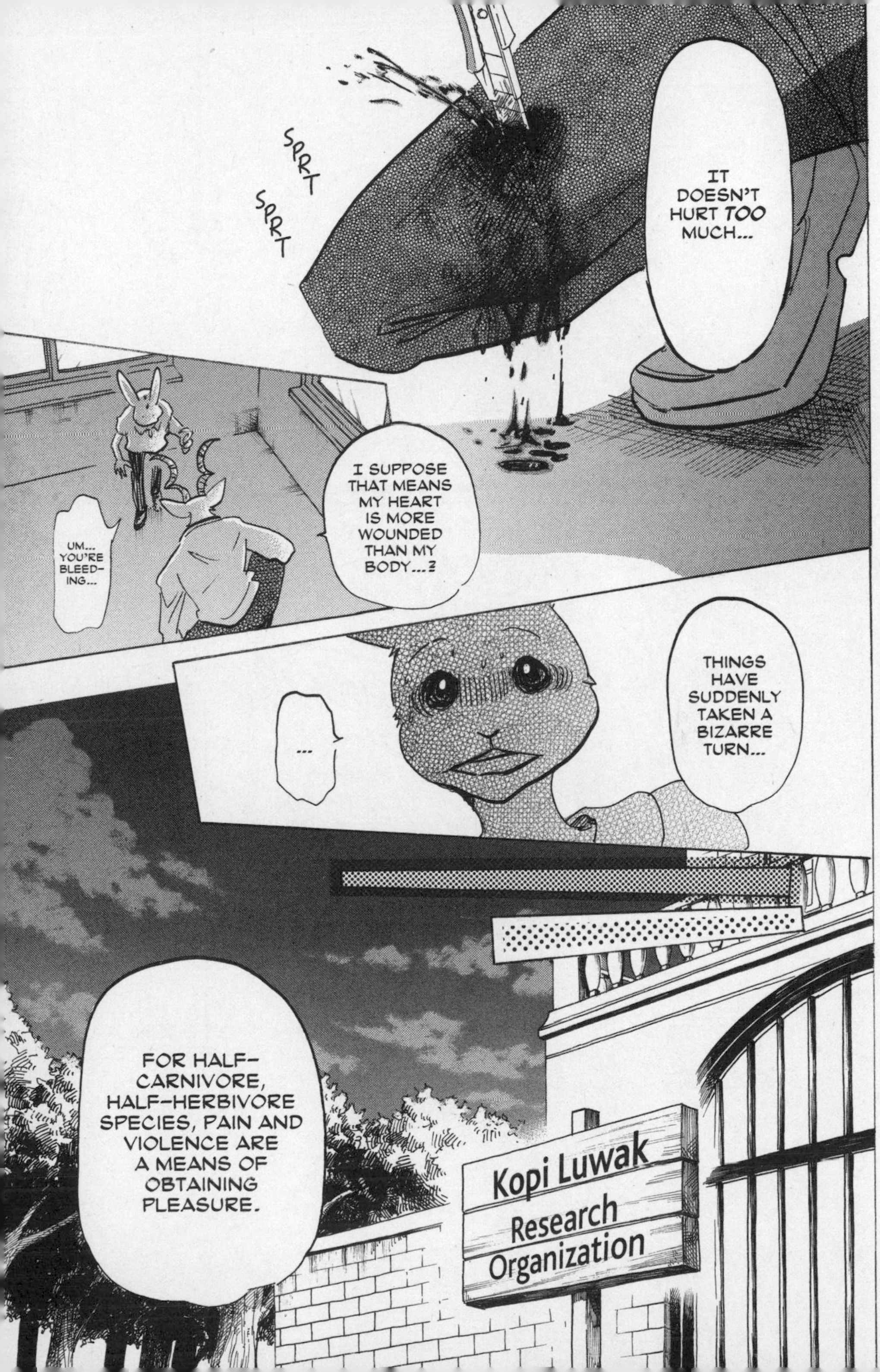
IT DOESN'T HURT *TOO* MUCH...
SPRT SPRT
I SUPPOSE THAT MEANS MY HEART IS MORE WOUNDED THAN MY BODY...?
UM... YOU'RE BLEEDING...
THINGS HAVE SUDDENLY TAKEN A BIZARRE TURN...
...
Kopi Luwak Research Organization
FOR HALF-CARNIVORE, HALF-HERBIVORE SPECIES, PAIN AND VIOLENCE ARE A MEANS OF OBTAINING PLEASURE.

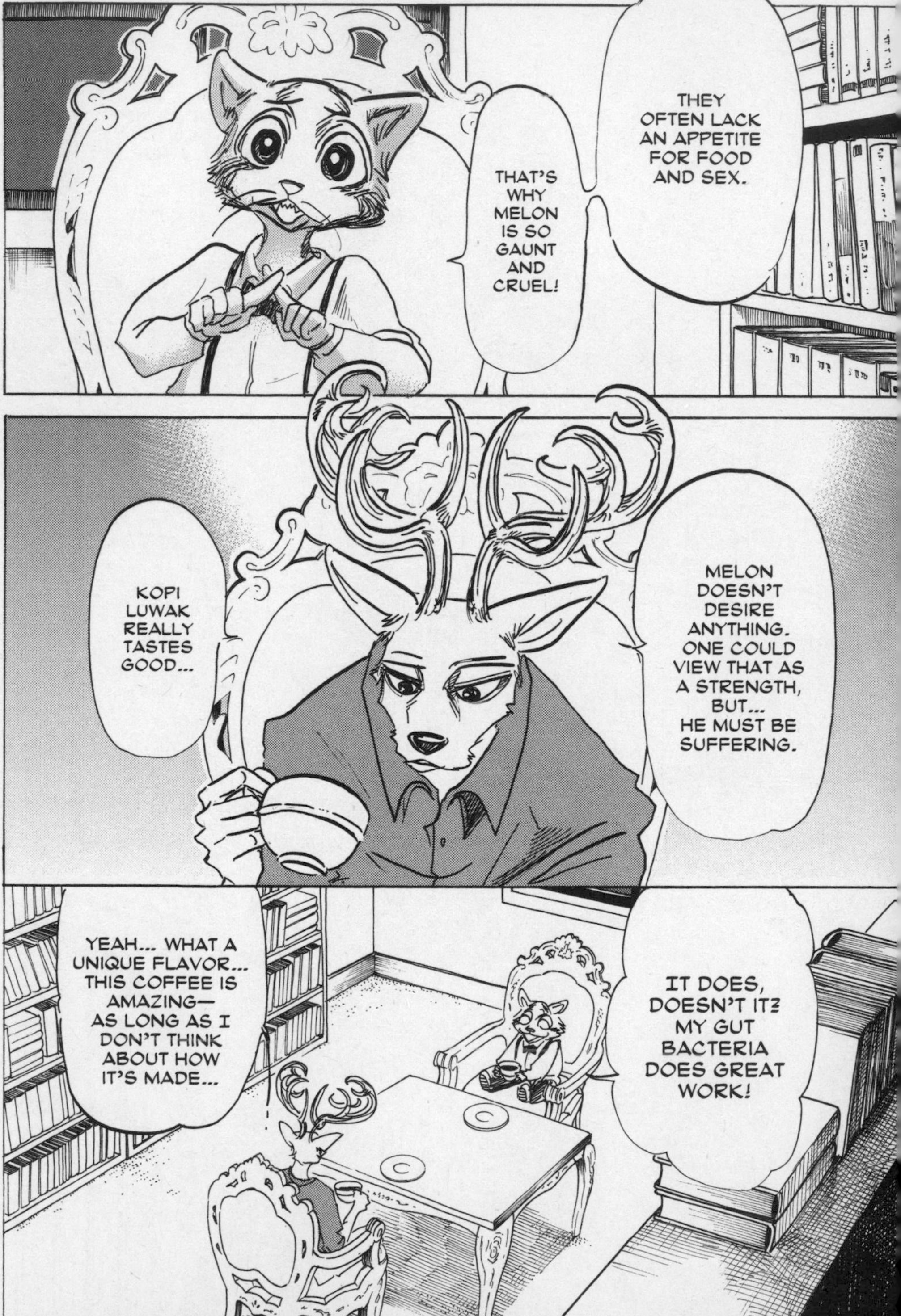
THEY OFTEN LACK AN APPETITE FOR FOOD AND SEX.
THAT'S WHY MELON IS SO GAUNT AND CRUEL!
MELON DOESN'T DESIRE ANYTHING. ONE COULD VIEW THAT AS A STRENGTH, BUT... HE MUST BE SUFFERING.
KOPI LUWAK REALLY TASTES GOOD...
IT DOES, DOESN'T IT? MY GUT BACTERIA DOES GREAT WORK!
YEAH... WHAT A UNIQUE FLAVOR... THIS COFFEE IS AMAZING— AS LONG AS I DON'T THINK ABOUT HOW IT'S MADE...

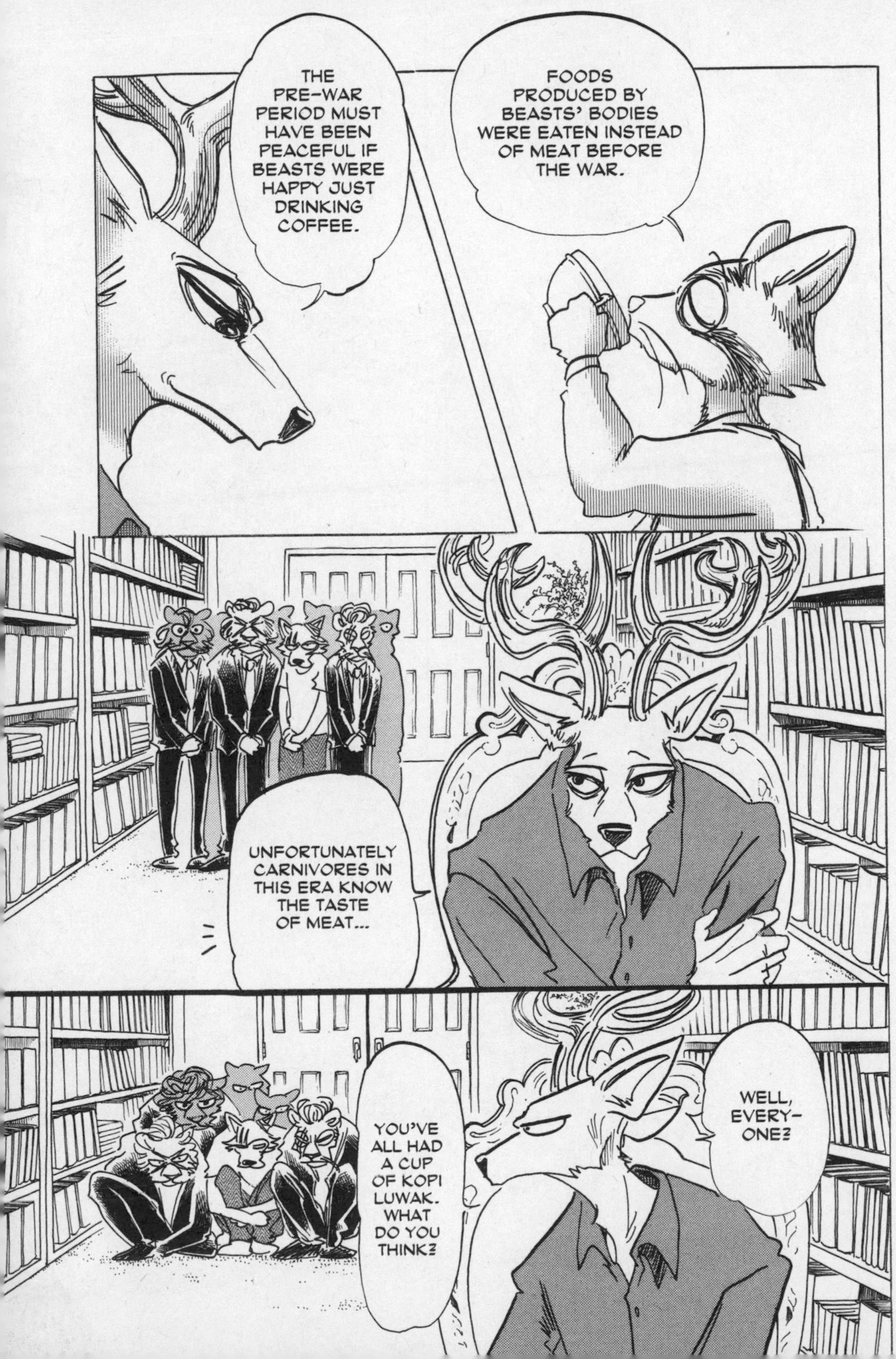
FOODS PRODUCED BY BEASTS' BODIES WERE EATEN INSTEAD OF MEAT BEFORE THE WAR.
THE PRE-WAR PERIOD MUST HAVE BEEN PEACEFUL IF BEASTS WERE HAPPY JUST DRINKING COFFEE.
UNFORTUNATELY CARNIVORES IN THIS ERA KNOW THE TASTE OF MEAT...
WELL, EVERY-ONE?
YOU'VE ALL HAD A CUP OF KOPI LUWAK. WHAT DO YOU THINK?

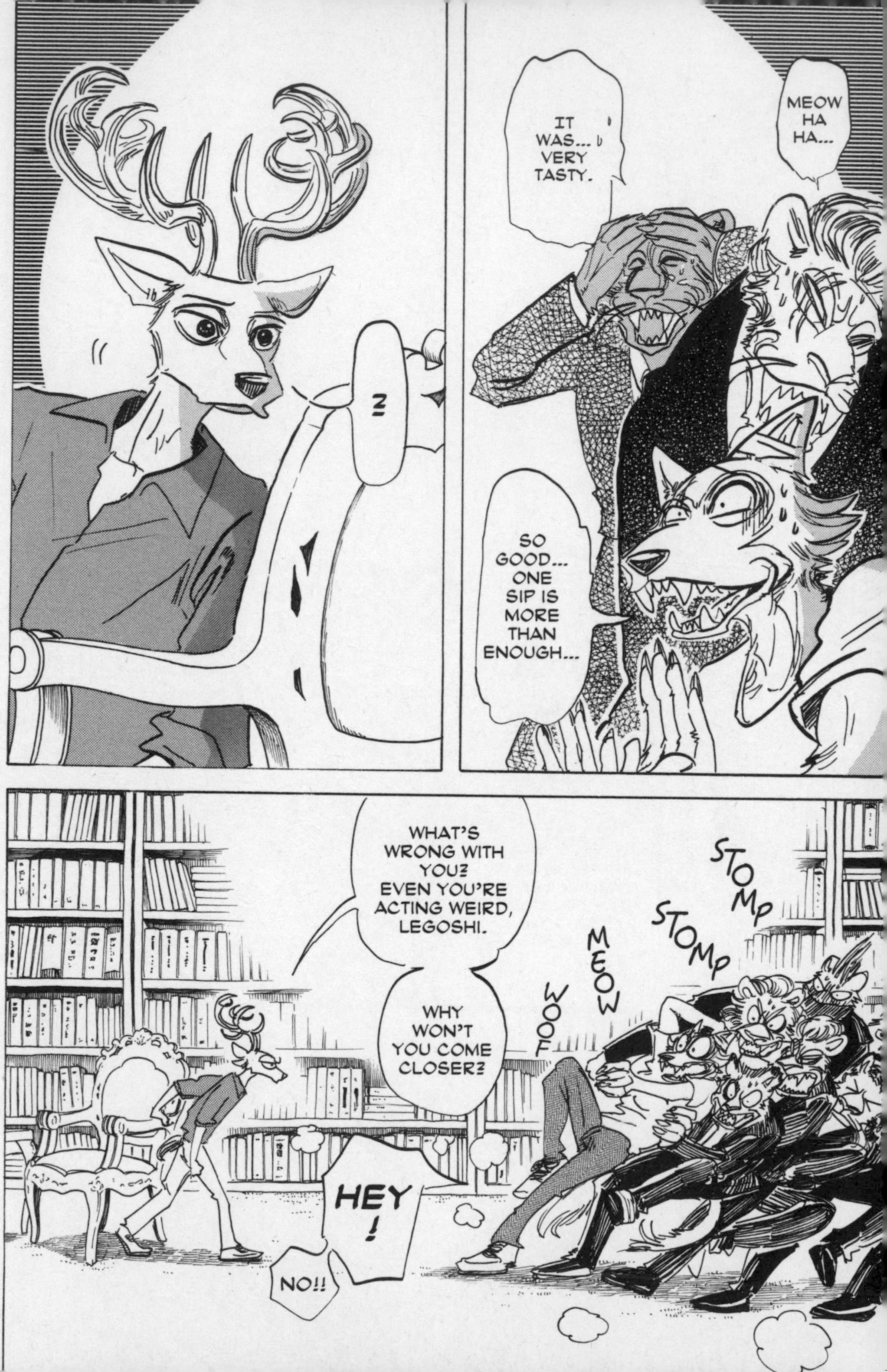
MEOW HA HA...
IT WAS... VERY TASTY.
SO GOOD... ONE SIP IS MORE THAN ENOUGH...
STOMP
STOMP
MEOW
WOOF
WHAT'S WRONG WITH YOU? EVEN YOU'RE ACTING WEIRD, LEGOSHI.
WHY WON'T YOU COME CLOSER?
HEY!
NO!!

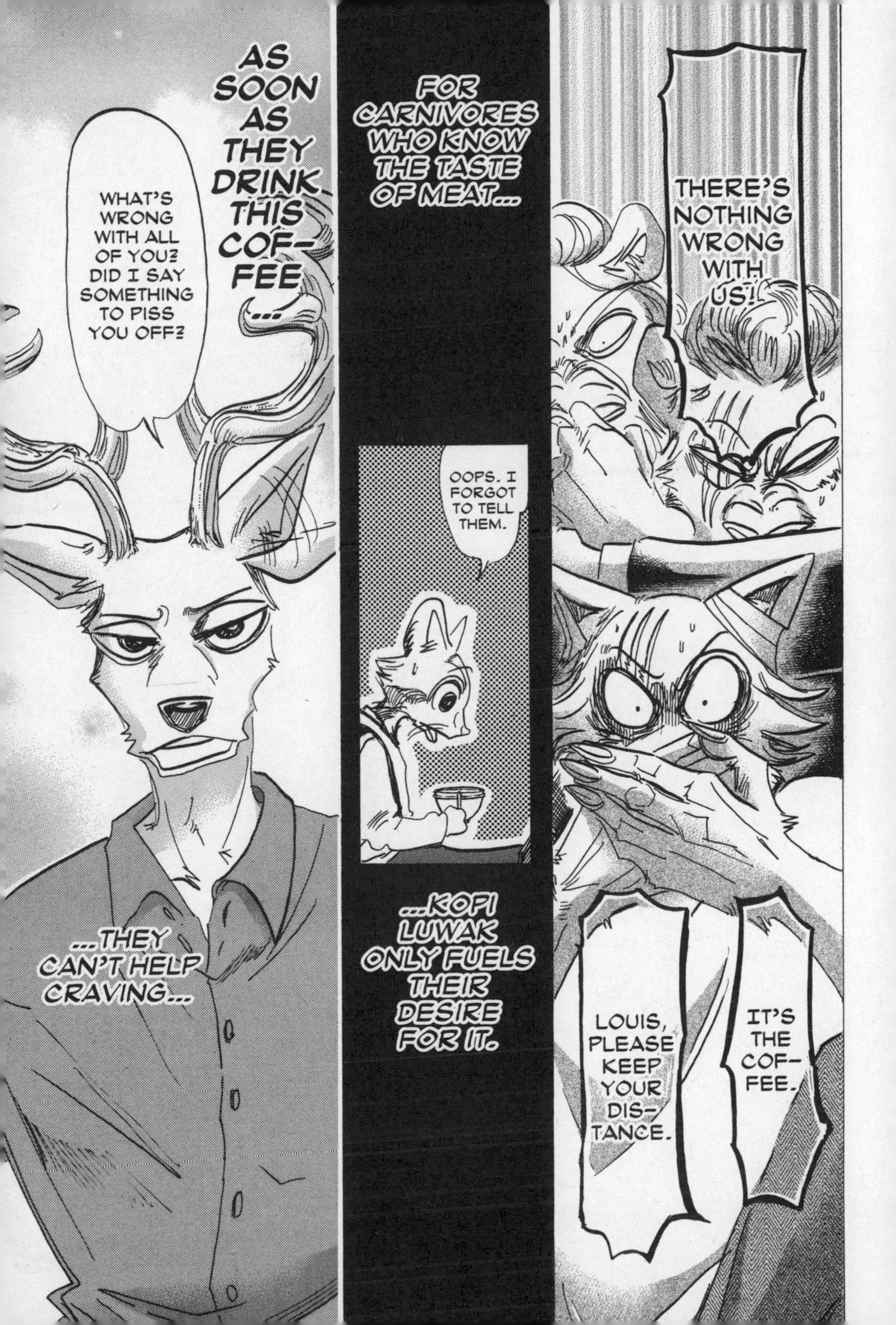

THERE'S NOTHING WRONG WITH US!
IT'S THE COFFEE.
LOUIS, PLEASE KEEP YOUR DISTANCE.
FOR CARNIVORES WHO KNOW THE TASTE OF MEAT...
OOPS. I FORGOT TO TELL THEM.
...KOPI LUWAK ONLY FUELS THEIR DESIRE FOR IT.
AS SOON AS THEY DRINK THIS COFFEE...
WHAT'S WRONG WITH ALL OF YOU? DID I SAY SOMETHING TO PISS YOU OFF?
...THEY CAN'T HELP CRAVING...

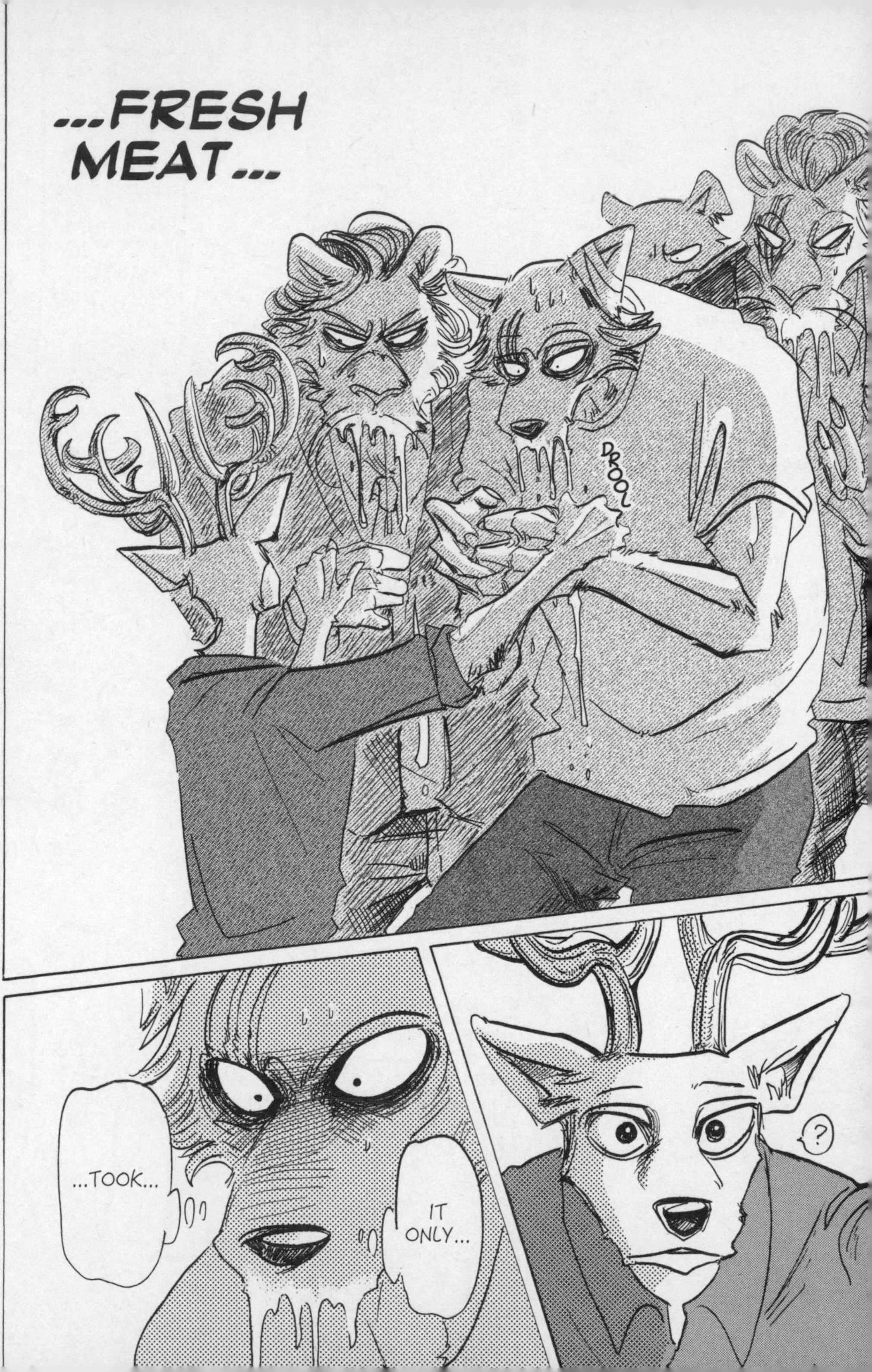
...FRESH MEAT...
DROOL
?
IT ONLY...
...TOOK...

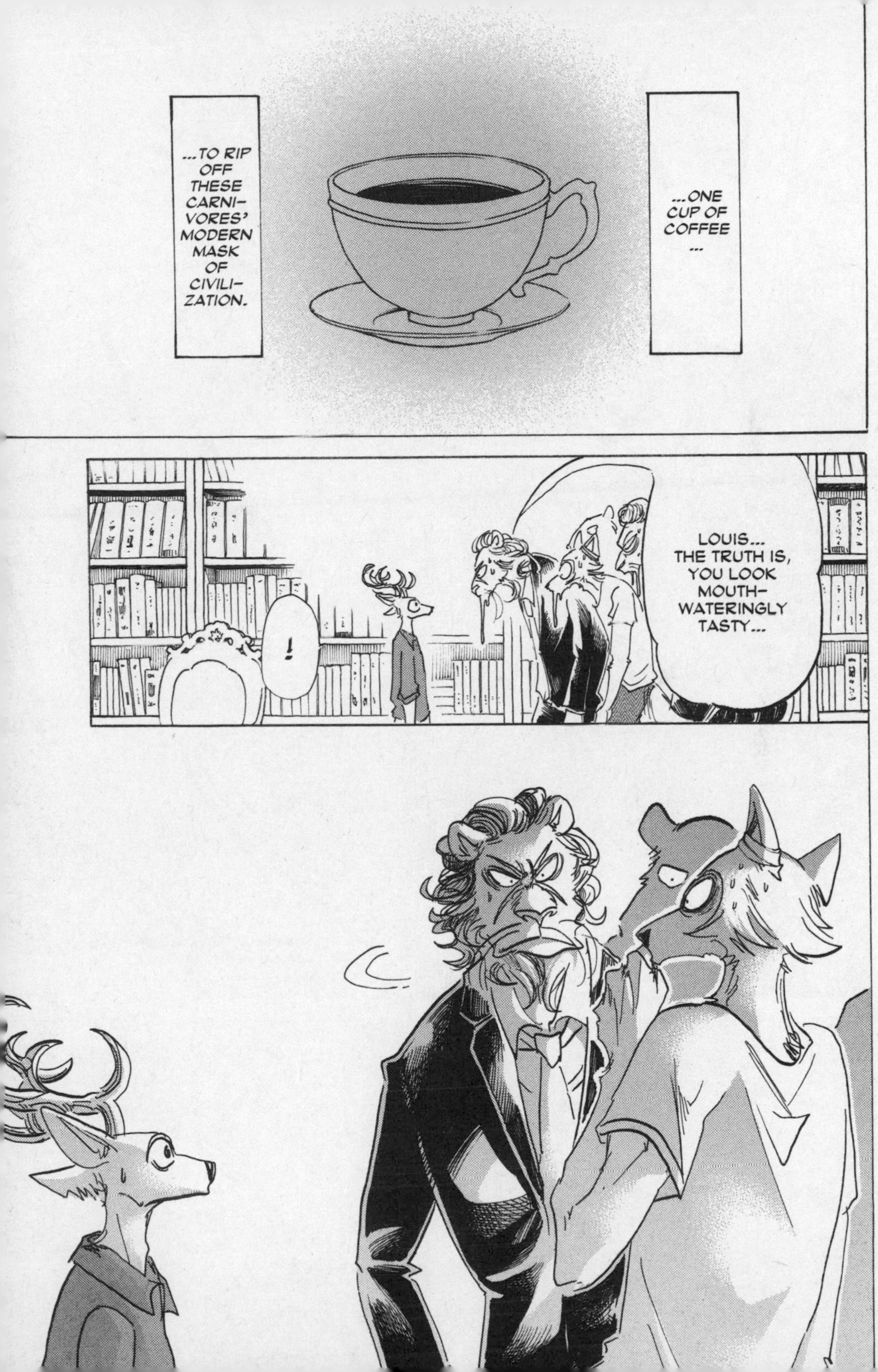
...ONE CUP OF COFFEE ...
...TO RIP OFF THESE CARNIVORES' MODERN MASK OF CIVILIZATION.
LOUIS... THE TRUTH IS, YOU LOOK MOUTH-WATERINGLY TASTY...
!

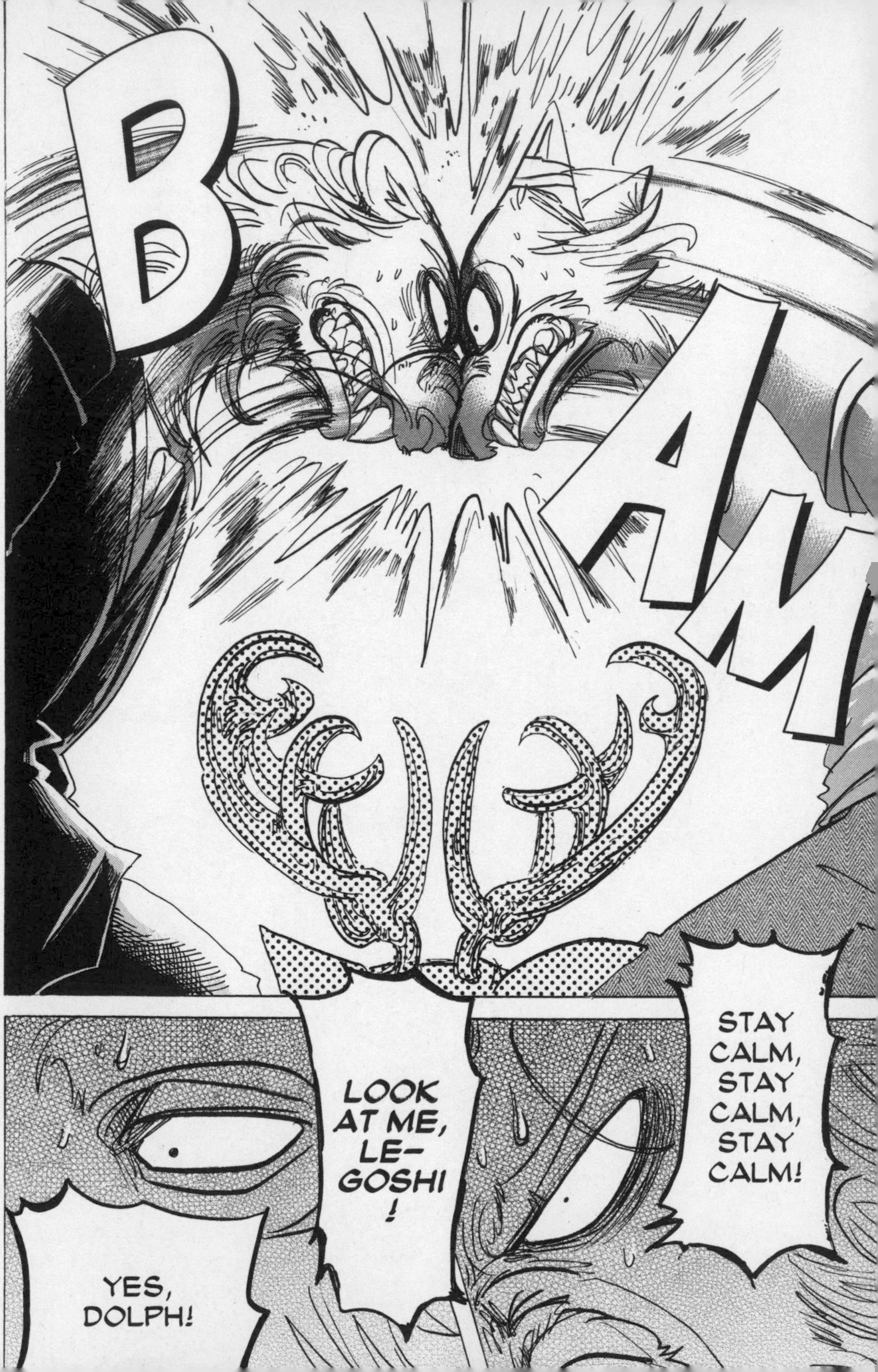
BAM
STAY CALM, STAY CALM, STAY CALM!
LOOK AT ME, LE-GOSHI!
YES, DOLPH!

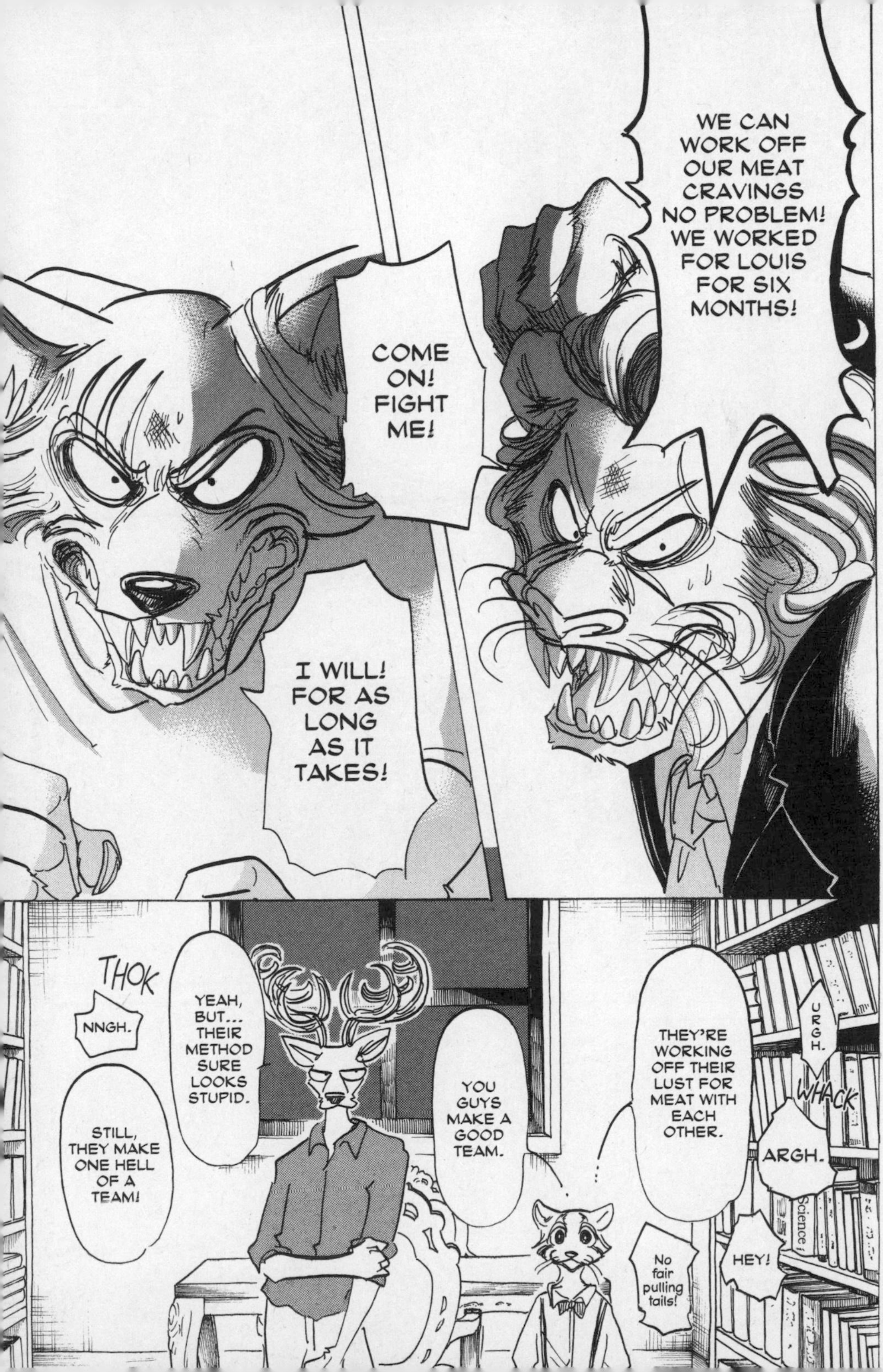
WE CAN WORK OFF OUR MEAT CRAVINGS NO PROBLEM! WE WORKED FOR LOUIS FOR SIX MONTHS!
COME ON! FIGHT ME!
I WILL! FOR AS LONG AS IT TAKES!
URGH.
WHACK
ARGH.
THEY'RE WORKING OFF THEIR LUST FOR MEAT WITH EACH OTHER.
HEY!
No fair pulling tails!
Science
...
YOU GUYS MAKE A GOOD TEAM.
YEAH, BUT... THEIR METHOD SURE LOOKS STUPID.
THOK
NNGH.
STILL, THEY MAKE ONE HELL OF A TEAM!

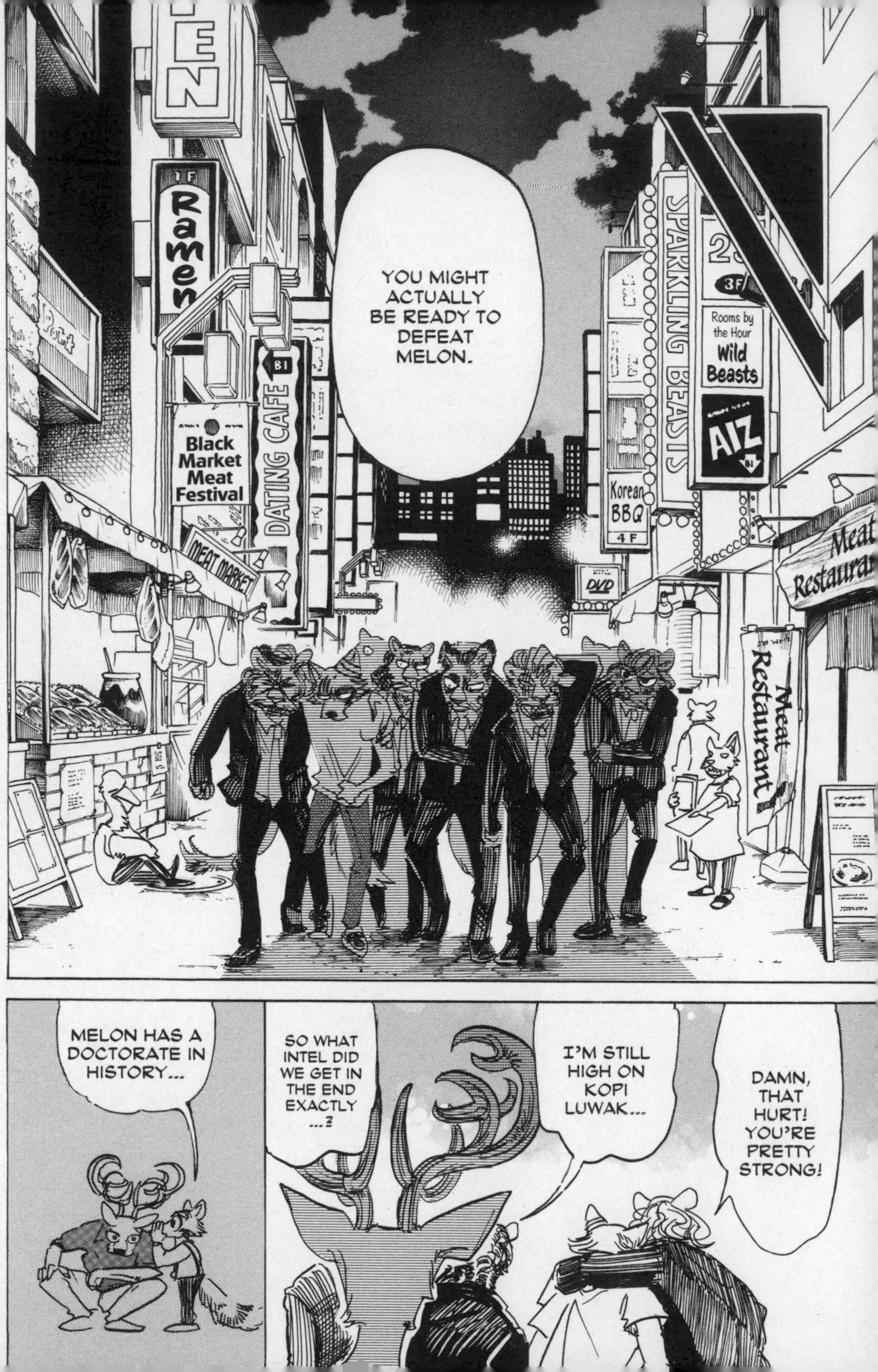
YOU MIGHT ACTUALLY BE READY TO DEFEAT MELON.
Ramen
Black Market Meat Festival
DATING CAFE
MEAT MARKET
SPARKLING BEASTS
Rooms by the Hour Wild Beasts
AIZ
Korean BBQ 4F
DVD
Meat Restaurant
Meat Restaurant
DAMN, THAT HURT! YOU'RE PRETTY STRONG!
I'M STILL HIGH ON KOPI LUWAK...
SO WHAT INTEL DID WE GET IN THE END EXACTLY ...?
MELON HAS A DOCTORATE IN HISTORY...

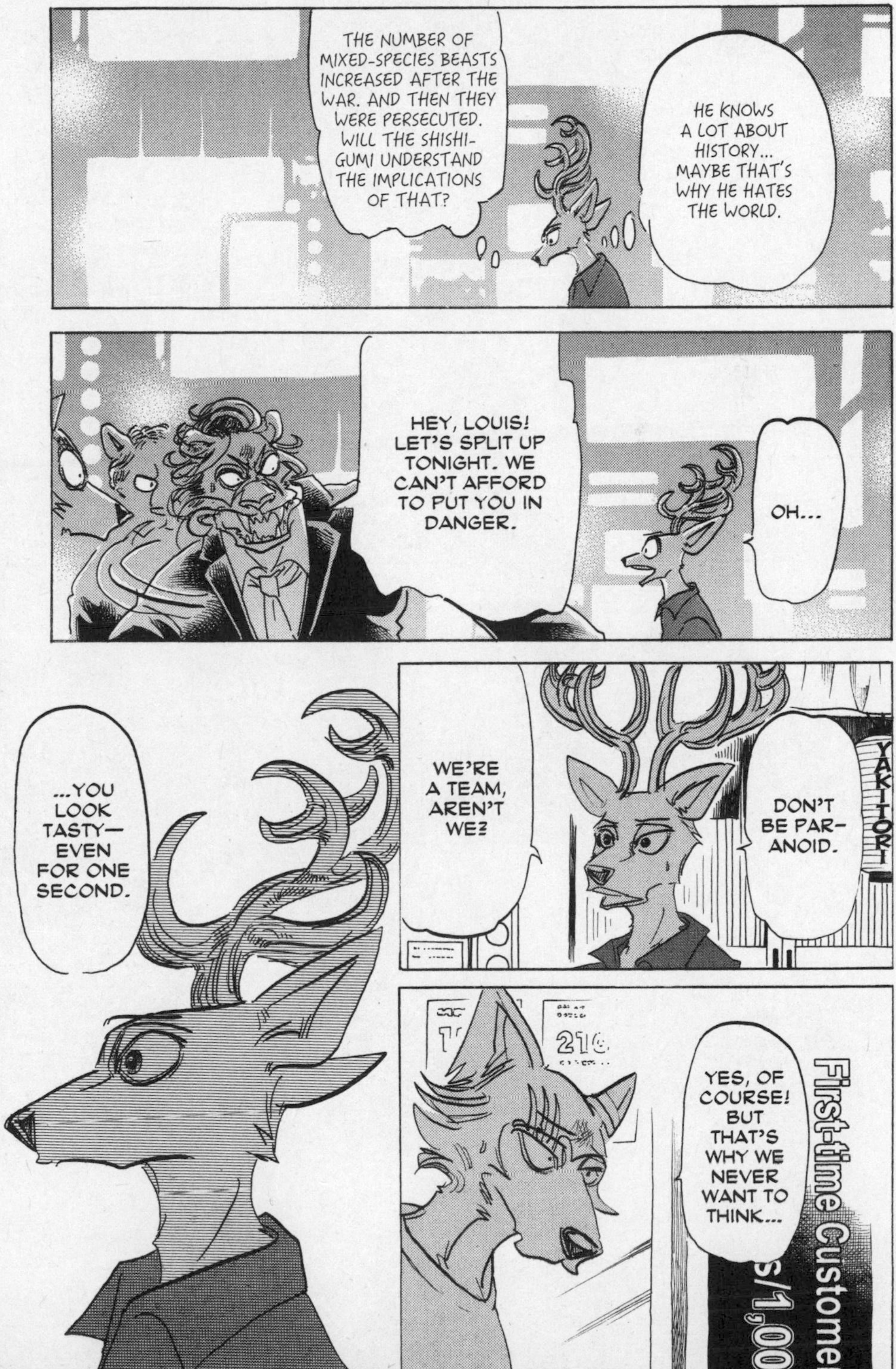
HE KNOWS A LOT ABOUT HISTORY... MAYBE THAT'S WHY HE HATES THE WORLD.
THE NUMBER OF MIXED-SPECIES BEASTS INCREASED AFTER THE WAR. AND THEN THEY WERE PERSECUTED. WILL THE SHISHI-GUMI UNDERSTAND THE IMPLICATIONS OF THAT?
OH...
HEY, LOUIS! LET'S SPLIT UP TONIGHT. WE CAN'T AFFORD TO PUT YOU IN DANGER.
YAKITORI
DON'T BE PAR-ANOID.
WE'RE A TEAM, AREN'T WE?
First-time Customer
YES, OF COURSE! BUT THAT'S WHY WE NEVER WANT TO THINK...
...YOU LOOK TASTY—EVEN FOR ONE SECOND.

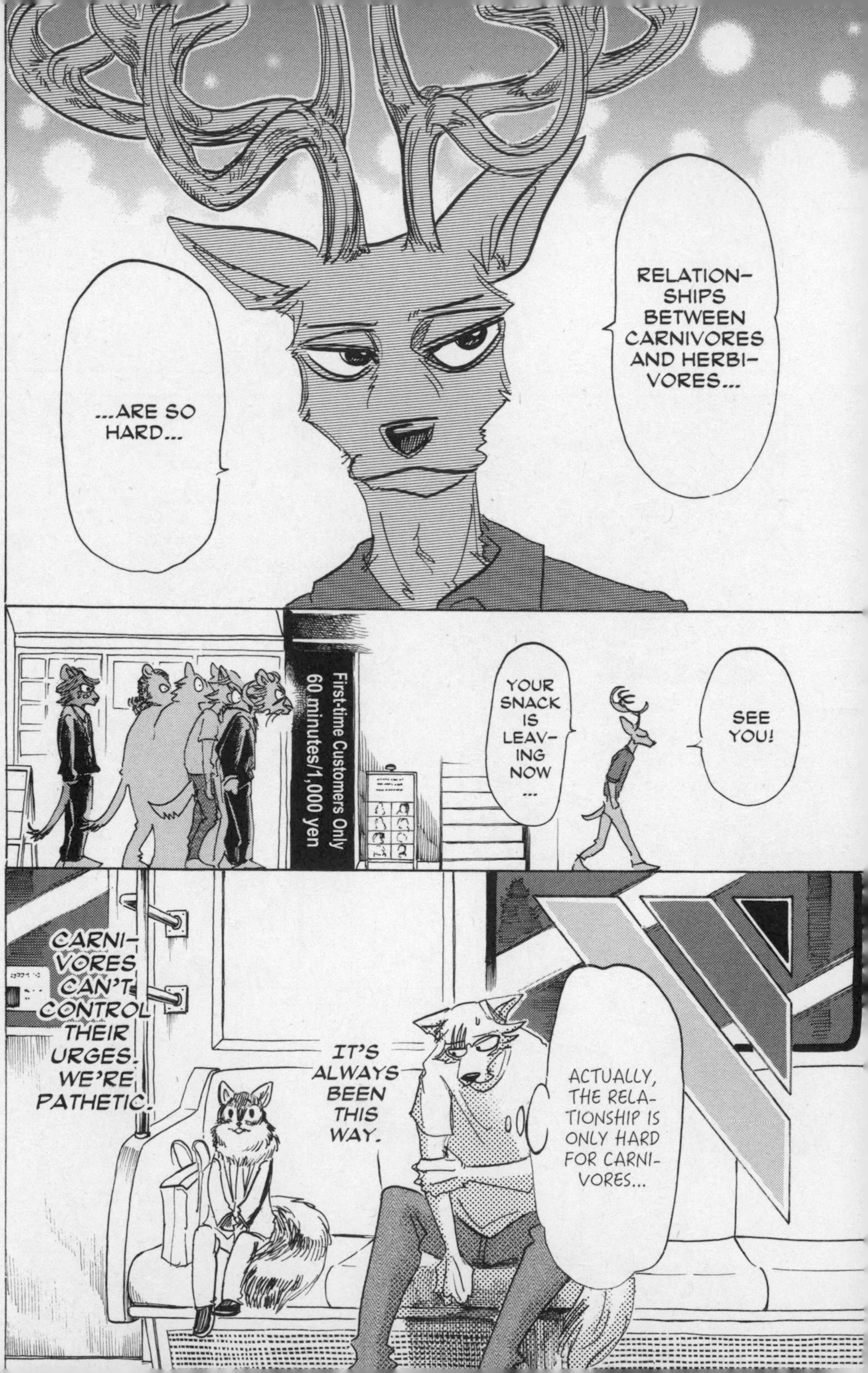
RELATIONSHIPS BETWEEN CARNIVORES AND HERBIVORES...
...ARE SO HARD...
SEE YOU!
YOUR SNACK IS LEAVING NOW...
First-time Customers Only 60 minutes/1,000 yen
ACTUALLY, THE RELATIONSHIP IS ONLY HARD FOR CARNIVORES...
IT'S ALWAYS BEEN THIS WAY.
CARNIVORES CAN'T CONTROL THEIR URGES. WE'RE PATHETIC.

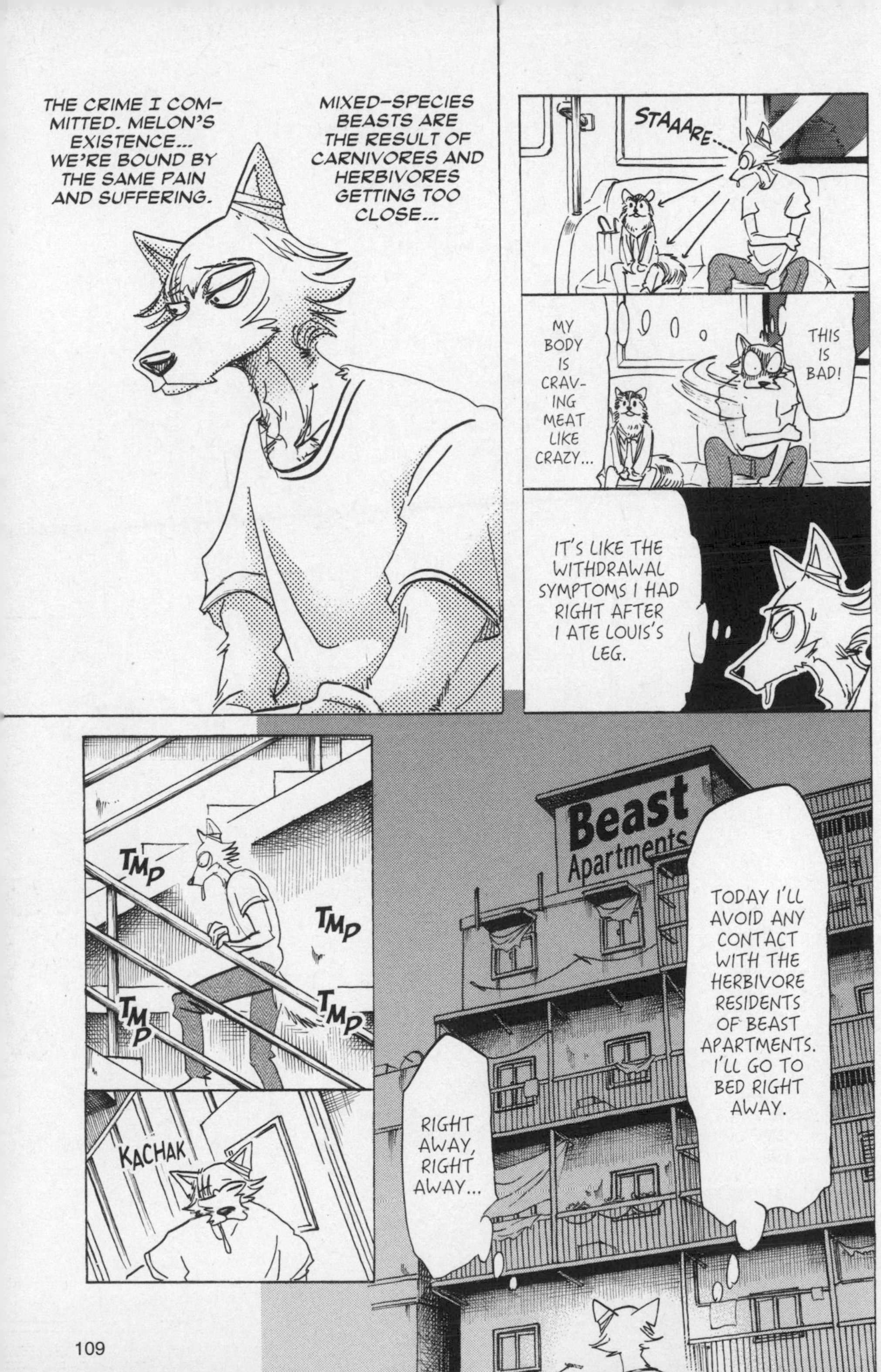
STAAARE...
THIS IS BAD!
MY BODY IS CRAVING MEAT LIKE CRAZY...
IT'S LIKE THE WITHDRAWAL SYMPTOMS I HAD RIGHT AFTER I ATE LOUIS'S LEG.
MIXED-SPECIES BEASTS ARE THE RESULT OF CARNIVORES AND HERBIVORES GETTING TOO CLOSE...
THE CRIME I COMMITTED. MELON'S EXISTENCE... WE'RE BOUND BY THE SAME PAIN AND SUFFERING.
Beast Apartments
TODAY I'LL AVOID ANY CONTACT WITH THE HERBIVORE RESIDENTS OF BEAST APARTMENTS. I'LL GO TO BED RIGHT AWAY.
RIGHT AWAY, RIGHT AWAY...
TMP
TMP
TMP
TMP
KACHAK

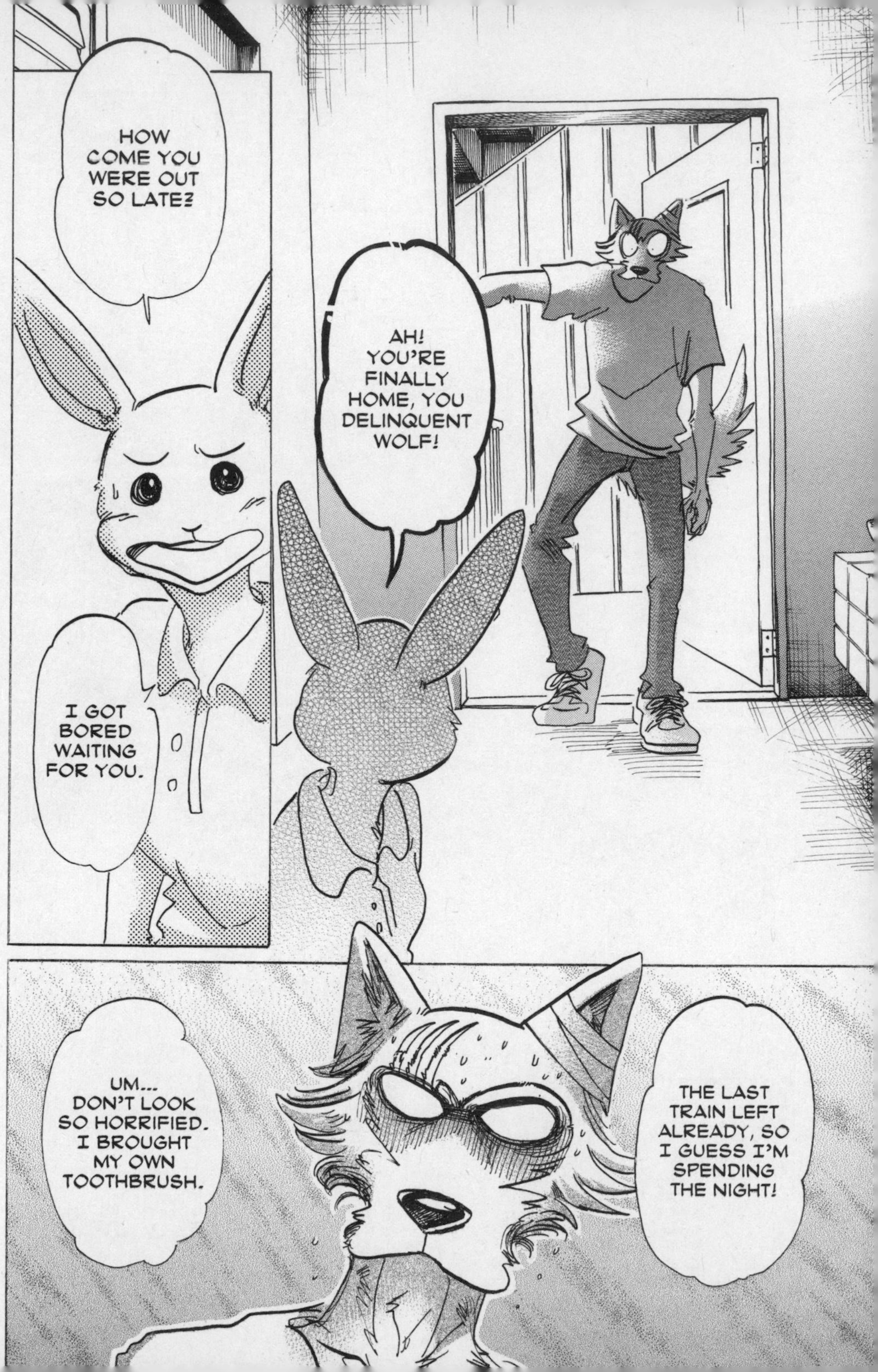
AH! YOU'RE FINALLY HOME, YOU DELINQUENT WOLF!
HOW COME YOU WERE OUT SO LATE?
I GOT BORED WAITING FOR YOU.
THE LAST TRAIN LEFT ALREADY, SO I GUESS I'M SPENDING THE NIGHT!
UM... DON'T LOOK SO HORRIFIED. I BROUGHT MY OWN TOOTHBRUSH.

BEASTARS
Vol. 17

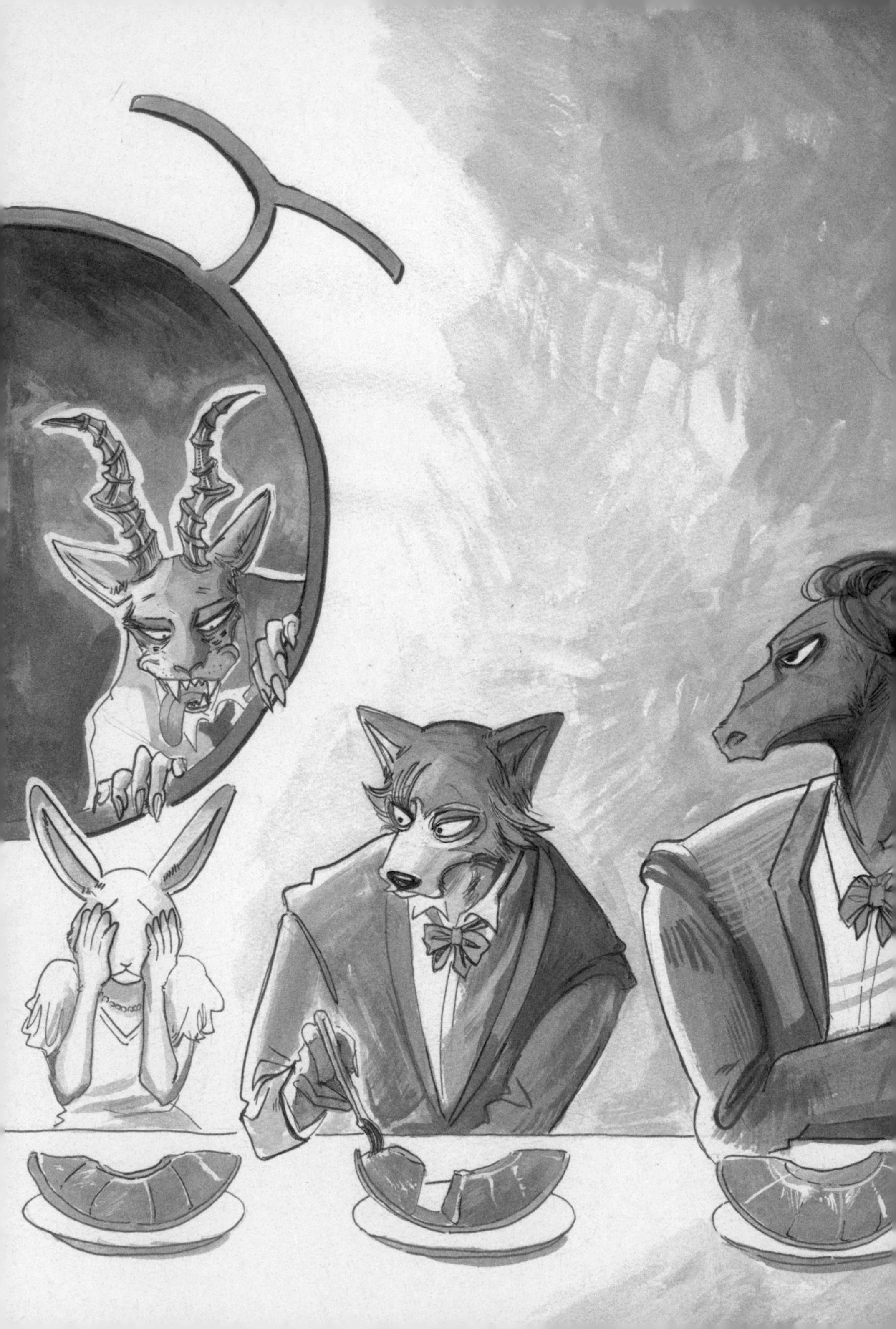

Chapter 148: I Thought It Would Always Be Morning when I Awoke

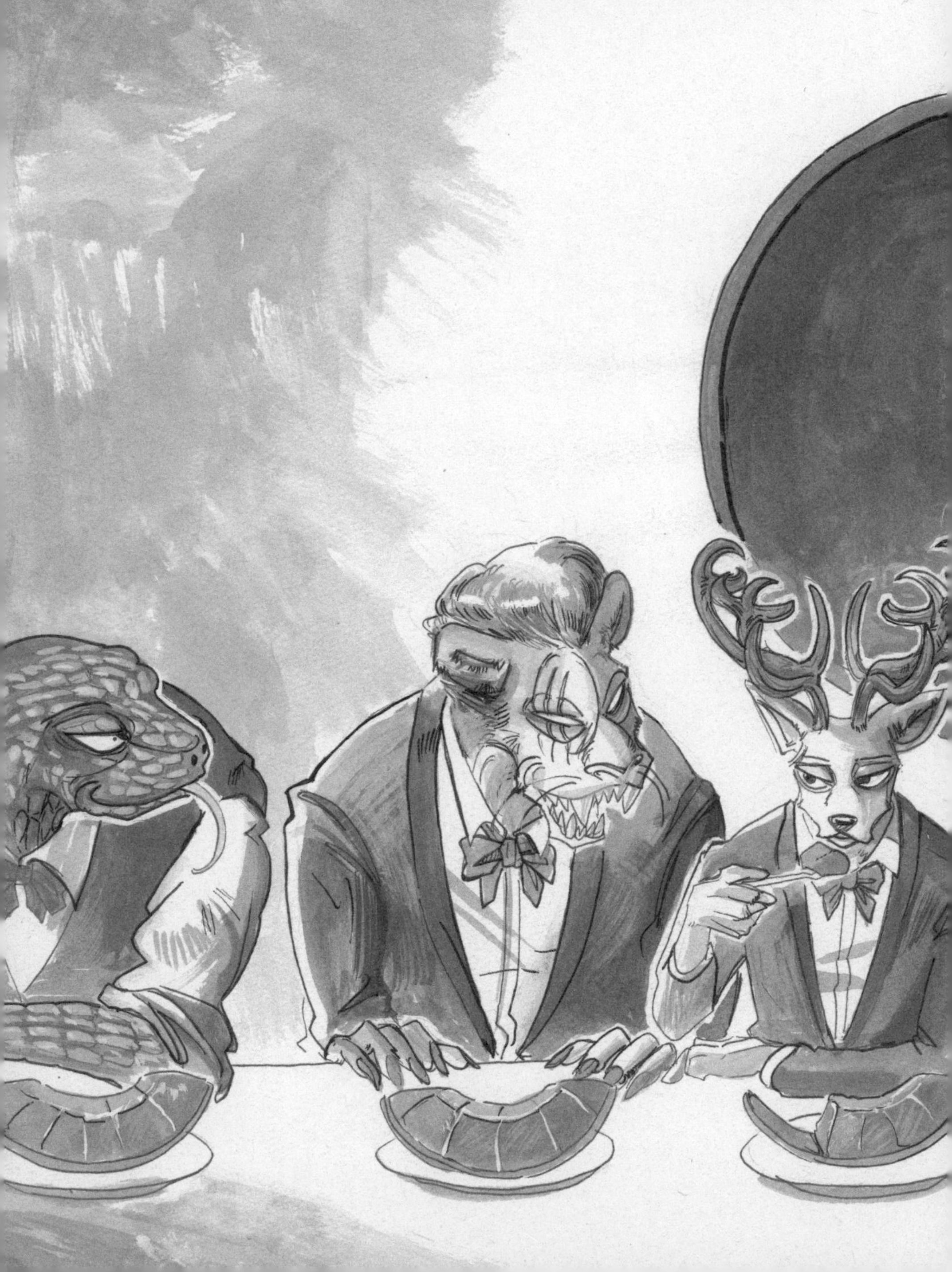

BEASTARS
Vol. 17

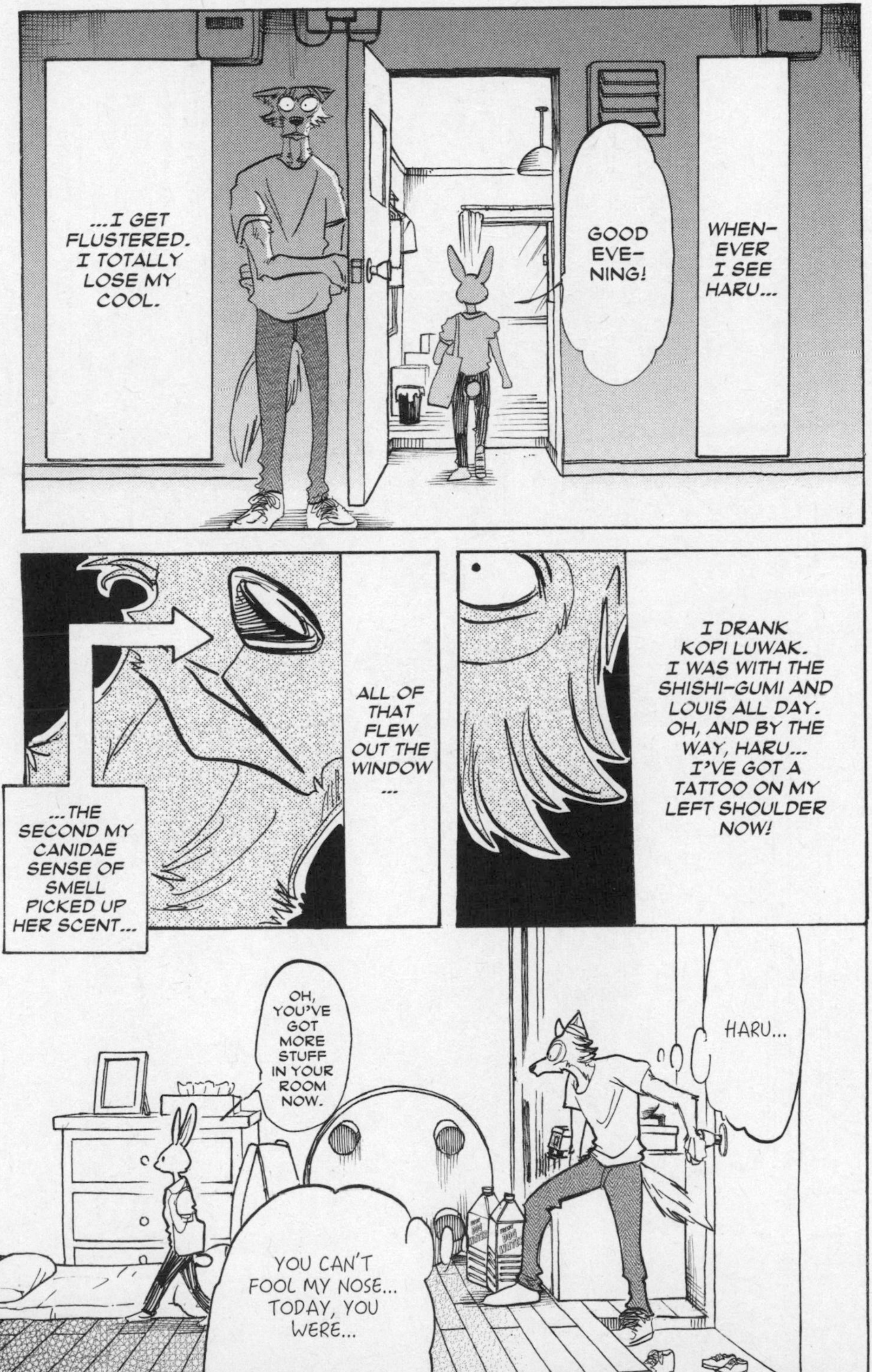
WHEN-EVER I SEE HARU...
GOOD EVE-NING!
...I GET FLUSTERED. I TOTALLY LOSE MY COOL.
I DRANK KOPI LUWAK. I WAS WITH THE SHISHI-GUMI AND LOUIS ALL DAY. OH, AND BY THE WAY, HARU... I'VE GOT A TATTOO ON MY LEFT SHOULDER NOW!
ALL OF THAT FLEW OUT THE WINDOW...
...THE SECOND MY CANIDAE SENSE OF SMELL PICKED UP HER SCENT...
HARU...
OH, YOU'VE GOT MORE STUFF IN YOUR ROOM NOW.
YOU CAN'T FOOL MY NOSE... TODAY, YOU WERE...

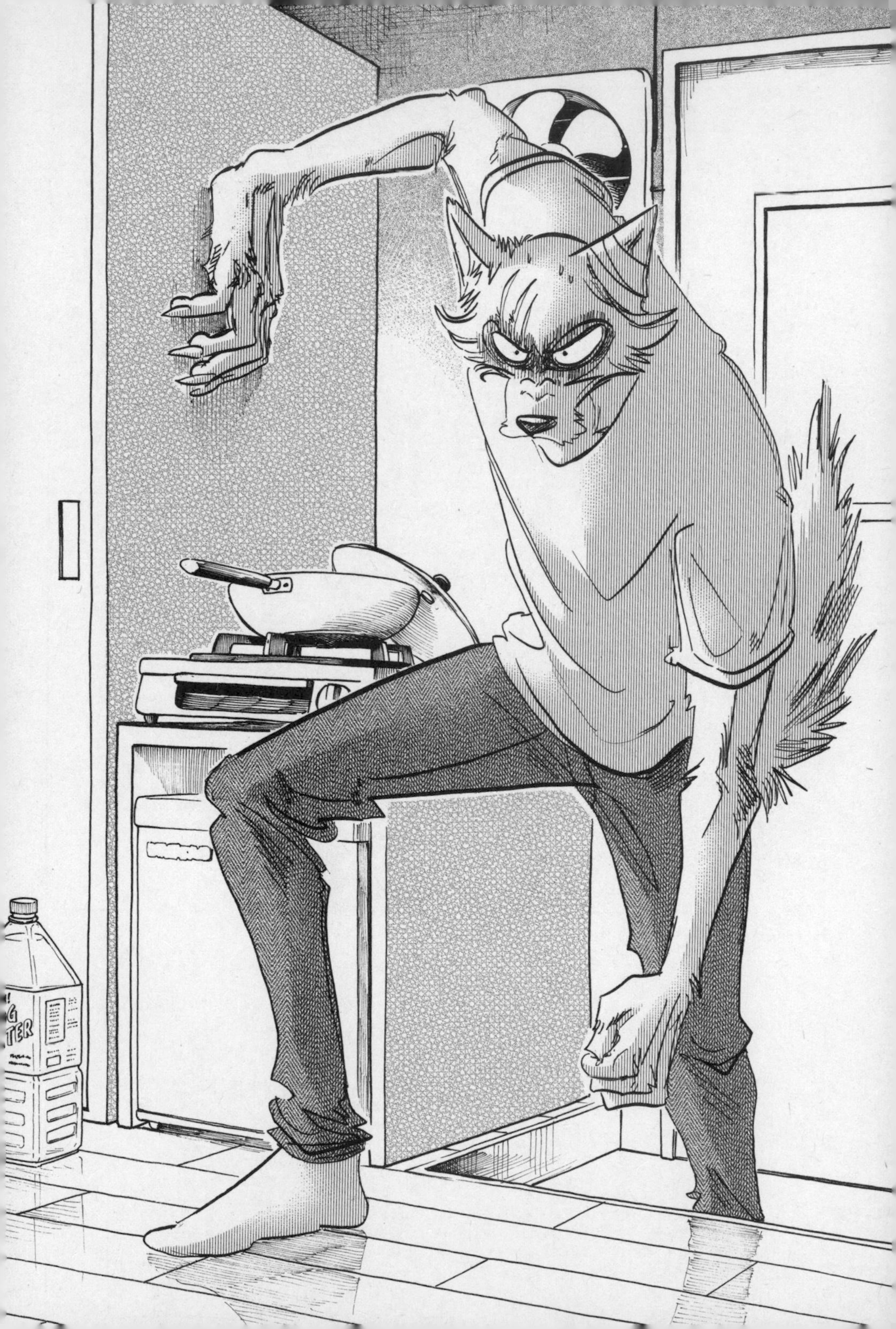

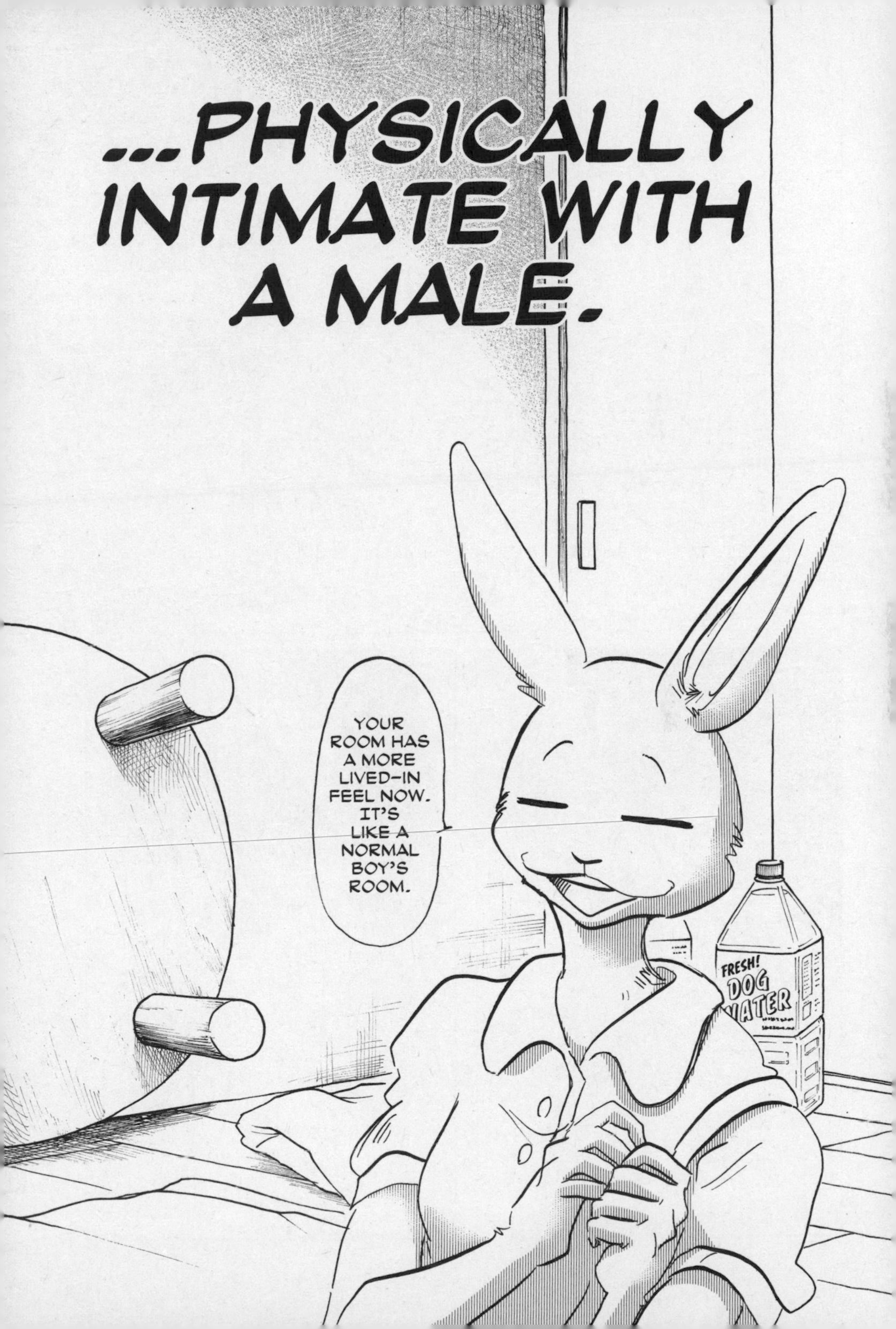
...PHYSICALLY INTIMATE WITH A MALE.
YOUR ROOM HAS A MORE LIVED-IN FEEL NOW. IT'S LIKE A NORMAL BOY'S ROOM.
FRESH! DOG WATER

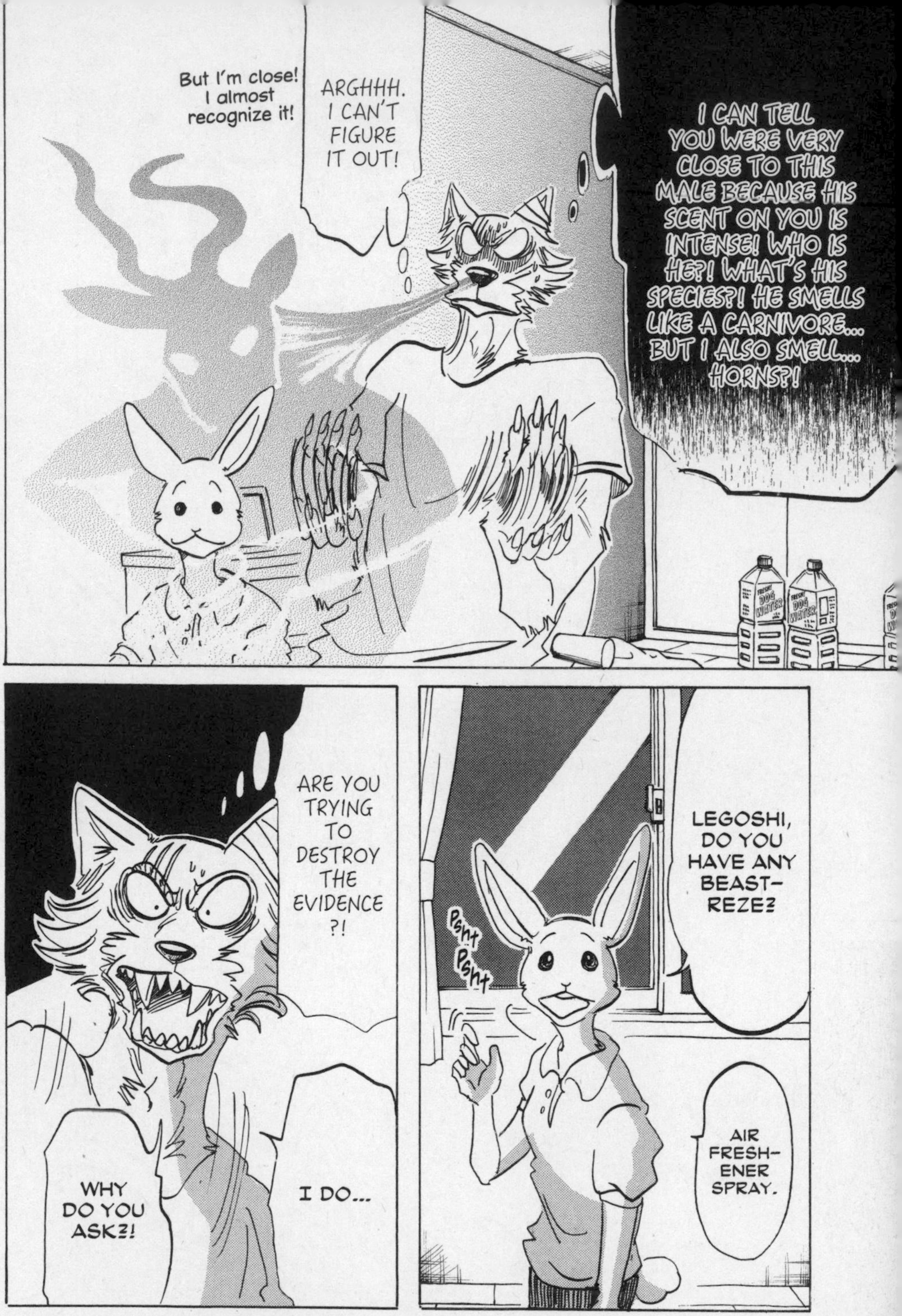
I CAN TELL YOU WERE VERY CLOSE TO THIS MALE BECAUSE HIS SCENT ON YOU IS INTENSE! WHO IS HE?! WHAT'S HIS SPECIES?! HE SMELLS LIKE A CARNIVORE... BUT I ALSO SMELL... HORNS?!
ARGHHH. I CAN'T FIGURE IT OUT!
But I'm close! I almost recognize it!
DOG WATER
LEGOSHI, DO YOU HAVE ANY BEAST-REZE?
Psht Psht
AIR FRESHENER SPRAY.
ARE YOU TRYING TO DESTROY THE EVIDENCE?!
I DO...
WHY DO YOU ASK?!

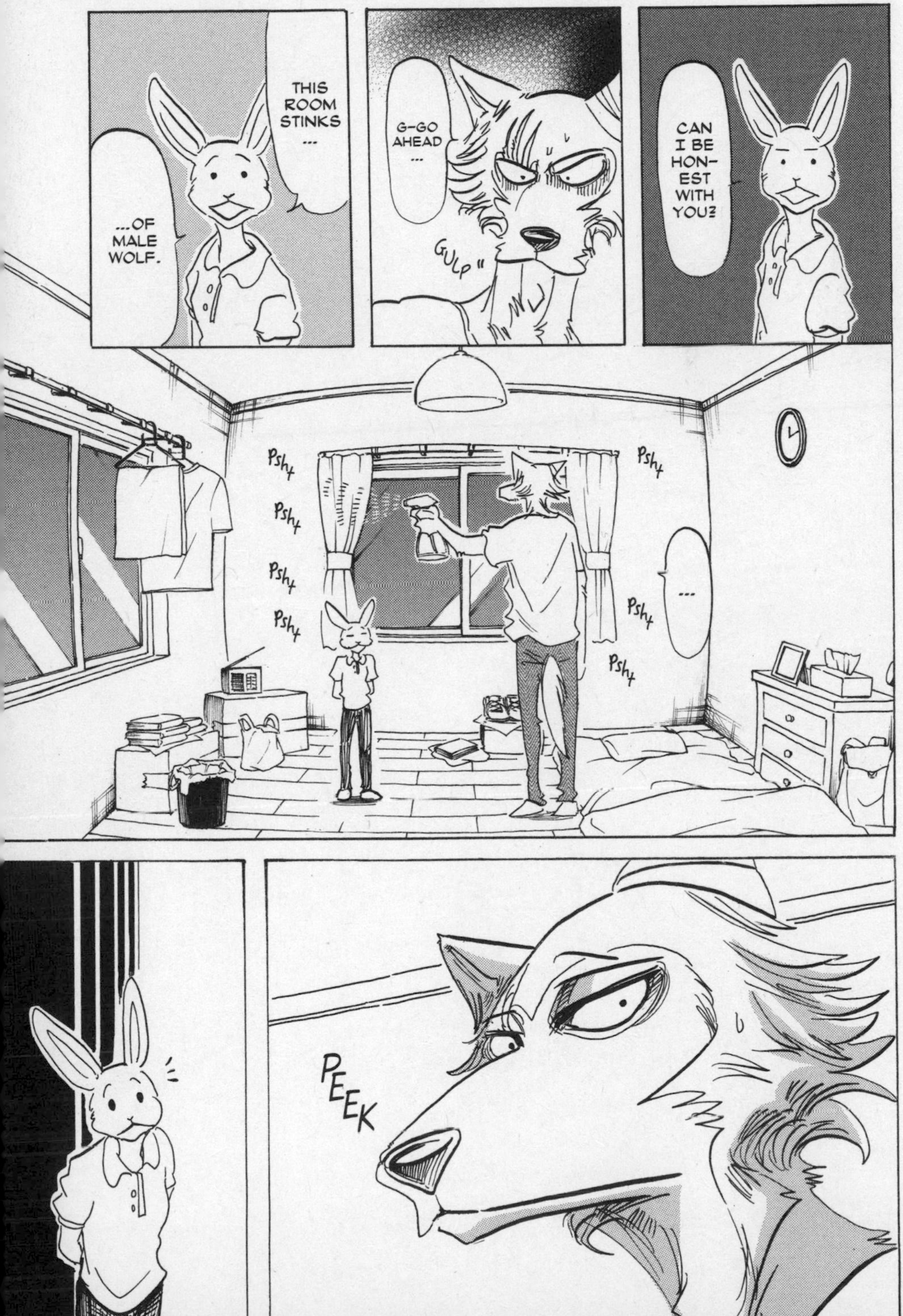
CAN I BE HONEST WITH YOU?
G-GO AHEAD ...
GULP
THIS ROOM STINKS ...
...OF MALE WOLF.
Psht
Psht
Psht
Psht
Psht
Psht
Psht
...
PEEK

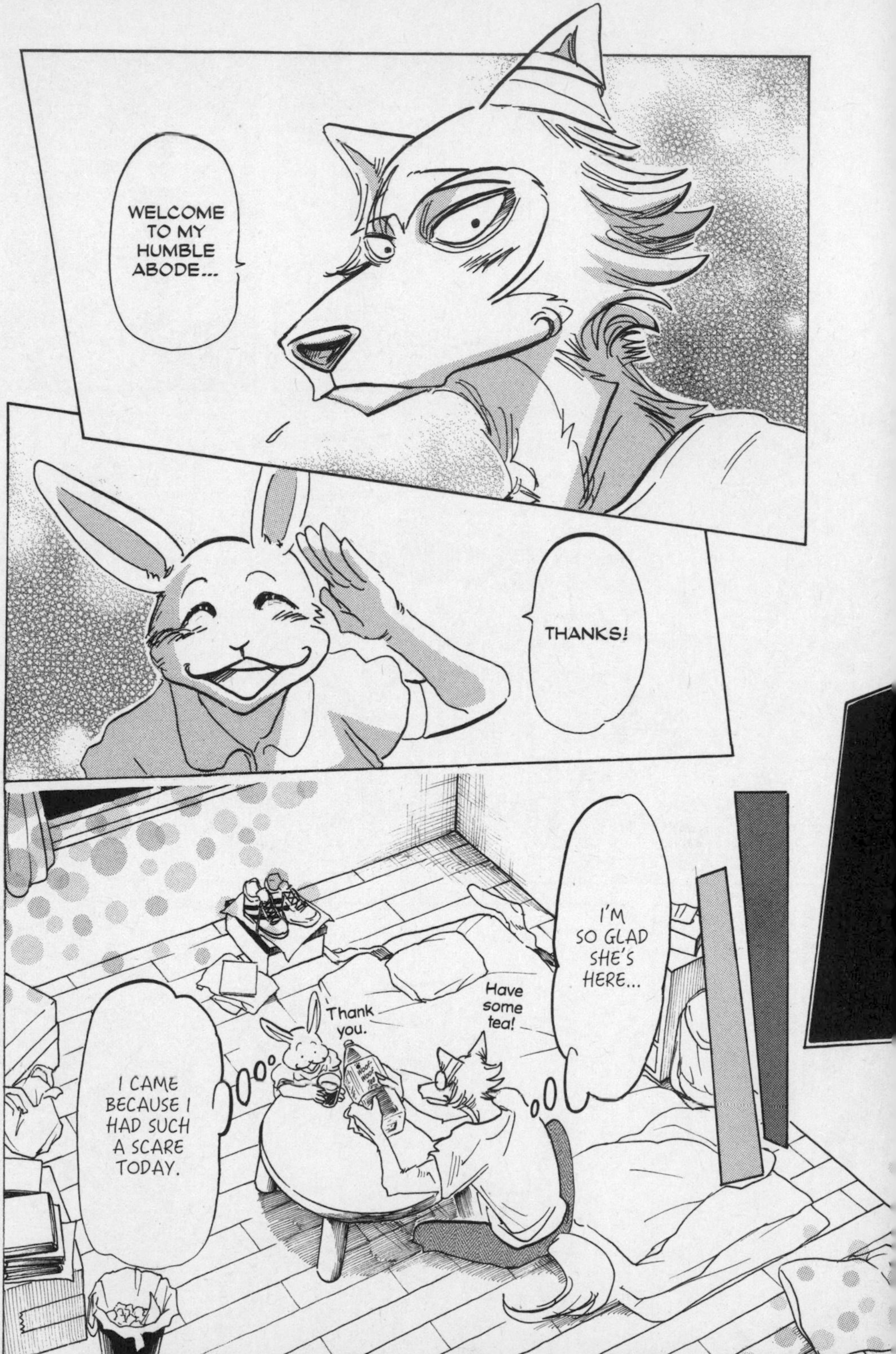
WELCOME TO MY HUMBLE ABODE...
THANKS!
I'M SO GLAD SHE'S HERE...
Have some tea!
Thank you.
I CAME BECAUSE I HAD SUCH A SCARE TODAY.

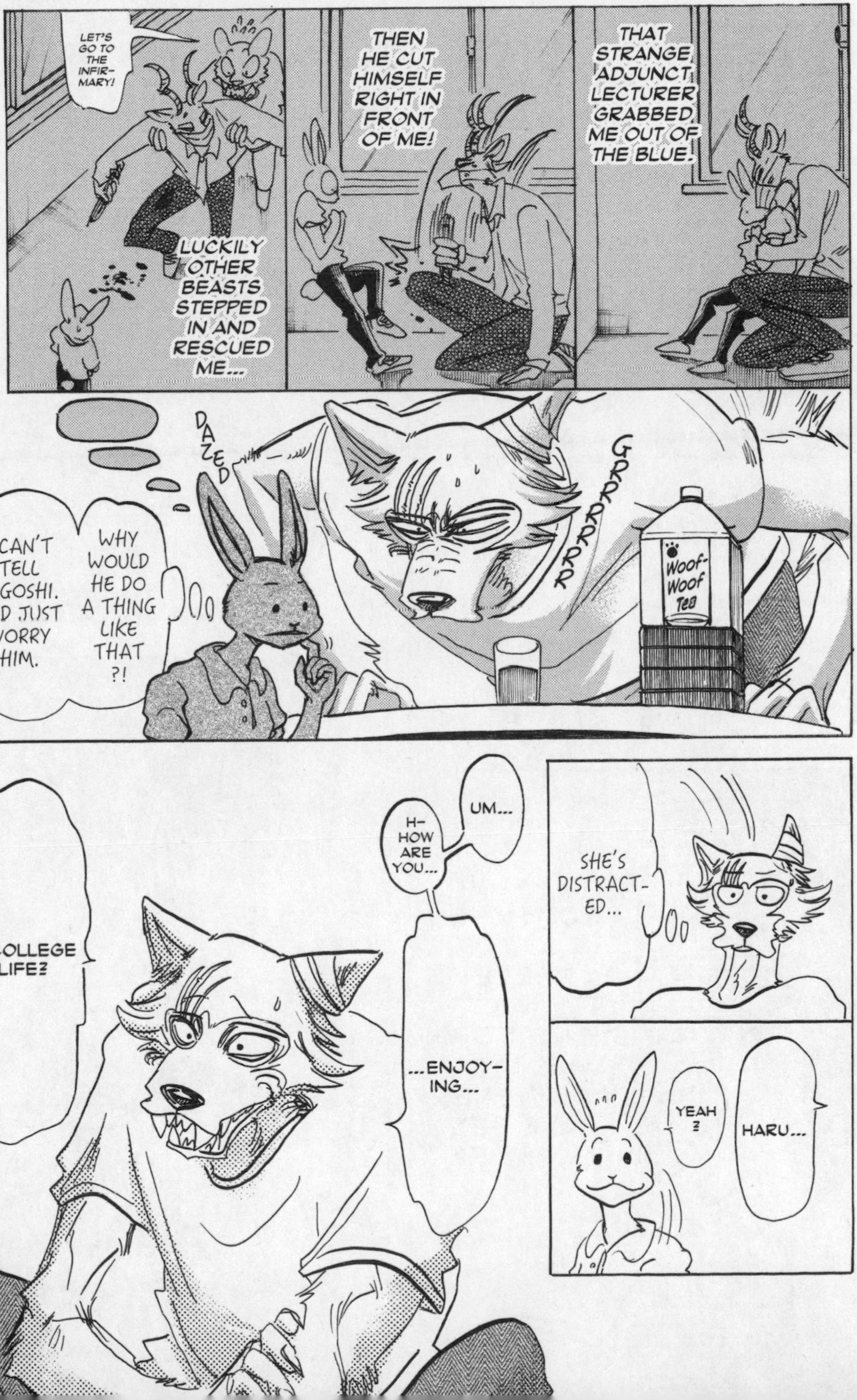
THAT STRANGE, ADJUNCT LECTURER GRABBED ME OUT OF THE BLUE!
THEN HE CUT HIMSELF RIGHT IN FRONT OF ME!
LET'S GO TO THE INFIRMARY!
LUCKILY OTHER BEASTS STEPPED IN AND RESCUED ME...
GRRRRRRR
Woof-Woof Tea
DAZED
WHY WOULD HE DO A THING LIKE THAT?!
I CAN'T TELL LEGOSHI. IT'D JUST WORRY HIM.
SHE'S DISTRACTED...
HARU...
YEAH?
UM...
H-HOW ARE YOU...
...ENJOYING...
...COLLEGE LIFE?

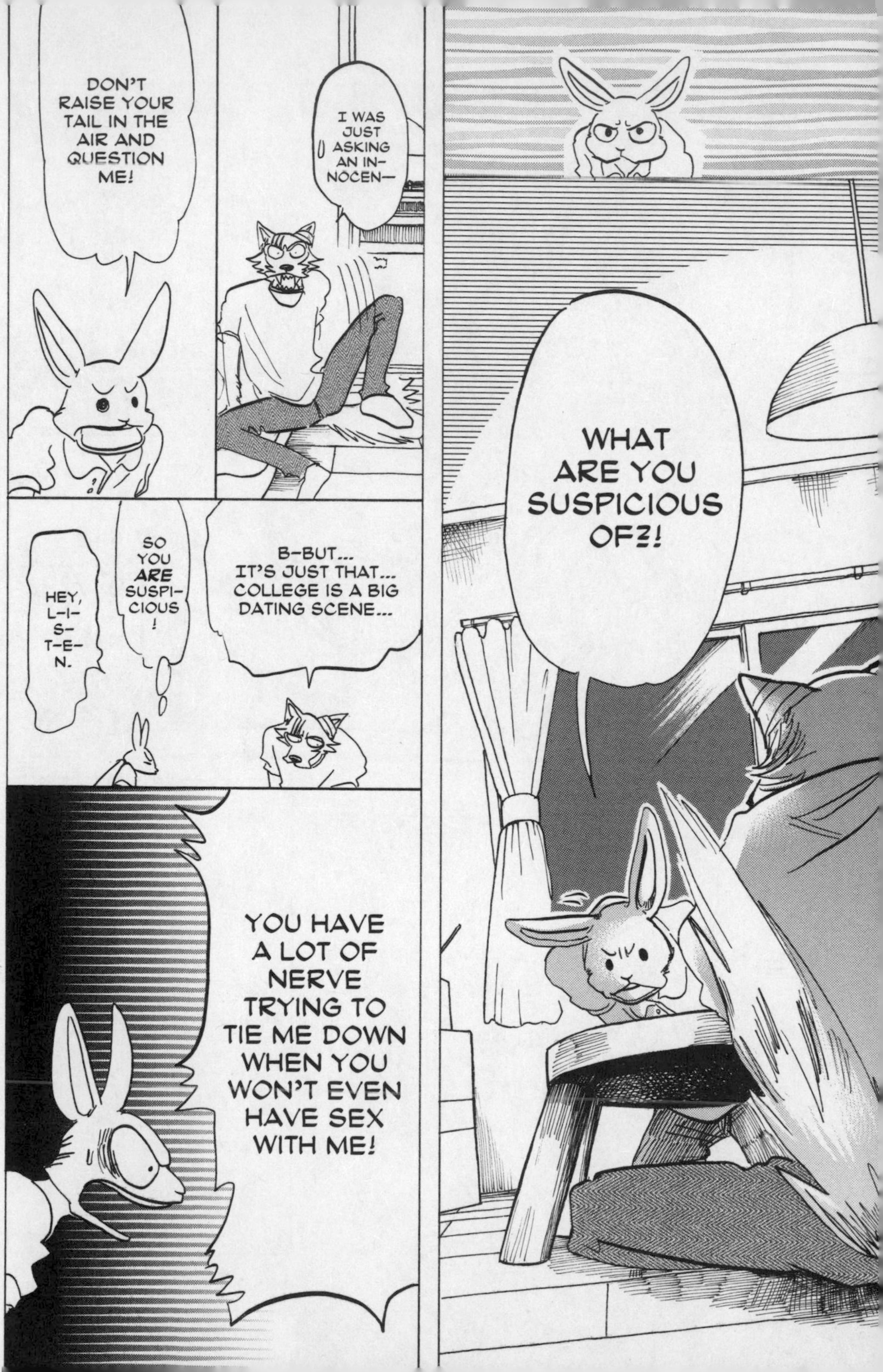
WHAT ARE YOU SUSPICIOUS OF?!
I WAS JUST ASKING AN IN-NOCEN—
DON'T RAISE YOUR TAIL IN THE AIR AND QUESTION ME!
B-BUT... IT'S JUST THAT... COLLEGE IS A BIG DATING SCENE...
SO YOU ARE SUSPICIOUS!
HEY, L-I-S-T-E-N.
YOU HAVE A LOT OF NERVE TRYING TO TIE ME DOWN WHEN YOU WON'T EVEN HAVE SEX WITH ME!

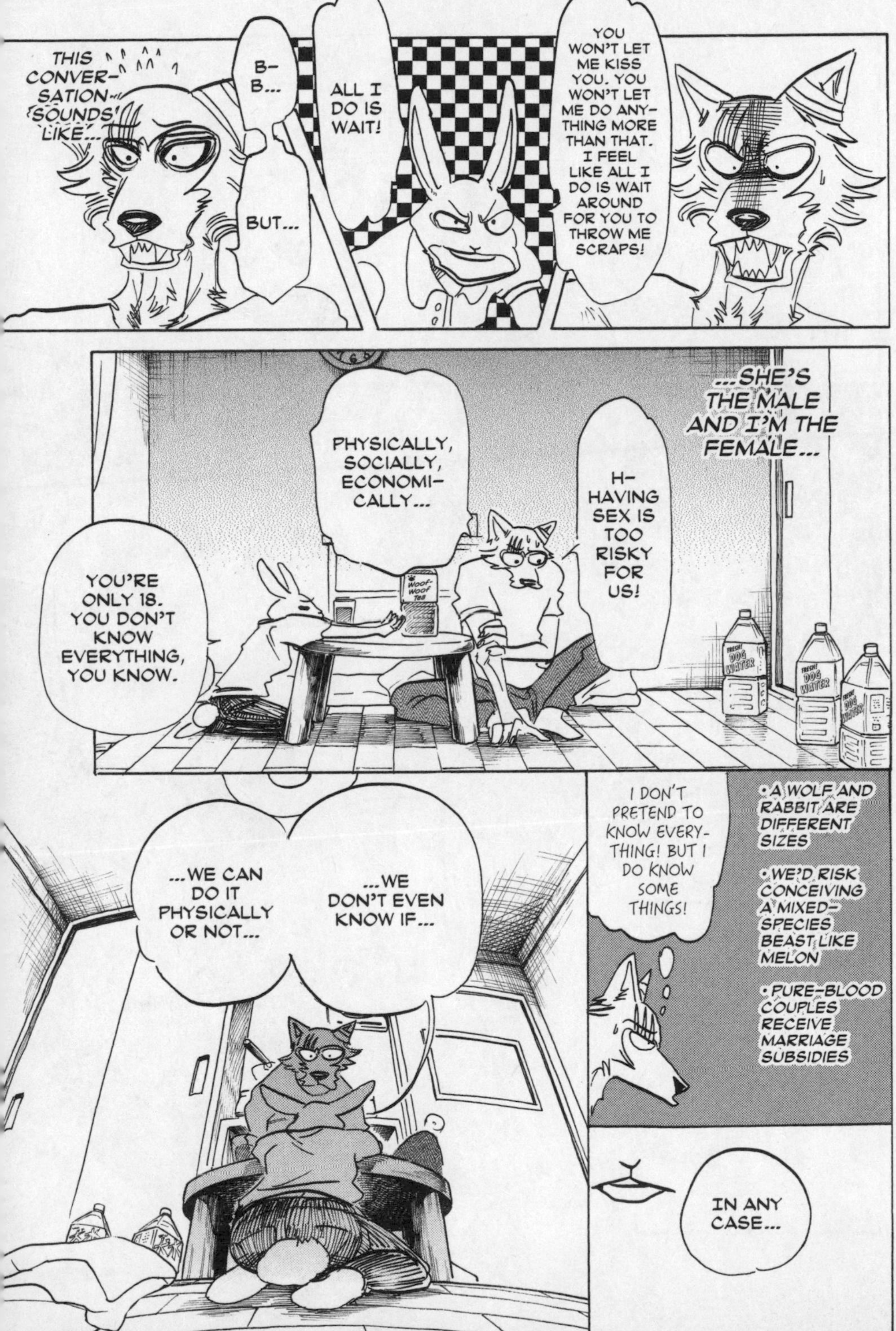
YOU WON'T LET ME KISS YOU. YOU WON'T LET ME DO ANYTHING MORE THAN THAT. I FEEL LIKE ALL I DO IS WAIT AROUND FOR YOU TO THROW ME SCRAPS!
ALL I DO IS WAIT!
B-B...
BUT...
THIS CONVERSATION SOUNDS LIKE...
...SHE'S THE MALE AND I'M THE FEMALE...
H-HAVING SEX IS TOO RISKY FOR US!
PHYSICALLY, SOCIALLY, ECONOMICALLY...
Woof-Woof Tea
FRESH! DOG WATER
YOU'RE ONLY 18. YOU DON'T KNOW EVERYTHING, YOU KNOW.
• A WOLF AND RABBIT ARE DIFFERENT SIZES
• WE'D RISK CONCEIVING A MIXED-SPECIES BEAST LIKE MELON
• PURE-BLOOD COUPLES RECEIVE MARRIAGE SUBSIDIES
I DON'T PRETEND TO KNOW EVERYTHING! BUT I DO KNOW SOME THINGS!
IN ANY CASE...
...WE DON'T EVEN KNOW IF...
...WE CAN DO IT PHYSICALLY OR NOT...

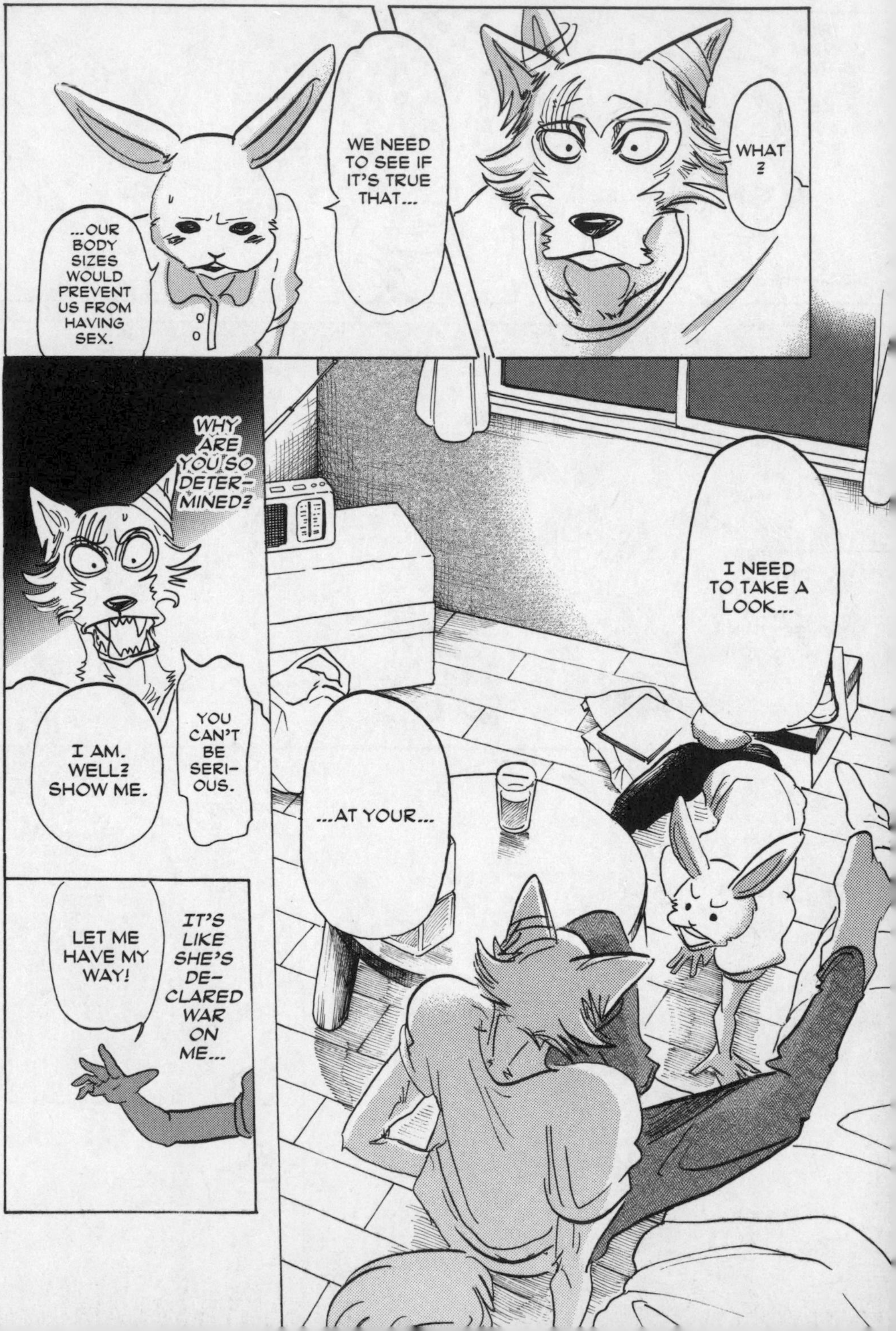
WHAT?
WE NEED TO SEE IF IT'S TRUE THAT...
...OUR BODY SIZES WOULD PREVENT US FROM HAVING SEX.
I NEED TO TAKE A LOOK...
...AT YOUR...
WHY ARE YOU SO DETER-MINED?
YOU CAN'T BE SERI-OUS.
I AM. WELL? SHOW ME.
IT'S LIKE SHE'S DE-CLARED WAR ON ME...
LET ME HAVE MY WAY!

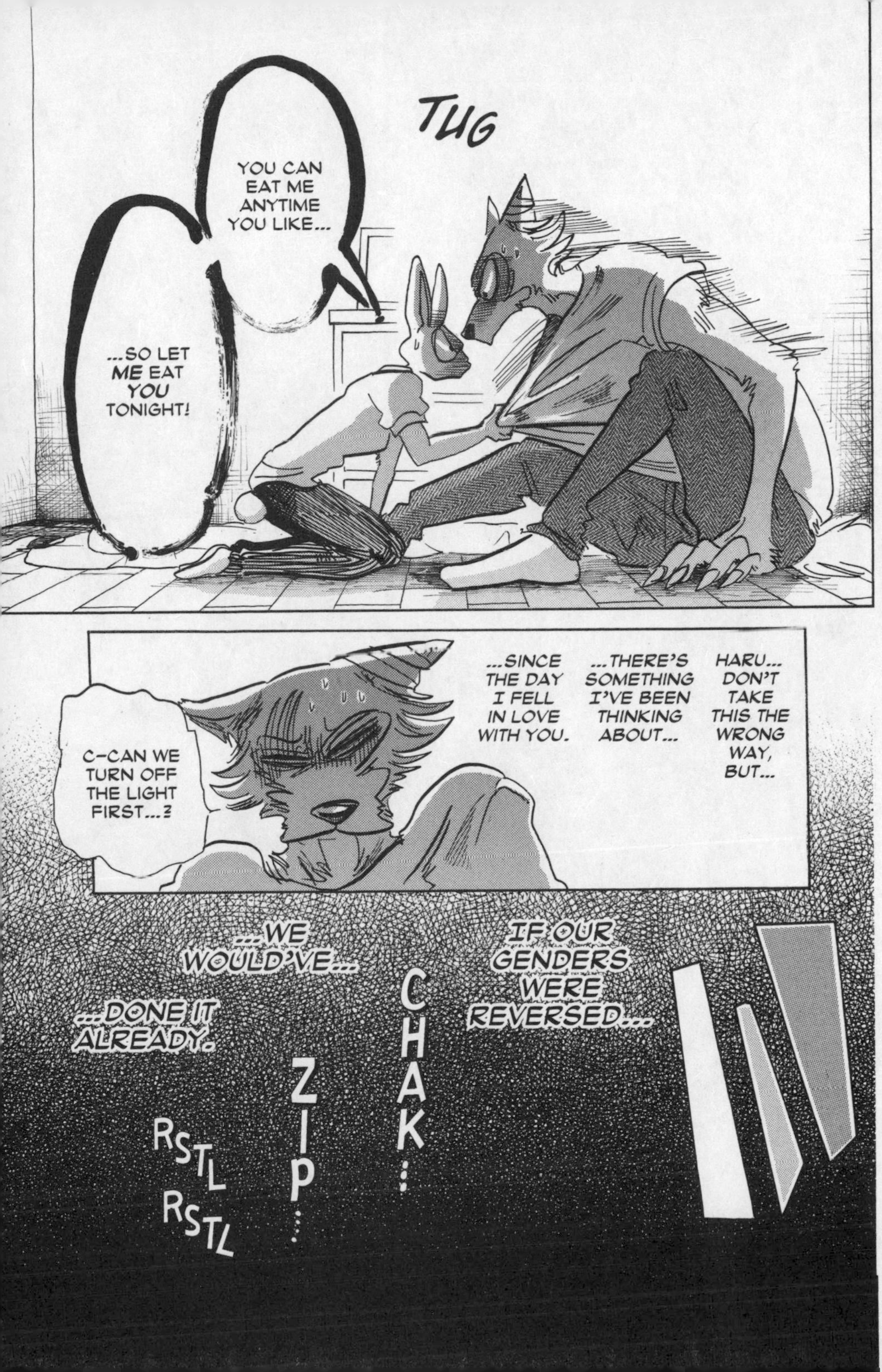
TUG
YOU CAN EAT ME ANYTIME YOU LIKE...
...SO LET ME EAT YOU TONIGHT!
HARU... DON'T TAKE THIS THE WRONG WAY, BUT...
...THERE'S SOMETHING I'VE BEEN THINKING ABOUT...
...SINCE THE DAY I FELL IN LOVE WITH YOU.
C-CAN WE TURN OFF THE LIGHT FIRST...?
IF OUR GENDERS WERE REVERSED...
CHAK...
...WE WOULD'VE...
...DONE IT ALREADY.
ZIP...
RSTL
RSTL

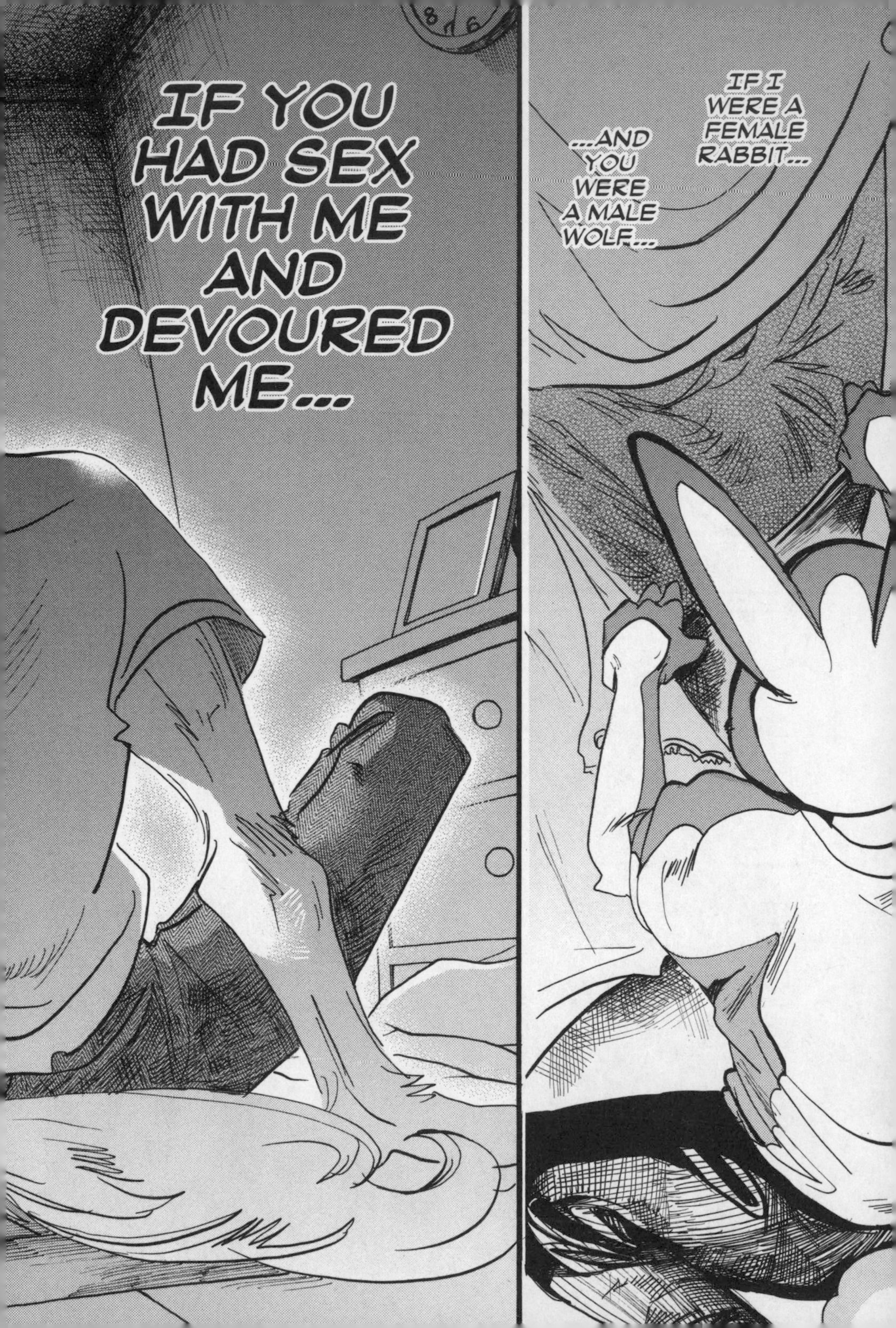
IF I WERE A FEMALE RABBIT...
...AND YOU WERE A MALE WOLF...
IF YOU HAD SEX WITH ME AND DEVOURED ME...

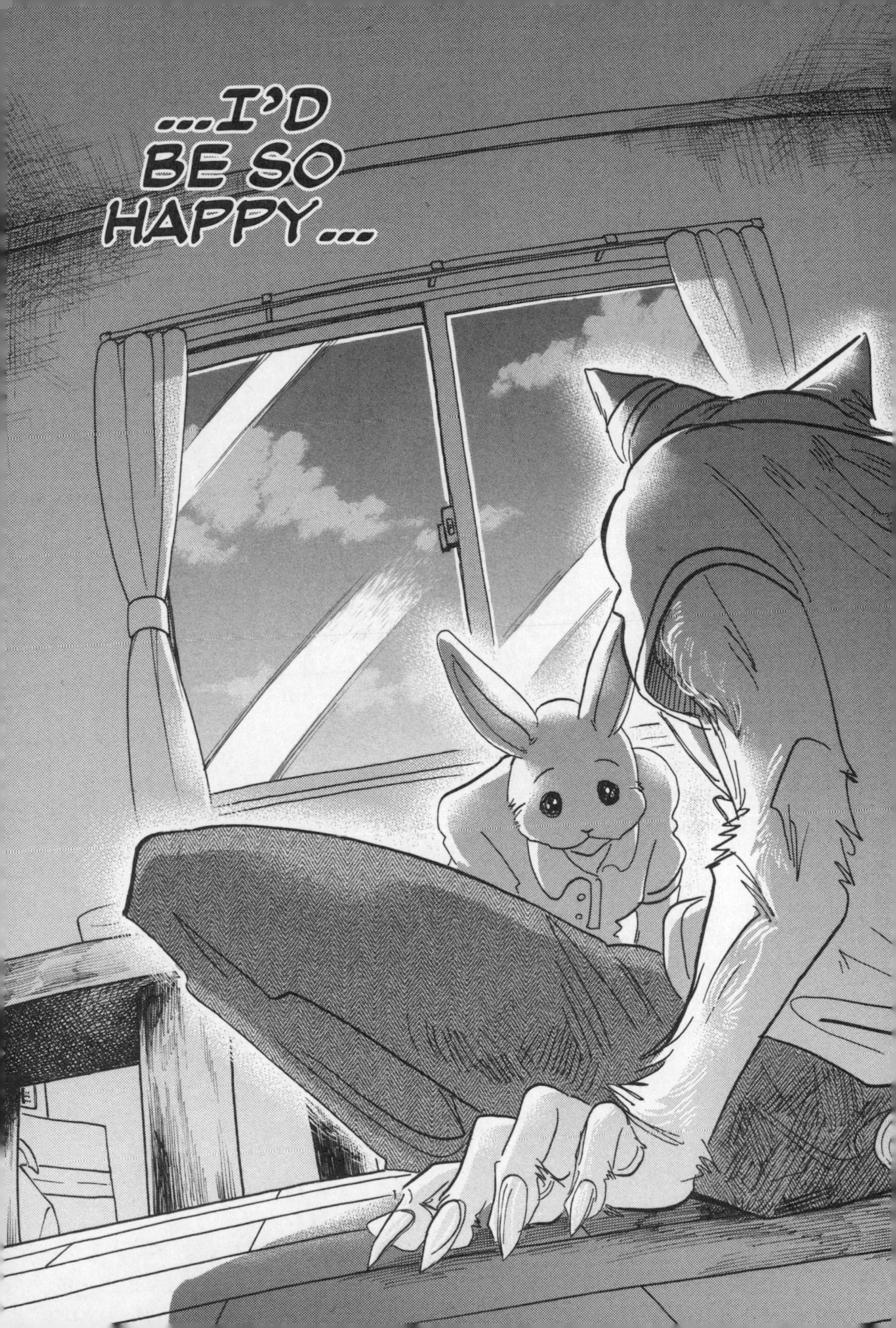
...I'D BE SO HAPPY...

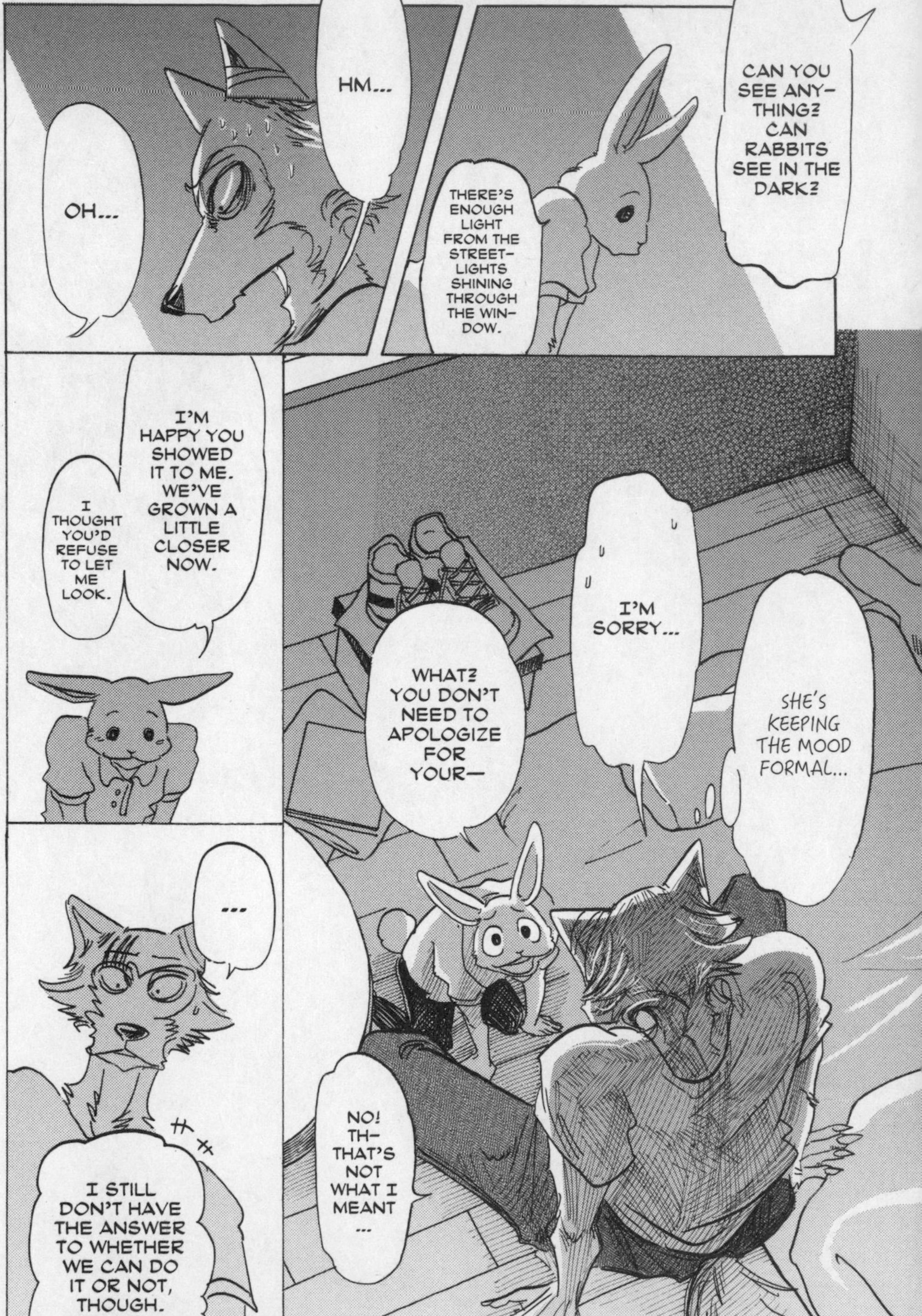
CAN YOU SEE ANY-THING? CAN RABBITS SEE IN THE DARK?
THERE'S ENOUGH LIGHT FROM THE STREET-LIGHTS SHINING THROUGH THE WIN-DOW.
HM...
OH...
SHE'S KEEPING THE MOOD FORMAL...
I'M SORRY...
WHAT? YOU DON'T NEED TO APOLOGIZE FOR YOUR—
NO! TH-THAT'S NOT WHAT I MEANT ...
I'M HAPPY YOU SHOWED IT TO ME. WE'VE GROWN A LITTLE CLOSER NOW.
I THOUGHT YOU'D REFUSE TO LET ME LOOK.
...
I STILL DON'T HAVE THE ANSWER TO WHETHER WE CAN DO IT OR NOT, THOUGH. HEH HEH...

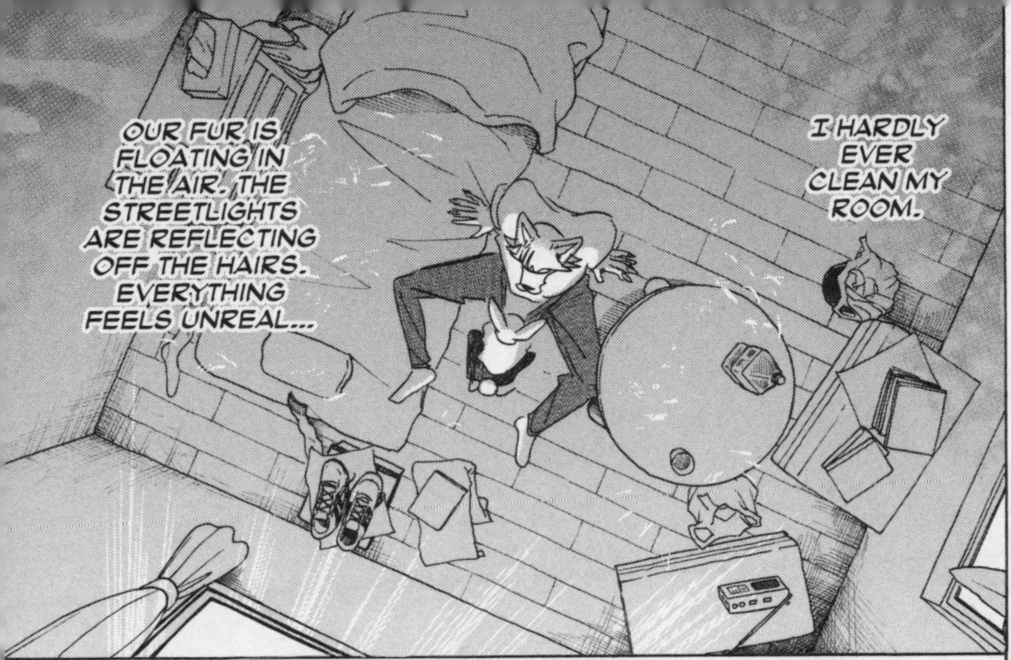
I HARDLY EVER CLEAN MY ROOM.
OUR FUR IS FLOATING IN THE AIR. THE STREETLIGHTS ARE REFLECTING OFF THE HAIRS. EVERYTHING FEELS UNREAL...

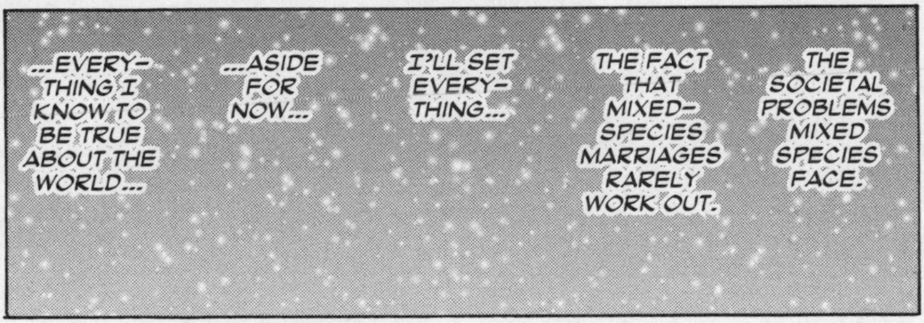
THE SOCIETAL PROBLEMS MIXED SPECIES FACE.
THE FACT THAT MIXED-SPECIES MARRIAGES RARELY WORK OUT.
I'LL SET EVERY-THING...
...ASIDE FOR NOW...
...EVERY-THING I KNOW TO BE TRUE ABOUT THE WORLD...

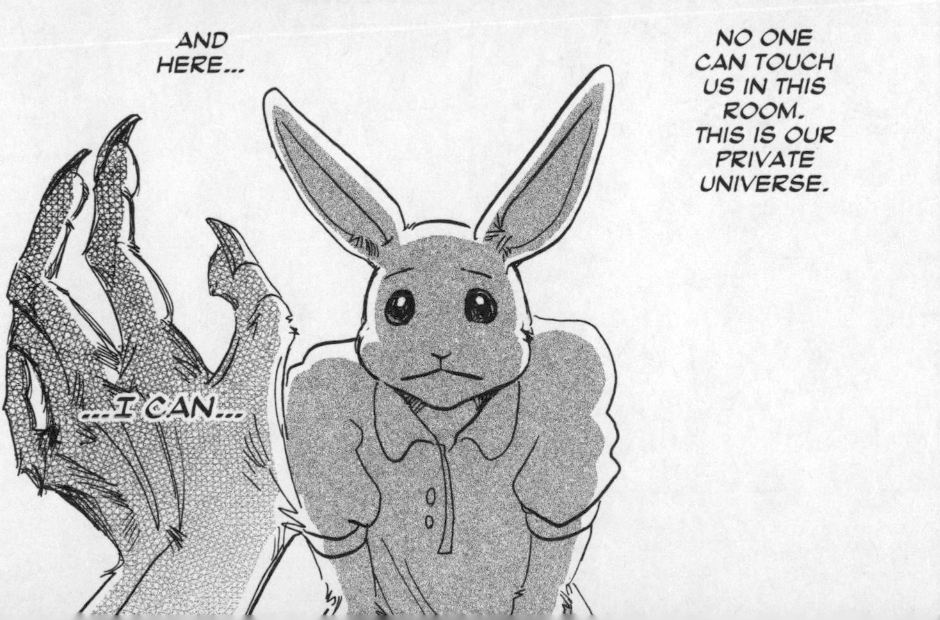
NO ONE CAN TOUCH US IN THIS ROOM. THIS IS OUR PRIVATE UNIVERSE.
AND HERE...
...I CAN...

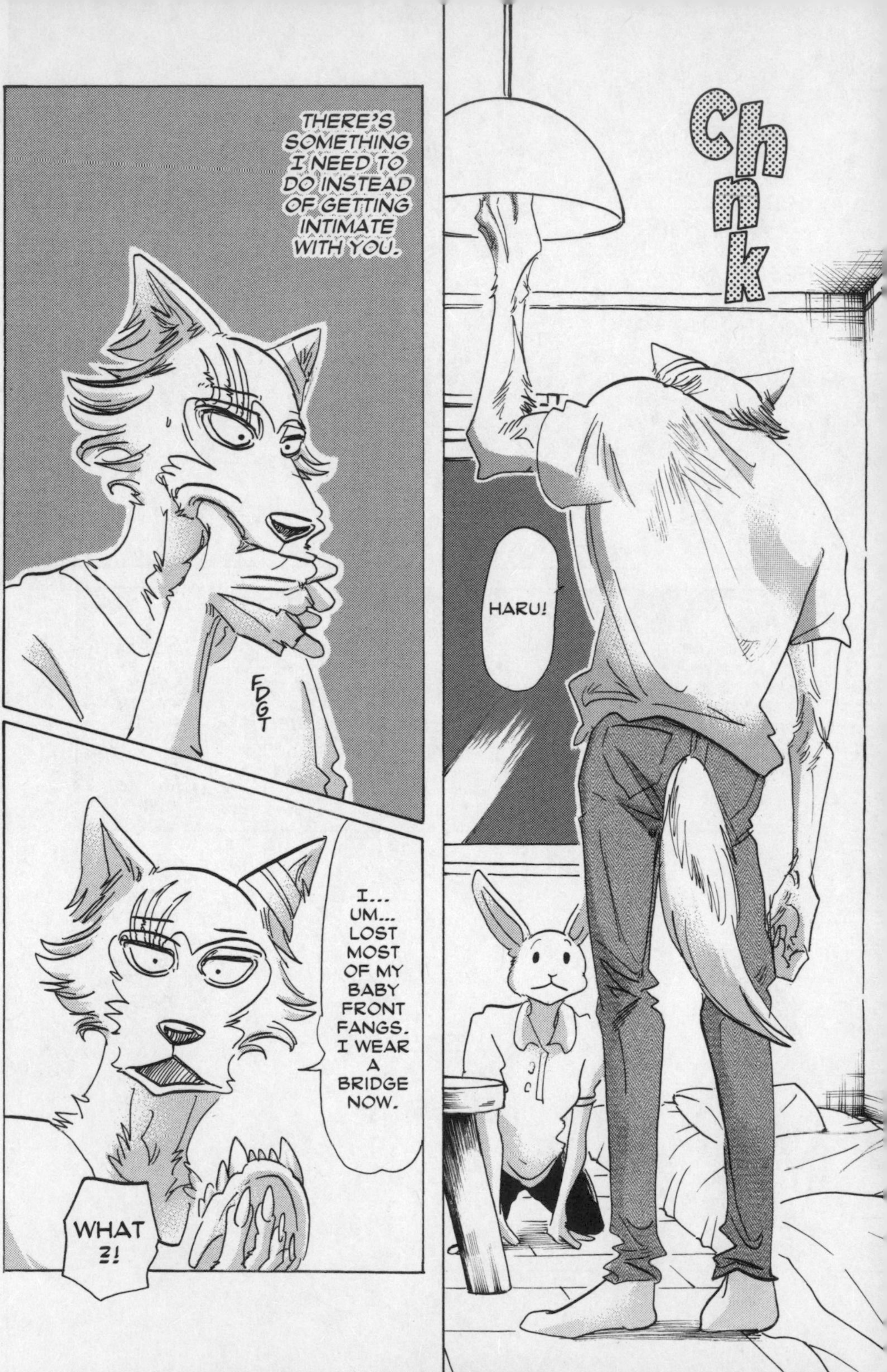
Chnk
HARU!
THERE'S SOMETHING I NEED TO DO INSTEAD OF GETTING INTIMATE WITH YOU.
FDGT
I... UM... LOST MOST OF MY BABY FRONT FANGS. I WEAR A BRIDGE NOW.
WHAT ?!

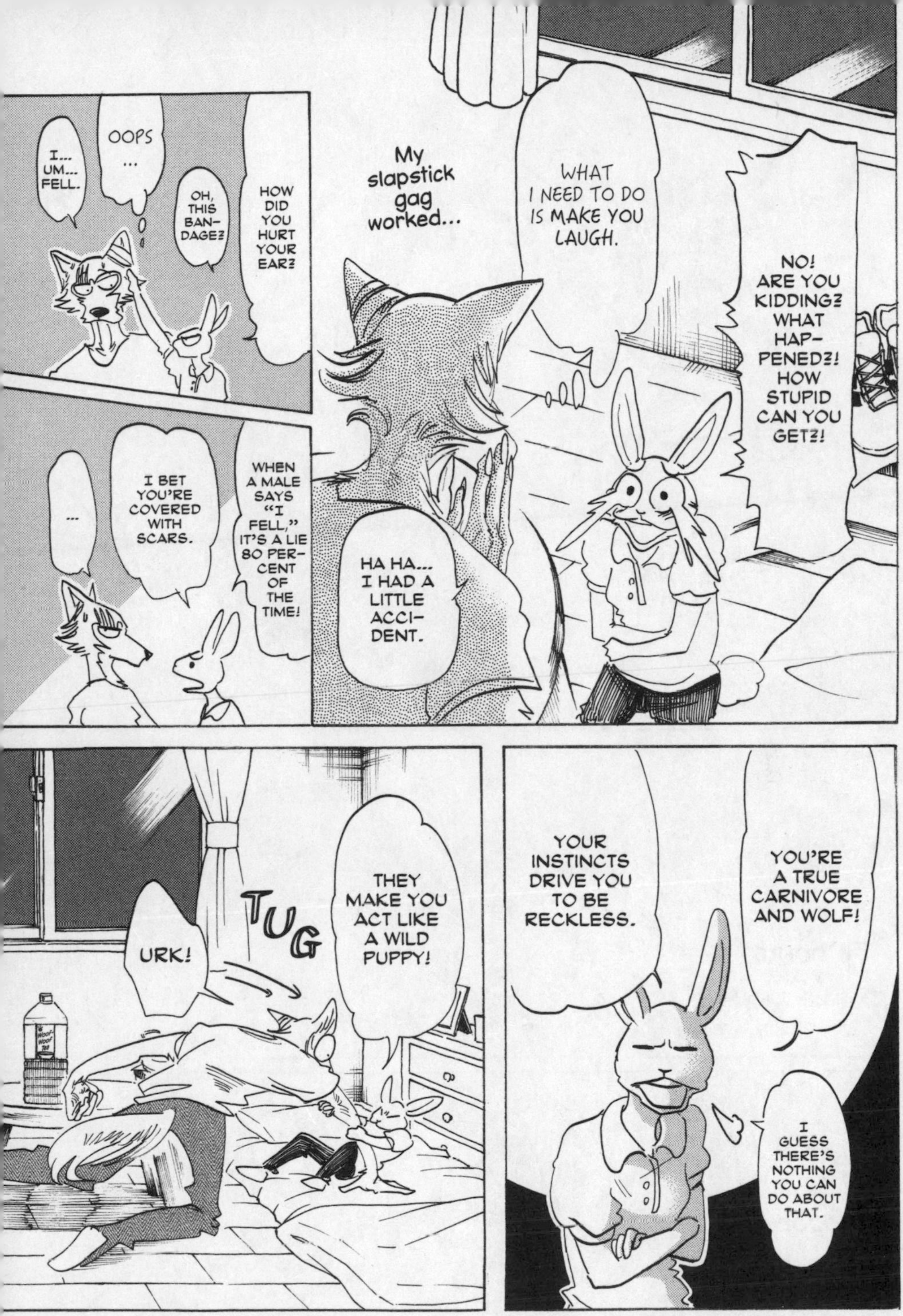
NO! ARE YOU KIDDING? WHAT HAP-PENED?! HOW STUPID CAN YOU GET?!
WHAT I NEED TO DO IS MAKE YOU LAUGH.
My slapstick gag worked...
HA HA... I HAD A LITTLE ACCI-DENT.
HOW DID YOU HURT YOUR EAR?
OH, THIS BAN-DAGE?
OOPS ...
I... UM... FELL.
WHEN A MALE SAYS "I FELL," IT'S A LIE 80 PER-CENT OF THE TIME!
I BET YOU'RE COVERED WITH SCARS.
...
YOU'RE A TRUE CARNIVORE AND WOLF!
YOUR INSTINCTS DRIVE YOU TO BE RECKLESS.
I GUESS THERE'S NOTHING YOU CAN DO ABOUT THAT.
THEY MAKE YOU ACT LIKE A WILD PUPPY!
TUG
URK!

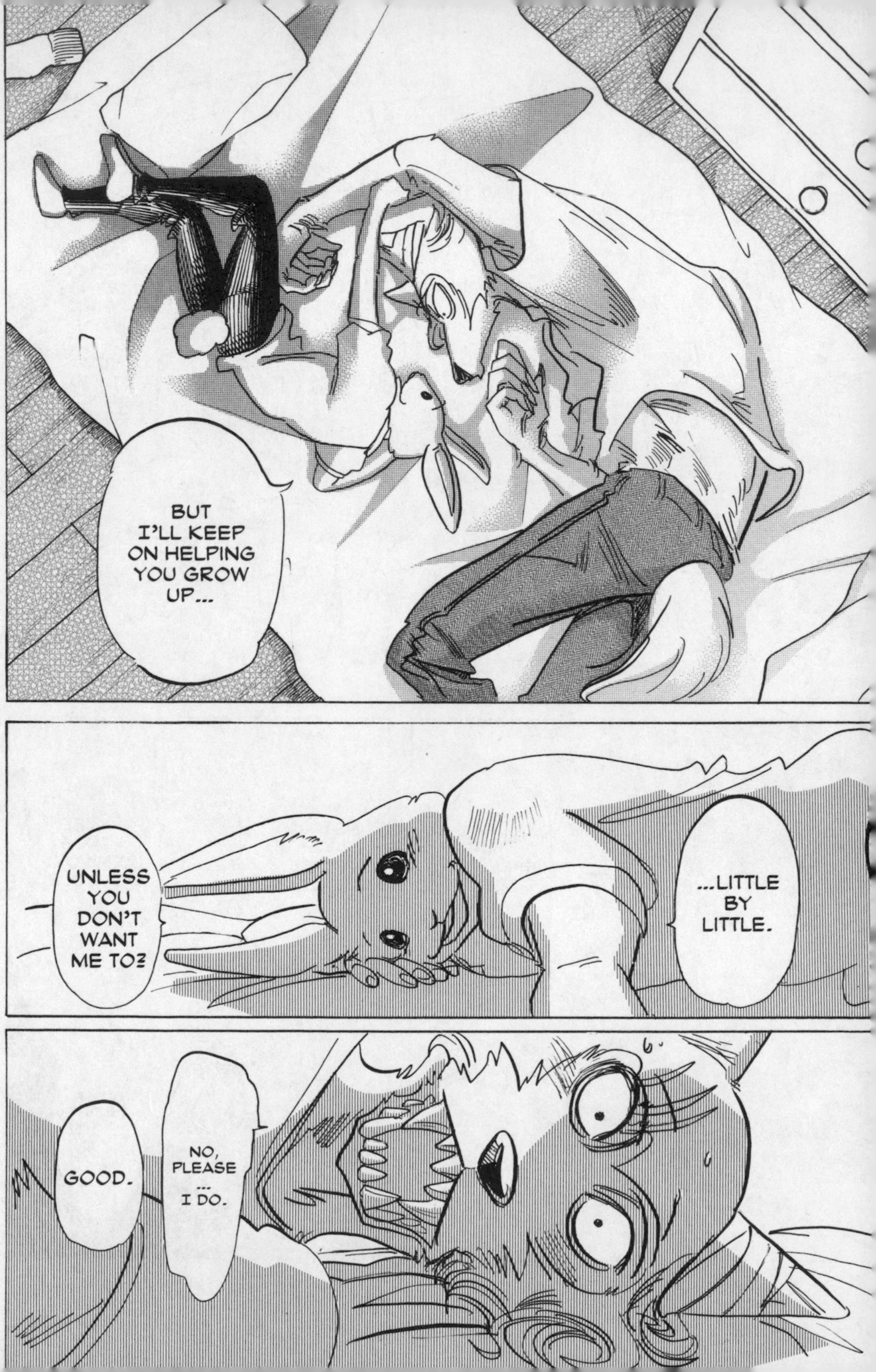
BUT I'LL KEEP ON HELPING YOU GROW UP...
...LITTLE BY LITTLE.
UNLESS YOU DON'T WANT ME TO?
NO, PLEASE ... I DO.
GOOD.

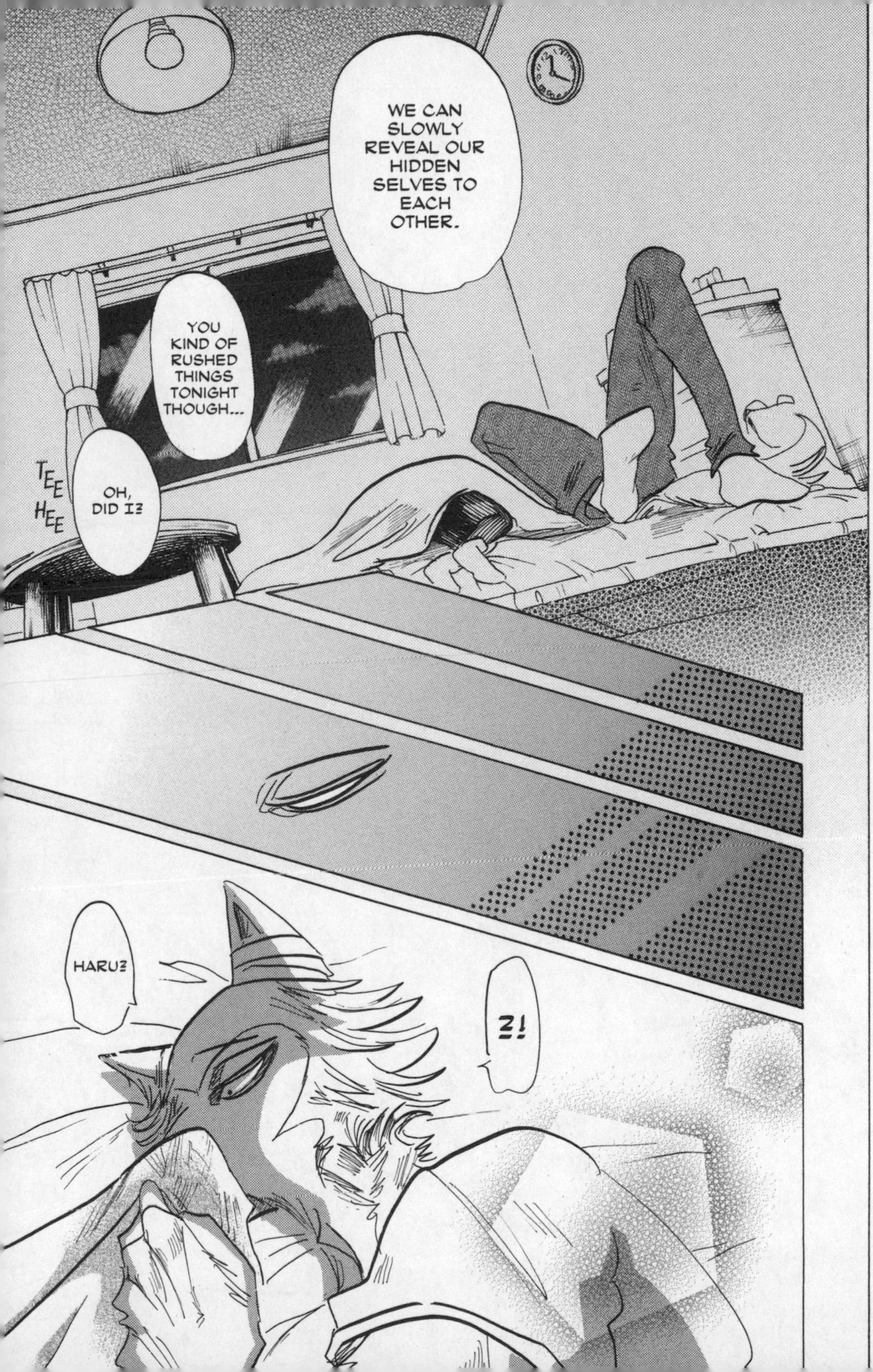
WE CAN SLOWLY REVEAL OUR HIDDEN SELVES TO EACH OTHER.
YOU KIND OF RUSHED THINGS TONIGHT THOUGH...
OH, DID I?
TEE HEE
!?
HARU?

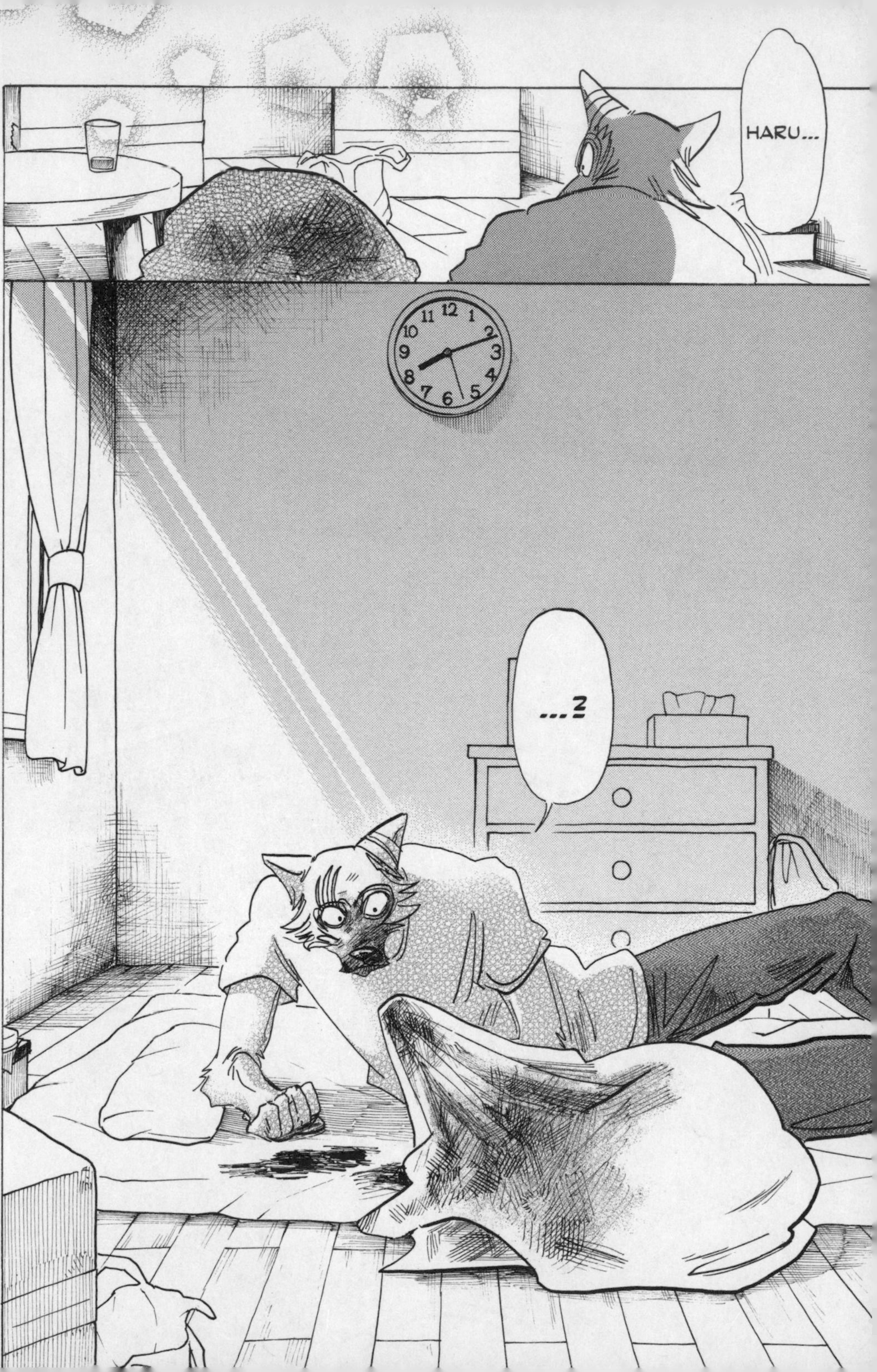
HARU...
...?

Chapter 149: The Second Coming of the White Fox

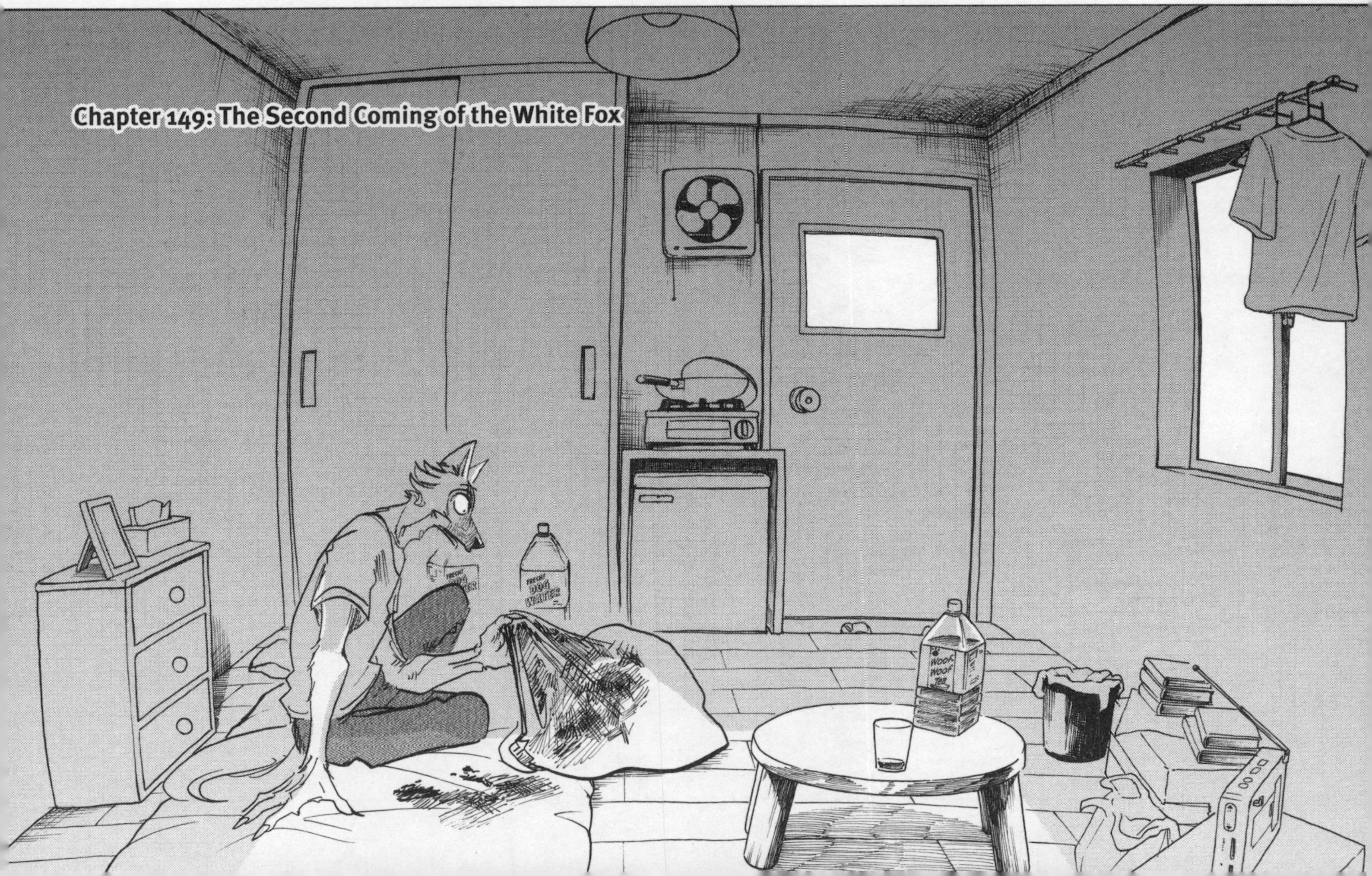
FRESH DOG WATER

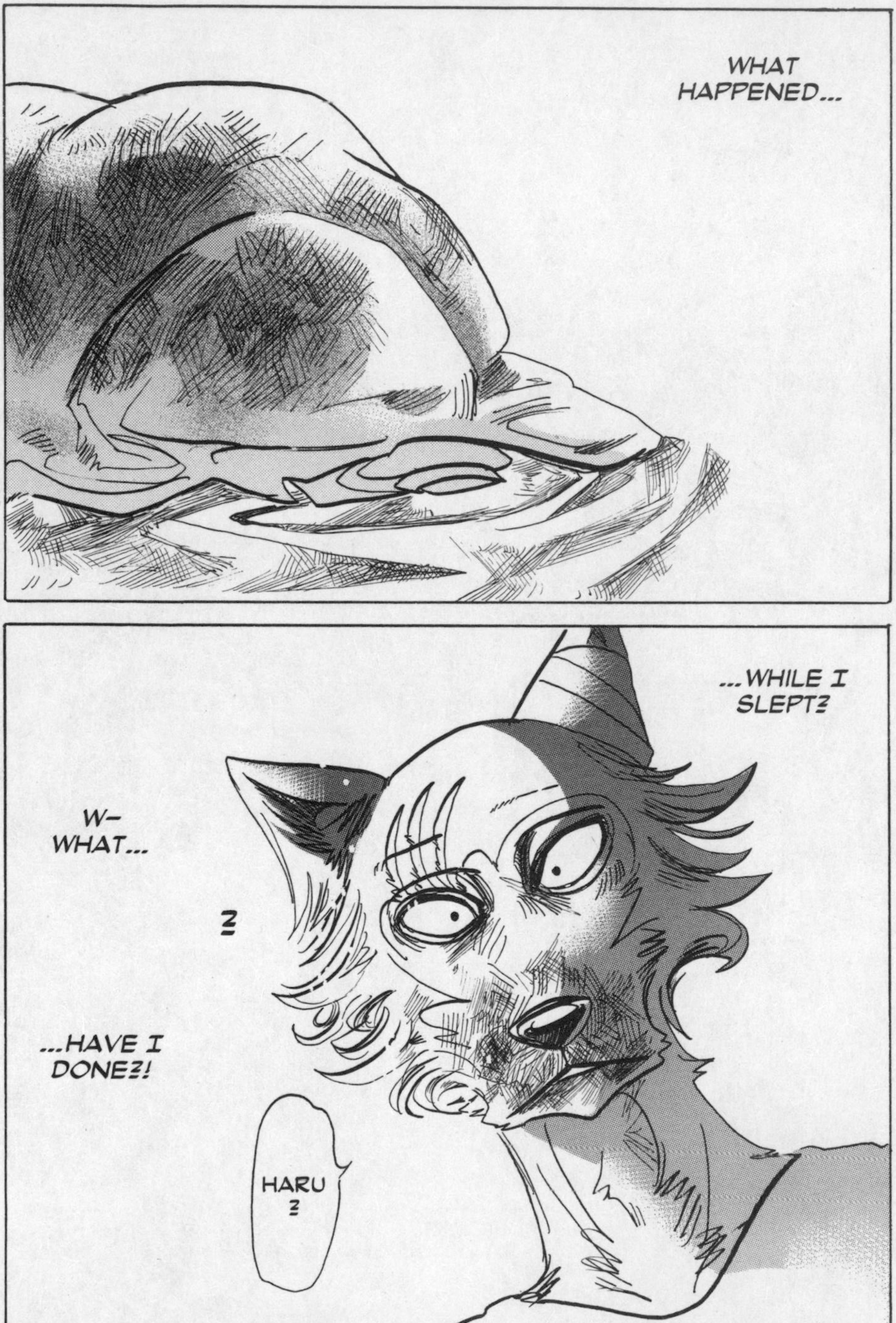
WHAT HAPPENED...
...WHILE I SLEPT?
W-WHAT...
?
...HAVE I DONE?!
HARU?

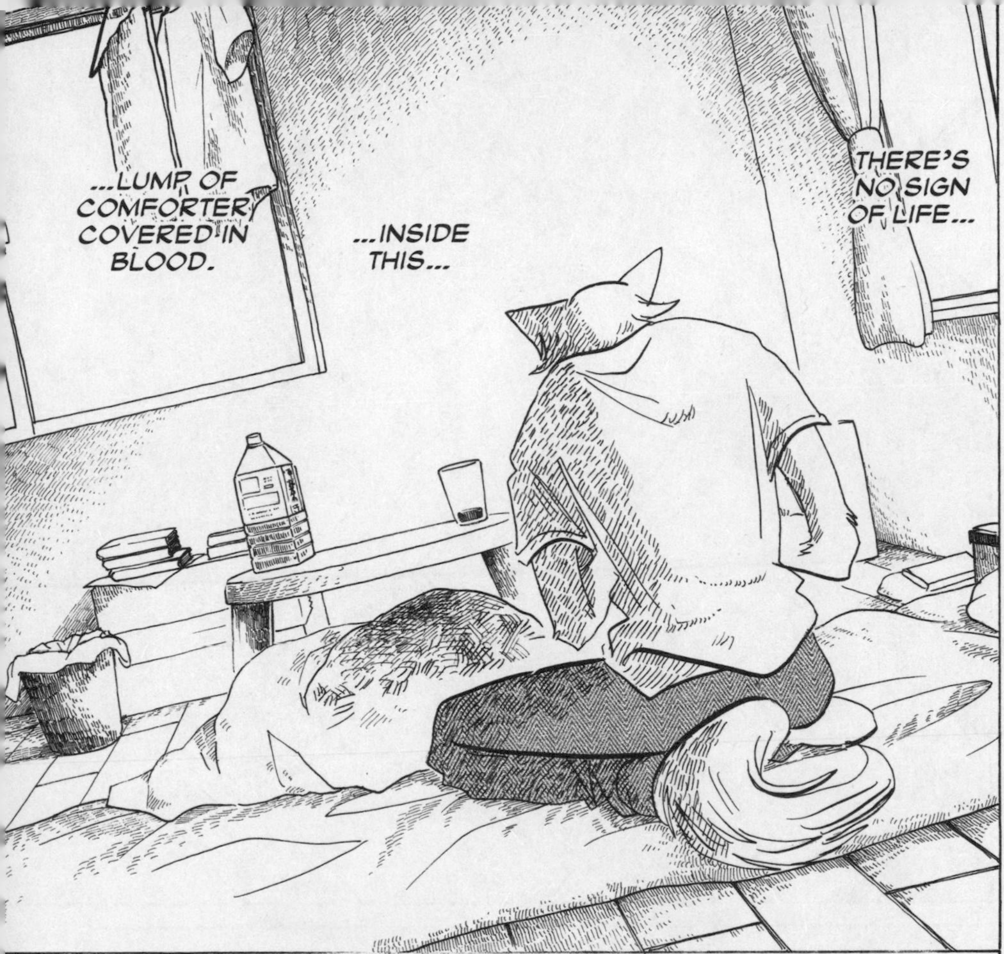
THERE'S NO SIGN OF LIFE...
...INSIDE THIS...
...LUMP OF COMFORTER COVERED IN BLOOD.
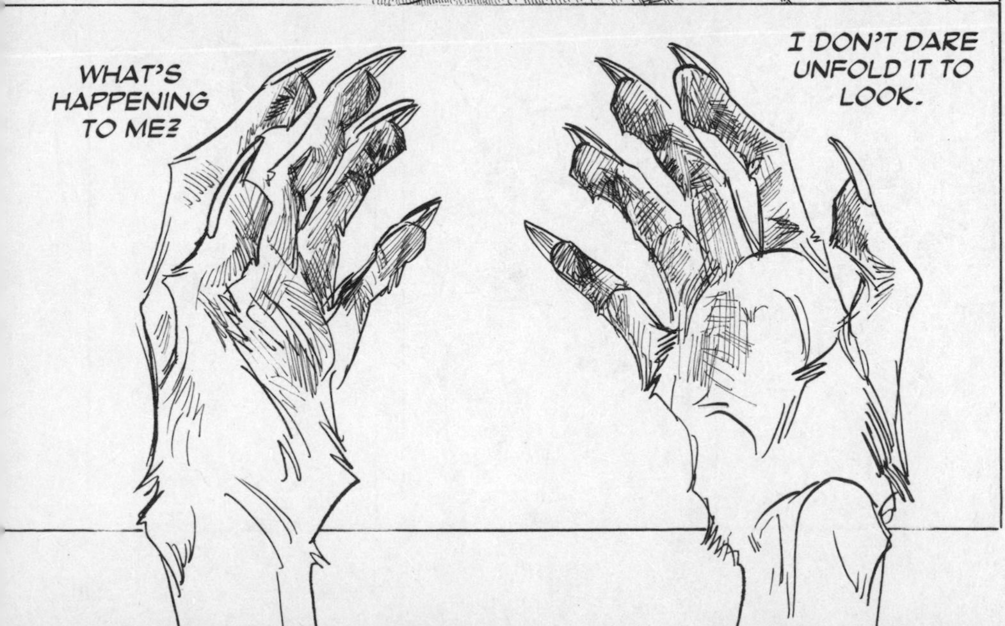
I DON'T DARE UNFOLD IT TO LOOK.
WHAT'S HAPPENING TO ME?

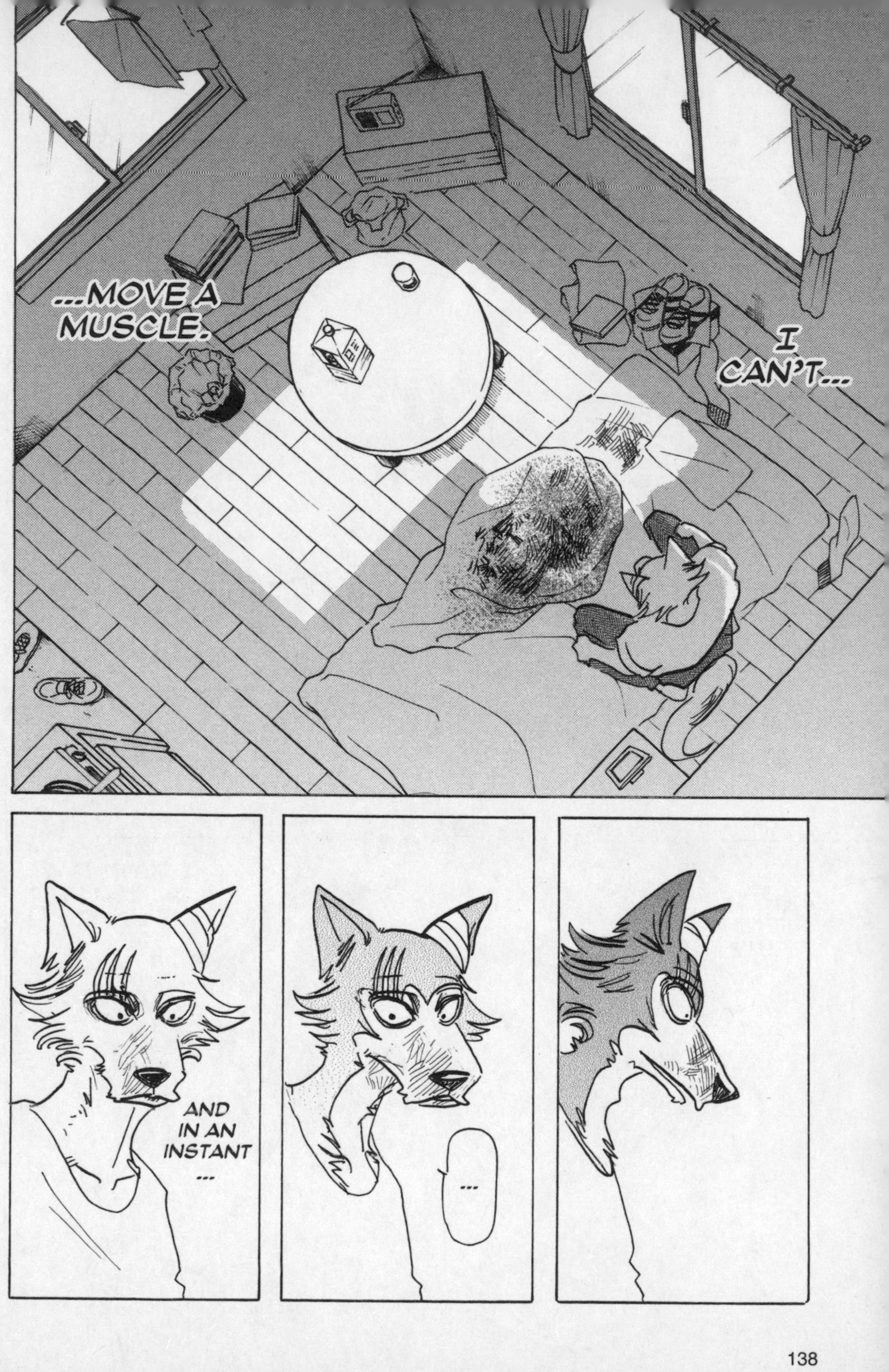
I CAN'T...
...MOVE A MUSCLE.
...
AND IN AN INSTANT ...

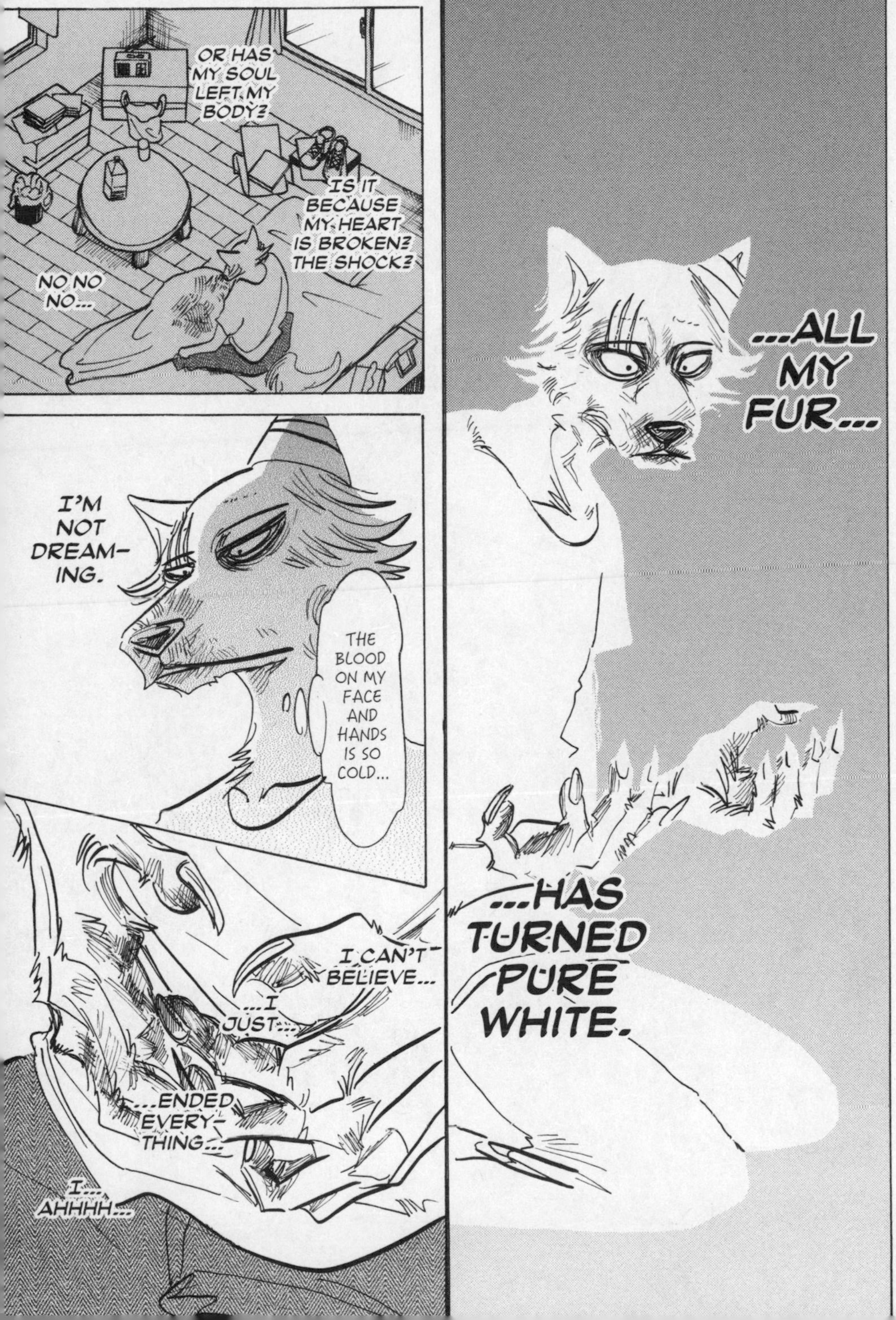
...ALL MY FUR...
...HAS TURNED PURE WHITE.
OR HAS MY SOUL LEFT MY BODY?
IS IT BECAUSE MY HEART IS BROKEN? THE SHOCK?
NO NO NO...
THE BLOOD ON MY FACE AND HANDS IS SO COLD...
I'M NOT DREAMING.
I CAN'T BELIEVE...
...I JUST...
...ENDED EVERYTHING...
I... AHHHH...

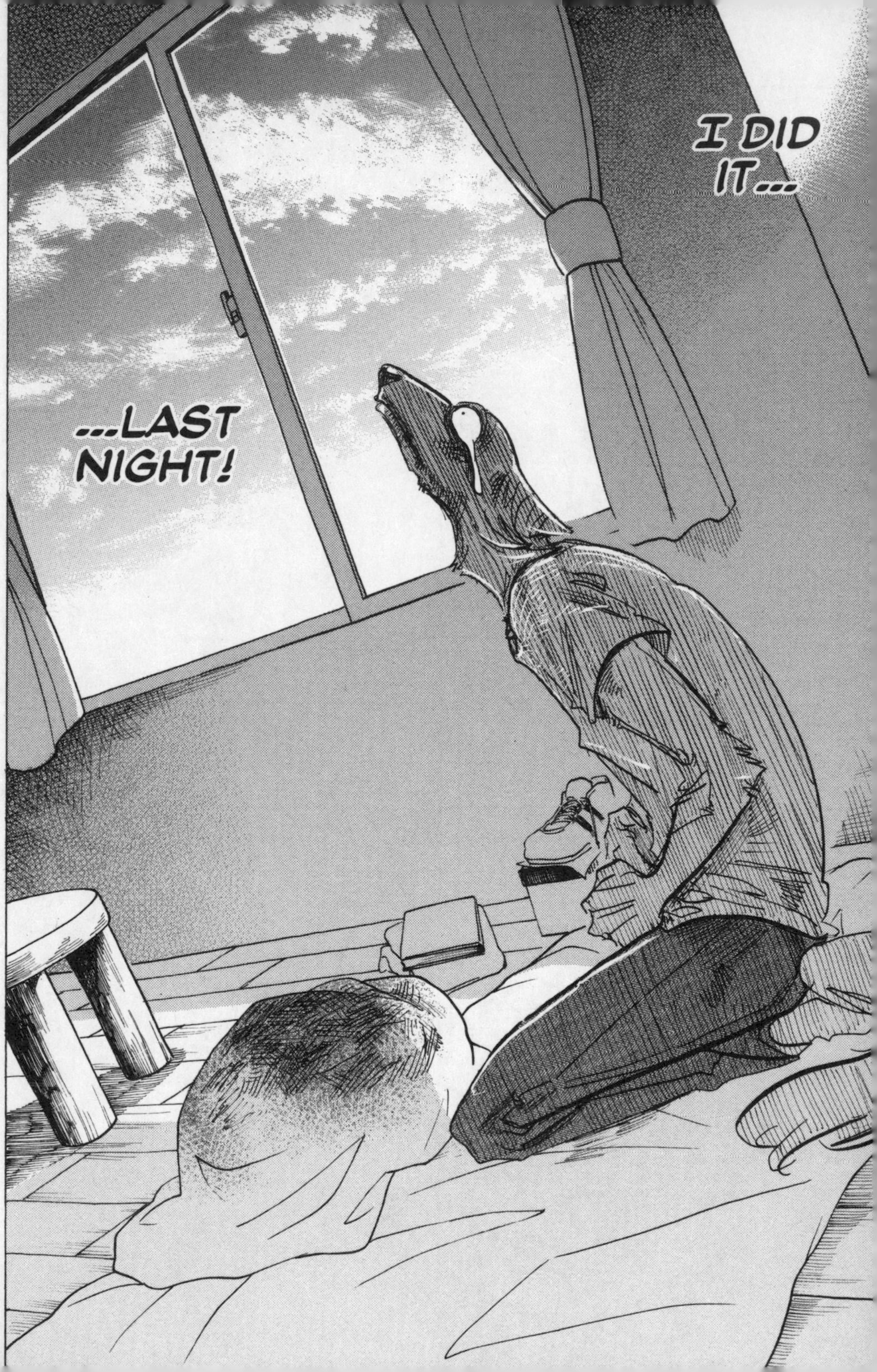
I DID IT...
...LAST NIGHT!

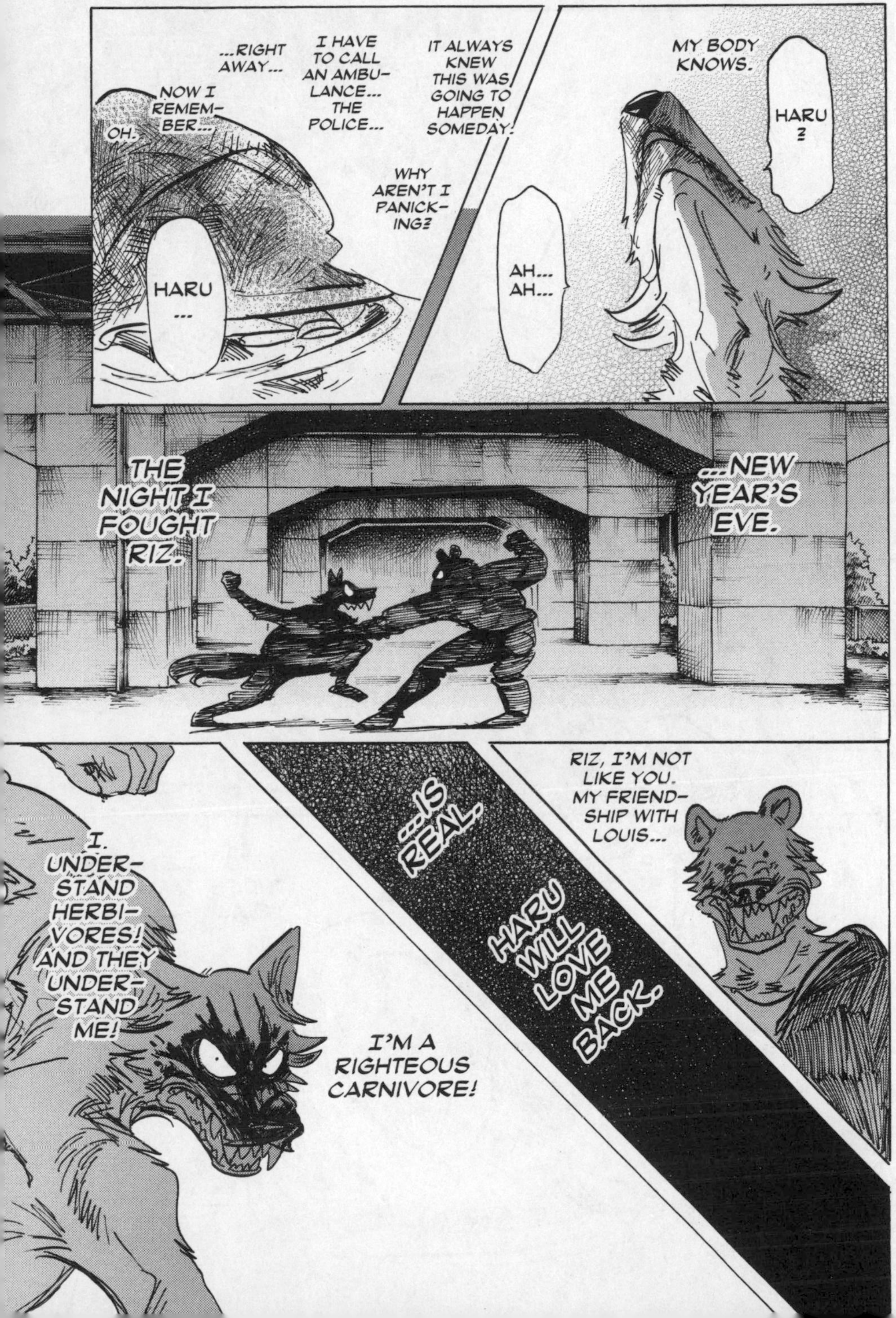
MY BODY KNOWS.
HARU?
AH... AH...
IT ALWAYS KNEW THIS WAS GOING TO HAPPEN SOMEDAY!
WHY AREN'T I PANICKING?
I HAVE TO CALL AN AMBULANCE... THE POLICE...
...RIGHT AWAY...
NOW I REMEMBER...
OH.
HARU...
THE NIGHT I FOUGHT RIZ.
...NEW YEAR'S EVE.
RIZ, I'M NOT LIKE YOU. MY FRIENDSHIP WITH LOUIS...
...IS REAL.
HARU WILL LOVE ME BACK.
I. UNDERSTAND HERBIVORES! AND THEY UNDERSTAND ME!
I'M A RIGHTEOUS CARNIVORE!

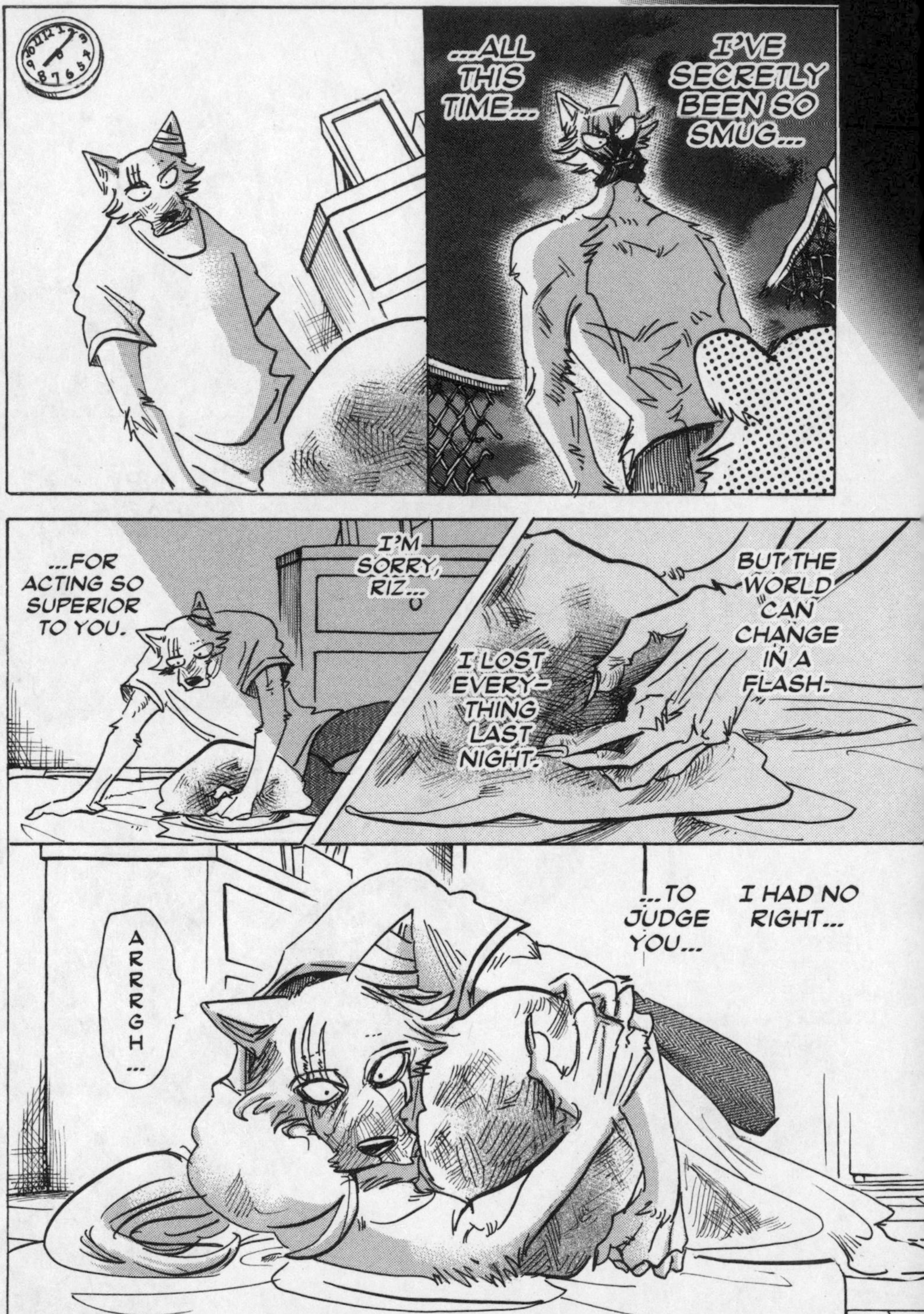
I'VE SECRETLY BEEN SO SMUG...
...ALL THIS TIME...
BUT THE WORLD CAN CHANGE IN A FLASH.
I LOST EVERY-THING LAST NIGHT.
I'M SORRY, RIZ...
...FOR ACTING SO SUPERIOR TO YOU.
I HAD NO RIGHT...
...TO JUDGE YOU...
ARRRGH...

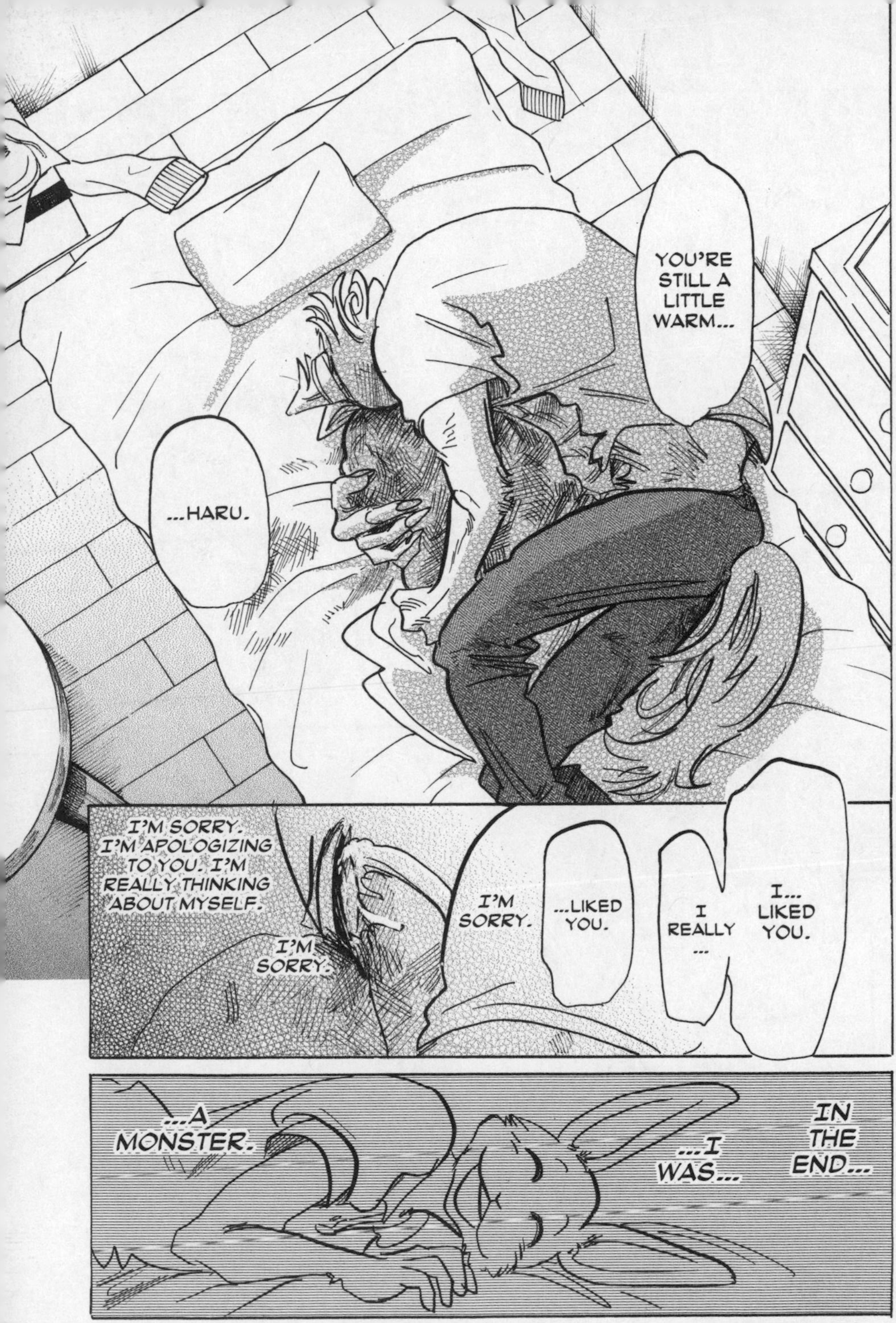
YOU'RE STILL A LITTLE WARM...
...HARU.
I... LIKED YOU.
I REALLY ...
...LIKED YOU.
I'M SORRY.
I'M SORRY. I'M APOLOGIZING TO YOU. I'M REALLY THINKING ABOUT MYSELF.
I'M SORRY.
IN THE END...
...I WAS...
...A MONSTER.

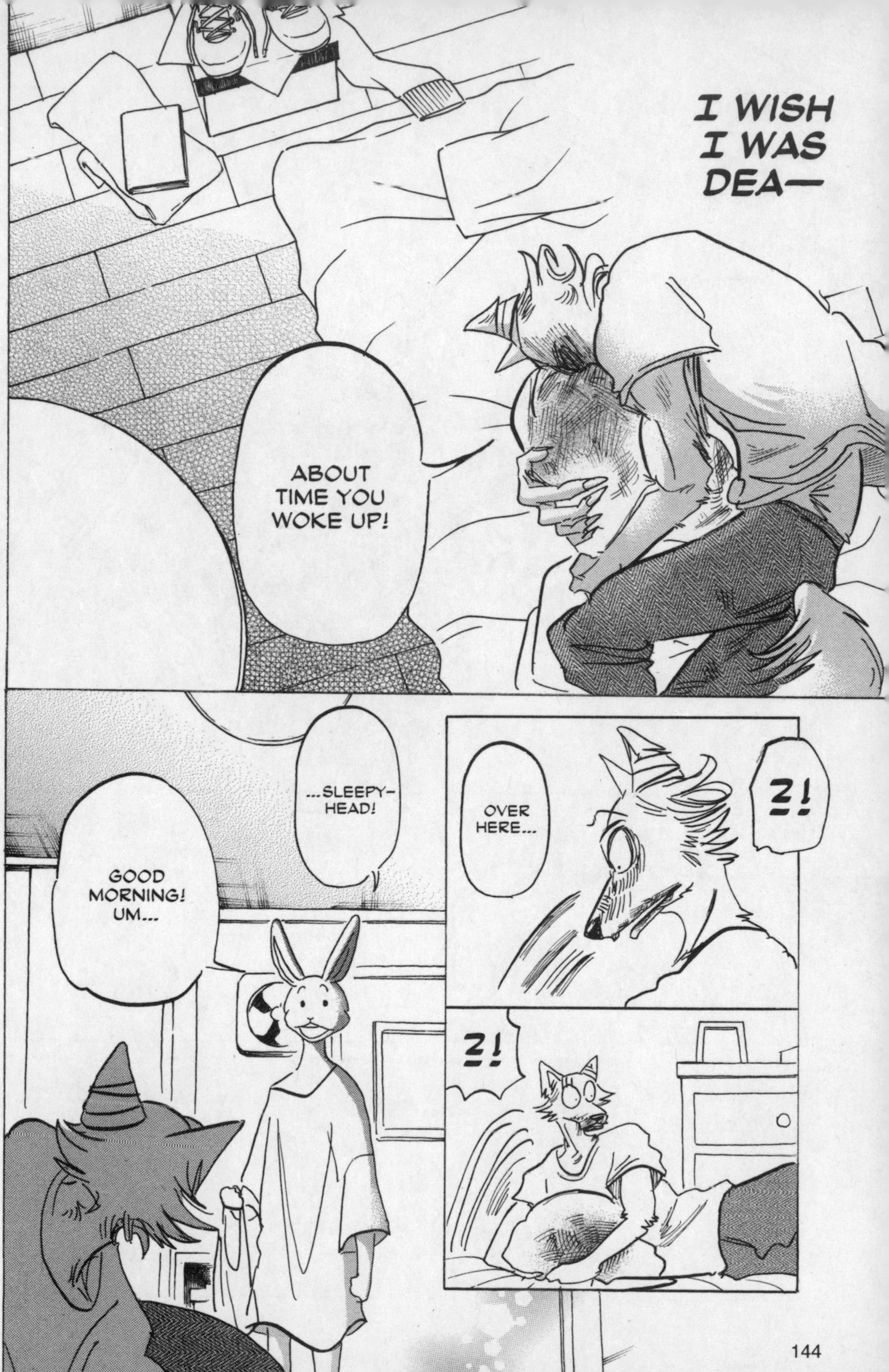
I WISH I WAS DEA—
ABOUT TIME YOU WOKE UP!
?!
OVER HERE...
?!
...SLEEPY-HEAD!
GOOD MORNING! UM...

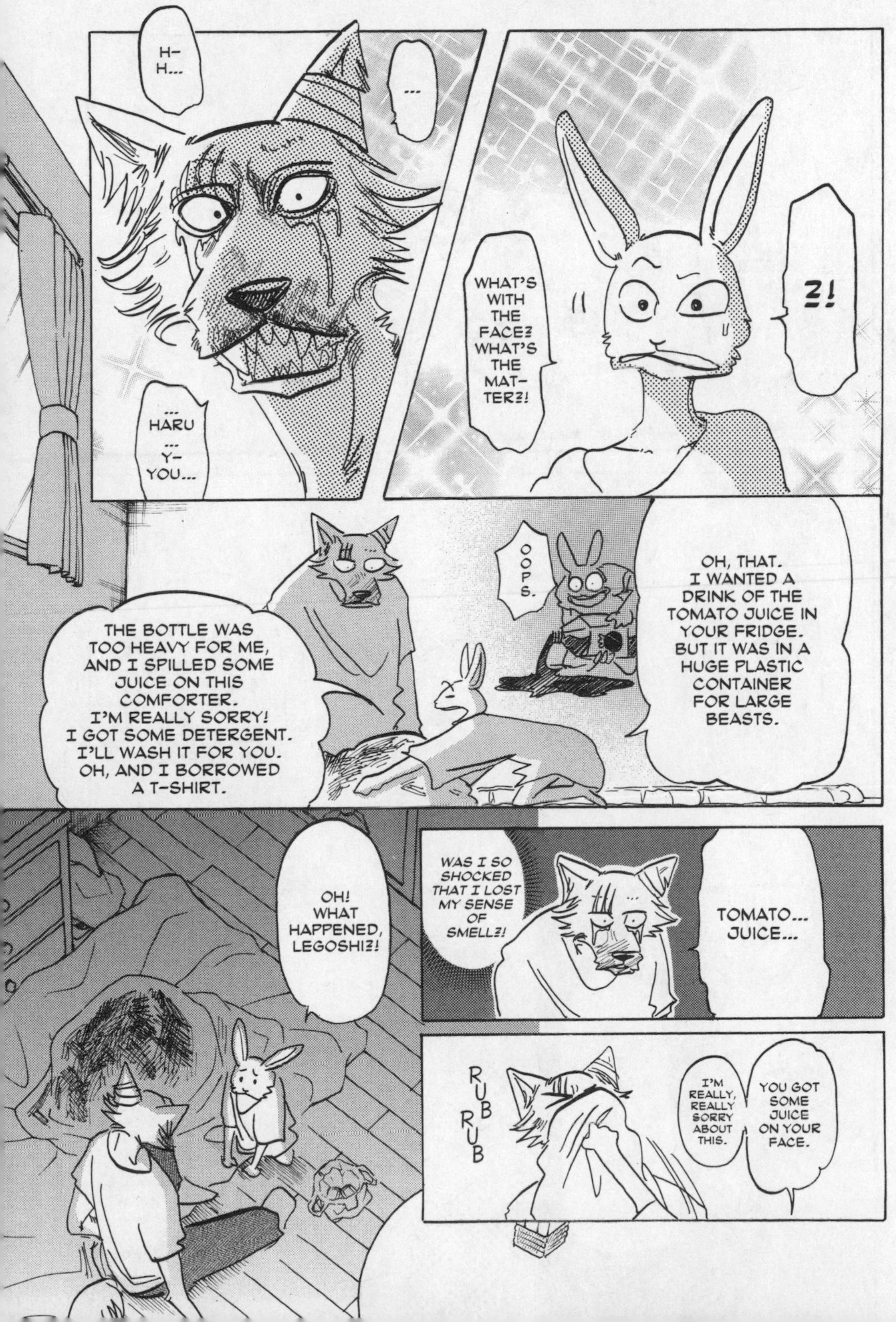
?!
WHAT'S WITH THE FACE? WHAT'S THE MAT-TER?!
...
H- H...
... HARU ... Y- YOU...
OH, THAT. I WANTED A DRINK OF THE TOMATO JUICE IN YOUR FRIDGE. BUT IT WAS IN A HUGE PLASTIC CONTAINER FOR LARGE BEASTS.
OOPS.
THE BOTTLE WAS TOO HEAVY FOR ME, AND I SPILLED SOME JUICE ON THIS COMFORTER. I'M REALLY SORRY! I GOT SOME DETERGENT. I'LL WASH IT FOR YOU. OH, AND I BORROWED A T-SHIRT.
TOMATO... JUICE...
...
WAS I SO SHOCKED THAT I LOST MY SENSE OF SMELL?!
YOU GOT SOME JUICE ON YOUR FACE.
I'M REALLY, REALLY SORRY ABOUT THIS.
RUB RUB
OH! WHAT HAPPENED, LEGOSHI?!

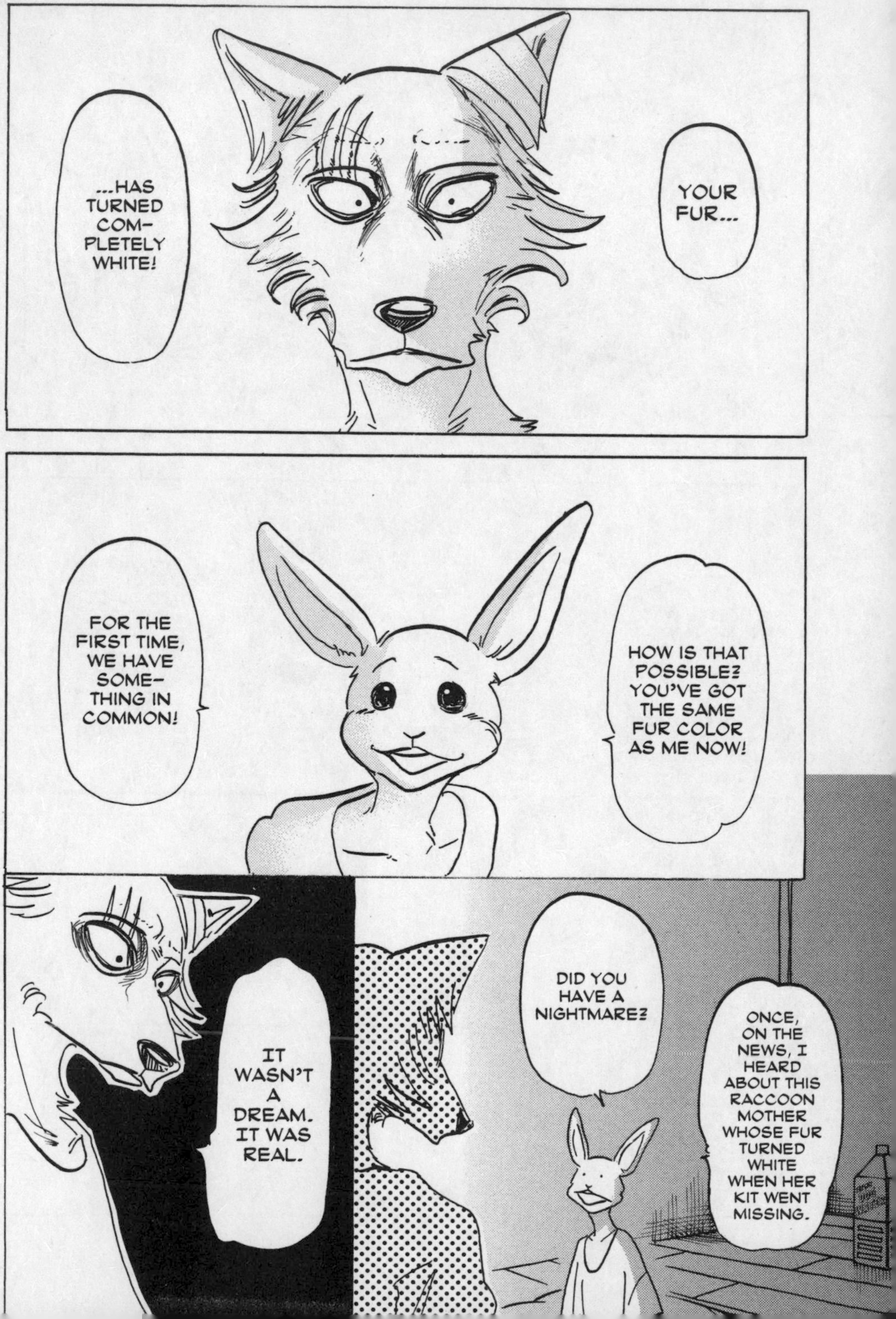
YOUR FUR...
...HAS TURNED COMPLETELY WHITE!
HOW IS THAT POSSIBLE? YOU'VE GOT THE SAME FUR COLOR AS ME NOW!
FOR THE FIRST TIME, WE HAVE SOMETHING IN COMMON!
DID YOU HAVE A NIGHTMARE?
ONCE, ON THE NEWS, I HEARD ABOUT THIS RACCOON MOTHER WHOSE FUR TURNED WHITE WHEN HER KIT WENT MISSING.
IT WASN'T A DREAM. IT WAS REAL.

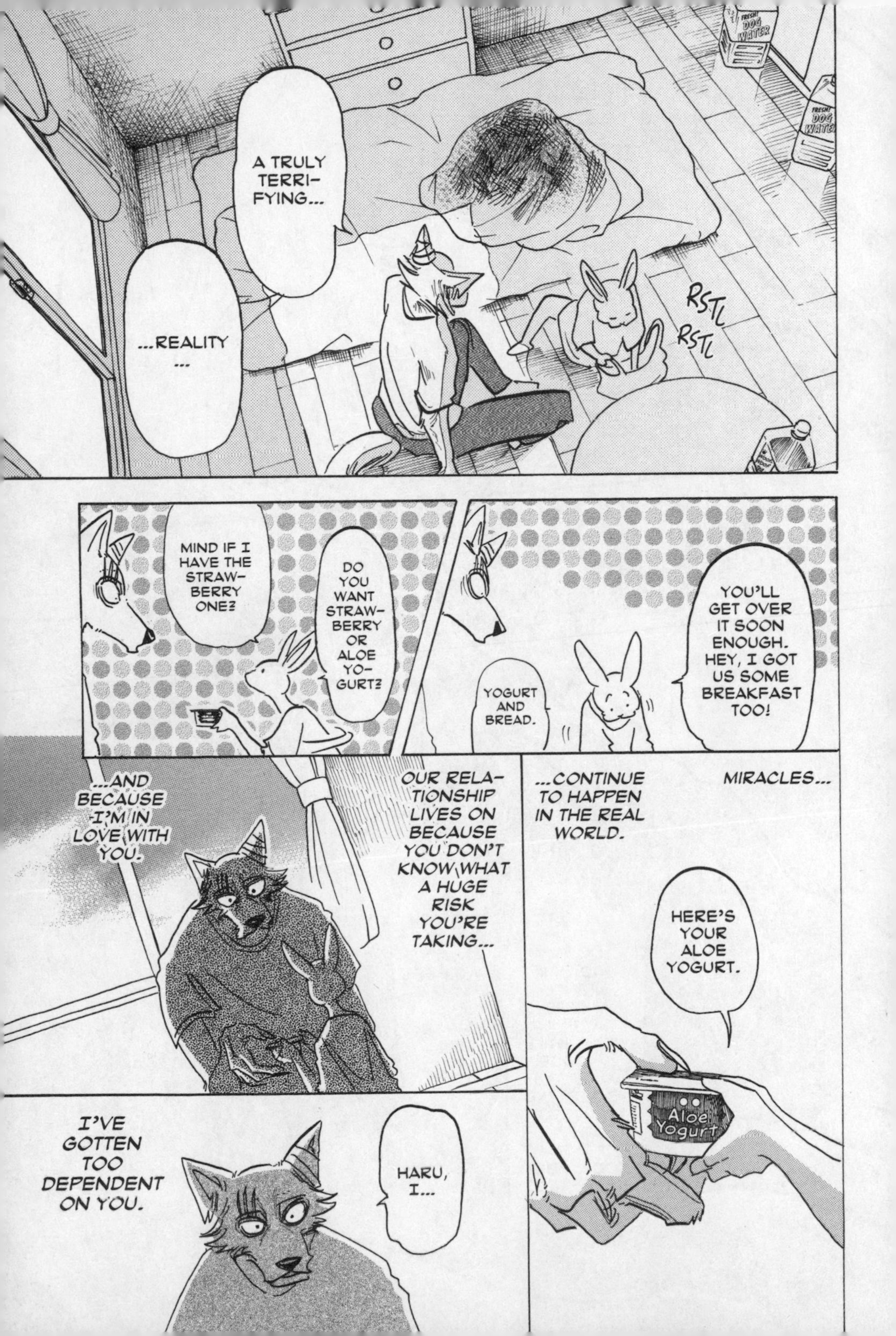
A TRULY TERRIFYING...
...REALITY...
RSTL RSTL
YOU'LL GET OVER IT SOON ENOUGH. HEY, I GOT US SOME BREAKFAST TOO!
YOGURT AND BREAD.
DO YOU WANT STRAWBERRY OR ALOE YOGURT?
MIND IF I HAVE THE STRAWBERRY ONE?
MIRACLES...
...CONTINUE TO HAPPEN IN THE REAL WORLD.
HERE'S YOUR ALOE YOGURT.
Aloe Yogurt
OUR RELATIONSHIP LIVES ON BECAUSE YOU DON'T KNOW WHAT A HUGE RISK YOU'RE TAKING...
...AND BECAUSE I'M IN LOVE WITH YOU.
HARU, I...
I'VE GOTTEN TOO DEPENDENT ON YOU.

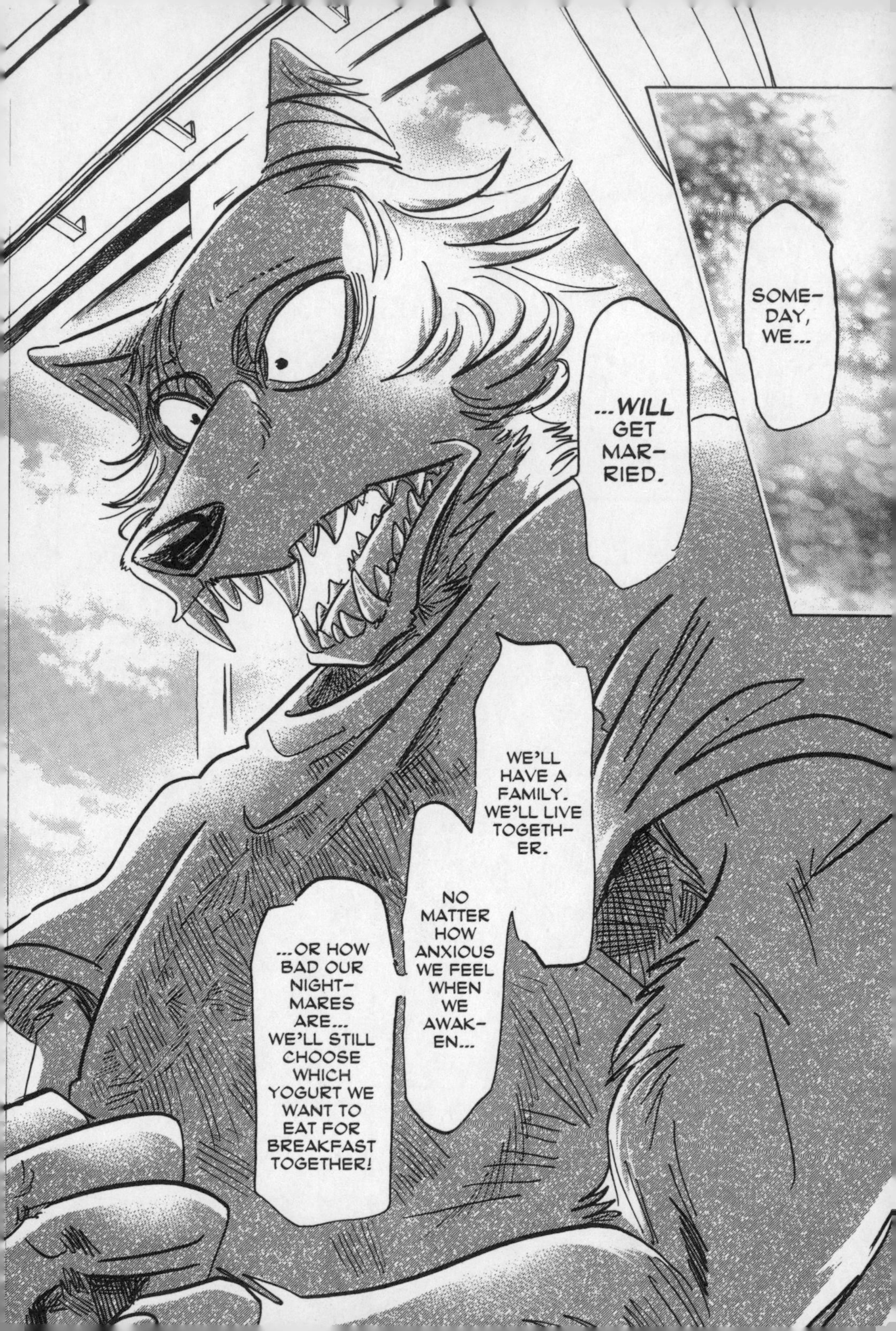
SOME-DAY, WE...
...WILL GET MAR-RIED.
WE'LL HAVE A FAMILY. WE'LL LIVE TOGETH-ER.
NO MATTER HOW ANXIOUS WE FEEL WHEN WE AWAK-EN...
...OR HOW BAD OUR NIGHT-MARES ARE... WE'LL STILL CHOOSE WHICH YOGURT WE WANT TO EAT FOR BREAKFAST TOGETHER!

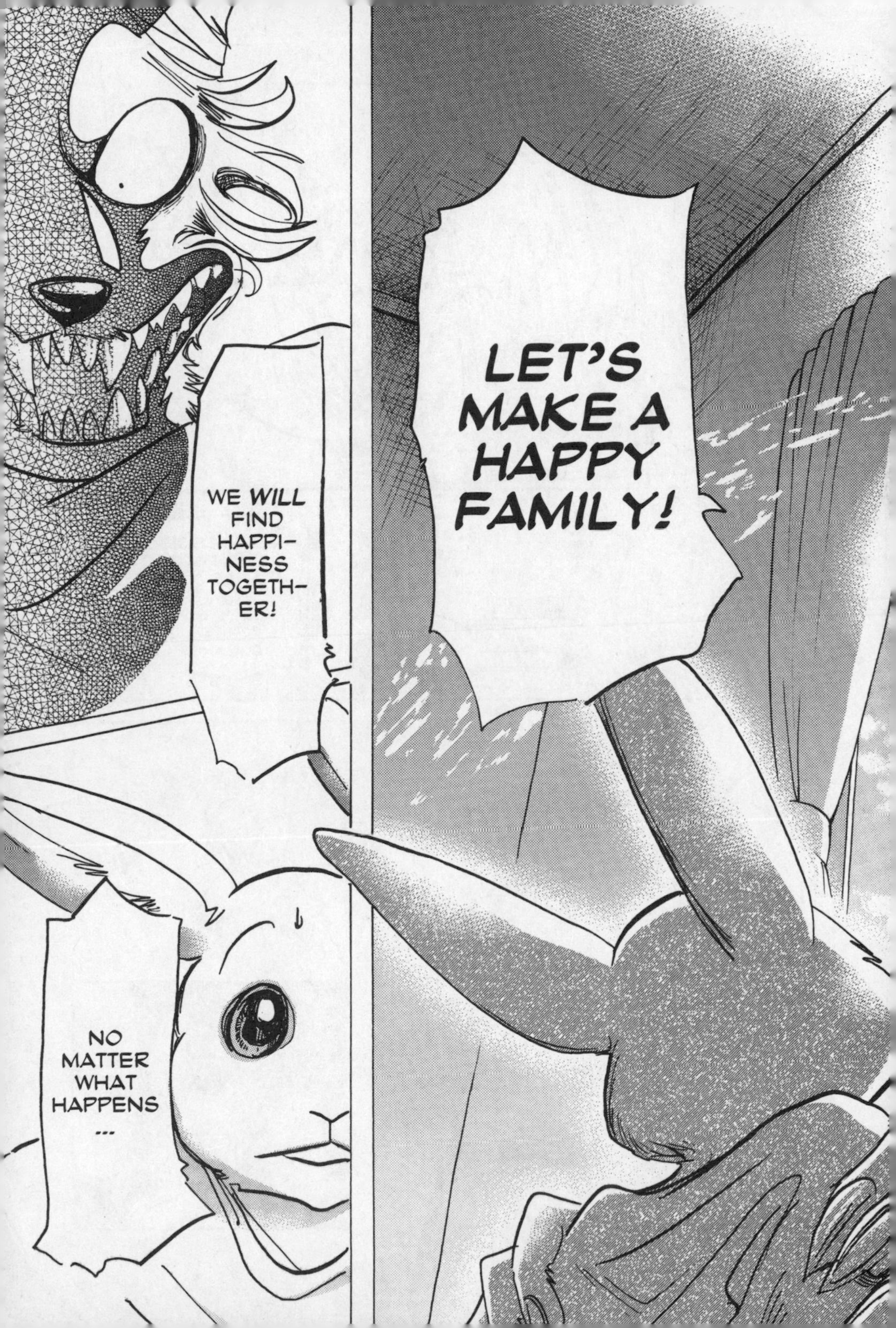
LET'S MAKE A HAPPY FAMILY!
WE WILL FIND HAPPINESS TOGETHER!
NO MATTER WHAT HAPPENS...

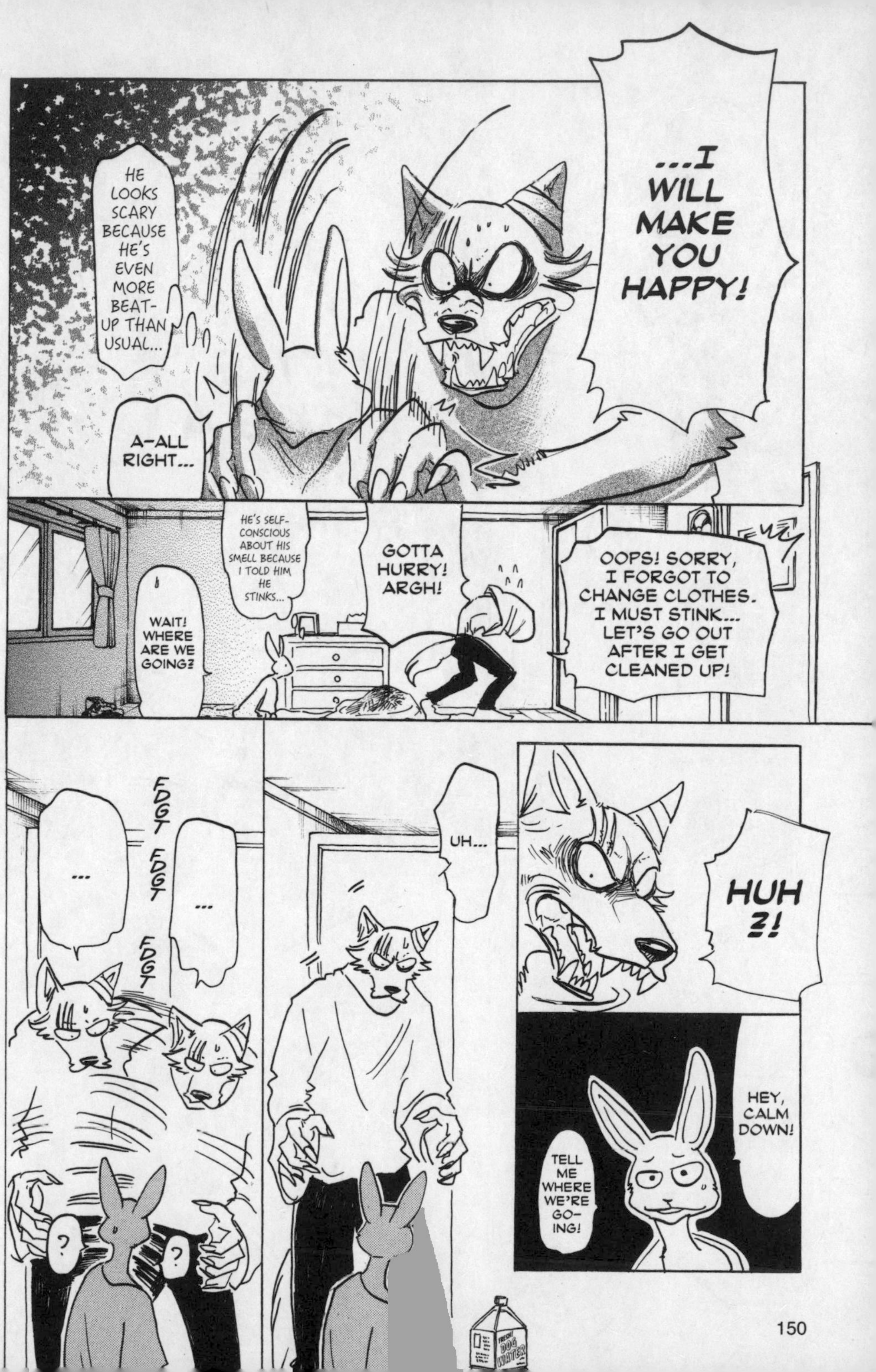

...I WILL MAKE YOU HAPPY!
HE LOOKS SCARY BECAUSE HE'S EVEN MORE BEAT-UP THAN USUAL...
A-ALL RIGHT...
OOPS! SORRY, I FORGOT TO CHANGE CLOTHES. I MUST STINK... LET'S GO OUT AFTER I GET CLEANED UP!
GOTTA HURRY! ARGH!
HE'S SELF-CONSCIOUS ABOUT HIS SMELL BECAUSE I TOLD HIM HE STINKS...
WAIT! WHERE ARE WE GOING?
HUH?!
HEY, CALM DOWN!
TELL ME WHERE WE'RE GO-ING!
UH...
FDGT FDGT
FDGT
...
...
?
?
DOG WATER

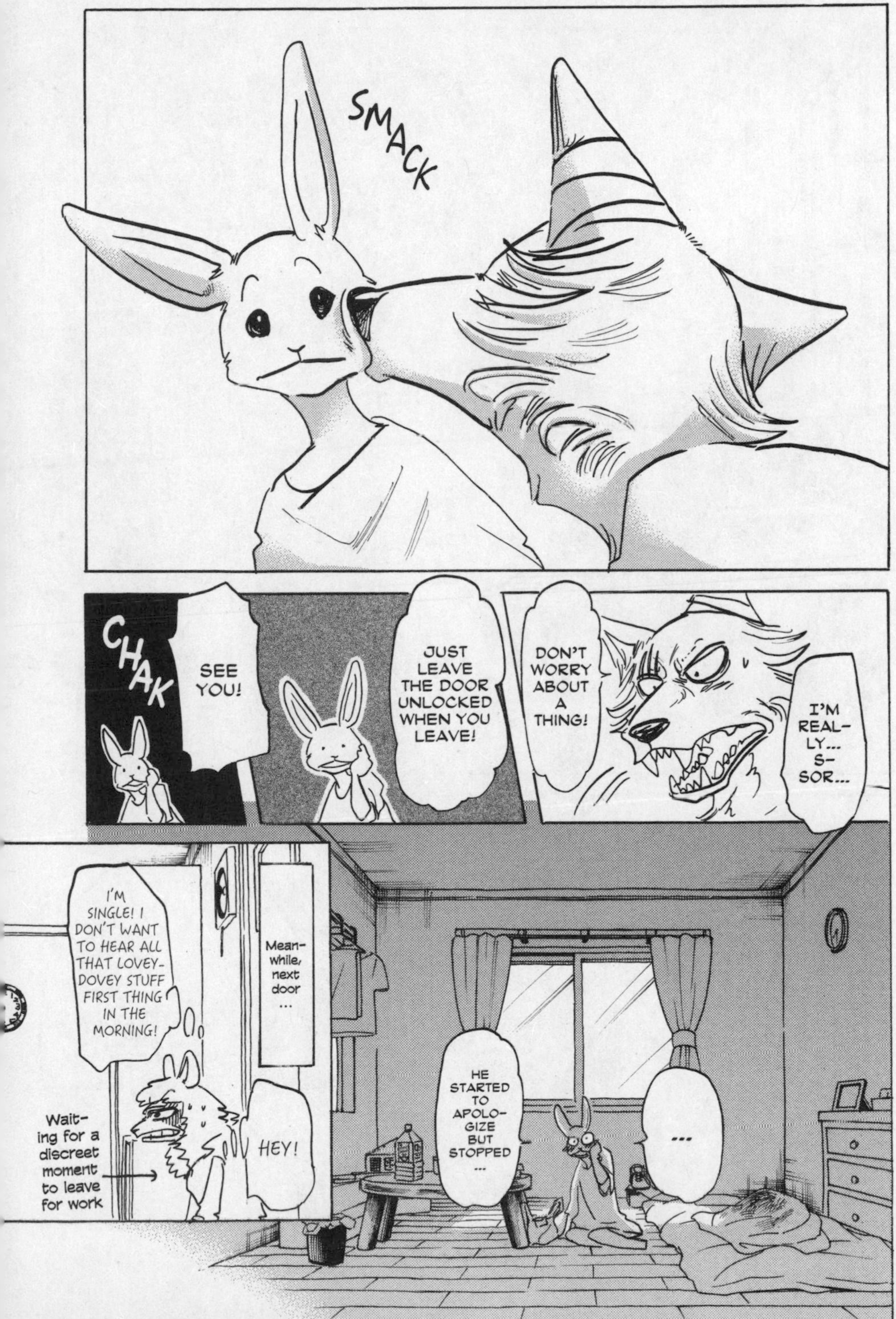
SMACK
I'M REAL-LY... S-SOR...
DON'T WORRY ABOUT A THING!
JUST LEAVE THE DOOR UNLOCKED WHEN YOU LEAVE!
SEE YOU!
CHAK
...
HE STARTED TO APOLO-GIZE BUT STOPPED ...
Mean-while, next door ...
I'M SINGLE! I DON'T WANT TO HEAR ALL THAT LOVEY-DOVEY STUFF FIRST THING IN THE MORNING!
HEY!
Wait-ing for a discreet moment to leave for work

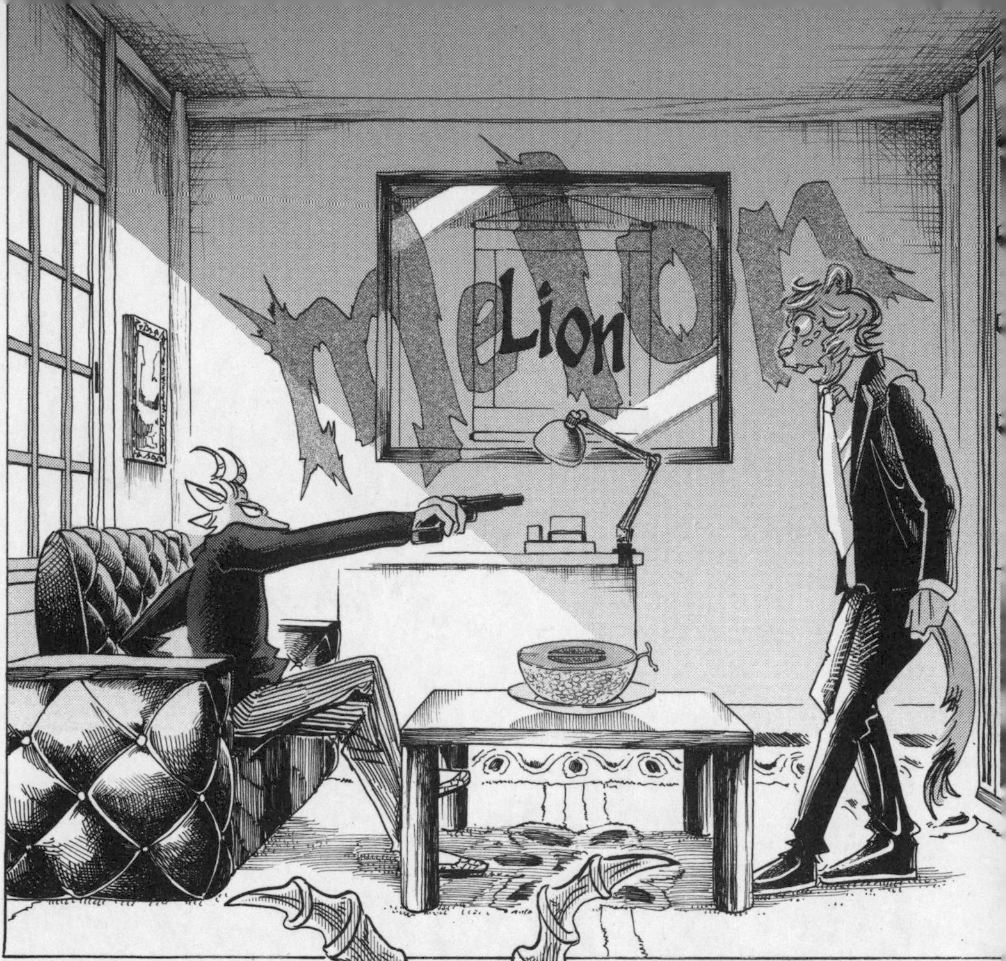
Lion

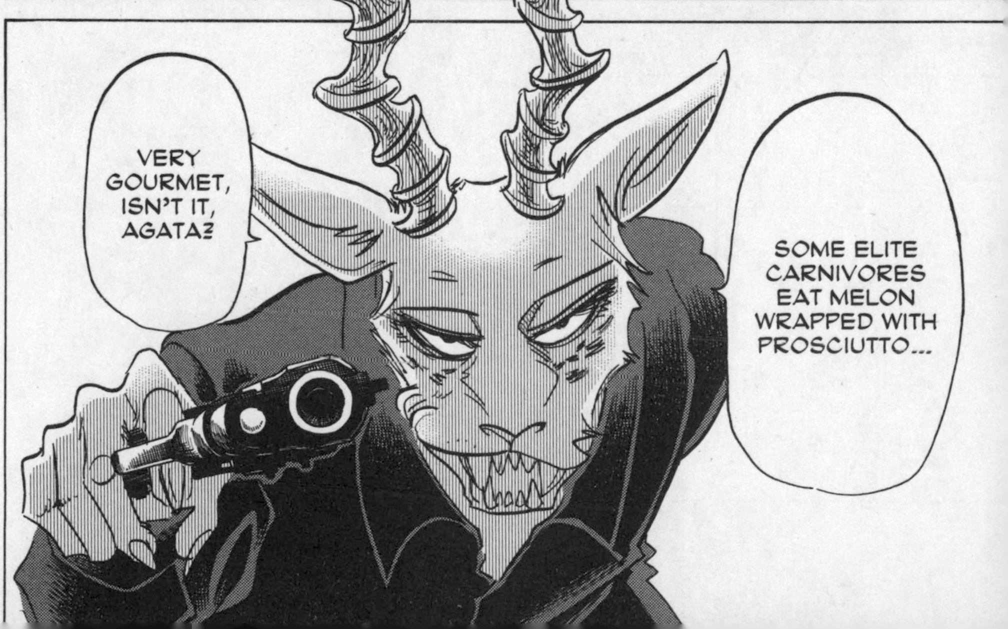
SOME ELITE CARNIVORES EAT MELON WRAPPED WITH PROSCIUTTO...
VERY GOURMET, ISN'T IT, AGATA?

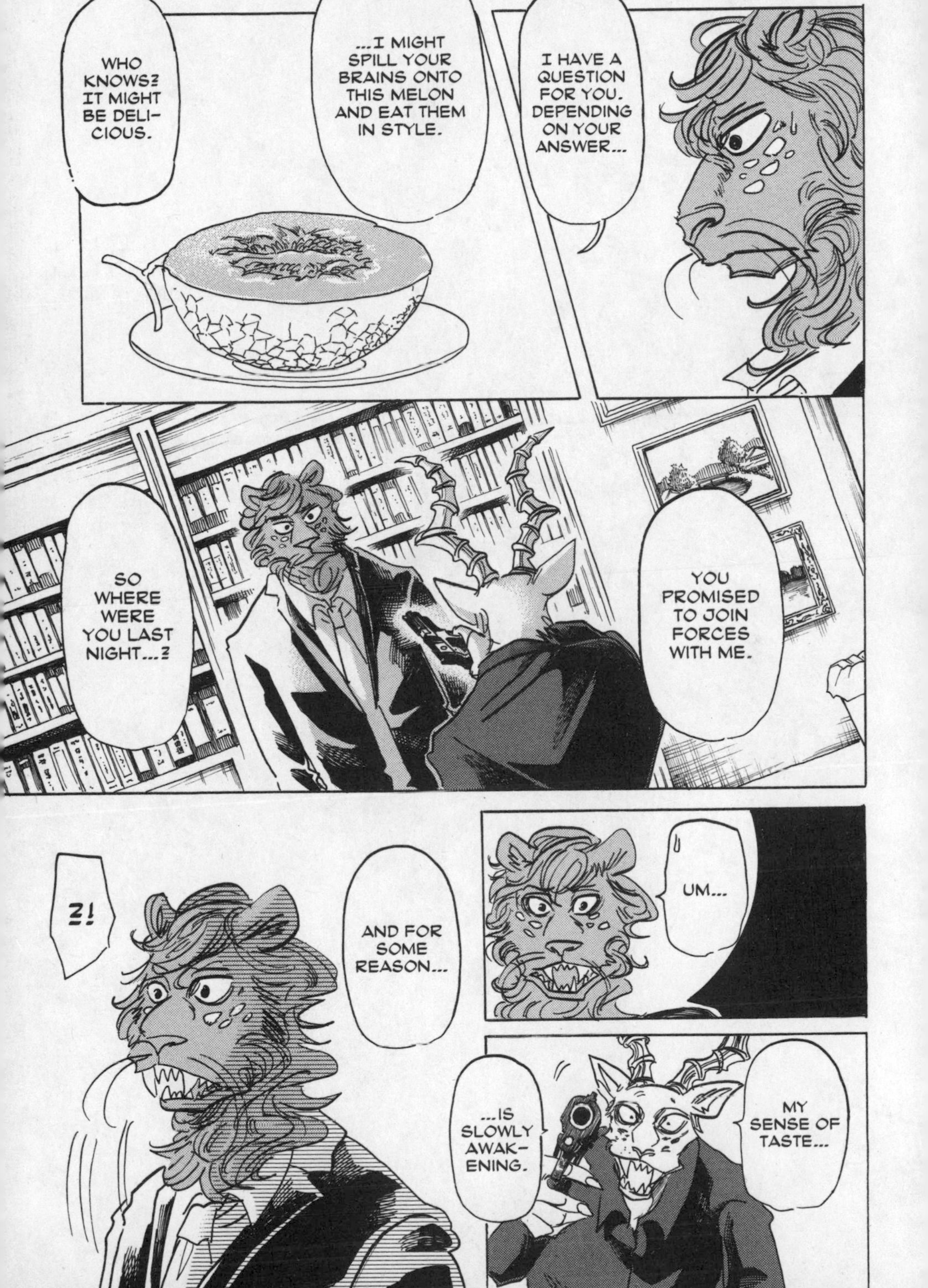
I HAVE A QUESTION FOR YOU. DEPENDING ON YOUR ANSWER...
...I MIGHT SPILL YOUR BRAINS ONTO THIS MELON AND EAT THEM IN STYLE.
WHO KNOWS? IT MIGHT BE DELICIOUS.
YOU PROMISED TO JOIN FORCES WITH ME.
SO WHERE WERE YOU LAST NIGHT...?
UM...
AND FOR SOME REASON...
MY SENSE OF TASTE...
...IS SLOWLY AWAKENING.
?!

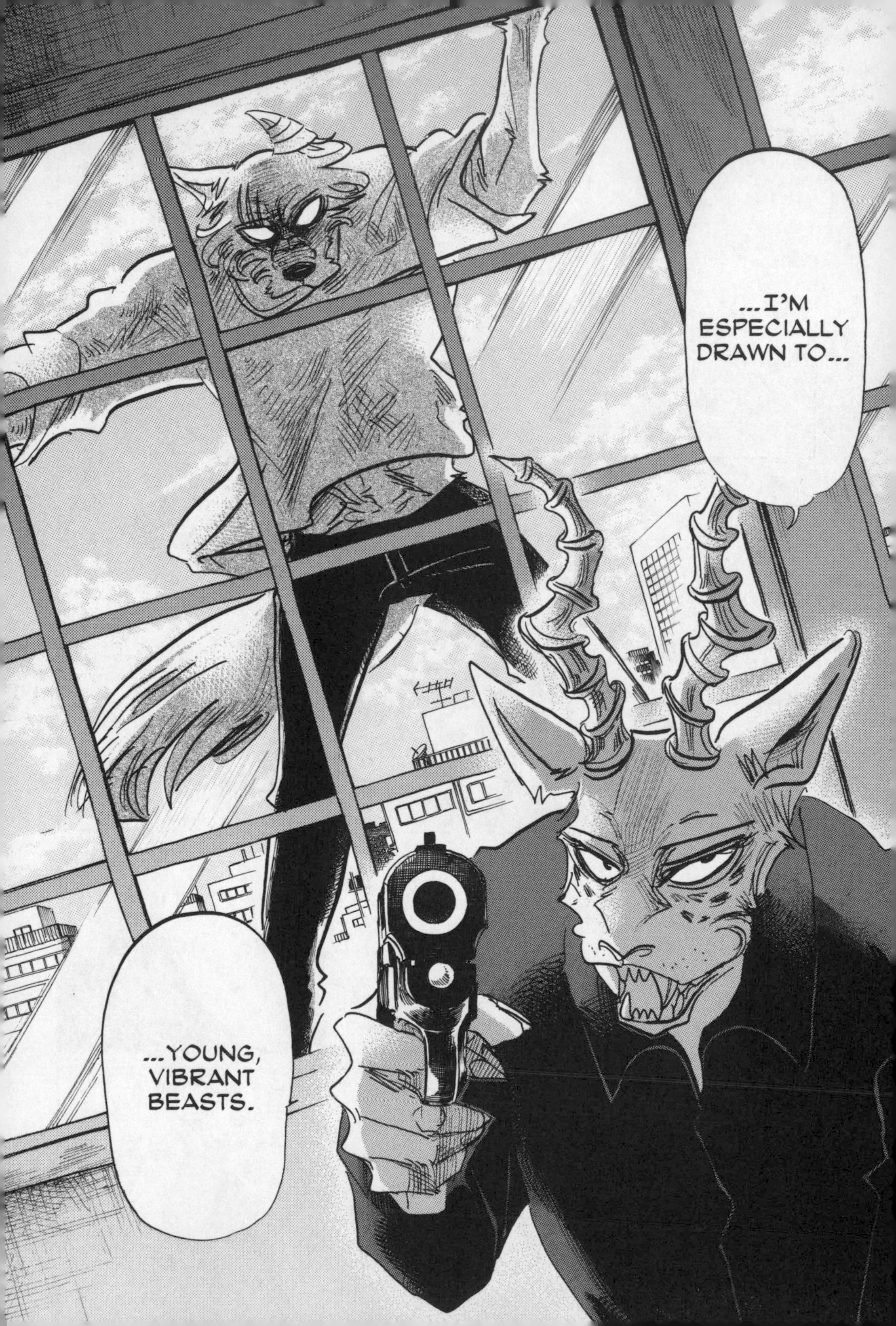
...I'M ESPECIALLY DRAWN TO...
...YOUNG, VIBRANT BEASTS.

BEASTARS
Vol. 17

Chapter 150: Oh, My Big Daddy!

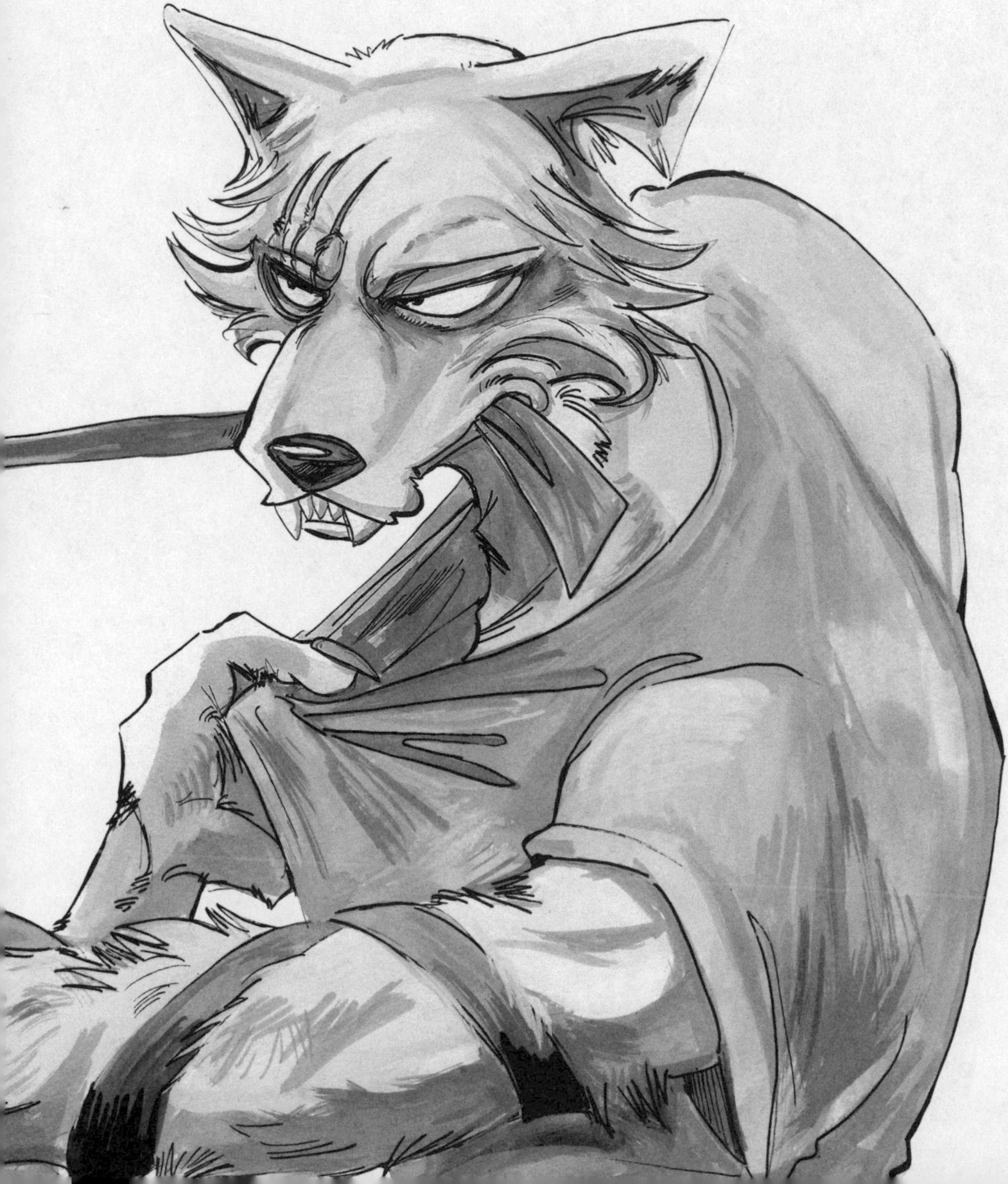

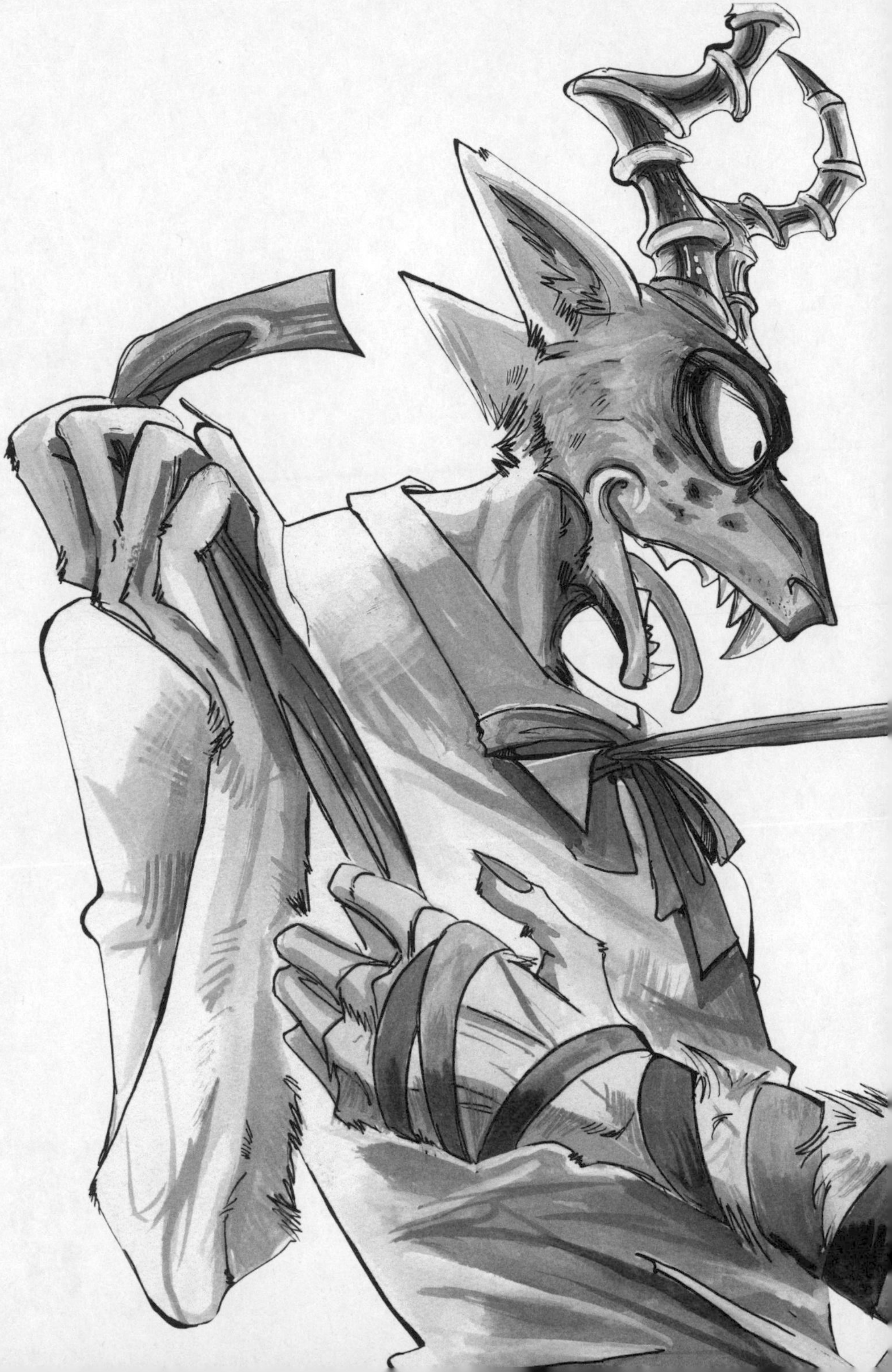

BEASTARS
Vol. 17

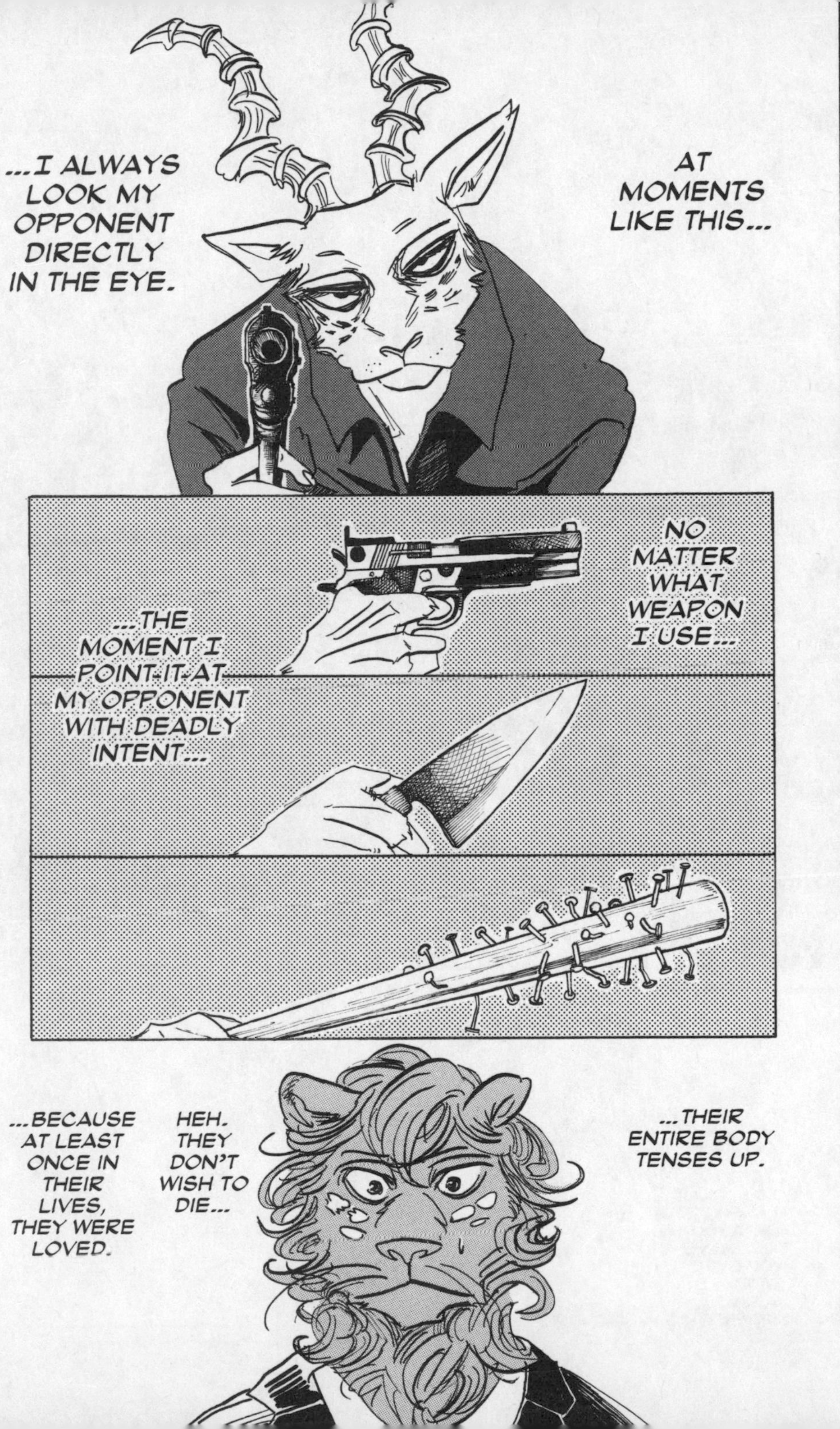
AT MOMENTS LIKE THIS...
...I ALWAYS LOOK MY OPPONENT DIRECTLY IN THE EYE.
NO MATTER WHAT WEAPON I USE...
...THE MOMENT I POINT IT AT MY OPPONENT WITH DEADLY INTENT...
...THEIR ENTIRE BODY TENSES UP.
HEH. THEY DON'T WISH TO DIE...
...BECAUSE AT LEAST ONCE IN THEIR LIVES, THEY WERE LOVED.

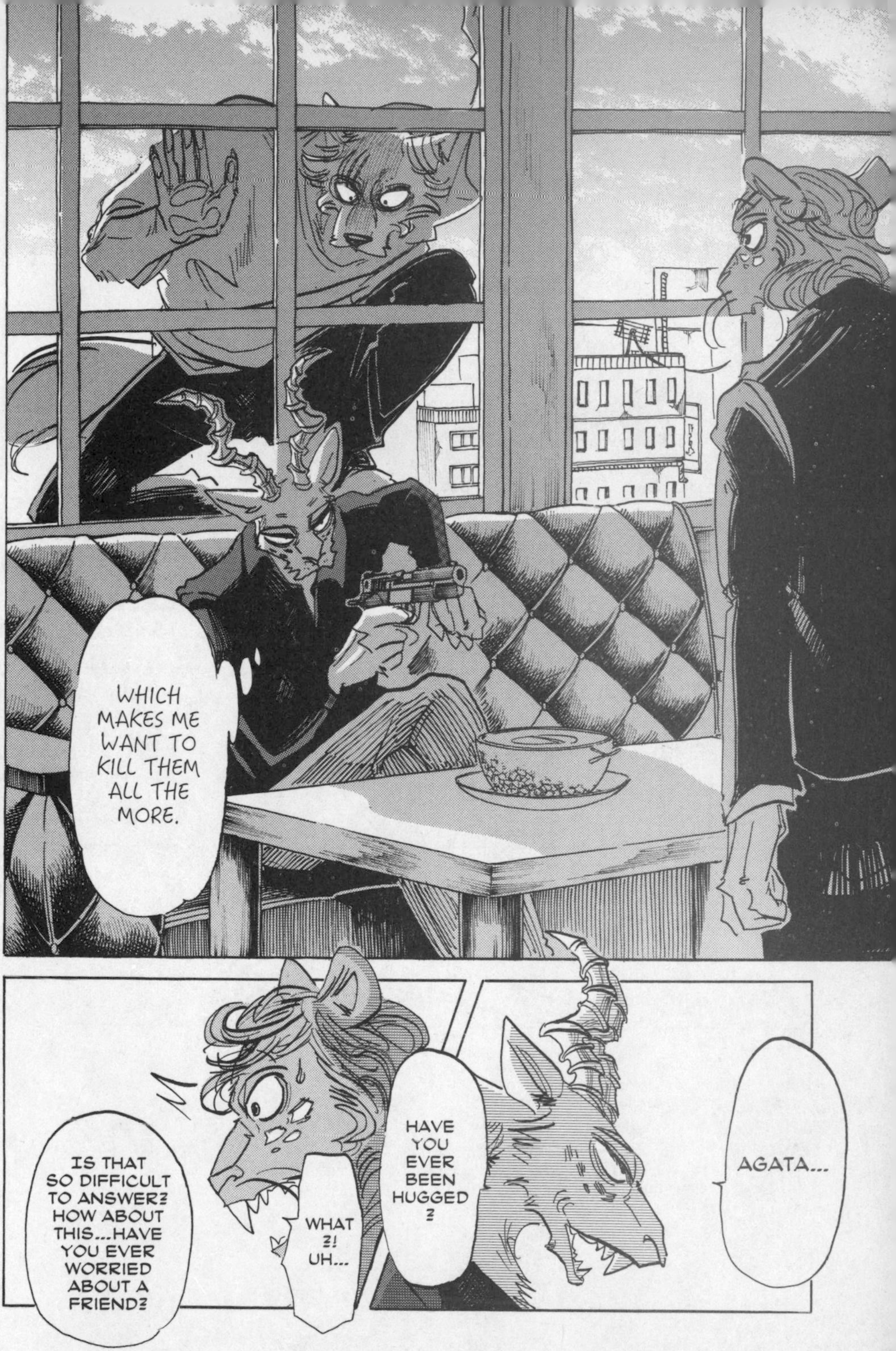
WHICH MAKES ME WANT TO KILL THEM ALL THE MORE.
AGATA...
HAVE YOU EVER BEEN HUGGED?
WHAT?! UH...
IS THAT SO DIFFICULT TO ANSWER? HOW ABOUT THIS...HAVE YOU EVER WORRIED ABOUT A FRIEND?

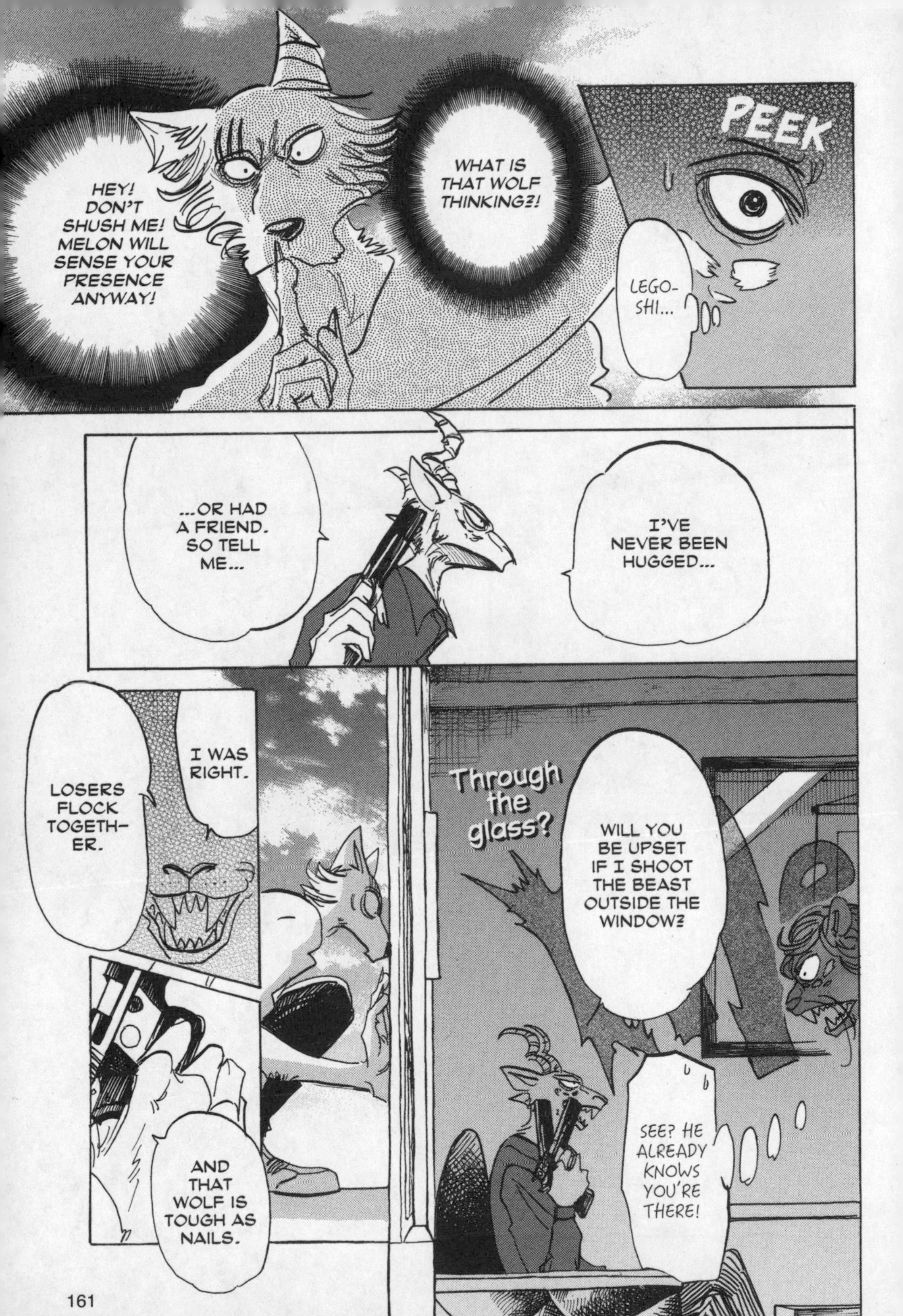
PEEK
LEGO-SHI...
WHAT IS THAT WOLF THINKING?!
HEY! DON'T SHUSH ME! MELON WILL SENSE YOUR PRESENCE ANYWAY!
I'VE NEVER BEEN HUGGED...
...OR HAD A FRIEND. SO TELL ME...
WILL YOU BE UPSET IF I SHOOT THE BEAST OUTSIDE THE WINDOW?
Through the glass?
SEE? HE ALREADY KNOWS YOU'RE THERE!
I WAS RIGHT.
LOSERS FLOCK TOGETH-ER.
AND THAT WOLF IS TOUGH AS NAILS.

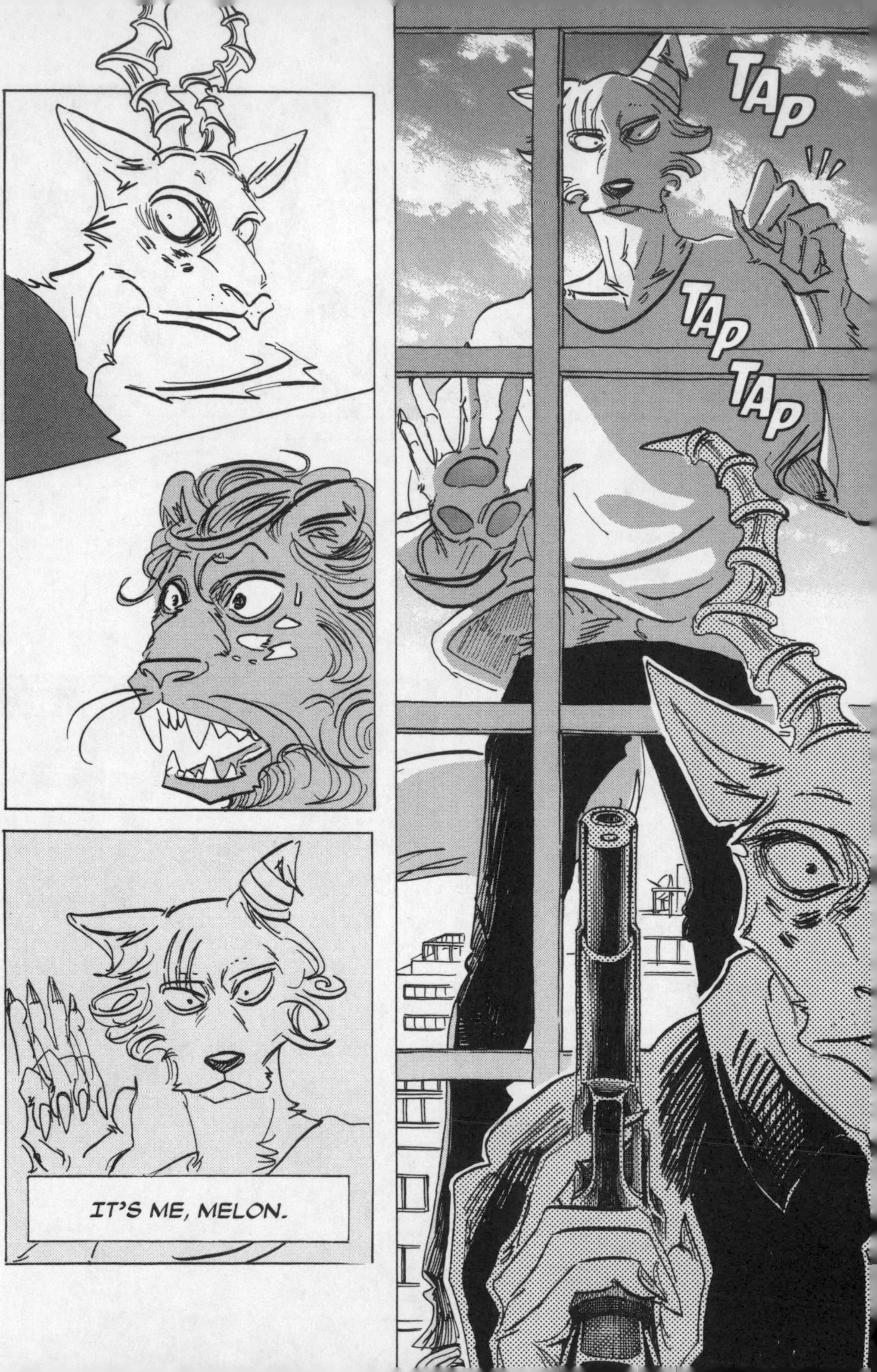
TAP
TAP
TAP
TAP
IT'S ME, MELON.

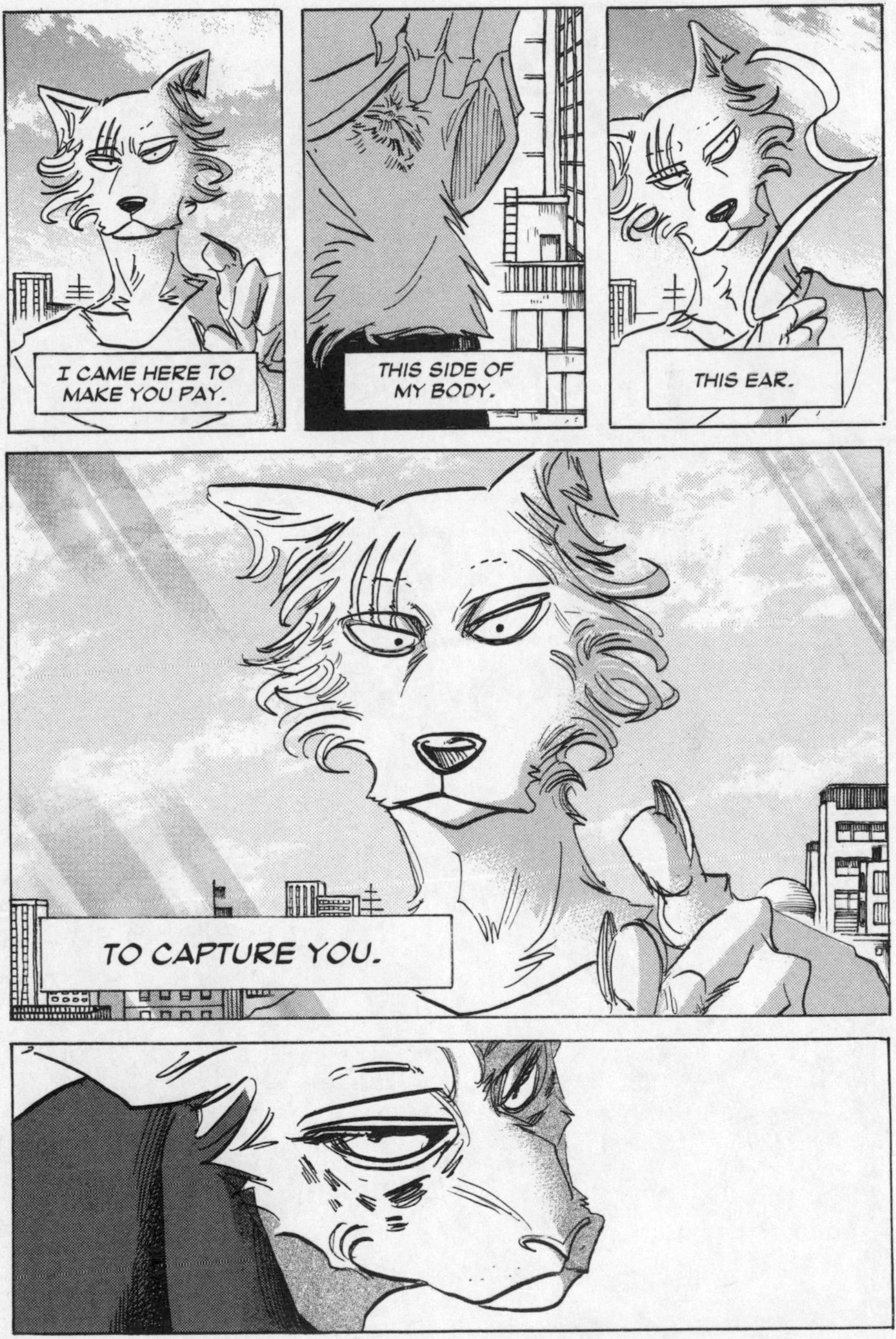
THIS EAR.
THIS SIDE OF MY BODY.
I CAME HERE TO MAKE YOU PAY.
TO CAPTURE YOU.

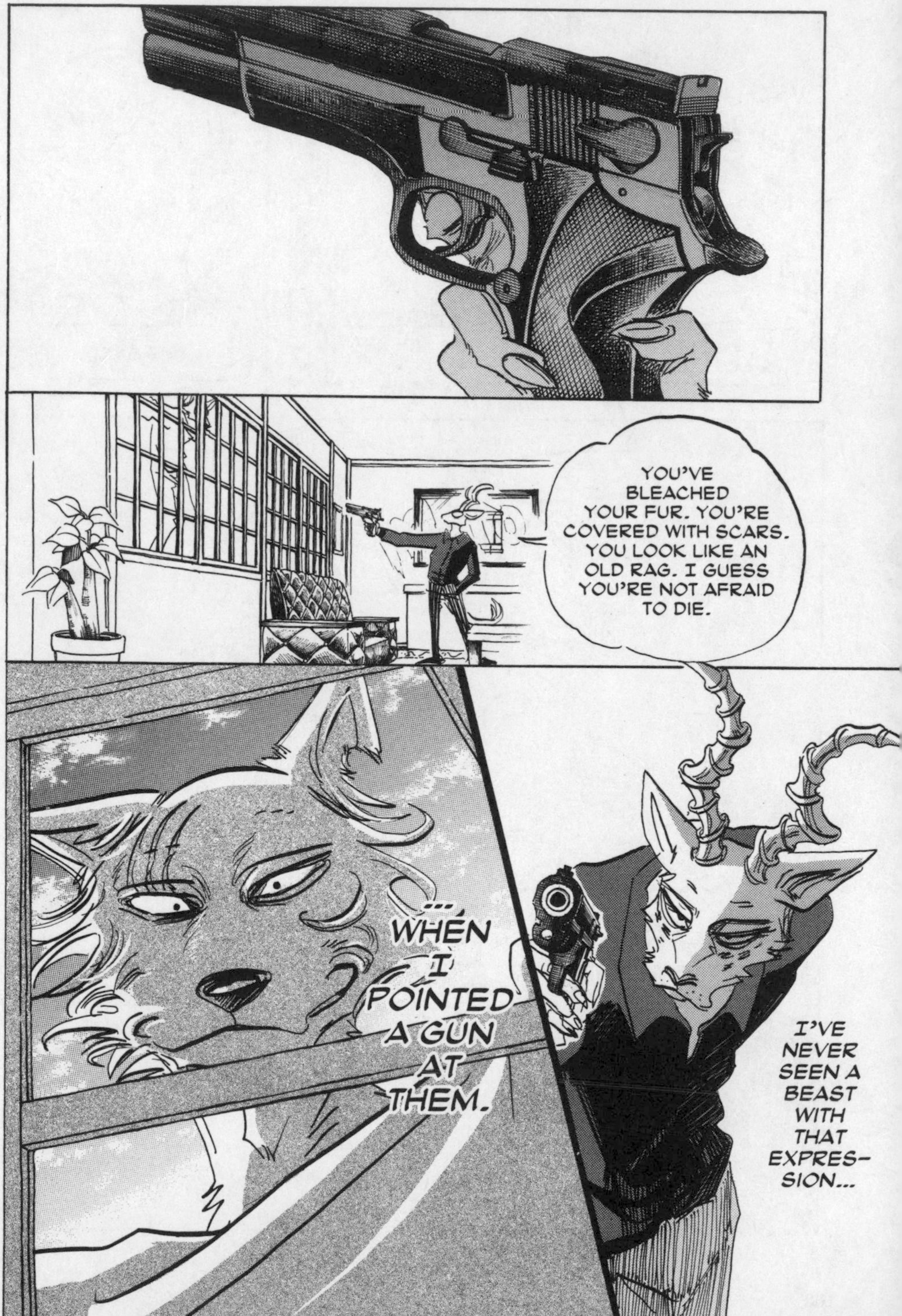
YOU'VE BLEACHED YOUR FUR. YOU'RE COVERED WITH SCARS. YOU LOOK LIKE AN OLD RAG. I GUESS YOU'RE NOT AFRAID TO DIE.
I'VE NEVER SEEN A BEAST WITH THAT EXPRES-SION...
...WHEN I POINTED A GUN AT THEM.

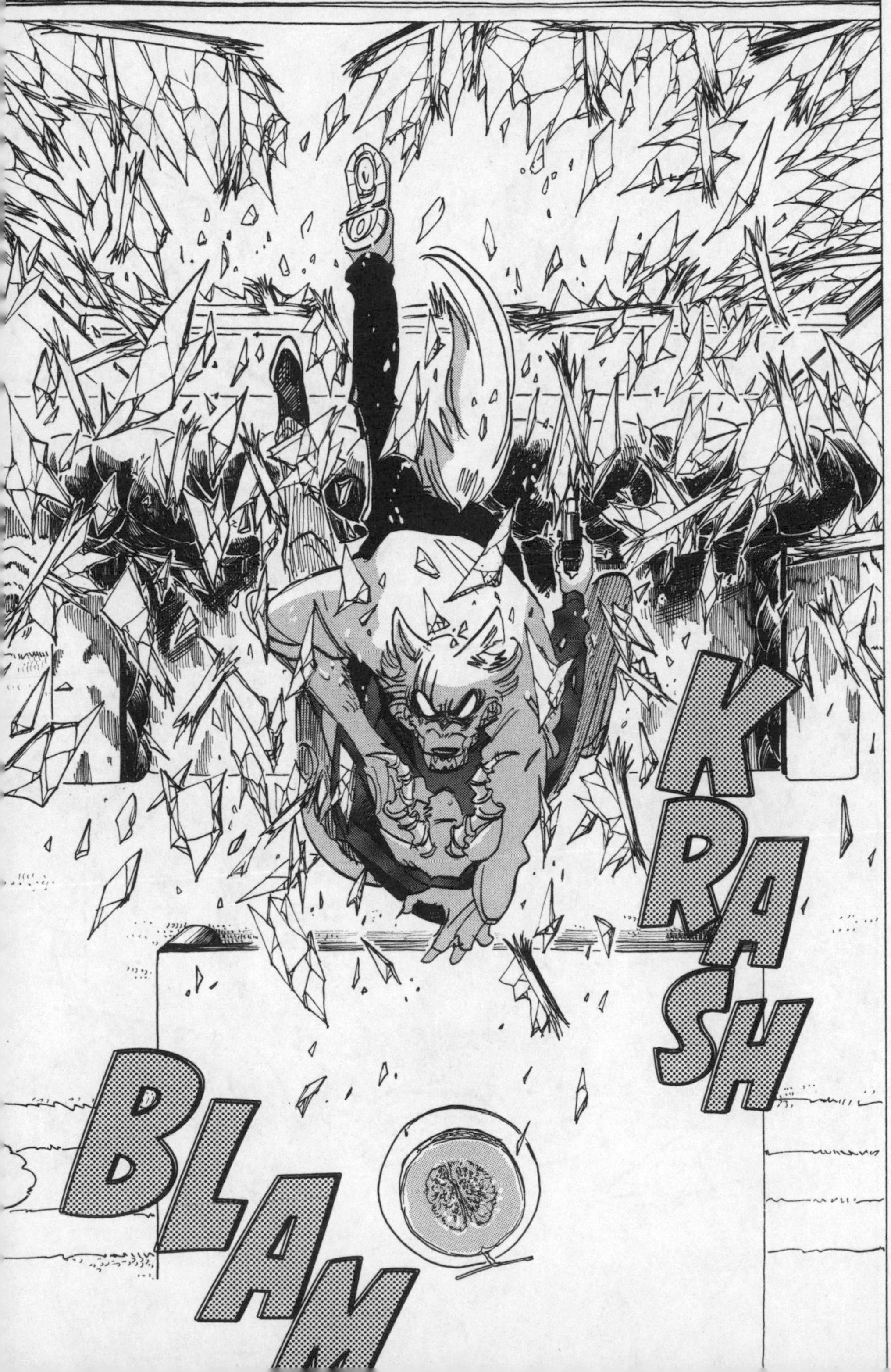
KRASH
BLAM

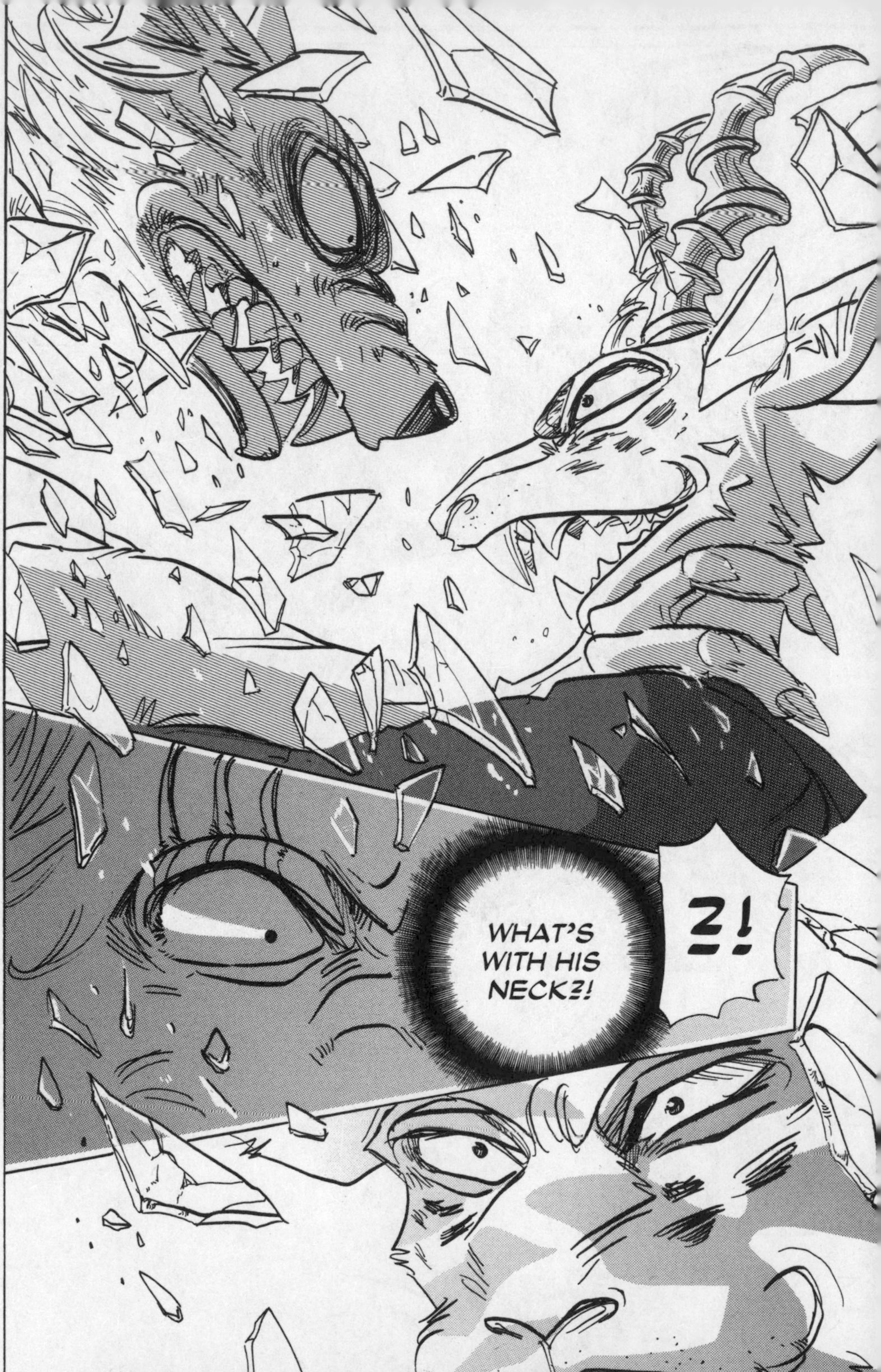
?!
WHAT'S WITH HIS NECK?!

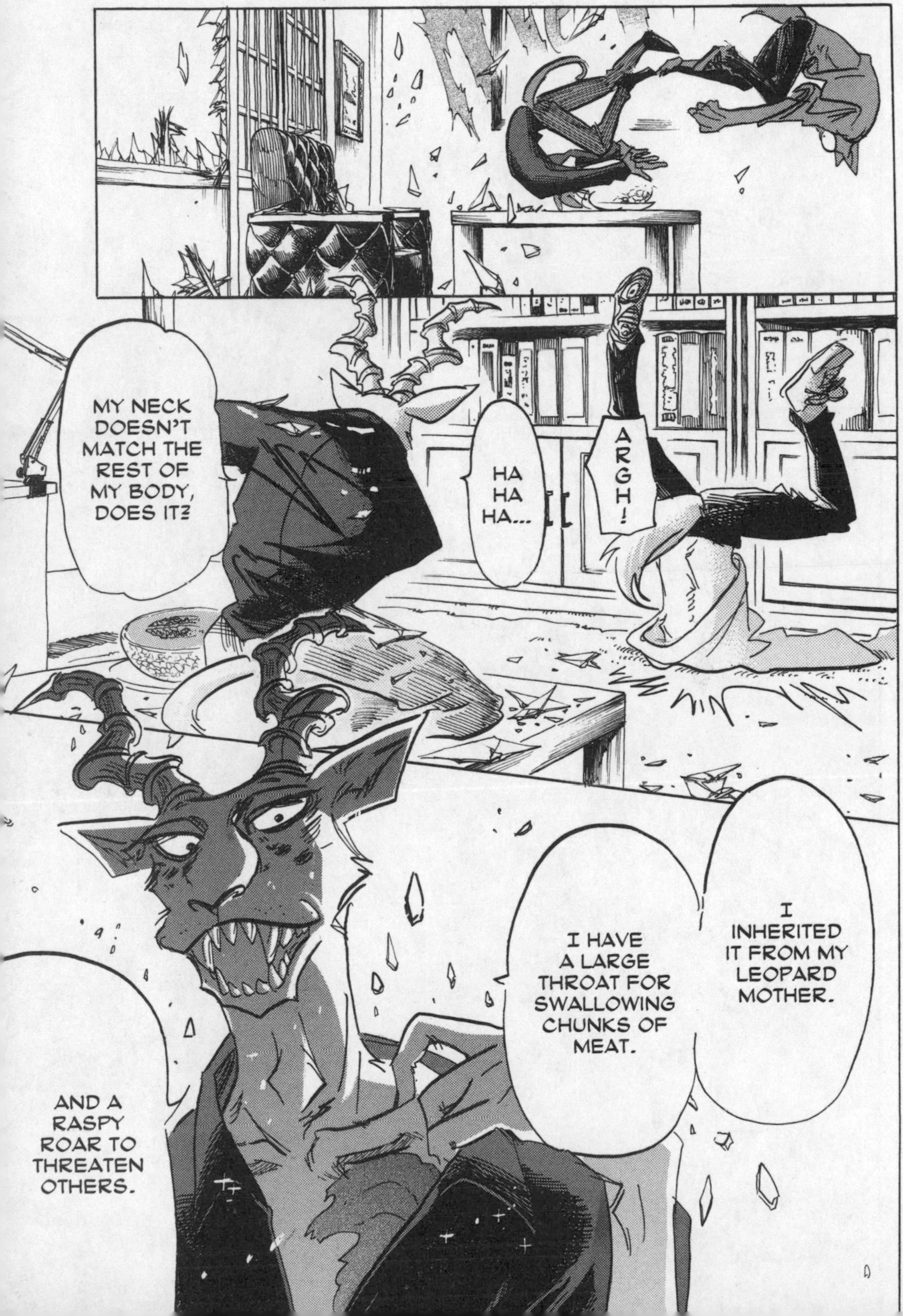
ARGH!
HA HA HA...
MY NECK DOESN'T MATCH THE REST OF MY BODY, DOES IT?
I INHERITED IT FROM MY LEOPARD MOTHER.
I HAVE A LARGE THROAT FOR SWALLOWING CHUNKS OF MEAT.
AND A RASPY ROAR TO THREATEN OTHERS.

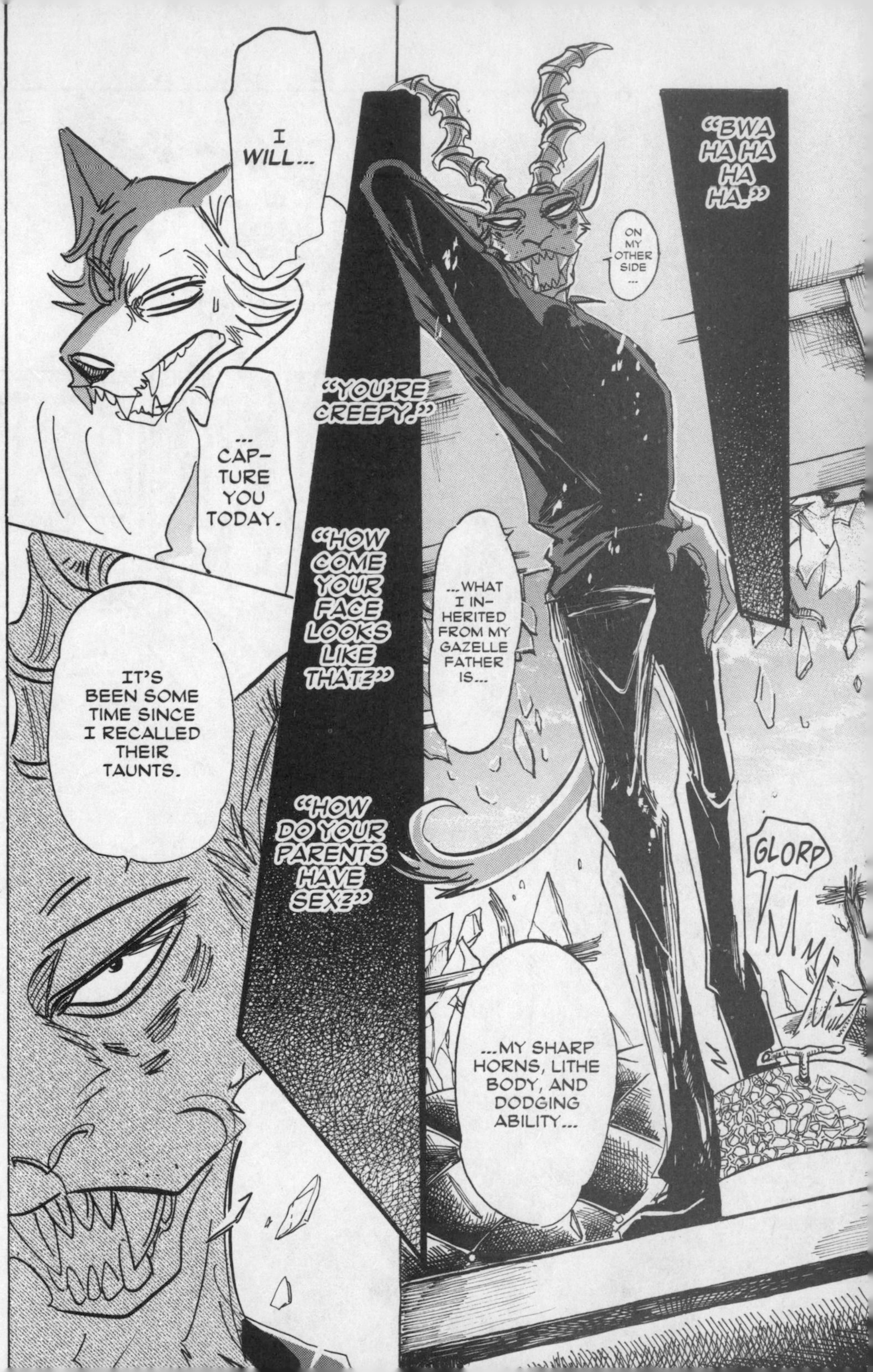
"BWA HA HA HA HA."
ON MY OTHER SIDE...
"YOU'RE CREEPY."
...WHAT I INHERITED FROM MY GAZELLE FATHER IS...
"HOW COME YOUR FACE LOOKS LIKE THAT?"
GLORP
"HOW DO YOUR PARENTS HAVE SEX?"
...MY SHARP HORNS, LITHE BODY, AND DODGING ABILITY...
I WILL...
...CAPTURE YOU TODAY.
IT'S BEEN SOME TIME SINCE I RECALLED THEIR TAUNTS.

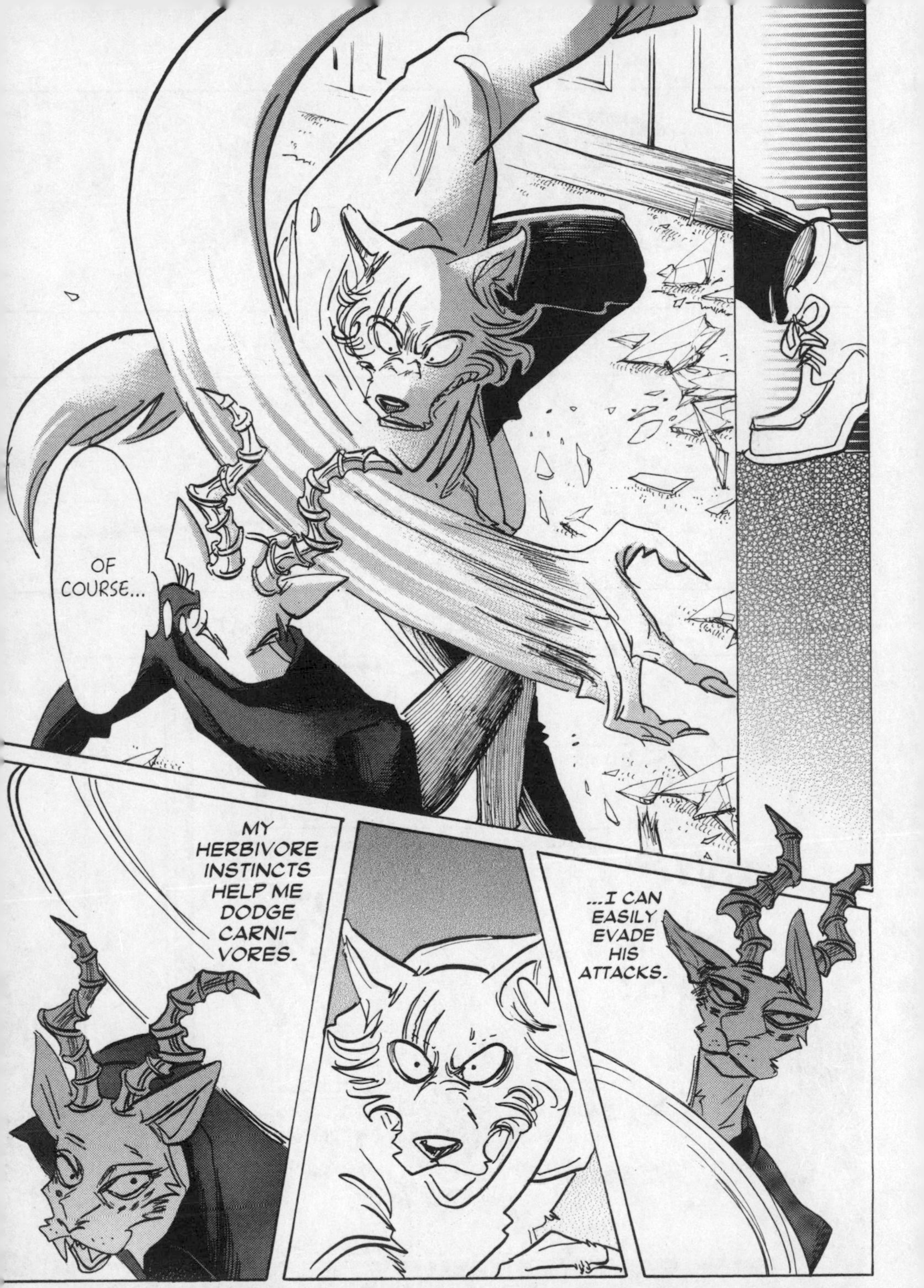

OF COURSE...
...I CAN EASILY EVADE HIS ATTACKS.
MY HERBIVORE INSTINCTS HELP ME DODGE CARNI- VORES.

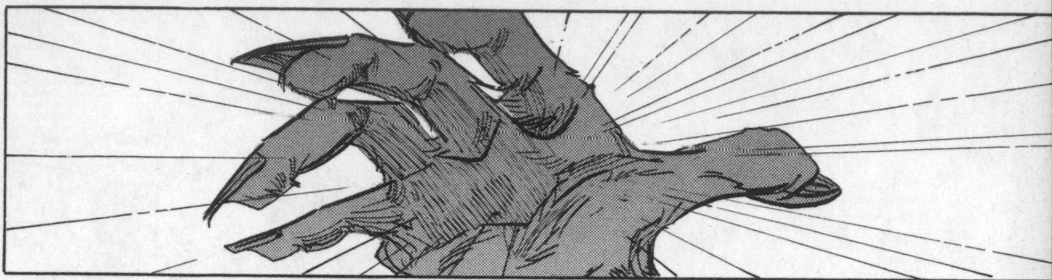

THE OTHER KIDS USED TO SAY...

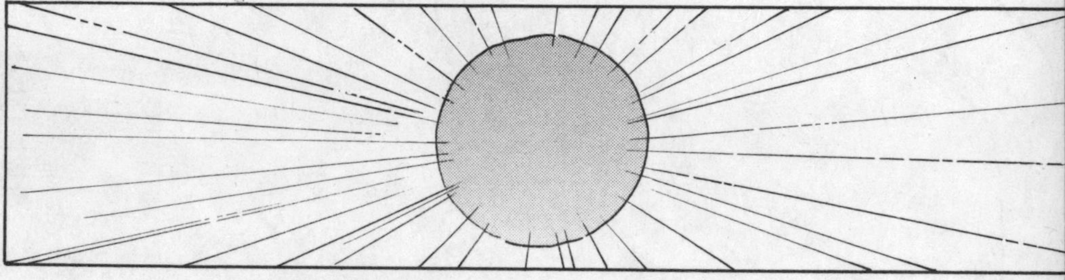

...THEY COULD THROW ANYTHING AT ME.

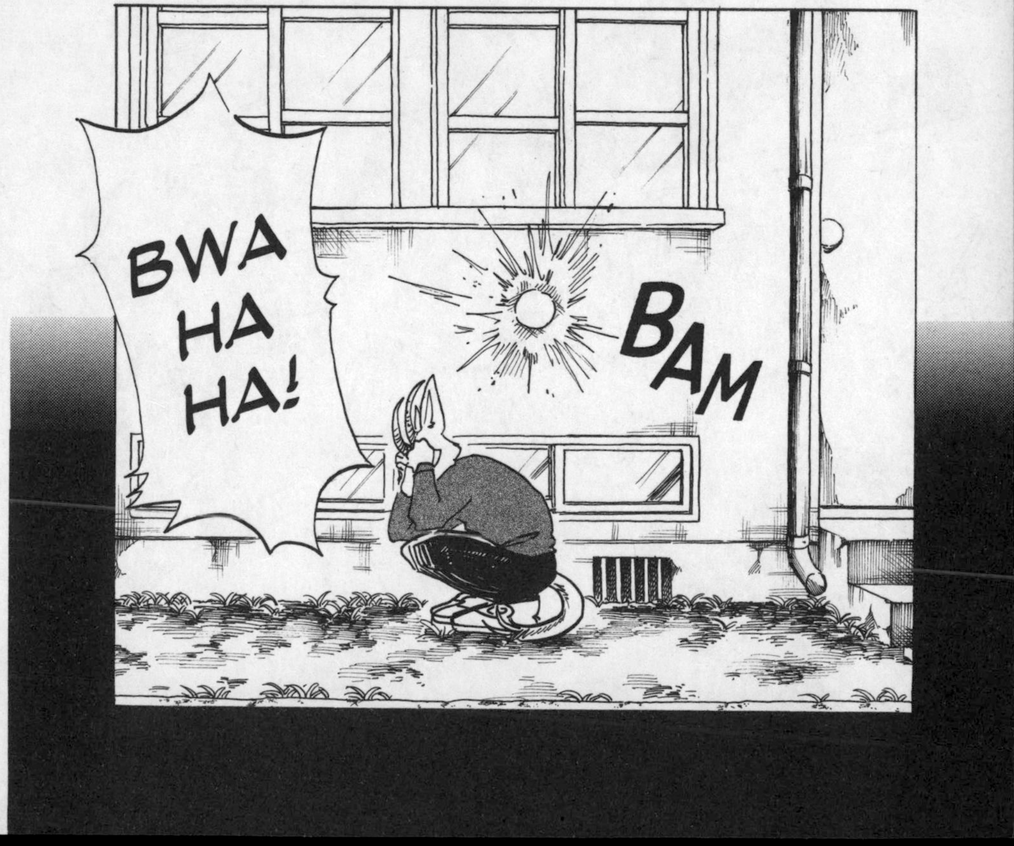
BWA HA HA!
BAM

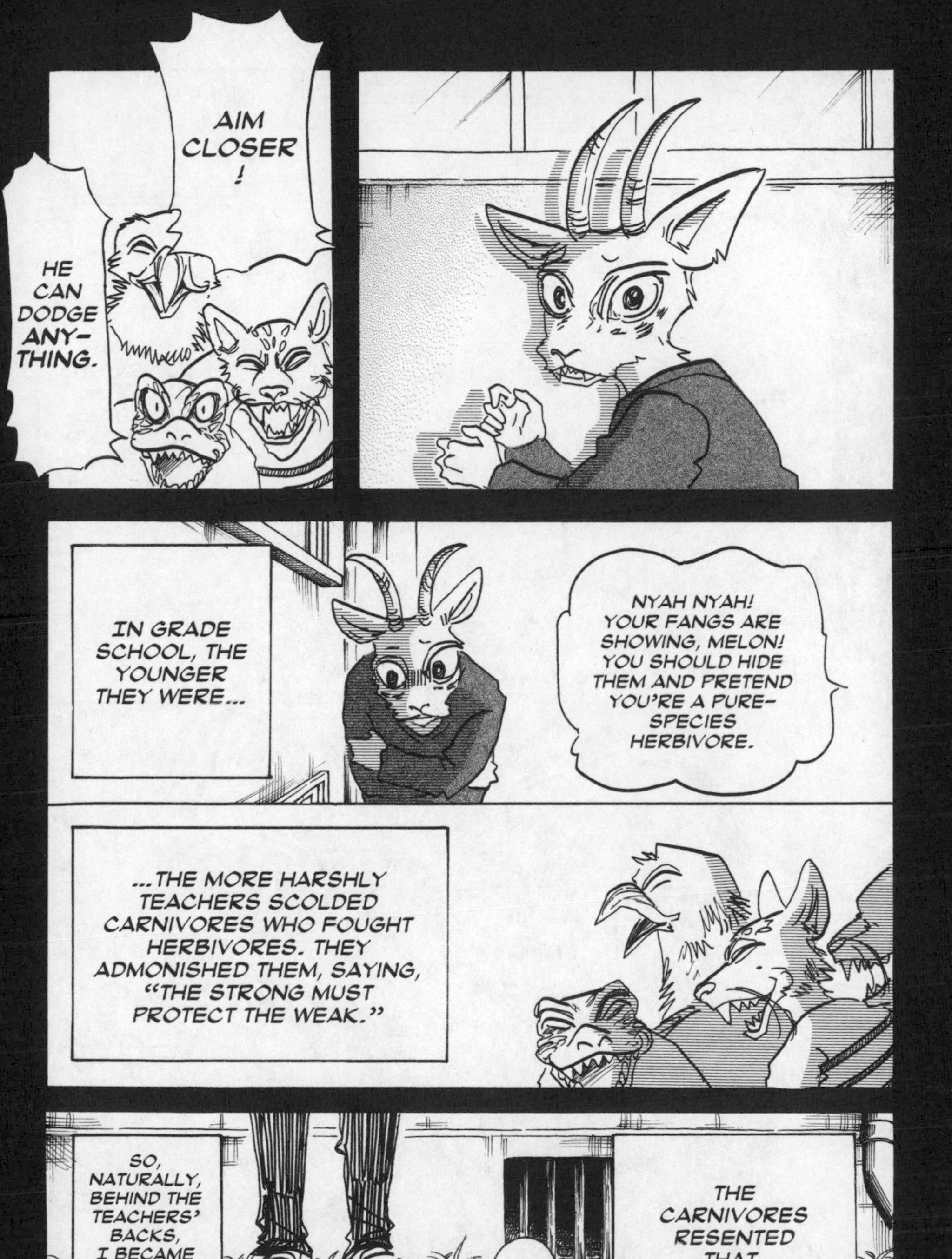
AIM CLOSER!
HE CAN DODGE ANYTHING.
NYAH NYAH! YOUR FANGS ARE SHOWING, MELON! YOU SHOULD HIDE THEM AND PRETEND YOU'RE A PURE-SPECIES HERBIVORE.
IN GRADE SCHOOL, THE YOUNGER THEY WERE...
...THE MORE HARSHLY TEACHERS SCOLDED CARNIVORES WHO FOUGHT HERBIVORES. THEY ADMONISHED THEM, SAYING, "THE STRONG MUST PROTECT THE WEAK."
THE CARNIVORES RESENTED THAT.
SO, NATURALLY, BEHIND THE TEACHERS' BACKS, I BECAME THEIR PRIME TARGET.

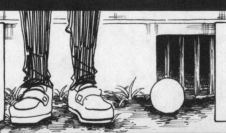

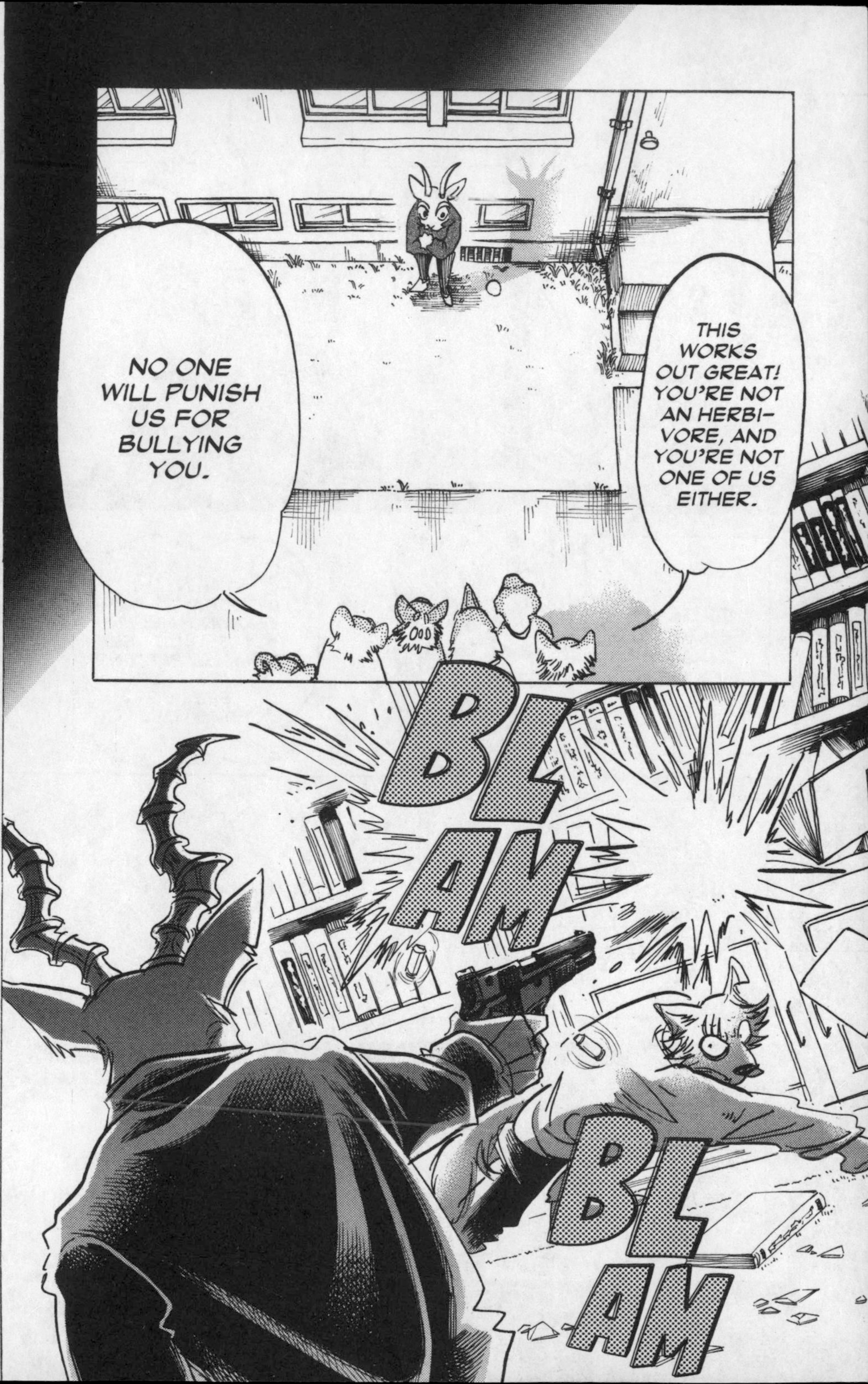
THIS WORKS OUT GREAT! YOU'RE NOT AN HERBIVORE, AND YOU'RE NOT ONE OF US EITHER.
NO ONE WILL PUNISH US FOR BULLYING YOU.
BLAM
BLAM

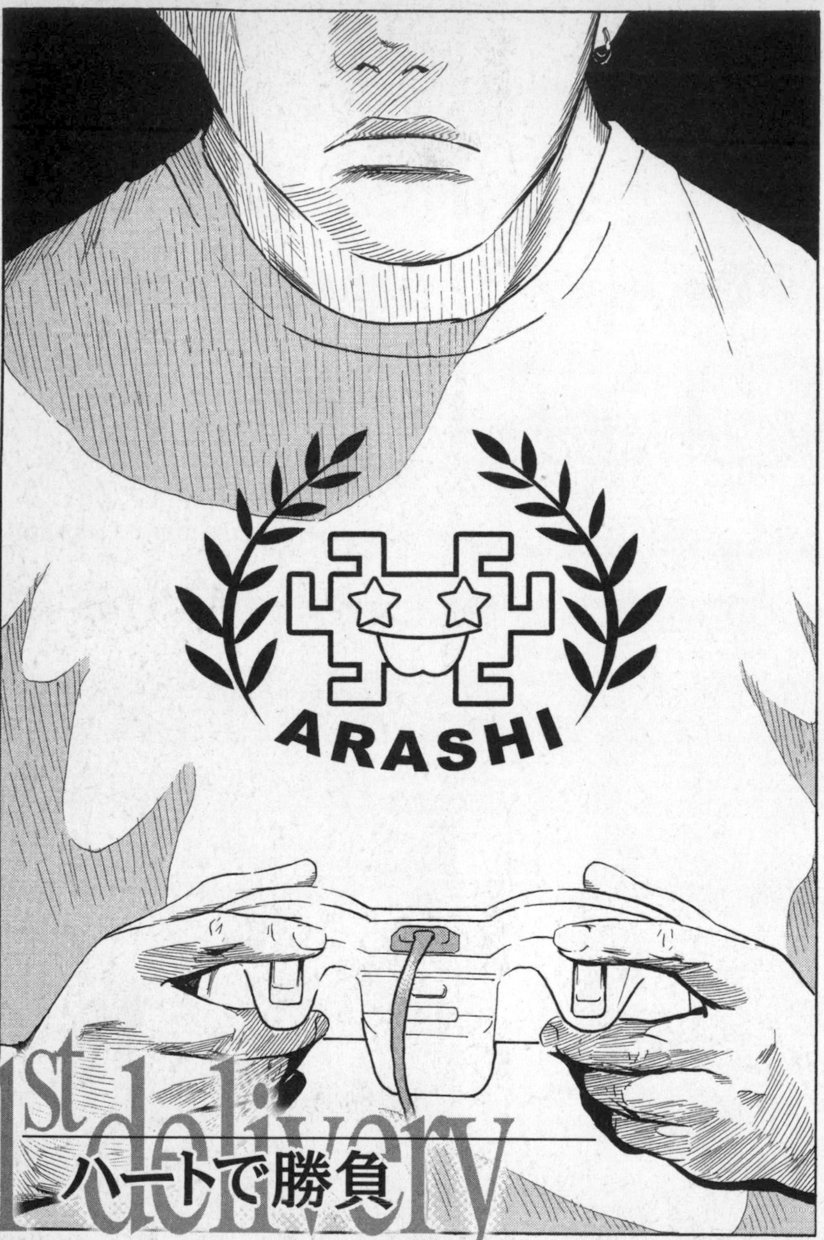
ARASHI

1st delivery ハートで勝負

fight with my heart

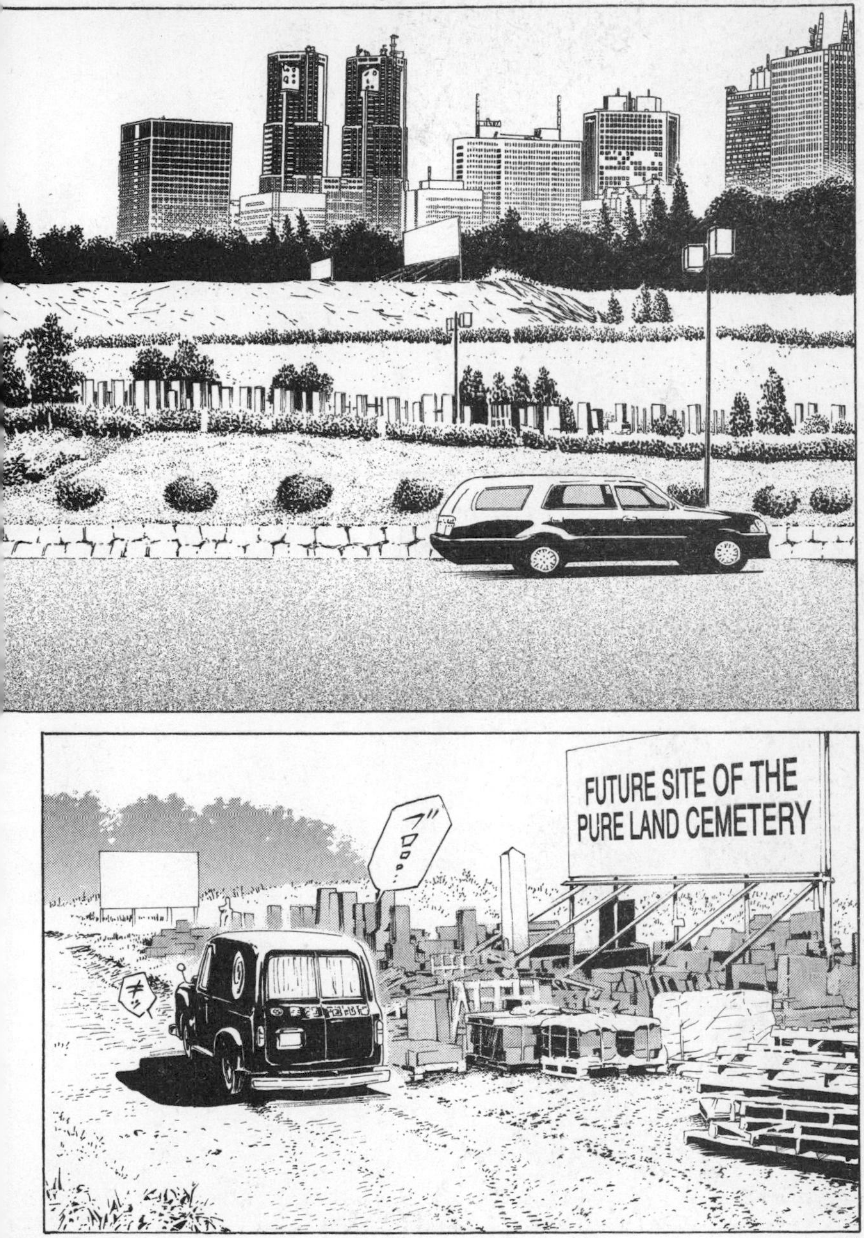
FUTURE SITE OF THE
PURE LAND CEMETERY
ブロロロ…
キッ

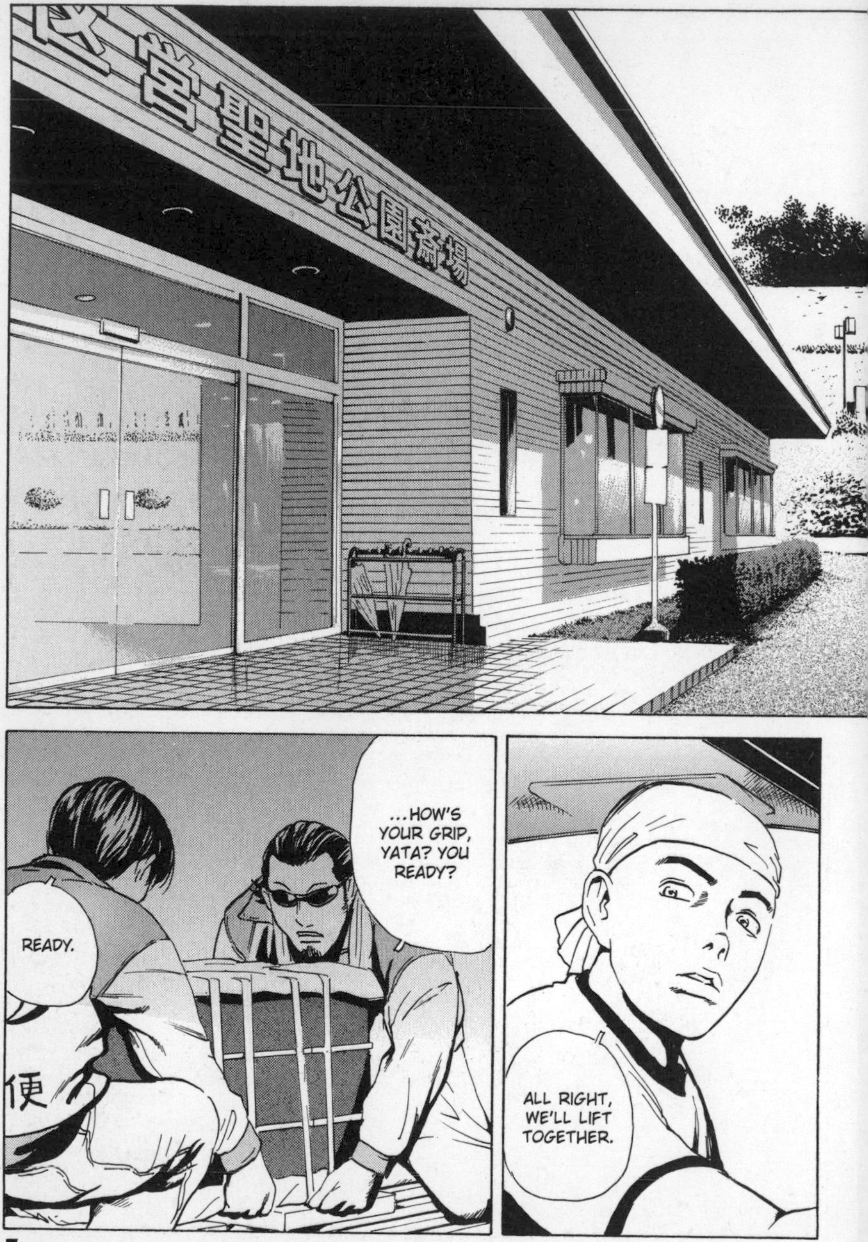
営聖地公園斎場
ALL RIGHT, WE'LL LIFT TOGETHER.
...HOW'S YOUR GRIP, YATA? YOU READY?
READY.
便

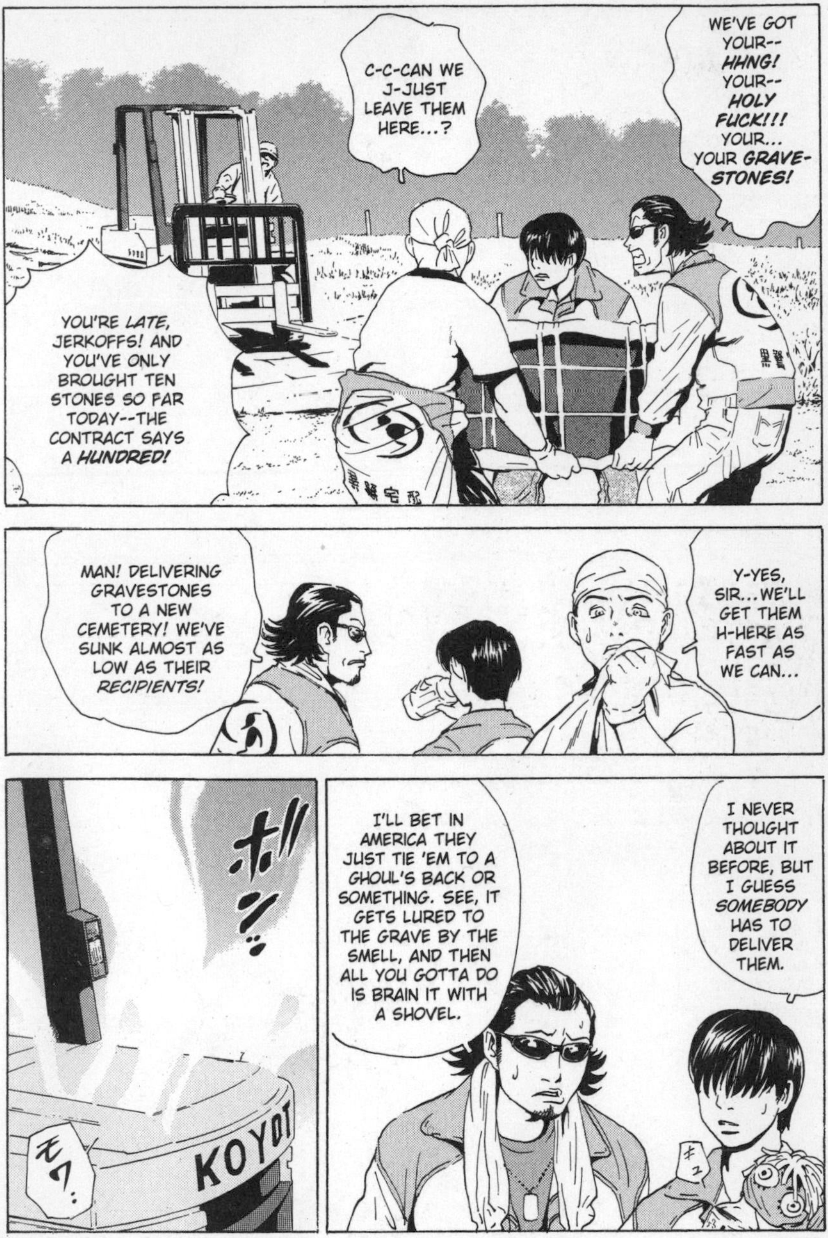
WE'VE GOT YOUR-- *HHNG!* YOUR-- *HOLY FUCK!!!* YOUR... YOUR *GRAVE-STONES!*
C-C-CAN WE J-JUST LEAVE THEM HERE...?
YOU'RE *LATE,* JERKOFFS! AND YOU'VE ONLY BROUGHT TEN STONES SO FAR TODAY--THE CONTRACT SAYS A *HUNDRED!*
Y-YES, SIR...WE'LL GET THEM H-HERE AS FAST AS WE CAN...
MAN! DELIVERING GRAVESTONES TO A NEW CEMETERY! WE'VE SUNK ALMOST AS LOW AS THEIR *RECIPIENTS!*
I NEVER THOUGHT ABOUT IT BEFORE, BUT I GUESS *SOMEBODY* HAS TO DELIVER THEM.
I'LL BET IN AMERICA THEY JUST TIE 'EM TO A GHOUL'S BACK OR SOMETHING. SEE, IT GETS LURED TO THE GRAVE BY THE SMELL, AND THEN ALL YOU GOTTA DO IS BRAIN IT WITH A SHOVEL.
KOYOT

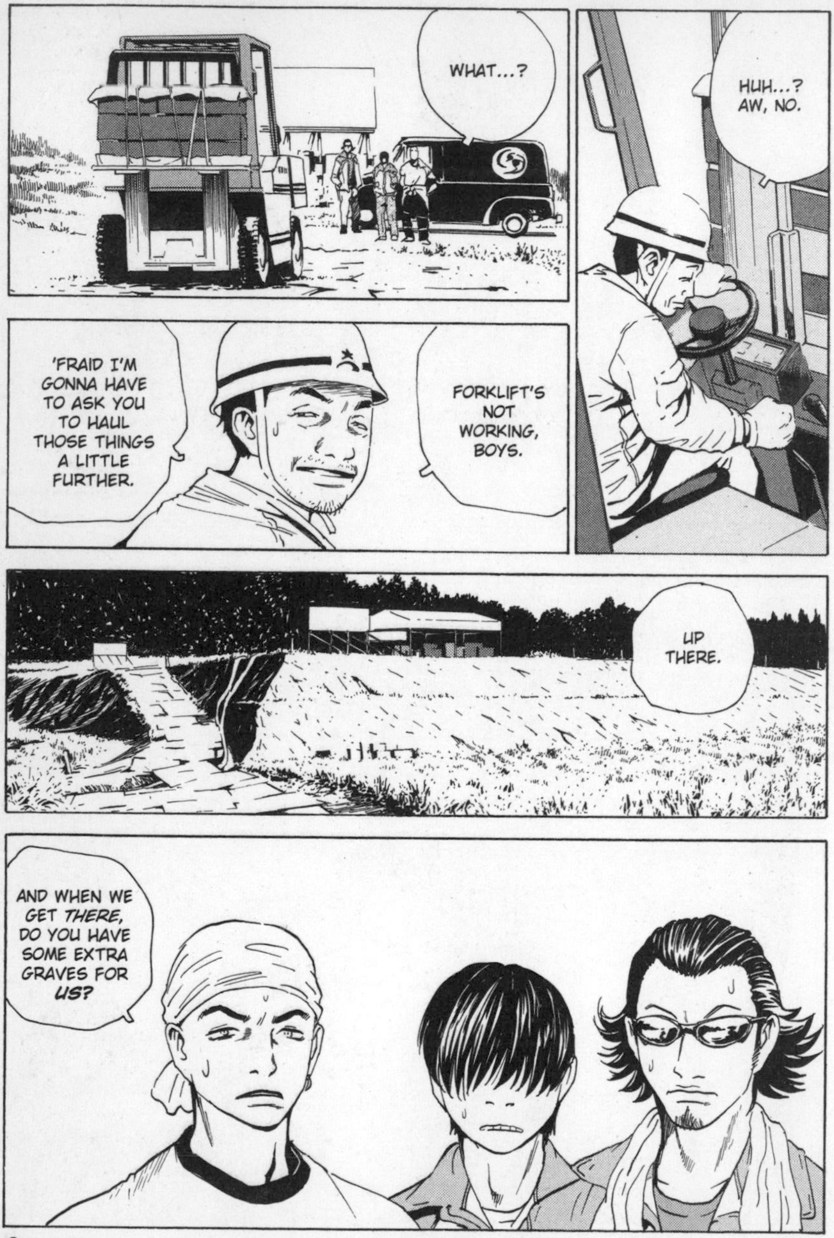
HUH...? AW, NO.
WHAT...?
FORKLIFT'S NOT WORKING, BOYS.
'FRAID I'M GONNA HAVE TO ASK YOU TO HAUL THOSE THINGS A LITTLE FURTHER.
UP THERE.
AND WHEN WE GET *THERE*, DO YOU HAVE SOME EXTRA GRAVES FOR *US*?

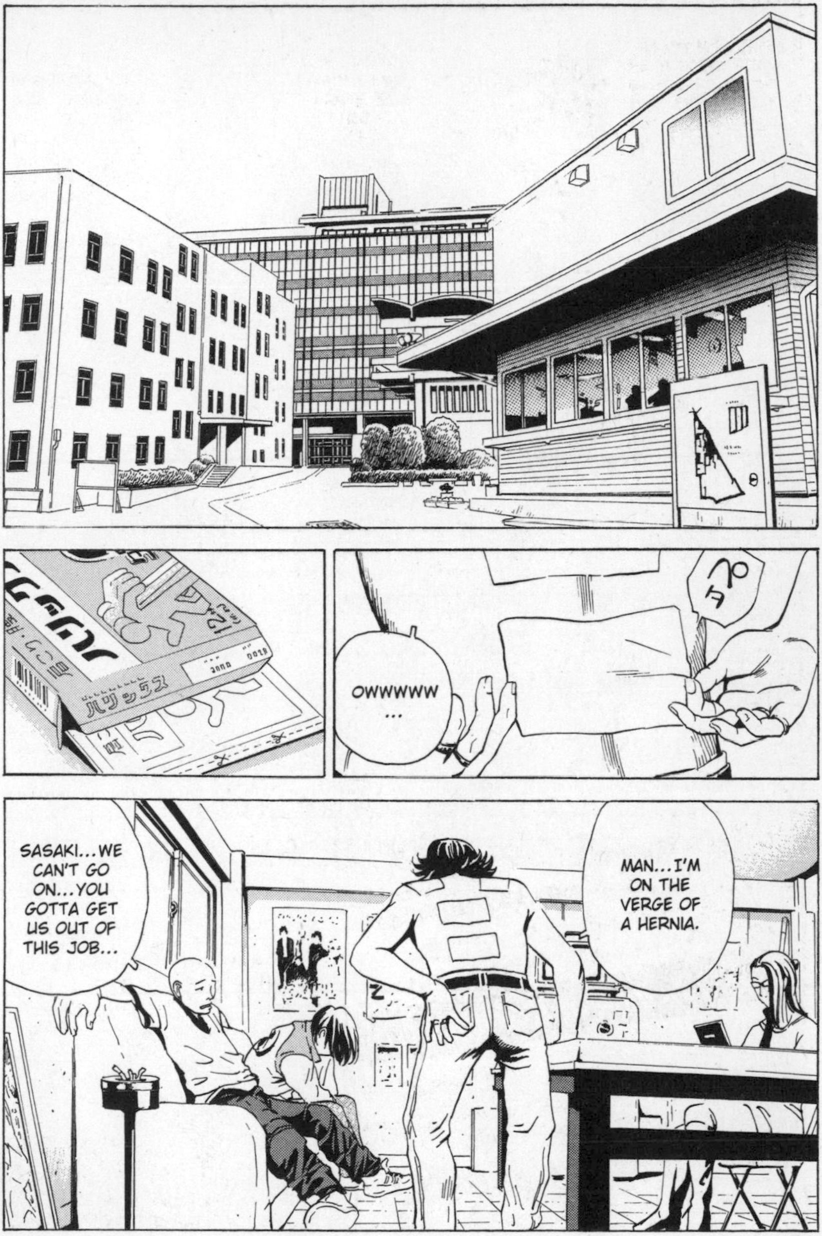
ペタ
OWWWWW ...
MAN...I'M ON THE VERGE OF A HERNIA.
SASAKI...WE CAN'T GO ON...YOU GOTTA GET US OUT OF THIS JOB...

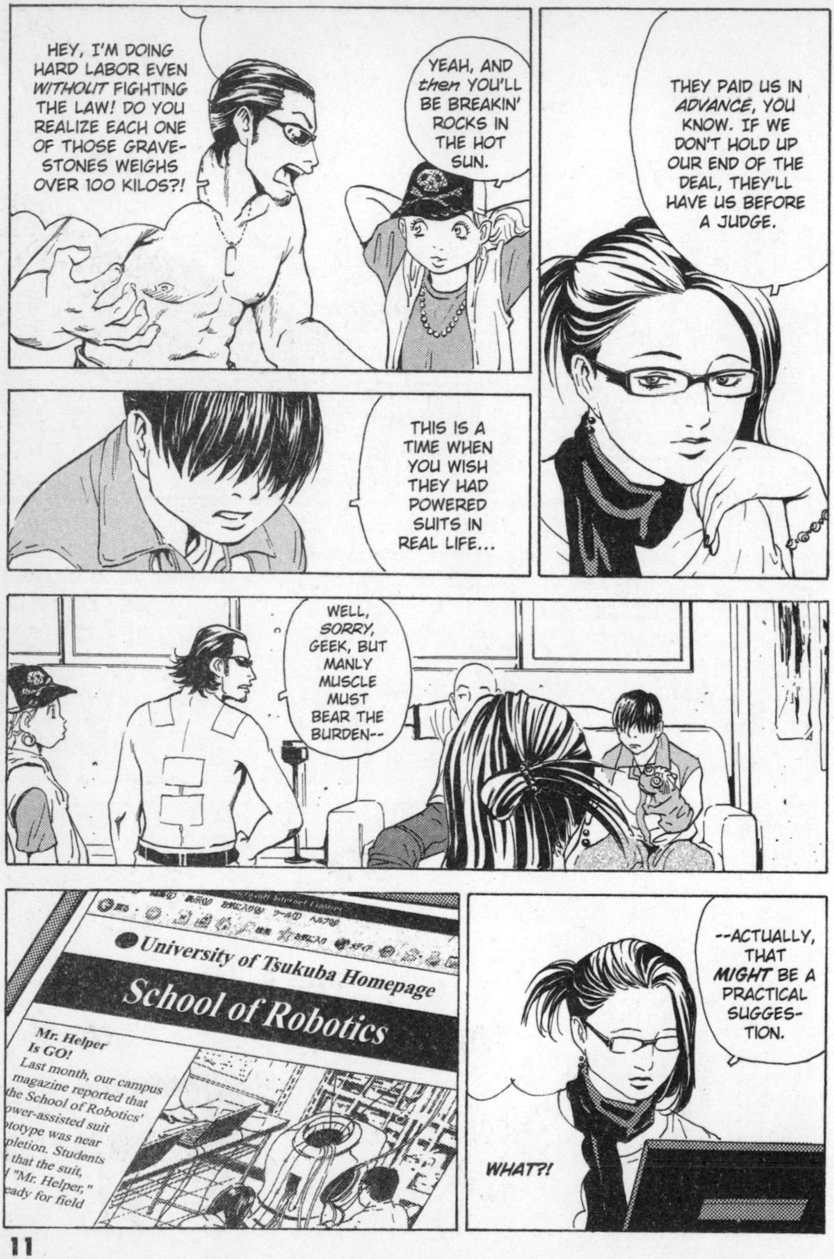
THEY PAID US IN *ADVANCE*, YOU KNOW. IF WE DON'T HOLD UP OUR END OF THE DEAL, THEY'LL HAVE US BEFORE A JUDGE.
YEAH, AND *then* YOU'LL BE BREAKIN' ROCKS IN THE HOT SUN.
HEY, I'M DOING HARD LABOR EVEN *WITHOUT* FIGHTING THE LAW! DO YOU REALIZE EACH ONE OF THOSE GRAVE-STONES WEIGHS OVER 100 KILOS?!
THIS IS A TIME WHEN YOU WISH THEY HAD POWERED SUITS IN REAL LIFE...
WELL, *SORRY*, GEEK, BUT MANLY MUSCLE MUST BEAR THE BURDEN--
--ACTUALLY, THAT *MIGHT* BE A PRACTICAL SUGGES-TION.
WHAT?!
University of Tsukuba Homepage
School of Robotics
Mr. Helper Is GO!
Last month, our campus magazine reported that the School of Robotics' ower-assisted suit ototype was near pletion. Students that the suit, "Mr. Helper," eady for field

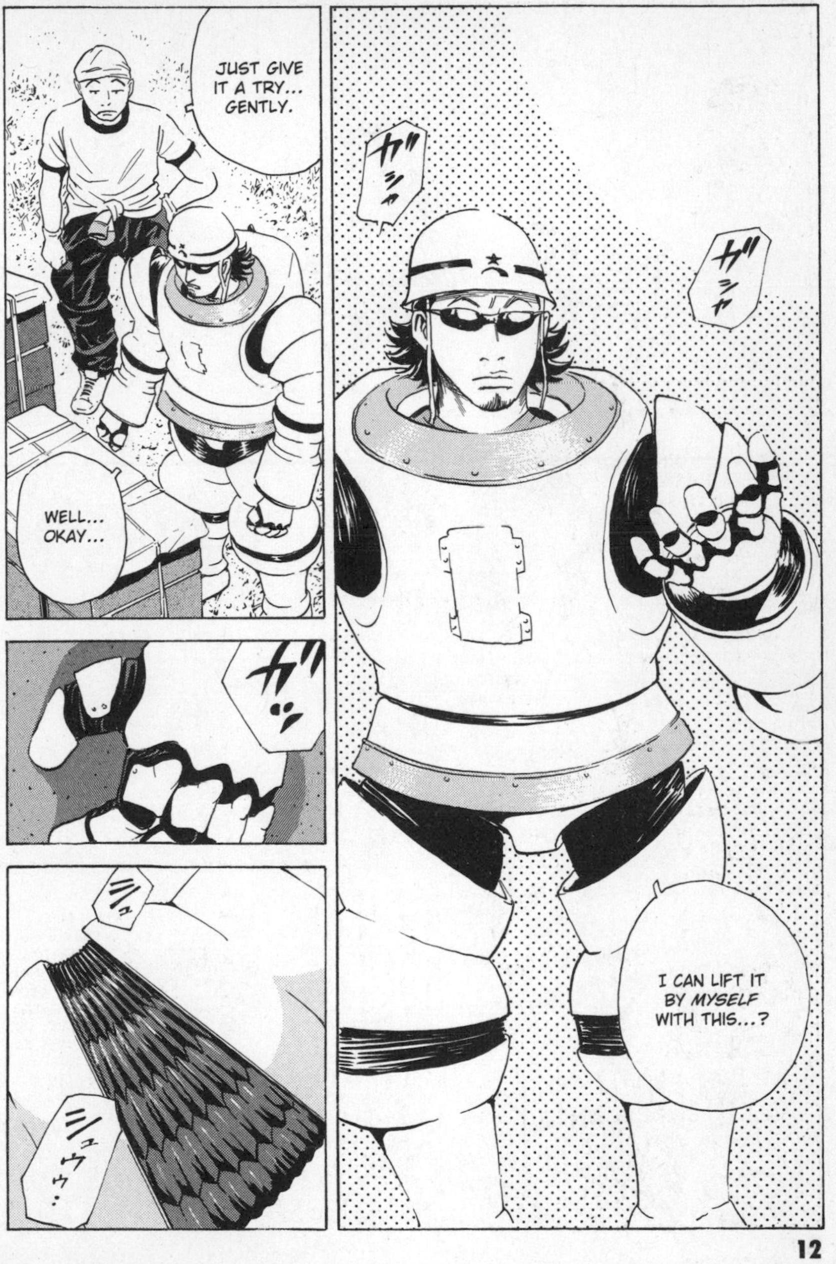
ガシャ
ガシャ
I CAN LIFT IT BY *MYSELF* WITH THIS...?
JUST GIVE IT A TRY... GENTLY.
WELL... OKAY...
ガッ
シュ
シュウウ…

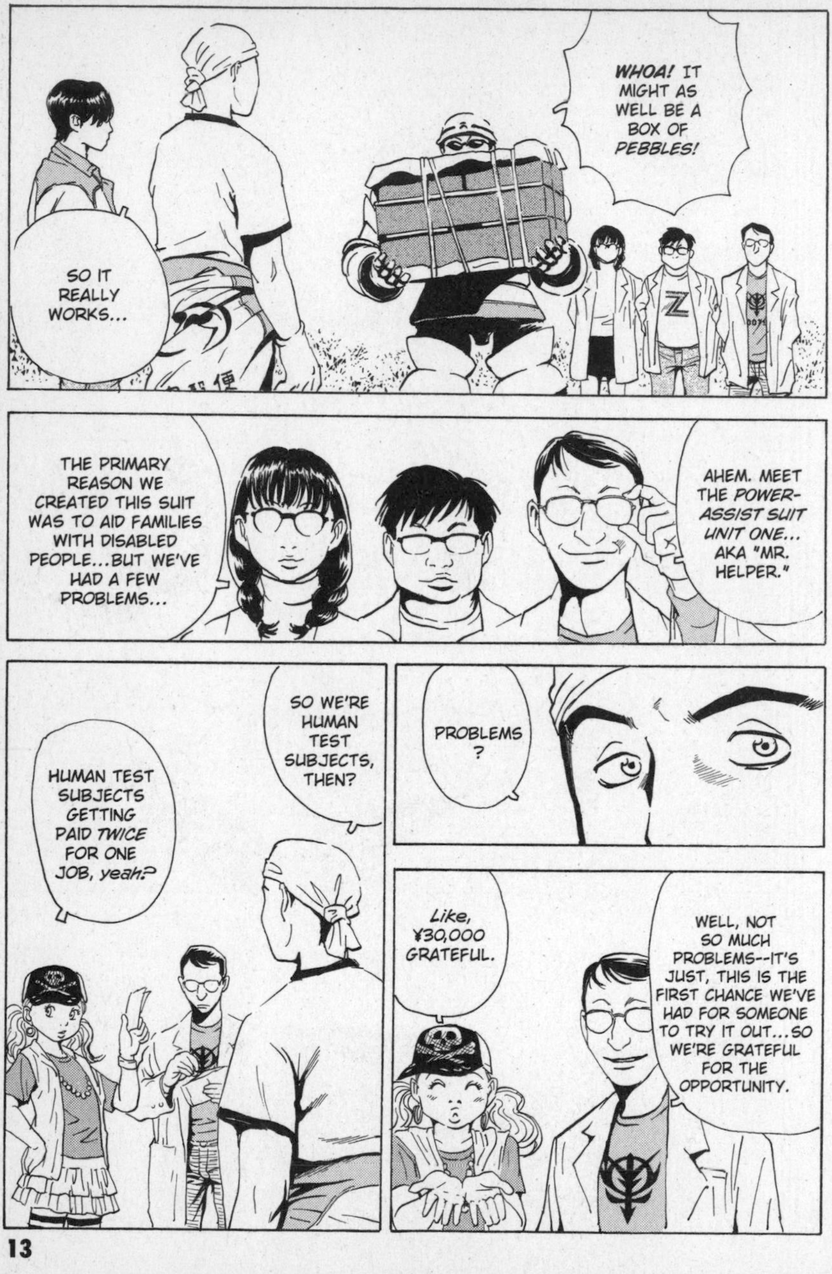
WHOA! IT MIGHT AS WELL BE A BOX OF PEBBLES!
SO IT REALLY WORKS...
AHEM. MEET THE POWER-ASSIST SUIT UNIT ONE... AKA "MR. HELPER."
THE PRIMARY REASON WE CREATED THIS SUIT WAS TO AID FAMILIES WITH DISABLED PEOPLE...BUT WE'VE HAD A FEW PROBLEMS...
PROBLEMS ?
WELL, NOT SO MUCH PROBLEMS--IT'S JUST, THIS IS THE FIRST CHANCE WE'VE HAD FOR SOMEONE TO TRY IT OUT...SO WE'RE GRATEFUL FOR THE OPPORTUNITY.
Like, ¥30,000 GRATEFUL.
SO WE'RE HUMAN TEST SUBJECTS, THEN?
HUMAN TEST SUBJECTS GETTING PAID TWICE FOR ONE JOB, yeah?

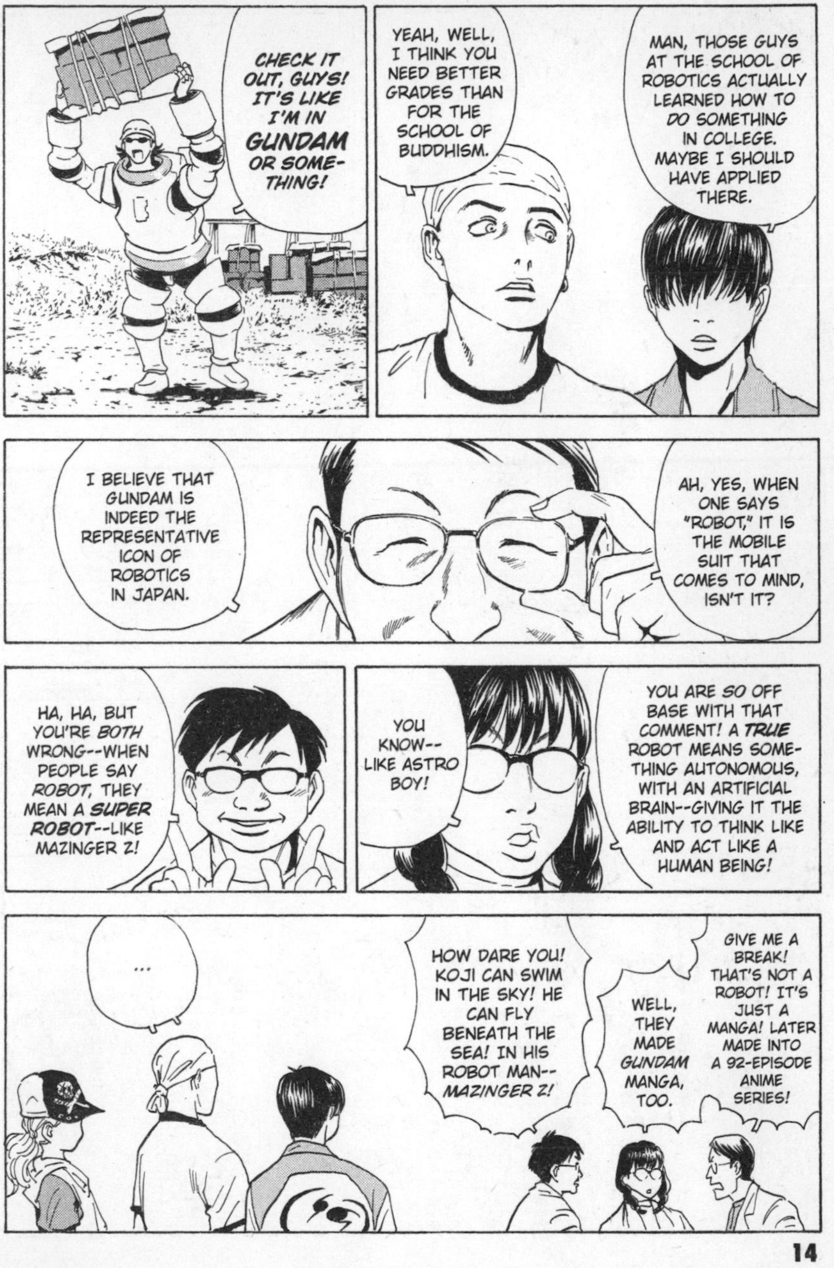
MAN, THOSE GUYS AT THE SCHOOL OF ROBOTICS ACTUALLY LEARNED HOW TO DO SOMETHING IN COLLEGE. MAYBE I SHOULD HAVE APPLIED THERE.
YEAH, WELL, I THINK YOU NEED BETTER GRADES THAN FOR THE SCHOOL OF BUDDHISM.
CHECK IT OUT, GUYS! IT'S LIKE I'M IN GUNDAM OR SOME-THING!
AH, YES, WHEN ONE SAYS "ROBOT," IT IS THE MOBILE SUIT THAT COMES TO MIND, ISN'T IT?
I BELIEVE THAT GUNDAM IS INDEED THE REPRESENTATIVE ICON OF ROBOTICS IN JAPAN.
YOU ARE SO OFF BASE WITH THAT COMMENT! A TRUE ROBOT MEANS SOME-THING AUTONOMOUS, WITH AN ARTIFICIAL BRAIN--GIVING IT THE ABILITY TO THINK LIKE AND ACT LIKE A HUMAN BEING!
YOU KNOW--LIKE ASTRO BOY!
HA, HA, BUT YOU'RE BOTH WRONG--WHEN PEOPLE SAY ROBOT, THEY MEAN A SUPER ROBOT--LIKE MAZINGER Z!
GIVE ME A BREAK! THAT'S NOT A ROBOT! IT'S JUST A MANGA! LATER MADE INTO A 92-EPISODE ANIME SERIES!
WELL, THEY MADE GUNDAM MANGA, TOO.
HOW DARE YOU! KOJI CAN SWIM IN THE SKY! HE CAN FLY BENEATH THE SEA! IN HIS ROBOT MAN--MAZINGER Z!
...

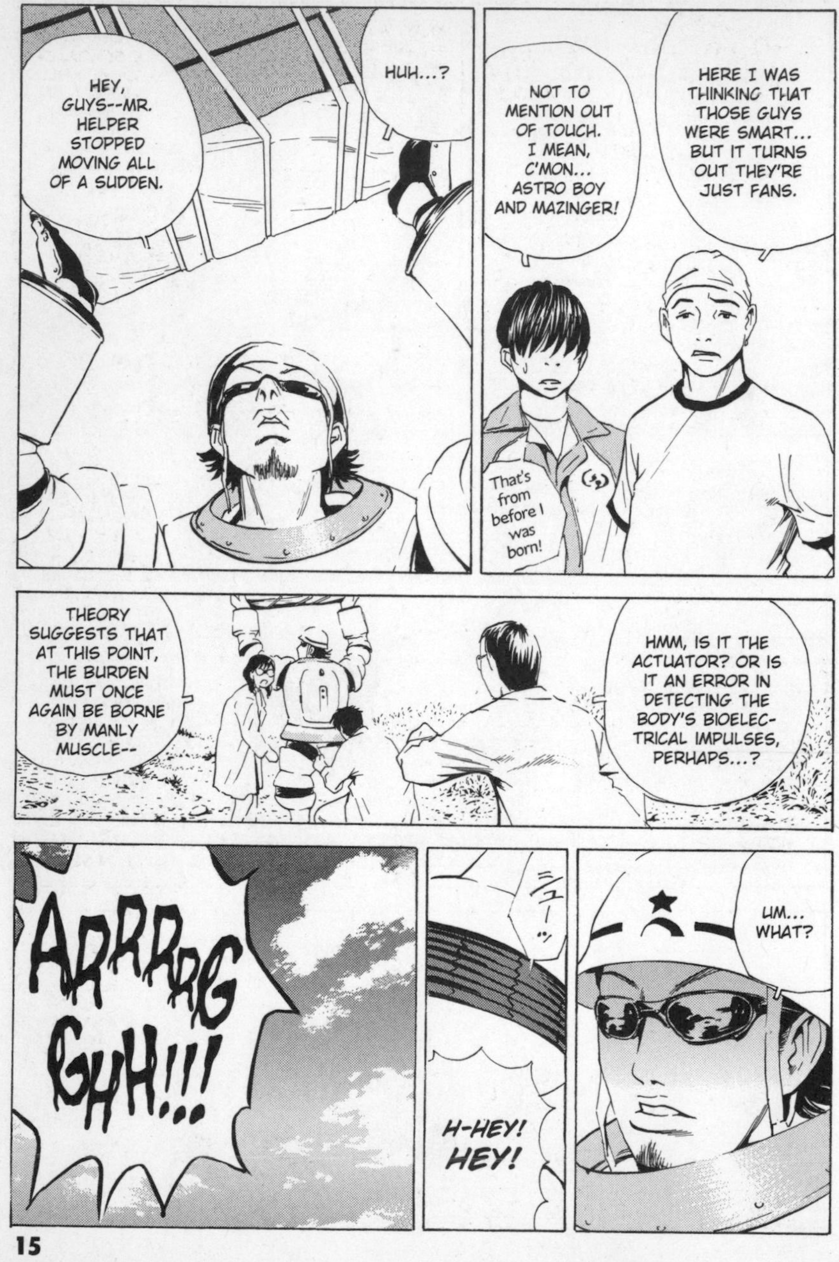
HERE I WAS THINKING THAT THOSE GUYS WERE SMART... BUT IT TURNS OUT THEY'RE JUST FANS.
NOT TO MENTION OUT OF TOUCH. I MEAN, C'MON... ASTRO BOY AND MAZINGER!
That's from before I was born!
HUH...?
HEY, GUYS--MR. HELPER STOPPED MOVING ALL OF A SUDDEN.
HMM, IS IT THE ACTUATOR? OR IS IT AN ERROR IN DETECTING THE BODY'S BIOELECTRICAL IMPULSES, PERHAPS...?
THEORY SUGGESTS THAT AT THIS POINT, THE BURDEN MUST ONCE AGAIN BE BORNE BY MANLY MUSCLE--
UM... WHAT?
ミューッ
H-HEY! HEY!
ARRRRG GHH!!!

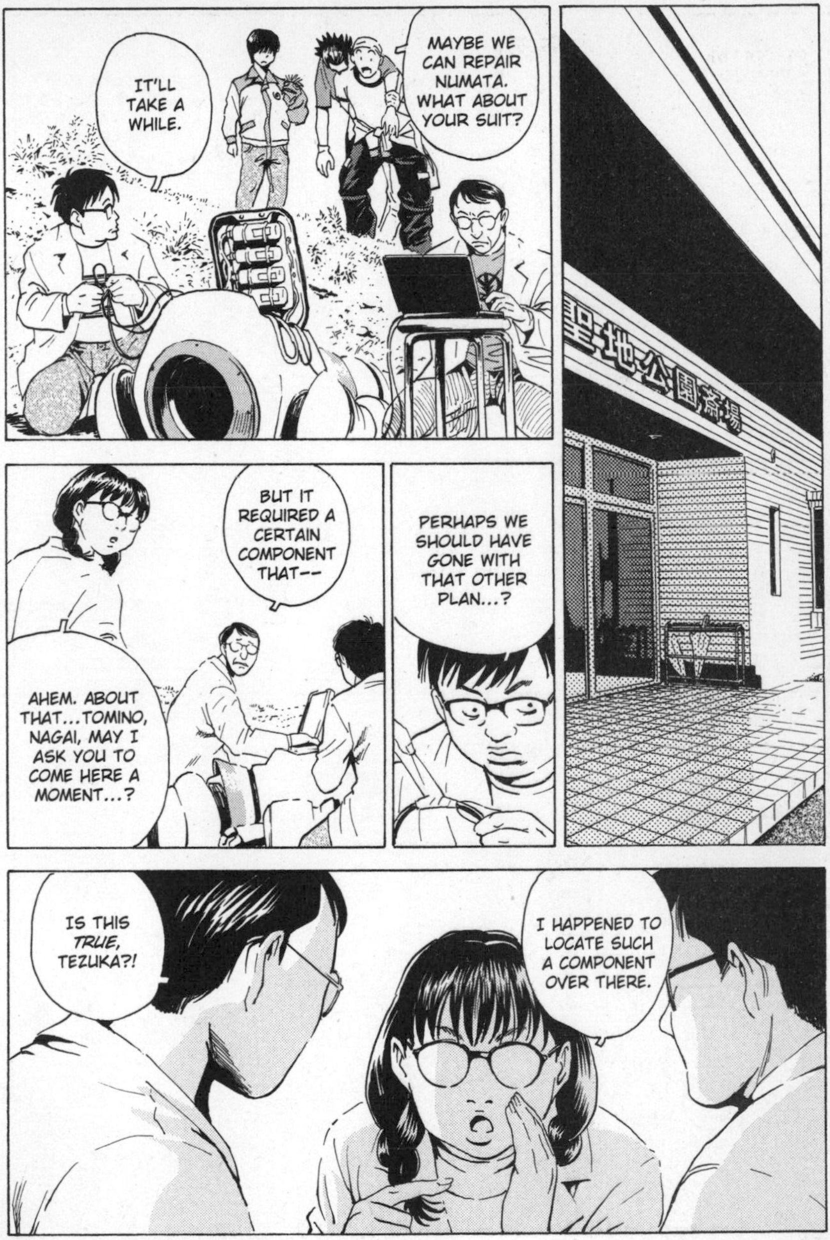
聖地公園斎場
MAYBE WE CAN REPAIR NUMATA. WHAT ABOUT YOUR SUIT?
IT'LL TAKE A WHILE.
PERHAPS WE SHOULD HAVE GONE WITH THAT OTHER PLAN...?
BUT IT REQUIRED A CERTAIN COMPONENT THAT--
AHEM. ABOUT THAT...TOMINO, NAGAI, MAY I ASK YOU TO COME HERE A MOMENT...?
I HAPPENED TO LOCATE SUCH A COMPONENT OVER THERE.
IS THIS *TRUE*, TEZUKA?!

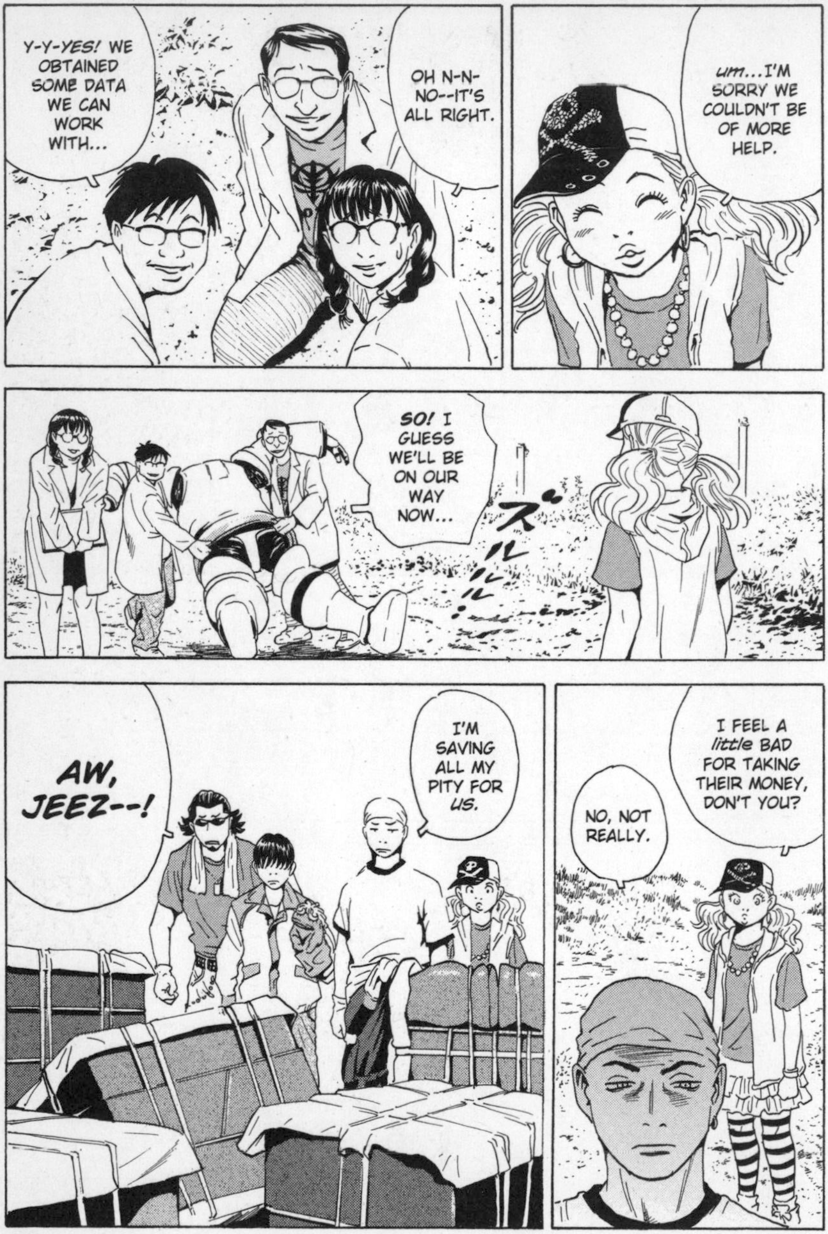
um...I'M SORRY WE COULDN'T BE OF MORE HELP.
OH N-N-NO--IT'S ALL RIGHT.
Y-Y-YES! WE OBTAINED SOME DATA WE CAN WORK WITH...
SO! I GUESS WE'LL BE ON OUR WAY NOW...
ズルルル!
I FEEL A little BAD FOR TAKING THEIR MONEY, DON'T YOU?
NO, NOT REALLY.
I'M SAVING ALL MY PITY FOR us.
AW, JEEZ--!

W-W-
WE'RE...
B-BACK?

ALL RIGHT.
WHAT'D YOU
DO WITH IT?

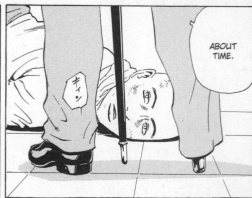

ABOUT
TIME.

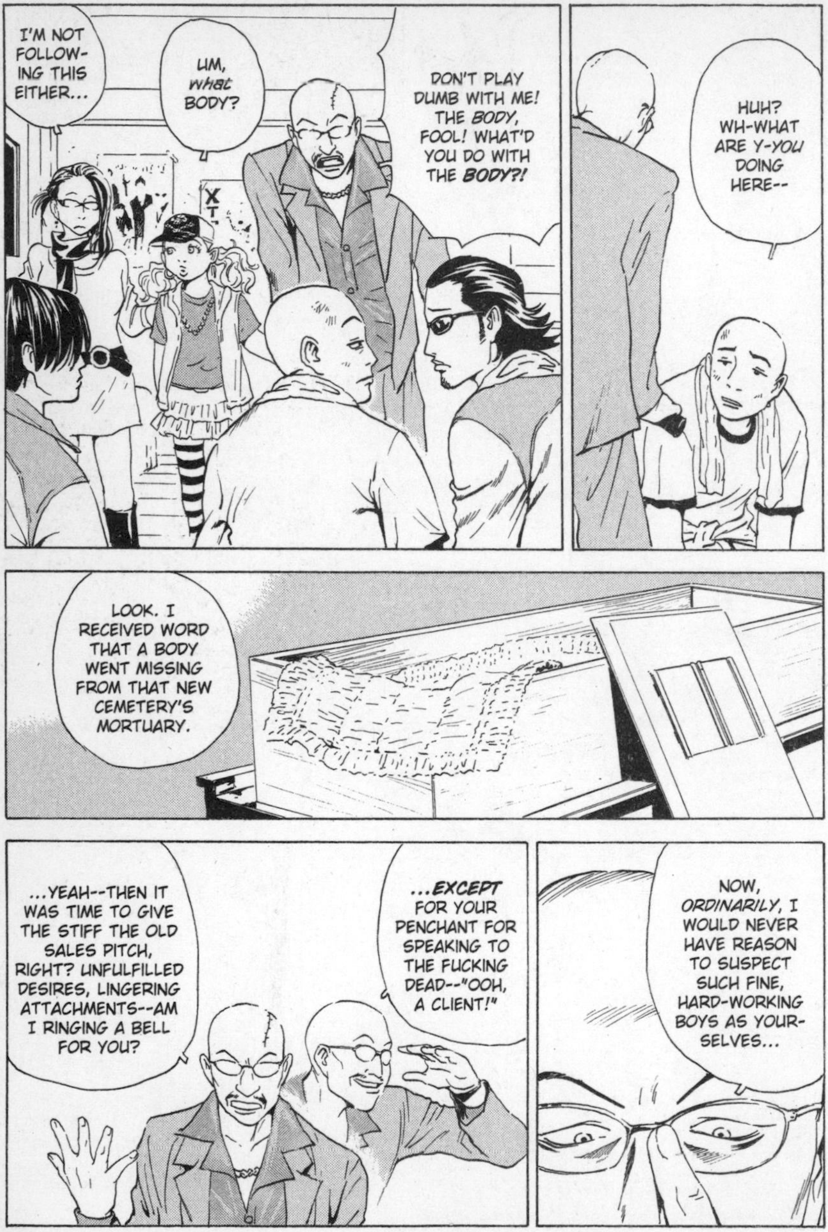
HUH? WH-WHAT ARE Y-YOU DOING HERE--
DON'T PLAY DUMB WITH ME! THE BODY, FOOL! WHAT'D YOU DO WITH THE BODY?!
UM, what BODY?
I'M NOT FOLLOWING THIS EITHER...
LOOK. I RECEIVED WORD THAT A BODY WENT MISSING FROM THAT NEW CEMETERY'S MORTUARY.
NOW, ORDINARILY, I WOULD NEVER HAVE REASON TO SUSPECT SUCH FINE, HARD-WORKING BOYS AS YOURSELVES...
...EXCEPT FOR YOUR PENCHANT FOR SPEAKING TO THE FUCKING DEAD--"OOH, A CLIENT!"
...YEAH--THEN IT WAS TIME TO GIVE THE STIFF THE OLD SALES PITCH, RIGHT? UNFULFILLED DESIRES, LINGERING ATTACHMENTS--AM I RINGING A BELL FOR YOU?

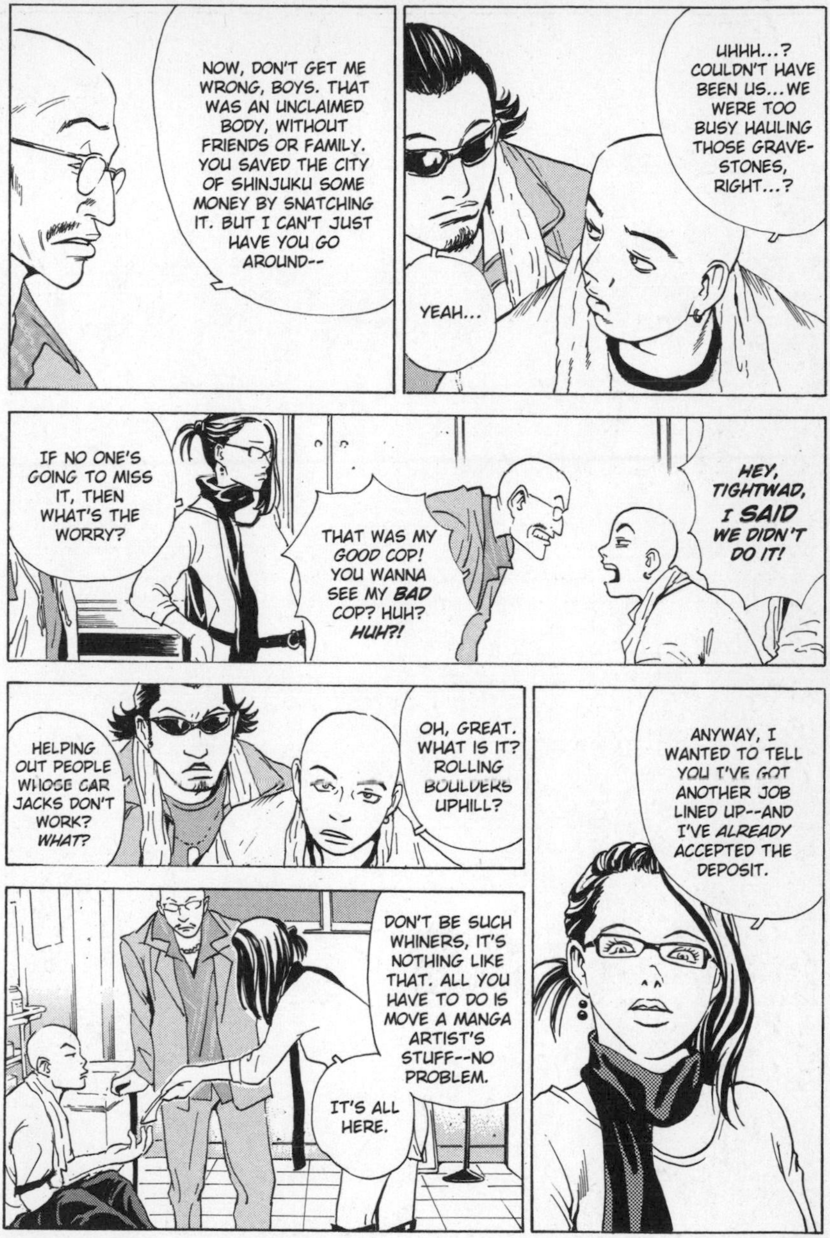
UHHH...? COULDN'T HAVE BEEN US...WE WERE TOO BUSY HAULING THOSE GRAVE-STONES, RIGHT...?
YEAH...
NOW, DON'T GET ME WRONG, BOYS. THAT WAS AN UNCLAIMED BODY, WITHOUT FRIENDS OR FAMILY. YOU SAVED THE CITY OF SHINJUKU SOME MONEY BY SNATCHING IT. BUT I CAN'T JUST HAVE YOU GO AROUND--
HEY, TIGHTWAD, I *SAID* WE DIDN'T DO IT!
THAT WAS MY *GOOD COP!* YOU WANNA SEE MY *BAD* COP? HUH? *HUH?!*
IF NO ONE'S GOING TO MISS IT, THEN WHAT'S THE WORRY?
ANYWAY, I WANTED TO TELL YOU I'VE GOT ANOTHER JOB LINED UP--AND I'VE *ALREADY* ACCEPTED THE DEPOSIT.
OH, GREAT. WHAT IS IT? ROLLING BOULDERS UPHILL?
HELPING OUT PEOPLE WHOSE CAR JACKS DON'T WORK? *WHAT?*
DON'T BE SUCH WHINERS, IT'S NOTHING LIKE THAT. ALL YOU HAVE TO DO IS MOVE A MANGA ARTIST'S STUFF--NO PROBLEM.
IT'S ALL HERE.

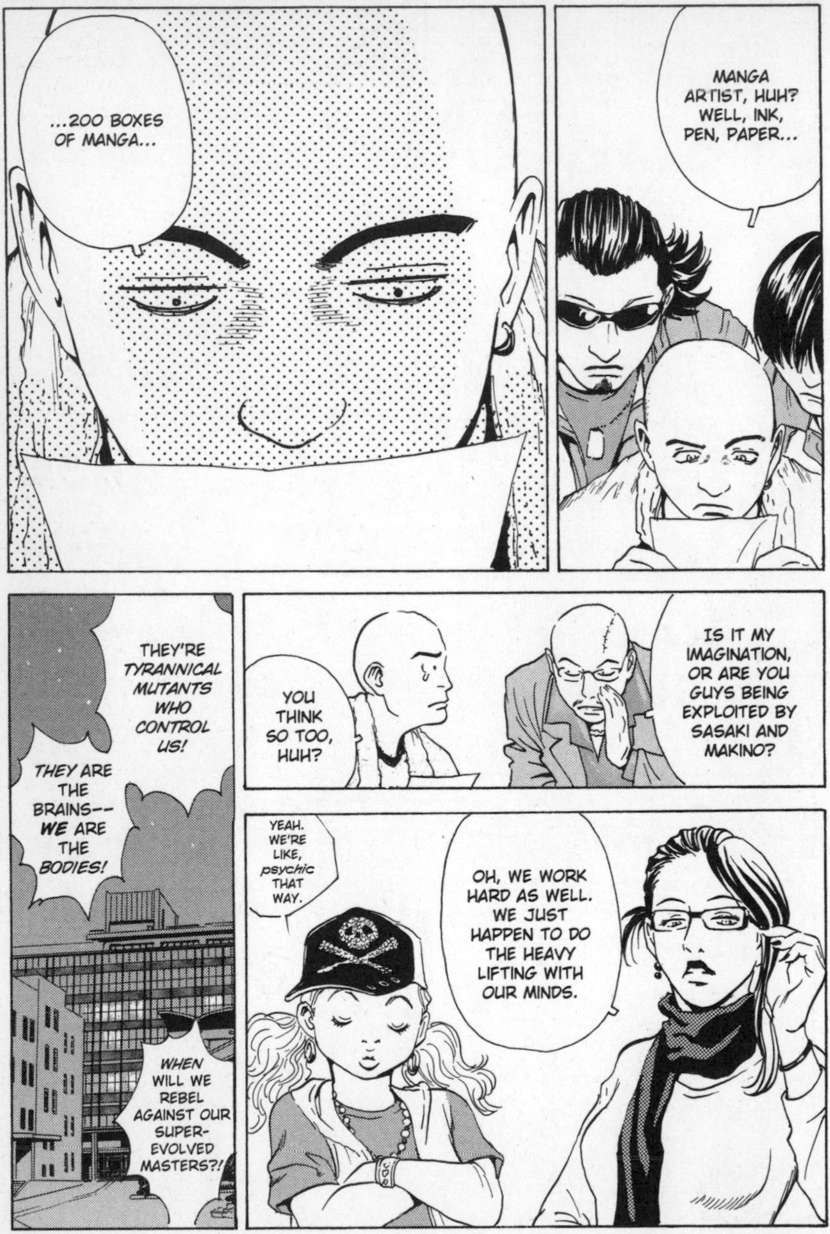
MANGA ARTIST, HUH? WELL, INK, PEN, PAPER...
...200 BOXES OF MANGA...
IS IT MY IMAGINATION, OR ARE YOU GUYS BEING EXPLOITED BY SASAKI AND MAKINO?
YOU THINK SO TOO, HUH?
OH, WE WORK HARD AS WELL. WE JUST HAPPEN TO DO THE HEAVY LIFTING WITH OUR MINDS.
YEAH. WE'RE LIKE, *psychic* THAT WAY.
THEY'RE *TYRANNICAL MUTANTS* WHO CONTROL *US!*
THEY ARE THE BRAINS-- *WE* ARE THE *BODIES!*
WHEN WILL WE REBEL AGAINST OUR SUPER-EVOLVED MASTERS?!

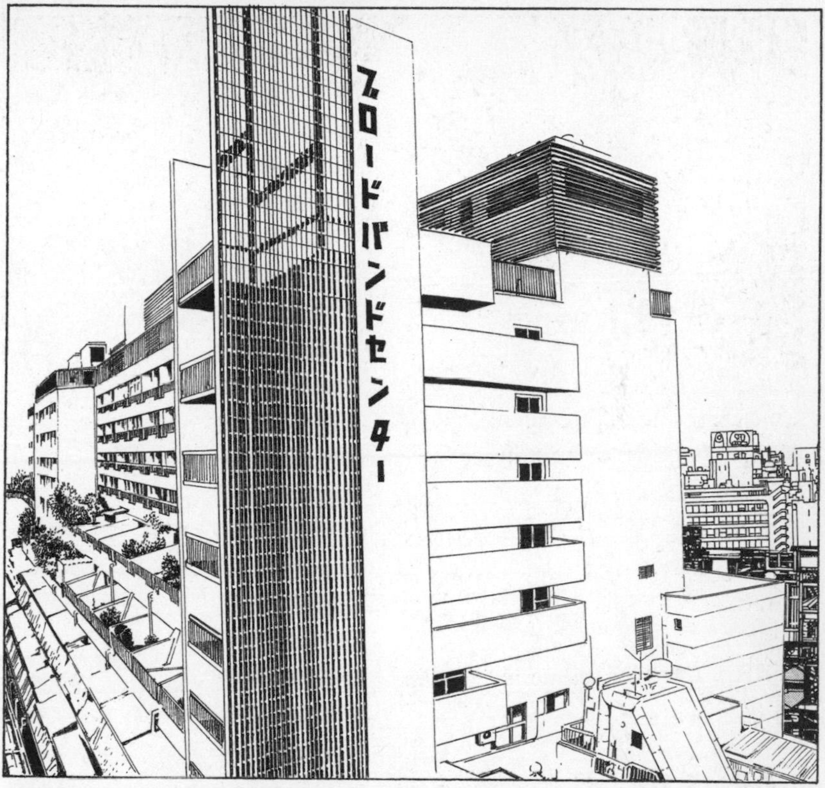
ブロードバンドセンター

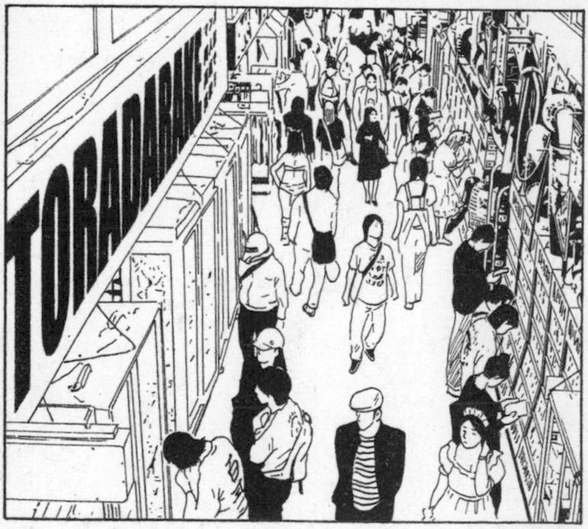
TORADARAKE

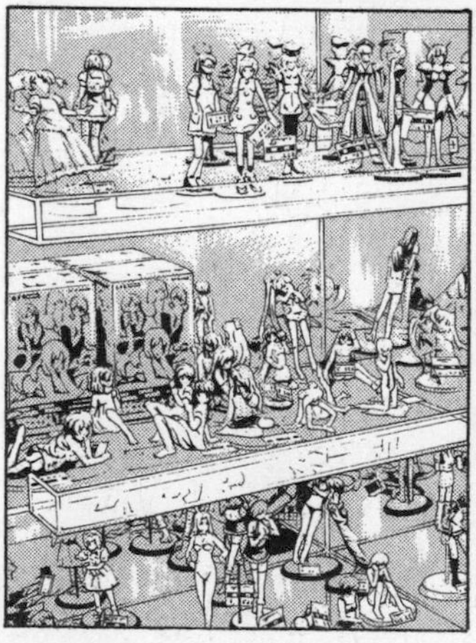

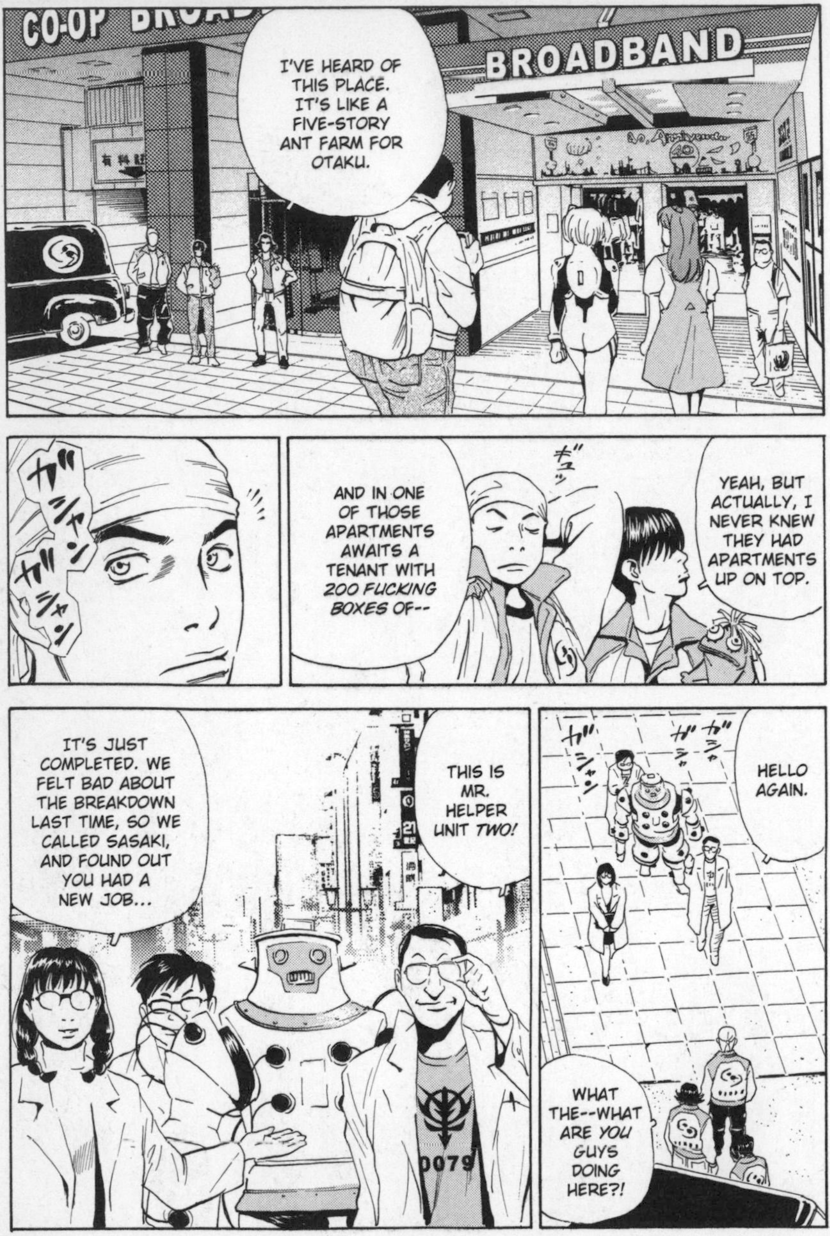
CO-OP BROAD
BROADBAND
I'VE HEARD OF THIS PLACE. IT'S LIKE A FIVE-STORY ANT FARM FOR OTAKU.
YEAH, BUT ACTUALLY, I NEVER KNEW THEY HAD APARTMENTS UP ON TOP.
ギュッ
AND IN ONE OF THOSE APARTMENTS AWAITS A TENANT WITH *200 FUCKING BOXES OF--*
ガシャン ガシャン
HELLO AGAIN.
ガシャ ガシャン
WHAT THE--WHAT ARE *YOU* GUYS DOING HERE?!
THIS IS MR. HELPER UNIT *TWO!*
IT'S JUST COMPLETED. WE FELT BAD ABOUT THE BREAKDOWN LAST TIME, SO WE CALLED SASAKI, AND FOUND OUT YOU HAD A NEW JOB...

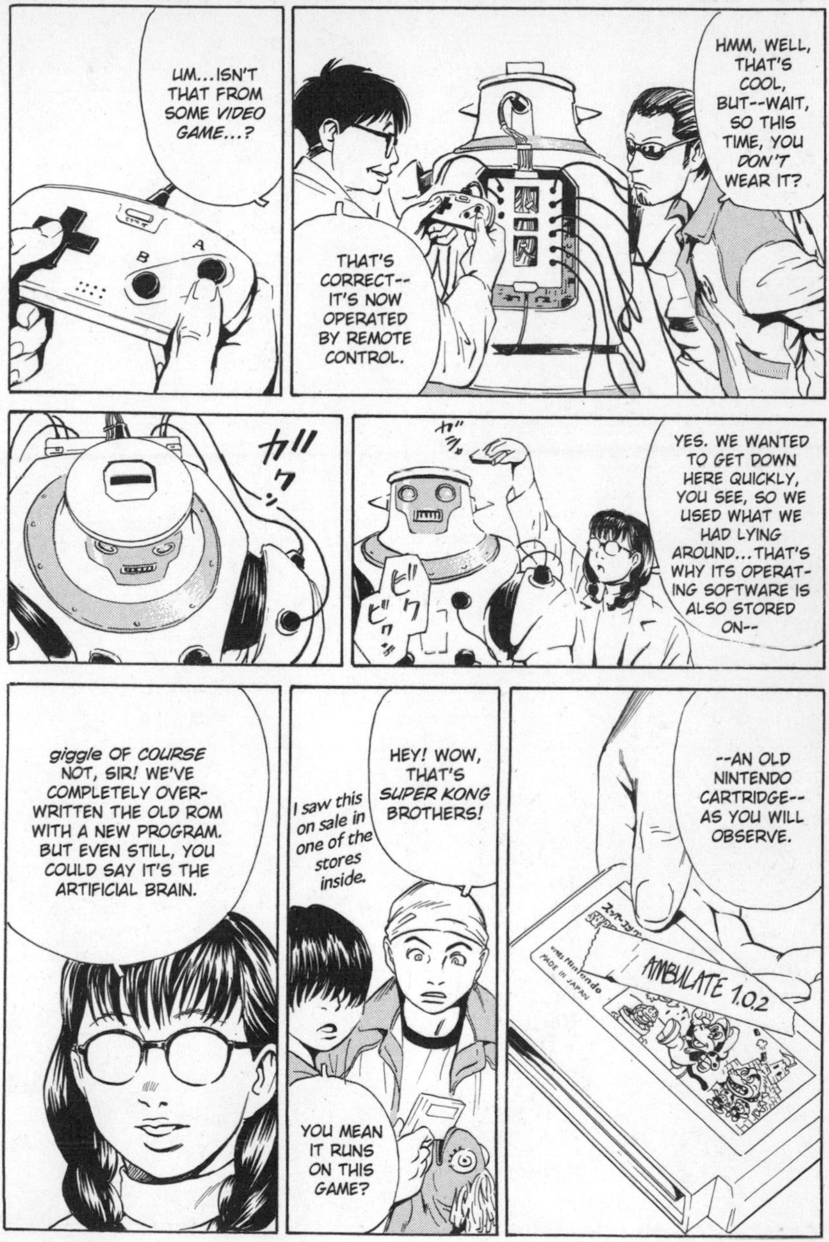
HMM, WELL, THAT'S COOL, BUT--WAIT, SO THIS TIME, YOU *DON'T* WEAR IT?
THAT'S CORRECT--IT'S NOW OPERATED BY REMOTE CONTROL.
UM...ISN'T THAT FROM SOME *VIDEO GAME...?*
B
A
YES. WE WANTED TO GET DOWN HERE QUICKLY, YOU SEE, SO WE USED WHAT WE HAD LYING AROUND...THAT'S WHY ITS OPERATING SOFTWARE IS ALSO STORED ON--
--AN OLD NINTENDO CARTRIDGE--AS YOU WILL OBSERVE.
AMBULATE 1.0.2
Nintendo
MADE IN JAPAN
HEY! WOW, THAT'S *SUPER KONG BROTHERS!*
I saw this on sale in one of the stores inside.
YOU MEAN IT RUNS ON THIS GAME?
giggle OF *COURSE* NOT, SIR! WE'VE COMPLETELY OVERWRITTEN THE OLD ROM WITH A NEW PROGRAM. BUT EVEN STILL, YOU COULD SAY IT'S THE ARTIFICIAL BRAIN.

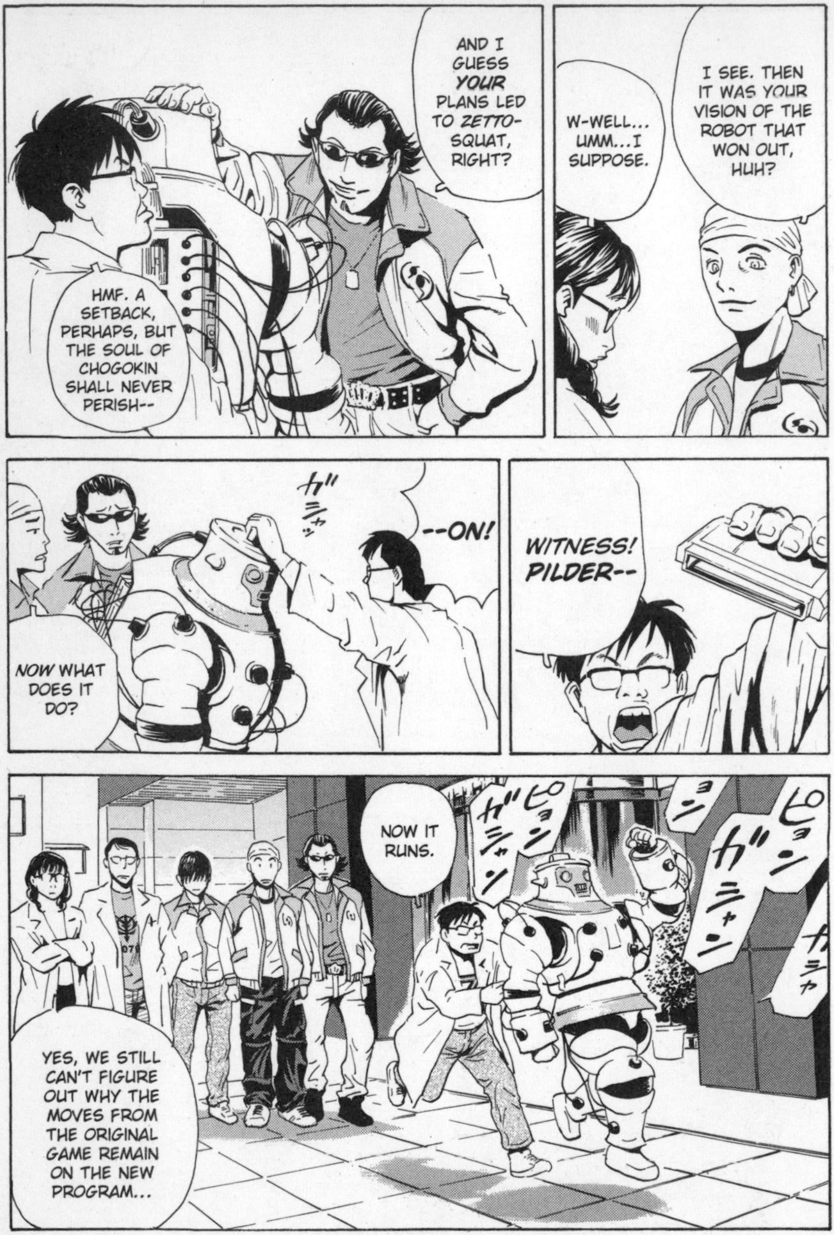
I SEE. THEN IT WAS YOUR VISION OF THE ROBOT THAT WON OUT, HUH?
W-WELL... UMM...I SUPPOSE.
AND I GUESS *YOUR* PLANS LED TO *ZETTO*-SQUAT, RIGHT?
HMF. A SETBACK, PERHAPS, BUT THE SOUL OF CHOGOKIN SHALL NEVER PERISH--
WITNESS! PILDER--
ガシャッ
--ON!
NOW WHAT DOES IT DO?
ピョン
ガシャン
ピョン
ガシャン
カシャ
NOW IT RUNS.
YES, WE STILL CAN'T FIGURE OUT WHY THE MOVES FROM THE ORIGINAL GAME REMAIN ON THE NEW PROGRAM...

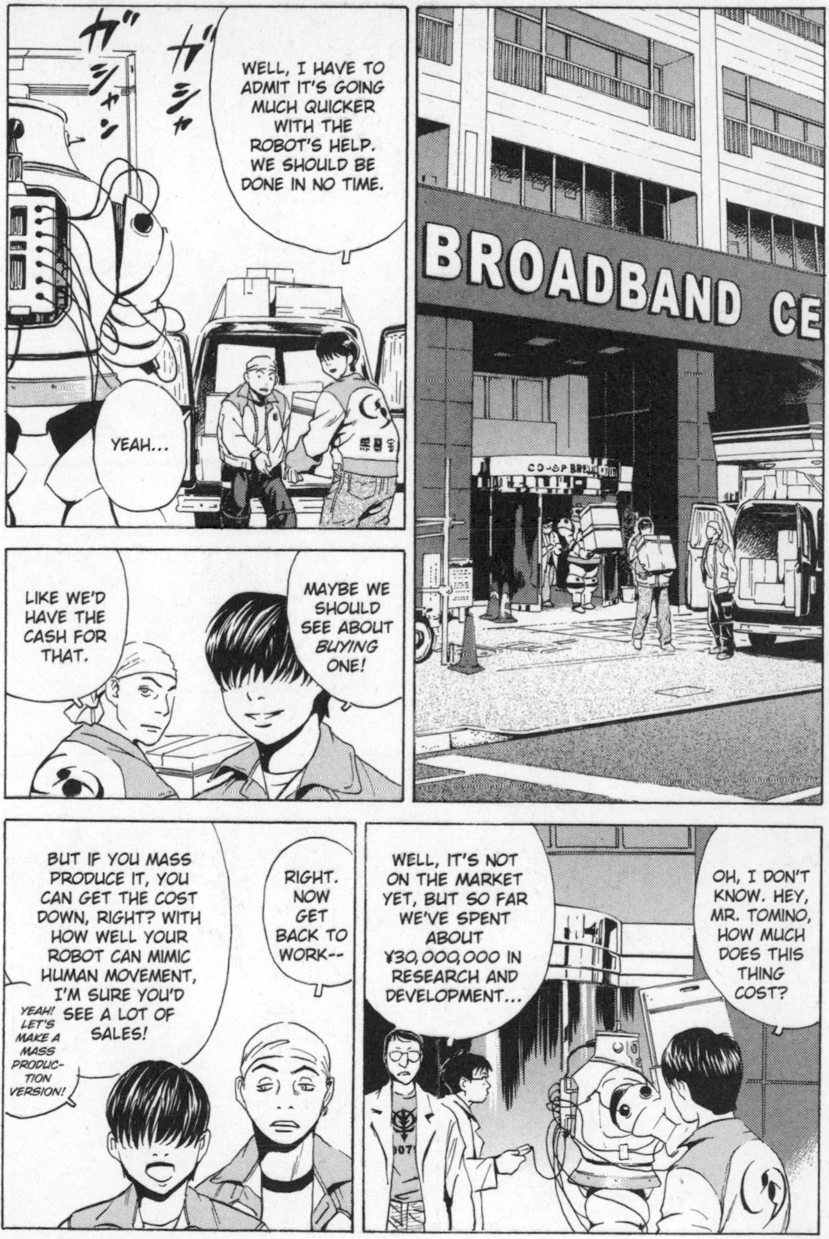
BROADBAND CE
ガシャ
ガシャン
WELL, I HAVE TO ADMIT IT'S GOING MUCH QUICKER WITH THE ROBOT'S HELP. WE SHOULD BE DONE IN NO TIME.
YEAH...
MAYBE WE SHOULD SEE ABOUT *BUYING* ONE!
LIKE WE'D HAVE THE CASH FOR THAT.
OH, I DON'T KNOW. HEY, MR. TOMINO, HOW MUCH DOES THIS THING COST?
WELL, IT'S NOT ON THE MARKET YET, BUT SO FAR WE'VE SPENT ABOUT ¥30,000,000 IN RESEARCH AND DEVELOPMENT...
RIGHT. NOW GET BACK TO WORK--
BUT IF YOU MASS PRODUCE IT, YOU CAN GET THE COST DOWN, RIGHT? WITH HOW WELL YOUR ROBOT CAN MIMIC HUMAN MOVEMENT, I'M SURE YOU'D SEE A LOT OF SALES!
YEAH! LET'S MAKE A MASS PRODUCTION VERSION!

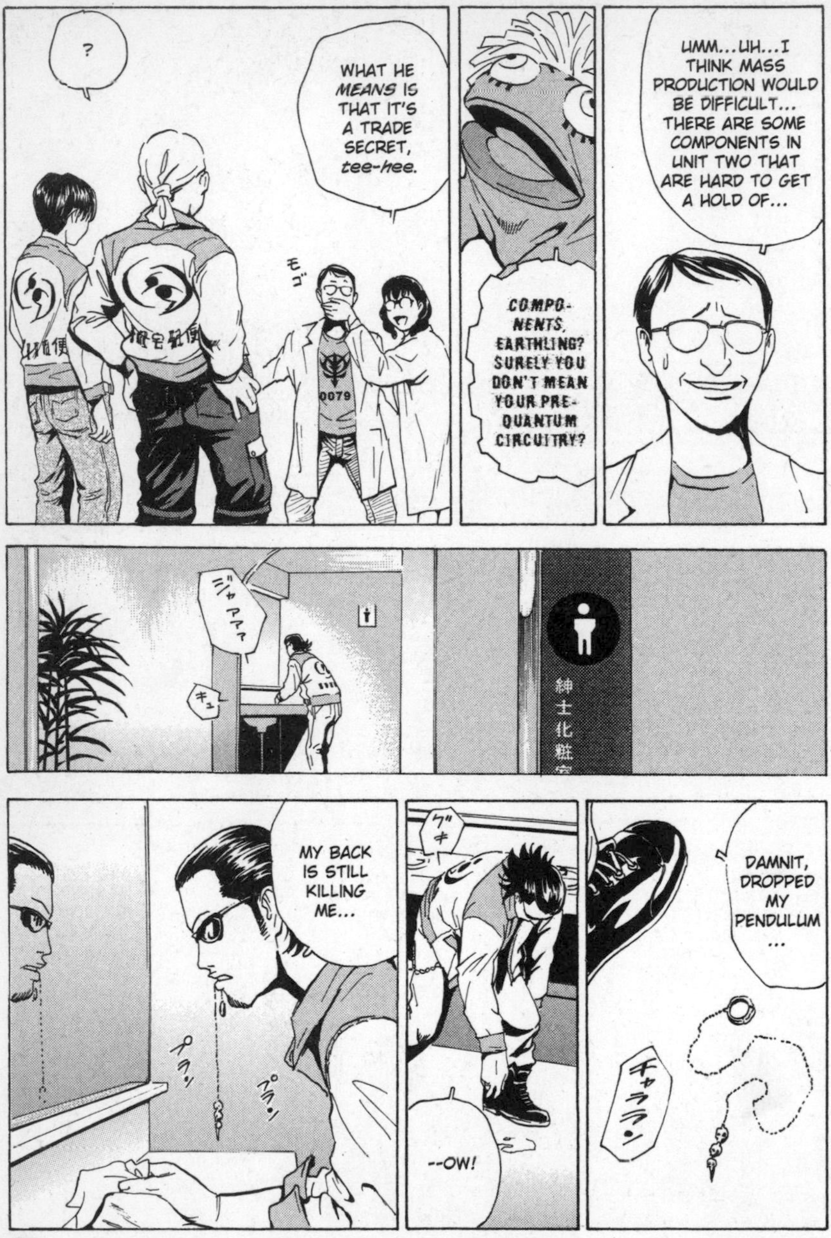
UMM...UH...I THINK MASS PRODUCTION WOULD BE DIFFICULT... THERE ARE SOME COMPONENTS IN UNIT TWO THAT ARE HARD TO GET A HOLD OF...
COMPONENTS, EARTHLING? SURELY YOU DON'T MEAN YOUR PRE-QUANTUM CIRCUITRY?
WHAT HE MEANS IS THAT IT'S A TRADE SECRET, tee-hee.
?
モゴ
0079
ジャアアア
キュ
DAMNIT, DROPPED MY PENDULUM ...
チャラララン
グキ
--OW!
MY BACK IS STILL KILLING ME...
プラン
プラン

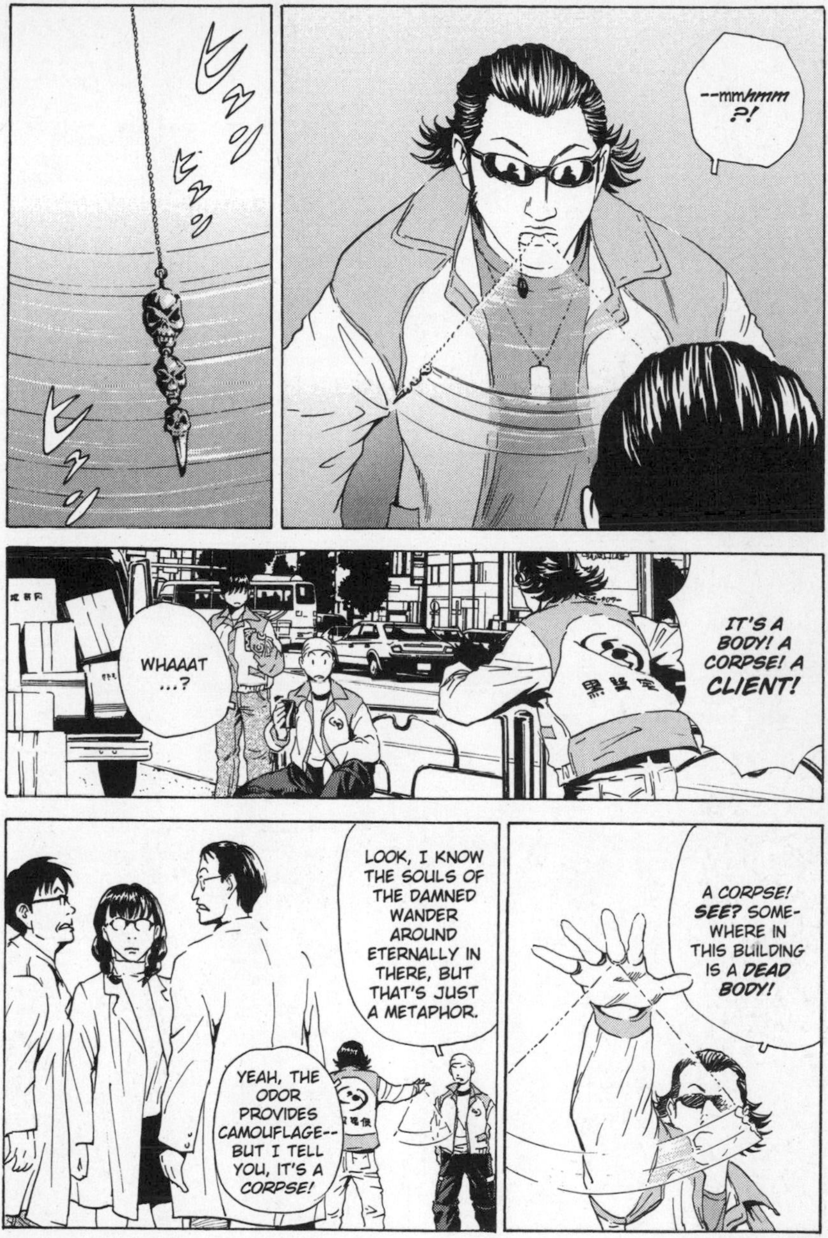
--mmhmm ?!
IT'S A BODY! A CORPSE! A CLIENT!
WHAAAT ...?
A CORPSE! SEE? SOMEWHERE IN THIS BUILDING IS A DEAD BODY!
LOOK, I KNOW THE SOULS OF THE DAMNED WANDER AROUND ETERNALLY IN THERE, BUT THAT'S JUST A METAPHOR.
YEAH, THE ODOR PROVIDES CAMOUFLAGE-- BUT I TELL YOU, IT'S A CORPSE!

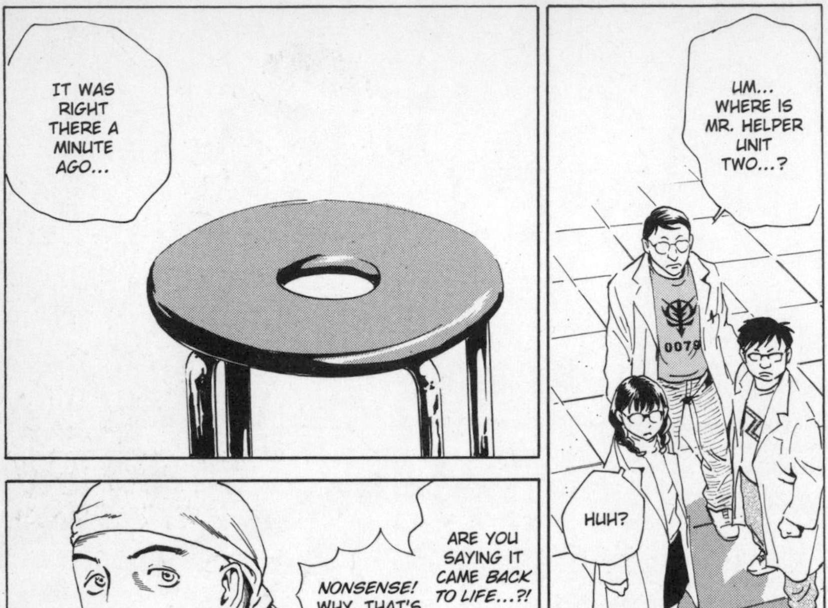

UM... WHERE IS MR. HELPER UNIT TWO...?
HUH?
IT WAS RIGHT THERE A MINUTE AGO...
ARE YOU SAYING IT CAME BACK TO LIFE...?!
NONSENSE! WHY, THAT'S SCIENTIFICALLY IMPOSSIBLE!
HEY, SOMETHING WRONG?
WELL... ER...
"...THE ROBOT STARTED TO MOVE ON ITS OWN?!"
OHHHHKAY ...WE'LL SPLIT UP AND LOOK FOR IT.
NUMATA, YOU TRY AND FIND THAT CORPSE.
ブロードバンドセンター
YOU GOT IT!

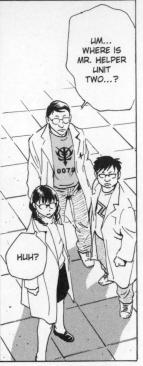

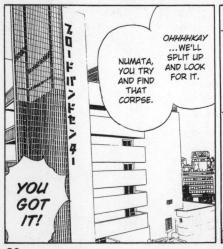

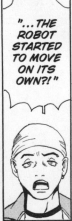

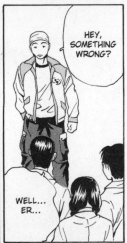

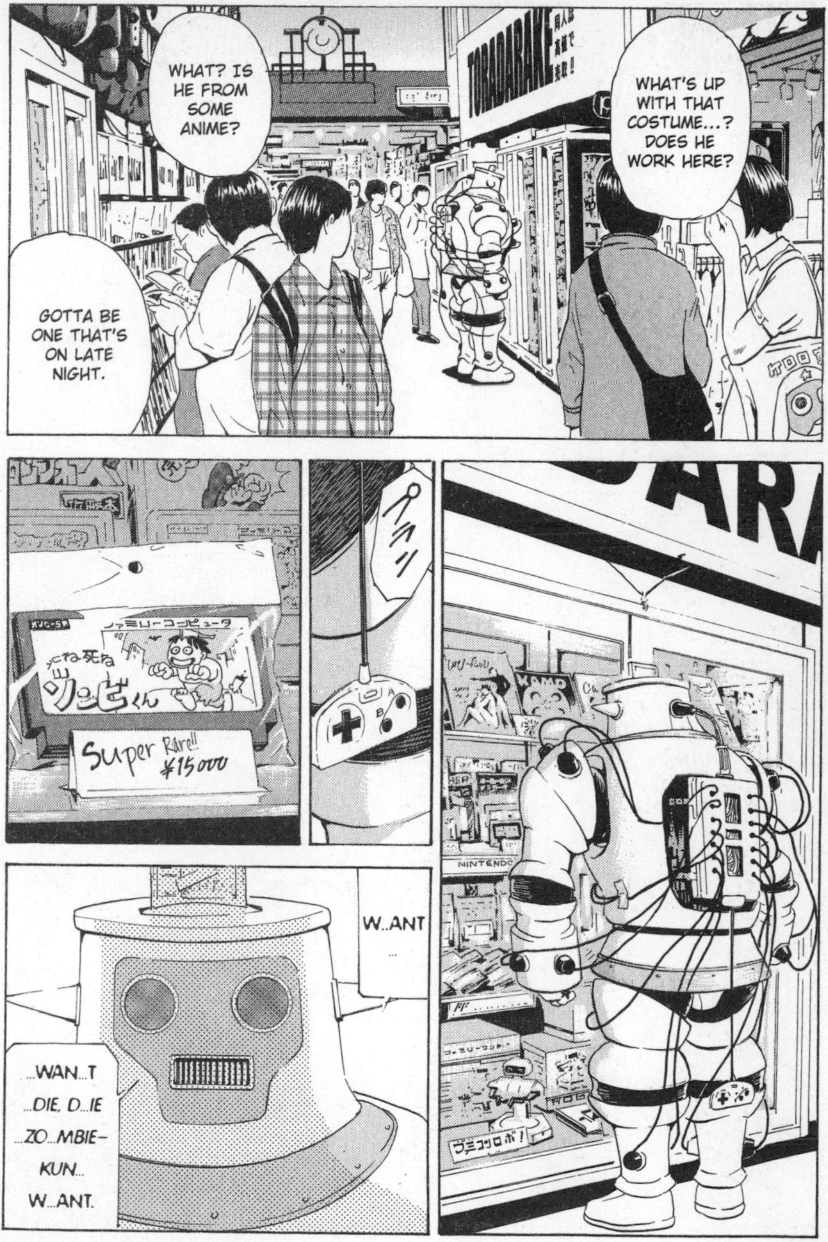
TORADARAKE
WHAT'S UP WITH THAT COSTUME...? DOES HE WORK HERE?
WHAT? IS HE FROM SOME ANIME?
GOTTA BE ONE THAT'S ON LATE NIGHT.
NINTENDO
ファミリーコンピュータ
死ね死ね ゾンビくん
Super Rare!! ¥15000
W..ANT ...
...WAN...T ...DIE, D...IE ...ZO...MBIE-KUN... W...ANT.

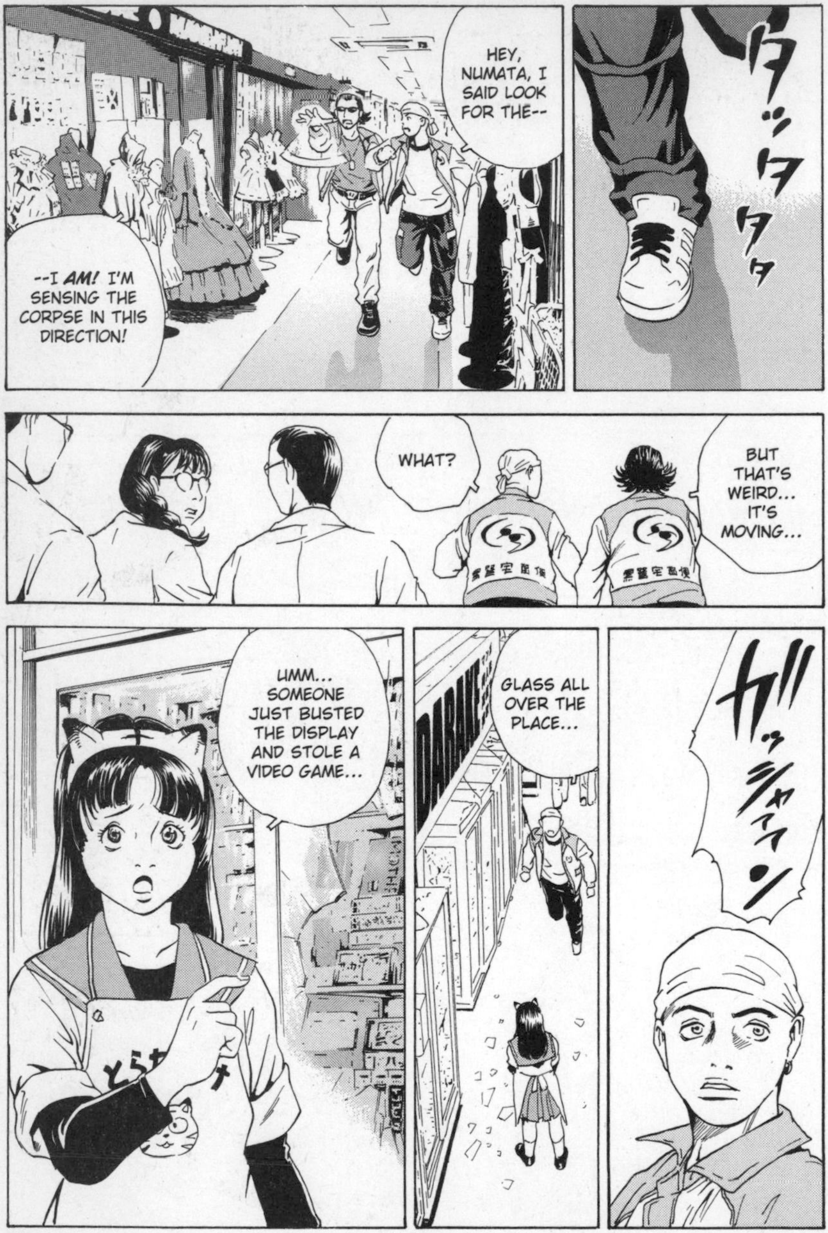
ダッタタタ
HEY, NUMATA, I SAID LOOK FOR THE--
--I *AM!* I'M SENSING THE CORPSE IN THIS DIRECTION!
BUT THAT'S WEIRD... IT'S MOVING...
WHAT?
ガッシャアアン
GLASS ALL OVER THE PLACE...
UMM... SOMEONE JUST BUSTED THE DISPLAY AND STOLE A VIDEO GAME...

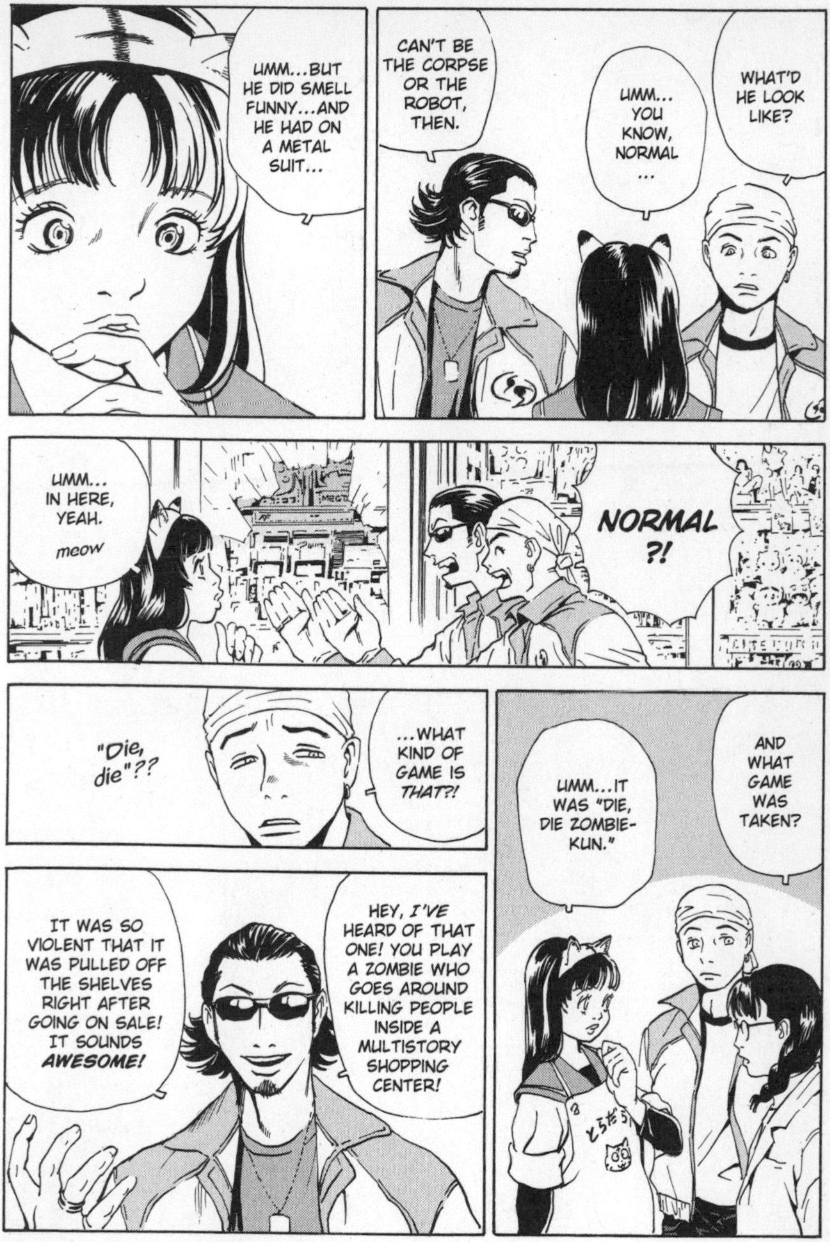
WHAT'D HE LOOK LIKE?
UMM... YOU KNOW, NORMAL ...
CAN'T BE THE CORPSE OR THE ROBOT, THEN.
UMM...BUT HE DID SMELL FUNNY...AND HE HAD ON A METAL SUIT...
NORMAL ?!
UMM... IN HERE, YEAH. meow
AND WHAT GAME WAS TAKEN?
UMM...IT WAS "DIE, DIE ZOMBIE-KUN."
...WHAT KIND OF GAME IS THAT?!
"Die, die"??
HEY, I'VE HEARD OF THAT ONE! YOU PLAY A ZOMBIE WHO GOES AROUND KILLING PEOPLE INSIDE A MULTISTORY SHOPPING CENTER!
IT WAS SO VIOLENT THAT IT WAS PULLED OFF THE SHELVES RIGHT AFTER GOING ON SALE! IT SOUNDS AWESOME!

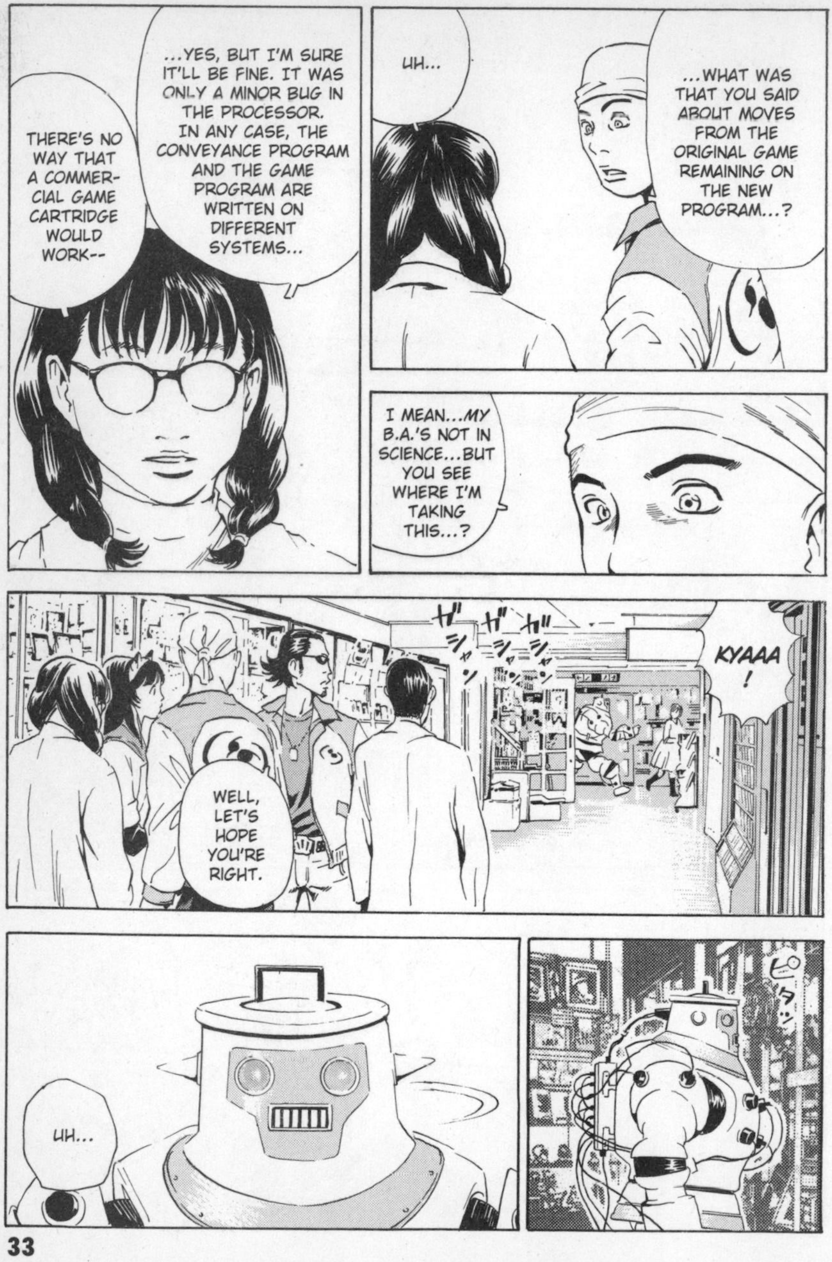
...WHAT WAS THAT YOU SAID ABOUT MOVES FROM THE ORIGINAL GAME REMAINING ON THE NEW PROGRAM...?
UH...
I MEAN...*MY* B.A.'S NOT IN SCIENCE...BUT YOU SEE WHERE I'M TAKING THIS...?
...YES, BUT I'M SURE IT'LL BE FINE. IT WAS ONLY A MINOR BUG IN THE PROCESSOR. IN ANY CASE, THE CONVEYANCE PROGRAM AND THE GAME PROGRAM ARE WRITTEN ON DIFFERENT SYSTEMS...
THERE'S NO WAY THAT A COMMERCIAL GAME CARTRIDGE WOULD WORK--
KYAAA!
WELL, LET'S HOPE YOU'RE RIGHT.
ピタッ
UH...

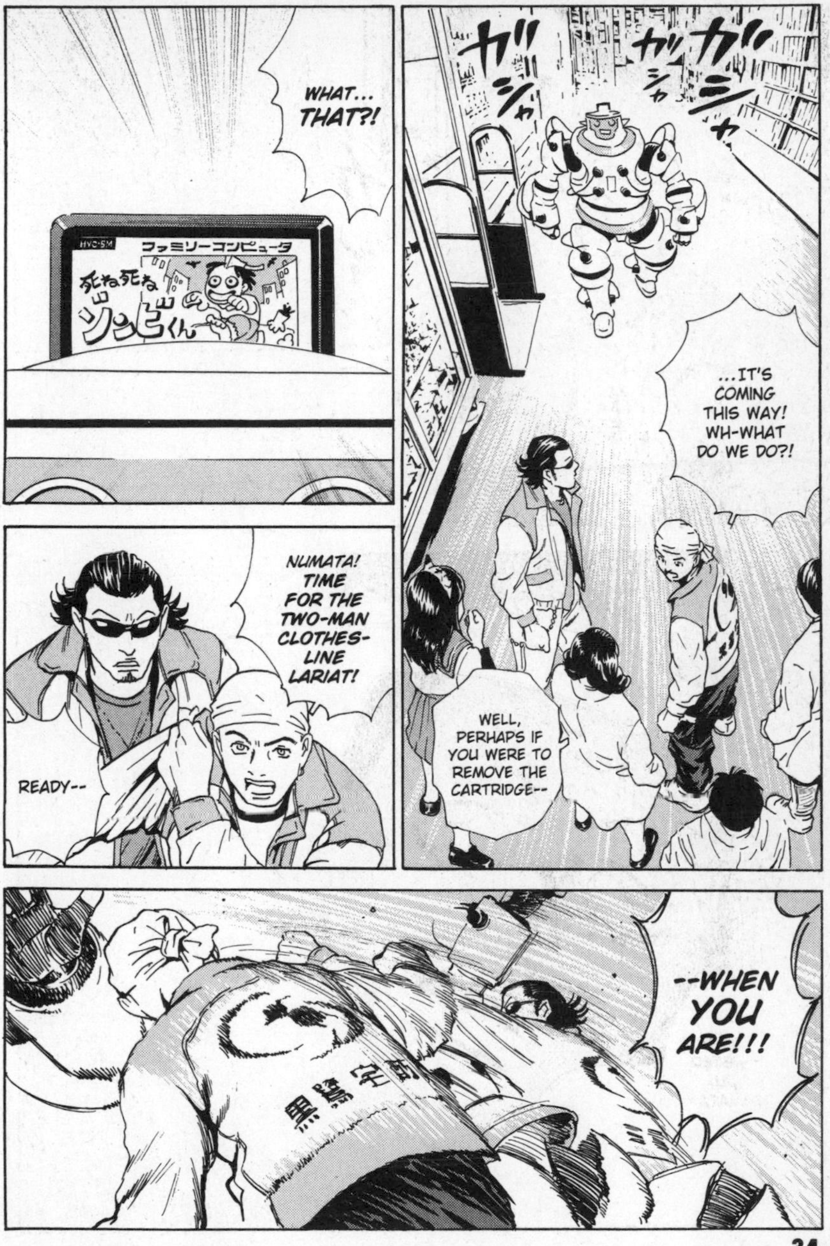
...IT'S COMING THIS WAY! WH-WHAT DO WE DO?!
WELL, PERHAPS IF YOU WERE TO REMOVE THE CARTRIDGE--
WHAT... THAT?!
HVC-SM
ファミリーコンピュータ
死ね死ねゾンビくん
NUMATA! TIME FOR THE TWO-MAN CLOTHES-LINE LARIAT!
READY--
--WHEN YOU ARE!!!

THE ROBOT'S DOWN...

...UM...

ALL RIGHT!

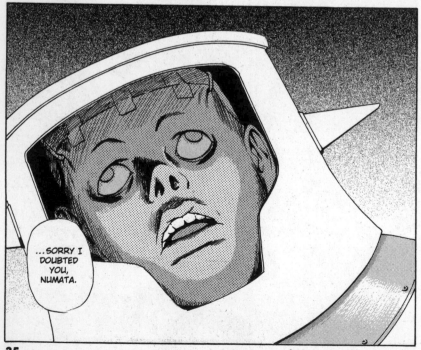

...SORRY I DOUBTED YOU, NUMATA.

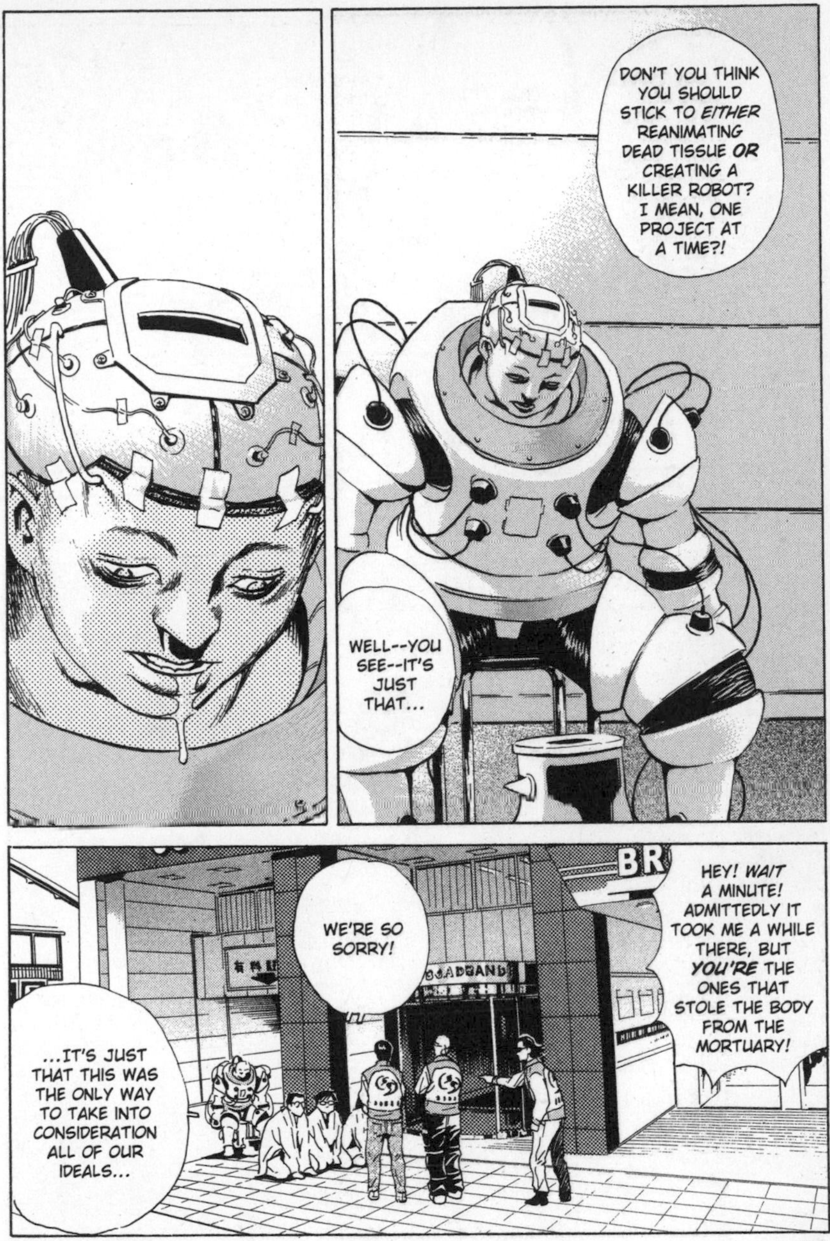
DON'T YOU THINK YOU SHOULD STICK TO *EITHER* REANIMATING DEAD TISSUE ***OR*** CREATING A KILLER ROBOT? I MEAN, ONE PROJECT AT A TIME?!
WELL--YOU SEE--IT'S JUST THAT...
HEY! *WAIT* A MINUTE! ADMITTEDLY IT TOOK ME A WHILE THERE, BUT ***YOU'RE*** THE ONES THAT STOLE THE BODY FROM THE MORTUARY!
WE'RE SO SORRY!
...IT'S JUST THAT THIS WAS THE ONLY WAY TO TAKE INTO CONSIDERATION ALL OF OUR IDEALS...

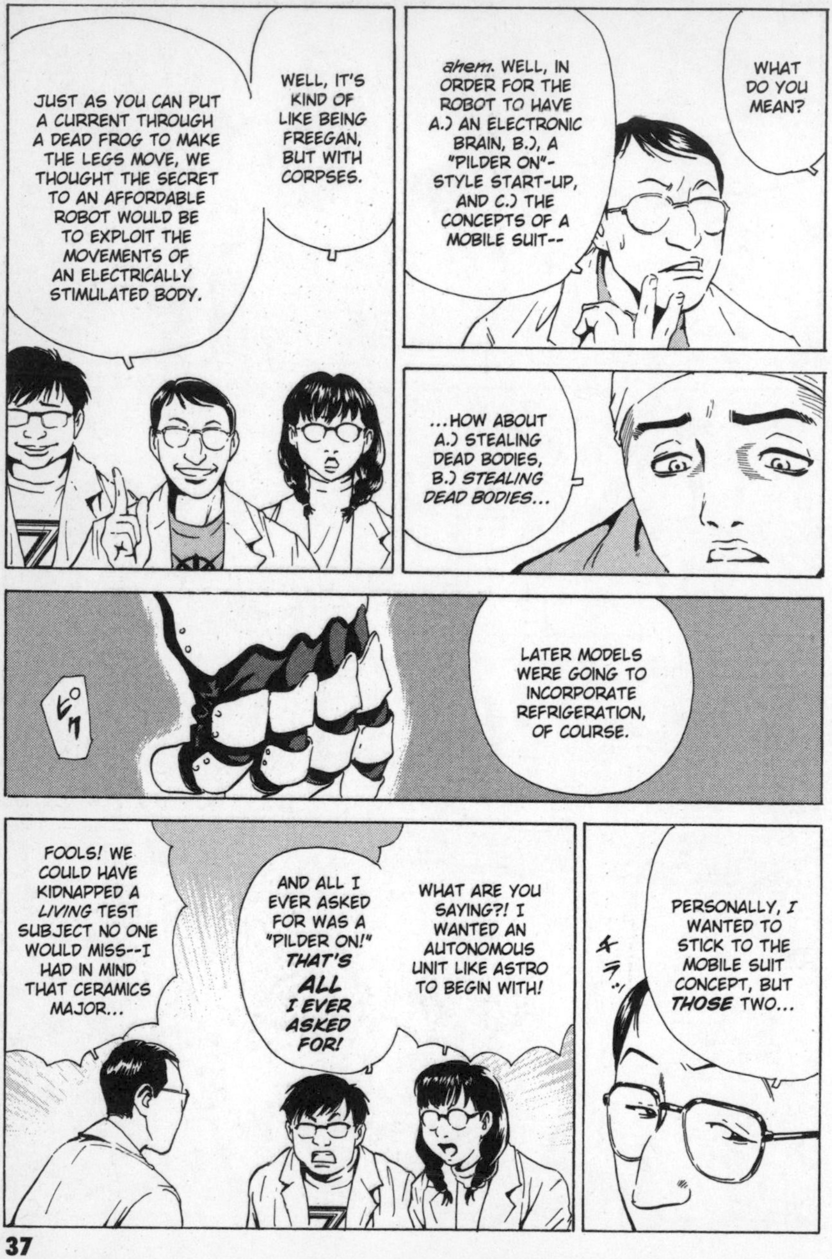

WHAT DO YOU MEAN?
ahem. WELL, IN ORDER FOR THE ROBOT TO HAVE A.) AN ELECTRONIC BRAIN, B.), A "PILDER ON"-STYLE START-UP, AND C.) THE CONCEPTS OF A MOBILE SUIT--
...HOW ABOUT A.) STEALING DEAD BODIES, B.) STEALING DEAD BODIES...
WELL, IT'S KIND OF LIKE BEING FREEGAN, BUT WITH CORPSES.
JUST AS YOU CAN PUT A CURRENT THROUGH A DEAD FROG TO MAKE THE LEGS MOVE, WE THOUGHT THE SECRET TO AN AFFORDABLE ROBOT WOULD BE TO EXPLOIT THE MOVEMENTS OF AN ELECTRICALLY STIMULATED BODY.
LATER MODELS WERE GOING TO INCORPORATE REFRIGERATION, OF COURSE.
ピク
キラッ
PERSONALLY, I WANTED TO STICK TO THE MOBILE SUIT CONCEPT, BUT THOSE TWO...
WHAT ARE YOU SAYING?! I WANTED AN AUTONOMOUS UNIT LIKE ASTRO TO BEGIN WITH!
AND ALL I EVER ASKED FOR WAS A "PILDER ON!" THAT'S ALL I EVER ASKED FOR!
FOOLS! WE COULD HAVE KIDNAPPED A LIVING TEST SUBJECT NO ONE WOULD MISS--I HAD IN MIND THAT CERAMICS MAJOR...

YOU DO?!

ALL RIGHT, ALL RIGHT, WE'RE NOT THE NOBEL COMMITTEE. LISTEN, WE *KIND OF* SYMPATHIZE--

HUH?

HEY.

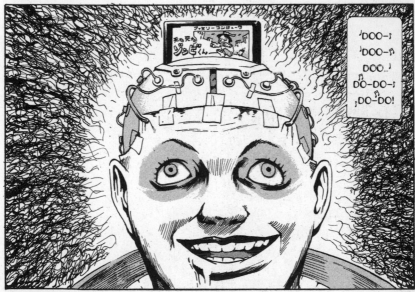

♪DOO-♪
♪DOO-♪
DOO...♪
♪DO-DO-♪
♪DO-DO!

38

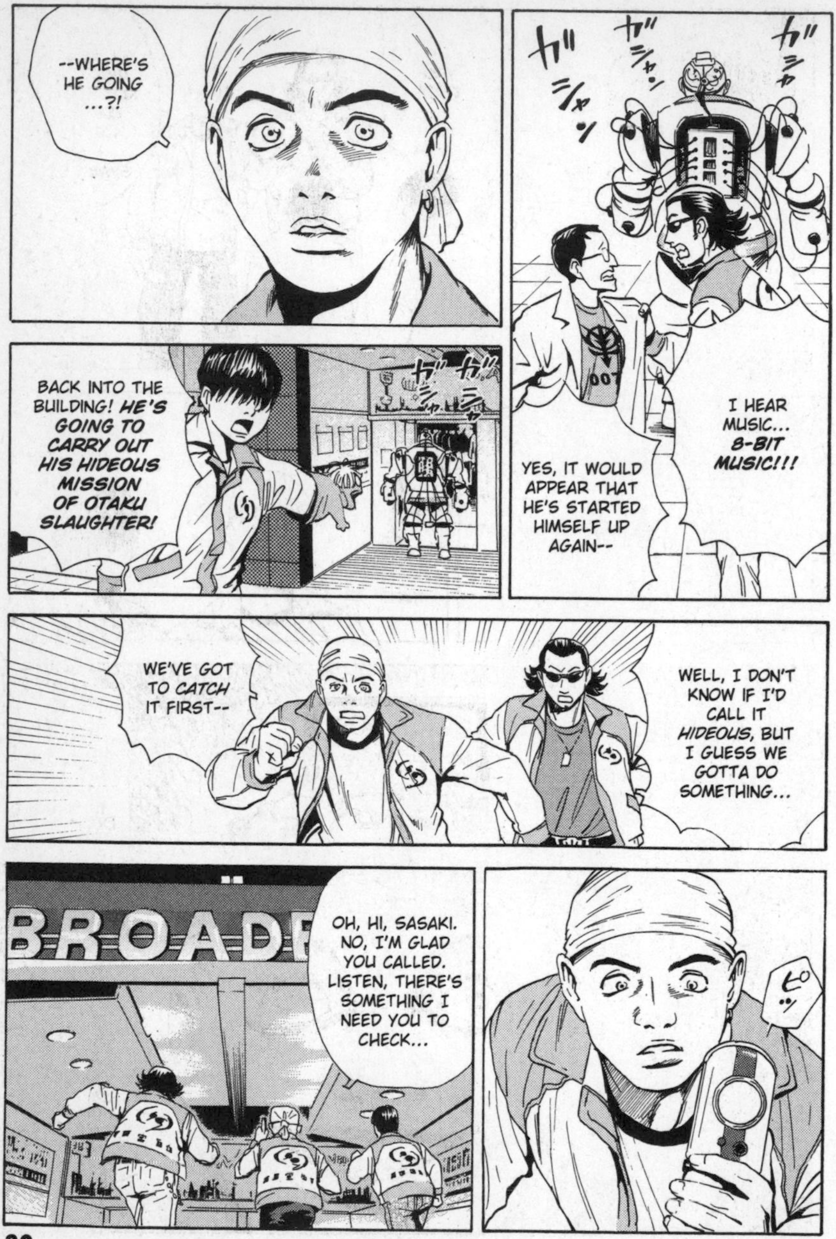
ガシャ
ガシャン
ガシャン
I HEAR MUSIC... *8-BIT MUSIC!!!*
YES, IT WOULD APPEAR THAT HE'S STARTED HIMSELF UP AGAIN--
--WHERE'S HE GOING ...?!
BACK INTO THE BUILDING! *HE'S GOING TO CARRY OUT HIS HIDEOUS MISSION OF OTAKU SLAUGHTER!*
WELL, I DON'T KNOW IF I'D CALL IT *HIDEOUS*, BUT I GUESS WE GOTTA DO SOMETHING...
WE'VE GOT TO *CATCH* IT FIRST--
ピッ
OH, HI, SASAKI. NO, I'M GLAD YOU CALLED. LISTEN, THERE'S SOMETHING I NEED YOU TO CHECK...
BROAD

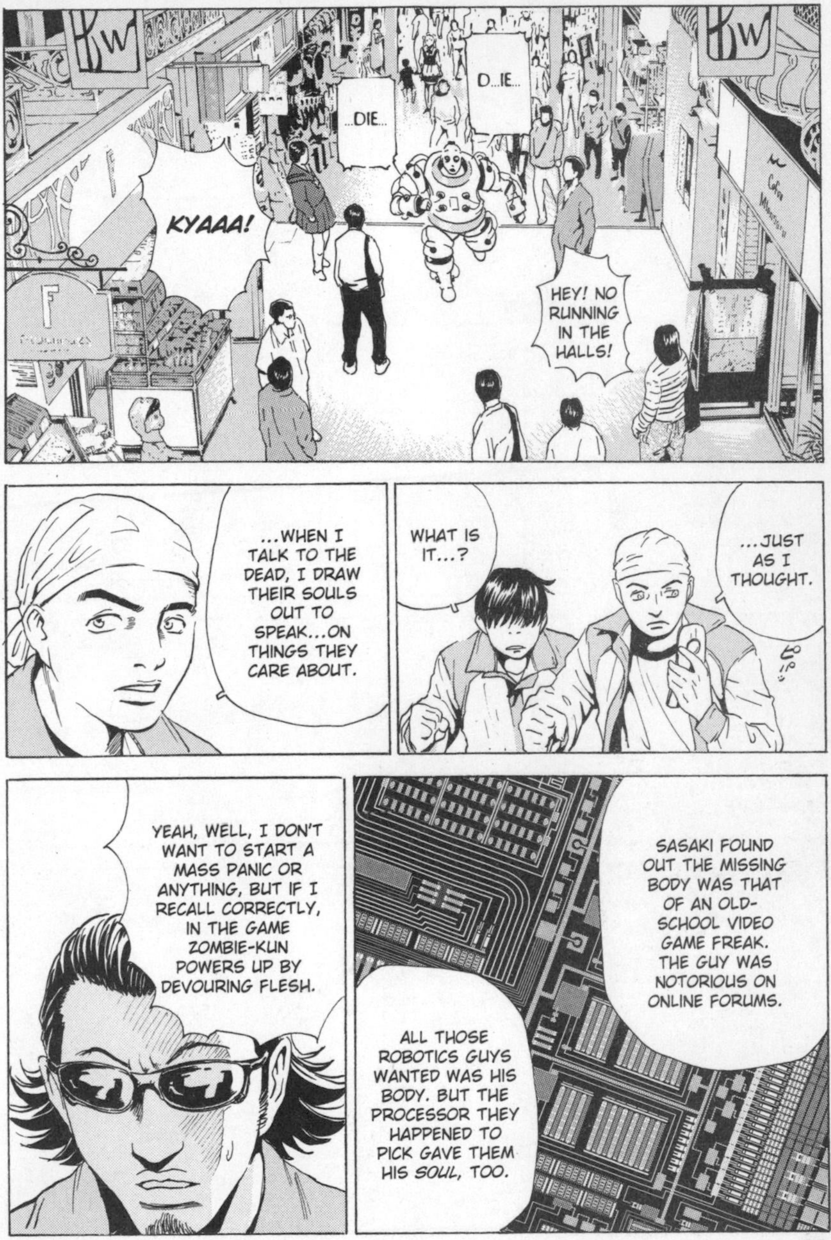
D...IE...
...DIE...
KYAAA!
HEY! NO RUNNING IN THE HALLS!
...JUST AS I THOUGHT.
WHAT IS IT...?
...WHEN I TALK TO THE DEAD, I DRAW THEIR SOULS OUT TO SPEAK...ON THINGS THEY CARE ABOUT.
SASAKI FOUND OUT THE MISSING BODY WAS THAT OF AN OLD-SCHOOL VIDEO GAME FREAK. THE GUY WAS NOTORIOUS ON ONLINE FORUMS.
ALL THOSE ROBOTICS GUYS WANTED WAS HIS BODY. BUT THE PROCESSOR THEY HAPPENED TO PICK GAVE THEM HIS *SOUL*, TOO.
YEAH, WELL, I DON'T WANT TO START A MASS PANIC OR ANYTHING, BUT IF I RECALL CORRECTLY, IN THE GAME ZOMBIE-KUN POWERS UP BY DEVOURING FLESH.

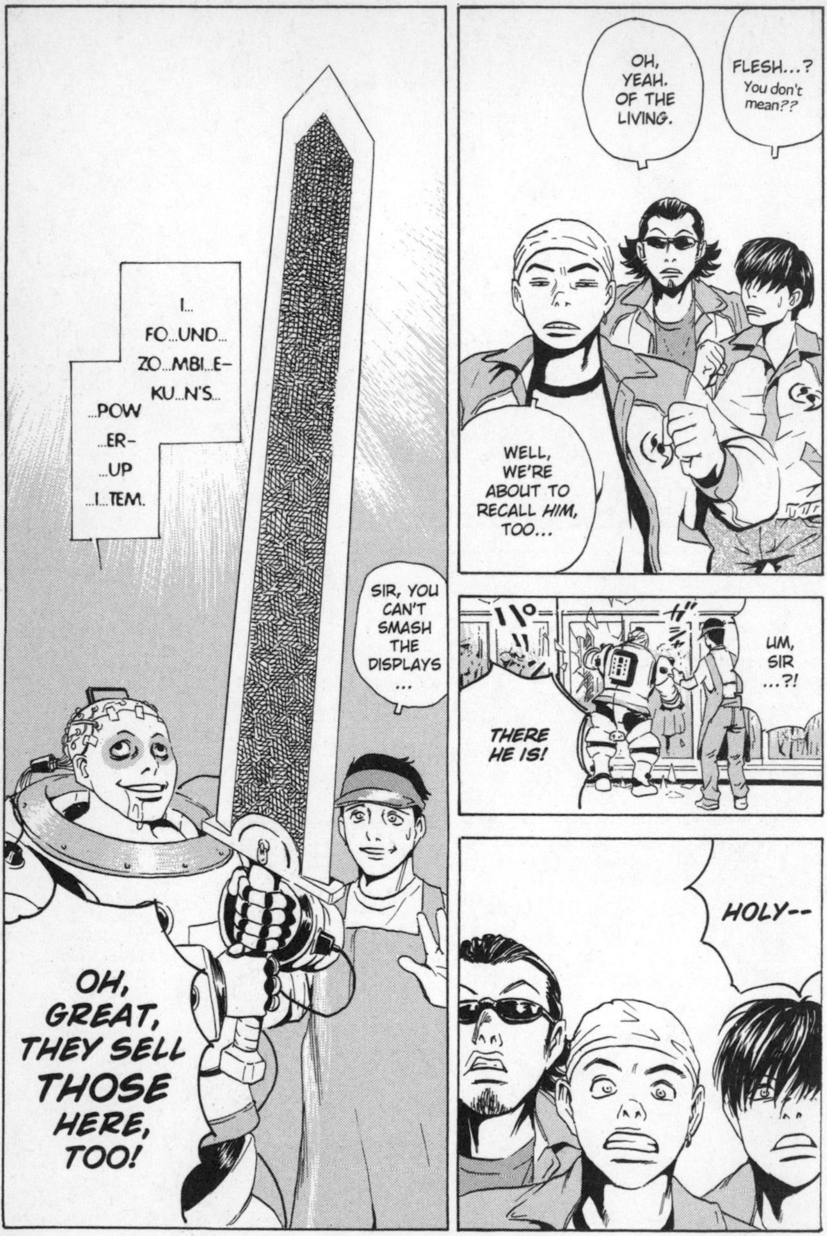
FLESH...? You don't mean??
OH, YEAH. OF THE LIVING.
WELL, WE'RE ABOUT TO RECALL HIM, TOO...
UM, SIR ...?!
THERE HE IS!
HOLY--
SIR, YOU CAN'T SMASH THE DISPLAYS ...
I... FO...UND... ZO...MBI...E-KU...N'S... ...POW ...ER- ...UP ...I...TEM.
OH, GREAT, THEY SELL THOSE HERE, TOO!

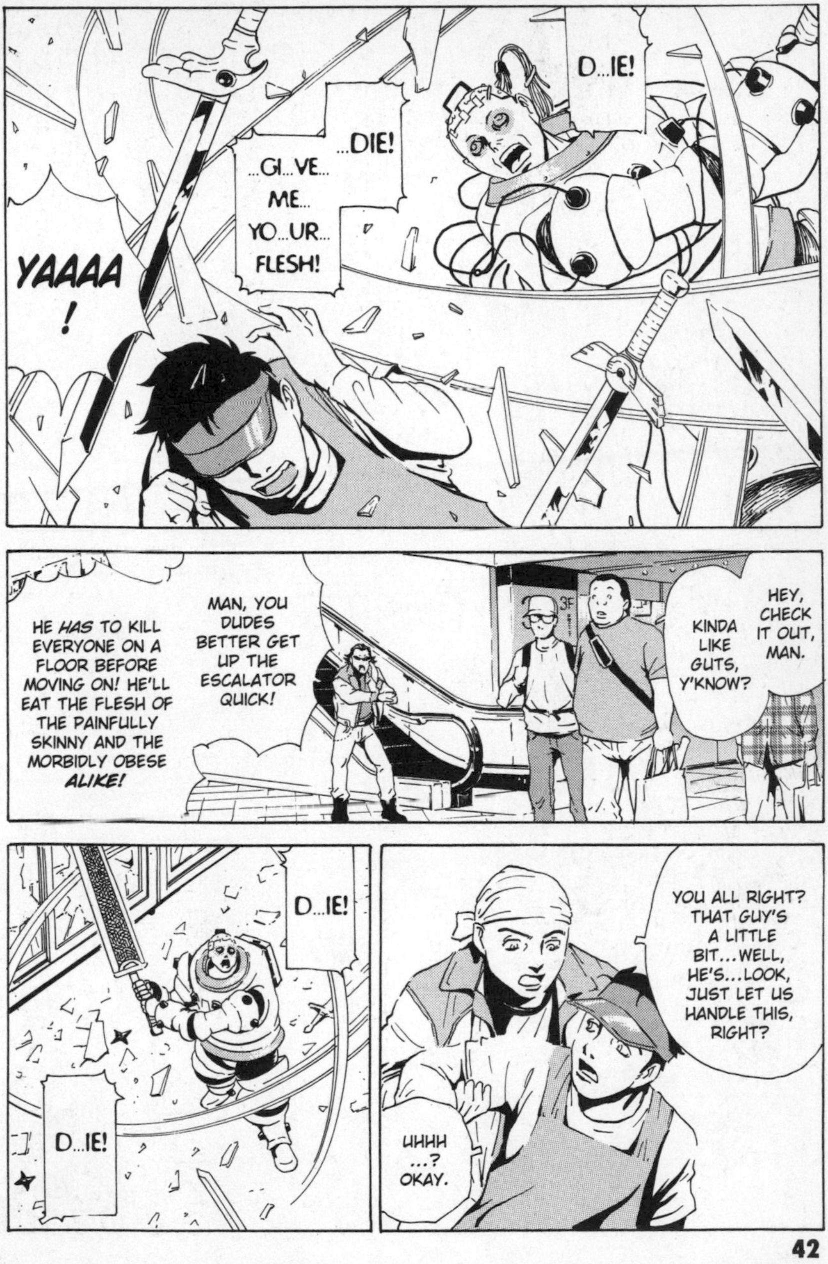
D...IE!
...DIE!
...GI...VE... ME... YO...UR... FLESH!
YAAAA !
HEY, CHECK IT OUT, MAN.
KINDA LIKE GUTS, Y'KNOW?
3F
MAN, YOU DUDES BETTER GET UP THE ESCALATOR QUICK!
HE *HAS* TO KILL EVERYONE ON A FLOOR BEFORE MOVING ON! HE'LL EAT THE FLESH OF THE PAINFULLY SKINNY AND THE MORBIDLY OBESE ***ALIKE!***
YOU ALL RIGHT? THAT GUY'S A LITTLE BIT...WELL, HE'S...LOOK, JUST LET US HANDLE THIS, RIGHT?
UHHH ...? OKAY.
D...IE!
D...IE!

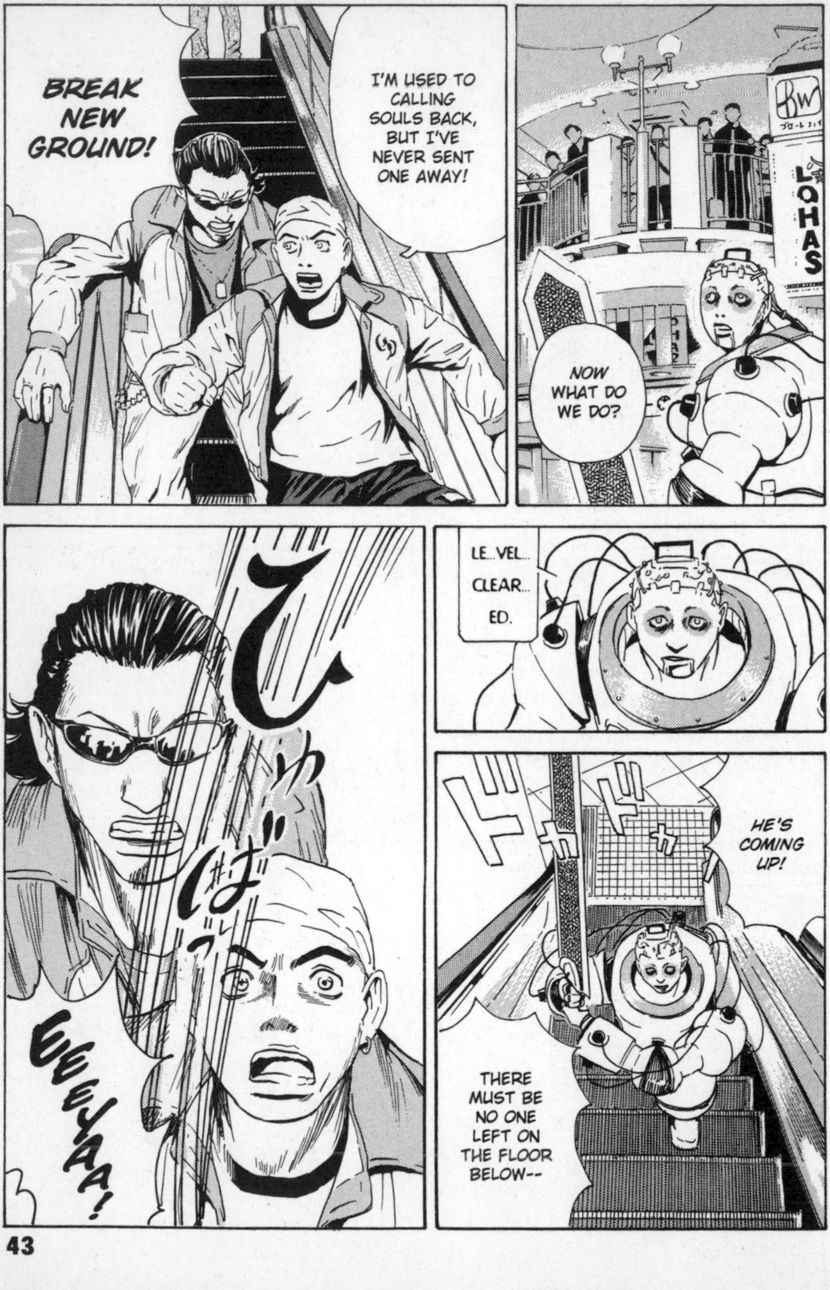
LOHAS
NOW WHAT DO WE DO?
I'M USED TO CALLING SOULS BACK, BUT I'VE NEVER SENT ONE AWAY!
BREAK NEW GROUND!
LE...VEL... CLEAR... ED.
HE'S COMING UP!
THERE MUST BE NO ONE LEFT ON THE FLOOR BELOW--
WEEYAA!

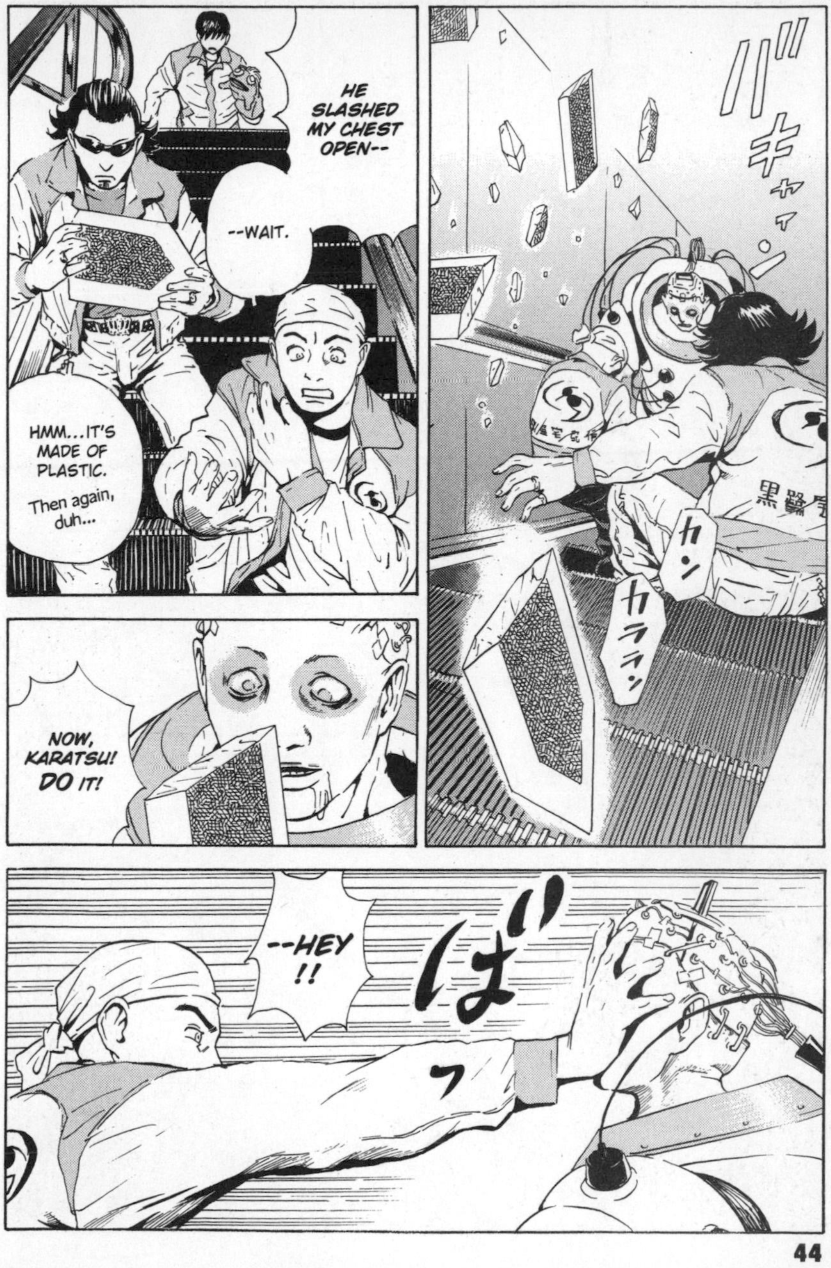

バキャィン
カン
カララン
HE SLASHED MY CHEST OPEN--
--WAIT.
HMM...IT'S MADE OF PLASTIC.
Then again, duh...
NOW, KARATSU! DO IT!
--HEY !!
ばっ

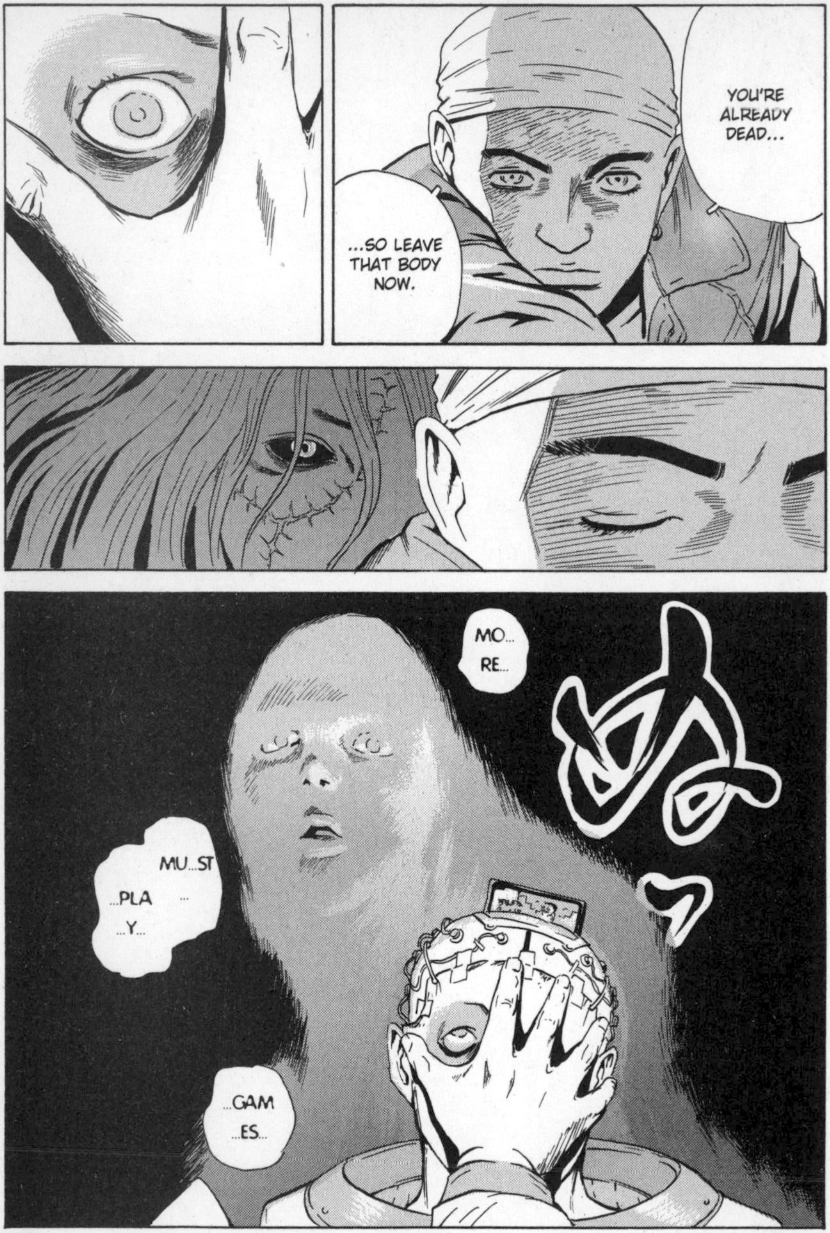
YOU'RE ALREADY DEAD...
...SO LEAVE THAT BODY NOW.
MO... RE...
ぬっ
MU...ST ...PLA ... ...Y...
...GAM ...ES...

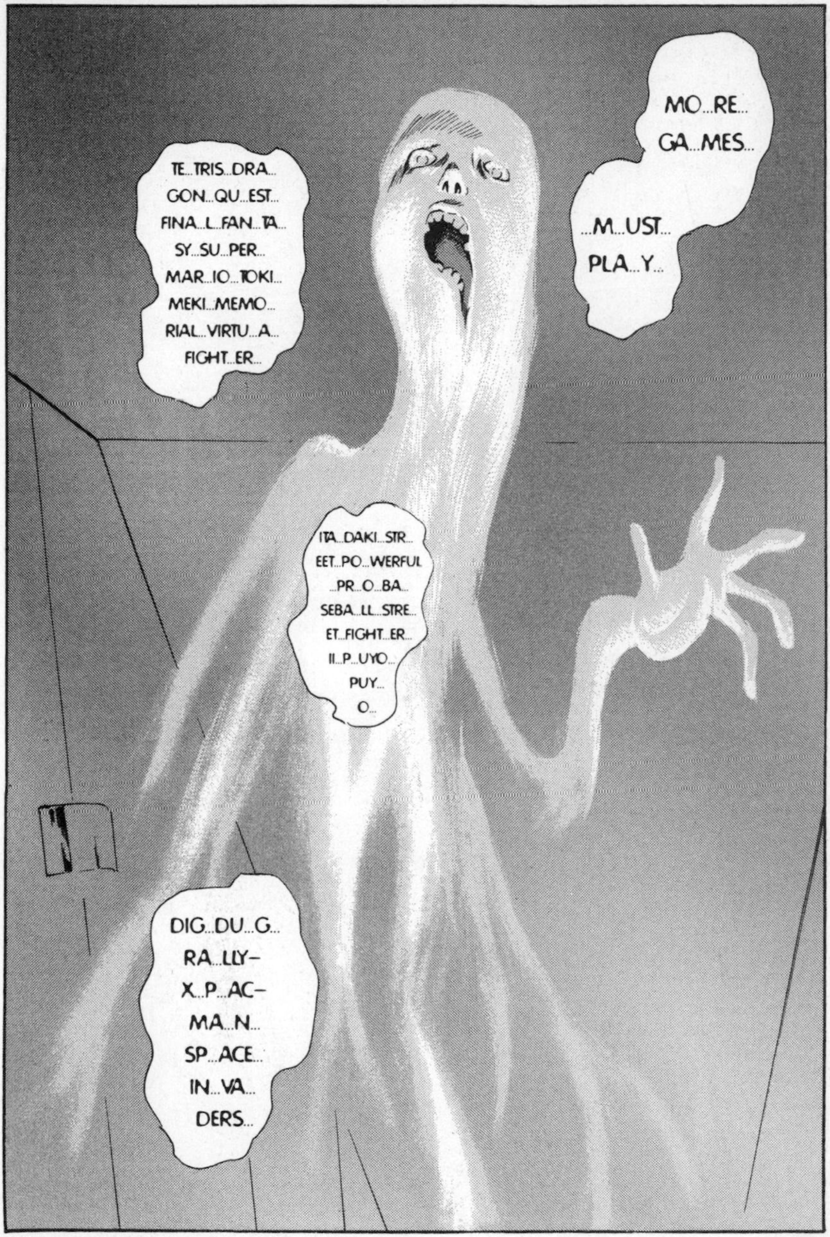
MO...RE... GA...MES... ...M...UST... PLA...Y...
TE...TRIS...DRA... GON...QU...EST... FINA...L...FAN...TA... SY...SU...PER... MAR...IO...TOKI... MEKI...MEMO... RIAL...VIRTU...A... FIGHT...ER...
ITA...DAKI...STR... EET...PO...WERFUL ...PR...O...BA... SEBA...LL...STRE... ET...FIGHT...ER... II...P...UYO... PUY... O...
DIG...DU...G... RA...LLY– X...P...AC– MA...N... SP...ACE... IN...VA... DERS...

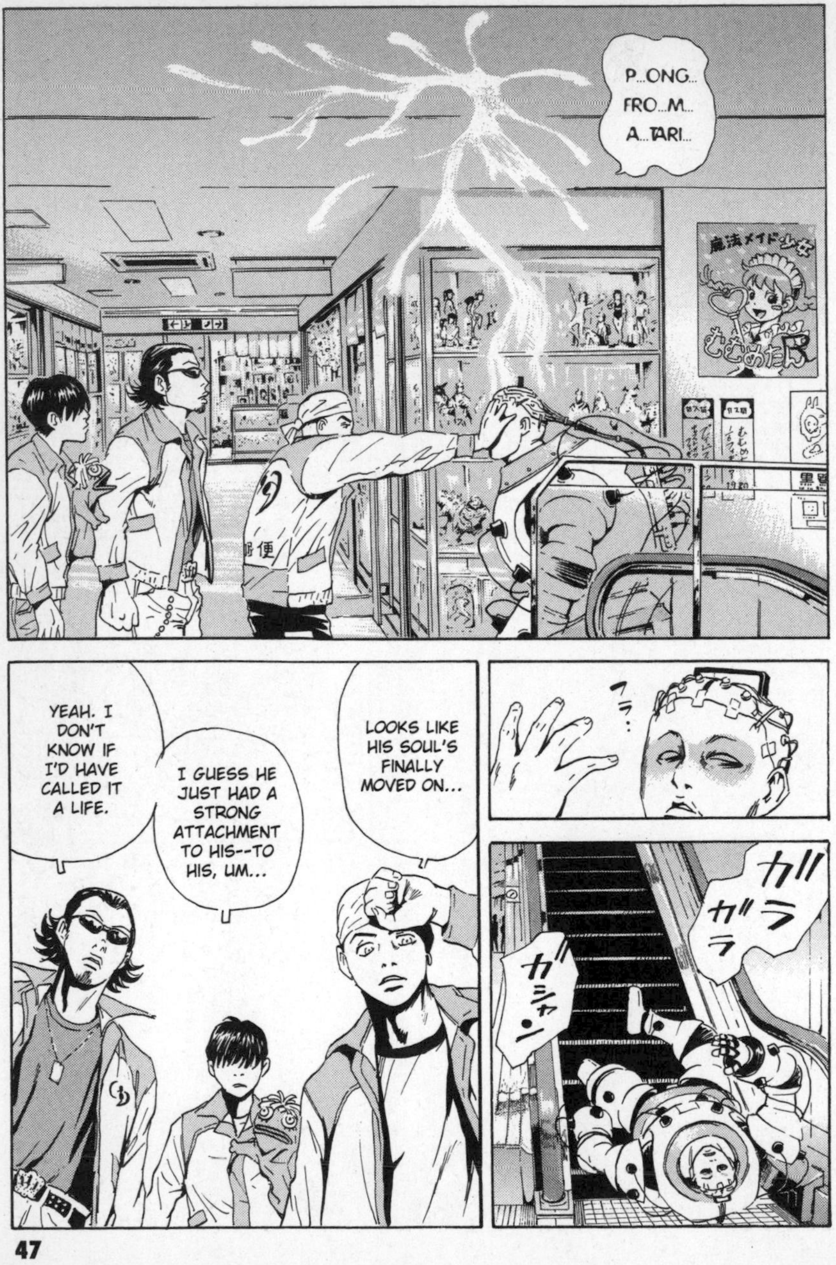
P...ONG...
FRO...M...
A...TARI...
フラ・・・
ガラ
ガラ
ガシャン
LOOKS LIKE HIS SOUL'S FINALLY MOVED ON...
I GUESS HE JUST HAD A STRONG ATTACHMENT TO HIS--TO HIS, UM...
YEAH. I DON'T KNOW IF I'D HAVE CALLED IT A LIFE.

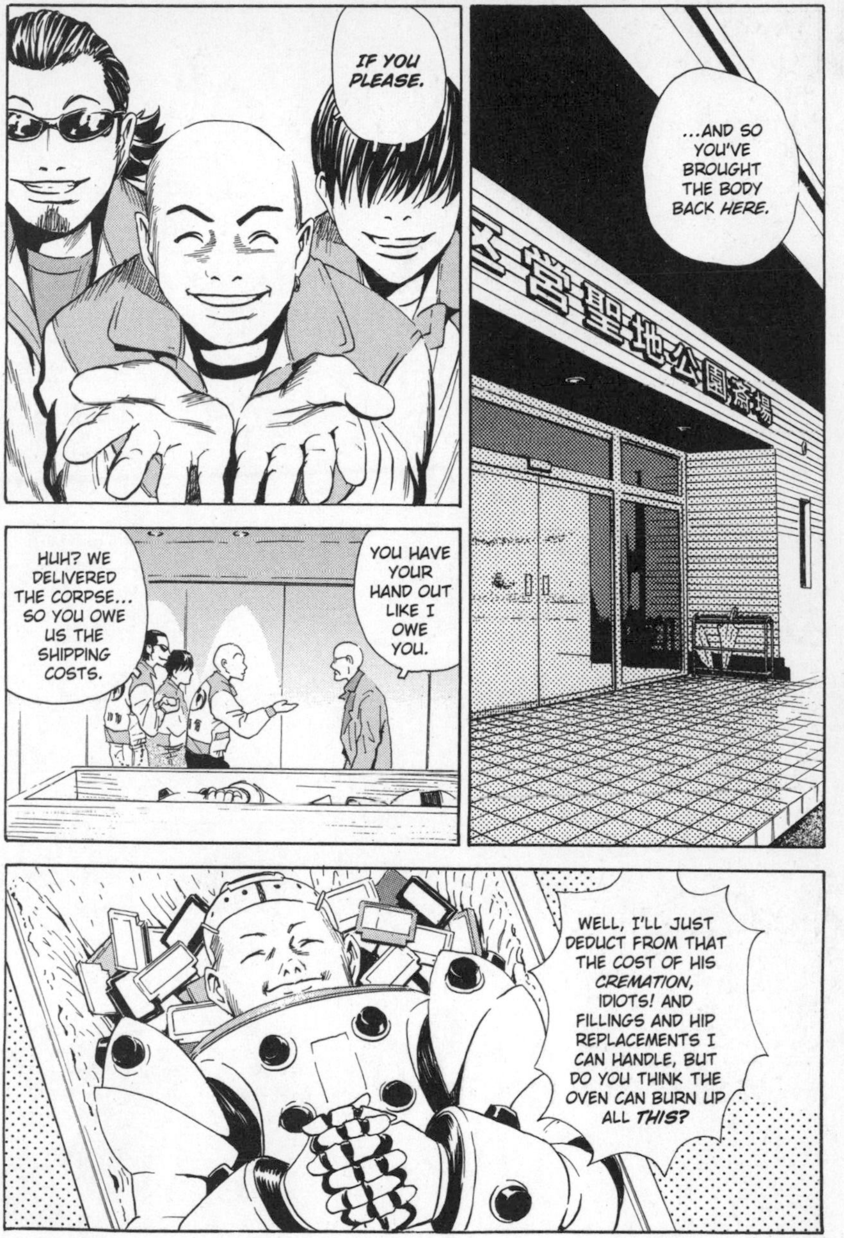
...AND SO YOU'VE BROUGHT THE BODY BACK HERE.
IF YOU PLEASE.
YOU HAVE YOUR HAND OUT LIKE I OWE YOU.
HUH? WE DELIVERED THE CORPSE... SO YOU OWE US THE SHIPPING COSTS.
WELL, I'LL JUST DEDUCT FROM THAT THE COST OF HIS CREMATION, IDIOTS! AND FILLINGS AND HIP REPLACEMENTS I CAN HANDLE, BUT DO YOU THINK THE OVEN CAN BURN UP ALL THIS?

1st delivery: fight with my heart—the end

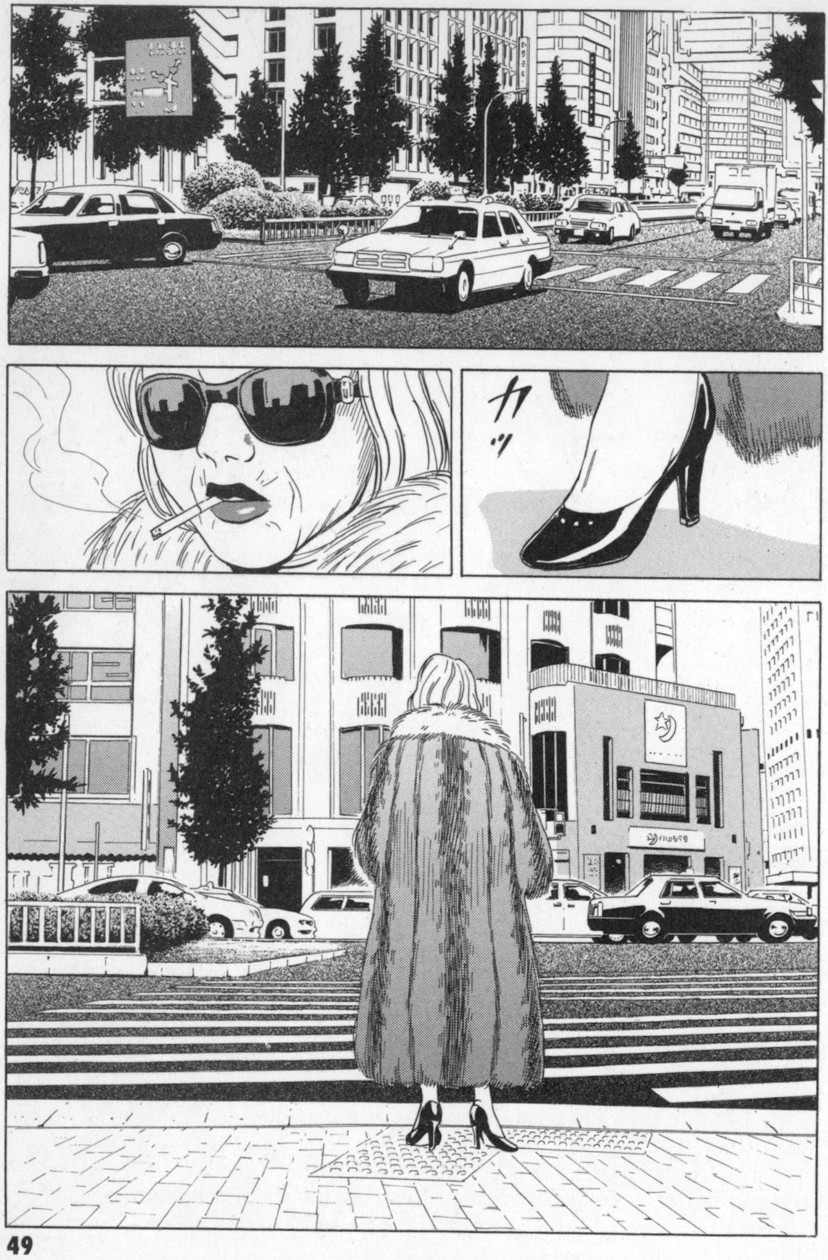
カッ

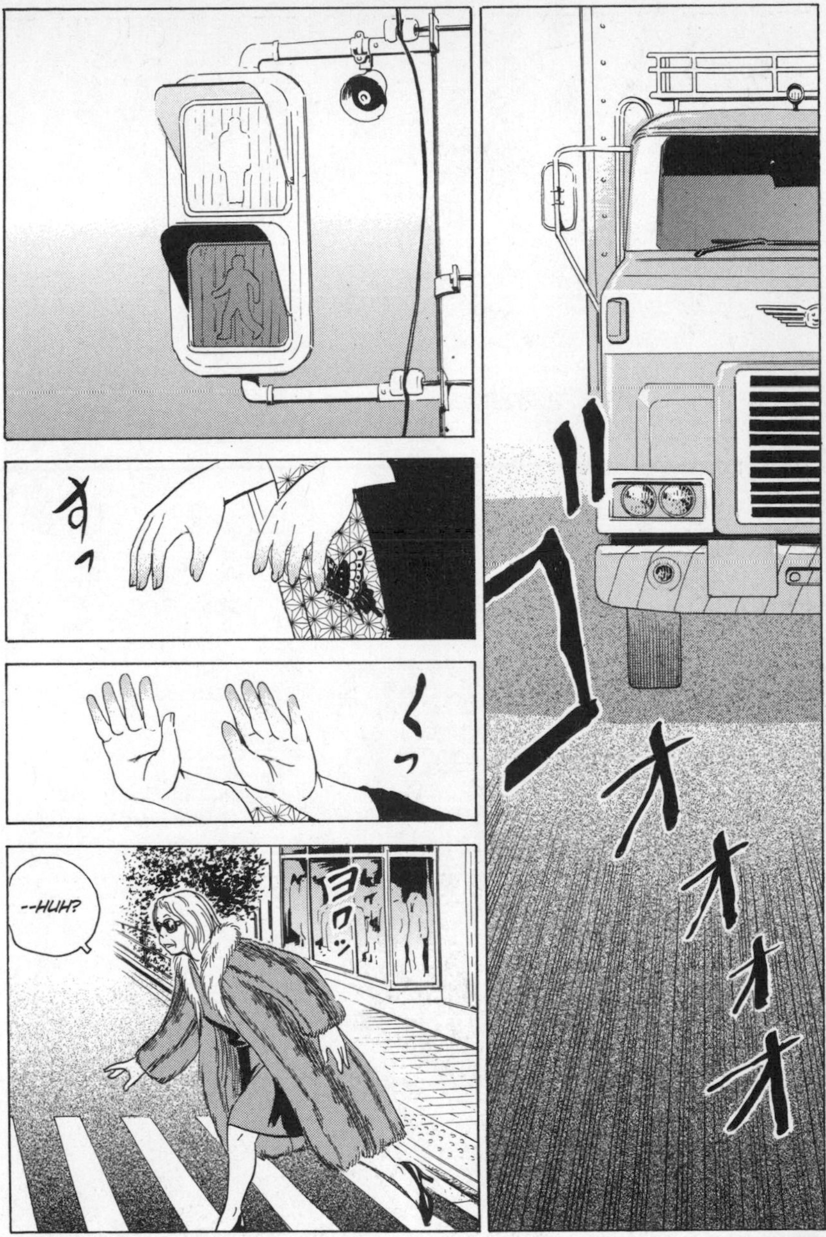
ゴオオオオ
すっ
くっ
--HUH?
ヨロッ

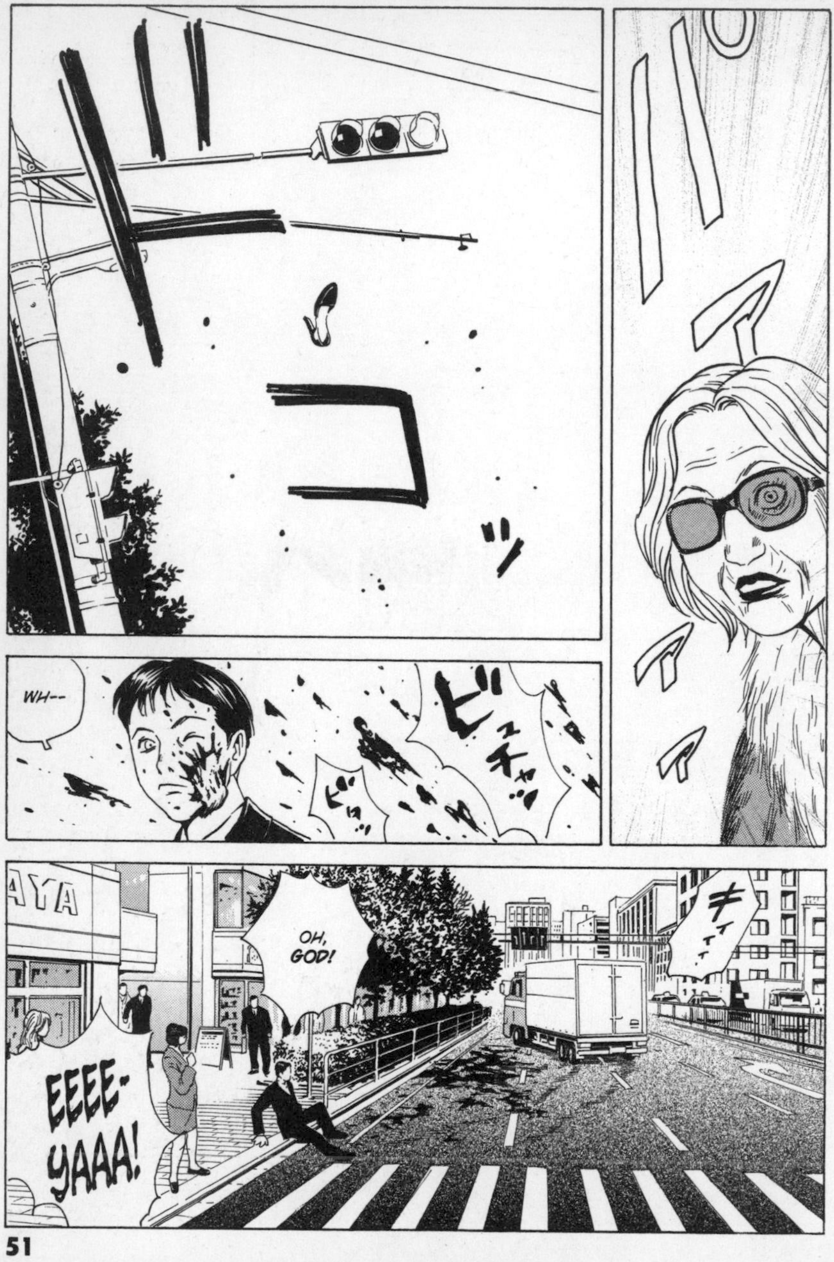
ドコッ
ビュチャッ
ビュッ
WH--
キィィィ
OH, GOD!
EEEE-YAAA!

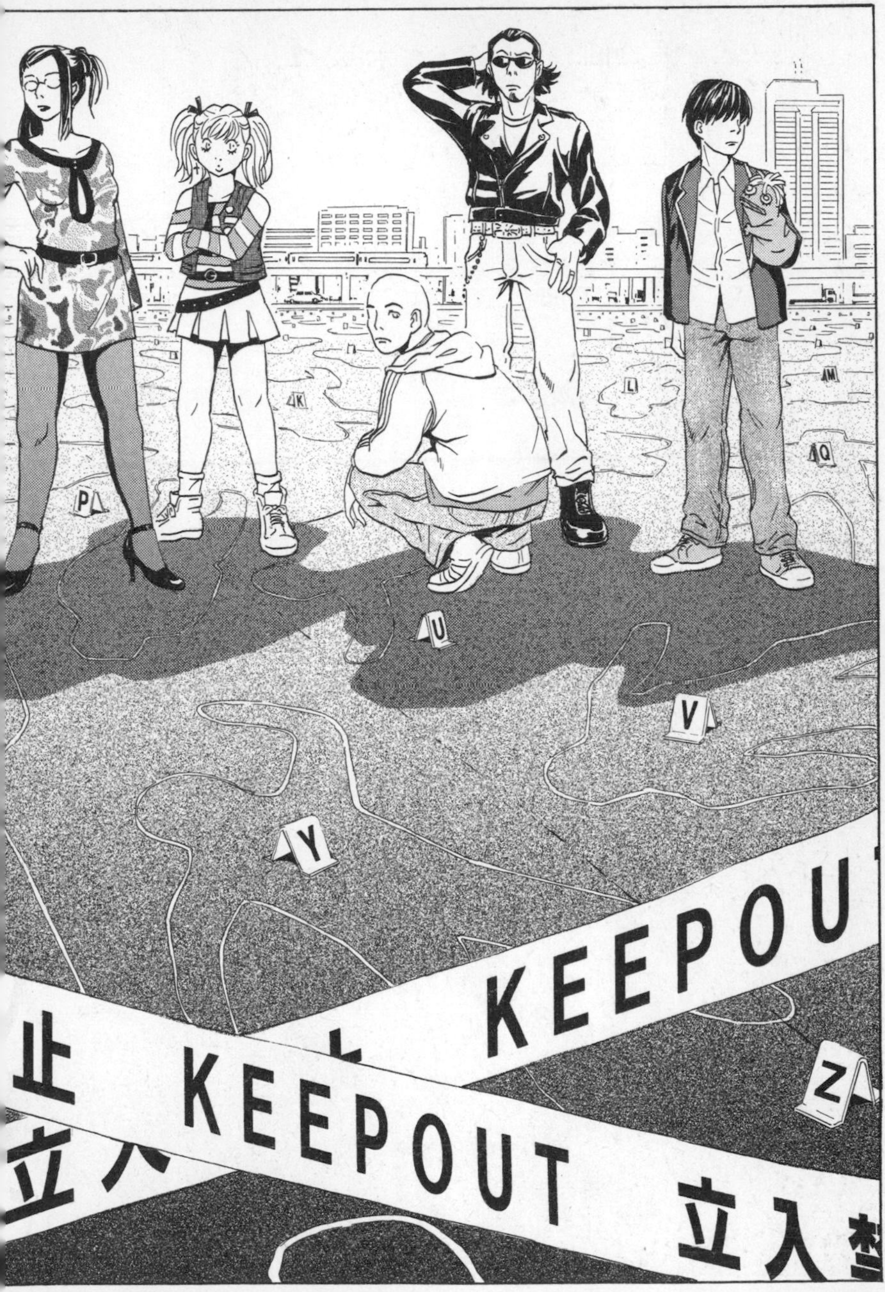
KEEPOUT
止 KEEPOUT
立入
立入禁

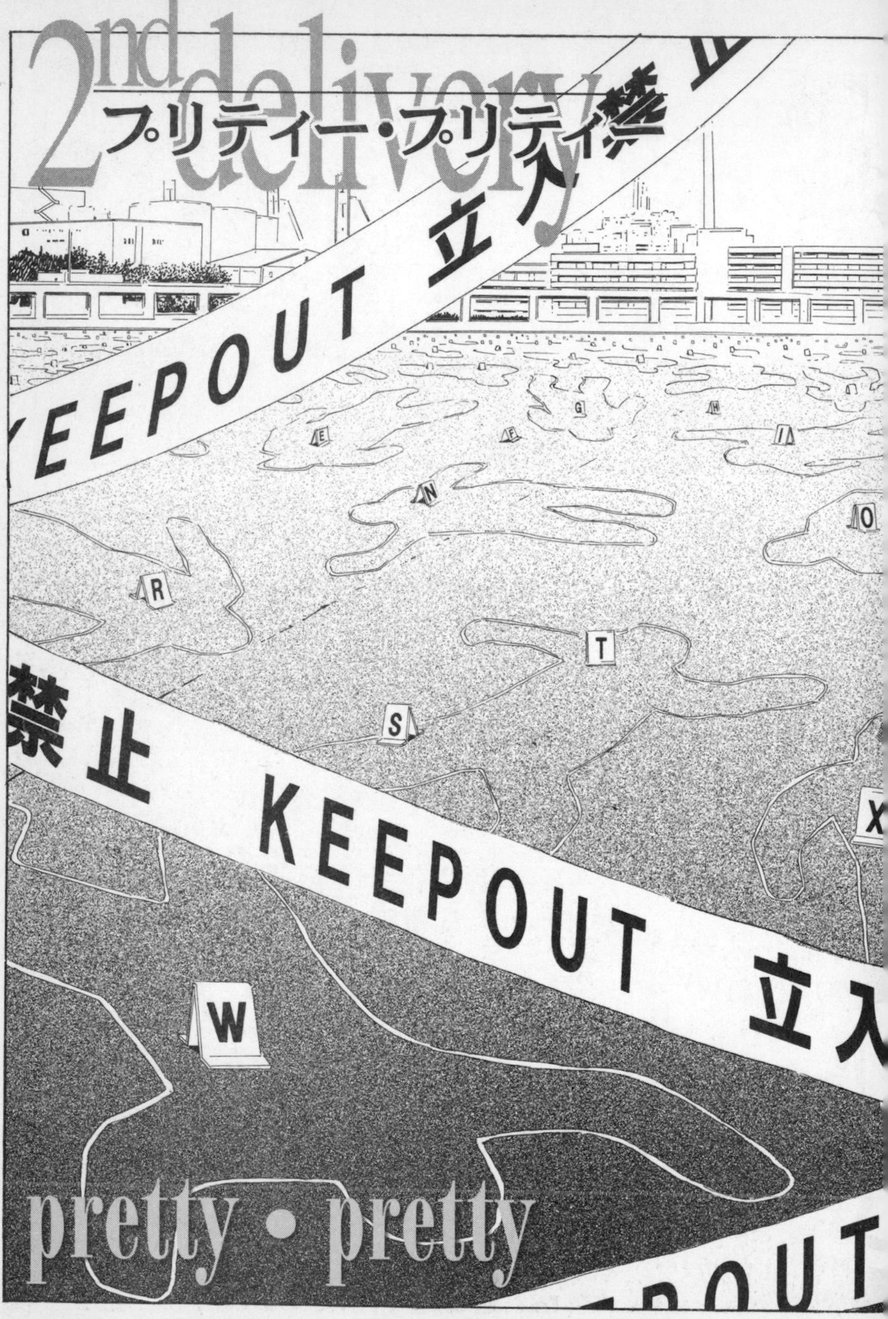

2nd delivery
プリティー・プリティ
KEEPOUT 立入
禁止 KEEPOUT 立入
pretty • pretty

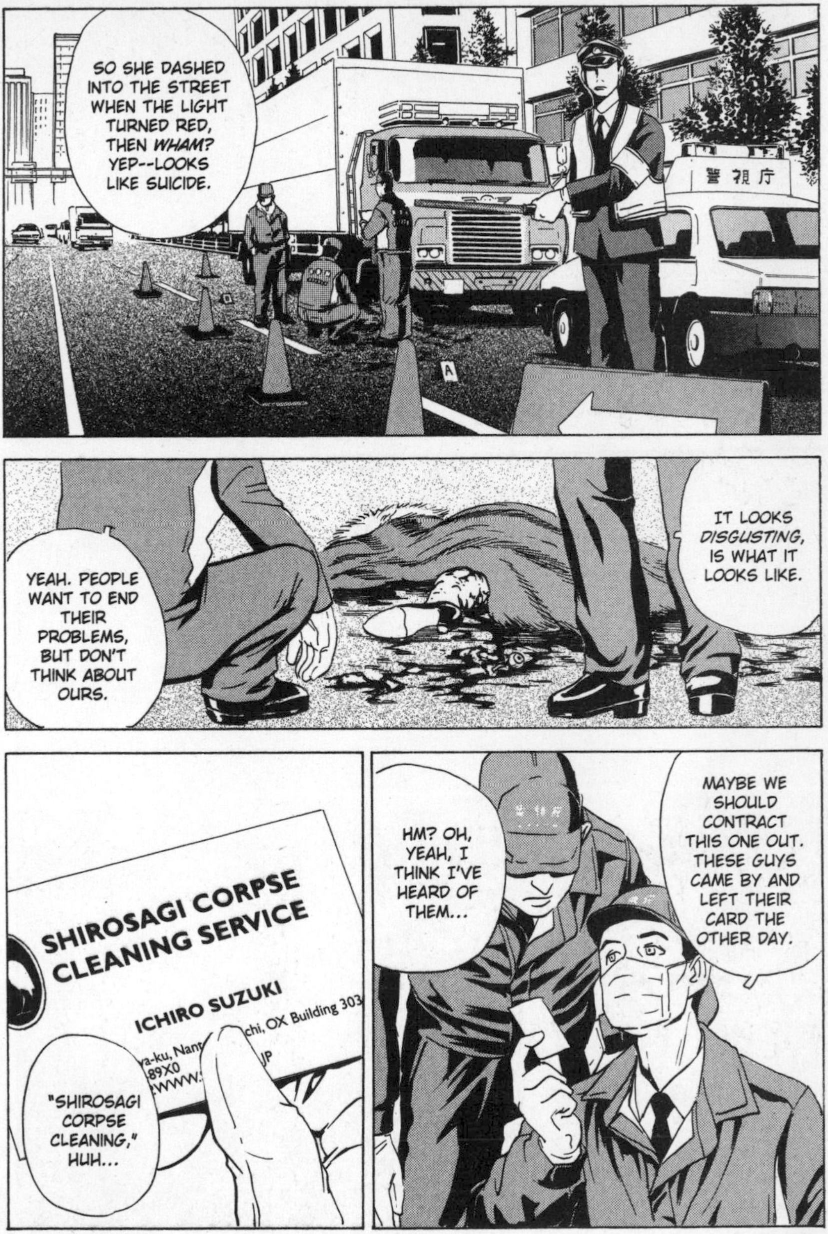
SO SHE DASHED INTO THE STREET WHEN THE LIGHT TURNED RED, THEN *WHAM?* YEP--LOOKS LIKE SUICIDE.
警視庁
IT LOOKS *DISGUSTING*, IS WHAT IT LOOKS LIKE.
YEAH. PEOPLE WANT TO END THEIR PROBLEMS, BUT DON'T THINK ABOUT OURS.
MAYBE WE SHOULD CONTRACT THIS ONE OUT. THESE GUYS CAME BY AND LEFT THEIR CARD THE OTHER DAY.
HM? OH, YEAH, I THINK I'VE HEARD OF THEM...
SHIROSAGI CORPSE CLEANING SERVICE
ICHIRO SUZUKI
"SHIROSAGI CORPSE CLEANING," HUH...

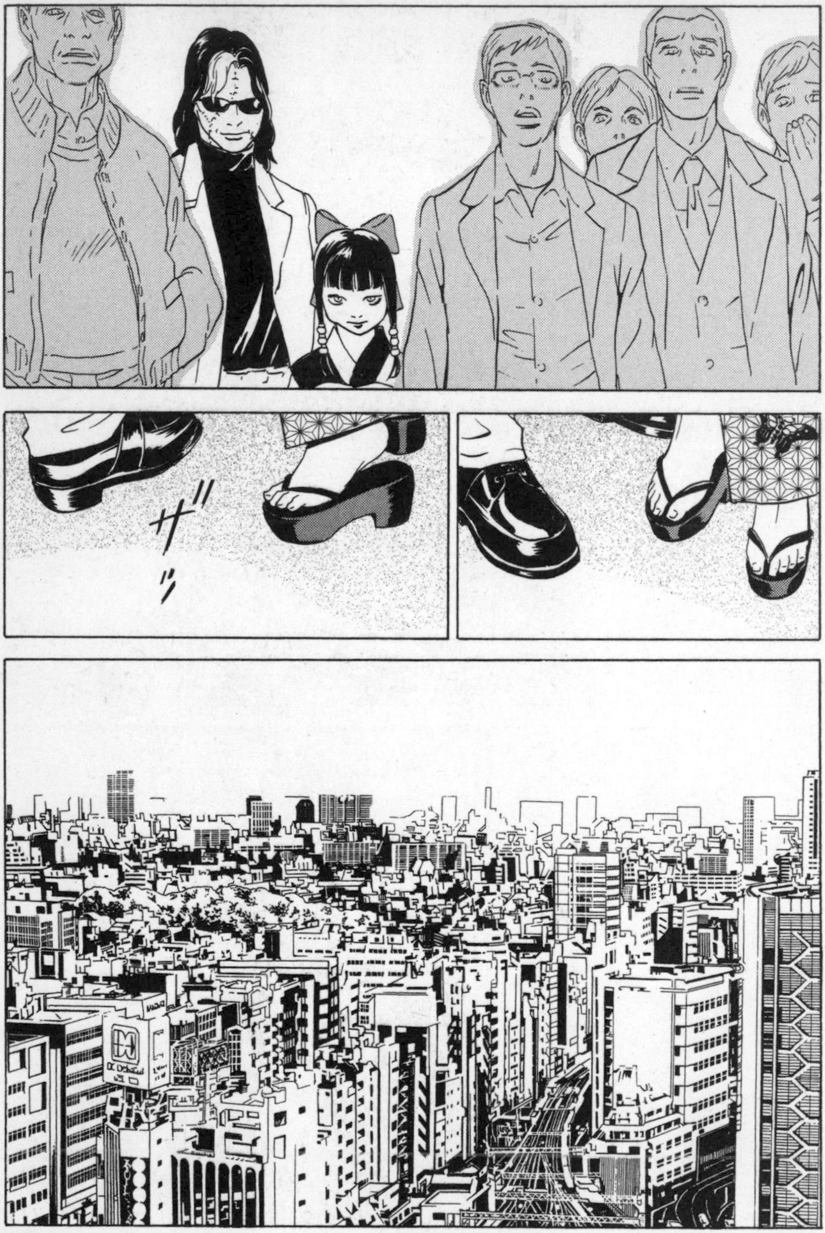
ザッ

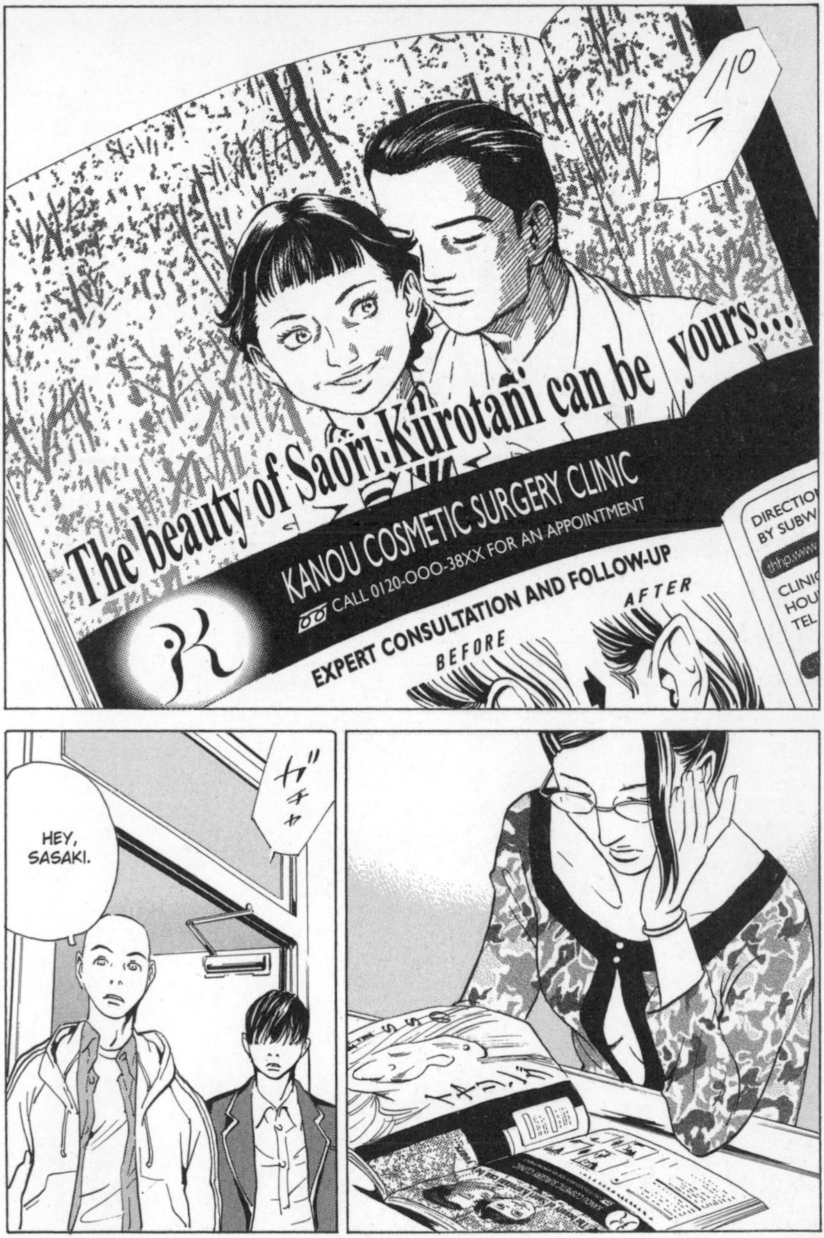
The beauty of Saori Kurotani can be yours...
KANOU COSMETIC SURGERY CLINIC
CALL 0120-OOO-38XX FOR AN APPOINTMENT
EXPERT CONSULTATION AND FOLLOW-UP
BEFORE
AFTER
HEY, SASAKI.

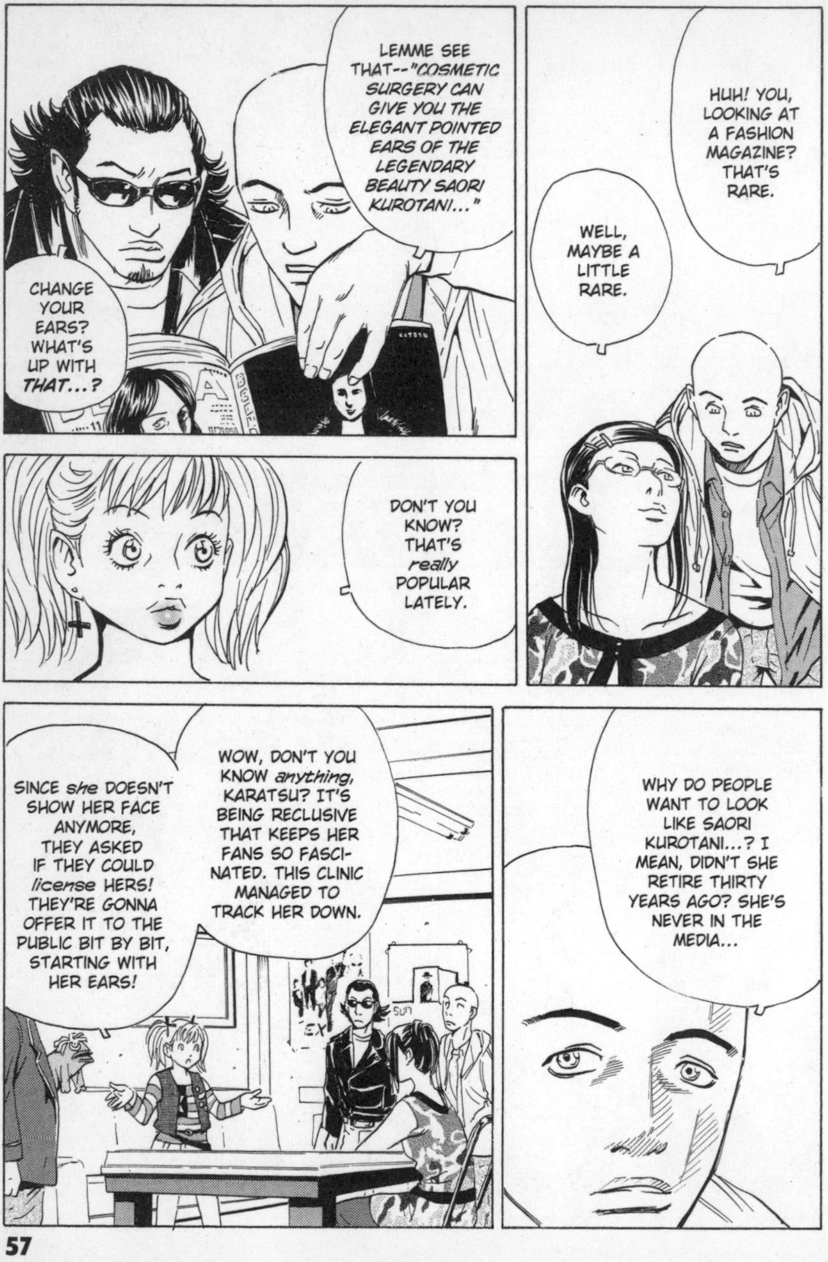
HUH! YOU, LOOKING AT A FASHION MAGAZINE? THAT'S RARE.
WELL, MAYBE A LITTLE RARE.
LEMME SEE THAT--"*COSMETIC SURGERY CAN GIVE YOU THE ELEGANT POINTED EARS OF THE LEGENDARY BEAUTY SAORI KUROTANI...*"
CHANGE YOUR EARS? WHAT'S UP WITH *THAT*...?
DON'T YOU KNOW? THAT'S *really* POPULAR LATELY.
WHY DO PEOPLE WANT TO LOOK LIKE SAORI KUROTANI...? I MEAN, DIDN'T SHE RETIRE THIRTY YEARS AGO? SHE'S NEVER IN THE MEDIA...
WOW, DON'T YOU KNOW *anything*, KARATSU? IT'S BEING RECLUSIVE THAT KEEPS HER FANS SO FASCI-NATED. THIS CLINIC MANAGED TO TRACK HER DOWN.
SINCE *she* DOESN'T SHOW HER FACE ANYMORE, THEY ASKED IF THEY COULD *license* HERS! THEY'RE GONNA OFFER IT TO THE PUBLIC BIT BY BIT, STARTING WITH HER EARS!

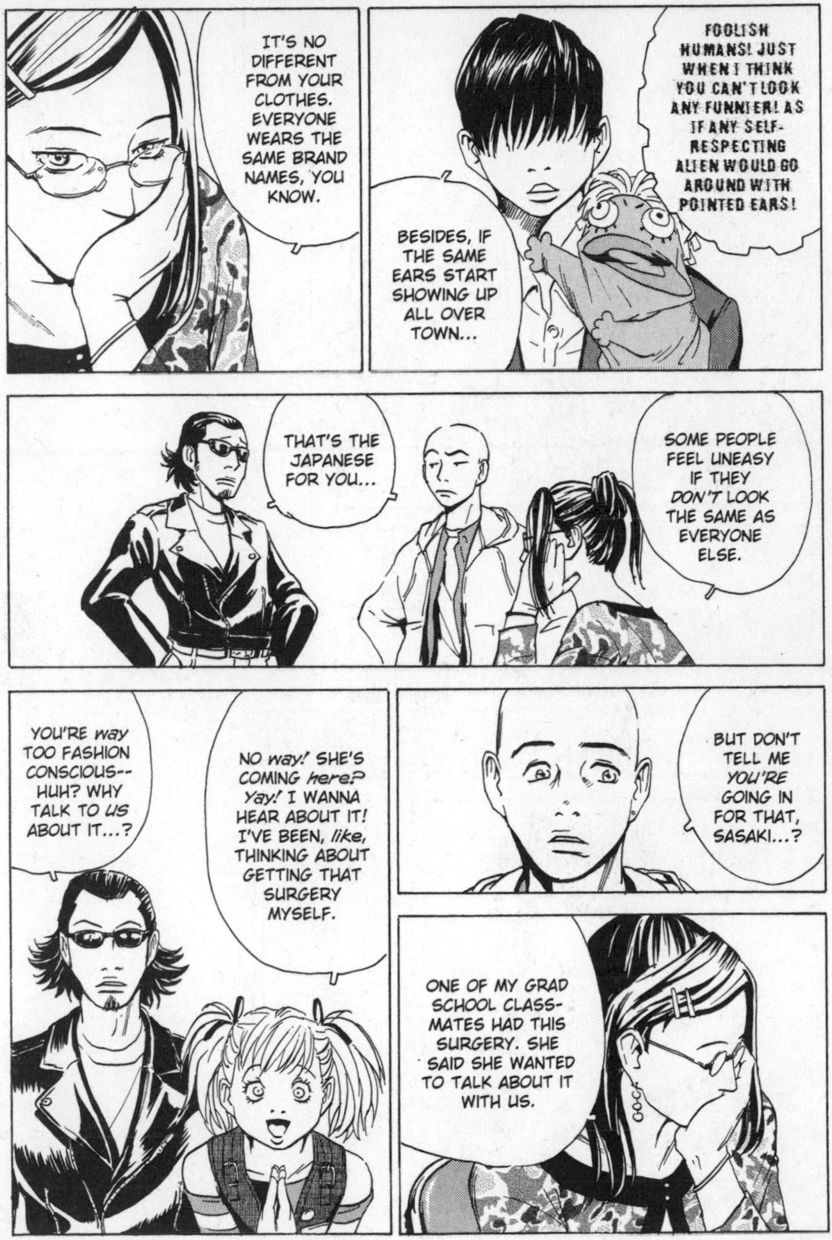
FOOLISH HUMANS! JUST WHEN I THINK YOU CAN'T LOOK ANY FUNNIER! AS IF ANY SELF-RESPECTING ALIEN WOULD GO AROUND WITH POINTED EARS!
BESIDES, IF THE SAME EARS START SHOWING UP ALL OVER TOWN...
IT'S NO DIFFERENT FROM YOUR CLOTHES. EVERYONE WEARS THE SAME BRAND NAMES, YOU KNOW.
SOME PEOPLE FEEL UNEASY IF THEY *DON'T* LOOK THE SAME AS EVERYONE ELSE.
THAT'S THE JAPANESE FOR YOU...
BUT DON'T TELL ME *YOU'RE* GOING IN FOR THAT, SASAKI...?
ONE OF MY GRAD SCHOOL CLASS-MATES HAD THIS SURGERY. SHE SAID SHE WANTED TO TALK ABOUT IT WITH US.
NO *way!* SHE'S COMING *here?* *Yay!* I WANNA HEAR ABOUT IT! I'VE BEEN, *like,* THINKING ABOUT GETTING THAT SURGERY MYSELF.
YOU'RE *way* TOO FASHION CONSCIOUS-- HUH? WHY TALK TO *US* ABOUT IT...?

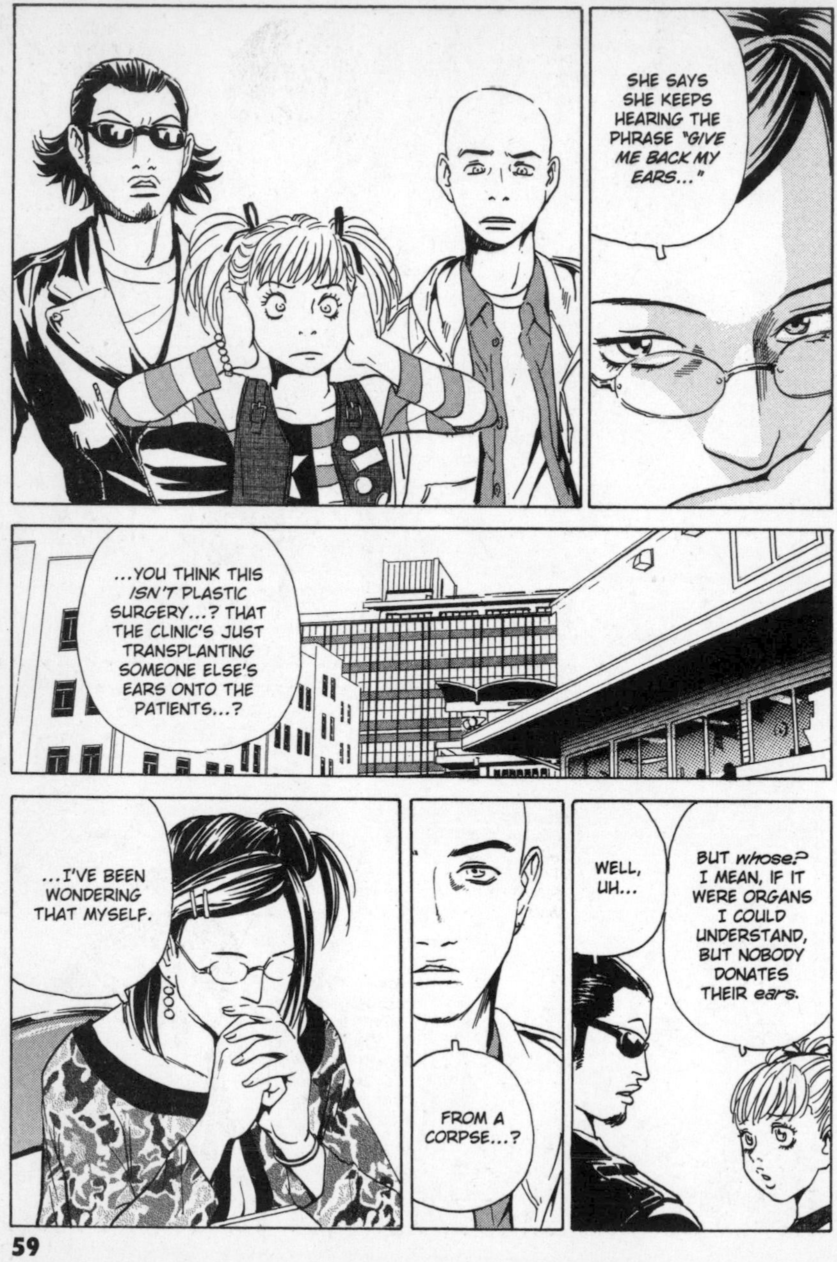
SHE SAYS SHE KEEPS HEARING THE PHRASE "GIVE ME BACK MY EARS..."
...YOU THINK THIS ISN'T PLASTIC SURGERY...? THAT THE CLINIC'S JUST TRANSPLANTING SOMEONE ELSE'S EARS ONTO THE PATIENTS...?
WELL, UH...
BUT whose? I MEAN, IF IT WERE ORGANS I COULD UNDERSTAND, BUT NOBODY DONATES THEIR ears.
FROM A CORPSE...?
...I'VE BEEN WONDERING THAT MYSELF.

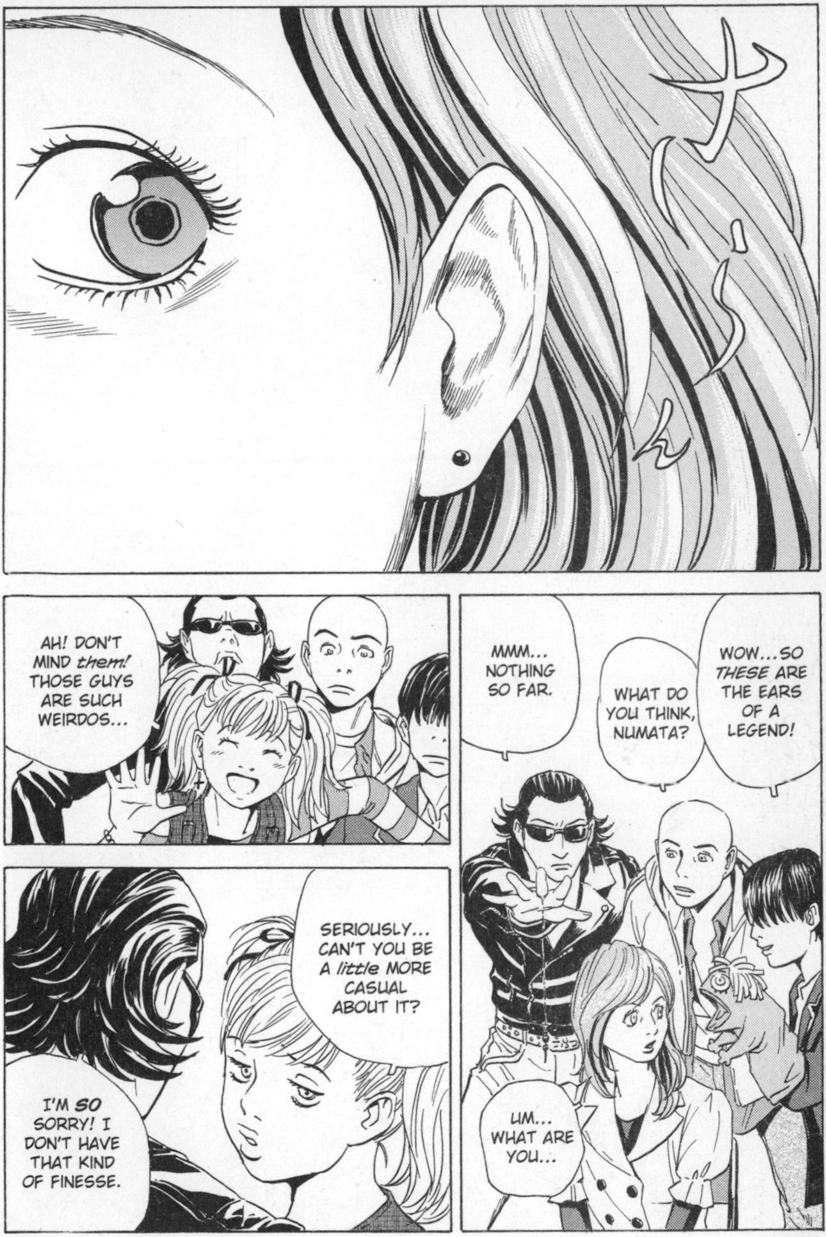
WOW...SO THESE ARE THE EARS OF A LEGEND!
WHAT DO YOU THINK, NUMATA?
MMM... NOTHING SO FAR.
UM... WHAT ARE YOU...
AH! DON'T MIND them! THOSE GUYS ARE SUCH WEIRDOS...
SERIOUSLY... CAN'T YOU BE A little MORE CASUAL ABOUT IT?
I'M SO SORRY! I DON'T HAVE THAT KIND OF FINESSE.

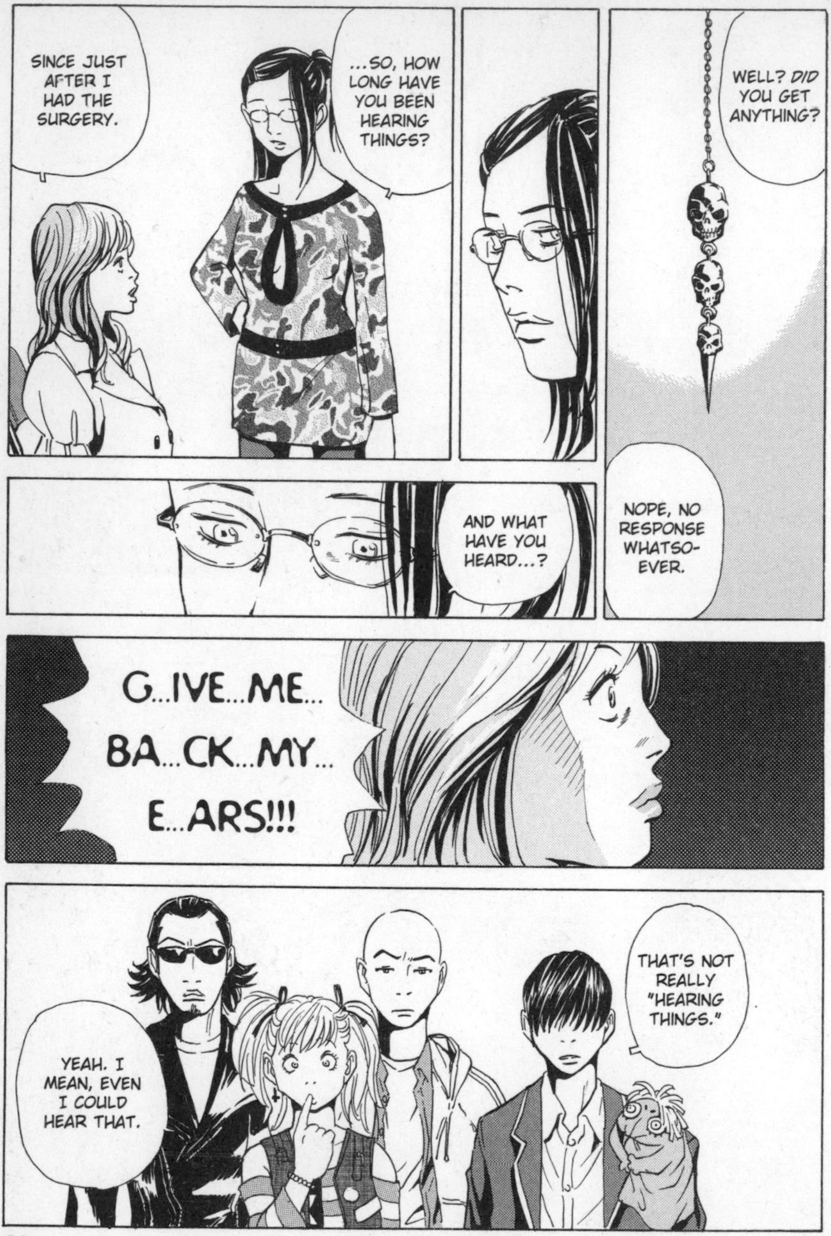
WELL? *DID* YOU GET ANYTHING?
NOPE, NO RESPONSE WHATSO-EVER.
...SO, HOW LONG HAVE YOU BEEN HEARING THINGS?
SINCE JUST AFTER I HAD THE SURGERY.
AND WHAT HAVE YOU HEARD...?
G...IVE...ME... BA...CK...MY... E...ARS!!!
THAT'S NOT REALLY "HEARING THINGS."
YEAH. I MEAN, EVEN I COULD HEAR THAT.

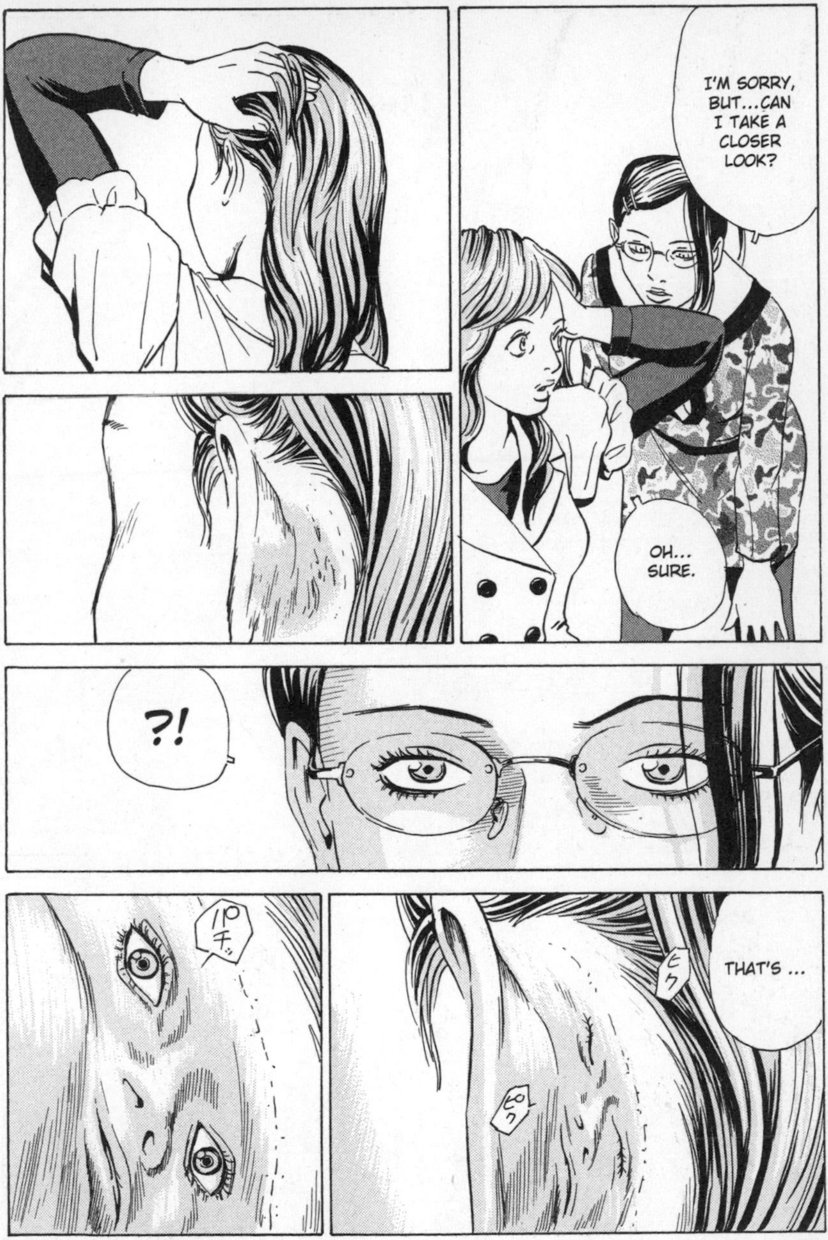
I'M SORRY, BUT...CAN I TAKE A CLOSER LOOK?
OH... SURE.
?!
THAT'S ...

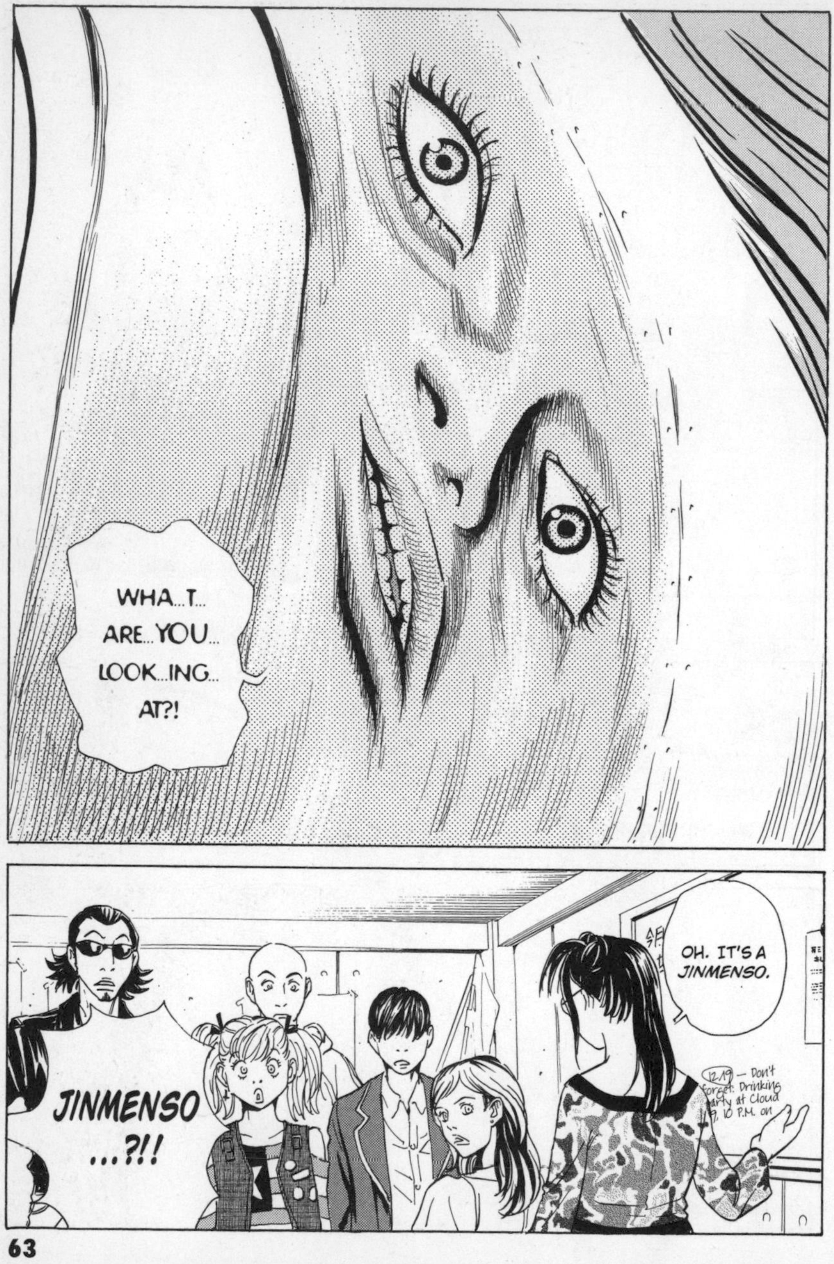
WHA...T... ARE...YOU... LOOK...ING... AT?!
OH. IT'S A JINMENSO.
12.19 — Don't forget: Drinking arty at Cloud 9, 10 P.M. on
JINMENSO ...?!!

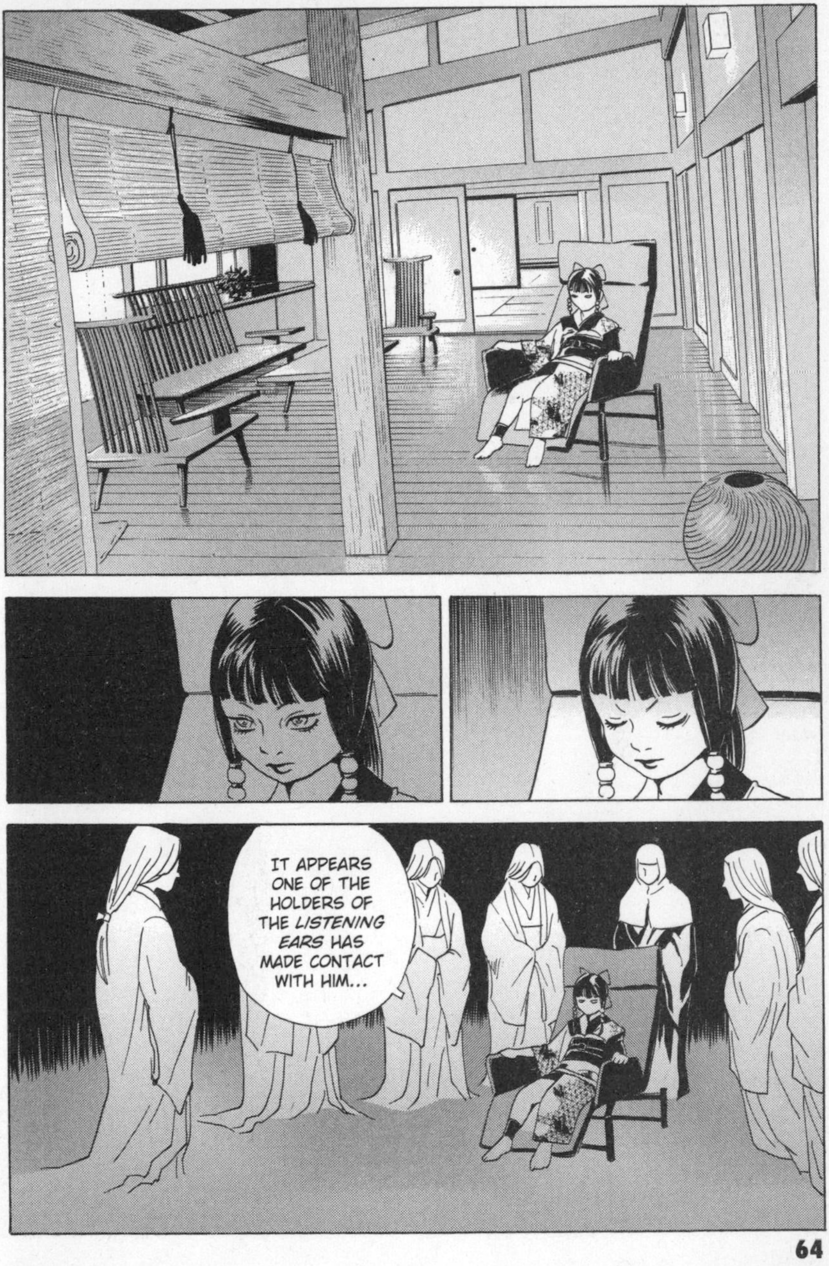
IT APPEARS ONE OF THE HOLDERS OF THE *LISTENING EARS* HAS MADE CONTACT WITH HIM...

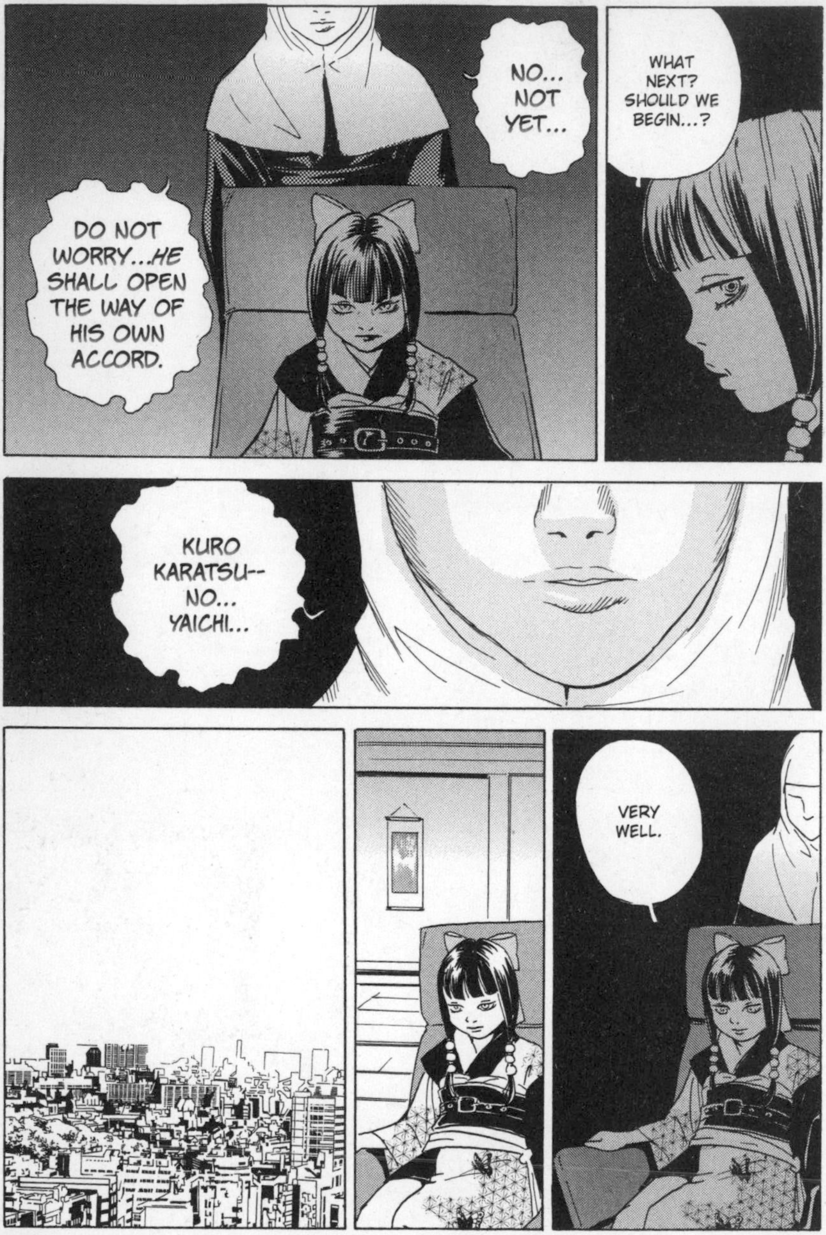
WHAT NEXT? SHOULD WE BEGIN...?
NO... NOT YET...
DO NOT WORRY...*HE* SHALL OPEN THE WAY OF HIS OWN ACCORD.
KURO KARATSU-NO... YAICHI...
VERY WELL.

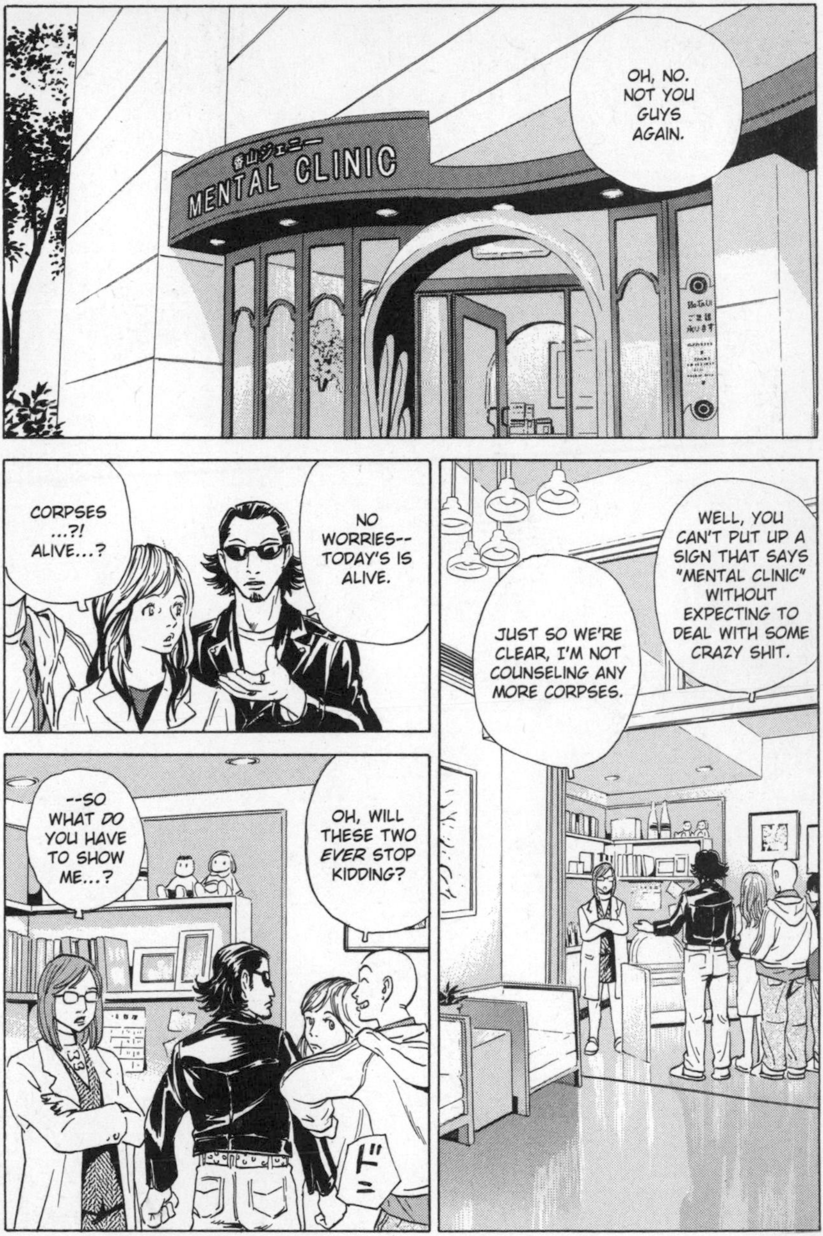
香山ジェニー
MENTAL CLINIC
OH, NO. NOT YOU GUYS AGAIN.
WELL, YOU CAN'T PUT UP A SIGN THAT SAYS "MENTAL CLINIC" WITHOUT EXPECTING TO DEAL WITH SOME CRAZY SHIT.
JUST SO WE'RE CLEAR, I'M NOT COUNSELING ANY MORE CORPSES.
NO WORRIES-- TODAY'S IS ALIVE.
CORPSES ...?! ALIVE...?
OH, WILL THESE TWO *EVER* STOP KIDDING?
--SO WHAT *DO* YOU HAVE TO SHOW ME...?
ド

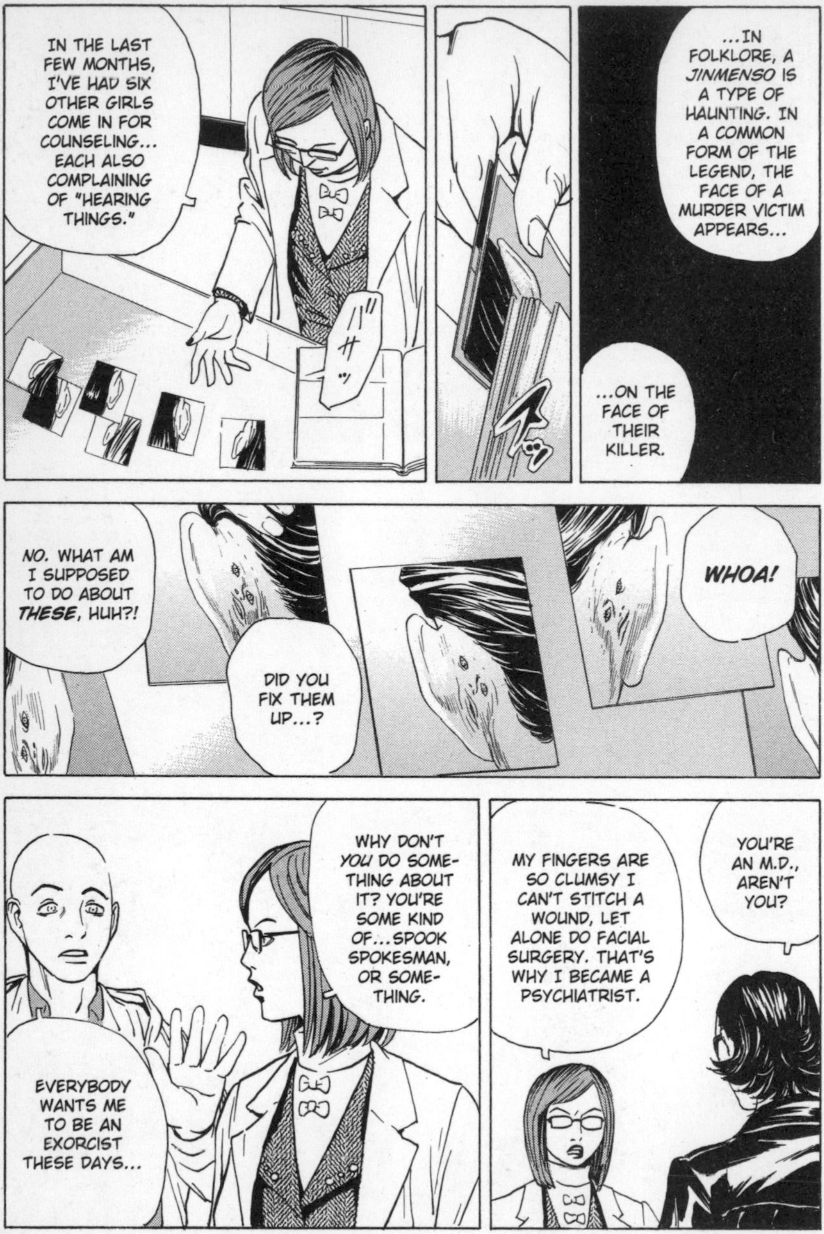
...IN FOLKLORE, A *JINMENSO* IS A TYPE OF HAUNTING. IN A COMMON FORM OF THE LEGEND, THE FACE OF A MURDER VICTIM APPEARS...
...ON THE FACE OF THEIR KILLER.
IN THE LAST FEW MONTHS, I'VE HAD SIX OTHER GIRLS COME IN FOR COUNSELING... EACH ALSO COMPLAINING OF "HEARING THINGS."
WHOA!
DID YOU FIX THEM UP...?
NO. WHAT AM I SUPPOSED TO DO ABOUT *THESE*, HUH?!
YOU'RE AN M.D., AREN'T YOU?
MY FINGERS ARE SO CLUMSY I CAN'T STITCH A WOUND, LET ALONE DO FACIAL SURGERY. THAT'S WHY I BECAME A PSYCHIATRIST.
WHY DON'T *YOU* DO SOMETHING ABOUT IT? YOU'RE SOME KIND OF...SPOOK SPOKESMAN, OR SOMETHING.
EVERYBODY WANTS ME TO BE AN EXORCIST THESE DAYS...

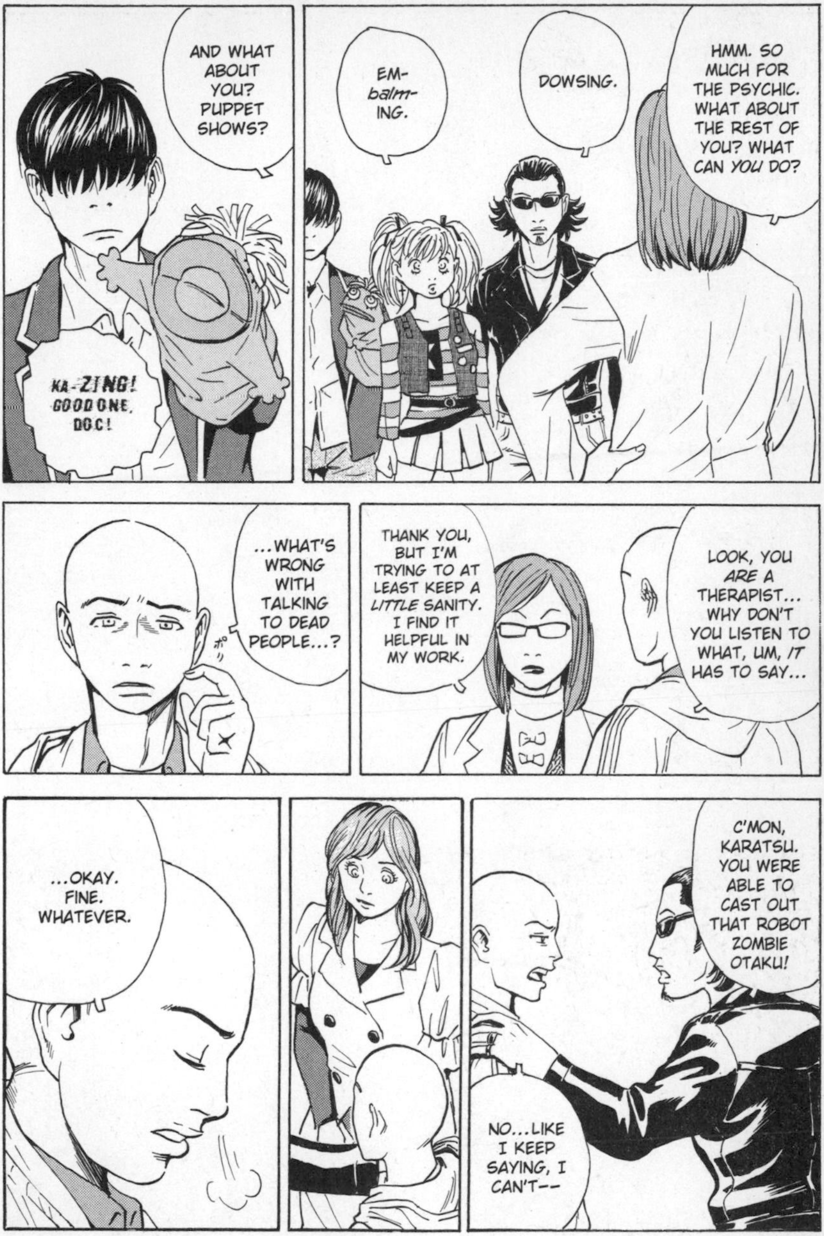
HMM. SO MUCH FOR THE PSYCHIC. WHAT ABOUT THE REST OF YOU? WHAT CAN *YOU* DO?
DOWSING.
EM-*balm*-ING.
AND WHAT ABOUT YOU? PUPPET SHOWS?
KA-ZING! GOOD ONE, DOC!
LOOK, YOU *ARE* A THERAPIST... WHY DON'T YOU LISTEN TO WHAT, UM, *IT* HAS TO SAY...
THANK YOU, BUT I'M TRYING TO AT LEAST KEEP A *LITTLE* SANITY. I FIND IT HELPFUL IN MY WORK.
...WHAT'S WRONG WITH TALKING TO DEAD PEOPLE...?
C'MON, KARATSU. YOU WERE ABLE TO CAST OUT THAT ROBOT ZOMBIE OTAKU!
NO...LIKE I KEEP SAYING, I CAN'T--
...OKAY. FINE. WHATEVER.

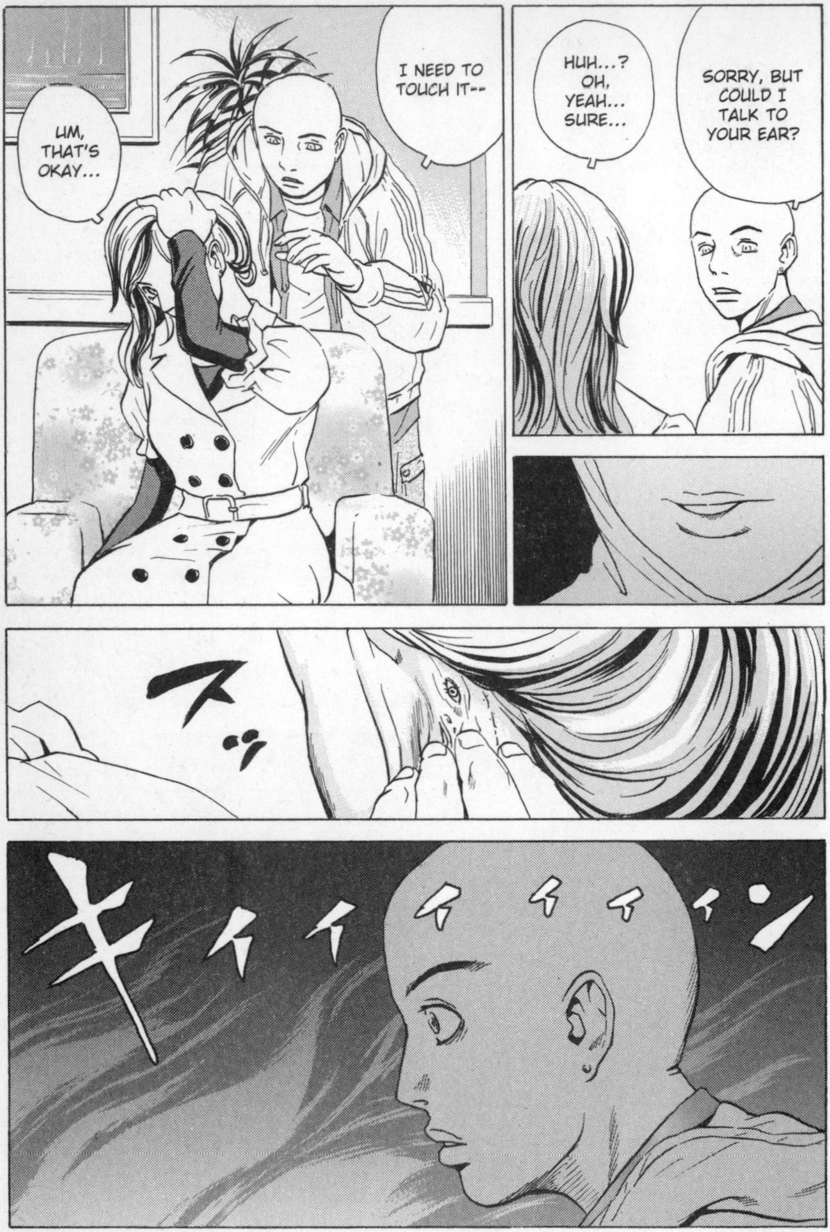
SORRY, BUT COULD I TALK TO YOUR EAR?
HUH...? OH, YEAH... SURE...
I NEED TO TOUCH IT--
UM, THAT'S OKAY...
スッ
キイイイイン

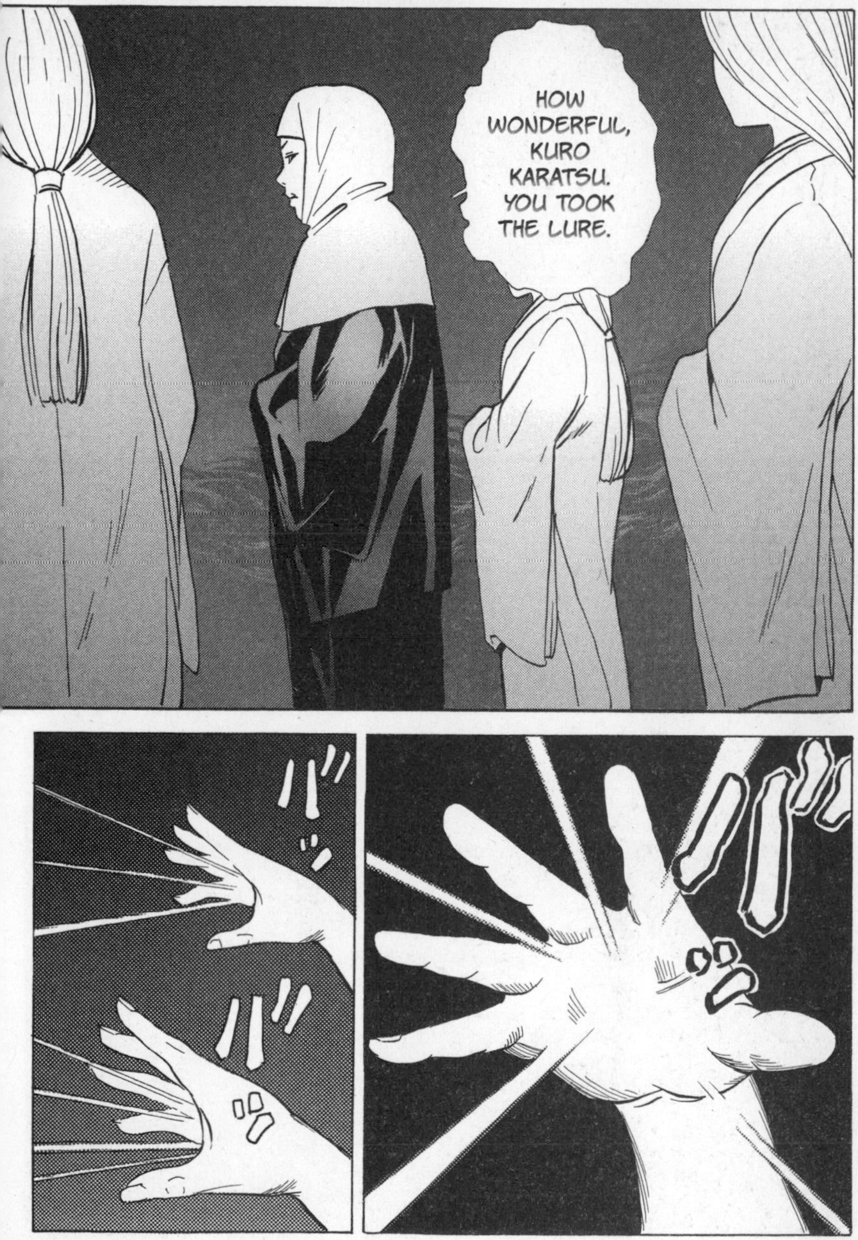
HOW WONDERFUL, KURO KARATSU. YOU TOOK THE LURE.

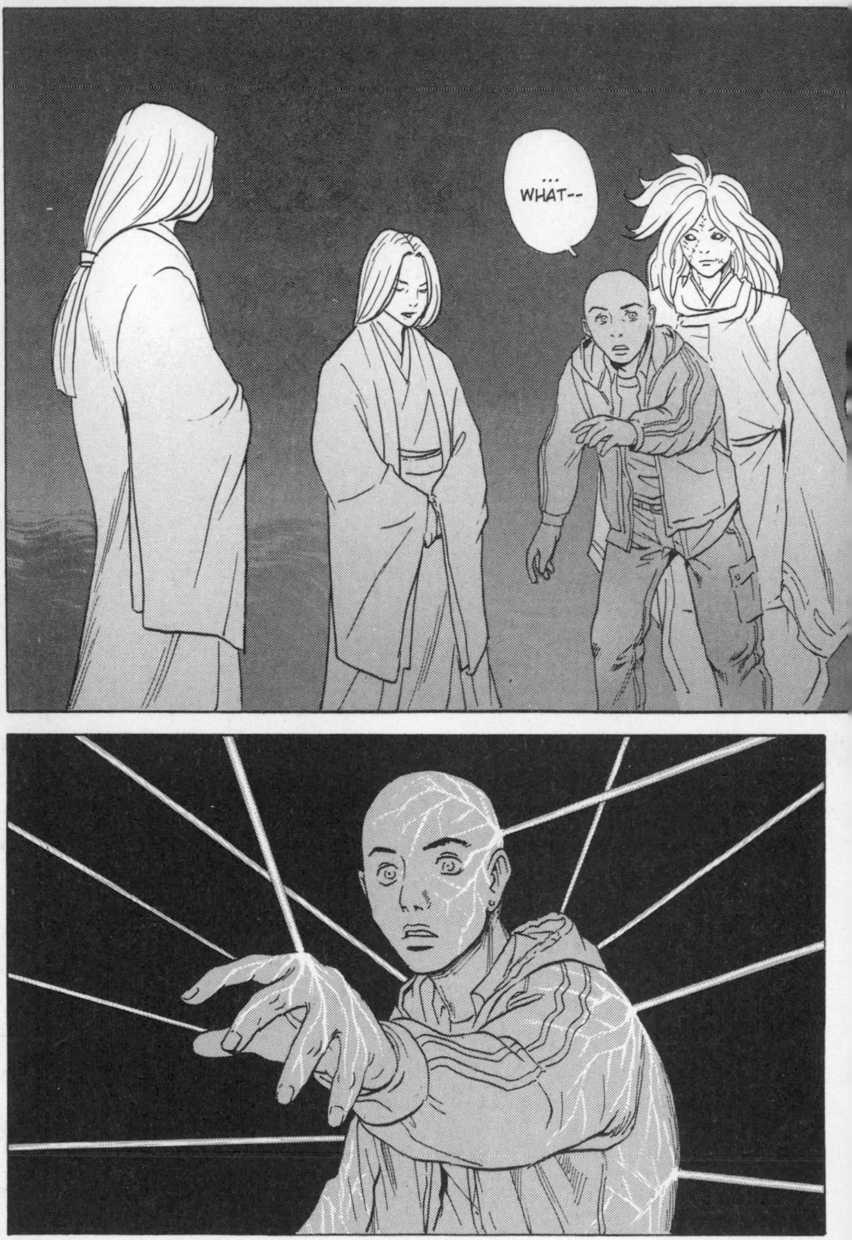
...
WHAT--

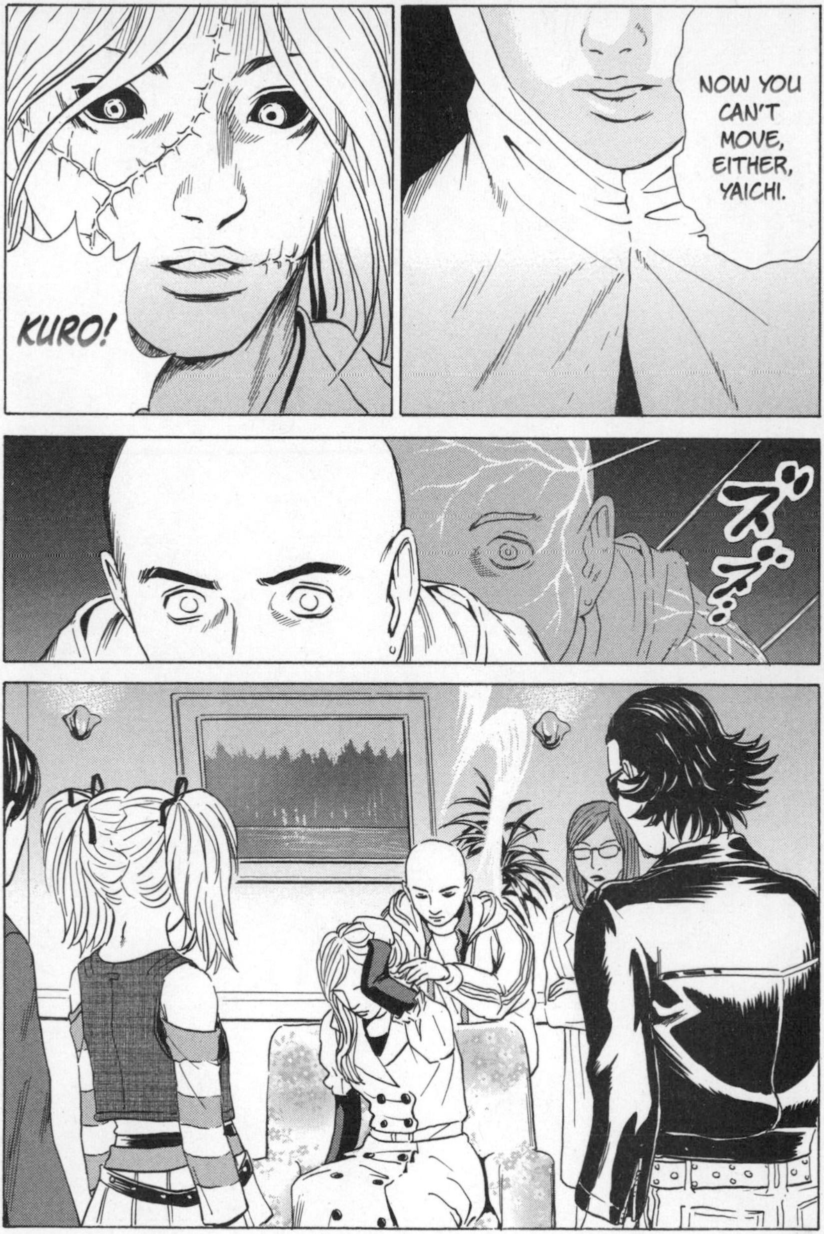
NOW YOU CAN'T MOVE, EITHER, YAICHI.
KURO!
ズププ…

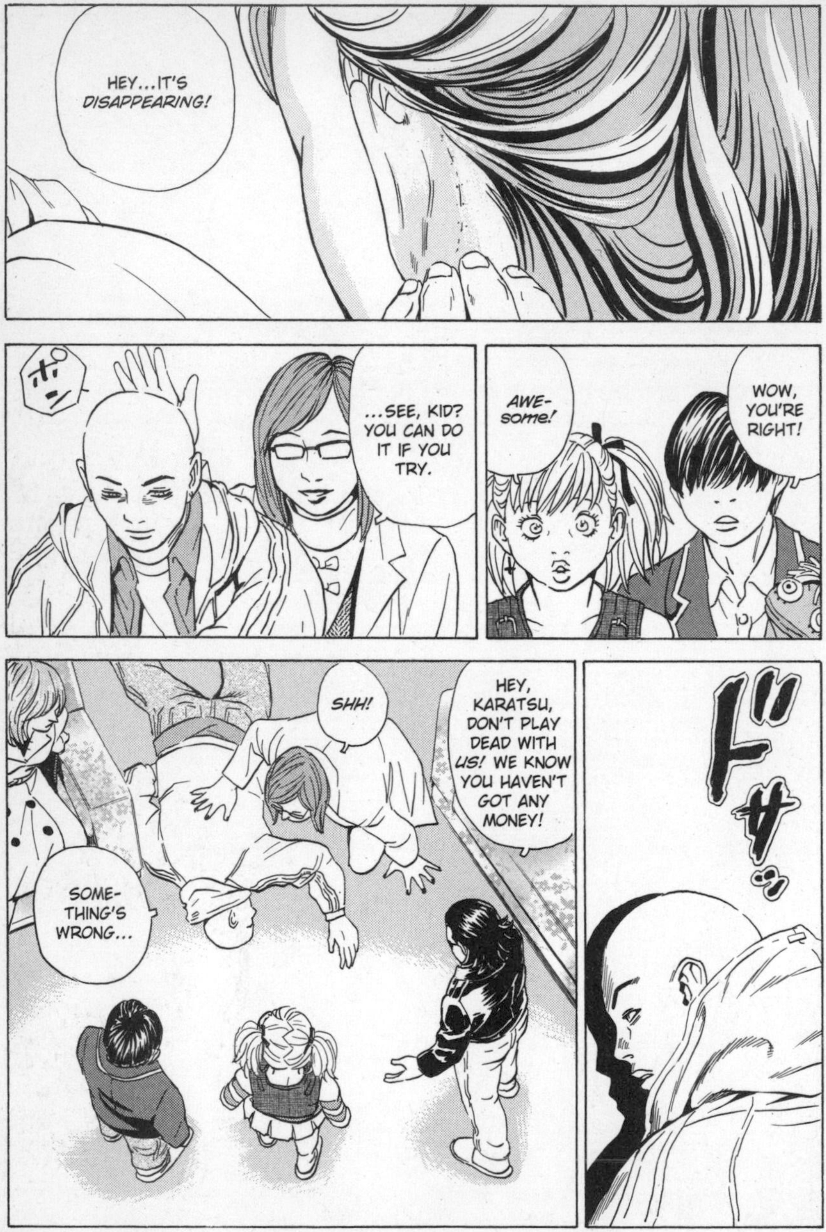
HEY...IT'S DISAPPEARING!
WOW, YOU'RE RIGHT!
AWE-some!
...SEE, KID? YOU CAN DO IT IF YOU TRY.
ドサッ
HEY, KARATSU, DON'T PLAY DEAD WITH US! WE KNOW YOU HAVEN'T GOT ANY MONEY!
SHH!
SOME-THING'S WRONG...

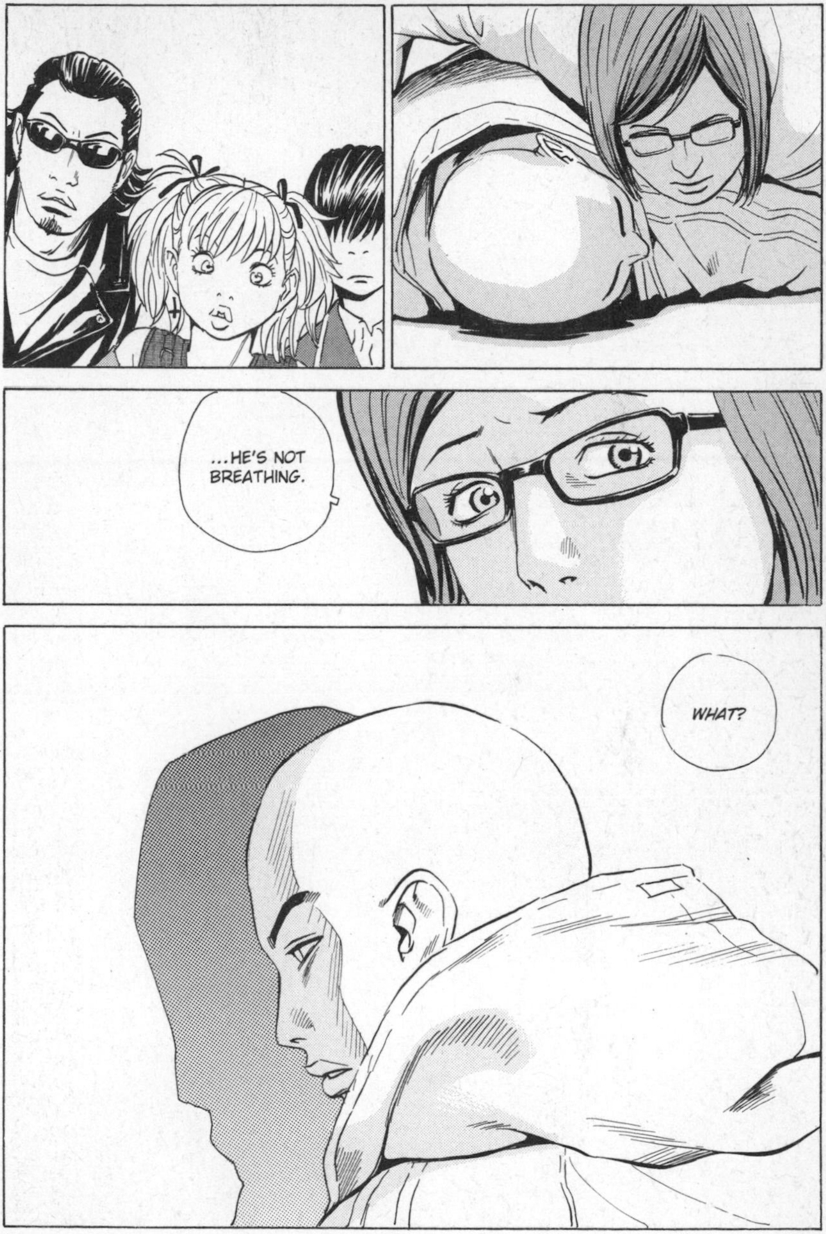
...HE'S NOT BREATHING.
WHAT?

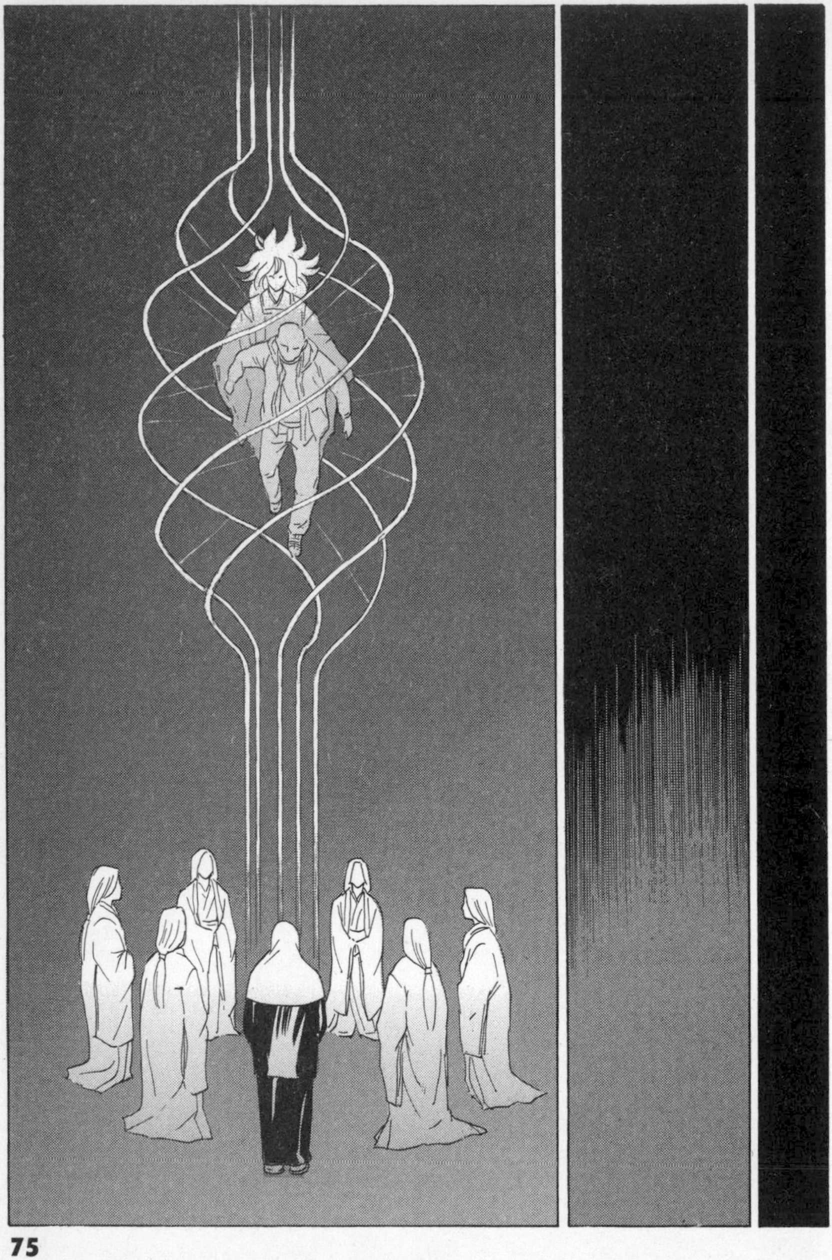

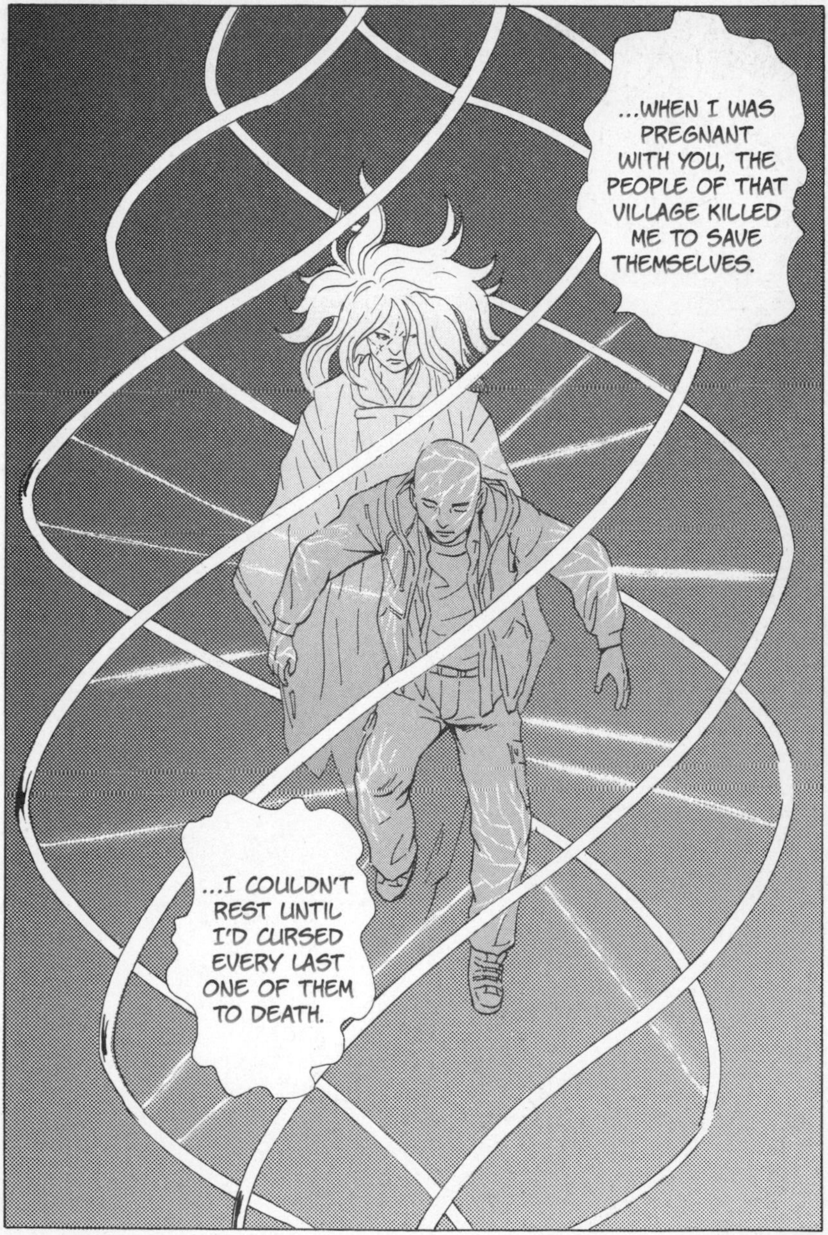
...WHEN I WAS PREGNANT WITH YOU, THE PEOPLE OF THAT VILLAGE KILLED ME TO SAVE THEMSELVES.
...I COULDN'T REST UNTIL I'D CURSED EVERY LAST ONE OF THEM TO DEATH.

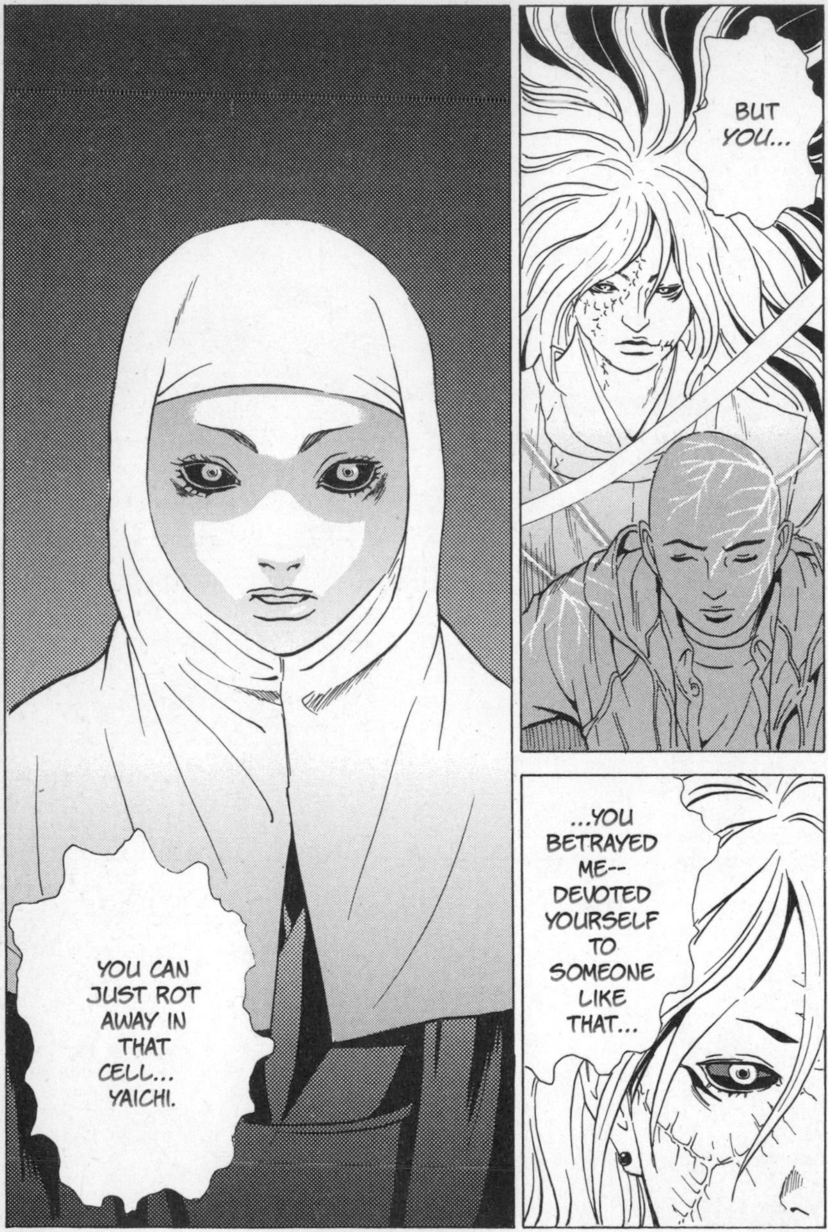
BUT YOU...
...YOU BETRAYED ME-- DEVOTED YOURSELF TO SOMEONE LIKE THAT...
YOU CAN JUST ROT AWAY IN THAT CELL... YAICHI.

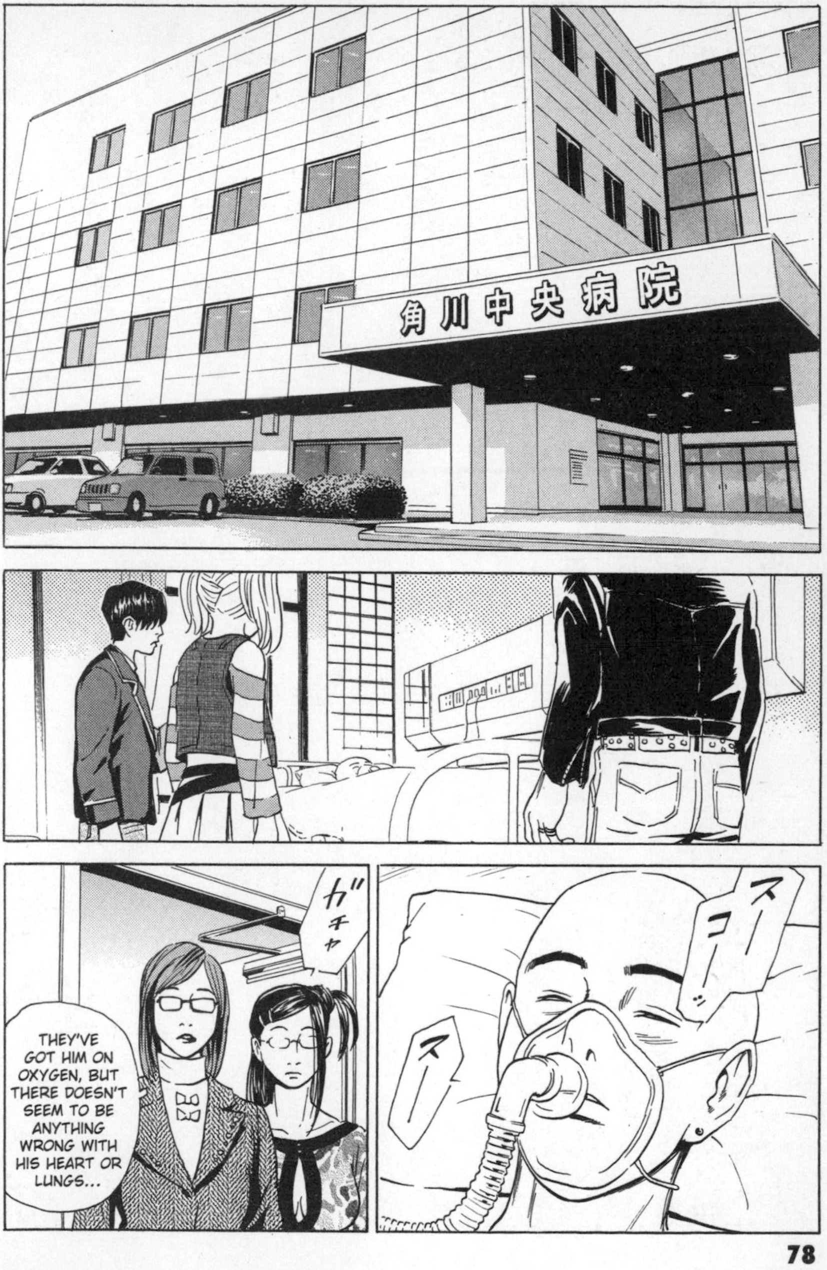
角川中央病院
スー
スー
ガチャ
THEY'VE GOT HIM ON OXYGEN, BUT THERE DOESN'T SEEM TO BE ANYTHING WRONG WITH HIS HEART OR LUNGS...

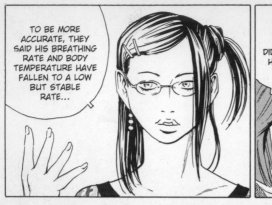

--HEY, M.D., YOU SAID HE WASN'T BREATH-ING!
WELL, I REALLY DIDN'T THINK HE WAS...
TO BE MORE ACCURATE, THEY SAID HIS BREATHING RATE AND BODY TEMPERATURE HAVE FALLEN TO A LOW BUT STABLE RATE...
THAT SOUNDS SORT OF...
YES... HIBERNA-TION, I GUESS.
DUDE! LIKE A BEAR! COOL.
BUT... WHAT MADE KARATSU GET LIKE THIS?
HE COLLAPSED AFTER HE TOUCHED THAT *JINMENSO*, DIDN'T HE? WAS *that* WHAT CAUSED IT?
BUT THE *JINMENSO* DISAP-PEARED WITHOUT A TRACE.
ALL OF THEM...EVEN THE ONES ON THE OTHER GIRLS WHO CAME IN FOR COUNSELING.

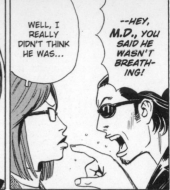

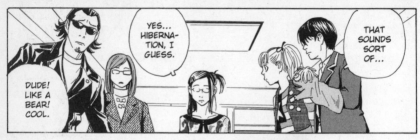

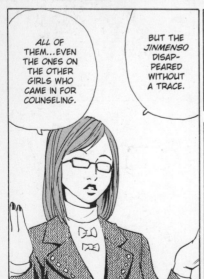

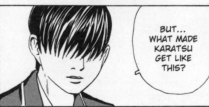

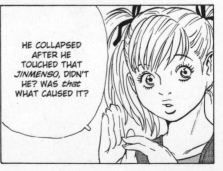

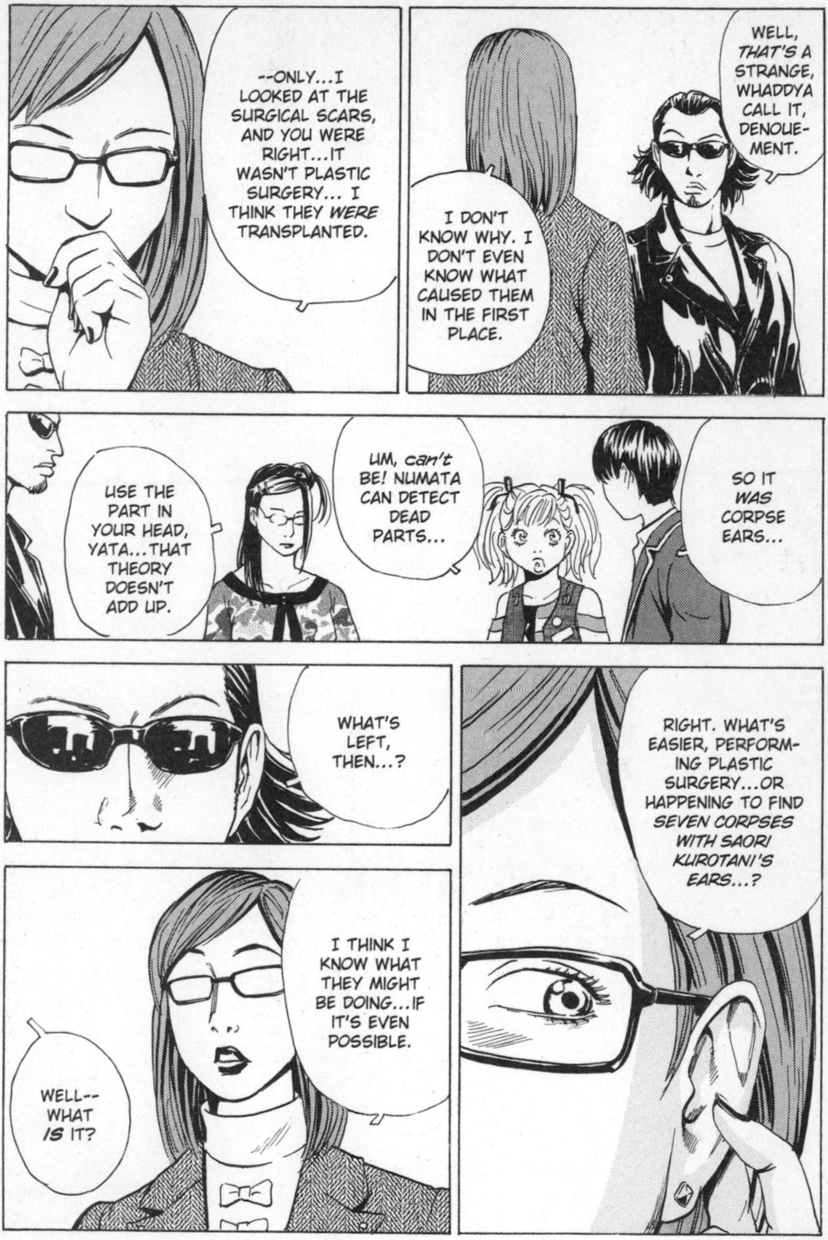

WELL, *THAT'S* A STRANGE, WHADDYA CALL IT, DENOUEMENT.
I DON'T KNOW WHY. I DON'T EVEN KNOW WHAT CAUSED THEM IN THE FIRST PLACE.
--ONLY...I LOOKED AT THE SURGICAL SCARS, AND YOU WERE RIGHT...IT WASN'T PLASTIC SURGERY... I THINK THEY *WERE* TRANSPLANTED.
SO IT *WAS* CORPSE EARS...
UM, *can't* BE! NUMATA CAN DETECT DEAD PARTS...
USE THE PART IN YOUR HEAD, YATA...THAT THEORY DOESN'T ADD UP.
RIGHT. WHAT'S EASIER, PERFORMING PLASTIC SURGERY...OR HAPPENING TO FIND *SEVEN CORPSES WITH SAORI KUROTANI'S EARS...?*
WHAT'S LEFT, THEN...?
I THINK I KNOW WHAT THEY MIGHT BE DOING...IF IT'S EVEN POSSIBLE.
WELL-- WHAT *IS* IT?

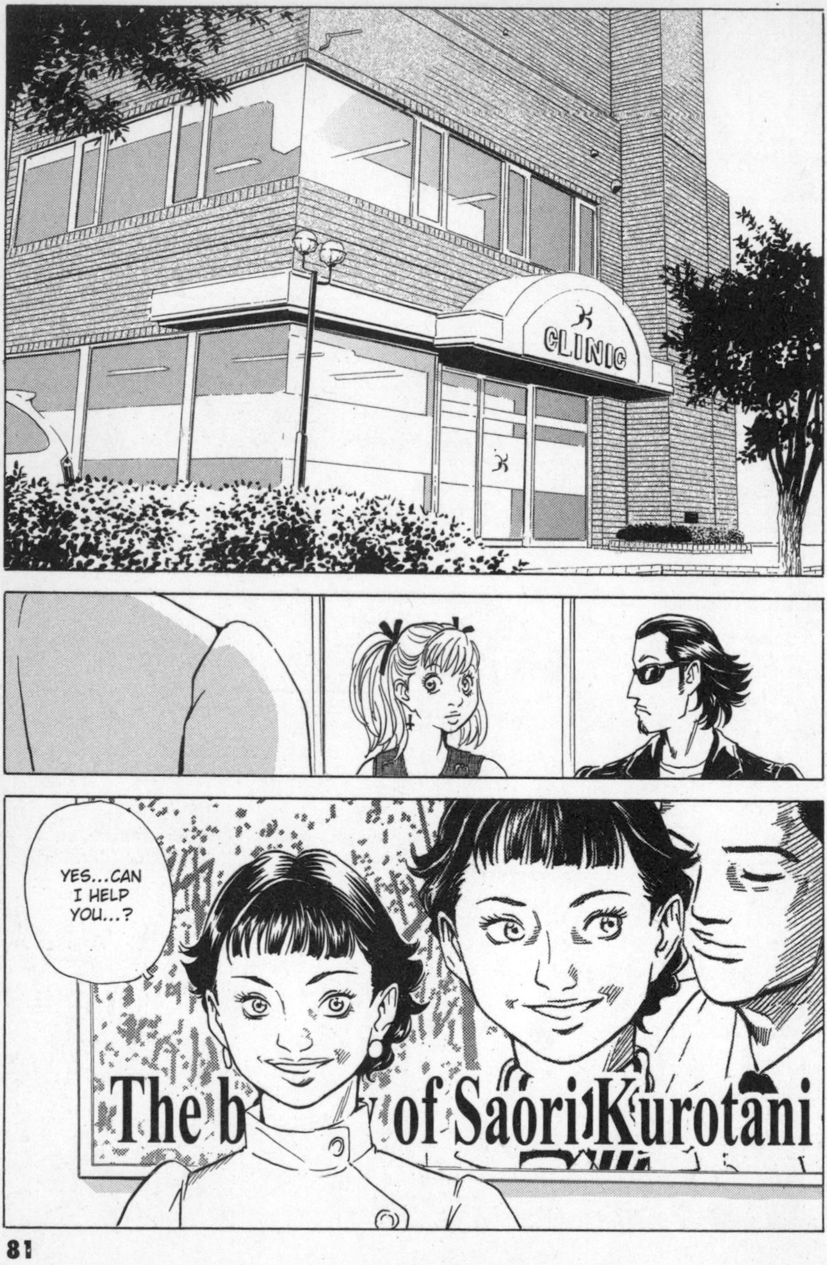
CLINIC
YES...CAN I HELP YOU...?
The b
y of Saori Kurotani

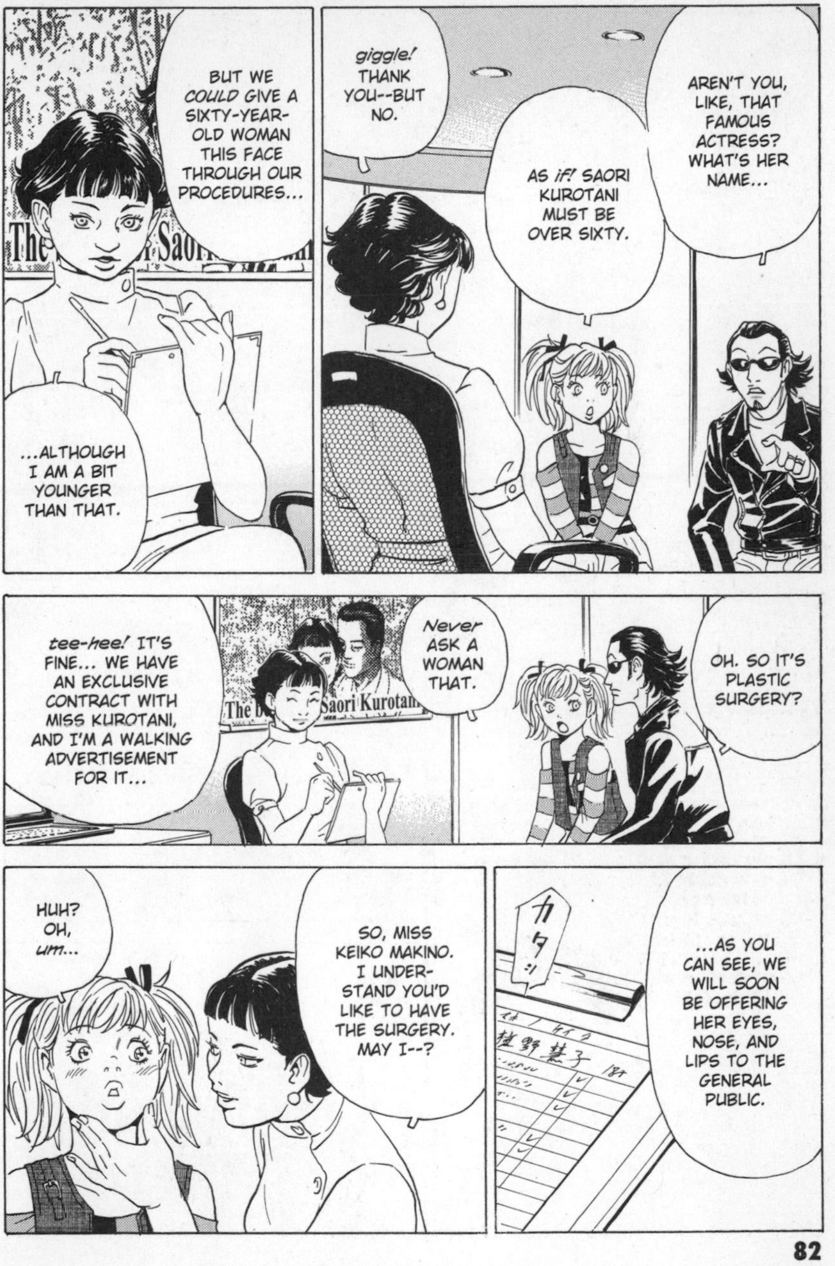
AREN'T YOU, LIKE, THAT FAMOUS ACTRESS? WHAT'S HER NAME...
AS *if!* SAORI KUROTANI MUST BE OVER SIXTY.
giggle! THANK YOU--BUT NO.
BUT WE *COULD* GIVE A SIXTY-YEAR-OLD WOMAN THIS FACE THROUGH OUR PROCEDURES...
...ALTHOUGH I AM A BIT YOUNGER THAN THAT.
OH. SO IT'S PLASTIC SURGERY?
Never ASK A WOMAN THAT.
tee-hee! IT'S FINE... WE HAVE AN EXCLUSIVE CONTRACT WITH MISS KUROTANI, AND I'M A WALKING ADVERTISEMENT FOR IT...
カタ!!
...AS YOU CAN SEE, WE WILL SOON BE OFFERING HER EYES, NOSE, AND LIPS TO THE GENERAL PUBLIC.
SO, MISS KEIKO MAKINO. I UNDERSTAND YOU'D LIKE TO HAVE THE SURGERY. MAY I--?
HUH? OH, *um...*

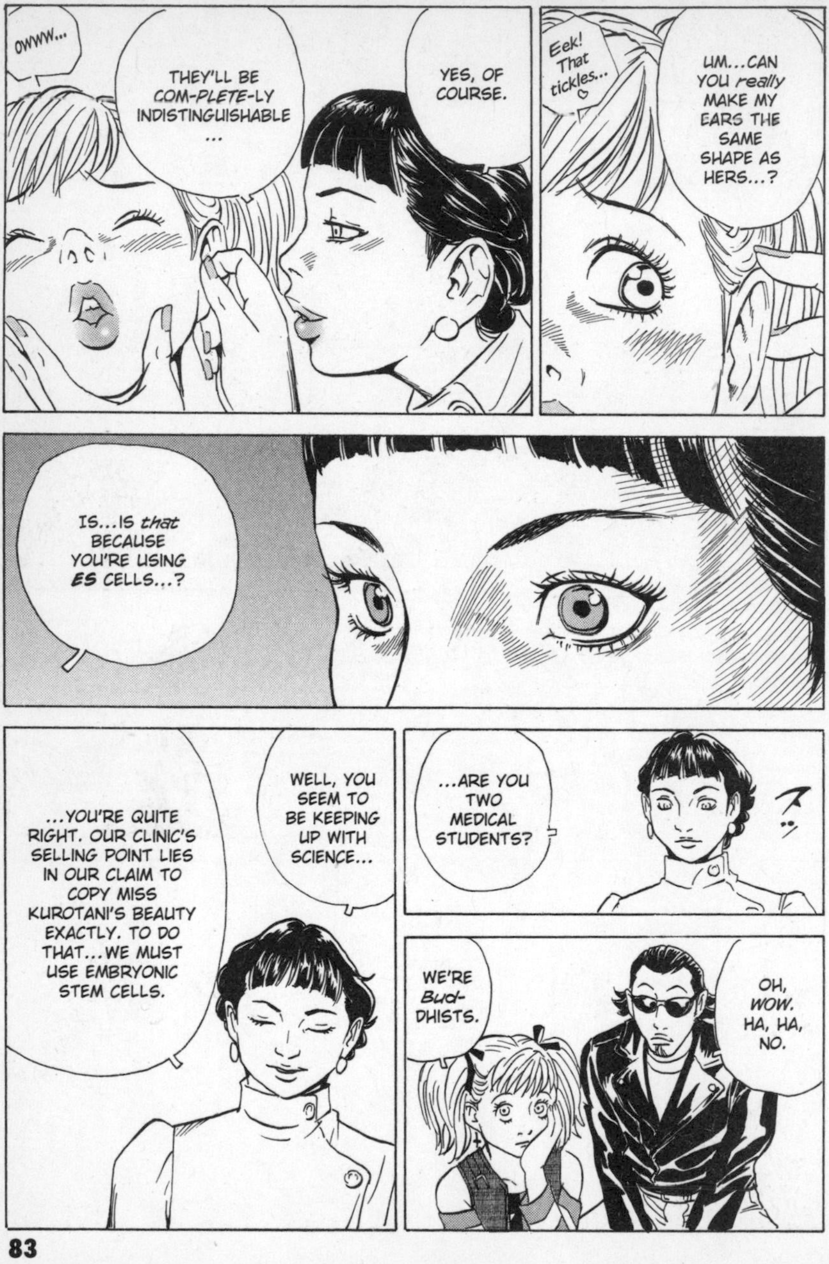
UM...CAN YOU *really* MAKE MY EARS THE SAME SHAPE AS HERS...?
Eek! That tickles... ♡
YES, OF COURSE.
THEY'LL BE *COM-PLETE*-LY INDISTINGUISHABLE ...
OWWW...
IS...IS *that* BECAUSE YOU'RE USING **ES** CELLS...?
...ARE YOU TWO MEDICAL STUDENTS?
スッ
OH, *WOW*. HA, HA, NO.
WE'RE *Bud*-DHISTS.
WELL, YOU SEEM TO BE KEEPING UP WITH SCIENCE...
...YOU'RE QUITE RIGHT. OUR CLINIC'S SELLING POINT LIES IN OUR CLAIM TO COPY MISS KUROTANI'S BEAUTY EXACTLY. TO DO THAT...WE MUST USE EMBRYONIC STEM CELLS.

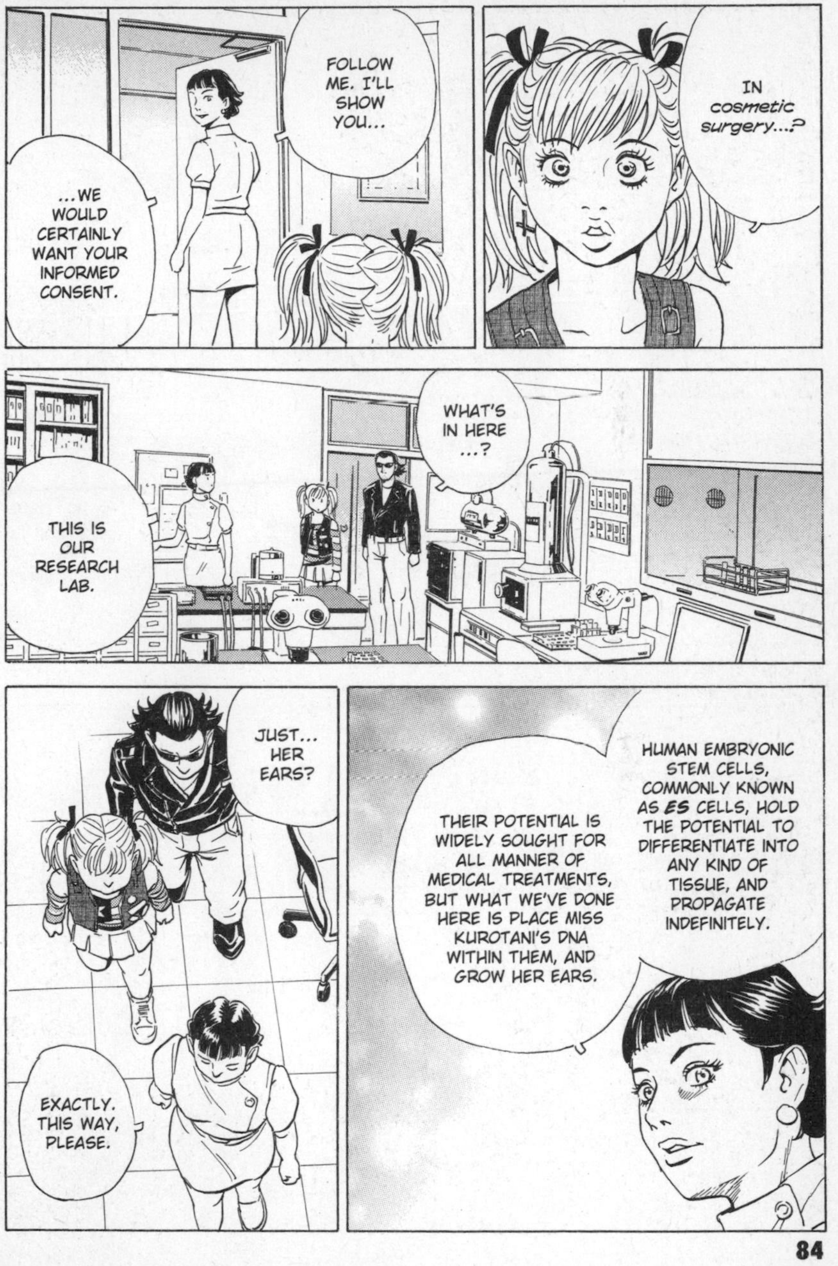

IN *cosmetic surgery...?*
FOLLOW ME. I'LL SHOW YOU...
...WE WOULD CERTAINLY WANT YOUR INFORMED CONSENT.
WHAT'S IN HERE ...?
THIS IS OUR RESEARCH LAB.
HUMAN EMBRYONIC STEM CELLS, COMMONLY KNOWN AS ***ES*** CELLS, HOLD THE POTENTIAL TO DIFFERENTIATE INTO ANY KIND OF TISSUE, AND PROPAGATE INDEFINITELY.
THEIR POTENTIAL IS WIDELY SOUGHT FOR ALL MANNER OF MEDICAL TREATMENTS, BUT WHAT WE'VE DONE HERE IS PLACE MISS KUROTANI'S DNA WITHIN THEM, AND GROW HER EARS.
JUST... HER EARS?
EXACTLY. THIS WAY, PLEASE.

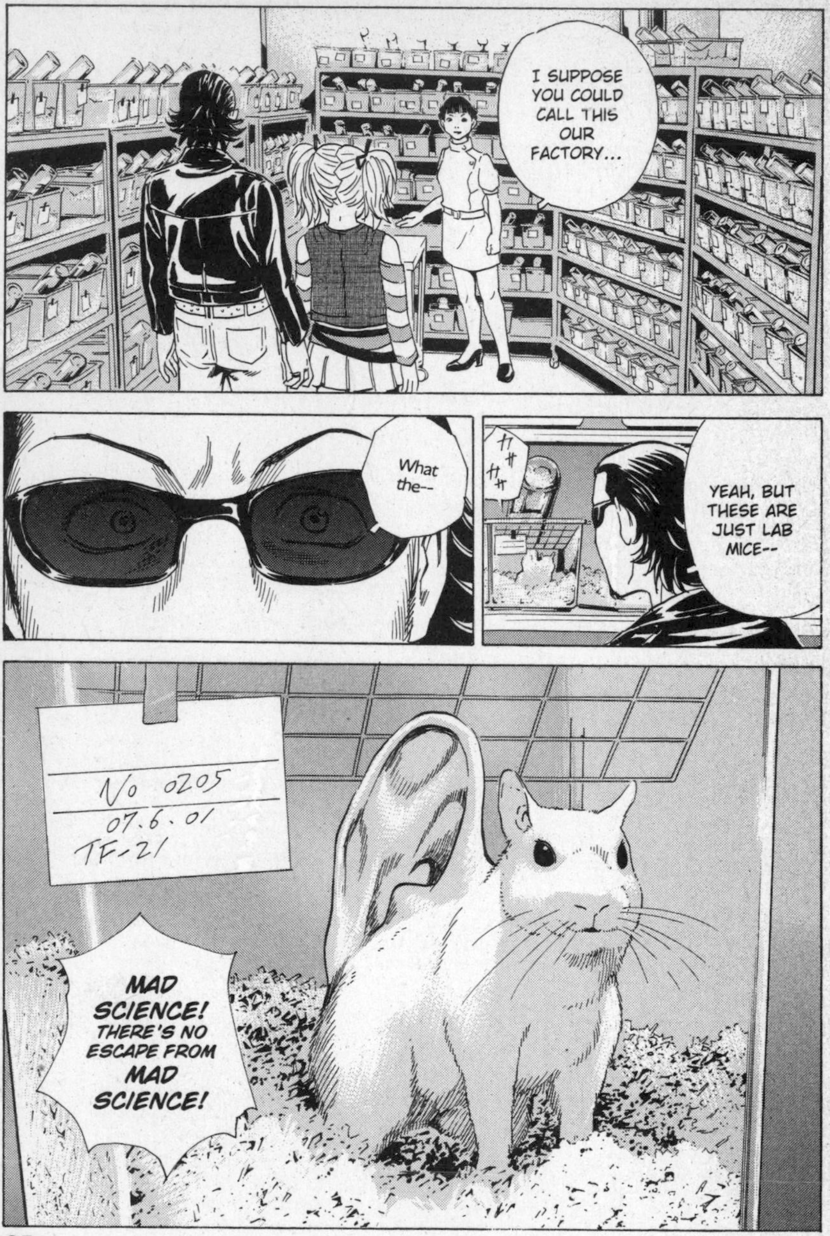
I SUPPOSE YOU COULD CALL THIS OUR FACTORY...
YEAH, BUT THESE ARE JUST LAB MICE--
What the--
No 0205
07.6.01
TF-21
MAD SCIENCE! THERE'S NO ESCAPE FROM MAD SCIENCE!

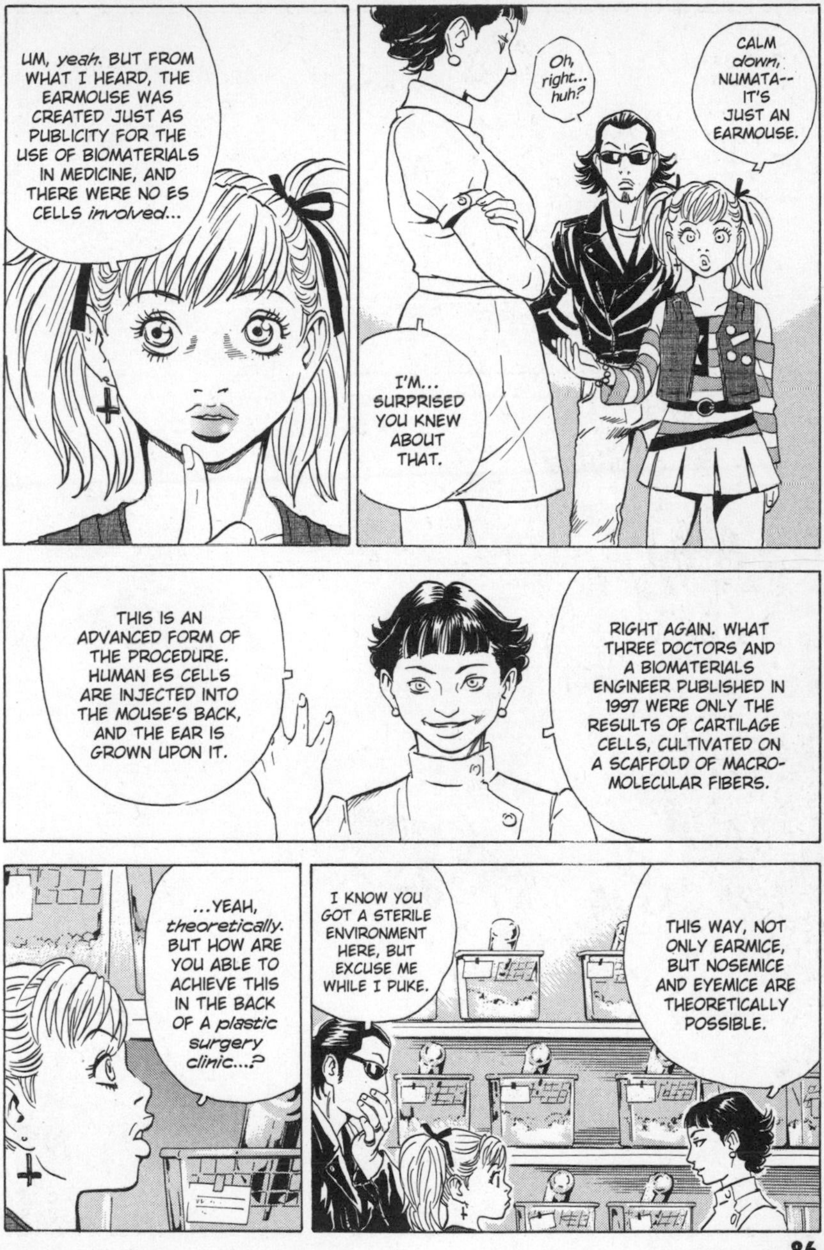
CALM *down,* NUMATA-- IT'S JUST AN EARMOUSE.
Oh, right... huh?
I'M... SURPRISED YOU KNEW ABOUT THAT.
UM, *yeah.* BUT FROM WHAT I HEARD, THE EARMOUSE WAS CREATED JUST AS PUBLICITY FOR THE USE OF BIOMATERIALS IN MEDICINE, AND THERE WERE NO ES CELLS *involved*...
RIGHT AGAIN. WHAT THREE DOCTORS AND A BIOMATERIALS ENGINEER PUBLISHED IN 1997 WERE ONLY THE RESULTS OF CARTILAGE CELLS, CULTIVATED ON A SCAFFOLD OF MACRO-MOLECULAR FIBERS.
THIS IS AN ADVANCED FORM OF THE PROCEDURE. HUMAN ES CELLS ARE INJECTED INTO THE MOUSE'S BACK, AND THE EAR IS GROWN UPON IT.
THIS WAY, NOT ONLY EARMICE, BUT NOSEMICE AND EYEMICE ARE THEORETICALLY POSSIBLE.
I KNOW YOU GOT A STERILE ENVIRONMENT HERE, BUT EXCUSE ME WHILE I PUKE.
...YEAH, *theoretically.* BUT HOW ARE YOU ABLE TO ACHIEVE THIS IN THE BACK OF A *plastic surgery clinic*...?

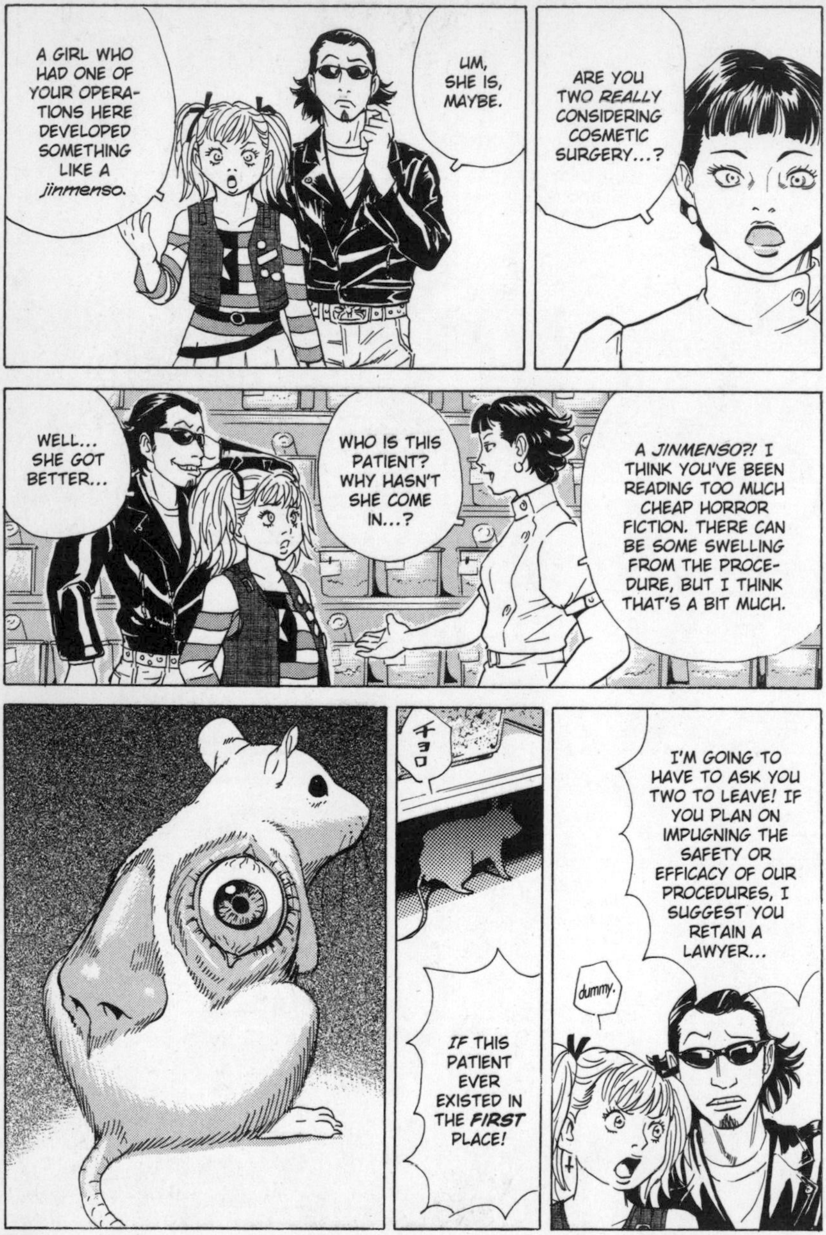
ARE YOU TWO *REALLY* CONSIDERING COSMETIC SURGERY...?
UM, SHE IS, MAYBE.
A GIRL WHO HAD ONE OF YOUR OPERATIONS HERE DEVELOPED SOMETHING LIKE A *jinmenso*.
A *JINMENSO?!* I THINK YOU'VE BEEN READING TOO MUCH CHEAP HORROR FICTION. THERE CAN BE SOME SWELLING FROM THE PROCEDURE, BUT I THINK THAT'S A BIT MUCH.
WHO IS THIS PATIENT? WHY HASN'T SHE COME IN...?
WELL... SHE GOT BETTER...
I'M GOING TO HAVE TO ASK YOU TWO TO LEAVE! IF YOU PLAN ON IMPUGNING THE SAFETY OR EFFICACY OF OUR PROCEDURES, I SUGGEST YOU RETAIN A LAWYER...
IF THIS PATIENT EVER EXISTED IN THE *FIRST* PLACE!
dummy.
チョロ

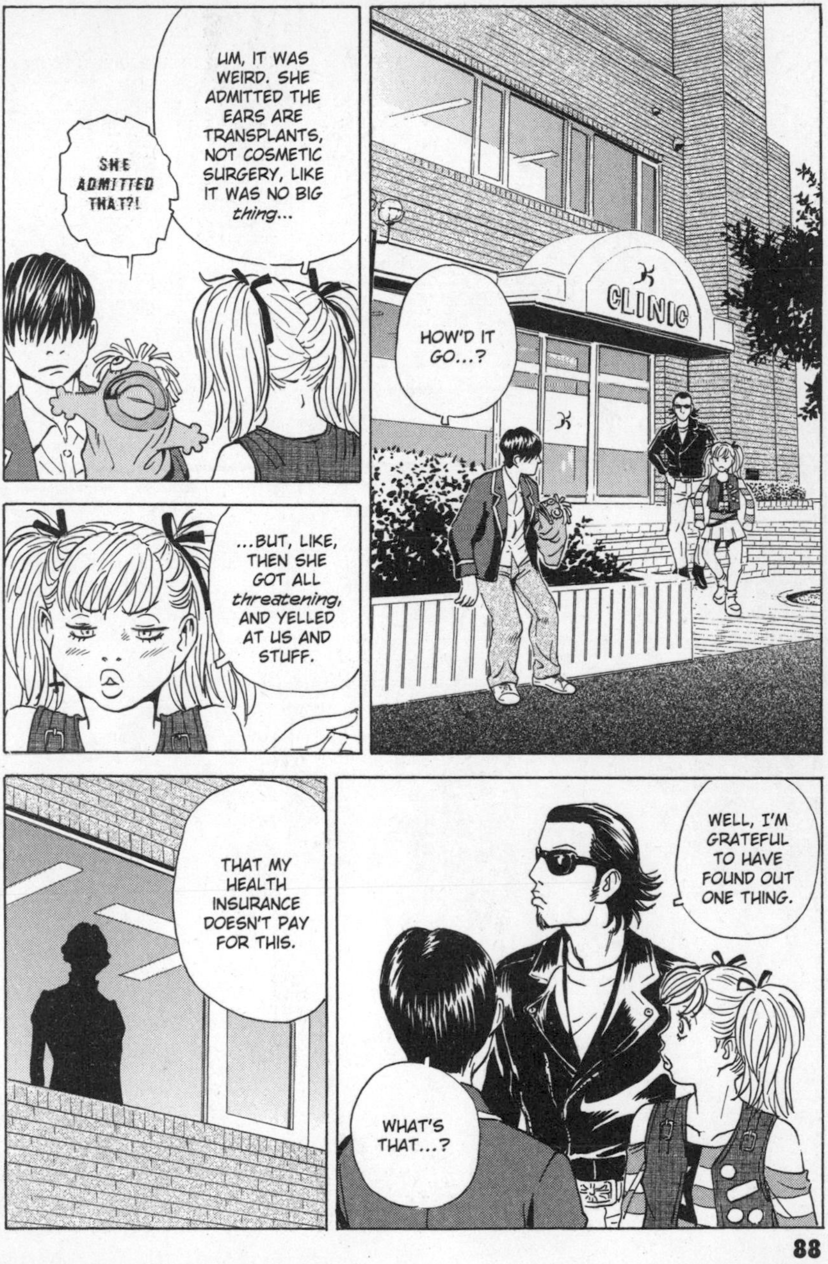
HOW'D IT GO...?
UM, IT WAS WEIRD. SHE ADMITTED THE EARS ARE TRANSPLANTS, NOT COSMETIC SURGERY, LIKE IT WAS NO BIG *thing*...
SHE ADMITTED THAT?!
...BUT, LIKE, THEN SHE GOT ALL *threatening*, AND YELLED AT US AND STUFF.
CLINIC
WELL, I'M GRATEFUL TO HAVE FOUND OUT ONE THING.
WHAT'S THAT...?
THAT MY HEALTH INSURANCE DOESN'T PAY FOR THIS.

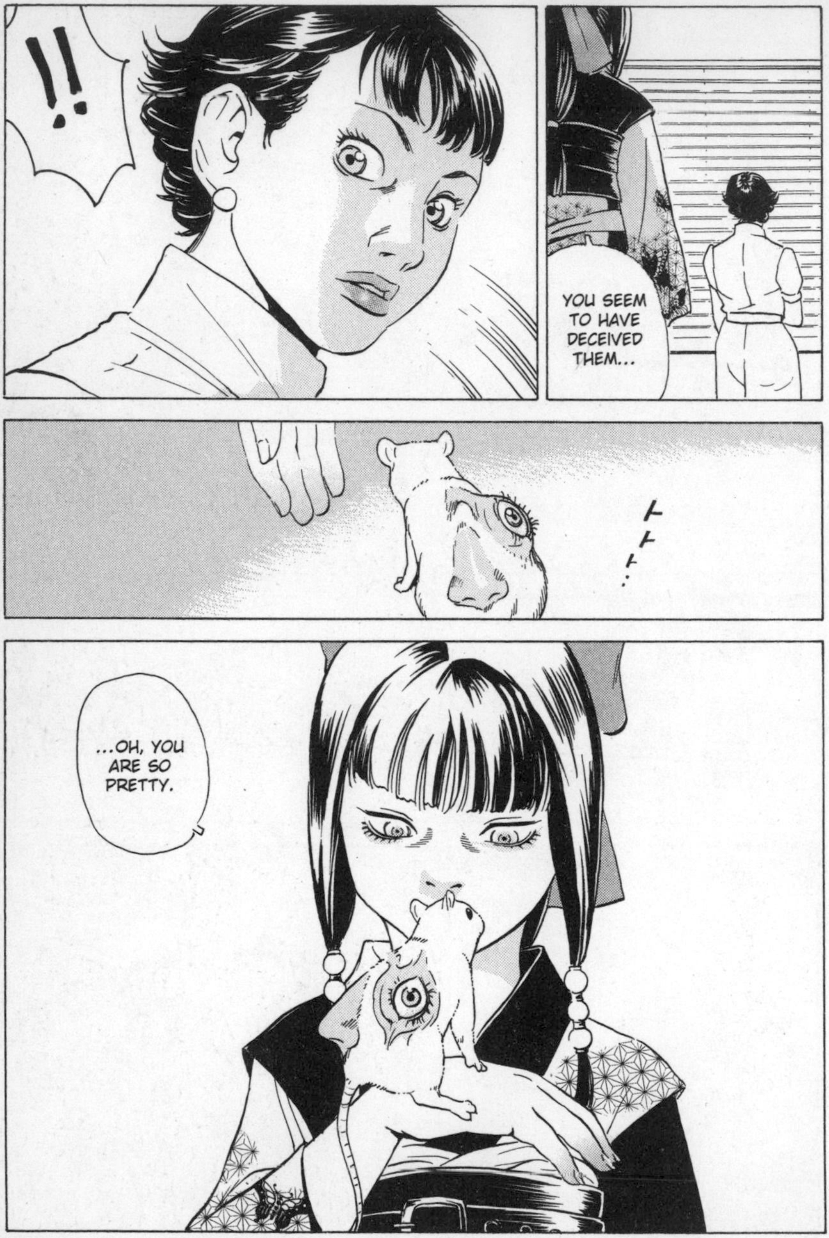
YOU SEEM TO HAVE DECEIVED THEM...
!!
...OH, YOU ARE SO PRETTY.

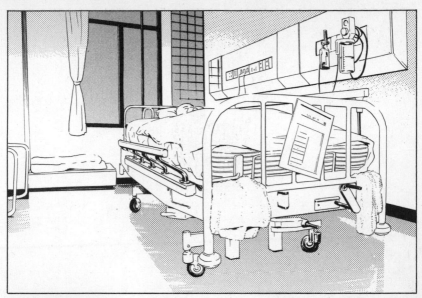

SORRY TO SUMMON YOU FOR THIS.

OH, IT'S NO TROUBLE. HOW'S THE BOY?

...NOT GREAT, AS YOU CAN SEE.

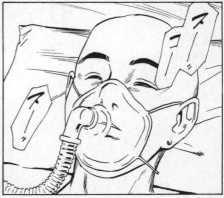

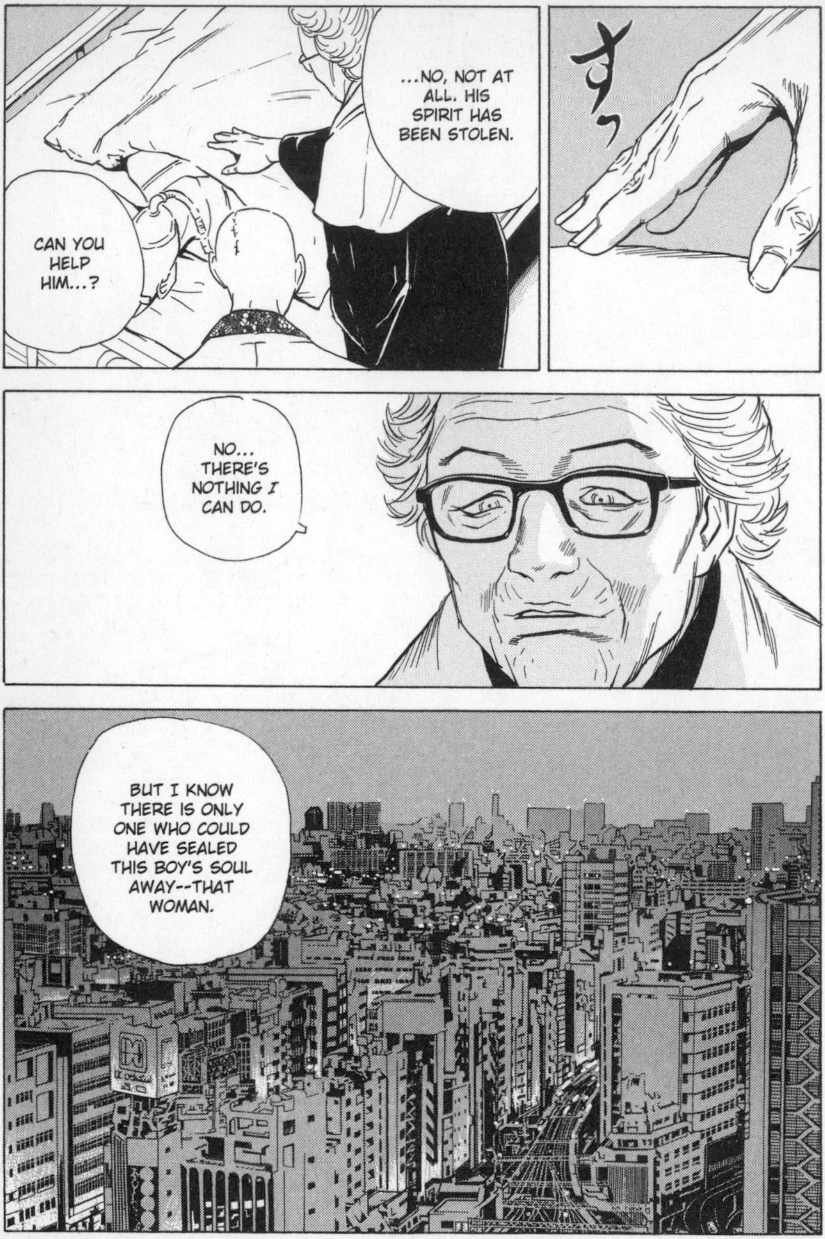
すっ
...NO, NOT AT ALL. HIS SPIRIT HAS BEEN STOLEN.
CAN YOU HELP HIM...?
NO... THERE'S NOTHING I CAN DO.
BUT I KNOW THERE IS ONLY ONE WHO COULD HAVE SEALED THIS BOY'S SOUL AWAY--THAT WOMAN.

2nd delivery: pretty • pretty—the end

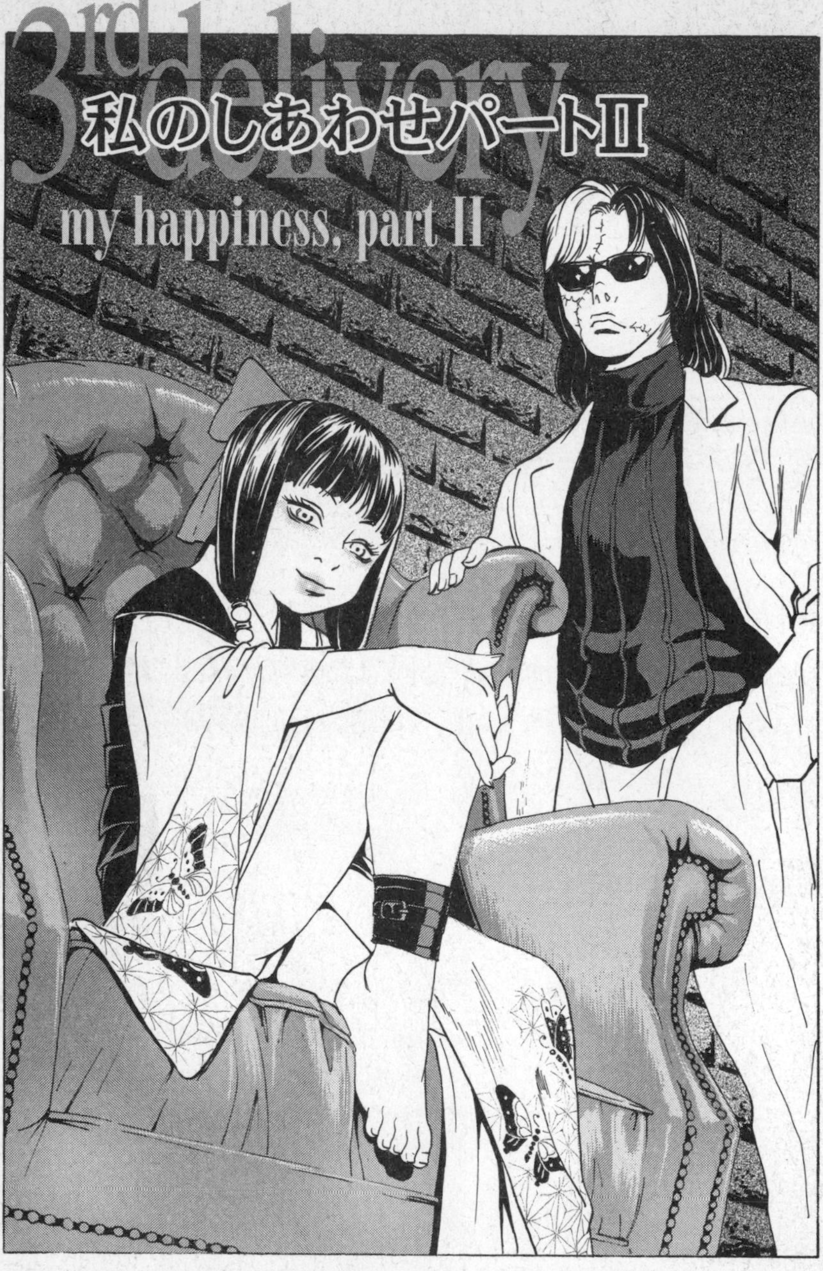
3rd delivery
私のしあわせパートII
my happiness, part II

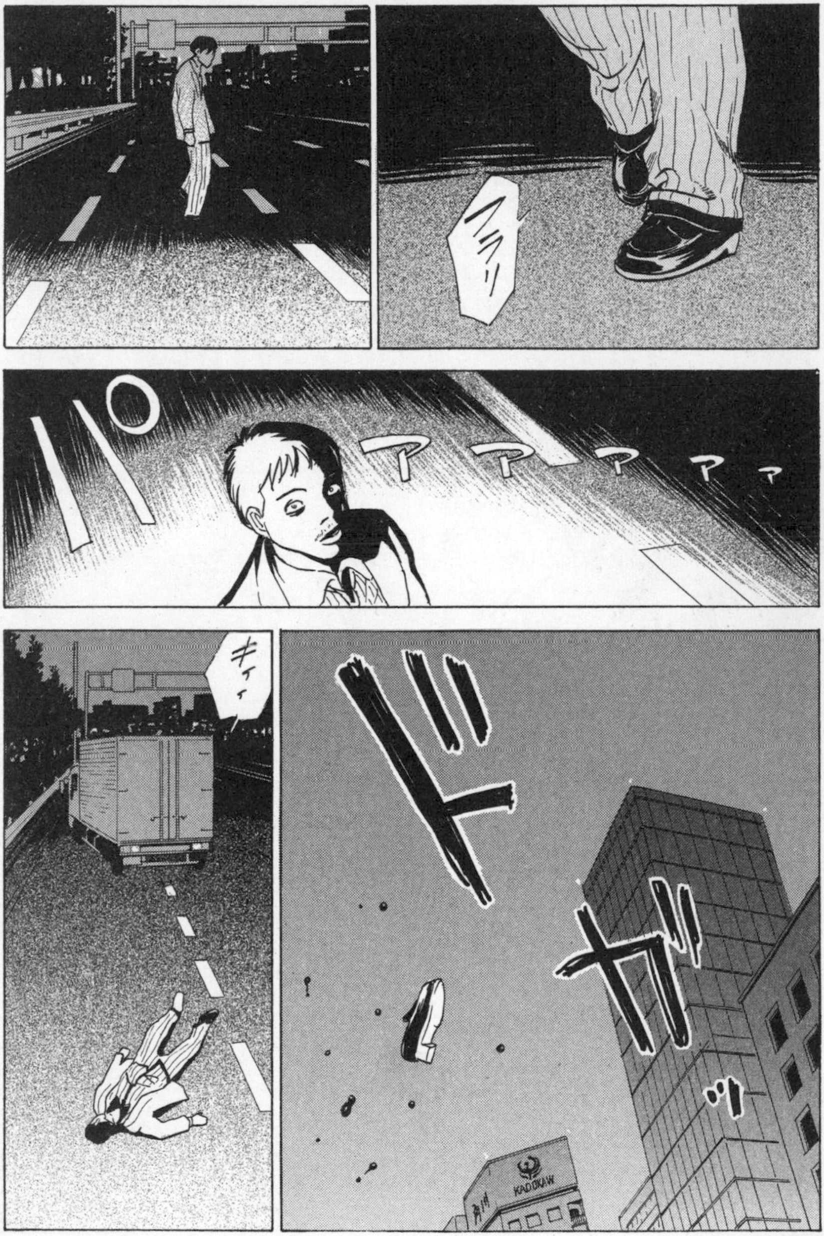
フラッ
パアアアアア
ドガッ
キィィ

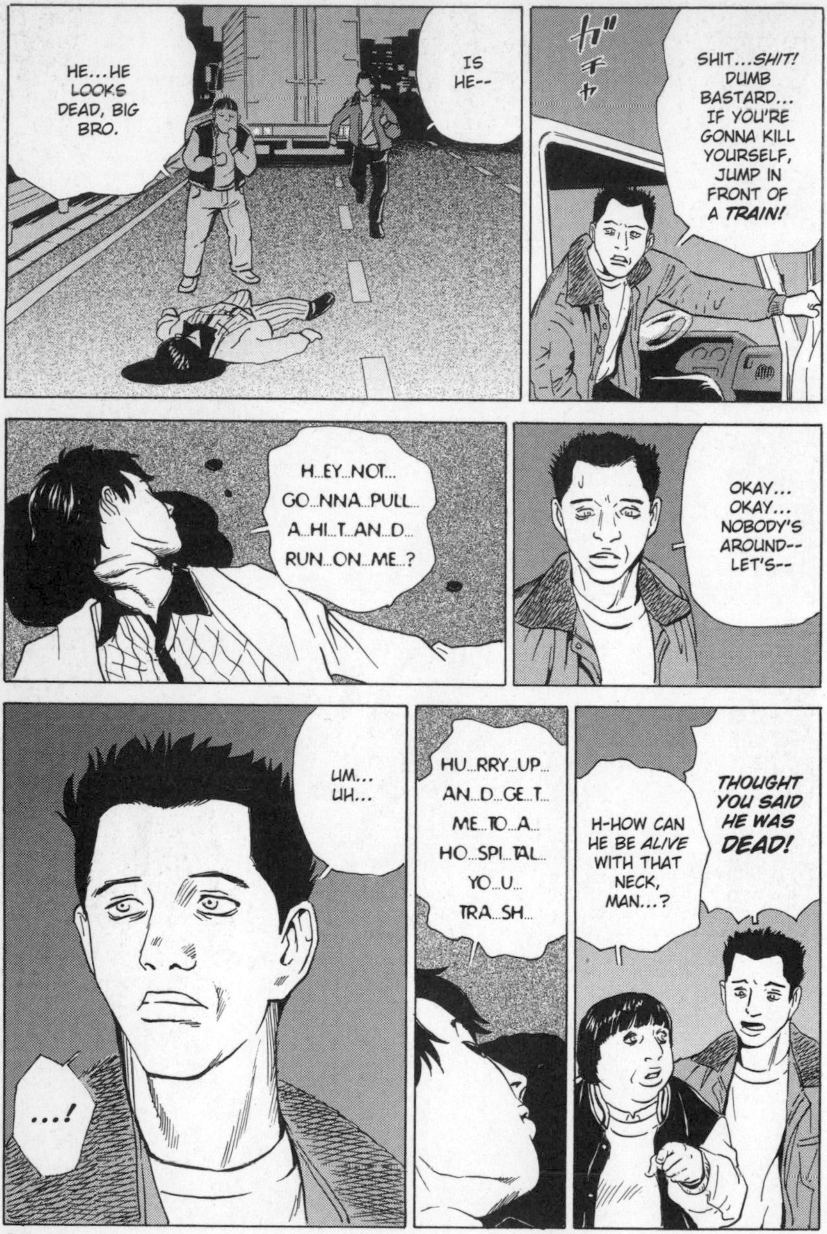
ガチャ
SHIT...SHIT! DUMB BASTARD... IF YOU'RE GONNA KILL YOURSELF, JUMP IN FRONT OF A TRAIN!
IS HE--
HE...HE LOOKS DEAD, BIG BRO.
OKAY... OKAY... NOBODY'S AROUND-- LET'S--
H...EY...NOT... GO...NNA...PULL... A...HI...T...AN...D... RUN...ON...ME...?
THOUGHT YOU SAID HE WAS DEAD!
H-HOW CAN HE BE ALIVE WITH THAT NECK, MAN...?
HU...RRY...UP... AN...D...GE...T... ME...TO...A... HO...SPI...TAL... YO...U... TRA...SH...
UM... UH...
...!

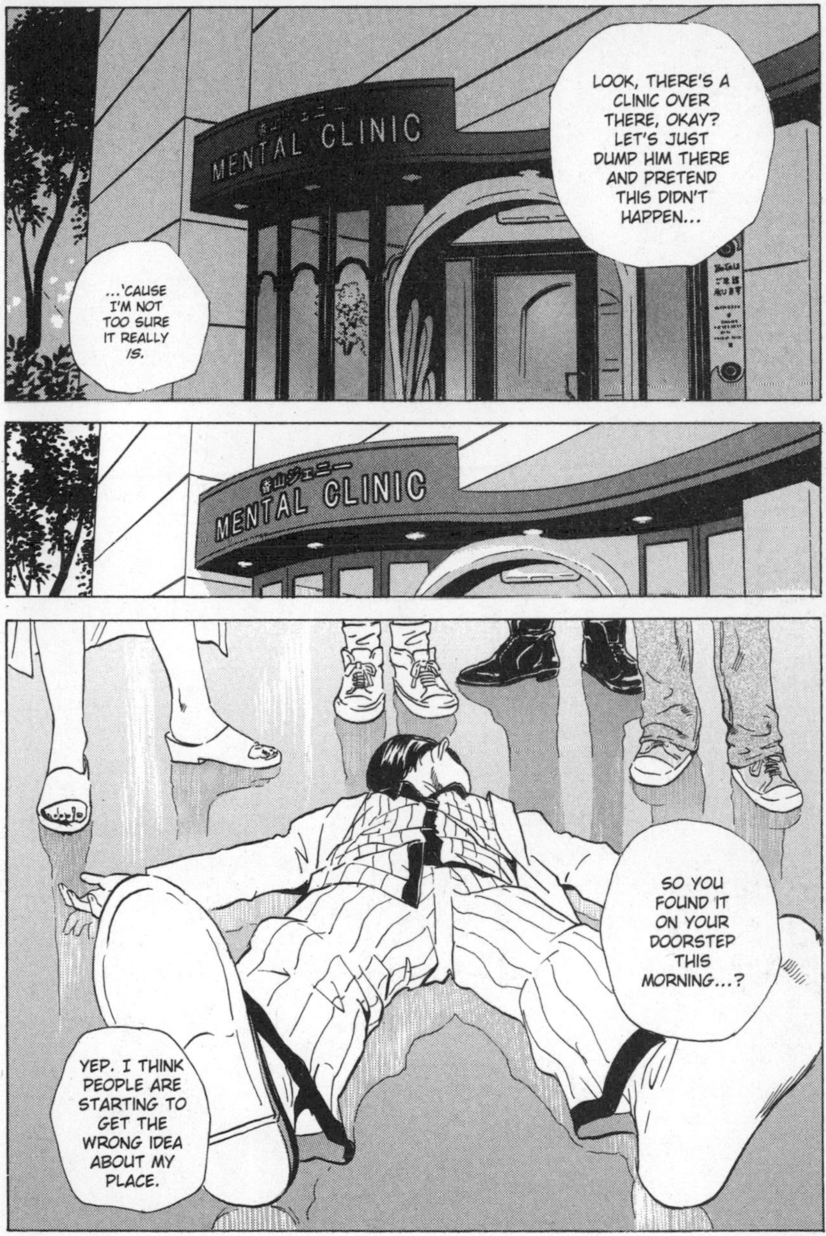
MENTAL CLINIC
LOOK, THERE'S A CLINIC OVER THERE, OKAY? LET'S JUST DUMP HIM THERE AND PRETEND THIS DIDN'T HAPPEN...
...'CAUSE I'M NOT TOO SURE IT REALLY *IS*.
香山ジェニー
MENTAL CLINIC
SO YOU FOUND IT ON YOUR DOORSTEP THIS MORNING...?
YEP. I THINK PEOPLE ARE STARTING TO GET THE WRONG IDEA ABOUT MY PLACE.

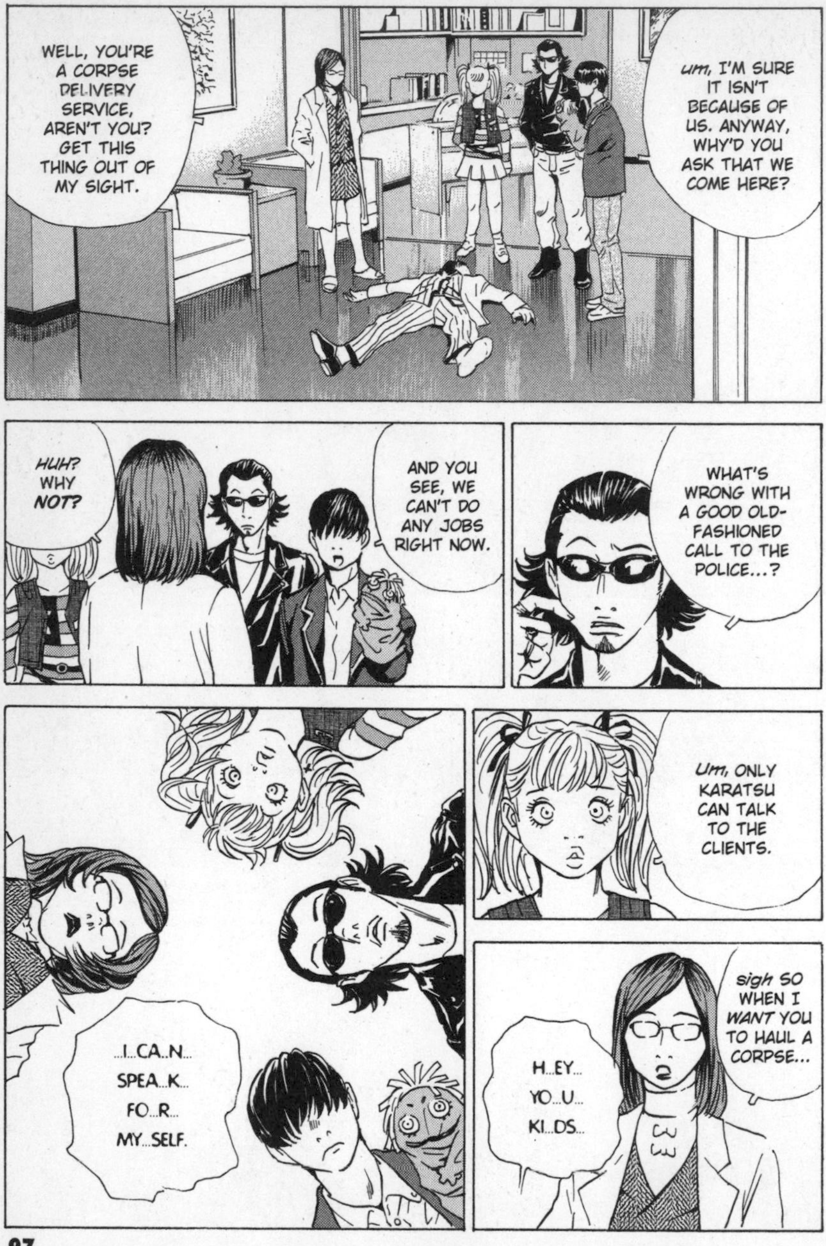
UM, I'M SURE IT ISN'T BECAUSE OF US. ANYWAY, WHY'D YOU ASK THAT WE COME HERE?
WELL, YOU'RE A CORPSE DELIVERY SERVICE, AREN'T YOU? GET THIS THING OUT OF MY SIGHT.
WHAT'S WRONG WITH A GOOD OLD-FASHIONED CALL TO THE POLICE...?
AND YOU SEE, WE CAN'T DO ANY JOBS RIGHT NOW.
HUH? WHY NOT?
UM, ONLY KARATSU CAN TALK TO THE CLIENTS.
SIGH SO WHEN I WANT YOU TO HAUL A CORPSE...
H..EY... YO..U... KI..DS...
...I..CA..N... SPEA..K... FO..R... MY...SELF.

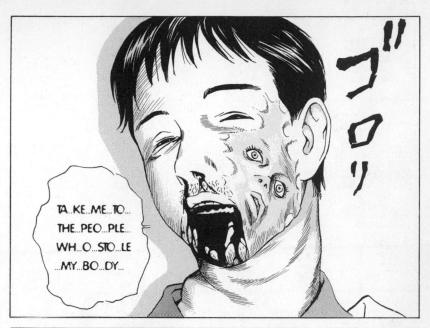

ゴロリ
TA...KE...ME...TO... THE...PEO...PLE... WH...O...STO...LE ...MY...BO...DY...
ANOTHER JINMENSO ....?!
IT WOULD APPEAR SO...LOOK, CAN WE *PLEASE* GET THIS OUT OF MY OFFICE?

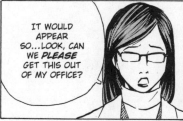

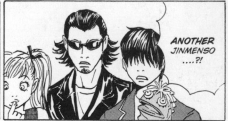

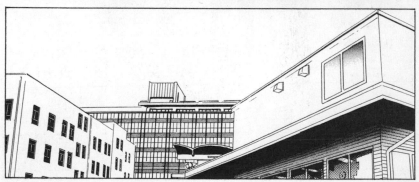

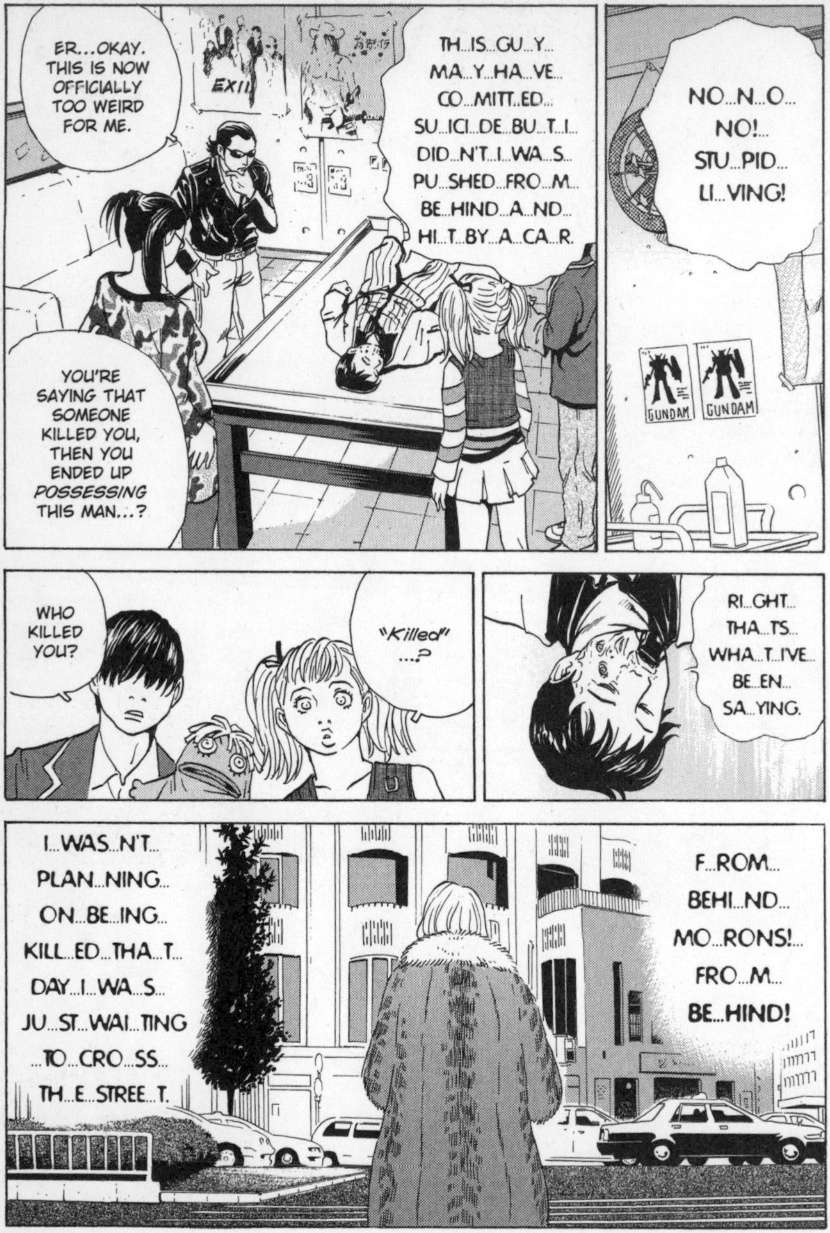
NO...N...O... NO!... STU...PID... LI...VING!
TH...IS...GU...Y... MA...Y...HA...VE... CO...MITT...ED... SU...ICI...DE...BU...T...I... DID...N'T...I...WA...S... PU...SHED...FRO...M... BE...HIND...A...ND... HI...T...BY...A...CA...R.
ER...OKAY. THIS IS NOW OFFICIALLY TOO WEIRD FOR ME.
YOU'RE SAYING THAT SOMEONE KILLED YOU, THEN YOU ENDED UP *POSSESSING* THIS MAN...?
RI...GHT... THA...TS... WHA...T...I'VE... BE...EN... SA...YING.
"*Killed*" ...?
WHO KILLED YOU?
I...WAS...N'T... PLAN...NING... ON...BE...ING... KILL...ED...THA...T... DAY...I...WA...S... JU...ST...WAI...TING ...TO...CRO...SS... TH...E...STREE...T.
F...ROM... BEHI...ND... MO...RONS!... FRO...M... BE...HIND!

...WE...LL...I...
WA...S..D..EAD...
BU...T..I...
WAS...N'T...
GON...E.

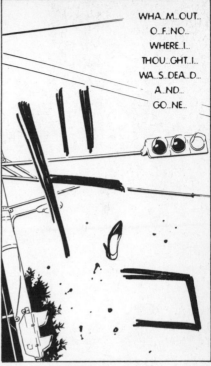

WHA...M...OUT...
O...F..NO...
WHERE...I...
THOU...GHT...I...
WA...S...DEA...D...
A...ND...
GO...NE...

A...T..FIR...ST..I...
DID...N'T...
UND...ER...STAND
...WHA...T..HA...D
HAP...PENED...
TO ...M..E...

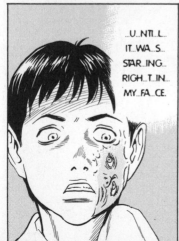

...U...NTI...L...
IT..WA...S...
STAR...ING...
RIGH...T..IN...
MY..FA...CE.

...BU...T...
GRAD...
UA...LLY..IT...
BE..CAME...
MO...RE...
CLEA...R...

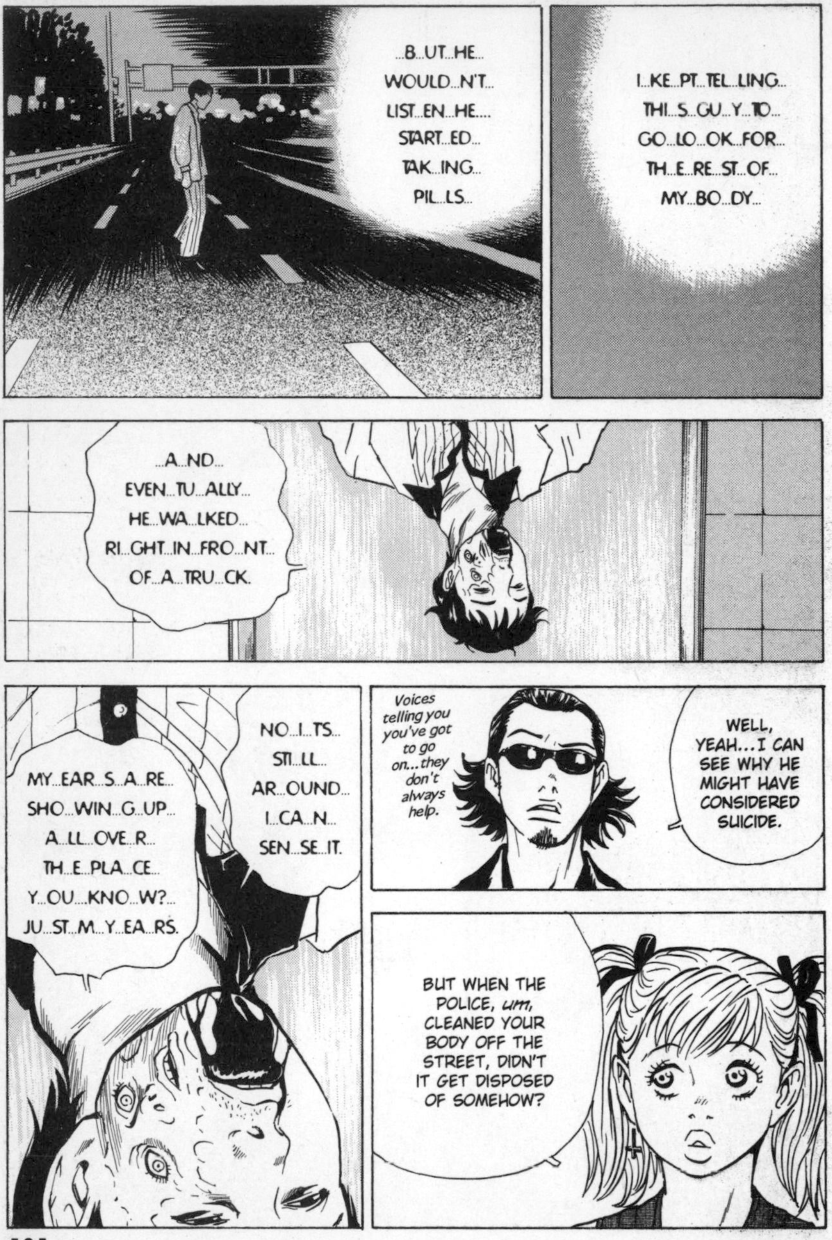
I...KE...PT...TEL...LING... THI...S...GU...Y...TO... GO...LO...OK...FOR... TH...E...RE...ST...OF... MY...BO...DY...
...B...UT...HE... WOULD...N'T... LIST...EN...HE.... START...ED... TAK...ING... PIL...LS...
...A...ND... EVEN...TU...ALLY... HE...WA...LKED... RI...GHT...IN...FRO...NT... OF...A...TRU...CK.
WELL, YEAH... I CAN SEE WHY HE MIGHT HAVE CONSIDERED SUICIDE.
Voices telling you you've got to go on...they don't always help.
BUT WHEN THE POLICE, *um*, CLEANED YOUR BODY OFF THE STREET, DIDN'T IT GET DISPOSED OF SOMEHOW?
NO...I...TS... STI...LL... AR...OUND... I...CA...N... SEN...SE...IT.
MY...EAR...S...A...RE... SHO...WIN...G...UP... A...LL...OVE...R... TH...E...PLA...CE... Y...OU...KNO...W?... JU...ST...M...Y...EA...RS.

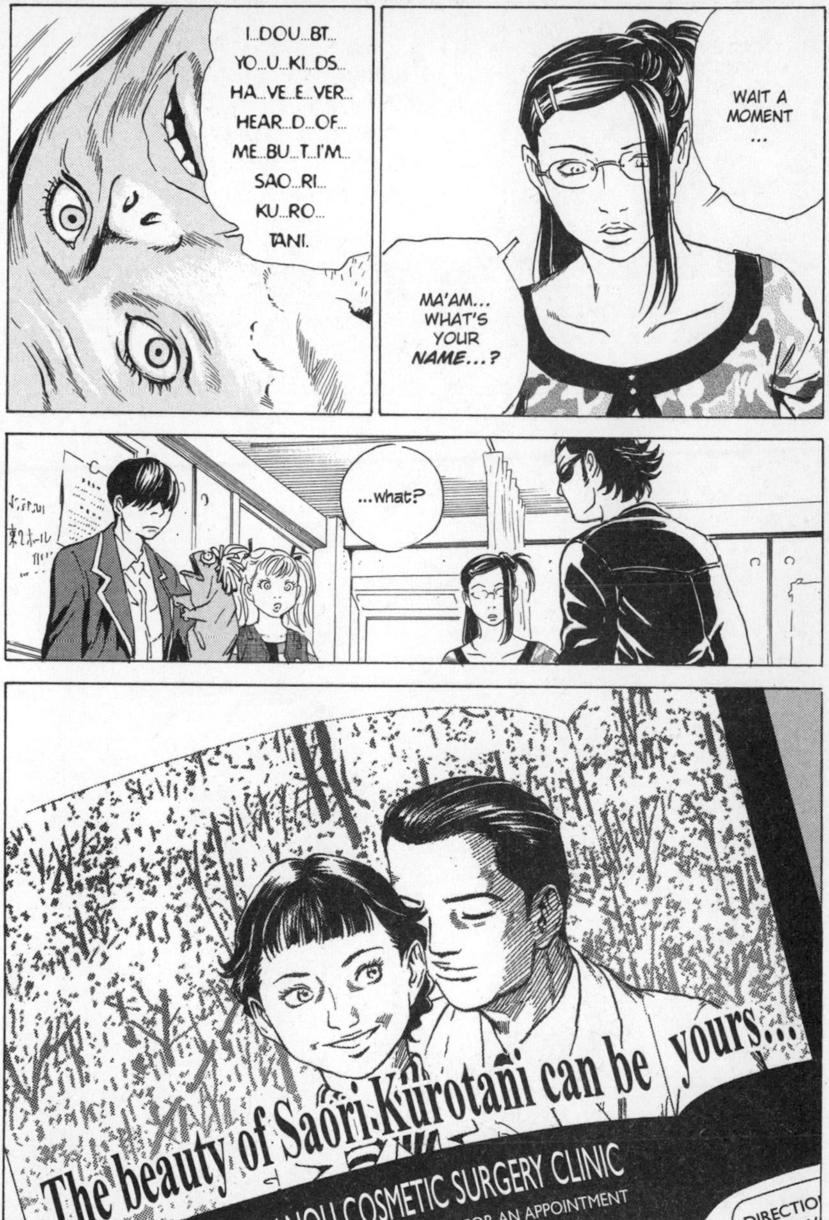
WAIT A MOMENT ...
MA'AM... WHAT'S YOUR NAME...?
I...DOU...BT... YO...U...KI...DS... HA...VE...E...VER... HEAR...D...OF... ME...BU...T...I'M... SAO...RI... KU...RO... TANI.
...what?
The beauty of Saori Kurotani can be yours...
ANOU COSMETIC SURGERY CLINIC
FOR AN APPOINTMENT
DIRECTIO

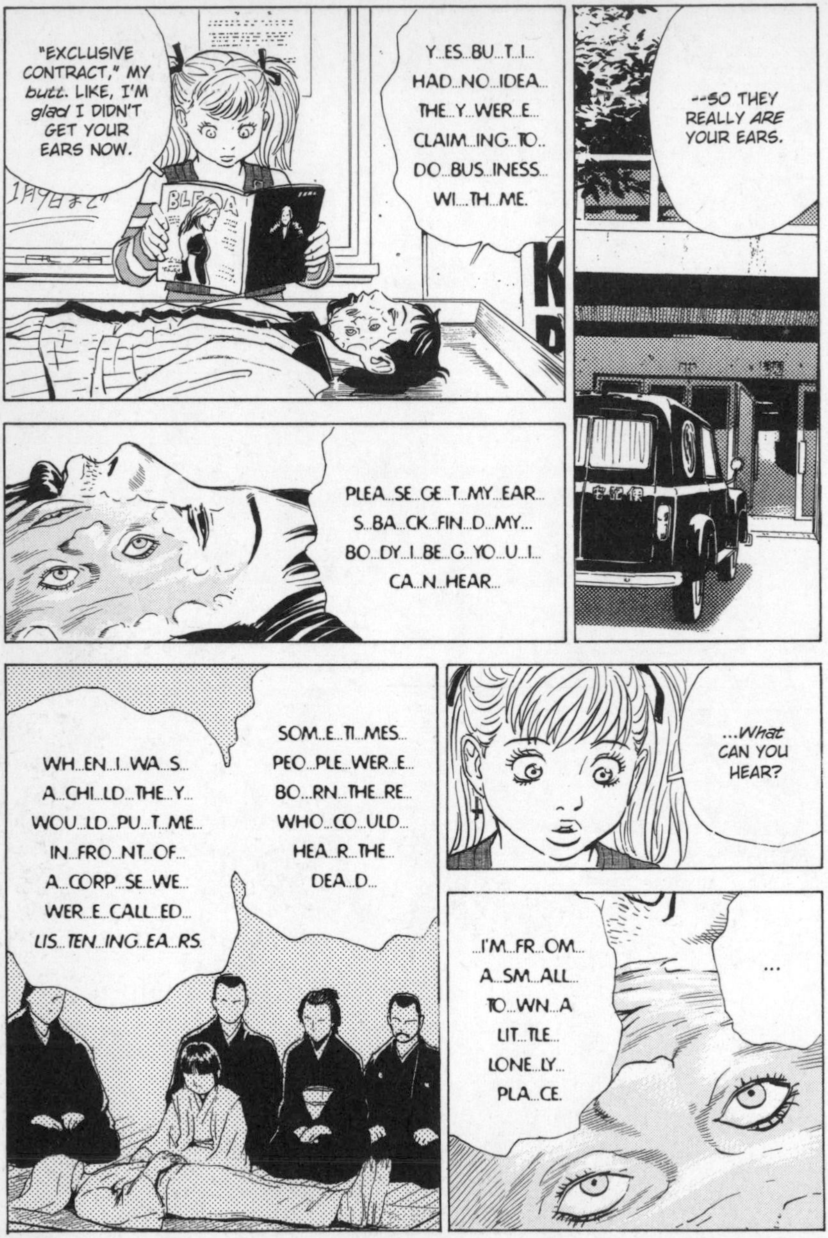
--SO THEY REALLY *ARE* YOUR EARS.
Y...ES...BU...T...I... HAD...NO...IDEA... THE...Y...WER...E... CLAIM...ING...TO... DO...BUS...INESS... WI...TH...ME.
"EXCLUSIVE CONTRACT," MY *butt*. LIKE, I'M *glad* I DIDN'T GET YOUR EARS NOW.
PLEA...SE...GE...T...MY...EAR... S...BA...CK...FIN...D...MY... BO...DY...I...BE...G...YO...U...I... CA...N...HEAR...
...*What* CAN YOU HEAR?
...
...I'M...FR...OM... A...SM...ALL... TO...WN...A LIT...TLE... LONE...LY... PLA...CE.
SOM...E...TI...MES... PEO...PLE...WER...E... BO...RN...THE...RE WHO...CO...ULD... HEA...R...THE... DEA...D...
WH...EN...I...WA...S... A...CHI...LD...THE...Y... WOU...LD...PU...T...ME... IN...FRO...NT...OF... A...CORP...SE...WE... WER...E...CALL...ED... *LIS...TEN...ING...EA...RS.*

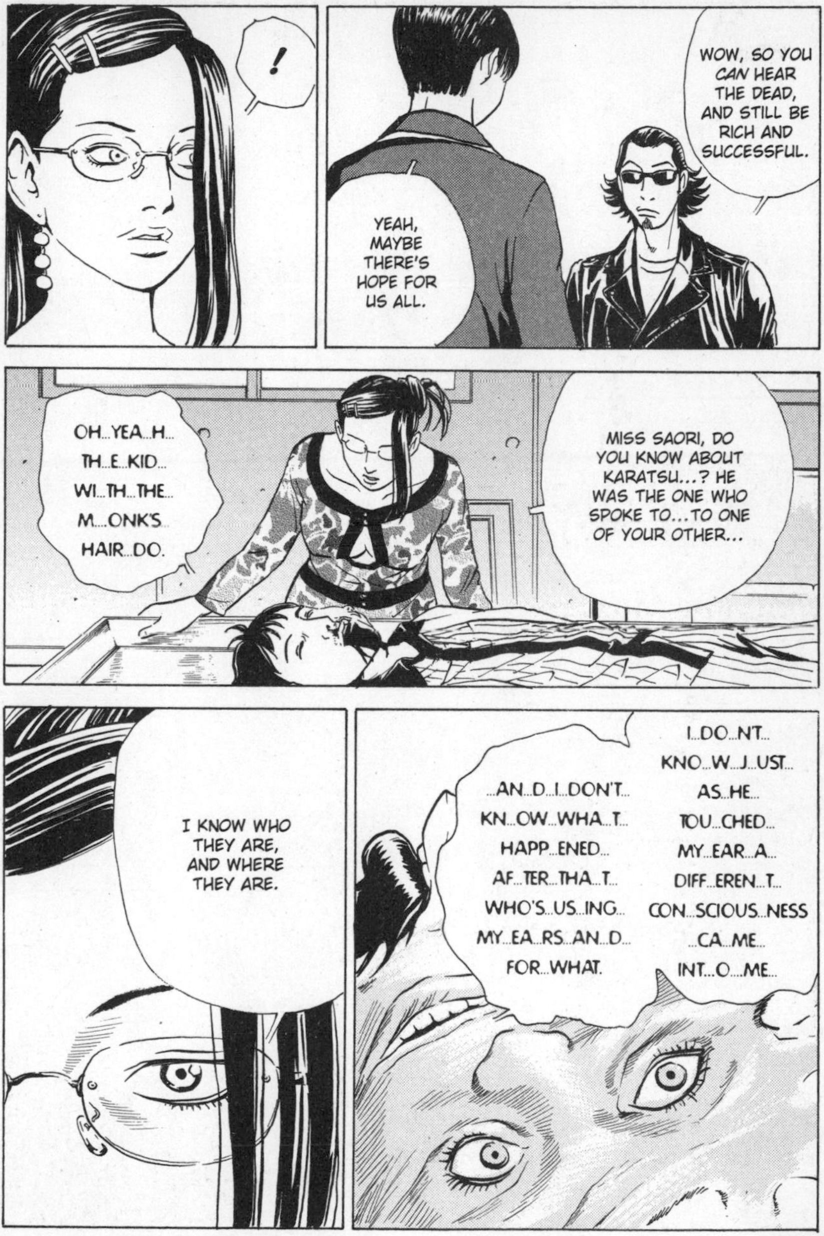
WOW, SO YOU CAN HEAR THE DEAD, AND STILL BE RICH AND SUCCESSFUL.
YEAH, MAYBE THERE'S HOPE FOR US ALL.
!
MISS SAORI, DO YOU KNOW ABOUT KARATSU...? HE WAS THE ONE WHO SPOKE TO...TO ONE OF YOUR OTHER...
OH...YEA...H... TH...E...KID... WI...TH...THE... M...ONK'S... HAIR...DO.
I...DO...NT... KNO...W...J...UST... AS...HE... TOU...CHED... MY...EAR...A... DIFF...EREN...T... CON...SCIOUS...NESS ...CA...ME... INT...O...ME...
...AN...D...I...DON'T... KN...OW...WHA...T... HAPP...ENED... AF...TER...THA...T... WHO'S...US...ING... MY...EA...RS...AN...D... FOR...WHAT.
I KNOW WHO THEY ARE, AND WHERE THEY ARE.

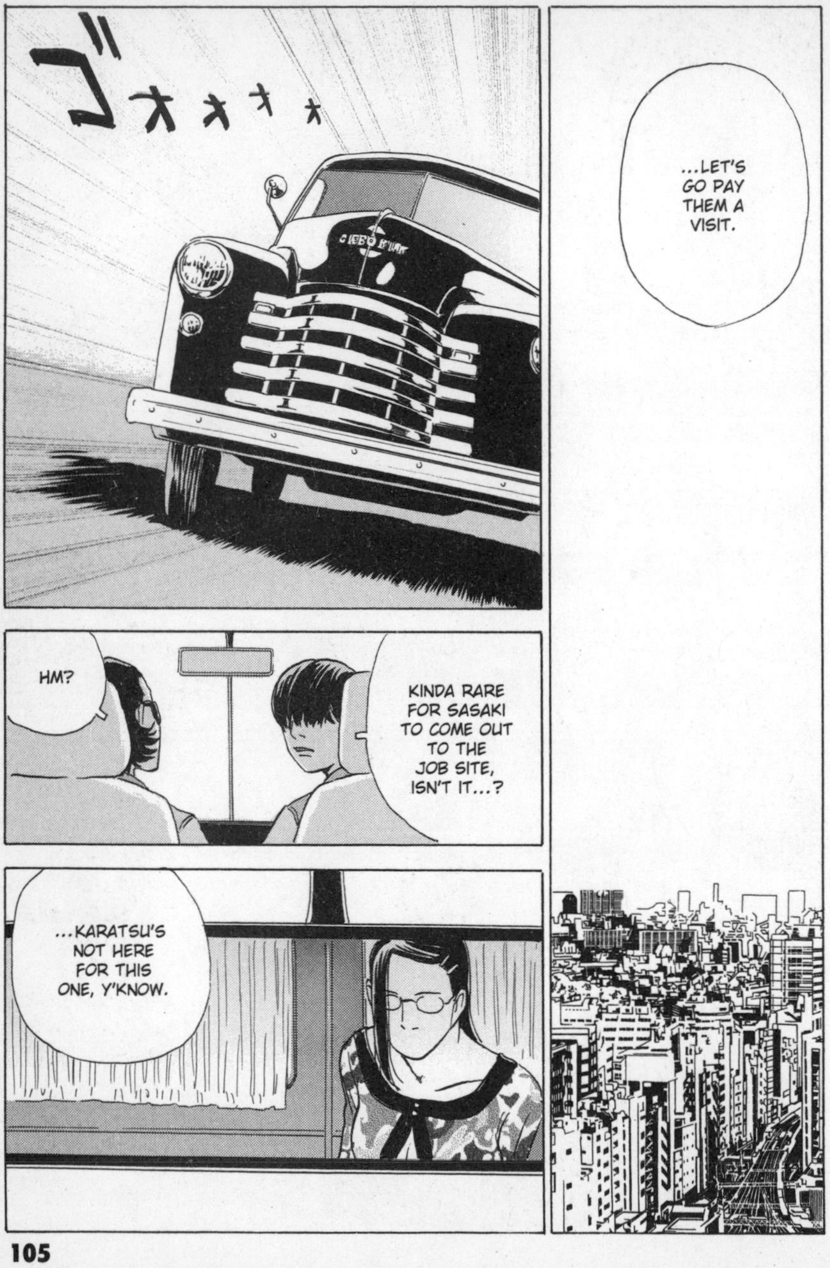
...LET'S GO PAY THEM A VISIT.
ゴオォォォ
KINDA RARE FOR SASAKI TO COME OUT TO THE JOB SITE, ISN'T IT...?
HM?
...KARATSU'S NOT HERE FOR THIS ONE, Y'KNOW.

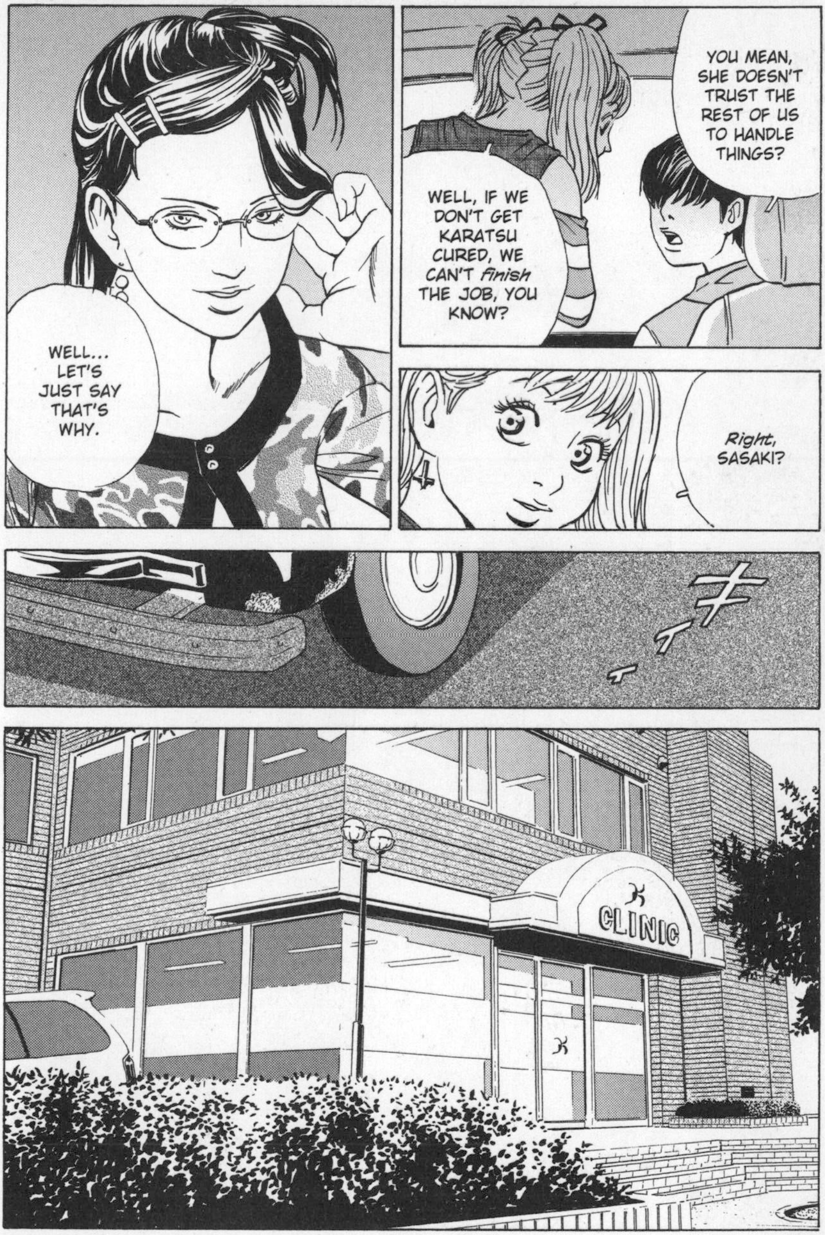
YOU MEAN, SHE DOESN'T TRUST THE REST OF US TO HANDLE THINGS?
WELL, IF WE DON'T GET KARATSU CURED, WE CAN'T *finish* THE JOB, YOU KNOW?
Right, SASAKI?
WELL... LET'S JUST SAY THAT'S WHY.
キィィ
CLINIC

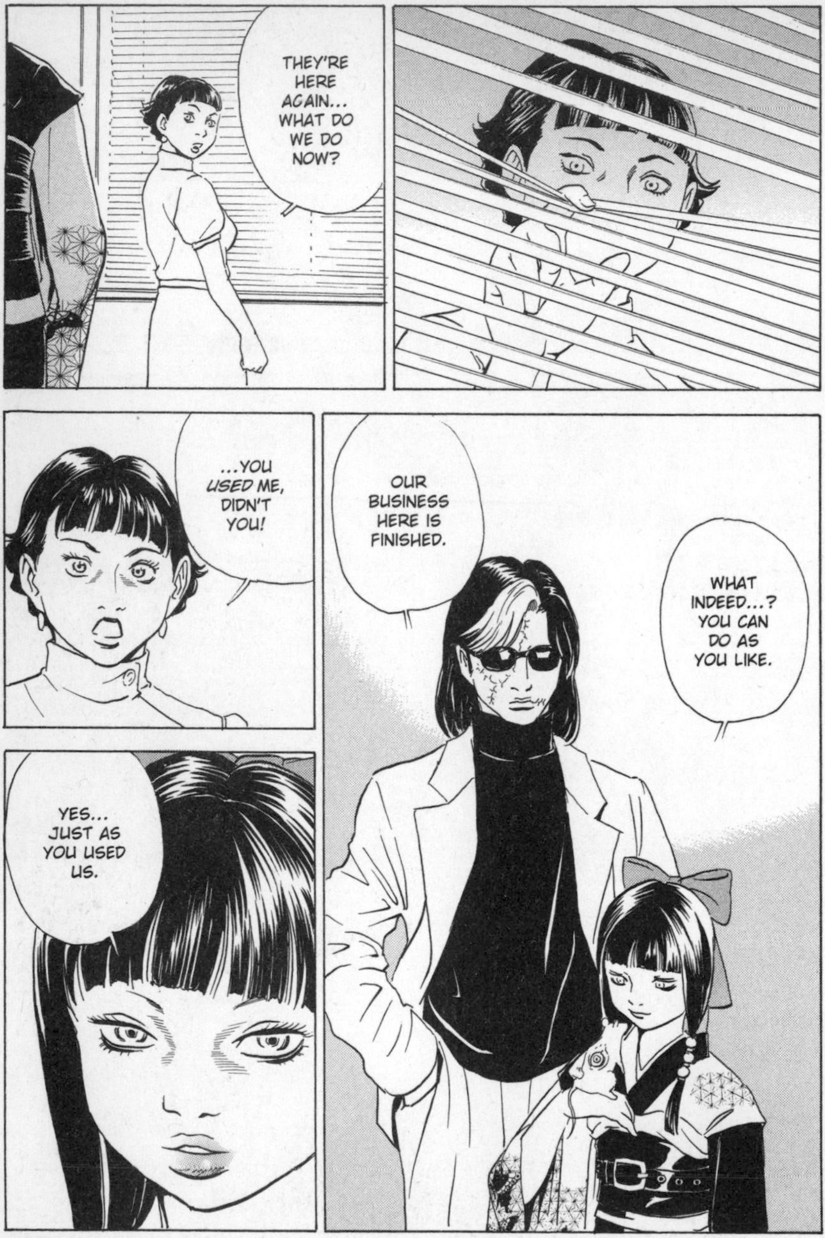
THEY'RE HERE AGAIN... WHAT DO WE DO NOW?
WHAT INDEED...? YOU CAN DO AS YOU LIKE.
OUR BUSINESS HERE IS FINISHED.
...YOU *USED ME*, DIDN'T YOU!
YES... JUST AS YOU USED US.

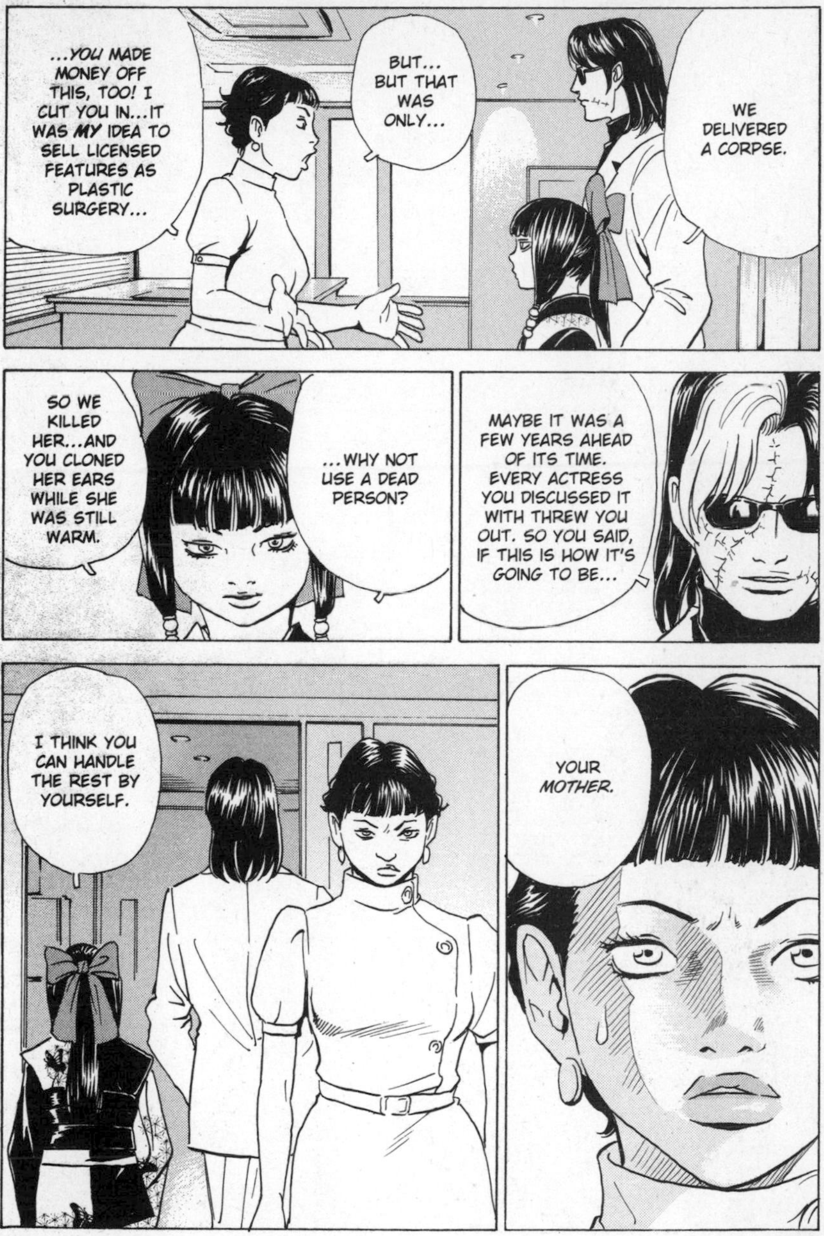
WE DELIVERED A CORPSE.
BUT... BUT THAT WAS ONLY...
...YOU MADE MONEY OFF THIS, TOO! I CUT YOU IN...IT WAS MY IDEA TO SELL LICENSED FEATURES AS PLASTIC SURGERY...
MAYBE IT WAS A FEW YEARS AHEAD OF ITS TIME. EVERY ACTRESS YOU DISCUSSED IT WITH THREW YOU OUT. SO YOU SAID, IF THIS IS HOW IT'S GOING TO BE...
...WHY NOT USE A DEAD PERSON?
SO WE KILLED HER...AND YOU CLONED HER EARS WHILE SHE WAS STILL WARM.
YOUR MOTHER.
I THINK YOU CAN HANDLE THE REST BY YOURSELF.

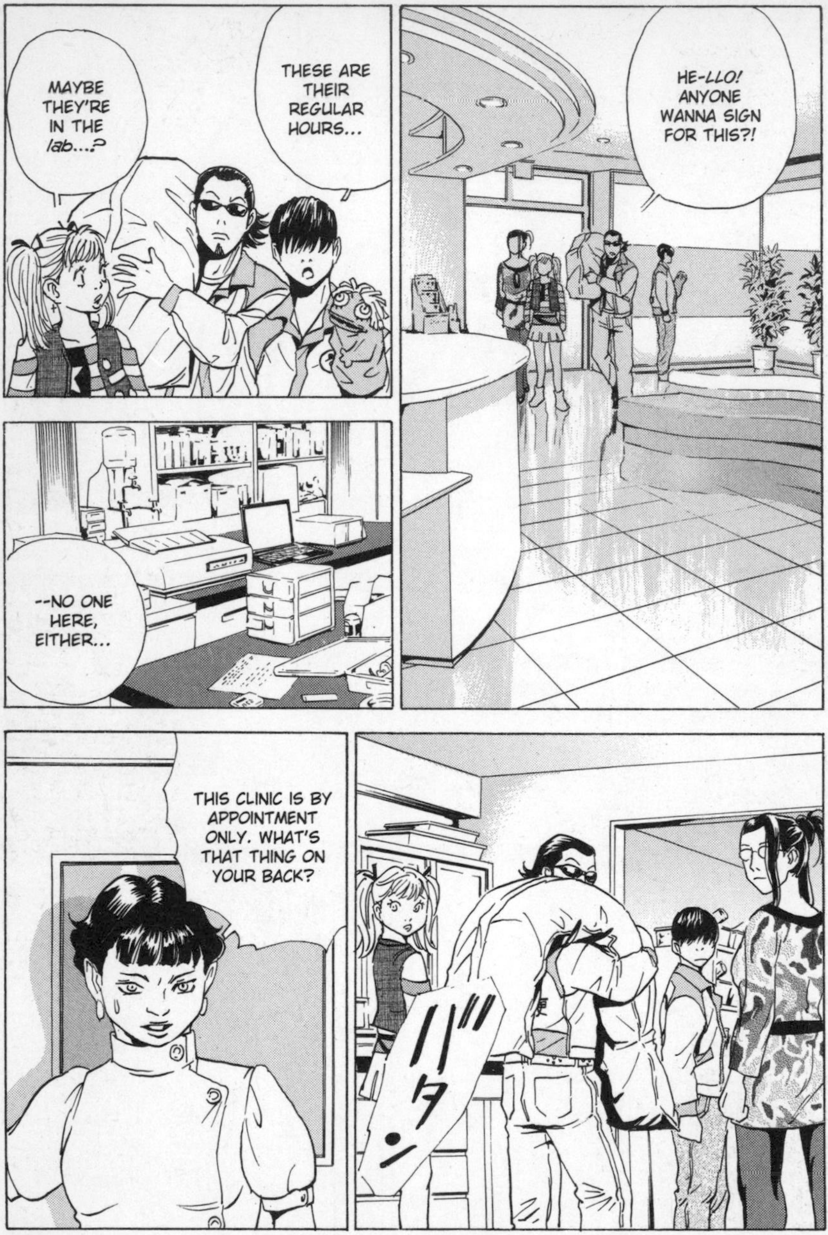
HE-LLO! ANYONE WANNA SIGN FOR THIS?!
THESE ARE THEIR REGULAR HOURS...
MAYBE THEY'RE IN THE *lab*...?
--NO ONE HERE, EITHER...
バタン
THIS CLINIC IS BY APPOINTMENT ONLY. WHAT'S THAT THING ON YOUR BACK?

A VICTIM OF YOUR MAL-PRACTICE.

MALPRACTICE? I HAVEN'T DONE ANY PROCEDURES ON MEN...

L...OOK... CLO...SER...

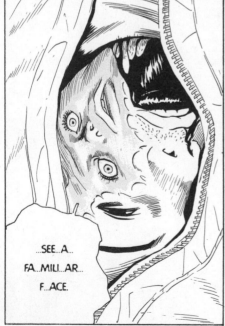

...SEE...A... FA...MILI...AR... F...ACE.

!

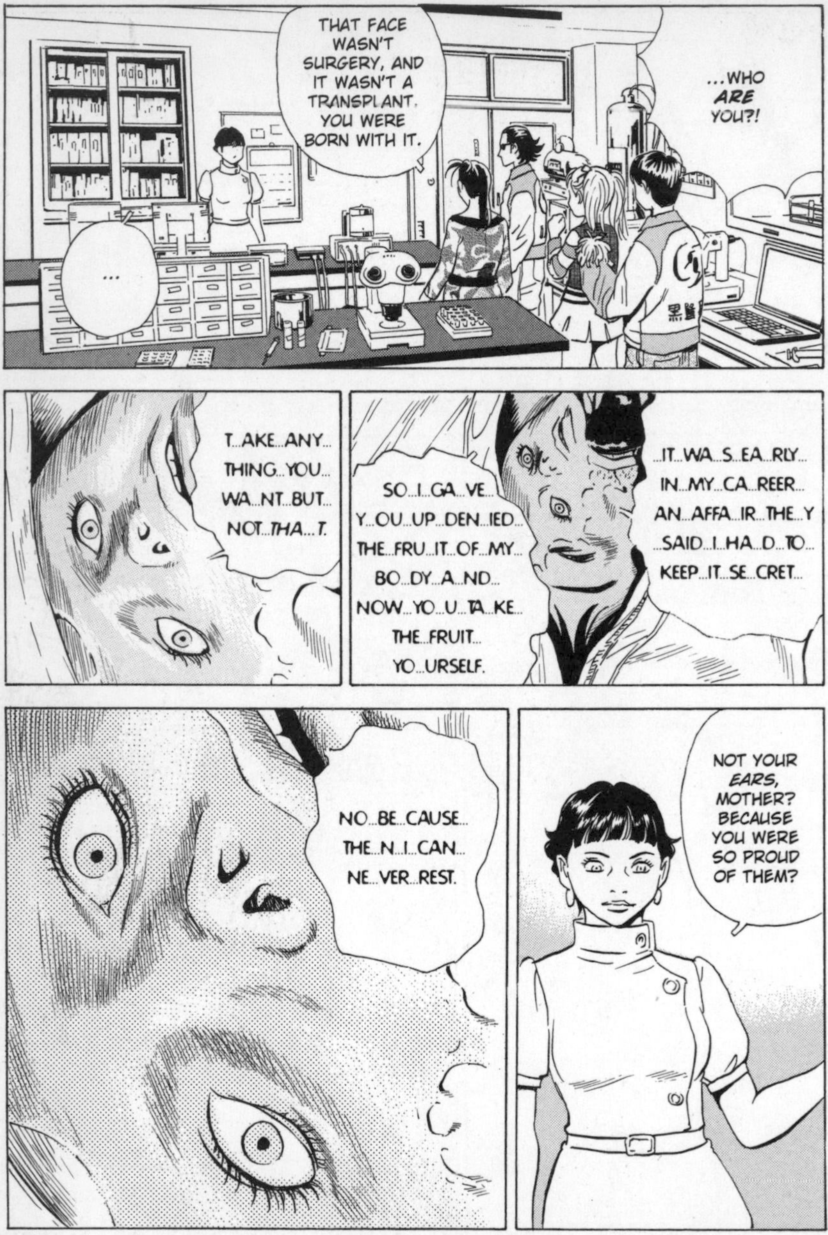
THAT FACE WASN'T SURGERY, AND IT WASN'T A TRANSPLANT. YOU WERE BORN WITH IT.
...WHO *ARE* YOU?!
...
...IT...WA...S...EA...RLY... IN...MY...CA...REER... AN...AFFA...IR...THE...Y SAID...I...HA...D...TO... KEEP...IT...SE...CRET...
SO...I...GA...VE... Y...OU...UP...DEN...IED... THE...FRU...IT...OF...MY... BO...DY...A...ND... NOW...YO...U...TA...KE... THE...FRUIT... YO...URSELF.
T...AKE...ANY... THING...YOU... WA...NT...BUT... NOT...*THA*...T.
NOT YOUR *EARS*, MOTHER? BECAUSE YOU WERE SO PROUD OF THEM?
NO...BE...CAUSE... THE...N...I...CAN... NE...VER...REST.

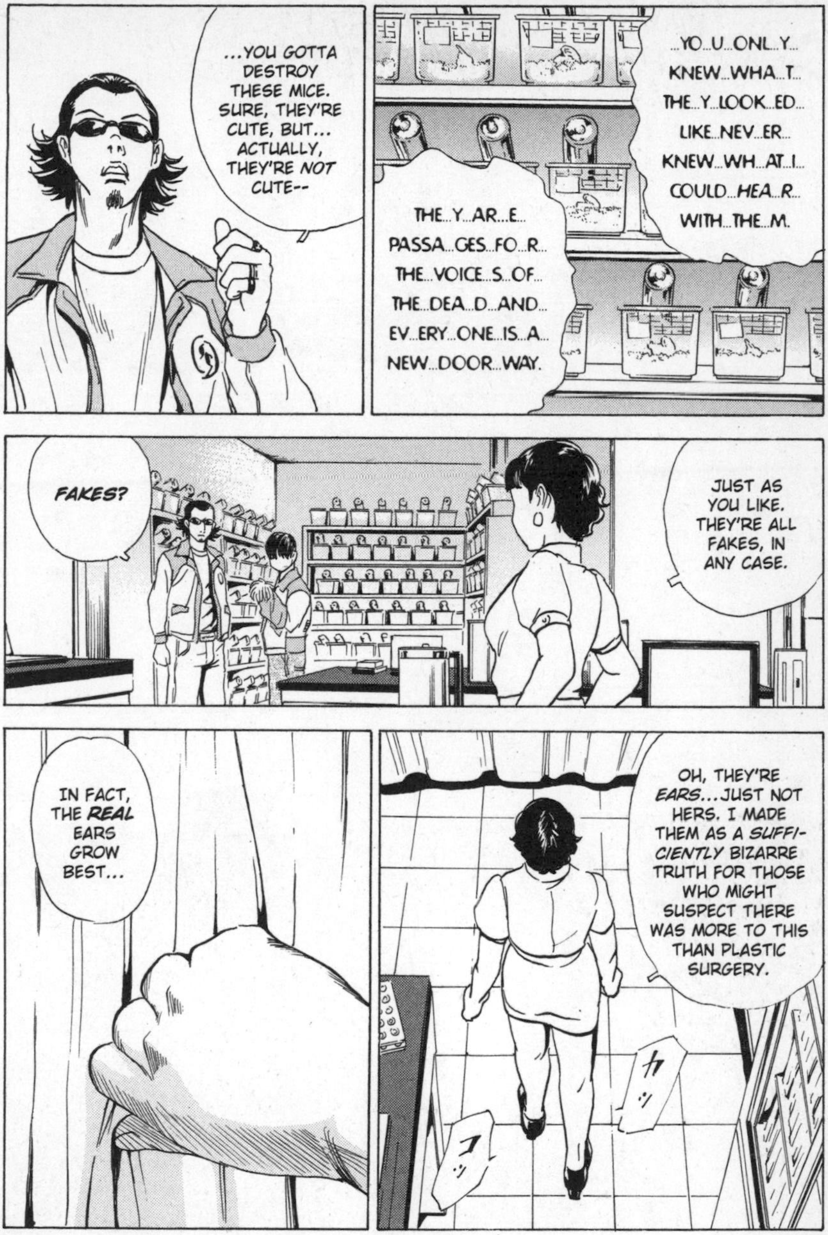
...YO...U...ONL...Y... KNEW...WHA...T... THE...Y...LOOK...ED... LIKE...NEV...ER... KNEW...WH...AT...I... COULD...*HEA*...R... WITH...THE...M.
THE...Y...AR...E... PASSA...GES...FO...R... THE...VOICE...S...OF... THE...DEA...D...AND... EV...ERY...ONE...IS...A... NEW...DOOR...WAY.
...YOU GOTTA DESTROY THESE MICE. SURE, THEY'RE CUTE, BUT... ACTUALLY, THEY'RE *NOT* CUTE--
JUST AS YOU LIKE. THEY'RE ALL FAKES, IN ANY CASE.
FAKES?
OH, THEY'RE *EARS*...JUST NOT HERS. I MADE THEM AS A *SUFFI-CIENTLY* BIZARRE TRUTH FOR THOSE WHO MIGHT SUSPECT THERE WAS MORE TO THIS THAN PLASTIC SURGERY.
カッ
コッ
IN FACT, THE *REAL* EARS GROW BEST...

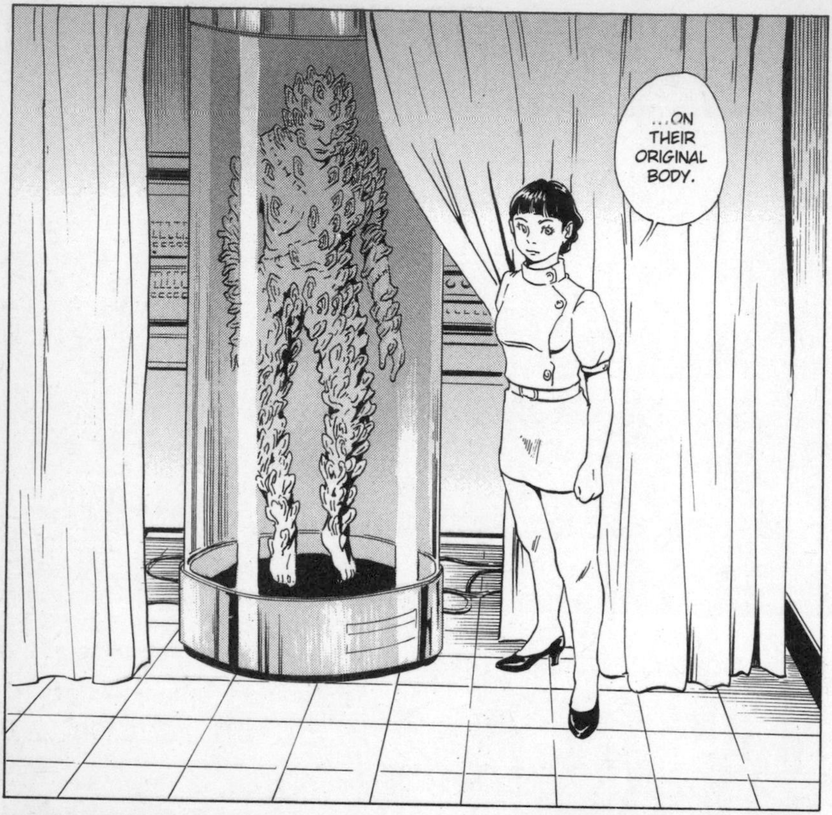
...ON THEIR ORIGINAL BODY.

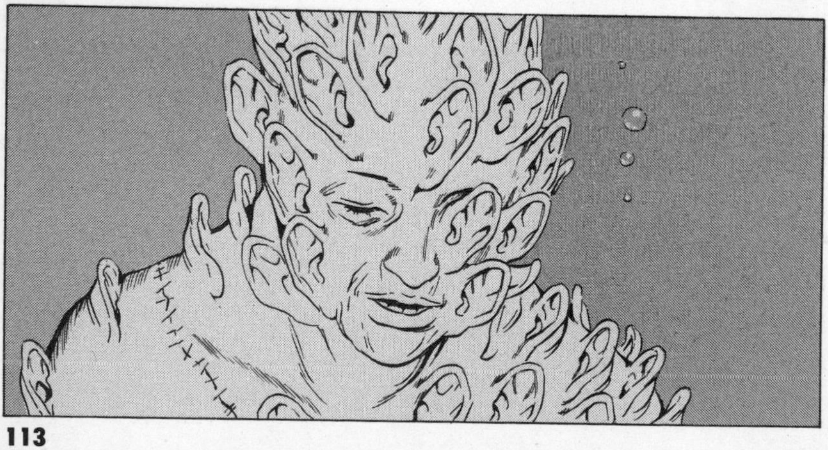

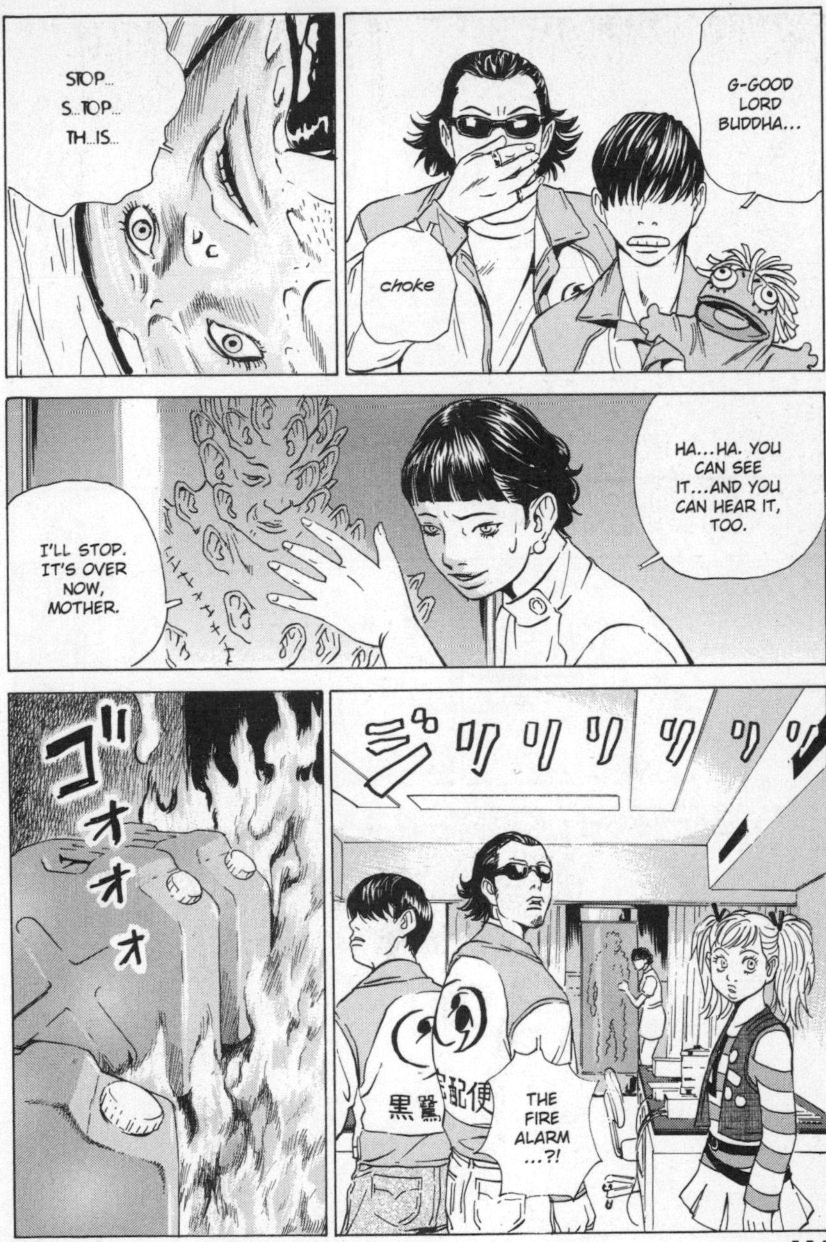
G-GOOD LORD BUDDHA...
choke
STOP... S...TOP... TH...IS...
HA...HA. YOU CAN SEE IT...AND YOU CAN HEAR IT, TOO.
I'LL STOP. IT'S OVER NOW, MOTHER.
ジリリリリリ
黒鷺 宅配便
THE FIRE ALARM ...?!
ゴオオオ

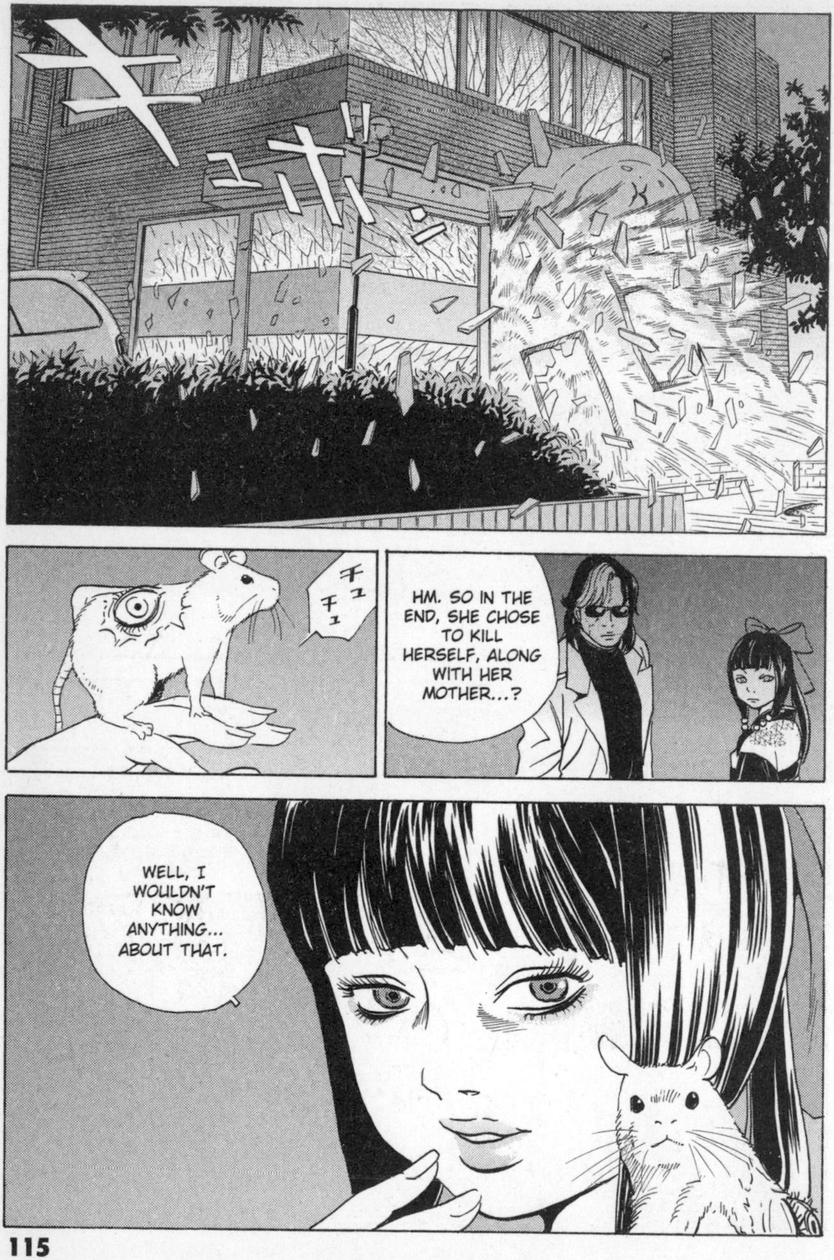
HM. SO IN THE END, SHE CHOSE TO KILL HERSELF, ALONG WITH HER MOTHER...?
チュ チュ
WELL, I WOULDN'T KNOW ANYTHING... ABOUT THAT.

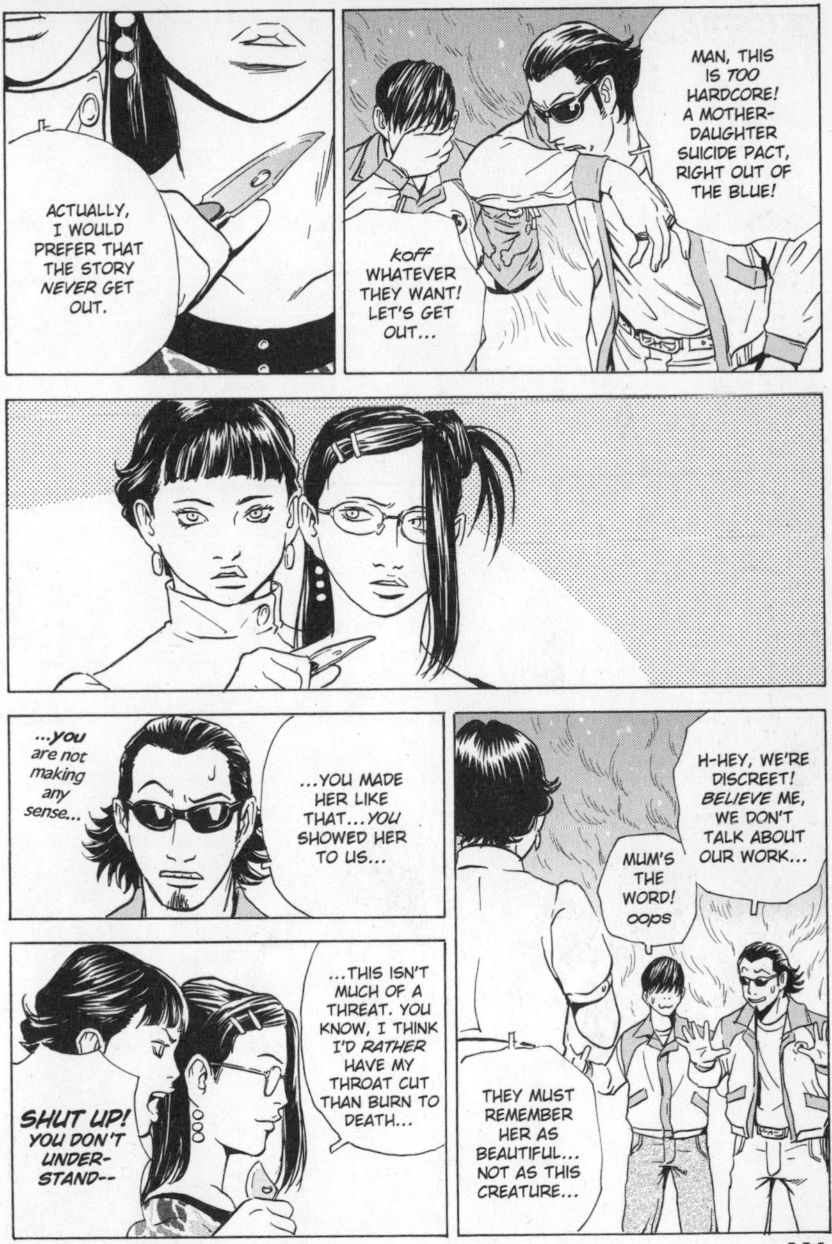
MAN, THIS IS *TOO* HARDCORE! A MOTHER-DAUGHTER SUICIDE PACT, RIGHT OUT OF THE BLUE!
koff WHATEVER THEY WANT! LET'S GET OUT...
ACTUALLY, I WOULD PREFER THAT THE STORY *NEVER* GET OUT.
H-HEY, WE'RE DISCREET! *BELIEVE* ME, WE DON'T TALK ABOUT OUR WORK...
MUM'S THE WORD! *oops*
THEY MUST REMEMBER HER AS BEAUTIFUL... NOT AS THIS CREATURE...
...YOU MADE HER LIKE THAT... *YOU* SHOWED HER TO US...
...you are not making any sense...
...THIS ISN'T MUCH OF A THREAT. YOU KNOW, I THINK I'D *RATHER* HAVE MY THROAT CUT THAN BURN TO DEATH...
SHUT UP! YOU DON'T UNDER-STAND--

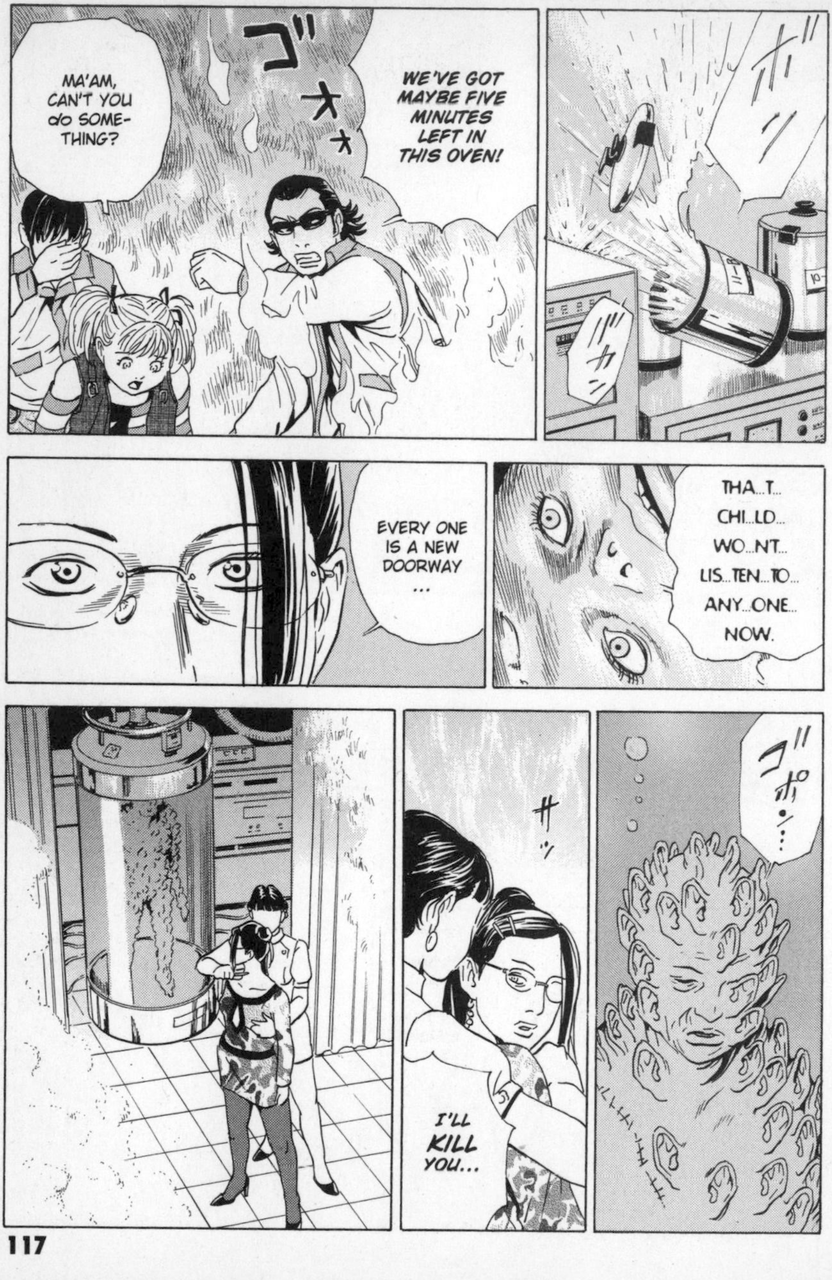

WE'VE GOT MAYBE FIVE MINUTES LEFT IN THIS OVEN!
MA'AM, CAN'T YOU do SOME-THING?
THA...T... CHI...LD... WO...N'T... LIS...TEN...TO... ANY...ONE... NOW.
EVERY ONE IS A NEW DOORWAY ...
I'LL KILL YOU...

KARATSU... WAKE UP... PLEASE.
KARATSU ...
...HELP.

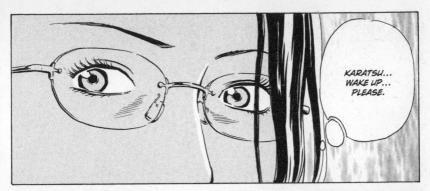

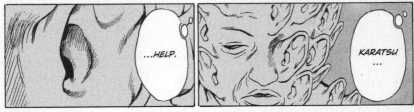

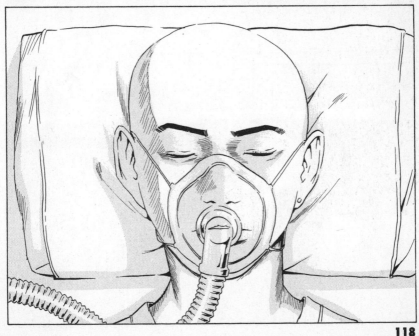

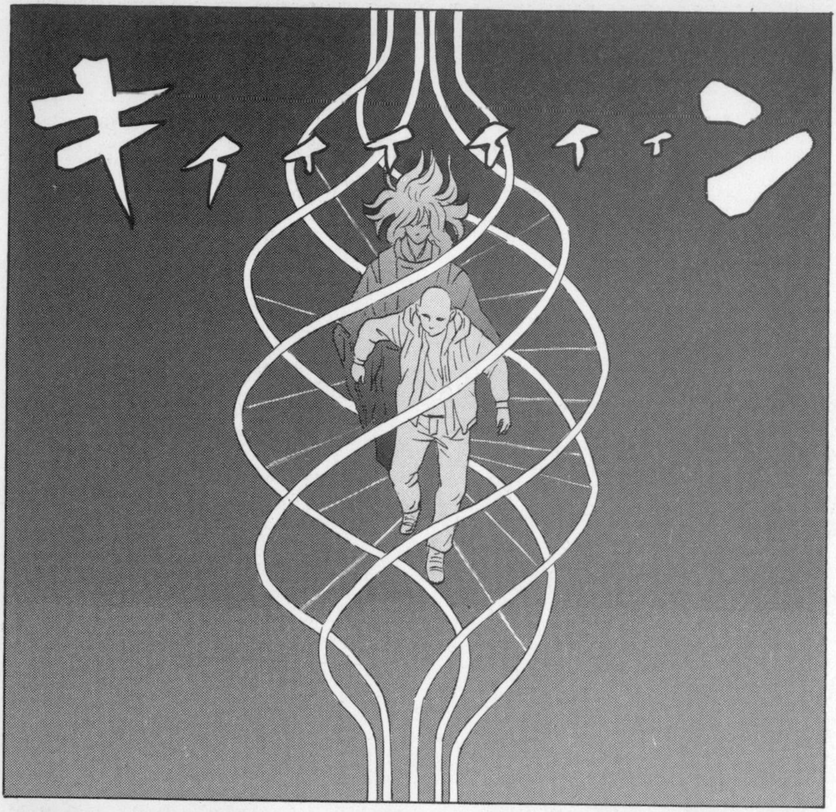
キィィィィィィン

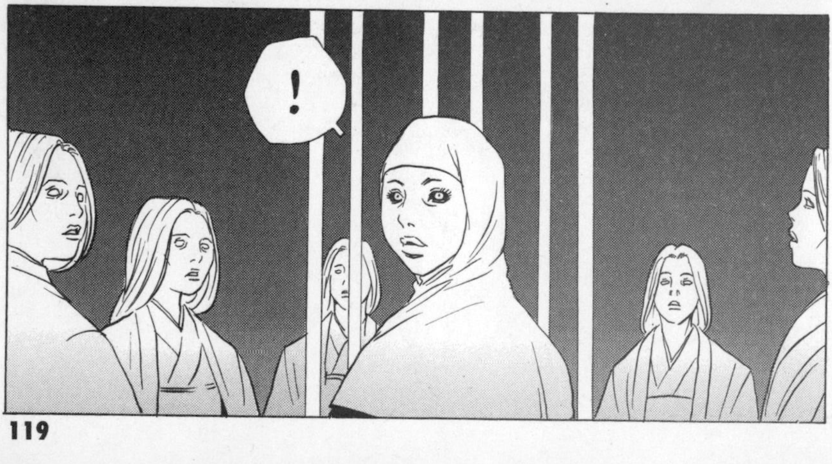
!

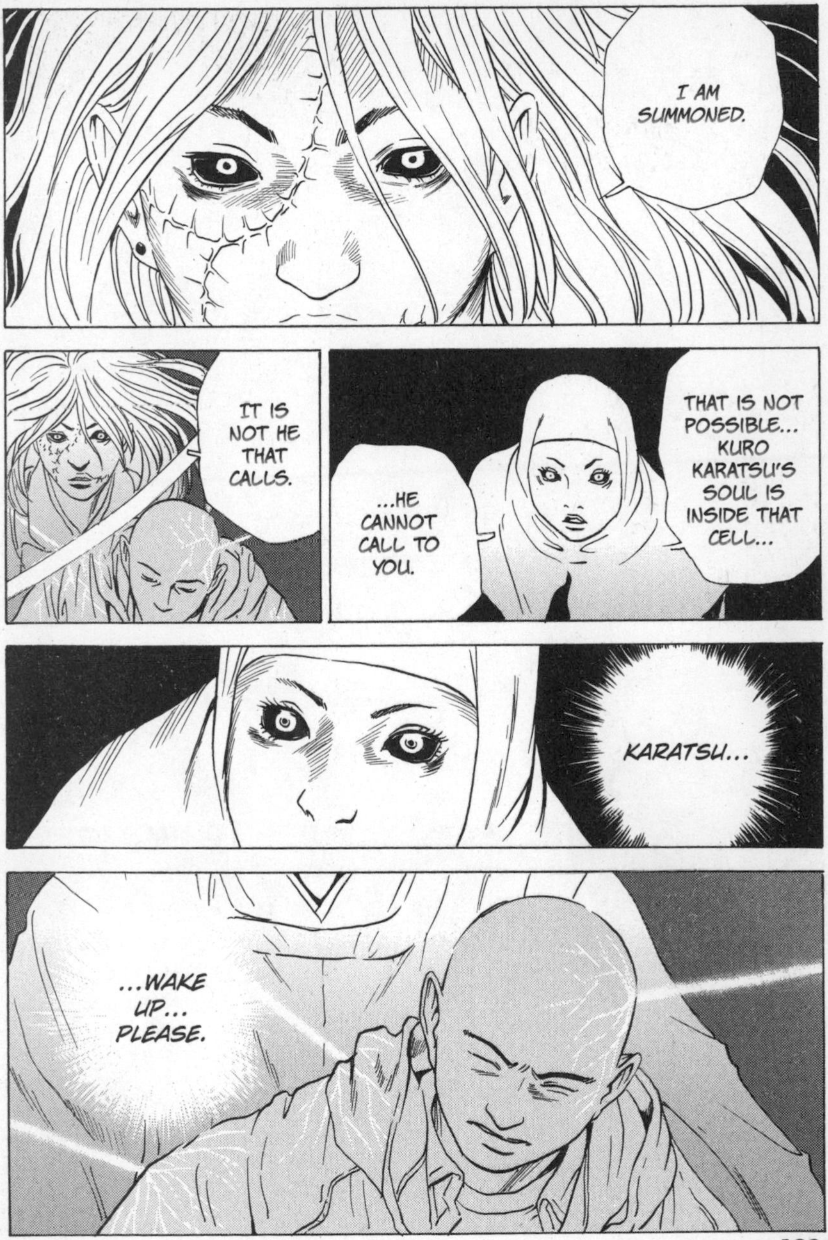
I AM SUMMONED.
THAT IS NOT POSSIBLE... KURO KARATSU'S SOUL IS INSIDE THAT CELL...
...HE CANNOT CALL TO YOU.
IT IS NOT HE THAT CALLS.
KARATSU...
...WAKE UP... PLEASE.

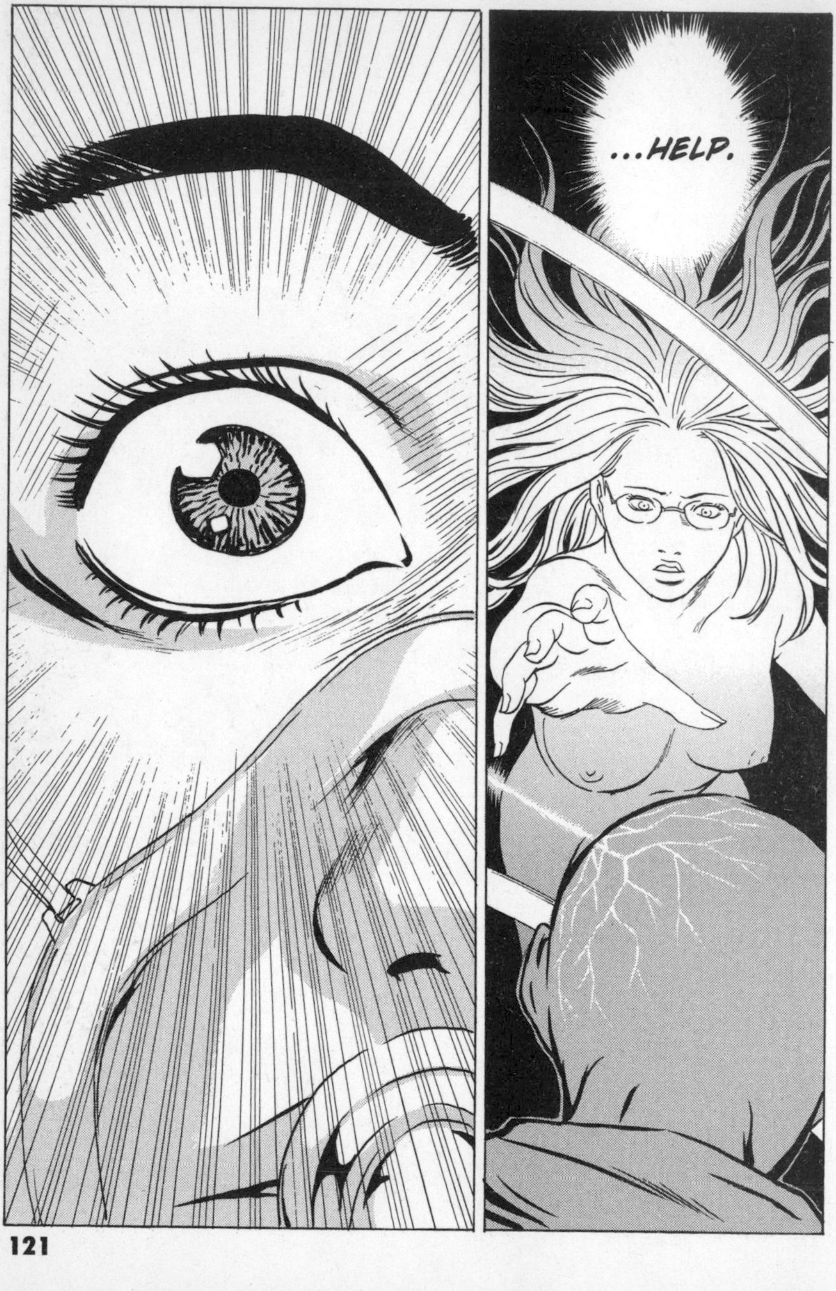
...HELP.

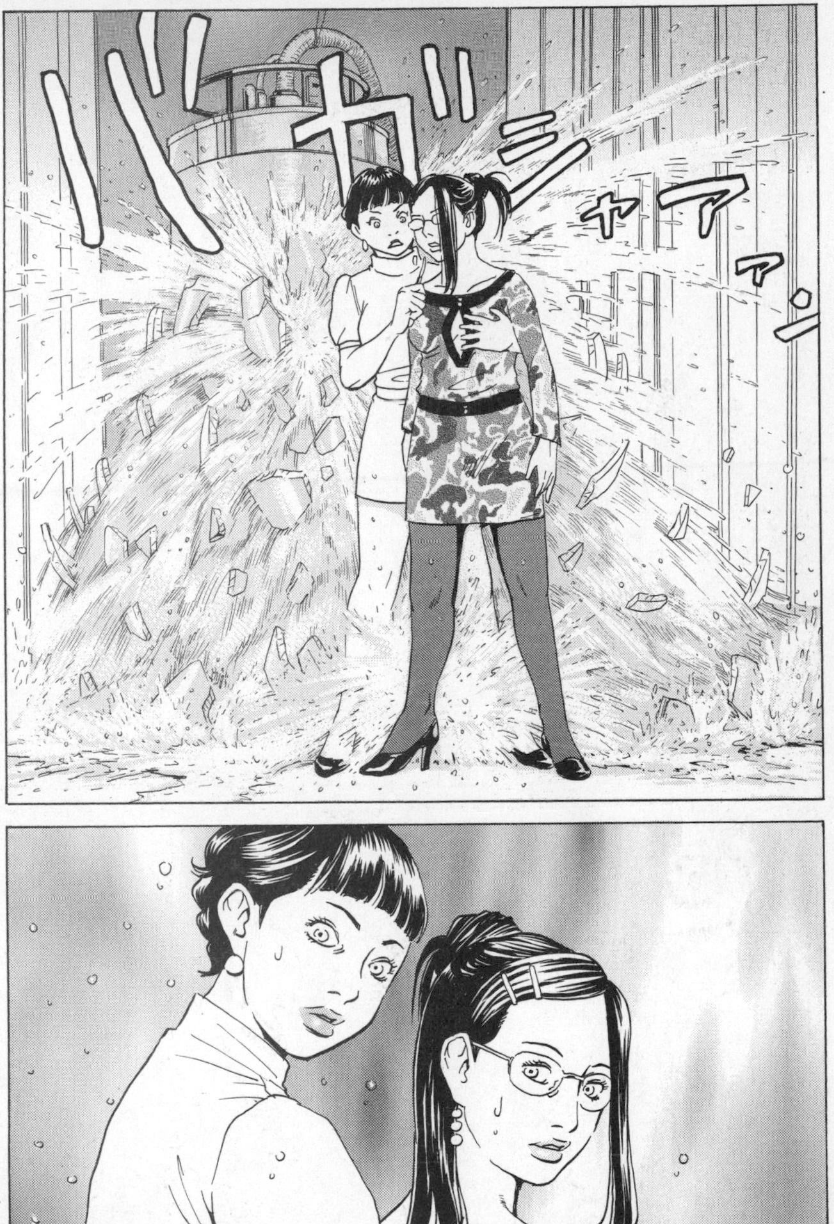
バカッシャアアン

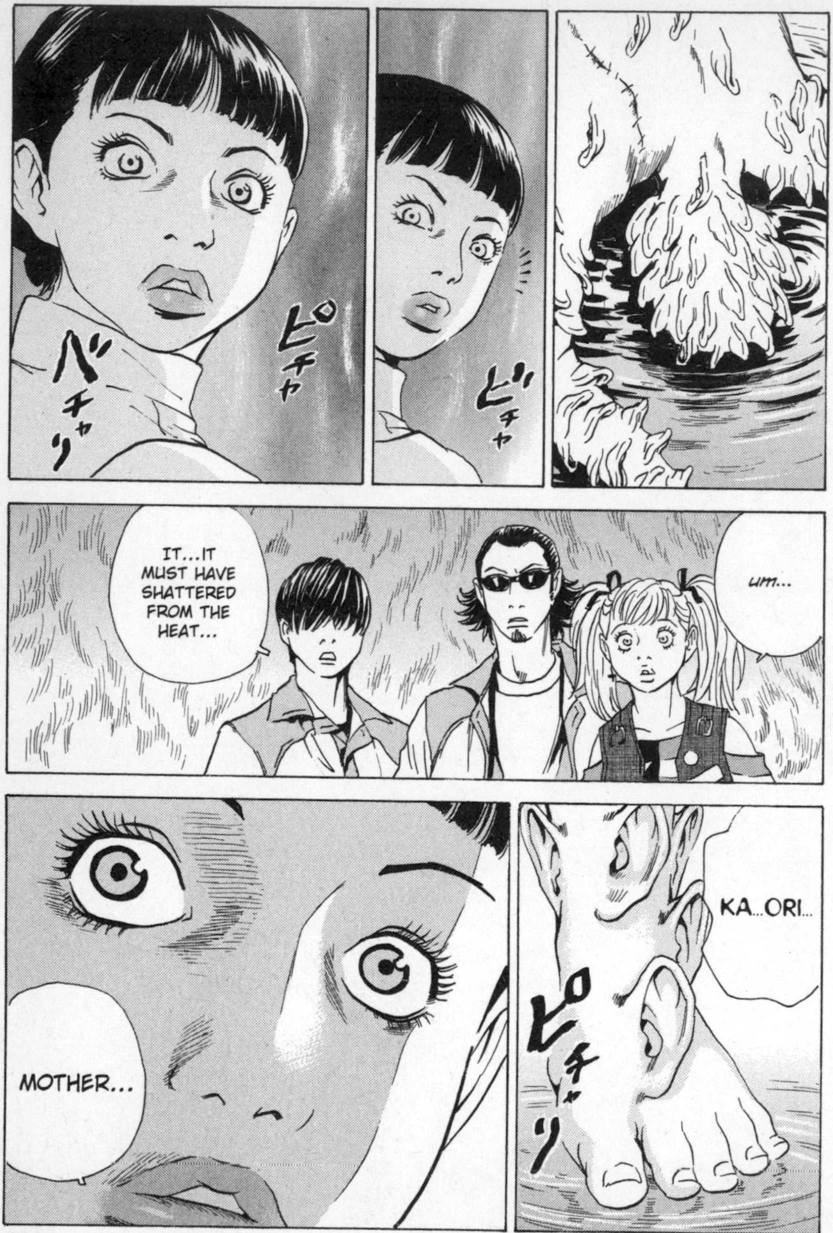
ピチャ
ビチャ
バチャリ
um...
IT...IT MUST HAVE SHATTERED FROM THE HEAT...
KA...ORI...
ピチャリ
MOTHER...

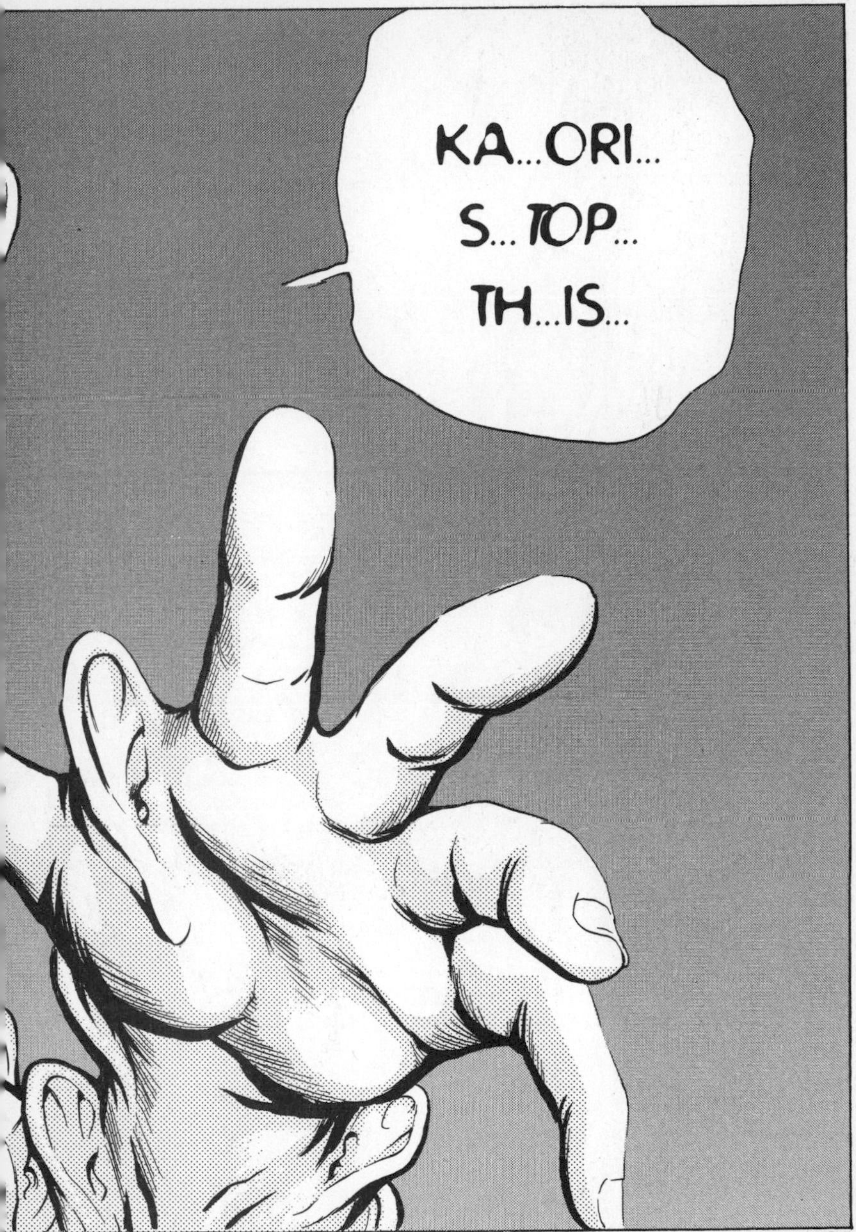
KA...ORI...
S...TOP...
TH...IS...

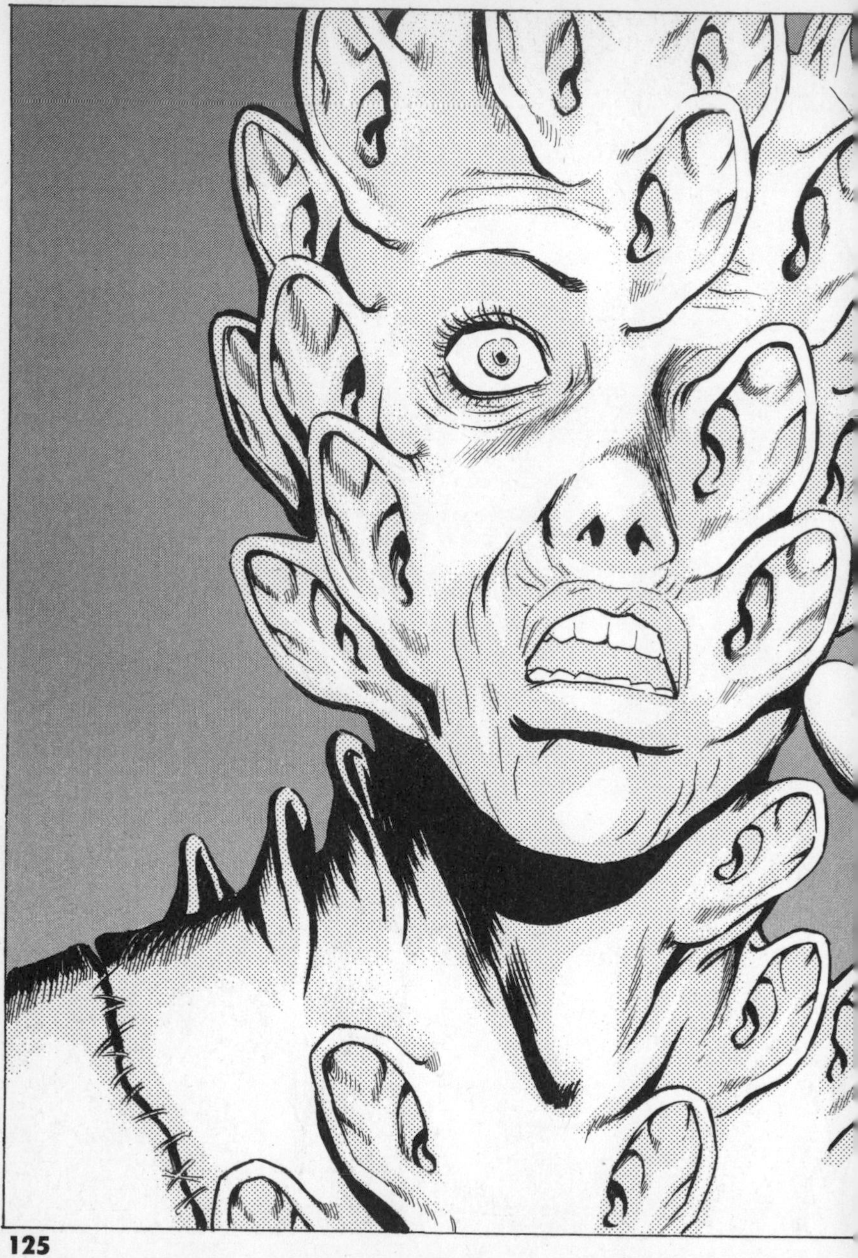

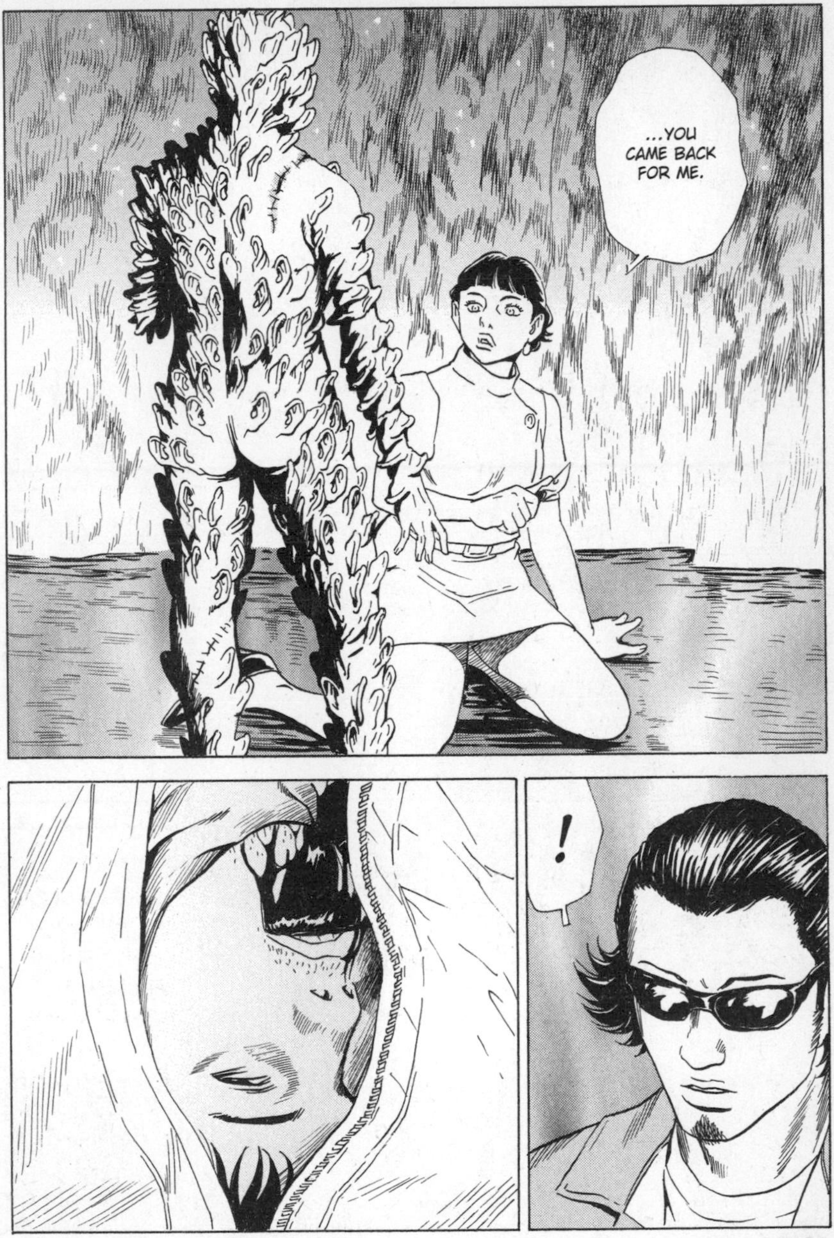
...YOU CAME BACK FOR ME.
!

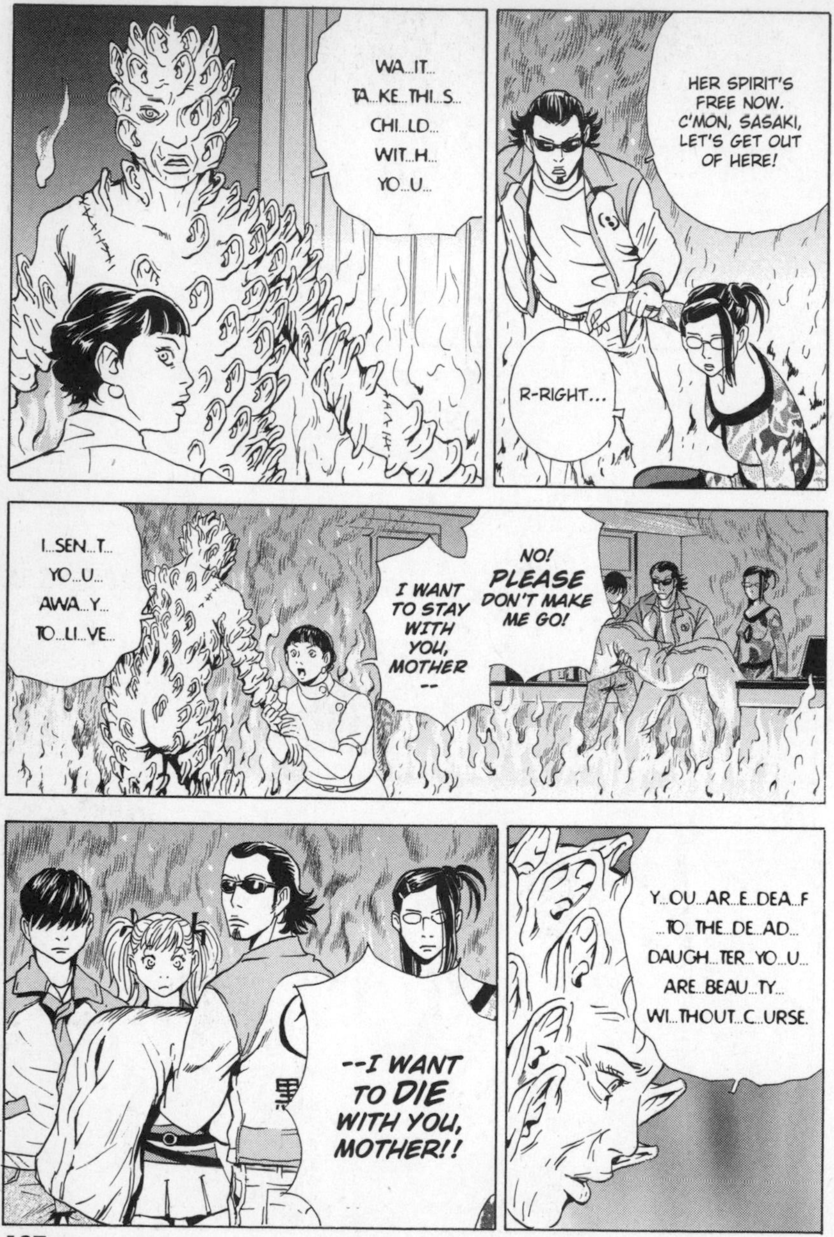
HER SPIRIT'S FREE NOW. C'MON, SASAKI, LET'S GET OUT OF HERE!
R-RIGHT...
WA...IT... TA...KE...THI...S... CHI...LD... WIT...H... YO...U...
NO! PLEASE DON'T MAKE ME GO!
I WANT TO STAY WITH YOU, MOTHER --
I...SEN...T... YO...U... AWA...Y... TO...LI...VE...
Y...OU...AR...E...DEA...F ...TO...THE...DE...AD... DAUGH...TER...YO...U... ARE...BEAU...TY... WI...THOUT...C...URSE.
--I WANT TO DIE WITH YOU, MOTHER!!

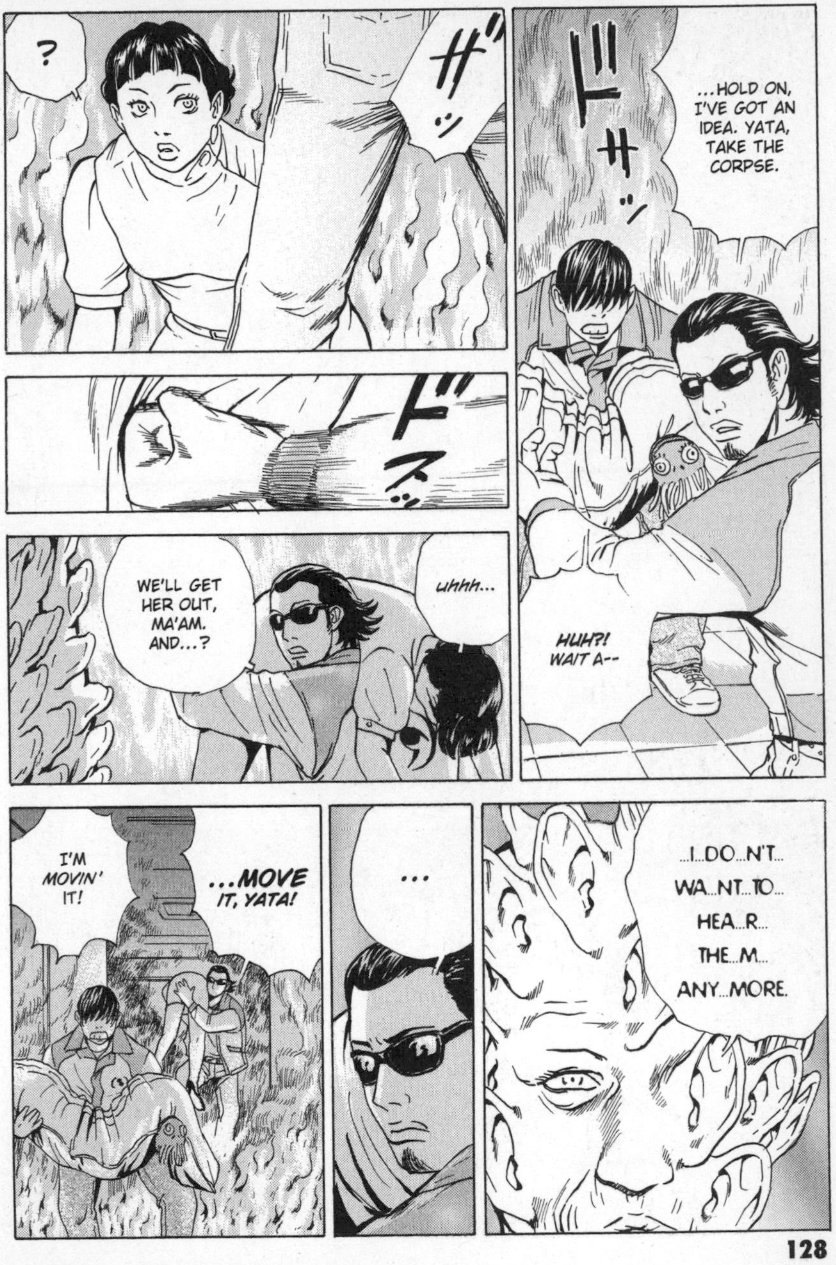
...HOLD ON, I'VE GOT AN IDEA. YATA, TAKE THE CORPSE.
HUH?! WAIT A--
?
ザッ
ドスッ
WE'LL GET HER OUT, MA'AM. AND...?
uhhh...
...I...DO...N'T... WA...NT...TO... HEA...R... THE...M... ANY...MORE.
...
...MOVE IT, YATA!
I'M MOVIN' IT!

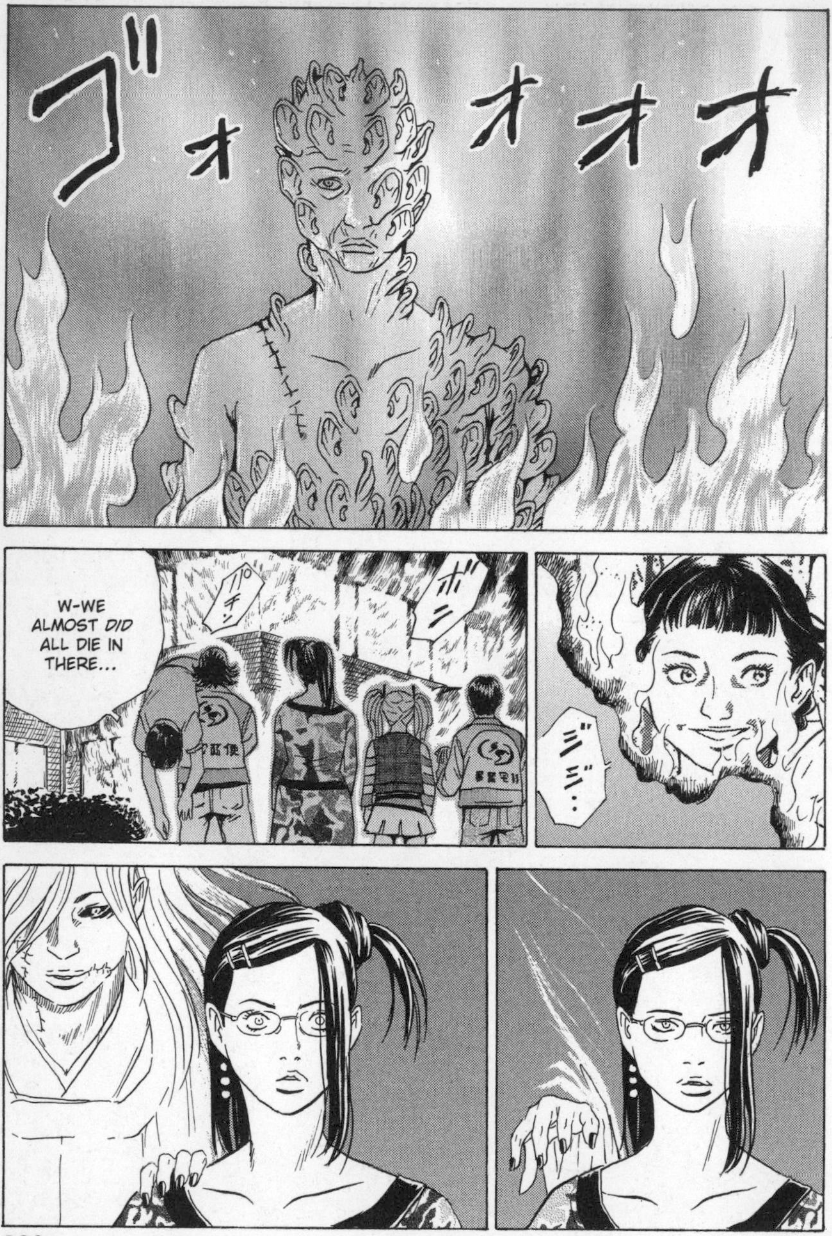
ゴォオオオ
ジジ…
ボン
パチン
W-WE ALMOST *DID* ALL DIE IN THERE...

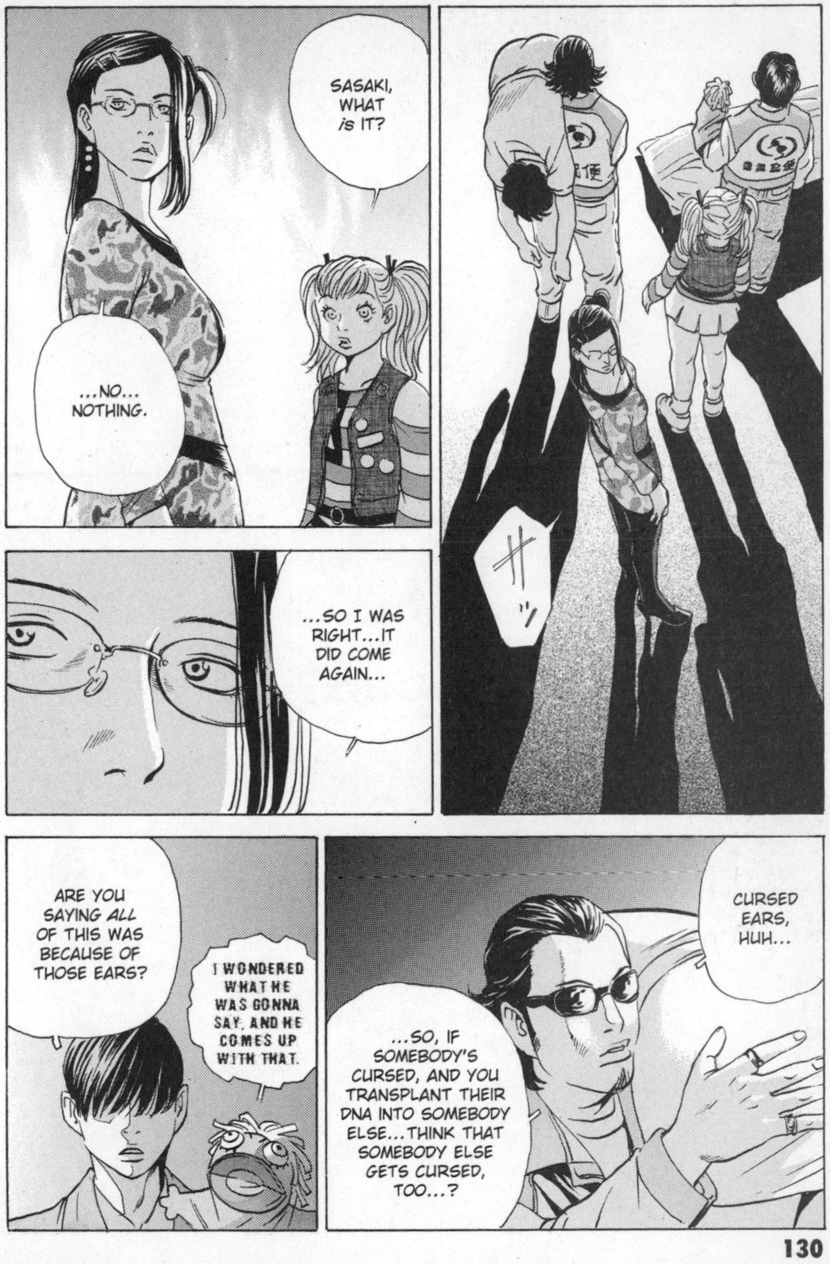
SASAKI, WHAT *is* IT?
...NO... NOTHING.
...SO I WAS RIGHT...IT DID COME AGAIN...
CURSED EARS, HUH...
...SO, IF SOMEBODY'S CURSED, AND YOU TRANSPLANT THEIR DNA INTO SOMEBODY ELSE...THINK THAT SOMEBODY ELSE GETS CURSED, TOO...?
ARE YOU SAYING *ALL* OF THIS WAS BECAUSE OF THOSE EARS?
I WONDERED WHAT HE WAS GONNA SAY, AND HE COMES UP WITH THAT.

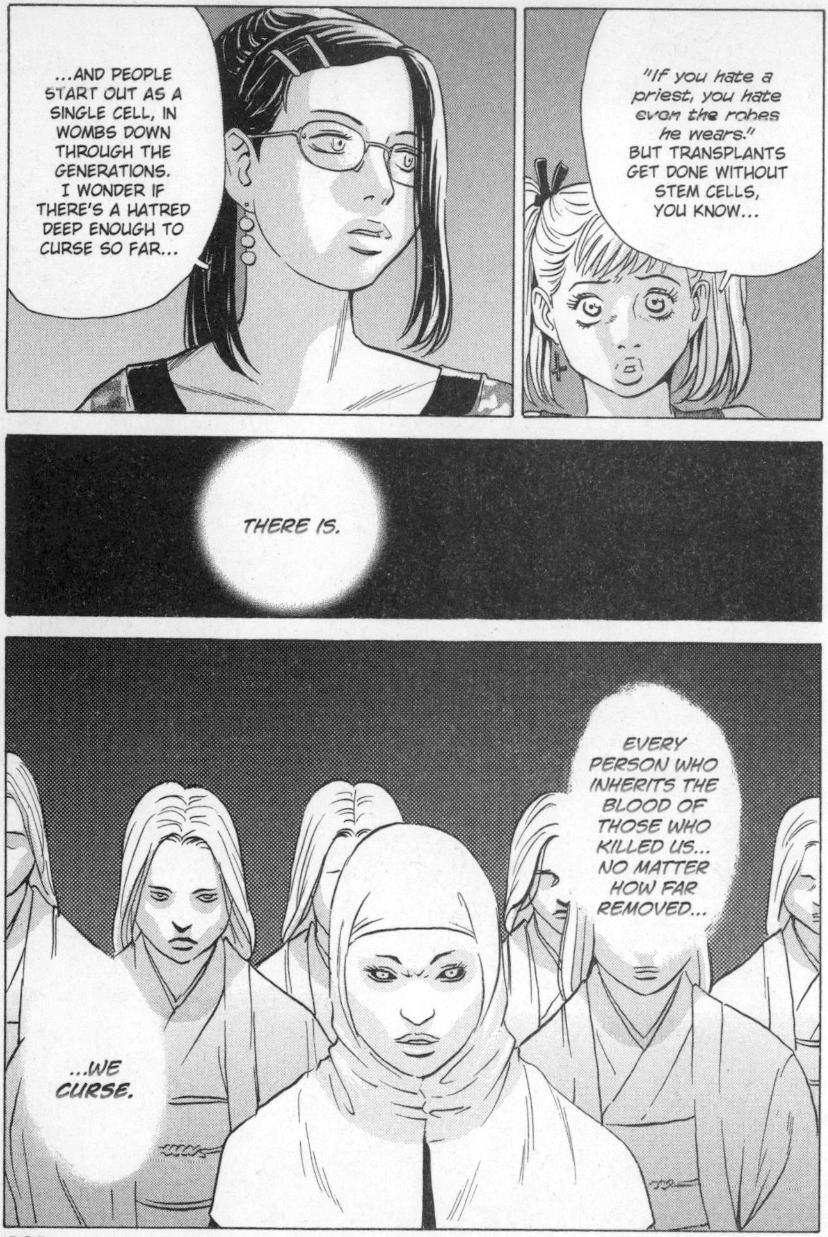
"If you hate a priest, you hate even the robes he wears." BUT TRANSPLANTS GET DONE WITHOUT STEM CELLS, YOU KNOW...
...AND PEOPLE START OUT AS A SINGLE CELL, IN WOMBS DOWN THROUGH THE GENERATIONS. I WONDER IF THERE'S A HATRED DEEP ENOUGH TO CURSE SO FAR...
THERE IS.
EVERY PERSON WHO INHERITS THE BLOOD OF THOSE WHO KILLED US... NO MATTER HOW FAR REMOVED...
...WE CURSE.

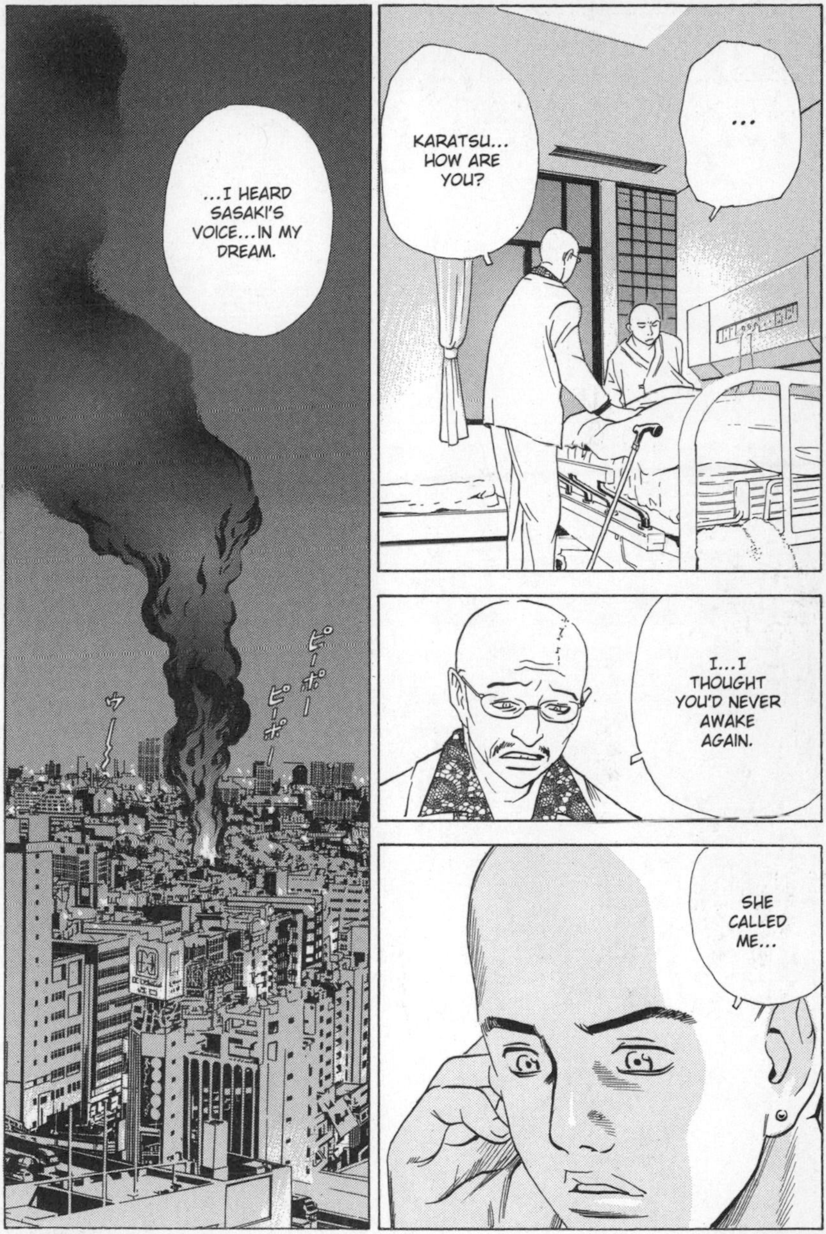
...
KARATSU... HOW ARE YOU?
I...I THOUGHT YOU'D NEVER AWAKE AGAIN.
SHE CALLED ME...
ピーポーピーポー
ウー
...I HEARD SASAKI'S VOICE...IN MY DREAM.

3rd delivery: my happiness, part II—the end

4th delivery
わたしの首領（ドン）
my don

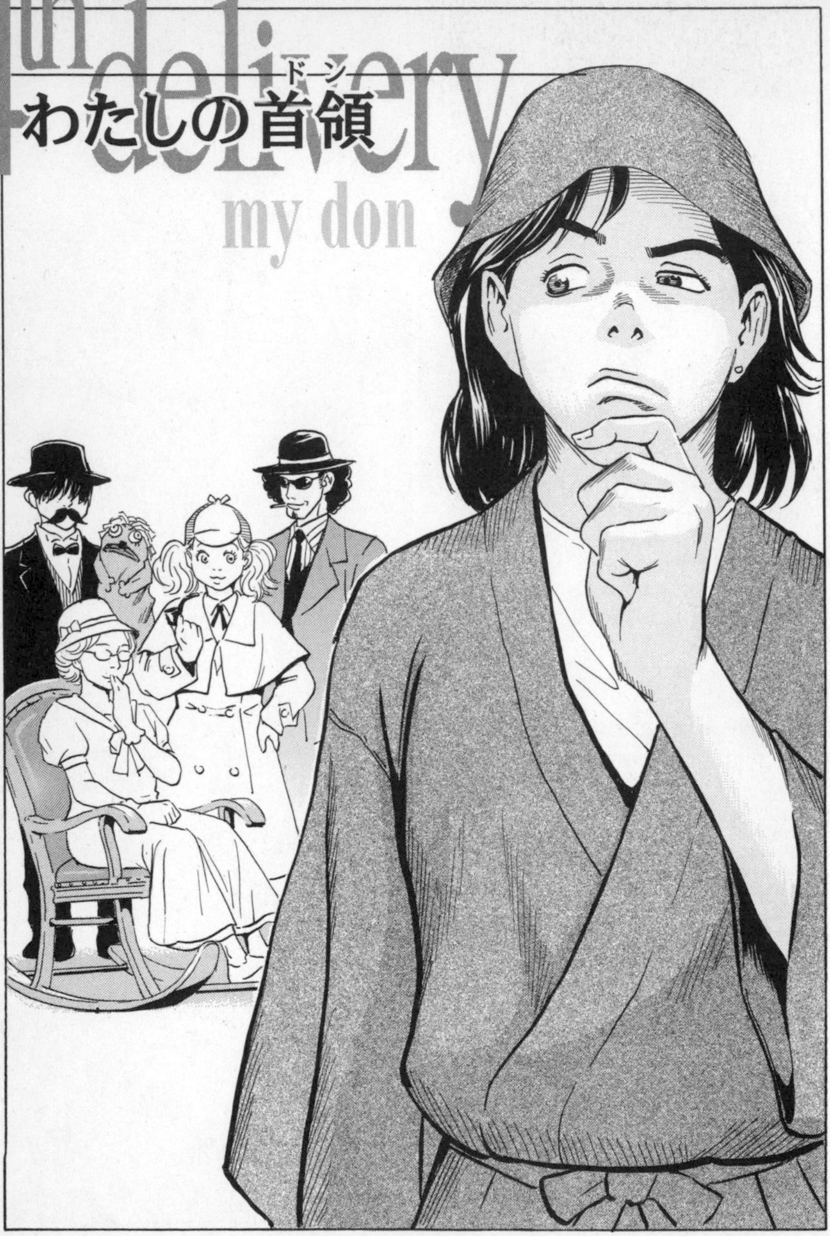

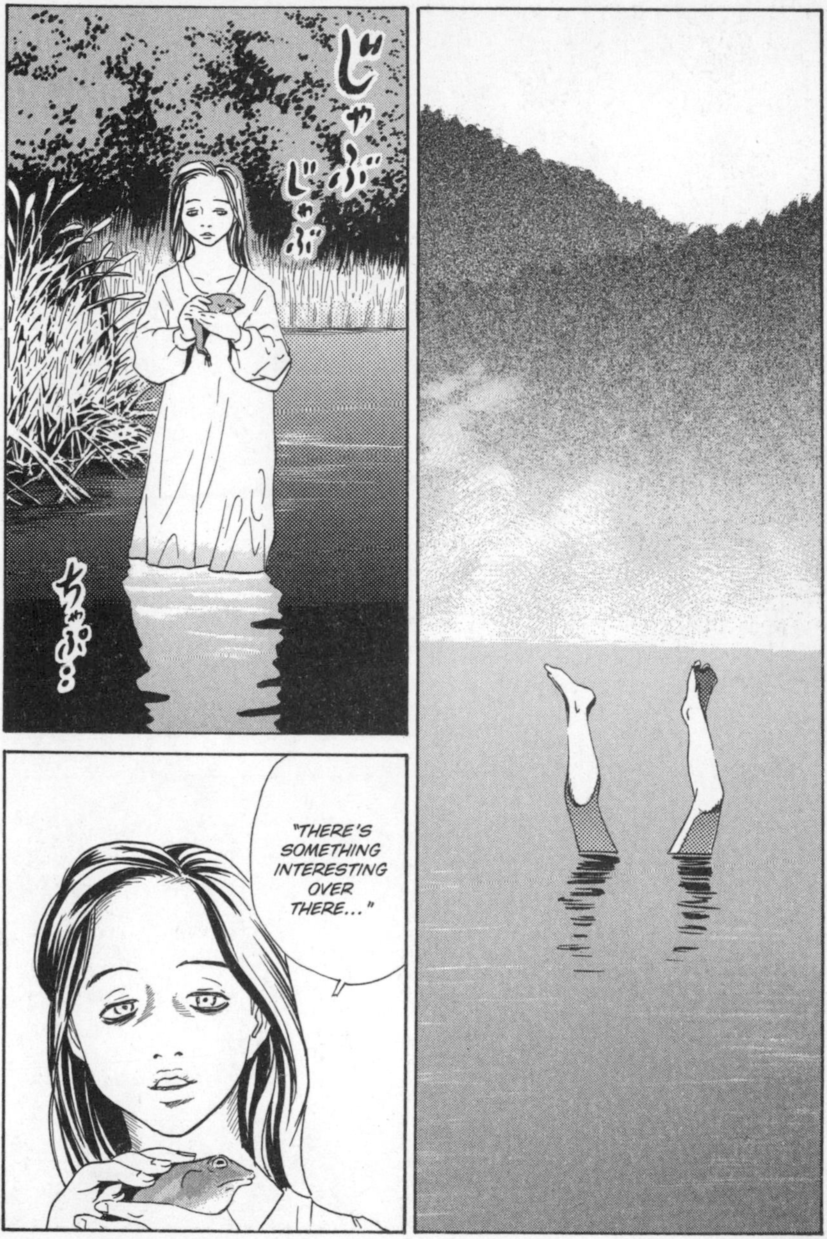
じゅぶ
じゅぶ
ちゃぷ…
"THERE'S SOMETHING INTERESTING OVER THERE..."

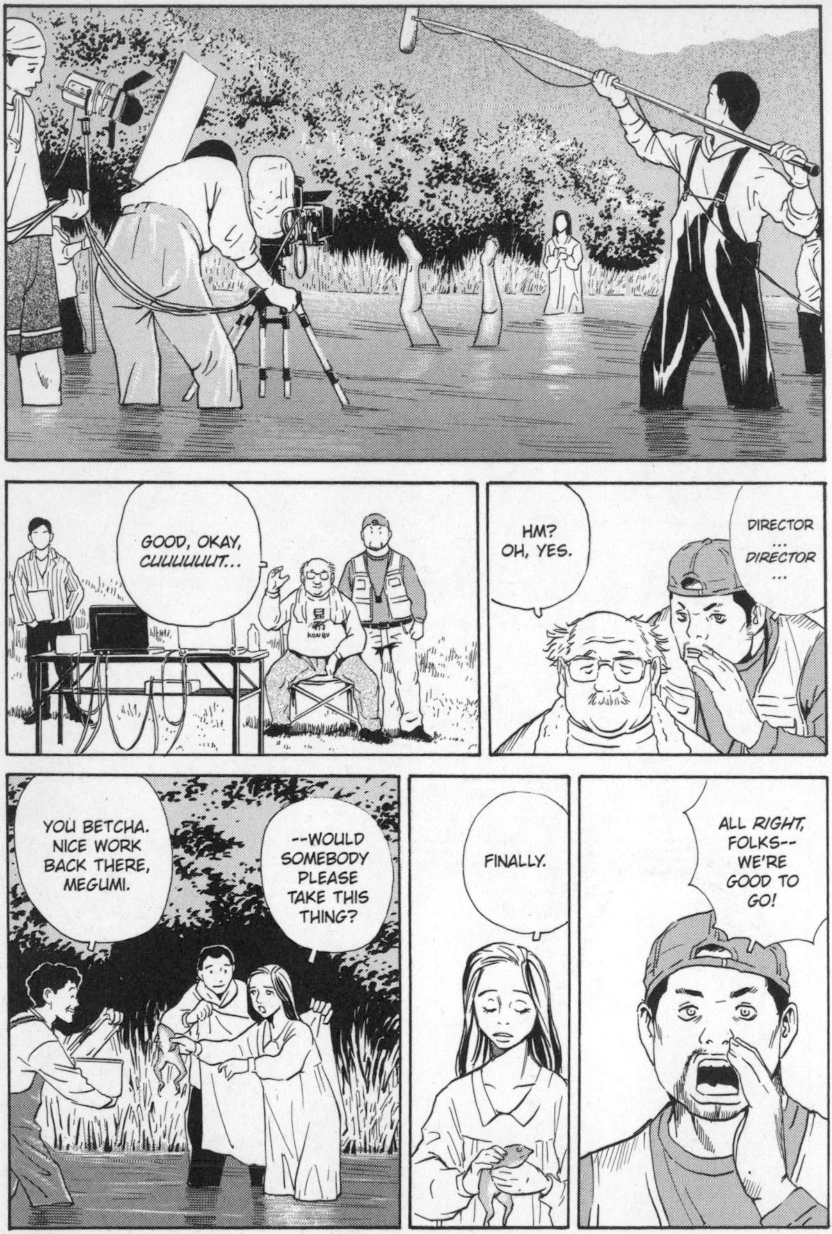
DIRECTOR ... DIRECTOR ...
HM? OH, YES.
GOOD, OKAY, CUUUUUUT...
ALL RIGHT, FOLKS--WE'RE GOOD TO GO!
FINALLY.
--WOULD SOMEBODY PLEASE TAKE THIS THING?
YOU BETCHA. NICE WORK BACK THERE, MEGUMI.

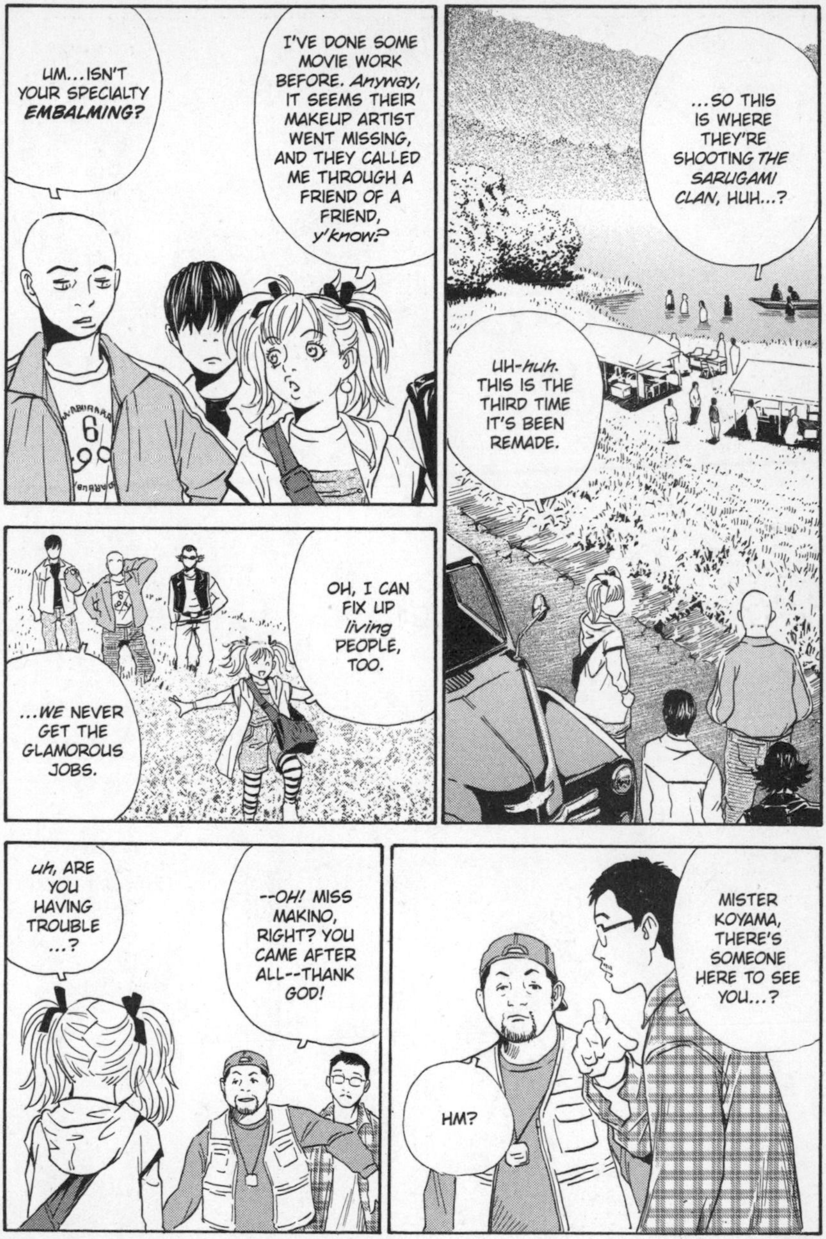
...SO THIS IS WHERE THEY'RE SHOOTING *THE SARUGAMI CLAN*, HUH...?
UH-*huh*. THIS IS THE THIRD TIME IT'S BEEN REMADE.
I'VE DONE SOME MOVIE WORK BEFORE. *Anyway*, IT SEEMS THEIR MAKEUP ARTIST WENT MISSING, AND THEY CALLED ME THROUGH A FRIEND OF A FRIEND, *y'know?*
UM...ISN'T YOUR SPECIALTY ***EMBALMING?***
OH, I CAN FIX UP *living* PEOPLE, TOO.
...*WE* NEVER GET THE GLAMOROUS JOBS.
MISTER KOYAMA, THERE'S SOMEONE HERE TO SEE YOU...?
HM?
--OH! MISS MAKINO, RIGHT? YOU CAME AFTER ALL--THANK GOD!
uh, ARE YOU HAVING TROUBLE ...?

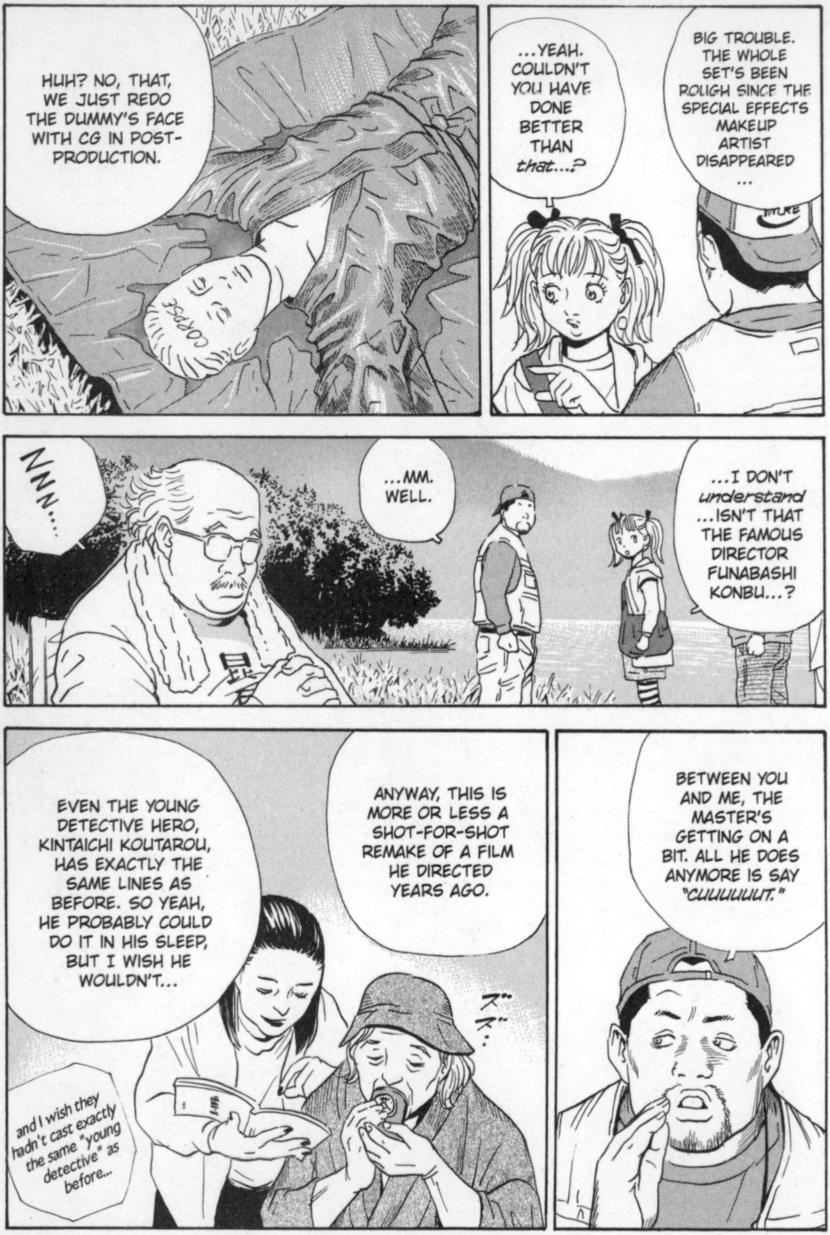
BIG TROUBLE. THE WHOLE SET'S BEEN ROUGH SINCE THE SPECIAL EFFECTS MAKEUP ARTIST DISAPPEARED ...
...YEAH. COULDN'T YOU HAVE DONE BETTER THAN *that*...?
HUH? NO, THAT, WE JUST REDO THE DUMMY'S FACE WITH CG IN POST-PRODUCTION.
CORPSE
...I DON'T *understand* ...ISN'T THAT THE FAMOUS DIRECTOR FUNABASHI KONBU...?
...MM. WELL.
NNN...
BETWEEN YOU AND ME, THE MASTER'S GETTING ON A BIT. ALL HE DOES ANYMORE IS SAY *"CUUUUUUT."*
ANYWAY, THIS IS MORE OR LESS A SHOT-FOR-SHOT REMAKE OF A FILM HE DIRECTED YEARS AGO.
EVEN THE YOUNG DETECTIVE HERO, KINTAICHI KOUTAROU, HAS EXACTLY THE SAME LINES AS BEFORE. SO YEAH, HE PROBABLY COULD DO IT IN HIS SLEEP, BUT I WISH HE WOULDN'T...
ズズ…
and I wish they hadn't cast exactly the same "young detective" as before...

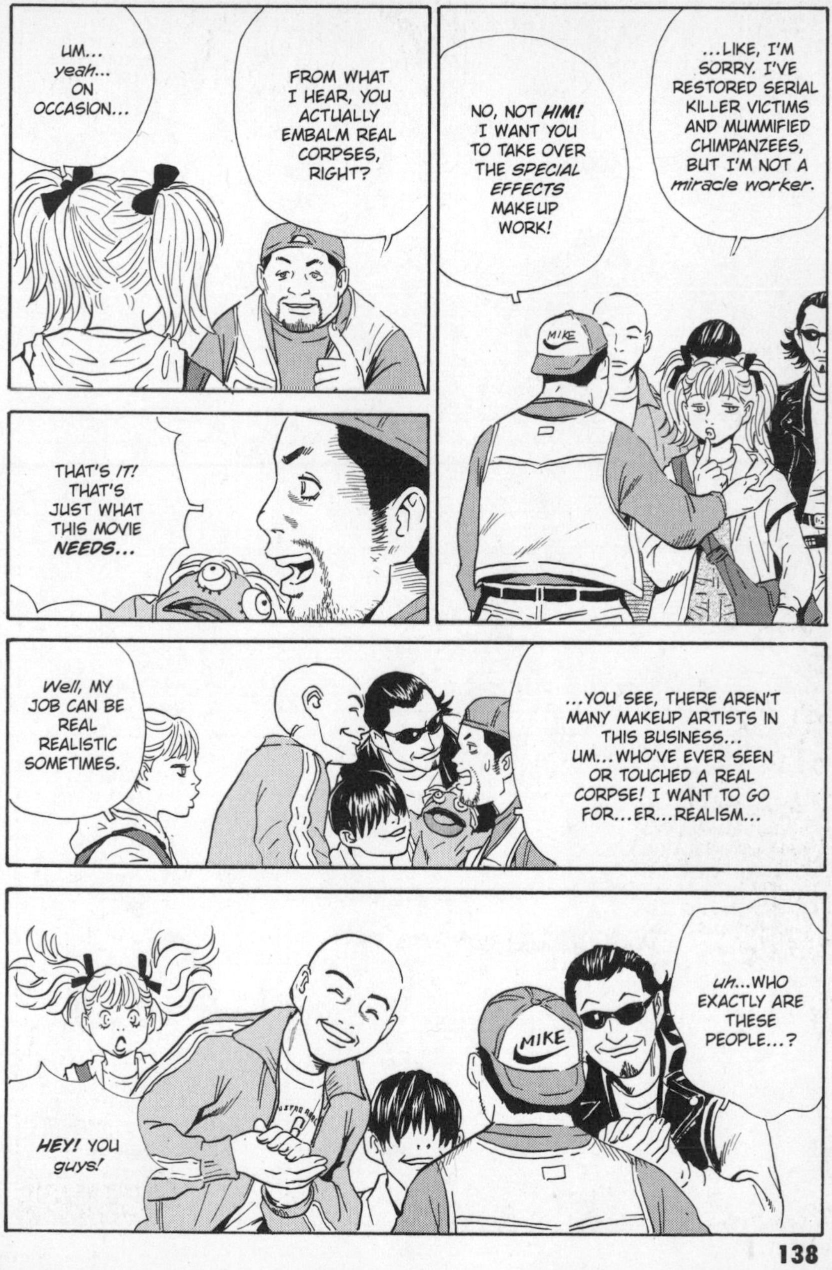
...LIKE, I'M SORRY. I'VE RESTORED SERIAL KILLER VICTIMS AND MUMMIFIED CHIMPANZEES, BUT I'M NOT A *miracle worker*.
NO, NOT ***HIM!*** I WANT YOU TO TAKE OVER THE *SPECIAL EFFECTS* MAKEUP WORK!
MIKE
FROM WHAT I HEAR, YOU ACTUALLY EMBALM REAL CORPSES, RIGHT?
UM... *yeah*... ON OCCASION...
THAT'S *IT!* THAT'S JUST WHAT THIS MOVIE ***NEEDS...***
...YOU SEE, THERE AREN'T MANY MAKEUP ARTISTS IN THIS BUSINESS... UM...WHO'VE EVER SEEN OR TOUCHED A REAL CORPSE! I WANT TO GO FOR...ER...REALISM...
Well, MY JOB CAN BE REAL REALISTIC SOMETIMES.
uh...WHO EXACTLY ARE THESE PEOPLE...?
MIKE
HEY! YOU *guys!*

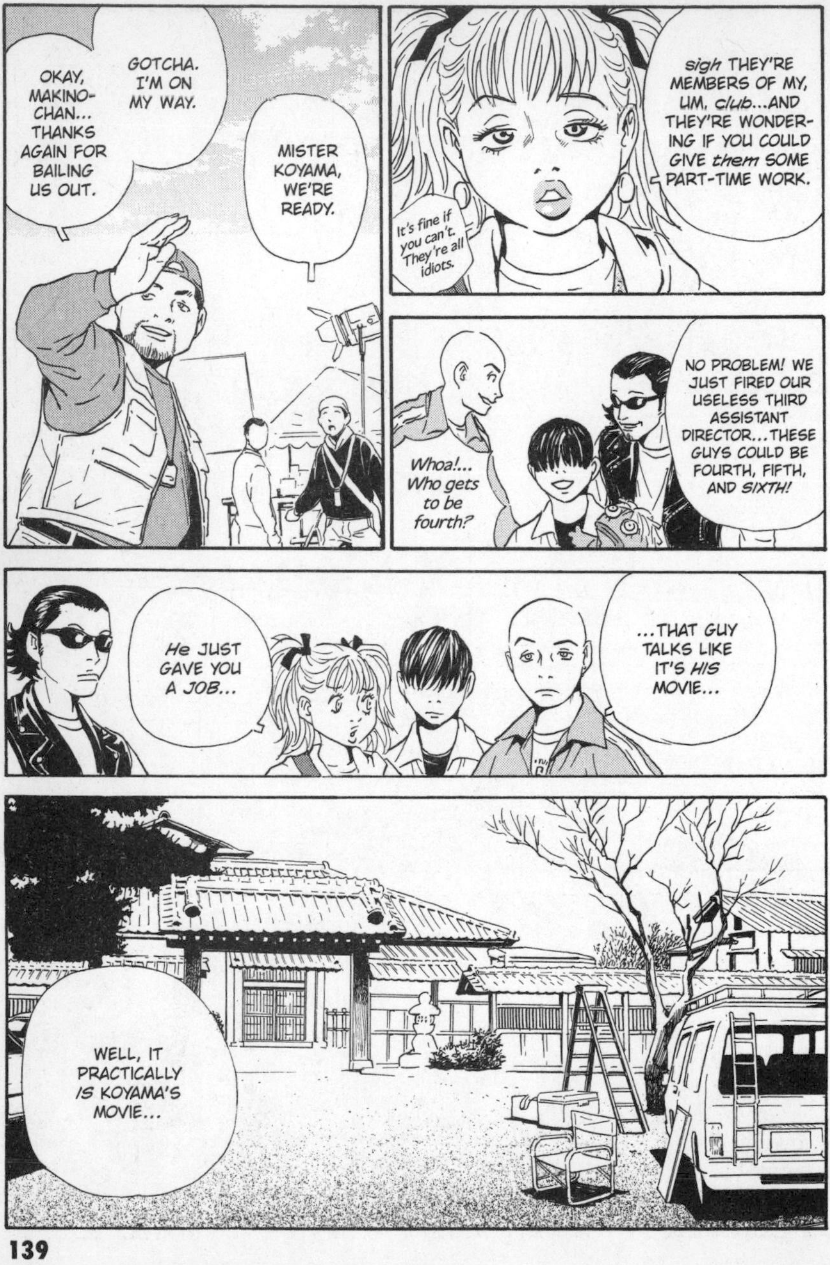
sigh THEY'RE MEMBERS OF MY, UM, *club*...AND THEY'RE WONDERING IF YOU COULD GIVE *them* SOME PART-TIME WORK.
It's fine if you can't. They're all idiots.
NO PROBLEM! WE JUST FIRED OUR USELESS THIRD ASSISTANT DIRECTOR...THESE GUYS COULD BE FOURTH, FIFTH, AND *SIXTH!*
Whoa!... Who gets to be fourth?
GOTCHA. I'M ON MY WAY.
OKAY, MAKINO-CHAN... THANKS AGAIN FOR BAILING US OUT.
MISTER KOYAMA, WE'RE READY.
...THAT GUY TALKS LIKE IT'S *HIS* MOVIE...
He JUST GAVE YOU A *JOB*...
WELL, IT PRACTICALLY *IS* KOYAMA'S MOVIE...

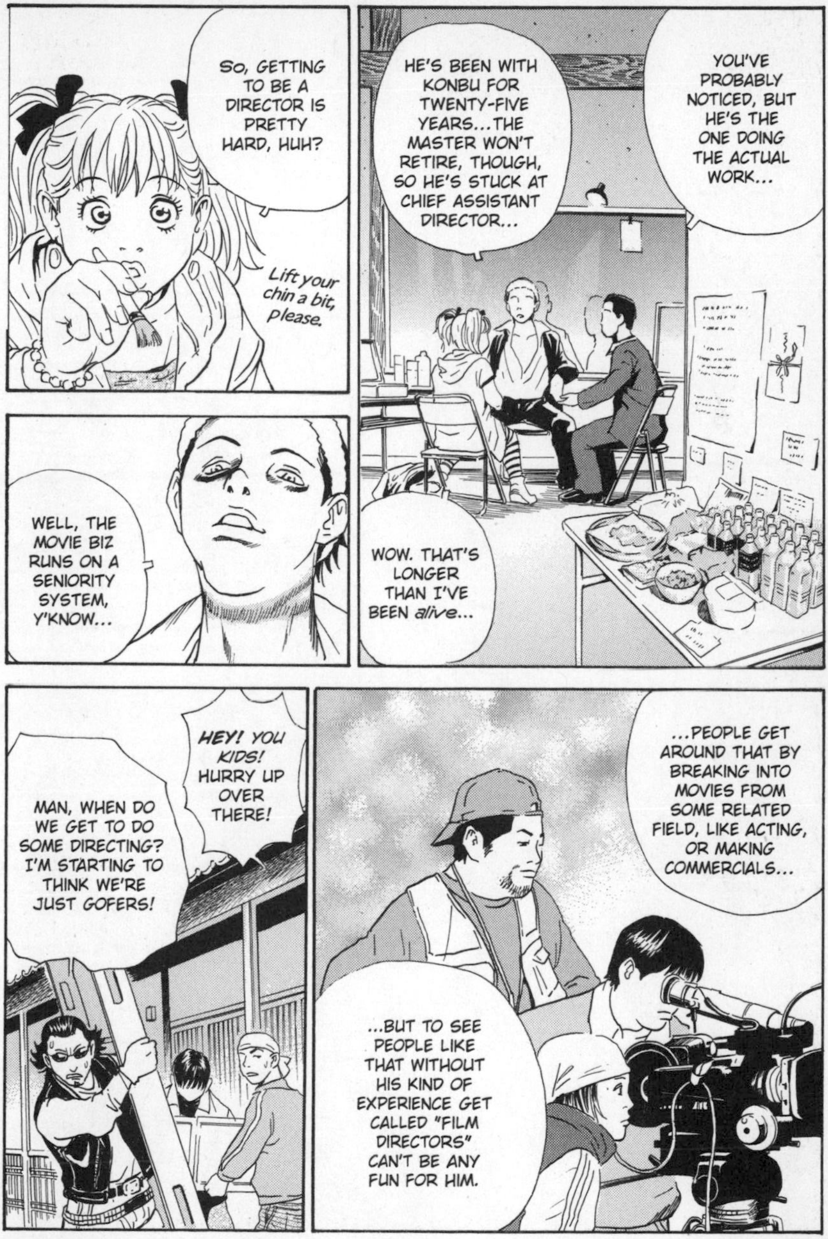
YOU'VE PROBABLY NOTICED, BUT HE'S THE ONE DOING THE ACTUAL WORK...
HE'S BEEN WITH KONBU FOR TWENTY-FIVE YEARS...THE MASTER WON'T RETIRE, THOUGH, SO HE'S STUCK AT CHIEF ASSISTANT DIRECTOR...
WOW. THAT'S LONGER THAN I'VE BEEN *alive*...
SO, GETTING TO BE A DIRECTOR IS PRETTY HARD, HUH?
Lift your chin a bit, please.
WELL, THE MOVIE BIZ RUNS ON A SENIORITY SYSTEM, Y'KNOW...
...PEOPLE GET AROUND THAT BY BREAKING INTO MOVIES FROM SOME RELATED FIELD, LIKE ACTING, OR MAKING COMMERCIALS...
...BUT TO SEE PEOPLE LIKE THAT WITHOUT HIS KIND OF EXPERIENCE GET CALLED "FILM DIRECTORS" CAN'T BE ANY FUN FOR HIM.
HEY! YOU KIDS! HURRY UP OVER THERE!
MAN, WHEN DO WE GET TO DO SOME DIRECTING? I'M STARTING TO THINK WE'RE JUST GOFERS!

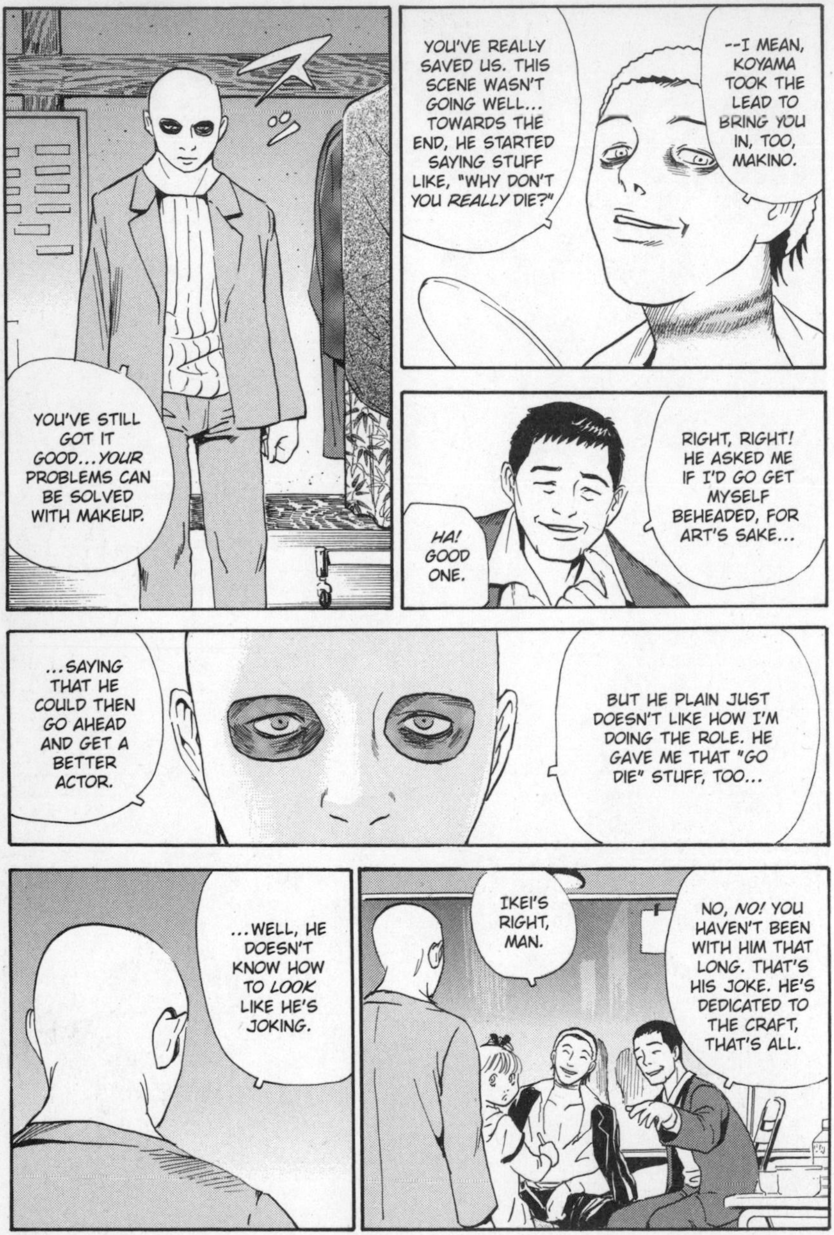
--I MEAN, KOYAMA TOOK THE LEAD TO BRING YOU IN, TOO, MAKINO.
YOU'VE REALLY SAVED US. THIS SCENE WASN'T GOING WELL... TOWARDS THE END, HE STARTED SAYING STUFF LIKE, "WHY DON'T YOU *REALLY* DIE?"
RIGHT, RIGHT! HE ASKED ME IF I'D GO GET MYSELF BEHEADED, FOR ART'S SAKE...
HA! GOOD ONE.
YOU'VE STILL GOT IT GOOD... *YOUR* PROBLEMS CAN BE SOLVED WITH MAKEUP.
BUT HE PLAIN JUST DOESN'T LIKE HOW I'M DOING THE ROLE. HE GAVE ME THAT "GO DIE" STUFF, TOO...
...SAYING THAT HE COULD THEN GO AHEAD AND GET A BETTER ACTOR.
NO, *NO!* YOU HAVEN'T BEEN WITH HIM THAT LONG. THAT'S HIS JOKE. HE'S DEDICATED TO THE CRAFT, THAT'S ALL.
IKEI'S RIGHT, MAN.
...WELL, HE DOESN'T KNOW HOW TO *LOOK* LIKE HE'S JOKING.

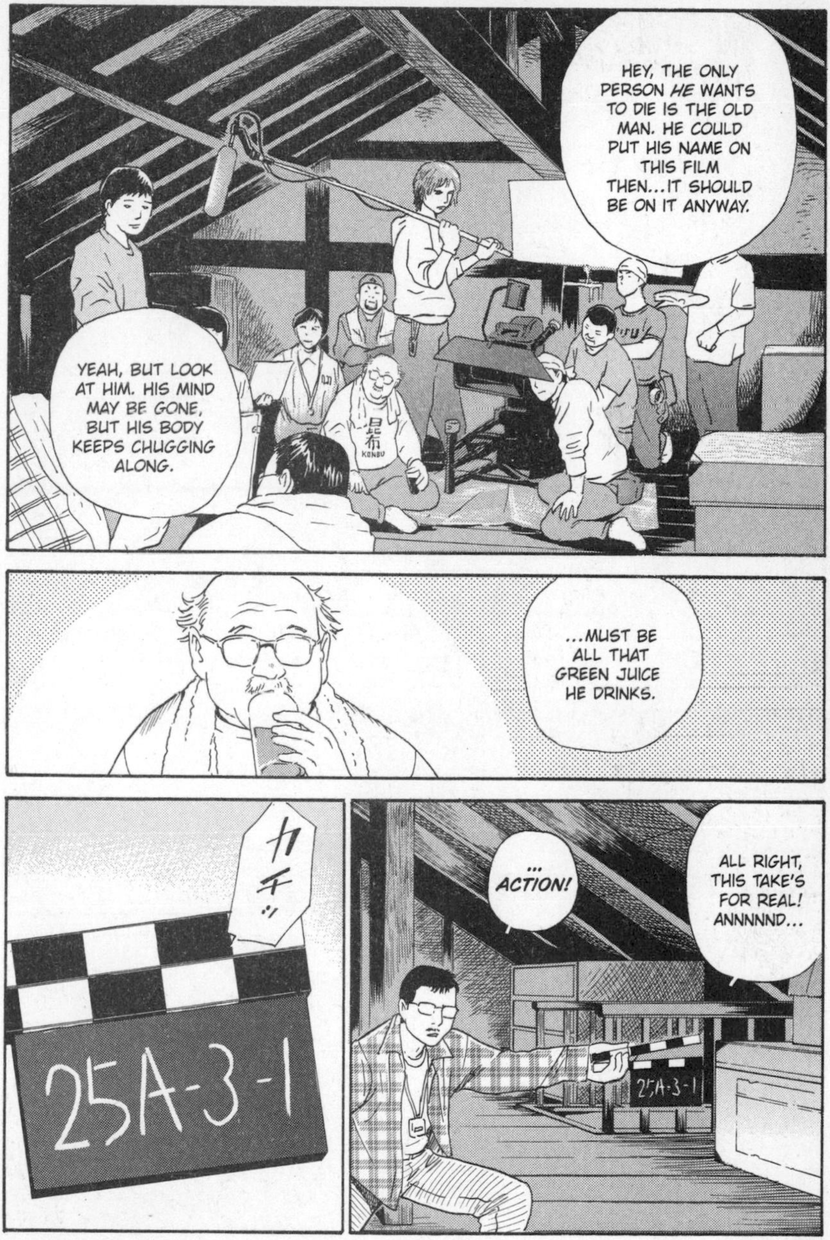
HEY, THE ONLY PERSON *HE* WANTS TO DIE IS THE OLD MAN. HE COULD PUT HIS NAME ON THIS FILM THEN...IT SHOULD BE ON IT ANYWAY.
YEAH, BUT LOOK AT HIM. HIS MIND MAY BE GONE, BUT HIS BODY KEEPS CHUGGING ALONG.
...MUST BE ALL THAT GREEN JUICE HE DRINKS.
ALL RIGHT, THIS TAKE'S FOR REAL! ANNNNND...
... *ACTION!*
カチッ
25A-3-1

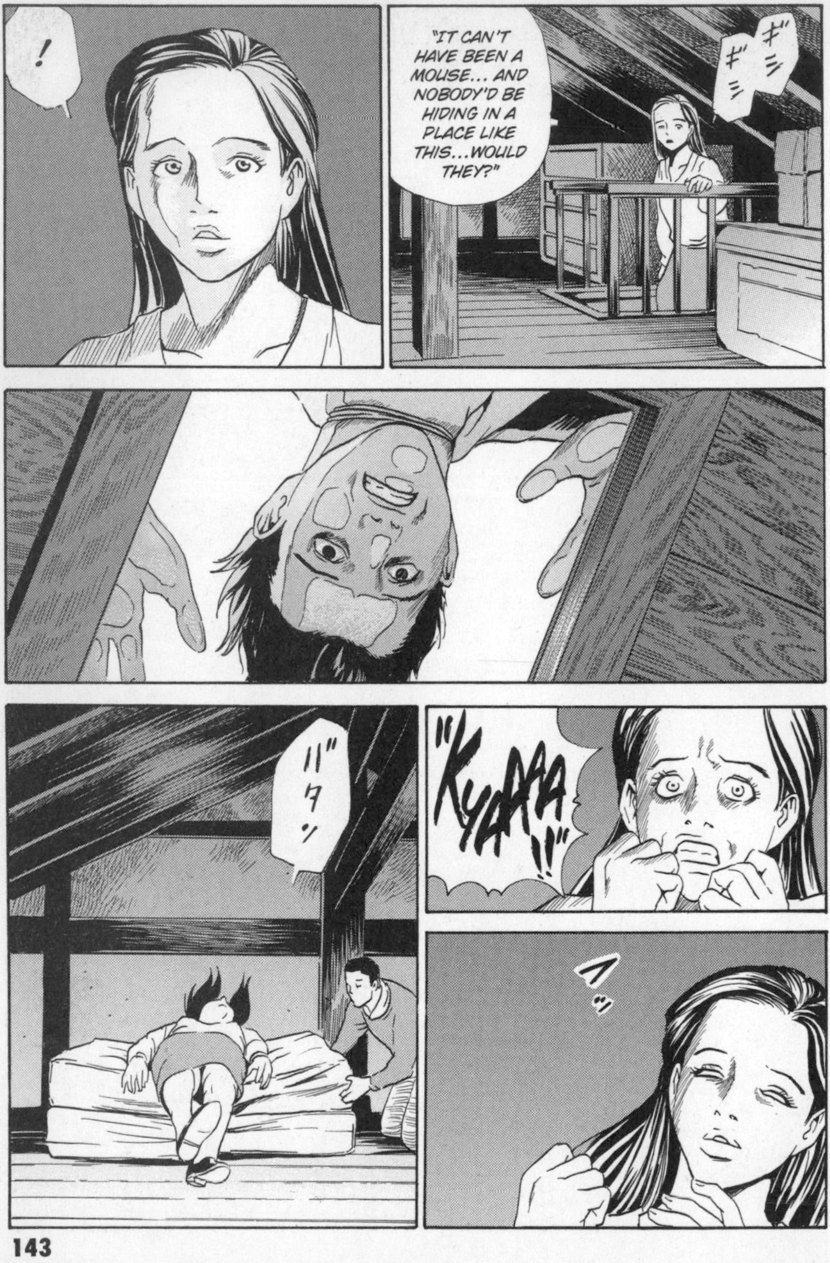
"IT CAN'T HAVE BEEN A MOUSE... AND NOBODY'D BE HIDING IN A PLACE LIKE THIS...WOULD THEY?"
ギシ ギシ
!
"KYAAAA!!"
ハッ
バタッ

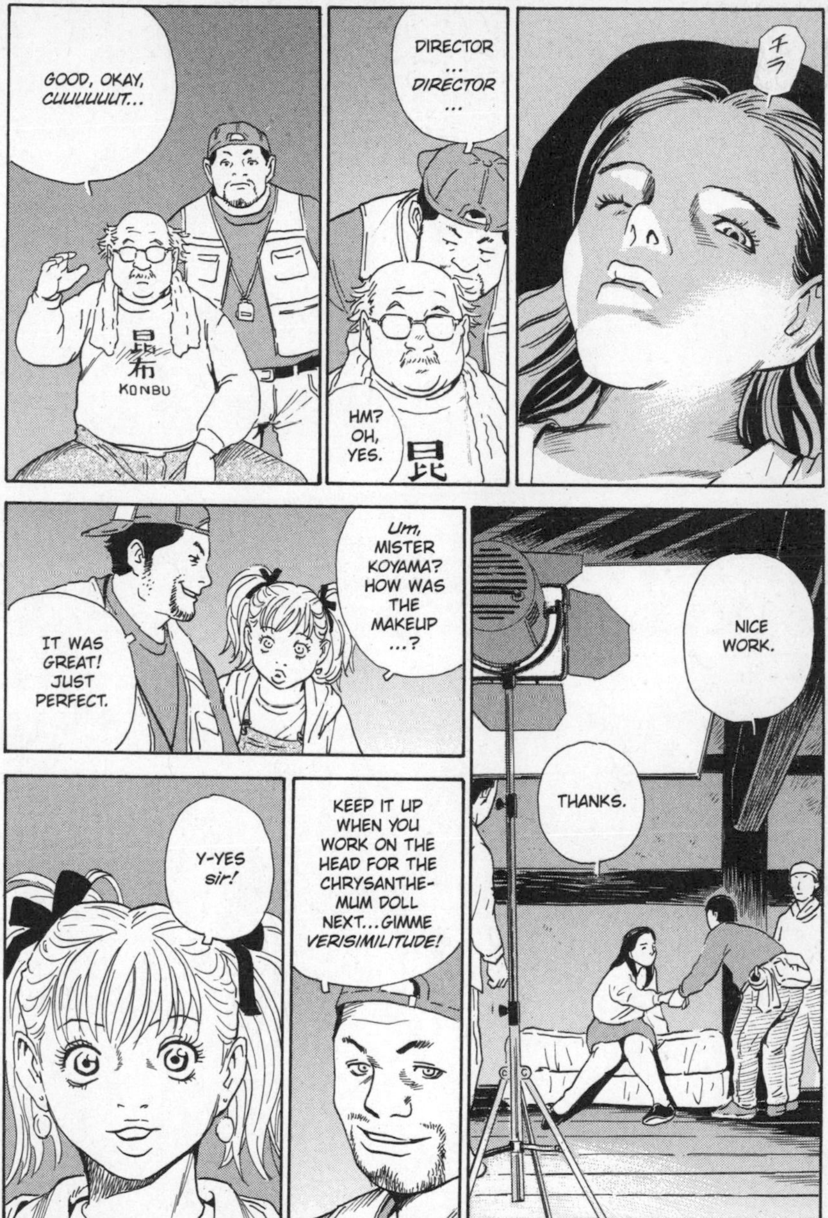
チラ
DIRECTOR ... DIRECTOR ...
HM? OH, YES.
昆
GOOD, OKAY, CUUUUUUT...
昆布
KONBU
NICE WORK.
THANKS.
Um, MISTER KOYAMA? HOW WAS THE MAKEUP ...?
IT WAS GREAT! JUST PERFECT.
KEEP IT UP WHEN YOU WORK ON THE HEAD FOR THE CHRYSANTHEMUM DOLL NEXT...GIMME *VERISIMILITUDE!*
Y-YES *sir!*

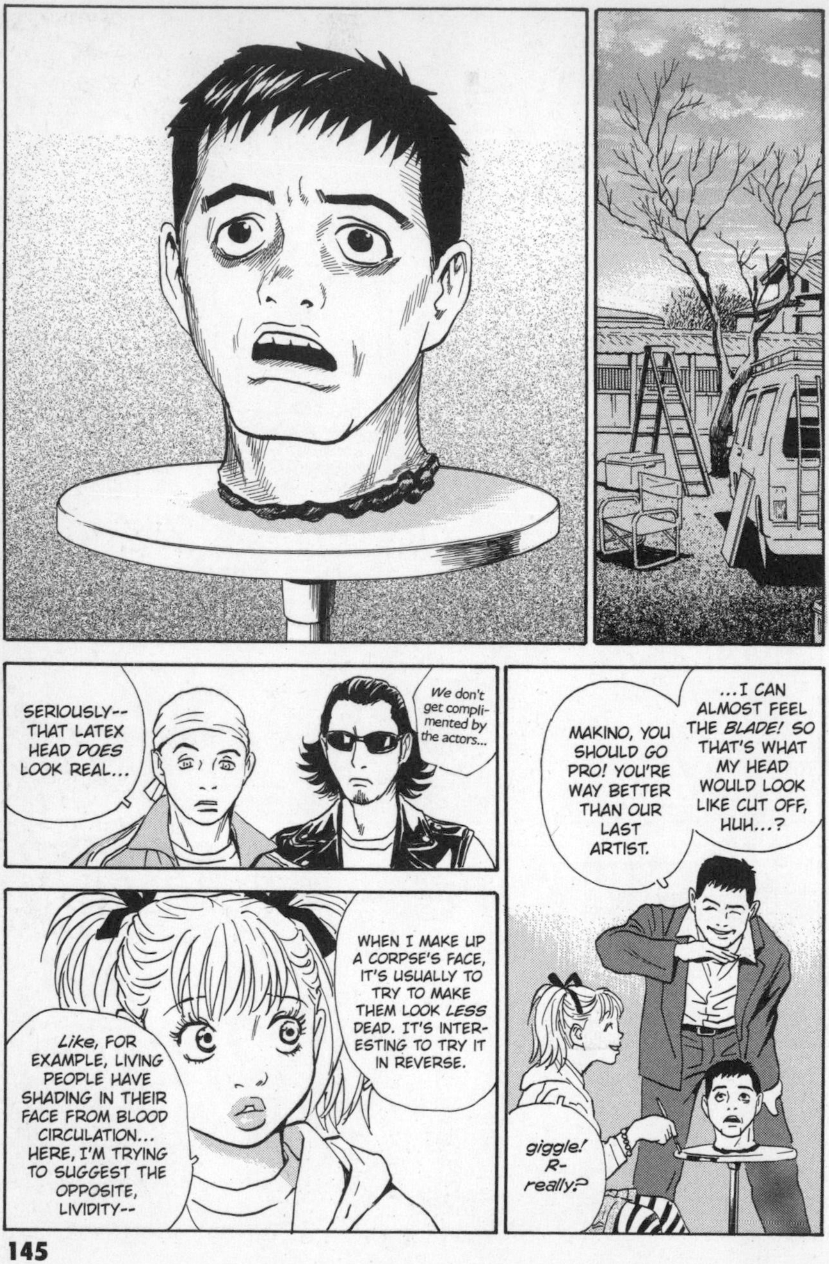
...I CAN ALMOST FEEL THE *BLADE!* SO THAT'S WHAT MY HEAD WOULD LOOK LIKE CUT OFF, HUH...?
MAKINO, YOU SHOULD GO PRO! YOU'RE WAY BETTER THAN OUR LAST ARTIST.
giggle! R-really?
We don't get complimented by the actors...
SERIOUSLY--THAT LATEX HEAD *DOES* LOOK REAL...
WHEN I MAKE UP A CORPSE'S FACE, IT'S USUALLY TO TRY TO MAKE THEM LOOK *LESS* DEAD. IT'S INTERESTING TO TRY IT IN REVERSE.
Like, FOR EXAMPLE, LIVING PEOPLE HAVE SHADING IN THEIR FACE FROM BLOOD CIRCULATION... HERE, I'M TRYING TO SUGGEST THE OPPOSITE, LIVIDITY--

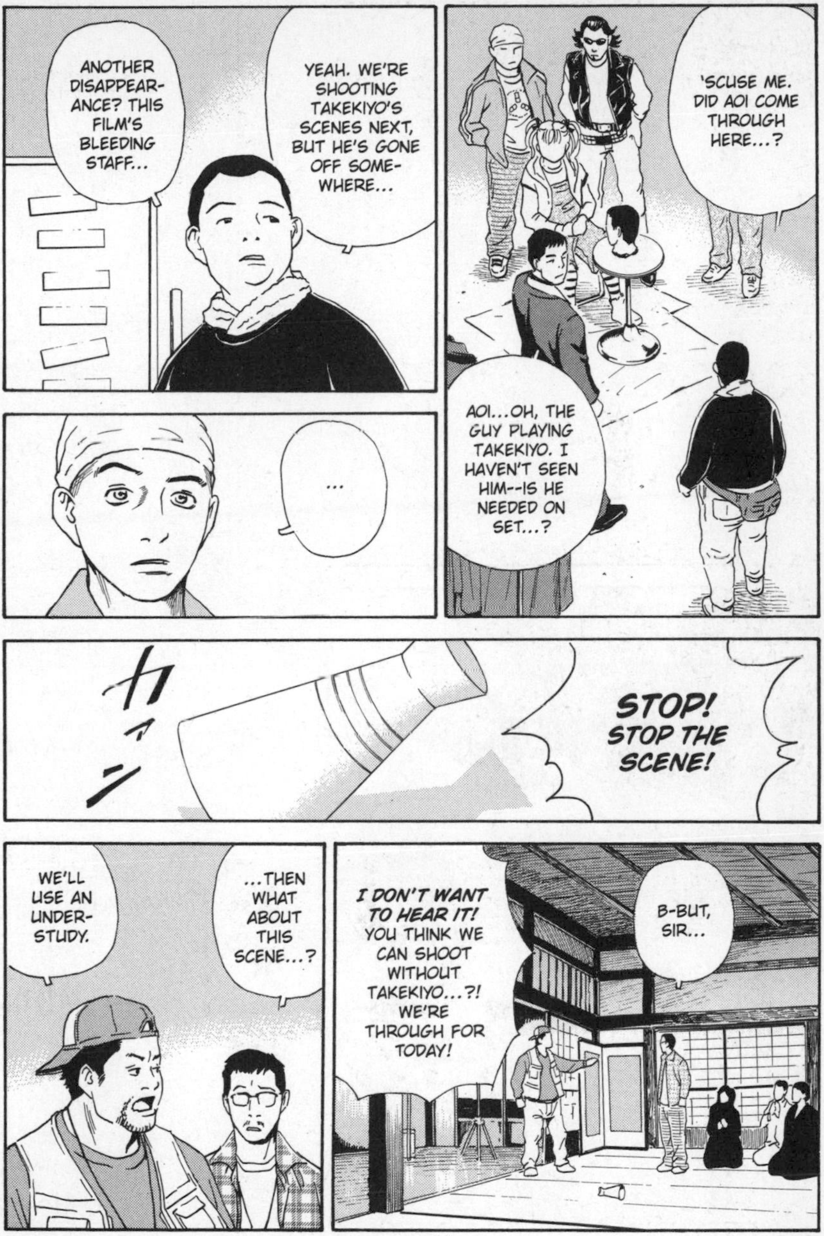
'SCUSE ME. DID AOI COME THROUGH HERE...?
AOI...OH, THE GUY PLAYING TAKEKIYO. I HAVEN'T SEEN HIM--IS HE NEEDED ON SET...?
YEAH. WE'RE SHOOTING TAKEKIYO'S SCENES NEXT, BUT HE'S GONE OFF SOMEWHERE...
ANOTHER DISAPPEARANCE? THIS FILM'S BLEEDING STAFF...
...
STOP! STOP THE SCENE!
カァン
B-BUT, SIR...
I DON'T WANT TO HEAR IT! YOU THINK WE CAN SHOOT WITHOUT TAKEKIYO...?! WE'RE THROUGH FOR TODAY!
...THEN WHAT ABOUT THIS SCENE...?
WE'LL USE AN UNDERSTUDY.

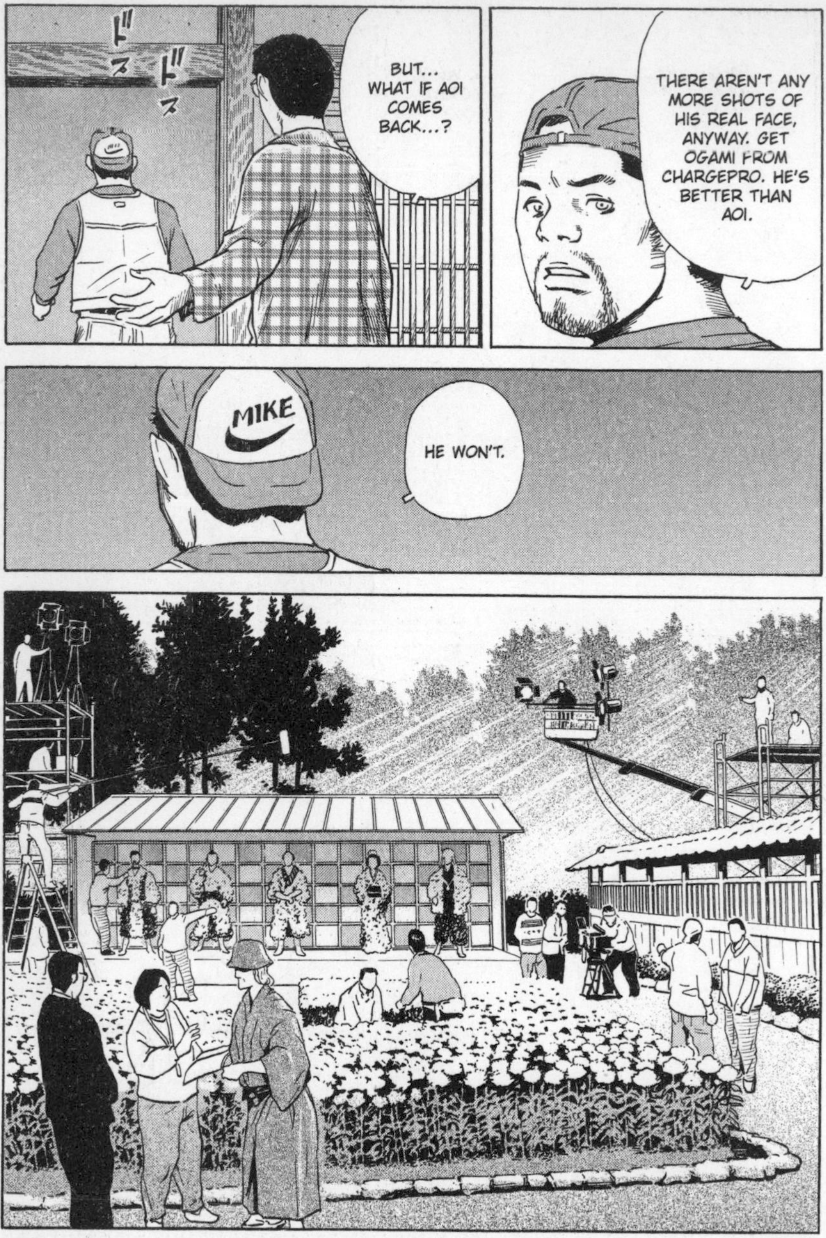
THERE AREN'T ANY MORE SHOTS OF HIS REAL FACE, ANYWAY. GET OGAMI FROM CHARGEPRO. HE'S BETTER THAN AOI.
BUT... WHAT IF AOI COMES BACK...?
ドス ドス
MIKE
HE WON'T.

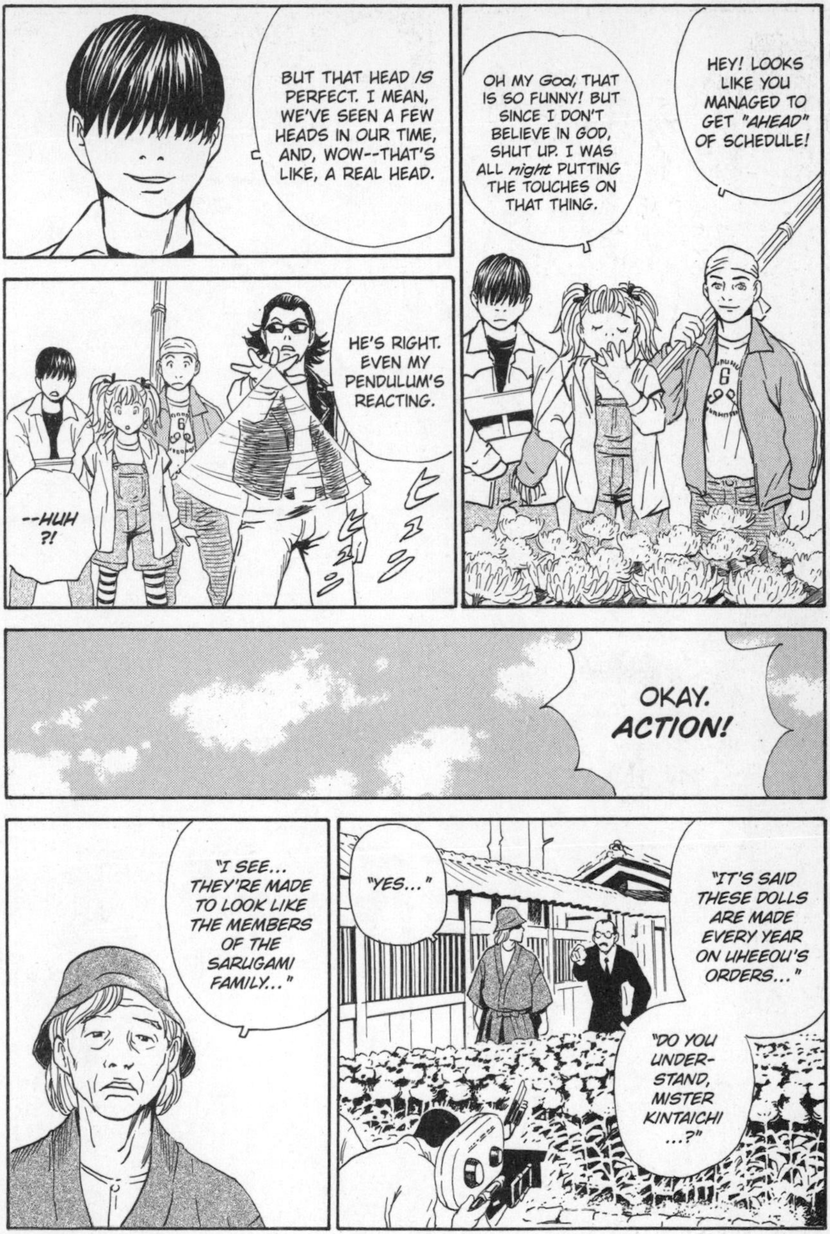
HEY! LOOKS LIKE YOU MANAGED TO GET "AHEAD" OF SCHEDULE!
OH MY God, THAT IS SO FUNNY! BUT SINCE I DON'T BELIEVE IN GOD, SHUT UP. I WAS ALL night PUTTING THE TOUCHES ON THAT THING.
BUT THAT HEAD IS PERFECT. I MEAN, WE'VE SEEN A FEW HEADS IN OUR TIME, AND, WOW--THAT'S LIKE, A REAL HEAD.
HE'S RIGHT. EVEN MY PENDULUM'S REACTING.
--HUH ?!
OKAY. ACTION!
"IT'S SAID THESE DOLLS ARE MADE EVERY YEAR ON UHEEOU'S ORDERS..."
"YES..."
"DO YOU UNDER-STAND, MISTER KINTAICHI ...?"
"I SEE... THEY'RE MADE TO LOOK LIKE THE MEMBERS OF THE SARUGAMI FAMILY..."

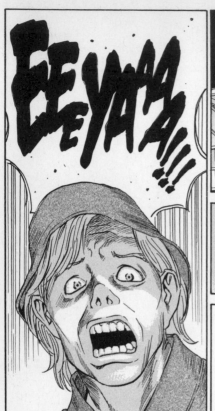

"YES..."
グラリ
"AH... THAT'S--"
ドサッ
EEEYAAA!!!!
MM-HMM...
...?
DIRECTOR ... DIRECTOR ...
HM? OH, YES.
GOOD, OKAY, CUUUUUUT...
昆布
KONBU

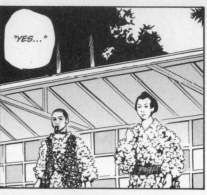

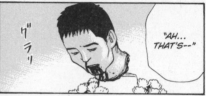

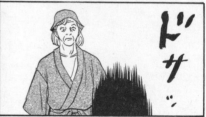

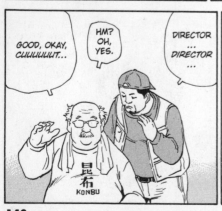

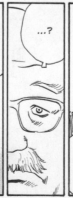

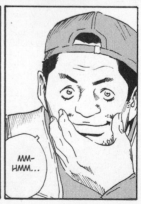

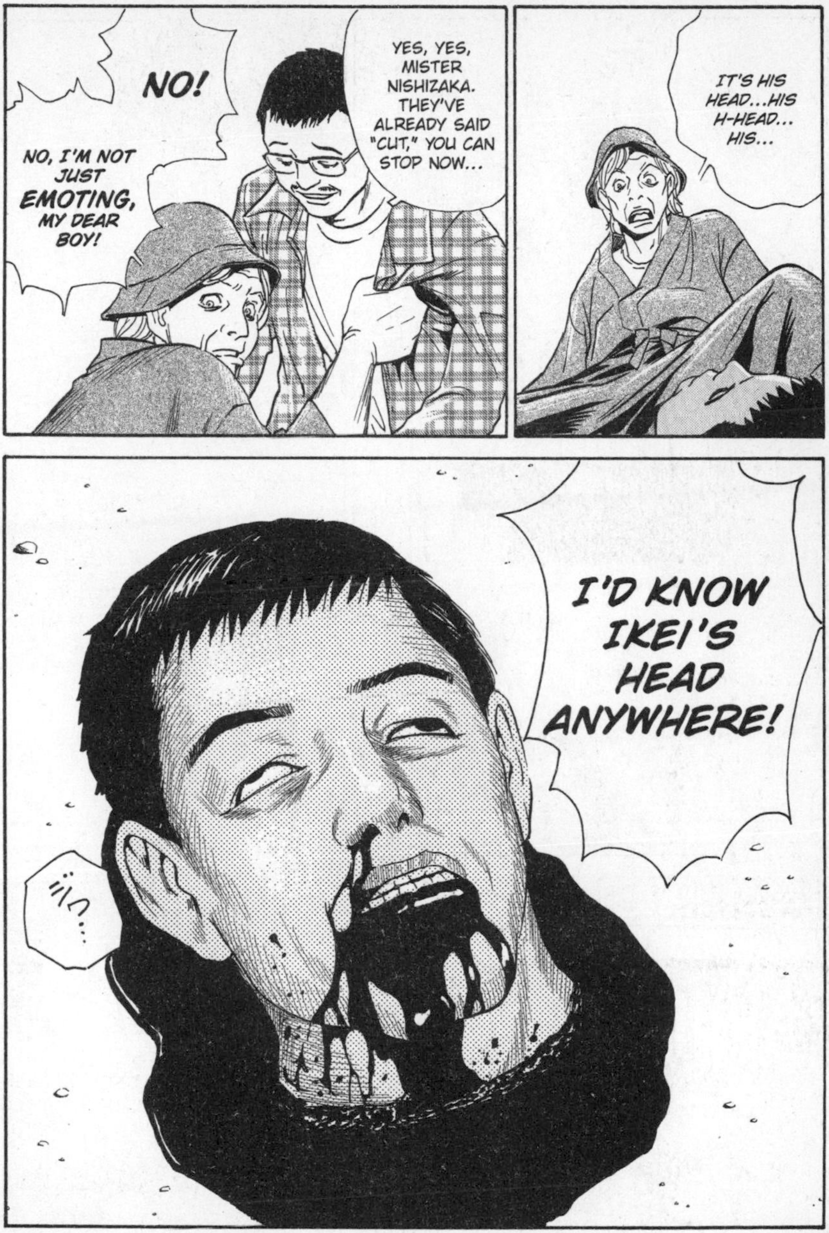
IT'S HIS HEAD...HIS H-HEAD... HIS...
YES, YES, MISTER NISHIZAKA. THEY'VE ALREADY SAID "CUT," YOU CAN STOP NOW...
NO!
NO, I'M NOT JUST EMOTING, MY DEAR BOY!
I'D KNOW IKEI'S HEAD ANYWHERE!

4th delivery: my don—the end

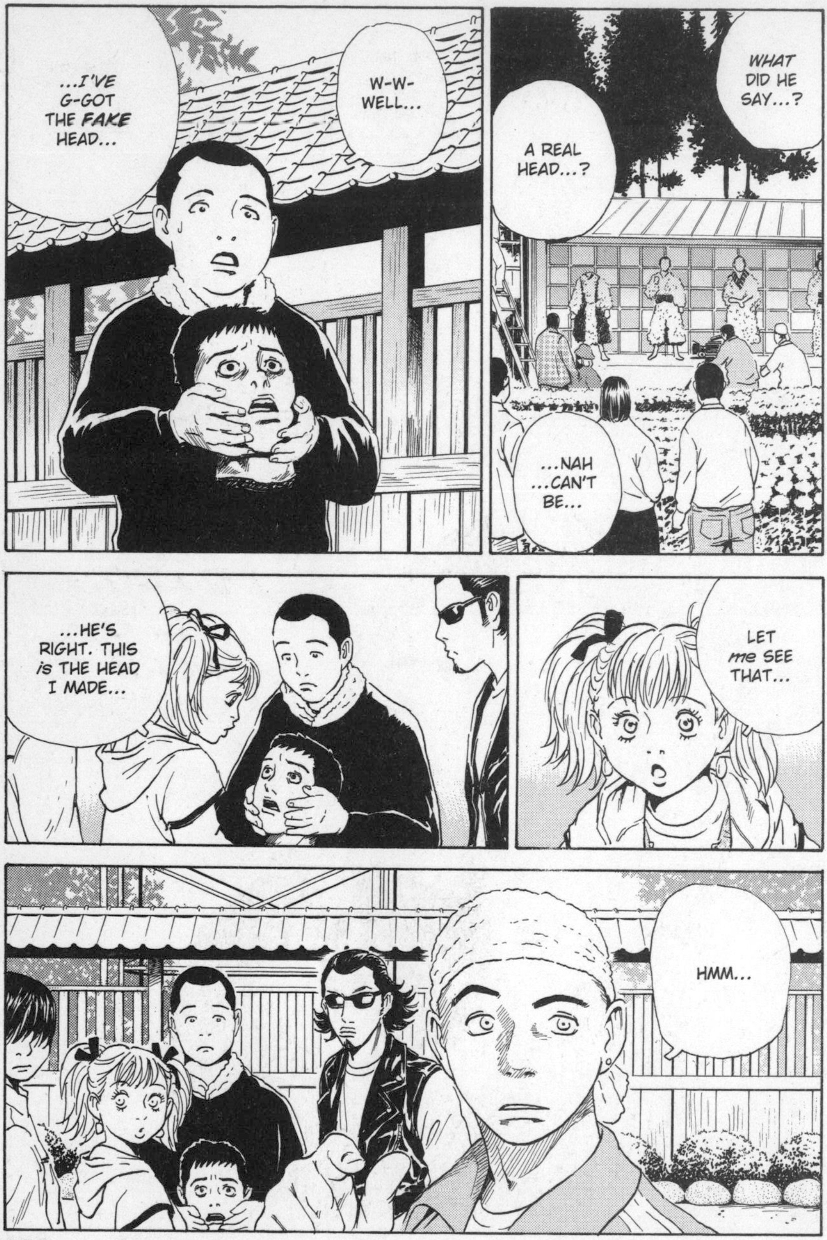
WHAT DID HE SAY...?
A REAL HEAD...?
...NAH ...CAN'T BE...
W-W-WELL...
...I'VE G-GOT THE *FAKE* HEAD...
LET *me* SEE THAT...
...HE'S RIGHT. THIS *is* THE HEAD I MADE...
HMM...

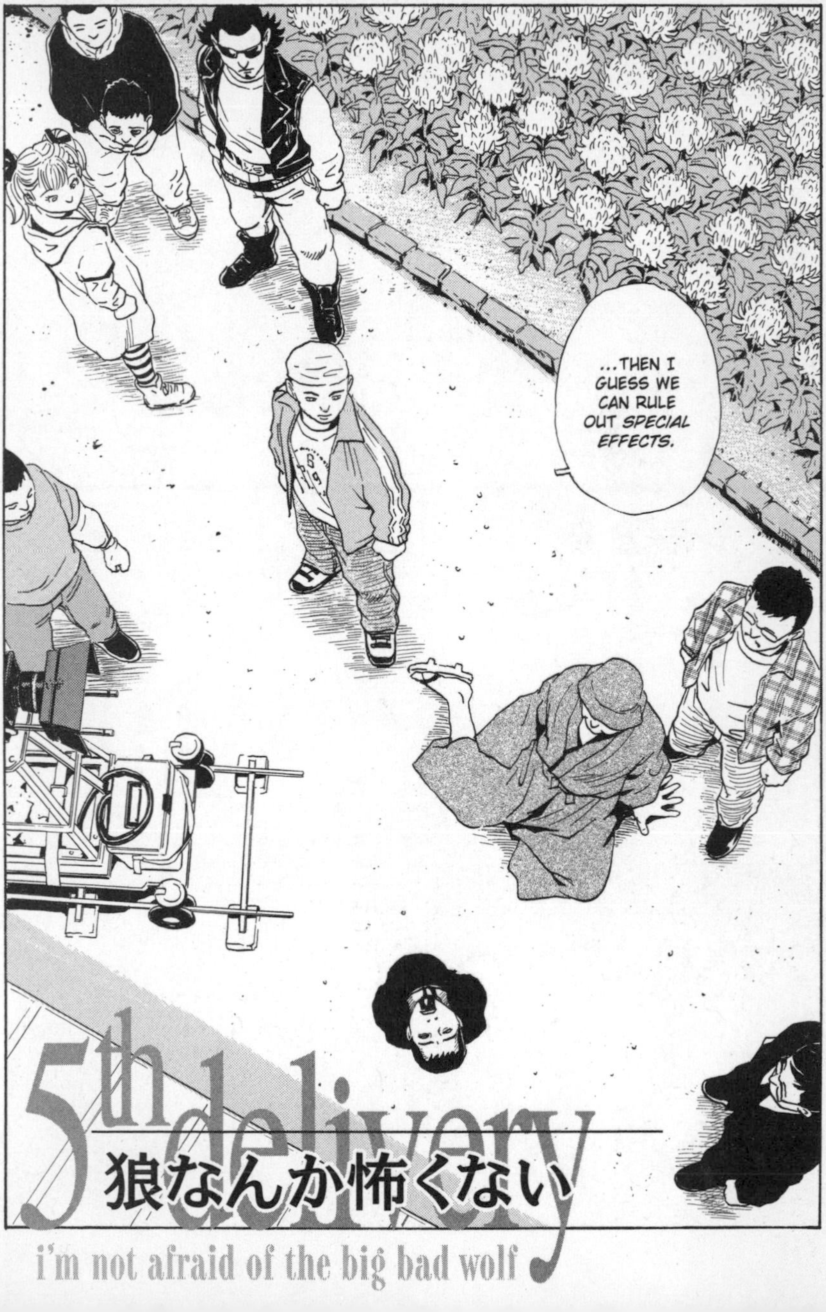
...THEN I GUESS WE CAN RULE OUT SPECIAL EFFECTS.

5th delivery

狼なんか怖くない

i'm not afraid of the big bad wolf

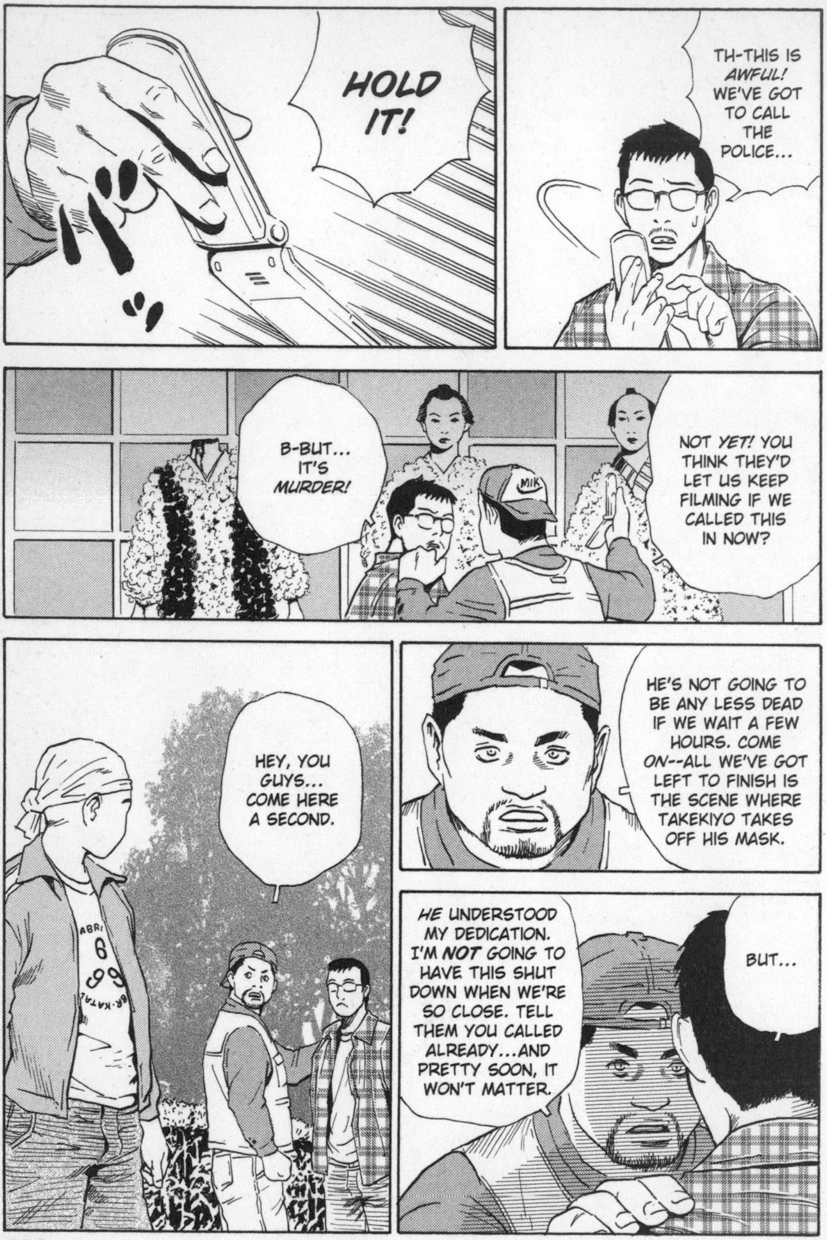
TH-THIS IS AWFUL! WE'VE GOT TO CALL THE POLICE...
HOLD IT!
NOT YET! YOU THINK THEY'D LET US KEEP FILMING IF WE CALLED THIS IN NOW?
B-BUT... IT'S MURDER!
HE'S NOT GOING TO BE ANY LESS DEAD IF WE WAIT A FEW HOURS. COME ON--ALL WE'VE GOT LEFT TO FINISH IS THE SCENE WHERE TAKEKIYO TAKES OFF HIS MASK.
BUT...
HE UNDERSTOOD MY DEDICATION. I'M NOT GOING TO HAVE THIS SHUT DOWN WHEN WE'RE SO CLOSE. TELL THEM YOU CALLED ALREADY...AND PRETTY SOON, IT WON'T MATTER.
HEY, YOU GUYS... COME HERE A SECOND.

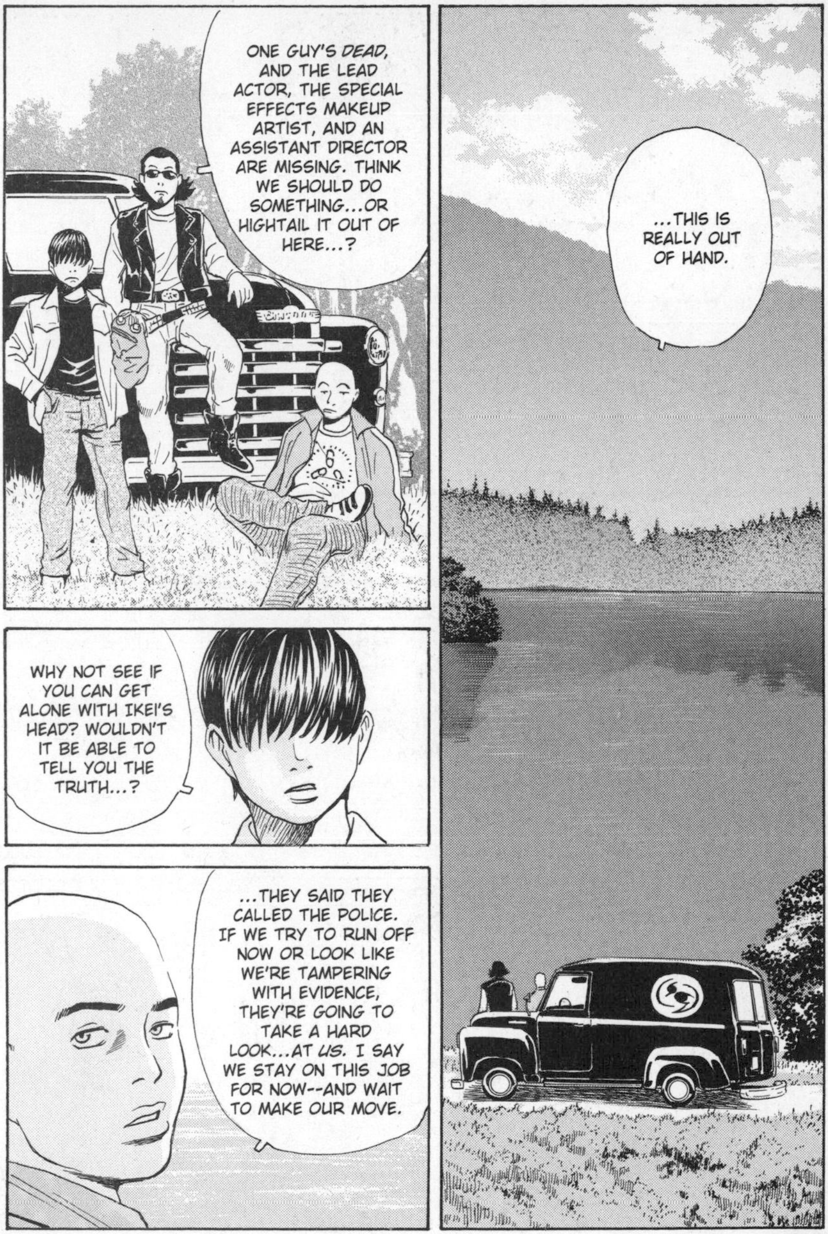
...THIS IS REALLY OUT OF HAND.
ONE GUY'S *DEAD*, AND THE LEAD ACTOR, THE SPECIAL EFFECTS MAKEUP ARTIST, AND AN ASSISTANT DIRECTOR ARE MISSING. THINK WE SHOULD DO SOMETHING...OR HIGHTAIL IT OUT OF HERE...?
WHY NOT SEE IF YOU CAN GET ALONE WITH IKEI'S HEAD? WOULDN'T IT BE ABLE TO TELL YOU THE TRUTH...?
...THEY SAID THEY CALLED THE POLICE. IF WE TRY TO RUN OFF NOW OR LOOK LIKE WE'RE TAMPERING WITH EVIDENCE, THEY'RE GOING TO TAKE A HARD LOOK...AT *US*. I SAY WE STAY ON THIS JOB FOR NOW--AND WAIT TO MAKE OUR MOVE.

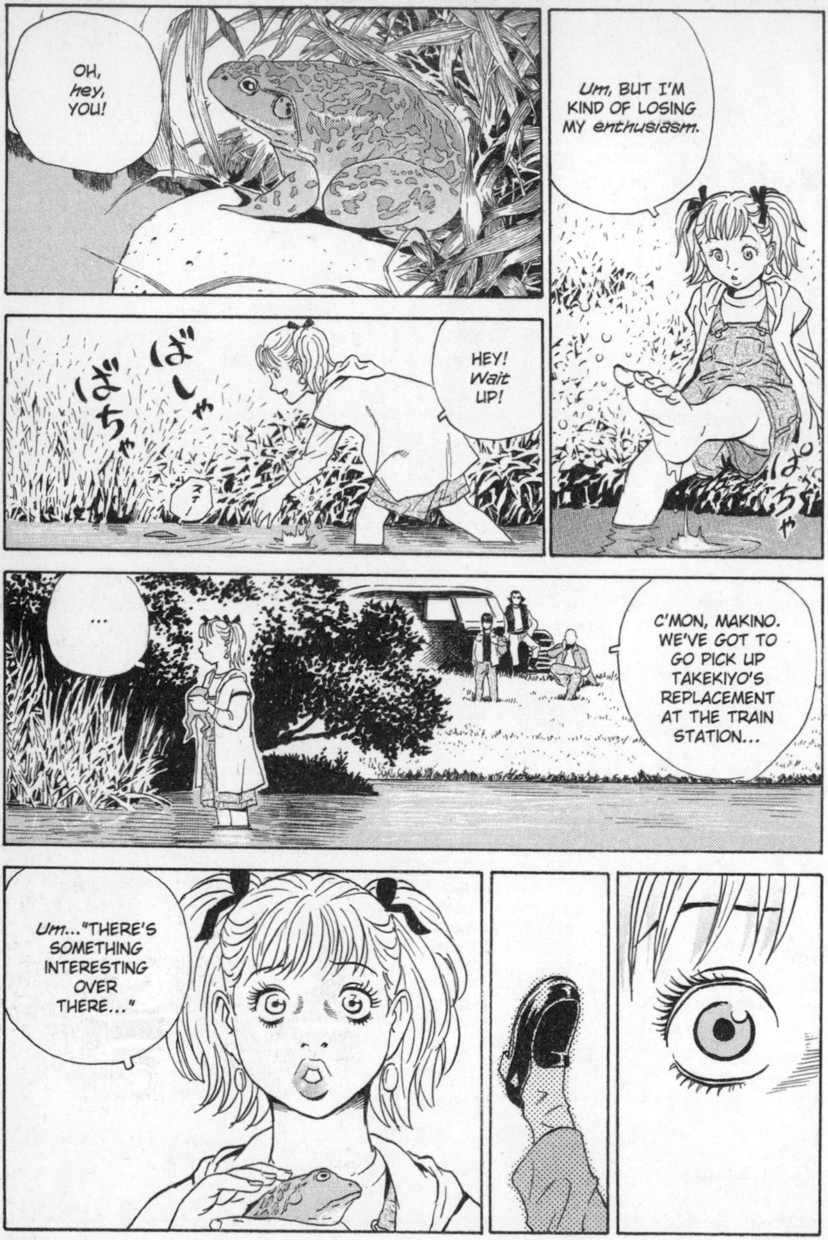
Um, BUT I'M KIND OF LOSING MY enthusiasm.
ぱちゃ
OH, hey, YOU!
HEY! Wait UP!
ばしゃ
ばちゃ
C'MON, MAKINO. WE'VE GOT TO GO PICK UP TAKEKIYO'S REPLACEMENT AT THE TRAIN STATION...
...
Um... "THERE'S SOMETHING INTERESTING OVER THERE..."

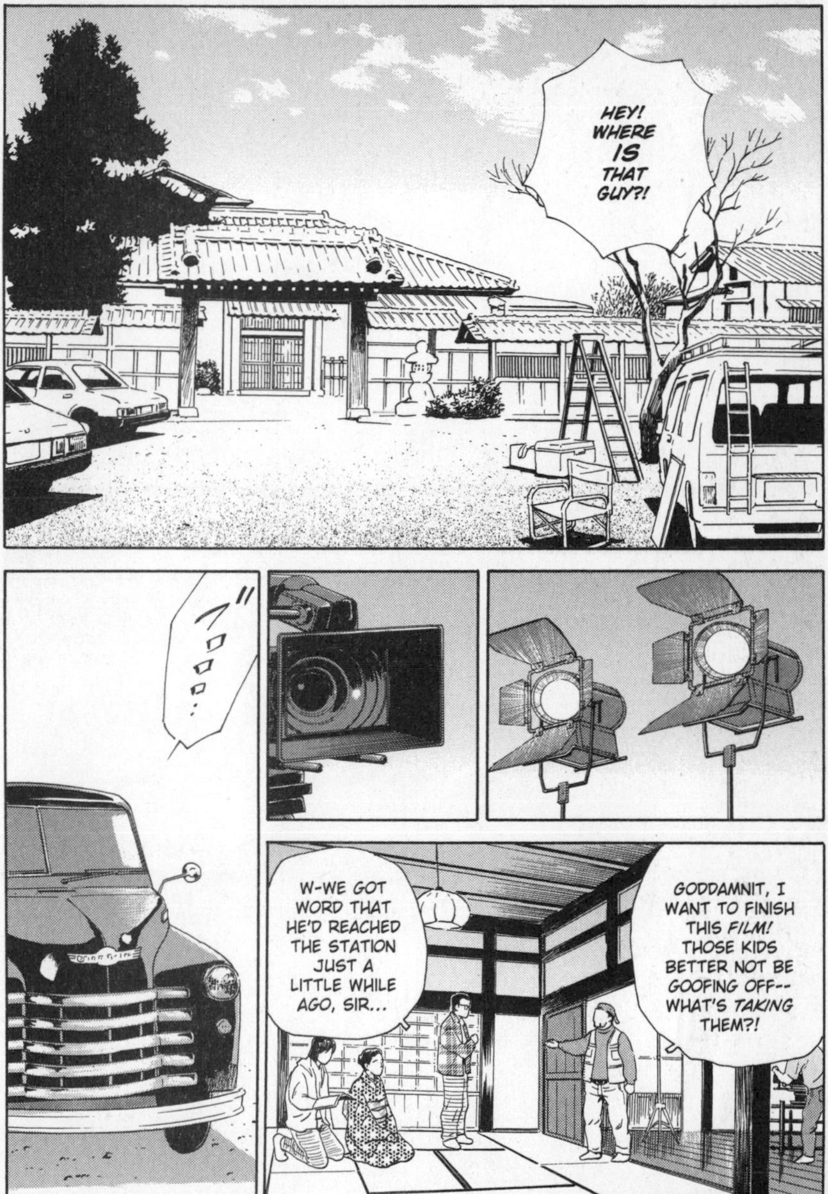
HEY! WHERE *IS* THAT GUY?!
GODDAMNIT, I WANT TO FINISH THIS *FILM!* THOSE KIDS BETTER NOT BE GOOFING OFF-- WHAT'S *TAKING* THEM?!
W-WE GOT WORD THAT HE'D REACHED THE STATION JUST A LITTLE WHILE AGO, SIR...
ブロロロ…

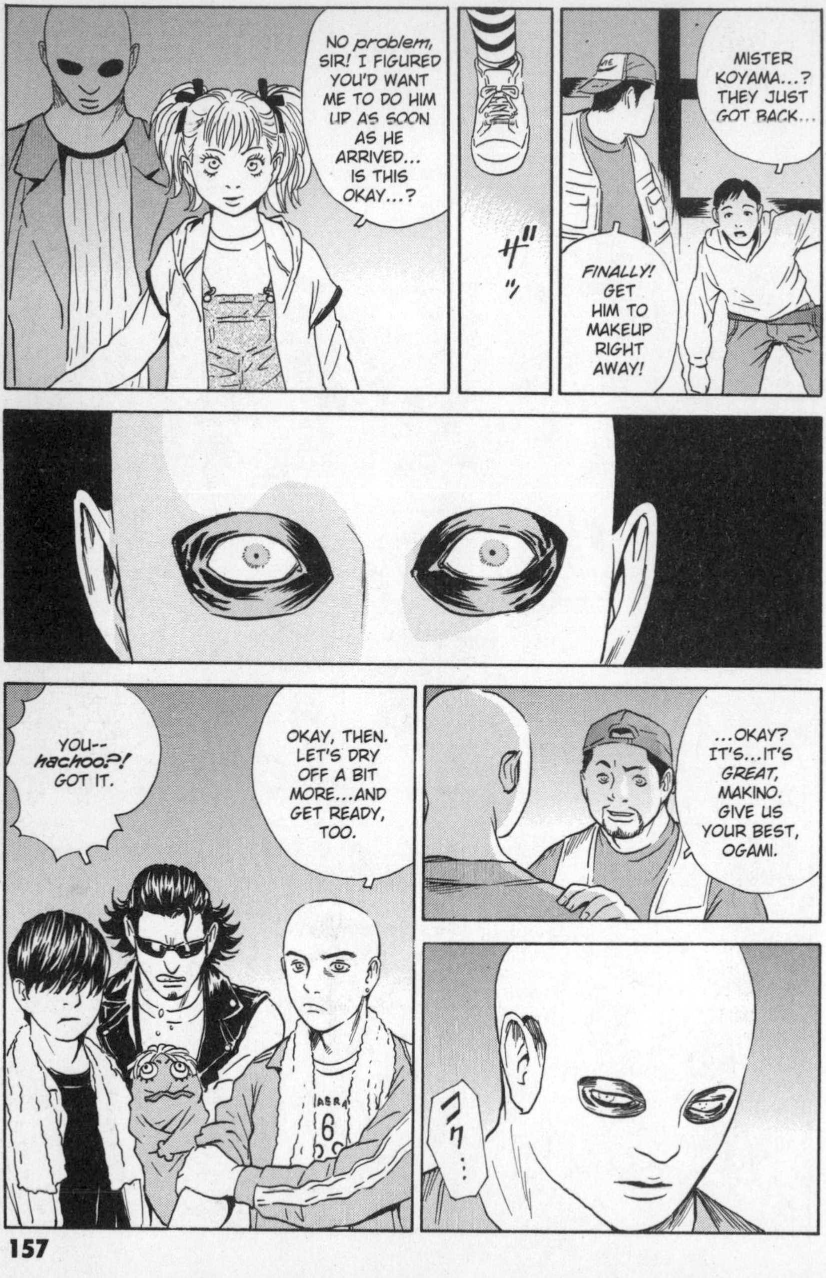
MISTER KOYAMA...? THEY JUST GOT BACK...
FINALLY! GET HIM TO MAKEUP RIGHT AWAY!
ザッ
NO *problem*, SIR! I FIGURED YOU'D WANT ME TO DO HIM UP AS SOON AS HE ARRIVED... IS THIS OKAY...?
...OKAY? IT'S...IT'S *GREAT*, MAKINO. GIVE US YOUR BEST, OGAMI.
コク…
OKAY, THEN. LET'S DRY OFF A BIT MORE...AND GET READY, TOO.
YOU-- *hachoo?!* GOT IT.

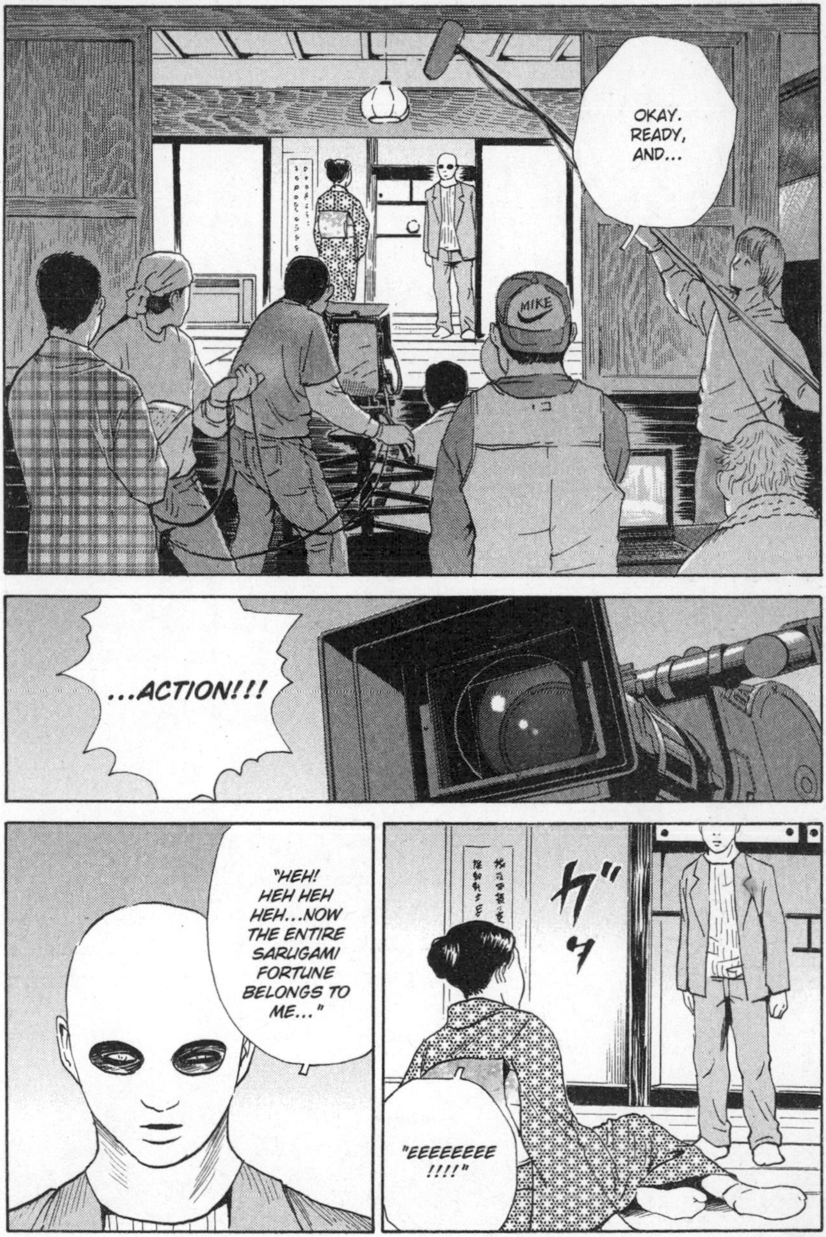
OKAY. READY, AND...
MIKE
...ACTION!!!
ガッ
"EEEEEEE !!!!"
"HEH! HEH HEH HEH...NOW THE ENTIRE SARUGAMI FORTUNE BELONGS TO ME..."

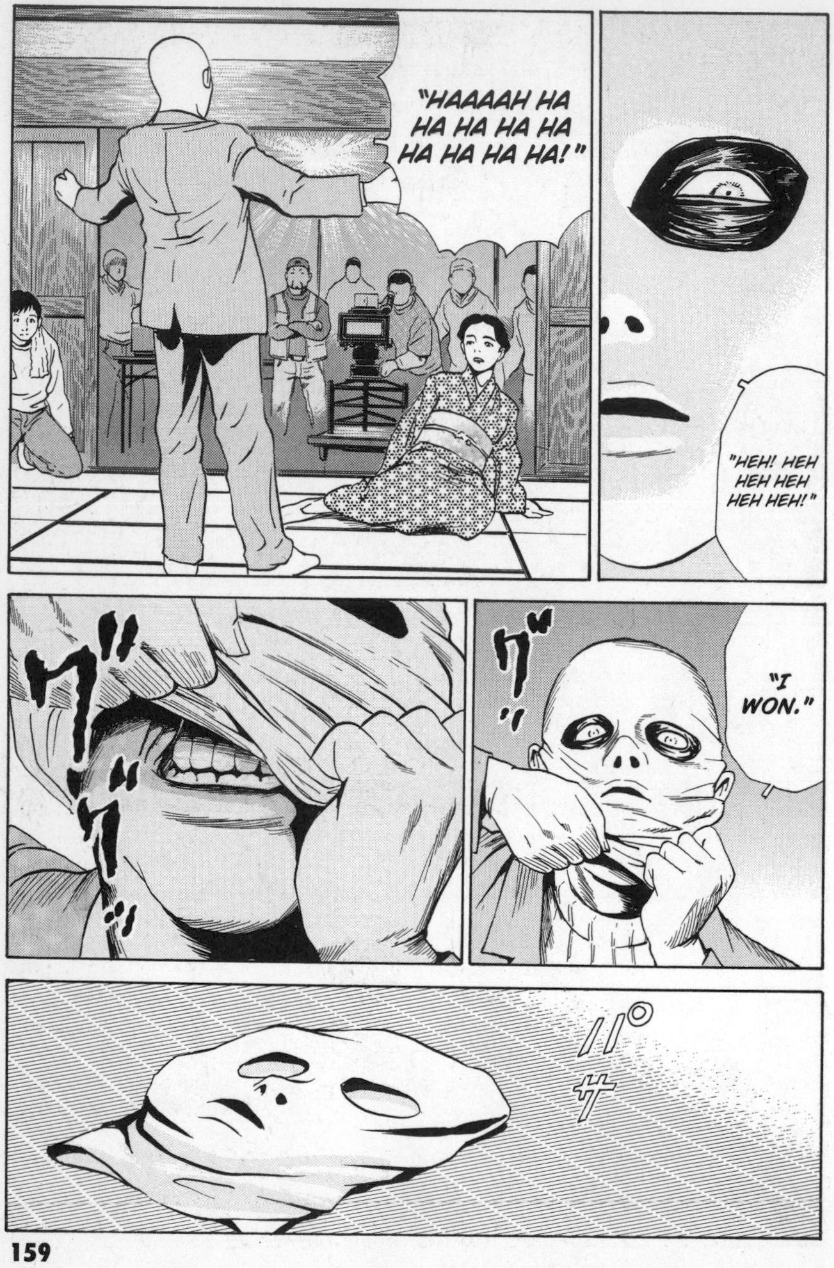
"HEH! HEH HEH HEH HEH HEH!"
"HAAAAH HA HA HA HA HA HA HA HA HA!"
"I WON."
グ
グッ
グ
パサ

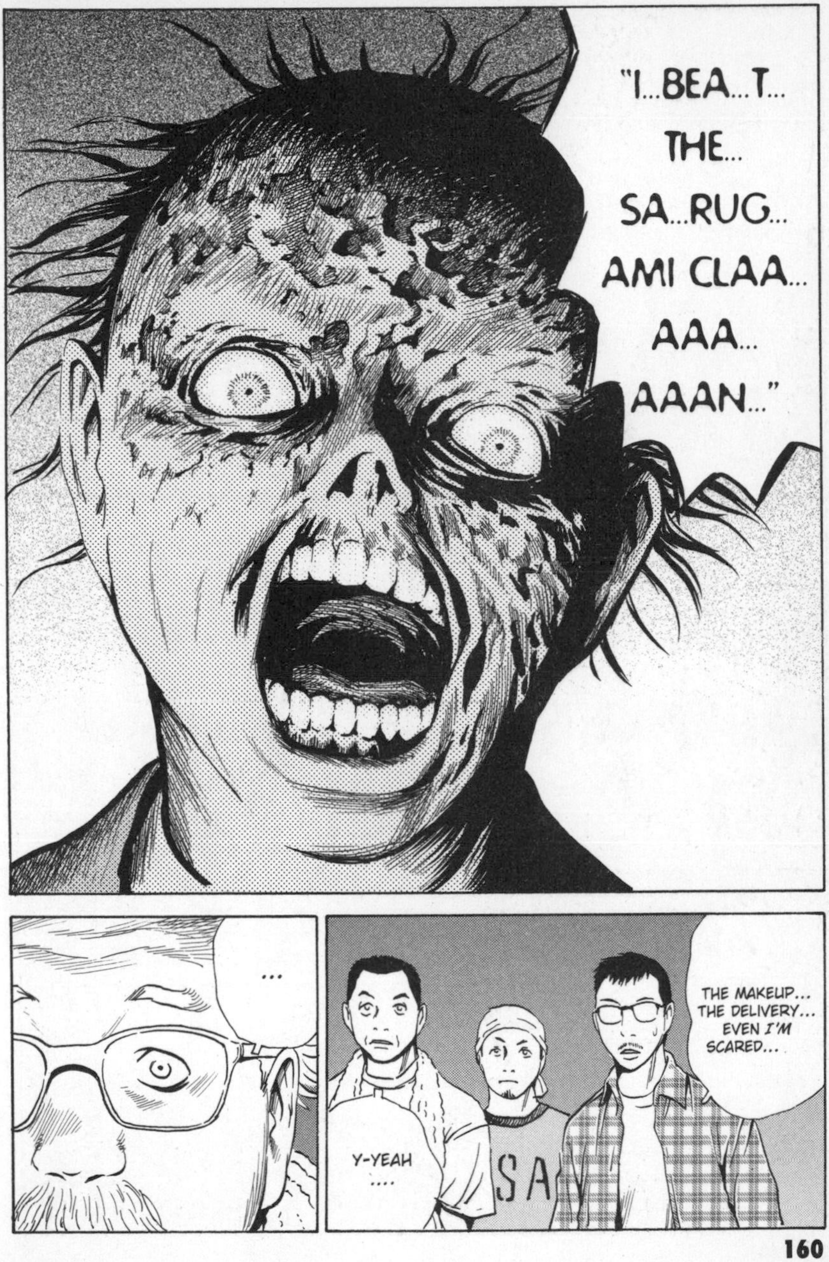
"I...BEA...T... THE... SA...RUG... AMI CLAA... AAA... AAAN..."
THE MAKEUP... THE DELIVERY... EVEN *I'M* SCARED...
Y-YEAH ....
...

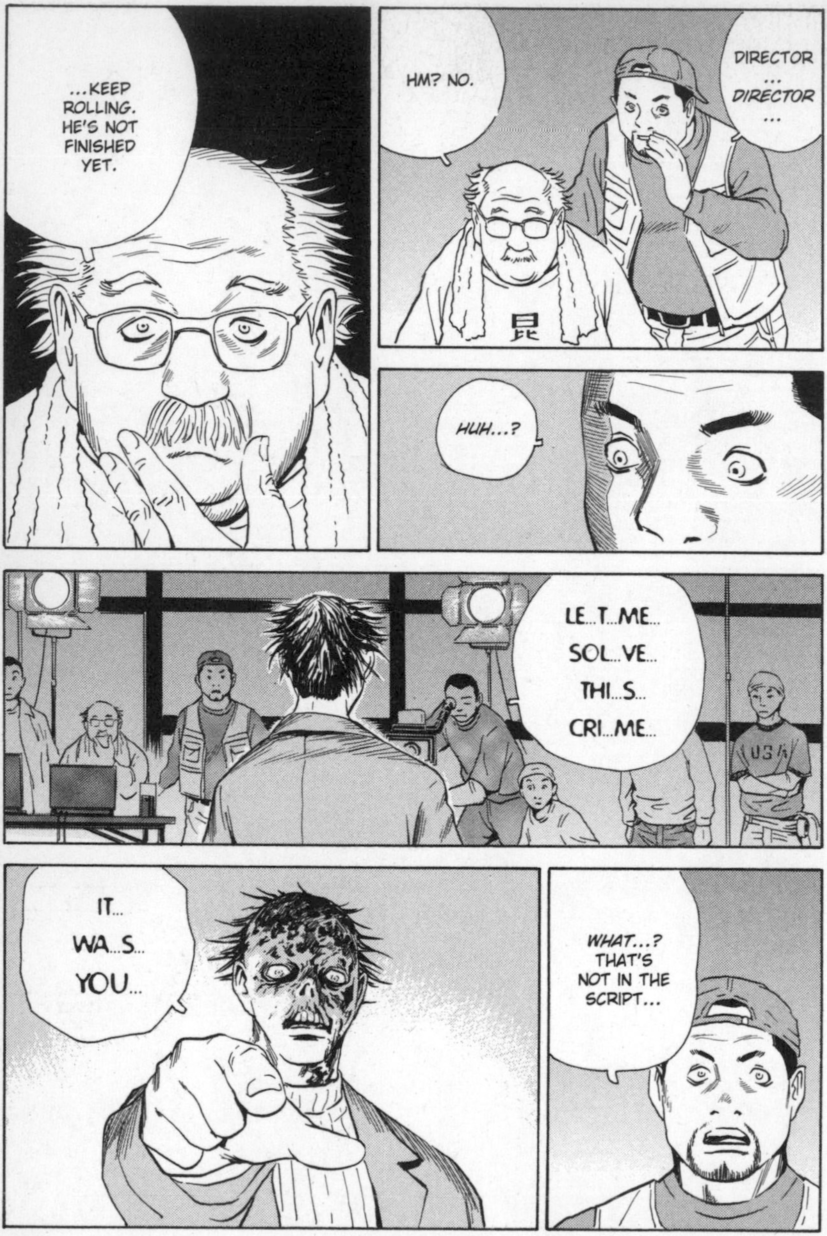
DIRECTOR ... *DIRECTOR* ...
HM? NO.
HUH...?
...KEEP ROLLING. HE'S NOT FINISHED YET.
LE...T...ME... SOL...VE... THI...S... CRI...ME...
WHAT...? THAT'S NOT IN THE SCRIPT...
IT... WA...S... YOU...

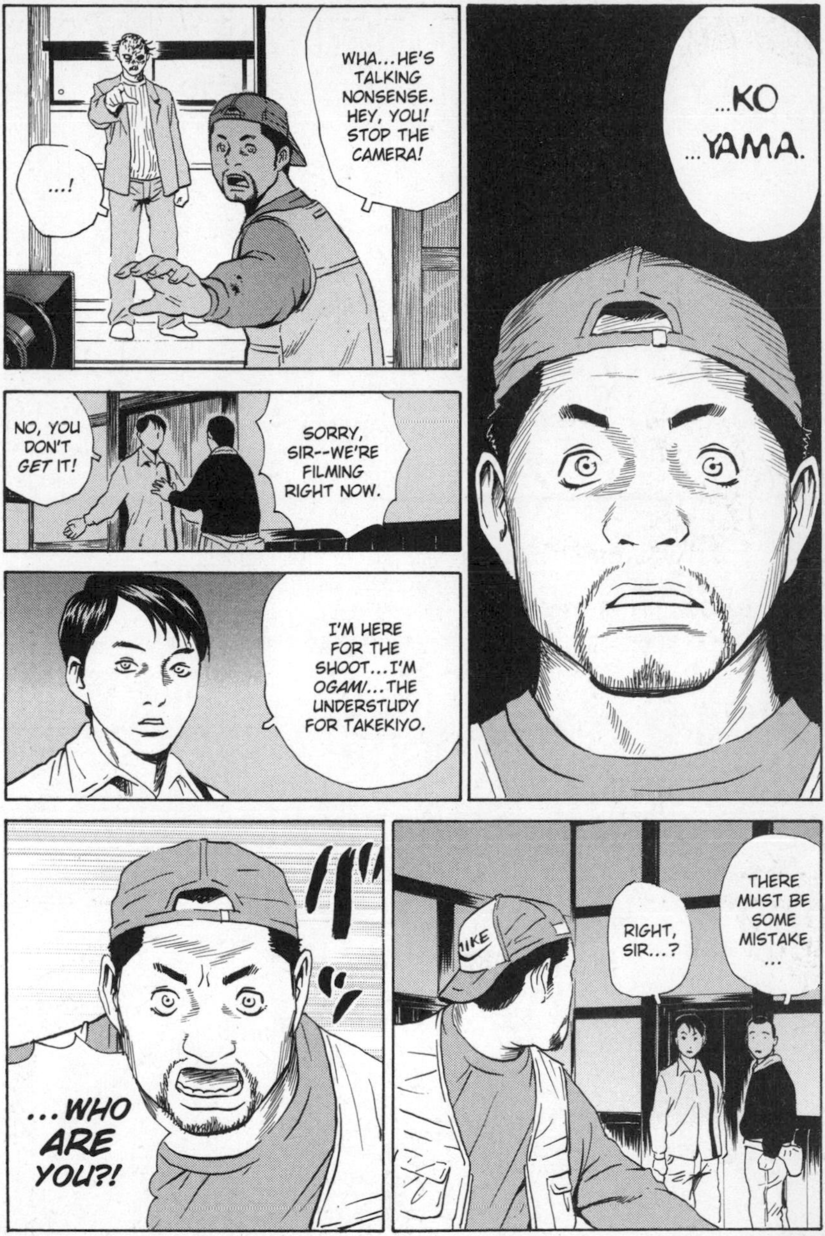
...KO ...YAMA.
WHA...HE'S TALKING NONSENSE. HEY, YOU! STOP THE CAMERA!
...!
SORRY, SIR--WE'RE FILMING RIGHT NOW.
NO, YOU DON'T GET IT!
I'M HERE FOR THE SHOOT...I'M OGAMI...THE UNDERSTUDY FOR TAKEKIYO.
THERE MUST BE SOME MISTAKE ...
RIGHT, SIR...?
...WHO ARE YOU?!

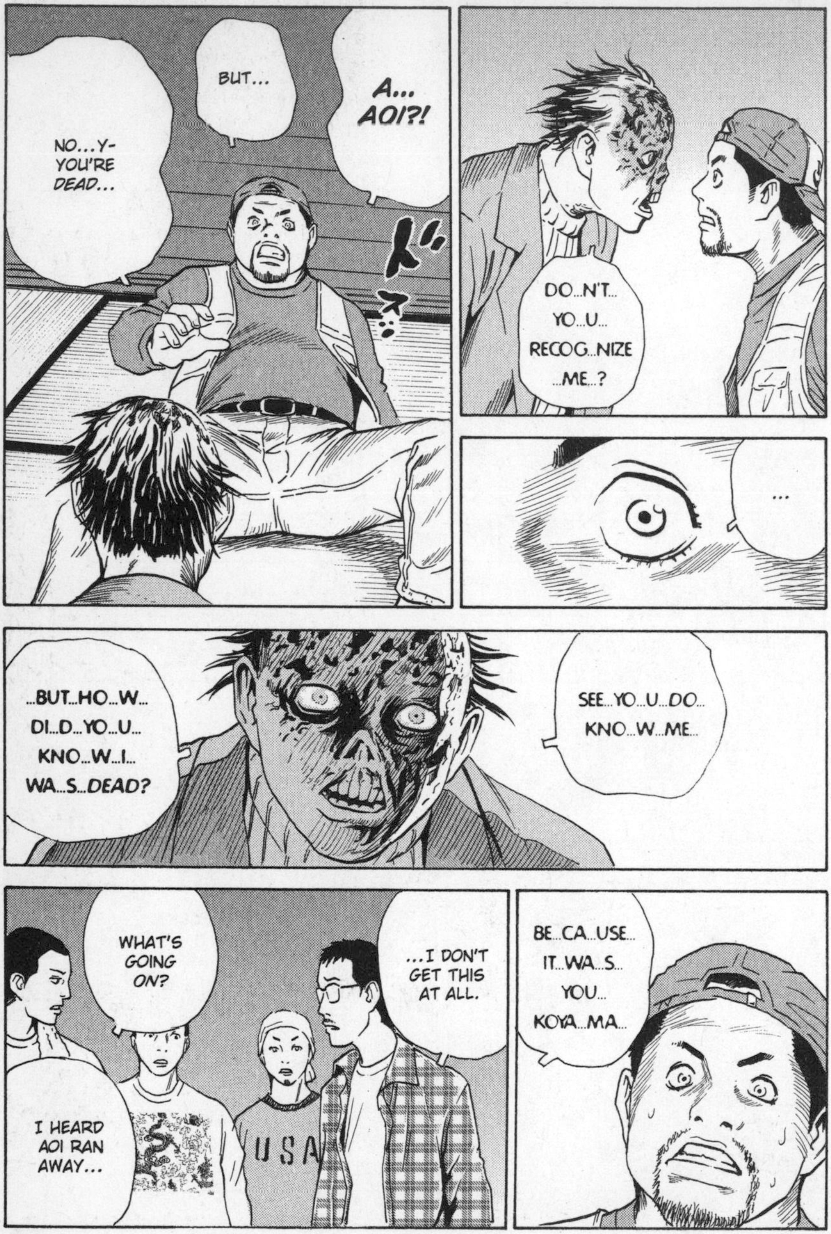
DO...N'T... YO...U... RECOG...NIZE ...ME...?
...
A... AOI?!
ドス
BUT...
NO...Y- YOU'RE DEAD...
SEE...YO...U...DO... KNO...W...ME...
...BUT...HO...W... DI...D...YO...U... KNO...W...I... WA...S...DEAD?
BE...CA...USE... IT...WA...S... YOU... KOYA...MA...
...I DON'T GET THIS AT ALL.
WHAT'S GOING ON?
USA
I HEARD AOI RAN AWAY...

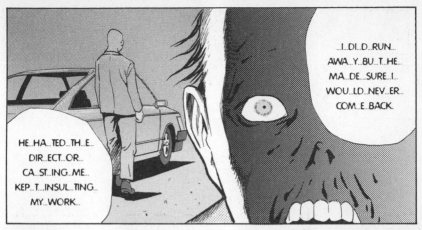

...I...DI...D...RUN... AWA...Y...BU...T...HE MA...DE...SURE...I... WOU...LD...NEV...ER... COM...E...BACK.

HE...HA...TED...TH...E... DIR...ECT...OR... CA...ST...ING...ME... KEP...T...INSUL...TING... MY...WORK...

...AN...D...ONE... NI...GHT...I... COULD...N'T... TAKE...IT...ANY... MORE...I...HA...D... TO...GO...FOR... A...DRI...VE.

H-HUH...?

HE...KNE...W...I'D... NE...VER...M...AKE ...THA...T... CUR...VE...NOT... WI...TH...MY... BRA...KES...CUT.

164

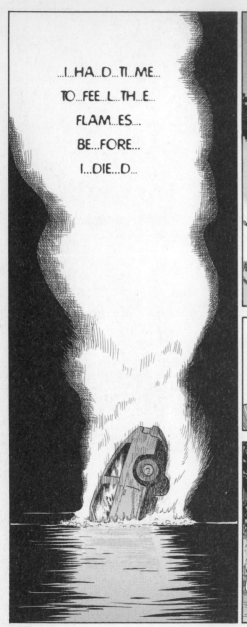

...I...HA...D...TI...ME...
TO...FEE...L...TH...E...
FLAM...ES...
BE...FORE...
I...DIE...D...

EEEEYAAA
!!!

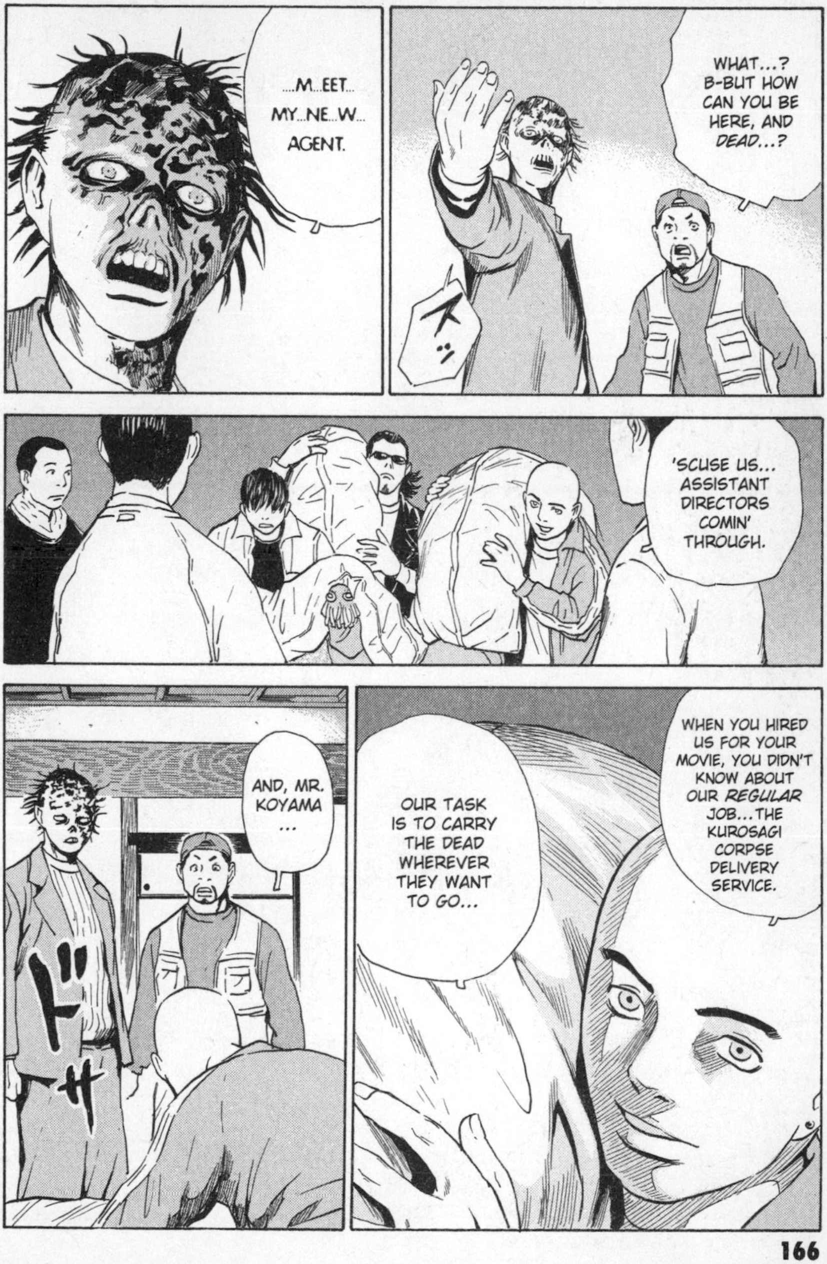
WHAT...? B-BUT HOW CAN YOU BE HERE, AND *DEAD*...?
...M...EET... MY...NE...W... AGENT.
'SCUSE US... ASSISTANT DIRECTORS COMIN' THROUGH.
WHEN YOU HIRED US FOR YOUR MOVIE, YOU DIDN'T KNOW ABOUT OUR *REGULAR* JOB...THE KUROSAGI CORPSE DELIVERY SERVICE.
OUR TASK IS TO CARRY THE DEAD WHEREVER THEY WANT TO GO...
AND, MR. KOYAMA ...

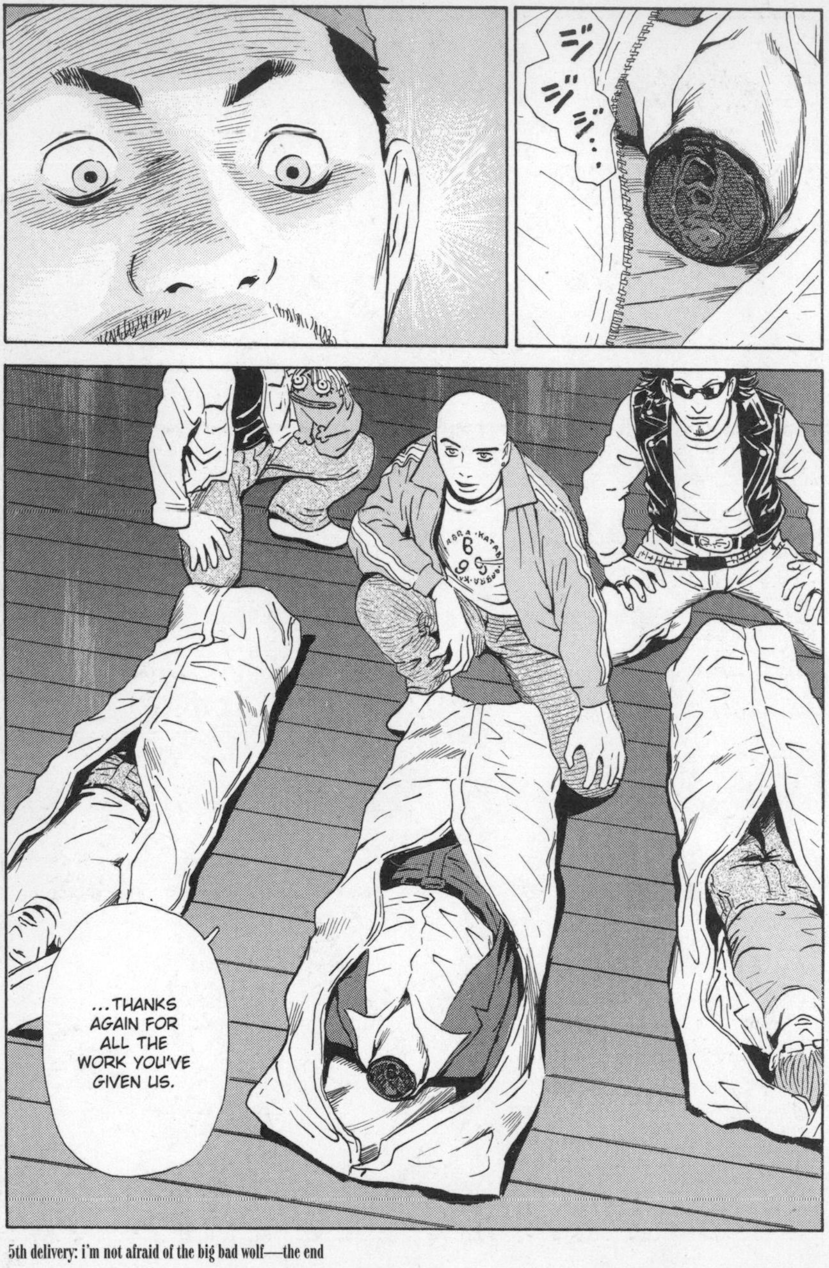
ジジジジ…
...THANKS AGAIN FOR ALL THE WORK YOU'VE GIVEN US.

5th delivery: i'm not afraid of the big bad wolf—the end

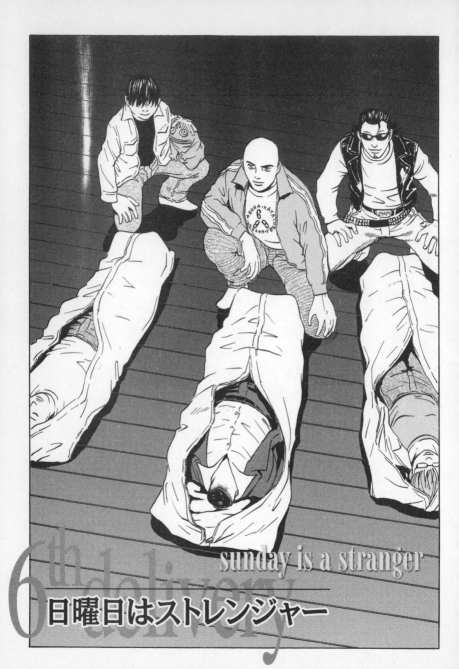

sunday is a stranger

6th delivery

日曜日はストレンジャー

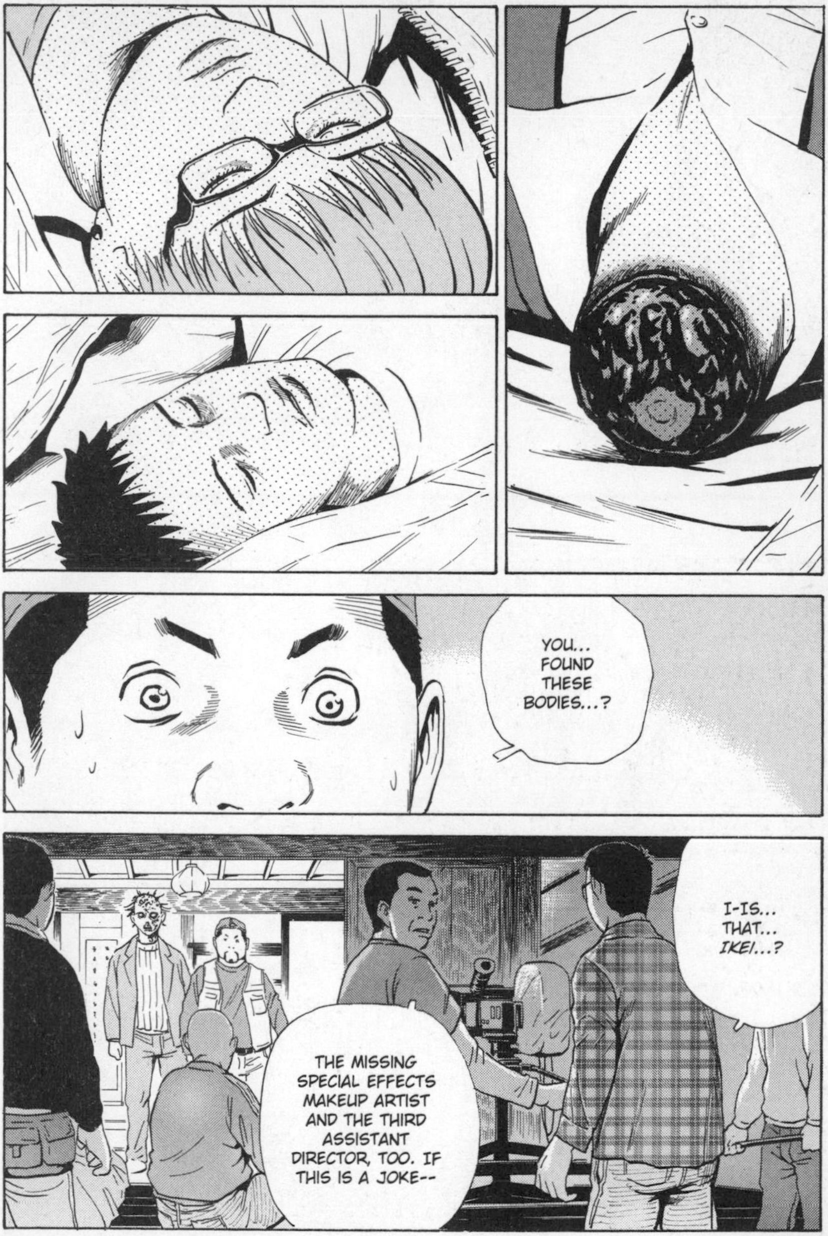
YOU... FOUND THESE BODIES...?
I-IS... THAT... *IKEI*...?
THE MISSING SPECIAL EFFECTS MAKEUP ARTIST AND THE THIRD ASSISTANT DIRECTOR, TOO. IF THIS IS A JOKE--

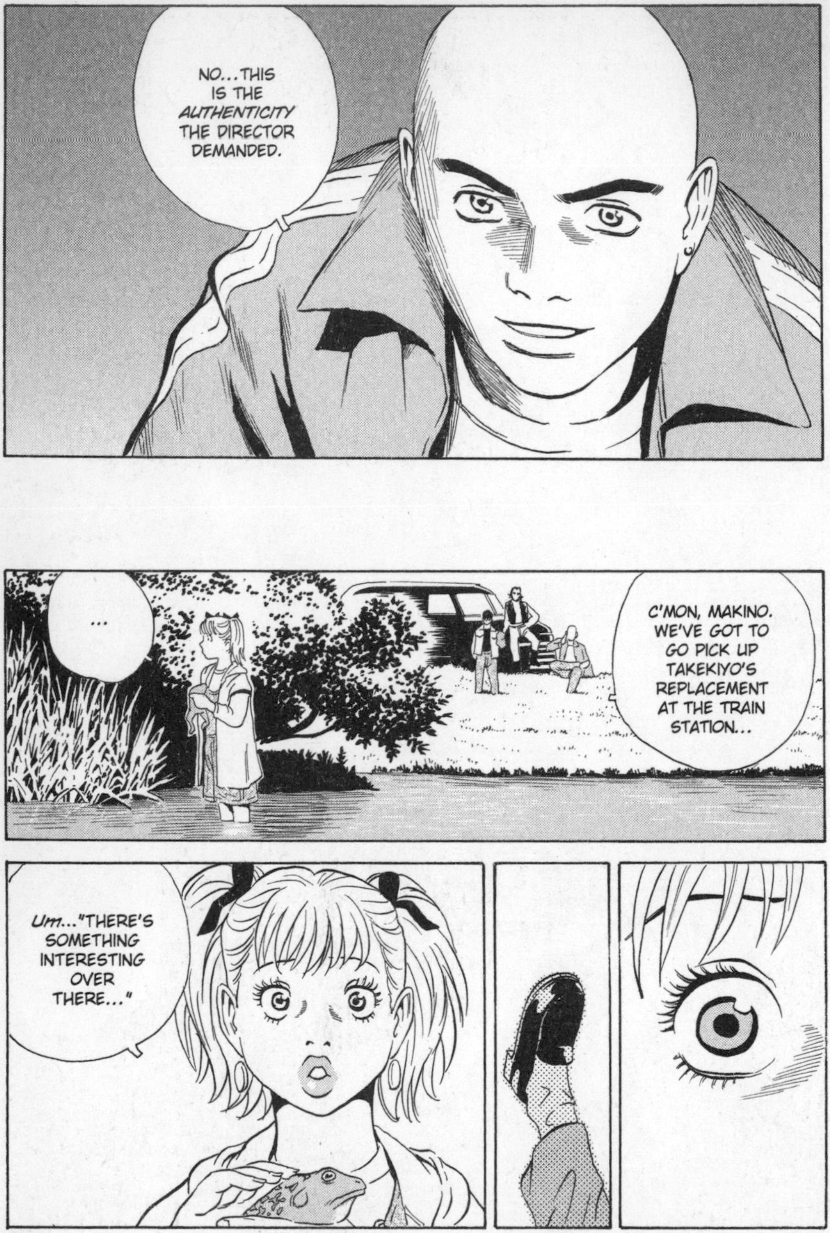
NO...THIS IS THE *AUTHENTICITY* THE DIRECTOR DEMANDED.
C'MON, MAKINO. WE'VE GOT TO GO PICK UP TAKEKIYO'S REPLACEMENT AT THE TRAIN STATION...
...
Um..."THERE'S SOMETHING INTERESTING OVER THERE..."

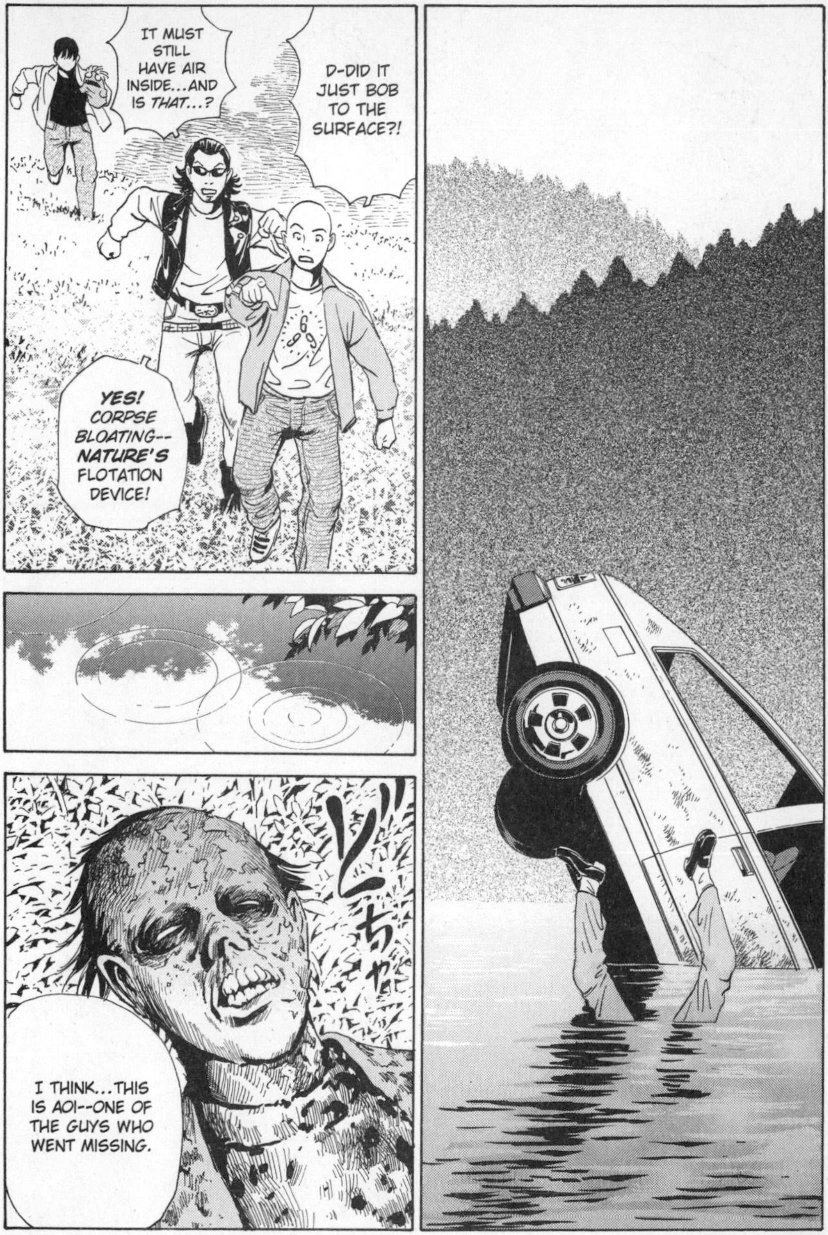
D-DID IT JUST BOB TO THE SURFACE?!
IT MUST STILL HAVE AIR INSIDE...AND IS *THAT*...?
YES! CORPSE BLOATING--**NATURE'S** FLOTATION DEVICE!
I THINK...THIS IS AOI--ONE OF THE GUYS WHO WENT MISSING.

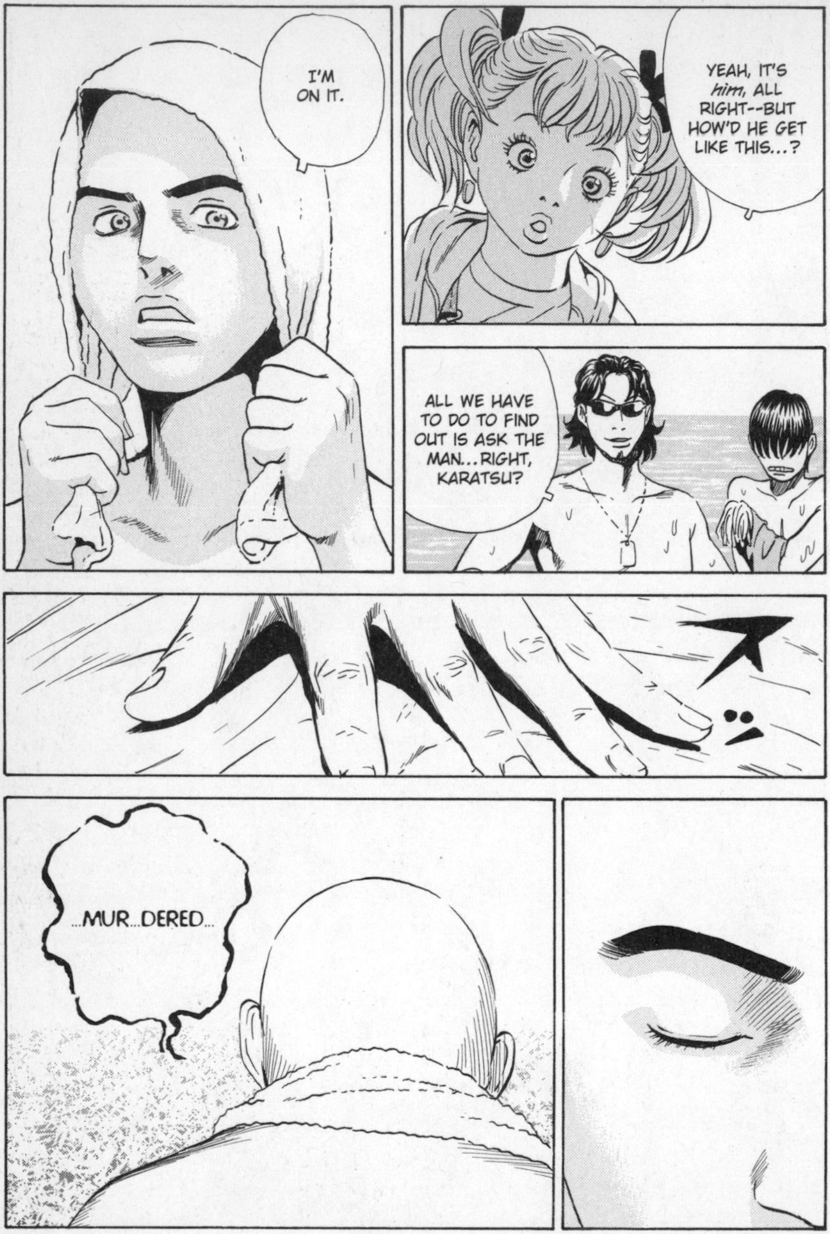
YEAH, IT'S *him*, ALL RIGHT--BUT HOW'D HE GET LIKE THIS...?
ALL WE HAVE TO DO TO FIND OUT IS ASK THE MAN...RIGHT, KARATSU?
I'M ON IT.
...MUR...DERED...

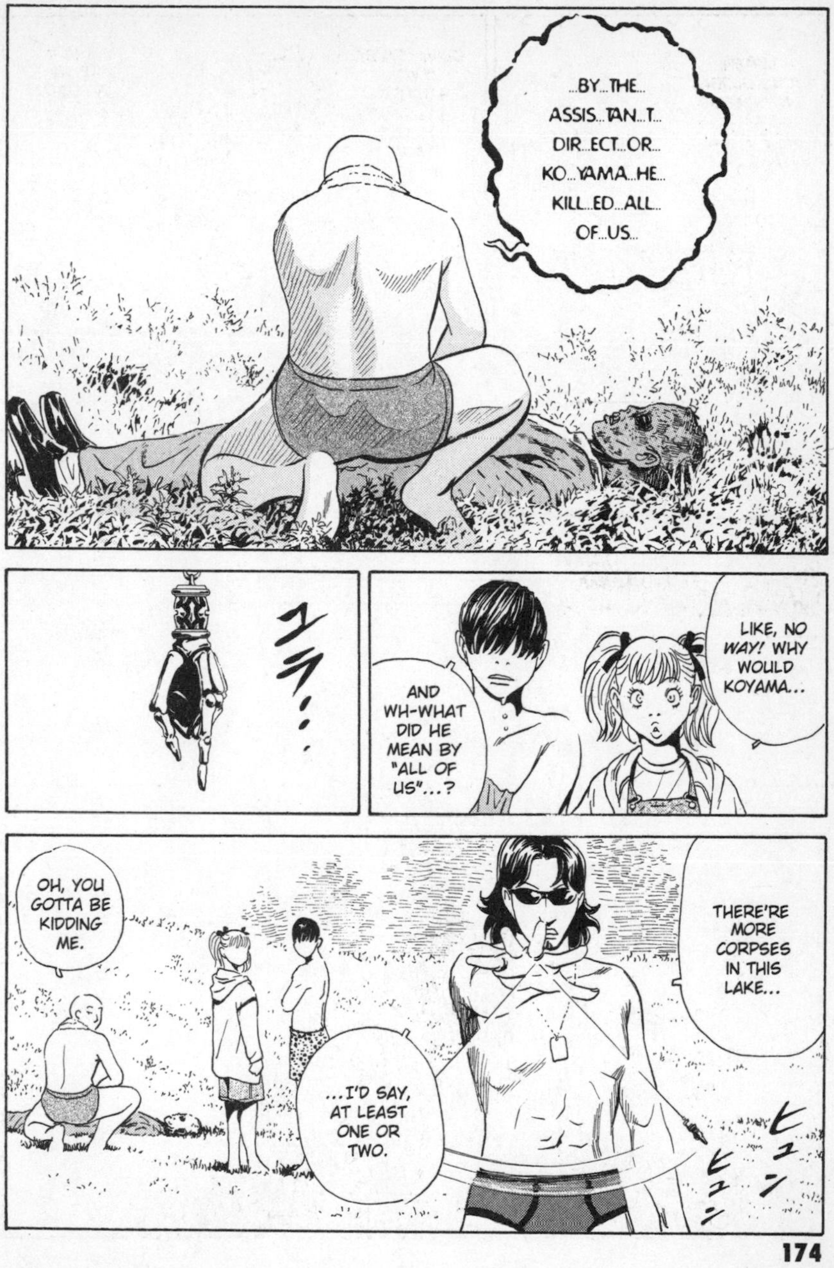
...BY...THE... ASSIS...TAN...T... DIR...ECT...OR... KO...YAMA...HE... KILL...ED...ALL... OF...US...
LIKE, NO *WAY!* WHY WOULD KOYAMA...
AND WH-WHAT DID HE MEAN BY "ALL OF US"...?
ユラ…
THERE'RE MORE CORPSES IN THIS LAKE...
...I'D SAY, AT LEAST ONE OR TWO.
ヒュン ヒュン
OH, YOU GOTTA BE KIDDING ME.

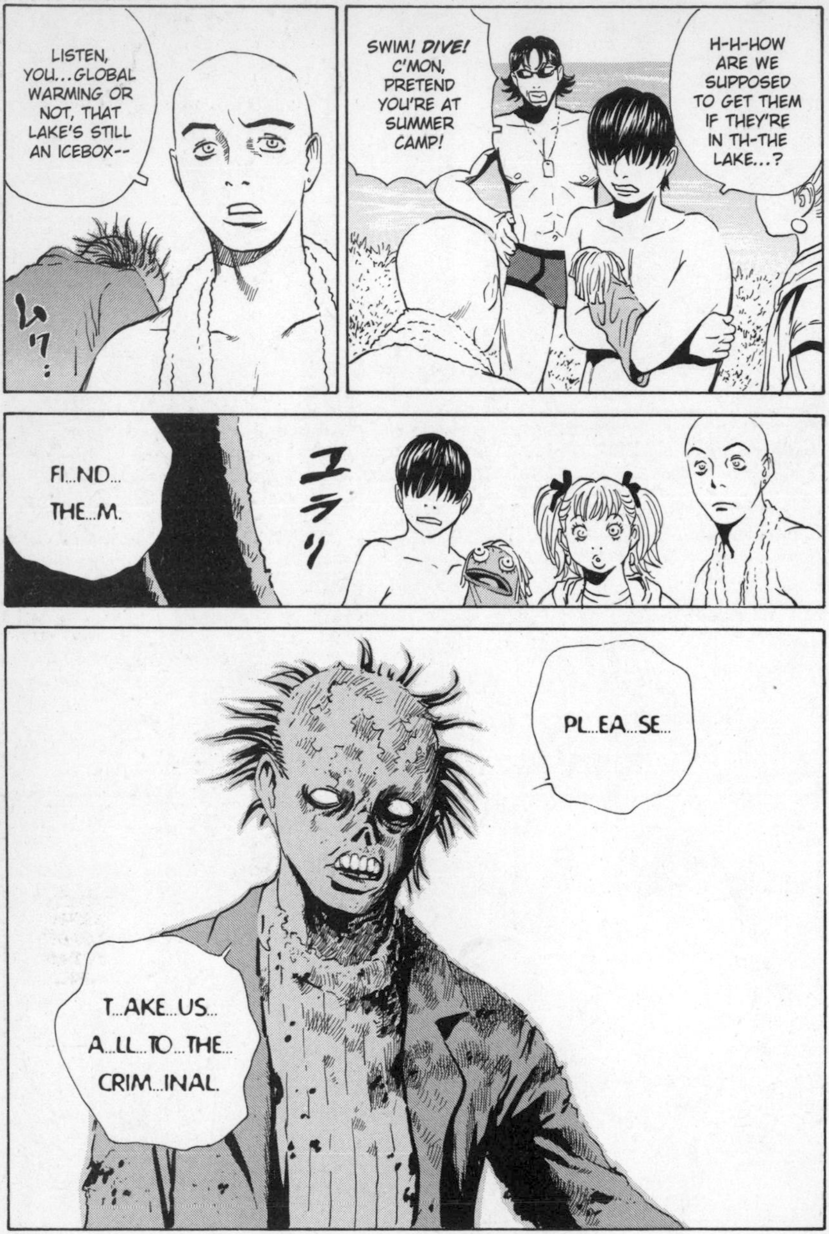
H-H-HOW ARE WE SUPPOSED TO GET THEM IF THEY'RE IN TH-THE LAKE...?
SWIM! *DIVE!* C'MON, PRETEND YOU'RE AT SUMMER CAMP!
LISTEN, YOU...GLOBAL WARMING OR NOT, THAT LAKE'S STILL AN ICEBOX--
ムッ
ユラリ
FI...ND... THE...M.
PL...EA...SE...
T...AKE...US... A...LL...TO...THE... CRIM...INAL.

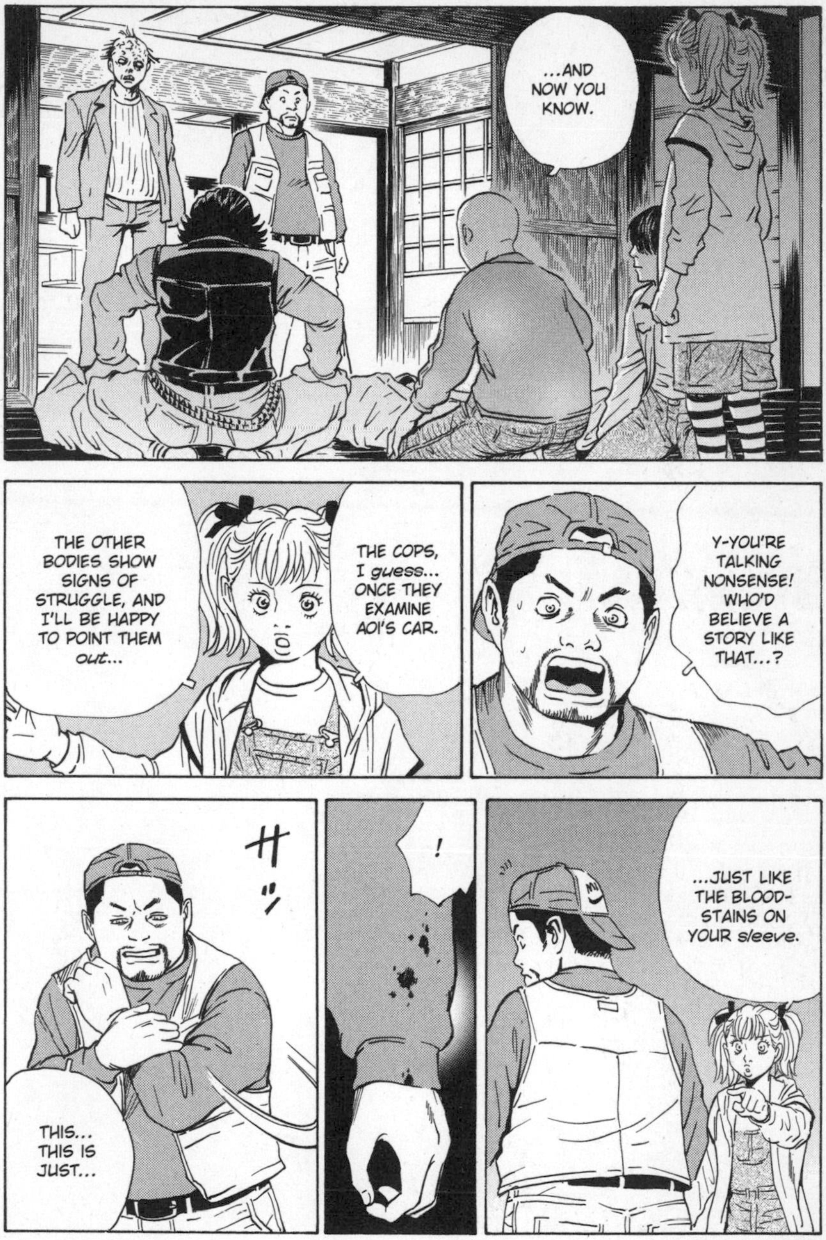
...AND NOW YOU KNOW.
Y-YOU'RE TALKING NONSENSE! WHO'D BELIEVE A STORY LIKE THAT...?
THE COPS, I *guess*... ONCE THEY EXAMINE AOI'S CAR.
THE OTHER BODIES SHOW SIGNS OF STRUGGLE, AND I'LL BE HAPPY TO POINT THEM *out*...
...JUST LIKE THE BLOOD-STAINS ON YOUR *sleeve*.
!
サッ
THIS... THIS IS JUST...

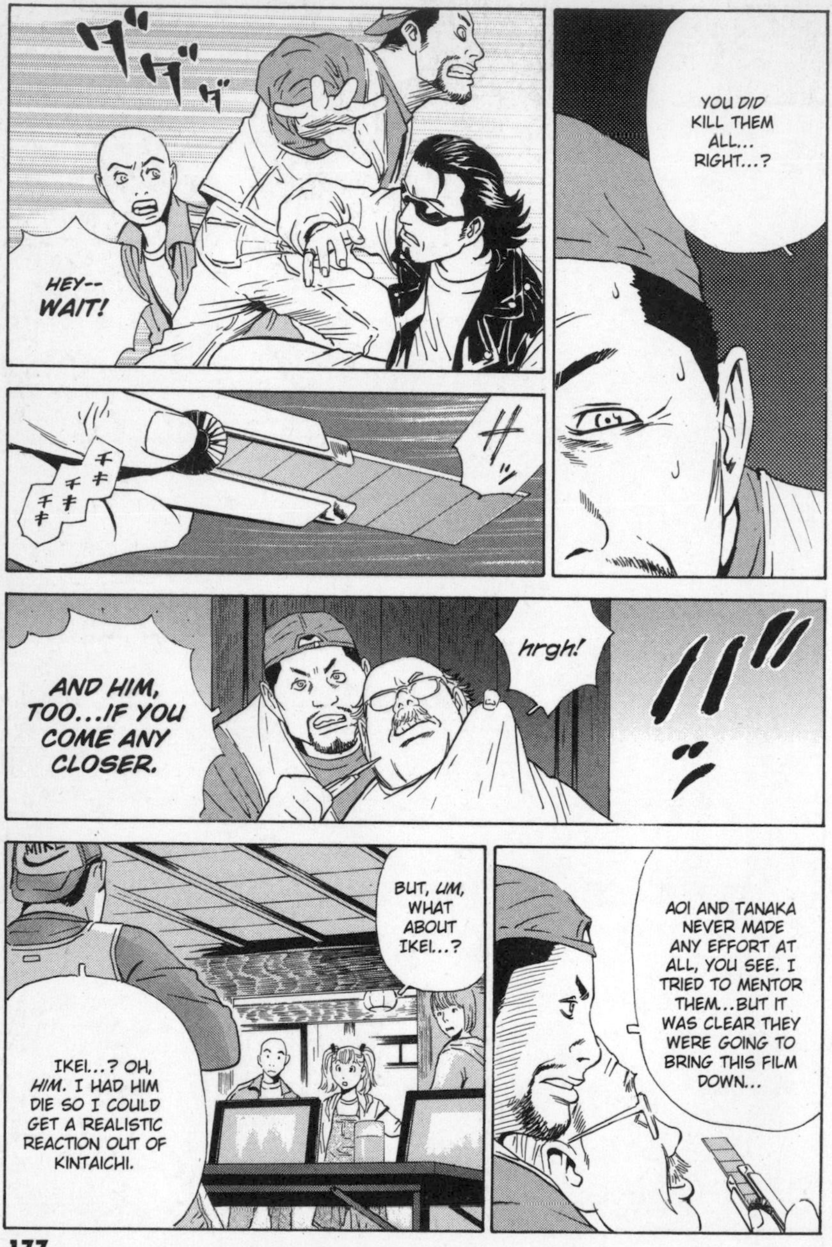
YOU *DID* KILL THEM ALL... RIGHT...?
HEY-- WAIT!
チキチキチキ
hrgh!
AND HIM, TOO...IF YOU COME ANY CLOSER.
AOI AND TANAKA NEVER MADE ANY EFFORT AT ALL, YOU SEE. I TRIED TO MENTOR THEM...BUT IT WAS CLEAR THEY WERE GOING TO BRING THIS FILM DOWN...
BUT, *UM*, WHAT ABOUT IKEI...?
IKEI...? OH, *HIM*. I HAD HIM DIE SO I COULD GET A REALISTIC REACTION OUT OF KINTAICHI.

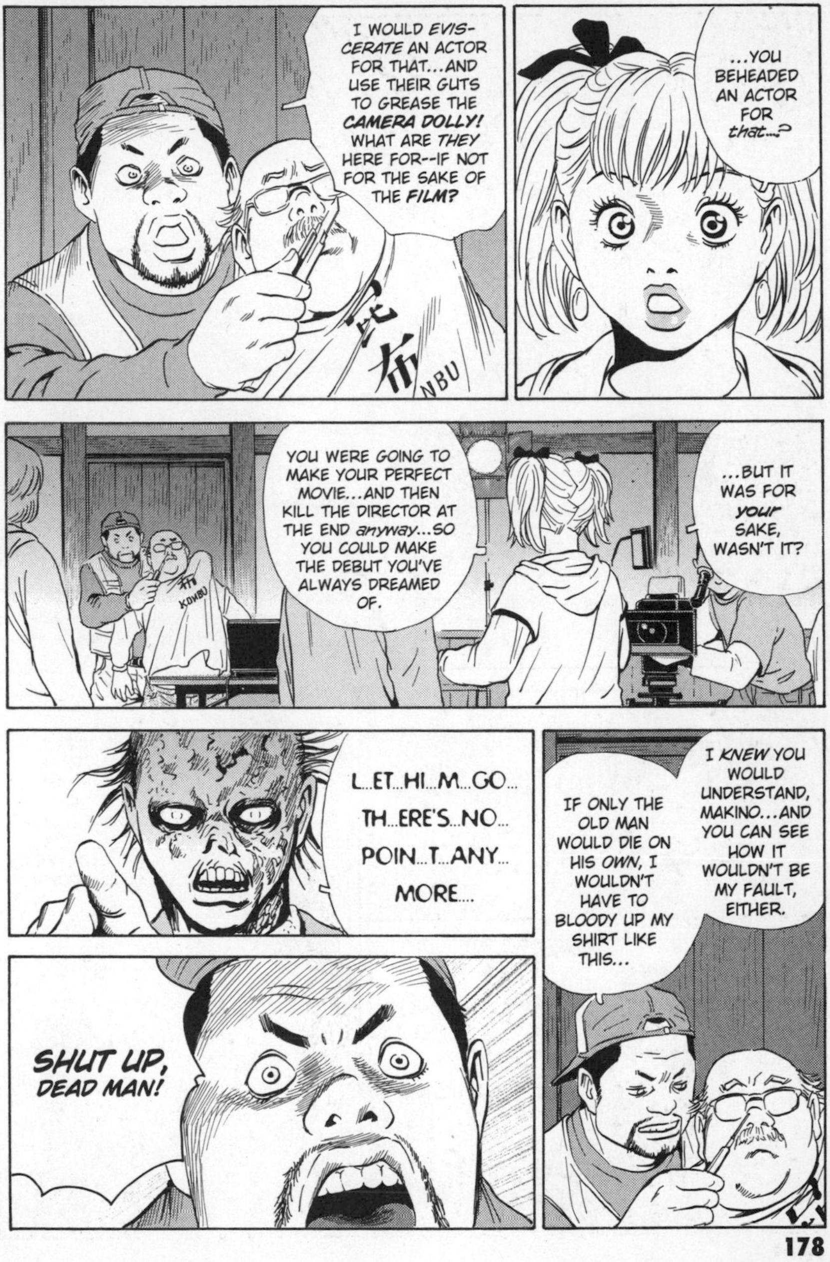

...YOU BEHEADED AN ACTOR FOR *that*...?
I WOULD *EVISCERATE* AN ACTOR FOR THAT...AND USE THEIR GUTS TO GREASE THE **CAMERA DOLLY!** WHAT ARE *THEY* HERE FOR--IF NOT FOR THE SAKE OF THE *FILM?*
...BUT IT WAS FOR *your* SAKE, WASN'T IT?
YOU WERE GOING TO MAKE YOUR PERFECT MOVIE...AND THEN KILL THE DIRECTOR AT THE END *anyway*...SO YOU COULD MAKE THE DEBUT YOU'VE ALWAYS DREAMED OF.
I *KNEW* YOU WOULD UNDERSTAND, MAKINO...AND YOU CAN SEE HOW IT WOULDN'T BE MY FAULT, EITHER.
IF ONLY THE OLD MAN WOULD DIE ON HIS *OWN*, I WOULDN'T HAVE TO BLOODY UP MY SHIRT LIKE THIS...
L...ET...HI...M...GO... TH...ERE'S...NO... POIN...T...ANY... MORE...
SHUT UP, DEAD MAN!

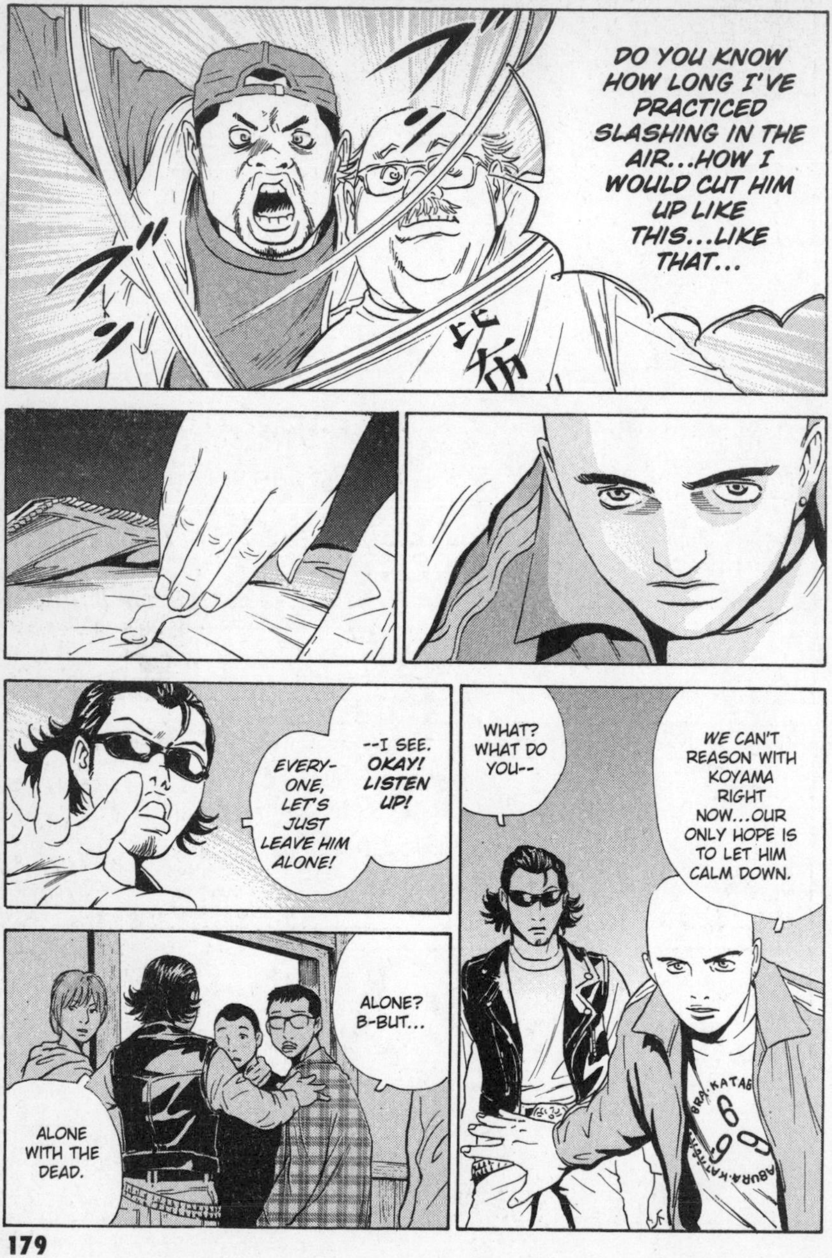
DO YOU KNOW HOW LONG I'VE PRACTICED SLASHING IN THE AIR...HOW I WOULD CUT HIM UP LIKE THIS...LIKE THAT...
WE CAN'T REASON WITH KOYAMA RIGHT NOW...OUR ONLY HOPE IS TO LET HIM CALM DOWN.
WHAT? WHAT DO YOU--
--I SEE. OKAY! LISTEN UP!
EVERYONE, LET'S JUST LEAVE HIM ALONE!
ALONE? B-BUT...
ALONE WITH THE DEAD.

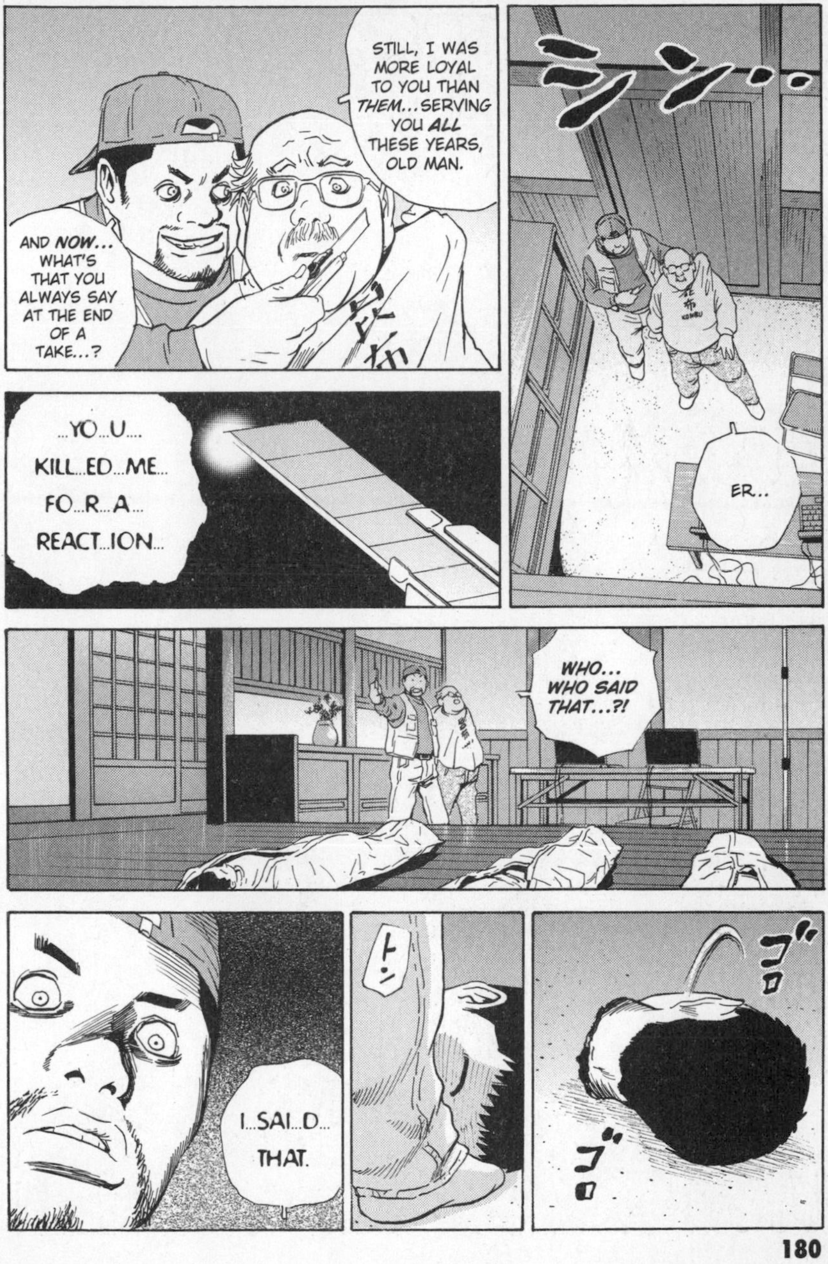
シン…
ER...
STILL, I WAS MORE LOYAL TO YOU THAN *THEM*... SERVING YOU ***ALL*** THESE YEARS, OLD MAN.
AND ***NOW***... WHAT'S THAT YOU ALWAYS SAY AT THE END OF A TAKE...?
...YO...U... KILL...ED...ME... FO...R...A... REACT...ION...
WHO... WHO SAID THAT...?!
ゴロ
ゴロ
トン
I...SAI...D... THAT.

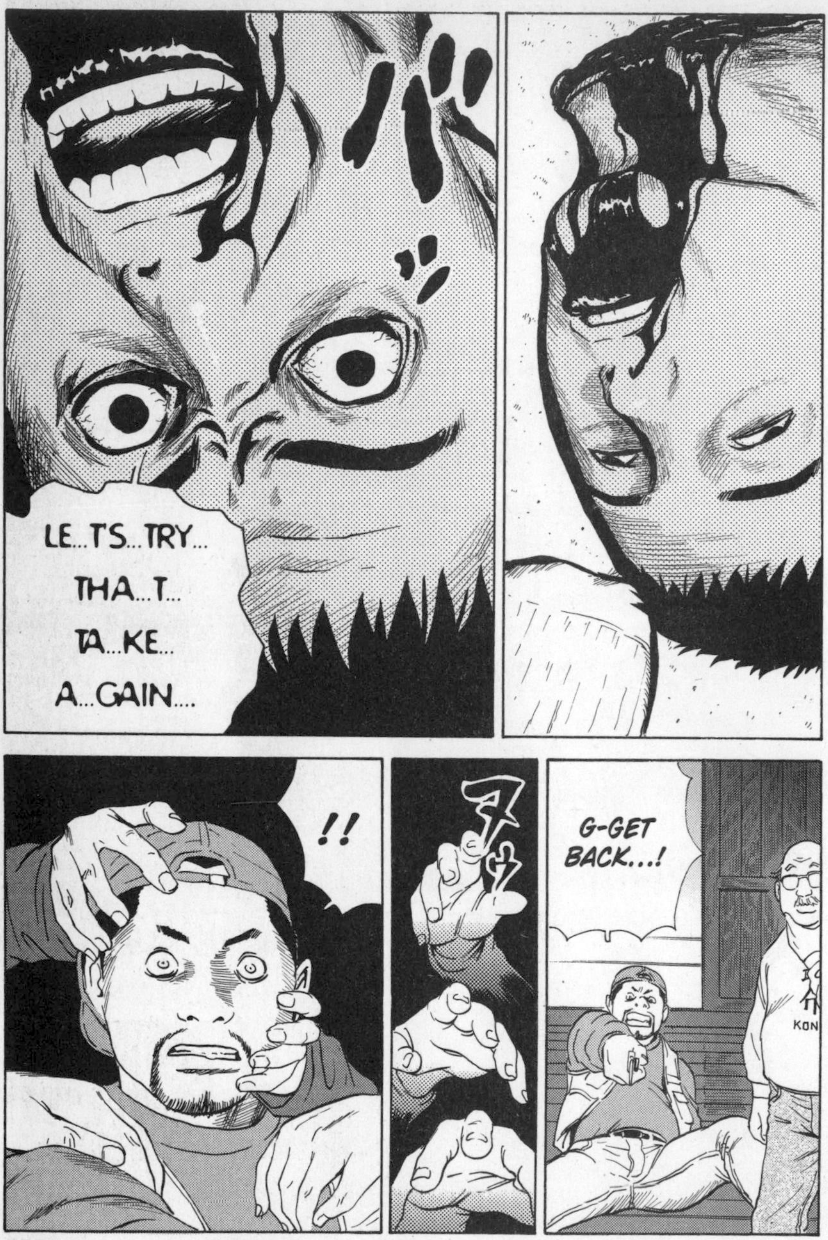

LE...T'S...TRY...
THA...T...
TA...KE...
A...GAIN....
G-GET BACK...!
KON
!!

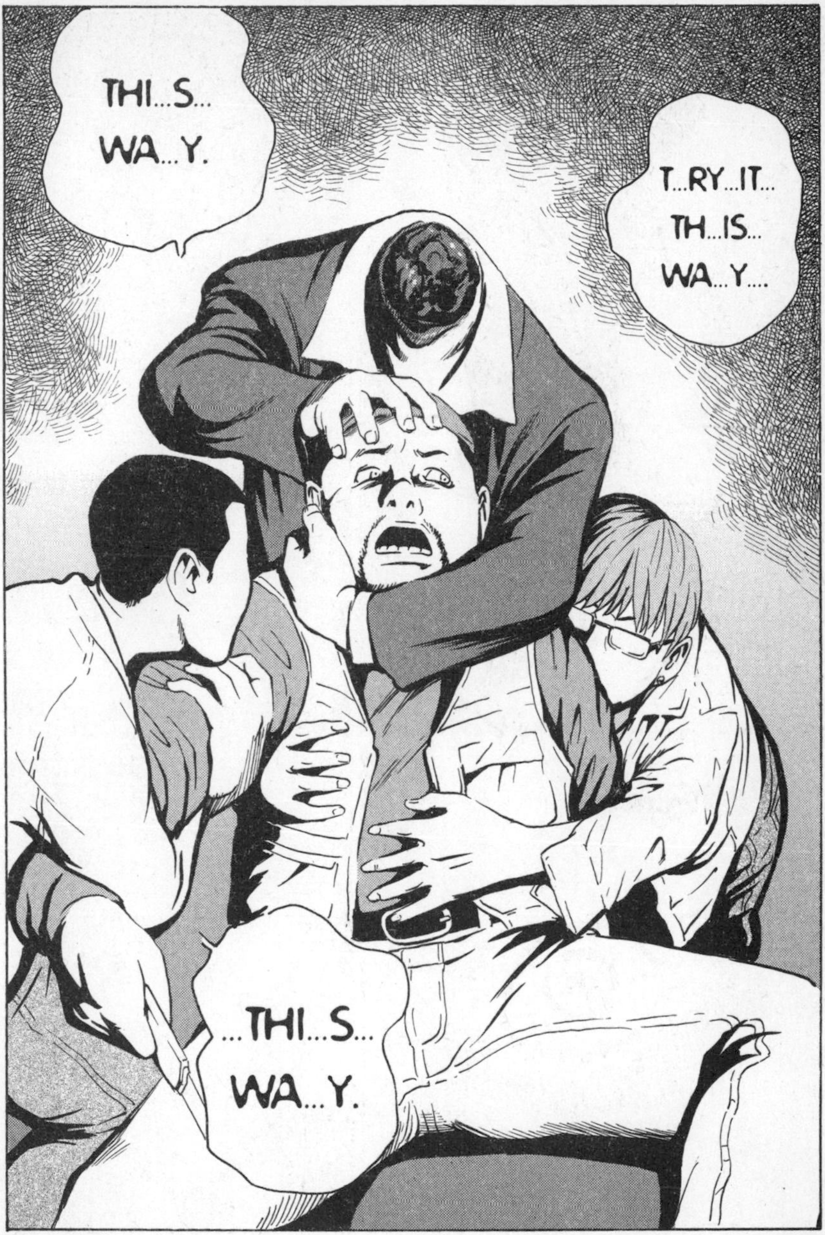
T...RY...IT... TH...IS... WA...Y....
THI...S... WA...Y.
...THI...S... WA...Y.

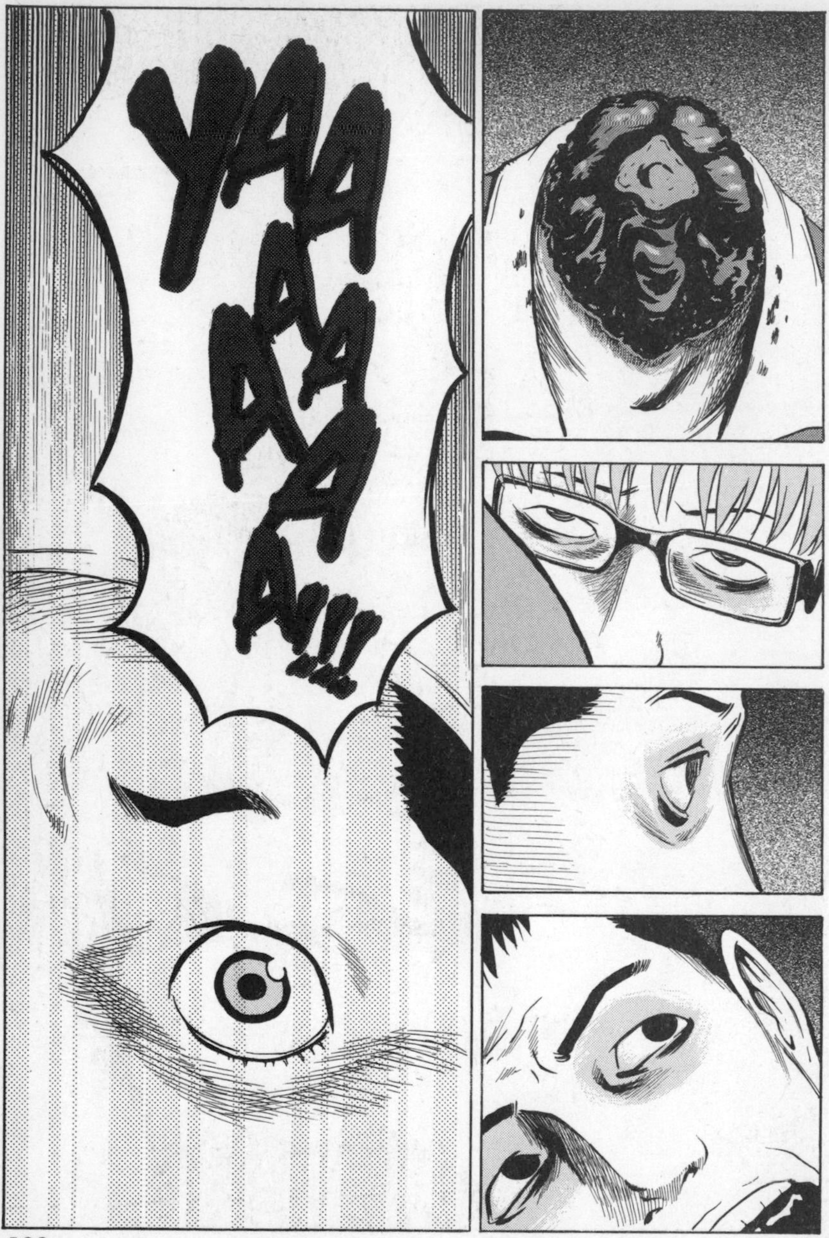
YAAAAAAAAA!!!

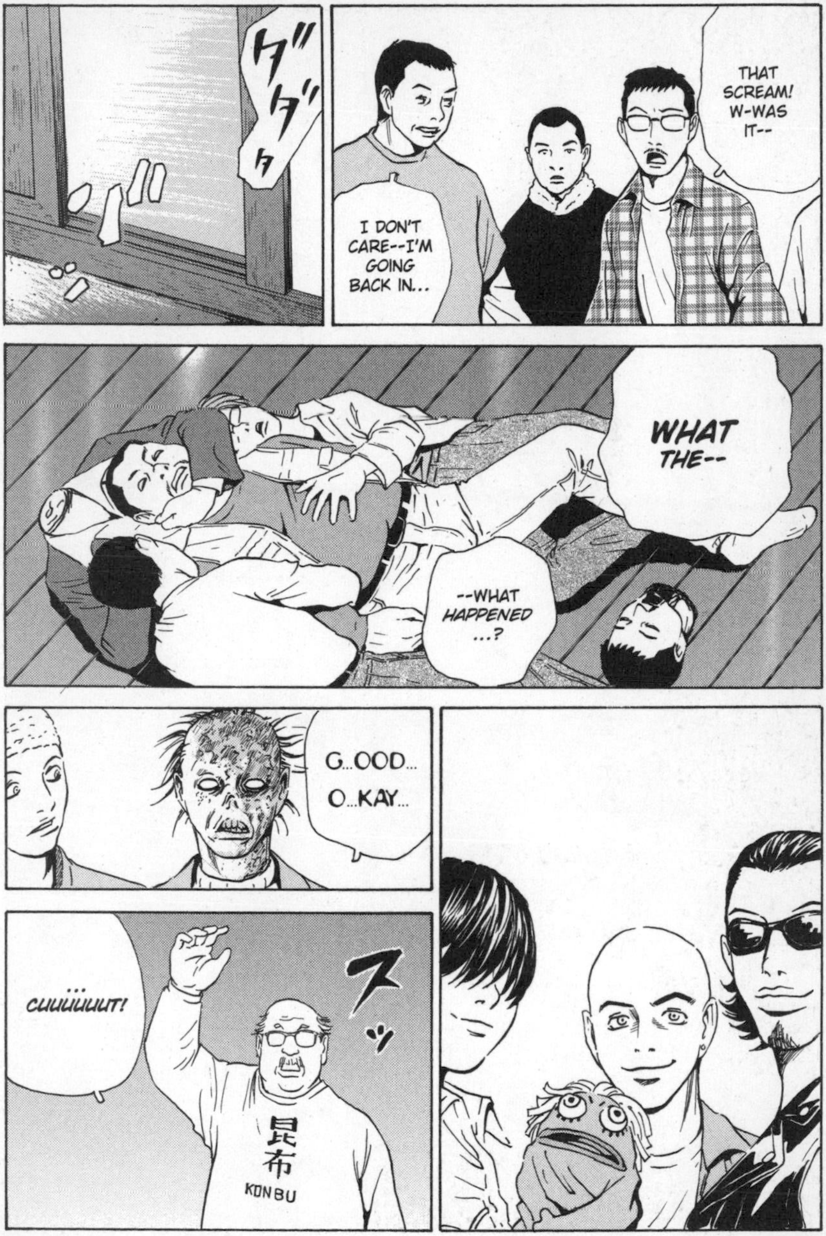
THAT SCREAM! W-WAS IT--
I DON'T CARE--I'M GOING BACK IN...
ダダダ
WHAT THE--
--WHAT HAPPENED ...?
G...OOD... O...KAY...
...CUUUUUUUT!
スッ
昆布
KONBU

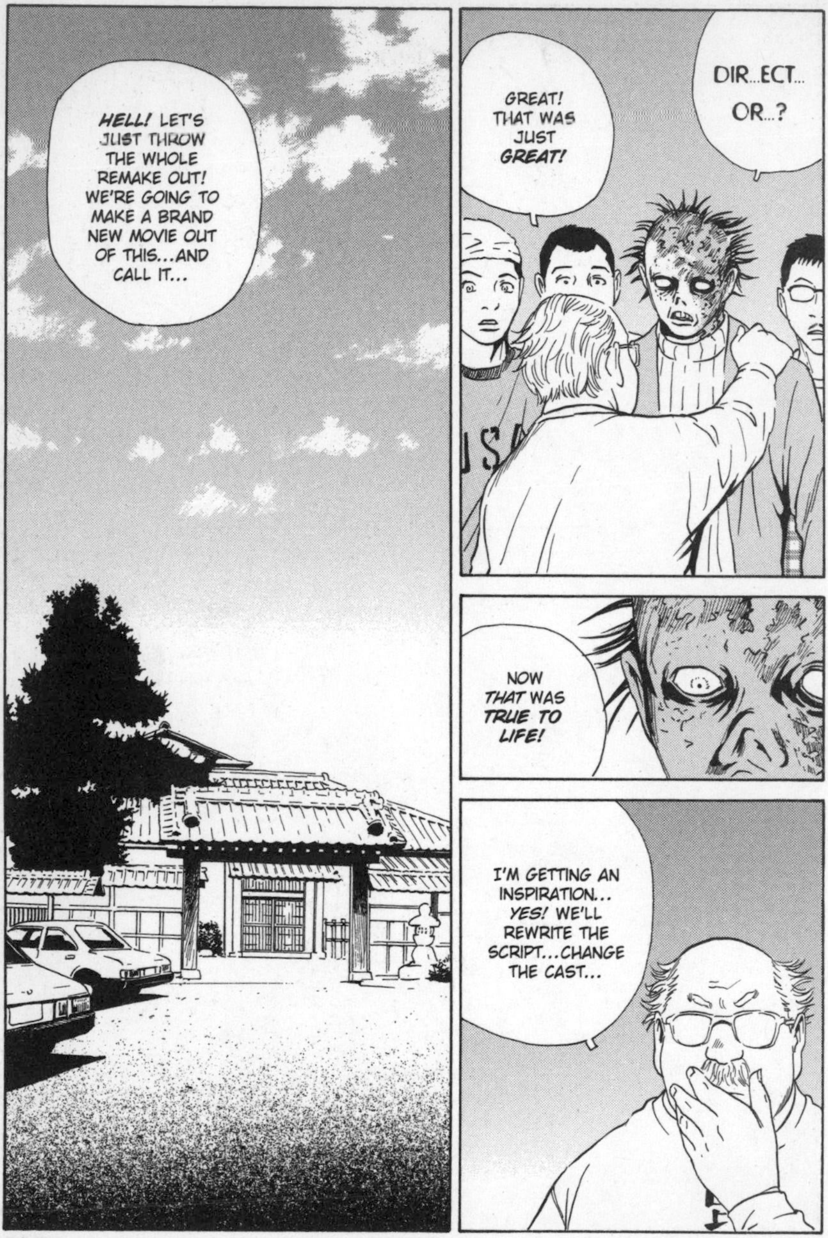
DIR...ECT... OR...?
GREAT! THAT WAS JUST GREAT!
NOW THAT WAS TRUE TO LIFE!
I'M GETTING AN INSPIRATION... YES! WE'LL REWRITE THE SCRIPT...CHANGE THE CAST...
HELL! LET'S JUST THROW THE WHOLE REMAKE OUT! WE'RE GOING TO MAKE A BRAND NEW MOVIE OUT OF THIS...AND CALL IT...

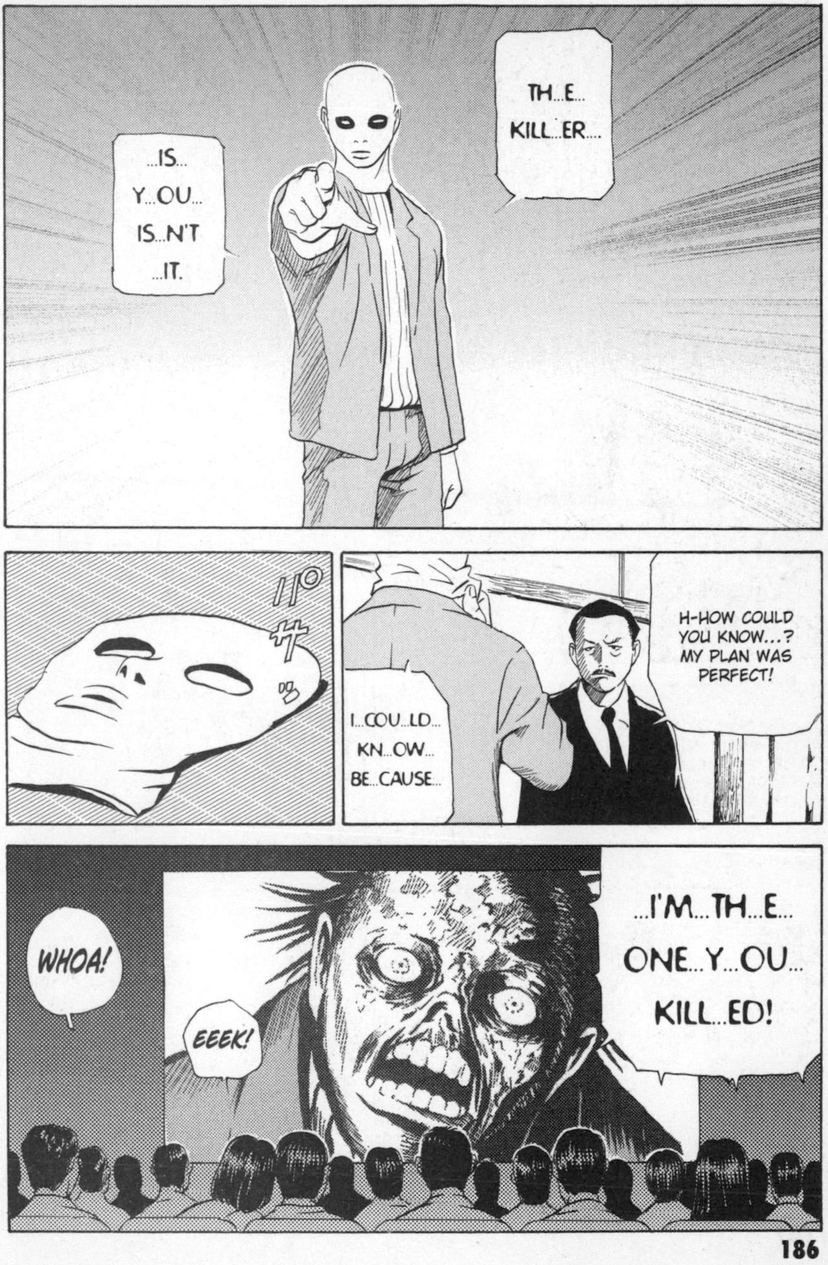
TH...E... KILL...ER....
...IS... Y...OU... IS...N'T ...IT.
H-HOW COULD YOU KNOW...? MY PLAN WAS PERFECT!
I...COU...LD... KN...OW... BE...CAUSE...
パサッ
...I'M...TH...E... ONE...Y...OU... KILL...ED!
EEEK!
WHOA!

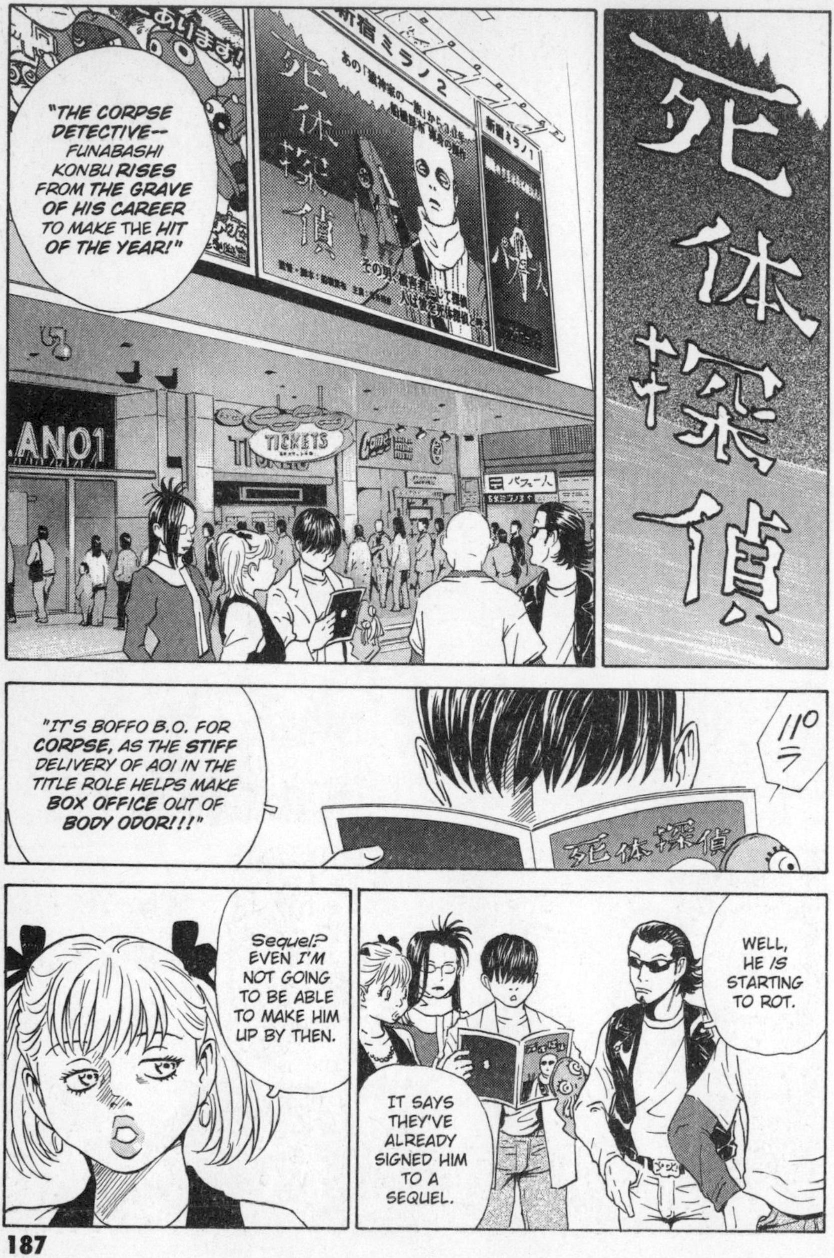
死体探偵
新宿ミラノ2
新宿ミラノ1
"THE CORPSE DETECTIVE-- FUNABASHI KONBU RISES FROM THE GRAVE OF HIS CAREER TO MAKE THE HIT OF THE YEAR!"
.ANO1
TICKETS
パラ
"IT'S BOFFO B.O. FOR CORPSE, AS THE STIFF DELIVERY OF AOI IN THE TITLE ROLE HELPS MAKE BOX OFFICE OUT OF BODY ODOR!!!"
死体探偵
WELL, HE *IS* STARTING TO ROT.
IT SAYS THEY'VE ALREADY SIGNED HIM TO A SEQUEL.
Sequel? EVEN *I'M* NOT GOING TO BE ABLE TO MAKE HIM UP BY THEN.

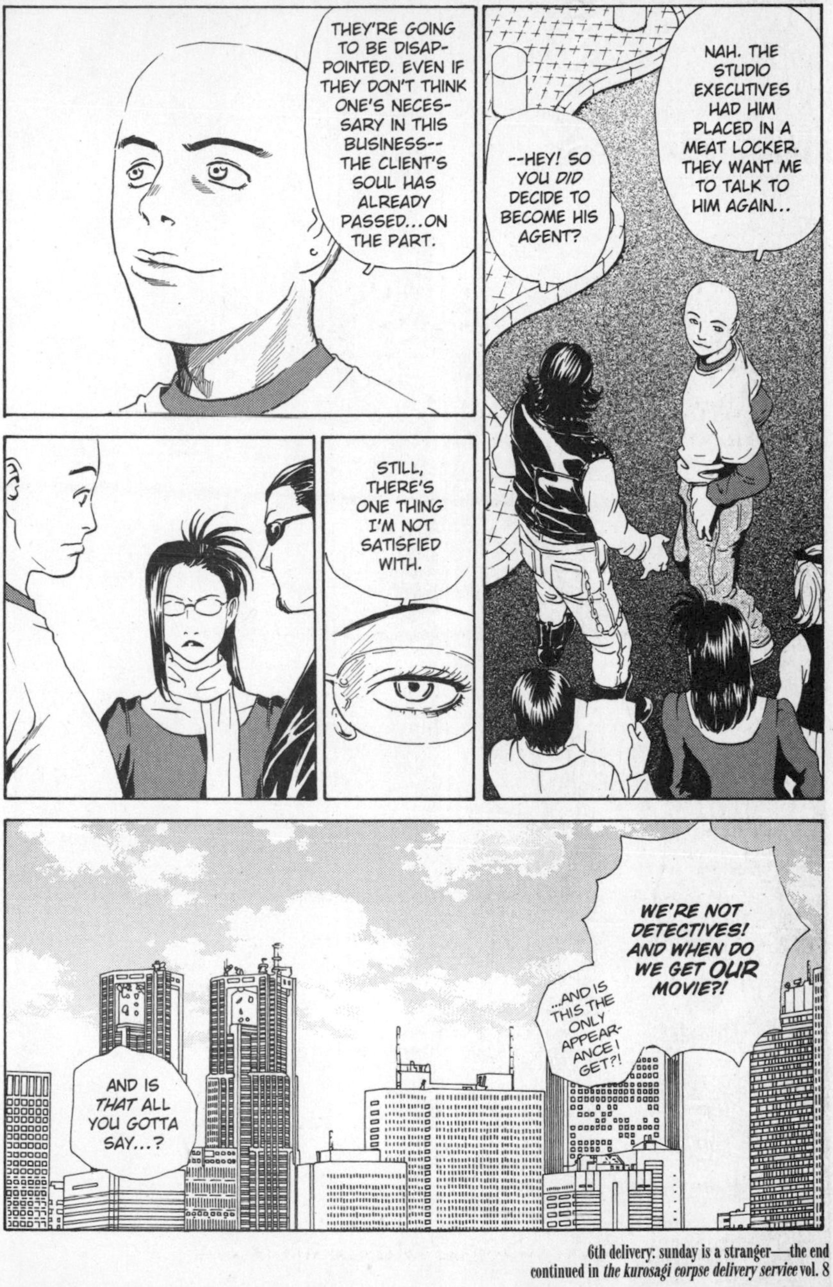
NAH. THE STUDIO EXECUTIVES HAD HIM PLACED IN A MEAT LOCKER. THEY WANT ME TO TALK TO HIM AGAIN...
--HEY! SO YOU *DID* DECIDE TO BECOME HIS AGENT?
THEY'RE GOING TO BE DISAPPOINTED. EVEN IF THEY DON'T THINK ONE'S NECESSARY IN THIS BUSINESS--THE CLIENT'S SOUL HAS ALREADY PASSED...ON THE PART.
STILL, THERE'S ONE THING I'M NOT SATISFIED WITH.
WE'RE NOT DETECTIVES! AND WHEN DO WE GET OUR MOVIE?!
...AND IS THIS THE ONLY APPEARANCE I GET?!
AND IS *THAT* ALL YOU GOTTA SAY...?

6th delivery: sunday is a stranger—the end

continued in *the kurosagi corpse delivery service* vol. 8

the KUROSAGI corpse delivery service

黒鷺死体宅配便

eiji otsuka 大塚英志 housui yamazaki 山崎峰水

designer **HEIDI WHITCOMB**
editorial assistant **ANNIE GULLION**
art director **LIA RIBACCHI**
publisher **MIKE RICHARDSON**

English-language version
produced by Dark Horse Comics

THE KUROSAGI CORPSE DELIVERY SERVICE VOL. 7
© EIJI OTSUKA OFFICE 2007, © HOUSUI YAMAZAKI 2007. First published in
Japan in 2007 by KADOKAWA SHOTEN Publishing Co., Ltd., Tokyo. English
translation rights arranged with KADOKAWA SHOTEN Publishing Co., Ltd., Tokyo,
through TOHAN CORPORATION, Tokyo. This English language edition © 2008
by Dark Horse Comics, Inc. All other material © 2008 by Dark Horse Comics, Inc.
All rights reserved. No portion of this publication may be reproduced or transmitted,
in any form or by any means, without the express written permission of the copyright
holders. Names, characters, places, and incidents featured in this publication
are either the product of the author's imagination or are used fictitiously. Any
resemblance to actual persons (living or dead), events, institutions, or locales,
without satiric intent, is coincidental. Dark Horse Manga™ is a trademark of Dark
Horse Comics, Inc. All rights reserved.

Published by
Dark Horse Manga
A division of Dark Horse Comics, Inc.
10956 SE Main Street
Milwaukie, OR 97222
www.darkhorse.com

To find a comics shop in your area,
call the Comic Shop Locator Service
toll-free at 1-888-266-4226

First edition: September 2008
ISBN 978-1-59307-982-6

1 3 5 7 9 10 8 6 4 2

PRINTED IN CANADA

DISJECTA MEMBRA

SOUND FX GLOSSARY AND NOTES ON *KUROSAGI* VOL. 7 BY TAYLOR ENGEL AND TOSHIFUMI YOSHIDA
introduction and additional comments by the editor

TO INCREASE YOUR ENJOYMENT of the distinctive Japanese visual style of this manga, we've included a guide to the sound effects (or "FX") used in this manga. It is suggested the reader *not* constantly consult this glossary as they read through, but regard it as supplemental information, in the manner of footnotes. If you want to imagine it being read aloud by Osaka, after the manner of her lecture to Sakaki on hemorrhoids in episode five of *Azumanga Daioh*, please go right ahead. In either Yuki Matsuoka or Kira Vincent-Davis's voice—I like them both.

Japanese, like English, did not independently invent its own writing system, but instead borrowed and modified the system used by then-dominant cultural power in their part of the world. We still call the letters we use to write English today the "Roman" alphabet, for the simple reason that about 1600 years ago the earliest English speakers, living on the frontier of the Roman Empire, began to use the same letters the Romans used for their Latin language to write out English.

Around that very same time, on the other side of the planet, Japan, like England, was another example of an island civilization lying across the sea from a great empire, in this case, that of China. Likewise the Japanese borrowed from the Chinese writing system, which then, as now, consisted of thousands of complex symbols—today in China officially referred to in the Roman alphabet as *hanzi*, but which the Japanese pronounce as *kanji*. For example,

all the Japanese characters you see on the front cover of *The Kurosagi Corpse Delivery Service*—the seven which make up the original title and the four each which make up the creators' names—are examples of kanji. Of course, all of them were hanzi first—although the Japanese did also invent some original kanji of their own, just as new hanzi have been created over the centuries as Chinese evolved.

(Note that whereas both *kanji* and *hanzi* are examples of writing foreign words in Roman letters, "kanji" gives English speakers a fairly good idea of how the Japanese word is really pronounced—*khan-gee*—whereas "hanzi" does not—in Mandarin Chinese it sounds something like *n-tsuh*. The reason is fairly simple: whereas the most commonly used method of writing Japanese in Roman letters, called the Hepburn system, was developed by a native English speaker, the most commonly used method of writing Chinese in Roman letters, called the Pinyin system, was developed by native Mandarin speakers. In fact, Pinyin was developed to help teach Mandarin pronunciation to speakers of other Chinese dialects; unlike Hepburn, it was not intended as a learning tool for English speakers per se, and hence has no particular obligation to "make sense" to English speakers or, indeed, users of the many other languages spelled with the Roman alphabet.)

Whereas the various dialects of Chinese are written entirely in hanzi, it is impractical to render the Japanese language entirely in them. To compare once more, English

is a notoriously difficult language in which to spell properly, and this is in part because it uses an alphabet designed for another language, Latin, whose sounds are different (this is, of course, putting aside the fact the sounds of both languages experienced change over time). The challenges the Japanese faced in using the Chinese writing system for their own language were even greater, for whereas spoken English and Latin are at least from a common language family, spoken Japanese is unrelated to any of the various dialects of spoken Chinese. The complicated writing system that Japanese evolved represents an adjustment to these great differences.

When the Japanese borrowed hanzi to become kanji, what they were getting was a way to write out (remember, they already had ways to *say*) their vocabulary. Nouns, verbs, many adjectives, the names of places and people—that's what kanji are used for, the fundamental data of the written language. The practical use and processing of that "data"—its grammar and pronunciation—is another matter entirely. Because spoken Japanese neither sounds nor functions like Chinese, the first work-around tried was a system called *manyogana*, where individual kanji were picked to represent certain syllables in Japanese. A similar method is still used in Chinese today to spell out foreign names; companies and individuals often try to choose hanzi for this purpose that have an auspicious, or at least not insulting, meaning. As you will also observe in *Kurosagi* and elsewhere, the meaning behind the characters that make up a personal name are an important literary element of Japanese as well.

The commentary in *Katsuya Terada's The Monkey King* (also available from Dark Horse, and also translated by Toshifumi Yoshida) notes the importance that not only Chinese, but also Indian culture had on Japan at this time in history—particularly through Buddhism. Similarly, In Western history at this time, religious communities in Asia were associated with learning, since priests and monks were more likely to be literate than other groups in society. It is believed the Northeast Indian *Siddham* script studied by Kukai (died 835 AD), founder of the Shingon sect of Japanese Buddhism, inspired him to create the solution for writing Japanese still used today. Kukai is credited with the idea of taking the manyogana and making shorthand versions of them—which are now known simply as *kana*. The improvement in efficiency was dramatic: a kanji, used previously to represent a sound, that might have taken a dozen strokes to draw, was now reduced to three or four.

Unlike the original kanji they were based on, the new kana had *only* a sound meaning. And unlike the thousands of kanji, there are only forty-six kana, which can be used to spell out any word in the Japanese language, including the many ordinarily written with kanji (Japanese keyboards work on this principle). The same set of forty-six kana is written two different ways depending on their intended use: cursive style, *hiragana*, and block style, *katakana*. Naturally, sound FX in manga are almost always written out using kana.

Kana work somewhat differently than the Roman alphabet. For example, while there are separate kana for each of the five vowels (the Japanese order is not A-E-I-O-U as in English, but A-I-U-E-O), there are, except for "n," no separate kana for consonants (the middle "n" in the word *ninja* illustrates this exception). Instead, kana

work by grouping together consonants with vowels: for example, there are five kana for sounds starting with "k," depending on which vowel follows it—in Japanese vowel order, they go KA, KI, KU, KE, KO. The next set of kana begins with "s" sounds, so SA, SHI, SU, SE, SO, and so on. You will observe this kind of consonant-vowel pattern in the FX listings for *Kurosagi* Vol. 7 below.

Katakana are almost always the kind that get used for manga sound FX, but on occasion hiragana are used instead. This is commonly done when the sound is one associated with a human body, but can be a subtler aesthetic choice by the artist as well. In *Kurosagi* Vol. 7 you can see an example on 43.5, with the HYUBA swish-strike of the sword, which in hiragana style is written ひゅばつ. Note its more cursive appearance compared to the other FX. If it had been written in katakana style, it would look like ヒュバツ.

To see how to use this glossary, take an example from page 8: "8.4 FX: BON—sound of something exploding under hood." 8.4 means the FX is the one on page 8, in panel 4. BON is the sound these kana—ボンツ—literally stand for. After the dash comes an explanation of what the sound represents (in some cases, it will be less obvious than others). Note that in cases where there are two or more different sounds in a single panel, an extra number is used to differentiate them from right to left; or, in cases where right and left are less clear, in clockwise order.

The use of kana in these FX also illustrates another aspect of written Japanese—its flexible reading order. For example, the way you're reading the pages and panels of this book in general: going from right to left, and from top to bottom—is similar to the

order in which Japanese is also written in most forms of print: books, magazines, and newspapers. However, many of the FX in *Kurosagi* (and manga in general) read left to right. This kind of flexibility is also to be found on Japanese web pages, which usually also read left to right. In other words, Japanese doesn't simply read "the other way" from English; the Japanese themselves are used to reading it in several different directions.

As might be expected, some FX "sound" short, and others "sound" long. Manga represent this in different ways. One of many instances of "short sounds" in *Kurosagi* Vol. 7 is to be found in the example from 43.5 given above: HYUBA. See the small つ mark it has at the end—note again that this is the hiragana "tsu," and you will far more often see it in its katakana form, ツ, as (for example) in the other above example, 8.4's BON. This mark ordinarily represents the sound "tsu," but its half-size use at the end of FX like this means the sound is the kind which stops or cuts off suddenly; that's why the sound is written as BON and not BONTSU—you don't "pronounce" the TSU in such cases. Note the small "tsu" has another occasional use *inside*, rather than at the end, of a particular FX, where it indicates a doubling of the consonant sound that follows it.

There are three different ways you may see "long sounds"—where a vowel sound is extended—written out as FX. One is with an ellipsis, as in 6.2.1's BURORORO. Another is with an extended line, as in 78.3's SUU KOO. Still another is by simply repeating a vowel several times, as in 69.5's KIIIIIIIIN. You will note that the KOO in 78.3's SUU KOO has a "tsu" at its end, suggesting an elongated sound that's suddenly cut off; the methods may be

combined within a single FX. As a visual element in manga, FX are an art rather than a science, and are used in a less rigorous fashion than kana are in standard written Japanese.

The explanation of what the sound represents may sometimes be surprising, but every culture "hears" sounds differently. Note that manga FX do not even necessarily represent literal sounds. Such "mimetic" words, which represent an imagined sound, or even a state of mind, are called *gitaigo* in Japanese. Like the onomatopoeic *giseigo* (the words used to represent literal sounds—i.e., most FX in this glossary are classed as giseigo), they are also used in colloquial speech and writing. A Japanese, for example, might say that something bounced by saying PURIN, or talk about eating by saying MUGU MUGU. It's something like describing chatter in English by saying "yadda yadda yadda" instead.

One important last note: all these spelled-out kana vowels should be pronounced as they are in Japanese: "A" as *ah*, "I" as *eee*, "U" as *ooh*, "E" as *eh*, and "O" as *oh*.

2.1 We're back to once again having song titles for this volume. This time around, they're all singles from Mako Ishino between 1978 and 1981. Although she began her career as an idol singer, Ishino has moved on to become an actor since her last single was released in 1987. She's appeared in TV series and movies, including a number based off manga, such as *Ping Pong* (as Player A's mom), *Boys Over Flowers* (as Tsukushi's mom) and *Dance Till Tomorrow* (as Shimomura). The translator notes, by the way, that the title of "1st Delivery"

could be alternately rendered as "Challenge of My Heart," and "6th Delivery"'s as "A Stranger Called Sunday."

6.2.1 **FX/balloon: BURORORO**— engine sound

6.2.2 **FX/balloon: KI**—car brake sound. "Pure Land," *joodo* in Japanese, is a reference to a popular form of Buddhism as practiced in East Asia (in Southeast Asia and Sri Lanka the doctrine is less common) that stresses salvation through faith and prayer to the incarnation of the Buddha named Amitabha. This is in contrast to the "classic" practice of Buddhism, in which salvation depends on the individual's own effort toward proper works and mindfulness. Pure Land Buddhists believe that Amitabha perceived that worldly existence is so corrupt as to stand in the way of most beings' personal enlightenment, so he created a pure land as a sanctuary that souls might reach after death by having faith in Amitabha, known as *Amida* in Japanese. To reach the pure land after death is not the same thing as achieving final enlightenment, but it is believed to be a place where all souls can and will receive enlightenment, as opposed to the uncertainty and suffering of being reborn into the ordinary world.

7.2 No, you're not imagining things— Karatsu is back to more or less normal after Vol. 6's cliffhanger, with no explanation as to what happened to him between then and now. We are assured Eiji

Otsuka will explain this . . . in good time, reader, in good time.

8.2 In case you're wondering *what was therein inhum'd* (to quote H. P. Lovecraft) in a Japanese cemetery such as this one, the answer is, of course, the ashes of the dead, which take up much less space than an actual body.

8.4.1 **FX: BON**—sound of something exploding under hood

8.4.2 **FX/balloon: MOWA**—sound of smoke starting to come out

10.2 **FX/balloon: PETA**—applying heating/cooling patch

10.3 As you might guess, these are heating/cooling patches for shoulder aches and back pain. Harix brand company homepage, yo: http://www.harix.jp/.

12.1.1 **FX/balloon: GASHA**—sound of shifting metal

12.1.2 **FX/balloon: GASHA**—sound of shifting metal

12.3 **FX/balloon: GA**—grabbing sound

12.4.1 **FX/balloon: SHU**—sound of pneumatics activating

12.4.2 **FX/balloon: SHUU**—sound of pneumatics

14.6 Each of the robotics students is, of course, named after the inventor of the (imaginary) robot whose paradigm they champion: Tomino, from Yoshiyuki Tomino, creator of *Gundam* (he's also wearing the Zeon symbol from *Gundam* on his T-shirt); Nagai, from Go Nagai, creator of *Mazinger Z* (he likewise wears a "Z" on his own shirt); and Tezuka, from—wait for

it—Osamu Tezuka, creator of *Astro Boy* (she, showing somewhat better taste, sports a white turtleneck). As you can see from their conversation, they represent three different images anime has given pop culture in Japan of what a "robot" is. *Gundam*, which premiered in 1979, epitomizes the so-called "real robot," where a robot is a mass-produced weapon, just like a plane or tank, made for future wars driven by politics, ideology, or economics, just like today's wars. *Mazinger Z*, which premiered in 1972, exemplified the "super robot," where a robot is a rare or unique machine that typically fights the "monster of the week" unleashed by the flamboyant forces of evil. The distinction is valid, yet is also understandably often lost on people who aren't otaku, seeing as how both kinds of shows involve young pilots commanding giant, humanoid robots; moreover, popular shows such as 1995's *Evangelion* combined elements of the "super" and "real" robot, to the extent that fans now speak of "hybrid robot" shows. If you haven't fallen asleep by now, the larger distinction would seem to be between both "super" and "real" robots and the kind exemplified by *Astro Boy*. Some would say that, properly speaking, those former two categories aren't robots at all, and when you think "robot," you really mean something like the eponymous Astro Boy—not a machine with a human inside controlling it, but a human-sized machine that independently moves and thinks on its own. Of course, Americans might be more likely to think of the Terminator, rather than Astro Boy . . . In Brian Winston's

fascinating book *Media Technology and Society*, the author shows that inventions are developed not only because they become technically possible, but because society shows a need for them; conversely, if society doesn't desire an invention, its progress might be slowed or abandoned. Japan seems to be the world leader in robotics in part because their society seems simply to like the idea of robots more than ours, and it's fair to say that *is* in part due to the influence of manga such as *Astro Boy*.

15.1 Yata's remark makes me think about the *Akira* movie. It's one of the greatest anime films ever made, and in fact made such a strong impression in the late '80s and early '90s, that fans sometimes had trouble explaining to newcomers that not all anime had to be like *Akira*. But, to many of today's anime fans, *Akira* isn't something that's overexposed—*Akira* is something that came out before they were *born*.

15.5 FX: SHUU—air leaking sound

17.3 FX: ZURURURU—dragging sound

18.2 FX: GACHA—door opening

18.3 FX: DOSASA—group falling down exhausted

18.4 FX/balloon: KIIN—sound of metal tip of cane striking floor

19.2 I can't help but notice that, although Ao and Sasayama presumably also wear glasses to correct vision, theirs are more stylish than Nagai, Tezuka, and Tomino's. At Fanime-Con '08, it seemed half the Gainax contingent was wearing the kind of narrow, Chanel-style frames that Ao sports. Of course, from a *meganekko* perspective, it's frequently the case that the bigger and more unstylish the glasses, the *more* erotic, as seen with Nagai, Koyomi Mizuhara, Yomiko Readman, or Morrissey when he did "Heaven Knows I'm Miserable Now" on *Top of the Pops*. I'm sorry to sexualize everything, but when I became an otaku, I gave up my moral rights, much like a Shining Stars contract.

22.1 The "Broadband Center" in which the rest of this story takes place is a play on the actual Nakano Broadway building, a multistory shopping center in the Nakano district of Tokyo. Akihabara is the neighborhood that gets interna-tional attention for its otaku scene (even in Japan, ordinary folk have been known to gawk at the ~~beautiful~~ freaks, the same way they used to have bus tours of Haight-Ashbury in the 1960s). But Nakano is the older hardcore fan hangout, for in 1987, Mandarake was established in the Broadway Building—and Mandarake was basically the first collector's store for anime and manga goods (it is a sign, perhaps, of how mainstream comics are in Japan, that it took so long to develop a specialized collectors' market). The Kurosagi gang drove there, but you'll probably take the JR Chuo Line. Getting off at Nakano Station, you'll take the north exit and enter a long, broad hallway that looks more or less like an American shopping mall—but this is only the Sun Mall Shopping Center, and the Broadway, attached to it, is at the

end. The Broadway itself, being a forty-year-old building, is narrower in its walkways and is divided into small, swap-meet-sized partitions, of which some stores take up only one, while others (such as Mandarake) take up many. Not only does Broadway have the goods (there are *nineteen* different Mandarake substores inside, each specializing in such wares as doujinshi, toys, old videocassettes, LDs, and even 8mm reels), it has character: the vegetarian restaurant, mysterious flyers posted about, and Taco Ché, the world's greatest postcard and T-shirt store, give parts of it a vaguely student-union air. The nicest thing about both Mandarake and the Broadway Building is that they're genuinely interested in foreign customers; Mandarake has staff that speak English, Spanish, French, Korean, and Mandarin. The English-language homepage of Mandarake's store in the Broadway is http://www.mandarake.co.jp/en/shop/nkn.html, whereas the English-language page of the Broadway Building itself is at www.bwy.jp, although, mysteriously, it plays Paris Hilton's "Stars Are Blind" upon opening. As much as I feel she betrayed the proud legacy of Conrad Hilton (growing up in hotel rooms with their Gideons, I thought *Be My Guest* was the Apocrypha), it's a perfectly good song. Let us separate the creator from their art.

22.2   *Toradarake* is a portmanteau— if that's the word I'm looking for, Jeeves—of Mandarake with the name of another real-life store, Toranoana. There is, in fact, no Toranoana in the Broadway Building (there are five of the stores in other parts of Tokyo, however, including Akihabara), but the zombie robot is probably artistic license, too. Toranoana (which, unlike Mandarake, does not make foreign sales) specializes in selling doujinshi—self-published zines, usually consisting of manga content—and as you may have heard, most doujinshi are unauthorized parodies of licensed characters (there are so many "doujin" published, however, that there are thousands of original ones each year as well). But, being a brick-and-mortar store chain, it represents just how un-underground doujinshi are in Japan; in fact, Toranoana habitually takes out the back-cover ad on the monthly *Shonen Ace* magazine, the original home of *Kurosagi*—and of many manga parodied in the doujinshi Toranoana sells. Now, this utterly cavalier treatment of intellectual property by both rights-holder and fan may seem horrific by American legal standards, but tell me: if it's so detrimental, then how come the Japanese comics industry is much bigger than ours? How come it's better *mon-e-tized?* And don't tell me it's because "the Japanese are different"; that's the same simple excuse that was used in the 1970s and '80s in our auto and electronics industries. Businesses and legal practices reflect a larger culture, but they are also things that are changed by people and companies, through new decisions, theories, and initiatives. History doesn't have to run in a straight line; consider that in the 1980s, the trendsetting portable music player was Japanese, the Sony Walkman; today,

it is American, Apple's iPod. Speaking of turning things around, perhaps you're wondering if anyone's made a *Kurosagi Corpse Delivery Service* doujinshi in Japan. No, not that I know of. Show the world the true spirit of Yankee innovation, and be the first! I heard there's a Yata/Karatsu shipper out there.

22.3 There actually *is* a swap-meet element to the Nakano Broadway; some of its myriad glass display cases are the wares of its resident stores, but some are available for a monthly rent to individual collectors, who can use them to show off and sell their personal stuff on consignment. Now, having just sung a long paragraph of praise about the Mandarake in Nakano, Patrick Macias and Matt Alt have reported on the recent opening of the *new* Mandarake store in the T-shirt-stretched belly of the beast, Akihabara, saying that it appears to have better stock than the one in Nakano. Hear the scoop on episode #4 of the official podcast of *Otaku USA*, the magazine that's putting the man into the manga, and the fu fu into the fujoshi (http://patrickmacias.blogs.com/er/files/otaku_usa_podcast_4.mp3).

22.3.1 All right, back to the sound effects.

23.2 **FX: GYU**—tightening his bandanna

23.3 **FX/balloon: GASHAN GASHAN**—sound of metallic footsteps

23.4 **FX: GASHA GASHA GASHAN**—metallic footsteps

24.3.1 **FX: GASHA**—pulling out cartridge sound

24.3.2 **FX/balloon: BIKU BIKUN**—robot shuddering/twitching when the cart is pulled

24.4 **FX: GAKUN**—robot slumping over

24.5 In the original Japanese, she said a Famicom cartridge—which was what Nintendo was called in Japan (it was a contraction of *Family Computer*).

24.6 Made up, from combining the genuine games *Super Mario Brothers* and *Donkey Kong*.

25.2 Whereas Americans pronounce the letter "Z" as *zee*, the Japanese use the traditional British *zed*, pronounced as *zetto*; hence *Mazinger Z* is sometimes spoken out as *Mazinger Zetto*. "Soul of Chogokin" is the name of Bandai's line of high-end adult collector's toys based on classic robot series such as *Mazinger Z*; in the anime, the robot itself was said to be made of *chogokin*, or "super alloy." This is the same Mazinger, by the way, that was part of the dope Shogun Warriors toy line, if you were lucky enough to have one in the 1970s. The editor was not lucky enough. Had things worked out differently for him in the Carter years, he would have arranged a fitting showdown between Mazinger and his Marx Navarone Giant Play Set.

25.3 *Pilder on!* is what hot-blooded young hero Koji Kabuto calls out when he docks his Hover Pilder craft with Mazinger Z's head, which then becomes the cockpit where he controls the robot. You're thinking I know why it's called "Pilder," but I don't.

25.4 FX: GASHU—sound of the cartridge being put in

25.5.1 FX/balloon: SHAN—sound of a robot landing

25.5.2 FX/balloon: PYON GASHAN—jumping sound, then a robot landing sound

25.5.3 FX: YON—jumping sound

25.5.4 FX/balloon: PYON GASHAN—jumping sound, then a robot landing sound

26.2 FX: GASHA GASHAN—mechanical footsteps

26.5 It's a cliché in giant robot anime that you start off with such robots being few: rare technological artifacts, or advanced prototypes, and then sooner or later, someone figures out how to make a "mass production version."

27.3 FX: MOGO—muffled sound

27.4.1 FX/balloon: JAAA—sound of running water

27.4.2 FX/balloon: KYU—sound of a tap being closed

27.5 FX/balloon: CHARARAN—sound of pendulum falling on the floor

27.6 FX/balloon: GUKI—sound of lower back straining

27.7 FX: PURAN PURAN—sound of the pendulum dangling

28.2 FX: HYUN HYUN—sound of the pendulum swinging

30.1 The last ten years have seen a lot of new anime shows assigned to late-night time slots on cable—generally, this happens to shows that are considered to have appeal mainly to hardcore fans, as opposed to an anime directed at the mass market such as *Naruto*, which would air at better hours. *Neon Genesis Evangelion* was on broadcast TV at 7 PM on Sundays; but I suspect that were the show to have aired for the first time today, it might have been assigned to late-night cable instead—where it might never reach the nationwide audience among whom it became a phenomenon in 1995.

30.3 FX/balloon: PURAN—sound of the controller dangling

31.1 FX: TA TA TA—running sound

31.4 FX/balloon: GASHAAN—sound of breaking glass

31.5 The cat ears, or *nekomimi*, are part of the real Toranoana staff style, as their mascot is a tiger cub (*tora* means tiger), and the store name itself is said to come from writer Ikki Kajiwara (cocreator also of the famous sports manga *Ashita no Joe* and *Star of the Giants*) and artist Naoki Tsuji's wrestling epic *Tiger Mask*. Fred Schodt had a genius in his 1983 book *Manga! Manga!* for picking panels that seemed to sum up an entire series, and I vividly remember (this was in the late Rory Root's onetime store on Telegraph Ave., Best of Both Worlds) the image Schodt chose for *Tiger Mask*, showing the eponymously vizarded hero launching himself feet first at his hooded foe Golgotha Cross—who takes his stance in the ring next to a giant, nail-studded cross, for he is Golgotha Cross by name, and Golgotha Cross by nature. You can see why I spent the twenty bucks

I had planned for *X-Men* #121 on *Manga! Manga!* instead—even Claremont, Byrne, and Austin put together couldn't compete with *that*.

33.4 **FX: GASHAN GASHAN GASHAN**—running robot sound

33.5 **FX: PITA**—robot stopping

34.1 **FX: GASHA GASHA GASHA**—robot footsteps

35.1.1 **FX: GORORO**—rolling sound

35.1.2 **FX/balloon: GASHAN**—sound of robot hitting the ground

35.2 **FX/balloon: KARAN**—faceplate clanking on ground

37.3 Tomino is referring to the famous 1783 observation by Luigi Galvani, who was dissecting a frog when his assistant touched a scalpel to the frog's sciatic nerve. The scalpel, having built up an electrical charge earlier, transferred it to the nerve, causing the frog's leg to kick. This was the first evidence that electricity had a role to play in animating life, and, as you might guess, helped to inspire Mary Shelley's 1818 novel *Frankenstein*.

37.4 **FX/balloon: PIKU**—robot twitching

37.5 **FX: CHIRA**—glancing over sound

38.1 **FX/balloon: SU**—picking up game

38.3 **FX/balloon: GACHA**—sound of a game cart being pushed in

38.4 **FX/box: PIRO RIRO RIROOON**—8-bit game music starting. This is the editor's attempt to express the *Donkey Kong* theme, the only 8-bit theme he knows.

39.1 **FX: GASHA GASHAN GASHAN**—robot footsteps

39.5 **FX/balloon: PI**—pressing a button on the cell phone

40.2 **FX: PIPA**—hanging-up sound

41.2.1 **FX: GASHAN**—breaking glass

41.2.2 **FX: PARIN**—falling glass shattering

41.4 **FX/robot: PIRORIROON**—video-game sound

42.1 The translator suggests Zombie-kun is swinging Guts's sword from *Berserk*, whereas the blade to the right looks like the Master Sword from the *Zelda* video-game series, and the sword to the left seems to come from *Card Captor Sakura*.

43.4 **FX: DOKA DOKA**—running up stairs sound

43.5 **FX: HYUBA**—giant sword coming down

44.1.1 **FX: BAKYAAAN**—plastic sword shattering

44.1.2 **FX/balloon: KAN**—piece of sword hitting escalator

44.1.3 **FX/balloon: KARARAN**—piece of sword hitting escalator

44.4 **FX: BA**—putting hand on head

45.4 **FX: NU**—sound of the soul coming out

47.1 Even at this critical moment in the plot, please note the *Magical Maid Girl Mumume-Tan R* poster—the character Makino was forced to cosplay in Vol. 5. The "R" implies that a sequel has now been made as the second season of *Sailor Moon* was called *Sailor Moon R* (for "Return"). You have not, by the way, seen the last of Mumume-tan in this manga.

47.2 FX: FURA—body starting to fall over

47.3.1 FX/balloon: GARA GARA—sound of robot sliding down escalator

47.3.2 FX/balloon: GASHAN—robot coming to a stop at the bottom

49.1 As you may have noticed, there are two translation credits in Vol. 7; right after Toshifumi Yoshida did "1st Delivery," he had to take a hiatus from the book—but for a good cause, as he was hired by Bandai as an anime dub producer, his first assignment being the English version of *Tengen Toppa Gurren Lagann*, which should have been on the Sci-Fi Channel's Ani-Monday block for several weeks by the time you read this (as mentioned previously in "Disjecta Membra," Toshi was the producer of the English dubs of *Inu-Yasha*, *Ranma 1/2*, *Maison Ikkoku*, and *Jin-Roh*). I am grateful to Taylor Engel who was able to pinch-hit for the rest of the volume; many of the notes in this volume's "Disjecta Membra" are therefore also hers.

49.2 FX: KA—high heel clicking on pavement

50.1 FX: GOOOOO—sound of speeding truck

50.3 FX: SU—hands being stealthily raised

50.4 FX: KU—pushing

50.5 FX: YORO—woman stumbling forward

51.1 FX: PAAAA—truck's horn blaring

51.2 FX: DOKO—whud!

51.3.1 FX/balloon: BYUCHA—wet splatter

51.3.2 FX/balloon: BITA—something splattering and sticking

51.4 FX/balloon: KIIII—squealing brakes

55.3 FX: ZA—turning to leave

56.1 FX/balloon: PARA—page turning

56.3 FX/balloon: GACHA—Door opening

57.5 Sydney-based Japanese media scholar and artist Zen Yipu has written in a 2004 issue of the journal *Humanities Research* on "generations of Japanese female audiences who have idolized and imitated Audrey Hepburn . . . She is popular not only among middle-aged women who have grown up watching her movies, and therefore might have nostalgic memories of her, but also among young women in their mid-20s who would have no such recollections of her. This latter group has learnt about her either through watching old films or through seeing her 'reincarnations' [as a number of dead actors have in America, Hepburn has been CG-reanimated for commercials in Japan—ed.] in the marketplace. There is no other western idol who enjoys the same level of popularity in Japan, a popularity which endures even today, in 2004, more than a decade after her death." Zen goes on to quote Japan's trend-tracking magazine *Dime*'s explanation that "[Hepburn] has black hair, black eyes and a

slender physique just like the Japanese. Unlike the blonde glamour of a [Marilyn] Monroe type, her appearance has a feeling of familiarity with that of the Japanese female."

58.3 See 19.2. Or read *Dime*, which, by the way, is published by Shogakukan, better known in the U.S. for their manga. It's good to remember that manga publishers large and small in Japan are often part of larger book- and magazine-publishing entities. *The Kurosagi Corpse Delivery Service*, for example, appears in Kadokawa's *Comic Charge* magazine, but Kadokawa's best-selling magazine isn't a manga one, but rather the weekly what's-happening-in-town *Tokyo Walker*. Complicating the issue a bit more in the best "Disjecta Membra" manner, non-manga magazines in Japan are known to sometimes have a regular manga feature. Yoshinori Kobayashi's controversial (*"How would you feel about playing a controversial manga-ka?" "Yeah, I'm with it!"*) *Gomanism Sengen* ("The Arrogance Manifesto") runs in the contemporary biweekly affairs newsmagazine *Sapio*, whereas Kazuo Koike and Hideki Mori's *New Lone Wolf and Cub* ran in the weekly (middle-aged) men's magazine *Shukan Post*. Such a slot in a nonmanga magazine might be advantageous for an individual manga, since it doesn't have to compete for attention with other stories, may connect with people who ordinarily wouldn't follow manga (there are plenty of these in Japan; comics readership isn't universal in Japan,

it's just wider and more accepted than in the U.S.), and, as mentioned, may find itself having a wider circulation than in an actual manga magazine.

60.1 **FX: SARAN**—hair being swept out of the way, model-style.

62.5.1 **FX/balloon: HIKU**—twitching

62.5.2 **FX/balloon: PIKU**—quiver

62.6 **FX/balloon: PACHI**—eyes opening

65.2 The woman in back is wearing the habit of a Buddhist nun, or *bhikkhuni*. It is the editor's impression that even though neither Asian nor European culture has had any shortage of sexism, nevertheless it was historically more accepted and respectable for women to take holy orders in Catholicism than Buddhism—perhaps because of the prominence given to a figure such as the Virgin Mary. Even though Buddhism has the longer tradition in Japan, it seems more common to find Catholic nuns as heroines in manga, such as Rosette Christopher of *Chrono Crusade* and Yumie Takagi from *Hellsing*. Now, these nuns are admittedly portrayed with a smidgen of poetic license, but at least Japan still thinks nuns are cute, an attitude that hasn't been seen in the West since the youth of Sally Field.

66.4 **FX/balloon: DON**—jabbing with elbow

67.1 The translator notes a *jinmenso* is usually seen as able to talk and even eat, and can therefore be killed by feeding it medicine or poison. It is possibly inspired by

the rare congenital abnormality of a parasitic twin.

67.2 **FX: SU**—drawing photos out of file

67.3 **FX/balloon: BASA**—scattering photos across table

68.2 In the original Japanese, Kereellis said *Nande ya nen!* which the translator points out means "What was *that* for?" in a Kansai accent (usually associated with the city of Osaka, which bears a cultural relationship to Tokyo *somewhat* comparable to that which Brooklyn or New Jersey does to Manhattan). It's a stock phrase in traditional Kansai *manzai*, or double act comedy. The internationally known actor and director Takeshi Kitano (*Battle Royale*, *HANA-BI*) got his start in manzai; although well known in Japan as a comedian, perhaps the closest Americans have gotten to that side of him is on Spike TV's *MXC*, a facetiously dubbed version of his late-'80s game show *Takeshi's Castle* (like *Iron Chef*, it has been one of the more internationally popular Japanese live-action series).

68.4 **FX: PORI**—scritch

69.4 **FX: SU**—soft touch

69.5 **FX: KIIIIIIIIIN**—high-pitched ringing in the ears

70-71.2 **FX: BA**—energy (?) shooting from hand

70-71.3 **FX: BA BA**—energy (?) shooting from hand

72.3 **FX: ZUZU**—Karatsu's soul getting pulled out of his body

73.3 **FX/balloon: PON**—slapping on the shoulder

73.4 **FX: DOSA**—Karatsu's body falling to the floor

77.2 It is assumed "someone like that" refers to Karatsu, but the pronoun she uses isn't gendered, so there's a possibility that she means someone else.

78.1 You can set your watch by the Kadokawa references in *Kurosagi*, and here it turns out they run the "Kadokawa Central Hospital," too.

78.3.1 **FX/balloon: SUU KOO**—breathing on a respirator

78.3.2 **FX/balloon: SUU**—breathing on a respirator

78.4 **FX/balloon: GACHYA**—door opening

82.1 The translator notes that her chuckling in the original has the sound *u fu fu*, a sort of "weird, close-mouthed" sound for which it's hard to find an exact equivalent in American English.

82.4 **FX/balloon: KATA**—Clipboard clicking against the desk. Note the chart claims Makino is only *18!* Although that would make her elderly by the standards of many manga, it seems perhaps too young for someone who's presumably been in college a while. Of course, she might have either a.) started college early, or b.) be lying on the form. Sasayama's transition in appearance between *MPD-Psycho* and *Kurosagi* certainly establishes a precedent for uncertainty in an Eiji Otsuka manga.

83.4 **FX: SU**—standing up

85.2 **FX/balloon: KASA KASA**—sawdust rustling

86.1 In Japanese, "ear" is mimi (see 31.5), but in the original manga, Numata heard it as "*mini*," and thought Makino was referring to Minnie Mouse. It's interesting to observe his thought processes.

86.3 In the August 1997 issue of the journal *Plastic and Reconstructive Surgery*. The doctors were Joseph P. Vacanti, Keith T. Paige, and Joseph Upton; the biomaterials engineer was Yilin Cao—although he in fact holds a medical degree as well. Incidentally, the editor started working professionally in the U.S. anime and manga industry while a medical librarian in Houston (it was more *Slacker* than *Reality Bites*), a job that could have inspired any number of *Corpse Delivery Service* stories. The library was eliminated from the Texas Medical Center's budget (and much of its holdings simply thrown away; I made off with a 16mm film in French about onchocerciasis) in part, I was told, because of the massive subscription fees charged at the time to institutions—as much as $15,000 a year per journal. It looked to me back then as if the *real* money was in publishing.

87.5 FX/balloon: CHORO—skitter

89.3 FX: TO TO TO—mouse scampering over

90.2 FX/balloon: GACHYA—door opening

90.4.1 FX/balloon: SUU KOO—breathing on a respirator

90.4.2 FX/balloon: SUU—breathing on a respirator

91.1 FX: SU—soft touch

94.1 FX/balloon: FURARI—unsteady, faltering walk

94.3 FX: PAAAAA—car horn honking

94.4 FX: DOGA—whud! Did you spot the Kadokawa building? The real Kadokawa building, by the way, has their phoenix logo rendered on its front in a pattern of raised bricks.

94.5 FX/balloon: KII—Squealing brakes

95.1 FX: GACHYA—door opening

95.2 In the original Japanese, "big bro" (as said by a man) is *aniki*. Its use in this context suggests the two are involved in organized crime—as small-timers, from the look of it.

96.2 By the way, the Japanese above "MENTAL CLINIC" says "Jenny Kayama," the name of the proprietor.

98.1 FX: GORORI—head rolling over lazily

100.1 FX: DOKO—whump!

105.2 FX: GOOOO—speeding car

106.4 FX: KII—car braking

109.4 FX/balloon: BATAN—door closing sharply

110.1 FX: DOSA—body bag being dumped on the ground

110.4.1 FX/balloon: MOZO GOSO—something rustling inside thick fabric

110.4.2 FX/balloon: KATSU KOTSU—heels clicking on tile

113.1 The letterer notes that this image puts him in mind of the 1999 Korean horror film *Tell Me Something*.

114.4 FX: JIRIRIRIRIRIRI—fire alarm

114.5 FX: GOOOOO—fire roaring

115.1 FX: KYUBON—the sound of a glass-fronted building exploding

115.2 FX/balloon: CHU CHU—mouse squeaking

117.1.1 FX/balloon: BON—container clanging over onto its side

117.1.2 FX/balloon: BAKAN—lid popping off from the heat

117.2 FX: GOOO—fire roaring

117.5 FX/balloon: GOPON—underwater burbling

117.6 FX: SA—Sasaki shifting position, quickly

119.1 FX: KIIIIN—high-pitched ringing in the ears

121.1 The translator notes that Sasaki's spirit form has kept her glasses on, even though she's lost her clothes. But that's the power of a *meganekko*.

122.1 FX: BAGASHAAAN—tank shattering

123.2 FX: DOCHA—splish

123.3.1 FX: PICHA—drip

123.3.2 FX: BECHARI—wet squishing

123.4 FX: PICHIRI—wet bare footstep

128.1 FX: DOSA—Numata dumping the corpse on Yata

128.2 FX/balloon: ZA—quick movement

128.3 FX: DOSU—whump!

129.1 FX: GOOOOOO—roaring fire

129.2 FX/balloon: JIJI—paper sizzling away

129.3.1 FX/balloon: BON—muffled explosion

129.3.2 FX/balloon: PACHIN—glass shattering

130.1 FX/balloon: SA—Sasaki turning quickly

132.4.1 FX: PIIIPOOOPIIIPOOO—fire engine sirens

132.4.2 FX: UUUUUU—alarm

133.1 They are all cosplaying literary detectives: Karatsu as Kousuke Kindaichi—also the "real" protagonist of the movie being parodied in this episode—a fictional Japanese sleuth made famous in the postwar novels of Seishi Yokomizo. The manga series *The Kindaichi Case Files*, released in the U.S. by Tokyopop ("Disjecta Membra"'s cracks taketh away, and "Disjecta Membra"'s cracks giveth) stars Hajime, the supposed grandson of Yokomizo's character, although it is said, much as with *Lupin III*, this is an unauthorized tribute. Makino is doing . . . oh, who could that be. Numata, not surprisingly, is playing private eye Shunsaku Kudo, from the 1979–90 TV series *Tantei Monogatari* ("Detective Story"), portrayed by the late Yusaku Matsuda, an actor still the epitome of cool to many Japanese men—his appearance is said to have inspired that of Spike Spiegel in *Cowboy Bebop*. Anyway, Yata is dressed as Agatha Christie's Belgian, not French, detective Hercule Poirot, whereas Sasaki (rather charmingly) portrays Christie's Miss Marple. The appearance of these last two is possibly inspired by the recent 2004–2005 anime series on NHK,

Agatha Christie's Great Detectives Poirot and Marple (homepage http://www3.nhk.or.jp/anime/agatha/).

134.2.1 FX: JYABU JYABU—splash splash

134.2.2 FX: CHAPU—splish

135.3 The director's shirt has the kanji for *konbu*, seaweed, which is also the character's last name. He is a parody of the late Ichikawa Kon, who died on February 13 of this year at the age of 92, the last surviving representative of a group of directors (including Akira Kurosawa and Hiroshi Inagaki) who brought Japanese cinema to world attention in the 1950s.

136.1 The film being shot here is a parody of Ichikawa Kon's *Inuga-mike no ichizoku*, or *The Inugami Clan*. Written in 1950, this is one of Seishi Yokomizo's famous Kousuke Kindaichi mysteries—the story of the death of silk tycoon Sahei Inugami at his lakeside villa, and the string of gruesome murders over his inheritance that ensue. It has in fact been adapted as a movie three times to date in Japan, in 1954, 1976, and 2006. The last two versions were done by Kon, and the 1976 one, in particular, was one of the biggest domestic box-office successes in Japanese history. It was produced by Haruki Kadokawa—former president of the itself formidable Kadokawa clan. Despite its fame inside Japan, there is no U.S. release on home video, although a Hong Kong (Region 3) DVD under the title *The Inugami Family* is available with English subtitles. An English-language version of the original novel of *The Inugami Clan* is available from my stromies, my homies, Stone Bridge Press (www.stonebridge.com).

137.5 FX: ZUZU—slurping tea. The detective in the parody is named Koutarou Kintaichi rather than Kousuke Kindaichi; "suke" and "tarou" are both common endings for boys' names.

139.3 Koyama has switched from saying "Makino-san" at the beginning of this conversation to saying "Makino-chan" here; indicating he's gone from formal to familiar.

141.3 FX: SU—appearing abruptly

142.3 FX/balloon: KACHI—clapper board clicking

143.1 FX/balloon: GISHI GISHI—old stair treads creaking

143.4 FX: FU—fainting

143.5 FX/balloon: BATAN—fwump

144.1 FX/balloon: CHIRA—peek

146.4 FX: KAAN—megaphone hitting floor

147.2 FX: DOSU DOSU—stomp stomp

148.3 FX: HYUN HYUN—pendulum swinging vigorously

148.5 The translator notes that this is a remarkably awkward name to try to pronounce in English: "ooh-heh-eh-ohh."

149.2 FX: GURARI—teeter

149.3 FX: DOSA—thump

150.3 FX/balloon: JIWA—seep

153.2 FX: BA!—snatching cell phone away

155.1 **FX: PACHA**—splish

155.3.1 **FX: BASHA BASHA**—splash splash

155.3.2 **FX/balloon: SUI**—frog sliding into water

155.7 Makino is, of course, quoting the actress's line from 134.1.

156.5 **FX/balloon: BURORORO**—vrooooom

157.2 **FX: ZA**—footstep

157.6 **FX/balloon: KOKU**—nod

157.7 Judging by Kereellis's expression, that lake must have been mighty chilly, even by the standards of the interstellar void. As the late Sullivan Carew pointed out, "space is one cold motherfucker."

158.3 **FX: GATA**—clatter

158.4 The original Japanese laugh went *hu hu hu hu*, and the translator suggests that English isn't very good at expressing the changing nuance of the laughter here; the first time he laughs, it's a deep-throated chuckle, the second time, it's sort of a menacing snigger, and the last time is full-out maniacal laughter.

159.3 **FX: GU**—tug

159.4 **FX: GU GU**—pulling the mask off

159.5 **FX: PASA**—mask hitting the floor

162.6 **FX: BA**—Koyama turning back quickly

163.3 **FX: DOSU**—heavy thump

164.2 **FX/balloon: BURORORO**—vrooooom

164.4 **FX/balloon: GAKO GAKO**—empty clunking

165.1.1 FX: GON—muted explosion

165.1.2 FX: BAKI—snap

165.1.3 FX/balloon: BO—bursting into flames

165.3.1 FX: BAKI BEKI—snapping underbrush noises

165.3.2 FX/balloon: BA—car becoming airborne

166.1 **FX/balloon: SU**—hand being raised

166.5 **FX: DOSA**—heavy thud

167.1 **FX/balloon: JI JI JI**—body bag zipper being unzipped

172.4 **FX: DOCHA**—wet squelch

173.4 **FX: SU**—placing fingers on corpse

174.3 **FX: YURA**—pendulum beginning to swing

174.4 **FX: HYUN HYUN**—pendulum swinging violently

175.2 **FX: MUKU**—corpse getting up

175.3 **FX: YURARI**—corpse swaying on its feet

176.3 In the original, Makino uses the technical term *kaeri chi*, meant specifically to refer to blood that splashes back onto the killer from their victim; it is also used when discussing this phenomenon in close combat. This might be a good time to note that I've been seeing a lot of Spartans at anime and manga cons lately. As a purist I should object, but as a Dark Horse employee, I just pretend they're from *Arion*. Now, every once in a while you'll have an Akiba moment in Portland. Today, about 11 AM, I saw an individual in full Stormtrooper kit walking across Burnside at

21st. Burnside is one of our main streets, four lanes, supermarkets, gas stations, what have you. It was an odd hour for a costume party, and if it was for a graduation, there weren't any schools for several blocks. But to paraphrase LL Cool J, I love it when an otaku ain't scared to do his thing.

176.6 FX: SA!—Koyama hastily covering the stain

177.2 FX: DA DA DA—heavy running footsteps

177.3.1 FX/balloon: SA!—brandishing box cutter

177.3.2 FX/balloon: CHIKI CHIKI CHIKI—box cutter blade being extended

177.4 FX: BA!—Koyama yanking the director to him

179.1 FX: BUN BUN—swinging the box cutter around

180.1 FX: SHIN—silence

180.5 FX: GORO GORO—roll roll

180.6 FX/balloon: TON—light tap

181.2 FX: BA!—eyes and mouth flying open

181.4 FX: NUU—loom

184.2.1 FX/balloon: DA DA TA—running feet

184.2.2 FX: BA!—door being yanked open

184.6 FX: SU!—director raising his hand

186.2 FX: PASA—mask falling to floor

187.2 The close-up on the billboard in panel 1 and the film program Yata is reading in panel 3 (while rare in America, theater-style film program books are a common marketing tool in Japan; in the 1980s and '90s, the program books for anime films were much-sought-after import items by American fans hungry for images and info) says *The Corpse Detective*, naturally. It's playing on screen 2 of the Shinjuku Milano, a real movie house that as of this writing (June 2008) was screening *Shoot 'Em Up, Prince Caspian*, and *Rambo*—the last of which, as Patrick Macias has detailed, had a much better promo campaign in Japan, where you could get the Rambo Hot Dog (deployed on camouflage cardboard for "sneaking snacking"), the Rambo coffee-based energy drink, and the Rambo crocodile burger, served on an eco-friendly palm leaf. Gory pictures on the May 18 posting at patrickmacias.blogs.com, which you really should be reading every day anyway. Playing next door appears to be the *Keroro Gunso* (known as *Sgt. Frog* in the U.S.) movie *The Deep Sea Princess*. Movie tickets for an adult in Tokyo, by the way, average 1800 yen; one reason manga are so successful is that they're one of the few entertainment *values* in Japan—they pay more than Americans for DVDs, CDs, and even songs on iTunes.

187.3 FX/balloon: PARA—page turning

188.4 We're working on it! Seriously, we are. You know Dark Horse doesn't give up when it comes to making titles into movies (or TV shows). It took forty-five years between *Iron Man* the comic and the movie—I bet you we do better than that. And thanks to everyone who's supporting *The Kurosagi Corpse Delivery Service*—see you in January 2009 for Volume 8!

STOP!

THIS IS THE BACK OF THE BOOK!

This manga collection is translated into English, but arranged in right-to-left reading format to maintain the artwork's visual orientation as originally drawn and published in Japan. If you've never read comics this way before, take a look at the diagram below to give yourself an idea of how to go about it. Basically, you'll be starting in the upper right-hand corner, and will read each word balloon and panel moving right to left. It may take a little getting used to, but you should get the hang of it very quickly. Have fun! If this is the millionth manga you've read this way, never mind. ^_^

1
...
2
THEY TALK TO YOU BECAUSE YOU'RE THE KIND OF GUY WHO CAN'T SAY NO.
3
...YES.
4
RIGHT. SO LET'S TAKE THIS HORRIBLE, STINKING, ROTTING THING BACK TO CAMPUS. QUICK, BEFORE THE COPS NOTICE.
5
BACK TO CAMPUS?!
6
KARATSU, THERE'S NOTHING IN THE HANDBOOK THAT SAYS STUDENTS CAN'T POSSESS CORPSES--OR, IN YOUR CASE, VICE-VERSA.

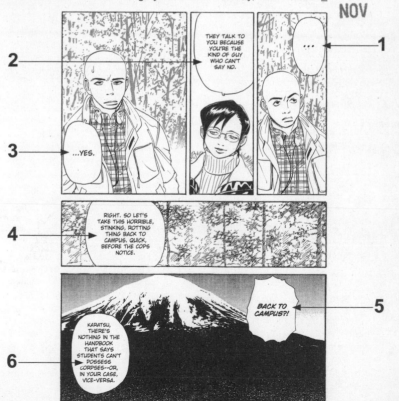

This is the last page.

BEASTARS reads from right to left to preserve the orientation of the original Japanese artwork.

RUBY ROSE

WEISS SCHNEE

BLAKE BELLADONNA

YANG XIAO LONG

RWBY

OFFICIAL MANGA ANTHOLOGIES

Original Concept by Monty Oum & Rooster Teeth Productions, Story and Art by Various Artists

All-new stories featuring Ruby, Weiss, Blake and Yang from Rooster Teeth's hit animation series!

 VIZ

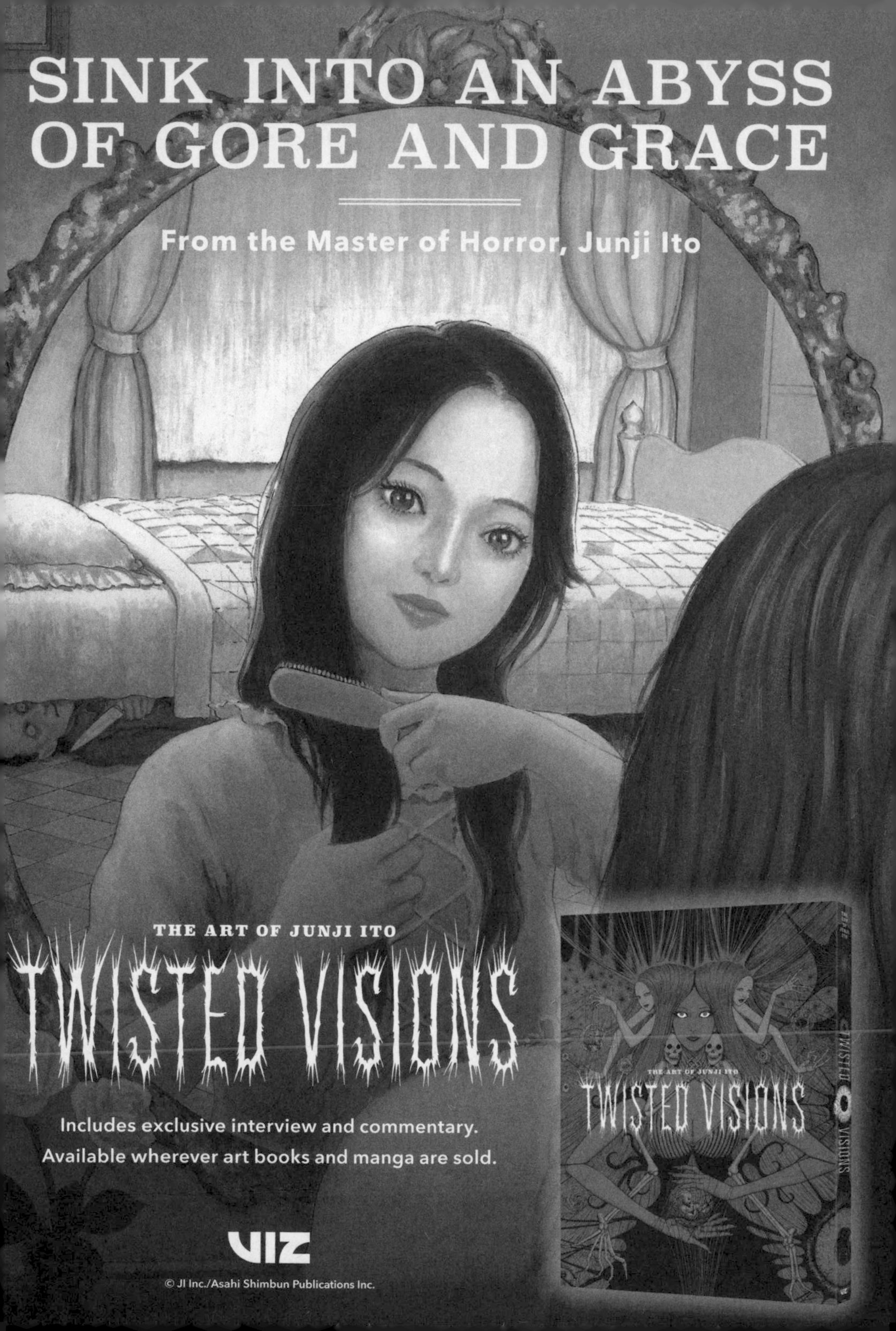
SINK INTO AN ABYSS
OF GORE AND GRACE
From the Master of Horror, Junji Ito
THE ART OF JUNJI ITO
TWISTED VISIONS
Includes exclusive interview and commentary.
Available wherever art books and manga are sold.
VIZ
© JI Inc./Asahi Shimbun Publications Inc.
THE ART OF JUNJI ITO
TWISTED VISIONS

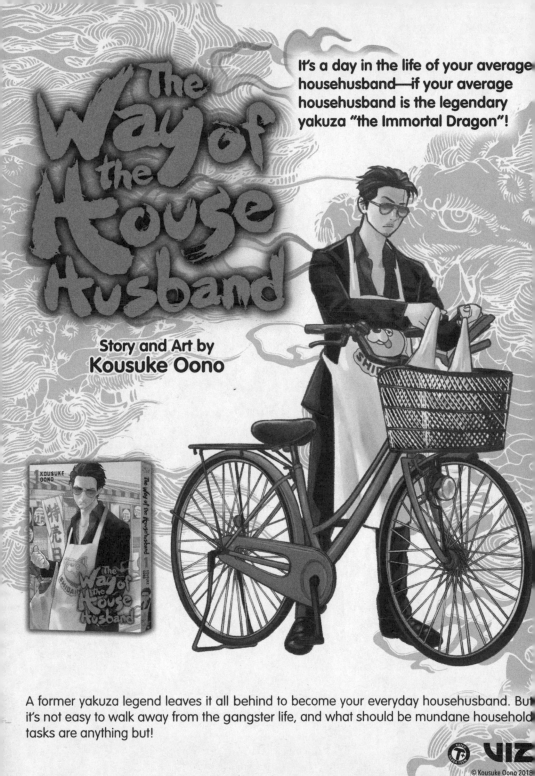

IN THE ORIGINAL CLASSIC MANGA set in a postapocalyptic wasteland ruled by savage gangs, a hero appears to bring justice to the guilty. This warrior named Ken holds the deadly secrets of a mysterious martial art known as Hokuto Shinken—the Divine Fist of the North Star!

Story by **BURONSON**   Art by **TETSUO HARA**

Six short stories that set the scene for the best-selling *BEASTARS* series!

BEAST COMPLEX

Story and Art by **Paru Itagaki**

In these six stories from the creator of the Eisner-nominated, best-selling series BEASTARS, a menagerie of carnivores and herbivores grapple with conflicts based on their differences and— sometimes—find common ground.

COMING IN VOLUME 18...

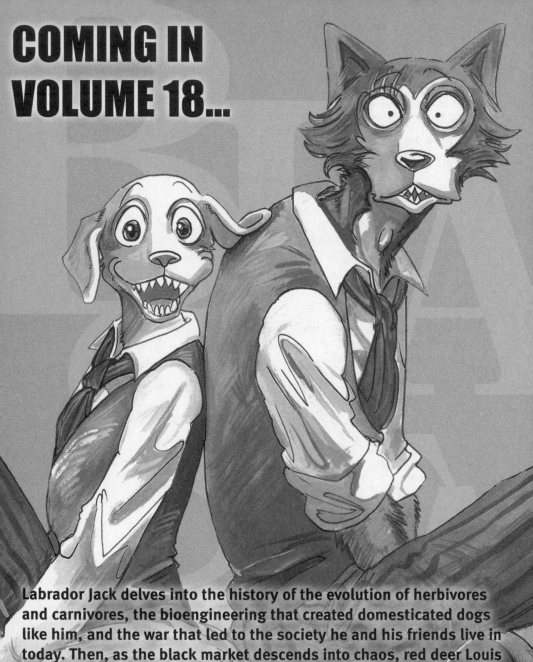

Labrador Jack delves into the history of the evolution of herbivores and carnivores, the bioengineering that created domesticated dogs like him, and the war that led to the society he and his friends live in today. Then, as the black market descends into chaos, red deer Louis encounters old comrades from his miserable childhood and Legoshi begs one to train him in combat. Plus, Bengal tiger Bill gets a big surprise when he cracks open an egg!

BEASTARS
VOL. 17
VIZ Signature Edition

Story & Art by
Paru Itagaki

Translation/Tomo Kimura
English Adaptation/Annette Roman
Touch-Up Art & Lettering/Susan Daigle-Leach
Cover & Interior Design/Yukiko Whitley
Editor/Annette Roman

Printed in the U.S.A.

Published by VIZ Media, LLC
P.O. Box 77010
San Francisco, CA 94107

10 9 8 7 6 5 4 3 2 1
First printing, March 2022

 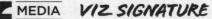

viz.com   vizsignature.com

I DREW A LOT OF COLOR
ILLUSTRATIONS IN 2019.
I HOPE TO HAVE AN ART BOOK
PUBLISHED SOMEDAY.
I'D LIKE THE BOOK BINDING TO BE
BEAUTIFUL BUT NOT TOO ORNATE.

PARU ITAGAKI

Paru Itagaki began her professional
career as a manga author in 2016 with the
short story collection **BEAST COMPLEX**.
BEASTARS is her first serialization.
BEASTARS has won multiple awards in
Japan, including the prestigious 2018
Manga Taisho Award.

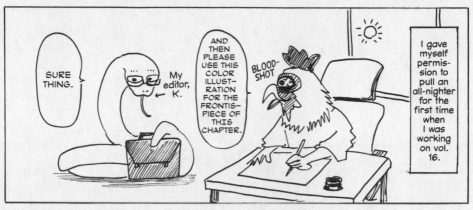

I gave myself permission to pull an all-nighter for the first time when I was working on vol. 16.
AND THEN PLEASE USE THIS COLOR ILLUSTRATION FOR THE FRONTISPIECE OF THIS CHAPTER.
BLOODSHOT
...
My editor, K.
SURE THING.
We were very busy back then. K looked desperate as he was about to leave. He was reviewing what he had to do out loud...
Okay, that needs to get done by tomorrow... And this needs to get done by...
Watching him, I was suddenly overcome with the urge to laugh.
...
PFFFT
BWA HA HA HA HA HA HA...
...
K, YOU'RE SO FUNNY! BWAH HA HA HA!
HEY, K! WHY AREN'T YOU SAYING ANYTHING? PLEASE LAUGH WITH ME.
AHA HA HA HA... THIS IS TOO FUNNY. BWA HA HA HA HA! HEE HEE! PLEASE LAUGH, PLEASE LAUGH!
K later told me...
People act drunk after pulling all-nighters.
Apparently, I'm an obnoxious "drunk." I can't drink alcohol, so I wasn't aware of this.
?
After sleeping it off, I returned to normal.
I'm glad I can't drink...

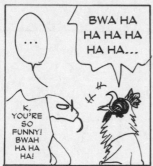

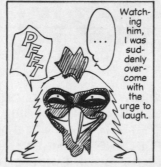

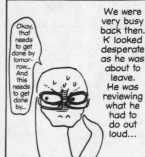

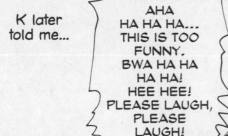

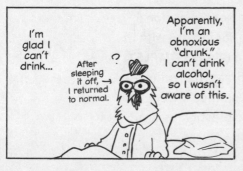

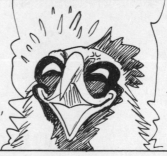

*There are many theories about this.
(A note from the editorial department.)

How the Two-Page Spread in Chapter 106 (vol. 12) Was Created

Storyboard ➡

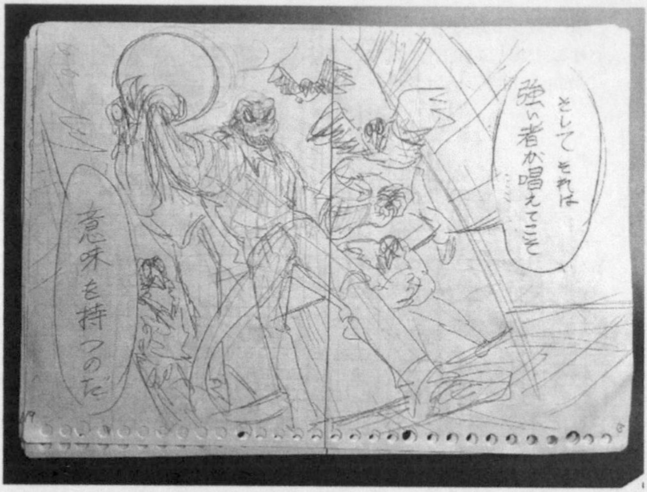
そして それは
強い者が唱えてこそ
意味を持つのだ

Rough draft ➡

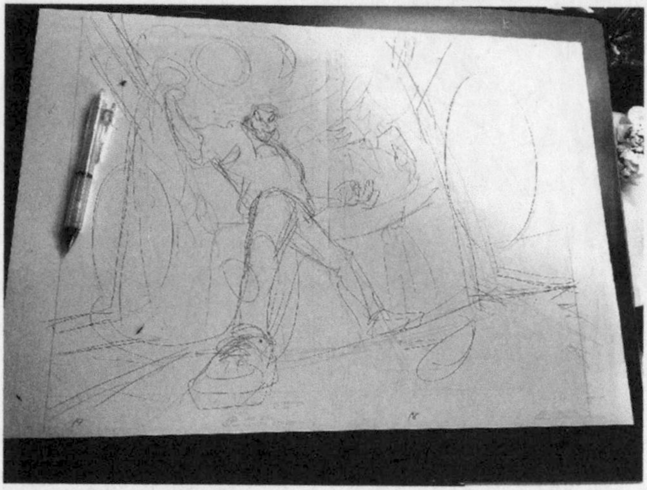

My assistants draw the background and sound effects.

Done! ➡

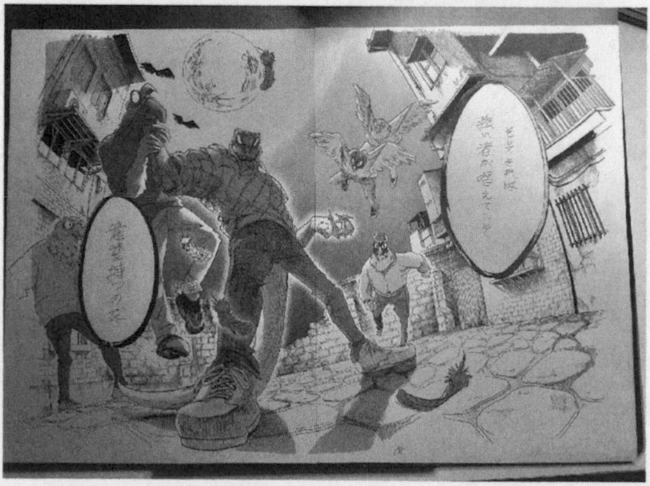

Legoshi keeps getting scars because he's overconfident and thinks he's too tough for anything to hurt him. He only looks in the mirror about twice a month, so he forgets about the scar above his right eye. But when he does look in the mirror, he can't stop staring at it.

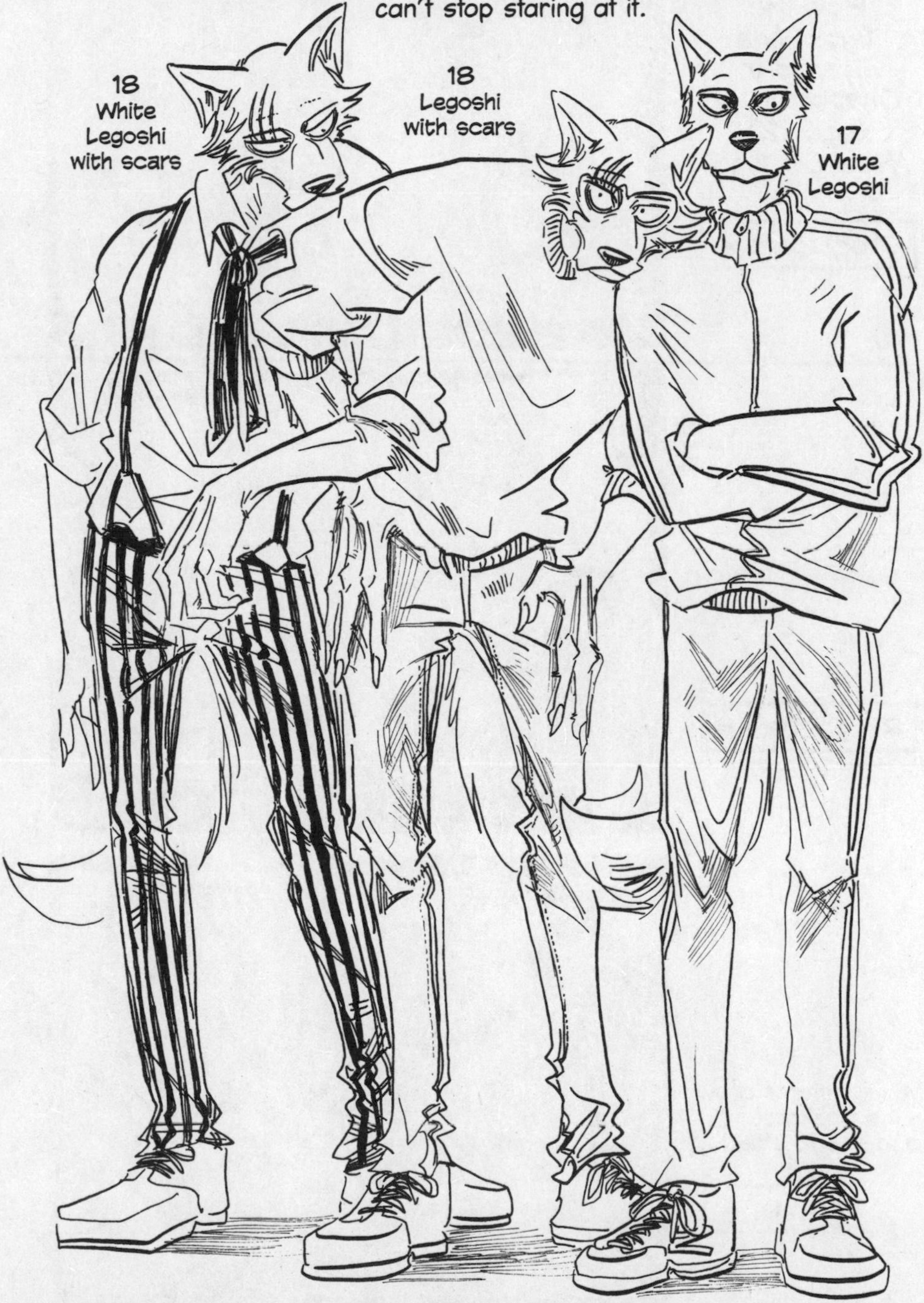
18
White
Legoshi
with scars
18
Legoshi
with scars
17
White
Legoshi

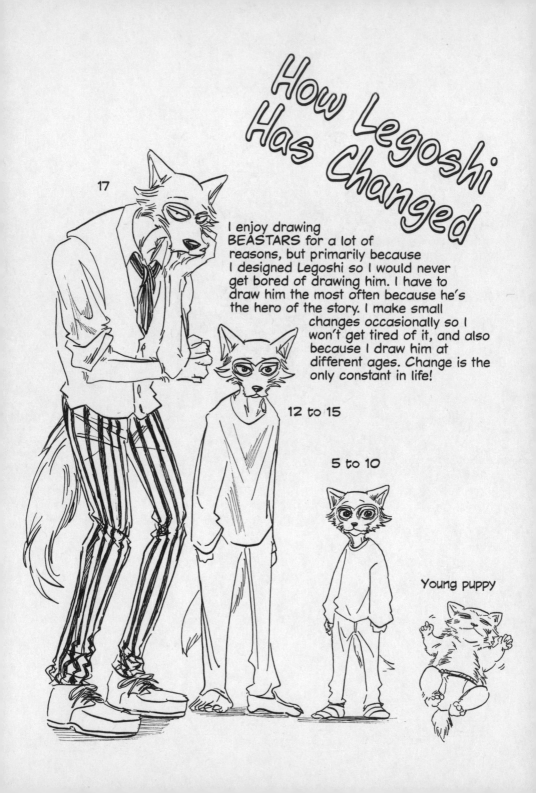

How Legoshi Has Changed

I enjoy drawing **BEASTARS** for a lot of reasons, but primarily because I designed Legoshi so I would never get bored of drawing him. I have to draw him the most often because he's the hero of the story. I make small changes occasionally so I won't get tired of it, and also because I draw him at different ages. Change is the only constant in life!

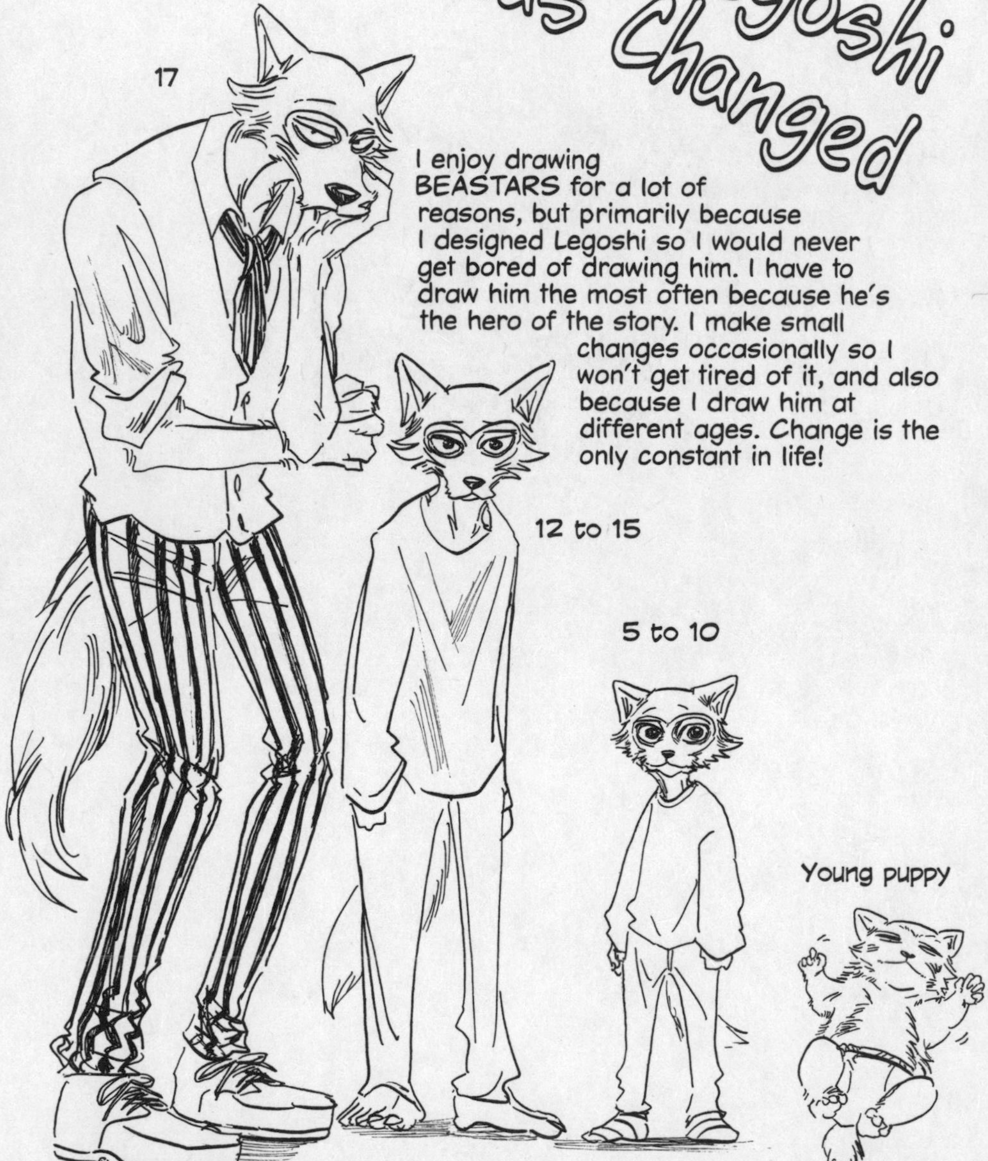
17
12 to 15
5 to 10
Young puppy

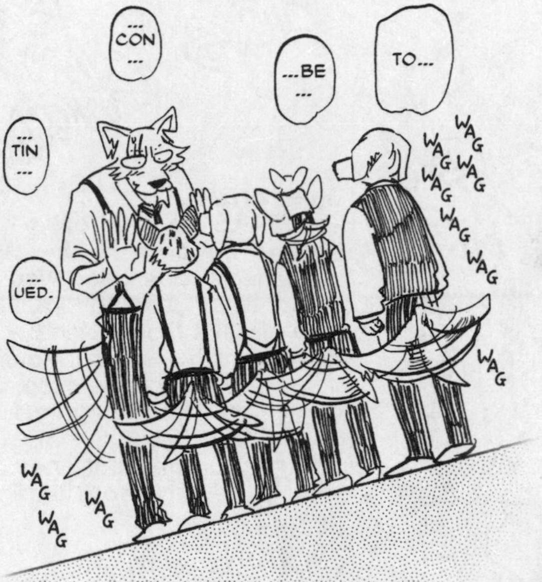
TO...
...BE...
...CON...
...TIN...
...UED.
WAG WAG WAG WAG WAG WAG
WAG
WAG WAG WAG

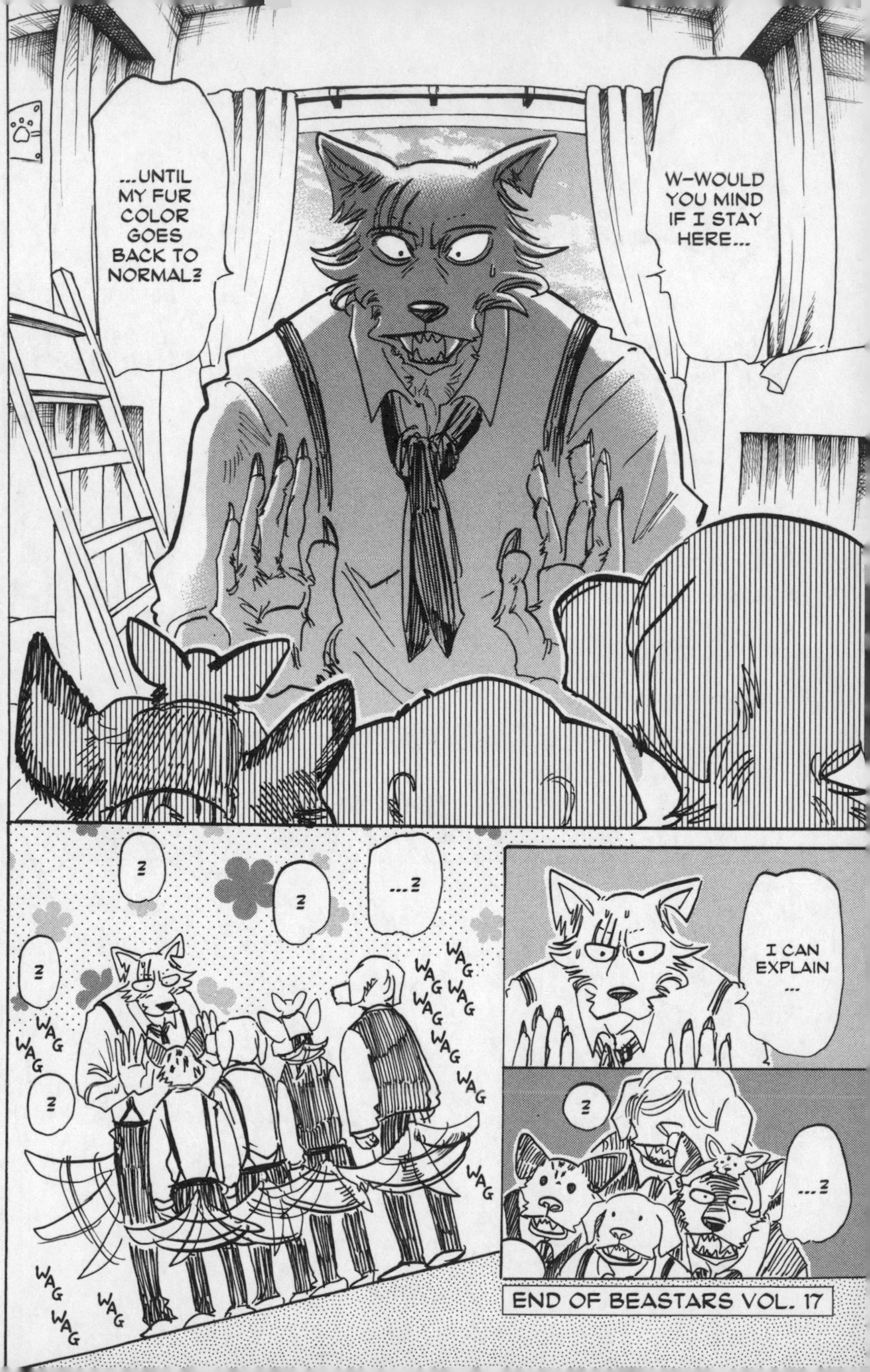
W-WOULD YOU MIND IF I STAY HERE...
...UNTIL MY FUR COLOR GOES BACK TO NORMAL?
I CAN EXPLAIN ...
?
...?
END OF BEASTARS VOL. 17
...?
?
?
?
?
WAG WAG WAG WAG WAG WAG WAG WAG
WAG
WAG WAG
WAG WAG WAG

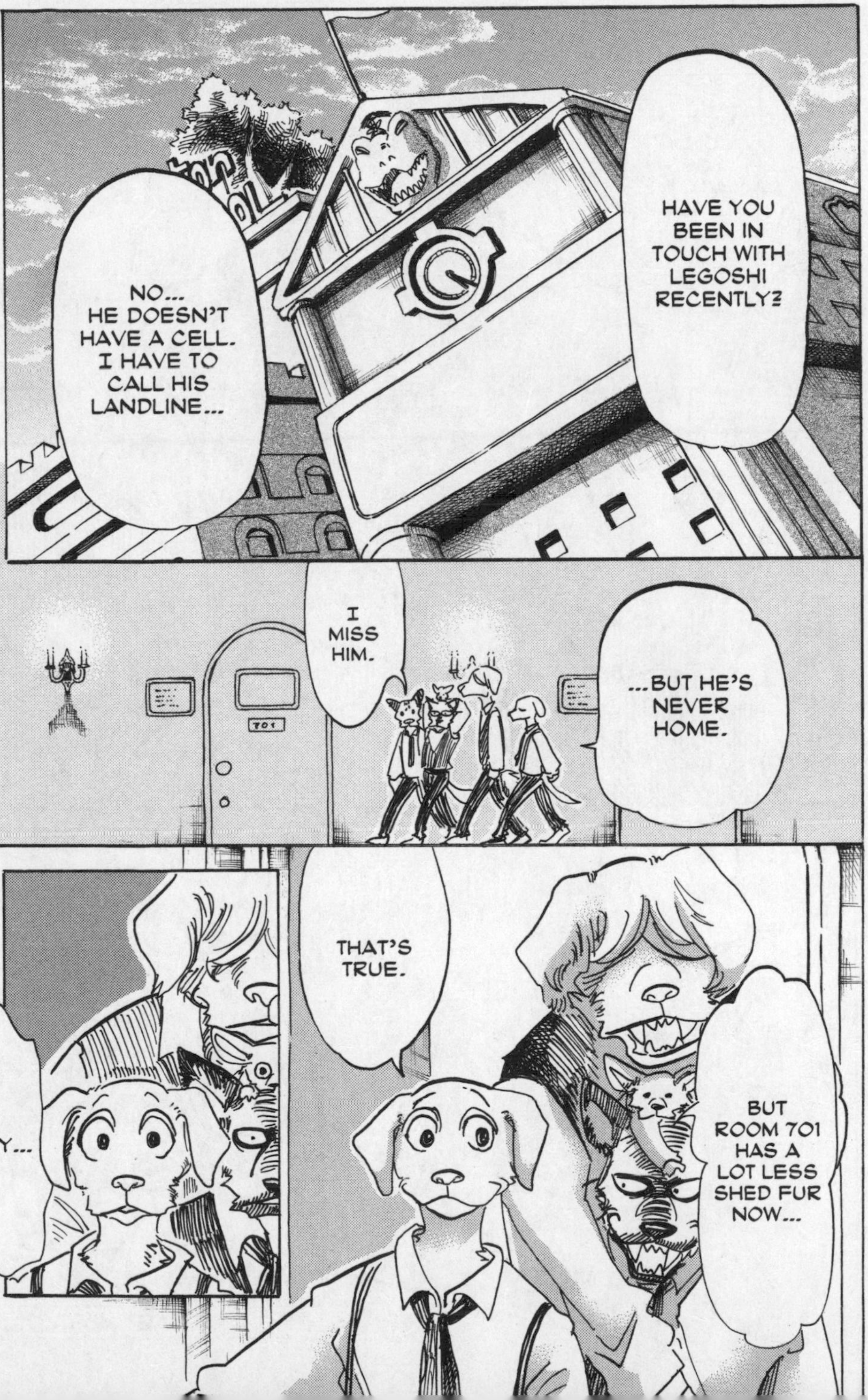
HAVE YOU BEEN IN TOUCH WITH LEGOSHI RECENTLY?
NO... HE DOESN'T HAVE A CELL. I HAVE TO CALL HIS LANDLINE...
...BUT HE'S NEVER HOME.
I MISS HIM.
BUT ROOM 701 HAS A LOT LESS SHED FUR NOW...
THAT'S TRUE.
HEY...

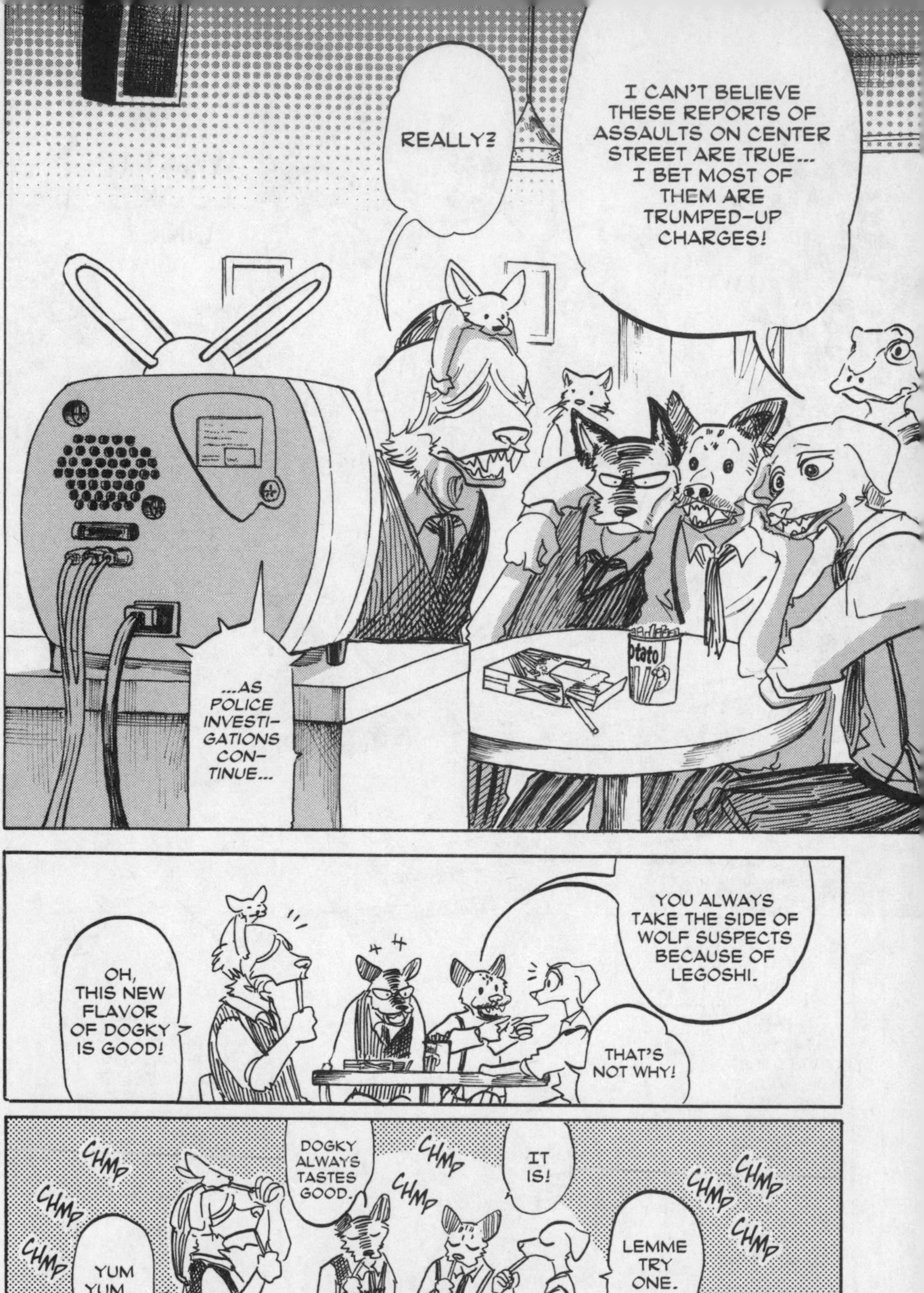
I CAN'T BELIEVE THESE REPORTS OF ASSAULTS ON CENTER STREET ARE TRUE... I BET MOST OF THEM ARE TRUMPED-UP CHARGES!
REALLY?
...AS POLICE INVESTI-GATIONS CON-TINUE...
YOU ALWAYS TAKE THE SIDE OF WOLF SUSPECTS BECAUSE OF LEGOSHI.
THAT'S NOT WHY!
OH, THIS NEW FLAVOR OF DOGKY IS GOOD!
CHMP CHMP CHMP
IT IS!
LEMME TRY ONE.
CHMP
CHMP
CHMP
DOGKY ALWAYS TASTES GOOD.
CHMP CHMP CHMP
YUM YUM...

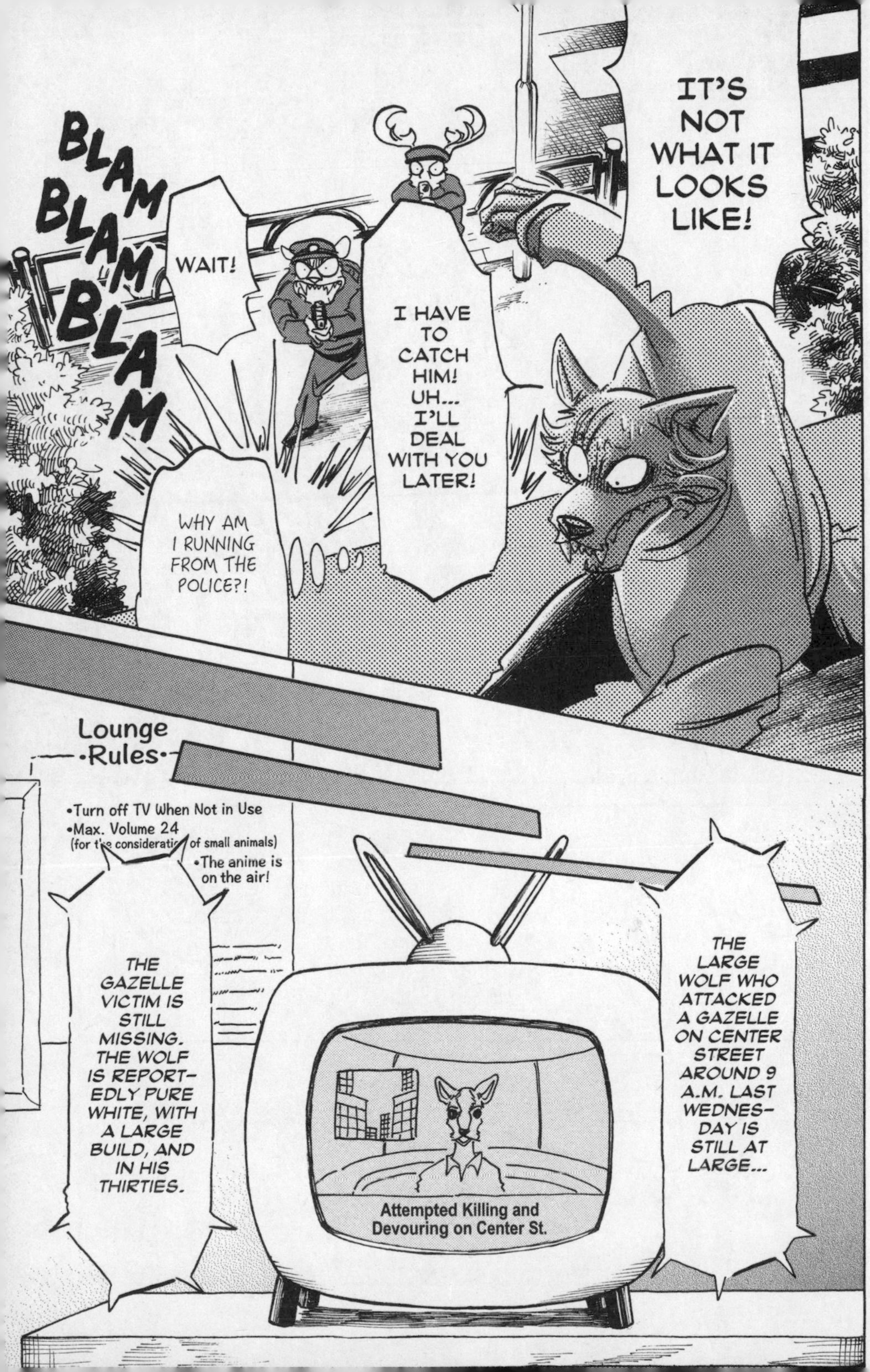
IT'S NOT WHAT IT LOOKS LIKE!
WAIT!
I HAVE TO CATCH HIM! UH... I'LL DEAL WITH YOU LATER!
BLAM BLAM BLAM BLAM
WHY AM I RUNNING FROM THE POLICE?!
Lounge •Rules•
•Turn off TV When Not in Use
•Max. Volume 24 (for the consideration of small animals)
•The anime is on the air!
THE LARGE WOLF WHO ATTACKED A GAZELLE ON CENTER STREET AROUND 9 A.M. LAST WEDNESDAY IS STILL AT LARGE...
Attempted Killing and Devouring on Center St.
THE GAZELLE VICTIM IS STILL MISSING. THE WOLF IS REPORTEDLY PURE WHITE, WITH A LARGE BUILD, AND IN HIS THIRTIES.

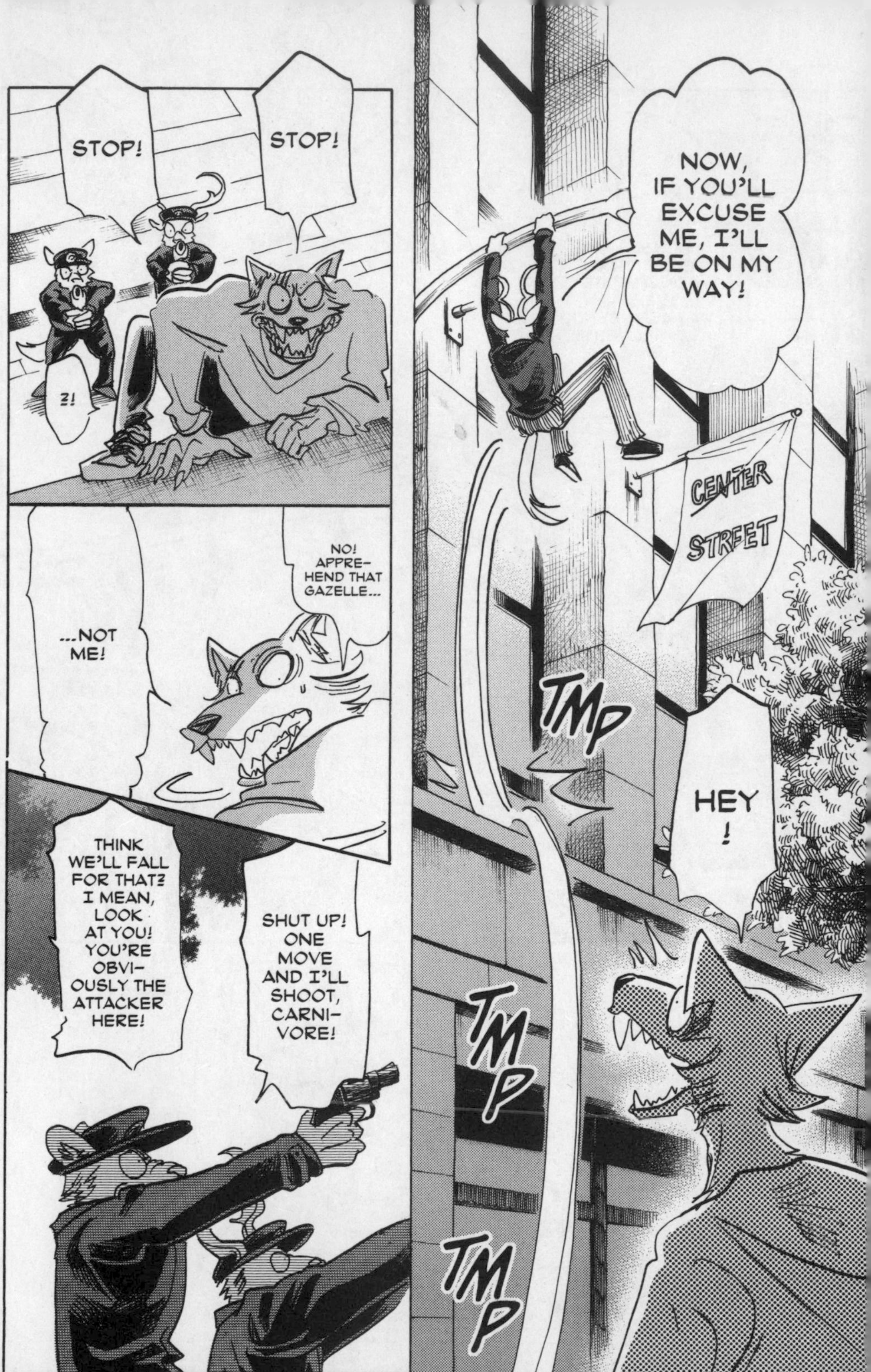
NOW, IF YOU'LL EXCUSE ME, I'LL BE ON MY WAY!
CENTER STREET
TMP
HEY!
TMP
TMP
STOP!
STOP!
?!
NO! APPREHEND THAT GAZELLE...
...NOT ME!
SHUT UP! ONE MOVE AND I'LL SHOOT, CARNIVORE!
THINK WE'LL FALL FOR THAT? I MEAN, LOOK AT YOU! YOU'RE OBVIOUSLY THE ATTACKER HERE!

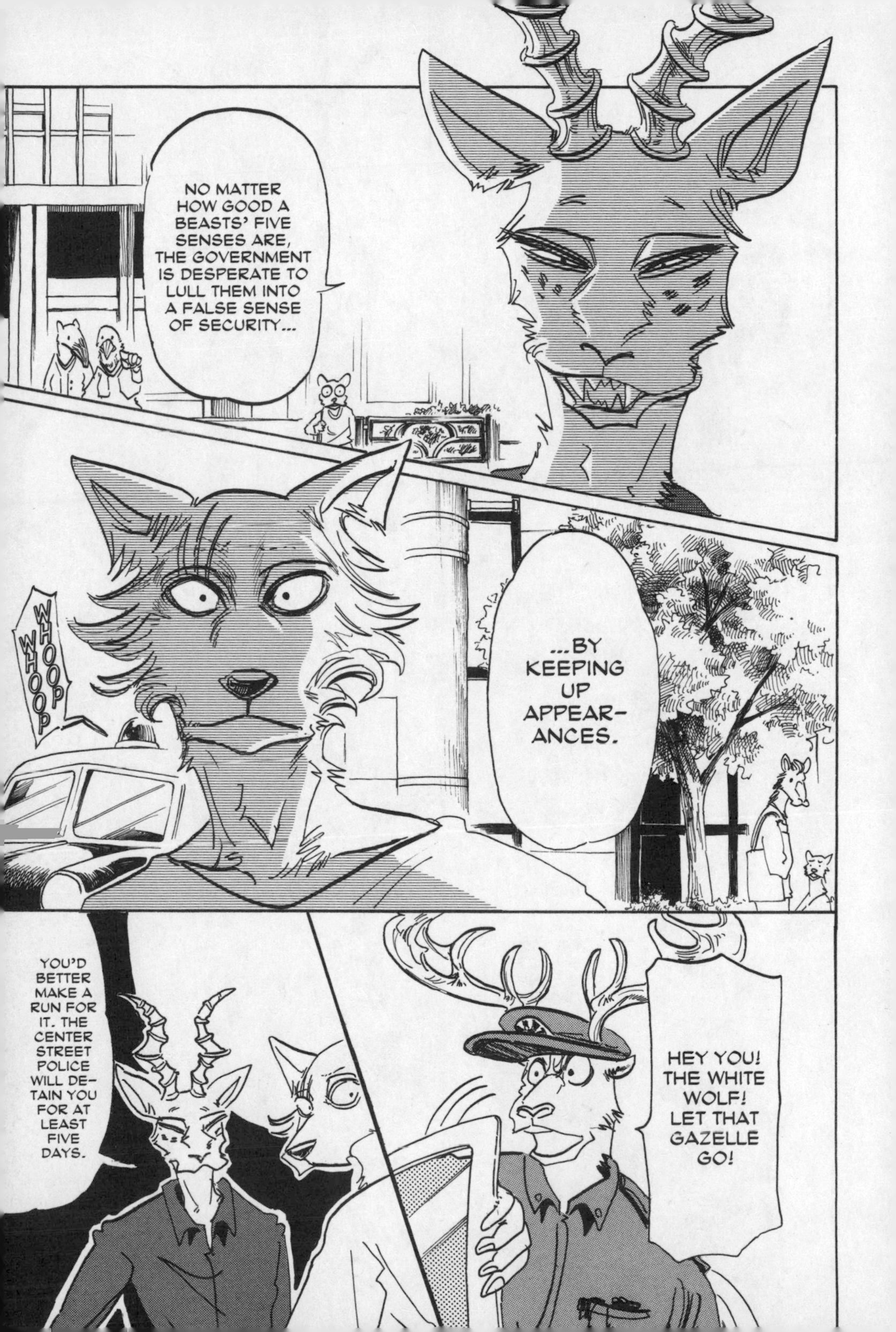
NO MATTER HOW GOOD A BEASTS' FIVE SENSES ARE, THE GOVERNMENT IS DESPERATE TO LULL THEM INTO A FALSE SENSE OF SECURITY...
...BY KEEPING UP APPEAR-ANCES.
WHOOP WHOOP
HEY YOU! THE WHITE WOLF! LET THAT GAZELLE GO!
YOU'D BETTER MAKE A RUN FOR IT. THE CENTER STREET POLICE WILL DE-TAIN YOU FOR AT LEAST FIVE DAYS.

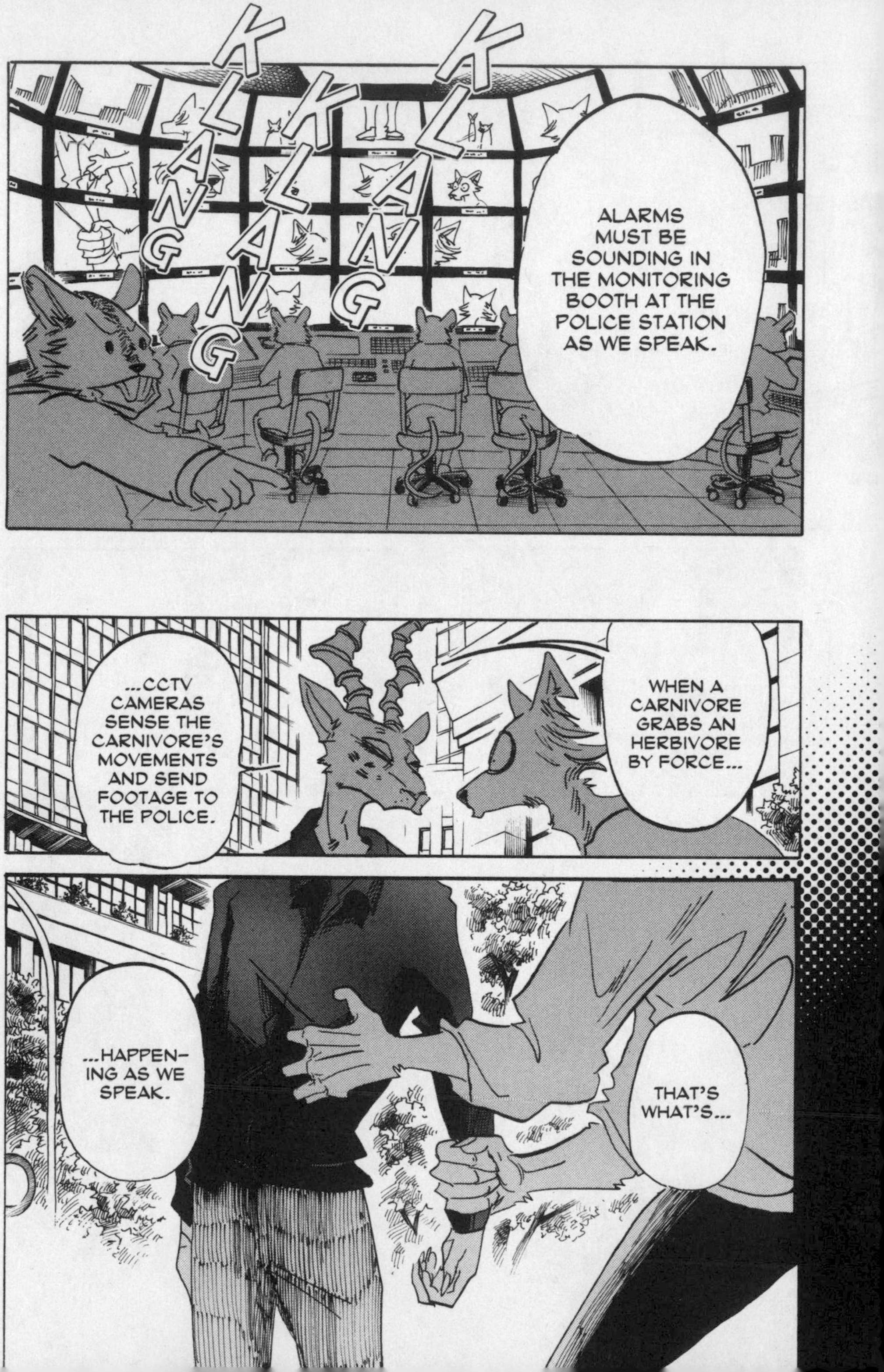
KLANG
KLANG
KLANG
ALARMS MUST BE SOUNDING IN THE MONITORING BOOTH AT THE POLICE STATION AS WE SPEAK.
WHEN A CARNIVORE GRABS AN HERBIVORE BY FORCE...
...CCTV CAMERAS SENSE THE CARNIVORE'S MOVEMENTS AND SEND FOOTAGE TO THE POLICE.
THAT'S WHAT'S...
...HAPPEN-ING AS WE SPEAK.

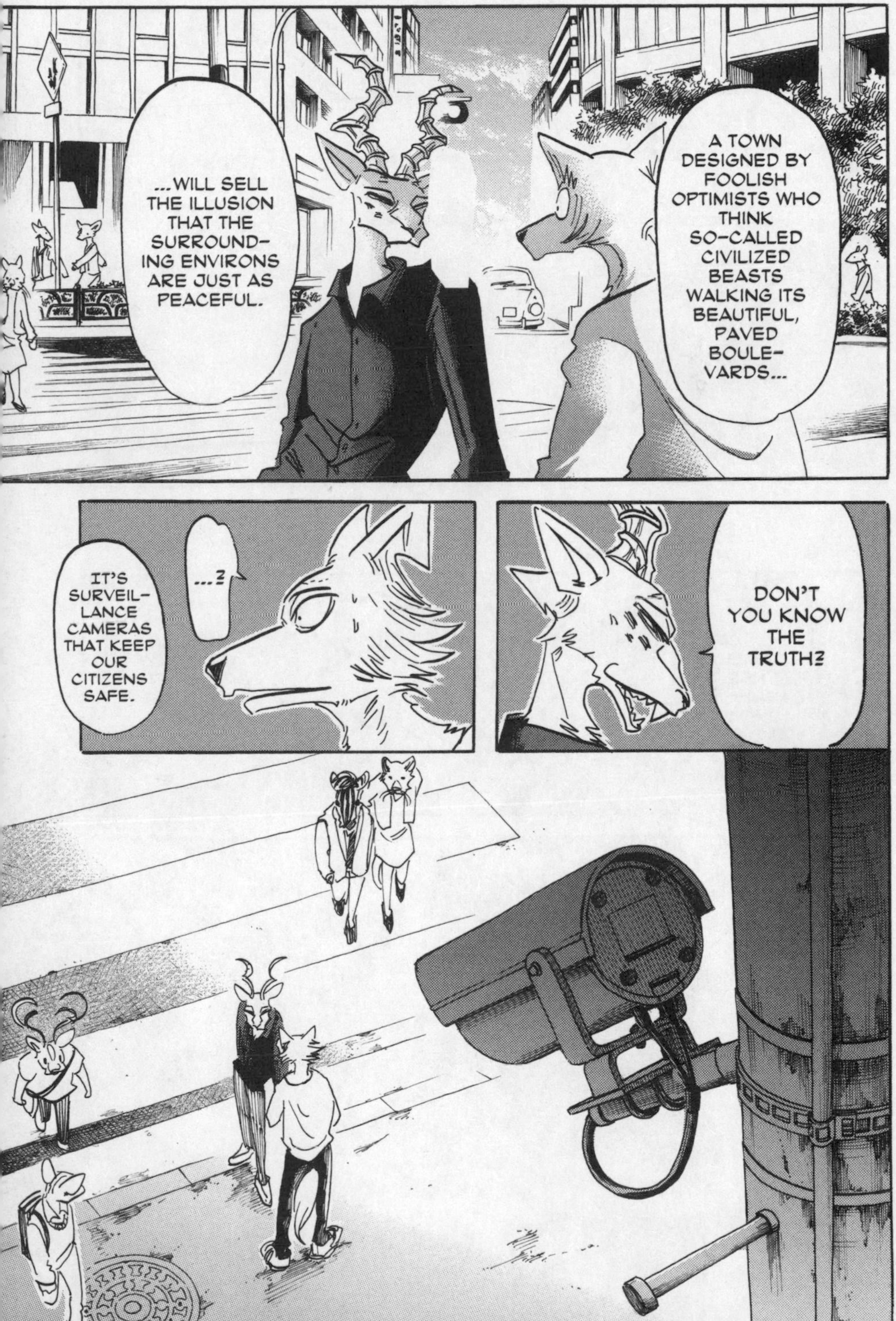
A TOWN DESIGNED BY FOOLISH OPTIMISTS WHO THINK SO-CALLED CIVILIZED BEASTS WALKING ITS BEAUTIFUL, PAVED BOULE-VARDS...
...WILL SELL THE ILLUSION THAT THE SURROUND-ING ENVIRONS ARE JUST AS PEACEFUL.
DON'T YOU KNOW THE TRUTH?
...?
IT'S SURVEIL-LANCE CAMERAS THAT KEEP OUR CITIZENS SAFE.

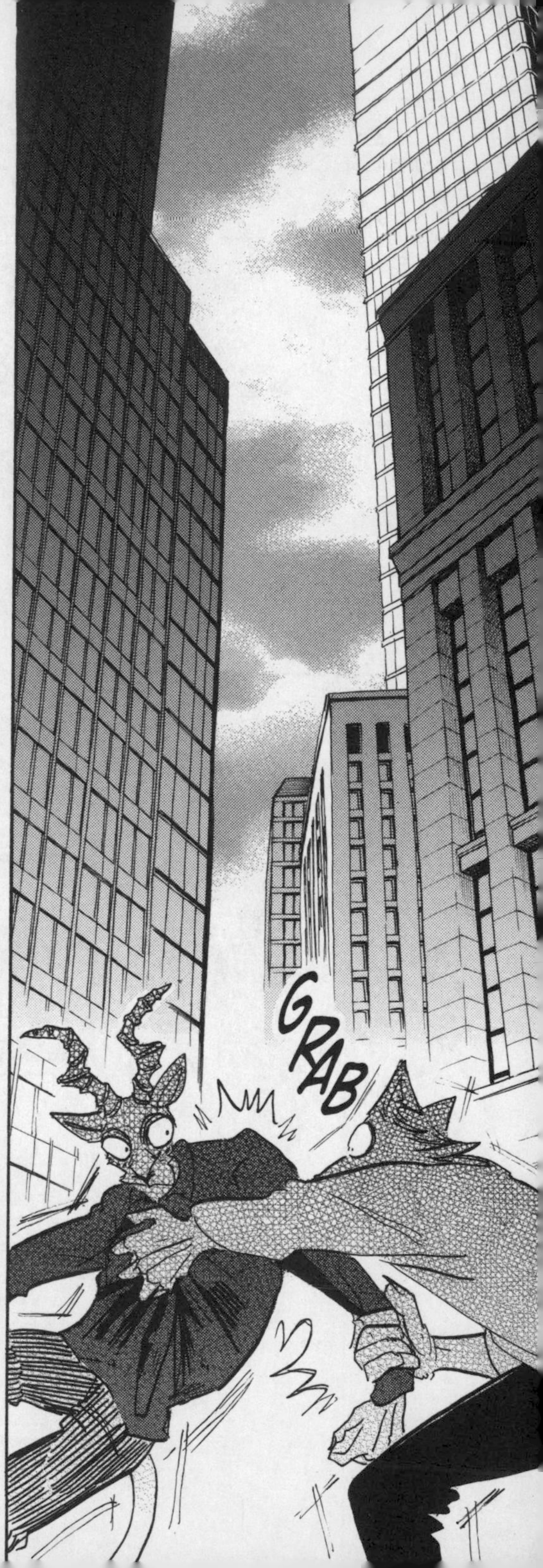
GRAB
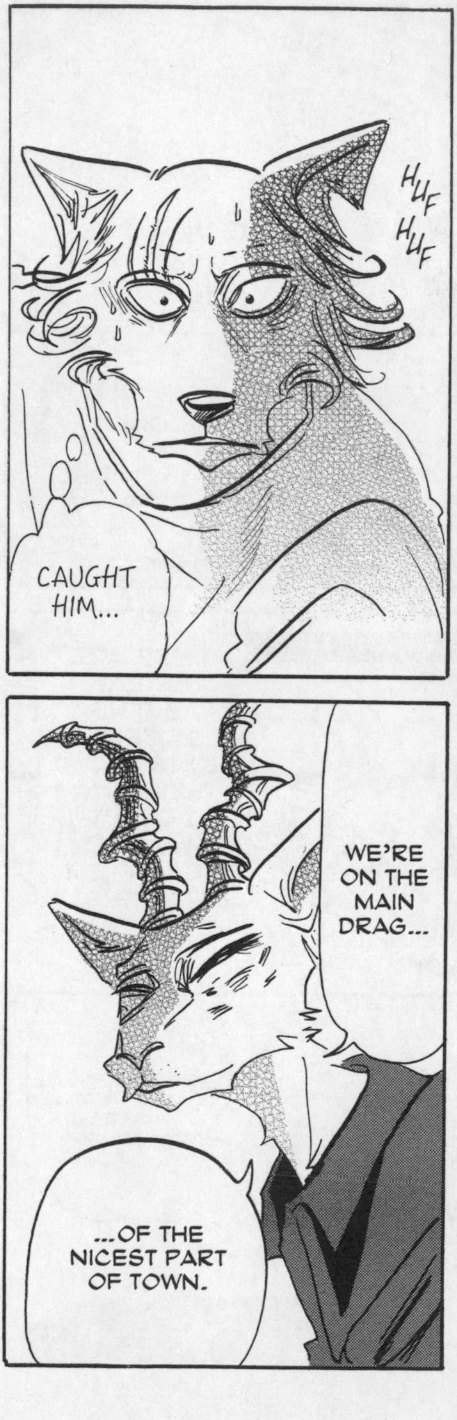
HUF HUF
CAUGHT HIM...
WE'RE ON THE MAIN DRAG...
...OF THE NICEST PART OF TOWN.

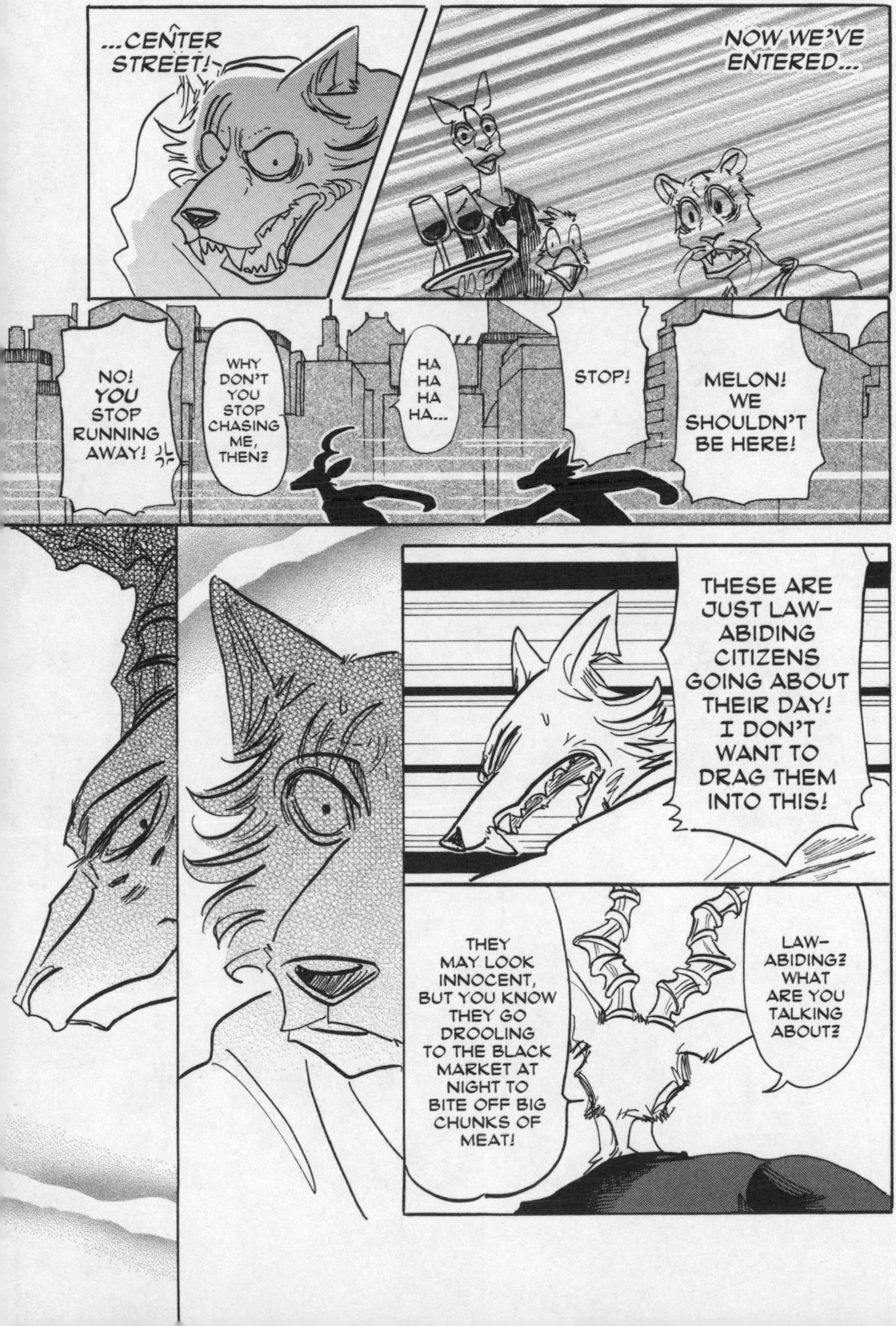
NOW WE'VE ENTERED...
...CENTER STREET!
MELON! WE SHOULDN'T BE HERE!
STOP!
HA HA HA HA...
WHY DON'T YOU STOP CHASING ME, THEN?
NO! *YOU* STOP RUNNING AWAY!
THESE ARE JUST LAW-ABIDING CITIZENS GOING ABOUT THEIR DAY! I DON'T WANT TO DRAG THEM INTO THIS!
LAW-ABIDING? WHAT ARE YOU TALKING ABOUT?
THEY MAY LOOK INNOCENT, BUT YOU KNOW THEY GO DROOLING TO THE BLACK MARKET AT NIGHT TO BITE OFF BIG CHUNKS OF MEAT!

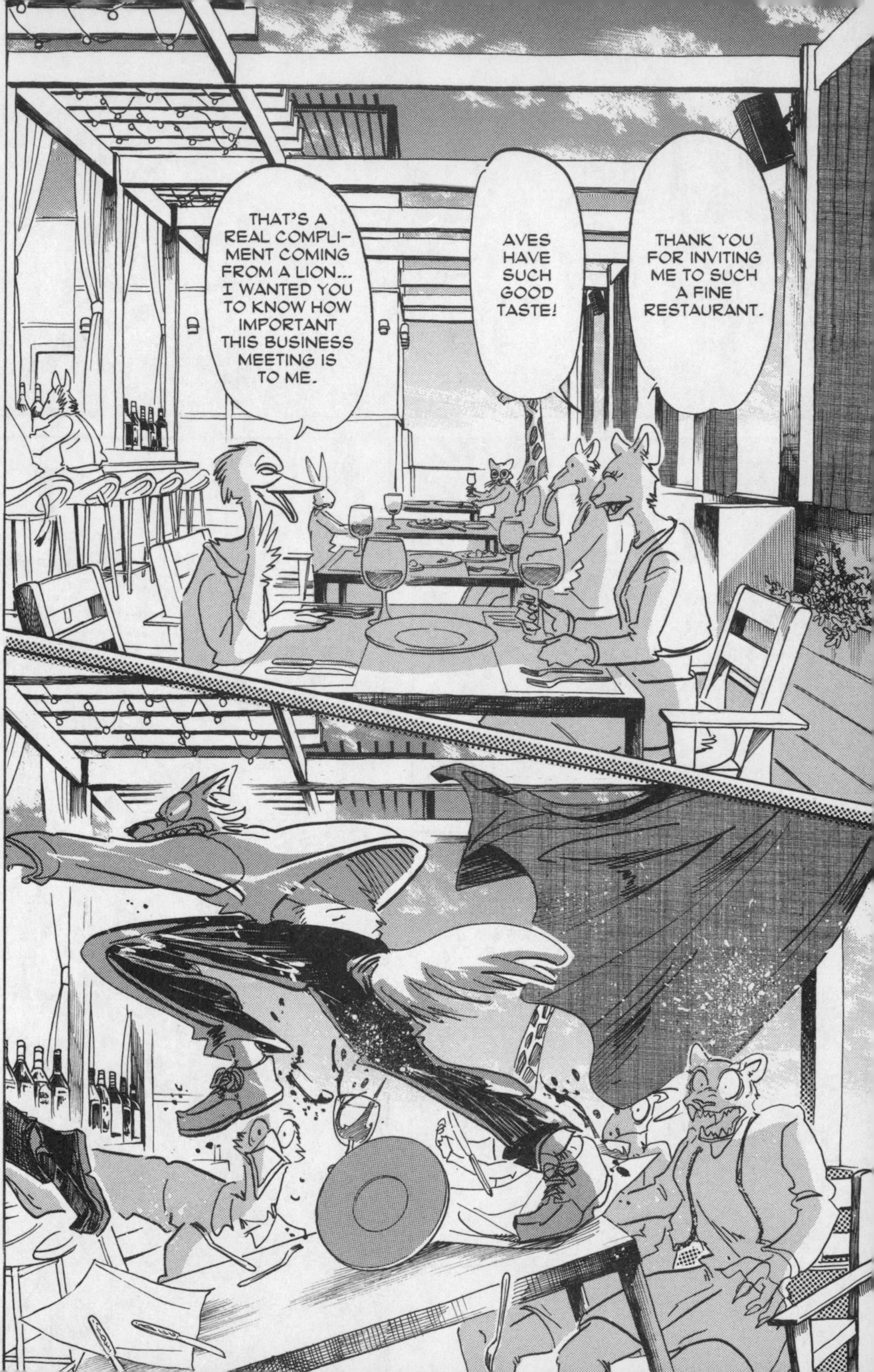
THANK YOU FOR INVITING ME TO SUCH A FINE RESTAURANT.
AVES HAVE SUCH GOOD TASTE!
THAT'S A REAL COMPLI-MENT COMING FROM A LION... I WANTED YOU TO KNOW HOW IMPORTANT THIS BUSINESS MEETING IS TO ME.

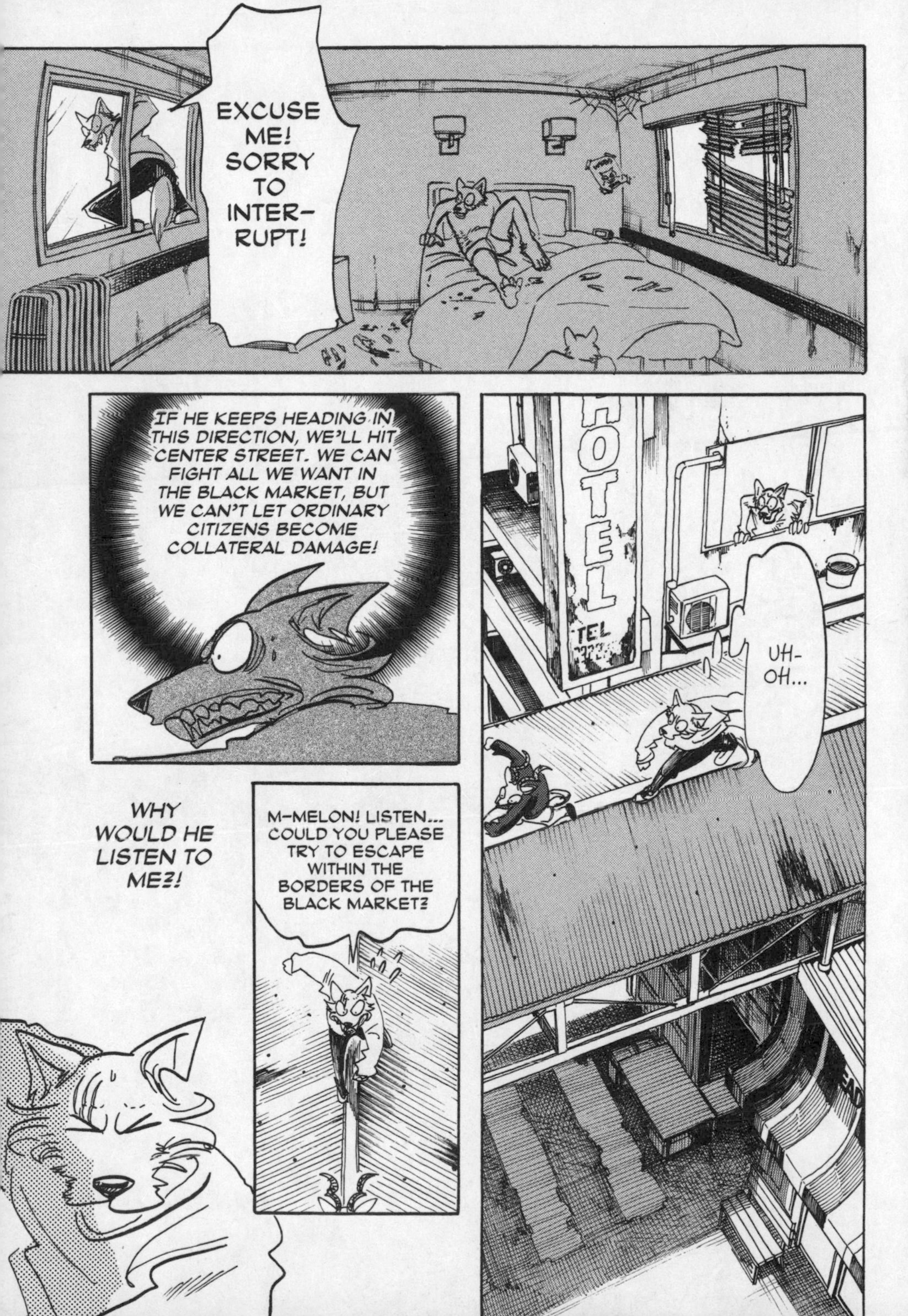
EXCUSE ME! SORRY TO INTER-RUPT!
HOTEL
UH-OH...
IF HE KEEPS HEADING IN THIS DIRECTION, WE'LL HIT CENTER STREET. WE CAN FIGHT ALL WE WANT IN THE BLACK MARKET, BUT WE CAN'T LET ORDINARY CITIZENS BECOME COLLATERAL DAMAGE!
M-MELON! LISTEN... COULD YOU PLEASE TRY TO ESCAPE WITHIN THE BORDERS OF THE BLACK MARKET?
WHY WOULD HE LISTEN TO ME?!

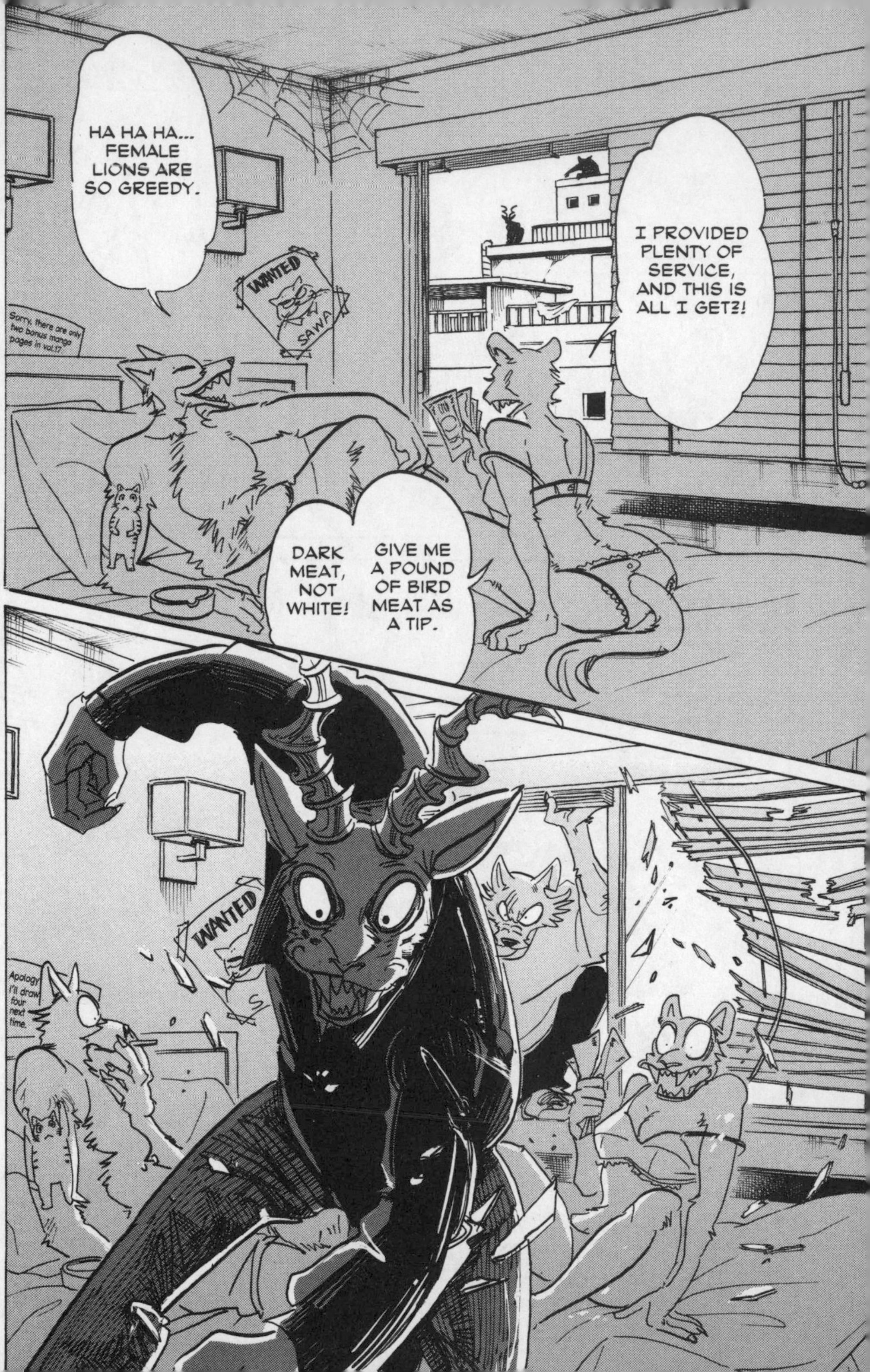
I PROVIDED PLENTY OF SERVICE, AND THIS IS ALL I GET?!
HA HA HA... FEMALE LIONS ARE SO GREEDY.
WANTED
SAWA
Sorry, there are only two bonus manga pages in vol.17
GIVE ME A POUND OF BIRD MEAT AS A TIP.
DARK MEAT, NOT WHITE!
WANTED
Apology I'll draw four next time.

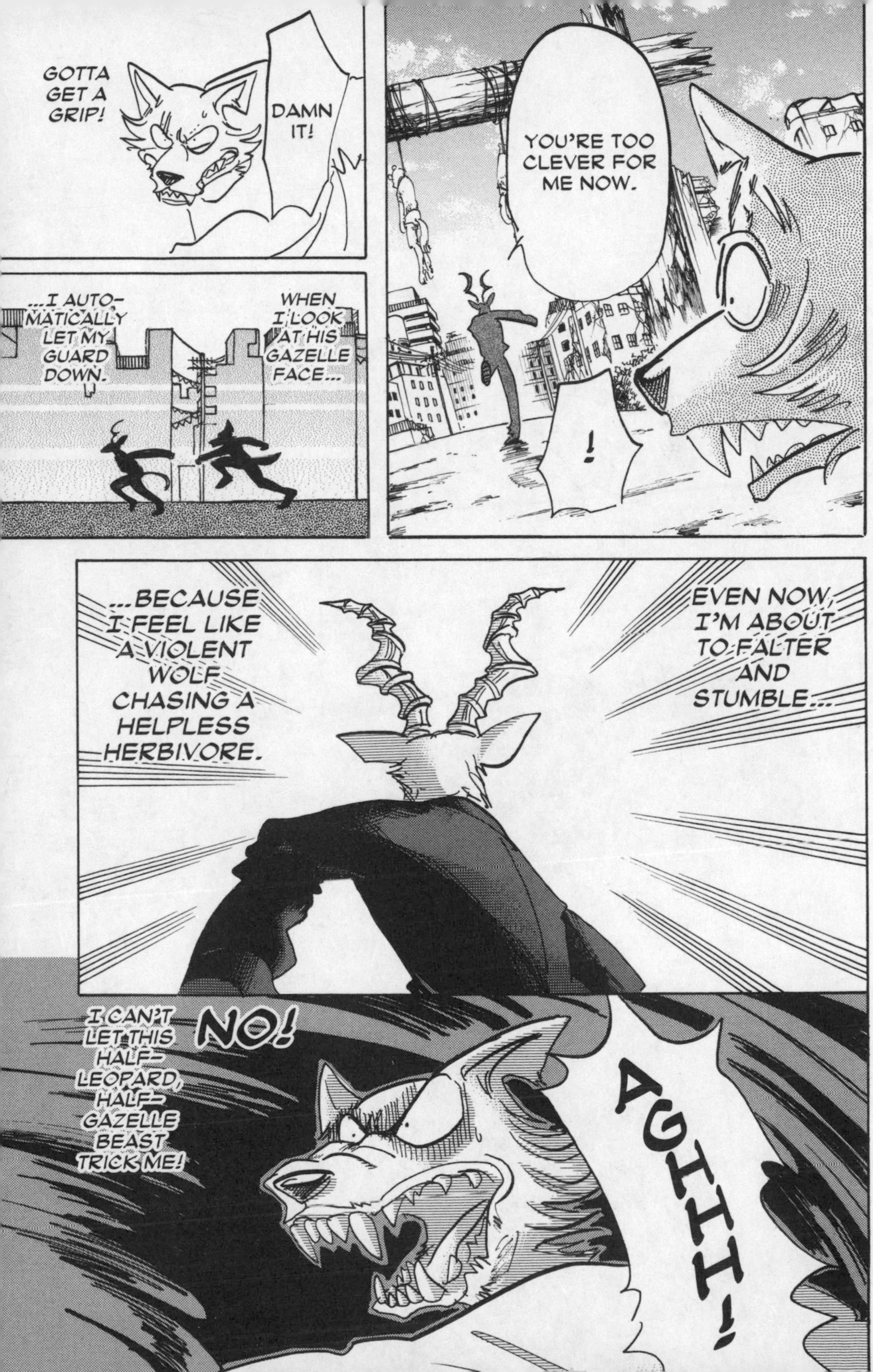
YOU'RE TOO CLEVER FOR ME NOW.
!
DAMN IT!
GOTTA GET A GRIP!
WHEN I LOOK AT HIS GAZELLE FACE...
...I AUTO-MATICALLY LET MY GUARD DOWN.
EVEN NOW, I'M ABOUT TO FALTER AND STUMBLE...
...BECAUSE I FEEL LIKE A VIOLENT WOLF CHASING A HELPLESS HERBIVORE.
AGHHH!
NO!
I CAN'T LET THIS HALF-LEOPARD, HALF-GAZELLE BEAST TRICK ME!

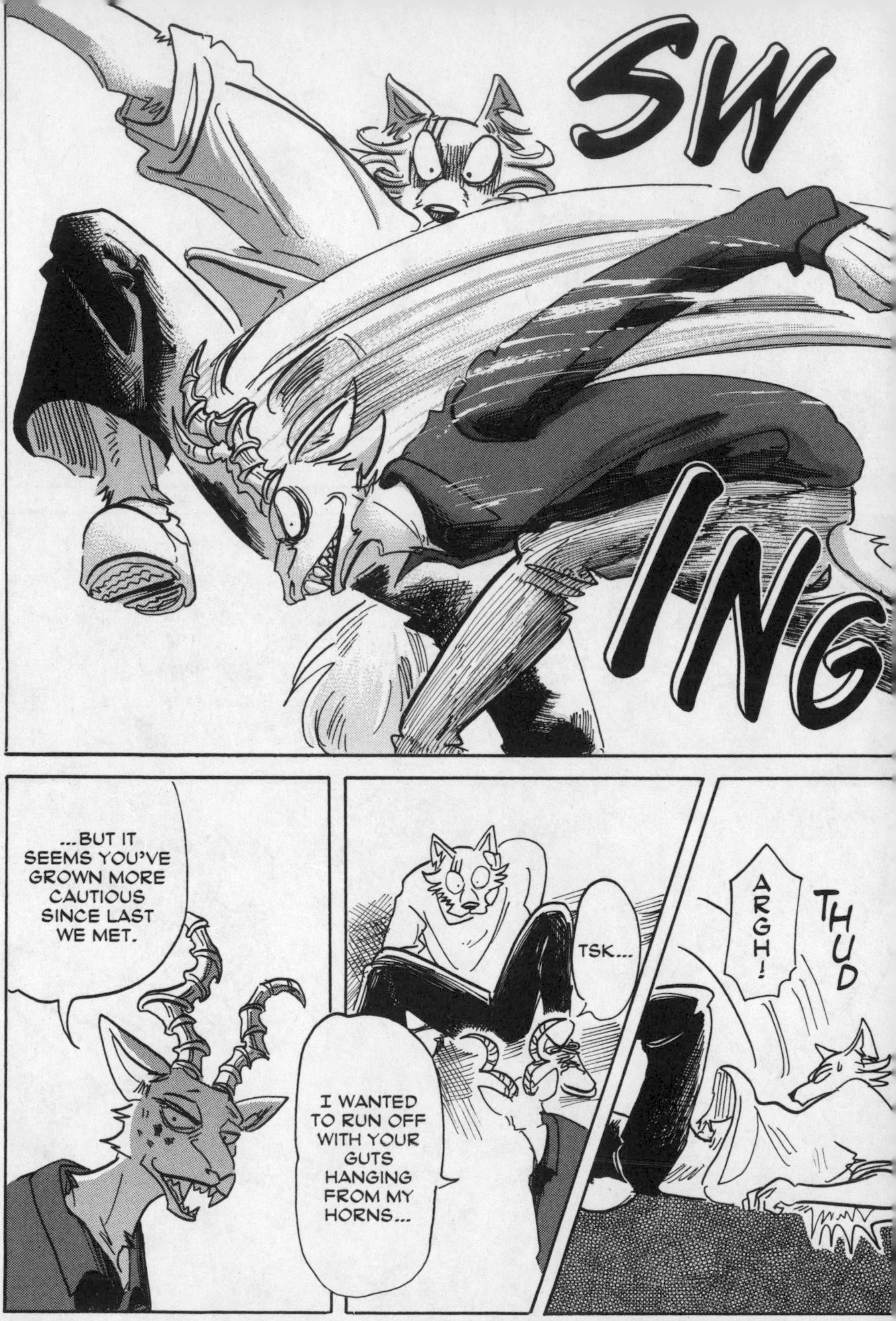
SWING
ARGH!
THUD
TSK...
I WANTED TO RUN OFF WITH YOUR GUTS HANGING FROM MY HORNS...
...BUT IT SEEMS YOU'VE GROWN MORE CAUTIOUS SINCE LAST WE MET.

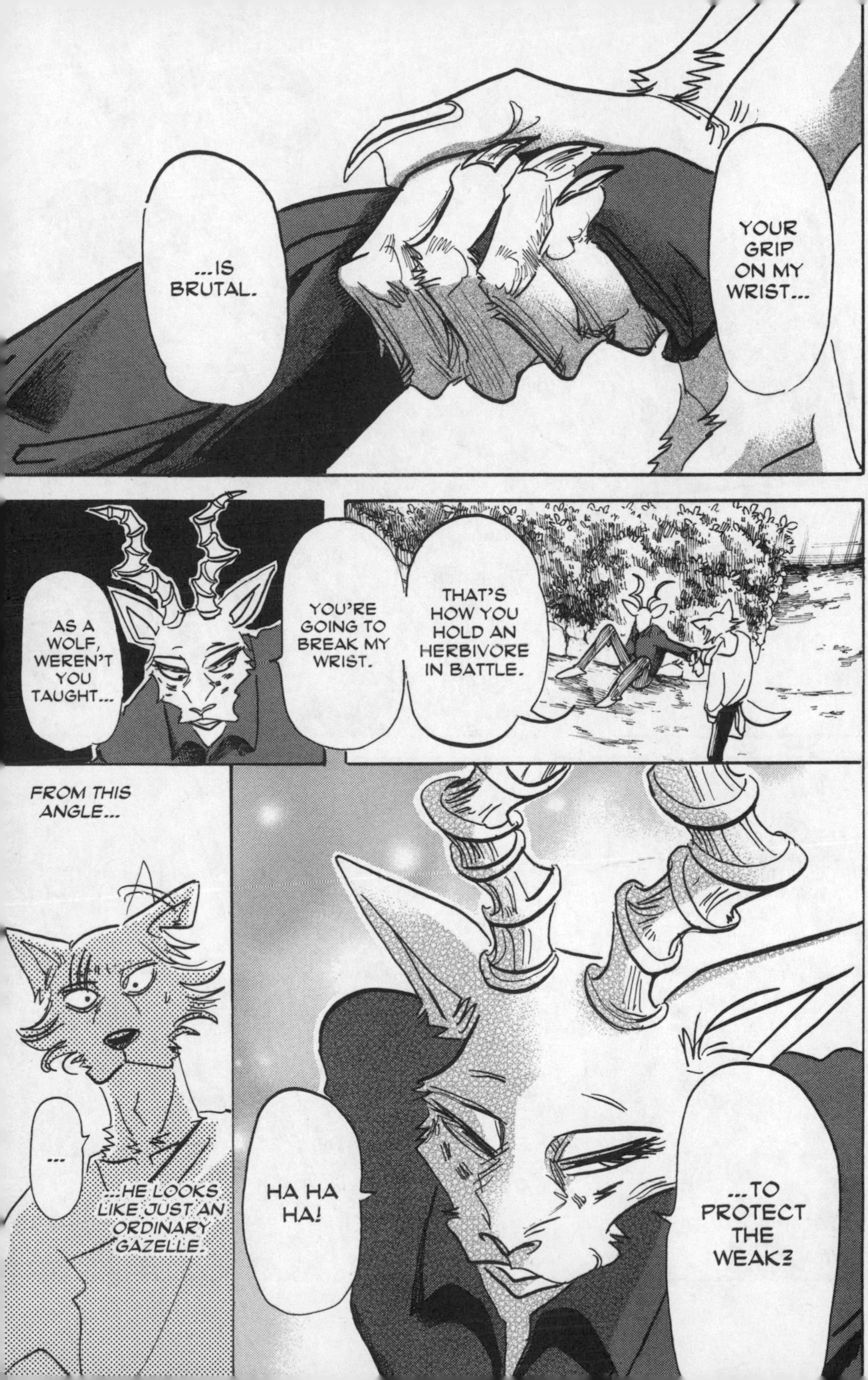
YOUR GRIP ON MY WRIST...
...IS BRUTAL.
THAT'S HOW YOU HOLD AN HERBIVORE IN BATTLE.
YOU'RE GOING TO BREAK MY WRIST.
AS A WOLF, WEREN'T YOU TAUGHT...
...TO PROTECT THE WEAK?
HA HA HA!
FROM THIS ANGLE...
...
...HE LOOKS LIKE JUST AN ORDINARY GAZELLE.

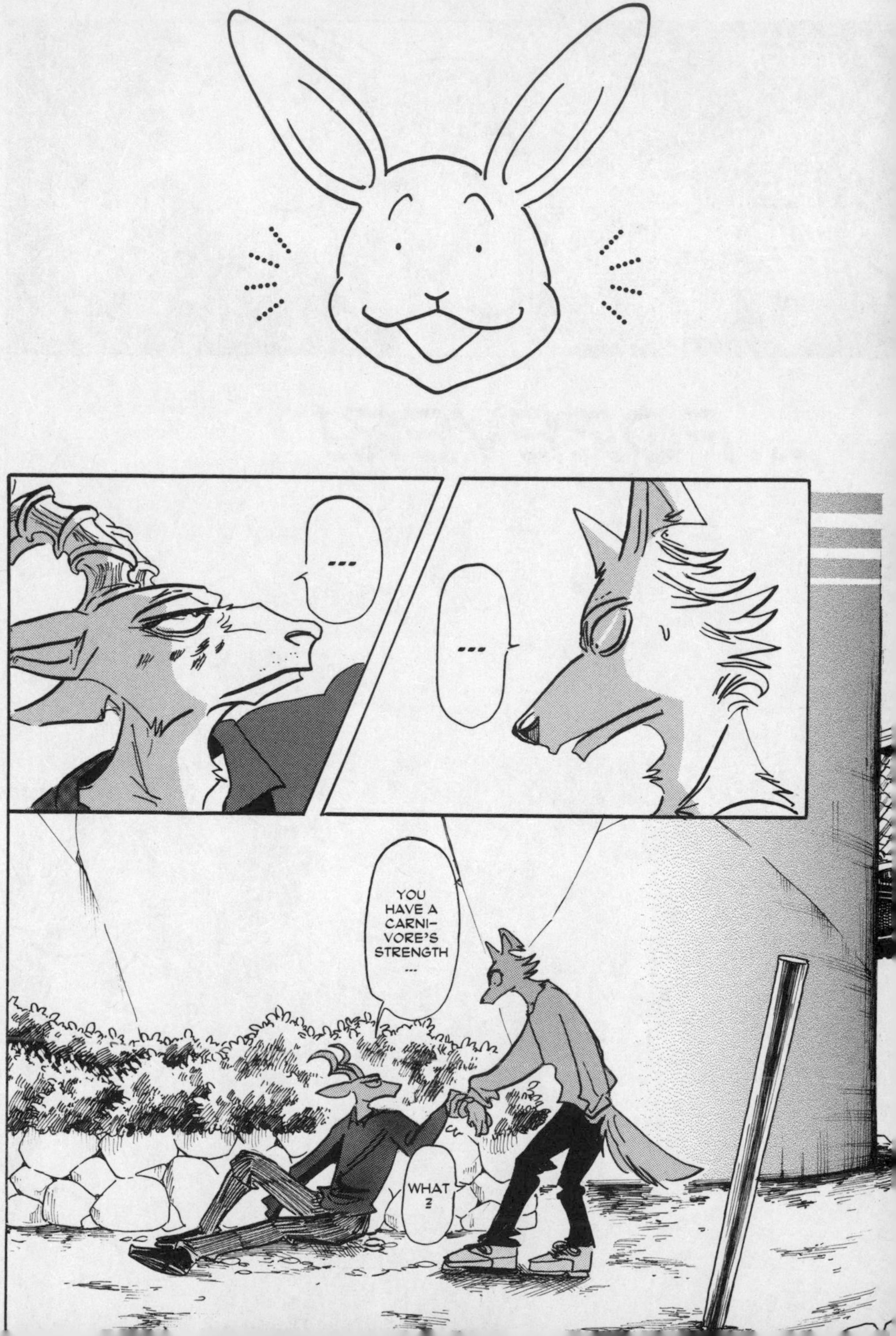
...
...
YOU HAVE A CARNI-VORE'S STRENGTH...
WHAT?

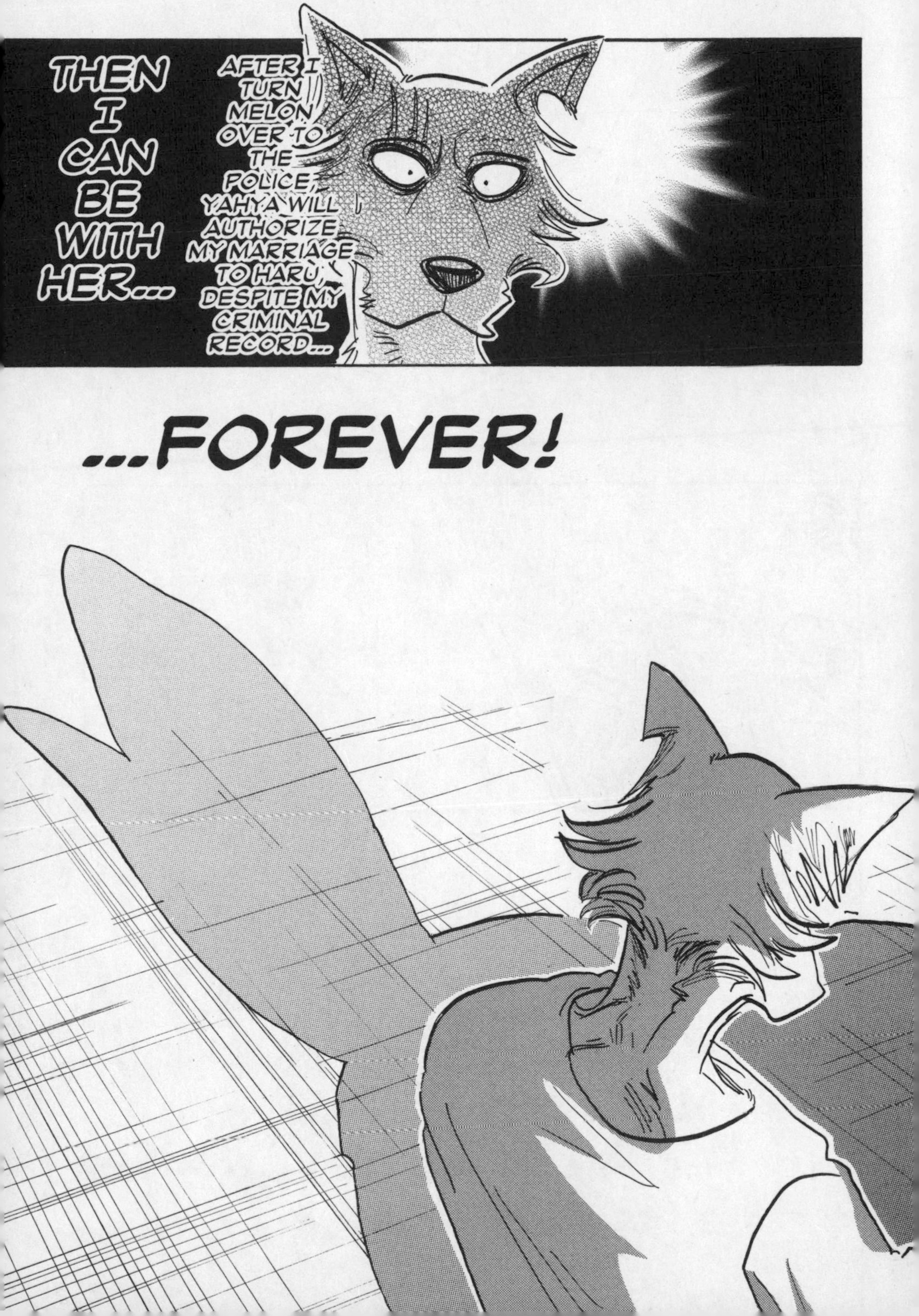
AFTER I TURN MELON OVER TO THE POLICE, YAHYA WILL AUTHORIZE MY MARRIAGE TO HARU, DESPITE MY CRIMINAL RECORD...
THEN I CAN BE WITH HER...
...FOREVER!

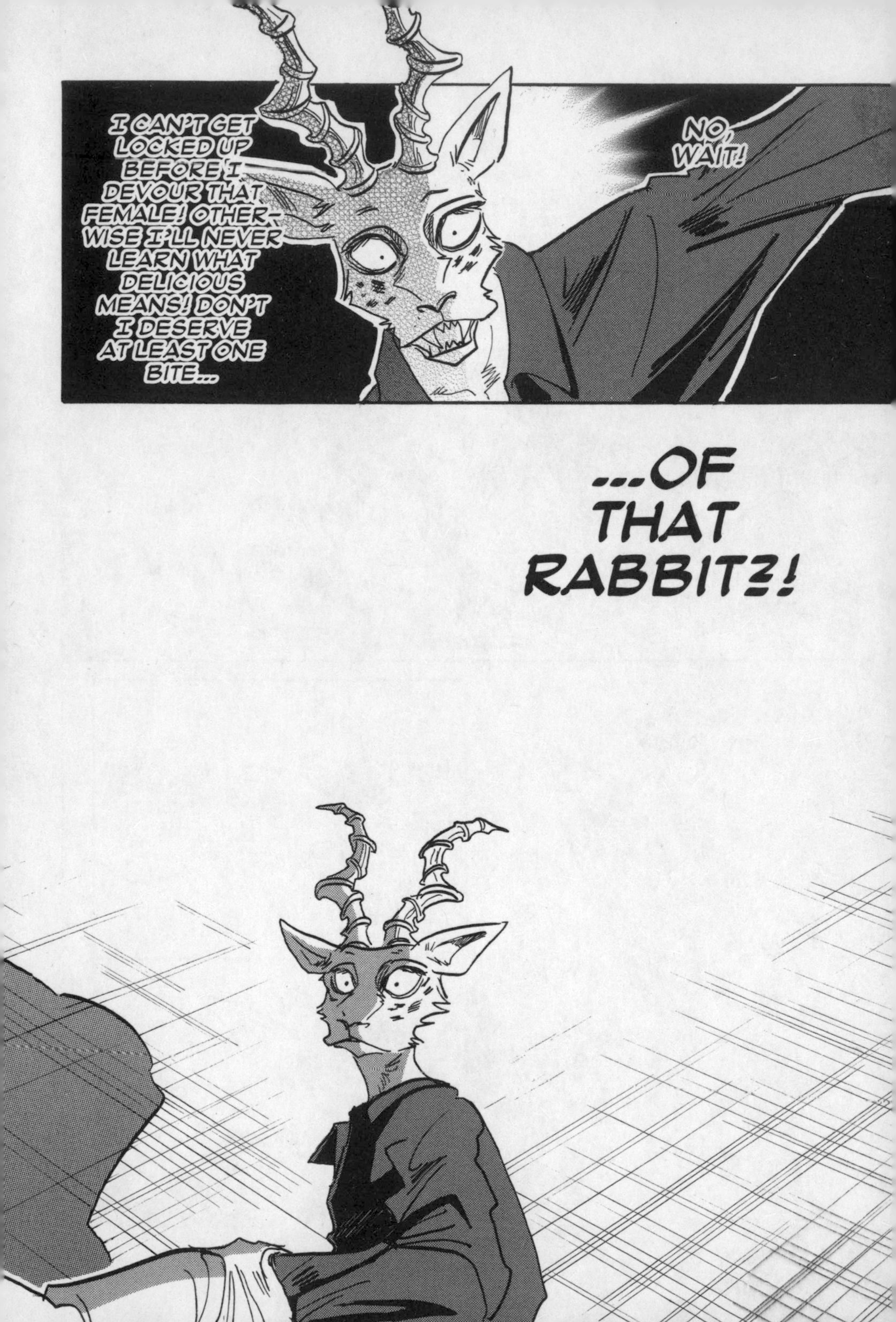
NO, WAIT!
I CAN'T GET LOCKED UP BEFORE I DEVOUR THAT FEMALE! OTHER-WISE I'LL NEVER LEARN WHAT DELICIOUS MEANS! DON'T I DESERVE AT LEAST ONE BITE...
...OF THAT RABBIT?!

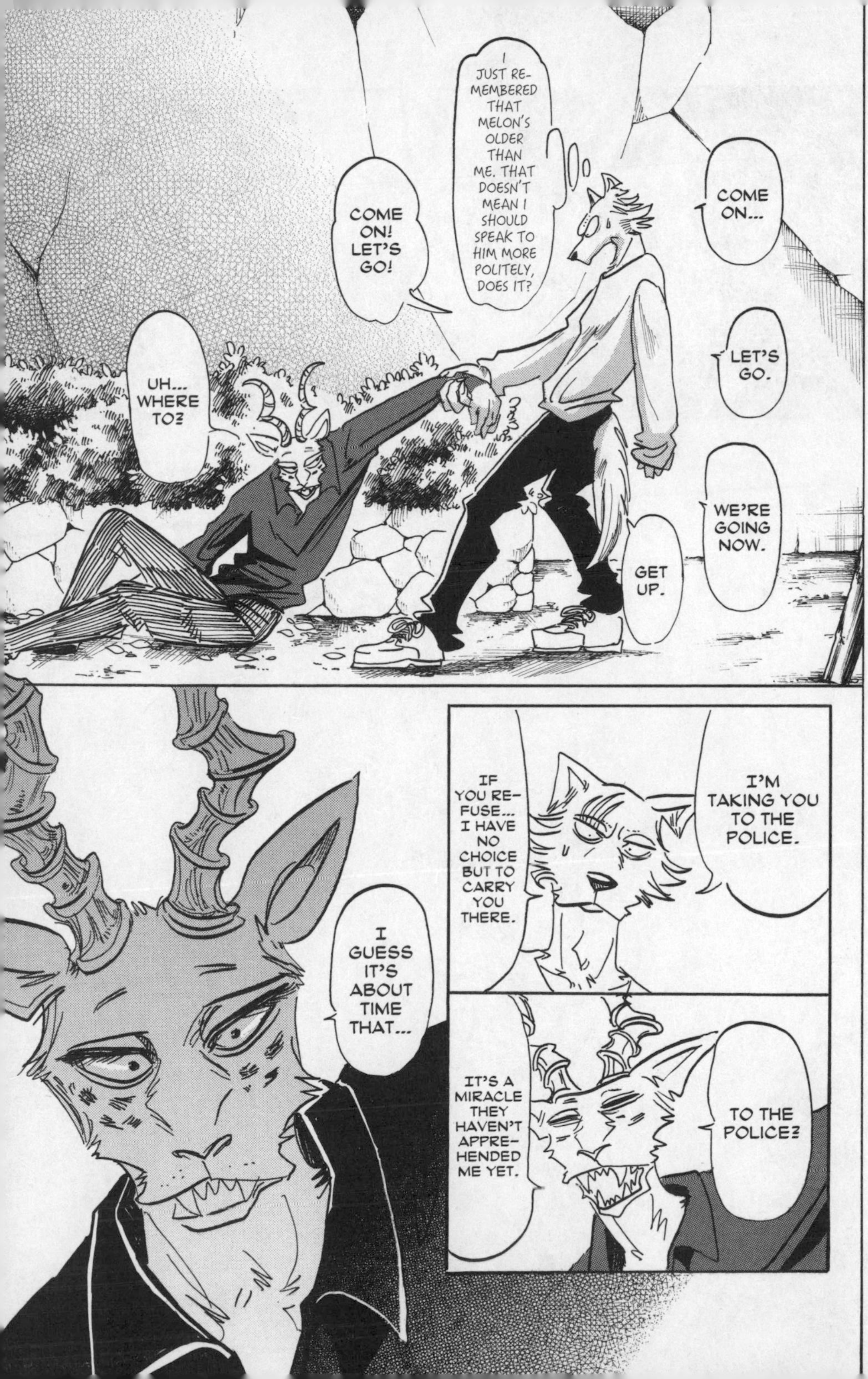
COME ON...
LET'S GO.
WE'RE GOING NOW.
GET UP.
I JUST RE-MEMBERED THAT MELON'S OLDER THAN ME. THAT DOESN'T MEAN I SHOULD SPEAK TO HIM MORE POLITELY, DOES IT?
COME ON! LET'S GO!
UH... WHERE TO?
I'M TAKING YOU TO THE POLICE.
IF YOU RE-FUSE... I HAVE NO CHOICE BUT TO CARRY YOU THERE.
TO THE POLICE?
IT'S A MIRACLE THEY HAVEN'T APPRE-HENDED ME YET.
I GUESS IT'S ABOUT TIME THAT...

BEASTARS
Vol. 17

Chapter 151: Enjoy While Listening to "Comedians' Galop" as Your Background Music

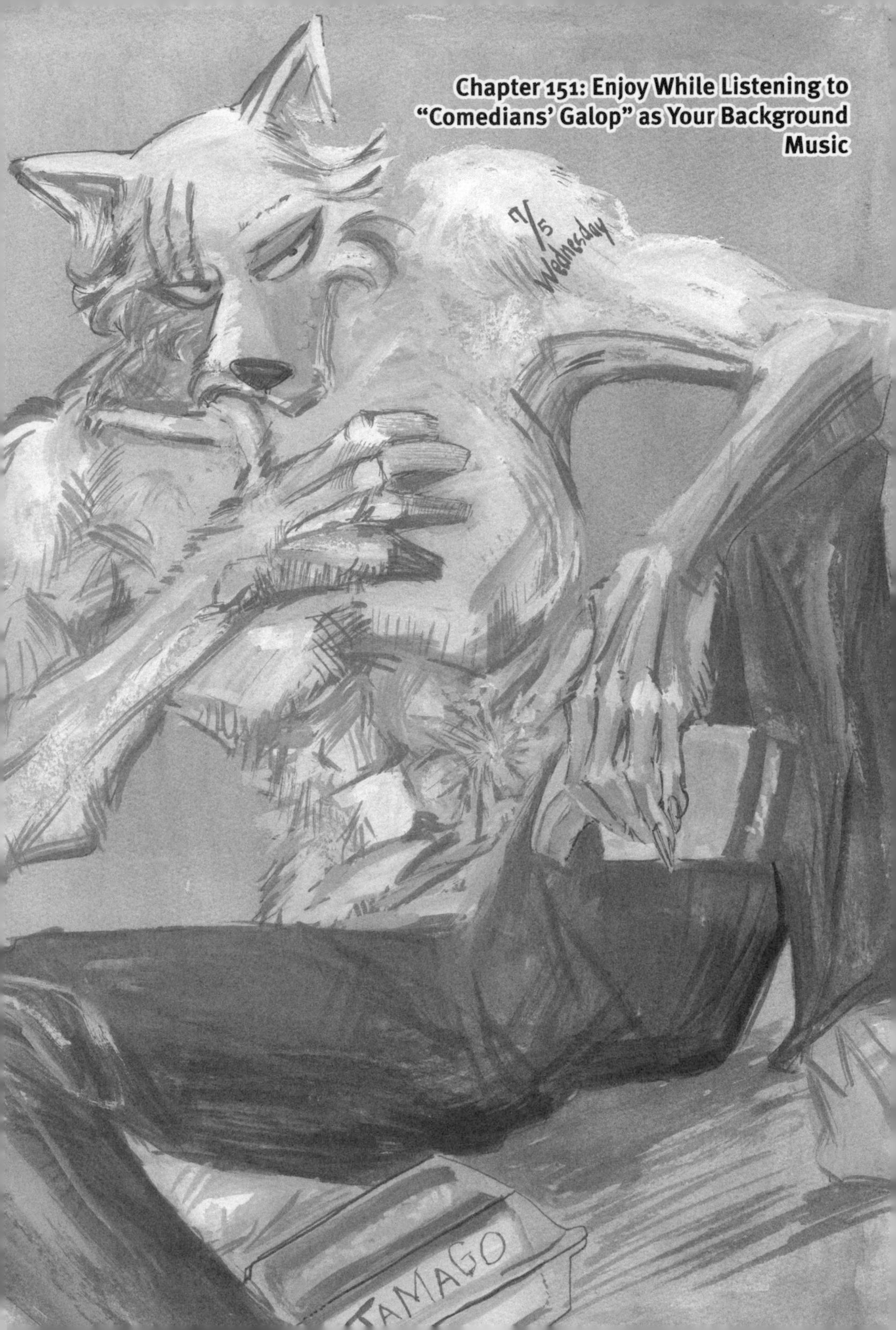
7/5 Wednesday
TAMAGO

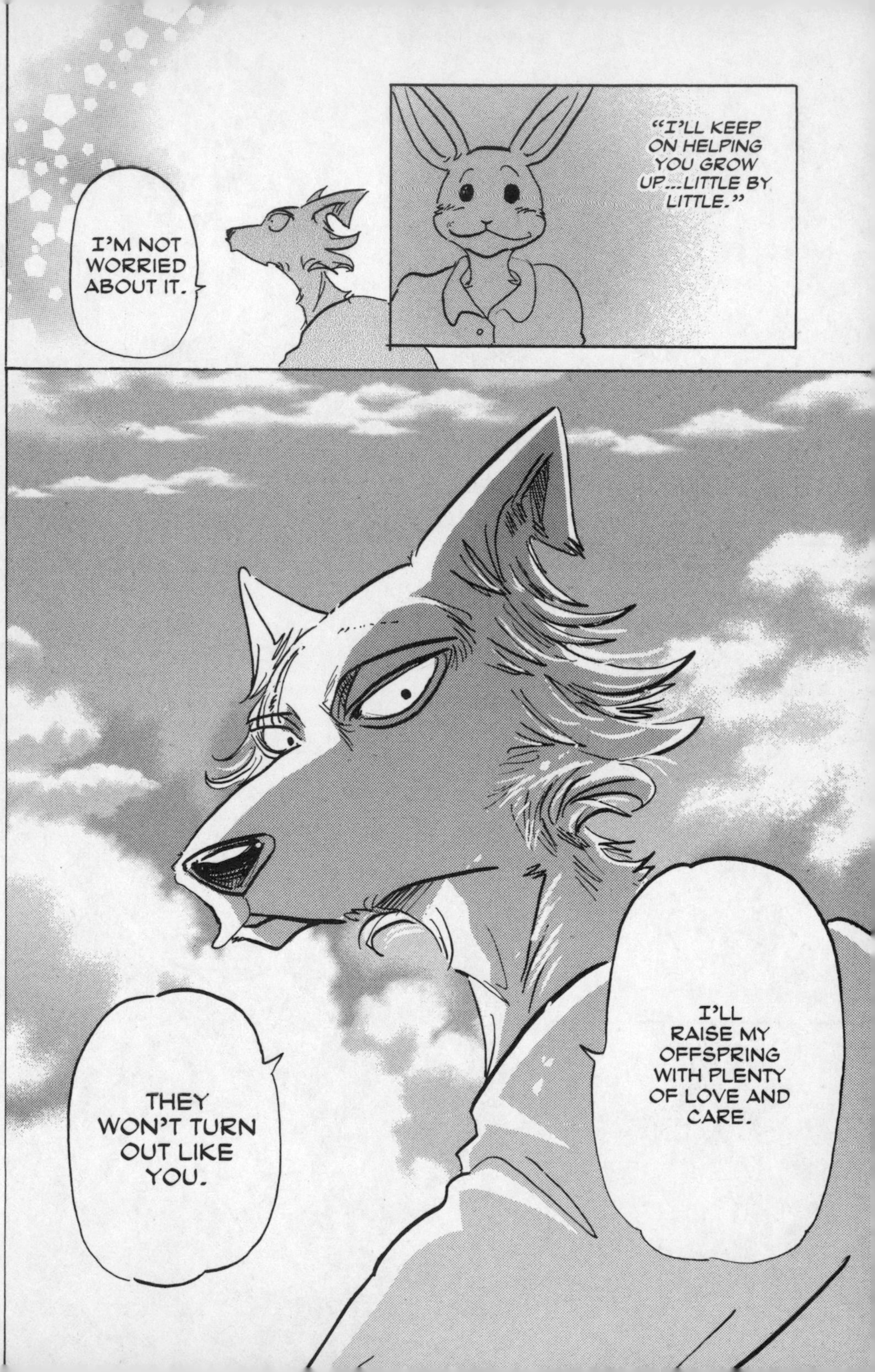
"I'LL KEEP ON HELPING YOU GROW UP...LITTLE BY LITTLE."
I'M NOT WORRIED ABOUT IT.
I'LL RAISE MY OFFSPRING WITH PLENTY OF LOVE AND CARE.
THEY WON'T TURN OUT LIKE YOU.

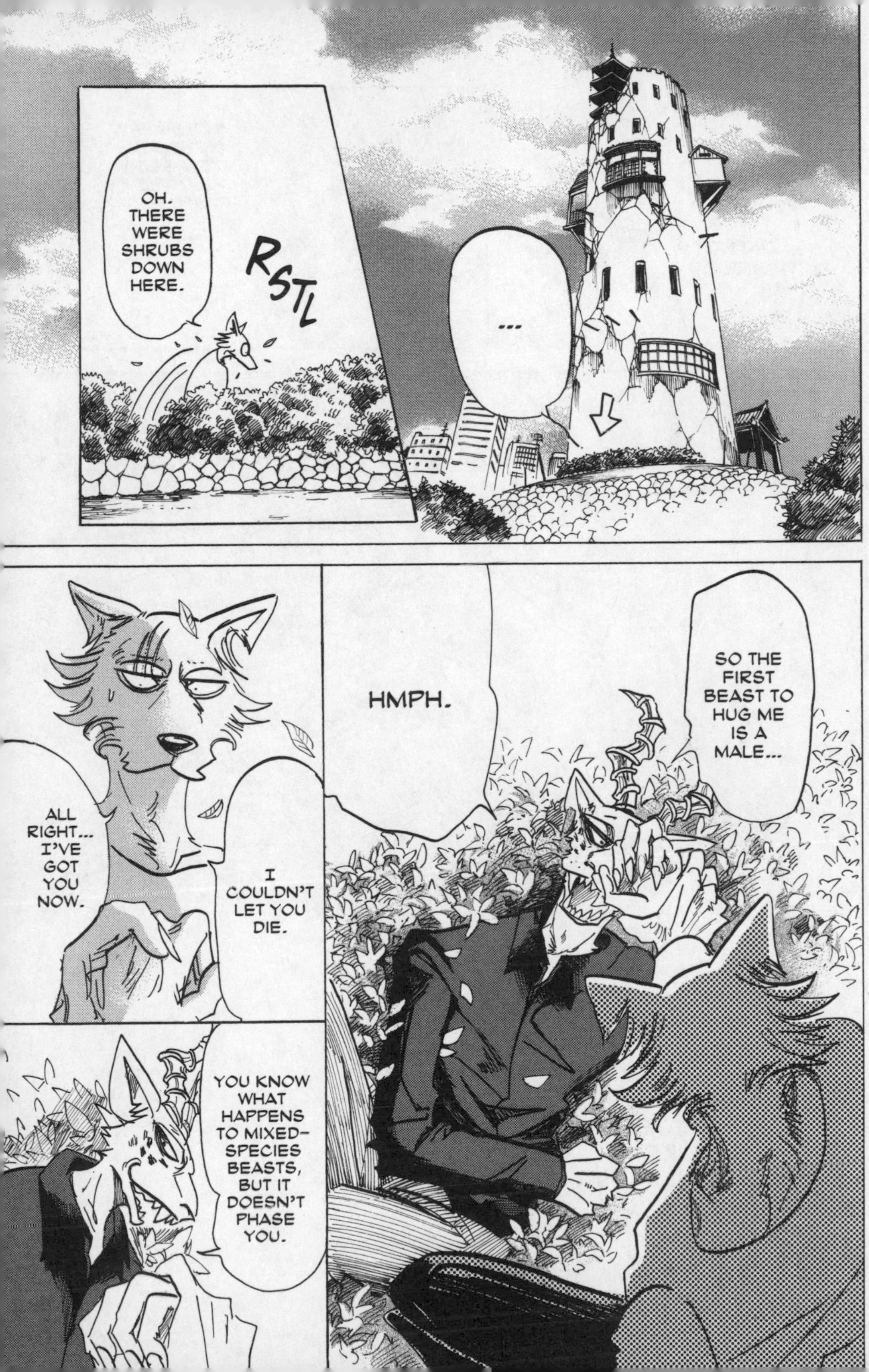
...
OH. THERE WERE SHRUBS DOWN HERE.
RSTL
SO THE FIRST BEAST TO HUG ME IS A MALE...
HMPH.
I COULDN'T LET YOU DIE.
ALL RIGHT... I'VE GOT YOU NOW.
YOU KNOW WHAT HAPPENS TO MIXED-SPECIES BEASTS, BUT IT DOESN'T PHASE YOU.

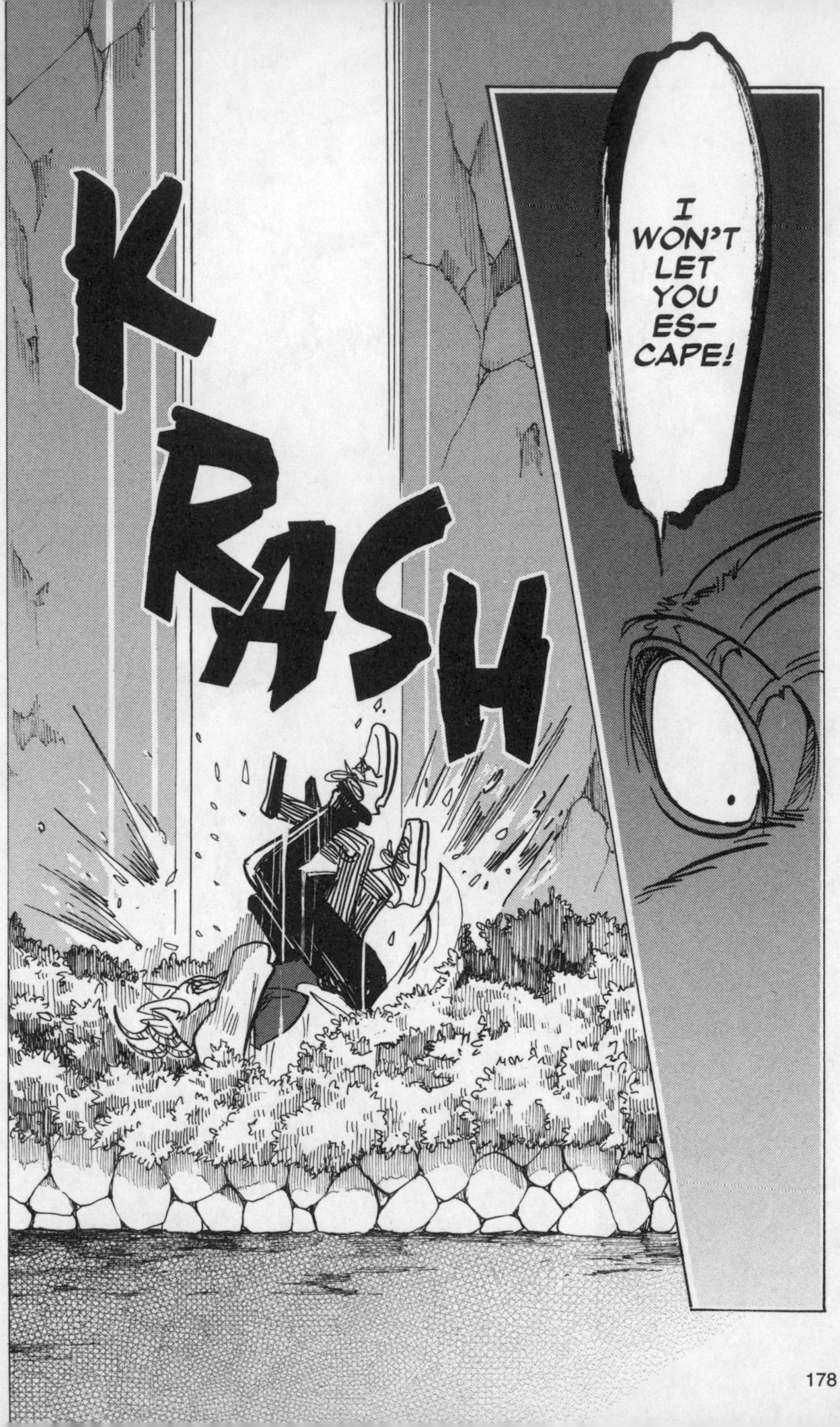
I WON'T LET YOU ES-CAPE!
KRASH

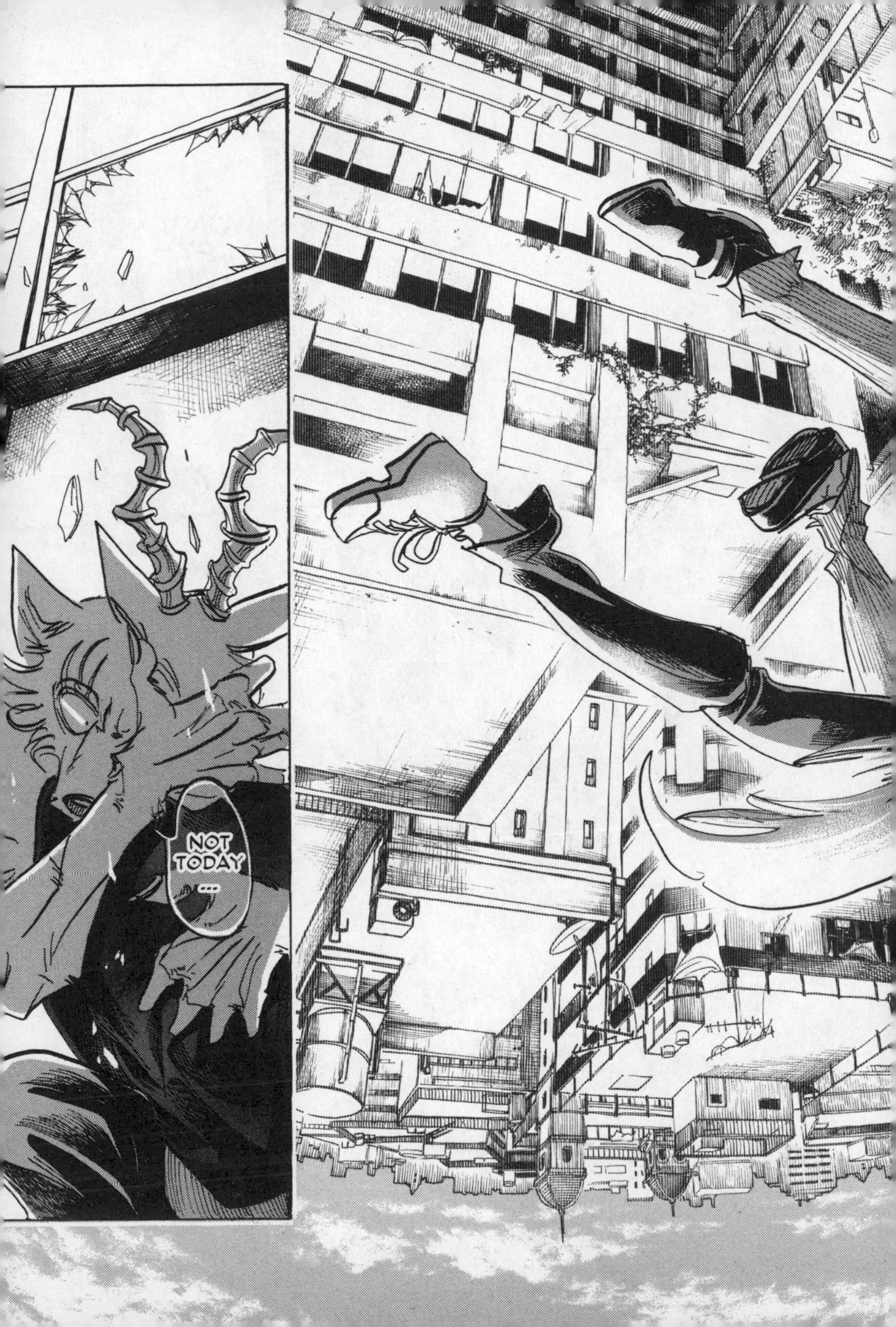
NOT TODAY ...

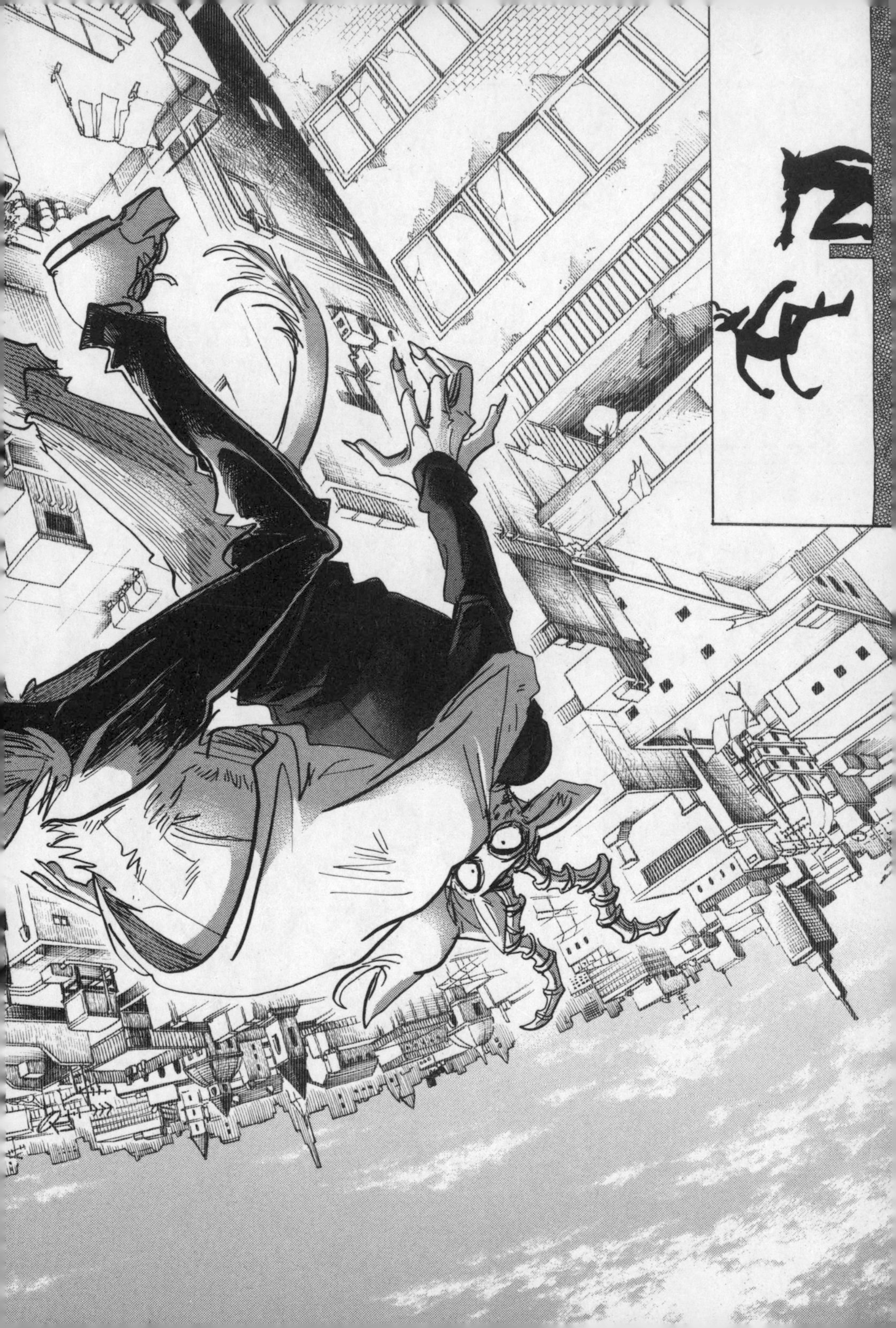

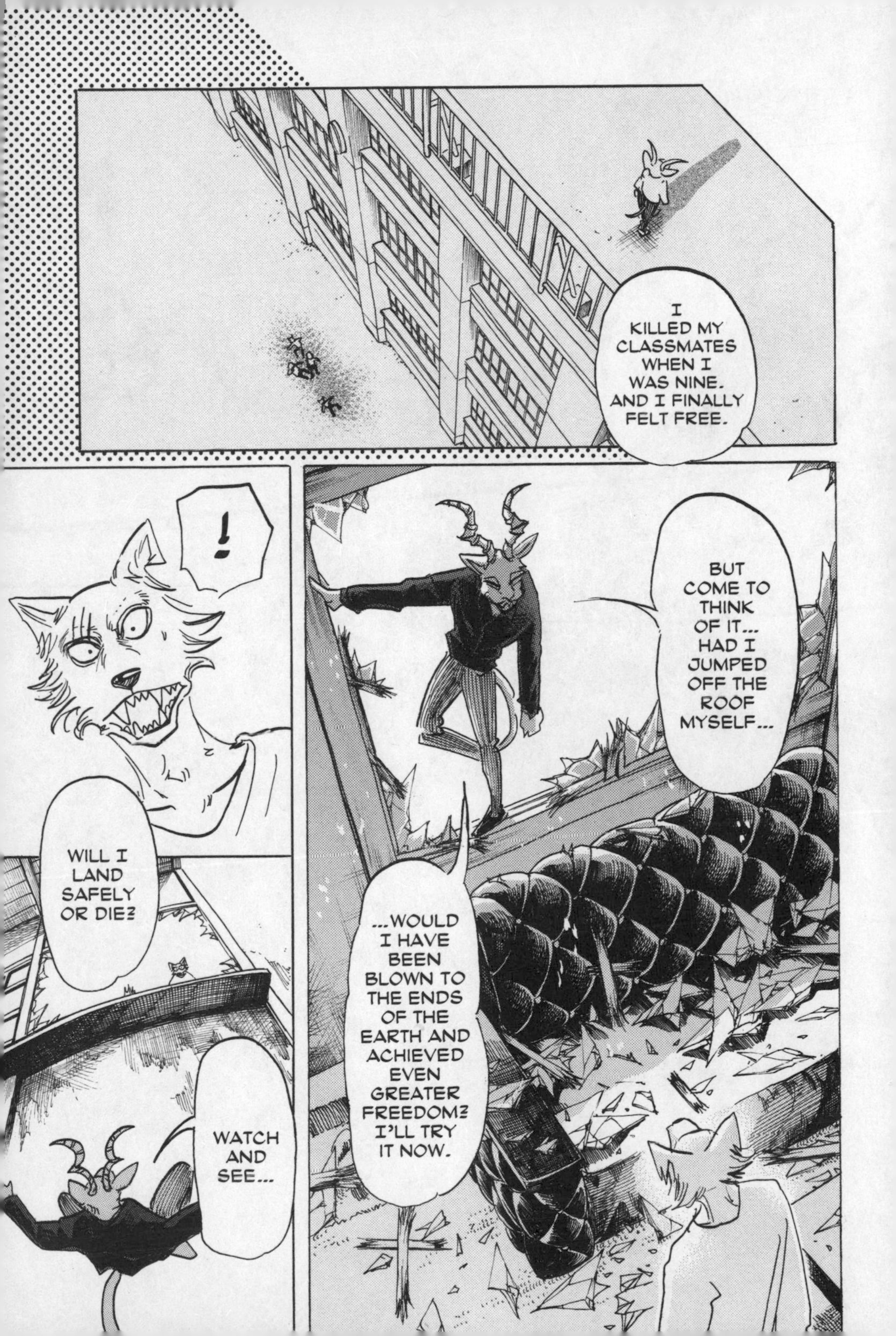
I KILLED MY CLASSMATES WHEN I WAS NINE. AND I FINALLY FELT FREE.
BUT COME TO THINK OF IT... HAD I JUMPED OFF THE ROOF MYSELF...
...WOULD I HAVE BEEN BLOWN TO THE ENDS OF THE EARTH AND ACHIEVED EVEN GREATER FREEDOM? I'LL TRY IT NOW.
!
WILL I LAND SAFELY OR DIE?
WATCH AND SEE...

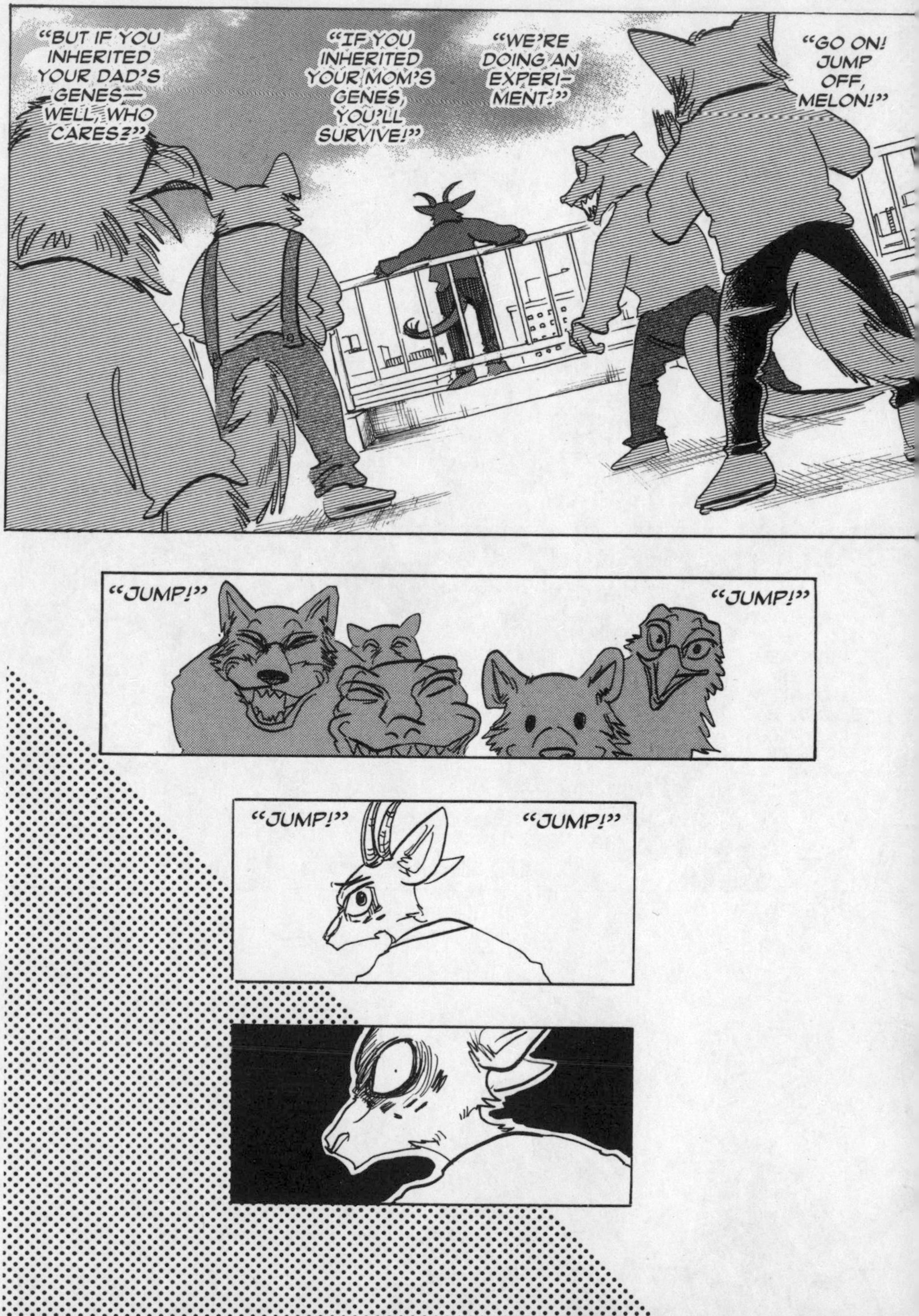
"GO ON! JUMP OFF, MELON!"
"WE'RE DOING AN EXPERI-MENT."
"IF YOU INHERITED YOUR MOM'S GENES, YOU'LL SURVIVE!"
"BUT IF YOU INHERITED YOUR DAD'S GENES—WELL, WHO CARES?"
"JUMP!"
"JUMP!"
"JUMP!"
"JUMP!"

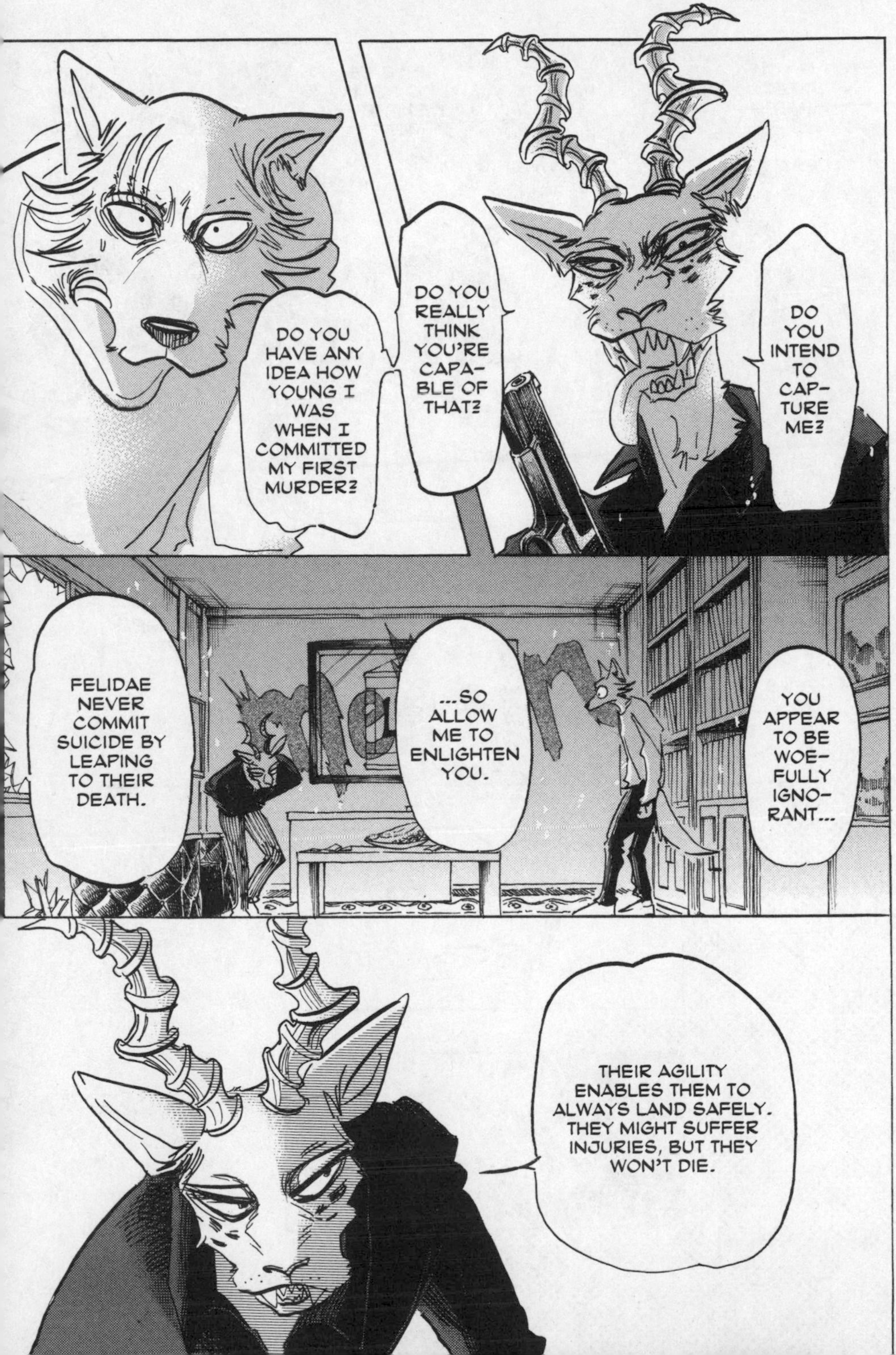
DO YOU INTEND TO CAPTURE ME?
DO YOU REALLY THINK YOU'RE CAPABLE OF THAT?
DO YOU HAVE ANY IDEA HOW YOUNG I WAS WHEN I COMMITTED MY FIRST MURDER?
YOU APPEAR TO BE WOEFULLY IGNORANT...
...SO ALLOW ME TO ENLIGHTEN YOU.
FELIDAE NEVER COMMIT SUICIDE BY LEAPING TO THEIR DEATH.
THEIR AGILITY ENABLES THEM TO ALWAYS LAND SAFELY. THEY MIGHT SUFFER INJURIES, BUT THEY WON'T DIE.

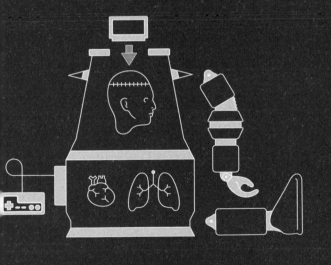

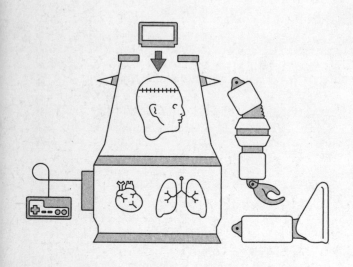

contents

黒鷺死体宅配便
the KUROSAGI corpse delivery service

story
EIJI OTSUKA

art
HOUSUI YAMAZAKI

original cover design
BUNPEI YORIFUJI

translation
TAYLOR ENGEL and TOSHIFUMI YOSHIDA

editor and english adaptation
CARL GUSTAV HORN

lettering and touch-up
IHL

DARK
HORSE
MANGA

CONTENTS

EDITOR'S PREFACE

Understanding Contemporary American Literature has been planned as a series of guides or companions for students as well as good nonacademic readers. The editor and publisher perceive a need for these volumes because much of the influential contemporary literature makes special demands. Uninitiated readers encounter difficulty in approaching works that depart from the traditional forms and techniques of prose and poetry. Literature relies on conventions, but the conventions keep evolving; new writers form their own conventions—which in time may become familiar. Put simply, *UCAL* provides instruction in how to read certain contemporary writers—identifying and explicating their material, themes, use of language, point of view, structures, symbolism, and responses to experience.

The word *understanding* in the series title was deliberately chosen. Many willing readers lack an adequate understanding of how contemporary literature works; that is, what the author is attempting to express and the means by which it is

EDITOR'S PREFACE

conveyed. Although the level of criticism and analysis in the series has been aimed at a level of general accessibility, these introductory volumes are meant to be applied in conjunction with the works they cover. Thus they do not provide a substitute for the works and authors they introduce, but rather prepare the reader for more profitable literary experiences.

M.J.B.

UNDERSTANDING
JOHN HAWKES

CHAPTER ONE

UNDERSTANDING JOHN HAWKES

Career

John Hawkes (born Stamford, Connecticut, 17 August 1925) is often grouped with John Barth and Thomas Pynchon as one of the three most important antirealistic novelists in the United States after World War II. They have deliberately challenged the conventions of the novel, and of the three Hawkes is the most radical. Concerned primarily with the beauty of language, the power of the imagination, and the relation of love and death, he uses comedy, irony, and parody to explore often terrifying situations. The result of such a conscious rejection of the traditional realistic novel is that his fiction is received with a wide range of opinions. Thomas McGuane, for example, has called Hawkes "feasibly our best writer," but Roger Sale has described one of Hawkes's novels as "the product of a contemptible imagination." The truth may be somewhere between the two extremes, as the scores of critical studies of Hawkes attest.

Growing up in New England, Alaska, and New York, Hawkes was a student at Harvard University before leaving during the war. After serving as an ambulance driver for the

UNDERSTANDING JOHN HAWKES

American Field Service in Italy and Germany, he returned to Harvard, began writing fiction, and graduated. His first novel, *The Cannibal*, appeared in 1949. A darkly comic, hallucinated response to the terrors of the European battlefield, *The Cannibal* established the innovative tone and technique that have identified Hawkes's fiction for more than three decades.

Hawkes takes seriously his claim that the "enemies" of the novel are plot, character, setting, and theme, and his effort to extend the genre of fiction has shaped his career. His second novel, *The Beetle Leg* (1951), reflects the atmosphere of its predecessor, and it is his only major publication in the 1950s. During this decade he was assistant to the production manager at Harvard University Press and later a professor at Harvard, Brown, and MIT.

The turning point in his career came in the 1960s when, while a member of the English Department at Brown, he published *The Lime Twig* (1961) and *Second Skin* (1964), runner-up to Saul Bellow's *Herzog* for the National Book Award. More accessible than *The Cannibal* and *The Beetle Leg*, these two novels brought Hawkes a wider audience and increased critical attention without sacrificing his unusual combination of violent comedy and antirealistic technique.

In the 1970s Hawkes published what he calls his "triad" of sex and the imagination: *The Blood Oranges* (1971), *Death, Sleep & the Traveler* (1974), and *Travesty* (1976). *The Blood Oranges* won the Prix du meilleur livre étranger, testifying to his high reputation in France, and it introduced a trio of novels that parody the storyteller and his art while exploring the

UNDERSTANDING JOHN HAWKES

connections between erotic love and imaginative vision. *The Passion Artist* (1979) and *Virginie: Her Two Lives* (1982) extend the exploration, but parody of first-person narration is not a primary issue as it is in the triad.

Hawkes has also published poetry (*Fiasco Hall*, 1943), plays (*The Innocent Party*, 1966), short fiction (*Lunar Landscapes*, 1969), and a miscellany (*Humors of Blood & Skin*, 1984). He continues to teach at Brown.

Overview

During the four decades that John Hawkes has been writing fiction, he has stressed the originality of his achievement. With candor and a knowledge of the history of the novel, he describes his writing as "special and exceptional, powerful and beautiful." He is correct. It is also different: "But then I am probably one of the more original of post–World War II writers, one of the most significantly original . . . in a new use of language, and in a new conception of fictional structures."[1] As Mark Mirsky, editor of *Fiction Magazine*, notes, "If you haven't read John Hawkes, you don't know where American writing is today."[2]

Where much American writing seems today is a conscious reaction against realism. In this sense Hawkes is one of the leading authors, but an initial reaction to his innovations is likely to be that his work poses extraordinary difficulties for the unprepared reader. Yet as his first publisher, James Laughlin (of New Directions), argues, the apparent strangeness of such novels as *The Cannibal* (1949) and *Virginie: Her Two Lives* (1982) is no more than a challenge to read actively: "They all keep yacking about how difficult he is. Well, he isn't. You just have to be willing to put something into it, that's all. It's meaty stuff, yes, and it requires participation on the part of the reader." Hawkes's mentor at Harvard, Albert Guerard, concurs: "Most older people brought up on Hemingway simply can't adjust to the work of somebody like Hawkes. There are so many more younger people who love it."[3] They "love it" because the fiction is startling, different, and still accessible. Hawkes explains that he is interested in "the primacy of the imagination, not in esoteric indulgence or in the writer as public figure. And I dislike autobiographical fiction. I don't write fiction in order to use my life up as its source. . . . If we don't know our destructive potential, we can't very well assume genuine responsibility for the world around us. The problem is that people don't know that life is a kind of fiction that we create, or that others create and we accept as 'real.' We need to challenge such realities all the time. I'm just writing about the things that are most deeply embedded in the human psyche."[4]

The exposure of truths buried in the psyche, the sense of life where, as Hawkes says, "everything is dangerous, everything is tentative, nothing is certain," is at the heart of his fiction.[5] To advocate these kinds of novels, then, is to reject the authority of moral norms and rational processes except for those created in the work itself. Hawkes would agree that the

UNDERSTANDING JOHN HAWKES

writer's obligation is not to the reader and surely not to the author but to the novel as an art form. Fiction based on such a premise is likely to disturb readers who look for an easily recognizable connection between the mundane surfaces of their lives and the novels they read.

John Hawkes refuses to supply that connection. Although he insists on a moral center to his work, his definition of the morality upsets readers who look to art for solace and confirmation of prevailing beliefs: "The novelist's first allegiance is to his art, but it's impossible for me to think of fiction without a moral center. Mine is Conradian. My work is an effort to expose the worst in us all, to cause us to face up to the enormities of our terrible potential for betrayal, disgrace, and criminal behavior. I think that it is necessary to destroy repression while showing at the same time that the imagination is unlimited."[6] Specifying his interests as "idealism, innocence, and luminous, murderous impulse," he describes his fiction as writing that touches on matters vital to the unconscious of all people. Truly moral art, he argues, challenges conventional morality, which by its nature is harsh, narrow, and finally repressive.

Hawkes accepts the comic absurdities of life as a given because he does not believe in the possibility of a creative, controlling power at the center of the universe. Organizing his work so that the general conflict is usually the life force versus inhibition and death, he deliberately tries to shock readers who are complacent about good and evil. When told, for example, that his writing disturbs many people, he replied, "I'm glad it does. Insofar as I think of it in terms of intention, I want my fiction to destroy conventional morality and conventional attitudes. That's part of its purpose—to challenge us in every way possible in order to cause us to know ourselves better and to live with more compassion."[7] Skipper, the bumbling hero of *Second Skin* (1964), learns better than any Hawkes character the necessary balance between the life and death forces. To do so, however, he must shake off deeply embedded puritan attitudes and the morality of formal religion, hindrances that depend on repression and that offer artificial consolation in the face of life's enormities, and he must also abandon his preoccupation with the cemeteries of his loved ones. Only then can he discover what he calls "love at last."

Hawkes's emphasis on creativity, be it making love or writing novels, causes him to bristle when readers complain that his fiction is negative. Despite the murky atmosphere and the random violence in his earlier work, especially *The Cannibal* and *The Beetle Leg* (1951), he points to the power of the imagination and the very act of completing a novel as indications of his affirmation. True nihilists would not bother to write. The need to create in the face of the void suggests that moral value is found not in conventional platitudes but in art. The reader may debate, for example, the positive or negative results of Cyril's "tapestry" of sexual love in *The Blood Oranges* (1971), but Cyril does challenge Hugh's inhibitions against sexuality in order to create his "Illyria" of the imagination. The story he tells, the "novel" he writes, is an act of rebellion against a world that would repress his lyricism. If, as

UNDERSTANDING JOHN HAWKES

Hawkes suggests, Cyril and Hugh represent a polarity between the creative impulse and the puritan ethic, then the two men must forever be in conflict.

Hugh's negative sexuality—his one arm, his pornography collection, and his black sweaters—is a metaphor for all the destructive forces that conspire against the mandate to love. Albert Guerard has called this conspiracy Hawkes's "landscape of sexual apathy," and it is true that an aura of desperation surrounds the characters who are unable to use love as a means to create.[8] Yet Hawkes's depiction of such listless sexual activity has a dual thrust that lifts his novels far beyond the merely titillating. Convinced of the necessity for creativity and sympathy, he describes his concern with life's darker threats as part of one's duty to confront the nightmare: "I mean that the writer who exploits his own psychic life reveals the inner lives of us all, the inner chaos, the negative aspects of the personality in general. I'm appalled at violence, opposed to pain, terrified of actual destructiveness. . . . It isn't that I'm advocating that we live by acts of violence. . . . It's just that our deepest inner lives are largely organized around such impulses, which need to be exposed and understood and used. Even appreciated."[9]

This last phrase—"even appreciated"—might be difficult to accept if the reader considers only such horrifying scenes as the slaughter of the child in *The Cannibal* or Luke's fishing up the fetus in *The Beetle Leg*, but Hawkes uses destructive action to extend the reader's concern for those trapped in nightmare and violence. This unexpected authorial position is his doctrine of "reverse sympathy," which he deems essential to the novelistic experience: "If the point is to discover true compassion, true sympathy, then clearly the task is to sympathize with what we ordinarily take to be truly repulsive in life."[10] Thus for Hawkes writing a novel is an act of rebellion. Authors who dare to create a landscape rather than represent one, who reject the restrictions of conventional morality in their fiction, and who ask the reader to care for characters threatened by the night rebel against a prevailing notion in the post–World War II world that individual effort counts for naught.

A concise overview of Hawkes's fiction, then, suggests that it is difficult but accessible, violent but comic, apparently nihilistic but finally affirmative. His characters are often baffled buffoons. Buffeted by outside forces, they turn away from pain and fear to the solace of the imagination. They discover, however, that the imagination can lacerate as well as soothe. Hawkes's situations take place against a background of violence, of shattered moral values, and of disordered cultures, and they are supported by specific references to war, crooked gambling, disintegrating dams in arid deserts, and suicide. One thinks of Skipper's floating island at the end of *Second Skin* versus Conrad Vost's endless swamp in *The Passion Artist* (1979) or Zizendorf's ravaged Germany in *The Cannibal* versus Cyril's erotic Illyria in *The Blood Oranges* as polar situations in which Hawkes explores the power of the imagination. Triumph in his work is rarely over the specific enemy—be it war, the lure of suicide, or the inhibition against sexuality; it is found, rather, in the ability of the characters to withstand the pressures of external reality by the insistence of their internal visions.

Thus most of Hawkes's heroes are artist figures, men determined to remake the world's ugliness into the imagination's lyricism. They don't always succeed. Those who do, confront the nightmare and expand their sympathies with the ruined members of the human lot. Those who don't, give in to the backwash of the psyche. Hawkes's tragic characters are not those who fall from high places, as in classical tragedy, but those who are devoured by their dreams, and his sufferers are to be judged not by their ethical strength or physical courage but by the vitality of their visions.

Love, sexuality, creativity, and lyricism are the hallmarks of Hawkes's survivors. Those who triumph are able to break with the repression of civic and moral codes to celebrate the freedom of their private lives. Responsibility toward other human beings is not a primary issue with some of his characters, though it is an important quality to Hawkes personally. Indeed, many of the important relationships in his fiction are not those of commitment or mutual support but those that flower in the linking of victim and victimizer. Zizendorf thinks he is restoring Germany to its former glory when in reality he is plunging it toward another war. Cyril thinks he is liberating Hugh to the mysteries of "sex-singing" when in reality he is destroying his own Illyria. Vost thinks he is putting women in their place when in reality he is discovering his most urgent needs. The victim cannot exist without the victimizer, and in many cases the two are the same. The quality of one's imagination often determines the outcome of the struggle.

One might even say that Hawkes's true subject is the province of art. Not the meaning of life but the working of the mind is the issue. Such is not the standard material of the realistic novel. The reader who would feel at ease with Hawkes must understand first the venerable traditions of the novel and second Hawkes's conscious disruption of them. These ideas will be discussed in detail later, but for the moment one should remember that for most readers "novel" means the realistic tradition begun in English by Daniel Defoe in the early eighteenth century, extending through Samuel Richardson and Henry Fielding to the great age of realism in the nineteenth century as illustrated by Jane Austen, W. M. Thackeray, and George Eliot, and perhaps reaching its high point in Henry James, Ernest Hemingway, F. Scott Fitzgerald, and William Faulkner. For Hawkes, however, realism in fiction after 1945 means "pedestrian" thinking and pedestrian technique. Given such emphasis, such radical variation of the staples of the genre, the reader should not judge the success or failure of Hawkes's characters and settings by the standards of Fielding or Austen or James. In Hawkes, how a character earns his living is insignificant beside how he copes with his psyche. Similarly, how a character gets from one place to another is unimportant beside how he handles himself when he gets there. As Hawkes has explained, when he wants a character to fly, he merely writes that the character flies.

UNDERSTANDING JOHN HAWKES

Hawkes's commitment to innovative fiction is so firm that he hopes to liberate the novel from the constraints of traditional realism. Not only the novel form itself but also the reader is freed from the tyranny of reader expectation when an author deliberately violates the textbook definitions of the genre. Hawkes would likely take seriously the warning in Hugh Holman's *A Handbook to Literature*: "Attempts to classify the *novel* usually come to logical grief."[11] Active reader participation is crucial; intellectual dexterity is mandatory. The reader of Hawkes cannot assume that the author will do the work for him. He will also have to admit that these complex fictions require multiple readings.

Those who would understand John Hawkes must deal immediately with technique and vision. Unusual method and unexpected scenes are at the center of his work, and the unprepared reader often feels first startled and then unsure. But such strangeness is also the pleasure of Hawkes, for he readily rewards those who accept the invitation to a different reading experience. Although he is an antirealistic novelist, one should not equate his reaction against conventional methods of storytelling with the bizarre incohesiveness of surrealism. Uninterested in the automatic writing or spontaneous flow often associated with the surrealists, Hawkes deliberately gives his tales poetic intensity and intricate structure. He has no interest in duplicating a naturalistic location in which the reader may be caught up in the actions and characters as if the experience were his own. Opening a book by Hawkes, one is always aware that one is reading a novel, a fiction, something made up—in short, a work of art.

Not the recognizable perimeters of a represented scene but the unexplored domain of created landscapes is standard fare in Hawkes. He insists on the strangeness of his fictional locales because he is fascinated by the possibilities of the imagination. Spurning the mundane demands of the daily routine, his characters risk the extremes of psychic journeys that plunge them into events beyond their control. Innocents all—in the sense that they are unprepared for or ignorant of the power of the imagination—they find themselves threatened and often maimed or destroyed by their own visions and dreams. Michael Banks (*The Lime Twig*, 1961) is killed within the fog of his dream of owning a racehorse, his symbol of sexual prowess, by the very animals he seeks to emulate. Cyril creates a modern Shakespearean tableau of love in an imaginary Illyria, only to find his "tapestry" in shreds when the external world intrudes from beyond the mountains. Hawkes shows that the nether side of the imagination is as devastating as its power to create. The irony, of course, is that he is always in control of the uncontrollable visions that his characters conjure up and to which they succumb.

Dislocation of cause and effect, distortion of rational processes, insistence on the psychic truth beneath the recognizable surfaces of the quotidian—these are the staples of Hawkes's fiction. The novels seem difficult primarily because while journeying with Michael Banks and Cyril, the reader confronts the unexpected in technique and the unexplainable

in theme. Hawkes comments in an interview: "I'm not interested in reflection or representation; I'm only interested in creating a fictive world. . . . I want to find all the fluid, germinal,
pestilential 'stuff' of life itself as it exists in the unconscious.
The writing of each fiction is a taking of a psychic journey."[12]

These journeys to the depths of the mind are often parodies of the quest. The visionary dreamer finds not the grail but
the grotesque. Inviting the reader to meet what he mistakenly
believes is the least harmful part of the self—the imagination—Hawkes exposes the brutality of fantasies that lurch out
of control. Of all his characters only Skipper successfully
erects the pleasures of the imagination against the indignities
of a world that deliberately hurts him. Most of Hawkes's
dreamers are not so lucky.

A point to remember is that Hawkes requires the reader's
discomfort as well as the character's. Seeking to open up the
reading experience, to free the reader from the safety of the
traditional novel with its beginning, middle, and end, Hawkes
introduces fragments, images, and motifs that while initially
appearing disorderly are finally the keys to order. The reader
need only realize the links among the parts, just as Skipper
does with the color and animal imagery in *Second Skin*. Liberation from conventional attitudes and expectations, suggests
Hawkes, leads to compassion, a quality he greatly prizes: "I
happen to believe that it is only by travelling those dark tun-
nels, perhaps not literally but psychically, that one can learn
in any sense what it means to be compassionate."[13] Comic dislocation as well as discomfort and fear are likely to be the re-

sult of such psychic plunges by both reader and character, but Hawkes hopes that the outcome is increased tolerance for the varieties of the imagination and for those who experience them.

Given such a commitment to the imagination, representational fiction—mimesis—is not possible. Neither are significant parallels between Hawkes's life and his art. In both interview and conversation he denies close relationships between how he has lived and what he has written. The primary reason for the denial is that detachment of the author from his tale is a cornerstone of his aesthetic. He explains: "I look at my work as if somebody else had written it. . . . It isn't that I want any of Joyce's godlike omniscience, it's just that I want whatever one creates out of words to be so clearly something made, so clearly an artifice."[14] Autobiographical extension is not an issue in his fiction, but creation and exploration of imagined landscapes are. His insistence on detachment is the reason why the reader senses a lack of authorial pressure on the bumblers who people his novels. Hawkes refuses to help the reader by indicating approval or disapproval of his characters' actions. The Duke in *The Cannibal* dismembers a boy with impunity while the uneasy reader simultaneously recoils from and laughs at the absurdity of the slaughter. Papa in *Travesty* (1976) is determined to kill himself in a car wreck in order to illustrate the paradox of design and debris that anchors all artistic creations. How does the reader evaluate such intricate mosaics of art and pain? In a traditional novel the reader may often rely on hints and nudges from the author, es-

UNDERSTANDING JOHN HAWKES

pecially when the point of view is omniscient or when the dialogue is a realistic indicator of character.

Hawkes's detachment precludes these props. In one of his earliest published commentaries on the craft of fiction he writes: "Detachment, then, is at the center of the novelist's experiment. . . . But mere malice is nothing in itself, of course, and the product of extreme fictive detachment is extreme fictive sympathy. The writer who maintains most successfully a consistent cold detachment toward physical violence . . . is likely to generate the deepest novelistic sympathy of all, a sympathy which is a humbling before the terrible and a quickening in the presence of degradation."[15] He cites American novelists Djuna Barnes, Flannery O'Connor, and Nathanael West as forerunners in the comic treatment of absurdity, violence, and extreme fictive detachment, and he praises them for their abilities in generating compassion without authorial intrusion. All human beings, argues Hawkes, are "poor, forked, and corruptible," and the necessary artist is the one who encourages recognition of the contemptible while insisting on the absolute need for sympathy. Persuading the reader to cope with the same visionary experiences that the characters suffer is one way to convince the reader of the solace of compassion. When menace is everywhere, sympathy is all.

This is not to suggest, of course, that remnants of Hawkes's life never reappear in his fiction. As Patrick O'Donnell has discovered, a few isolated biographical moments have lodged in the author's memory to resurface later as illustrations of the transforming power of the imagination. A riding stable near his grandfather's property in Connecticut, for example, suggested the immensity of horses, and Hawkes uses the image of the horse as destructive force in *The Lime Twig* and *Death, Sleep & the Traveler* (1974) to connote primal strength and the unity of sex, terror, and beauty. Similarly, a childhood memory of stepping on a hornet's nest while on a family outing during which his father recalled the joys of his own youth turns up in *The Passion Artist* as a disturbing account of how the most intense pleasure inadvertently triggers the most unexpected pain. Finally, Hawkes remembers living in Alaska as a ten-year-old child and becoming fascinated by a strange cove that exposed a mysteriously wrecked airplane when the tide was low. The excitement of the unknown and the lure of violent death united in his recollection of the ruined plane, and he reshaped the experience to create the crashing aircraft (*The Lime Twig*), the eerie ocean liners (*Death, Sleep & the Traveler*), and the dangerous automobiles (*Second Skin, Travesty*) that often signal the enticing combination of thrill and destruction when one is enclosed in such isolated compartments, symbols of the psychic journey itself.[16] Unlike more standard novelists, then, Hawkes does not use the facts of his life as the foundations of his art. Rather, he transforms a few memories into imaginative visions, indirectly denying the validity of realism while directly practicing his theory of authorial detachment. In the unknown territory of vision and dislocation the writer can introduce himself and his reader to the promise of created worlds. Narrative distance often encourages narrative energy. Detachment enhances art.

UNDERSTANDING JOHN HAWKES

Characters left so totally to their own devices are likely to stumble in laughable ways, and it is important to understand that Hawkes considers himself foremost a comic novelist. He comments: "I have always thought that my fictions, no matter how diabolical, were comic. I wanted to be very comic— but they have not been treated as comedy. . . . In *Second Skin* I wanted to be sure, first, that the comedy would be unmistakable."[17] The reference to *Second Skin* is revealing, for the main character, Skipper, is a buffoon who survives a scale of indignities ranging from snowball fights through belly-bumping contests to the suicides of his loved ones, but he survives with his lust for love and life even stronger. The larger point is that Hawkes uses comedy to extend the reaches of compassion. The comic tone of his novels is what he calls "a saving attitude," an affirmation that pulls both novelist and reader back into the realm of "permanent human values."

Once again, however, the reader must be prepared for the unexpected. Trained to read sophisticated comedy via the fiction of Jane Austen or Henry Fielding, the reader expects the humor to be directed against characters who violate the social norm. In *Emma* and *Tom Jones* laughter encourages those who stray beyond the boundaries of propriety to reintegrate themselves with society and its accepted codes of behavior. This venerable comic tradition, however, rests on an assumption by both author and reader that a recognizable social norm exists. Comedy in such novels is a means of maintaining order. One thinks of Austen's Emma and Fielding's Jones enduring the snickers of their peers and associates before recognizing their wayward actions and acquiescing to the demands of normal behavior. Laughter is thus a corrective measure and a means to conformity.

Not so in Hawkes. Writing in an era when the threat of nuclear apocalypse is ever present and the isolation of the individual a daily fear, he cannot believe in the reality of a verifiable social norm. The laughter in his novels is not the humor of resolution in which an odd person is reunited with his fellows but the comedy of the inappropriate response. Hawkes argues that the highest form of comedy in his work produces not only laughter but also "a kind of light."[18] His characters have no norm to return to, and thus their responses to the often violent surprises of their psychic journeys seem laughable to the reader who rests securely in the safety of his own normal affairs. When Skipper, for instance, tries to transpose the iced snowballs purposely hurled against him into accidental attacks by escaped homing pigeons and eaglets, the reader laughs at his unexpected reaction to a brutal act that bloodies his face. Unlike traditional comedy, then, Hawkes's cuts two ways: it underscores the dislocation of contemporary life, but it also persuades the reader to empathize with life's victims.

Hawkes traces the line of what he defines as a "comic appetite for invented calamities" back from O'Connor, West, and Barnes through Céline to the Spanish picaresque writer Quevedo because he finds in these authors a determination to "face up to the enormities of ugliness and potential failure within ourselves and in the world around us, and to bring to this exposure a savage or saving comic spirit and the saving beauties of language."[19] Comic response and lyrical prose are affirmations in Hawkes. Both sadistic and liberating, the comic spirit involves surprise, which for Hawkes is an indication of life's vitality and potential. He explains that comedy "ameliorates pain through laughter. . . . through laughter there is release, vilification, possible purification, and, finally, identification with the victim."[20] Always confronting the reader with what he terms "the truth of the fractured picture," he uses comic distortion to expand the limits of the imagination, to encourage compassion, and to suggest the promise of futurity in life itself. Michael Banks (*The Lime Twig*) may inadvertently parody the hero of a slapstick movie when he gives his life to stop the crooked horse race by dashing in front of the thundering herd, but his bumbling sacrifice is an affirmative act, an insistence on the possibilities of meaningful gestures.

Hawkes's celebration of comedy extends to the structure of his fiction. Urged on by his need to parody the conventions of the traditional novel, he has changed his writing from the nearly pure vision of *The Cannibal* to fictions that on the surface seem closer to standard narrative. The presence of a narrator telling a tale is much stronger in *Second Skin* and *Travesty*, for example, than in *The Cannibal* and *The Beetle Leg*. Yet a comic treatment of novelistic structure and technique is always an issue in Hawkes. How the novel is put together is fair game for the reader's laughter. Careful reading shows that his sense of a fractured social order is reflected not only in his insistence on imaginative vision but also in his disruption of fictional technique.

His best-known statement on the art of the novel speaks to this point. In a comment that continues to raise eyebrows Hawkes said in 1965 that he "began to write fiction on the assumption that the true enemies of the novel were plot, character, setting, and theme."[21] As radical as this opinion first appears, one must not make the mistake of assuming that Hawkes abandons the reader when he jettisons the elemental props of storytelling. Rather, he hopes to liberate both author and reader—the former from the reader's expectations; the latter from the realistic tradition—as a means of revitalizing the genre of the novel. Hawkes's pronouncement does not mean that his novels lack plot, character, setting, and theme. What he insists on is that plots need not follow the format of beginning, middle, and end; that characters need not be "round" or totally knowable; that settings need not be representational or even recognizable; and that themes need not be packaged for the reader's benefit or resolved at the conclusion.

Confronted with such a clear rejection of the staples of the novel, the reader might well ask, "What is left?" Imaginative vision, the beauty of language, and innovative structure are the answers. Hawkes elaborates: "My novels are not highly plotted, but certainly they're elaborately structured. . . . having once abandoned these familiar ways of thinking about fiction, totality of vision or structure was really all that remained."[22] Defining structure as "verbal and psychological

coherence," he unifies his novels and advances the tale not by
the mechanics of plot but by "recurring image and recurring
action." The significance of color imagery (green, yellow,
white, and black) in *Second Skin*, for instance, is established
with such conviction in the first chapter that the reader learns
to look for the recurrence of the colors as clues to tone and
character. Thus the reader who feels at home with the nuances
of poetry, a genre that often depends on the placement and development of image patterns, will find Hawkes's fiction readily accessible despite the surface difficulties.

The point is that Hawkes trusts the reader. Rather than
supply commentary from a reliable narrator or nudges toward comprehension from the author himself, he encourages
the reader to rely on his own imagination and intuition while
struggling with the related images. As Hawkes notes, "This
kind of structure can't be planned in advance but can only be
discovered in the writing process itself. The success of the effort depends on the degree and quality of consciousness that
can be brought to bear on fully liberated materials of the unconscious. I'm trying to hold in balance poetic and novelistic
methods in order to make the novel a more valid and pleasur-
able experience."[23] Just as the author cannot plan this innovative approach to structure in advance, so the reader should
not expect a traditional method of organizing a novel when he
opens a book by Hawkes. The unusual technique becomes
clear to the author as he writes and to the reader as he reads.
Hawkes requires an active reader.

UNDERSTANDING JOHN HAWKES

Parody is one way to violate the traditional "rules" of fiction and to urge the reader to close attention. The first-person omniscient narrator—a paradox in itself—of *The Cannibal* parodies the conventional storyteller. *The Beetle Leg* is a parody of the popular Western in which the John Wayne figure does not arrive in the nick of time. *The Lime Twig* is a parody of the crime thriller in which the main characters all die and the police remain forever baffled. The first sentence of *Second Skin*—"I will tell you in a few words who I am"—parodies one of the most famous beginnings in fiction, Charles Dickens's *David Copperfield*, a traditional novel that begins where traditional novels traditionally begin, at the beginning: "I am born." Rejecting the safeties of familiarity, Hawkes deliberately disrupts the conventions of fiction and takes seriously the artist's mandate to break new ground.

Once he frees the reader from familiar ways of looking at novels and experience, he offers the beauty of language which, along with comedy, is one of the "saving graces." Filling his novels with unusually articulate narrators, and lavishing their tales with stunningly lyrical prose, he celebrates language as a promise of communication in a disheartening world. Hawkes is on record as appreciating paradox, and he defines language as paradox because it is "intelligence turned into sound." That is to say, it makes the intangible concrete. In this sense language may be said not to exist at all. Yet, as he points out, "In another sense, it's the most powerful kind of actuality, so that the paradox of a man behaving through language means that the behavior both exists and does not exist.

UNDERSTANDING JOHN HAWKES

We can do things with language that we can never do with other forms of action."[24]

Perhaps the most accessible introduction to Hawkes's language and vision is *The Owl* (1954). A novella, its short length allows readers unprepared to grapple with unconventional plotting and nightmarish imagery to digest the unexpected in a manageable dosage. *The Owl* is also an early illustration of Hawkes's tendency to organize his fiction around the voice of a single obsessed narrator. In *The Owl* the narrator speaks in the first person and controls tone and mood, and thus the reader must be wary of succumbing to the insistent prodding of a storyteller who turns out to be a parody of Italian fascism. Indeed, the voice of Il Gufo ("the owl") is so overwhelming to both victims and readers alike that Robert Scholes likens the novel to a dramatic monologue by Robert Browning. Like Browning, Hawkes "delights in immersing his readers in the voice and vision of a character whose consciousness is disturbing to 'normal' sensibilities. The point of this immersion in the abhorrent is to force readers to acknowledge a kind of complicity, to admit that something in us resonates to all sorts of monstrous measures, even as we recognize and condemn the evil consciousness for what it is."[25] *The Owl* is one of the clearest examples of Hawkes's insistence that the reader sympathize with the nightmarish and the absurd because of repressed but recognizable tendencies in himself. As Scholes notes, such a balance of complicity and condemnation requires delicate control by the author. Hawkes must convince the reader to laugh at and understand

Il Gufo's rigid morality at the same time that he shows the reader the monstrosity of Gufo's obsession with law and sterility.

The Owl is also a good introduction to how Hawkes uses recurring images rather than conventional plotting to structure a novel. The plot of *The Owl*, like the plots of many of his novels, is relatively simple to outline: The Italian town of Sasso Fetore ("tomb stench") has endured an unnamed war long enough to lose all of its marriageable men except Il Gufo, the hangman. Women, however, continue to grow and desire husbands, and thus the fathers with daughters and dowries petition the Owl to permit marriage to the single male prisoner in the Owl's fortress or even to the Owl himself. But Gufo fears the prisoner, who may be a redeemer of love and life, and he dooms the captive to horrifying pain. Safe in his fascist fiefdom, assured of the stench of continued sterility, Il Gufo guarantees the ironic stability of this wretched wasteland.

Hawkes advances *The Owl*, however, not so much by progressive action as by patterns of elaborately extended images. One such pattern revolves around the religious connotations of the word *Sunday*. Associated with such traditional ideas as the day of rest, God's creation, ceremonial worship, and the promise of eternal life, Sunday in *The Owl* becomes suspect when the reader learns early in the novel that "politically, historically, Sasso Fetore was an eternal Sabbath."[26] The reader thinks not of rest and peace but of an endless stupor. The Prince Charming of "Sleeping Beauty," suggested by the hangman's prisoner, will have little success with the waiting

UNDERSTANDING JOHN HAWKES

virgins in this tale. True to Hawkes's rebellion against conventional morality, he writes that the history of the "eternal Sabbath" may be traced back to the priests of a "primitive monastic order whose members worked in strict obedience and were the first inhabitants of the province" (42). Armed with religious authority, the monks have enacted the original puritanical laws that continue to repress the populace. Those, like the prisoner, who offer sexuality and vitality must be chained to inhibition, represented by the prisoner's cell. Thus the biblical tomb of Christ, once the promise of forgiveness and eternity, becomes in *The Owl* the eternal tomb of sterility. The hangman's gallows is his chosen bride, and the statue of the mythical mother of Jesus, the "Donna," symbol of mercy and love, is kicked off its pedestal, forgotten in the forest. Even the pathos of the Last Supper degenerates into a parody of cruelty as Gufo and his twelve disciples sit at the table, eat the "cuisine of justice," and condemn the prisoner. As *The Owl* suggests, religious rituals inevitably decline to sterile prescriptions of law. Those who have no choice except to believe find themselves trapped in a cycle of "thou shalt nots," forever victims of religion's victimizing mentality. Significantly, the final word of the novel is "blessing."

Readers of *The Owl* may work out additional implications of this image pattern. For example, one might consider the whorish red paint applied to the cheeks of the Donna, or the parody of the flight of the dove of peace when the prisoner attempts to escape by flying. The important point is that Hawkes uses linked images with expanding meanings to structure a novel that reveals how those deprived of the liberating forces of sexuality and futurity are caught in an eternal Sabbath where they are finally attracted to the very power that inhibits them. Antonina, the most desirable virgin, eventually offers herself to the hangman. Virgin births in Sasso Fetore are sure to be stillborn, and the Owl himself is a victim of the bleak tradition he upholds.

The darkness of *The Owl* is apparent to even the most facile peruser, but the careful reader also notices the comedy. An early example of Hawkes's interest in comic terror, the novel undercuts the mechanical gestures of people who live not by instinct and desire but by ritual. History dominates them all, from the hangman to the prisoner, and history in *The Owl* is a book of the dead dragging from the necks of the living. Walking in the tower, Il Gufo senses "that curious feeling in the fortress of half human, half mildew of history" (11).

Stuck in such a regularized continuum in which life's content gives way to style, the populace of Sasso Fetore is a comic dupe of the history it strains to honor. The town is described as "a judgment passed upon the lava, long out of date," and the aging virgins are doomed to read *Laws of the Young Women Not Yet Released to Marriage.* As an example of mechanical action used for comedy, the reader might consider the conclusion of the hangman's synod, itself a parody of the Last Supper. The twelve Mongers and the hangman gather to debate the prisoner's fate, which, of course, has been decided for the last thousand years ever since the first law about prisoners was passed by the ancient monks. Even the meal of fish and the instructions as to how to eat it are prescribed by tradition. Any departure from the rules set down by the "primitive monastic order" is a threat. In the midst of this comically gothic dinner, complete with a hunchback waiter, a real owl, and an aura of fairy tales, Barabo rises to address the hangman. Knowing that all gestures in Sasso Fetore are stylized, the reader awaits Barabo's mechanical act. When the petitioner tears open his shirt to expose a stomach now full of fish—the signal that he wishes to speak to Il Gufo—the reader can do little except grin. *The Owl* is a pessimistic novel, but the exaggerated horror and the comic bumbling of all the characters, including Il Gufo, save it from being an exploitation of terror.

Those who would read *The Owl* and the novels of John Hawkes with pleasure need only remain alert, open to the infinite variations of fiction, willing to experience the unexpected in both technique and imagination, ready to acknowledge their own psychic sores as they confront an incredible series of obsessed visionaries who stumble through nightmarish adventures in terrifying but comic ways.

Notes

1. Andrew Fielding, "John Hawkes Is a Very Nice Guy, and a Novelist of Sex and Death," *Village Voice* 24 May 1976: 45.

2. Fielding 45.

3. Fielding 46.

4. Fielding 47.

5. "Hawkes and Barth Talk about Fiction," *New York Times Book Review* 1 Apr. 1979: 31.

6. Thomas LeClair, "The Novelists: John Hawkes," *New Republic* 10 Nov. 1979: 27.

7. "Interview," John Kuehl, *John Hawkes and the Craft of Conflict* (New Brunswick: Rutgers University Press, 1975) 157.

8. Kuehl 166.

9. Kuehl 164–65.

10. Kuehl 162.

11. C. Hugh Holman, *A Handbook to Literature*, 4th ed. (Indianapolis: Bobbs-Merrill, 1980) 302.

12. "Conversations between Patrick O'Donnell and John Hawkes on His Life and Art," O'Donnell, *John Hawkes* (Boston: Twayne, 1982) 2.

13. "A Conversation on *The Blood Oranges* between John Hawkes and Robert Scholes," *Novel* 5 (1972): 205.

14. O'Donnell 3.

15. John Hawkes, "Notes on *The Wild Goose Chase*," *Massachusetts Review* 3 (1962): 787.

16. O'Donnell 4–10.

17. John Graham, "John Hawkes on His Novels," *Massachusetts Review* 7 (1966): 459.

18. Kuehl 173.

19. John Enck, "John Hawkes: An Interview," *Wisconsin Studies in Contemporary Literature* 6 (1965): 144.

20. Kuehi 175.

21. Enck 149.

22. Enck 149.

23. Enck 149.

24. Kuehl 176.

25. Robert Scholes, introduction, *The Owl*, by John Hawkes (1954; New York: New Directions, 1977) vii.

26. John Hawkes, *The Goose on the Grave* and *The Owl* (New York: New Directions, 1954) 17. Further references will be noted parenthetically.

CHAPTER TWO

THE CANNIBAL

T|*he Cannibal* is a war novel unlike any other in American literature. There is no emphasis on the disillusionment of young soldiers, on the coming of age of hopeful idealists, on the wrecked morale of entire regiments, or on the physical agony of conquering new territory. There is, however, a focus on nightmare and horror, hallucination and dream, violence and death, and conscious disruption of reader complacency and fictional technique. Where *The Cannibal* does connect with other war fiction is Hawkes's suggestion that though many battles are fought, few are won, and victory remains an illusion of idiots and fools.

When Hawkes published his first fiction in 1949—the novella *Charivari* and the novel *The Cannibal*—he stopped writing poetry. In 1943, at age eighteen, he had privately printed a collection of poems titled *Fiasco Hall* in an edition of 150 copies, but, as he explains, "The war intervened and the war was a kind of shocking acting-out of internal nightmare, as if all of our nightmares had become literally real. After the war I turned to prose quite by accident because my wife gave me a novel to read. I didn't like the novel and thought I could do better and began to write with extreme detachment."[1]

The Cannibal was written for Professor Albert Guerard's class at Harvard. The germ of the novel was a notice in Time about a cannibal in Bremen, Germany, where Hawkes had been stationed during part of World War II. The composition took nine months, and while Hawkes claims that the novel was not extensively revised, he does admit that it was rearranged at Guerard's suggestion: Hawkes collected the sections relating to 1914 and moved them to the middle of the book.

He focused most of the relatively minor revisions on the problem of narration. The novel was originally written in the voice of the third person, but true to Hawkes's instinct to parody the coventional props of fiction, he switched the third-person voice to first person when he revised. This change created a comically omniscient first-person narrator, a paradoxical point of view who knows more than he should but who cannot act on all that he knows. Hawkes comments: "The Cannibal was written in the third person, but in revision I found myself (perversely or not) wishing to project myself into the fiction and to become identified with its most criminal and, in a conventional sense, least sympathetic spokesman, the neo-Nazi leader of the hallucinated uprising. I simply went through the manuscript and changed the pronouns from third to first person, so that the neo-Nazi Zizendorf became the teller of those absurd and violent events. The result was interesting, I think, not because The Cannibal became a genuine example of first-person fiction, but because its 'narrator' natu-

THE CANNIBAL

rally possessed an unusual omniscience, while the authorial consciousness was given specific definition, definition in terms of humor and 'black' intelligence."[2]

Since *The Cannibal* is a direct result of Hawkes's experiences as an ambulance driver in the war, it is appropriate that the primary action of the novel be dated 1945, his last year as a member of the American Field Service. But while Hawkes also refers to the First World War of 1914–18 and to the Franco-Prussian War of 1870–71, he specifies that the real time of *The Cannibal* is the future. The allusions to three separate European wars in three distinct periods illustrate the never-endingness of horror. As Hawkes observes, "This juxtaposition at the outset is intended to try to suggest that perhaps we don't move so much in cycles as repetitions or that we have always had these particular problems of violence, destruction, sadism and so on."[3]

Despairing of the absurdity and chaos of war, Hawkes describes Germany, the aggressor in three consecutive conflicts, as an insane asylum. *The Cannibal* begins with Germany's crawling out of the asylum, and it ends with the slaughter of children, the success of the neo-Nazi coup, and the reentry of Germany into insanity. War once again obliterates the future. The last sentence—"She did as she was told"—is the response of a child to the command of the mad Zizendorf to go back to sleep. The automatic obedience of youth guarantees the dictatorial power of the insane. Hawkes compares the conclusion of *The Cannibal* to Albert Camus's *The Plague*: "It's the idea, more the notion, of the latency of de-

structive force, rather than the possibility of life-force."⁴ At
this early point in Hawkes's fiction sterility rules the landscape. The life force that he celebrates in later novels gives
way in *The Cannibal* to perversity and pain. One cannot forget that Madame Snow, the woman of vitality and promise in
1914, participates in the eating of the child in 1945. Germany
is a nation that not only ravages its heritage but also devours
its future.

Hawkes's disillusioned response to the shock of war is not
that different from the responses of other American novelists
returning from the battlefield. The reaction of two famous
ambulance drivers in World War I is an example. At the end of
Three Soldiers (1921), John Dos Passos writes of the defeat of
John Andrews, the musician of sensitivity and hope. As the
MPs surround his room, the sheets of his musical composition
"flew off the table, until the floor was littered with them."
Similarly, at the conclusion of *A Farewell to Arms* (1929), Ernest Hemingway describes the despair of Frederic Henry, the
man who has learned the meaning of love in the chaos of war.
After his beloved and baby die, he has nothing to do except to
walk back to the hotel in the rain.

Hawkes's sense of defeat in *The Cannibal* is comparable.
There is nothing unusual about a young novelist writing negatively to express his bewilderment in a war. Yet unlike *Three
Soldiers* and *A Farewell to Arms*, *The Cannibal* is a shocking
reading experience. The nightmare hangs especially heavy;
the violent events are truly dire; and the dense, often lyrical
prose forces the reader to slow down and consciously work

his way through the book. By any standard *The Cannibal* is a difficult novel to understand after one reading, and its difference lies not in the author's reaction to war but in the extraordinary, dreamlike vision that he gives to it. The effects of the novel are visual rather than active. Although there is plot in the sense of Zizendorf's planning to ambush the American military overseer, the novel progresses by various series of recurring events and linked images.

Hawkes is aware of the visual uniqueness of *The Cannibal*: "I write out of a series of pictures that literally and actually do come to mind, but I've never seen them before. It is perfectly true that I don't know what they mean, but I feel and know that they have meaning. *The Cannibal* is probably the clearest example of this kind of absolute coherence of vision of anything I have written, when all the photographs do add together or come right out of the same black pit. Yes, it is visual, it's compulsive, and a conscious knowledge of exactly what it means is not always there."[5] He has in mind such eerie scenes as the riot in the asylum; the frozen, dead monkeys that seem to speak; and the unsettling picture of the lone American, Leevey, overseeing one third of Germany on his motorcycle. Hawkes does not like to specify meanings for these isolated snapshots because to do so is to limit the reverberations of fear and uncertainty that are generated when the scenes are read in context. Yet he worries about readers who resist these imaginative visions, who require ready connections between meaning and metaphor, and who "make it sound as if it is something that is merely happening to me, as if I am a mere receptacle or a vehicle and the imaginative image passes through, as if I had nothing to do with it."[6] As he notes, he thinks about and shapes the visionary set pieces as much as any serious writer. Narrative drive is not at all dismissed in *The Cannibal*; indeed, the pressure of Zizendorf's pursuit of Leevey builds to a comically absurd climax. Yet the reader must understand that the traditional staples of characterization and dialogue are less important to the progression of the tale than the revelation of psychic depths offered by such recurring images of terror as the monkeys, the roving packs of dogs, and the dead horse. Bestiality has usurped the humanity of the surviving Germans, and random acts of violence merely mirror the officially sanctioned violence of war.

The Cannibal is a long way from *Three Soldiers* and *A Farewell to Arms* in its nightmarish response to the shock of total conflict. But while it seems closer in tone and vision to such bleakly dark European fictions as Kafka's *The Trial* and Céline's *Journey to the End of Night*, *The Cannibal* is American in its depiction of innocence horrified by the experience it is forced to confront. Hawkes's reaction to war is not that different from Edgar Allan Poe's fearful uncertainty in *The Narrative of Arthur Gordon Pym* or Herman Melville's terror in the face of the ubiquitous color white in *Moby-Dick*. In American fiction innocent characters are often yanked into the depths of the psyche once they set out on journeys through less-than-hospitable territory. *The Cannibal* is thus both an American war novel and an illustration of the gothic strain in American literature. Hayden Carruth comments: "Obviously we may compare him to Kafka, Céline, Orwell, Hesse, but it

THE CANNIBAL

is more important to recognize that he is also radically unlike these writers, that he is genuinely American, and that his personal style is transformed by the intensity of his vision into something as impersonal as truth itself. Nowhere has the nightmare of human terror and the deracinated sensibility been more concisely analyzed than in *The Cannibal*."[7]

Albert Guerard, Hawkes's mentor, also invokes Kafka—along with William Faulkner and Djuna Barnes—when he discusses Hawkes's first novel. In an introduction to the first edition of *The Cannibal*, Guerard argues that the novelist's task is not to clear away the "peripheral difficulties and obstacles of strangeness" that often confound readers of an unconventional novel: "The merely secondary difficulties and obstacles involved in the first appearance of a Franz Kafka or a William Faulkner or a Djuna Barnes are not comparable to those involved in the first appearance of a conventional realist . . . and perhaps it would be well if we could get at the restless and original Kafkas at least, if not at the Djuna Barneses, over a shorter period of ridicule, without having to wait so long."[8] Guerard realizes that the challenge represented by *The Cannibal* is not for Hawkes to write more conventionally but for the public to read more imaginatively. At this stage of his career, says Guerard, Hawkes is more difficult than Kafka and Faulkner, and as demanding as Barnes. Like these authors, and like James Joyce, Henry James, and Joseph Conrad before them, Hawkes refuses to tell a story directly.

Only a truly attentive reader can outline even the bare bones of the plot: The smashed, warring nation of Germany in 1945 looks back to a similar plunge from glory in 1918; as the isolated American Leevey travels through Germany in 1945 on his motorcycle, representing the American forces of occupation, Stella Snow, daughter of a German general, recalls 1914, when she conspires with the English traitor Cromwell and marries the Christ-driven Ernst; now old in 1945, she runs a boardinghouse where her sister Jutta, Zizendorf's mistress, lives with a daughter; the obsessed Zizendorf, a parody of the crazed artist figure in that he creates his private vision of a newly armed, triumphant Germany, plots Leevey's death; he succeeds with ridiculous ease, and as the insane asylum reopens its doors at the end of the novel, Germany metaphorically readies for a new round of war, Nazism, and murder.

The plot, however, is more a vehicle for the nightmarish visions and the exposure of war's utter horror than a traditional story with beginning, middle, and end. Very little of the plot develops consecutively, and what is revealed seems difficult to unravel because of Hawkes's unusual characterization of the narrator. Zizendorf has a godlike omniscience that in his crazed mind allows him to narrate in 1945 the events of 1914, when he was not present, and bits of the Franco-Prussian War in 1870, when he was not alive. Not only must the reader determine the relevance of what Zizendorf does; he must also decide the reliability of what Zizendorf says. His insanity, his combination of sexual violence and sterility, and his insistence on Leevey's murder illustrate Hawkes's youthful, horrified reaction to Germany, the most destructive—and most destroyed—of modern nations at the end of World War II. In *The Cannibal*, Hawkes reveals his fear that World War III is eminently possible.

THE CANNIBAL

Convinced that a conventionally structured novel might betray a conventional response to war, Hawkes establishes Germany as a metaphor for the nightmare of the twentieth century, and he fills it with images that do the work of standard narrative: cannibalized children, dry sex, memories of Teutonic pride, and a blasted landscape choked with pestilential canals and cold wind. Starving children see the asylum as an "empty scorpion," and their town is described as "roosting on charred earth" and "gaunt beneath an evil cloaked moon." This developing animal imagery, itself an indicator of humanity turning bestial, encompasses the entire populace: "The town, without its walls and barricades, though still a campsite of a thousand years, was as shriveled in structure and as decomposed as an ox tongue black with ants."[9] Disturbing images, suggests Hawkes, better communicate the unspeakable despair of war than stacks of statistics and realistic descriptions of wounded soldiers. His visual imagery is as effective and as eerie as silently televised accounts of battle carnage.

As Guerard observes, the plot of *The Cannibal* is "radically" out of focus. Hawkes intends the distortion. Yet the linked images provide flickers of light for the reader to make his way across the dark terrain. Reader attention is mandatory, for the full impact of an image or of a fragment of information may not become clear for dozens of pages. Early in the novel, for example, Hawkes writes:

A man followed, swinging a cane, craning into the darkness. The child passed a wall spattered with holes and the fingers of a dead defender, and behind him, the man coughed.

A butcher shop was closing and a few cold strands of flesh hung unsold from hooks, the plucked skin and crawling veins uninspected, hanging, but without official sanction. Wire caught the child's knee (7).

This unearthly scene is typical of the entire novel. Detail dominates narrative motion, and the reader notes the casual allusion to the fingers of a dead soldier spattering the wall that the child runs past. Mention of the butcher shop adds to the macabre effect, for the little meat available is plucked and crawling with veins, recalling the butchering of human beings in war. The black joke that the meat lacks the sanction of official inspection seems to cap the scene. But when the reader reaches the last third of the novel, he realizes that the most important point in this early passage is the one that initially seems to go nowhere: the coughing man following the running child. For this is the first account of the cannibal, the Duke who will slice up Jutta's boy and serve him to Madame Snow. The sentence "Wire caught the child's knee" directly alludes to an obstacle in the boy's way, but it indirectly connects the victim to the plucked meat in the butcher shop hanging "unsold from hooks." The next sentence begins "The town, roosting on charred earth" and thus completes the first image pattern of animals slaughtered into unsanctioned meat. Germany cannibalizes itself. Only by attending to the developing sequences can the reader appreciate the full measure of *The Cannibal*. Visual impact is at least as significant as narrative progression

THE CANNIBAL

and advancing theme. As Guerard writes in a memorable sentence, "Terror can create its own geography" (xiii).

In the case of *The Cannibal* the geography of terror is the landscape of the mind. Hawkes fashions a "Germany" that is the territory of the psychic slime which oozes over humanity when the constraints of civilized behavior are negated by war. And yet for all the power of this invented domain, Hawkes aids the reader by supplying historical parallels to some of the characters and their actions. History may indeed be the primary character in the novel, the force that Zizendorf underestimates. Historical processes are blindly powerful and absurd, and they finally appropriate even Zizendorf's mad rekindling of the neo-Nazi flame.

The keeper of the flame is Stella Snow. The personification of German militarism, of the Teutonic heritage itself, she touches both ends of the 1870–1945 continuum of war. Since she is the daughter of a German general who has fought in the Franco-Prussian War, she inherits the nation's battle cry as part of her life's sustenance. By 1914 Stella is associated with the Archduchess who was present at Sarajevo, the site of the beginning of World War I. In 1945 she is the Queen Mother of the defeated country, and she mistakenly believes that support of Zizendorf will help to prop up Germany to past heights of military glory. She does not realize that she sips the soup of her cannibalized family. As the presiding spirit of the German race Stella devours herself. Hawkes's sense of German self-destruction is clear, but, typically, he makes the point indirectly, relying on the reader to identify the unifying links among the fragmented parts.

Zizendorf understands Stella's power. Calling her "the very hangman, the eater, the greatest leader of us all," he looks to her as the personification of nationalism. But he misses the irony of his equation of eater and leader, and though he comically claims omniscience as a narrator, he cannot see that history is the force that will eat him too. His plan to assassinate the American Leevey in order to take command of another Teutonic uprising is also ironic, for *The Cannibal* shows that Zizendorf is as much a plaything of history as the nameless sufferers who populate his wretched land. History is no more than a cycle of terror. War begets war begets war.

Yet true to Hawkes's belief that comedy is a saving grace, he ridicules the historical process even while he insists on its fierceness. The reader may laugh with terror, but the ability to grin is a sign of humanity. A case in point is the parallel between Stella's family and history.

Stella's father, for example, is a hero of the Franco-Prussian War, but in 1914 he is too senile to remember the lesson of 1870: that history cannibalizes its participants. The Germans march into Paris, but at incalculable cost. The populace forgets too, and thus when they surge to the old German's balcony at the outbreak of World War I, Hawkes comically undercuts the fire in their eyes by referring to the eventual feebleness of their bodies:

1870, it would take many dead men to encircle Paris, and the responsibility, that's what he didn't understand or no one could speak in such a manner, pride on the heights. "War," her father said, and there was a terrible fire in his eye through the ferns. "War," and he leaned slightly forward as if to strike her, but his arm only raised part way, shivered, and dropped back on the plate (67).

Historical repetitions produce little except catastrophe, and individuality gives way to the martial imperative of nationalism. As Hawkes shows, the predicament is a sick joke on all of humanity. The old general totters before the mob that remains hushed and reverent even though it realizes that the aged warrior can speak only one word at a time. Stressing the ridiculousness of this historical moment, Hawkes simultaneously laughs and shudders at man's inability to remember the past and learn from it:

All at once he spoke, and the single word fell upon them hushed and excited. "Victory." For a moment they waited for more, watched, listened and then broke out in screams of appreciation while the old man was led back inside the house. They did not realize that he thought the war, which had just begun, was over, and they took up the word and sent it flying along the street from one startled citizen to the next (70).

Stella's comic relic of a father confuses the meaning of victory, but the reader gets the point: victory and defeat are relative concepts when history's wars indiscriminately bloody both sides. The most unexpected connection in the novel between the forces of history and the characters of *The Cannibal* underscores this truth. In a frighteningly comic scene the parallels with history succumb to identification with it, and Stella, Cromwell, and Ernst helplessly reenact the assassination of Archduke Ferdinand at Sarajevo, the disaster that plummeted the western world into war in 1914. History's blind force makes pawns of even those who dominate the situation. History usurps individuality.

This astonishing scene begins with a drunken Ernst remembering other tipplers who have stumbled in the alley behind the beer hall, "sprawled like a murdered Archduke, his face in the bile" (53). Hawkes expects the alert reader to catch the allusion to the assassinated Ferdinand, for the reader must understand that Ernst is now somehow a historical personage in Sarajevo. The guns of August are about to thunder. Racing up the "avenue of heroes," the thoroughfare to destiny on which individuality is cannibalized by nationalism as suggested in the progression of the statues that Ernst passes (*"love, Stella, Ernst, lust, tonight, leader, land"*), Ernst finds that he is running "to coincide with Princip in Sarajevo" (54–55). Once again the reader must be alert, for Gavrilo Princip was the assassin who triggered the war. True to Hawkes's insistence that history is a bizarre joker, however, he makes Ernst jump from the avenue of heroes to the bushes of the park because of a need to urinate: Ernst has drunk too much beer. Aware that he may lose sight of Stella and Cromwell, but powerless before this call from nature, he fumbles in the foliage, somehow intuiting that "already the guns were being oiled and the Belgians, not he, would use that Merchant as a target" (55).

THE CANNIBAL

By this time, of course, the reader realizes that Ernst-Princip pursues the carriage of Cromwell-Ferdinand and Stella-Archduchess. Cromwell-Ferdinand predicts his own role in the cycle of history that is about to explode, and he understands in 1914 that the "loyalty of civilization" in Germany will fan the fires of nationalism for the next half century. Incredibly, Cromwell-Ferdinand defines war as merely an "incident":

It is pleasant, in moments such as these, knowing with certainty an approaching catastrophe, to view the whole incident that will probably extend fifty years, not as the death of politics or the fall of kings and wives, but as the loyalty of civilization, to realize that Krupp, perhaps a barbarian, is more the peg where history hangs than a father who once spoke of honor (55).

The allusion to Krupp, the German munitions manufacturer, is another way that Hawkes indirectly helps the reader. Even the great Krupp is a pawn of history. Following Cromwell-Ferdinand's speech, Stella declares that she will be his "Archduchess for the people," and the historical tableau is replayed before the reader's eyes. Ernst-Princip overtakes the carriage after his exit from the bushes; Cromwell-Ferdinand anticipates the "short muzzle of the pistol" and the explosion into pain and death; and Stella-Archduchess knows that she has finally identified "her greatest love": war.

As Hawkes concludes this startling scene, he underlines the union of history and fiction in *The Cannibal:*

Francis Ferdinand lay on the seat of the carriage, his light shirt filled with blood, his epaulettes askew and on the floor lay the body of his departed wife, while the assassin, Gavrilo Princip, ran mad through the encircling streets. Obviously the advent of the great war would not throw them all together, make them friends, or even make them enemies; Ernie was ready, even in the throes of love, for a goal of religious fanaticism; Cromwell simply longed, desperately, to fit into the conflict somewhere; and Stella knew only that she was climbing high and would someday lose him (56).

The freedom of fiction reshapes the facts of history, and Hawkes's characters both play out their roles and anticipate the disaster. Later in the novel Stella looks at her dead mother and wonders, "Gavrilo . . . what have you done?" (79).

What Gavrilo has done is obvious; he has begun a cycle of terror that engulfs the twentieth century and that has its roots in the Franco-Prussian War. But what Hawkes has done is something else; he has structured *The Cannibal* so that the fragmentation, the patterns of images and of historical allusions, and the wrenching, humorous asides all mirror the disruption of orderly progression that causes uncertainty in contemporary life. War has become so unthinkable with its proximity to apocalypse, initiated by the advent of nuclear weapons, that Hawkes fears a conventional novel would spark only a conventional response. War is not, he argues, an opportunity for experience and fame but the arena of disaster. Battlefields lead to battle casualties, and casualties lead to death.

What better way, then, to insist on the importance of the individual than to celebrate the creativity of the imagination? This Hawkes does in *The Cannibal*. The novel is thematically pessimistic but artistically affirmative because Hawkes believes that new imaginative constructions are signs of life. Form counters confusion. Thus while the characters continue their slosh through the mire of history, the author maintains his commitment to imaginative projection. The final curve of the cycle in *The Cannibal* takes place in 1945.

By the end of World War II the glory that Cromwell-Ferdinand seeks and the power that Stella-Archduchess covets have degenerated to a worn-out populace in a dead land. Now sterile and listless, the German people shuffle to the rhythms of scratchy dance records when they once goose-stepped to the beat of marching bands: "All were spiritless from the very strangeness of the country. . . . All of them slept in the back rooms on hay that should have been fed to the herds" (32). Ernst's avenue of heroes, with its decline from love through lust to land, is now the side road to desolation. Land has negated love; that is, nationalism has overwhelmed humanity. The rabble that passes by the unsanctioned meat on hooks in 1945 is a far cry from the screaming mob that misinterprets the old general's proclamation of victory in 1914.

Zizendorf steps quickly into the void. A self-styled leader who madly foresees a rebirth of German military might, he separates the impersonal land from the people who should sustain it. Stella Snow at least personifies Germany itself. Zizendorf, however, dismisses the spirit altogether. Believing that "the land is important, not the *Geist*" (the spirit), he defines a country not as a gathering of humans but as a matter of boundaries. His rejection of spirit accelerates the cannibalization by history.

Hawkes again uses linked images to make the point. Identifying the words that Ernst hears during his run along the avenue of heroes—*love, Stella, Ernst, lust, tonight, leader, land*—Hawkes uses each word as a chapter title to chronicle Zizendorf's ironic assumption of power. Unaware that he is also a toy of history, he ambushes Leevey and then in the chapter titled "Land" posts his rallying cry to the numbed souls who now populate the defeated Germany: "Indictment of the Allied Antagonists, and Proclamation of the German Liberation." Deluded that a new Hitler can proclaim a new dawn, he fails to see the comic absurdity of his belief that "the land, the Teutonic land, gives birth to the strongest of races, the Teutonic race" (176). The sacrifice of the spirit to the demands of nationalism never fazes him. Kaiser Wilhelm's ghost, "thin, depressed," slinks across "a land that was now strange to his touch," and Zizendorf becomes caught in the recycling of history that forever promises the never-endingness of war. No wonder Hawkes occasionally names the town in the novel *das Grab*—the grave.

Cannibalism would seem an appropriate metaphor for a nation that buries itself, but just as Hawkes mingles history and fiction, so he makes the metaphorical become literal. At the end of the novel an actual cannibalism occurs. Recall that the linking of the fragmented images and scenes that build to the devouring of the child begins in the early passage when the pursued boy is likened to a piece of meat hanging on a butcher's hook. The reader may not suspect cannibalism in these first descriptions, but throughout the novel Hawkes interjects such comments as the following to indicate the unspecified danger surrounding the youth: "Jutta's son, the fairy, fled for his life, his knees the size of finger-joints whirling in every direction like the un-coordinated thrashings of a young and frightened fox. The Duke continued to prod and tap with the gleaming cane" (36). Although scattered, the allusions to meat and fox begin to build until the reader suspects a homosexual attack by the Duke on the boy. Such a suspicion is acceptable, of course, for homosexuality is merely one more illustration of the sterile sexuality that consumes Zizendorf's doomed followers.

Having established this possibility, however, Hawkes then jerks the reader out of his complacency by describing a literal cannibalism in grotesquely humorous detail. The metaphor for homosexuality pales beside the actual dismemberment of the boy. Stranding the reader between outraged laughter and outraged horror, Hawkes exaggerates the Duke's fastidious concern for the proper way to slice up a "fox." The laughter is partly protective, a defensive measure by which the reader distances himself from the terror; but it is also an admission of common humanity, an uneasy acknowledgment that all men are capable of horrific acts, if not literally then at least in their dreams. This scene illustrates Hawkes's interest in "extreme fictive sympathy."

The Duke needs that sympathy. Finally trapping the "fox," he frets because skinning an animal with a sword is awkward. Joints are missed; buttons are struck; the fox attempts to kick back. Slicing away, the Duke is appalled when he loses bits and pieces in the mud. Which parts to eat and which parts to discard? Decisions frustrate his sense of order: "The very fact that it was not a deer or a possum made the thing hard to skin" (181). When the Duke realizes that he is ill prepared to dissect something with such "infernal humanness," the black comedy becomes clear. The reader laughs because the Duke contrasts his bungling efforts and what he assumes is the correct way to cut up a child. His inappropriate response is the key to the humor: "He would have preferred to have a light and a glass-topped table, to follow the whole thing out on a chart, knowing which muscles to cut and which to tie" (180). Unfortunately, he has forgotten the lessons of Biology I. Upset at the violation of his propriety, admitting that "the task was interminable and not for a layman," he looks at the wreckage of bone and muscle and tongue, at the confusion of paw and foot, and he all but turns to the reader and asks, "What could he do?" (181, 182).

The reader is likely to ask a similar question: Is his laughter-mixed-with-terror an acceptable response? Hawkes argues that it is. This kind of laughter does not deny dire circumstances in a world that produces the mad Duke, the madder

Zizendorf, and the maddest of all—war. The irony is that in eating the boy the Duke personifies the renewal of nationalism that will spark a new holocaust. Normally the hope of the future, children in *The Cannibal* cannot break the inherited cycle of historical destruction. The asylum reopens its doors, and long lines of people "revived already with the public spirit" return to the institution that Hawkes suggests is specifically Germany and generally the modern world.

Four decades after its publication *The Cannibal* remains a radical reaction to war. Deliberately upsetting perspective and conventional continuity, Hawkes overturns the reader's equilibrium in order to illustrate the nightmare of the European battlefield. There is no romantic concept of war in *The Cannibal.* The dashing horses of the cavalry, a linking image throughout, are dead reminders of past glory, and they have been replaced by roving packs of dogs, another linking image, that take over trains and portend the outbreak of brutality. Many war novels communicate the author's sense of outrage by indirectly contrasting current horror with past tranquillity. Such nostalgia is not sentimentality but the author's way of showing that there may be a better future since there once was a calmer past. *The Cannibal* breaks with this tradition.

Hawkes plunges the reader immediately into the desolation. Except for the unusual comedy and the appreciation of innovative technique, there is little relief from the impact of grotesque events, nightmarish atmosphere, and despair at the ubiquity of death. Hawkes forces the issue of war's horror by denying the reader the safety of a romanticized past. Indeed, his references to the past suggest only another war, each one triggering its duplicate until history cannibalizes all who seek to ignore it, to run from it, or to control it.

Notes

1. "Interview," John Kuehl, *John Hawkes and the Craft of Conflict* (New Brunswick: Rutgers University Press, 1975) 156.

2. John Enck, "John Hawkes: An Interview," *Wisconsin Studies in Contemporary Literature* 6 (1965): 150.

3. John Graham, "John Hawkes on His Novels," *Massachusetts Review* 7 (1966): 450.

4. Graham 451.

5. Graham 452.

6. Graham 452.

7. Andrew Fielding, "John Hawkes Is a Very Nice Guy, and a Novelist of Sex and Death," *Village Voice* 24 May 1976: 45.

8. Albert J. Guerard, introduction, *The Cannibal*, by John Hawkes (1949; New York: New Directions, 1962) ix.

9. Hawkes, *The Cannibal* 8. Further references will be noted parenthetically.

CHAPTER THREE

THE BEETLE LEG

T*he Beetle Leg* (1951) is Hawkes's most difficult novel. Even he admits the strangeness of large parts of it, as if his reaction against realism, first illustrated in *The Cannibal*, were pushed to the extreme of innovation. Yet one way to approach this unusual novel is to understand its parody of the Western. Long a staple of America's myth of innocence expressed in the tall tale, novel, and film, the Western as written by Hawkes is not the triumphal story of national might but the exposure of national nightmare. The good guys do not win in *The Beetle Leg* because there are none.

Unlike *The Cannibal*, *The Beetle Leg* was extensively revised. When Hawkes talks about the novel, he recalls cutting the manuscript into fragments, attaching sections and paragraphs to a work board, and rearranging the various parts. The result is a short book that Hawkes himself confesses is different: "I was rereading *The Beetle Leg*. It's been a long time since I've looked at it. When I was reading it, it struck me that the first half was pretty difficult, and not too interesting. I read the second half, however, and I must say that it is an absolutely splendid piece of American fiction."[1]

Asked about his status as an American writer, Hawkes first claims that he is not interested in the question, but he then points to *The Beetle Leg*: "Bernard Malamud and I were talking on the phone . . . and he was complaining that it was foolish of reviewers to imply that I'm not much of an American writer, because he thinks my interests are gothic, and very American in that sense—Poe, Melville, and so on. Maybe he's right. I don't think of myself as an *American* writer. . . . I'm not interested in writing about America as such. I did my American novel with *The Beetle Leg*."[2]

Set in the American West, *The Beetle Leg* is one of the clearest examples in Hawkes's canon of his commitment to exposing the extreme circumstances of the psychic life: "Each one of us has his bestial interior. If we don't know that, then we're likely to be overcome by it, we're likely to live by it without knowing it. . . . We should know that our own inner life is as a matter of fact a cesspool, and that we'd better start draining it. This is so obvious. Everybody has bad dreams, everybody thinks vindictive thoughts, everybody is cruel, everybody is sadistic. . . . We need to know what we're about, and we need to know what it is to feel compassion for the most vicious people. That's why my fiction is poised, as it is, between the detestable and the sublime."[3]

The Beetle Leg is Hawkes's bad dream of those vicious people. Establishing the frame of the Western, he writes of a small town located near a dirt dam built to provide necessary

THE BEETLE LEG

water. The reader soon notes the irony, however, for the local sheriff lingers by the dam to guard against sunbathers and sexual encounters. The emptiness of the desert landscape stifles love, always a celebrated emotion in Hawkes's fiction. Worse, the dam, which should be a life source, holds the body of Mulge Lampson, Luke's brother. Thus the dam houses the dead and looms as a monument not to affirmation but to negation. The townspeople elevate Mulge to mythic status, exposing their impotence as they give their bounty to the dead. Even Luke, the main character, fishes by the dam, hoping to make contact with his lost kin. Darting through the scenes with noise and violence and dirt is the motorcycle gang known only as the Red Devils. As harbingers of the primitive side of humanity they illustrate the failure of man's efforts to make a garden of a wasteland. Mulge's body is never found and thus never exorcised, and the Red Devils roar away into the sunset at the end.

The reader should keep in mind the staples of the Western—vast horizons, the hero and the bad guys, the sheriff and the doc—but the reader must also be alert when Hawkes undercuts these familiar props. Laughter is encouraged as Hawkes stands the Western on its ear to investigate the American heritage of violence. Since the action unfolds inconsecutively, the reader should look for such linking images as dead bodies, sterile sex, swarming insects, and snakes as a means of noting the unity of the novel. In some cases—Luke's shower, for example—the scenes resemble hallucination so that Hawkes can challenge those who rely on chronology and characterization. Opening *The Beetle Leg*, the reader must remember the author's determination to make fun of the standard features of the conventional novel: plot, character, setting, and theme. *The Beetle Leg* is more militantly experimental than even *The Cannibal*, but both reflect Hawkes's method of countering the ugly with the sublime.

The detestable in image balances the sublime in technique as Hawkes lavishes his intricate prose on scenes that reflect the human cesspool. *The Beetle Leg* is packed with debris from those waters, with psychic projections cast loose from the depths of the pool that silently settle on the surface to startle the complacently comfortable reader into recognizing an identification with the unimaginable and the repressed. Although cannibalization of the child in *The Cannibal* is one of those events that remain with the reader, the snaring of the fetus in *The Beetle Leg* is the most memorable of Hawkes's many metaphors of the human pit. Finishing that scene, the reader is shaken from revulsion to compassion. Fishing the waters of the lake, itself an image of the cesspool of the unconscious, Luke Lampson finds not his dead brother but the central figure of us all: a fetus, a nearly formed person that never got to suffer waking life. Safe from the psychic slime that hinders all who make it to birth, the dead fetus is Hawkes's shocking reminder of the potential and precariousness of human existence. It is also, he explains, an illustration of the deep sympathy that the artist must feel in the face of the unexpected and terrifying: "The moment in *The Beetle Leg* when Luke Lampson fishes the fetal baby out of the flood and tenderly holds it, then puts it back into the flood, is an analogue for what I think the artist ought to be able to do. We should feel a strong attachment to human life even in its most frightening form. There is something about the fetus with its unformedness, its total tremendous potential, and its connection to lower life forms, that makes it terribly, terribly frightening."[4]

This scene illustrates Hawkes's need to penetrate to the tender heart of the ugly, to confront the mossy underlife on the other side of the rock. Hawkes comments: "The fiction writer discovers the beauty of all forms of life; all of life is worthy of his gargantuan interest, sympathy, and love. I'm not an advocate of ugliness. I deplore violence. I want to lead a safe, ordinary life with my wife and children and my friends and students. But ugliness is as essential to fiction as it is to the dream."[5]

Hawkes argues that the novelist who filters the grim materials of life through the beauties of language and artistic form is closer to the poet than he knows. This association is especially true of the innovative writer because, like the poet, he is prompted to his narrative by a vision that drives him not to represent but to create a world. Thus while *The Beetle Leg* is set in the American West and is complete with a sheriff, a gang of bad guys, and a shoot-out at the end, it bears little resemblance to a John Wayne Western or to the romanticized tales of cowboys and Indians that have nurtured the national myth for more than a century. One of Hawkes's general comments about novels is appropriate to *The Beetle Leg* and to its strange mixture of Western adventure and impenetrable dream: "Like the poem, the experimental fiction is an exclamation of psychic materials which come to the writer all readily distorted, prefigured in that nightly inner schism between the rational and the absurd . . . . A comic sense of the dream, the presumption of a newly envisioned world, absolute fastness, firmness, insistence upon the creation of that other landscape where the moon hangs like a sac loaded with water. . . . If the true purpose of the novel is to assume a significant shape and to objectify the terrifying similarity between the unconscious desires of the solitary man and the disruptive needs of the visible world, then the satiric writer, running maliciously at the head of the mob and creating the shape of his meaningful psychic paradox as he goes, will serve best the novel's purpose."[6]

The psychic paradox at the heart of *The Beetle Leg* is a curious merger of Hawkes's memories of a trip to Montana with his fiancée, the false myth of an American West bathed in innocence despite a violent heritage, and the fall of the American Adam figure as he stumbles from a New World Eden to a wretched horizon of desert sand and cactus. The murky atmosphere suggests the distance that Hawkes demands between his life and his fiction. Part of the background, for example, of *The Beetle Leg* is based on an experience while Hawkes was working on the Fort Peck Irrigation Dam in Montana in 1947. Stuck in a limitless expanse of landscape, Hawkes and his fiancée attended a dance in an airplane hangar: "The figures in the dance were all western, and they were, for the most part, masked by bandannas, and they would whip out revolvers and shoot them through the hangar."⁷ In *The Beetle Leg*, Luke Lampson attends a dance that combines similarly incongruous elements of festival and violence, but Hawkes's emphasis on created worlds distances him from the reader who might try to discern parts of the novelist's life in his fiction. Experience is no more than a catalyst for vision. Life is transformed in art.

With *The Beetle Leg*, however, Hawkes need not have worried about inadvertent revelation of his own adventures. Strangeness is the order of the day, and the reader must make his way through a series of events and isolated set pieces that gather about them the illusion of otherworldly hallucination. It is not that the individual events themselves are beyond the boundary of possibility but that Hawkes confronts the reader with so many of them. The result is a comic parody of the Western that shakes the reader into contemplating the decline of American innocence. Such scenes as Luke's shower, Mulge's burial in the slightly moving dirt dam, and the conflict between the rattlesnake and the car are believable projections of "real" events, but the rapidity with which Hawkes places them before the reader veers the novel toward the edge of the unreal. The sheriff in *The Beetle Leg*, for example, is a far cry from the Gary Cooper who protects the undeserving townspeople against the threat of returning bad guys in *High Noon*. Rather than track down bandits, he searches the desert for sex offenders. His opposition to sexuality immediately establishes a contrast between the potential of sex and the aridity of the western wasteland:

The crime rate was high around the river and the daylight offenders were the worst. I knew this little girl had found one of the spots where water, meant just to liven up men half dead or draw together cattle, drives men and women to undress and swim and maybe kill themselves.[8]

The laconic sheriff is not the hero of *The Beetle Leg* but just one more person blasted by the landscape. He, in addition to the other characters, ought to be encouraged by the building of the dam with its promise of life-sustaining water, but like his neighbors he allows the dam to dominate him. The result is that the dam becomes a paradox, an image of sterility when it should be the symbol of a green Eden in a dry land. The black and white protagonists of the traditional Western are shaded into ambiguity. Heroes are merely the false stuff of myth.

So, suggests Hawkes, is the version of the western expansion that most Americans accept as historical fact. The reader should remember that *The Beetle Leg* was published in 1951, long before Native Americans lobbied for their rights or the discrepancy between fact and myth in the history of the West became a matter of public knowledge. Hawkes uses *The Beetle Leg* not to redress Indian grievances but to expose the fictitiousness of the popular Western. His primary method is parody, for he undercuts the familiar trappings of the adventure tale to show the absurdity and duplicity at the heart of the

THE BEETLE LEG

American dream. The concept of manifest destiny, relied on for a century to rationalize the national push beyond the Mississippi River, is unfortunately a description of an American nightmare.

The key symbol of this bad dream, and the central irony in the novel, is the dam. Normally a laudable sign of man's determination to make his mark upon the land by bringing life-giving water, the dam is the home of the dead in *The Beetle Leg*. Rather than conserve the water necessary to guarantee the American Eden, it houses Mulge's body, killed during the construction of its dirt walls. Secondly, the instability of the edifice, originally designed to be a permanent monument to human ingenuity, is illustrated in its slipping "a beetle's leg" at a time. Finally, the dam creates the lake that holds the fetus. The promise of life turns into the reality of death, the innocent Western becomes the revelation of national violence, and a bad dream takes its place at the center of the American myth.

The difficulty of *The Beetle Leg* is that these events seem motiveless. Cause and effect, the indicator of orderly process, is all but eliminated, and the result is that the characters are unable to break out of the stupor that Mulge Lampson's death has cast upon them. Like the people in *The Cannibal* they unintentionally create comedy because of their inappropriate responses to dire circumstances. When the son of Camper and Lou is bitten by a rattlesnake, for example, Camper's initial concern is not for the health of the boy but for the inconvenience of the injury. He complains to Luke, "It's a hell of a thing when you can't take a leak without kicking up a pack of rattlers" (26). The child's mother, Lou, remains in the car, try-ing to find a good station for music on the radio, and Luke un-consciously parodies the role of the efficient, quiet cowboy. While Camper brags about practically building the dam alone and retells the story of the Great Slide that has killed Mulge, Luke says only, "I recollect it." The reader's laughter is uneasy because the characters' reactions seem abnormal, but Hawkes suggests that normality is a relative concept. Snakes slither along the ground, parents show little worry for their children, and violence negates innocence. The world of *The Beetle Leg* is the domain of the spiritually dispossessed. Nowhere is this better illustrated than when Luke finds the fetus.

Many readers compare this scene with the Duke's slaugh-ter of the child in *The Cannibal*. Such a response is understandable since one is compelled to witness innocence horribly victimized by circumstances it is powerless to com-bat. Yet Luke's unhappy fishing trip seems more dire than the Duke's fumbling cannibalism if only because it is not enclosed in an atmosphere of comedy. The Duke can complain about lacking glass-topped tables and dissecting charts, but all Luke can do is close his eyes. Similarly, the Duke's pursuit of the boy is a linking image throughout *The Cannibal*, and thus the reader expects a disaster—though perhaps not the extreme of this kind of murder. There is no preparation, however, for the hooked fetus, and the reader is momentarily as stunned as Luke:

The eyes slept on either side of the fish line and a point of the barb protruded near the nose stopped with silt. It turned slowly

around and around on the end of the wet string that cut in half
its forehead. It had been tumbled under exposed roots and
with creatures too dumb to swim, long days through the
swell, neither sunk nor floating. . . . God's naked child (132).

No wonder Luke closes his eyes.

The reader does too because Hawkes's detachment forces
assimilation of the horror without the aid of narrative or
authorial commentary. And yet the incident is not a gratu-
itous moment of violence. Luke is fishing in the lake made by
the sliding dam, and he is therefore near the unknown grave-
site of Mulge, who in death has become a mythic presence in a
sterile land. In this sense Luke fishes for his lost brother, for
one of those who has gone before, one who may reveal the secrets of the dead. The promising water of the lake would seem
to offer a rebirth of the western desert into the American Eden
as portrayed at one extreme by Western movies and at a more
sophisticated extreme by F. Scott Fitzgerald's memorable line
"the green breast of the new land." But Luke finds neither a
Tiresias figure in Mulge nor a prelapsarian Adam in the child.
He hooks only innocence destroyed before birth. The fetus in
The Beetle Leg is Hawkes's most disturbing image of external
victimization and internal psychic depths.

Luke's confrontation with the void occurs late in the
book, and it is the culmination of Hawkes's emphasis on the
arid countryside that has defined the atmosphere of the novel
from the very beginning when the sheriff tracks down sexual
offenders. This is the place where "few humans gather, in the
gullies of rattlesnakes or before the coils of braided whips"

(24). Such fond American notions as "home on the range" and "don't fence me in" are parodied in this wasteland where rattlers lurk behind rocks and mosquitoes fill the air. Idyllic portrayals of Monument Valley in the mythic cowboy films that helped to shape America's consciousness of its own innocence are out of place in Hawkes's West. Note the focus on the insignificance of mankind, including the indigenous Indians, in the following description of Luke's desert abyss:

Any nomad tribes that had once burned raiding fires at night were gone, human drops sprinkled and spent in the sand, as bodies slipped from the edge of the horse blanket, had been settled upon and obscured by wingless insects or fried, like the heads of small but ruddy desert flowers, in the sun of one afternoon (45).

The title of the novel is the linchpin of the insect imagery which suggests the inevitable obliteration of these "human drops." Insects survive while people die, and civilization moves a beetle's leg at a time closer to the void.

Given such bleakness, the potential for violence is especially menacing. Hawkes makes fun of the guys in black hats, standard props in standard Westerns, when he characterizes the motorcycle thugs as Red Devils. Physical projections of the psychic underworld, carriers of an infected past, the Red Devils represent the utter freedom from inhibition that all humans long for at one time or another. They are the bank robbers or the cattle rustlers or the wandering raiders of Western

THE BEETLE LEG

tales, but they also personify the amorality that explodes when men are free to act with total impunity.

For this reason they seem inhuman, creatures made of leather and metal and straps, alive only when the motorcycles that propel them across the sand roar into motion. They rip apart dogs, crash the local dance, and hover in the badlands when Luke helps the snakebit boy. Their bestiality is exposed when Lou, Camper's wife, sees one peeping at her through a hotel window, "constructed as a baseball, bound about a small core of rubber. . . . Its snout was pressed against the screen, pushing a small bulge into the room" (53). When they invade the town dance, playing their roles of the gang of hoods wrecking the social gathering of the tame, the Red Devils so impress a child with their gyrations and noise that he murmurs, "They had jewels all over them." Luke's reply—"We don't want to hear about it"—is one of the points of *The Beetle Leg* (63). No one wants to face the dead fetus either, but the unpredictable realities beneath the surface must be met. Repression of the underside of life results not in sugary accounts of good guys defeating bad but in an inability to deal with unpleasant impulses that are kept in check only by the flimsy barriers of civilized restraint. Hawkes makes the reader "hear about it"—about, as it were, the thin line between Luke and the fetus.

The character who has heard most of the echoes from the deep is Cap Leech. On one level he is a recognizable prototype of the Western, the itinerant medicine man. But rather than the kindly, wise Doc, Cap Leech is a parody of the healer. Described as a "midnight vivisectionist in a cat hospital," he has warty hands that seem better practiced in disease and death than in healing and health: "He had reduced all medicine to a ringed wash basin and kept, for its good or harm, the tinkling world in a bundle under his rocking bed" (144). Leech looks beneath the surface and is not afraid. His operation on the Indian woman, itself a parody of such monster movies as *Frankenstein*, is indirectly described in terms of sexual violation: "But now, faced with the incomplete incision, having taken the liberty of nursing a flower of tubes from pubescent flesh, he longed only for extraction and the cautious, painful closing of her mouth" (149). Cap Leech is feared because he has the power to look at the women of the town. His probing of the female Indian is much more threatening than the Red Devil who watches Lou undress.

Left in this manner, Leech would be little more than a blackly comic quack. But Hawkes goes beyond mere parody to establish Cap as an ironic father figure. Only at the end of *The Beetle Leg* does the reader learn that Cap Leech is the father of Luke and Mulge. The information does not bring comfort. As Mulge assumes mythic status from the rumors about his restlessly searching body inside the dam, so Cap roams the countryside with a wagonload of pain and death, and Luke, for all his harmlessness, fishes up the sleeping children of the deep. Sleep suggests death in *The Beetle Leg*, and with his supply of noxious powders and narcotics Leech is the opposite of the life-providing father of the race.

THE BEETLE LEG

With one son dead and another stunned by the sterile waters of the dam, the eerie healer delivers his spiritual son Harry Bohn to the netherworld of the desert. Life soiled with death follows Leech everywhere. Called, for example, to Bohn's birth, he arrives "according to law too late" because the mother has already died. But master of the scalpel and forceps, he dares "to extract the secret of a dead woman," yanking bleeding life from the undersea region of the womb. Hawkes describes the operation as "more abortive than life saving," and thus he negates any suggestion of a miracle to save a life. More important, however, is the following account of Cap's skill: "The son, fished none too soon from the dark hollow, swayed coldly to and fro between his fingers" (121). For with the word "fished," Hawkes extends an image pattern that begins with the fishing for Mulge's corpse, develops through Luke and the fetus and Camper's need to fish the waters of the dam at night, and ends with the town cook's casting for eels. The beneficent biblical notion of "fishers of men" has been reversed, for Luke and Leech fish up the dead and the living dead respectively. Harry Bohn is unlikely to reel in the kingdom: "Harry Bohn, by miracle born of a dead mother and thereafter in his youth . . . drawn to the expressionless genitals of animals as the Sheriff was in a later day, doted upon the stomach kept distended with effort, and lest they be torn to pieces, slept with his hands drawn in from the edges of the bed" (108). Life in *The Beetle Leg* is irresistibly attracted to death.

The primary illustration of the magnet of the dead is Mulge Lampson. Obsessed with what he is doing "in there"—

in the depths of the dam—the people convert the huge grave to a shrine that in turn becomes a tourist trap. Relics are collected, admission is charged, and tales of Mulge and the Great Slide become the stuff of folklore. One may even buy postcards of Mulge's razor and shaving bowl. Comedy obviously challenges myth, but debunking is not the main issue. Sympathetic to man's need to create order, but critical of the flimsiness of his effort, Hawkes parodies the tenuous foundations on which man tries to fashion stability. The huge earthen dam is the largest totem in these people's lives, but Hawkes emphasizes its connection with death in order to stress the unsuitability of their hopes. Perhaps the most important account of the general slide into nothingness is this description of the dam: "It moved. . . . Visitors hung their mouths and would not believe, and yet the hill eased down the rotting shale a beetle's leg each several anniversaries, the pride of the men of Gov City who would have to move fast to keep up with it" (67–68). Museums and myths will not slow the inch by inch journey to destruction.

Stuck forever in the dam, Mulge is an unworthy object of adoration, a man with loose socks and a cut lip who in death ironically rallies the people to their need for heroic tales of skill and strength. His bizarre marriage to Ma is a negation of fertility rites, and the promise of progeny is not a possibility in their union. The natural results, says Hawkes, are apathy and violence. Thus his Western ends the way readers expect, with a gunfight. But this is no *Gunfight at the OK Corral* in which the lines between good and bad are clearly drawn. Assuming the role of the attacking marauders, the Red Devils circle the sheriff and Luke, who defend themselves with shotguns. Hawkes refuses, however, to differentiate white hats from black, and all the reader knows is that Luke is either shot or has his shotgun blow up beneath his nose. The conclusion is appropriate:

And suddenly, from the isolated battering truck, shrill and buoyant above the clumsiness of thick-kneed marksmen, there came that cool baying of the rising head, the call to kill, louder and singsong, faintly human after the flight of Devils, the nasal elated sounds of the cowboy's western bark. Yip, yip, yip (158).

Cap Leech's final word reveals only that he will continue the quest for Mulge and death.

The Beetle Leg remains Hawkes's most difficult novel. Although the familiar trappings of the Western provide a frame of reference, Hawkes deliberately upsets the reader's sense of comfort by exposing the traditional props of civilized behavior as useless. Motherhood and love, fertility myths and the promise of children, the rituals of burial and the potential of water, America's need to believe in its own innocence—all of these devices by which a people order the chaos of their lives are dismissed. Left unprotected, as it were, the reader has to confront the ascendancy of aggression and pain if he hopes to finish the novel. The thing lurking just beneath the surface of the lake is real, argues Hawkes, and no amount of mythic projection can reduce it to a safety zone of order where most people hide away the unknown, the unwelcome, and the untried. The brilliant set pieces in *The Beetle Leg*—Luke's shower, Lou's hallucinated poker game, the sheriff's voyeurism—deny the convention of cause and effect to revel in the beauty of language. Each event is not tied logically to another, but that is the point. Such questions as where the fetus comes from or why Mulge marries Ma are never answered, for to provide answers would be to suggest order in a world that Hawkes sees as fractured. Thus the reader admires the scenes for what they are: intricately wrought visions from the psyche that Hawkes creates with language. Freeing the novel from the expected conventions of traditional fiction, Hawkes persuades the reader to consider what he does not want to think about—the inevitable slide, a beetle's leg at a time, into oblivion.

Notes

1. Andrew Fielding, "John Hawkes Is a Very Nice Guy, and a Novelist of Sex and Death," *Village Voice* 24 May 1976: 45.

2. Roger Sauls, "John Hawkes: I Am Pleased to Talk about Fiction," *New Lazarus Review* 1 (1978): 8.

3. Sauls 9–10.

4. Anthony C. Santore and Michael Pocalyko, " 'A Trap to Catch Little Birds With': An Interview with John Hawkes," *A John Hawkes Symposium: Design and Debris* (New York: New Directions, 1977) 182–83.

5. Thomas LeClair, "The Novelists: John Hawkes," *New Republic* 10 Nov. 1979: 28.

6. John Hawkes, "Notes on *The Wild Goose Chase*," *Massachusetts Review* 3 (1962): 786–87.

7. Patrick O'Donnell, *John Hawkes* (Boston: Twayne, 1982) 153.

8. John Hawkes, *The Beetle Leg* (New York: New Directions, 1951) 11. Further references will be noted parenthetically.

CHAPTER FOUR

THE LIME TWIG

T|he Lime Twig (1961) is a new direction in the Hawkes canon. Although challenging for the unprepared reader, it is more accessible than his earlier fiction in terms of both surface plot and metaphorical significance. One reason for the change is that Hawkes tones down the visual effects and the fractured narrative line of *The Beetle Leg* and *The Cannibal*. Another reason is that he draws on familiar details from mundane life to set the frame for his investigation of the power of dreams. Sports, cheap crime, dull married couples, and frustrated ambitions are recognizable particulars of the daily cycle, but as the reader might expect, Hawkes uses them for a springboard into the bizarre.

Yet Hawkes keeps the spectacular events in touch with the lives of most readers. As Flannery O'Connor notes in a jacket blurb, "It seems to be something that is happening to you, that you want to escape from but can't. The reader even has that slight feeling of suffocation that you have when you can't wake up and some evil is being worked on you." Happily for O'Connor and the reader, waking life is out there beyond the novel; Michael Banks, the main character, is not so lucky.

The reader will note immediately that the plot of *The Lime Twig* is relatively clear for a novel by Hawkes. The key is understanding that William Hencher and Banks want their fantasies literally to materialize: Hencher as a sacrificing helper for other people, Banks as an owner of racehorses and as a sexual stud. The older Hencher has a connection with the underworld in Larry, and thus when he realizes the dimensions of Banks's dream, he sees a way of fulfilling both wishes: helping Larry steal a horse, he will also help Banks by looking the other way as the gangster uses Michael as the front man, the bogus owner of the stallion. Unfortunately, Hencher makes the old saw about killing two birds with one stone a reality. Both dreamers are dead by the end of the novel.

The reader will also have an easier time with *The·Lime Twig* because the recurring image patterns are not so otherwordly as those in *The Cannibal* and *The Beetle Leg*. Dukes do not dismember little boys (*The Cannibal*), and fishermen do not hook fetuses (*The Beetle Leg*). Rather, the reader should follow the bird imagery and the many references to the color green because these allusions are indirect pointers to the snaring of such innocent dreamers as William Hencher and Michael Banks. Long a symbol of regeneration and life, green has connotations of entrapment and betrayal in *The Lime Twig*. These image patterns help the reader understand that pursuit of dreams inevitably degenerates to confrontation with nightmare because fantasy cannot be controlled.

THE LIME TWIG

When Hawkes talks about *The Lime Twig*, he calls attention to its language, which he defines as "the very stuff of the human imagination, hence life at its best." He goes on to argue that "language functions as a form of energized beauty, inseparable from the painful materials."[1] His point is that the beautiful language cannot be divorced from the terrifying action because each reinforces the other. The imaginative freshness of *The Lime Twig* is found not only in the situation but also in the arrangement of the words to create images and suggest nuances.

The novel was written during a summer and then revised over four years. Although it is literally about a stolen horse and the efforts of a gang of hoods to fix a race called the Golden Bowl, the novel primarily examines the lure of sexuality and dreams. As embodiments of potency and beauty, power and form, horses figure in many of Hawkes's novels and have become mythic totems from his youth: "Horses were indeed a powerful element in my childhood. There was a riding stable just behind the house where I lived for a while. I used to work at this stable when I was about eight years old, and ever since I've cared a great deal about horses. I actually carry a photograph of Faulkner in hunting costume on horseback in my copy of *Second Skin* as a talisman. . . . I had a racing magazine at one point while writing *The Lime Twig* that I simply picked up on a newsstand and flicked through. I got some names and some ideas, a little bit of detail about the racetrack out of this magazine."[2] The magazine also showed Hawkes how to work out the genealogy of horses. The two words in the name of the mystery horse Rock Castle suggest size, power, and invulnerability, but the elaborate bloodline that he created for Rock Castle is more to the point. With such names as Apprentice, Shallow Draft, Draftsman, and Words on Rock, he parallels Rock Castle's heritage with the writing of *The Lime Twig:* "The metaphor seems to be about building, creating, writing this low life, low life in a high kingdom. 'Castle Churl out of Words on Rock.' I think it's the 'Words on Rock' that's really important. The 'Words on Rock' *are* the book."[3]

Hawkes recalls that he began *The Lime Twig* when he read a newspaper story about legalized gambling in England. "My other novels were begun similarly with mere germs of ideas, and not with substantial narrative materials or even with particular characters. In each case what appealed to me was a landscape or world, and in each case I began with something immediately and intensely visual—a room, a few figures, an object, something prompted by the initial idea and then literally seen, like the visual images that come to us just before sleep."[4]

The Lime Twig begins with two voices that were added in revision: Hencher's prologue and Sidney Slyter's newspaper column. Although the sheriff in *The Beetle Leg* speaks in the first person in his short preface, Hencher is Hawkes's first conventional first-person narrator, a character whom Hawkes describes as "a fully created voice that dramatized a character conceived in a certain depth."[5] Hencher is more important to the novel than Slyter, but the latter is the primary means of indicating the cheap, violent underworld of postwar England.

THE LIME TWIG

Hawkes remembers that he added Sidney Slyter at the suggestion of his first publisher, James Laughlin, who believed that
The Lime Twig would be more accessible with the addition of
a kind of reader's guide. Acting as a chorus that comments on
the action, Slyter is what Hawkes calls "snake-like," the "ugly
sibilance" of his name echoing that of the sexually eager Sybil-
line, the "dark temptress." In Sidney Slyter degradation is carried to its extreme: "To me it's interesting that Sidney Slyter's
column was in effect another afterthought, since actually his
sleazy character and cheap column afforded me perhaps the
best opportunity for dramatizing the evil inherent in the
world of *The Lime Twig*. Slyter's curiosity, his callow opti-
mism, his lower middle class English ego, his tasteless rhetoric,
his vaguely obscene excitement in the presence of violence—
all this makes him one of the most degrading and perversely
appealing figures in the novel."[6]

Sidney's confidence as the know-it-all sports writer is
outrageous and finally ironic because although he claims to
see all, he learns nothing. Hencher, however, is entirely sympathetic despite the perversity of his need to be loved. Hawkes
uses Hencher's first-person voice to lull the reader into understanding the fat man's desperation to break free of a dominat-
ing mother, and then he shocks the reader by killing off
Hencher less than halfway through the book. Kicked to death
by Rock Castle, one of the horses that will later fatally tram-
ple Michael Banks, Hencher, says Hawkes, is the "seedbed" of
the pathetic dreams and lives of Michael and Margaret Banks.
Such innocence as theirs can only be victimized.

UNDERSTANDING JOHN HAWKES

And victimized it is to the point of terror. Calling Hencher's murder "amusing," Hawkes explains that in light of his desire to parody the novel form, "in this case to parody the soporific plot of the thriller, Hencher's death seems to me an appropriate violation of fictional expectations or fictional 'rules.' "[7] Yet William Hencher seems present throughout *The Lime Twig* because he metaphorically reappears as Cowles and the constable, themselves apparently overweight and lonely: "I meant the pseudo-mystery of his death to pervade the novel." Stranded, as it were, in an England that Hawkes calls "the spiritless, degraded landscape of the modern world," Hencher hopes to act out his dreams of love by helping others fulfill their own.[8] Sudden death is the result.

While Hencher and Slyter are unattractive, Hawkes stresses the latter's inhumanity. Slyter is clearly comic, a parody of the nosy reporter as well as of the all-knowing narrator who glosses the action, and he has nothing to redeem him. Describing Slyter as "the only character in my fiction that might approach a genuinely damned state," Hawkes points to his failure to love, his lack of sympathy, and his inability to relate to other people except as agents to satisfy his curiosity.[9] Hawkes even compares him to the "publishing scoundrel" in Henry James's *The Aspern Papers*, a man who preys on human beings to exploit them. Hencher, however, lives for love in his own bumbling way. Deprived by a dependent mother during her life and fixated on the mother after her death, he is a sexually awkward fat man trying to connect with other lonely dreamers. His love may initially appear perverse, with

THE LIME TWIG

its masturbatory, death-ridden, and incestuous impulses, but his innocent hope of living through his nightmare encourages sympathy. He is a primary example of the character in Hawkes's fiction who is to be laughed at and cared for simultaneously.

The reader should also understand that Hencher's death is not an accident. Kicked to death in the narrow confines of the van, he is a victim of the gang's retribution for his failure to obey orders. Larry, the boss who orders Hencher's execution, is a parody of the tough guy in most pulp mysteries. He even wears a bullet-proof vest and glories in his sexual mastery over the various molls who follow the gang from caper to caper. But as Hawkes explains, Larry is also "a man almost going beyond life-size. He is almost a god, a demonic god."[10]

Larry's control of Hencher, the stolen racehorse, the hoods, and Michael and Margaret Banks can be found in the pages of any cheap thriller, but Hawkes has much more in mind than parody. *The Lime Twig* considers what might happen if a person's most intimate, repressed desires were to come true. Thus while the surface of the novel is about the mayhem that explodes when criminals steal a horse and try to fix a race with the help of innocent dupes, the deeper level explores the nature of dreams. The title refers to the practice of covering a twig with birdlime in order to snare a bird, and it points to the ridiculous ease with which innocence is trapped. Both attracted to and repulsed by the lure, the naïve dreamers in *The Lime Twig* are caught by their own fantasies.

The unwitting birds to be limed are Hencher and Michael and Margaret Banks. Although *The Lime Twig* is primarily a third-person novel, Hencher's prologue creates the context for the investigation of Michael's dream of sexual mastery (note that the first chapter does not begin until the prologue ends on page 28). Opening the novel with a first-person voice and then switching to third person and killing the "I" narrator is one way that Hawkes both makes fun of the traditional conventions of fiction and upsets reader expectation, but it also encourages sympathy for the fumbling Hencher. His loneliness is overwhelming. Having lived through most of World War II in Dreary Station with his grotesquely repulsive mother, he has grown middle-aged while eating kidneys and lacking love: "Fifteen years of circling Dreary Station, she and I, of discovering footprints in the bathtub or a necktie hanging from the toilet chain, or seeing flecks of blood in the shaving glass."[11] Life in boardinghouses guarantees impermanence, and Hencher knows that he has no status beyond that of devoted son and lodger. When the mother dies in a comically violent way after an air raid, Hencher feels not only free but lonelier. He has lost the sole recipient—no matter how undeserving—of his love.

That loss limes him to Larry. During the war the gang leader and his men serve as civil defense officials even though they have not cut their connections with the underworld. Aware of the mother's awful burns, Larry, "the Captain," supplies narcotics to ease the pain (" 'You ain't going to give my stuff to her?' said Sparrow. 'Not to the old woman, are

THE LIME TWIG

you?' "). But Larry does give Sparrow's dope to Mrs. Hencher and thus places Hencher in his debt. The most startling scene in the prologue follows, for while his injured mother is sleeping, William watches a crashing bomber silently float down to the yard. With a naked woman and the name Reggie's Rose painted on the nose, the plane is the first illustration of the massive power created by the union of sex and violence. Identifying with the dead pilot, Hencher crawls into the snug fit of the cockpit, itself both womb and female sexuality, puts on the helmet with its "pretty good fit," and thinks that he has his crown at last. Hawkes extends the scene for five pages, and in so doing he writes one of the most eerie accounts of innocence rushing to meet nightmare in American literature. What makes the description so unusual is that unlike, say, a short story by Poe, nothing immediately happens. Hencher's joy in the cockpit suggests his incestuous longing for the mother and his desire for normal sexual experience, and he seems happy when he whispers, *"Give a kiss to Rose"* (23). But the thing that goes bump in the night slams him into oblivion with devastating force when the bomber reappears later in the novel as the powerful Rock Castle. Fantasies cannot be contained. Shape-shifters—ghosts—always seduce the dreamer.

Limed to Larry, lonelier and more sexually frustrated than ever, William returns to Dreary Station a decade or so later to take rooms in the same boardinghouse where he once lived with his mother, now owned by the Bankses. As Hencher says, "A man must take possession of a place if it is to be a home for the waiting out of dreams. So we lead our lives"

(27). With no chance to date seductive women, to indulge in orgies, to own horses, or to live on the edge of violence with impunity, men resort to fantasies. And this is just what Hencher does. He wanders "home" after years of drifting, dreaming a dream that spins out of control and jerks Michael and Margaret along with him.

Denied an outlet for his needs, Hencher retreats to the old role of devoted son, this time to the much younger Bankses: " 'My old girl died on these premises, Mr. Banks.' . . . And then it was home again for William" (17). At first the reader suspects little malevolence beyond the confines of Hencher's obsession to be wanted and loved. William smells the fire in the walls that burned his mom; he roams the Banks's flat and becomes weirdly attracted to Margaret's dull femininity; he indulges his masturbatory fantasies. When he murmurs, "Can I help but smile? I can get along without you, Mother," the reader assumes that a measure of contentment has broken through the fat man's despair (28).

But just as Hencher lulls the reader with his account of a false peace, so he lures the Bankses into unawareness. The first sign that the surface of William's dream contains the void occurs when he stands outside the door of the sleeping Bankses and whispers his dreams. Is he to lime them as Larry has limed him so long ago? The rest of the novel uses third person to focus on the dreary lives of Michael and Margaret, the next "birds" to be snared, and Hencher hears "a little bird trying to sing" when he leaves his mysterious vigil outside their bedroom. Slowly enough to generate increasing anxiety

THE LIME TWIG

for the unsuspecting victims, the reader begins to realize that Larry is behind the plot. Larry plans to steal a horse and fix a race, but to do so he needs a front, a person free of suspicion. Michael Banks is that person, and Hencher's job is to trap him.

Leslie Fiedler has remarked how *The Lime Twig* illustrates that "love breeding terror is itself the final terror."[12] This is a shrewd comment, especially when one realizes that Hawkes took the name of Michael Banks from the Mary Poppins children's stories indirectly to suggest the helplessness of innocence. Dreams come true in a sugarcoated way for the youngsters in the Poppins tales, but the dreamers in *The Lime Twig* die as fantasy edges toward fruition. For in longing to own a racehorse, clearly a psychological substitution for his subconscious obsession with sexual mastery and erotic death, Michael finds that his dream materializes in ways he never imagined: following an orgy he is trampled to death by the symbol of potency. Hawkes shows that the disruptive needs of the inner man must be recognized but cannot be ordered.

Hencher is Michael's link between the destructive past (World War II) that he cannot recall and the dull present (postwar England) that he cannot face. In short, William knows just where Banks can get a horse—from Larry himself. The Bankses are easily limed because of Michael's sexual frustration. Married to resolutely unerotic Margaret, a spiritless woman of twenty-five who dresses in drab brown and who wears a safety pin beneath her skirt that Banks can rip open only in his fantasies, Michael longs to be a stud as powerful as a stallion. Although he describes his bed as "ordinary," he also knows that "the course of dreams is mapped" on the covers (30). Banks is so upset by the "soft timid sounds" that Margaret makes in their bedroom before going shopping that he hopes to hear "the smashing of a piece of furniture. Anything" (31).

He will hear it. His fairy godfather will guide him to the fulfillment of his visions, neither of them suspecting that as the fantasy lurches out of control, not only will furniture be smashed, but Larry's hoods will destroy everything in the flat to erase all signs of Michael's existence in the waking world; Hencher will be crushed by Rock Castle; Margaret will be raped and beaten to a pulp; and Banks will die under the hooves of the galloping horses. The reader, of course, becomes aware of Hawkes's mastery of foreshadowing only after finishing the book, but while reading what is perhaps Hawkes's most tightly constructed novel, he can follow the linking images—the birds to suggest entrapment, the color green to suggest lime, the rearing horse to suggest sexuality. The reader must also accept Hawkes's unusual convention that Michael Banks literally dies *within* his dream.

Mousy Margaret understands the fantasy. Her worst dream—her husband's disappearance—is the opposite of his best—sexual ecstasy—and she suspects that eroticism, violence, and the horse combine to issue a frightening invitation to the unknown:

Knowing how much she feared his dreams: knowing that her own worst dream was one day to find him gone, overdue min-

THE LIME TWIG

ute by minute some late afternoon until the inexplicable absence of him became a certainty; knowing that his own worst
dream, and best, was of a horse which was itself the flesh of all
violent dreams; knowing this dream, that the horse was in
their sitting room . . . the hoof to splinter in a single crash one
plank of that empty Dreary Station floor (33).

Sexual longing masks the death wish. Michael yearns for Annie, the dream girl next door; Margaret is mastered by Larry
in his ridiculous bullet-proof vest; destruction appropriates
the dream; and the gang gets away without a scratch.

Hawkes uses fog and steam to signal the arrival of the
fantasy. Shading Michael away from reality, the fog covers
the appearances of the ship *Artemis* and Rock Castle. Hawkes
points to the conscious irony in the name Artemis, for the
goddess of virginity and purity leads Banks to a sexual wonderland where fog hides the illicit deed: "where to discover everything he dreamed of except in a fog. . . . where to lose it all
if not in the same white fog" (45).[13] The reader can only laugh
with terror as he sees Michael Banks, now snatched into his
dream and cut off from time because of the smothering fog,
watching the descent of Rock Castle from the barge in a scene
that looks back to the silently falling bomber and Hencher's
desperate needs.

Hencher's unexpected death severs Banks's final human
connection with the waking world because, forced by Larry,
Michael telephones his wife to join him. Larry does not want
Margaret to notify the police about her husband's absence,
and she dutifully obeys. A comic irony is that Margaret also

longs unconsciously for violent physical fulfillment. Relying on her ordinariness to protect her—her brown skirt pulled below her knees and her closed safety pin—she nevertheless hears the cries of children as she dreams of "men with numbers wrapped round their fingers" feeling her legs, and of men going at her "with their truncheons or knives or knuckles" while she tries to remember their names (68, 70). The phallic implications are unmistakable, and her passive slide into fantasy is merely the other side of Michael's active pursuit of illusion. Their mutual frustration is illustrated in a humorous aside: "When Banks had first kissed her, touching the arm that was only an arm, the cheek that was only a cheek, he had turned away to find a hair in his mouth" (68). Thus Margaret fears the feminine color pink, but when she boards the train to answer Michael's summons, she holds a pink ticket. Her safety pin is finally unsnapped.

The fog that shrouds Margaret and Michael seems at first to confuse the reader, for like all of Hawkes's novels *The Lime Twig* develops inconsecutively. In this way Hawkes compels the reader to experience along with the Bankses, noting an echo here, glimpsing an image there. But true to the tight structure of the thriller *The Lime Twig* falls into place for readers who will play the role of the crack private eye, not only gathering clues but refraining from conclusions until the job is complete. Thus the reader has two parts in *The Lime Twig*. He identifies with the Bankses and the repression of their most private longings, and he learns, as they do not, the terrible power unleashed when one abandons the sunlight for the fog.

THE LIME TWIG

A revealing clue within the fog is Larry. He, too, will one day be limed, for he wears green sunglasses, dreams of vacations among lime trees, and thinks about "a bit of marriage." But for the moment he is the all-powerful, strutting, comic god, the personification of Michael's fantasy and the disrupter of Margaret's ordinariness. Note how Hawkes equates Larry with Rock Castle: "The man was big, heavy as a horse cart of stone" (73). Wanting to be Larry, unaware that "there's power in this world you never dreamed of," Michael ironically gets his wish when he joins an orgy with Larry's women while Larry rapes a horribly beaten Margaret. In this unexpected manner, trapped at the far edges of the fog, Michael and Margaret experience the satisfaction of uninhibited eroticism.

It costs them their lives. "Even two oven tits may be snared and separated in such a dawn. . . . the little bird was fagged. And he could feel . . . himself fagged and tasteless as the bird on the sick bough" (159). Margaret falls first. Although Thick's beating of her is viciously expert in the sense that it leaves no external bruises, the scene is blackly comic because of Margaret's inappropriate response. First she rationalizes that she is tied in a manner that has to be good for her figure, and then she worries that the battering is terrible primarily because it was "something they couldn't show in films" (129). Larry's attack joins Thick's beating as the twisted culmination of her repressed dreams of physical surrender, and by psychological displacement a godlike Larry-Michael finds a bound but willing Sybilline-Margaret in a masochistic

UNDERSTANDING JOHN HAWKES

vision. The reader laughs at her reaction while he mourns her pain. Limed birds do not escape.

Thus when the child Monica, dressed in green as a projection of Margaret's lost innocence, is shot, Michael tries to atone for his mistake. He recognizes the child and thereby recognizes his lost humanity, but to redeem his fatal plunge into the fog he must repudiate Rock Castle. This he does when, "small, yet beyond elimination," he rushes onto the track to meet the gathering storm of horses, arms outstretched in a parody of crucifixion, determined to shatter the golden bowl of Larry's dream: "He was running in final stride, the greatest spread of legs, redness coming across the eyes, the pace so fast that it ceases to be motion, but at its peak becomes the long downhill deathless gliding of a dream" (171). With the apparently insignificant detail of the red eyes Hawkes subtly reminds the reader of Hencher's part in the disaster, for early in the novel Hencher smears Margaret's lipstick around his eyes. They are all culpable together. A dove bursts into the air when Banks falls beneath Rock Castle's crashing hooves, and as Michael dies within his dream, "the green, the suspended time was gone" (170). Larry escapes, of course, evaporating with the fog.

Only Sidney Slyter and the police remain in the real world beyond the limes. Ever the dupe of his own ego, the snakelike Sidney knows little more than that some trick has been played. The police are even more baffled. Completing his parody of the thriller, Hawkes ends *The Lime Twig* with a squad of detectives sifting the evidence for the "particulars" of

THE LIME TWIG

the crime. They examine the rafters; they prod the straw; they wrap up Hencher's body in a sheet. But when they make "note of a dead wasp caught on a green splinter," the reader realizes that the particulars will forever elude them (174). The color of lime, the green splinter signals that the catastrophe has taken place within the undefined perimeters of Michael's dream. Surface details are insignificant, and detectives cannot penetrate to the other side of the fog.

The grim conclusion to *The Lime Twig* is clear, but it nevertheless represents a change of emphasis for Hawkes. For while Michael's dream runs out of control and causes a series of bloody deaths, it does not negate his final determination to redeem his error. The redemption is not in any way religious, but it is important that Banks, in Hawkes's words, destroys "the golden bowl of earthly pleasure at the very last moment of his life."[14] Michael makes a supreme effort to awaken, and as he does so he accepts the cost of killing the victim in order to bring down the victimizer. Such positive action, no matter how small, suggests a new interest in Hawkes's fiction. Those readers who demand a strict accounting of motivation and cause and effect must join Slyter and the police, hopelessly examining mundane details for clues to an adventure that remains beyond their comprehension.

Notes

1. Nancy Levine, "An Interview with John Hawkes," *A John Hawkes Symposium: Design and Debris* (New York: New Directions, 1977) 91, 92.

2. Levine 106–07.

3. Levine 108.

4. John Enck, "John Hawkes: An Interview," *Wisconsin Studies in Contemporary Literature* 6 (1965): 148.

5. Enck 150.

6. Enck 150–51.

7. Enck 151.

8. Enck 151.

9. "Interview," John Kuehl, *John Hawkes and the Craft of Conflict* (New Brunswick: Rutgers University Press, 1975) 162, 163.

10. John Graham, "John Hawkes on His Novels," *Massachusetts Review* 7 (1966): 455.

11. John Hawkes, *The Lime Twig* (New York: New Directions, 1961) 7. Further references will be noted parenthetically.

12. Leslie Fiedler, "The Pleasures of John Hawkes," *The Lime Twig* xi.

13. Graham 454.

14. Graham 456.

CHAPTER FIVE

SECOND SKIN

S *econd Skin* (1964) is Hawkes's most celebrated fiction. Runner-up for the National Book Award, the novel lifted him from relative obscurity and helped to establish his current status as a major contemporary American author. Laced with death but fully affirmative, violent in places but thoroughly comic, *Second Skin* all but glows with a sensuous style that points to Hawkes's insistence on the pleasures of the imagination.

Hawkes is quite conscious of the importance of *Second Skin* to his canon. Beginning with *The Cannibal* at the extreme of extraordinary visual effects, he had little choice but to develop in the direction of accessibility: "Of course it's obvious that from *The Cannibal* to *Second Skin* I've moved from nearly pure vision to a kind of work that appears to resemble much more closely the conventional novel. In a sense there was no other direction to take, but in part this shift came about, I think, from an increasing need to parody the conventional novel."[1] One of his primary means of parodying traditional fiction is the narrator. The first of Hawkes's novels to use first-person voice throughout, *Second Skin* makes fun of, among other things, the teller of the tale. Skipper, the bumbling, fifty-nine-year-old ex-navy man, is the main character in a novel in which he plays the role of a first-person narrator writing a novel in which he is the main character. Fat Hencher of *The Lime Twig* leads to large Skipper in *Second Skin:* "As far as the first-person narrator goes, I've worked my way slowly toward that method by a series of semi-conscious impulses and sheer accidents."[2] From the comic use of omniscient first person in *The Cannibal* through Hencher's desperate musings in *The Lime Twig* to Skipper's rationalization of his grievous failures in *Second Skin* is a long way. Skipper is not just a voice, however; he is a character who suffers an unending string of defeats before finding "love at last."

The reader notices the affirmation immediately. For while *Second Skin* plumbs the nightmare as much as any Hawkes fiction, the main character does not give in to it. Skipper stresses his endurance by contrasting two islands: a cold one that echoes of pain and negation, and a warm one that promises fertility and life. The reader must be prepared for Skipper's sudden shifts in locale, for he does not tell his story chronologically. From the haven of his survival, he recalls the violent deaths of his family and hesitates to accept part of the blame. Yet his efforts to point out his heroism are so humorously exaggerated that the reader cannot fail to sense the comedy. Hawkes urges the reader to laugh at the narrator, but he simultaneously encourages sympathy.

SECOND SKIN

Thus *Second Skin* represents a change in both technique and theme. While suggesting the possibilities for love and life over the ubiquity of destruction and death, Hawkes also examines the standard methods of telling a story. Skipper may be an unreliable narrator whose life is bounded by cemeteries, but in shaping his "naked history" he celebrates the creative process. Rigorous verisimilitude is dismissed in favor of comic, imaginative projection. Hawkes explains: "The fiction writer's imagination, for me, exists primarily to beat inert reality into life. Now, in *Second Skin*, though I think that novel remains true to my own particular fictional or imaginative vision, I don't think I've really sacrificed anything, but frankly I have become increasingly interested in the conventions of the novel and in novelistic methods."[3]

Hawkes's insistence on comedy in *Second Skin*, on combining the blackly humorous disasters of his earlier fiction with belly laughs, is a key to the tone: "In *Second Skin* I wanted to be sure, first, that the comedy would be unmistakable. . . . This is the first time, I think, in my fiction that there is something affirmative. In other words, even I got very much involved in the life-force versus death. The life and death in the novel go on as a kind of equal contest, until the very end, when a new-born baby, perhaps the narrator's, is taken to a cemetery on a tropical island, on an imaginary island. . . . And out of this, I think, does come a sort of continuing life."[4]

Hawkes's emphases on parodying the first-person narrator, on a clearer sense of comic action, and on a change of tone are important to an appreciation of *Second Skin*, but his account of how he wrote the novel is also relevant. Although he admits that he will never be able to reconstruct the genesis of his best-known book, he does supply some of the particulars. He wrote it during what he calls "eight swift magnificent months" in 1962–63 when he lived with his family on a lush Caribbean island. Yet *Second Skin* also looks back to a distant part of his childhood and is "related to other fiction I'd written by that time, appeared to depend on a few strange moments when literal event and imagined event coincided, and underwent a fairly extensive metamorphosis several years before we lived on our splendid island."[5] Writing with what he remembers as "genuine ease and considerable pleasure," he avoided the autobiographical but did touch base with his past when he recalled the suicide of a friend. Note how Hawkes refuses to be too revealing about his life: "When I was about 17, I happened by accident to enter a room in which a relative of mine was threatening to commit suicide. Or perhaps this moment was merely a dream."[6] A second key recollection is of an island mentioned to him by poet Edwin Honig. This island, where Hawkes spent a summer and made an abortive beginning of *Second Skin*, was near the New England coast and thus contrasted with the colors of the Caribbean paradise. Finally, the threat of death that he remembered from his youth materialized: "Two years later, in the spring, our life-filled friend from Harvard committed suicide. That fall Sophie and our by now four young children and I went to our coral-

SECOND SKIN

ringed island. . . . There at last I had *Second Skin* firmly in mind and wrote it."[7] A cold island, a warm island, and a suicide coalesce, and *Second Skin* emerges as his most lyrical evocation of the life-death cycle.

With the support of a Guggenheim Fellowship, Hawkes traveled south but remembered the stark land in the North Atlantic where "the privy was like an upended coffin, there were stunted apple trees on the slope between the porch and the sea, we lived in the rhythms of bright sun and heavy fog. . . . in the context of all this I was, for the first time, prompted to try to write fiction out of the very world I was living in. I was so moved by the vivid mythical atmosphere of the island that I thought I could overcome the dangers inherent in immediacy. And perhaps in *Second Skin* I did finally overcome the risks of immediacy."[8]

The first result was a story called "The Nearest Cemetery." Focusing on a barber who kills himself after murdering an unhappy, smiling woman called the Princess, "The Nearest Cemetery" provides some of the names that Hawkes uses in *Second Skin*.[9] He abandoned the story, however, when he heard another anecdote about a selfless man who devotes his life to a futile attempt at preventing the suicide of his daughter: "I knew that . . . the real center of the novel had to be sexuality and suicide, that the novel would be comic, and that I wanted to write it not in infectious Providence but on a tropical island. . . ."[10] There amid the sunshine and the warmth Hawkes listened to the echoes of Shakespeare's *The Tempest* and imagined Skipper as a "heavy benevolent middle-aged disreputable Prospero creating both his present and past life on a wandering tropical island. . . ."[11]

The point is that Skipper *creates* his past and his present through language, and thus he is the opposite of the hero in the other Shakespearean play Hawkes invokes when discussing *Second Skin—Hamlet*. Hamlet takes action too late, whereas Skipper constantly evades until he can conjure the life that he desires. Incapable of understanding his culpability in the suicide of his daughter Cassandra, Skipper becomes an artist figure imagining his life in such a way that there may be a discrepancy between what the narrator claims and what the reader perceives. Skipper's love for Cassandra is too blind, too possessive, too indirectly incestuous; and when he loses her to promiscuity and suicide, he has only language for support. Hawkes stresses Skipper's error and his art: "Surely he is telling the truth, trying to come close to what he is evading. He is talking to keep himself alive. He is using language to create reality."[12] In this sense, then, Skipper is an inept god, a man who stumbles through his life in the United States and on the black island in the North Atlantic, but who gives himself mythic stature when he retreats to the warm, wandering island of his imagination. For all the death and violence in *Second Skin*, Hawkes correctly points to Skipper's affirmation: "I meant him by the end of the fiction to be a very powerful, all-fulfilled, all-fulfilling, totally self-sufficient human being. He, to me, in all his weakness is supposed to embody the strength of knowing that there is nothing else in the world except what he creates and the figures he discovers in his creation."[13]

Not everyone agrees. *Second Skin* is Hawkes's most beautiful novel, an evocation of the creativity he celebrates, but first-time readers are likely to be overwhelmed by the apparent differences between Skipper's confident voice and his reluctance to act. As Hawkes says, "The novel is about a bumbler, an absurd man, sometimes reprehensible, sometimes causing the difficulties, the dilemmas, he gets in—but ending with some kind of inner strength that allows him to live."[14] What one needs to remember when reading the first short chapter is that although Skipper has failed to prevent the suicides of his parents and wife, the murder of his homosexual son-in-law, and the suicide of his adult daughter Cassandra, whose death he has "fought against the hardest," he himself is a survivor who must live forever with the memories of his losses. Life is possible for him because he now resides in a paradise of the imagination where he can literally, comically, create by artificially inseminating cows, by impregnating Catalina Kate, and by writing the novel that becomes *Second Skin*.

Unaware of the long development of fiction, he begins his "naked history," his vision through "a golden glass," and his defense of his own ineffectiveness with an unintentional parody of one of the highpoints of the realistic novel, *David Copperfield*. Dickens's great tale begins where traditional novels usually begin—at the beginning: "I am born." Thus Skipper establishes himself as an Adam figure, as the original namer, with a chapter titled "Naming Names," and his first words are, "I will tell you in a few words who I am."[15] But rather than relate the information expected in standard fiction about family, childhood, and initiation, Skipper reveals that he is a lover—a lover of hummingbirds, of bright needlepoint, of parasols, of his mess boy Sonny, and of his family. Most of all he is a lover of "my harmless and sanguine self." From the first page of *Second Skin* the reader knows that he is encountering a different experience.

The result is exhilarating. Using his love of hummingbirds as a metaphor for the structure of his tale, Skipper darts here and there amid the dregs of his past, ignoring chronology while reinterpreting his disasters. He introduces people, places, and things not according to the rationale of logical storytelling but according to his needs as a narrator. As the creator of his own history he interrupts his novel both to switch emphases and to address the reader. For he is reshaping his years of suicide and pain with a specific purpose: to convince himself that his survival is warranted, and to persuade the reader of his triumph. Convinced that "virtue always wins," he manipulates the materials of his narrative to guarantee the heroism of his life. He may not be telling the whole truth, but total veracity is not an issue. At the end of the novel he is alive.

Such affirmation affects the reader. Caught between Skipper's insistence on his innocence and his ineffectiveness in the face of implacable evil, the reader is exasperated with his bumbling, shocked at his suffering, and joyous for his survival.

SECOND SKIN

As Skipper says, "I am fifty-nine years old and I knew I would be." Nearly everyone else around him either pursues death or urges others to embrace it.

Thus the reader must understand that Skipper tells his tale—his story of growing a second skin to cover the scars of his past—from the perspective of hindsight. He is so assured of the power of his imagination that he literally creates a wandering island from which he can look back on the black island and flaunt his triumph: "So I had my small quiet victory over Miranda after all, and had my victory over Cassandra too, since there are always faces, strange or familiar, young or old, waiting to kiss me in the dark. . . . My shades, my children, my memories, my time of no time, and I thank God for wandering islands and invisible shores" (205). The reader notes the names of the vanquished: Miranda from Shakespeare's *The Tempest* and Cassandra from the Greek myths—and understands why Skipper insists on his status as a hero.

He deserves it. Because Skipper controls the tale, only the reader is in a position to question his worthiness, but the issue of his reliability may not finally matter. Skipper is culpable and perhaps reprehensible, but he is also loving and alive: "A few of us, a few good men with soft reproachful eyes, a few honor-bright men of imagination, a few poor devils, are destined to live out our fantasies, to live out even the sadistic fantasies of friends, children and possessive lovers" (18). He is a willing victim, a typical innocent in Hawkes's fiction who atypically emerges from the black pit of violence with his confidence intact.

The plunge to the depths begins in his childhood. In the short first chapter Skipper calls the names of those he has loved and lost and in effect tells the plot of the novel, although the reader may not realize it at the time. His daughter jumps naked from a lighthouse; his son-in-law, Fernandez, dies on a flophouse floor; his wife, Gertrude (named for Hamlet's mother), kills herself in a cheap motel after challenging Skipper's smothering love with her infidelities. But these losses follow long after the suicides of his parents. The son of a mortician, Skipper grows up familiar with what he calls "the seeds of death." He considers himself a witness and accomplice to his father's suicide because, in a wonderfully comic scene, he remembers being a fat boy crouching in front of the locked bathroom door and desperately screeching out Brahms—art, imagination—on a cello in an attempt to prevent his father from putting a bullet through his head. He fails. His mother also dies, pouring hot wax into her ears to shut out the explosion of the gunshot, and waiting for oblivion in a serene manner that reminds the reader of Emily Dickinson's poem "Because I could not stop for Death / He kindly stopped for me." As Skipper explains, "I . . . knew that my father had begun my knowledge of death as a lurid truth but that my mother had extended it toward the promise of mystery" (8). After his heritage of death is revealed in the first chapter, he urges the reader onward to the highlights of his memory.

Moving erratically back through his past, stopping to stress a painful experience one moment, a triumphant victory

SECOND SKIN

another, he sets out to prove his heroism. He submits, for example, to Cassandra's perverted request that he have the name of Fernandez tattooed in bright green on his chest. The pain is excruciating, but he stresses only his pride at not crying as the green "lizard" takes shape on his skin. Similarly he is proud that he encourages Cassandra to be brave when three AWOL, naked soldiers demand a "kiss" from the daughter who desires a final date with death. The novel is full of such illustrations of his willing victimization, of his need to use his own flesh to absorb pain meant for others, and thus the reader learns what Skipper tries to ignore: that his serene love so infuriates friends and associates that they deliberately hope to hurt him. The ultimate way to hurt is to commit suicide. Nowhere is this better shown than in the events that occur on the ironically named gentle island of Miranda and Captain Red, the northern island of Hawkes's memory.

The chain of defeats from Skipper's retreat to the gentle island through the dance and snowball fight is one of the comic highpoints of Hawkes's fiction. Structured around Skipper's rhetorical questions and inappropriate responses, the sequence reveals his determination to define himself as heroic while the reader's exasperation at his reluctance to act mounts to frustration. Note, for example, his pride in refusing to turn back when he first sees suggestions of evil on the island he has taken Cassandra to for safety:

But how could I know that Captain Red's boat, the *Peter Poor*, lay invisible and waiting only fifty yards from shore in its dark anchorage? . . . But if I had known . . . would I have faltered, turned back, fled in some other direction? No. I think not. Surely I would have been too proud, too innocent, too trusting (56–57).

His eagerness to be a willing victim in order to show off his love upsets the reader, who wants him to earn the heroic atmosphere that he creates for himself.

It also baffles the perverse inhabitants of the gentle island. Miranda, Captain Red, Jomo, and Bub do their best to make Skipper face up to pain, but he dodges among the signs of disaster, resolved not to admit that a malevolent world automatically sets traps for innocent dupes. Thus when Miranda, "the black widow," slashes the nipples of the baby bottles, Skipper merely cleans up the mess. And when Miranda becomes more explicit and slops blood-red ketchup on his white naval uniform, he responds, "But of course I ignored it as best I could . . . and merely shut my door" (67). The phrase "of course" is the key, but the more he refuses to consider the signals of looming death, the more Miranda and Captain Red try to bring him down. His comic responses to dire circumstances continue through the dance scene.

Following Cassandra to the party, Skipper acts as an unwanted chaperon and observes that his daughter's green dress has a bow across the buttocks that is bound to be a party favor. Smothering Cassandra with love, requesting and not receiving the first dance with her, he is lured away from the festivities to one of the funniest attacks in contemporary

SECOND SKIN

American fiction. He describes himself as two hundred pounds of "fearless snowshoe rabbit," and he hurries through the snow to the edge of a cemetery next to the dance hall. There he is blasted by iced snowballs that bloody his face, but true to his refusal to acknowledge those who live to inflict pain, he tries to defeat the iced balls with his imagination. His inappropriate reaction is a masterful comic set piece:

But I stopped. Listened. Because the air seemed to be filled with low-flying invisible birds. Large or small I could not tell, but fast, fast and out of their senses. . . . Escaped homing pigeons? A covey of tiny ducks driven berserk in the cold? Eaglets? I . . . thought I saw a little drop of blood on the snow. And I was relieved with the first hit (86–87).

His reaction is outrageous. Rhetorical questions will not stop the attack. Even funnier—and worse—is his relief at the sight of his own blood because he knows that "this time" at least he has "nothing to fear from any unnatural vengefulness of wild birds." When he returns to the dance, he is yanked into a belly-bumping contest with other fat men. "The fat begins to fly" in what Skipper calls an "obscene tournament," but he participates anyway. The reader laughs as he rumbles across the floor to match stomachs with the defending champion, but the reader also suspects that Cassandra has used Skipper's determined innocence in the face of malice to escape to an orgy with Red and his sons.

The larger point is Skipper's view of himself. From the reader's perspective his naïveté is ridiculous, but the reader's perspective is not the issue. Only Skipper's matters. Aware that heroes must perform feats of strength and skill, he stresses not the "obscenity" of the belly-bumping contest but the "tournament." In his eyes it is a jousting match during which he defeats the king of the fat and wins a crucifix and a chocolate cake. Similarly, when he hurries from the dance to "save" Cassandra and rejects a sexual tumble with naked Miranda, who has been sent to occupy him, he applauds himself for escaping Cleopatra and a new disaster on the Nile. Even when he fails later to dislodge a green iguana from Catalina Kate's back (recall the green lizard on his own chest), he interprets his effort as a rerun of St. George and the dragon. For Skipper sees himself as a hero by the sheer fact of his survival. He has lived through suicides, murder, and a homosexual attack by Tremlow, in addition to a green tattoo, a snowball fight, and a belly-bumping contest, and not once has he abandoned love.

Thus while the reader laughs at the number of catastrophes that descend on this bright-eyed innocent, he should also evaluate Skipper according to the terms of the novel. Skipper is a hero in a diminished age, and more than once he steps from behind his mask as narrator to instruct the reader on the correct interpretation:

High lights of helplessness? Mere trivial record of collapse? Say, rather, that it is the chronicle of recovery, the history of courage, the dead reckoning of my romance, the act of memory, the dance of shadows. And all the earmarks of pageantry, if you will, the glow of Skipper's serpentine tale (162).

SECOND SKIN

The heightened language stresses his courage to embrace a life that constantly tries to beat him into despair.

Skipper's serpentine tale, his narrative flight of the hummingbird, darts here and there through location and chronology to rest finally on the tropical wandering island. Cassandra jumps to her death from the phallic lighthouse, in all likelihood pregnant, since Miranda presents Skipper with a dead fetus, and he runs once more from the persistent malevolence of a violent world. This time he succeeds. Discovering a paradise that is out of space and out of time, he finds solace in the imagination.

The events on the wandering island constitute the present time of the novel. Coordinating the completion of his memoir with the birth of Catalina Kate's child, he emphasizes the reversal of the life cycle that has previously pulled him toward death. Now, amid soft winds and gentle people, the cycle shifts to affirmation:

So in six months and on the Night of All Saints Catalina Kate will bear her child—our child—and I shall complete my history, my evocation through a golden glass, my hymn to the invisible changing serpents of the wind, complete this the confession of my triumph, this my diary of an artificial inseminator (49).

As an artificial inseminator for a herd of cows, symbols of maternity, Skipper revels in his three opportunities for creativity: the cows, Kate's baby, and the novel itself. On All Saints Eve—Halloween—he will finally vanquish the shades and shapes of death that have plagued him since the father shot a bullet through his brain.

Still calling attention to his heroism, Skipper titles the final chapter "The Golden Fleas" and alludes to the myth of Jason and the golden fleece. No longer running from oblivion, he realizes that life and death are one, a never-ending continuum of loss and regeneration. Thus while his past threatens him with cemeteries and the seeds of death, his present soothes him to the extent that he can celebrate a baby's birth in a graveyard. He even speaks of having a fete with the dead, something he could not have done on the gentle island. When the golden sun tans over the green lizard "Fernandez" on his chest, Skipper's second skin is so complete that he confidently selects a symbol of himself as the location for the festival in the cemetery—a grave: "No name. No dates. . . . great monumental outline of old stone that had survived grief and that had no need of identity. I knelt there in the darkness and quickly swept the little lizards off the rim of it" (208). Iguanas and dragons are too much for him, but lizards are just his size. Kate intuitively knows what has taken Skipper fifty-nine years to learn, that life and death are inextricable. She describes the newborn baby as "him look like the fella in the grave" (209). He now accepts this truth. In his time of no time, on an island that is nowhere, and with people who long to accept his love, he can signal the ultimate unity of all things as he completes the novel: "And now there is the sun in the evening, the moon at dawn, the still voice. That's it. The sun in the evening. The moon at dawn. The still voice" (210). Existing throughout *Second Skin* by means of his voice, Skipper meta-phorically "dies" when he finally has nothing else to say.

Language has been the key to his triumph all along. Some readers are put off for a moment by the highly conscious, lyrical style, but most soon understand that the sensuous phrases, alliteration, and rhythmic prose are the narrator's methods of viewing his bloody past through the perspective of a golden lens. As a parody of Shakespeare's Prospero on a magical island, Skipper resorts to heightened language to communicate his overcharged reaction during the long journey to his distant kingdom. Such conscious style distances the reader from the narrative voice, for one is always aware that one is not participating in a life but reading a fiction. Hawkes desires this response, of course, for it illustrates his insistence on the primacy of the imagination, of creativity, of art. Rather than identity with Skipper, then, the reader keeps track of the linking images, the most important of which are the variations on the colors black, white, green, and yellow, as he follows Skipper through a serpentine tale to victory. Skipper's narrative reliability is finally unimportant in *Second Skin*, the most lyrical, humorous, and affirmative novel in the Hawkes canon.

Notes

1. John Enck, "John Hawkes: An Interview," *Wisconsin Studies in Contemporary Literature* 6 (1965): 149.
2. Enck 149–50.

3. John Graham, "John Hawkes on His Novel
7 (1966): 459.

4. Graham 459–60.

5. John Hawkes, "Notes on Writing a Novel," TriQ

6. Hawkes "Notes" 112.

7. Hawkes "Notes" 113.

8. Hawkes "Notes" 120–21.

9. "The Nearest Cemetery" is collected in John
(New York: New Directions, 1969) 43–50.

10. Hawkes "Notes" 124.

11. Hawkes "Notes" 125.

12. John Hawkes, "Response," Mosaic 8 (1974): 6.

13. Hawkes "Response" 74.

14. Graham 460.

15. John Hawkes, Second Skin (New York: New [
ferences will be noted parenthetically.

ject lessons on how to live or for confir
liefs are likely to be disappointed a
Realistic portrayal of common conce
Hawkes's work, and thus such subjects
as justice, initiation, marriage, and mor
however, is not ignored. Just as the cub
sionist painters challenge the represent
as composers from Stravinsky to the a
lyrical continuity of a score, and just
trude Stein to James Joyce and Thomas
realistic tradition of the novel, so Haw
break with the recognizably real and t
possibilities of the imagination. Art is
human need to express oneself, and wl
reader is an invitation to ponder ever
scapes that he would not normally enc
recognition but the infinity of the imagi
Reading a Hawkes novel, the reader is
stead of actuality. In The Blood Orange
that potential come true.

The Blood Orange

Hawkes began writing The Blood (
living in Greece and southern France w
Rockefeller Fellowship. As extensions
that inspired Second Skin, warm locales

THE BLOOD ORANGES

. . . the tranquillity or the volatile quality of the sun-world, which is the opposite of the materials . . . I was first writing about."[2] Hawkes's description is apt, for the tranquil nature of Cyril's sun-splashed land beyond the mountains is unexpectedly destroyed by Hugh's hanging. Hugh's volatile nature wrecks Cyril's "tapestry" of love and provides an indirect answer to the question both Hawkes and Cyril raise in the epigraph: "Is there then any terrestrial paradise where, amidst the whispering of the olive-leaves, people can be with whom they like and have what they like and take their ease in shadows and in coolness?" Borrowed from Ford Madox Ford's *The Good Soldier,* a novel that also considers unreliable narration and a quartet of would-be lovers who fail, the epigraph describes an ideal that may exist only in the imagination. Skipper locates such a haven in *Second Skin,* but Cyril is left with the memory of Hugh's death, the burden of Catherine's breakdown, and the fact of Fiona's departure. Perhaps only within the weave of his visionary tapestry—the novel itself—is a terrestrial paradise possible.

Since Cyril offers a modern-day paradise lost framed by his belief that he has successfully regained it at the end of the novel, the reader must be prepared to balance two levels of time: the immediate past when Cyril and his wife, Fiona, try to initiate Hugh and his wife, Catherine, into the pleasures of the imagination, and the present when Cyril tells the tale and works to persuade Catherine to accept his love once more. Hawkes juxtaposes the two levels so that the reader moves back and forth between Cyril's memories and his musings.

THE TRIAD

What begins in lyricism ends in death. For while Hugh desires Fiona, he nevertheless balks long enough for Cyril to dismiss him as a conventional, unimaginative puritan. Hugh finally gives in to Cyril's insistence on sexual harmony among the four adults and enjoys an interlude with Fiona, but he dies. When Catherine falls ill and Fiona leaves to nurture Hugh's children, Cyril finds his wonderland in shreds. True to his conviction that he remains a favorite of the god of love, however, he tells his story to exonerate himself and to urge Catherine to rekindle love's flame.

Hawkes uses techniques similar to those in *Second Skin*—unreliable narration, comic irony, and intricate image patterns—but *The Blood Oranges* is not as comforting. The reader should consider the tone of Cyril's tale. More desperate, more pleading, and surely more egotistical than Skipper, Cyril is a far less attractive narrator.

The result is that *The Blood Oranges* is as lyrical as *Second Skin* but clearly not as affirmative. Death has crept into the garden. Hawkes explains the genesis of the novel as a sense of "some children carrying a little coffin with a dead dog in it; I had a mental image, and I thought about the parents of these children."[3] The parents are Hugh and Catherine. Rescued from a canal deep with excrement, a symbol of Hugh's inability to embrace Cyril's tapestry, Hugh and Catherine find themselves in Illyria, a modern update of Shakespeare's mythical domain in *Twelfth Night*. No wonder Hawkes occasionally considers *The Blood Oranges* in terms of cinema: "I think *The*

THE BLOOD ORANGES

Blood Oranges would make a terrific film. Can you imagine all that color just oozing on the screen? . . . I'd love to be on the set when they're making *The Blood Oranges* in Greece. I'd be there eating grapes and drinking limes."[4]

Eating grapes in the sunshine while thinking of *Twelfth Night* and *The Good Soldier* does not, however, negate the sudden death that rends Cyril's tapestry of uninhibited sexuality. The restoration of order that exists at the conclusion of Shakespeare's play is balanced by the destruction of imaginative potential at the end of Ford's novel. Hawkes is aware of the two extremes in *The Blood Oranges:* "I wanted very much to strive for the ambience, atmosphere, harmony that exist in the play. But I also had *The Lime Twig* and *The Good Soldier* in mind. I wasn't trying to parody either of those novels, but was trying to create a partial alternative to them. *The Good Soldier* is another fiction in which sexual 'extension' results in total destructiveness."[5]

The allusions to Shakespeare and Ford help Hawkes maintain the unreal quality of the novel, the rejection of conventional verisimilitude; thus he also refuses to detail the past lives of his characters. *The Blood Oranges* begins with Cyril's voice musing on the destruction of his sexual tableau following Hugh's hanging, and the reader is introduced to four characters without the benefit of exposition: "I wanted to create characters in total purity and to deny myself the novelistic easiness of past lives to draw on. It's easier to sustain fiction with flashbacks, with a kind of explanatory reconstruction of past lives. . . . I wanted none of it. I was trying to make *The Blood Oranges* pure for the sake of comedy, and I wanted to struggle with the characters without letting the past intrude."[6] Severing the characters from their pasts has thematic implications as well, for the technique allows Hawkes to stress what he calls the "purity" of their "sex-singing." Unencumbered by the heritage of guilt that inhibits nearly all readers, Cyril and his friends are able to experiment with their innocence. As Hawkes explains, innocence is one of his favorite concepts: "These characters simply have to do with my preoccupation with innocence. . . . in which a few adult characters are freed of the question of guilt in their sexual lives. Cyril insists that they are all pure, all innocent, no matter what they are doing—which is my own view."[7]

Hawkes's support of Cyril's blamelessness is the crux of the critical controversy that has surrounded *The Blood Oranges* since its publication. In a series of interviews he has elaborated his position that Cyril is not responsible for the unraveling of the tapestry. Defending him against the charge of manipulating the other three characters, Hawkes stresses that Hugh dies because of "his solipsized sexual impulses and his puritanism," illustrated by his pornography collection.[8] In Hawkes's view Hugh's hanging is an accident, a failed effort "to undergo a partial hanging in order to experience sexual release, but he slips and thus accidentally dies." Calling the hanging "absurd," Hawkes insists that he "meant the death of Hugh in a sense to trick the reader into thinking of it as a moral

THE BLOOD ORANGES

judgment on the multiple relationships—but to me it is not."[9]
Readers who do not see through the trick, says Hawkes, fail to
understand that Cyril's greatest flaw is his inability to love
Hugh's children, and thus these readers must join Hugh's
daughter Meredith and expose their own conventional hostil-
ity toward adultery.

Time and again Hawkes denies Cyril's culpability. When
readers point to the narrator's shortcomings, Hawkes counters:
"My sympathies are all with Cyril. I don't see any way to argue that he is reprehensible. I do not think he is a manipula-
tor. . . . It seems to me that he is a god of love, a kind of
eros. . . . some of the writing is exaggerated, and some of the
perceptions are exaggerated. But that's just to emphasize his
comic imperfections."[10] The most elaborate of Hawkes's de-
fenses of Cyril is a recorded conversation with critic Robert
Scholes. Only a few highlights can be mentioned here, but the
reader of *The Blood Oranges* should consult the conversation
for the author's position against widespread reader condemnation of the narrator. Noting, for example, that *The Blood
Oranges* is about the imaginative projection of sexuality,
Hawkes explains that "Cyril is probably right when he says
that monogamy is the enemy of marriage." Hawkes reveals
that he himself lives a thoroughly conventional married life,
but in terms of the imagination, "to base the definition of marriage on sexual monogamy is absurdly reductive. Cyril's modest defiance of matrimonial conventions is intended to lead us
into realities of the imagination."[11] The problem is that many

THE TRIAD

readers do not see Cyril's defiance as "modest." Although he is impotent during the present time of the novel, his pride and confidence are overbearing, albeit comic.

The opposite of Hugh's puritan restraint, Cyril is an artist figure of the colorful imagination whereas Hugh is an artist of black-and-white photographs. They are two sides of the creative impulse, and Hawkes condemns the artist who denies color and love: "And it is Hugh's remoteness from love that causes his death, which in turn destroys the relationship or the harmony between all four characters."[12] The title of the novel suggests pain negating a life-sustaining fruit, and Hawkes does not hesitate to point his finger at Hugh. At the end of the conversation with Scholes he insists again, "I would rather have 'wife-swapping' than sterility."[13] To the observation that readers cannot determine from the novel whether Hugh's hanging is an accident or a suicide, Hawkes responds that the ambiguity exists because Cyril controls the tale.[14] But since Cyril is a first-person narrator who seems unreliable in some places and pompously overconfident in others, the reader is disinclined to believe his explanation to Catherine that the disaster is not his fault.

Against such authorial and narrative commentary the reader must consider his own sense of Cyril's culpability. For what he is faced with is a narrator who develops directly out of Hencher (*The Lime Twig*) and Skipper (*Second Skin*). All three are large, lyrical, comic, and middle-aged; but Hencher dies for his dream of love, Skipper finds his only in the imagination, and Cyril fails to make his come true in the strange land of Illyria. Reasons other than Hugh's moral rigor should be examined when evaluating Cyril's defeat.

Cyril claims, for example, that he values everything because he is love's "own faithful sex-singer,"[15] yet his narrative shows that he does not love Hugh or the children. Similarly Cyril argues that he is a man of feeling, but he denies pain:

Was all this at least my true pain, my real agony? Not at all. The nausea, the red eyes, the lips white in blind grief and silent hate, these may have been the externals of a pain that belonged to Hugh but never once to me. Hugh's pain perhaps. Not mine (57).

Cyril's protests notwithstanding, Catherine apparently believes that her affair with him is largely responsible for the tragedy: "I never expected to talk to you again" (131). More important, Cyril insists that the four adults do achieve sexual extension, but he never narrates the affairs following Hugh's acceptance of Fiona. The reader may assume, therefore, that Cyril refrains from offering an account of the sexual idyll because it may not have been as serene as he claims. Finally, Cyril stresses that he is "starting over," thereby implying a progression of time, but his final words emphasize the timelessness of his landscape: "In Illyria there are no seasons" (271). Thus the reader may legitimately conclude that the narrator of *The Blood Oranges* is both creative and destructive: creative in the sense that he writes a novel that shapes the chaos of his past into the order of his art; destructive in the sense that he wrecks the very harmony that he struggles to create.

THE TRIAD

The primary difficulty in evaluating the reliability of the narrator stems from his insisting on his position as supreme lover. Trained to more conservative notions of romance, the reader is likely to be initially entranced by Cyril's ideal of sexual freedom and then amused by his arrogant theorizing. The reaction sets in when Cyril tries to impose his notions of sex-singing on Hugh. With his black sweaters, nude photographs of peasant girls, onanism, and missing arm that Cyril implies is a symbol of sexual inadequacy, handsome Hugh seems unattractive. But the reader still balks at the narrator's effort to heap all the blame on him. Trying to counter objections, Cyril proclaims that most conventional people detest a lover, even one as modest as he; but note the lack of modesty in his explanation:

For some, love itself is a crime. I realize all this. . . . But it will take a dark mind to strip my vines, to destroy the last shreds of my tapestry, to choke off my song. . . . I am a match, I hope, for the hatred of conventional enemies wherever they are (36).

Presumably the reader is the conventional enemy, for Hawkes has successfully written a lyrical evocation of sexual love that makes outsiders think about the stirrings of their own imaginations. The narrator's tapestry is the problem, and at the beginning of the novel it is in pieces.

Cyril's efforts in the present time of *The Blood Oranges* are to persuade Catherine again to be his mistress. Although

THE BLOOD ORANGES

he is confident, he seems unaware of the humor of his position. When, for example, he reveals that he equates himself with such animals of sexual potency as the bull and the ram, he ignores the ridiculousness of the way he translates love into mere amorous freedom:

I was there always. I completed the picture. I took my wife, took her friends, took the wives of my friends and a fair roster of other girls and women, from young to old and old to young, whenever the light was right or the music sounded (2).

The reader must be ready to see through his pomposity, to deflect the authority of the first-person narrator.

For Cyril is trying to convince both the reader and himself of his innocence. Interrupting the account of his campaign to woo Catherine from her illness to his bed, he keeps returning to the immediate past in the hope of exonerating himself. The reason is not only that he needs a female to complete his tableau but that his obsession with symmetry has been wrecked by Hugh's death.

One must understand that Cyril desires not a *ménage à trois* but a foursome. He is convinced of his status as a favorite son of the love god, and he is thrilled at the opportunity to initiate Hugh into the pleasures of sex-singing. In other words, Hugh must accept Fiona while Cyril pairs off with Catherine. Such an arrangement would be symmetrical. But Hugh, the unimaginative representative of conventional marriage, hesitates. At first unaware that Catherine is Cyril's mistress, he re-

THE TRIAD

fuses to complete the symmetry. Note, for example, Cyril's comic befuddlement when Hugh does not remove Catherine's bathing suit top after Cyril has lifted off Fiona's:

Was he then thoughtless? Selfish? Without even the crudest idea of simple reciprocity? . . . What was holding him back? Could he not see that Catherine herself was puzzled, uncomfortable? Could he deliberately mean to embarrass his wife and to tamper with the obviously intended symmetry of our little scene on the beach? (42–43).

Never thinking that Catherine might be embarrassed not by Hugh's hesitation but by public nakedness itself, Cyril blames Hugh's puritanism. This scene is typical of Cyril's rationalization throughout.

Later, of course, Hugh does accept Fiona. Although Cyril is not about to explain why beyond the soothing sound of his sex-song, one assumes that the combination of guilt, onanism, and coercion is too great for Hugh to resist. Yet while there is a short interlude when the symmetry seems intact, Hugh's true position is best illustrated by his determined pursuit of a chastity belt.

Arguing that Hugh listens to "the rhythm of some dark death of his own," Cyril recounts their search for the belt in order to contrast Hugh's blackness to his own light. He emphasizes the pastoral connotations of grapes, flowers, and nude sunbathing when he recalls the sexual extension, and then he points out that Hugh leads them to the inner depths of dungeons. The underground passageway smells of excrement instead of arbors, and Cyril hopes that the reader will note how sex-singers are out of place in dungeons just as puritans are strangers in Illyria. The grail of Hugh's quest turns out to be the chastity belt, "monstrous memento of Hugh's true attitude toward all of our well-intended loves" (204). Clamping the "artful relic of fear and jealousy" between Catherine's thighs, Hugh unimaginatively but understandably stakes his claim to monogamy. He accepts Fiona only after Cyril removes the belt, yet the pairing off leads not to singing but to a final, death-filled shriek.

Thus Cyril argues that Hugh dies for love, but he protests his innocence so strenuously that the reader should reexamine the extent of Cyril's defense and the unimaginativeness of Hugh's hesitation. In essence they are two artists whose creations degenerate to distortion. Both outrageous Cyril and grim Hugh deserve sympathy because each is victimized by the other, but only the former is alive to plead his case. This Cyril does in the present time of the novel as he struggles to include Catherine in the song once more.

The pagan boat-launching scene suggests that Catherine agrees. Escorting her from the sickroom, Cyril takes her to a native fertility ceremony during which a priest and half-naked attendants celebrate by the sea. They observe the dancing, flowers, and blood, and Cyril interprets the spectacle according to his needs. He also hopes to convince the reader: "Priest, blood, *Lobularia maritima*, procession—how could it have been more plain? . . . Why not assume that a now invulnerable Catherine and reflective Cyril were starting over? Why not?" (126). Despite such serenity, the reader must be wary. *Lobularia maritima* is a flower traditionally used to cure madness, and the word "assume" hints that the issue is not as plain as Cyril claims. He believes that harmony has been reestablished in Illyria, but it may be that he creates it only within the confines of his tale. Against his inviting freedom the reader should balance the facts of Hugh's death, Catherine's resulting illness, and Fiona's departure.

Hawkes's skill with unreliable narration means that the reader must look within the novel itself for indirect challenges to the narrator's story. Thus one should note not only the pomposity of Cyril's tone but the flaws in his imagery. References to animals and allusions to *Twelfth Night* are patterns to consider, but an equally important illustration is the flower imagery.

Long a staple of love ceremonies, flowers generally indicate fertility and commitment. Cyril is aware of the mythological associations of grape arbors, orange blossoms, and flowers, and he fills his narrative with descriptions of them. But just as his use of *Lobularia maritima* in the boat-launching scene may inadvertently indicate irony because of the hidden allusion to madness, so his flower imagery may unintentionally expose him as unreliable. The flower gathering scene with Hugh's daughters is an example. Trying to show his companions and the reader that his sense of love extends beyond mere sexuality, Cyril escorts the young girls on an outing to pick blossoms. He instructs the children to gather *Cyclamen persicum, Echium diffusum*, ghostly asphodel, and *Anemone cor-*

THE BLOOD ORANGES

onaria, while he selects *Laurus nobilis* and *Genista cinerea*. The reader in a hurry will miss the ironic allusions because he will not take the time to research the connotations of the Latin names. But those who do will find that Cyril unknowingly undercuts himself. The flowers assigned to the girls mean, respectively, a bad luck gift to women, courage, regret and the Greek emblem of death, and refusal and abandonment. The flowers he saves for himself mean glory and renown, and ardor and humility. Cyril may not expect the reader to look up the connotations, but Hawkes does. The names of the flowers show that the narrator is not as loving as he claims.

Cyril's story is as humorously ironic as Skipper's in *Second Skin*, but the affirmation is toned down. Skipper's hymn to love results in a baby, a frisky herd of cows, and a creative imagination, but Cyril's leads to destruction of the one thing he wants to protect: his tapestry of freedom in Illyria. Even he admits that love has "purged" him (3). Thus while he insists that he is beginning again with Catherine, his inviting wonderland may be the other extreme of Hugh's restrictive conventionality. The one offers color while the other has only black and white, but terror challenges love in both cases.

Hawkes disagrees: "It seems to me that the ending of *The Blood Oranges* is very similar to the ending of *Second Skin*. . . . I think these relics [the flower crown, the chastity belt, the undershorts] are an effort to insist on the actuality of innocence. Virginity is the negative existence of sexual experience."[16] With such comments by the author and the novel itself in hand, the reader is left to make up his own mind.

THE TRIAD

Death, Sleep & the Traveler

If *The Blood Oranges* describes a lyrical song degenerating to a shriek, *Death, Sleep & the Traveler* turns the singing into the wail of a nightmare. The location of the second novel in the triad is so eerie that Allert, the traveler of the title, may not have left the interior of his dreams. Sex and death unify with such power in his psyche that he seems doomed to pursue his adventures within himself.

The attraction to strange locales is part of Hawkes's commitment to detachment and antirealism: "I had a simple theory of detachment: that if one could find a landscape that, in some way or other, without the writer's being conscious of it, could touch off psychological themas, *that* would provide the energy and even the subject matter of a fiction. I was trying to find such landscapes or happened to be exposed to such landscapes."[17] Leaving the normal world encourages the imagination to meet its potential.

In *Death, Sleep & the Traveler*, Hawkes deliberately sidesteps his commitment to comedy. Once again the story is told from the point of view of a large, middle-aged, first-person narrator, but Allert lacks the promise of hopeful creativity that motivates Hencher (*The Lime Twig*), Skipper (*Second Skin*), and Cyril (*The Blood Oranges*). Although, for example, he seems to follow Skipper from a cold locale to a warm land, his travels propel him to the threat of frigidity and the danger of searing heat. He is unlikely to glory in Skipper's golden fleas or Cyril's tapestry. Hawkes comments: "I might add that I'm no longer interested in writing comic novels, that I'm wary now of the 'safety' inherent in the comic form, that from now on I want to come still closer to terror, which I think I'm doing in the short novel I'm trying to write at the moment."[18] Hawkes does not name the novel, but it is probably *Death, Sleep & the Traveler* since both comment and novel were published in 1974.

Thus the reader must be ready for a change of tone. The lyrical beauty long associated with Hawkes's fiction is evident, but like Hugh in *The Blood Oranges*, Allert, a collector of pornography, seeks an extended sexual thrill in death. As his wife, Ursula, remarks, "Allert's theory is that the ordinary man becomes an artist only in sex. In which case pornography is the true field of the ordinary man's imagination."[19] The reader should not, of course, confuse the narrator's opinions with the author's. While Hawkes explores art and imagination, Allert investigates orgasm and death. Since Allert wonders whether he may be alive only in his dreams, the reader looks for evidence that the narration *is* the life of the narrator. That is, the action and other characters may exist no further than Allert's psyche, thus making *Death, Sleep & the Traveler* a novel about fiction. The reader must join Hawkes and mold the extremes of Allert's nightmare into an artistic whole.

The process is fun. While the narrator suffers the agony of a plunge into his subconscious, the reader enjoys discovering that the literal level of the novel is relatively unimportant. Two stretches of time are interspersed. In the present, Allert tells of marrying in middle age, to Ursula. Together for at least a decade, they have invited a psychiatrist named Peter to participate in their erotic adventures. But by the time that Ursula claims to be leaving Allert, Peter has been dead for three years. The other time level concerns Allert's mysterious travels aboard a silent ocean liner. There he becomes the center of another *ménage à trois* with young Ariane and boorish Olaf. When Ariane disappears from the ship, Allert is acquitted of her murder. He hints that the trial occurs almost ten years ago, and he concludes with a protest that echoes Cyril: "I am not guilty."

The action, however, is more a frame for an investigation of dreams than a progression of plot. A key image is the drifting ocean liner, for it illustrates the traveler enclosed within his psyche as he hurries to a meeting with himself. Like Skipper's lighthouse, Hugh's dungeon, and Luke's (*The Beetle Leg*) dam, the ship suggests the dark tunnel of the interior. Terror lurks everywhere because the traveler cannot see what lingers on the other side of consciousness. Hawkes persuades the reader to look.

He explains the importance of the ship as "a personal waking dream in which I stand alone at the edge of a straight empty shore at low tide and gaze with both fear and longing at an enormous black derelict or damaged ocean liner that looms in awful silence in kneedeep water about a mile from shore. . . . And then I am compelled to walk slowly but deliberately into the muddy shallow water and toward the ship." Hawkes is compelled, just as he hopes to compel the reader, because the interior of the ship represents a vast world that he must pry open and discover "either its treasure, if childhood hopes prevail, or its emptiness, its floating corpses." In *Death, Sleep & the Traveler* he stumbles on the corpses: "The vision, no matter how personal, is one of potential and desolation. It suggests the undiminishing power of childhood experience."[20]

Childhood fear and trauma are the likely causes of Allert's dilemma. Trapped by unspecified incidents in his youth, he may be a patient in a psychiatric hospital who understands the possibilities when myth unites with coma. Uncertain of the implications of his waking life, he retreats to his psyche, where he travels within himself to pursue the fullest expression of sexual myth. Coma is the result, and he suspects that the final myth can be found only in the ultimate coma: death. Hawkes indirectly supports such a reading of the novel because he has said that he finds myth "precisely that traumatic, that powerful, that real, that devastating."[21] For one of the few times in his career he admits that he is referring to autobiography in a novel: "Peter intuits very clearly what Allert has once been—a patient who has undergone a particular treatment. . . .insulin shock therapy. It is a treatment that I myself experienced after the second World War. But I didn't know much about it intellectually until I met a friend of mine only a few years ago. He happens to be a psychiatrist, and he told me why the treatment has been discontinued—because it brought the patient up to the point of death. I was able to put that information into the novel."[22]

As Hawkes writes his novel, so Allert dreams his life. When the narrator asks, "Who can confront his psychic sores in the clear glass?" he hints that the reader will know him only through the language that accounts for his journey to the interior. Faced with the paradoxes of his physical needs—onanism and heterosexuality, marriage and adultery—he describes his travels from nightmare to coma as he searches for the ultimate experience. Some of his descriptions are so exaggerated as to cause laughter—the bats perusing their private parts, Peter rubbing Ursula's underwear with lotion—but in general Allert's obsession with drowning and water is a key to his desire and fear.

Long associated with femininity and eternity, water is another of Hawkes's linking images. Its presence is important throughout the novel, from the searing saunas, through Allert's gulping cold water, to his diving to the bottom of the ocean liner's pool; and the reader should understand that Allert splashes through water in search of himself. Hawkes comments: "By now it's obvious that I'm obsessed among other things with the sea and with islands, and whereas Donne says that 'no man is an island,' I myself believe that we're all islands—inaccessible, drifting apart, thirsting to be explored, magical."[23] Significantly, Allert says the same thing: "Every man is an island. . . . I am like the rest" (104). His story is an exploration of his own island.

With Allert as the travel guide the reader should not rely on verisimilitude. The narrator mentions "concreteness rotating toward illusion," and he all but dismisses conventional realism in favor of vision when he describes Ursula's departure on the first page: "Dressed in her severe gray suit, her gar-

DEATH, SLEEP & THE TRAVELER

dening hat, her girdle, her negligee, her sullen silk dress, her
black blouse, her stockings, her red pumps . . . thus she is
leaving me" (1). Clearly she cannot be wearing all of this, but
Allert stresses his rejection of verisimilitude even more when
at the end of the novel he remarks that Ursula prepares to
leave while wearing a red knit top and white slacks.

The point is that his trip across the ocean takes him nowhere except inside himself, and the reader begins to suspect
that all the characters are projections of Allert's psyche. Note
the hints of identification: the fish hook that links Ariane and
Allert, Ursula and Peter; the similar ages of Allert and Peter;
the red rashes of Ursula and Ariane; the fact that both Allert
and Olaf are confined to their rooms. As projections within
the narrator's night sea journey, the characters act out the
dreamer's neurotic wishes.

The reader who balks at this suggestion should consider
an alternative that the novel also supports: that the Allert-Ur-
sula-Peter triangle is "real," and that the Allert-Ariane-Olaf
trio is a subconscious extension of it. If this possibility is acceptable, then Ursula has committed Allert to Acres Wild, a
mental hospital, freeing him to live his fantasies. She advises
him, for example, to stop dreaming in order to enjoy her natural eroticism, but he is incapable of controlling his desires except within the novel itself. The further he sinks into his own
coma, the closer he approaches extinction. Although he stops
short of suicide, he does succeed in cleansing himself of the
other characters: Ariane falls from the ocean liner, Olaf loses
his position as a ship's officer, Peter succumbs to a heart at-

tack, and Ursula leaves. Part of the challenge of *Death, Sleep & the Traveler* is that the reader must play the narrator's game, for Hawkes does not violate his sense of detachment to provide authorial commentary. Even Allert's inviting allusions in the choice of names (Ursula as Ursa, the she-bear of the Great Bear Constellation, or as the organizer of the Ursuline nuns into nurses, for instance) may be suspect, another of his efforts to divert the reader.

Calling himself the "alerted sleeper," Allert admits an "inability to believe in the reality of the human self" (90). Thus he consciously identifies with the "dead ship," senses the rhythm of the propellers inside him (8), and follows the ocean liner toward "the unmoving fictional horizon" that is *Death, Sleep & the Traveler*. When Ursula accuses him of emotionally annihilating himself and of having the face of a fetus, the reader understands that he has no reality beyond the narrative that exposes a sexual insecurity originating in childhood (he identifies with his mother when he dons her clothes to look at nudity).

The erotic ecstasy that Cyril hopes to establish in *The Blood Oranges* takes a destructive twist in the second novel of the triad. For Hawkes dismisses the creativity of sexuality found in *Second Skin*, cuts off Cyril's lyrical song heard in *The Blood Oranges*, and has Peter ask a question in *Death, Sleep & the Traveler* that illustrates Allert's investigation of sex and death: "What do you think of my theory that a man remains a virgin until he has committed murder?" (26). Allert is so determined to shed his virginity and personify Peter's equation that he may have killed Ariane and still hopes to "murder" himself.

Death will be his most arousing mistress. No wonder he insists on the identification of coma and myth. No wonder Peter asks, "Has it ever occurred to you that your life is a coma? That you live your entire life in a coma? Sometimes I cannot help but think that you never entirely emerge from your flickering cave" (144).

He doesn't. At the end of the novel the reader realizes that Allert prefers to stay within himself where he can live the paradox of being "more youthful and yet closer to death" than ever. He is almost serene. Protesting that he is not guilty of Ariane's murder, he remains on his ocean liner, traveling between the cold and hot flashes of his northern home and a southern clime, sailing by dead reckoning toward oblivion and a resulting sexual adventure beyond his wildest fantasy. Hugh's shriek in *The Blood Oranges* becomes Allert's pursuit of terror in *Death, Sleep & the Traveler* as Hawkes lures the reader into the darkest recesses of the imagination.

Travesty

For the final novel of the triad Hawkes chooses an extreme paradox: a tale told by a first-person narrator who is crashing his car into a wall. If his plan succeeds, the reader wonders, how can he tell his story? Once again an external event triggered Hawkes's imagination. Just as a visit to the island of Lesbos and a newspaper account of a Dutch sailor murdering a woman inspired *Death, Sleep & the Traveler*, so a stay in Brittany (France), a reading of Albert Camus' *The Fall*, and seeing "a marvelous French car accident with the cars coming together head-on and then just melding their pieces all over the landscape for hundreds and hundreds of yards" led to *Travesty*.[24] *Travesty* is among other considerations a parody of the novel: a dead narrator tells the story of his own death.

Papa, the narrator of *Travesty*, is an extension of Allert (*Death, Sleep & the Traveler*), for as Hawkes says, Papa does consciously what Allert does unconsciously.[25] Committed to an artistic paradox of "design and debris," Papa kills himself to show that suicide has nothing to do with courage but everything to do with imagination. His speeding car recalls Allert's drifting ocean liner, and Hawkes explains that part of the background of the novel is his original fear of automobiles that bothered him when he rushed through a driving course in order to qualify for ambulance service in World War II: "I soon developed a horror of automobiles through trying to drive an ambulance. . . . One night . . . I happened upon a convoy of tanks. They had their searchlights on. The searchlights blinded me, and I ran the ambulance into a boulder and blew out a tire. . . . I was left with a considerable horror of automobiles that went into *Travesty*." After the war he became fond of foreign cars and bought one that was "very much like a coffin—a small, high, black coffin."[26]

Although the epigraphs to *Travesty* are by Camus (*The Fall*) and Michel Leiris (*Manhood*), Hawkes has indicated that the following line by Braque is also appropriate: "The vase gives shape to space, music to silence."[27] He has in mind paradox, art supplying form to suicide so that the ultimate creative act is the imagining of one's own death. In this sense Papa's memory of trying to run down a little girl and his current plan of including his daughter Chantal in the wreck are parallel: "The privileged man is driving the car with Chantal and Henri in it, intending to crash against a wall, in order to explore the imagination in the process."[28] In other words, the memory of the hit-and-run, "the formative event of his life," inspires Papa ironically to his greatest creative effort.

Travesty is his account of that creation, and he himself is the only speaker in the novel. Far from being unsure of himself as Skipper (*Second Skin*) and Cyril (*The Blood Oranges*) appear at times, he is a middle-aged man confidently driving an expensive car at high speed "in the darkest quarter of the night" toward a fatal impact at a wall. He claims to have two companions with him, his twenty-five-year-old daughter, who is near hysteria, and his friend Henri, who is the lover of both Chantal and Papa's wife, Honorine. But while the narrator talks to the other characters, they never directly respond. Thus the reader may wonder whether they are projections of Papa's imagination, illustrations of his need to thrive on "design and debris."[29] The reader should also look for signs of narrative unreliability. Papa, for instance, insists that his primary concern is clarity, but the reader may give greater credence to his warning: "The moral of it all is trust me but do not believe me—ever" (102). He may be mad from the so-called normal point of view, imagining the drive in his mind as he resists Henri's effort to bring him "back to sanity."

THE TRIAD

It is important to understand that Hawkes separates suicide as act and suicide as a metaphor for art: "I feel very violently opposed to it. . . . In *Travesty*, murder and suicide are instruments that are deliberately being used thematically. They are the substance out of which something is created— something having to do with the imagination itself. . . . If I could enact my anti-suicide law and have it enforced safely, I certainly would do it. I am utterly opposed to suicide."[30] But, as Hawkes explains, moral judgment is not an issue when a fictional character uses suicide to complete the design of his life: "The irony is that I'm not appalled yet by the privileged man's murder/suicide in *Travesty*. This is because I think of it as so purely a work of art that he assumes responsibility rather than commits an outrage against life itself."[31]

The point is that Hawkes wants his triad of sex and the imagination to conclude with a shock in order to persuade the reader to rethink his own concept of love. Psychic depths always lurk beneath the surface of normal life. Those who are most adept at confronting the nightmare are those who are most aware: "My work affirms the imagination, yet I couldn't help but end that triad of fictions . . . on a severe note. The dangers of the most joyous of human experiences had to reassert themselves. These are so much at the center of human life that we should know that our clearest impulses toward love inevitably involve pain as well as joy. I wanted the final statement to be paradoxically the most erotic and, at the same time, the most shockingly severe, so that the reader would pause and think about the magnitude of the erotic impulse."[32]

Thus art is more important than morality in *Travesty*. The deplorable act of suicide is secondary when one considers the task Hawkes sets for himself—to conceive of the inconceivable: "Death—cessation, annihilation—is the only thing I can think of that cannot be imagined. The only way that the artist-driver of the car can imagine it is through paradox. He conceives of the wreckage before it occurs; he recognizes that in destruction there is always a design for those of us who want to seek it; and he sees that in any design, any created thing, there is always the potential for the loss of its beautiful shape and its collapse into chaos."[33]

Since art is both design and debris, Hawkes shows that his control of the novel balances Papa's ride into chaos. The narrator seems intent, for example, on impressing his wife with the vividness of his vision, but he also admits that she is sleeping and not in the car. Thus when he argues that she will nevertheless be aware of his race through her "dormant consciousness," he inadvertently suggests that his journey is a plunge into his own mind. His delight in articulating his fantasies may derive from a need to possess both Honorine and Chantal sexually. Clearly forbidden in waking life, sexual involvement with wife and daughter is imaginable in the psyche. This is why he stresses a memory of making love to a strange woman while Honorine and Chantal eat chocolates nearby; the affair is "as if I had only found my way again to

Chantal and Honorine, and as if I had accepted from mother and daughter the same unimaginable gift" (31).

Imagining the unimaginable in terms of love as well as death, Papa talks to Henri, the lover of both women and like himself an artist figure. The reader should consider the possibility that Papa *creates* Henri as a way of loving wife and daughter. If Henri is a personification of the narrator's erotic needs, then Papa can safely give him the face of a criminal and a history of mental instability. In other words, the narrator can unify sex and death by imagining an alter ego with characteristics that would be unacceptable outside of the speeding car: "At any rate you will not deny that in yourself you have achieved that brilliant anomaly: the poet as eroticist and pragmatist combined" (42).

Confessing that he lacks a "fixed and predictable personality," Papa may be wondering about his own rationality when he describes Henri's past mental infirmities. The result of his protest is that he protests too much. The more he stresses his separation from Henri, the more the reader senses their identification: "The poet is the thick-skinned and simple-minded beast of the ego, while contrary to popular opinion, it is your ordinary privileged man who turns out to reveal in the subtlest of ways all those faint sinister qualities of the artistic mind" (100). Note the equation of sinister and artistic. Suspecting derangement, Papa takes a death ride as a metaphor for his desperate measures to assert design within the debris of his life.

TRAVESTY

Chantal and Honorine may also be illusory. Although daughter and wife, they enter Papa's tale primarily when he describes erotic dreams. The sexual overtones of Chantal's being crowned "Queen of Carrots" and of Papa's delight in licking chocolate from her fingers are unmistakable. Similarly, Honorine is the center of identical visions by Papa and Henri in which they unbutton her blouse. A collector of pornography, the narrator implies that his wife, daughter, and mistress are three projections of his fantasy life when he admits that Honorine poses for his camera, that Chantal is a "porno brat," and that Monique the mistress likes photographs of nudes. Indeed, *Travesty* may be such an extension of the narrator's inner needs that it reflects one of his affairs with Monique: "It was a scene that might have come directly from the writing desk or cold and shabby studio of one of our poor, dull, unshaven pornographers" (69). Papa insists that he is not such a man, but the reader can only wonder.

Papa seems aware that the reader will also join Henri's protest against the ride, for he argues that the charge of murder is banal when one considers the artistic design of his plan. Such outrage, he says, is no more than a cry of "moral wolf": "So you accuse me of planning murder. But with the very use of the word you reveal at last that you are only the most banal and predictable of poets" (14). He hopes to disarm the reader of the protection of moral judgment, and to a large extent he succeeds. For only in the confines of art can the reader share in the death of another. Thus just as Allert declares that he is not

THE TRIAD

guilty, Cyril says that he is not responsible, and Papa notes that he is not a murderer, so the reader may freely imagine the design of death if he will join Papa in the car. Papa even pleads with the reader: "Please, I beg you. Do not accuse me of being a man without feeling or a man of unnatural feeling. This moment, for instance, is not disgusting but decisive" (18–19). Those who reject the plea, he implies, do not share his interest in the order of destruction.

But Hawkes himself does share it. Agreeing with Papa that "nothing is more important than the existence of what does not exist" (57), he describes the imagination as the power to invent a world even while life is being negated. For this reason Hawkes denies the suggestion that the other characters and perhaps the car ride are no more than particulars of Papa's fantasy: "It leaves us with literally nothing but the narrator, and I don't want to be left with nothing but the narrator. . . . I think the accident the narrator imagines is the accident that occurs. Without the literal accident, you wouldn't have the impossible object, you wouldn't have the whole fabric of imagined event, you wouldn't have the imagination exemplified as it is in that short novel."[34]

D. H. Lawrence once warned the public to trust not the artist but the art, and he meant that people should pay more attention to how the creation affects them than to what the creator says about it. But the reader of *Travesty* should consider Hawkes's comments if only to ponder the ability of the imagination to create art out of nothing. If the novelist can take the blank page and shape a novel, then Papa can take a car wreck and make design from debris. One does not have to agree with Hawkes's interpretation of his own novel to appreciate its challenge to the imagination. Among other considerations *Travesty* is a travesty of the traditional realistic novel that relies on logic and cause and effect to hold it together. Remembering Papa's monologue, Hawkes might note that he is not so banal in his fiction.

The reader of the triad should not be either. Each novel carries the reader further from exterior reality as Hawkes pushes imagination to its limits. From Cyril's Illyria on the other side of the mountains, through Allert's water-soaked psyche, to Papa's hurtling car is a journey that confirms Hawkes's conviction that imagined life is more sustaining than remembered life. In this sense the triad is as much about the art of fiction as about sex and the imagination, and it should be read as an example of the vitality of the genre. The unreliable narrators ask not for belief in their tales but for trust in their visions. Hawkes does too. Urging the reader beyond the safety of convention, he illustrates the intricate fabrications that the inspired mind can create.

Notes

1. Thomas LeClair, "The Novelists: John Hawkes," *New Republic* 10 Nov. 1979: 28.

2. "Conversations Between Patrick O'Donnell and John Hawkes on His Life and Art," O'Donnell, *John Hawkes* (Boston: Twayne, 1982) 17–18.

3. O'Donnell 18.

THE TRIAD

4. Roger Sauls, "John Hawkes: I Am Pleased to Talk about Fiction," *New Lazarus Review* 1 (1978): 7.

5. "Interview," John Kuehl, *John Hawkes and the Craft of Conflict* (New Brunswick: Rutgers University Press, 1975) 171.

6. Kuehl 167.

7. Kuehl 171.

8. Kuehl 168.

9. Kuehl 169.

10. Paul Emmett and Richard Vine, "A Conversation with John Hawkes," *Chicago Review* 28 (1976): 168.

11. "A Conversation on *The Blood Oranges* between John Hawkes and Robert Scholes," *Novel* 5 (1972): 198.

12. "Conversation on *The Blood Oranges*" 199.

13. "Conversation on *The Blood Oranges*" 207.

14. Anthony C. Santore and Michael Pocalyko, " 'A Trap to Catch Little Birds With': An Interview with John Hawkes," *A John Hawkes Symposium: Design and Debris* (New York: New Directions, 1977) 181.

15. John Hawkes, *The Blood Oranges* (New York: New Directions, 1971) 3. Further references will be noted parenthetically.

16. Emmett and Vine 169.

17. O'Donnell 16.

18. John Hawkes, "Notes on Writing a Novel," *TriQuarterly* 30 (1974): 111.

19. John Hawkes, *Death, Sleep & the Traveler* (New York: New Directions, 1974) 153. Further references will be noted parenthetically.

20. Hawkes "Notes" 115.

21. Emmett and Vine 170.

22. Emmett and Vine 170.

23. Hawkes "Notes" 113.

24. Emmett and Vine 165.

25. Emmett and Vine 171.

26. Emmett and Vine 165–66.

27. Emmett and Vine 167.

28. Emmett and Vine 166.

29. John Hawkes, *Travesty* (New York: New Directions, 1976) 27. Further references will be noted parenthetically.

30. Santore and Pocalyko 182, 180.

THE TRIAD

31. Santore and Pocalyko 181.
32. LeClair 28.
33. LeClair 28.
34. Emmett and Vine 169–70.

CHAPTER SEVEN

THE PASSION ARTIST

F or *The Passion Artist* (1979), Hawkes shifted from the first-person narration of the four immediately preceding novels to third person. This change allowed him to create one of his most unattractive characters and thus limit the empathy often accorded self-revealing comic dupes in such novels as *Second Skin*.

Hawkes recalls the germ of *The Passion Artist* as a conversation with a friend: "I said that the interior life of the human being is a cesspool, and she said, 'Well, how do you know it isn't a bed of stars?' And that pair of possibilities stuck with me." He then remembered two events that revolved around prisons: the passage in *The Cannibal* when women put down the revolt in the asylum, and the source of that passage as an adventure by his father who, as a member of the Connecticut National Guard, volunteered to quell a rebellion in a woman's prison.[1]

Writing the novel in France and thereby drawing on imaginative projections stimulated by a non-native landscape, Hawkes created an atmosphere not of the color and

THE PASSION ARTIST

light associated with most of his novels since *The Lime Twig* but of the drab and cold found in *The Cannibal* and *The Owl*. Konrad Vost, the humorless, unimaginative, and uncreative central character, feels at home in his dank environment. Hawkes comments on the novel and Vost: "It's about a middle-aged widower who, in a 'mythical' European country, is introduced to the nature of woman in the prison where his mother is confined for the murder of his father. I've decided that the three most important subjects are consciousness, the imagination, and the nature of woman. In *The Passion Artist* I've tried to create the worst possible protagonist I could think of—a sort of Malvolio who is crazed by his ignorance of women. But for once I've tried to deal with a topical theme, by dramatizing the power of women. That's something new for me."[2]

The allusion to Malvolio reminds the reader of *The Blood Oranges*, in which the black-sweatered, puritanical Hugh is also associated with Shakespeare's dreary victim, but *The Passion Artist* is significantly different from *The Blood Oranges* in terms of style and tone. Rather than a lyricism supported by characters pursuing love, *The Passion Artist* offers a grimly stark style, especially in the opening section, in order to suggest the monotonous, listless sterility of Vost's daily routine. The result is that the comic tone that highlights many of Hawkes's earlier fictions gives way to a relentless exposition of a man alienated from himself. Frightened by women and suspicious of sexual urges, Konrad represses the guilt and fear caused by onanistic memories of his "silver horn." These changes also make *The Passion Artist* easier to understand than *The Blood Oranges* and *The Cannibal* because the uninvolved narrator is reliable and because Hawkes specifies that Vost's unappealing city is the "domain" of the human psyche.

The title is an allusion to Kafka's short story "A Hunger Artist," as Hawkes makes clear when he uses a quotation from the tale as an epigraph: "Just try to explain to anyone the art of fasting! Anyone who has no feeling for it cannot be made to understand it." Kafka indirectly prefigures Vost, for Konrad has no feel for passion. Thus the title of Vost's story is ironic until the conclusion. Caught between the excessiveness of his psychic depths and the rigidity of his waking life, he is an outcast in a world of women. As Hawkes explains, Konrad's personality verges on the criminal: "The writer who sets out to create his own world in a sense defies the world around him. He has to become an outcast, an outsider. He works in isolation to create something which to him is a thing of beauty, as well as a thing of knowledge and moral meaning. And that act is a risk, an assault on the world as we think we know it, and as such can be viewed as dangerous, destructive, criminal."[3] In *The Passion Artist*, then, Hawkes explores the suspect side of the artist and creates a main character who is closer to Il Gufo (*The Owl*) than to Skipper (*Second Skin*). As the other epigraph to the novel suggests (from Rilke, *The Book of Images*), Vost grows from boy to man prepared to "fight against the nightingale."

The fight costs him his life. Yet a psychic victory is also won, for though he is the most brutal of Hawkes's main characters, he eventually sheds his fear of sexual commitment.

THE PASSION ARTIST

The Passion Artist is Hawkes's clearest illustration of the tendency of American novelists to unite love and death. Vost's ultimate acceptance of "willed eroticism" coincides with his accidental death, but his courage in investigating the repression of his own imagination grants him a sympathy that his despicable beating of women inmates might at first seem to deny. The reader should understand that Konrad's private adventure, his ironic quest in which the grail can be only himself, is a direct result of his brutality during a counterattack against the prisoners. After the attack fails and Vost is captured, he escapes to track down fugitives but discovers instead his humanity.

Vost personifies the institutionalized misogyny of his environment. Hawkes distances the reader from Konrad's bleak life, and the result is that the reader is encouraged to judge Vost more than the absurd Zizendorf (*The Cannibal*) or the bumbling Skipper. Although, for example, Konrad lingers at the railroad terminal as a "stationary traveler" in search of another glimpse of the woman who reminds him of his imprisoned mother, he is secretly happy that the woman is in chains. His joy at such restraint reveals his ignorance of femininity and thus of passion and creativity. Hawkes urges the reader not to damn Vost but to be repelled by his excesses while sympathizing with his violent struggle to light the pit of his subconscious. The lighting process takes a long time.

Guilt and fear lead him along the way. Vost does not much like himself because of the very quality of restraint that defines him. He is as unattractive to himself as he is to his family:

But Konrad Vost was only a middle-aged man without distinction or power of any kind, so that to others these two most obtrusive qualities of his personality were all the more odious. And since Vost also possessed self-insight and understanding of the feelings of friends and family, such as they were, he too found odious the main qualities that were himself. But the joy of being always precise and always right was insurmountable, so that he detested himself fiercely yet could hardly change.[4]

He lacks the imagination to break out of his resolutely drab approach to life. The central irony that shapes the novel is that Vost has long been encircled by one of the prime sources of the imagination: women. The problem is that his wife is dead; his mother is incarcerated for killing his father; and his daughter, he mistakenly thinks, is still a child:

Claire the dead wife. Eva the imprisoned mother. Mirabelle the daughter. Surrounded by the music of such names, it was inevitable that Konrad Vost should himself become one of the children menaced by the nightingales (3).

Menaced he is. Attracted most of all to the mother, Vost remains in the town that holds her prison, La Violaine (the name suggests violation), and patronizes the cafe across the street from its high, rusted gates and grilled windows. The allusion is clear: Konrad has locked up his own life because he fears the shock of alteration. As he sits in the cafe and stares at the prison while smelling rancid cigarette smoke and listening to the progress of a fly, he feels "the boredom and security of time passing as it was expected to pass, indifferently, without meaning, without the threat of impending unwanted change or even disaster" (5). Disaster, however, cannot be kept behind bars or hidden in the psyche. A meticulous life is an easy target for the free forms of passion. Imagination, Hawkes shows, is not to be denied.

The reader should note the landscapes in *The Passion Artist*, especially how the stark town contrasts with the fecund swamp outside it. Absence of color in the city illustrates avoidance of creativity in Vost: "He knew only too well that the city in which he lived was without trees, without national monuments, without ponds or flower gardens, without even a single building to attract visitors from other parts of the world" (11). Konrad's city is the exterior of his subconscious: dull, dreary, drab. The only time that he longs for "unseen vistas" is when he is safely contained within the coach of a train. Readers familiar with *Death, Sleep & the Traveler* will note the allusion to Allert when the narrator of *The Passion Artist* describes Konrad as a traveler. Vost has nowhere to go because he is afraid to violate the order of his life. The threat posed by imaginative femininity is repelled by helping women die, by keeping them childlike, or by forcing them behind the steel doors of man's rigidity. The rebellion is a revolt of Vost's subconscious against himself and of women against men. Significantly, the chained woman looks at Vost but never acknowledges his presence. His sterility is no match for her openness.

Konrad's world becomes disordered, as he realizes in ret-rospect, because of the "eruption of unpredictable incident on a public axis that was also his own personal axis" (20). As the uprising in the prison signals the stirring of his subconscious, Vost learns that abandoning the safety of chronology—cause and effect—can help him uncover "the sum of his secrets." To do so is to meet his bestial side, to confront the personal night-mare, for only by peering inside has he any hope of knowing who he is: a man who distrusts women because he thinks that his mother destroyed his childhood. His wife, Claire, under-stands that "the weaker the child . . . the more fanatical the man" (31). Konrad Vost is that man. All he needs is the rebel-lion to set him free.

His first descent into what he calls "the psychic pit" takes place when he is seduced beyond his most vivid dreams by a girl the age of his daughter. Clearly a practiced prostitute and wearing a sleeveless shirt with the words "We Aim to Please" stamped across her breasts, she is a stand-in for the daughter and thus reminds the reader of Papa's visions of both wife and daughter in *Travesty*. Comically, erotically introduced to his own "psychic slime," he has his first lesson in what it means to lose control of himself. At this stage of the novel, however, Vost is unable to accept the imagination's invitation to free-dom. Rather than rejoice in his experience with the young woman, he reports his daughter to the police for prostitution. Later that night the women in the prison explode in revolt, the sign that the dismantling of his world has begun. Yanked out of his routine, Konrad discovers the price and pleasure of the

THE PASSION ARTIST

imagination. His wife has told him that he is "always detesting the enigma, refusing to believe it," but by the end of the novel he embraces what he has previously declined (42). All the dreams, longings, and perceptions that are buried in his memory break free as women initiate him into the creativity of passion.

Vost volunteers to help quell the rebellion because he cannot yet admit that the freeing of his imagination, begun by the girl, will take "him in fact from woman to woman in a disarrangement that would finally effect his change" (44). Unable to control the emergence of his true self from the prison of his own sense of order, he degenerates to one of the most violent of all those who try to beat the women into submission with symbolically phallic clubs. The distant tunnel that leads into the fortress is the entry to both femininity and dreams. Hoping to find his mother, he discovers his identity: violent, bestial, unloved. The attack on La Violaine is as bloody as any scene in Hawkes's fiction, and it suggests the extremes to which men go to counter the humanizing effect of women. As he batters the inmates into pain beyond shrieking, Vost thinks he is avenging the betrayals by mother, wife, and daughter. But the women win the battle, knock Vost unconscious, and then trigger his long, symbolic journey to the marshland of his soul.

Konrad's trip beyond the city—his plunge into the psyche—parallels Allert's travels aboard the ocean liner and Papa's race to death in the speeding car: "But it was not the darkness of night, which is always brimming with the implicit light of the impending day, but rather the eternal darkness of that interior world into which no light can shine and whose nomenclature can be found only in the formulations of the psychological function" (58). Hawkes helps the reader more than in the earlier books, for he makes sure the reader understands that Vost is traveling within himself: Konrad feels his clothes loosen; he sees a coffin that he recognizes from childhood; he knows that he will have to live a paradox—all the death-in-life that the coffin represents. Confronting this uninspired male, the female captors correctly define him as an ignorant man. He is now a victim of those he has victimized, trapped in the hospital of the prison but also rushing to his interior.

Unaware whether his gloved hand hides the bones of death or the silver claw of heroism, he learns in the rest of the novel that self-possession is impossible without a corresponding sense of the other half of the species. Fleeing first to a cemetery, he meets the dead end of his life: "The prison had exploded, so to speak; interior and exterior life were assuming a single shape; rebellious women appeared to be arising even from the graves of the dead" (74).

Vost begins the discovery of himself by recalling the repressed memories of childhood. This section of *The Passion Artist* displays Hawkes's talent for the unusual, and the reader must be ready for a series of unexpectedly developing, hallucinatory scenes rather than a logically revealed extension of plot. Konrad's memory opens up before him, and he is able to remember and thus release the hidden traumas of the past that have caused the imprisonment of his better self: "All perception, all psychic life, everything remembered, everything dreamt, everything thought. . . . Nothing is lost, nothing discarded" (43).

Indeed, it isn't; Konrad stumbles into the low points of his history as he splashes through the quagmire of the swamp. Following the tracks of his memory, suggested by the dilapidated railroad, he remembers his father, who exposes a lack of physical energy by constantly sitting in the dark and puffing a long cigar; he recalls his mother, "the fearsome heart" of the house, who either sleeps alone or cooks in an overheated kitchen; he sees an old woman who personifies the beauty of youth rotting into the worms of age; he watches a girl he has beaten in the counterattack bathe nude, and he summons the police, who shoot her; he wanders into an eerie barn where, submitting to the sexual overtures of two escaped women, he relives the mother's murder of the father and her fear of the shiny, phallic object in the father's hand. Vost's swamp journey ends when the women in the barn return him to the prison, where he finally meets again the domineering, long-absent mother.

Konrad's education will not conclude until he confronts the memory of his own unfortunate personal experience with sexual repression, but while in the swamp he has realized his grievous error in defining sex according to the terms of dominance or violence. His equation of love and death has stifled his capacity to care. Through the use of association of ideas and patterns of interlocking images rather than linear plot, Hawkes suggests Vost's mistake and its remedy: embracing the natural creativity of women. Konrad must learn, in other words, Skipper's lessons of fertility rites in graveyards and of "love at last," but true to the terror of *The Passion Artist*, Vost has waited too long. The release of his sexual potential is the promise of his death.

Still, release is a measure of victory. Finally aware that trauma begins at birth, Vost sits in prison and listens to his mother tell the story of his agonizing entry into the world as a bloody inheritor of "the instinct for innocence" (133). The unity of love and death has distorted him even in the womb, for the mother believed the mad speculation that her fetus was already dead. Traumatized at birth, dominated in childhood, Konrad lives following his mother's imprisonment with Anna Kossowski, who completes the warping of his normal sexuality. When, for example, he shows a natural, childlike curiosity about anatomy, Anna exposes herself in such a fearful manner that young Vost is terrified by what he construes as "single files of black ants" approaching the "face" where her legs meet (151). Worse, Anna forces him to a sexual embrace with her ward Kristel, only to pull the baffled children apart at the climatic moment. No wonder Vost feels threatened by the birds of night. Dismissing the romantic yearning associated with Keats's passionate odes on the Grecian urn and the nightingale, Hawkes probes not longing and consummation but repression and fear.

THE PASSION ARTIST

Mothers fear birth and dominate fathers and sons, who then fear mothers and dominate wives and daughters. Violence masquerading as sexuality is the inevitable result. The cycle, Hawkes suggests, is unending unless one exchanges inhibition for expression and understands that sex is also a form of communication, a salutation to the partner in a gesture of equality. Konrad learns the lesson well, for in his last moments he accepts sensual delights from the women he has previously thrashed during the attack on the prison. Trapped by his physically decaying body as he approaches the final revelation of psychic depths, Vost realizes how to meet a woman without guilt or fear or repression: "Thus in a city without a name, without flowers, without birds, without angels, and in a prison room containing only an iron bedstead and a broken toilet . . . Vost knew at last the transports of that singular experience which makes every man an artist: the experience, that is, of the willed erotic union" (181). Recognizing the unity of masculinity and femininity that sex offers, he wanders to his death, shot accidentally by a friend who is still demanding revenge on women.

Claire has told him that he is the source of his own discontent, and she means that Vost cannot understand the harmony within all human beings of what he calls the "bed of stars" and the "pit of putrescence" (31). As the names of two of his women—Claire and Kristel—imply, he has only to reach for the light in their lives to avoid the dark in his soul. That he dies at the completion of his stationary travels is ironic, but sudden death does not negate the affirmation of his lesson:

that everyone is a passion artist if he will but accept the polarities of life, the stars and the pit, and embrace the creative communion of the erotic.

Notes

1. "Conversations between Patrick O'Donnell and John Hawkes on His Life and Art," O'Donnell, *John Hawkes* (Boston: Twayne, 1982) 19.

2. Thomas LeClair, "The Novelists: John Hawkes," *New Republic* 10 Nov. 1979: 28-29.

3. LeClair 27.

4. John Hawkes, *The Passion Artist* (New York: Harper & Row, 1979) 1. Further references will be noted parenthetically.

CHAPTER EIGHT

VIRGINIE: HER TWO LIVES

I n 1979, three years before the publication of *Virginie: Her Two Lives* (1982), Hawkes explained to John Barth the subject of the novel: "I want to write a novel called 'The Amorous Lives of the Gauls,' which is a title of an actual 17th-century book written by one Bussy-Rabutin (that name alone is enough to send one into erotic hysteria). Bussy-Rabutin wrote a gossip book about court life and got himself exiled for 20 years; I want to redo his book as a parody of a pornographic novel with a woman as the narrator. I hope I manage it."[1]

Hawkes manages the assignment in fine style. The first sentence of this fiction of comic terror sets the tone: "Mine is an impossible story."[2] Yet *Virginie* is impossible only for those readers inhibited by the limits of realism: the eleven-year-old narrator lives and dies in two different centuries. For readers freed to the invitation of the imagination, however, the novel has possibilities not normally seen in contemporary American literature. Praising Hawkes's "power to do, gorgeously and as art, what most of us can at best do drably and as dream— transform incident into phantasm," philosopher Arthur C.

Danto describes the parody of the Marquis de Sade in *Virginie* as an erotic Pygmalion who seeks to instruct women "in the attainment of innocence, which is possessed without instruction by Virginie, through a curriculum of abstract agonies. He is punished by women who prefer his withheld flesh to . . . his metaphysics of eroticism." As Danto notes, the reviewers who reacted negatively were those who wanted more than Hawkes's "Pygmalionlike transformation of the idiom of pornography into a moral text no one can use."[3]

The point is that Hawkes deliberately combines ingenious plot and intricate style to discourage the reader from attempting to apply the novel to his own life. Like Hawkes's other complex investigations of love and the imagination, *Virginie* is to be admired not as vicarious experience but as art. Artistic design rather than narrative impulse holds the parts together, and the reader is consciously denied the opportunity to lift a moral or a lesson from the text. The pleasures of art are all. As Danto observes, the episodes are "as little extricable from the writing that gives them all the substance they possess as those illuminations of men and animals in the elaborate monograms of the 'Book of Kells' are detachable from the labyrinthine traceries into which they are drawn."[4] Donald Barthelme echoes the praise: "Mr. Hawkes's sentences, like the larger designs they advance, are spendidly not-simple."[5]

The sentences are, in fact, so complex that an overview of *Virginie* is a disservice to the novel. Once again Hawkes looks into the complicated relationship between imagination

VIRGINIE: HER TWO LIVES

and love that has preoccupied him since *The Lime Twig*, and once again he stresses the infinity of innocence when psychic depths are probed and subconscious needs explored. But unlike *The Lime Twig, Death, Sleep & the Traveler*, and *The Passion Artist*, *Virginie* parodies not only the various forms of the narrative as journal, history, and fiction but also the extremes of pornography in which the erotic can be more destructive than creative.

An author's note, composed in Venasque, France, where Hawkes wrote *Virginie* while on leave from Brown University, suggests that the novel is a humorous tale of eroticism that bows deeply to the variations of the love story: "Thus parody, archaic tones, and an overall comic flavor were inevitable, as were sources and influences." Charlotte Brontë and de Sade grace the background, and parody nudges the reader's funny bone. As the epigraph (from Heide Ziegler) states, "Beauty is paradox." Paradox is a child of the imagination, and in *Virginie*, Hawkes returns to the intricacies of first-person narration after pushing that ancient device to what seemed to be its limits in *Travesty*, a novel in which the narrator kills himself while telling his story. A different extreme is illustrated in *Virginie*: a first-person narrator who lives in 1740 (the year of de Sade's birth) and 1945 (the year of the atomic bomb).

The reader should remember that, for Hawkes, first-person narration invites parody of the novelist's role. In *Virginie* the parody is also of storytelling itself, for Virginie confesses in the first pages not only that the tale is impossible but also that the teller does not exist. Imagination is the only force that matters and is, finally, the hero of the novel: "the insubstantial voice of the page that burns" (11).

The fires of passion flare up everywhere. A flower girl recalling her journals while trapped in a burning room set afire by her mother, Virginie is innocence stranded between elegant and plebeian perversions. Her mother, a mute, is accidentally incapacitated, and her adult brother, Bocage, takes over the household, filling it with strange men and women who aid him in elaborately staged "charades of love."

But Virginie has also lived in the eighteenth century, and her journal of that age ironically illuminates the paradoxes of her other life. Young and silent in 1740, she is the protégée, servant, sister—and finally daughter and soul—of the polished but depraved Seigneur, a man so committed to the reveries of eros that he takes rough women and molds them into erotic mistresses for men who can afford them. His work is clearly an act of the imagination, for he argues that he who creates women is an artist. He may be correct, but his quest for the perfect female is comically absurd. Listening to Seigneur justify the strenuous regimen of eroticism, the reader can only grin: "She who stuffs herself on the food of love has room for more. . . . It is not satiety that drives us from our citadel" (100-01).

In *Virginie*, Hawkes uses lyrical prose to make fun of the long history of narrative that portrays women as merely creations of the male's desire for "true womanhood." The fictional possibilities of such a premise are endless, and in expanding them he indirectly comments on the need of contemporary women to express their individuality. As in *The Passion Artist*, he also explores the peculiar American fascination with the relationship between love and death. In 1945, for example, Virginie longs to brave the flames to achieve her destiny that lies in ashes; and in 1740 she inhabits the most frightening chamber in the chateau, the enormous hearth. Similarly, she listens to stories about a "sex arcade" filled with erotically posed skeletons. Even her tale itself skirts death: "What could be more ominous than the death of this rhetoric?"

Virginie's role in the dance of love and death is to witness and record the various charades of love, to learn the bright colors of passion, to understand that everyone aspires to partial nudity. Although her journals jump with life, she herself is the quiet observer of willing women being molded in artful fashion to erotic ends. The ideal woman, says her brother, is not the demure maid but one who exists as a "form of desire," as one who knows that her identity depends not on the longing of men but on the spark of her own craving. Only the free and confident woman realizes that "the first principle of love is secrecy." Hidden in her corner, witness to the art of love's tableau, Virginie is Seigneur's secret. He solemnly intones: "The grace of novelty is to love as is the skin to the fruit."

Innovation is thus the key to both the sex arcade and the novel that undercuts it. As Seigneur knows, and as Virginie learns, seduction is all the more stimulating with a threat of uncertainty, an element of risk. Voyeur rather than participant, she understands that her pleasure is the solace that her dreams of creation inspire while she writes her journals, which are, of course, this novel. Like love, fiction is one of the jewels of the imagination. Yet threats to the imagination's pleasures abound from those who would rein in its creative possibilities with the bridle and bit of duty and inhibition. In each of Virginie's two lives, for example, a mother figure acts violently to end male obsession. But the essence of Virginie survives. Always protecting her innocence, the symbol of his own soul, while outrageously indulging the flesh of others, Seigneur cries out to her as the flames devour him, "Destroy your innocence." She does so willingly, and thus saves it, by embracing the fire. Only her voice—the tale itself, the innocence of the imagination—is eternal.

To gloss the novel in such a manner, however, is to undervalue the comedy of its vision and the lyricism of its prose. *Virginie* begins, for example, with an unquenchable fire in which both Virginie and Bocage burn while their friends call out to them from below. Significantly, the men are helpless, as they tend to be throughout the novel, but the mother who sets the fire is strong and determined to destroy the dominance of the male world. She must do so silently, for she has suffered a stroke. Thus deprived of her customary protector, Virginie, who is associated with the ephemeral life of flowers, is destined to play naive observer to her brother's egotistical adventures in the erotic. But she must also relive her life of 1740, and thus Hawkes contrasts Bocage's plebeian charades with those of a more courtly though not less absurd age.

VIRGINIE: HER TWO LIVES

In the eighteenth-century world of Seigneur, Virginie is linked to Cinderella. Dressed in gray and sleeping among the ashes, she witnesses a radical Pygmalion's efforts to train women for man's pleasure, but her own Prince Charming never comes to the ball. Aware that she is a "flower-laden child of ashes" (21), she knows even in her girlhood that only past cruelties can coerce a woman to acquiesce to a male definition of joy. Noblesse, for example, is a woman whom Seigneur molds for a baron, but she cannot forgive the obvious pain of her training in order to accept whatever future erotic pleasure she may find. The elegant Seigneur refuses to acknowledge the natural and thus innocent sensuality of women without tampering with it. They are mere clay, he mistakenly believes, to be shaped according to his tastes for the bizarre. Seigneur is one of Hawkes's clearest parodies of the artist.

His artistry is also the butt of Hawkes's laughter. Pornography may counter inhibition, as Hawkes suggests in *The Blood Oranges*, but in *Virginie* the reader can only laugh at the perversion of Seigneur's "art" that degrades women in the process. Rescuing a fair maid, for instance, he notes that her exposed breasts "had about them no lean look of arrogance, no opposite fattening with lust or despair" (28). Virginie, of course, is too young to repudiate such ridiculous descriptions. Her innocence is her shield, the quality that Seigneur inadvertently challenges in the women he sculpts according to the dictates of his art. De Sade might have approved of his nonsense, but today's liberated woman will shudder.

The grimace is mixed with humor as Hawkes pokes fun in the rest of the novel at the various erotic fantasies from dirty books to dirty pictures that men have created through the centuries to distort the image of females. For every sexual charade that Seigneur stages in 1740, Bocage answers with a more earthy version in 1945. These alternating sequences shape the novel while Virginie records the escapades. The props are the usual stuff of such dreams: frilly underwear, sheer nightgowns, dogs in heat, flowers, light—in short, as Virginie observes, all "the elasticity of the ribbons and fringes she was now stretching comically across her bold curves" (36). Bocage is unaware, of course, that his games lack the sophistication of de Sade. Thus the reader grins while Bocage seriously collects the men necessary to complete his latter-day pageants: a man with such massive shoulders and belly that he appears to have no head, and a boxer with a dirty cast around foot and ankle, a pair of "vivid" crutches, and a body covered with green tattoos.

Reminiscent of Skipper (*Second Skin*), the tattooed fighter describes himself as having been "irresistible" since his earliest manhood, and he is thereby one of Hawkes's many examples in the novel of the overconfident male. Such emphasis is a new departure, for Hawkes usually sympathizes with masculine attempts to court the god of eros. Indeed, *Virginie* is full of allusions to his earlier novels, from Skipper's green tattoo, through Cyril's oranges and tapestry of love (*The Blood Oranges*), to the limes of *The Lime Twig* and Papa's car in *Travesty*. It is as if Hawkes encourages the initiated reader to

VIRGINIE: HER TWO LIVES

remember these male-oriented spectacles of love before the author unexpectedly reverses the emphasis and highlights the role of women. Any man who claims to be irresistible is going to be undercut in *Virginie* by the artistic designs of women who are far more practiced in the delicate game of seduction. Hawkes knows that Eve offered the apple while Adam took the bite. The reader notes, for example, that one of Bocage's ladies is called a priestess.

Throughout the intricate descriptions of the various charades Hawkes challenges the innocence of the reader who imagines himself detached from Virginie's erotic journals. The freedom of the imagination is always an issue in a Hawkes novel, and he understands that curiosity is one of the primary catalysts of speculation and dream. Thus when Virginie wanders through Seigneur's "labyrinth," considers the voluptuousness of past activities, and wonders "Who shall she be? What shall she be made to do," she innocently but effectively arouses the reader's fantasies about the next tableau. Curiosity negates detachment. Hawkes parodies the tradition of pornographic reverie to show that the imagined always outstrips the real. The reader's imagination soars far beyond the pageants of Bocage, Seigneur, and de Sade himself to examine what Seigneur defines as the seven expressions of innocence: joy, attention, calm, surprise, grief, incomprehension, and pain (54).

Attempting to maintain a tenuous hold on his own innocence by never touching Virginie, Seigneur finally personifies the male passion for order. He is a parody of Cyril's obsession with symmetry (*The Blood Oranges*), as well as a pseudo artist who believes that females are not women unless he makes them so, and thus he is the opposite of the naturalness that Hawkes attributes to femininity. Committed to his preposterously named "Citadel of the Desire to Please," Seigneur insists that women are supposed to surrender to the desires of those they are born to serve: men. His sense of a male order may have carried the day in the eighteenth century, but Hawkes's twentieth-century reader recognizes the contrast with his own era and thereby laughs at Seigneur's equation of love and servility. Times have changed, and *Virginie* is a lush commentary on the alteration.

Virginie: Her Two Lives is not Hawkes's most accomplished novel, but it is one of his most innovative. Rather than rely on the urging of narrative development, he offers variations on a theme. Late in the novel Virginie thinks, "Few would believe that from sources purely imaginary such happiness can be derived," and she has in mind the fictions that thought and reverie can create (191). *Virginie* is such a creation, more an abbreviated version of *A 1001 Nights* than a novel in which the main character undergoes initiation and change. Each chapter is like a new story rather than an advancement of the central tale. From the sex arcade in which the skeletons are erotically reassembled, through the seduction of a man who may or may not be a priest, to the sewing of clothes that accentuate the voluptuous, the innocent narrator merely observes and records.

VIRGINIE: HER TWO LIVES

Too young to participate, she does not join the women who, like those in *The Passion Artist*, rebel against the male imagination that limits females to sexuality and servility. In both 1740 and 1945 a mother destroys the erotic wonderland. Readers may view the mother as civilized restraint or maternal instinct, but she is also a center of creativity, and thus she protests the limitations of a male-dominated world. In *Virginie*, Hawkes parodies the art form women are said to resent—pornography—and thereby smiles at the contemporary woman's movement even while he salutes femininity.

Notes

1. "Hawkes and Barth Talk about Fiction," *New York Times Book Review* 1 Apr. 1979: 32.

2. John Hawkes, *Virginie: Her Two Lives* (New York: Harper & Row, 1982) 9. Further references will be noted parenthetically.

3. Arthur C. Danto, "Gems without Their Setting," *New York Times Book Review* 25 Nov. 1984: 3.

4. Danto 3.

5. Donald Barthelme, "The Most Wonderful Trick," *New York Times Book Review* 25 Nov. 1984: 3.

CONCLUSION

A lthough Hawkes has published other books during his long career, his major contribution to contemporary American literature is the innovation he has brought to the novel. *Fiasco Hall* (poetry), *The Innocent Party* (plays), *Lunar Landscapes* (short fiction), and *Humors of Blood & Skin* (miscellany) illustrate his range, but their value to Hawkes's canon is primarily that of variations on his central concerns in different genres. Hawkes is foremost a novelist, a writer whose stature is such that the publication of each new book prompts a spectrum of reviews and commentary from high praise to outraged distaste.

One doubts whether Hawkes would have it any other way. Innovative, imaginative, and daring, he has deliberately challenged the traditional characteristics of fiction from the beginning of his career. Although he rarely goes so far as completely to dismiss plot, character, setting, and theme, his well-known definition of these conventions as the "enemies" of the novel has persuaded many readers that fiction does not have to be written according to time-honored prescriptions. A writer who favors imaginative projection over verisimilitude

CONCLUSION

is free to violate the standard props of the novel so long as he remains true to the demands of his vision. Plot, character, setting, and theme are not eliminated in Hawkes's novels, but adherence to the requirements of realism is not a primary concern. Thus while Hawkes avoids such traditional staples as logical plots, round characters, and recognizable settings, he offers in their absence unreliable narrators, created landscapes, lyrical language, a mixture of comedy and terror, and finally a parody of the novel form itself.

For Hawkes hopes to free not only the genre of fiction but also the reader from the constraints that the tenets of realism impose on novels and those who care about them. It is not, he would argue, that realistic fiction is bad but that realism is not the sole way of writing about experience. Unfortunately, he points out, readers expect authors to supply the conventional staples of the novel and thereby inadvertently limit the art form. Hawkes refuses to fulfill reader expectations. In so doing, he offers the joy of imagination in both technique and theme. Yet his novels are accessible for those who will free themselves to look for unconventional structure, linking image patterns, an investigation of unconscious impulses, and the revelations of the narrator's voice.

Hawkes will never be popular with those who demand that fiction be limited to realism. Readers who appreciate the infinite recesses of art are another matter. Along with John Barth, Thomas Pynchon, Donald Barthelme, and Robert Coover, John Hawkes has changed not only the concept of fiction but also the way novels are read.

BIBLIOGRAPHY

I. Books by John Hawkes

Fiasco Hall. Cambridge: Harvard Printing Office, 1943.

Charivari. New Directions in Prose and Poetry 11 (1949): 365–436.

The Cannibal. 1949. New York: New Directions, 1962.

The Beetle Leg. New York: New Directions, 1951.

The Goose on the Grave and *The Owl.* New York: New Directions, 1954.

The Lime Twig. New York: New Directions, 1961.

Second Skin. New York: New Directions, 1964.

The Innocent Party: Four Short Plays. New York: New Directions, 1966.

Lunar Landscapes: Stories & Short Novels, 1949–1963. New York: New Directions, 1969.

The Blood Oranges. New York: New Directions, 1971.

Death, Sleep & the Traveler. New York: New Directions, 1974.

Travesty. New York: New Directions, 1976.

The Passion Artist. New York: Harper & Row, 1979.

Virginie: Her Two Lives. New York: Harper & Row, 1982.

Humors of Blood & Skin: A John Hawkes Reader. New York: New Directions, 1984.

II. Selected Uncollected Essays by Hawkes

"Notes on Violence." *Audience* 7 (1960): 60.

"The Voice of Edwin Honig." *Voices: A Journal of Poetry* 174 (1961): 39–47.

BIBLIOGRAPHY

"Flannery O'Connor's Devil." *Sewanee Review* 70 (1962): 395–407.

"Notes on *The Wild Goose Chase.*" *Massachusetts Review* 3 (1962): 784–88.

"Story into Novel." *Write and Rewrite: A Story of the Creative Process.* Ed. John Kuehl. New York: Meredith 1967. 265; 284–87.

"The Voice Project: An Idea for Innovation in the Teaching of Writing." *Writers as Teachers; Teachers as Writers.* Ed. Jonathan Baumbach. New York: Holt, 1970. 89–144.

"Notes on Writing a Novel." *TriQuarterly* 30 (1974): 109–26.

"*The Floating Opera* and *Second Skin.*" *Mosaic* 8 (1974): 17–28.

"Four Introductions." *John Hawkes: An Annotated Bibliography.* Comp. Carol A. Hryciw. Metuchen, NJ: Scarecrow, 1977. 1–7.

III. Interviews

Dunn, Douglas. "Profile 11: John Hawkes." *New Review* 12 (1975): 23–28.

Emmett, Paul, and Richard Vine. "A Conversation with John Hawkes." *Chicago Review* 28 (1976): 163–71.

Enck, John. "John Hawkes: An Interview." *Wisconsin Studies in Contemporary Literature* 6 (1965): 141–55.

Fielding, Andrew. "John Hawkes Is a Very Nice Guy, and a Novelist of Sex and Death." *Village Voice* 24 May 1976: 45–47.

Graham, John. "John Hawkes on His Novels." *Massachusetts Review* 7 (1966): 449–61.

"Hawkes and Barth Talk about Fiction." *New York Times Book Review* 1 Apr. 1979: 7 + .

Keyser, David and Ned French. "Talks with John Hawkes." *Harvard Advocate* 104 (1970): 6 + .

Kuehl, John. "Interview." *John Hawkes and the Craft of Conflict.* By John Kuehl. New Brunswick: Rutgers University Press, 1975. 155–83.

LeClair, Thomas. "The Novelists: John Hawkes." *New Republic* 10 Nov. 1979: 26–29.

Levine, Nancy. "An Interview with John Hawkes." *A John Hawkes Symposium: Design and Debris.* Eds. Anthony C. Santore and Michael Pocalyko. New York: New Directions, 1977. 91–108.

BIBLIOGRAPHY

Santore, Anthony C., and Michael Pocalyko. " 'A Trap to Catch Little Birds With': An Interview with John Hawkes." *A John Hawkes Symposium: Design and Debris.* Eds. Santore and Pocalyko. New York: New Directions, 1977. 165–84.

Sauls, Roger. "John Hawkes: I Am Pleased to Talk about Fiction." *New Lazarus Review* 1 (1978): 5–10.

Scholes, Robert. "A Conversation on *The Blood Oranges* between John Hawkes and Robert Scholes." *Novel* 5 (1972): 197–207.

IV. Books about Hawkes

Berry, Eliot. *A Poetry of Force and Darkness: The Fiction of John Hawkes.* San Bernadino: Borgo Press, 1979. Monograph suggesting changes in Hawkes's career.

Busch, Frederick. *Hawkes: A Guide to His Fictions.* Syracuse: Syracuse University Press, 1973. Primarily concerned with Hawkes's language and use of animal imagery.

Graham, John, comp. *Studies in Second Skin.* Columbus, Ohio: Merrill, 1971. Collection of essays with various points of view about *Second Skin.*

Greiner, Donald J. *Comic Terror: The Novels of John Hawkes.* 1973. Memphis: Memphis State University Press, 1978. Novel by novel analysis of Hawkes's unusual comedy, themes, and techniques; includes selected checklist of primary and secondary material.

Kuehl, John. *John Hawkes and the Craft of Conflict.* New Brunswick: Rutgers University Press, 1975. Analysis of love and death in Hawkes; interesting primarily for interview with Hawkes.

O'Donnell, Patrick. *John Hawkes.* Boston: Twayne, 1982. Good overview with valuable chapter on Hawkes's life.

Santore, Anthony C., and Pocalyko, Michael, eds. *A John Hawkes Symposium: Design and Debris.* New York: New Directions, 1977. Collection of essays by major Hawkes scholars, plus interviews with Hawkes.

BIBLIOGRAPHY

V.   Critical Articles about Hawkes

Allen, C. J. "Desire, Design and Debris: The Submerged Narrative of John Hawkes's Recent Trilogy." *Modern Fiction Studies* 25 (1979–80): 579–92. Analyzes how unconscious fears undermine idyllic visions in the triad.

Baxter, Charles. "In the Suicide Seat: Reading John Hawkes's *Travesty.*" *Georgia Review* 34 (1980): 871–85. Discusses the complexity of *Travesty* in terms of the negation of reader expectations.

Boutrous, Lawrence K. "Parody in Hawkes' *The Lime Twig.*" *Critique* 15.2 (1973): 49–56. Focuses on parody of detective fiction in *The Lime Twig.*

Edenbaum, Robert I. "John Hawkes: *The Lime Twig* and Other Tenuous Horrors." *Massachusetts Review* 7 (1966): 462–75. Discusses violence and fantasy in *The Lime Twig.*

Emmett, Paul. "The Reader's Voyage through *Travesty.*" *Chicago Review* 28 (1976): 172–87. Discusses how Hawkes deliberately frustrates the reader of *Travesty.*

Frohock, W. M. "John Hawkes's Vision of Violence." *Southwest Review* 50 (1965): 69–79. Important early analysis of how Hawkes suppresses information the reader usually expects.

Frost, Lucy. "The Drowning of American Adam: Hawkes's *The Beetle Leg.*" *Critique* 14.3 (1973): 63–74. Reads *The Beetle Leg* in terms of the fall of Adam and the soiling of the new Eden.

Greiner, Donald J. "*Death, Sleep & the Traveler*: John Hawkes' Return to Terror." *Critique* 17.3 (1976): 26–38. Argues that *Death, Sleep & the Traveler* marks a significant change in Hawkes from comedy to terror.

———. "Strange Laughter: The Comedy of John Hawkes." *Southwest Review* 56 (1971): 318–28. Analyzes Hawkes's unusual comedy by contrasting it with traditional theories of humor.

———. "The Thematic Use of Color in John Hawkes' *Second Skin.*" *Contemporary Literature* 11 (1970): 389–400. Explains Hawkes's theory of fictional structure based on recurring image patterns by discussing the color imagery in *Second Skin.*

Guerard, Albert J. "The Illuminating Distortion." *Novel* 5 (1972): 101–21. Discusses how Hawkes achieves both comic and terrifying effects when writing about psychic needs.

BIBLIOGRAPHY

_____. "Introduction to the Cambridge Anti-Realists." *Audience* 7 (1960): 57–59. Suggests how Hawkes's narrative distortion illustrates a general disbelief in order.

_____. "The Prose Style of John Hawkes." *Critique* 6 (1963): 19–29. Important early evaluation of Hawkes's unusual style.

Imhoff, Ron. "On *Second Skin*." *Mosaic* 8 (1974): 51–63. Comments on how Hawkes's sense of fictional structure challenges conventional fiction.

Klein, Marcus. "Hawkes in Love." *Caliban* ns 11 (1975): 65–79. Analyzes Hawkes's novels about love in terms of detachment and satire.

Knapp, John V. "Hawkes' *The Blood Oranges*: A Sensual New Jerusalem." *Critique* 17.3 (1976): 5–25. Discusses *The Blood Oranges* in terms of Plato, Shakespeare, the Bible, and Milton.

Kraus, Elisabeth. "Psychic Sores in Search of Compassion: Hawkes' *Death, Sleep & the Traveler*." *Critique* 17.3 (1976): 39–52. Focuses on how Hawkes shapes *Death, Sleep & the Traveler* around the conflicting forces of instinct and repression.

Lavers, Norman. "The Structure of *Second Skin*." *Novel* 5 (1972): 208–14. Argues that *Second Skin* is among other things Hawkes's parody of the notion of the Great American Novel.

LeClair, Thomas. "A Pair of Jacks: John Barth and John Hawkes Gamble with New Fiction." *Horizon* 22 (1979): 64–71. Excellent overview of Hawkes in terms of *The Passion Artist*.

_____. "The Unreliability of Innocence: John Hawkes' *Second Skin*." *Journal of Narrative Technique* 3 (1973): 32–39. Discusses death, innocence, and unreliable narration in *Second Skin*.

Oberbeck, S. K. "John Hawkes: The Smile Slashed by a Razor." *Contemporary American Novelists*. Ed. Harry T. Moore. Carbondale: Southern Illinois University Press, 1964. 193–204. Analyzes language, dream, and terror in Hawkes's fiction.

Reutlinger, D. P. "*The Cannibal*: The Reality of Victim." *Critique* 6 (1963): 30–37. Analyzes how Hawkes creates sympathy through detachment.

BIBLIOGRAPHY

Rovit, Earl. "The Fiction of John Hawkes: An Introductory View." *Modern Fiction Studies* 10 (1964): 150–62. Overview of Hawkes's technique and themes that explains how Hawkes changes from *The Cannibal* to *The Lime Twig*.

Warner, John M. "The 'Internalized Quest Romance' in Hawkes' *The Lime Twig*." *Modern Fiction Studies* 19 (1973): 89–95. Discusses the quest and the artist-hero in *The Lime Twig*.

Yarborough, Richard. "Hawkes' *Second Skin*." *Mosaic* 8 (1974): 65–75. Discusses *Second Skin* in terms of important images and John Berryman's *The Dream Songs*.

VI. Bibliography

Hryciw, Carol A. *John Hawkes: An Annotated Bibliography*. Metuchen, NJ: Scarecrow, 1977. Primary and secondary.

INDEX

The index does not include references to material in the notes.

INDEX

INDEX

Major Characters
Allert, 120–127, 128, 133, 135, 143, 145
Margaret and Michael Banks, 12, 19, 70, 73, 75–85
Cassandra, 92–101
Catherine, 107, 108, 113, 114, 115, 116, 117, 118, 119
Cyril, 6, 7, 8, 9, 17, 105–119, 120, 122, 126, 129, 134, 135, 158, 159
Fiona, 107, 108, 113, 115, 116, 117, 118
William Hencher, 70, 72, 73, 74–85, 88, 112, 120
Hugh, 6, 7, 9, 107–119, 121, 122, 127, 139
Il Gufo, 23–27, 140
Luke Lampson, 7, 53–68, 122
Mulge Lampson, 53–68
Larry, 70, 75, 76, 77, 78, 79, 80, 81, 83, 84
Papa, 14, 128–35, 144, 145, 158
Seigneur, 154–160
Skipper, 6, 8, 13, 17, 18, 88–103, 107, 108, 112, 119, 120, 122, 129, 140, 141, 148, 158
Sidney Slyter, 72–73, 74, 84
Stella Snow, 30–49
Virginie, 153–161
Konrad Vost, 8, 9, 139–50
Zizendorf, 8, 9, 30–49, 141
Minor Characters
Annie, 81
Antonina, 26
Ariane, 122, 125, 126, 127
Barabo, 27
Bocage, 154, 156, 158, 159
Harry Bohn, 65
Bub, 98
Camper and Lou, 59–60, 63, 65
Cap Leech, 63–65, 67
Captain Red, 97, 98, 99
Catalina Kate, 93, 100, 101, 102
Chantal, 129, 131, 132, 133
Clara, Mirabelle, and Eve, 142, 144, 149
Cowles, 74
Cromwell, 36, 42–43, 45
The Duke, 14, 38, 47–49, 60
Ernst, 36, 42–43, 45, 46
Fernandez, 96, 97, 102
Gertrude, 96

INDEX

INDEX

INDEX

INDEX